STRATEGIC MANAGEMENT 12e

AN INTEGRATED APPROACH

THEORY & CASES

CHARLES W. L. HILL
University of Washington – Foster School of Business

MELISSA A. SCHILLING
New York University – Stern School of Business

GARETH R. JONES

Australia • Brazil • Mexico • Singapore • United Kingdom • United States

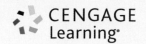
CENGAGE
Learning®

Strategic Management: An Integrated Approach, Theory & Cases, 12e
Charles W. L. Hill
Melissa A. Schilling
Gareth R. Jones

Vice President, General Manager, Social
   Science & Qualitative Business:
   Erin Joyner

Product Director: Jason Fremder

Senior Product Manager: Scott Person

Content/Media Developer: Tara Singer

Product Assistant: Brian Pierce

Marketing Director: Kristen Hurd

Marketing Manager: Emily Horowitz

Marketing Coordinator:
   Christopher Walz

Senior Content Project Manager:
   Kim Kusnerak

Manufacturing Planner:
   Ron Montgomery

Production Service: MPS Limited

Senior Art Director: Linda May

Cover/Internal Designer: Mike Stratton

Cover Image: mbbirdy/Getty Images

Intellectual Property

   Analyst: Diane Garrity

   Project Manager: Sarah Shainwald

Strategy in Action Sailboat Image:
   © Steve Bly/Getty Images

Part 5 Nautical Compass Image:
   holbox/Shutterstock.com

For product information and technology assistance, contact us at
Cengage Learning Customer & Sales Support, 1-800-354-9706

For permission to use material from this text or product,
submit all requests online at **www.cengage.com/permissions**
Further permissions questions can be emailed to
permissionrequest@cengage.com

Unless otherwise noted all items © Cengage Learning.

Library of Congress Control Number: 2015953360

ISBN: 978-1-305-50227-7

Cengage Learning
20 Channel Center Street
Boston, MA 02210
USA

Cengage Learning is a leading provider of customized learning solutions with employees residing in nearly 40 different countries and sales in more than 125 countries around the world. Find your local representative at **www.cengage.com.**

Cengage Learning products are represented in Canada by Nelson Education, Ltd.

To learn more about Cengage Learning Solutions, visit **www.cengage.com**

Purchase any of our products at your local college store or at our preferred online store **www.cengagebrain.com**

Printed in Canada
Print Number: 01   Print Year: 2016

BRIEF CONTENTS

CONTENTS

PART THREE   STRATEGIES

PART FOUR   IMPLEMENTING STRATEGY

Chapter 11   Corporate Governance, Social Responsibility,
and Ethics   348

PREFACE

Consistent with our mission to provide students with the most current and up-to-date account of the changes taking place in the world of strategy and management, there have been some significant changes in the 12th edition of *Strategic Management: An Integrated Approach.*

First, our new co-author, Melissa Schilling has taken on a major role in this edition. Melissa is a Professor of Management and Organization at the Leonard Stern School of Business at New York University, where she teaches courses on strategic management, corporate strategy, and technology and innovation management. She has published extensively in top-tier academic journals and is recognized as one of the leading experts on innovation and strategy in high-technology industries. We are very pleased to again have Melissa on the book team. Melissa made substantial contributions to the prior edition, and that continues with this edition. She has revised several chapters and written seven high-caliber case studies. We believe her input has significantly strengthened the book.

Second, a number of chapters have been extensively revised. In the 11th edition, Chapter 5, "Business-Level Strategy," was rewritten from scratch. In addition to the standard material on Porter's generic strategies, this chapter now includes discussion of *value innovation* and *blue ocean strategy* following the work of W. C. Kim and R. Mauborgne. Chapter 6, "Business-Level Strategy and the Industry Environment," was also extensively rewritten and updated to clarify concepts and bring it into the 21st century. For the 12th edition, we significantly revised and updated Chapter 3, building discussion of resources and competitive advantage around Jay Barney's popular VRIO model. We also combined Chapters 12 and 13 into a single chapter on implementing strategy through organization. We think this more streamlined approach greatly strengthens the book and enhances readability, particularly for students.

Third, the examples and cases contained in each chapter have been revised. Every chapter has a new *Opening Case* and a new *Closing Case*. There are also many new *Strategy in Action* features. In addition, there has been significant change in the examples used in the text to illustrate content. In making these changes, our goal has been to make the book relevant for students reading it in the second decade of the 21st century.

Fourth, we have a substantially revised selection of cases for this edition. All of the cases are either new to this edition or are updates of cases that adopters have indicated they like to see in the book. For this edition, we made the decision to use only our own cases. Over the years, it has been increasingly difficult to find high-quality, third-party cases, while we have received consistently positive feedback about the quality of cases that we have written; so we decided that from this point forward we would only use our own cases. We have also received feedback that many professors like to use shorter cases, instead of or in addition to the longer cases normally included in our book. Consequently, in this edition of the book we have included 30 cases, 20 of which are the traditional long-form cases, and 10 of which are shorter cases. Many of the cases are current as of 2015. We have made an effort to include cases that have high name recognition with students, and that they will enjoy reading and working on. These include cases on Boeing, Staples, Trader Joe's, Tesla Motors, Uber, Google, Microsoft, and 3M.

Practicing Strategic Management: An Interactive Approach

We have received a lot of positive feedback about the usefulness of the end-of-chapter exercises and assignments in the Practicing Strategic Management sections of our book. They offer a wide range of hands-on and digital learning experiences for students. We are thrilled to announce that we have moved some of these elements into the MindTap digital learning solution to provide a seamless learning experience for students and instructors. We have enhanced these features to give students engaging, multimedia learning experiences that teach them the case analysis framework and provide them multiple opportunities to step into the shoes of a manager and solve real-world strategic challenges. For instructors, MindTap offers a fully customizable, all-in-one learning suite including a digital gradebook, real-time data analytics, and full integration into your LMS. Select from assignments including:

- **Cornerstone to Capstone Diagnostic** assesses students' functional area knowledge and provides feedback and remediation so that students are up to speed and prepared for the strategic management course material.
- **Multimedia Quizzes** assess students' basic comprehension of the reading material to help you gauge their level of engagement and understanding of the content.
- **Directed Cases** engage students by presenting businesses facing strategic challenges, placing concepts in real-world context, and making for great points of discussion. As they complete these activities, students receive instruction and feedback that teaches them the case analysis methodology and helps them build critical thinking and problem-solving skills.
- **Experiential Exercises** are based on the "Practicing Strategic Management" assignments in the end-of-chapter materials in previous editions. They have been updated for the MindTap and challenge students to work in teams using the YouSeeU app in our one-of-a-kind collaborative environment to solve real-world managerial problems and begin to experience firsthand what it's like to work in management.
- **Branching Activities** present challenging problems that cannot be solved with one specific, correct answer. Students are presented with a series of decisions to be made based upon information they are given about a company and are scored according to the quality of their decisions.
- **Case Analysis Projects** are delivered in our online collaborative environment via the YouSeeU app so that students can work together synchronously to complete their comprehensive case analysis projects, papers, and presentations. Offered in conjunction with robust cases written exclusively by Charles Hill and Melissa Schilling, these activities challenge students to think and act like tomorrow's strategic leaders. Use our default activity, written by seasoned strategic management instructors, or customize the project to suit your class.
- **Strategy Sign-On** projects are back by popular demand. They are designed to provide students the opportunity to explore the latest data through digital research activities. Students first research a company that is facing a strategic management problem, and students then follow the company throughout the semester and complete various case analysis assignments.

It is not our intention to suggest that *all* of these exercises should be used for *every* chapter. Strategic management is taught at both undergraduate and graduate levels, and therefore we offer a variety of pedagogically designed activities with numerous challenge levels so that instructors can customize MindTap to best suit their teaching style and the objectives of the course.

We have found that our interactive approach to teaching strategic management appeals to students. It also greatly improves the quality of their learning experience. Our approach is more fully discussed in the *Instructor's Resource Manual*.

Strategic Management Cases

The 30 cases that we have selected for this edition will appeal, we are certain, to students and professors alike, both because these cases are intrinsically interesting and because of the number of strategic management issues they illuminate. The organizations discussed in the cases range from large, well-known companies, for which students can do research to update the information, to small, entrepreneurial businesses that illustrate the uncertainty and challenge of the strategic management process. In addition, the selections include many international cases, and most of the other cases contain some element of global strategy. Refer to the Contents for a complete listing of the cases.

To help students learn how to effectively analyze and write a case study, we continue to include a special section on this subject. It has a checklist and an explanation of areas to consider, suggested research tools, and tips on financial analysis. Additionally, the MindTap learning activities include Directed Cases that ask students to complete the steps and offer in-depth explanations to guide them through the process, as well as case-based Branching Activities that place students in the shoes of a manager and require them to move through strategic decisions; students are assessed on the quality of their analysis in making their choices, and the activity concludes with a discussion question for you to implement in class.

We feel that our entire selection of cases is unrivaled in breadth and depth.

Teaching and Learning Aids

Taken together, the teaching and learning features of *Strategic Management* provide a package that is unsurpassed in its coverage and that supports the integrated approach that we have taken throughout the book.

- **Instructor Website.** Access important teaching resources on this companion website. For your convenience, you can download electronic versions of the instructor supplements from the password-protected section of the site, including Instructor's Resource Manual, Comprehensive Case Notes, Cognero Testing, Word Test Bank files, PowerPoint® slides, and Video Segments and Guide. To access these additional course materials and companion resources, please visit www.cengagebrain.com.
- The **Instructor's Resource Manual.** For each chapter, we provide a clearly focused synopsis, a list of teaching objectives, a comprehensive lecture outline, teaching notes for the Ethical Dilemma feature, suggested answers to discussion questions, and comments on the end-of-chapter activities. Each Opening Case, Strategy in Action boxed feature, and Closing Case has a synopsis and a corresponding teaching note to help guide class discussion.
- **Case Teaching Notes.** These include a complete list of case discussion questions, as well as comprehensive teaching notes for each case, which give a complete analysis of case issues.
- **Cognero Test Bank.** A completely online test bank allows the instructor the ability to create comprehensive, true/false, multiple-choice, and essay questions for each chapter in the book. The mix of questions has been adjusted to provide fewer fact-based or simple memorization items and to provide more items that rely on synthesis or application.

- **PowerPoint Presentation Slides.** Each chapter comes complete with a robust PowerPoint presentation to aid with class lectures. These slides can be downloaded from the text website.
- **Cengage Learning Write Experience 3.0.** This new technology is the first in higher education to offer students the opportunity to improve their writing and analytical skills without adding to your workload. Offered through an exclusive agreement with Vantage Learning, creator of the software used for GMAT essay grading, Write Experience evaluates students' answers to a select set of writing assignments for voice, style, format, and originality.
- **Video Segments.** A collection of 13 BBC videos have been included in the MindTap Learning Path. These new videos are short, compelling, and timely illustrations of today's management world. Available on the DVD and Instructor website, and detailed case write-ups including questions and suggested answers appear in the Instructor's Resource Manual and Video Guide.
- **MindTap**. MindTap is the digital learning solution that helps instructors engage students and help them become tomorrow's strategic leaders. All activities are designed to teach students to problem-solve and think like management leaders. Through these activities and real-time course analytics, and an accessible reader, MindTap helps you turn cookie cutter into cutting edge, apathy into engagement, and memorizers into higher-level thinkers.
- **Micromatic Strategic Management Simulation** (for bundles only). The Micromatic Business Simulation Game allows students to decide their company's mission, goals, policies, and strategies. Student teams make their decisions on a quarter-by-quarter basis, determining price, sales and promotion budgets, operations decisions, and financing requirements. Each decision round requires students to make approximately 100 decisions. Students can play in teams or play alone, compete against other players or the computer, or use Micromatic for practice, tournaments, or assessment. You can control any business simulation element you wish, leaving the rest alone if you desire. Because of the number and type of decisions the student users must make, Micromatic is classified as a medium-to-complex business simulation game. This helps students understand how the functional areas of a business fit together, without being bogged down in needless detail, and provides students with an excellent capstone experience in decision making.
- **Smartsims** (for bundles only). MikesBikes Advanced is a premier strategy simulation providing students with the unique opportunity to evaluate, plan, and implement strategy as they manage their own company while competing online against other students within their course. Students from the management team of a bicycle manufacturing company make all the key functional decisions involving price, marketing, distribution, finance, operations, HR, and R&D. They formulate a comprehensive strategy, starting with their existing product, and then adapt the strategy as they develop new products for emerging markets. Through Smartsims' easy-to-use interface, students are taught the cross-functional disciplines of business and how the development and implementation of strategy involves these disciplines. The competitive nature of MikesBikes encourages involvement and learning in a way that no other teaching methodology can, and your students will have fun in the process!

ACKNOWLEDGMENTS

This book is the product of far more than three authors. We are grateful to our Senior Product Manager, Scott Person; our Content Developer, Tara Singer; our Content Project Manager, Kim Kusnerak; and our Marketing Manager, Emily Horowitz, for their help in developing and promoting the book and for providing us with timely feedback and information from professors and reviewers, which allowed us to shape the book to meet the needs of its intended market. We also want to thank the departments of management at the University of Washington and New York University for providing the setting and atmosphere in which the book could be written, and the students of these universities who react to and provide input for many of our ideas. In addition, the following reviewers of this and earlier editions gave us valuable suggestions for improving the manuscript from its original version to its current form:

Andac Arikan, *Florida Atlantic University*

Ken Armstrong, *Anderson University*

Richard Babcock, *University of San Francisco*

Kunal Banerji, *West Virginia University*

Kevin Banning, *Auburn University- Montgomery*

Glenn Bassett, *University of Bridgeport*

Thomas H. Berliner, *The University of Texas at Dallas*

Bonnie Bollinger, *Ivy Technical Community College*

Richard G. Brandenburg, *University of Vermont*

Steven Braund, *University of Hull*

Philip Bromiley, *University of Minnesota*

Geoffrey Brooks, *Western Oregon State College*

Jill Brown, *Lehigh University*

Amanda Budde, *University of Hawaii*

Lowell Busenitz, *University of Houston*

Sam Cappel, *Southeastern Louisiana University*

Charles J. Capps III, *Sam Houston State University*

Don Caruth, *Texas A&M Commerce*

Gene R. Conaster, *Golden State University*

Steven W. Congden, *University of Hartford*

Catherine M. Daily, *Ohio State University*

Robert DeFillippi, *Suffolk University Sawyer School of Management*

Helen Deresky, *SUNY—Plattsburgh*

Fred J. Dorn, *University of Mississippi*

Gerald E. Evans, *The University of Montana*

John Fahy, *Trinity College, Dublin*

Patricia Feltes, *Southwest Missouri State University*

Bruce Fern, *New York University*

Mark Fiegener, *Oregon State University*

Chuck Foley, *Columbus State Community College*

Isaac Fox, *Washington State University*

Craig Galbraith, *University of North Carolina at Wilmington*

Scott R. Gallagher, *Rutgers University*

Eliezer Geisler, *Northeastern Illinois University*

Gretchen Gemeinhardt, *University of Houston*

Lynn Godkin, *Lamar University*

Sanjay Goel, *University of Minnesota—Duluth*

Robert L. Goldberg, *Northeastern University*

James Grinnell, *Merrimack College*

Russ Hagberg, *Northern Illinois University*

Allen Harmon, *University of Minnesota—Duluth*

Ramon Henson, *Rutgers University*

David Hoopes, *California State University—Dominguez Hills*

Todd Hostager, *University of Wisconsin—Eau Claire*

David Hover, *San Jose State University*

Graham L. Hubbard, *University of Minnesota*

Miriam Huddleston, *Harford Community College*

Tammy G. Hunt, *University of North Carolina at Wilmington*

James Gaius Ibe, *Morris College*

W. Grahm Irwin, *Miami University*

Homer Johnson, *Loyola University—Chicago*

Jonathan L. Johnson, *University of Arkansas Walton College of Business Administration*

Marios Katsioloudes, *St. Joseph's University*

Robert Keating, *University of North Carolina at Wilmington*

Geoffrey King, *California State University—Fullerton*

Rico Lam, *University of Oregon*

Robert J. Litschert, *Virginia Polytechnic Institute and State University*

Franz T. Lohrke, *Louisiana State University*

Paul Mallette, *Colorado State University*

Daniel Marrone, *SUNY Farmingdale*

Lance A. Masters, *California State University—San Bernardino*

Robert N. McGrath, *Embry-Riddle Aeronautical University*

Charles Mercer, *Drury College*

Van Miller, *University of Dayton*

Debi Mishra, *Binghamton University*

Tom Morris, *University of San Diego*

Joanna Mulholland, *West Chester University of Pennsylvania*

James Muraski, *Marquette University*
John Nebeck, *Viterbo University*
Jeryl L. Nelson, *Wayne State College*
Louise Nemanich, *Arizona State University*
Francine Newth, *Providence College*
Don Okhomina, *Fayetteville State University*
Phaedon P. Papadopoulos, *Houston Baptist University*
John Pappalardo, *Keen State College*
Paul R. Reed, *Sam Houston State University*
Rhonda K. Reger, *Arizona State University*
Malika Richards, *Indiana University*
Simon Rodan, *San Jose State*
Stuart Rosenberg, *Dowling College*
Douglas Ross, *Towson University*
Ronald Sanchez, *University of Illinois*
Joseph A. Schenk, *University of Dayton*
Brian Shaffer, *University of Kentucky*
Leonard Sholtis, *Eastern Michigan University*
Pradip K. Shukla, *Chapman University*
Mel Sillmon, *University of Michigan—Dearborn*
Dennis L. Smart, *University of Nebraska at Omaha*
Barbara Spencer, *Clemson University*
Lawrence Steenberg, *University of Evansville*
Kim A. Stewart, *University of Denver*
Ted Takamura, *Warner Pacific College*
Scott Taylor, *Florida Metropolitan University*
Thuhang Tran, *Middle Tennessee University*
Bobby Vaught, *Southwest Missouri State*
Robert P. Vichas, *Florida Atlantic University*
John Vitton, *University of North Dakota*
Edward Ward, *St. Cloud State University*
Kenneth Wendeln, *Indiana University*
Daniel L. White, *Drexel University*
Edgar L. Williams, Jr., *Norfolk State University*
Donald Wilson, *Rochester Institute of Technology*
Jun Zhao, *Governors State University*

Charles W. L. Hill
Melissa A. Schilling
Gareth R. Jones

DEDICATION

To my daughters Elizabeth, Charlotte, and Michelle

— Charles W. L. Hill

For my children, Julia and Conor

— Melissa A. Schilling

For Nicholas and Julia and Morgan and Nia

— Gareth R. Jones

PART 1

INTRODUCTION TO STRATEGIC MANAGEMENT

Photomax/Shutterstock.com

CHAPTER 1

STRATEGIC LEADERSHIP: MANAGING THE STRATEGY-MAKING PROCESS FOR COMPETITIVE ADVANTAGE

1.1 Explain what is meant by "competitive advantage"

1.2 Discuss the strategic role of managers at different levels within an organization

1.3 Identify the primary steps in a strategic planning process

1.4 Discuss the common pitfalls of planning, and how those pitfalls can be avoided

1.5 Outline the cognitive biases that might lead to poor strategic decisions, and explain how these biases can be overcome

1.6 Discuss the role strategic leaders play in the strategy-making process

OPENING CASE

The Rise of Lululemon

In 1998, self-described snowboarder and surfer dude Chip Wilson took his first yoga class. The Vancouver native loved the exercises, but hated doing them in the cotton clothing that was standard yoga wear at the time. For Wilson, who had worked in the sportswear business and had a passion for technical athletic fabrics, wearing cotton clothes to do sweaty, stretchy, power yoga exercises seemed inappropriate. Thus the idea for Lululemon was born.

Wilson's vision was to create high-quality, stylishly designed clothing for yoga and related sports activities using the very best technical fabrics. He built a design team, but outsourced manufacturing to low-cost producers in South East Asia. Rather than selling clothing through existing

iStockphoto/Mlenny

2

retailers, Wilson elected to open his own stores. The idea was to staff the stores with employees who were themselves passionate about exercise, and could act as ambassadors for healthy living through yoga and related sports such as running and cycling.

The first store, opened in Vancouver, Canada, in 2000, quickly became a runaway success, and other stores followed. In 2007, the company went public, using the capital raised to accelerate its expansion plans. By late 2014, Lululemon had over 290 stores, mostly in North America, and sales in excess of $1.7 billion. Sales per square foot were estimated to be around $1,800—more than four times that of an average specialty retailer. Lululemon's financial performance was stellar. Between 2007 and 2104, average return on invested capital—an important measure of profitability—was 31%, far outpacing that of other well-known specialty retailers, while earnings per share grew by a staggering 3,183% (see Table 1.1).

How did Lululemon achieve this? It started with a focus on an unmet consumer need: the latent desire among yoga enthusiasts for high-quality, stylish, technical athletic wear. Getting the product offering right was a central part of the company's strategy. An equally important part of the strategy was to stock a limited supply of an item. New colors and seasonal items, for example, get a 3- to 12-week lifecycle, which keeps the product offerings feeling fresh. The goal is to sell gear at full price, and to condition customers to buy it when they see it, rather than wait, because if they do it may soon be "out of stock." The company only allows product returns if the clothes have not been worn and still have the price tags attached. The scarcity strategy has worked. Lululemon never holds sales, and its clothing sells for a premium price. For example, its yoga pants are priced from $78 to $128 a pair, whereas low-priced competitors like Gap Inc.'s Athleta sell yoga pants on their websites for $25 to $50.

To create the right in-store service, Lululemon hires employees who are passionate about fitness. Part of the hiring process involves taking prospective employees to a yoga or spin class. Some 70% of store managers are internal hires; most started on the sales floor and grew up in the culture. Store managers are given funds to repaint their stores, any color, twice a year. The interior design of each store is largely up to its manager. Each store is also given $2,700 a year for employees to contribute to a charity or local event of their own choosing. One store manager in Washington, D.C., used the funds to create, with regional community leaders, a global yoga event in 2010. The result, Salutation Nation, is now an annual event in which over 70 Lululemon stores host a free, all-level yoga practice at the same time.

Employees are trained to eavesdrop on customers, who are called "guests." Clothes-folding tables are placed on the sales floor near the fitting rooms rather than in a back room so that employees can overhear complaints. Nearby, a large chalkboard lets customers write suggestions or complaints that are sent back to headquarters. This feedback is then incorporated into the product design process.

Table 1.1 Lululemon's Financial Performance

	Lululemon	Gap Inc.	Urban Outfitters	Abercrombie & Fitch
Average ROIC 2007–2014	31%	21%	19%	14%
EPS Growth 2007–2014	3183%	295%	274%	15%

Despite the company's focus on providing a quality product, it has not all been clear sailing. In 2010, Wilson caused a stir when he emblazoned the company's tote bags with the phrase "Who is John Galt?" the opening line from Ayn Rand's 1957 novel, *Atlas Shrugged*. *Atlas Shrugged* has become a libertarian bible, and the underlying message that Lululemon supported Rand's brand of unregulated capitalism did not sit well with many of the stores' customers. After negative feedback, the bags were quickly pulled from stores. Wilson himself stepped down from day-to-day involvement in the company in January 2012 and resigned his chairman position in 2014.

In early 2013, Lululemon found itself dealing with another controversy when it decided to recall black yoga pants that were too sheer, and effectively "see through," when stretched due to the lack of "rear-end coverage." In addition to the negative fallout from the product itself, some customers report being mistreated by employees who demanded that customers put the pants on and bend over to determine whether the clothing was see-through enough to warrant a refund. One consequence of this PR disaster was the resignation of then CEO Christine Day. The company is also facing increasing competition from rivals such as Gap's Athleta Urban Outfitters' Without Walls, and Nike Stores. Notwithstanding these challenges, most observers in the media and financial community believe that the company can handle these issues and should be able to continue on its growth trajectory.

Sources: D. Mattoili, "Lululemon's Secret Sauce," *The Wall Street Journal*, March 22, 2012; C. Leahey, "Lululemon CEO: How to Build Trust Inside Your Company," *CNN Money*, March 16, 2012; T. Hsu, "'Pantsgate' to Hurt Lululemon Profit: Customer Told to Bend Over," *latimes.com*, March 21, 2013; C. O'Commor, "Billionaire Founder Chip Wilson Out at Yoga Giant Lululemon," *Forbes*, January 9, 2012; B. Weishaar, "No-moat Lululemon faces increasing competition but is regaining its customer base," *Morningstar*, December 17, 2014.

◤ OVERVIEW

Why do some companies succeed, whereas others fail? Why has Lululemon been able to persistently outperform most other specialty retailers? In the airline industry, how has Southwest Airlines managed to keep increasing its revenues and profits through both good times and bad, whereas rivals such as United Airlines have had to seek bankruptcy protection? What explains the persistent growth and profitability of Nucor Steel, now the largest steelmaker in the United States, during a period when many of its once-larger rivals disappeared into bankruptcy?

In this book, we argue that the strategies that a company's managers pursue have a major impact on the company's performance relative to that of its competitors. A **strategy** is a set of related actions that managers take to increase their company's performance. For most, if not all, companies, achieving superior performance relative to rivals is the ultimate challenge. If a company's strategies result in superior performance, it is said to have a competitive advantage.

Lululemon's strategies produced superior performance from 2007 to 2014; as a result, Lululemon enjoyed a competitive advantage that was translated into stellar financial performance. As described in the Opening Case, Lululemon's strategies included

strategy
A set of related actions that managers take to increase their company's performance.

focusing on a market niche where there was an unmet need for stylish, well-designed, high-quality athletic wear, satisfying that need through excellence in product design, and managing product inventory to limit supply, spur impulse purchases, and keep prices high. Lululemon's founder, Chip Wilson, clearly had a compelling strategic vision, and that vision was well executed.

This book identifies and describes the strategies that managers can pursue to achieve superior performance and provide their companies with a competitive advantage. One of its central aims is to give you a thorough understanding of the analytical techniques and skills necessary to formulate and implement strategies successfully. The first step toward achieving this objective is to describe in more detail what superior performance and competitive advantage mean and to explain the pivotal role that managers play in leading the strategy-making process.

Strategic leadership is about how to most effectively manage a company's strategy-making process to create competitive advantage. The strategy-making process is the process by which managers select and then implement a set of strategies that aim to achieve a competitive advantage. **Strategy formulation** is the task of selecting strategies. **Strategy implementation** is the task of putting strategies into action, which includes designing, delivering, and supporting products; improving the efficiency and effectiveness of operations; and designing a company's organizational structure, control systems, and culture. Lululemon was successful not just because managers formulated a viable strategy, but because that strategy was for the most part very well implemented.

By the end of this chapter, you will understand how strategic leaders can manage the strategy-making process by formulating and implementing strategies that enable a company to achieve a competitive advantage and superior performance. Moreover, you will learn how the strategy-making process can sometimes go wrong, as it did at one point for Lululemon, and what managers can do to make this process more effective.

strategic leadership
Creating competitive advantage through effective management of the strategy-making process.

strategy formulation
Selecting strategies based on analysis of an organization's external and internal environment.

strategy implementation
Putting strategies into action.

STRATEGIC LEADERSHIP, COMPETITIVE ADVANTAGE, AND SUPERIOR PERFORMANCE

Strategic leadership is concerned with managing the strategy-making process to increase the performance of a company, thereby increasing the value of the enterprise to its owners, its shareholders. As shown in Figure 1.1, to increase shareholder value, managers must pursue strategies that increase the profitability of the company and ensure that profits grow (for more details, see the Appendix to this chapter). To do this, a company must be able to outperform its rivals; it must have a competitive advantage.

Superior Performance

Maximizing shareholder value is the ultimate goal of profit-making companies, for two reasons. First, shareholders provide a company with the risk capital that enables managers to buy the resources needed to produce and sell goods and services. **Risk capital** is capital that cannot be recovered if a company fails and goes bankrupt. For

risk capital
Equity capital invested with no guarantee that stockholders will recoup their cash or earn a decent return.

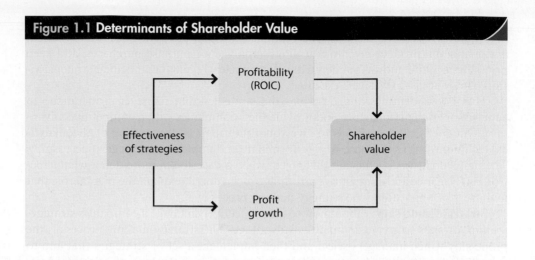

Figure 1.1 Determinants of Shareholder Value

example, when Lululemon went public in 2007, shareholders provided Chip Wilson's company with capital it used to build out its network of stores. Had Lululemon failed to execute, its shareholders would have lost their money—their shares would have been worthless. Thus, shareholders will not provide risk capital unless they believe that managers are committed to pursuing strategies that provide a good return on their capital investment. Second, shareholders are the legal owners of a corporation, and their shares therefore represent a claim on the profits generated by a company. Thus, managers have an obligation to invest those profits in ways that maximize shareholder value.

That being said, as explained later in this book, managers must behave in a legal, ethical, and socially responsible manner while working to maximize shareholder value. Moreover, as we shall see, there is good evidence that the best way to maximize the *long-run* return to shareholders is to focus on customers and employees. Satisfying customer needs, and making sure that employees are fairly treated and work productively, typically translates into better financial performance and superior long-run returns for shareholders. Alternatively, ignoring customer needs, and treating employees unfairly, may boost short-run profits and returns to shareholders, but it will also damage the long-run viability of the enterprise and ultimately depress shareholder value. This is why many successful managers argue that if a company focuses on its customers, and creates incentives for its employees to work productivity, shareholder returns will take care of themselves.

shareholder value
Returns that shareholders earn from purchasing shares in a company.

By **shareholder value**, we mean the returns that shareholders earn from purchasing shares in a company. These returns come from two sources: (a) capital appreciation in the value of a company's shares and (b) dividend payments. For example, during 2014 a share of Microsoft increased in price from $37.35 to $46.73. Each share of Microsoft also paid a dividend of $1.15 to its owners during 2014. Thus, in 2014, shareholders in Microsoft earned a return of 28.2%, 25.1% of which came from capital appreciation in the value of the share and 3.1% of which came in the form of a dividend payout.

profitability
The return a company makes on the capital invested in the enterprise.

One way to measure the **profitability** of a company is by its return on the capital invested in the enterprise.[1] The return on invested capital (ROIC) that a company earns is defined as its net profit over the capital invested in the firm (profit/capital invested). By net profit, we mean net income after tax. By capital, we mean the sum of money invested in the company: that is, stockholders' equity plus debt owed to creditors. So defined, *profitability is the result of how efficiently and effectively managers use the capital at their disposal to produce goods and services that satisfy customer needs.* A company that uses its capital efficiently and effectively makes a positive return on invested capital. Between 2007 and 2014, Lululemon earned an average **return on invested capital** (ROIC) of 31%, far above that of most other specialty retailers, which indicated that its strategies resulted in the very efficient and effective use of its capital.

A company's **profit growth** can be measured by the increase in net profit over time. A company can grow its profits if it sells products in rapidly growing markets, gains market share from rivals, increases sales to existing customers, expands overseas, or diversifies profitably into new lines of business. For example, between 2007 and 2012, Lululemon increased its net profits from $8 million to $280 million by rapidly growing the market for high-end, yoga-inspired clothing. Due to its dramatic profit growth, Lululemon's earnings per share increased from $0.06 to $1.91 over this period, resulting in appreciation in the value of each share in Lululemon.

profit growth
The increase in net profit over time.

Together, profitability and profit growth are the principal drivers of shareholder value (see the Appendix to this chapter for details). *To both boost profitability and grow profits over time, managers must formulate and implement strategies that give their company a competitive advantage over rivals.* This is what Lululemon achieved between 2007 and 2014. As a result, investors who purchased Lululemon shares on July 27, 2007, when it went public, and held on to them until December 31, 2014, saw the value of their shares increase from $14 to $55.79, a capital appreciation of almost 400%. By pursuing strategies that lead to high, sustained profitability and profit growth, Lululemon's managers rewarded shareholders for their decision to invest in the company.

One key challenge managers face is how best to simultaneously generate high profitability and increase profits. Companies that have high profitability but no profit growth will often be less valued by shareholders than companies that have both high profitability and rapid profit growth (see the Appendix for details). At the same time, managers need to be aware that if they grow profits but profitability declines, that too will be less highly valued by shareholders. What shareholders want to see, and what managers must try to deliver through strategic leadership, is *profitable growth*: that is, high profitability and sustainable profit growth. This is not easy, but some of the most successful enterprises of our era have achieved it—companies such as Apple, Google, and Lululemon.

Competitive Advantage and a Company's Business Model

Managers do not make strategic decisions in a competitive vacuum. Their company is competing against other companies for customers. Competition is a rough-and-tumble process in which only the most efficient, effective companies win out. It is a race without end. To maximize long-run shareholder value, managers must formulate and implement strategies that enable their company to outperform rivals—that give it a competitive advantage. A company is said to have a **competitive advantage** over its rivals when its profitability and profit growth are greater than the average of other companies competing for the same set of customers. The higher its profitability and profit growth relative to rivals, the greater its competitive advantage will be. A company has a **sustained competitive advantage** when its strategies enable it to maintain above-average profitability and profit growth for a number of years. This was the case for Lululemon between 2007 and 2014.

competitive advantage
The achieved advantage over rivals when a company's profitability is greater than the average profitability of firms in its industry.

sustained competitive advantage
A company's strategies enable it to maintain above-average profitability for a number of years.

business model

The conception of how strategies should work together as a whole to enable the company to achieve competitive advantage.

The key to understanding competitive advantage is appreciating how the different strategies managers pursue over time can create activities that fit together to make a company unique and able to consistently outperform them. A **business model** is managers' conception of how the set of strategies their company pursues work together as a congruent whole, enabling the company to gain a competitive advantage and achieve superior profitability and profit growth. In essence, a business model is a kind of mental model, or gestalt, of how the various strategies and capital investments a company makes fit together to generate above-average performance. A business model encompasses the totality of how a company will:

- Select its customers.
- Define and differentiate its product offerings.
- Create value for its customers.
- Acquire and keep customers.
- Produce goods or services.
- Increase productivity and lower costs.
- Deliver goods and services to the market.
- Organize activities within the company.
- Configure its resources.
- Achieve and sustain a high level of profitability.
- Grow the business over time.

The business model at discount stores such as Wal-Mart, for example, is based on the idea that costs can be lowered by replacing a full-service retail format for with a self-service format and a wider selection of products sold in a large-footprint store that contains minimal fixtures and fittings. These savings are passed on to consumers in the form of lower prices, which in turn grow revenues and help the company achieve further cost reductions from economies of scale. Over time, this business model has proved superior to the business models adopted by smaller, full-service, "mom-and-pop" stores, and by traditional, high-service department stores such as Sears. The business model—known as the self-service supermarket business model—was first developed by grocery retailers in the 1950s and later refined and improved on by general merchandisers such as Wal-Mart in the 1960s and 1970s. Subsequently, the same basic business model was applied to toys (Toys "R" Us), office supplies (Staples, Office Depot), and home-improvement supplies (Home Depot and Lowes).

Industry Differences in Performance

It is important to recognize that in addition to its business model and associated strategies, a company's performance is also determined by the characteristics of the industry in which it competes. Different industries are characterized by different competitive conditions. In some industries, demand is growing rapidly, and in others it is contracting. Some industries might be beset by excess capacity and persistent price wars, others by strong demand and rising prices. In some, technological change might be revolutionizing competition; others may be characterized by stable technology. In some industries, high profitability among incumbent companies might induce new companies to enter the industry, and these new entrants might subsequently depress prices and profits in the industry. In other industries, new entry might be difficult, and periods of high profitability might persist for a considerable time.

Thus, the different competitive conditions prevailing in different industries may lead to differences in profitability and profit growth. For example, average profitability might be higher in some industries and lower in other industries because competitive conditions vary from industry to industry.

Figure 1.2 shows the average profitability, measured by ROIC, among companies in several different industries between 2002 and 2011. The computer software industry had a favorable competitive environment: demand for software was high and competition was generally not based on price. Just the opposite was the case in the air transport industry, which was extremely price competitive.

Exactly how industries differ is discussed in detail in Chapter 2. For now, it is important to remember that the profitability and profit growth of a company are determined by two main factors: *its relative success in its industry and the overall performance of its industry relative to other industries.*[2]

Performance in Nonprofit Enterprises

A final point concerns the concept of superior performance in the nonprofit sector. By definition, nonprofit enterprises such as government agencies, universities, and charities are not in "business" to make profits. Nevertheless, they are expected to use their resources efficiently and operate effectively, and their managers set goals to measure their performance. The performance goal for a business school might be to

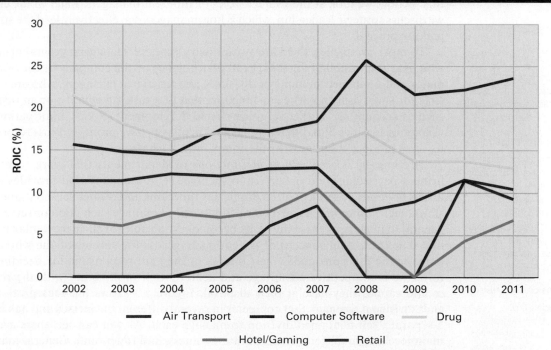

Figure 1.2 Return on Invested Capital (ROIC) in Selected Industries, 2002–2011

Source: Value Line Investment Survey.

get its programs ranked among the best in the nation. The performance goal for a charity might be to prevent childhood illnesses in poor countries. The performance goal for a government agency might be to improve its services while reducing its need for taxpayer funds. The managers of nonprofits need to map out strategies to attain these goals. They also need to understand that nonprofits compete with each other for scarce resources, just as businesses do. For example, charities compete for scarce donations, and their managers must plan and develop strategies that lead to high performance and demonstrate a track record of meeting performance goals. A successful strategy gives potential donors a compelling message about why they should contribute additional donations. Thus, planning and thinking strategically are as important for managers in the nonprofit sector as they are for managers in profit-seeking firms.

◢ STRATEGIC MANAGERS

Managers are the linchpin in the strategy-making process. Individual managers must take responsibility for formulating strategies to attain a competitive advantage and for putting those strategies into effect through implementation. They must lead the strategy-making process. The strategies that made Lululemon so successful were not chosen by some abstract entity known as "the company"; they were chosen by the company's founder, Chip Wilson, and the managers he hired. Lululemon's success was largely based on how well the company's managers performed their strategic roles. In this section, we look at the strategic roles of different managers. Later in the chapter, we discuss strategic leadership, which is how managers can effectively lead the strategy-making process.

general managers

Managers who bear responsibility for the overall performance of the company or for one of its major self-contained subunits or divisions.

functional managers

Managers responsible for supervising a particular function, that is, a task, activity, or operation, such as accounting, marketing, research and development (R&D), information technology, or logistics.

multidivisional company

A company that competes in several different businesses and has created a separate, self-contained division to manage each.

In most companies, there are two primary types of managers: **general managers**, who bear responsibility for the overall performance of the company or for one of its major, self-contained subunits or divisions, and **functional managers**, who are responsible for supervising a particular function; that is, a task, an activity, or an operation such as accounting, marketing, research and development (R&D), information technology, or logistics. Put differently, general managers have profit-and-loss responsibility for a product, a business, or the company as a whole.

A company is a collection of functions or departments that work together to bring a particular good or service to the market. A company that provides several different goods or services often duplicates functions and creates self-contained divisions (each containing its own set of functions) to manage each good or service. The general managers of these divisions become responsible for their particular product line. The overriding concern of general managers is the success of the whole company or the divisions under their direction; they are responsible for deciding how to create a competitive advantage and achieve high profitability with the resources and capital they have at their disposal. Figure 1.3 shows the organization of a **multidivisional company** that competes in several different businesses and has created a separate, self-contained division to manage each. As you can see, there are three main levels of management: corporate, business, and functional. General managers are found at the first two of these levels, but their strategic roles differ depending on their sphere of responsibility.

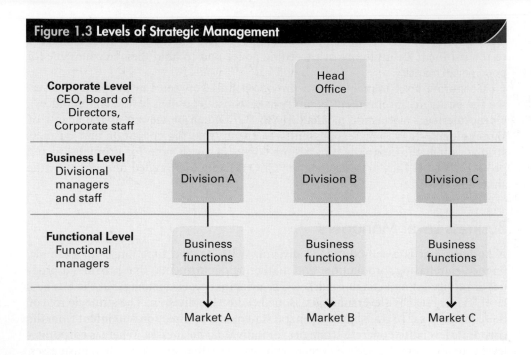

Figure 1.3 Levels of Strategic Management

Corporate Level
CEO, Board of Directors, Corporate staff

Head Office

Business Level
Divisional managers and staff

Division A   Division B   Division C

Functional Level
Functional managers

Business functions   Business functions   Business functions

Market A   Market B   Market C

Corporate-Level Managers

The corporate level of management consists of the chief executive officer (CEO), other senior executives, and corporate staff. These individuals occupy the apex of decision making within the organization. The CEO is the principal general manager. In consultation with other senior executives, the role of corporate-level managers is to oversee the development of strategies for the whole organization. This role includes defining the goals of the organization, determining what businesses it should be in, allocating resources among the different businesses, formulating and implementing strategies that span individual businesses, and providing leadership for the entire organization.

Consider General Electric (GE) as an example. GE is active in a wide range of businesses, including lighting equipment, motor and transportation equipment, turbine generators, construction and engineering services, industrial electronics, medical systems, aerospace, aircraft engines, and financial services. The main strategic responsibilities of its CEO, Jeffrey Immelt, are setting overall strategic goals, allocating resources among the different business areas, deciding whether the firm should divest itself of any of its businesses, and determining whether it should acquire any new ones. In other words, it is up to Immelt to develop strategies that span individual businesses; his concern is with building and managing the corporate portfolio of businesses to maximize corporate profitability.

It is not the CEO's (in this example, Immelt's) specific responsibility to develop strategies for competing in individual business areas such as financial services. The development of such strategies is the responsibility of the general managers in these different businesses, or business-level managers. However, it is Immelt's responsibility to probe the strategic thinking of business-level managers to make sure that

they are pursuing robust business models and strategies that will contribute to the maximization of GE's long-run profitability, to coach and motivate those managers, to reward them for attaining or exceeding goals, and to hold them accountable for poor performance.

Corporate-level managers also provide a link between the people who oversee the strategic development of a firm and those who own it (the shareholders). Corporate-level managers, particularly the CEO, can be viewed as the agents of shareholders.[3] It is their responsibility to ensure that the corporate and business strategies that the company pursues are consistent with superior profitability and profit growth. If they are not, then the CEO is likely to be called to account by the shareholders.

Business-Level Managers

business unit

A self-contained division that provides a product or service for a particular market.

A **business unit** is a self-contained division (with its own functions—for example, finance, purchasing, production, and marketing departments) that provides a product or service for a particular market. The principal general manager at the business level, or the business-level manager, is the head of the division. The strategic role of these managers is to translate the general statements of direction and intent from the corporate level into concrete strategies for individual businesses. Whereas corporate-level general managers are concerned with strategies that span individual businesses, business-level general managers are concerned with strategies that are specific to a particular business. At GE, a major corporate goal is to be a market leader in every business in which the corporation competes. The general managers in each division work out for their business the details of a business model that is consistent with this objective.

Functional-Level Managers

Functional-level managers are responsible for the specific business functions or operations (human resources, purchasing, product development, logistics, production, customer service, and so on) found within a company or one of its divisions. Thus, a functional manager's sphere of responsibility is generally confined to one organizational activity, whereas general managers oversee the operation of an entire company or division. Although they are not responsible for the overall performance of the organization, functional managers nevertheless have a major strategic role: to develop functional strategies in their areas that help fulfill the strategic objectives set by business- and corporate-level general managers.

In GE's aerospace business, for instance, production managers are responsible for developing manufacturing strategies consistent with corporate objectives. Moreover, functional managers provide most of the information that makes it possible for business- and corporate-level general managers to formulate realistic and attainable strategies. Indeed, because they are closer to the customer than is the typical general manager, functional managers may generate important ideas that subsequently become major strategies for the company. Thus, it is important for general managers to listen closely to the ideas of their functional managers. An equally great responsibility for managers at the operational level is strategy implementation: the execution of corporate- and business-level plans.

▼ THE STRATEGY-MAKING PROCESS

We can now turn our attention to the process by which managers formulate and implement strategies. Many writers have emphasized that strategy is the outcome of a formal planning process and that top management plays the most important role in this process.[4] Although this view has some basis in reality, it is not the whole story. As we shall see later in the chapter, valuable strategies often emerge from deep within the organization without prior planning. Nevertheless, a consideration of formal, rational planning is a useful starting point for our journey into the world of strategy. Accordingly, we consider what might be described as a typical, formal strategic planning model.

A Model of the Strategic Planning Process

The formal strategic planning process has five main steps:

1. Select the corporate mission and major corporate goals.
2. Analyze the organization's external competitive environment to identify opportunities and threats.
3. Analyze the organization's internal operating environment to identify the organization's strengths and weaknesses.
4. Select strategies that build on the organization's strengths and correct its weaknesses in order to take advantage of external opportunities and counter external threats. These strategies should be consistent with the mission and major goals of the organization. They should be congruent and constitute a viable business model.
5. Implement the strategies.

The task of analyzing the organization's external and internal environments and then selecting appropriate strategies constitutes strategy formulation. In contrast, as noted earlier, strategy implementation involves putting the strategies (or plan) into action. This includes taking actions consistent with the selected strategies of the company at the corporate, business, and functional levels; allocating roles and responsibilities among managers (typically through the design of organizational structure); allocating resources (including capital and money); setting short-term objectives; and designing the organization's control and reward systems. These steps are illustrated in Figure 1.4 (which can also serve as a roadmap for the rest of this book).

Each step in Figure 1.4 constitutes a sequential step in the strategic planning process. At step 1, each round, or cycle, of the planning process begins with a statement of the corporate mission and major corporate goals. The mission statement is followed by the foundation of strategic thinking: external analysis, internal analysis, and strategic choice. The strategy-making process ends with the design of the organizational structure and the culture and control systems necessary to implement the organization's chosen strategy. This chapter discusses how to select a corporate mission and choose major goals. Other aspects of strategic planning are reserved for later chapters, as indicated in Figure 1.4.

Some organizations go through a new cycle of the strategic planning process every year. This does not necessarily mean that managers choose a new strategy each year. In many instances, the result is simply to modify and reaffirm a strategy and structure already in place. The strategic plans generated by the planning process generally

Figure 1.4 Main Components of the Strategic Planning Process

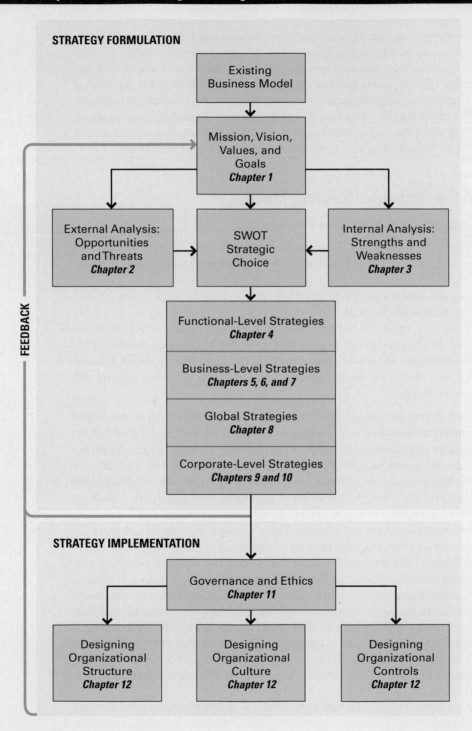

project over a period of 1 to 5 years, and the plan is updated, or rolled forward, every year. The results of the annual strategic planning process should be used as input into the budgetary process for the coming year so that strategic planning shapes resource allocation within the organization.

Mission Statement

The first component of the strategic management process is crafting the organization's mission statement, which provides the framework—or context—within which strategies are formulated. A mission statement has four main components: a statement of the organization's reason for existence—normally referred to as the mission; a statement of some desired future state, usually referred to as the vision; a statement of the key values to which the organization is committed; and a statement of major goals.

The Mission   A company's **mission** describes what the company does. For example, the mission of Google is *to organize the world's information and make it universally accessible and useful*.[5] Google's search engine is the method that is employed to "organize the world's information and make it accessible and useful." In the view of Google's founders, Larry Page and Sergey Brin, information includes not just text on websites, but also images, video, maps, products, news, books, blogs, and much more. You can search through all of these information sources using Google's search engine.

According to the late Peter Drucker, an important first step in the process of formulating a mission is to come up with a definition of the organization's business. Essentially, the definition answers these questions: "What is our business? What will it be? What should it be?"[6] The responses to these questions guide the formulation of the mission. To answer the question, "What is our business?" a company should define its business in terms of three dimensions: who is being satisfied (what customer groups), what is being satisfied (what customer needs), and how customers' needs are being satisfied (by what skills, knowledge, or distinctive competencies).[7] Figure 1.5 illustrates these dimensions.

This approach stresses the need for a *customer-oriented* rather than a *product-oriented* business definition. A product-oriented business definition focuses on the characteristics of the products sold and the markets served, not on the customer needs the products satisfy. Such an approach obscures the company's true mission, because a product is only the physical manifestation of applying a particular skill to satisfy a particular need for a particular customer group. In practice, that need may be served in many different ways, and a broad, customer-oriented business definition that identifies these ways can safeguard companies from being caught unaware by major shifts in demand.

Google's mission statement is customer oriented. Google's product is search. Its production technology involves the development of complex search algorithms and vast databases that archive information. But Google does not define its self as a search engine company. Rather, it sees itself as organizing information to make it accessible and useful *to customers*.

The need to take a customer-oriented view has often been ignored. History is peppered with the ghosts of once-great corporations that did not define their businesses, or defined them incorrectly, and so ultimately declined. In the 1950s and 1960s, many office equipment companies such as Smith Corona and Underwood defined their businesses as being the production of typewriters. This product-oriented definition ignored the fact that they were really in the business of satisfying customers' needs

mission
The purpose of the company, or a statement of what the company strives to do.

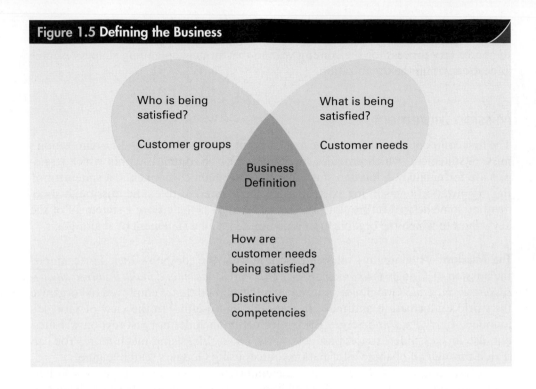

Figure 1.5 Defining the Business

Who is being satisfied?

Customer groups

What is being satisfied?

Customer needs

Business Definition

How are customer needs being satisfied?

Distinctive competencies

for information processing. Unfortunately for those companies, when a new form of technology appeared that better served customer needs for information processing (computers), demand for typewriters plummeted. The last great typewriter company, Smith Corona, went bankrupt in 1996, a victim of the success of computer-based word-processing technology.

In contrast, IBM correctly foresaw what its business would be. In the 1950s, IBM was a leader in the manufacture of typewriters and mechanical tabulating equipment using punchcard technology. However, unlike many of its competitors, IBM defined its business as providing a means for *information processing and storage*, rather than only supplying mechanical tabulating equipment and typewriters.[8] Given this definition, the company's subsequent moves into computers, software systems, office systems, and printers seem logical.

vision

The articulation of a company's desired achievements or future state.

Vision   The **vision** of a company defines a desired future state; it articulates, often in bold terms, what the company would like to achieve. In its early days, Microsoft operated with a very powerful vision of a computer on every desk and in every home. To turn this vision into a reality, Microsoft focused on producing computer software that was cheap and useful to business and consumers. In turn, the availability of powerful, inexpensive software such as Windows and Office helped to drive the penetration of personal computers into homes and offices.

values

A statement of how employees should conduct themselves and their business to help achieve the company mission.

Values   The **values** of a company state how managers and employees should conduct themselves, how they should do business, and what kind of organization they should build. Insofar as they help drive and shape behavior within a company, values are commonly seen as the bedrock of a company's organizational culture: the set of values, norms, and standards that control how employees work to achieve an organization's mission and goals. An organization's culture is commonly seen as an important source of its competitive advantage.[9] (We discuss the issue of organizational culture in depth in Chapter 12.) For example, Nucor Steel is one of the most productive and profitable steel firms in the world. Its competitive advantage is based, in part, on the extremely high productivity of its workforce, which the company maintains is a direct result of its cultural values, which in turn determine how it treats its employees. These values are as follows:

- "Management is obligated to manage Nucor in such a way that employees will have the opportunity to earn according to their productivity."
- "Employees should be able to feel confident that if they do their jobs properly, they will have a job tomorrow."
- "Employees have the right to be treated fairly and must believe that they will be."
- "Employees must have an avenue of appeal when they believe they are being treated unfairly."[10]

At Nucor, values emphasizing pay for performance, job security, and fair treatment for employees help to create an atmosphere within the company that leads to high employee productivity. In turn, this has helped Nucor achieve one of the lowest cost structures in its industry, and it helps to explain the company's profitability in a very price-competitive business.

In one study of organizational values, researchers identified a set of values associated with high-performing organizations that help companies achieve superior financial performance through their impact on employee behavior.[11] These values included respect for the interests of key organizational stakeholders: individuals or groups that have an interest, claim, or stake in the company, in what it does, and in how well it performs.[12] They include stockholders, bondholders, employees, customers, the communities in which the company does business, and the general public. The study found that deep respect for the interests of customers, employees, suppliers, and shareholders was associated with high performance. The study also noted that the encouragement of leadership and entrepreneurial behavior by mid- and lower-level managers and a willingness to support change efforts within the organization contributed to high performance. The same study identified the attributes of poorly performing companies—as might be expected, these are not articulated in company mission statements: (1) arrogance, particularly in response to ideas from outside the company; (2) lack of respect for key stakeholders; and (3) a history of resisting change efforts and "punishing" mid- and lower-level managers who showed "too much leadership."

◤ MAJOR GOALS

Having stated the mission, vision, and key values, strategic managers can take the next step in the formulation of a mission statement: establishing major goals. A goal is a precise, measurable, desired future state that a company attempts to realize. In this context, the purpose of goals is to specify with precision what must be done if the company is to attain its mission or vision.

Well-constructed goals have four main characteristics:[13]

- They are precise and measurable. Measurable goals give managers a yardstick or standard against which they can judge their performance.
- They address crucial issues. To maintain focus, managers should select a limited number of major goals to assess the performance of the company. The goals that are selected should be crucial or important ones.
- They are challenging but realistic. They give all employees an incentive to look for ways of improving the operations of an organization. If a goal is unrealistic in the challenges it poses, employees may give up; a goal that is too easy may fail to motivate managers and other employees.[14]
- They specify a time period in which the goals should be achieved, when that is appropriate. Time constraints tell employees that success requires a goal to be attained by a given date, not after that date. Deadlines can inject a sense of urgency into goal attainment and act as a motivator. However, not all goals require time constraints.

Well-constructed goals also provide a means by which the performance of managers can be evaluated.

As noted earlier, although most companies operate with a variety of goals, the primary goal of most corporations is to maximize shareholder returns, and doing this requires both high profitability and sustained profit growth. Thus, most companies operate with goals for profitability and profit growth. However, it is important that top managers do not make the mistake of overemphasizing current profitability to the detriment of long-term profitability and profit growth.[15] The overzealous pursuit of current profitability to maximize short-term ROIC can encourage such misguided managerial actions as cutting expenditures judged to be nonessential in the short run—for instance, expenditures for research and development, marketing, and new capital investments. Although cutting current expenditures increases current profitability, the resulting underinvestment, lack of innovation, and diminished marketing can jeopardize long-run profitability and profit growth.

To guard against short-run decision making, managers need to ensure that they adopt goals whose attainment will increase the long-run performance and competitiveness of their enterprise. Long-term goals are related to such issues as product development, customer satisfaction, and efficiency, and they emphasize specific objectives or targets concerning such details as employee and capital productivity, product quality, innovation, customer satisfaction, and customer service.

External Analysis

The second component of the strategic management process is an analysis of the organization's external operating environment. The essential purpose of the external analysis is to identify strategic opportunities and threats within the organization's operating environment that will affect how it pursues its mission. Strategy in Action 1.1 describes how an analysis of opportunities and threats in the external environment led to a strategic shift at Time Inc.

Three interrelated environments should be examined when undertaking an external analysis: the industry environment in which the company operates, the country or national environment, and the wider socioeconomic or macroenvironment. Analyzing

1.1 STRATEGY IN ACTION

Strategic Analysis at Time Inc.

Time Inc., the magazine publishing division of media conglomerate Time Warner, has a venerable history. Its magazine titles include *Time*, *Fortune*, *Sports Illustrated*, and *People*, all long-time leaders in their respective categories. By the mid-2000s, however, Time Inc. was confronted with declining subscription rates.

An external analysis revealed what was happening. The readership of Time's magazines was aging. Increasingly, younger readers were getting what they wanted from the Web. This was both a *threat* for Time Inc., as its Web offerings were not strong, and an *opportunity*, because with the right offerings, Time Inc. could capture this audience. Time also realized that advertising dollars were migrating rapidly to the Web, and if the company was going to maintain its share, its Web offerings had to be every bit as good as its print offerings.

An internal analysis revealed why, despite multiple attempts, Time had failed to capitalize on the opportunities offered by the emergence of the Web. Although Time had tremendous *strengths*, including powerful brands and strong reporting, development of its Web offerings had been hindered by a serious *weakness*— an editorial culture that regarded Web publishing as a backwater. At *People*, for example, the online operation used to be "like a distant moon," according to managing editor Martha Nelson. Managers at Time Inc. had also been worried that Web offerings would cannibalize print offerings and accelerate the decline in the circulation of magazines, with dire financial consequences for the company. As a result of this culture, efforts to move publications onto the Web were underfunded or were stymied entirely by a lack of management attention and commitment.

Martha Nelson showed the way forward for the company. Her *strategy* for overcoming the *weakness* at Time Inc., and better exploiting *opportunities* on the Web, started in 2003 with merging the print and online newsrooms at *People*, removing the distinction between them. Then, she relaunched the magazine's online site, made major editorial commitments to Web publishing, stated that original content should appear on the Web, and emphasized the importance of driving traffic to the site and earning advertising revenues. Over the next 2 years, page views at People.com increased fivefold.

Ann Moore, then the CEO at Time Inc., formalized this strategy in 2005, mandating that all print offerings should follow the lead of People.com, integrating print and online newsrooms and investing significantly more resources in Web publishing. To drive this initiative home, Time hired several well-known bloggers to write for its online publications. The goal of Moore's strategy was to neutralize the cultural *weakness* that had hindered online efforts in the past and to redirect resources to Web publishing.

In 2006, Time made another strategic move designed to exploit the opportunities associated with the Web. It partnered with the 24-hour news channel CNN to put all of its financial magazines onto a jointly owned site, CNNMoney .com. The site, which offers free access to *Fortune*, *Money*, and *Business 2.0*, quickly took the third spot in online financial websites, behind Yahoo Finance and MSN. This was followed with a redesigned website for *Sports Illustrated* that has rolled out video downloads for iPods and mobile phones.

In 2007, to further its shift to Web-centric publishing, Time Inc. announced another change in strategy: It would sell off 18 magazine titles that, although good performers, did not appear to have much traction on the Web.

Also in 2007, Ann Moore stated that, going forward, Time Inc. would focus its energy, resources, and investments on the company's largest, most profitable brands, those that have demonstrated an ability to draw large audiences in digital form. Since then, the big push has been to develop magazine apps for tablet computers, most notably Apple's iPad and tablets that use the Android operating system.

(continued)

By early 2012, Time Inc. had its entire magazine catalog on every major tablet platform. As of 2014, revenues from digital editions were growing rapidly, while print subscriptions were in a secular decline, which underlined the wisdom of Moore's digitalization strategy.

Sources: A. Van Duyn, "Time Inc. Revamp to Include Sale of 18 Titles," *Financial Times* (September 13, 2006): 24; M. Karnitsching, "Time Inc. Makes New Bid to Be Big Web Player," *The Wall Street Journal* (March 29, 2006): B1; M. Flamm, "Time Tries the Web Again," *Crain's New York Business* (January 16, 2006): 3; T. Carmody, "Time Warner Bringing Digital Magazines, HBO to More Platforms," *Wired* (July 3, 2011); "Time Inc. Q3 2014 Review: Digitalization Underway," Seeking Alpha, November 5, 2014; http://seekingalpha.com/.

the industry environment requires an assessment of the competitive structure of the company's industry, including the competitive position of the company and its major rivals. It also requires analysis of the nature, stage, dynamics, and history of the industry. Because many markets are now global, analyzing the industry environment also means assessing the impact of globalization on competition within an industry. Such an analysis may reveal that a company should move some production facilities to another nation, that it should aggressively expand in emerging markets such as China, or that it should beware of new competition from emerging nations. Analyzing the macroenvironment consists of examining macroeconomic, social, governmental, legal, international, and technological factors that may affect the company and its industry. We look at external analysis in Chapter 2.

Internal Analysis

Internal analysis, the third component of the strategic planning process, focuses on reviewing the resources, capabilities, and competencies of a company in order to identify its strengths and weaknesses. For example, as described in Strategy in Action 1.1, an internal analysis at Time Inc. revealed that although the company had strong, well-known brands such as *Fortune*, *Money*, *Sports Illustrated*, and *People* (a strength), and strong reporting capabilities (another strength), it suffered from a lack of editorial commitment to online publishing (a weakness). We consider internal analysis in Chapter 3.

SWOT Analysis and the Business Model

The next component of strategic thinking requires the generation of a series of strategic alternatives, or choices of future strategies to pursue, given the company's internal strengths and weaknesses and its external opportunities and threats. The comparison of strengths, weaknesses, opportunities, and threats is normally referred to as a **SWOT analysis**.[16] The central purpose is to identify the strategies to exploit external opportunities, counter threats, build on and protect company strengths, and eradicate weaknesses.

At Time Inc., managers saw the move of readership to the Web as both an *opportunity* that they must exploit and a *threat* to Time's established print magazines. Managers recognized that Time's well-known brands and strong reporting capabilities were *strengths* that would serve it well online, but that an editorial culture that marginalized

SWOT analysis

The comparison of strengths, weaknesses, opportunities, and threats.

online publishing was a *weakness* that had to be fixed. The *strategies* that managers at Time Inc. devised included merging the print and online newsrooms to remove distinctions between them; investing significant financial resources in online sites; and entering into a partnership with CNN, which already had a strong online presence.

More generally, the goal of a SWOT analysis is to create, affirm, or fine-tune a company-specific business model that will best align, fit, or match a company's resources and capabilities to the demands of the environment in which it operates. Managers compare and contrast various alternative possible strategies and then identify the set of strategies that will create and sustain a competitive advantage. These strategies can be divided into four main categories:

- *Functional-level strategies*, directed at improving the efficiency and effectiveness of operations within a company, such as manufacturing, marketing, materials management, product development, and customer service. We review functional-level strategies in Chapter 4.
- *Business-level strategies*, which encompass the business's overall competitive theme, the way it positions itself in the marketplace to gain a competitive advantage, and the different positioning strategies that can be used in different industry settings—for example, cost leadership, differentiation, focusing on a particular niche or segment of the industry, or some combination of these. We review business-level strategies in Chapters 5, 6, and 7.
- *Global strategies*, which address how to expand operations outside the home country in order to grow and prosper in a world where competitive advantage is determined at a global level. We review global strategies in Chapter 8.
- *Corporate-level strategies*, which answer the primary questions: What business or businesses should we be in to maximize the long-run profitability and profit growth of the organization, and how should we enter and increase our presence in these businesses to gain a competitive advantage? We review corporate-level strategies in Chapters 9 and 10.

The strategies identified through a SWOT analysis should be congruent with each other. Thus, functional-level strategies should be consistent with, or support, the company's business-level strategies and global strategies. Moreover, as we explain later in this book, corporate-level strategies should support business-level strategies. When combined, the various strategies pursued by a company should constitute a complete, viable business model. In essence, a SWOT analysis is a methodology for choosing between competing business models, and for fine-tuning the business model that managers choose. For example, when Microsoft entered the videogame market with its Xbox offering, it had to settle on the best business model for competing in this market. Microsoft used a SWOT-type analysis to compare alternatives, and settled on a business model referred to as "razor and razor blades," in which the Xbox console is priced at cost to build sales (the "razor"), while profits are generated from royalties on the sale of games for the Xbox (the "blades").

Strategy Implementation

Once managers have chosen a set of congruent strategies to achieve a competitive advantage and increase performance, those strategies have to be implemented. Strategy implementation involves taking actions at the functional, business, and corporate levels to execute a strategic plan. Implementation can include, for example, putting quality improvement programs into place, changing the way a product is designed, positioning the product differently in the marketplace, segmenting the marketing and offering different versions of the product to different consumer groups, implementing price increases or decreases, expanding through mergers and acquisitions, or downsizing the company by closing down or selling off parts of the company. These and other topics are discussed in detail in Chapters 4 through 10.

Strategy implementation also entails designing the best organizational structure and the best culture and control systems to put a chosen strategy into action. In addition, senior managers need to put a governance system in place to make sure that everyone within the organization acts in a manner that is not only consistent with maximizing profitability and profit growth, but also legal and ethical. We look at the topic of governance and ethics in Chapter 11; in Chapter 12 we discuss the organizational structure, culture, and controls required to implement business-level strategies.

The Feedback Loop

The feedback loop in Figure 1.4 indicates that strategic planning is ongoing: it never ends. Once a strategy has been implemented, its execution must be monitored to determine the extent to which strategic goals and objectives are actually being achieved, and to what degree competitive advantage is being created and sustained. This information and knowledge is returned to the corporate level through feedback loops, and becomes the input for the next round of strategy formulation and implementation. Top managers can then decide whether to reaffirm the existing business model and the existing strategies and goals, or suggest changes for the future. For example, if a strategic goal proves too optimistic, a more conservative goal is set. Or, feedback may reveal that the business model is not working, so managers may seek ways to change it. In essence, this is what happened at Time Inc. (see Strategy in Action 1.1).

◤ STRATEGY AS AN EMERGENT PROCESS

The planning model suggests that a company's strategies are the result of a plan, that the strategic planning process is rational and highly structured, and that top management orchestrates the process. Several scholars have criticized the formal planning model for three main reasons: (1) the unpredictability of the real world, (2) the role that lower-level managers can play in the strategic management process, and (3) the fact that many successful strategies are often the result of serendipity, not rational strategizing. These scholars have advocated an alternative view of strategy making.[17]

Strategy Making in an Unpredictable World

Critics of formal planning systems argue that we live in a world in which uncertainty, complexity, and ambiguity dominate, and in which small chance events can have a large and unpredictable impact on outcomes.[18] In such circumstances, they claim, even the most carefully thought-out strategic plans are prone to being rendered useless by rapid and unforeseen change. In an unpredictable world, being able to respond quickly to changing circumstances, and to alter the strategies of the organization accordingly, is paramount. The dramatic rise of Google, for example, with its business model based on revenues earned from advertising links associated with search results (the so-called "pay-per-click" business model), disrupted the business models of companies that made money from more traditional forms of online advertising. Nobody could foresee this development or plan for it, but companies had to respond to it, and rapidly. Companies with a strong online advertising presence, including Yahoo.com and Microsoft's MSN network, rapidly changed their strategies to adapt to the threat Google posed. Specifically, both companies developed their own search engines and copied Google's pay-per-click business model. According to critics of formal systems, such a flexible approach to strategy making is not possible within the framework of a traditional strategic planning process, with its implicit assumption that an organization's strategies only need to be reviewed during the annual strategic planning exercise.

Autonomous Action: Strategy Making by Lower-Level Managers

Another criticism leveled at the rational planning model of strategy is that too much importance is attached to the role of top management, particularly the CEO.[19] An alternative view is that individual managers deep within an organization can—and often do—exert a profound influence over the strategic direction of the firm.[20] Writing with Robert Burgelman of Stanford University, Andy Grove, the former CEO of Intel, noted that many important strategic decisions at Intel were initiated not by top managers but by the autonomous action of lower-level managers deep within Intel who, on their own initiative, formulated new strategies and worked to persuade top-level managers to alter the strategic priorities of the firm.[21] These strategic decisions included the decision to exit an important market (the DRAM memory chip market) and to develop a certain class of microprocessors (RISC-based microprocessors) in direct contrast to the stated strategy of Intel's top managers.

Another example of autonomous action occurred at Starbucks. Anyone who has walked into a Starbucks cannot help but notice that in addition to various coffee beverages and food, the company also sells music CDs. Most Starbucks stores now have racks displaying anywhere between 5 and 20 CDs nearby the cash register. You can also purchase Starbucks music CDs on the company's website, and music published by the company's Hear Music label is available for download via iTunes. The interesting thing about Starbucks' entry into music retailing and publishing is that it was not the result of a formal planning process. The company's journey into music started in the late 1980s, when Tim Jones, then the manager of a Starbucks in Seattle's University Village, started to bring his own mix tapes into the store to play. Soon Jones was getting requests for copies from customers. Jones reported this to Starbucks' CEO, Howard Schultz, and suggested that Starbucks sell music. At first, Schultz was skeptical, but after repeated lobbying efforts by Jones he eventually took up the suggestion. In the late 1990s, Starbucks purchased Hear Music, a small publishing company, so that it could sell and distribute its own music CDs. Today, Starbucks' music business represents a small but healthy part of its overall product portfolio. For some artists, sales through Starbucks can represent an important revenue stream. Although it shifts titles regularly, sales of a CD over, say, 6 weeks, typically accounts for 5 to 10% of the album's overall sales.

Autonomous action may be particularly important in helping established companies deal with the uncertainty created by the arrival of a radical new technology that changes the dominant paradigm in an industry.[22] Top managers usually rise to preeminence by successfully executing the established strategy of the firm. Therefore, they may have an emotional commitment to the status quo and are often unable to see things from a different perspective. In this sense, they can be a conservative force that promotes inertia. Lower-level managers are less likely to have the same commitment to the status quo and have more to gain from promoting new technologies and strategies. They may be the first ones to recognize new strategic opportunities and lobby for strategic change. As described in Strategy in Action 1.2, this seems to have been the case at discount stockbroker Charles Schwab, which had to adjust to the arrival of the Web in the 1990s.

Serendipity and Strategy

Business history is replete with examples of accidental events that helped push companies in new and profitable directions. These examples suggest that many successful strategies are not the result of well-thought-out plans, but of serendipity—stumbling across good outcomes unexpectedly. One such example occurred at 3M during the 1960s. At that time, 3M was producing fluorocarbons for sale as coolant liquid in air-conditioning equipment. One day, a researcher working with fluorocarbons in a 3M lab spilled some of the liquid on her shoes. Later that day when she spilled coffee over her shoes, she watched with interest as the coffee formed into little beads of liquid and then ran off her shoes without leaving a stain. Reflecting on this phenomenon, she realized that a fluorocarbon-based liquid might turn out to be useful for protecting fabrics from liquid stains, and so the idea for Scotchgard was born. Subsequently, Scotchgard became one of 3M's most profitable products and took the company into the fabric protection business, an area within which it had never planned to participate.[23]

Serendipitous discoveries and events can open all sorts of profitable avenues for a company. But some companies have missed profitable opportunities because serendipitous discoveries or events were inconsistent with their prior (planned) conception of their strategy. In one classic example of such myopia, in the 19th century, the telegraph company Western Union turned down an opportunity to purchase the rights to an invention by Alexander Graham Bell. The invention was the telephone, the technology that subsequently made the telegraph obsolete.

Intended and Emergent Strategies

Henry Mintzberg's model of strategy development provides a more encompassing view of strategy. According to this model, illustrated in Figure 1.6, a company's realized strategy is the product of whatever planned strategies are actually put into action (the company's deliberate strategies) and any unplanned, or emergent, strategies. In Mintzberg's view, many planned strategies are not implemented because of unpredicted changes in the environment (they are unrealized). Emergent strategies are the unplanned responses to unforeseen circumstances. They arise from autonomous action by individual managers deep within the organization, from serendipitous discoveries or events, or from an unplanned strategic shift by top-level managers in response to changed circumstances. They are not the product of formal, top-down planning mechanisms.

1.2 STRATEGY IN ACTION

A Strategic Shift at Charles Schwab

In the mid-1990s, Charles Schwab was the most successful discount stockbroker in the world. Over 20 years, it had gained share from full-service brokers like Merrill Lynch by offering deep discounts on the commissions charged for stock trades. Although Schwab had a nationwide network of branches, most customers executed their trades through a telephone system, TeleBroker. Others used online proprietary software, Street Smart, which had to be purchased from Schwab. It was a business model that worked well—then along came E*Trade.

Bill Porter, a physicist and inventor, started the discount brokerage firm E*TRADE in 1994 to take advantage of the opportunity created by the rapid emergence of the World Wide Web. E*TRADE launched the first dedicated website for online trading: E*TRADE had no branches, no brokers, and no telephone system for taking orders, and thus it had a very-low-cost structure. Customers traded stocks over the company's website. Due to its low-cost structure, E*TRADE was able to announce a flat $14.95 commission on stock trades, a figure significantly below Schwab's average commission, which at the time was $65. It was clear from the outset that E*TRADE and other online brokers, such as Ameritrade, which soon followed, offered a direct threat to Schwab. Not only were their cost structures and commission rates considerably lower than Schwab's, but the ease, speed, and flexibility of trading stocks over the Web suddenly made Schwab's Street Smart trading software seem limited and its telephone system antiquated.

Deep within Schwab, William Pearson, a young software specialist who had worked on the development of Street Smart, immediately saw the transformational power of the Web. Pearson believed that Schwab needed to develop its own Web-based software, and quickly. Try as he might, though, Pearson could not get the attention of his supervisor. He tried a number of other executives but found little support. Eventually he approached Anne Hennegar, a former Schwab manager who now worked as a consultant to the company. Hennegar suggested that Pearson meet with Tom Seip, an executive vice president at Schwab who was known for his ability to think outside the box. Hennegar approached Seip on Pearson's behalf, and Seip responded positively, asking her to set up a meeting. Hennegar and Pearson arrived, expecting to meet only Seip, but to their surprise, in walked Charles Schwab, his chief operating officer, David Pottruck, and the vice presidents in charge of strategic planning and electronic brokerage.

As the group watched Pearson's demo, which detailed how a Web-based system would look and work, they became increasingly excited. It was clear to those in the room that a Web-based system using real-time information, personalization, customization, and interactivity all advanced Schwab's commitment to empowering customers. By the end of the meeting, Pearson had received a green light to start work on the project. A year later, Schwab launched its own Web-based offering, eSchwab, which enabled Schwab clients to execute stock trades for a low, flat-rate commission. eSchwab went on to become the core of the company's offering, enabling it to stave off competition from deep discount brokers like E*TRADE.

Sources: J. Kador, *Charles Schwab: How One Company Beat Wall Street and Reinvented the Brokerage Industry* (New York: John Wiley Sons, 2002); E. Schonfeld, "Schwab Puts It All Online," *Fortune* (December 7, 1998): 94–99.

Mintzberg maintains that emergent strategies are often successful and may be more appropriate than intended strategies. In the classic example of this process, Richard Pascale described the entry of Honda Motor Co. into the U.S. motorcycle market.[24] When a number of Honda executives arrived in Los Angeles from Japan in

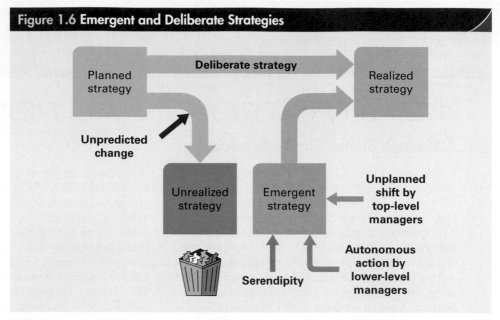

Figure 1.6 Emergent and Deliberate Strategies

Source: Adapted from H. Mintzberg and A. McGugh, Administrative Science Quarterly 30:2 (June 1985).

1959 to establish a U.S. operation, their original aim (intended strategy) was to focus on selling 250-cc and 350-cc machines to confirmed motorcycle enthusiasts rather than 50-cc Honda Cubs, which were a big hit in Japan. Their instinct told them that the Honda 50s were not suitable for the U.S. market, where everything was bigger and more luxurious than in Japan.

However, sales of the 250-cc and 350-cc bikes were sluggish, and the bikes themselves were plagued by mechanical failure. It looked as if Honda's strategy was going to fail. At the same time, the Japanese executives who were using the Honda 50s to run errands around Los Angeles were attracting a lot of attention. One day, they got a call from a Sears, Roebuck and Co. buyer who wanted to sell the 50-cc bikes to a broad market of Americans who were not necessarily motorcycle enthusiasts. The Honda executives were hesitant to sell the small bikes for fear of alienating serious bikers, who might then associate Honda with "wimpy" machines. In the end, however, they were pushed into doing so by the failure of the 250-cc and 350-cc models.

Honda had stumbled onto a previously untouched market segment that would prove huge: the average American who had never owned a motorbike. Honda had also found an untried channel of distribution: general retailers rather than specialty motorbike stores. By 1964, nearly one out of every two motorcycles sold in the United States was a Honda.

The conventional explanation for Honda's success is that the company redefined the U.S. motorcycle industry with a brilliantly conceived intended strategy. The fact was that Honda's intended strategy was a near-disaster. The strategy that emerged did so not through planning but through unplanned action in response to unforeseen circumstances. Nevertheless, credit should be given to the Japanese management for recognizing the strength of the emergent strategy and for pursuing it with vigor.

The critical point demonstrated by the Honda example is that successful strategies can often emerge within an organization without prior planning, and in response to unforeseen circumstances. As Mintzberg has noted, strategies can take root wherever people have the capacity to learn and the resources to support that capacity.

In practice, the strategies of most organizations are likely a combination of the intended and the emergent. The message for management is that it needs to recognize the process of emergence and to intervene when appropriate, relinquishing bad emergent strategies and nurturing potentially good ones.[25] To make such decisions, managers must be able to judge the worth of emergent strategies. They must be able to think strategically. Although emergent strategies arise from within the organization without prior planning—that is, without completing the steps illustrated in Figure 1.5 in a sequential fashion—top management must still evaluate emergent strategies. Such evaluation involves comparing each emergent strategy with the organization's goals, external environmental opportunities and threats, and internal strengths and weaknesses. The objective is to assess whether the emergent strategy fits the company's needs and capabilities. In addition, Mintzberg stresses that an organization's capability to produce emergent strategies is a function of the kind of corporate culture that the organization's structure and control systems foster. In other words, the different components of the strategic management process are just as important from the perspective of emergent strategies as they are from the perspective of intended strategies.

STRATEGIC PLANNING IN PRACTICE

Despite criticisms, research suggests that formal planning systems do help managers make better strategic decisions. A study that analyzed the results of 26 previously published studies came to the conclusion that, on average, strategic planning has a positive impact on company performance.[26] Another study of strategic planning in 656 firms found that formal planning methodologies and emergent strategies both form part of a good strategy-formulation process, particularly in an unstable environment.[27] For strategic planning to work, it is important that top-level managers plan not only within the context of the current competitive environment but also within the context of the future competitive environment. To try to forecast what that future will look like, managers can use scenario-planning techniques to project different possible futures. They can also involve operating managers in the planning process and seek to shape the future competitive environment by emphasizing strategic intent.

Scenario Planning

One reason that strategic planning may fail over longer time periods is that strategic managers, in their initial enthusiasm for planning techniques, may forget that the future is entirely unpredictable. Even the best-laid plans can fall apart if unforeseen contingencies occur, and that happens all the time. The recognition that uncertainty makes it difficult to forecast the future accurately led planners at Royal Dutch Shell to pioneer the scenario approach to planning.[28] **Scenario planning** involves formulating plans that are based upon "what-if" scenarios about the future. In the typical scenario-planning exercise, some scenarios are optimistic and some are pessimistic. Teams of

scenario planning
Formulating plans that are based upon "what-if" scenarios about the future.

managers are asked to develop specific strategies to cope with each scenario. A set of indicators is chosen as signposts to track trends and identify the probability that any particular scenario is coming to pass. The idea is to allow managers to understand the dynamic and complex nature of their environment, to think through problems in a strategic fashion, and to generate a range of strategic options that might be pursued under different circumstances.[29] The scenario approach to planning has spread rapidly among large companies. One survey found that over 50% of the *Fortune* 500 companies use some form of scenario-planning methods.[30]

The oil company Royal Dutch Shell has, perhaps, done more than most companies to pioneer the concept of scenario planning, and its experience demonstrates the power of the approach.[31] Shell has been using scenario planning since the 1980s. Today, it uses two primary scenarios to anticipate future demand for oil and refine its strategic planning. The first scenario, called "Dynamics as Usual," sees a gradual shift from carbon fuels (such as oil) to natural gas, and, eventually, to renewable energy. The second scenario, "The Spirit of the Coming Age," looks at the possibility that a technological revolution will lead to a rapid shift to new energy sources.[32] Shell is making investments that will ensure profitability for the company, regardless of which scenario comes to pass, and it is carefully tracking technological and market trends for signs of which scenario will become more likely over time.

The great virtue of the scenario approach to planning is that it pushes managers to think outside the box, to anticipate what they might need to do in different situations. It reminds managers that the world is complex and unpredictable, and to place a premium on flexibility rather than on inflexible plans based on assumptions about the future (which may or may not be correct). As a result of scenario planning, organizations might pursue one dominant strategy related to the scenario that is judged to be most likely, but they make investments that will pay off if other scenarios come to the fore (see Figure 1.7). Thus, the current strategy of Shell is based on the assumption that the world will gradually shift away from carbon-based fuels

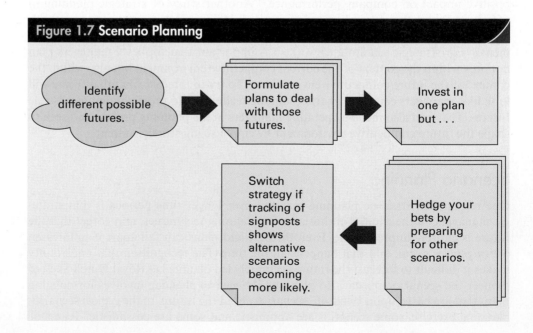

Figure 1.7 Scenario Planning

Identify different possible futures.

Formulate plans to deal with those futures.

Invest in one plan but . . .

Switch strategy if tracking of signposts shows alternative scenarios becoming more likely.

Hedge your bets by preparing for other scenarios.

(its "Dynamics as Usual" scenario), but the company is hedging its bets by investing in new energy technologies and mapping out a strategy should the second scenario come to pass.

Decentralized Planning

Some companies constructing a strategic planning process erroneously treat planning exclusively as a top-management responsibility. This "ivory tower" approach can result in strategic plans formulated in a vacuum by top managers who may be disconnected from current operating realities. Consequently, top managers may formulate suboptimal strategies. For example, when demographic data indicated that houses and families were shrinking, planners at GE's appliance group concluded that smaller appliances were the wave of the future. Because they had little contact with homebuilders and retailers, they did not realize that kitchens and bathrooms were the two rooms that were not shrinking. Nor did they appreciate that two-income families wanted large refrigerators to cut down on trips to the supermarket. GE wasted a lot of time designing small appliances for which there was limited demand.

The ivory tower concept of planning can also lead to tensions between corporate-, business-, and functional-level managers. The experience of GE's appliance group is again illuminating. Many of the corporate managers in the planning group were recruited from consulting firms or top-flight business schools. Many of the functional managers took this pattern of recruitment to mean that the corporate managers did not believe they were smart enough to think through strategic problems. They felt shut out of the decision-making process, which they believed to be unfairly constituted. From this perceived lack of procedural justice sprang an us-versus-them mindset that quickly escalated into hostility. As a result, even when the planners were correct, operating managers would not listen to them. For example, the planners correctly recognized the importance of the globalization of the appliance market and the emerging Japanese threat. However, operating managers, who then saw Sears, Roebuck and Co. as the competition, paid them little heed. Finally, ivory tower planning ignores both the important, strategic role of autonomous action by lower-level managers and the role of serendipity.

Correcting the ivory tower approach to planning requires recognizing that successful strategic planning encompasses managers at all levels of the corporation. Much of the best planning can and should be done by business and functional managers who are closest to the facts; in other words, planning should be decentralized. Corporate-level planners should be facilitators who help business and functional managers do the planning by setting the broad strategic goals of the organization and providing the resources necessary to identify the strategies required to attain those goals.

▼ STRATEGIC DECISION MAKING

Even the best-designed strategic-planning systems will fail to produce the desired results if managers do not effectively use the information at their disposal. Consequently, it is important that strategic managers use that information to understand why they sometimes make poor decisions. One important way to do is to understand how common cognitive biases can result in poor decision making.[33]

Cognitive Biases and Strategic Decision Making

The rationality of decision making is bound by one's cognitive capabilities.[34] Humans are not supercomputers—it is difficult for us to absorb and process large amounts of information effectively. As a result, when we make decisions, we tend to fall back on certain rules of thumb, or heuristics, that help us make sense out of a complex and uncertain world. Sometimes these rules lead to severe, systematic errors in the decision-making process.[35] Systematic errors are those that appear time and time again. They seem to arise from a series of **cognitive biases** in the way we process information and reach decisions. Cognitive biases cause many managers to make poor strategic decisions.

Numerous cognitive biases have been verified repeatedly in laboratory settings, so we can be reasonably sure that these biases exist and that all people are prone to them.[36] The **prior hypothesis bias** refers to the fact that decision makers who have strong prior beliefs about the relationship between two variables tend to make decisions on the basis of these beliefs, even when presented with evidence that their beliefs are incorrect. Moreover, they tend to seek and use information that is consistent with their prior beliefs while ignoring information that contradicts these beliefs. To place this bias in a strategic context, it suggests that a CEO who has a strong prior belief that a certain strategy makes sense might continue to pursue that strategy despite evidence that it is inappropriate or failing.

Another well-known cognitive bias, **escalating commitment**, occurs when decision makers, having already committed significant resources to a project, commit even more resources even if they receive feedback that the project is failing.[37] A more logical response would be to abandon the project and move on (that is, to cut your losses and exit), rather than escalate commitment.

A third bias, **reasoning by analogy**, involves the use of simple analogies to make sense out of complex problems. The problem with this heuristic is that the analogy may not be valid. A fourth bias, **representativeness**, is rooted in the tendency to generalize from a small sample or even a single, vivid anecdote. This bias violates the statistical law of large numbers, which states that it is inappropriate to generalize from a small sample, let alone from a single case. In many respects, the dot-com boom of the late 1990s was based on reasoning by analogy and representativeness. Prospective entrepreneurs saw some early dot-com companies such as Amazon and Yahoo! achieve rapid success, at least as judged by some metrics. Reasoning by analogy from a very small sample, they assumed that any dot-com could achieve similar success. Many investors reached similar conclusions. The result was a massive wave of start-ups that attempted to capitalize on perceived Internet opportunities. The vast majority of these companies subsequently went bankrupt, proving that the analogy was wrong and that the success of the small sample of early entrants was no guarantee that all dot-coms would succeed.

A fifth cognitive bias is referred to as **the illusion of control**, or the tendency to overestimate one's ability to control events. General or top managers seem to be particularly prone to this bias: having risen to the top of an organization, they tend to be overconfident about their ability to succeed. According to Richard Roll, such overconfidence leads to what he has termed the *hubris hypothesis of takeovers*.[38] Roll argues that top managers are typically overconfident about their ability to create value by acquiring another company. Hence, they make poor acquisition decisions, often paying far too much for the companies they acquire. Subsequently, servicing the debt taken on to finance such an acquisition makes it all but impossible to profit from the acquisition.

cognitive biases
Systematic errors in decision making that arise from the way people process information.

prior hypothesis bias
A cognitive bias that occurs when decision makers who have strong prior beliefs tend to make decisions on the basis of these beliefs, even when presented with evidence that their beliefs are wrong.

escalating commitment
A cognitive bias that occurs when decision makers, having already committed significant resources to a project, commit even more resources after receiving feedback that the project is failing.

reasoning by analogy
Use of simple analogies to make sense out of complex problems.

representativeness
A bias rooted in the tendency to generalize from a small sample or even a single, vivid anecdote.

illusion of control
A cognitive bias rooted in the tendency to overestimate one's ability to control events.

Availability error is yet another common bias. Availability error arises from our predisposition to estimate the probability of an outcome based on how easy the outcome is to imagine. For example, more people seem to fear a plane crash than a car accident, yet statistically one is far more likely to be killed in a car on the way to the airport than in a plane crash. People overweigh the probability of a plane crash because the outcome is easier to imagine, and because plane crashes are more vivid events than car crashes, which affect only small numbers of people at one time. As a result of availability error, managers might allocate resources to a project with an outcome that is easier to imagine, rather than to one that might have the highest return.

availability error
A bias that arises from our predisposition to estimate the probability of an outcome based on how easy the outcome is to imagine.

Techniques for Improving Decision Making

The existence of cognitive biases raises a question: How can critical information affect the decision-making mechanism so that a company's strategic decisions are realistic and based on thorough evaluation? Two techniques known to enhance strategic thinking and counteract cognitive biases are devil's advocacy and dialectic inquiry.[39]

Devil's advocacy requires the generation of a plan and a critical analysis of that plan. One member of the decision-making group acts as the devil's advocate, emphasizing all the reasons that might make the proposal unacceptable. In the process, decision makers become aware of the possible perils of recommended courses of action.

devil's advocacy
A technique in which one member of a decision-making team identifies all the considerations that might make a proposal unacceptable.

Dialectic inquiry is more complex because it requires the generation of a plan (a thesis) and a counterplan (an antithesis) that reflect plausible but conflicting courses of action.[40] Strategic managers listen to a debate between advocates of the plan and counterplan and then decide which plan will lead to higher performance. The purpose of the debate is to reveal the problems with the definitions, recommended courses of action, and assumptions of both plans. As a result of this exercise, strategic managers are able to form a new and more encompassing conceptualization of the problem, which then becomes the final plan (a synthesis). Dialectic inquiry can promote strategic thinking.

dialectic inquiry
The generation of a plan (a thesis) and a counterplan (an antithesis) that reflect plausible but conflicting courses of action.

Another technique for countering cognitive biases is the outside view, which has been championed by Nobel Prize winner Daniel Kahneman and his associates.[41] The **outside view** requires planners to identify a reference class of analogous past strategic initiatives, determine whether those initiatives succeeded or failed, and evaluate the project at hand against those prior initiatives. According to Kahneman, this technique is particularly useful for countering biases such as illusion of control (hubris), reasoning by analogy, and representativeness. For example, when considering a potential acquisition, planners should look at the track record of acquisitions made by other enterprises (the reference class), determine if they succeeded or failed, and objectively evaluate the potential acquisition against that reference class. Kahneman argues that such a reality check against a large sample of prior events tends to constrain the inherent optimism of planners and produce more realistic assessments and plans.

outside view
Identification of past successful or failed strategic initiatives to determine whether those initiatives will work for project at hand.

◤ STRATEGIC LEADERSHIP

One key strategic role of both general and functional managers is to use all their knowledge, energy, and enthusiasm to provide strategic leadership for their subordinates and develop a high-performing organization. Several authors have identified key characteristics of strong strategic leaders that lead to high performance: (1) vision, eloquence, and consistency; (2) articulation of a business model; (3) commitment; (4) being well informed; (5) willingness to delegate and empower; (6) astute use of power; and (7) emotional intelligence.[42]

Vision, Eloquence, and Consistency

One key task of leadership is to give an organization a sense of direction. Strong leaders have a clear, compelling vision of where the organization should go, eloquently communicate this vision to others within the organization in terms that energize people, and consistently articulate their vision until it becomes part of the organization's culture.[43]

In the political arena, John F. Kennedy, Winston Churchill, Martin Luther King, Jr., and Margaret Thatcher are regarded as visionary leaders. Think of the impact of Kennedy's summons, "Ask not what your country can do for you, ask what you can do for your country," of King's "I have a dream" speech, of Churchill's declaration that "we will never surrender", and of Thatcher's statement that "the problem with socialism is that you eventually run out of other peoples' money." Kennedy and Thatcher used their political office to push for governmental actions that were consistent with their visions. Churchill's speech galvanized a nation to defend itself against an aggressor. King pressured the government from outside to make changes within society.

Historic examples of strong business leaders include Microsoft's Bill Gates; Jack Welch, the former CEO of General Electric; and Sam Walton, Wal-Mart's founder. For years, Bill Gates's vision of a world in which there would be a Windows-based personal computer on every desk was a driving force at Microsoft. More recently, that vision has evolved into one of a world in which Windows-based software can be found on any computing device, from PCs and servers to videogame consoles (Xbox), cell phones, and handheld computers. At GE, Jack Welch was responsible for articulating the simple but powerful vision that GE should be first or second in every business in which it competed, or it should exit from that business. Similarly, Wal-Mart founder Sam Walton established and articulated the vision that has been central to Wal-Mart's success: passing on cost savings from suppliers and operating efficiencies to customers in the form of everyday low prices.

Articulation of the Business Model

Another key characteristic of good strategic leaders is their ability to identify and articulate the business model the company will use to attain its vision. A business model is the managers' conception of how the various strategies that the company pursues fit together into a congruent whole. At Dell, for example, Michael Dell identified and articulated the basic business model of the company: the direct sales business model. The various strategies that Dell has pursued over the years have refined this basic model, creating one that is very robust in terms of its efficiency and effectiveness. Although individual strategies can take root in many different places in an organization, and although their identification is not the exclusive preserve of top management, only strategic leaders have the perspective required to make sure that the various strategies fit together into a congruent whole and form a valid and compelling business model. If strategic leaders lack a clear conception of the company's business model (or what it should be), it is likely that the strategies the firm pursues will not fit together, and the result will be lack of focus and poor performance.

Commitment

Strong leaders demonstrate their commitment to their visions and business models by actions and words, and they often lead by example. Consider Nucor's former CEO, Ken Iverson. Nucor is a very efficient steelmaker with perhaps the lowest cost structure in the steel industry. It has achieved 30 years of profitable performance in an industry where most other companies have lost money due to a relentless focus on cost minimization. In his tenure as CEO, Iverson set the example: he answered his own phone, employed only one secretary, drove an old car, flew coach class, and was proud of the fact that his base salary was the lowest of the *Fortune* 500 CEOs (Iverson made most of his money from performance-based pay bonuses). This commitment was a powerful signal to employees that Iverson was serious about doing everything possible to minimize costs. It earned him the respect of Nucor employees and made them more willing to work hard. Although Iverson has retired, his legacy lives on in Nucor's cost-conscious organizational culture or, and like all other great leaders, his impact will last beyond his tenure.

Being Well Informed

Effective strategic leaders develop a network of formal and informal sources who keep them well informed about what is going on within the company. At Starbucks, the first thing that former CEO Jim Donald did every morning was call 5 to 10 stores, talk to the managers and other employees there, and get a sense for how their stores were performing. Donald also stopped at a local Starbucks every morning on the way to work to buy his morning coffee. This allowed him to get to know individual employees very well. Donald found these informal contacts to be a useful source of information about how the company was performing.[44]

Similarly, Herb Kelleher, the founder of Southwest Airlines, was able to gauge the health of his company by dropping in unannounced on aircraft maintenance facilities and helping workers perform their tasks. Herb Kelleher would also often help airline attendants on Southwest flights, distributing refreshments and talking to customers. One frequent flyer on Southwest Airlines reported sitting next to Kelleher three times in 10 years. Each time, Kelleher asked him (and others sitting nearby) how Southwest Airlines was doing in a number of areas, in order to spot trends and inconsistencies.[45]

Using informal and unconventional ways to gather information is wise because formal channels can be captured by special interests within the organization or by gatekeepers—managers who may misrepresent the true state of affairs to the leader. People like Donald and Kelleher who constantly interact with employees at all levels are better able to build informal information networks than leaders who closet themselves and never interact with lower-level employees.

Willingness to Delegate and Empower

High-performance leaders are skilled at delegation. They recognize that unless they learn how to delegate effectively, they can quickly become overloaded with responsibilities. They also recognize that empowering subordinates to make decisions is a good motivational tool and often results in decisions being made by those who must implement them. At the same time, astute leaders recognize that they need to maintain control over certain key decisions. Thus, although they will delegate many important decisions to lower-level employees, they will not delegate those that they judge to be of critical importance to the future success of the organization, such as articulating the company's vision and business model.

The Astute Use of Power

In a now-classic article on leadership, Edward Wrapp noted that effective leaders tend to be very astute in their use of power.[46] He argued that strategic leaders must often play the power game with skill and attempt to build consensus for their ideas rather than use their authority to force ideas through; they must act as members of a coalition or its democratic leaders rather than as dictators. Jeffery Pfeffer articulated a similar vision of the politically astute manager who gets things done in organizations through the intelligent use of power.[47] In Pfeffer's view, power comes from control over resources that are important to the organization: budgets, capital, positions, information, and knowledge. Politically astute managers use these resources to acquire another critical resource: critically placed allies who can help them attain their strategic objectives. Pfeffer stresses that one does not need to be a CEO to assemble power in an organization. Sometimes junior functional managers can build a surprisingly effective power base and use it to influence organizational outcomes.

Emotional Intelligence

Emotional intelligence, a term coined by Daniel Goleman, describes a bundle of psychological attributes that many strong, effective leaders exhibit[48]:

- Self-awareness—the ability to understand one's own moods, emotions, and drives, as well as their effect on others.
- Self-regulation—the ability to control or redirect disruptive impulses or moods; that is, to think before acting.
- Motivation—a passion for work that goes beyond money or status and a propensity to pursue goals with energy and persistence.
- Empathy—the ability to understand the feelings and viewpoints of subordinates and to take those into account when making decisions.
- Social skills—friendliness with a purpose.

According to Goleman, leaders who exhibit a high degree of emotional intelligence tend to be more effective than those who lack these attributes. Their self-awareness and self-regulation help to elicit the trust and confidence of subordinates. In Goleman's view, people respect leaders who, because they are self-aware, recognize their own limitations and, because they are self-regulating, consider decisions carefully. Goleman also argues that self-aware, self-regulating individuals tend to be more self-confident and therefore are better able to cope with ambiguity and are more open to change. A strong motivation exhibited in a passion for work can be infectious, persuading others to join together in pursuit of a common goal or organizational mission. Finally, strong empathy and social skills help leaders earn the loyalty of subordinates. Empathetic, socially adept individuals tend to be skilled at remedying disputes between managers, are better able to find common ground and purpose among diverse constituencies, and are better able to move people in a desired direction compared to leaders who lack these skills. In short, Goleman argues that the psychological makeup of a leader matters.

KEY TERMS

TAKEAWAYS FOR STRATEGIC MANAGERS

1. The major goal of companies is to maximize the returns that shareholders receive from holding shares in the company. To maximize shareholder value, managers must pursue strategies that result in high and sustained profitability and also in profit growth.

2. The profitability of a company can be measured by the return that it makes on the capital invested in the enterprise. The profit growth of a company can be measured by the growth in earnings per share. Profitability and profit growth are determined by the strategies managers adopt.

3. A company has a competitive advantage over its rivals when it is more profitable and has greater profit growth than the average for all firms in its industry. It has a sustained competitive advantage when it is able to maintain above-average performance over a number of years.

4. General managers are responsible for the overall performance of the organization, or for one of its major self-contained divisions. Their overriding strategic concern is for the health of the total organization under their direction.

5. Functional managers are responsible for a particular business function or operation. Although they lack general management responsibilities, they play a very important strategic role.

6. Formal strategic planning models stress that an organization's strategy is the outcome of a rational planning process.

7. The major components of the strategic management process are defining the mission, vision, and major goals of the organization; analyzing the external and internal environments of the organization; choosing a business model and strategies that align an organization's strengths and weaknesses with external environmental opportunities and threats; and adopting organizational structures and control systems to implement the organization's chosen strategies.

8. Strategy can emerge from deep within an organization in the absence of formal plans as lower-level managers respond to unpredicted situations.

9. Strategic planning may fail because executives do not plan for uncertainty and because ivory tower planners lose touch with operating realities.

10. In spite of systematic planning, companies may adopt poor strategies if cognitive biases are allowed to intrude into the decision-making process.

11. Devil's advocacy, dialectic inquiry, and the outside view are techniques for enhancing the effectiveness of strategic decision making.

12. Good leaders of the strategy-making process have a number of key attributes: vision, eloquence, and consistency; ability to craft a business model; commitment; being well informed; willingness to delegate and empower; political astuteness; and emotional intelligence.

DISCUSSION QUESTIONS

1. What do we mean by strategy? How is a business model different from a strategy?
2. What do you think are the sources of sustained superior profitability?
3. What are the strengths of formal strategic planning? What are its weaknesses?
4. Can you think of an example in your own life where cognitive biases resulted in you making a poor decision? How might that mistake have been avoided?

5. Discuss the accuracy of the following statement: Formal strategic planning systems are irrelevant for firms competing in high-technology industries where the pace of change is so rapid that plans are routinely made obsolete by unforeseen events.
6. Pick the current or a past president of the United States and evaluate his performance against the leadership characteristics discussed in the text. On the basis of this comparison, do you think that the president was/is a good strategic leader? Why or why not?

CLOSING CASE

The Evolution of Wal-Mart

Wal-Mart is one of the most extraordinary success stories in business history. Started in 1962 by Sam Walton, Wal-Mart has grown to become the world's largest corporation. In 2014, the discount retailer—whose mantra is "Everyday low prices"—had sales of more than $475 billion, close to 11,000 stores in 27 countries, and more than 2.2 million employees. Some 8% of all retail sales in the United States are made at a Wal-Mart store. Wal-Mart is not only large; it is also very profitable. Between 2005 and 2014, the company's average ROIC was 14.1%–better than its well–managed rivals, Costco and Target, which earned 11.8% and 11%, respectively.

Wal-Mart's persistently superior profitability is based on a number of factors. In 1962, Wal-Mart was one of the first companies to apply the self-service supermarket business model developed by grocery chains to sell general merchandise. Unlike rivals such as K-Mart and Target that focused on urban and suburban locations, Sam Walton's Wal-Mart concentrated on small, southern towns that were ignored by its rivals and which had enough demand to support one large discount store. Walton realized that, in rural America, people would drive an hour to Wal-Mart in a small town rather than

drive 2 to 3 hours to a major city. This meant that a small town with a population of 25,000 actually had a catchment area containing 100,000 people.

Wal-Mart grew quickly by pricing its products lower than those of local retailers, often putting them out of business. By the time its rivals realized that many small towns could support one large discount general merchandise store, Wal-Mart had already pre-empted them and had spread out to small towns across America.

Over time, the company became an innovator in information systems, logistics, and human resource practices. Actions taken in these functional areas resulted in higher productivity and lower costs as compared to rivals, which enabled the company to earn a high ROIC while charging low prices. Wal-Mart led the way among U.S. retailers in developing and implementing sophisticated product-tracking systems using bar-code technology and checkout scanners. This information technology enabled Wal-Mart to track what was selling and adjust its inventory accordingly so that the products found in each store matched local demand. By avoiding over-stocking, Wal-Mart did not have to hold periodic sales to shift unsold inventory. Over time, Wal-Mart linked its information system to a nationwide network of distribution centers in which inventory was shipped from vendors, and then shipped out on a daily basis to stores within a 400-mile radius. The combination of distribution centers and information systems enabled Wal-Mart to reduce the amount of inventory it held in stores, and thus to devote valuable space to selling and to reduce the amount of capital it had tied up in inventory.

With regard to human resources, Sam Walton set the tone. He held a strong belief that employees should be respected and rewarded for helping to improve the profitability of the company. Underpinning this belief, Walton referred to employees as "associates." He established a profit-sharing plan for all employees and, after the company went public in 1970, a program that allowed employees to purchase Wal-Mart stock at a discount to its market value. Wal-Mart was rewarded for this approach by high employee productivity, which translated into lower operating costs and higher profitability.

As Wal-Mart grew, its sheer size and purchasing power enabled it to drive down the prices that it paid suppliers and to pass on those savings to customers in the form of lower prices–which enabled Wal-Mart to gain more market share and hence lower prices even further. To take the sting out of the persistent demands for lower prices, Wal-Mart shared its sales information with suppliers on a daily basis, enabling them to gain efficiencies by configuring their own production schedules for sales at Wal-Mart.

By the 1990s, Wal-Mart was already the largest seller of general merchandise in the United States. To keep growing, it started to diversify into the grocery business, opening 200,000-square-foot supercenter stores that sold groceries and general merchandise under the same roof. Wal-Mart also diversified into the warehouse club business with the establishment of Sam's Club. The company began expanding internationally in 1991 with its entry into Mexico. Today, Wal-Mart generates $175 billion in foreign sales.

For all its success, Wal-Mart is now encountering very real limits to profitable growth. The U.S. market is saturated, and growth overseas has proved more difficult than the company hoped. The company was forced to exit Germany and South Korea after losing money there, and it has faced difficulties in several developed nations. Moreover, rivals Target and Costco have continued to improve their performance, and Costco in particular is now snapping at Wal-Mart's heels.

Sources: "How Big Can It Grow?" *The Economist* (April 17, 2004): 74–78; "Trial by Checkout," *The Economist* (June 26, 2004): 74–76; Wal-Mart 10-K, 2013, www.walmartstores.com; R. Slater, *The Wal-Mart Triumph* (New York: Portfolio Trade Books, 2004); "The Bulldozer from Bentonville Slows; Wal-Mart," *The Economist* (February 17, 2007): 70; K. Perkins, "Wal-Mart still faces challenges, but its scale should allow it to compete amid fierce rivalry," Morningstar, December 2, 2014.

CASE DISCUSSION QUESTIONS

1. What was Sam Walton's original strategic vision for Wal-Mart? How did this enable the company to gain a competitive advantage?
2. How did Wal-Mart continue to strengthen its competitive advantage over time? What does this teach you about the source of a long-term competitive advantage?
3. By the early 1990s, Wal-Mart was encountering limits to growth in the US. How did it overcome these limits to growth? Explain how the expansion moves that Wal-Mart made in the 1990s made economic sense and helped to create value for the company's shareholders.
4. Wal-Mart is once again encountering limits to growth. Why do you think this is the case? What might Wal-Mart do to push back these limits?
5. How much of Wal-Mart's strategy do you think was planned at the outset, and how much evolved over time in response to circumstances? What does this suggest to you about the nature of strategy development?

APPENDIX TO CHAPTER 1: Enterprise Valuation, ROIC, and Growth

The ultimate goal of strategy is to maximize the value of a company to its shareholders (subject to the important constraints that this is done in a legal, ethical, and socially responsible manner). The two main drivers of enterprise valuation are return on invested capital (ROIC) and the growth rate of profits, g.[49]

ROIC is defined as net operating profits less adjusted taxes (NOPLAT) over the invested capital of the enterprise (IC), where IC is the sum of the company's equity and debt (the method for calculating adjusted taxes need not concern us here). That is:

$$ROIC = NOPLAT/IC$$

where:

$$NOPLAT = revenues - cost of goods sold - $$
$$operating expenses - depreciation$$
$$charges - adjusted taxes$$
IC = value of shareholders' equity + value of debt

The growth rate of profits, g, can be defined as the percentage increase in net operating profits (NOPLAT) over a given time period. More precisely:

$$g = [(NOPLAT_{t+1} - NOPLAT_t)/NOPLAT_t] \times 100$$

Note that if NOPLAT is increasing over time, earnings per share will also increase so long as (a) the number of shares stays constant or (b) the number of shares outstanding increases more slowly than NOPLAT.

The valuation of a company can be calculated using discounted cash flow analysis and applying it to future expected free cash flows (free cash flow in a period is defined as NOPLAT − net investments). It can be shown that the valuation of a company so calculated is related to the company's weighted average cost of capital (WACC), which is the cost of the equity and debt that the firm uses to finance its business, and the company's ROIC. Specifically:

- If ROIC > WACC, the company is earning more than its cost of capital and it is creating value.
- If ROIC = WACC, the company is earning its cost of capital and its valuation will be stable.

- If ROIC < WACC, the company is earning less than its cost of capital and it is therefore destroying value.

A company that earns more than its cost of capital is even more valuable if it can grow its net operating profits less adjusted taxes (NOPLAT) over time. Conversely, a firm that is not earning its cost of capital destroys value if it grows its NOPLAT. This critical relationship between ROIC, g, and value is shown in Table A1.

In Table A1, the figures in the cells of the matrix represent the discounted present values of future free cash flows for a company that has a starting NOPLAT of $100, invested capital of $1,000, a cost of capital of 10%, and a 25-year time horizon after which ROIC = cost of capital.

Table A1 ROIC, Growth, and Valuation

NOPLAT Growth, g	ROIC 7.5%	ROIC 10.0%	ROIC 12.5%	ROIC 15.0%	ROIC 20%
3%	887	1000	1058	1113	1170
6%	708	1000	1117	1295	1442
9%	410	1000	1354	1591	1886

The important points revealed by this exercise are as follows:

1. A company with an already high ROIC can create more value by increasing its profit growth rate rather than pushing for an even higher ROIC. Thus, a company with an ROIC of 15% and a 3% growth rate can create more value by increasing its profit growth rate from 3 to 9% than it can by increasing ROIC to 20%.
2. A company with a low ROIC destroys value if it grows. Thus, if ROIC = 7.5%, a 9% growth rate for 25 years will produce less value than a 3% growth rate. This is because unprofitable growth requires capital investments, the cost of which cannot be covered. Unprofitable growth destroys value.
3. The best of both worlds is high ROIC and high growth.

Very few companies are able to maintain an ROIC > WACC and grow NOPLAT over time, but there are some notable examples, including Dell, Microsoft, and Wal-Mart. Because these companies have generally been able to fund their capital investment needs from internally generated cash flows, they have not had to issue more shares to raise capital. Thus, growth in NOPLAT has translated directly into higher earnings per share for these companies, making their shares more attractive to investors and leading to substantial share-price appreciation. By successfully pursuing strategies that result in a high ROIC and growing NOPLAT, these firms have maximized shareholder value.

NOTES

[1]There are several different ratios for measuring profitability, such as return on invested capital, return on assets, and return on equity. Although these different measures are highly correlated with each other, finance theorists argue that the return on invested capital is the most accurate measure of profitability. See T. Copeland, T. Koller, and J. Murrin, *Valuation: Measuring and Managing the Value of Companies* (New York: Wiley, 1996).

[2]Trying to estimate the relative importance of industry effects and firm strategy on firm profitability has been one of the most important areas of research in the strategy literature during the past decade. See Y. E. Spanos and S. Lioukas, "An Examination of the Causal Logic of Rent Generation," *Strategic Management* 22:10 (October 2001): 907–934; R. P. Rumelt, "How Much Does Industry Matter?" *Strategic Management* 12 (1991): 167–185. See also A. J. Mauri and M. P. Michaels, "Firm and Industry Effects Within Strategic Management: An Empirical Examination," *Strategic Management* 19 (1998): 211–219.

[3]This view is known as "agency theory." See M. C. Jensen and W. H. Meckling, "Theory of the Firm: Managerial Behavior, Agency Costs and Ownership Structure," *Journal of Financial Economics* 3 (1976): 305–360; E. F. Fama, "Agency Problems and the Theory of the Firm," *Journal of Political Economy* 88 (1980): 375–390.

[4]K. R. Andrews, *The Concept of Corporate Strategy* (Homewood, Ill.: Dow Jones Irwin, 1971); H. I. Ansoff, *Corporate Strategy* (New York: McGraw-Hill, 1965); C. W. Hofer and D. Schendel, *Strategy Formulation: Analytical Concepts* (St. Paul, Minn.: West, 1978). See also P. J. Brews and M. R. Hunt, "Learning to Plan and Planning to Learn," *Strategic Management* 20 (1999): 889–913; R. W. Grant, "Planning in a Turbulent Environment," *Strategic Management* 24 (2003): 491–517.

[5]www.google.com/about/company/.

[6]P. F. Drucker, *Management: Tasks, Responsibilities, Practices* (New York: Harper & Row, 1974), pp. 74–94.

[7]D. F. Abell, *Defining the Business: The Starting Point of Strategic Planning* (Englewood Cliffs, N.J.: Prentice-Hall, 1980).

[8]P. A. Kidwell and P. E. Ceruzzi, *Landmarks in Digital Computing* (Washington, D.C.: Smithsonian Institute, 1994).

[9]J. C. Collins and J. I. Porras, "Building Your Company's Vision," *Harvard Business Review* (September–October 1996): 65–77.

[10]www.nucor.com.

[11]See J. P. Kotter and J. L. Heskett, *Corporate Culture and Performance* (New York: Free Press, 1992); Collins and Porras, "Building Your Company's Vision."

[12]E. Freeman, *Strategic Management: A Stakeholder Approach* (Boston: Pitman Press, 1984).

[13]M. D. Richards, *Setting Strategic Goals and Objectives* (St. Paul, Minn.: West, 1986).

[14]E. A. Locke, G. P. Latham, and M. Erez, "The Determinants of Goal Commitment," *Academy of Management Review* 13 (1988): 23–39.

[15]R. E. Hoskisson, M. A. Hitt, and C. W. L. Hill, "Managerial Incentives and Investment in R&D in Large Multiproduct Firms," *Organization Science* 3 (1993): 325–341.

[16]Andrews, *Concept of Corporate Strategy;* Ansoff, *Corporate Strategy;* Hofer and Schendel, *Strategy Formulation.*

[17]For details, see R. A. Burgelman, "Intraorganizational Ecology of Strategy Making and Organizational Adaptation: Theory and Field Research," *Organization Science* 2 (1991): 239–262; H. Mintzberg,

"Patterns in Strategy Formulation," *Management Science* 24 (1978): 934–948; S. L. Hart, "An Integrative Framework for Strategy Making Processes," *Academy of Management Review* 17 (1992): 327–351; G. Hamel, "Strategy as Revolution," *Harvard Business Review* 74 (July–August 1996): 69–83; R. W. Grant, "Planning in a Turbulent Environment," *Strategic Management Journal* 24 (2003): 491–517. See also G. Gavetti, D. Levinthal, and J. W. Rivkin, "Strategy Making in Novel and Complex Worlds: The Power of Analogy," *Strategic Management Journal* 26 (2005): 691–712.

[18]This is the premise of those who advocate that complexity and chaos theory should be applied to strategic management. See S. Brown and K. M. Eisenhardt, "The Art of Continuous Change: Linking Complexity Theory and Time Based Evolution in Relentlessly Shifting Organizations," *Administrative Science Quarterly* 29 (1997): 1–34; R. Stacey and D. Parker, *Chaos, Management and Economics* (London: Institute for Economic Affairs, 1994). See also H. Courtney, J. Kirkland, and P. Viguerie, "Strategy Under Uncertainty," *Harvard Business Review* 75 (November–December 1997): 66–79.

[19]Hart, "Integrative Framework"; Hamel, "Strategy as Revolution."

[20]See Burgelman, "Intraorganizational Ecology," and Mintzberg, "Patterns in Strategy Formulation."

[21]R. A. Burgelman and A. S. Grove, "Strategic Dissonance," *California Management Review* (Winter 1996): 8–28.

[22]C. W. L. Hill and F. T. Rothaermel, "The Performance of Incumbent Firms in the Face of Radical Technological Innovation," *Academy of Management Review* 28 (2003): 257–274.

[23]Personal communication to the author by George Rathmann, former head of 3M's research activities.

[24]Richard T. Pascale, "Perspectives on Strategy: The Real Story Behind Honda's Success," *California Management Review* 26 (1984): 47–72.

[25]This viewpoint is strongly emphasized by Burgelman and Grove, "Strategic Dissonance."

[26]C. C. Miller and L. B. Cardinal, "Strategic Planning and Firm Performance: A Synthesis of More Than Two Decades of Research," *Academy of Management Journal* 37 (1994): 1649–1665. See also P. R. Rogers, A. Miller, and W. Q. Judge, "Using Information Processing Theory to Understand Planning/Performance Relationships in the Context of Strategy," *Strategic Management* 20 (1999): 567–577.

[27]P. J. Brews and M. R. Hunt, "Learning to Plan and Planning to Learn," *Strategic Management Journal* 20 (1999): 889–913.

[28]P. Cornelius, A. Van de Putte, and M. Romani, "Three Decades of Scenario Planning at Shell," *California? Management Review* 48 (2005): 92–110.

[29]H. Courtney, J. Kirkland, and P. Viguerie, "Strategy Under Uncertainty," *Harvard Business Review* 75 (November–December 1997): 66–79.

[30]P. J. H. Schoemaker, "Multiple Scenario Development: Its Conceptual and Behavioral Foundation," *Strategic Management Journal* 14 (1993): 193–213.

[31]P. Schoemaker, P. J. H. van der Heijden, and A. J. M. Cornelius, "Integrating Scenarios into Strategic Planning at Royal Dutch Shell," *Planning Review* 20:3 (1992): 41–47; I. Wylie, "There Is No Alternative to…" *Fast Company* (July 2002): 106–111.

[32]"The Next Big Surprise: Scenario Planning," *The Economist* (October 13, 2001): 71.

[33]See C. R. Schwenk, "Cognitive Simplification Processes in Strategic Decision Making," *Strategic Management* 5 (1984): 111–128; K. M. Eisenhardt and M. Zbaracki, "Strategic Decision Making," *Strategic Management* 13 (Special Issue, 1992): 17–37.

[34]H. Simon, *Administrative Behavior* (New York: McGraw-Hill, 1957).

[35]The original statement of this phenomenon was made by A. Tversky and D. Kahneman, "Judgment Under Uncertainty: Heuristics and Biases," *Science* 185 (1974): 1124–1131. See also D. Lovallo and D. Kahneman, "Delusions of Success: How Optimism Undermines Executives' Decisions," *Harvard Business Review* 81 (July 2003): 56–67; J. S. Hammond, R. L. Keeny, and H. Raiffa, "The Hidden Traps in Decision Making," *Harvard Business Review* 76 (September–October 1998): 25–34.

[36]Schwenk, "Cognitive Simplification Processes," pp. 111–128.

[37]B. M. Staw, "The Escalation of Commitment to a Course of Action," *Academy of Management Review* 6 (1981): 577–587.

[38]R. Roll, "The Hubris Hypotheses of Corporate Takeovers," *Journal of Business* 59 (1986): 197–216.

[39]See R. O. Mason, "A Dialectic Approach to Strategic Planning," *Management Science* 13 (1969): 403–414; R. A. Cosier and J. C. Aplin, "A Critical View of Dialectic Inquiry in Strategic Planning,"

Strategic Management 1 (1980): 343–356; I. I. Mintroff and R. O. Mason, "Structuring III—Structured Policy Issues: Further Explorations in a Methodology for Messy Problems," *Strategic Management* 1 (1980): 331–342.

[40] Mason, "A Dialectic Approach," pp. 403–414.

[41] Lovallo and Kahneman, "Delusions of Success."

[42] For a summary of research on strategic leadership, see D. C. Hambrick, "Putting Top Managers Back into the Picture," *Strategic Management* 10 (Special Issue, 1989): 5–15; D. Goldman, "What Makes a Leader?" *Harvard Business Review* (November–December 1998): 92–105; H. Mintzberg, "Covert Leadership," *Harvard Business Review* (November–December 1998): 140–148; R. S. Tedlow, "What Titans Can Teach Us," *Harvard Business Review* (December 2001): 70–79.

[43] N. M. Tichy and D. O. Ulrich, "The Leadership Challenge: A Call for the Transformational Leader," *Sloan Management Review* (Fall 1984): 59–68; F. Westley and H. Mintzberg, "Visionary Leadership and Strategic Management," *Strategic Management* 10 (Special Issue, 1989): 17–32.

[44] Comments made by Jim Donald at a presentation to University of Washington MBA students.

[45] B. McConnell and J. Huba. *Creating Customer Evangelists* (Chicago: Dearborn Trade Publishing, 2003).

[46] E. Wrapp, "Good Managers Don't Make Policy Decisions," *Harvard Business Review* (September–October 1967): 91–99.

[47] J. Pfeffer, *Managing with Power* (Boston: Harvard Business School Press, 1992).

[48] D. Goleman, "What Makes a Leader?" *Harvard Business Review* (November–December 1998): 92–105.

[49] C. Y. Baldwin, *Fundamental Enterprise Valuation: Return on Invested Capital*, Harvard Business School Note 9-801-125, July 3, 2004; T. Copeland et al., *Valuation: Measuring and Managing the Value of Companies* (New York: Wiley, 2000).

CHAPTER **2**

EXTERNAL ANALYSIS: THE IDENTIFICATION OF OPPORTUNITIES AND THREATS

OPENING CASE

Competition in the U.S. Market for Wireless Telecommunications

Over the last two decades, the wireless telecommunications industry in the United States has been characterized by strong growth as demand for mobile phones—and, since 2007 smartphones—drove industry revenues forward. In 2000, there were 109 million wireless subscribers in the United States. By 2014, the number had risen to almost 360 million, representing a penetration rate of 108% (some people had multiple phones). Moreover, smartphone penetration had risen from 37% of the population in 2010 to 83% by 2014.

As the market has grown, the competitive structure of the industry has become increasingly consolidated. Today four companies dominate the

Zhang Peng/Getty Images

industry: Verizon with 38% of the market, AT&T with 33%, Sprint with 15%, and T-Mobile also with 15%. Much of the consolidation has been achieved through mergers and acquisitions. In 2004, AT&T bought Cingular for $41 billion; in 2005, Sprint and Nextel closed a $36-billion merger; and in 2009, Verizon bought Alltel for $28.1 billion. Since then regulatory authorities have stymied further merger attempts between large players. In 2011, AT&T tried to purchase T-Mobile, but was blocked by regulators. A 2014 merger proposal between T-Mobile and Sprint was also scuttled by objections from regulators.

The merger wave was driven by a realization among wireless companies that only the largest firms can reap the scale economies necessary to be profitable in this capital-intensive industry. Building out network infrastructure such as cell towers, and constantly upgrading that infrastructure to deliver fast, reliable voice and data service, has consumed over $400 billion in capital spending since 1985; $330 billion of that has been spent since 2000. By 2014, capital expenditures in the industry were running at $35 billion a year. Wireless companies have also spent $53 billion so far to acquire from the government the right to use the wireless spectrum. The government periodically auctions off the spectrum, and competition among wireless providers typically drives up the price. Companies in the industry have also had to spend heavily on marketing to establish their brands, and on building out a nationwide network of retail stores to provide point-of-sale service to their customers.

Until recently, competition in the industry primarily focused on non-price factors such as service coverage and reliability, handset equipment, service packages, and brand. Verizon, for example, emphasized its superior coverage and the high speed of its network; AT&T gained share when it signed a deal in 2007 to be the exclusive supplier of Apple's iPhone for one year; and T-Mobile branded itself as the hip network for young people looking for value. To reduce customer churn and limit price competition, service providers required customers to enter into 2-year contracts with early termination fees in exchange for new equipment (the cost of which was heavily subsidized), or purchase updated service plans.

However, with the market now saturated, and regulators blocking further merger attempts, competition is increasingly based on price. The shift began in early 2013, when T-Mobile broke ranks with the industry and began discarding 2-year contracts and early-termination fees, and eliminating subsidies of several hundred dollars for new phones, instead offering customers the option to pay for new devices in monthly installments. When merger talks broke down between Sprint and T-Mobile in mid-2014, Sprint quickly shifted its strategy and went after market share by offering customers who switch from rivals lower prices and more data. T-Mobile responded with a similar offering of its own, and the price war started to accelerate in the industry. In December 2014, T-Mobile upped the stakes with further price cuts that would save a family of four 50% in their monthly payments compared to a similar plan from Verizon (Verizon continues to subsidize the cost of handsets, T-Mobile does not). Both AT&T and Sprint rolled out their own offers to keep pace with T-Mobile. In signs that the price war is starting to hurt the industry, in December both AT&T and Verizon warned investors that their profits might take a hit going forward due to declining average revenues per customer and high capital expenditures.

Sources: C. Lobello, "Wireless merger madness," *The Week*, April 25, 2013; M. De la Merced and B. Chen, "No merger of Sprint and T-Mobile," *New York Times*, August 6, 2014; "Number of wireless subscribers in the United States," *Statista*, www.statista.com; *CTIA* Wireless Industry Association Survey Results, 1985-2013, CTIA, archived at www.ctia.org; P. Dave, "Wireless price wars drive down costs for consumers, sales for carriers," *Los Angeles Times*, December 9, 2014.

◤OVERVIEW

opportunities

Elements and conditions in a company's environment that allow it to formulate and implement strategies that enable it to become more profitable.

threats

Elements in the external environment that could endanger the integrity and profitability of the company's business.

Strategy formulation begins with an analysis of the forces that shape competition within the industry in which a company is based. The goal is to understand the opportunities and threats confronting the firm, and to use this understanding to identify strategies that will enable the company to outperform its rivals. **Opportunities** arise when a company can take advantage of conditions in its industry environment to formulate and implement strategies that enable it to become more profitable. For example, as discussed in the Opening Case, the growth of demand for smartphone data services created an enormous opportunity for wireless companies to grow their revenues during the 2007–2013 time period. **Threats** arise when conditions in the external environment endanger the integrity and profitability of the company's business. The biggest threats confronting wireless service providers today are market saturation and the acceleration of price wars that began in late 2014 (see the Opening Case).

This chapter begins with an analysis of the external industry environment. First, it examines concepts and tools for analyzing the competitive structure of an industry and identifying industry opportunities and threats. Second, it analyzes the competitive implications that arise when groups of companies within an industry pursue similar or different kinds of competitive strategies. Third, it explores the way an industry evolves over time, and the changes present in competitive conditions. Fourth, it looks at the way in which forces in the macroenvironment affect industry structure and influence opportunities and threats. By the end of the chapter, you will understand that, in order to succeed, a company must either fit its strategy to the external environment in which it operates or be able to reshape the environment to its advantage through its chosen strategy.

◤DEFINING AN INDUSTRY

industry

A group of companies offering products or services that are close substitutes for each other.

An **industry** can be defined as a group of companies offering products or services that are close substitutes for each other—that is, products or services that satisfy the same basic customer needs. A company's closest competitors—its rivals—are those that serve the same basic customer needs. For example, carbonated drinks, fruit punches, and bottled water can be viewed as close substitutes for each other because they serve the same basic customer needs for refreshing, cold, nonalcoholic beverages. Thus, we can talk about the soft drink industry, whose major players are Coca-Cola, PepsiCo, and Cadbury Schweppes. Similarly, desktop and laptop computers and tablets satisfy the same basic need that customers have for computer hardware devices on which to run personal productivity software, browse the Internet, send e-mail, play games, music and video, and store, display, or manipulate digital images. Thus, we can talk about the computer hardware device industry, whose participants include Apple, Dell, Hewlett-Packard, Lenovo, Microsoft, and Samsung.

External analysis begins by identifying the industry within which a company competes. To do this, managers must start by looking at the basic customer needs their company is serving—that is, they must take a customer-oriented view of their business rather than a product-oriented view (see Chapter 1). The basic customer needs that are served by a market define an industry's boundaries. It is very important for managers to realize this, for if they define industry boundaries incorrectly, they may be caught off-guard by the rise of competitors that serve the same basic customer needs but with different product offerings. For example, Coca-Cola long saw itself as part of the soda industry—meaning carbonated soft drinks—whereas it actually was part of the soft drink industry, which includes noncarbonated soft drinks. In the mid-1990s, the rise of customer demand for bottled water and fruit drinks began to cut into the demand for sodas, which caught Coca-Cola by surprise. Coca-Cola moved quickly to respond to these threats, introducing its own brand of water, Dasani, and acquiring several other beverage companies, including Minute Maid and Glaceau (the owner of the Vitamin Water brand). By defining its industry boundaries too narrowly, Coke almost missed the rapid rise of noncarbonated soft drinks within the soft-drinks market.

It is important to realize that industry boundaries may change over time as customer needs evolve, or as emerging new technologies enable companies in unrelated industries to satisfy established customer needs in new ways. We have noted that during the 1990s, as consumers of soft drinks began to develop a taste for bottled water and noncarbonated fruit-based drinks, Coca-Cola found itself in direct competition with the manufacturers of bottled water and fruit-based soft drinks: All were in the same industry.

For another example of how technological change can alter industry boundaries, consider the convergence that has taken place between the computer and telecommunications industries. Historically, the telecommunications equipment industry has been considered an entity distinct from the computer hardware industry. However, as telecommunications equipment moved from analog technology to digital technology, this equipment increasingly resembled computers. The result is that the boundaries between these once distinct industries has been blurred. A smartphone such as Apple's iPhone is nothing more than a small, handheld computer with a wireless connection and telephone capabilities. Thus, Samsung and HTC, which manufacture wireless phones, are now competing directly with traditional computer companies such as Apple and Microsoft.

◤ PORTER'S COMPETITIVE FORCES MODEL

Once the boundaries of an industry have been identified, managers face the task of analyzing competitive forces within the industry environment in order to identify opportunities and threats. Michael E. Porter's well-known framework, the Five Forces model, helps managers with this analysis.[1] An extension of his model, shown in Figure 2.1, focuses on *six* forces that shape competition within an industry: (1) the risk of entry by potential competitors, (2) the intensity of rivalry among established companies within an industry, (3) the bargaining power of buyers, (4) the bargaining power of suppliers, (5) the closeness of substitutes to an industry's products, and (6) the power of complement providers (Porter did not recognize this sixth force).

As each of these forces grows stronger, it limits the ability of established companies to raise prices and earn greater profits. Within this framework, a strong competitive force can be regarded as a threat because it depresses profits. A weak competitive force can be viewed as an opportunity because it allows a company to earn greater profits. The strength of the six forces may change over time as industry conditions change. Managers face the task of recognizing how changes in the six forces give rise to new opportunities and threats, and formulating appropriate strategic responses. In addition, it is possible for a company, through its choice of strategy, to alter the strength of one or more of the forces to its advantage. This is discussed in the following chapters.

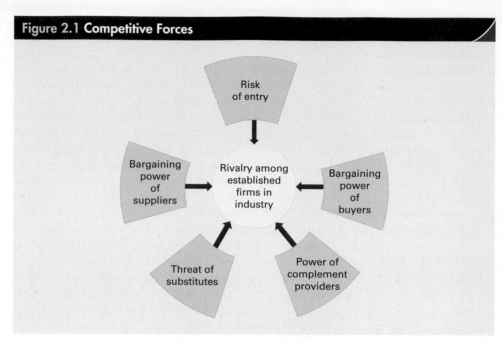

Figure 2.1 Competitive Forces

Source: Based on How Competitive Forces Shape Strategy, by Michael E. Porter, Harvard Business Review, March/April 1979.

Risk of Entry by Potential Competitors

potential competitors
Companies that are currently not competing in the industry but have the potential to do so.

Potential competitors are companies that are not currently competing in an industry but have the capability to do so if they choose. For example, in the last decade, cable television companies emerged as potential competitors to traditional phone companies. New digital technologies have allowed cable companies to offer telephone and Internet service over the same cables that transmit television shows.

Established companies already operating in an industry often attempt to discourage potential competitors from entering the industry because their entry makes it more difficult for the established companies to protect their share of the market and generate profits. A high risk of entry by potential competitors represents a threat to the profitability of established companies.

The risk of entry by potential competitors is a function of the height of the barriers to entry; that is, those factors that make it costly for companies to enter an industry. The greater the costs potential competitors must bear to enter an industry, the greater the barriers to entry, and the weaker this competitive force. High entry barriers may keep potential competitors out of an industry even when industry profits are high. Important barriers to entry include economies of scale, brand loyalty, absolute cost advantages, customer switching costs, and government regulation.[2] An important strategy is building barriers to entry (in the case of incumbent firms) or finding ways to circumvent those barriers (in the case of new entrants). We shall discuss this topic in more detail in subsequent chapters.

economies of scale
Reductions in unit costs attributed to large output.

Economies of Scale **Economies of scale** arise when unit costs fall as a firm expands its output. Sources of scale economies include: (1) cost reductions gained through mass-producing a standardized output; (2) discounts on bulk purchases of raw material inputs and component parts; (3) the advantages gained by spreading fixed production costs over a large production volume; and (4) the cost savings associated with distributing, marketing, and advertising costs over a large volume of output. For example, as discussed in the Opening Case, the economies of scale enjoyed by incumbent firms in the wireless telecommunications industry are large, and this constitutes a significant barrier to new entry into the market. More generally, if the cost advantages from economies of scale are significant, a new company that enters the industry and produces on a small scale suffers a significant cost disadvantage relative to established companies. If the new company decides to enter on a large scale in an attempt to obtain these economies of scale, it must raise the capital required to build large-scale production facilities and bear the high risks associated with such an investment. In addition, an increased supply of products will depress prices and result in vigorous retaliation by established companies, which constitutes a further risk of large-scale entry. For these reasons, the threat of entry is reduced when established companies achieve economies of scale.

Brand Loyalty   **Brand loyalty** exists when consumers have a preference for the products of established companies. A company can create brand loyalty by continuously advertising its brand-name products and company name, patent protection of its products, product innovation achieved through company research and development (R&D) programs, an emphasis on high-quality products, and exceptional after-sales service. Significant brand loyalty makes it difficult for new entrants to take market share away from established companies. Thus, it reduces the threat of entry by potential competitors; they may see the task of breaking down well-established customer preferences as too costly. In the smartphone business, for example, Apple has generated such strong brand loyalty with its iPhone offering and related products that Microsoft is finding it very difficult to attract customers away from Apple and build demand for its Windows phone, introduced in late 2011. Despite its financial might, three years after launching the Windows phone, Microsoft's U.S. market share remained mired at around 3.6%, whereas Apple led the market with a 42% share.[3]

brand loyalty
Preference of consumers for the products of established companies.

Absolute Cost Advantages   Sometimes established companies have an **absolute cost advantage** relative to potential entrants, meaning that entrants cannot expect to match the established companies' lower cost structure. Absolute cost advantages arise from three main sources: (1) superior production operations and processes due to accumulated experience, patents, or trade secrets; (2) control of particular inputs required for production, such as labor, materials, equipment, or management skills, that are limited in supply; and (3) access to cheaper funds because existing companies represent lower risks than new entrants. If established companies have an absolute cost advantage, the threat of entry as a competitive force weakens.

absolute cost advantage
A cost advantage that is enjoyed by incumbents in an industry and that new entrants cannot expect to match.

Customer Switching Costs   **Switching costs** arise when a customer invests time, energy, and money switching from the products offered by one established company to the products offered by a new entrant. When switching costs are high, customers can be locked in to the product offerings of established companies, even if new entrants offer better products.[4] A familiar example of switching costs concerns the costs associated with switching from one computer operating system to another. If a person currently uses Microsoft's Windows operating system and has a library of related software applications and document files, it is expensive for that person to switch to another computer operating system. To effect the change, this person would need to purchase a new set of software applications and convert all existing document

switching costs
Costs that consumers must bear to switch from the products offered by one established company to the products offered by a new entrant.

files to the new system's format. Faced with such a commitment of money and time, most people are unwilling to make the switch unless the competing operating system offers a substantial leap forward in performance. Thus, the higher the switching costs, the higher the barrier to entry for a company attempting to promote a new computer operating system. Similarly, as we saw in the Opening Case, wireless service companies have traditionally created high switching costs by requiring customers to enter into 2-year contracts with early-termination fees whenever they upgrade their equipment.

Government Regulations Government regulation can constitute a major entry barrier for many industries. For example, until the mid-1990s, U.S. government regulation prohibited providers of long-distance telephone service from competing for local telephone service, and vice versa. Other potential providers of telephone service, including cable television service companies such as Time Warner and Comcast (which could have used their cables to carry telephone traffic as well as TV signals), were prohibited from entering the market altogether. These regulatory barriers to entry significantly reduced the level of competition in both the local and long-distance telephone markets, enabling telephone companies to earn higher profits than they might have otherwise. All this changed in 1996, when the government significantly deregulated the industry. In the months that followed, local, long-distance, and cable TV companies all announced their intention to enter each other's markets, and a host of new players entered the market as well. The competitive forces model predicts that falling entry barriers due to government deregulation will result in significant new entry, an increase in the intensity of industry competition, and lower industry profit rates, and that is what occurred here.

In summary, if established companies have built brand loyalty for their products, have an absolute cost advantage over potential competitors, have significant scale economies, are the beneficiaries of high switching costs, or enjoy regulatory protection, the risk of entry by potential competitors is greatly diminished; it is a weak competitive force. Consequently, established companies can charge higher prices, and industry profits are therefore higher. Evidence from academic research suggests that the height of barriers to entry is one of the most important determinants of profit rates within an industry.[5] Clearly, it is in the interest of established companies to pursue strategies consistent with raising entry barriers to secure these profits. Additionally, potential new entrants must find strategies that allow them to circumvent barriers to entry.

Rivalry Among Established Companies

The second competitive force is the intensity of rivalry among established companies within an industry. Rivalry refers to the competitive struggle between companies within an industry to gain market share. The competitive struggle can be fought using price, product design, advertising and promotional spending, direct-selling efforts, and after-sales service and support. Intense rivalry implies lower prices or more spending on non-price-competitive strategies, or both. Because intense rivalry lowers prices and raises costs, it squeezes profits out of an industry. Thus, intense rivalry among established companies constitutes a strong threat to profitability. Alternatively, if rivalry is less intense, companies may have the opportunity to raise prices or reduce spending on non-price-competitive strategies, leading to higher industry profits. Four factors have a major impact on the intensity of rivalry among established companies within an industry: (1) industry competitive structure, (2) demand conditions, (3) cost conditions, and (4) the height of exit barriers in the industry.

2.1 STRATEGY IN ACTION

Circumventing Entry Barriers into the Soft Drink Industry

Two companies have long dominated the carbonated soft drink industry: Coca-Cola and PepsiCo. By spending large sums of money on advertising and promotion, these two giants have created significant brand loyalty and made it very difficult for new competitors to enter the industry and take away market share. When new competitors have tried to enter, both companies have responded by cutting prices, forcing new entrants to curtail expansion plans.

However, in the early 1990s, the Cott Corporation, then a small Canadian bottling company, worked out a strategy for entering the carbonated soft drink market. Cott's strategy was deceptively simple. The company initially focused on the cola segment of the market. Cott struck a deal with Royal Crown (RC) Cola for exclusive global rights to its cola concentrate. RC Cola was a small player in the U.S. cola market. Its products were recognized as high quality, but RC Cola had never been able to effectively challenge Coke or Pepsi. Next, Cott entered an agreement with a Canadian grocery retailer, Loblaw, to provide the retailer with its own, private-label brand of cola. The Loblaw private-label brand, known as "President's Choice," was priced low, became very successful, and took shares from both Coke and Pepsi.

Emboldened by this success, Cott tried to convince other retailers to carry private-label cola. To retailers, the value proposition was simple because, unlike its major rivals, Cott spent almost nothing on advertising and promotion. This constituted a major source of cost savings, which Cott passed on to retailers in the form of lower prices. Retailers found that they could significantly undercut the price of Coke and Pepsi colas and still make better profit margins on private-label brands than on branded colas.

Despite this compelling value proposition, few retailers were willing to sell private-label colas for fear of alienating Coca-Cola and Pepsi, whose products were a major draw for grocery store traffic. Cott's breakthrough came when it signed a deal with Wal-Mart to supply the retailing giant with a private-label cola, "Sam's Choice" (named after Wal-Mart founder Sam Walton). Wal-Mart proved to be the perfect distribution channel for Cott. The retailer was just beginning to appear in the grocery business, and consumers shopped at Wal-Mart not to buy branded merchandise, but to get low prices. As Wal-Mart's grocery business grew, so did Cott's sales. Cott soon added other flavors to its offerings, such as lemon-lime soda, which would compete with 7-Up and Sprite. Moreover, by the late 1990s, other U.S. grocers pressured by Wal-Mart had also started to introduce private-label sodas and often turned to Cott to supply their needs.

By 2014, Cott's private-label customers included Wal-Mart, Kroger, Costco, and Safeway. Cott had revenues of $2.33 billion and accounted for 60% of all private-label sales of carbonated beverages in the United States, and 6 to 7% of overall sales of carbonated beverages in grocery stores, its core channel. Although Coca-Cola and PepsiCo remain dominant, they have lost incremental market share to Cott and other companies that have followed Cott's strategy.

Sources: A. Kaplan, "Cott Corporation," *Beverage World*, June 15, 2004, p. 32; J. Popp, "2004 Soft Drink Report," *Beverage Industry*, March 2004, pp. 13–18; L. Sparks, "From Coca-Colonization to Copy Catting: The Cott Corporation and Retailers Brand Soft Drinks in the UK and US," *Agribusiness* 13:2 (March 1997): 153–167; E. Cherney, "After Flat Sales, Cott Challenges Pepsi, Coca-Cola," *The Wall Street Journal*, January 8, 2003, pp. B1, B8; "Cott Corporation: Company Profile," *Just Drinks*, August 2006, pp. 19–22; Cott Corp. 2011 Annual Report, www.cott.com.

Industry Competitive Structure   The competitive structure of an industry refers to the number and size distribution of companies within it, something that strategic managers determine at the beginning of an industry analysis. Industry structures vary, and different structures have different implications for the intensity of rivalry. A fragmented industry consists of a large number of small or medium-sized companies, none of which is in a position to determine industry price. A consolidated industry is dominated by a small number of large companies (an oligopoly) or, in extreme cases, by just one company (a monopoly), and such companies often are in a position to determine industry prices. Examples of fragmented industries are agriculture, dry cleaning, health clubs, real estate brokerage, and sun-tanning parlors. Consolidated industries include the aerospace, soft drink, wireless service (see the Opening Case), and small-package express delivery industries. In the small-package express delivery industry, two firms, UPS and FedEx, account for over 85% of industry revenues in the United States.

Low-entry barriers and commodity-type products that are difficult to differentiate characterize many fragmented industries. This combination tends to result in boom-and-bust cycles as industry profits rapidly rise and fall. Low-entry barriers imply that new entrants will flood the market, hoping to profit from the boom that occurs when demand is strong and profits are high. The number of video stores, health clubs, and sun-tanning parlors that exploded onto the market during the 1980s and 1990s exemplifies this situation.

Often, the flood of new entrants into a booming, fragmented industry creates excess capacity, and consequently companies cut prices. The difficulty of differentiating their products from those of competitors can exacerbate this tendency. The result is a price war, which depresses industry profits, forces some companies out of business, and deters potential new entrants. For example, after a decade of expansion and booming profits, many health clubs are now finding that they have to offer large discounts in order to maintain their memberships. In general, the more commodity-like an industry's product, the more vicious the price war will be. The bust phase of this cycle continues until overall industry capacity is brought into line with demand (through bankruptcies), at which point prices may stabilize again.

A fragmented industry structure, then, constitutes a threat rather than an opportunity. Economic boom times in fragmented industries are often relatively short-lived because the ease of new entry can soon result in excess capacity, which in turn leads to intense price competition and the failure of less-efficient enterprises. Because it is often difficult to differentiate products in these industries, minimizing costs is the best strategy for a company that strives to be profitable in a boom and survive any subsequent bust. Alternatively, companies might try to adopt strategies that change the underlying structure of fragmented industries and lead to a consolidated industry structure in which the level of industry profitability is increased. (We shall consider how companies can do this is sider in later chapters.)

In consolidated industries, companies are interdependent because one company's competitive actions (for instance, changes in price or quality) directly affect the market share of its rivals and thus their profitability. One company making a move can force a response from its rivals, and the consequence of such competitive interdependence can be a dangerous competitive spiral. Rivalry increases as companies attempt to undercut each other's prices or offer customers more value, pushing industry profits down in the process. This seems to be happening today in the wireless telecommunications industry (see the Opening Case).

Companies in consolidated industries sometimes seek to reduce this threat by matching the prices set by the dominant company in the industry.[6] However, care must be taken, for explicit, face-to-face, price-fixing agreements are illegal. (Tacit, indirect agreements, arrived at without direct or intentional communication, are legal.) For the most part, though, companies set prices by watching, interpreting, anticipating, and responding to one another's strategies. However, tacit price-leadership agreements often break down under adverse economic conditions, as has occurred in the breakfast cereal industry, profiled in Strategy in Action 2.2.

Industry Demand The level of industry demand is another determinant of the intensity of rivalry/among established companies. Growing demand from new customers or additional purchases by existing customers tend to moderate competition by providing greater scope for companies to compete for customers. Growing demand tends to reduce rivalry because all companies can sell more without taking market share away from other companies. High industry profits are often the result. This was the case in the U.S. wireless telecommunications industry until recently (see the Opening Case). Conversely, stagnant or declining demand results in increased rivalry as companies fight to maintain market share and revenues (see Strategy in Action 2.2). Demand stagnates when the market is saturated and replacement demand is not enough to offset the lack of first-time buyers. Demand declines when customers exit the marketplace, or when each customer purchases less. When demand is stagnating or declining, a company can grow only by taking market share away from its rivals, as is now occurring in the U.S. wireless telecommunications industry, where aggressive price cuts by T-Mobile and Sprint are designed to grab market share from rivals. Stagnant or declining demand constitutes a threat because for it increases the extent of rivalry between established companies.

Cost Conditions The cost structure of firms in an industry is a third determinant of rivalry. In industries where fixed costs are high, profitability tends to be highly leveraged to sales volume, and the desire to grow volume can spark intense rivalry. Again, this is the case in the U.S. wireless telecommunications industry (see Opening Case). Fixed costs are costs that must be paid before the firm makes a single sale. For example, before they can offer service, cable TV companies must lay cable in the ground; the cost of doing so is a fixed cost. Similarly, to offer express courier service, a company such as FedEx must first invest in planes, package-sorting facilities, and delivery trucks—all fixed costs that require significant capital investment. In industries where the cost of production is high, firms cannot cover their fixed costs and will not be profitable if sales volume is low. Thus, they have an incentive to cut their prices and/or increase promotional spending to drive up sales volume in order to cover fixed costs. In situations where demand is not rapidly growing and many companies are simultaneously engaged in the same pursuits, the result can be intense rivalry and lower profits. Research suggests that the weakest firms in an industry often initiate such actions precisely because they are struggling to cover their fixed costs.[7]

Exit Barriers Exit barriers are economic, strategic, and emotional factors that prevent companies from leaving an industry.[8] If exit barriers are high, companies become locked into an unprofitable industry where overall demand is static or declining. The result is often excess productive capacity, leading to even more intense rivalry and price competition as companies cut prices, attempting to obtain the customer orders needed to use their idle capacity and cover their fixed costs.[9] Common exit barriers include:

- Investments in assets such as specific machines, equipment, or operating facilities that are of little or no value in alternative uses, or cannot be later sold. If the company wishes to leave the industry, it must write off the book value of these assets.
- High fixed costs of exit such as severance pay, health benefits, or pensions that must be paid to workers who are being made laid off when a company ceases to operate.

2.2 STRATEGY IN ACTION

Price Wars in the Breakfast Cereal Industry

For decades, the breakfast cereal industry was one of the most profitable in the United States. The industry has a consolidated structure dominated by Kellogg's, General Mills, and Kraft Foods with its Post brand. Strong brand loyalty, coupled with control over the allocation of supermarket shelf space, helped to limit the potential for new entry. Meanwhile, steady demand growth of about 3% per annum kept industry revenues expanding. Kellogg's, which accounted for over 40% of the market share, acted as the price leader in the industry. Every year, Kellogg's increased cereal prices, its rivals followed, and industry profits remained high.

This favorable industry structure began to change in the 1990s, when growth in demand slowed—and then stagnated—as a latte and bagel or muffin replaced cereal as the American morning fare. Then came the rise of powerful discounters such as Wal-Mart (which entered the grocery industry in 1994) that began to aggressively promote their own cereal brands and priced them significantly below the brand-name cereals. As the decade progressed, other grocery chains such as Kroger's started to follow suit, and brand loyalty in the industry began to decline as customers realized that a $2.50 bag of wheat flakes from Wal-Mart tasted about the same as a $3.50 box of cornflakes from Kellogg's. As sales of cheaper, store-brand cereals began to take off, supermarkets, no longer as dependent on brand names to bring traffic into their stores, began to demand lower prices from the branded cereal manufacturers.

For several years, manufacturers of brand-name cereals tried to hold out against these adverse trends, but in the mid-1990s, the dam broke. In 1996, Kraft (then owned by Philip Morris) aggressively cut prices by 20% for its Post brand in an attempt to gain market share. Kellogg's soon followed with a 19% price cut on two-thirds of its brands, and General Mills quickly did the same. The decades of tacit price collusion were officially over.

If breakfast cereal companies were hoping that price cuts would stimulate demand, they were wrong.

Instead, demand remained flat while revenues and margins followed price decreases, and operating margins at Kellogg's dropped from 18% in 1995 to 10.2% in 1996, a trend also experienced by the other brand-name cereal manufacturers.

By 2000, conditions had only worsened. Private-label sales continued to make inroads, gaining over 10% of the market. Moreover, sales of breakfast cereals started to contract at 1% per annum. To cap it off, an aggressive General Mills continued to launch expensive price-and-promotion campaigns in an attempt to take away share from the market leader. Kellogg's saw its market share slip to just over 30% in 2001, behind the 31% now held by General Mills. For the first time since 1906, Kellogg's no longer led the market. Moreover, profits at all three major producers remained weak in the face of continued price discounting.

In mid-2001, General Mills finally blinked and raised prices a modest 2% in response to its own rising costs. Competitors followed, signaling—perhaps—that after a decade of costly price warfare, pricing discipline might once more emerge in the industry. Both Kellogg's and General Mills tried to move further away from price competition by focusing on brand extensions, such as Special K containing berries and new varieties of Cheerios. Efforts with Special K helped Kellogg's recapture market leadership from General Mills, and, more important, the renewed emphasis on non-price competition halted years of damaging price warfare.

After a decade of relative peace, price wars broke out in 2010 once more in this industry. The trigger, yet again, appears to have been falling demand for breakfast cereals due to substitutes such as a quick trip to the local coffee shop. In the third quarter of 2010, prices fell by 3.6% and unit volumes by 3.4%, leading to falling profit rates at Kellogg's. Both General Mills and Kellogg's introduced new products in an attempt to boost demand and raise prices.

Sources: G. Morgenson, "Denial in Battle Creek," *Forbes*, October 7, 1996, p. 44; J. Muller, "Thinking out of the Cereal Box," *Business Week*, January 15, 2001, p. 54; A. Merrill, "General Mills Increases Prices," *Star Tribune*, June 5, 2001, p. 1D; S. Reyes, "Big G, Kellogg's Attempt to Berry Each Other," *Brandweek*, October 7, 2002, p. 8; M. Andrejczak, "Kellogg's Profit Hurt by Cereal Price War," *Market Watch*, November 2, 2010.

- Emotional attachments to an industry, such as when a company's owners or employees are unwilling to exit an industry for sentimental reasons or because of pride.
- Economic dependence because a company relies on a single industry for its entire revenue and all profits.
- The need to maintain an expensive collection of assets at or above a minimum level in order to participate effectively in the industry.
- Bankruptcy regulations, particularly in the United States, where Chapter 11 bankruptcy provisions allow insolvent enterprises to continue operating and to reorganize under this protection. These regulations can keep unprofitable assets in the industry, result in persistent excess capacity, and lengthen the time required to bring industry supply in line with demand.

As an example of exit barriers and effects in practice, consider the small-package express mail and parcel delivery industry. Key players in this industry such as FedEx and UPS rely entirely upon the delivery business for their revenues and profits. They must be able to guarantee their customers that they will deliver packages to all major localities in the United States, and much of their investment is specific to this purpose. To meet this guarantee, they need a nationwide network of air routes and ground routes, an asset that is required in order to participate in the industry. If excess capacity develops in this industry, as it does from time to time, FedEx cannot incrementally reduce or minimize its excess capacity by deciding not to fly to and deliver packages in Miami, for example, because that portion of its network is underused. If it did, it would no longer be able to guarantee to its customers that packages could be delivered to all major locations in the United States, and its customers would switch to another carrier. Thus, the need to maintain a nationwide network is an exit barrier that can result in persistent excess capacity in the air-express industry during periods of weak demand.

The Bargaining Power of Buyers

The third competitive force is the bargaining power of buyers. An industry's buyers may be the individual customers who consume its products (end-users) or the companies that distribute an industry's products to end-users, such as retailers and wholesalers. For example, although soap powder made by Procter & Gamble (P&G) and Unilever is consumed by end-users, the principal buyers of soap powder are supermarket chains and discount stores, which resell the product to end-users. The bargaining power of buyers refers to the ability of buyers to bargain down prices charged by companies in the industry, or to raise the costs of companies in the industry by demanding better product quality and service. By lowering prices and raising costs, powerful buyers can squeeze profits out of an industry. Powerful buyers, therefore, should be viewed as a threat. Alternatively, when buyers are in a weak bargaining position, companies in an industry can raise prices and perhaps reduce their costs by lowering product quality and service, thus increasing the level of industry profits. Buyers are most powerful in the following circumstances:

- When buyers have choice. If the industry is a monopoly, buyers obviously lack choice. If there are two or more companies in the industry, the buyers clearly have choice.
- When the buyers purchase in large quantities, they can use their purchasing power as leverage to bargain for price reductions.

- When the supply industry depends upon buyers for a large percentage of its total orders.
- When switching costs are low and buyers can pit the supplying companies against each other to force down prices.
- When it is economically feasible for buyers to purchase an input from several companies at once, they can pit one company in the industry against another.
- When buyers can threaten to enter the industry and independently produce the product, thus supplying their own needs, they can force down industry prices.

The automobile component supply industry, whose buyers are large manufacturers such as GM, Ford, Honda, and Toyota, is a good example of an industry in which buyers have strong bargaining power, and thus pose a strong competitive threat. Why? The suppliers of auto components are numerous and typically smaller in scale; their buyers, the auto manufacturers, are large in size and few in number. Additionally, to keep component prices down, historically both Ford and GM have used the threat of manufacturing a component themselves rather than buying it from a supplier. The automakers use their powerful position to pit suppliers against one another, forcing down the prices for component parts, and to demand better quality. If a component supplier objects, the automaker can use the threat of switching to another supplier as a bargaining tool.

The Bargaining Power of Suppliers

The fourth competitive force is the bargaining power of suppliers—the organizations that provide inputs into the industry, such as materials, services, and labor (which may be individuals, organizations such as labor unions, or companies that supply contract labor). The bargaining power of suppliers refers to the ability of suppliers to raise input prices, or to raise the costs of the industry in other ways—for example, by providing poor-quality inputs or poor service. Powerful suppliers squeeze profits out of an industry by raising the costs of companies in the industry. Thus, powerful suppliers are a threat. Conversely, if suppliers are weak, companies in the industry have the opportunity to force down input prices and demand higher-quality inputs (such as more productive labor). As with buyers, the ability of suppliers to make demands on a company depends on their power relative to that of the company. Suppliers are most powerful in these situations:

- The product that suppliers sell has few substitutes and is vital to the companies in an industry.
- The profitability of suppliers is not significantly affected by the purchases of companies in a particular industry; in other words, when the industry is not an important customer to the suppliers.
- Companies in an industry would experience significant switching costs if they moved to the product of a different supplier because a particular supplier's products are unique or different. In such cases, the company depends upon a particular supplier and cannot pit suppliers against each other to reduce prices.
- Suppliers can threaten to enter their customers' industry and use their inputs to produce products that would compete directly with those of companies already in the industry.
- Companies in the industry cannot threaten to enter their suppliers' industry and make their own inputs as a tactic for lowering the price of inputs.

An example of an industry in which companies are dependent upon a powerful supplier is the PC industry. Personal computer firms are heavily dependent on Intel, the world's largest supplier of microprocessors for PCs. Intel's microprocessor chips are the industry standard for personal computers. Intel's competitors, such as Advanced Micro Devices (AMD), must develop and supply chips that are compatible with Intel's standard. Although AMD has developed competing chips, Intel still supplies approximately 85% of the chips used in PCs primarily because only Intel has the manufacturing capacity required to serve a large share of the market. It is beyond the financial resources of Intel's competitors to match the scale and efficiency of its manufacturing systems. This means that although PC manufacturers can purchase some microprocessors from Intel's rivals, most notably AMD, they still must turn to Intel for the bulk of their supply. Because Intel is in a powerful bargaining position, it can charge higher prices for its microprocessors than if its competitors were stronger and more numerous (that is, if the microprocessor industry were fragmented).

Substitute Products

The final force in Porter's model is the threat of substitute products: the products of different businesses or industries that can satisfy similar customer needs. For example, companies in the coffee industry compete indirectly with those in the tea and soft drink industries because all three serve customer needs for nonalcoholic, caffeinated drinks. The existence of close substitutes is a strong competitive threat because it limits the price that companies in one industry can charge for their product, which also limits industry profitability. If the price of coffee rises too much relative to that of tea or soft drinks, coffee drinkers may switch to those substitutes.

If an industry's products have few close substitutes (making substitutes a weak competitive force), then companies in the industry have the opportunity to raise prices and earn additional profits. There is no close substitute for microprocessors, which thus gives companies like Intel and AMD the ability to charge higher prices than if there were available substitutes.

Complementors

Andrew Grove, the former CEO of Intel, has argued that Porter's original formulation of competitive forces ignored a sixth force: the power, vigor, and competence of complementors.[10] Complementors are companies that sell products that add value to (complement) the products of companies in an industry because, when used together, the combined products better satisfy customer demands. For example, the complementors to the PC industry are the companies that make software applications. The greater the supply of high-quality software applications running on these machines, the greater the value of PCs to customers, the greater the demand for PCs, and the greater the profitability of the PC industry.

Grove's argument has a strong foundation in economic theory, which has long argued that both substitutes and complements influence demand in an industry.[11] Research has emphasized the importance of complementary products in determining demand and profitability in many high-technology industries such as the computer industry, where Grove made his mark.[12] When complements are an important determinant of demand for an industry's products, industry profits critically depend upon an adequate supply of complementary products. When the number of complementors is increasing and producing attractive complementary products, demand increases and profits in the industry can broaden opportunities for creating value. Conversely, if complementors are weak, and are not producing attractive complementary products, they can become a threat, slowing industry growth and limiting profitability.

It is also possible for complementors to gain so much power that they are able to extract profit from the industry to which they provide complements. Complementors this strong can be a competitive threat. For example, in the videogame industry, the companies that produce the consoles—Nintendo, Microsoft (Xbox), and Sony (PS3)—have historically made the most money in the industry. They have done so by charging game-development companies (the complement providers) a royalty fee for every game sold that runs on their consoles. For example, Nintendo used to charge third-party game developers a 20% royalty fee for every game they sold that was written to run on a Nintendo console. However, two things have changed over the last decade. First, game developers have choices. They can, for example, decide to write for Microsoft Xbox first, and Sony PS3 a year later. Second, some game franchises are now so popular that consumers will purchase whichever platform runs the most recent version of the game. Madden NFL, which is produced by Electronic Arts, has an estimated 5 to 7 million dedicated fans that will purchase each new release. The game is in such demand that Electronic Arts can bargain for lower royalty rates from Microsoft and Sony in return for writing it to run on their gaming platforms. Put differently, Electronic Arts has gained bargaining power over the console producers, and it uses this to extract profit from the console industry in the form of lower royalty rates paid to console manufacturers. The console manufacturers have responded by trying to develop their own powerful franchises that are exclusive to their platforms. Nintendo has been successful here with its long-running Super Mario series, and Microsoft has had a major franchise hit with its Halo series, which is now in its fourth version.

Summary: Why Industry Analysis Matters

The analysis of competition in the industry environment using the competitive forces framework is a powerful tool that helps managers think strategically. It is important to recognize that one competitive force often affects others, and all forces need to be considered when performing industry analysis. For example, if new entry occurs due to low entry barriers, this will increase competition in the industry and drive down prices and profit rates, other things being equal. If buyers are powerful, they may take advantage of the increased choice resulting from new entry to further bargain down prices, increasing the intensity of competition and making it more difficult to make a decent profit in the industry. Thus, it is important to understand how one force might impact upon another.

Industry analysis inevitably leads managers to think systematically about strategic choices. For example, if entry barriers are low, managers might ask themselves, "how can we raise entry barriers into this industry, thereby reducing the threat of new competition?" The answer often involves trying to achieve economies of scale, build brand loyalty, create switching costs, and so on, so that new entrants are at a disadvantage and find it difficult to gain traction in the industry. Or they could ask, "How can we modify the intensity of competition in our industry?" They might do this by emphasizing brand loyalty in an attempt to differentiate their products, or by creating switching costs that reduce buyer power in the industry. As noted in the Opening Case for example, wireless service providers have required their customers to sign a new 2-year contract with early termination fees that may run into hundreds of dollars whenever they upgrade their phone equipment. This action effectively increases the costs of switching to a different wireless provider, thus making it more difficult for new entrants to gain traction in the industry. The increase in switching costs also moderates the intensity of rivalry in the industry by making it less likely that consumers will switch from one provider to another in an attempt to lower the price they pay for their service.

For another example, consider what happened when Coca-Cola looked at its industry environment in the early 2000s. It noticed a disturbing trend—per capita consumption of carbonated beverages had started to decline as people switched to noncarbonated soft drinks. In other words, substitute products were becoming a threat. This realization led to a change in the strategy at Coca-Cola. The company started to develop and offer its own noncarbonated beverages, effectively turning the threat into a strategic opportunity. Similarly, in the 2000s, demand for traditional newspapers began to decline as people increasingly started to consume news content on the Web. In other words, the threat from a substitute product was increasing. Several traditional newspapers responded by rapidly developing their own Web-based content.

In all of these examples, an analysis of industry opportunities and threats led directly to a change in strategy by companies within the industry. This, of course, is the crucial point—analyzing the industry environment in order to identify opportunities and threats leads logically to a discussion of what strategies should be adopted to exploit opportunities and counter threats. We will return to this issue again in Chapters 5, 6, and 7 when we look at the different business-level strategies firms can pursue, and how they can match strategy to the conditions prevailing in their industry environment.

◤STRATEGIC GROUPS WITHIN INDUSTRIES

Companies in an industry often differ significantly from one another with regard to the way they strategically position their products in the market. Factors such as the distribution channels they use, the market segments they serve, the quality of their products, technological leadership, customer service, pricing policy, advertising policy, and promotions affect product position. As a result of these differences, within most industries, it is possible to observe groups of companies in which each company follows a strategy that is similar to that pursued by other companies in the group, but different from the strategy pursued by companies in other groups. These different groups of companies are known as strategic groups.[13]

For example, in the commercial aerospace industry there has traditionally been two main strategic groups: the manufacturers of regional jets and the manufacturers of large commercial jets (see Figure 2.2). Bombardier and Embraer are the standouts in the regional jet industry, whereas Boeing and Airbus have lone dominated the market for large commercial jets. Regional jets have less than 100 seats and limited range. Large jets have anywhere from 100 to 550 seats, and some models are able to fly across the Pacific Ocean. Large jets are sold to major airlines, and regional jets to small regional carriers. Historically, the companies in the regional jet group have competed against each other, but not against Boeing and Airbus (the converse is also true).

Normally, the basic differences between the strategies that companies in different strategic groups use can be captured by a relatively small number of factors. In the case of commercial aerospace, the differences are primarily in terms of product

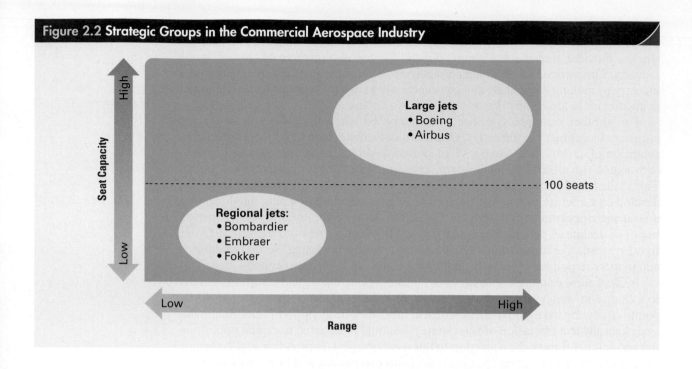

Figure 2.2 Strategic Groups in the Commercial Aerospace Industry

attributes (seat capacity and range), and customer set (large airlines versus smaller regional airlines). For another example, consider the pharmaceutical industry. Here two primary strategic groups stand out.[14] One group, which includes such companies as Merck, Eli Lilly, and Pfizer, is characterized by a business model based on heavy R&D spending and a focus on developing new, proprietary, blockbuster drugs. The companies in this proprietary strategic group are pursuing a high-risk, high-return strategy because basic drug research is difficult and expensive. Bringing a new drug to market can cost up to $800 million in R&D funding and a decade of research and clinical trials. The risks are high because the failure rate in new drug development is very high: only one out of every five drugs entering clinical trials is eventually approved by the U.S. Food and Drug Administration. However, this strategy has potential for a high return because a single successful drug can be patented, giving the innovator a monopoly on the production and sale of the drug for the life of the patent (patents are issued for 20 years). This allows proprietary companies to charge a high price for the drug, earning them millions, if not billions, of dollars over the lifetime of the patent.

The second strategic group might be characterized as the generic-drug strategic group. This group of companies, which includes Forest Labs, Mylan, and Watson Pharmaceuticals, focuses on the manufacture of generic drugs: low-cost copies of drugs that were developed by companies in the proprietary group, which now have expired patents. Low R&D spending, production efficiency, and an emphasis on low prices characterize the business models of companies in this strategic group. They are pursuing a low-risk, low-return strategy. It is low risk because these companies are not investing millions of dollars in R&D, and low return because they cannot charge high prices for their products.

Implications of Strategic Groups

The concept of strategic groups has a number of implications for the identification of opportunities and threats within an industry. First, because all companies in a strategic group are pursuing a similar strategy, customers tend to view the products of such enterprises as direct substitutes for each other. Thus, a company's closest competitors are those in its strategic group, not those in other strategic groups in the industry. The most immediate threat to a company's profitability comes from rivals within its own strategic group. For example, in the retail industry, there is a group of companies that might be characterized as general merchandise discounters. Included in this group are Wal-Mart, K-mart, Target, and Fred Meyer. These companies compete vigorously with each other, rather than with other retailers in different groups, such as Nordstrom or The Gap. K-Mart, for example, was driven into bankruptcy in the early 2000s, not because Nordstrom or The Gap took its business, but because Wal-Mart and Target gained share in the discounting group by virtue of their superior strategic execution of the discounting business model for general merchandise.

A second competitive implication is that different strategic groups can have different relationships to each of the competitive forces; thus, each strategic group may face a different set of opportunities and threats. Each of the following can be a relatively strong or weak competitive force depending on the competitive positioning approach adopted by each strategic group in the industry: the risk of new entry by potential competitors; the degree of rivalry among companies within a group; the bargaining power of buyers; the bargaining power of suppliers; and the competitive force of substitute and complementary products. For example, in the pharmaceutical industry, companies in the proprietary group historically have been in a very powerful position in relation to buyers because their products are patented and there are no substitutes. Also, rivalry based on price competition within this group has been low because competition in the industry depends upon which company is first to patent a new drug ("patent races"), not on drug prices. Thus, companies in this group have been able to charge high prices and earn high profits. In contrast, companies in the generic group have been in a much weaker position because many companies are able to produce different versions of the same generic drug after patents expire. Thus, in this strategic group, products are close substitutes, rivalry has been high, and price competition has led to lower profits than for the companies in the proprietary group.

The Role of Mobility Barriers

It follows from these two issues that some strategic groups are more desirable than others because competitive forces open up greater opportunities and present fewer threats for those groups. Managers, after analyzing their industry, might identify a strategic group where competitive forces are weaker and higher profits can be made. Sensing an opportunity, they might contemplate changing their strategy and move to compete in that strategic group. However, taking advantage of this opportunity may be difficult because of mobility barriers between strategic groups.

Mobility barriers are within-industry factors that inhibit the movement of companies between strategic groups. They include the barriers to entry into a group and the barriers to exit from an existing group. For example, attracted by the promise of higher returns, Forest Labs might want to enter the proprietary strategic group in the pharmaceutical industry, but it might find doing so difficult because it lacks the requisite R&D skills, and building these skills would be an expensive proposition. Over time, companies in different groups develop different cost structures, skills, and competencies that allow them different pricing options and choices. A company contemplating entry into another strategic group must evaluate whether it has the ability to imitate, and outperform, its potential competitors in that strategic group. Managers must determine if it is cost-effective to overcome mobility barriers before deciding whether the move is worthwhile.

At the same time, managers should be aware that companies based in another strategic group within their industry might ultimately become their direct competitors if they can overcome mobility barriers. This now seems to be occurring in the commercial aerospace industry, where two of the regional jet manufacturers, Bombardier and Embraer, have started to move into the large commercial jet business with the development of narrow-bodied aircraft in the 100- to 150-seat range. This implies that Boeing and Airbus will be seeing more competition in the years ahead, and their managers need to prepare for this.

◤ INDUSTRY LIFE-CYCLE ANALYSIS

Changes that take place in an industry over time are an important determinant of the strength of the competitive forces in the industry (and of the nature of opportunities and threats). The similarities and differences between companies in an industry often become more pronounced over time, and its strategic group structure frequently changes. The strength and nature of each competitive force also changes as an industry evolves, particularly the two forces of risk of entry by potential competitors and rivalry among existing firms.[15]

A useful tool for analyzing the effects of industry evolution on competitive forces is the industry life-cycle model. This model identifies five sequential stages in the evolution of an industry that lead to five distinct kinds of industry environment: embryonic, growth, shakeout, mature, and decline (see Figure 2.3). The task managers face is to anticipate how the strength of competitive forces will change as the industry environment evolves, and to formulate strategies that take advantage of opportunities as they arise and that counter emerging threats.

Embryonic Industries

An embryonic industry is one that is just beginning to develop (for example, personal computers and biotechnology in the 1970s, wireless communications in the 1980s, Internet retailing in the 1990s, and nanotechnology today). Growth at this stage is slow because of factors such as buyers' unfamiliarity with the industry's product, high prices due to the inability of companies to leverage significant scale economies, and poorly developed distribution channels. Barriers to entry tend to be based on access to key technological knowhow rather than cost economies or brand loyalty. If the core knowhow required to compete in the industry is complex and difficult to grasp, barriers to entry can be quite high, and established companies will

Figure 2.3 Stages in the Industry Life Cycle

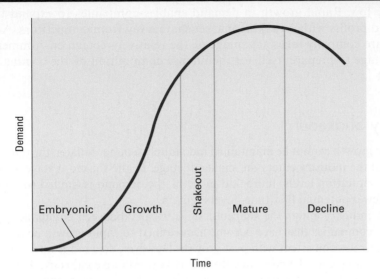

be protected from potential competitors. Rivalry in embryonic industries is based not so much on price as on educating customers, opening up distribution channels, and perfecting the design of the product. Such rivalry can be intense, and the company that is the first to solve design problems often has the opportunity to develop a significant market position. An embryonic industry may also be the creation of one company's innovative efforts, as happened with microprocessors (Intel), vacuum cleaners (Hoover), photocopiers (Xerox), small-package express delivery (FedEx), and Internet search engines (Google). In such circumstances, the developing company has a major opportunity to capitalize on the lack of rivalry and build a strong hold on the market.

Growth Industries

Once demand for an industry's product begins to increase, it develops the characteristics of a growth industry. In a growth industry, first-time demand is expanding rapidly as many new customers enter the market. Typically, an industry grows when customers become familiar with the product, prices fall because scale economies have been attained, and distribution channels develop. The U.S. wireless telephone industry remained in the growth stage for most of the 1985–2012 period. In 1990, there were only 5 million cellular subscribers in the nation. In 1997, there were 50 million. By 2014, this figure had increased to about 360 million, or roughly 1.08 accounts per person, implying that the market is now saturated and the industry is mature.

Normally, the importance of control over technological knowledge as a barrier to entry has diminished by the time an industry enters its growth stage. Because few companies have yet to achieve significant scale economies or built brand loyalty, other entry barriers tend to be relatively low early in the growth stage. Thus, the threat from potential competitors is typically highest at this point. Paradoxically, high growth usually means that new entrants can be absorbed into an industry without a marked increase in the intensity of rivalry. Thus, rivalry tends to be relatively low. Rapid growth in demand enables companies to expand their revenues and profits without taking market share away from competitors. A strategically aware company takes advantage of the relatively benign environment of the growth stage to prepare itself for the intense competition of the coming industry shakeout.

Industry Shakeout

Explosive growth cannot be maintained indefinitely. Sooner or later, the rate of growth slows, and the industry enters the shakeout stage. In the shakeout stage, demand approaches saturation levels: more and more of the demand is limited to replacement because fewer potential first-time buyers remain.

As an industry enters the shakeout stage, rivalry between companies can build. Typically, companies that have become accustomed to rapid growth continue to add capacity at rates consistent with past growth. However, demand is no longer growing at historic rates, and the consequence is excess productive capacity. This condition is illustrated in Figure 2.4, where the solid curve indicates the growth in demand over time and the broken curve indicates the growth in productive capacity over time. As you can see, past time t_1, demand growth slows as the industry matures. However, capacity continues to grow until time t_2. The gap between the solid and broken lines signifies excess capacity. In an attempt to use this capacity, companies often cut prices. The result can be a price war that drives inefficient companies into bankruptcy and deters new entry.

Figure 2.4 Growth in Demand and Capacity

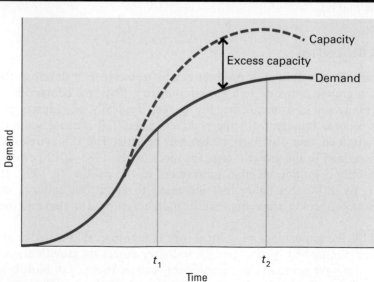

Mature Industries

The shakeout stage ends when the industry enters its mature stage: The market is totally saturated, demand is limited to replacement demand, and growth is low or zero. Typically, the growth that remains comes from population expansion, bringing new customers into the market, or increasing replacement demand.

As an industry enters maturity, barriers to entry increase, and the threat of entry from potential competitors decreases. As growth slows during the shakeout, companies can no longer maintain historic growth rates merely by holding on to their market share. Competition for market share develops, driving down prices and often producing a price war, as has happened in the airline and PC industries. To survive the shakeout, companies begin to focus on minimizing costs and building brand loyalty. The airlines, for example, tried to cut operating costs by hiring nonunion labor, and to build brand loyalty by introducing frequent-flyer programs. Personal computer companies have sought to build brand loyalty by providing excellent after-sales service and working to lower their cost structures. By the time an industry matures, the surviving companies are those that have secured brand loyalty and efficient, low-cost operations. Because both these factors constitute a significant barrier to entry, the threat of entry by potential competitors is often greatly diminished. High entry barriers in mature industries can give companies the opportunity to increase prices and profits, although this does not always occur.

As a result of the shakeout, most industries in the maturity stage consolidate and become oligopolies. Examples include the beer industry, breakfast cereal industry, and wireless service industry. In mature industries, companies tend to recognize their interdependence and try to avoid price wars. Stable demand gives them the opportunity to enter into tacit price-leadership agreements. The net effect is to reduce the threat of intense rivalry among established companies, thereby allowing greater profitability. Nevertheless, the stability of a mature industry is always threatened by further price wars. A general slump in economic activity can depress industry demand. As companies fight to maintain their revenues in the face of declining demand, price-leadership agreements break down, rivalry increases, and prices and profits fall. The periodic price wars that occur in the airline industry appear to follow this pattern.

Declining Industries

Eventually, most industries enter a stage of decline: growth becomes negative for a variety of reasons, including technological substitution (air travel instead of rail travel), social changes (greater health consciousness impacting tobacco sales), demographics (the declining birthrate constricting the market for products for babies and children), and international competition (low-cost, foreign competition pushing the U.S. steel industry into decline). Within a declining industry, the degree of rivalry among established companies usually increases. Depending on the speed of the decline and the height of exit barriers, competitive pressures can become as fierce as in the shakeout stage.[16] The largest problem in a declining industry is that falling demand leads to the emergence of excess capacity. In trying to use this capacity, companies begin to cut prices, thus sparking a price war. The U.S. steel industry experienced these problems during the 1980s and 1990s because steel companies tried to use their excess capacity despite falling demand. The same problem occurred in the airline industry in the 1990–1992 period, in 2001–2005, and again in 2008–2009 as companies cut prices to ensure that they would not be flying with half-empty planes (that is, they would not be operating with substantial excess capacity). Exit barriers play a part in adjusting excess capacity. The higher the exit barriers, the harder it is for companies to reduce capacity, and the greater the threat of severe price competition.

Summary

A third task of industry analysis is to identify the opportunities and threats that are characteristic of different kinds of industry environments in order to develop effective strategies. Managers have to tailor their strategies to changing industry conditions. They must also learn to recognize the crucial points in an industry's development, so they can forecast when the shakeout stage of an industry might begin, or when an industry might be moving into decline. This is also true at the level of strategic groups, for new embryonic groups may emerge because of shifts in customer needs and tastes, or because some groups may grow rapidly due to changes in technology, whereas others will decline as their customers defect.

◤ LIMITATIONS OF MODELS FOR INDUSTRY ANALYSIS

The competitive forces, strategic groups, and life-cycle models provide useful ways of thinking about and analyzing the nature of competition within an industry to identify opportunities and threats. However, each has its limitations, and managers must be aware of these.

Life-Cycle Issues

It is important to remember that the industry life-cycle model is a generalization. In practice, industry life cycles do not always follow the pattern illustrated in Figure 2.3. In some cases, growth is so rapid that the embryonic stage is skipped altogether. In others, industries fail to get past the embryonic stage. Industry growth can be revitalized after long periods of decline through innovation or social change. For example, the health boom brought the bicycle industry back to life after a long period of decline.

The time span of these stages can vary significantly from industry to industry. Some industries can remain mature almost indefinitely if their products are viewed as basic necessities, as is the case for the car industry. Other industries skip the mature stage and go straight into decline, as in the case of the vacuum-tube industry. Transistors replaced vacuum tubes as a major component in electronic products despite that the vacuum tube industry was still in its growth stage. Still other industries may go through several shakeouts before they enter full maturity, as appears to currently be happening in the telecommunications industry.

Innovation and Change

Over any reasonable length of time, in many industries competition can be viewed as a process driven by innovation.[17] Innovation is frequently the major factor in industry evolution and propels a company's movement through the industry life cycle. Innovation is attractive because companies that pioneer new products, processes, or strategies often earn enormous profits. Consider the explosive growth of Toys "R" Us, Dell, and Wal-Mart. In a variety of ways, all of these companies were innovators. Toys "R" Us pioneered a new way of selling toys (through large, discount warehouse-type stores), Dell pioneered an entirely new way of selling personal computers (directly via telephone, and then the Web), and Wal-Mart pioneered the low-price discount superstore concept.

Successful innovation can transform the nature of industry competition. In recent decades, one frequent consequence of innovation has been to lower the fixed costs of production, thereby reducing barriers to entry and allowing new, smaller enterprises to compete with large established organizations. Four decades ago, large, integrated steel companies such as U.S. Steel, LTV, and Bethlehem Steel dominated the steel industry. The industry was an oligopoly, dominated by a small number of large producers, in which tacit price collusion was practiced. Then along came a series of efficient, mini-mill producers such as Nucor and Chaparral Steel, which used a new technology: electric arc furnaces. Over the past 40 years, they have revolutionized the structure of the industry. What was once a consolidated industry is now fragmented and price competitive. U.S. Steel now has only a 12% market share, down from 55% in the mid-1960s. In contrast, the mini-mills as a group now hold over 40% of the market, up from 5% 20 years ago.[18] Thus, the mini-mill innovation has reshaped the nature of competition in the steel industry.[19] A competitive forces model applied to the industry in 1970 would look very different from a competitive forces model applied in 2014.

Michael Porter sees innovation as "unfreezing" and "reshaping" industry structure. He argues that after a period of turbulence triggered by innovation, the structure of an industry once more settles into a fairly stable pattern, and the competitive forces and strategic group concepts can once more be applied.[20] This view of the evolution of industry structure, often referred to as "punctuated equilibrium,"[21] holds that long periods of equilibrium (refreezing), when an industry's structure is stable, are punctuated by periods of rapid change (unfreezing), when industry structure is revolutionized by innovation.

Figure 2.5 depicts punctuated equilibrium for a key dimension of industry structure: competitive structure. From time t_0 to t_1, the competitive structure of the industry is a stable oligopoly, and few companies share the market. At time t_1, a major new innovation is pioneered either by an existing company or a new entrant. The result is a period of turbulence between t_1 and t_2. Afterward, the industry settles into a new state of equilibrium, but now the competitive structure is far more fragmented. Note that the opposite could have happened: the industry could have become more consolidated, although this seems to be less common. In general, innovation seems to lower barriers to entry, allow more companies into the industry, and, as a result, lead to fragmentation rather than consolidation.

During a period of rapid change when industry structure is being revolutionized by innovation, value typically migrates to business models based on new positioning strategies.[22] In the stockbrokerage industry, value migrated from the full-service broker

Figure 2.5 Punctuated Equilibrium and Competitive Structure

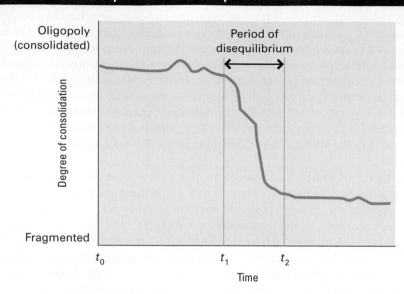

model to the online trading model. In the steel industry, electric arc technology led to a migration of value away from large, integrated enterprises and toward small mini-mills. In the bookselling industry, value has migrated first away from small boutique "bricks-and-mortar" booksellers toward large bookstore chains like Barnes & Noble, and more recently toward online bookstores such as Amazon.com. Because the competitive forces and strategic group models are static, they cannot adequately capture what occurs during periods of rapid change in the industry environment when value is migrating.

Company Differences

Another criticism of industry models is that they overemphasize the importance of industry structure as a determinant of company performance, and underemphasize the importance of variations or differences among companies within an industry or a strategic group.[23] As we discuss in the next chapter, the profit rates of individual companies within an industry can vary enormously. Research by Richard Rumelt and his associates suggests that industry structure explains only about 10% of the variance in profit rates across companies.[24] This implies that individual company differences account for much of the remainder. Other studies have estimated the explained variance at closer to 20%.[25] Similarly, a numbers of studies have found only weak evidence linking strategic group membership and company profit rates, despite that the strategic group model predicts a strong link.[26] Collectively these studies suggest that a company's individual resources and capabilities may be more important determinants of its profitability than the industry or strategic group of which the company is a member. In other words, there are strong companies in tough industries where average profitability is low (Nucor in the steel industry), and weak companies in industries where average profitability is high.

Although these findings do not invalidate the competitive forces and strategic group models, they do imply that the models are imperfect predictors of enterprise profitability. A company will not be profitable just because it is based in an attractive industry or strategic group. As we will discuss in subsequent chapters, much more is required.

THE MACROENVIRONMENT

Just as the decisions and actions of strategic managers can often change an industry's competitive structure, so too can changing conditions or forces in the wider macroenvironment, that is, the broader economic, global, technological, demographic, social, and political context in which companies and industries are embedded (see Figure 2.6). Changes in the forces within the macroenvironment can have a direct impact on any or all of the forces in Porter's model, thereby altering the relative strength of these forces as well as the attractiveness of an industry.

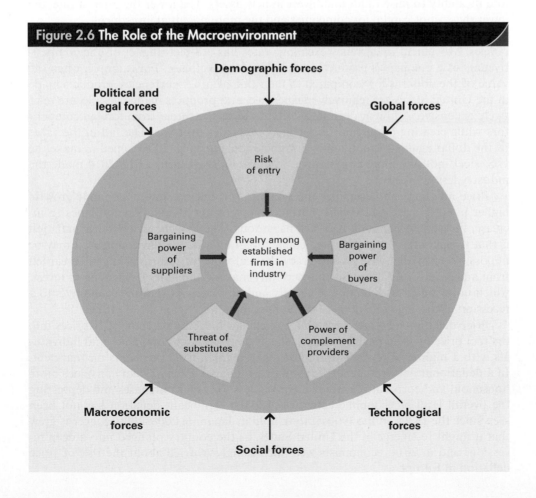

Figure 2.6 The Role of the Macroenvironment

Macroeconomic Forces

Macroeconomic forces affect the general health and well-being of a nation and the regional economy of an organization, which in turn affect companies' and industries' ability to earn an adequate rate of return. The four primary macroeconomic forces are the growth rate of the economy, interest rates, currency exchange rates, and inflation (or deflation) rates. Economic growth, because it leads to an expansion in customer expenditures, tends to ease competitive pressures within an industry. This gives companies the opportunity to expand their operations and earn higher profits. Because economic decline (a recession) leads to a reduction in customer expenditures, it increases competitive pressures. Economic decline frequently causes price wars in mature industries.

Interest rates can determine the demand for a company's products and thus are important whenever customers routinely borrow money to finance their purchase of these products. The most obvious example is the housing market, where mortgage rates directly affect demand. Interest rates also have an impact on the sale of autos, appliances, and capital equipment, to give just a few examples. For companies in such industries, rising interest rates are a threat, and falling rates an opportunity. Interest rates are also important because they influence a company's cost of capital, and therefore its ability to raise funds and invest in new assets. The lower the interest rate, the lower the cost of capital for companies and the more potential investment.

Currency exchange rates define the comparative value of different national currencies. Movement in currency exchange rates has a direct impact on the competitiveness of a company's products in the global marketplace. For example, when the value of the dollar is low compared to the value of other currencies, products made in the United States are relatively inexpensive, and products made overseas are relatively expensive. A low or declining dollar reduces the threat from foreign competitors while creating opportunities for increased sales overseas. The fall in the value of the dollar against several major currencies during 2004–2008 helped to make the U.S. steel industry more competitive, whereas its rise during 2012–2014 made the industry less competitive.

Price inflation can destabilize the economy, producing slower economic growth, higher interest rates, and volatile currency movements. If inflation continues to increase, investment planning becomes hazardous. The key characteristic of inflation is that it makes the future less predictable. In an inflationary environment, it may be impossible to predict with any accuracy the real value of returns that can be earned from a project 5 years later. Such uncertainty makes companies less willing to invest, which in turn depresses economic activity and ultimately pushes the economy into a recession. Thus, high inflation is a threat to companies.

Price deflation also has a destabilizing effect on economic activity. If prices fall, the real price of fixed payments rises. This is damaging for companies and individuals with a high level of debt who must make regular, fixed payments on that debt. In a deflationary environment, the increase in the real value of debt consumes more household and corporate cash flows, leaving less for other purchases and depressing the overall level of economic activity. Although significant deflation has not been seen since the 1930s, in the 1990s it took hold in Japan; in 2008–2009, concerns grew that it might re-emerge in the United States, as the country plunged into a deep recession; and in 2014, economists were increasingly worried about the risk of price deflation in Europe.

Global Forces

The last half-century has seen enormous changes in the world's economic system. We review these changes in some detail in Chapter 8, where we discuss global strategy. For now, the important points to note are that barriers to international trade and investment have tumbled, and more and more countries have enjoyed sustained economic growth. Economic growth in Brazil, China, and India has created large, new markets for companies' goods and services and is giving companies an opportunity to grow their profits faster by entering these nations. Falling barriers to international trade and investment have made it much easier to enter foreign nations. For example, 20 years ago, it was almost impossible for a Western company to set up operations in China. Today, Western and Japanese companies are investing approximately $100 billion annually in China. By the same token, falling barriers to international trade and investment have made it easier for foreign enterprises to enter the domestic markets of many companies (by lowering barriers to entry), thereby increasing the intensity of competition and lowering profitability. Because of these changes, many formerly isolated domestic markets have now become part of a much larger, more competitive global marketplace, creating both threats and opportunities for companies.

Technological Forces

Over the last few decades, the pace of technological change has accelerated.[27] This has unleashed a process that has been called a "perennial gale of creative destruction."[28] Technological change can render established products obsolete overnight and simultaneously create a host of new product possibilities. Thus, technological change is both creative and destructive—both an opportunity and a threat.

Most important, the impacts of technological change can affect the height of barriers to entry and therefore radically reshape industry structure. For example, the Internet lowered barriers to entry into the news industry. Providers of financial news must now compete for advertising dollars and customer attention with new, Internet-based media organizations that developed during the 1990s and 2000s, such as TheStreet .com, The Motley Fool, Yahoo Finance, and most recently, Google News. Advertisers now have more choices due to the resulting increase in rivalry, enabling them to bargain down the prices that they must pay to media companies.

Demographic Forces

Demographic forces result from changes in the characteristics of a population such as age, gender, ethnic origin, race, sexual orientation, and social class. Like the other forces in the general environment, demographic forces present managers with opportunities and threats and can have major implications for organizations. Changes in the age distribution of a population are an example of a demographic force that affects managers and organizations. Currently, most industrialized nations are experiencing the aging of their populations as a consequence of falling birth and death rates and the aging of the Baby-Boom generation. As the population ages, opportunities for organizations that cater to older people are increasing; the home-health-care and recreation industries, for example, are seeing an upswing in demand for their services. As the Bab-Boom generation from the late 1950s to the early 1960s has aged, it has created a host of opportunities and threats. During the 1980s, many Baby Boomers were getting married and creating an upsurge in demand for the customer appliances normally purchased by couples marrying for the first time. Companies such as Whirlpool Corporation and GE capitalized on the resulting upsurge in demand for washing machines, dishwashers, dryers, and the like. In the 1990s, many of these same baby boomers began to save for retirement, creating an inflow of money into mutual fund, and creating a surge in the mutual fund industry. Today many of these same baby boomers are retiring, creating a boom in retirement communities.

Social Forces

Social forces refer to the way in which changing social mores and values affect an industry. Like other macroenvironmental forces, social change creates opportunities and threats. One major social movement of recent decades has been the trend toward greater health consciousness. Its impact has been immense, and companies that recognized the opportunities early have often reaped significant gains. Philip Morris, for example, capitalized on the growing health consciousness trend when it acquired Miller Brewing Company, and then redefined competition in the beer industry with its introduction of low-calorie beer (Miller Lite). Similarly, PepsiCo was able to gain market share from its rival, Coca-Cola, by being the first to introduce diet colas and fruit-based soft drinks. At the same time, the health trend has created a threat for many industries. The tobacco industry, for example, is in decline as a direct result of greater customer awareness of the health implications of smoking.

Political and Legal Forces

Political and legal forces are outcomes of changes in laws and regulations, and significantly affect managers and companies. Political processes shape a society's laws, which constrain the operations of organizations and managers and thus create both opportunities and threats.[29] For example, throughout much of the industrialized world, there has been a strong trend toward deregulation of industries previously controlled by the state, and privatization of organizations once owned by the state. In the United States, deregulation of the airline industry in 1979 allowed 29 new airline companies to enter the industry between 1979 and 1993. The increase in passenger-carrying capacity after deregulation led to excess capacity on many routes, intense competition, and fare wars. To respond to this more competitive task environment, airlines needed to look for ways to reduce operating costs. The development of hub-and-spoke systems, the rise of nonunion airlines, and the introduction of no-frills discount service are all responses to increased competition in the airlines' task environment. Despite these innovations, the airline industry still experiences intense fare wars, which have lowered profits and caused numerous airline-company bankruptcies. The global telecommunications service industry is now experiencing the same kind of turmoil following the deregulation of that industry in the United States and elsewhere.

KEY TERMS

opportunities 44	potential	brand loyalty 47	switching costs 47
threats 44	competitors 46	absolute cost	
industry 44	economies of scale 46	advantage 47	

TAKEAWAYS FOR STRATEGIC MANAGERS

1. An industry is a group of companies offering products or services that are close substitutes for each other. Close substitutes are products or services that satisfy the same basic customer needs.

2. The main technique used to analyze competition in the industry environment is the competitive forces model. The forces are: (1) the risk of new entry by potential competitors, (2) the extent of rivalry among established firms, (3) the bargaining power of buyers, (4) the bargaining power of suppliers, (5) the threat of substitute products, and (6) the power of complement providers. The stronger each force is, the more competitive the industry and the lower the rate of return that can be earned.

3. The risk of entry by potential competitors is a function of the height of barriers to entry. The higher the barriers to entry are, the lower the risk of entry and the greater the potential profits in the industry.

4. The extent of rivalry among established companies is a function of an industry's competitive structure, demand conditions, cost conditions, and barriers to exit. Strong demand conditions moderate the competition among established companies and create opportunities for expansion. When demand is weak, intensive competition can develop, particularly in consolidated industries with high exit barriers.

5. Buyers are most powerful when a company depends on them for business, but they are not dependent on the company. In such circumstances, buyers are a threat.

6. Suppliers are most powerful when a company depends on them for business but they are not dependent on the company. In such circumstances, suppliers are a threat.

7. Substitute products are the products of companies serving customer needs similar to the needs served by the industry being analyzed. When substitute products are very similar to one another, companies can charge a lower price without losing customers to the substitutes.

8. The power, vigor, and competence of complementors represent a sixth competitive force. Powerful, vigorous complementors may have a strong positive impact on demand in an industry.

9. Most industries are composed of strategic groups of companies pursuing the same or a similar strategy. Companies in different strategic groups pursue different strategies.

10. The members of a company's strategic group constitute its immediate competitors. Because different strategic groups are characterized by different opportunities and threats, a company may improve its performance by switching strategic groups. The feasibility of doing so is a function of the height of mobility barriers.

11. Industries go through a well-defined life cycle: from an embryonic stage through growth, shakeout, and maturity, and eventually decline. Each stage has different implications for the competitive structure of the industry, and each gives rise to its own opportunities and threats.

12. The competitive forces, strategic group, and industry life-cycles models all have limitations. The competitive forces and strategic group models present a static picture of competition that deemphasizes the role of innovation. Yet innovation can revolutionize industry structure and completely shift the strength of different competitive forces. The competitive forces and strategic group models have been criticized for deemphasizing the importance of individual company

differences. A company will not be profitable just because it is part of an attractive industry or strategic group; much more is required. The industry life-cycle model is a generalization that is not always followed, particularly when innovation revolutionizes an industry.

13. The macroenvironment affects the intensity of rivalry within an industry. Included in the macroenvironment are the macroeconomic environment, the global environment, the technological environment, the demographic and social environment, and the political and legal environment.

DISCUSSION QUESTIONS

1. Under what environmental conditions are price wars most likely to occur in an industry? What are the implications of price wars for a company? How should a company try to deal with the threat of a price war?

2. Discuss the competitive forces model with reference to what you know about the US market for wireless telecommunications services (see the Opening Case). What does the model tell you about the level of competition in this industry?

3. Identify a growth industry, a mature industry, and a declining industry. For each industry, identify the following: (a) the number and size distribution of companies, (b) the nature of barriers to entry, (c) the height of barriers to entry, and (d) the extent of product differentiation. What do these factors tell you about the nature of competition in each industry? What are the implications for the company in terms of opportunities and threats?

4. Assess the impact of macroenvironmental factors on the likely level of enrollment at your university over the next decade. What are the implications of these factors for the job security and salary level of your professors?

CLOSING CASE

The Market for Large Commercial Aircraft

Two companies, Boeing and Airbus, have long dominated the market for large commercial jet aircraft. Today Boeing planes account for 50% of the world's fleet of commercial jet aircraft, and Airbus planes account for 31%. The reminder of the global market is split between several smaller players, including Embraer of Brazil and Bombardier of Canada, both of which have a 7% share. Embraer and Bombardier, however, have to date focused primarily on the regional jet market, building planes of less than 100 seats. The market for aircraft with more than 100 seats has been totally dominated by Boeing and Airbus.

The overall market is large and growing. In 2014, Boeing delivered 723 aircraft and Airbus delivered 620 aircraft. Demand for new aircraft is driven primarily by demand for air travel, which has grown at 5% per annum compounded since 1980. Looking forward, Boeing predicts that over the next 20 years the world economy will grow at 3.2% per annum, and airline traffic will continue to grow at 5% per annum as more and more people from the world's emerging economies take to the air for business and pleasure trips. Given the anticipated growth in demand, Boeing believes the world's airlines will need 37,000 new aircraft between 2013 and 2033 with a market value of $5.2 trillion dollars in today's prices.

Clearly, the scale of future demand creates an enormous profit opportunity for the two main incumbents, Boeing and Airbus. Given this, many observers wonder if the industry will see new entries. Historically, it has been assumed that the high development cost associated with bringing new commercial jet aircraft to market, and the need to realize substantial economies of scale to cover those costs, has worked as a very effective deterrent to new entries. For example, estimates suggest that it cost Boeing some $18 to $20 billion to develop its latest aircraft, the wide bodied Boeing 787, and that the company will have to sell 1,100 787s to break even, which will take 10 years. Given the costs, risks, and long time horizon here, it has been argued that only Boeing and Airbus can afford to develop new large commercial jet aircraft.

However, in the last few years, three new entrants have appeared. All three are building smaller narrow-bodied jets with a seat capacity between 100 and 190. Boeing's 737 and the Airbus A320 currently dominate the narrow-bodied segment. The Commercial Aircraft Corporation of China (Comac) is building a 170- to 190-seat narrow-bodied jet, scheduled for introduction in 2018. To date, Comac has 430 firm orders for the aircraft, mostly from Chinese domestic airlines. Bombardier is developing a 100- to 150-seat plane that will bring it into direct competition with Boeing and Airbus for the first time. Scheduled for introduction in late 2015, Bombardier has 243 firm orders and another 100 commitments for these aircraft. Embraer too, has developed a 108- to 125-seat plane to compete in

the narrow-bodied segment, the E-190/195. It has taken orders for 720 of these aircraft, 640 of which had been delivered by late 2014. The new entry is occurring because all three producers believe that the market for narrow-bodied aircraft is now large enough to support more than Boeing and Airbus. Bombardier and Embraer can leverage the know-how they developed manufacturing regional jets to help them move upmarket. For its part, Comac can count on orders from Chinese airlines and the tacit support of the Chinese government to help it get off the ground.

In response to these competitive threats, Boeing and Airbus are developing new, more fuel-efficient versions of their own narrow-bodied planes, the 737 and A320. Although they hope their new offerings will keep entrants in check, one thing seems clear: with potentially five producers rather than two in the market, it seems likely that competition will become more intense in the narrow-bodied segment of the industry, which could well drive prices and profits down for the big two incumbent producers.

Sources: R. Marowits, "Bombardier's C Series Drought Ends," *The Montreal Gazette*, December 20, 2012; D. Gates, "Boeing Projects Break-Even on 787 Manufacturing in 10 Years," *Seattle Times*, October 26, 2011; Boeing Corporation, "Current Market Outlook 2014–2033," www.boeing.com/commercial/cmo/; D. Cameron, "Boeing delivers record number of jets in 2014," *The Wall Street Journal*, January 6, 2015.

CASE DISCUSSION QUESTIONS

1. Explain why the wide-bodied segment of the large commercial jet aircraft industry can only profitably support two players at present. What are the implications of your answer for barriers to entry into this segment?

2. Are entry barriers into the narrow-bodied segment the same as those into the wide-bodied segment? Explain your answer?

3. Given future projections for demand, how do you think the industry as a whole will do over the next twenty years? How might

your forecast differ for the wide-bodied and narrow-bodied segments?

4. If you were a new entrant into the bottom part of the narrow-bodied industry, as are Comac and Bombardier, what would be your long-term development strategy?

5. What can Boeing and Airbus do to deter further entry into this industry, and/or keep new entrants boxed into the bottom end of the market (that is, smaller, narrow-bodied jets)?

NOTES

[1]M. E. Porter, *Competitive Strategy* (New York: Free Press, 1980).

[2]J. E. Bain, *Barriers to New Competition* (Cambridge, Mass.: Harvard University Press, 1956). For a review of the modern literature on barriers to entry, see R. J. Gilbert, "Mobility Barriers and the Value of Incumbency," in R. Schmalensee and R. D. Willig (eds.), *Handbook of Industrial Organization,* vol. 1 (Amsterdam: North-Holland, 1989). See also R. P. McAfee, H. M. Mialon, and M. A. Williams, "What Is a Barrier to Entry?" *American Economic Review* 94 (May 2004): 461–468.

[3]"comScore reports September 2014 U.S. smartphone subscriber market share," comScore, November 6, 2014.

[4]A detailed discussion of switching costs can be found in C. Shapiro and H. R. Varian, *Information Rules: A Strategic Guide to the Network Economy* (Boston: Harvard Business School Press, 1999).

[5]Most information on barriers to entry can be found in the industrial organization economics literature. See especially Bain, *Barriers to New Competition;* M. Mann, "Seller Concentration, Barriers to Entry and Rates of Return in 30 Industries," *Review of Economics and Statistics* 48 (1966): 296–307; W. S. Comanor and T. A. Wilson, "Advertising, Market Structure and Performance," *Review of Economics and Statistics* 49 (1967): 423–440; Gilbert, "Mobility Barriers"; K. Cool, L. H. Roller, and B. Leleux, "The Relative Impact of Actual and Potential Rivalry on Firm Profitability in the Pharmaceutical Industry," *Strategic Management Journal* 20 (1999): 1–14.

[6]For a discussion of tacit agreements, see T. C. Schelling, *The Strategy of Conflict* (Cambridge, Mass.: Harvard University Press, 1960).

[7]M. Busse, "Firm Financial Condition and Airline Price Wars," *Rand Journal of Economics* 33 (2002): 298–318.

[8]For a review, see F. Karakaya, "Market Exit and Barriers to Exit: Theory and Practice," *Psychology and Marketing* 17 (2000): 651–668.

[9]P. Ghemawat, *Commitment: The Dynamics of Strategy* (Boston: Harvard Business School Press, 1991).

[10]A. S. Grove, *Only the Paranoid Survive* (New York: Doubleday, 1996).

[11]In standard microeconomic theory, the concept used for assessing the strength of substitutes and complements is the cross elasticity of demand.

[12]For details and further references, see Charles W. L. Hill, "Establishing a Standard: Competitive Strategy and Technology Standards in Winner Take All Industries," *Academy of Management Executive* 11 (1997): 7–25; Shapiro and Varian, *Information Rules.*

[13]The development of strategic group theory has been a strong theme in the strategy literature. Important contributions include R. E. Caves and M. E. Porter, "From Entry Barriers to Mobility Barriers," *Quarterly Journal of Economics* (May 1977): 241–262; K. R. Harrigan, "An Application of Clustering for Strategic Group Analysis," *Strategic Management Journal* 6 (1985): 55–73; K. J. Hatten and D. E. Schendel, "Heterogeneity Within an Industry: Firm Conduct in the U.S. Brewing Industry, 1952–71," *Journal of Industrial Economics* 26 (1977): 97–113; M. E. Porter, "The Structure Within Industries and Companies' Performance," *Review of Economics and Statistics* 61 (1979): 214–227. See also K. Cool and D. Schendel, "Performance Differences Among Strategic Group Members," *Strategic Management Journal* 9 (1988): 207–233; A. Nair and S. Kotha, "Does Group Membership Matter? Evidence from the Japanese Steel Industry," *Strategic Management Journal* 20 (2001): 221–235; G. McNamara, D. L. Deephouse, and R. A. Luce, "Competitive Positioning Within and Across a Strategic Group Structure," *Strategic Management Journal* 24 (2003): 161–180.

[14]For details on the strategic group structure in the pharmaceutical industry, see K. Cool and I. Dierickx, "Rivalry, Strategic Groups, and Firm Profitability," *Strategic Management Journal* 14 (1993): 47–59.

[15]C. W. Hofer argued that life-cycle considerations may be the most important contingency when formulating business strategy. See Hofer, "Towards a Contingency Theory of Business Strategy," *Academy of Management Journal* 18 (1975): 784–810. For empirical evidence to support this view, see C. R. Anderson and C. P. Zeithaml,

"Stages of the Product Life Cycle, Business Strategy, and Business Performance," *Academy of Management Journal* 27 (1984): 5–24; D. C. Hambrick and D. Lei, "Towards an Empirical Prioritization of Contingency Variables for Business Strategy," *Academy of Management Journal* 28 (1985): 763–788. See also G. Miles, C. C. Snow, and M. P. Sharfman, "Industry Variety and Performance," *Strategic Management Journal* 14 (1993): 163–177; G. K. Deans, F. Kroeger, and S. Zeisel, "The Consolidation Curve," *Harvard Business Review* 80 (December 2002): 2–3.

[16]The characteristics of declining industries have been summarized by K. R. Harrigan, "Strategy Formulation in Declining Industries," *Academy of Management Review* 5 (1980): 599–604. See also J. Anand and H. Singh, "Asset Redeployment, Acquisitions and Corporate Strategy in Declining Industries," *Strategic Management Journal* 18 (1997): 99–118.

[17]This perspective is associated with the Austrian school of economics, which goes back to Schumpeter. For a summary of this school and its implications for strategy, see R. Jacobson, "The Austrian School of Strategy," *Academy of Management Review* 17 (1992): 782–807; C. W. L. Hill and D. Deeds, "The Importance of Industry Structure for the Determination of Industry Profitability: A Neo-Austrian Approach," *Journal of Management Studies* 33 (1996): 429–451.

[18]"A Tricky Business," *Economist,* June 30, 2001, pp. 55–56.

[19]D. F. Barnett and R. W. Crandall, *Up from the Ashes* (Washington, D.C.: Brookings Institution, 1986).

[20]M. E. Porter, *The Competitive Advantage of Nations* (New York: Free Press, 1990).

[21]The term *"punctuated equilibrium"* is borrowed from evolutionary biology. For a detailed explanation of the concept, see M. L. Tushman, W. H. Newman, and E. Romanelli, "Convergence and Upheaval: Managing the Unsteady Pace of Organizational Evolution," *California Management Review* 29:1 (1985): 29–44; C. J. G. Gersick, "Revolutionary Change Theories: A Multilevel Exploration of the Punctuated Equilibrium Paradigm," *Academy of Management Review* 16 (1991): 10–36; R. Adner and D. A. Levinthal, "The Emergence of Emerging Technologies, *California Management Review* 45 (Fall 2002): 50–65.

[22]A. J. Slywotzky, *Value Migration: How to Think Several Moves Ahead of the Competition* (Boston: Harvard Business School Press, 1996).

[23]Hill and Deeds, "Importance of Industry Structure."

[24]R. P. Rumelt, "How Much Does Industry Matter?" *Strategic Management Journal* 12 (1991): 167–185. See also A. J. Mauri and M. P. Michaels, "Firm and Industry Effects Within Strategic Management: An Empirical Examination," *Strategic Management Journal* 19 (1998): 211–219.

[25]R. Schmalensee, "Inter-Industry Studies of Structure and Performance," in Schmalensee and Willig (eds.), *Handbook of Industrial Organization.* Similar results were found by A. N. McGahan and M. E. Porter, "How Much Does Industry Matter, Really?" *Strategic Management Journal* 18 (1997): 15–30.

[26]For example, see K. Cool and D. Schendel, "Strategic Group Formation and Performance: The Case of the U.S. Pharmaceutical Industry, 1932–1992," *Management Science* (September 1987): 1102–1124.

[27]See M. Gort and J. Klepper, "Time Paths in the Diffusion of Product Innovations," *Economic Journal* (September 1982): 630–653. Looking at the history of 46 products, Gort and Klepper found that the length of time before other companies entered the markets created by a few inventive companies declined from an average of 14.4 years for products introduced before 1930 to 4.9 years for those introduced after 1949.

[28]The phrase was originally coined by J. Schumpeter, *Capitalism, Socialism and Democracy* (London: Macmillan, 1950), p. 68.

[29]For a detailed discussion of the importance of the structure of law as a factor explaining economic change and growth, see D. C. North, *Institutions, Institutional Change, and Economic Performance* (Cambridge: Cambridge University Press, 1990).

2

THE NATURE OF COMPETITIVE ADVANTAGE

CHAPTER **3**

INTERNAL ANALYSIS: RESOURCES AND COMPETITIVE ADVANTAGE

3.1 Discuss the source of competitive advantage

3.2 Utilize the VRIO model to assess the quality of resources

3.3 Understand the link between competitive advantage and profitability

3.4 Explain the concept of the value chain

3.5 Identify and explore the role of efficiency, quality, innovation, and customer responsiveness in building and maintaining a competitive advantage

OPENING CASE

Southwest Airlines

Southwest Airlines has long been the standout performer in the U.S. airline industry. It is famous for its fares, which are often some 30% lower than those of its major rivals. These low fares are balanced by an even lower cost structure, which has enabled Southwest to record superior profitability even in its down years. Indeed, Southwest has been profitable for 41 consecutive years, making it the envy of an airline industry that has seen more than 180 bankruptcies since 1978. Even during 2001 to 2005–quite possibly the worst four years in the history of the airline industry–when every other major airline lost money, Southwest made money each year and earned a return on invested capital of 5.8 percent.

Southwest operates differently than many of its competitors. While operators like American Airlines and Delta route passengers through hubs, Southwest Airlines flies point-to-point, often through smaller airports. By operating this way, Southwest has found that it can reduce total travel

time for its passengers. They are not routed through hubs and spend less time on the ground—something that most passengers value. This boosts demand and keeps planes full. Moreover, because it avoids many hubs, Southwest has experienced fewer long delays, which again helps to reduce total travel time. In 2014, a delayed flight at Southwest was on average 48.79 minutes late leaving the gate, compared to 58.9 minutes at Delta and 60.53 minutes at American Airlines. Southwest's high reliability translates into a solid brand reputation and strong demand, which further helps to fill its planes and consequently, reduce costs.

Furthermore, because Southwest because flies point to point rather than through congested airport hubs, there is no need for dozens of gates and thousands of employees to handle banks of flights that come arrive and depart within a 2-hour window, leaving the hub empty until the next flights arrive a few hours later. The result: Southwest operates with far fewer employees than do airlines that fly through hubs

To further reduce costs and boost reliability, Southwest flies only one type of plane, the Boeing 737. This reduces training costs, maintenance costs, and inventory costs while increasing efficiency in crew and flight scheduling. The operation is nearly ticketless and there is no seat assignment, which reduces costs associated with back-office functions. There are no in-flight meals or movies, and the airline will not transfer baggage to other airlines, reducing the need for baggage handlers. Southwest also has high employee productivity, which means fewer employees per passenger. All of this helps to keep costs low. In 2014, for example, Southwest's cost per available seat miles flown was 13.76 cents, compared to 16.80 cents at Delta and 15.84 cents at American Airlines.

To help maintain high employee productivity, Southwest devotes enormous attention to its staff. On average, the company hires only 3% of candidates interviewed in a year. When hiring, it emphasizes teamwork and a positive attitude. Southwest reasons that skills can be taught, but a positive attitude and a willingness to pitch in cannot. Southwest also creates incentives for its employees to work hard. All employees are covered by a profit-sharing plan, and at least 25% of each employee's share in the plan must to be invested in Southwest Airlines stock. This gives rise to a simple formula: The harder employees work, the more profitable Southwest becomes and the more well off the employees become. The results are clear. At other airlines, one would never see a pilot helping to check passengers onto the plane. At Southwest, pilots and flight attendants have been known to help clean the aircraft and check in passengers at the gate in order to get a plane back into the air as quickly as possible, because no plane makes money when it is sitting on the ground. This flexible, motivated workforce leads to higher productivity and reduces the need for more employees.

Sources: M. Brelis, "Simple Strategy Makes Southwest a Model for Success," *Boston Globe*, November 5, 2000, p. F1; M. Trottman, "At Southwest, New CEO Sits in the Hot Seat," *The Wall Street Journal*, July 19, 2004, p. B1; J. Helyar, "Southwest Finds Trouble in the Air," *Fortune*, August 9, 2004, p. 38; Southwest Airlines 10-K 2013; N. Dihora, "Southwest launched international routes on July 1st," Morningstar, July 24, 2014; Bureau of Transportation Statistics at www.transtats.bts.gov/.

◤OVERVIEW

Why, within a particular industry or market, do some companies outperform others? What is the basis of their sustained competitive advantage? The Opening Case provides some clues. For more than four decades, Southwest Airlines has outperformed its rivals in the U.S. airline industry because it offers a more reliable service that delivers more value to its customers at a lower cost than its rivals. Southwest was an *innovator* with regard to strategy, flying point to point between smaller airports. It was *responsive to the needs of its customers*, pursuing strategies that reduced total travel time and increased the *reliability* of its service. It has done all of this in a very *efficient* way that has lowered the costs of the business and enabled Southwest to offer lower prices and still make profits when its rivals have been losing money. As you will see in this chapter, responding to customer needs by offering them more *value* through innovative and reliable goods and services, and doing so efficiently, are common themes seen in many enterprises that have established a sustainable competitive advantage over their rivals.

This chapter focuses on internal analysis, which is concerned with identifying the strengths and weaknesses of a company. At Southwest, for example, its point-to-point route structure, its investments in employee productivity, and its utilization of only one type of aircraft can all be seen as strengths. Internal analysis, coupled with an analysis of the company's external environment, gives managers the information they need to choose the strategy that will enable their company to attain a sustained competitive advantage.

As explained in this chapter, internal analysis is a three-step process. First, managers must understand the role of rare, valuable, and hard-to-imitate resources in the establishment of competitive advantage. Second, they must appreciate how such resources lead to superior efficiency, innovation, quality, and customer responsiveness. Third, they must be able to analyze the sources of their company's competitive advantage to identify what drives the profitability of their enterprise, and just as importantly, where opportunities for improvement might lie. In other words, they must be able to identify how the strengths of the enterprise boost its profitability and how its weaknesses result in lower profitability.

After reading this chapter, you will understand the nature of competitive advantage and why managers need to perform internal analysis (just as they must conduct industry analysis) in order to achieve superior performance and profitability.

◤COMPETITIVE ADVANTAGE

A company has a *competitive advantage* over its rivals when its profitability is greater than the average profitability of all companies in its industry. It has a *sustained competitive advantage* when it is able to maintain above-average profitability over a number of years (as Southwest has done in the airline industry). The primary objective of strategy is to achieve a sustained competitive advantage, which in turn results in superior profitability and profit growth. What are the sources of competitive advantage, and what is the link between strategy, competitive advantage, and profitability?

Distinctive Competencies

It has long been argued that competitive advantage is based upon the possession of distinctive competencies. **Distinctive competencies** are firm-specific strengths that allow a company to differentiate its products from those offered by rivals and/or achieve substantially lower costs than its rivals. Apple, for example, has a distinctive competence in design. Customers want to own the beautiful devices that Apple markets. Similarly, it can be argued that Toyota, which historically has been the standout performer in the automobile industry, has distinctive competencies in the development and operation of manufacturing processes. Toyota pioneered an entire range of manufacturing techniques such as just-in-time inventory systems, self-managing teams, and reduced setup times for complex equipment. These competencies, collectively known as the "Toyota lean production system," helped the company attain superior efficiency and product quality as the basis of its competitive advantage in the global automobile industry.[1]

distinctive competencies
Firm-specific strengths that allow a company to differentiate its products and/or achieve substantially lower costs to achieve a competitive advantage.

Resources

Distinctive competencies also can be rooted in one or more of a company's resources.[2] **Resources** refer to the factors of production that a company uses to transform inputs into outputs that it can sell in the marketplace. Resources include basic factors of production such as labor, land, management, physical plant, and equipment.

However, any enterprise is more than just a combination of the basic factors of production. Another important factor of production is **process knowledge** about how to develop, produce, and sell a company's output. Process knowledge can be thought of as the organizational equivalent of human skills. Process knowledge resides in the rules, routines, and procedures of an organization; that is, in the style or manner in which managers make decisions and utilize the company's internal processes to achieve organizational objectives.[3] Process knowledge is accumulated by the organization over time and through experience. Organizations, like people, learn by doing, often through trial and error. Process knowledge is often **socially complex**, which means that it diffused among many different individuals, teams, departments, and functions within the company, no one of which possesses all of the knowledge required to develop, produce, and sell its products. Process knowledge also often has an important **tacit** component, meaning that some of it is not documented or codified, but instead is learned by doing and is transmitted to new employees through the culture of the organization.[4]

The organizational architecture of a company is another very important factor of production. By **organizational architecture** we mean the combination of the organizational structure of a company, its control systems, its incentive systems, its organizational culture, and the human capital strategy of the enterprise, particularly with regard to its hiring and employee development and retention strategies. We will explore the concept of organizational architecture in depth in Chapter 12. For now, it is important to understand that companies with well-designed organizational architecture generally outperform those with poorly designed organizational architecture. Getting the organizational structure, control systems, incentives, culture, and human capital strategy of a company right is extremely important. Differences in the efficacy of organizational architecture are a major reason for performance differentials across companies.

resources
Assets of a company.

process knowledge
Knowledge of the internal rules, routines, and procedures of an organization that managers can leverage to achieve organizational objectives.

socially complex
Something that is characterized by, or is the outcome of, the interaction of multiple individuals.

tacit
A characteristic of knowledge or skills such that they cannot be documented or codified but may be understood through experience or intuition.

organizational architecture
The combination of the organizational structure of a company, its control systems, its incentive systems, its organizational culture, and its human-capital strategy.

intellectual property

Knowledge, research, and information that is owned by an individual or organization.

The codified **intellectual property** that a company has created over time represents another important factor of production. Intellectual property takes many forms, such as engineering blueprints, the molecular structure of a new drug, proprietary software code, and brand logos. Companies establish ownership rights over their intellectual property through patents, copyright, and trademarks. For example, Apple has built a powerful brand based on its reputation for high-quality, elegantly designed computing devices. The Apple logo displayed on its hardware products symbolizes that brand. That logo is Apple's intellectual property. It assures the consumer that this is a genuine Apple product. It is protected from imitation by trademark law.

In sum, a company's resources include not just *basic* factors of production such as land, labor, managers, property, and equipment. They also include more *advanced* factors of production such as process knowledge, organizational architecture, and intellectual property. For example, Coca-Cola has been very successful over a prolonged period in the carbonated beverage business. Coke's factors of production include not just labor, land, management, plants, and equipment, but also the *process knowledge* about how to develop, produce, and sell carbonated beverages. Coke is in fact a very strong marketing company—it really knows how to sell its product. Furthermore, Coke has an *organizational architecture* that enables it to manage its functional process well. Coke also has valuable *intellectual property* such as the recipes for its leading beverages (which Coke keeps secret) and its brand, which is protected from imitation by trademark law.

Similarly, Apple is more than just a combination of land, labor, management, plants, and equipment. Apple has world-class *process knowledge* when it comes to developing, producing, and selling its products. Most notably, Apple probably has the best industrial-design group in the computer business. This design group is ultimately responsible for the format, features, look, and feel of Apple's innovative products, including the iPod, iPhone, iPad, and its striking line of desktop and laptop computers. Apple also has a strong *organizational architecture* that enables it to manage the enterprise productively. In particular, the industrial-design group has a very powerful position within Apple's organizational structure. It initiates and coordinates the core product development processes. This includes ensuring that hardware engineering, software engineering, and manufacturing all work to achieve the product specifications mapped out by the design group. Apple is probably unique among computing-device companies in terms of the power and influence granted to its design group. Furthermore, Apple has created extremely valuable *intellectual property*, including the patents underlying its products and the trademark that protects the logo symbolizing the Apple brand.

basic factors of production

Resources such as land, labor, management, plants, and equipment.

advanced factors of production

Resources such as process knowledge, organizational architecture, and intellectual property that contribute to a company's competitive advantage.

Thus, as in the Coke and Apple examples, the resources (or factors of production) of any enterprise include not just **basic factors of production** but also **advanced factors of production**. The important point to understand is that advanced factors of production are not endowments; they are human creations. Skilled managers can and do create these advanced factors of production, often out of little more than thin air, vision, and drive. Apple founder and CEO Steve Jobs, in combination with his handpicked head of industrial design, Jonny Ive, created the process knowledge that underlies Apple's world-class skills in industrial design, and he built an organizational structure that gave the design group a powerful central role.

To summarize: An expanded list of resources includes labor, land, management, plants, equipment, process knowledge, organizational architecture, and intellectual property. As shown in Figure 3.1, a company is in effect a bundle of resources

Figure 3.1 The Firm as a Bundle of Resources

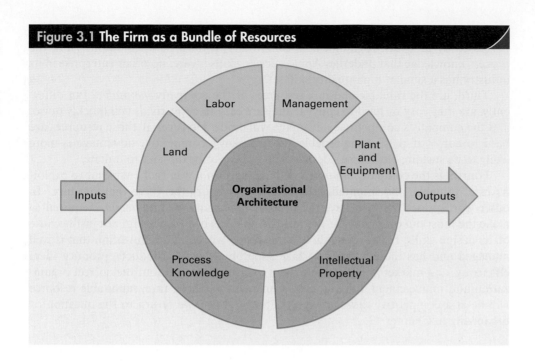

(factors of production) that transforms inputs (e.g., raw materials) into outputs (goods or services). The efficiency and effectiveness with which a company performs this transformation process depends critically upon the *quality* of its resources, and most significantly, upon the quality of its advanced factors of production—process knowledge, organizational architecture, and intellectual property. This insight gives rise to other, very important questions. What determines the quality of a company's resources? How do we know if its resources constitute and strength or a weaknesses?

Resource Quality: The VRIO Framework

Jay Barney and Bill Hesterly have developed a framework that represents a useful way for managers to think about the quality of resources.[5] They refer to this framework as the **VRIO framework**, where *V* stands for value, *R* for rarity, *I* for inimitability, and *O* for organization. They encourage managers to ask themselves the following questions when performing an internal analysis:

First, are the company's resources *valuable* in the sense that they enable the enterprise to exploit opportunities and counter threats in the external environment? For example, Apple's product-design skills constitute a valuable resource that has helped the company exploit opportunities to develop new product categories in the computer-device industry with its touch screen iPhone and iPad offerings. At the same time, those skills have also enabled Apple to keep rivals at bay, thereby countering threats. More generally, resources can be judged as valuable if they (a) enable a company to create strong demand for its products, and/or (b) lower the costs of producing those products.

Second, are those resources *rare*? If they are not rare and rivals also have access to them, by definition they cannot be a source of competitive advantage. For a company

VRIO framework

A framework managers use to determine the quality of a company's resources, where *V* is value, *R* is rarity, *I* is inimitability, and *O* is for organization.

to gain a competitive advantage, it must have some resource that is superior to that possessed by its rivals. It cannot be a commodity; it must be uncommon. Thus, the process knowledge that underlies Apple's design skills is rare; no other enterprise in its industry has a similar, high-quality skill set.

Third, are the valuable and rare resources of the company *inimitable*? Put differently, are they easy or hard to copy? If they are easy to copy, rivals will quickly do so, and the company's competitive advantage will erode. However, if those resources are hard to copy—if they are inimitable–the company's competitive advantage is more likely to be sustainable. Apple's design skills appear to be difficult to imitate.

Fourth, is the company *organized* and managed in a way that enables it to exploit its rare, valuable, and inimitable resources and capture the value they produce? In other words, does the firm have the broader *organizational architecture* required to make the most out of its unique strengths? Apple has been successful not just because of its design skills, but because those skills reside within an organization that is well managed and has the capability to take superbly designed products, produce them efficiently, and market and distribute them to customers. Without the correct organization and management systems, even firms with valuable, rare, inimitable resource will be at a competitive disadvantage. As noted above, we return to the question of organizing in Chapter 12.

Resources and Sustained Competitive Advantage

This discussion leads logically to another very important question: Which valuable resources are most likely to result in a long-term, *sustainable* competitive advantage? The quick answer is process knowledge, organizational architecture, and intellectual property. As we shall argue below, these resources or advanced factors of production are more likely to be rare and are in general more difficult for rivals to imitate.

Rare Resource   Consider the issue of rareness or scarcity with regard to basic factors of production. In general, land, labor, management, plants, and equipment are purchased on the open market. Of course, these resources are not homogenous; some employees are more productive than others; some land has more value; some managers have better skills. Over time, however, this becomes evident and the more productive resources will command a higher price for their services. You simply have to pay more for the best land, employees, managers, and equipment. Indeed, in a free market the price of such resources will be bid up to reflect their economic value, and the sellers of those resources, as opposed to the firm, will capture much of that value.

Now consider process knowledge and organizational architecture. These are likely to be heterogeneous. No two companies are exactly the same. Each has its own history, which impacts the way activities are organized and processes managed within the enterprise. The way in which product development is managed at Apple, for example, differs from the way it is managed at Microsoft or Samsung. Marketing at Coca Cola might differ in subtle but important ways from marketing at Pepsi Cola. The human resource function at Nucor Steel might be organized in such a way that it raises employee productivity above the level achieved by U.S. Steel. Each organization has its own culture, its own way of doing certain things. As a result of strategic vision, systematic process-improvement efforts, trial and error, or just blind luck, some companies will develop process knowledge and organizational architecture that is of higher quality than that of their rivals. By definition, such resources will be rare, since they are a *path-dependent* consequence of the history of the company. Moreover, the firm "owns" its process knowledge and organizational architecture. It does not buy these from a provider, so it is in a position to capture the full economic value of these resources.

Intellectual property that is protected by patents, copyright, or trademarks is also by definition rare. You can only patent something that no-one else has patented. A copyright protects the *unique* creation of an individual, or a company, and prevents anyone from copying it. The software code underlying Microsoft Windows, for example, is copyrighted, so no one else can use the same code without express permission from Microsoft. Similarly, a trademark protects the *unique* symbols, names, or logos of a company, preventing them from being copied and in effect making them rare. Rivals cannot use the Apple logo; it is Apple's unique property—thus it is rare.

Barriers to Imitation   Now let's consider the issue of inimitability. If a company develops a rare, valuable resource that enables it to create more demand, charge a higher price, and/or lower its costs, how easy will it be for rivals to copy that resource? Put differently, what are the **barriers to imitation**?[6]

Consider first intellectual property. The ability of rivals to copy a firm's intellectual property depends foremost upon the efficacy of the intellectual property regime in a nation state. In advanced nations such as the United States or the member states of the European Union, for example, where there is a well-established body of intellectual property law, direct imitation is outlawed and violators are likely to be sued for damages. This legal protection prevents most enterprises from engaging in direct copying of intellectual property. However, in developing nations with no well-established body of intellectual property law, copying may be widespread given the absence of legal sanctions. This used to be the case in China, for example, but it is becoming less common as the Chinese legal system adopts international norms with regard to patents, copyrights, and trademarks.

Even though direct copying is outlawed, it is certainly possible for companies to invent their way around their rivals' intellectual property through reverse engineering, producing a functionally similar piece of technology that works in a slightly different way to produce the same result. This seems to be a particular problem with regard to patented knowledge. Patents accord the inventor 20 years of legal protection from direct imitation, but research suggests that rivals invent their way around 60% of patent innovations within 4 years.[7] On the other hand, trademarks are initially protected from imitation for 10 years but can be renewed every 10 years. Moreover, it is almost impossible for a rival to copy a company's trademark protected logo and brand name without violating the law. This is important, for logos and brand names are powerful symbols. As such trademarks can insulate a company's brand from direct attack by rivals, which builds something of an economic moat around companies with strong brands.

A company's rare and valuable process knowledge can be very hard for rivals to copy; the barriers to imitation are high. There are two main reasons for this. First, process knowledge is often (1) partly tacit, (2) hidden from view within the firm, and (3) socially complex. As such, it is difficult for outsiders to identify with precision the nature of a company's rare and valuable process knowledge. We refer to this problem as **causal ambiguity**.[8] Moreover, the socially complex nature of such knowledge means that hiring individual employees away from a successful firm to gain access to its process knowledge may be futile, because each individual only has direct experience with part of the overall knowledge base.

barriers to imitation
Factors or characteristics that make it difficult for another individual or company to replicate something.

causal ambiguity
When the way that one thing, A, leads to an outcome (or "causes"), B, is not clearly understood.

Second, even if a rival were able to identify with precision the form of a company's valuable and rare process knowledge, it still has to implement that knowledge within its own organization. This not easy to do; it requires changing the way the imitating company currently operates. Such change can be stymied by organizational inertia. We discuss organizational inertia in more detail in Chapter 12, but for now note that organizational structure, routines, and culture are notoriously hard to change. The reasons include opposition from organizational members whose power and influence will be reduced as a result of the change, and the difficulties associated with changing the culture of an organization, particularly old habits, old ways of doing things, and old ways of perceiving the world. Typically, process change takes a sustained effort over several years, during which time the company that is the target of imitation efforts may have accumulated new knowledge and moved on.

An inability to imitate valuable process knowledge seems to have been a problem in the U.S. automobile industry, where attempts by Ford and GM to imitate Toyota's lean production systems were held back for years, if not decades, by their own internal inertia. These included objections from unions to proposals to change work practices, the legacy of decades of investment in factories configured to mass production rather than lean production, and an organizational culture that resisted change that altered the balance of power and influence within the company.

Organizational architecture that is rare and valuable can also be very hard for rivals to imitate, for many of the same reasons that process knowledge is hard to imitate. Specifically, even if the would-be imitator can identify with precision the features of a successful company's value creating organizational architecture, adopting that architecture might require wholesale organizational change, which is both risky and difficult to do given internal inertia.

Implications   In sum, we have demonstrated how *advanced* factors of production such as intellectual property, process knowledge, and organizational architecture are more likely to be rare, and will be harder to imitate due to high barriers to imitation, than more basic factors of production. Put differently, advanced factors of production are more likely to constitute the unique strengths of an organization. A number of implications flow from this insight.

First, it is clearly important for managers to vigorously protect their intellectual property from imitation both by establishing their intellectual property rights (e.g., by filing for patent, copyright or trademark protection), and by asserting those rights, legally challenging rivals who try to violate them. This said, it is sometimes best not to patent valuable technology but instead keep it as a trade secret, because that can make imitation more difficult. Coca Cola, for example, has never patented the recipe underlying its core Coke brand, because filing a patent would reveal valuable information about the recipe.

Second, given that process knowledge is often an important source of sustainable competitive advantage, managers would be well advised to devote considerable attention to optimizing their processes. They might, for example, invest time and effort in process improvement methodologies such as Six Sigma (which we shall discuss in Chapter 4). Similarly, given the importance of organizational architecture, it is crucial for managers to assure that their company's organization is optimal. Thinking critically and proactively about organizational design becomes a very important task (as we discuss in Chapter 12).

Third, it is important to protect knowledge about superior processes and practices from leaking out. For example, Intel, a very efficient manufacturer of microprocessors, has developed valuable technology to improve its manufacturing processes but has chosen not to patent it. Instead, it treats the underlying knowledge as a trade secret. Intel's reasoning is that if the technology were patented, the patent filing would make available crucial information about the technology, making imitation by rivals more likely.

Fourth, if a company has developed rare and valuable process knowledge in core functional activities of the firm, it would be unwise for the firm to outsource those activities to a third-party producer in pursuit of a perceived short-term cost saving or other transitory benefit. Some observers believed that Boeing made this mistake when it decided to outsource production for horizontal stabilizers for its 737 aircraft to Chinese subcontractors. Horizontal stabilizers are the horizontal winglets on the tail section of an aircraft. Historically, Boeing designed and built these and as a consequence it accumulated rare and valuable design and manufacturing process knowledge. In the late 1990s, Boeing outsourced production of horizontal stabilizers in exchange for the tacit promise for more orders from Chinese airlines. Although this benefitted Boeing in the short run, it gave Chinese manufacturers the chance to develop their own process knowledge, while Boeing stopped accumulating important process knowledge. Today, Chinese aircraft manufacturers are building a competitor to Boeing's 737 aircraft, and Boeing may well have helped them do that through outsource decisions that diminished the company's long-run competitive advantage.

▌VALUE CREATION AND PROFITABILITY

We have discussed how competitive advantage based upon valuable, rare, inimitable resources that reside within a well-organized, well-managed firm constitute unique strengths that lead to a sustained competitive advantage. In this section, we take a deeper look at how such resources (strengths) translate into superior profitability.

At the most basic level, a company's profitability depends on three factors: (1) the value customers place on the company's products, (2) the price that a company charges for its products, and (3) the costs of creating those products. The value customers place on a product reflects the *utility* they derive from it, or the happiness or satisfaction gained from consuming or owning it. Value must be distinguished from price. Value is something that customers receive from a product. It is a function of the attributes of the product such as its performance, design, quality, and point-of-sale and after-sale service. For example, most customers would place a much higher value on a top-end Lexus from Toyota than on a low-end, basic economy car from Kia, precisely because they perceive Lexus to have better performance and superior design, quality, and service. A company that strengthens the value of its products in the eyes of customers enhances its brand and has more pricing options: It can raise prices to reflect that value, or keep prices lower to induce more customers to purchase its products, thereby expanding unit sales volume.

Regardless of the pricing option a company chooses, that price is typically less than the value placed upon the good or service by the customer. This is because the customer captures some of that value in the form of what economists call a *consumer surplus*.

This occurs because it is normally impossible to segment the market to such a degree that the company can charge each customer a price that reflects that individual's unique assessment of the value of a product—what economists refer to as a customer's *reservation price*. In addition, because the company is competing against rivals for customers, it has to charge a lower price than it could were it a monopoly. For these reasons, the point-of-sale price tends to be less than the value placed on the product by many customers. Nevertheless, remember this basic principle: The more value that consumers derive from a company's goods or services, the more pricing options that company has.

These concepts are illustrated in Figure 3.2. V is the *average* value per unit of a product to a customer; P is the average price per unit that the company decides to charge for that product; and C is the average unit cost of producing that product (including actual production costs and the cost of capital investments in production systems). The company's average profit per unit is equal to $P - C$, and the consumer surplus is equal to $V - P$. In other words, $V - P$ is a measure of the value the consumer captures, and $P - C$ is a measure of the value the company captures. The company makes a profit so long as P is more than C, and its profitability will be greater the lower C is relative to P. Bear in mind that the difference between V and P is in part determined by the intensity of competitive pressure in the marketplace; the lower the competitive pressure's intensity, the higher the price that can be charged relative to V, but the difference between V and P is also determined by the company's pricing choice.[9]

As we shall see, a company may choose to keep prices low relative to volume because lower prices enable the company to sell more products, attain scale economies, and boost its profit margin by lowering C relative to P.

Also, note that the *value created by a company* is measured by the difference between the value or utility a consumer gets from the product (V) and the costs of production (C), that is, $V - C$. A company creates value by converting inputs that cost C into a good or service from which customers derive a value of V. A company can create more value for its customers by lowering C or making the product more attractive through superior design, performance, quality, service, and other factors. When customers assign a greater value to the product (V increases), they are willing to pay a higher price (P increases). This discussion suggests that a company

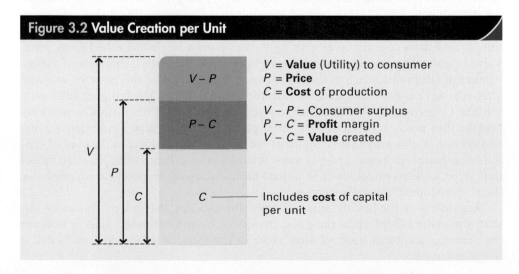

Figure 3.2 Value Creation per Unit

$V - P$

$P - C$

V

P

C

C

V = **Value** (Utility) to consumer
P = **Price**
C = **Cost** of production

$V - P$ = Consumer surplus
$P - C$ = **Profit** margin
$V - C$ = **Value** created

C ———— Includes **cost** of capital per unit

has a competitive advantage and high profitability when it creates more value for its customers than rivals.[10]

The company's pricing options are captured in Figure 3.3. Suppose a company's current pricing option is the one pictured in the middle column of Figure 3.3. Imagine that the company decides to pursue strategies to increase the utility of its product offering from V to V^* in order to boost its profitability. Increasing value initially raises production costs because the company must spend money in order to increase product performance, quality, service, and other factors. Now there are two different pricing options that the company can pursue. Option 1 is to raise prices to reflect the higher value: the company raises prices more than its costs increase, and profit per unit $(P - C)$ increases. Option 2 involves a very different set of choices: The company lowers prices in order to expand unit volume. Generally, customers recognize that they are getting a great bargain because the price is now much lower than the value (the consumer surplus has increased), so they rush out to buy more (demand has increased). As unit volume expands due to increased demand, the company is able to realize scale economies and reduce its average unit costs. Although creating the extra value initially costs more, and although margins are initially compressed by aggressive pricing, ultimately profit margins widen because the average per-unit cost of production falls as volume increases and scale economies are attained.

Managers must understand the dynamic relationships among value, pricing, demand, and costs in order to make decisions that will maximize competitive advantage and profitability. Option 2 in Figure 3.3, for example, may not be a viable strategy if demand did not increase rapidly with lower prices, or if few economies of scale will result by increasing volume. Managers must understand how value creation and pricing decisions affect demand, as well as how unit costs change with increases in volume. In other words, they must clearly comprehend the demand for their company's product and its cost structure at different levels of output if they are to make decisions that maximize profitability.

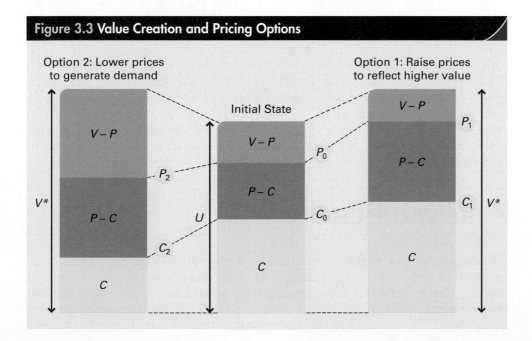

Figure 3.3 Value Creation and Pricing Options

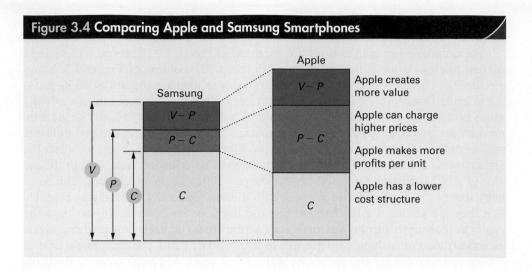

Figure 3.4 Comparing Apple and Samsung Smartphones

The most beneficial position for a company occurs when it can utilize its valuable, rare, inimitable resources and capabilities to deliver a product offering that consumers value more highly than that of rivals (that is, they derive more utility from it), and which can be produced at a lower cost than that of rivals. This is an outcome that many companies strive to achieve. Consider again the example of Apple and its successful iPhone offering. Apple creates value for consumers with the elegance of its design for the iPhone, its intuitive, easy-to-use interface, its onboard applications such as iTunes and iCloud, and the fact that Apple has encouraged a healthy ecosystem of developers to write third-party applications that run on the phone. Apple has been so successful at differentiating its product along these dimensions that it is able to charge a premium price for its iPhone relative to offerings from Samsung, HTC, and the like. At the same time, it sells so many iPhones that the company has been able to achieve enormous economies of scale in production and the purchasing of components, which has driven down the average unit cost of the iPhone. Thus, even though the iPhone makes use of expensive materials such as brushed aluminum casing and a gorilla-glass screen, Apple has been able to charge a higher price *and* has lower costs than its rivals. Hence, although Samsung sold more units than Apple in 2013, Apple was able to capture 75% of all profit in the global smartphone industry for that year. Samsung captured the remaining 25%, with no other smartphone supplier making money.

THE VALUE CHAIN

value chain

The concept that a company consists of a chain of activities that transforms inputs into outputs.

All functions of a company—production, marketing, product development, service, information systems, materials management, and human resources—have a role in lowering the cost structure and increasing the perceived value of products through differentiation. To explore this idea, consider the concept of the value chain illustrated in Figure 3.5.[11] The term **value chain** refers to the idea that a company is a chain of

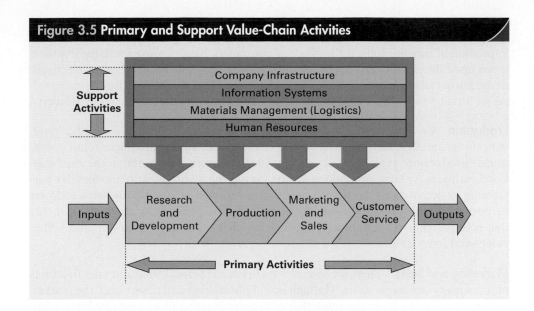

Figure 3.5 Primary and Support Value-Chain Activities

functional activities that transforms inputs into outputs. The transformation process involves both primary activities and support activities. Value is added to the product at each stage in the chain. Valuable, rare, inimitable resources can be found within one or more of a company's value-chain activities.

Primary Activities

Primary activities include the design, creation, and delivery of the product, the product's marketing, and its support and after-sales service. In the value chain illustrated in Figure 3.5, the primary activities are broken down into four functions: research and development, production, marketing and sales, and customer service.

Research and Development   Research and development (R&D) refers to the design of products and production processes. We may think of R&D as being associated with the design of physical products such as an iPhone or a Toyota, and/or production processes in manufacturing enterprises, service companies also undertake R&D. For example, banks compete with each other by developing new financial products and new ways of delivering those products to customers. Online banking and smart debit cards are examples of the fruits of new-product development in the banking industry. Earlier innovations in the banking industry include ATM machines, credit cards, and debit cards.

By creating superior product design, R&D can increase the functionality of products, making them more attractive to customers and thereby adding value. Alternatively, R&D may result in more efficient production processes, thereby lowering production costs. Either way, R&D can lower costs or raise a product's value, thus permitting a company to charge higher prices. At Intel, R&D creates value by developing ever-more powerful microprocessors and pioneering ever-more efficient manufacturing processes (in conjunction with equipment suppliers).

primary activities

activities related to the design, creation, and delivery of the product, its marketing, and its support and after-sales service.

It is important to emphasize that R&D is not just about enhancing the features and functions of a product; it is also about the elegance of product design, which can create an impression of superior value in the minds of consumers. Apple's success with the iPhone is based upon the elegance and appeal of the iPhone design, which has turned an electronic device into a fashion accessory. For another example of how design elegance can create value, see Strategy in Action 3.1, which discusses value creation at the fashion house Burberry.

Production Production refers to the creation of a good or service. For tangible products, this generally means manufacturing. For services such as banking or retail operations, "production" typically takes place while the service is delivered to the customer. For Southwest Airlines, production occurs every time a Southwest plane flies. By performing its activities efficiently, the production function of a company helps to lower its cost structure. The production function can also perform its activities in a way that is consistent with high product quality, which leads to differentiation (and higher value) and lower costs.

Marketing and Sales There are several ways in which the marketing and sales functions of a company can create value. Through brand positioning and advertising, the marketing function can increase the value that customers perceive to be contained in a company's product (and thus the utility they attribute to the product). Insofar as these help to create a favorable impression of the company's product in the minds of customers, they increase utility. For example, the French company Perrier persuaded U.S. customers that slightly carbonated, bottled water was worth $2.50 per bottle rather than a price closer to the $1.00 that it cost to collect, bottle, and distribute the water. Perrier's marketing function increased the perception of value that customers ascribed to the product. Similarly, by helping to rebrand the company and its product offering, the marketing department at Burberry helped to create value (see Strategy in Action 3.1). Marketing and sales can also create value by discovering customer needs and communicating them back to the R&D function , which can then design products that better match those needs.

Customer Service The role of the service function of an enterprise is to provide after-sales service and support. This function can create superior utility by solving customer problems and supporting customers after they have purchased the product. For example, Caterpillar, the U.S.-based manufacturer of heavy earth-moving equipment, can ship spare parts to any location in the world within 24 hours, thereby minimizing the amount of downtime its customers face if their Caterpillar equipment malfunctions. This is an extremely valuable support capability in an industry where downtime is very expensive. The extent of customer support has helped to increase the utility that customers associate with Caterpillar products, and therefore the price that Caterpillar can charge for them.

Support Activities

support activities

Activities of the value chain that provide inputs that allow the primary activities to take place.

The **support activities** of the value chain provide inputs that allow the primary activities to take place. These activities are broken down into four functions: materials management (or logistics), human resources, information systems, and company infrastructure (see Figure 3.5).

Materials Management (Logistics) The materials-management (or logistics) function controls the transmission of physical materials through the value chain, from

3.1 STRATEGY IN ACTION

Value Creation at Burberry

When Rose Marie Bravo, the highly regarded president of Saks Fifth Avenue, announced in 1997 that she was leaving to become CEO of ailing British fashion house Burberry, people thought she was crazy. Burberry, best known as a designer of raincoats with a trademark tartan lining, had been described as an outdated, stuffy business with a fashion cachet of almost zero. When Bravo stepped down in 2006, she was heralded in Britain and the United States as one of the world's best managers. In her tenure at Burberry, she had engineered a remarkable turnaround, leading a transformation of Burberry into what one commentator called an "achingly hip" high-end fashion brand whose famous tartan bedecks everything from raincoats and bikinis to handbags and luggage in a riot of color from pink to blue to purple. In less than a decade, Burberry had become one of the most valuable luxury fashion brands in the world.

When asked how she achieved the transformation, Bravo explained that there was hidden value in the brand, which was unleashed by constant creativity and innovation. Bravo hired world-class designers to redesign Burberry's tired fashion line and bought in Christopher Bailey, one of the very best, to lead the design team. The marketing department worked closely with advertisers to develop hip ads that would appeal to a younger, well-heeled audience. The ads featured supermodel Kate Moss promoting the line, and Burberry hired a top fashion photographer to shoot Moss in Burberry. Burberry exercised tight control over distribution, pulling its products from stores whose image was not consistent with the Burberry brand, and expanding its own chain of Burberry stores.

Bravo also noted that "creativity doesn't just come from designers ... ideas can come from the sales floor, the marketing department, even from accountants, believe it or not. People at whatever level they are working have a point of view and have something to say that is worth listening to." Bravo emphasized the importance of teamwork: "One of the things I think people overlook is the quality of the team. It isn't one person, and it isn't two people. It is a whole group of people— a team that works cohesively toward a goal—that makes something happen or not." She notes that her job is to build the team and then motivate the team, "keeping them on track, making sure that they are following the vision."

Sources: Quotes from S. Beatty, "Bass Talk: Plotting Plaid's Future," *The Wall Street Journal*, September 9, 2004, p. B1; C. M. Moore and G. Birtwistle, "The Burberry Business Model," *International Journal of Retail and Distribution Management* 32 (2004): 412–422; M. Dickson, "Bravo's Legacy in Transforming Burberry," *Financial Times*, October 6, 2005, p. 22.

procurement through production and into distribution. The efficiency with which this is carried out can significantly lower cost, thereby generating profit. A company that has benefited from very efficient materials management, the Spanish fashion company Zara, is discussed in Strategy in Action 3.2, see Figure 3.4.

Human Resources   There are numerous ways in which the human resource function can help an enterprise create more value. This function ensures that the company has the right combination of skilled people to perform its value creation activities effectively. It is also the job of the human resource function to ensure that people are adequately trained, motivated, and compensated to perform their value creation tasks. If the human resources are functioning well, employee productivity rises (which lowers costs) and customer service

3.2 STRATEGY IN ACTION

Competitive Advantage at Zara

Fashion retailer Zara is one of Spain's fastest-growing and most successful companies, with sales of some $10 billion and a network of 6,500 stores in 88 countries. Zara's competitive advantage centers around one thing: speed. Whereas it takes most fashion houses 6 to 9 months to go from design to delivering merchandise to a store, Zara can complete the entire process in just 5 weeks. This competitive advantage enables Zara to quickly respond to changing fashion trends.

Zara achieves this by breaking many of the rules of operation in the fashion business. Whereas most fashion houses outsource production, Zara has its own factories and keeps approximately half of its production in-house. Zara also has its own designers and its own stores. Its designers, who are in constant contact with the stores, track what is selling on a real-time basis through information systems and talk to store managers weekly to get their impressions of what is "hot." This information supplements data gathered from other sources such as fashion shows.

Drawing on this information, Zara's designers create approximately 40,000 new designs a year, 10,000 of which are selected for production. Zara then purchases basic textiles from global suppliers, but performs capital-intensive production activities in its own factories. These factories use computer-controlled machinery to cut pieces for garments. Zara does not produce in large volumes to attain economies of scale; instead, it produces in small lots. Labor-intensive activities such as sewing are performed by subcontractors located close to Zara's factories. Zara makes a practice of retaining more production capacity than necessary, so that when a new fashion trend emerges it can quickly respond by designing garments and ramping up production.

Completed garments are delivered to one of Zara's own warehouses, and then shipped to its own stores once a week. Zara deliberately underproduces products, supplying small batches of products in hot demand before quickly shifting to the next fashion trend. Often, its merchandise sells out quickly. The empty shelves in Zara stores create a scarcity value—which helps to generate demand. Customers quickly snap up products they like because they know these styles may soon be out of stock and never produced again.

As a result of this strategy, which is supported by competencies in design, information systems, and logistics management, Zara carries less inventory than its competitors (Zara's inventory equals about 10% of sales, compared to 15% at rival stores such as The Gap and Benetton). This means fewer price reductions to move products that haven't sold, and higher profit margins.

Sources: "Shining Examples," *The Economist: A Survey of Logistics,* June 17, 2006, pp. 4–6; K. Capell et al., "Fashion Conquistador," *Business Week,* September 4, 2006, pp. 38–39; K. Ferdows et al., "Rapid Fire Fulfillment," *Harvard Business Review* 82 (November 2004): 101–107; "Inditex is a leader in the fast fashion industry," *Morningstar,* December 15, 2009; "Pull based centralized manufacturing yields cost efficiencies for Zara," *Morningstar,* June 19, 2014.

improves (which raises value to consumers), thereby enabling the company to create more value. This has certainly been the case at Southwest Airlines, and it helps to explain the persistently low cost structure and high reliability of that company (see the Opening Case).

Information Systems Information systems are, primarily, the digital systems for managing inventory, tracking sales, pricing products, selling products, dealing with customer service inquiries, and so on. Modern information systems, coupled with the communications features of the Internet, have enabled many enterprises to significantly improve the efficiency and effectiveness with which they manage their other value creation activities. World-class information systems are an aspect of Zara's competitive advantage (see Strategy in Action 3.2).

Company Infrastructure   Company infrastructure is the companywide context within which all the other value creation activities take place. This includes organizational structure, control systems, incentive systems, and organizational culture—what we refer to as the organizational architecture of a company. The company infrastructure also includes corporate-level legal, accounting, and finance functions. Because top management can exert considerable influence upon shaping all of these aspects of a company, top management should also be viewed as part of the infrastructure. Indeed, through strong leadership, top management can shape the infrastructure of a company and, through that, the performance of all other value creation activities that take place within it. A good example of this process is given in Strategy in Action 3.1, which looks at how Rose Marie Bravo helped to engineer a turnaround at Burberry.

Value-Chain Analysis: Implications

The concept of the value chain is useful because, when performing an internal analysis, managers can look at the different value-chain activities of the firm, identifying which activities result in the creation of the most value and which are not performing as well as they might be. In other words, value-chain analysis is a useful tool that helps managers identify the company's strengths and weaknesses. Furthermore, it helps managers pinpoint where valuable, rare, and inimitable resources reside within the company.

If managers are to perform a rigorous value-chain analysis, they need to do several things. First, they must analyze how efficiently and effectively each activity is being performed. This should go beyond a qualitative assessment to include an in-depth analysis of quantitative data. For example, the efficiency of the materials-management function might be measured by inventory turnover; the effectiveness of the customer service function might be measured by the speed with which customer complaints are satisfactorily resolved; and ability of the enterprise to deliver reliable products might be measured by customer returns and warranty costs. Managers need to identify those quantitative measures that are important for their business, collect data on them, and assess how well the firm is performing.

Second, as an aid to this process, whenever possible managers should benchmark each activity against a similar activity performed by rivals to see how well the company is doing. **Benchmarking** requires a company to measure how well it is performing against other enterprises using strategically relevant data. An airline, for example, can benchmark its activities against rivals by using publically available data that covers important aspects of airline performance such as departure and arrival delays, revenue per seat mile, and cost per seat mile. Government agencies, industry associations, or third-party providers may collect such data. The Department of Transportation and the Air Transport Industry Association collect a wealth of valuable information on the airline industry. Similarly, the market research company J.D. Power provides important information on product quality and customer satisfaction for companies operating in a number of industries, including automobiles and wireless telecommunications. With regard to Web-based businesses, comScore.com collects a trove of valuable information on web traffic, search-engine performance, advertising conversions, and so on.

Third, in addition to benchmarking performance against rivals, it can be valuable to benchmark performance against best-in-class companies in other industries.

benchmarking
Measuring how well a company is doing by comparing it to another company, or to itself, over time.

For example, Apple is known for excellent customer services in its stores (through the Genius Bar). Comcast has a reputation for poor customer service. Thus, managers at Comcast might want to benchmark their customer service activities against Apple. Although Apple and Comcast are very different organizations, the comparison might yield useful insights that could help Comcast improve its performance.

Fourth, there are a number of process improvement methodologies that managers can and should use to analyze how well value creation activities are performing, and to identify opportunities for improving the efficiency and effectiveness of those activities. One of the most famous process improvement tools, *Six Sigma*, is discussed in more detail in Chapter 4. Finally, whenever there is potential for improvement within a value-chain activity, leaders within the company need to (a) empower managers to take the necessary actions, (b) measure performance improvements over time against goals, (c) reward managers for meeting or exceeding improvement goals, and (d) when goals are not met, analyze why this is so and take corrective action if necessary.

THE BUILDING BLOCKS OF COMPETITIVE ADVANTAGE

Four factors help a company build and sustain competitive advantage: superior efficiency, quality, innovation, and customer responsiveness. We call these factors the building blocks of competitive advantage. Each factor is the *result* of the way the various value-chain activities within an enterprise are performed. By performing value-chain activities to achieve superior efficiency, quality, innovation, and customer responsiveness, a company can (1) differentiate its product offering, and hence offer more value to its customers, and (2) lower its cost structure (see Figure 3.6). Although each factor

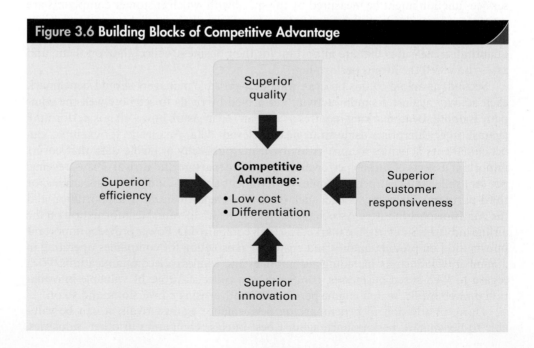

Figure 3.6 Building Blocks of Competitive Advantage

is discussed sequentially below, all are highly interrelated, and the important ways in which these building blocks affect each other should be noted. For example, superior quality can lead to superior efficiency, and innovation can enhance efficiency, quality, and responsiveness to customers.

Efficiency

The simplest measure of efficiency is the quantity of inputs required to produce a given output; that is, efficiency = outputs/inputs. The more efficient a company is, the fewer inputs it requires to produce a particular output, and the lower its costs.

One common measure of efficiency is employee productivity. **Employee productivity** refers to the output produced per employee. For example, if it takes General Motors 30 hours of employee time to assemble a car, and it takes Ford 25 hours, we can say that Ford has higher employee productivity than GM and is more efficient. As long as other factors such as wage rates are equal, we can assume from this information that Ford will have a lower cost structure than GM. Thus, employee productivity helps a company attain a competitive advantage through a lower cost structure.

employee productivity
The output produced per employee.

Another important measure of efficiency is capital productivity. **Capital productivity** refers to the output produced by a dollar of capital invested in the business. Firms that use their capital very efficiently and don't waste it on unproductive assets or activities will have higher capital productivity. For example, a firm that adopts just-in-time inventory systems to reduce both its inventory and its need for warehouse facilities will use less working capital (have less capital tied up in inventory) and less fixed capital (have less capital tied up in warehouses). Consequently, its capital productivity will increase.

capital productivity
The sales produced by a dollar of capital invested in the business.

Quality as Excellence and Reliability

A product can be thought of as a bundle of attributes.[12] The attributes of many physical products include their form, features, performance, durability, reliability, style, and design.[13] A product is said to have *superior quality* when customers perceive that its attributes provide them with higher utility than the attributes of products sold by rivals. For example, a Rolex watch has attributes such as design, styling, performance, and reliability that customers perceive as being superior to the same attributes in many other watches. Thus, we can refer to a Rolex as a high-quality product: Rolex has differentiated its watches by these attributes.

When customers evaluate the quality of a product, they commonly measure it against two kinds of attributes: those related to *quality as excellence* and those related to *quality as reliability*. From a quality-as-excellence perspective, the important attributes are a product's design and styling, its aesthetic appeal, its features and functions, the level of service associated with delivery of the product, and so on. For example, customers can purchase a pair of imitation-leather boots for $20 from Wal-Mart, or they can buy a handmade pair of butter-soft, leather boots from Nordstrom for $500. The boots from Nordstrom will have far superior styling, feel more comfortable, and look much better than those from Wal-Mart. The value consumers get from the Nordstrom boots will in all probability be much greater than the value derived from the Wal-Mart boots, but of course they will have to pay far more for them. That is the point: When excellence is built into a product offering, consumers must pay more to own or consume it.

With regard to quality as reliability, a product can be said to be reliable when it consistently performs the function it was designed for, performs it well, and rarely, if ever, breaks down. As with excellence, reliability increases the value (utility) a consumer derives from a product, and thus affects the price the company can charge for that product and/or the demand for that product.

The position of a product against two dimensions, reliability and other attributes, can be plotted as shown in Figure 3.7. For example, Verizon has the most reliable network in the wireless service industry as measured by factors such as coverage, number of dropped calls, dead zones, and so on. Verizon also has the best ratings when it comes to excellence, as measured by download speeds, customer care, and the like. According to J.D. Power surveys, T-Mobile has the worst position in the industry as measured by reliability and excellence.

The concept of quality applies whether we are talking about Toyota automobiles, clothes designed and sold by Zara, Verizon's wireless service, the customer service department of Citibank, or the ability of airlines to arrive on time. Quality is just as relevant to services as it is to goods.[14]

The impact of high product quality on competitive advantage is twofold.[15] First, providing high-quality products increases the value (utility) those products provide to customers, which gives the company the option of charging a higher price for the products. In the automobile industry, for example, Toyota has historically been able to charge a higher price for its cars because of the higher quality of its products.

Second, greater efficiency and lower unit costs associated with reliable products of high quality impact competitive advantage. When products are reliable, less employee time is wasted making defective products, or providing substandard services, and less time has to be spent fixing mistakes—which means higher employee productivity and lower unit costs. Thus, high product quality not only enables a company to differentiate its product from that of rivals, but, if the product is reliable, it also lowers costs.

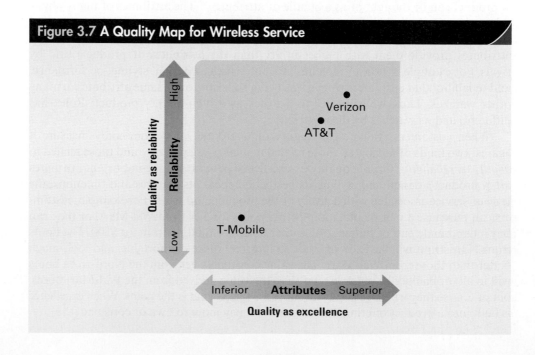

Figure 3.7 A Quality Map for Wireless Service

The importance of reliability in building competitive advantage has increased dramatically over the past 30 years. The emphasis many companies place on reliability is so crucial to achieving high product reliability that it can no longer be viewed as just one way of gaining a competitive advantage. In many industries, it has become an absolute imperative for a company's survival.

Innovation

There are two main types of innovation: product innovation and process innovation. **Product innovation** is the development of products that are new to the world or have superior attributes to existing products. Examples are Intel's invention of the microprocessor in the early 1970s, Cisco's development of the router for routing data over the Internet in the mid-1980s, and Apple's development of the iPod, iPhone, and iPad in the 2000s. **Process innovation** is the development of a new process for producing and delivering products to customers. Examples include Toyota, which developed a range of new techniques collectively known as the "Toyota lean production system" for making automobiles: just-in-time inventory systems, self-managing teams, and reduced setup times for complex equipment.

product innovation
Development of products that are new to the world or have superior attributes to existing products.

process innovation
Development of a new process for producing and delivering products to customers.

Product innovation generates value by creating new products, or enhanced versions of existing products, that customers perceive as having more value, thus increasing the company's pricing options. Process innovation often allows a company to create more value by lowering production costs. Toyota's lean production system helped boost employee productivity, thus giving Toyota a cost-based competitive advantage.[16] Similarly, Staples dramatically lowered the cost of selling office supplies by applying the supermarket business model to retail office supplies. Staples passed on some of this cost savings to customers in the form of lower prices, which enabled the company to increase its market share rapidly.

In the long run, innovation of products and processes is perhaps the most important building block of competitive advantage.[17] Competition can be viewed as a process driven by innovations. Although not all innovations succeed, those that do can be a major source of competitive advantage because, by definition, they give a company something unique that its competitors lack (at least until they imitate the innovation). Uniqueness can allow a company to differentiate itself from its rivals and charge a premium price for its product, or, in the case of many process innovations, reduce its unit costs far below those of competitors.

Customer Responsiveness

To achieve superior responsiveness to customers, a company must be able to do a better job than competitors of identifying and satisfying its customers' needs. Customers will then attribute more value to its products, creating a competitive advantage based on differentiation. Improving the quality of a company's product offering is consistent with achieving responsiveness, as is developing new products with features that existing products lack. In other words, achieving superior quality and innovation is integral to achieving superior responsiveness to customers.

Another factor that stands out in any discussion of responsiveness to customers is the need to customize goods and services to the unique demands of individuals or groups. For example, the proliferation of soft drinks and beers can be viewed partly as a response to this trend. An aspect of responsiveness to customers that has drawn increasing attention is **customer response time**: the time that it takes for a good to be

customer response time
Time that it takes for a good to be delivered or a service to be performed.

delivered or a service to be performed.[18] For a manufacturer of machinery, response time is the time it takes to fill customer orders. For a bank, it is the time it takes to process a loan, or the time that a customer must stand in line to wait for a free teller. For a supermarket, it is the time that customers must stand in checkout lines. For a fashion retailer, it is the time required to take a new product from design inception to placement in a retail store (see Strategy in Action 3.2 for a discussion of how the Spanish fashion retailer Zara minimizes this). Customer survey after customer survey has shown slow response time to be a major source of customer dissatisfaction.[19]

Other sources of enhanced responsiveness to customers are superior design, superior service, and superior after-sales service and support. All of these factors enhance responsiveness to customers and allow a company to differentiate itself from its less responsive competitors. In turn, differentiation enables a company to build brand loyalty and charge a premium price for its products. Consider how much more people are prepared to pay for next-day delivery of Express Mail, compared to delivery in 3 to 4 days. In 2012, a two-page letter sent by overnight Express Mail within the United States cost about $10, compared to $0.48 for regular mail. Thus, the price premium for express delivery (reduced response time) was $9.52, or a premium of 1983% over the regular price.

◤ ANALYZING COMPETITIVE ADVANTAGE AND PROFITABILITY

In order to perform a solid internal analysis and dig into how well different value-chain activities are performed, managers must be able to analyze the financial performance of their company, identifying how its strategies contribute (or not) to profitability. To identify strengths and weaknesses effectively, they must be able to compare, or benchmark, the performance of their company against competitors, as well as against the historic performance of the company itself. This will help them determine whether they are more or less profitable than competitors and whether the performance of the company has been improving or deteriorating through time; whether their company strategies are maximizing the value being created; whether their cost structure is out of alignment compared to competitors; and whether they are using the company resources to the greatest effect.

As we noted in Chapter 1, the key measure of a company's financial performance is its profitability, which captures the return that a company is generating on its investments. Although several different measures of profitability exist, such as return on assets and return on equity, many authorities on the measurement of profitability argue that return on invested capital (ROIC) is the best measure because "it focuses on the true operating performance of the company."[20] (However, return on assets is very similar in formulation to return on invested capital.)

ROIC is defined as net profit over invested capital, or ROIC = net profit/invested capital. Net profit is calculated by subtracting the total costs of operating the company from its total revenues (total revenues – total costs). *Net profit* is what is left over after the government takes its share in taxes. *Invested capital* is the amount that is invested in the operations of a company: property, plants, equipment, inventories, and other assets. Invested capital comes from two main sources: interest-bearing debt and shareholders' equity. *Interest-bearing debt* is money the company borrows from banks and those who purchase its bonds. *Shareholders' equity* is money raised from selling shares to the public, plus earnings that the company has retained in prior years (and that are available to fund current investments). ROIC measures the effectiveness with which a company is using the capital funds that it has available for investment. As such, it is recognized to be an excellent measure of the value a company is creating.[21]

A company's ROIC can be algebraically divided into two major components: return on sales and capital turnover.[22] Specifically:

$$\text{ROIC} = \text{net profits/invested capital}$$
$$= \text{net profits/revenues} \times \text{revenues/invested capital}$$

where net profits/revenues is the return on sales, and revenues/invested capital is capital turnover. Return on sales measures how effectively the company converts revenues into profits. Capital turnover measures how effectively the company employs its invested capital to generate revenues. These two ratios can be further divided into some basic accounting ratios, as shown in Figure 3.8 and defined in Table 3.1.[23]

Figure 3.8 notes that a company's managers can increase ROIC by pursuing strategies that increase the company's return on sales. To increase the company's return on sales, they can pursue strategies that reduce the cost of goods sold (COGS) for a given level of sales revenues (COGS/sales); reduce the level of spending on sales force, marketing, general, and administrative expenses (SG&A) for a given level of sales revenues (SG&A/sales); and reduce R&D spending for a given level of sales revenues (R&D/sales). Alternatively, they can increase return on sales by pursuing strategies that increase sales revenues more than they increase the costs of the business as measured by COGS, SG&A, and R&D expenses. That is, they can increase the return on sales by pursuing strategies that lower costs or increase value through differentiation, and thus allow the company to increase its prices more than its costs.

Figure 3.8 also tells us that a company's managers can boost the profitability of their company by obtaining greater sales revenues from their invested capital, thereby increasing capital turnover. They do this by pursuing strategies that reduce the amount of working capital, such as the amount of capital invested in inventories, needed to generate a given

Figure 3.8 Drivers of Profitability (ROIC)

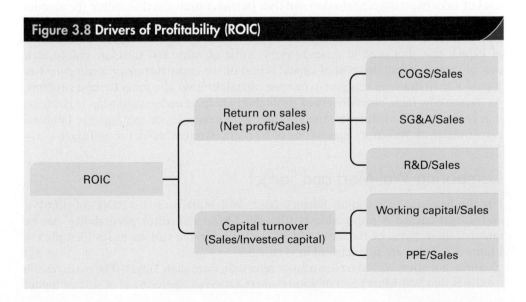

Table 3.1 Definitions of Basic Accounting Terms

Term	Definition	Source
Cost of goods sold (COGS)	Total costs of producing products	Income statement
Sales, general, and administrative expenses (SG&A)	Costs associated with selling products and administering the company	Income statement
Research and development (R&D) expenses	Research and development expenditure	Income statement
Working capital	The amount of money the company has to "work" with in the short term: Current assets – current liabilities	Balance sheet
Property, plant, and equipment (PPE)	The value of investments in the property, plant, and equipment that the company uses to manufacture and sell its products; also known as *fixed capital*	Balance sheet
Return on sales (ROS)	Net profit expressed as a percentage of sales; measures how effectively the company converts revenues into profits	Ratio
Capital turnover	Revenues divided by invested capital; measures how effectively the company uses its capital to generate revenues	Ratio
Return on invested capital (ROIC)	Net profit divided by invested capital	Ratio
Net profit	Total revenues minus total costs before tax	Income statement
Invested capital	Interest-bearing debt plus shareholders' equity	Balance sheet

level of sales (working capital/sales) and then pursuing strategies that reduce the amount of fixed capital that they have to invest in property, plant, and equipment (PPE) to generate a given level of sales (PPE/sales). That is, they pursue strategies that reduce the amount of capital that they need to generate every dollar of sales, and therefore reduce their cost of capital. Recall that cost of capital is part of the cost structure of a company (see Figure 3.2), so strategies designed to increase capital turnover also lower the cost structure.

To see how these basic drivers of profitability help us understand what is going on in a company and identify its strengths and weaknesses, let us compare the financial performance of Wal-Mart against one of its more effective competitors, Target.

Comparing Wal-Mart and Target

For the financial year ending January 2012, Wal-Mart earned a ROIC of 13.61%, and Target earned a respectable 10.01%. Wal-Mart's superior profitability can be understood in terms of the impact of its strategies on the various ratios identified in Figure 3.8. These are summarized in Figure 3.9.

First, note that Wal-Mart has a *lower* return on sales than Target. The main reason for this is that Wal-Mart's cost of goods sold (COGS) as a percentage of sales is higher

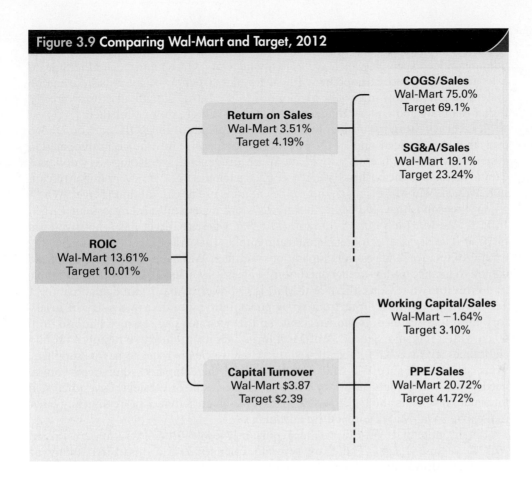

Figure 3.9 Comparing Wal-Mart and Target, 2012

than Target's (75% versus 69.1%). For a retailer, the COGS reflects the price that Wal-Mart pays to its suppliers for merchandise. The lower COGS/sales ratio implies that Wal-Mart does not mark up prices much as Target—its profit margin on each item sold is lower. Consistent with its long-time strategic goal, Wal-Mart passes on the low prices it gets from suppliers to customers. Wal-Mart's higher COGS/sales ratio reflects its strategy of being the lowest-price retailer.

On the other hand, you will notice that Wal-Mart spends less on sales, general, and administrative (SG&A) expenses as a percentage of sales than Target (19.1% versus 22.24%). There are three reasons for this. First, Wal-Mart's early strategy was to focus on small towns that could only support one discounter. In small towns, the company does not have to advertise heavily because it is not competing against other discounters. Second, Wal-Mart has become such a powerful brand that the company does not need to advertise as heavily as its competitors, even when its stores are located close to them in suburban areas. Third, because Wal-Mart sticks to its low-price philosophy, and because the company manages its inventory so well, it does not usually have an overstocking problem. Thus, the company does not need to hold periodic sales—and nor bear the costs of promoting those sales (e.g., sending out advertisements and coupons in local newspapers). Reducing spending on sales promotions reduces Wal-Mart's SG&A/sales ratio.

In addition, Wal-Mart operates with a flat organizational structure that has very few layers of management between the head office and store managers. This reduces administrative expenses (which are a component of SG&A) and hence the SG&A/sales ratio. Wal-Mart can operate with such a flat structure because its information systems allow its top managers to monitor and control individual stores directly, rather than rely upon intervening layers of subordinates to do that for them.

It is when we turn to consider the capital turnover side of the ROIC equation, however, that the financial impact of Wal-Mart's competitive advantage in information systems and logistics becomes apparent. Wal-Mart generates $3.87 for every dollar of capital invested in the business, whereas Target generates $2.39 for every dollar of capital invested. Wal-Mart is much more efficient in its use of capital than Target. Why?

One reason is that Wal-Mart has a lower working capital/sales ratio than Target. In fact, Wal-Mart has a *negative* ratio (–1.64%), whereas Target has a positive ratio (3.10%). The negative working capital ratio implies that Wal-Mart does not need any capital to finance its day-to-day operations—in fact, Wal-Mart is using its *suppliers'* capital to finance its day-to-day operations. This is very unusual, but Wal-Mart is able to do this for two reasons. First, Wal-Mart is so powerful that it can demand and get very favorable payment terms from its suppliers. It does not take ownership of inventory until it is scanned at the checkout, and it does not pay for merchandise until 60 days after it is sold. Second, Wal-Mart turns over its inventory so rapidly—around eight times a year—that it typically sells merchandise *before* it has to pay its suppliers. Thus, suppliers finance Wal-Mart's inventory and the company's short-term capital needs. Wal-Mart's high inventory turnover is the result of strategic investments in information systems and logistics. It is these value-chain activities more than any other that explain Wal-Mart's competitive advantage.

Finally, note that Wal-Mart has a significantly lower PPE/sales ratio than Target: 20.72% versus 41.72%. There are several explanations for this. First, many of Wal-Mart's stores are still located in small towns where land is cheap, whereas most Target stores are located in more expensive, suburban locations. Thus, on average, Wal-Mart spends less on a store than Target—again, strategy has a clear impact on financial performance. Second, because Wal-Mart turns its inventory over so rapidly, it does not need to devote as much space in stores to holding inventory. This means that more floor space can be devoted to selling merchandise. Other things being equal, this will result in a higher PPE/sales ratio. By the same token, efficient inventory management means that it needs less space at a distribution center to support a store, which again reduces total capital spending on property, plant, and equipment. Third, the higher PPE/sales ratio may also reflect the fact that Wal-Mart's brand is so powerful, and its commitment to low pricing so strong, that store traffic is higher than at comparable discounters such as Target. The stores are simply busier and the PPE/sales ratio is higher.

In sum, Wal-Mart's high profitability is a function of its strategy, and the resources and distinctive competencies that its strategic investments have built over the years, particularly in the area of information systems and logistics. As in the Wal-Mart example, the methodology described in this section can be very useful for analyzing why and how well a company is achieving and sustaining a competitive advantage. It highlights a company's strengths and weaknesses, showing where there is room for improvement and where a company is excelling. As such, it can drive strategy formulation. Moreover, the same methodology can be used to analyze the performance of competitors, and gain a greater understanding of their strengths and weakness, which in turn can inform strategy.

KEY TERMS

distinctive
    competencies   81
resources   81
process
    knowledge   81
socially complex   81
tacit   81

organizational
    architecture   81
intellectual property   82
basic factors of
    production   82
advanced factors of
    production   82

VRIO framework   83
barriers to imitation   85
causal ambiguity   85
value chain   90
primary activities   91
support activities   92
benchmarking   95

employee productivity   97
capital productivity   97
product innovation   99
process innovation   99
customer response
    time   99

TAKEAWAYS FOR STRATEGIC MANAGERS

1. Distinctive competencies are the firm-specific strengths of a company. Valuable distinctive competencies enable a company to earn a profit rate that is above the industry average.
2. The distinctive competencies of an organization arise from its resources. Resources include land, labor, management, plants, equipment, process knowledge, intellectual property, and organizational architecture.
3. Resources are likely to result in a competitive advantage when they are valuable, rare, and inimitable, and when the firm is organized to exploit them.
4. Advanced factors of production (resources) such as intellectual property, process knowledge, and organizational architecture are most likely to result in a sustained competitive advantage. Valuable advanced resources are more likely to be rare and inimitable.
5. In order to achieve a competitive advantage, a company needs to pursue strategies that build on its existing resources and formulate strategies that create additional resources (and thus develop new competencies).

6. The amount of value a company creates is measured by the difference between the value (utility) consumers derive from its goods or services and the cost of creating that value.
7. To create more value a company must lower its costs or differentiate its product so that it creates more utility for consumers and can charge a higher price, or do both simultaneously.
8. The four building blocks of competitive advantage are efficiency, quality, innovation, and responsiveness to customers. Superior efficiency enables a company to lower its costs; superior quality allows it to charge a higher price and lower its costs; and superior customer service lets it charge a higher price. Superior innovation can lead to higher prices in the case of product innovations, or lower unit costs in the case of process innovations.
9. In order to perform a solid internal analysis, managers need to be able to analyze the financial performance of their company, identifying how the strategies of the company relate to its profitability as measured by the return on invested capital.

DISCUSSION QUESTIONS

1. What are the primary implications of the material discussed in this chapter for strategy formulation?
2. When is a company's competitive advantage most likely to be sustained over time?
3. It is possible for a company to be the lowest-cost producer in its industry and simultaneously have an output that is the most valued by customers. Discuss this statement.

4. Why is it important to understand the drivers of profitability as measured by the return on invested capital?
5. Which is more important in explaining the success and failure of companies: strategizing to create valuable resources, or luck?

CLOSING CASE

Verizon Wireless

Established in 2000 as a joint venture between Verizon Communications and Britain's Vodafone, over the last 12 years Verizon Wireless has emerged as the largest and consistently most profitable enterprise in the fiercely competitive U.S. wireless service market (see the Chapter 2 Opening Case for details on the industry). Today, the company has almost 136 million subscribers and a 38% market share.

One of the most significant facts about Verizon is that it has the lowest churn rate in the industry. Customer churn refers to the number of subscribers who leave a service within a given time period. Churn is important because it costs between $400 and $600 to acquire a customer (with phone subsidies accounting for a large chunk of that). It can take months just to recoup the fixed costs of a customer acquisition. If churn rates are high, profitability is eaten up by the costs of acquiring customers who do not stay long enough to provide a profit to the service provider.

The risk of churn increased significantly in the United States after November 2003, when the Federal Communications Commission (FCC) allowed wireless subscribers to transfer their phone numbers when they switched to a new service provider. Over the next few years, Verizon Wireless emerged as the clear winner in the battle to limit customer defections. For example, in late 2014, Verizon's churn rate was 1.28% per month, compared to a rate of 1.36% at AT&T, 2.75% at Sprint, and 2.83% at T-Mobile. Verizon's low churn rate has enabled the company to grow its subscriber base faster than its rivals, which allows the company to better achieve economies of scale by spreading the fixed costs of building a wireless network over a larger customer base.

The low customer churn at Verizon is due to a number of factors. First, it has the most extensive network in the United States, blanketing 95% of the nation. This means fewer dropped calls and dead zones as compared to its rivals. For years, Verizon communicated its coverage and quality advantage to customers with its "Test Man" advertisements. In these ads, a Verizon Test Man wearing horn-rimmed glasses and a Verizon uniform wanders around remote spots in the nation asking on his Verizon cell phone, "Can you hear me now?" Verizon claims that the Test Man was actually the personification of a crew of 50 Verizon employees who each drive some 100,000 miles annually in specially outfitted vehicles to test the reliability of Verizon's network.

Second, the company has invested aggressively in high-speed wireless networks, including 3G and now 4G LTE, enabling fast download rates on smartphones. Complementing this, Verizon has a high-speed, fiber-optic backbone for transporting data between cell towers. Verizon has invested some $100 billion in its wireless and fiber-optic network since 2000. For customers, this means a high-quality user experience when accessing data such as streaming video on their smartphones. To drive this advantage home, in 2011, Verizon started offering Apple's market-leading iPhone in addition to the full range of Android smartphones it was already offering (the iPhone was originally exclusive to AT&T).

To further reduce customer churn, Verizon has invested heavily in its customer care function. Its automated software programs analyze the call habits of individual customers. Using that information, Verizon representatives will contact customers and suggest alternative plans that might better suit their needs. For example, Verizon might contact a customer and say, "We see that because of your heavy use of data, an alternative plan might make more sense for you and help reduce your monthly bills."

The goal is to anticipate customer needs and pro-actively satisfy them, rather than have the customer take the initiative and possibly switch to another service provider.

Surveys by J.D. Power have repeatedly confirmed Verizon's advantages. A recent J.D. Power study ranked Verizon best in the industry in terms of overall network performance. The ranking was based on a number of factors, including dropped calls, late text message notifications, Web connection errors, and slow download rates. Another J.D. Power study looked at customer care in three customer contact channels—telephone, walk-in (retail store), and online. Again, Verizon had the best score in the industry, reflecting faster service and greater satisfaction with the efficiency with which costumer service reps resolved problems.

Sources: R. Blackden, "Telecom's Giant Verizon Is Conquering America," *The Telegraph*, January 6, 2013; S. Woolley, "Do You Fear Me Now?" *Forbes*, November 10, 2003, pp. 78–80; A. Z. Cuneo, "Call Verizon Victorious," *Advertising Age*, March 24, 2004, pp. 3–5; M. Alleven, "Wheels of Churn," *Wireless Week*, September 1, 2006; J.D. Power, "2012 U.S. Wireless Customer Care Full-Service Performance Study," July 7, 2012; J.D. Power, "2012 U.S. Wireless Network Quality Performance Study," August 23, 2012; Statista, "Average monthly churn rate for wireless carriers in the United States," January 2015, www.statista.com.

CASE DISCUSSION QUESTIONS

1. What resources underlie Verizon's strong competitive position in the U.S. wireless telecommunications industry?
2. Explain how these resources enable Verizon to improve one or more of the following: efficiency, quality, customer responsiveness, and innovation.
3. Apply the VRIO framework and describe to what extent these resources can be considered valuable, rare, inimitable, and well organized.
4. What must Verizon do to maintain its competitive advantage going forward in the increasingly competitive U.S. wireless telecommunications industry (you might want to reread the Chapter 2 Opening Case)?

NOTES

[1]M. Cusumano, *The Japanese Automobile Industry* (Cambridge, Mass.: Harvard University Press, 1989); S. Spear and H. K. Bowen, "Decoding the DNA of the Toyota Production System," *Harvard Business Review* (September-October 1999): 96–108.

[2]The material in this section relies on the resource-based view of the company. For summaries of this perspective, see J. B. Barney, "Company Resources and Sustained Competitive Advantage," *Journal of Management* 17 (1991): 99–120; J. T. Mahoney and J. R. Pandian, "The Resource-Based View Within the Conversation of Strategic Management," *Strategic Management Journal* 13 (1992): 63–380.

[3]R. Amit and P. J. H. Schoemaker, "Strategic Assets and Organizational Rent," *Strategic Management Journal* 14 (1993): 33–46; M. A. Peteraf, "The Cornerstones of Competitive Advantage: A Resource-Based View," *Strategic Management Journal* 14 (1993): 179–191; B. Wernerfelt, "A Resource-Based View of the Company," *Strategic Management Journal* 15 (1994): 171–180; K. M. Eisenhardt and J. A. Martin, "Dynamic Capabilities: What Are They?" *Strategic Management Journal* 21 (2000): 1105–1121.

[4]For a discussion of organizational capabilities, see R. R. Nelson and S. Winter, *An Evolutionary Theory of Economic Change* (Cambridge, Mass.: Belknap Press, 1982).

[5]J. B. Barney and W. S. Hesterly, *Strategic Management and Competitive Advantage* (Boston: Pearson, 2005).

[6]The concept of barriers to imitation is grounded in the resource-based view of the company. For details, see R. Reed and R. J. DeFillippi, "Causal Ambiguity, Barriers to Imitation, and Sustainable Competitive Advantage," *Academy of Management Review* 15 (1990): 88–102.

[7]E. Mansfield, "How Economists See R&D," *Harvard Business Review* (November-December 1981): 98–106.

[8]R. Reed and R. J. DeFillippi, "Causal Ambiguity, Barriers to Imitation, and Sustainable Competitive Advantage," *Academy of Management Review* 15 (1990): 88–102.

[9]However, $P = V$ only in the special case when the company has a perfect monopoly and can charge each customer a unique price that reflects the utility of the product to that customer (i.e., where perfect price discrimination is possible). More generally, except in the limiting case of perfect price discrimination, even a monopolist will see most customers capture some of the value of a product in the form of a consumer surplus.

[10]This point is central to the work of Michael Porter. See M. E. Porter, *Competitive Advantage* (New York: Free Press, 1985). See also P. Ghemawat, *Commitment: The Dynamic of Strategy* (New York: Free Press, 1991), Chapter 4.

[11]Porter, *Competitive Advantage*.

[12]This approach goes back to the pioneering work by K. Lancaster, *Consumer Demand: A New Approach* (New York: Columbia University Press, 1971).

[13]D. Garvin, "Competing on the Eight Dimensions of Quality," *Harvard Business Review* (November-December 1987): 101–119; P. Kotler, *Marketing Management* (Millennium Ed.) (Upper Saddle River, N.J.: Prentice-Hall, 2000).

[14]C. K. Prahalad and M. S. Krishnan, "The New Meaning of Quality in the Information Age," *Harvard Business Review* (September-October 1999): 109–118.

[15]See D. Garvin, "What Does Product Quality Really Mean?" *Sloan Management Review* 26 (Fall 1984): 25–44; P. B. Crosby, *Quality Is Free* (New York: Mentor, 1980); A. Gabor, *The Man Who Discovered Quality* (New York: Times Books, 1990).

[16]M. Cusumano, *The Japanese Automobile Industry* (Cambridge, Mass.: Harvard University Press, 1989); S. Spear and H. K. Bowen, "Decoding the DNA of the Toyota Production System," *Harvard Business Review* (September-October 1999): 96–108.

[17]W. C. Kim and R. Mauborgne, "Value Innovation: The Strategic Logic of High Growth," *Harvard Business Review* (January–February 1997): 102–115.

[18]G. Stalk and T. M. Hout, *Competing Against Time* (New York: Free Press, 1990).

[19]Ibid.

[20]T. Copeland, T. Koller, and J. Murrin, *Valuation: Measuring and Managing the Value of Companies* (New York: Wiley, 1996). See also S. F. Jablonsky and N. P. Barsky, *The Manager's Guide to Financial Statement Analysis* (New York: Wiley, 2001).

[21]Copeland, Koller, and Murrin, *Valuation*.

[22]This is done as follows. Signifying net profit by $=$, invested capital by K, and revenues by R, then ROIC $= =/K$. If we multiply through by revenues, R, this becomes $R = (K) = (= = R)/(K = R)$, which can be rearranged as $=/R = R/K$, where $=/R$ is the return on sales and R/K is capital turnover.

[23]Figure 3.8 is a simplification that ignores other important items that enter the calculation, such as depreciation/sales (a determinant of ROS) and other assets/sales (a determinant of capital turnover).

CHAPTER 4

COMPETITIVE ADVANTAGE THROUGH FUNCTIONAL-LEVEL STRATEGIES

Christopher Halloran/Shutterstock.com

OPENING CASE

Trouble at McDonald's

For most of its history McDonald's has been an extraordinarily successful enterprise. It began in 1955, when the legendary Ray Kroc decided to franchise the McDonald brothers' fast-food concept. Since its inception, McDonald's has grown into the largest restaurant chain in the world, with almost 32,000 stores in 120 countries.

For decades, McDonald's success was grounded in a simple formula: give consumers value for money, good quick service, and consistent quality in a clean environment, and they will return time and time again. To deliver value for money and consistent quality, McDonalds standardized the process of order taking, making food, and providing service. Standardized processes raised employee productivity while ensuring that customers had the same experience in all branches of the restaurant. McDonald's also developed close ties with wholesalers and food producers, managing its supply chain to reduce costs. As it became

Najlah Feanny/Corbis

LEARNING OBJECTIVES

4.1 Explain how an enterprise can use functional-level strategies to increase its efficiency

4.2 Explain how an enterprise can use functional-level strategies to increase its quality

4.3 Explain how an enterprise can use functional-level strategies to increase its innovation

4.4 Explain how an enterprise can use functional-level strategies to increase its customer responsiveness

larger, buying power enabled McDonald's to realize economies of scale in purchasing and pass on cost savings to customers in the form of low-priced meals, which drove increased demand. There was also the ubiquity of McDonald's; their restaurants could be found everywhere. This accessibility, coupled with the consistent experience and low prices, built brand loyalty.

The formula worked well until the early 2000s. By then, McDonald's was under attack for contributing to obesity. Its low-priced, high-fat foods were dangerous, claimed critics. By 2002, sales were stagnating and profits were falling. It seemed that McDonald's had lost its edge. The company responded with a number of steps. It scrapped its supersize menu and added healthier options such as salads and apple slices. Executives mined data to discover that people were eating more chicken and less beef. So McDonald's added grilled chicken sandwiches, chicken wraps, Southern-style chicken sandwiches, and most recently, chicken for breakfast to their menu. Chicken sales doubled at McDonald's between 2002 and 2008, and the company now buys more chicken than beef.

McDonald's also shifted its emphasis on beverages. For decades, drinks were an afterthought, but executives couldn't help but note the rapid growth of Starbucks. In 2006, McDonald's decided to offer better coffee, including lattes. McDonald's improved the quality of its coffee by purchasing high-quality beans, using better equipment, and filtering its water. The company did not lose sight of the need to keep costs low and service quick, however, and continues to add coffee-making machines that produce lattes and cappuccinos in 45 seconds, at the push of a button. Starbucks it is not, but for many people a latte from the McDonald's drive-through window is comparable. Today, the latte machines have been installed in almost half of the stores in the United States.

All of these strategies seemed to work. Revenues, net profits and profitability all improved between 2002 and 2013. By 2014, however, McDonald's was once more running into headwinds. Same-store sales declined in 2014, impacting profitability. Among the problems that analysts identified at McDonald's was an inability to attract customers in the 19- to 30-year-old age group. Rivals offering healthier alternatives, such as Chipotle Mexican Grill, and "better burger" chains that appeal to this demographic, such as Smashburger, are gaining ground at the expense of McDonald's. A recent *Consumer Reports* survey ranked McDonald's burgers the worst among its peers. Another problem is that the quality of customer service at McDonald's seems to have slipped. Many customers say that employees at McDonalds are rude and unprofessional. One reason why McDonald's employees might be feeling stressed out is that the menu has grown quite large in recent years, and many restaurants are not longer staffed given the diversity of the menu. Management at McDonalds has promised to fix these problems, but how they will do this remains to be seen.

Sources: Jonathan Beer, "5 Reasons McDonald's Has Indigestion," *CBS Money Watch*, August 12, 2014; A. Martin, "McDonald's, the Happiest Meal is Hot Profits," *New York Times*, January 11, 2009; M. Vella, "A New Look for McDonald's," *Business Week Online*, December 4, 2008; M. Warner, "Salads or No, Cheap Burgers Revive McDonald's," *New York Times*, April 19, 2006.

OVERVIEW

In Chapter 3, we saw how valuable, rare, inimitable resources that are well organized within an enterprise form the foundation of competitive advantage. These resources reside in the value creation activities (functions) of a company. In this chapter, we take a close look at how a firm can use functional-level strategies to build valuable resources that enable it to attain superior efficiency, quality, innovation, and customer responsiveness (see Figure 4.1). **Functional-level strategies** are actions that managers take to improve the efficiency and effectiveness of one or more of value creation activities (see Figure 3.5 in the previous chapter).

functional-level strategies

Actions that managers take to improve the efficiency and effectiveness of one or more value creation activities.

The Opening Case illustrates some of these relationships. Historically, McDonald's has been a standout performer in the fast-food industry. McDonald's was a fast-food *innovator*, developing many of the practices that have become standard in the industry. It was *responsive to customer needs* for inexpensive fast food, good, quick service, and a clean environment. By standardizing the process of making fast food and working closely with its suppliers, McDonald's improved its *efficiency*, thereby lowering costs and prices, while offering a product of *reliable quality* that was the same no matter where it was purchased.

However, by the early 2000s, the company's distinctive competence in providing inexpensive fast food of reliable quality was under attack. Eating habits were changing. McDonald's responded to shifting customer needs by changing its menu, and for a few years this seemed to work. By 2014, however, same-store sales and profits were once more declining. This time, the problem was not only McDonald's menu but also a perception that the quality of customer service had declined. To fix these problems, McDonald's will have to take many actions at the functional level to enhance the perceived quality of its product offering, reconfigure the menu, and improve in-store customer service, all while keeping costs under control through efficient operations.

Figure 4.1 The Roots of Competitive Advantage

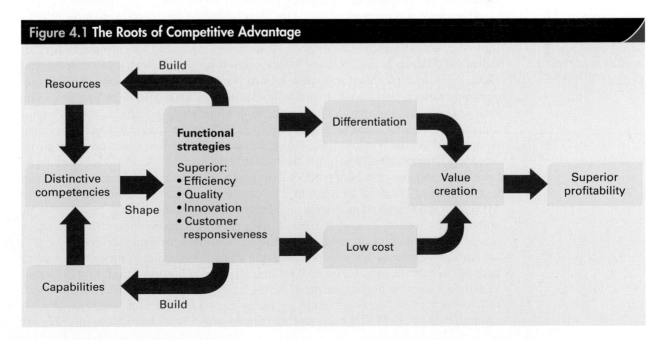

McDonald's, in other words, needs to adjust many of its functional strategies. The content in this chapter is germane to the problems McDonald's is facing today, for much of it is devoted to looking at the basic strategies that can be adopted at the functional level to improve efficiency, quality, innovation, and customer responsiveness of the enterprise. By the end of this chapter, you will understand how functional-level strategies can be used to build a sustainable competitive advantage.

◢ ACHIEVING SUPERIOR EFFICIENCY

A company is a device for transforming inputs (labor, land, capital, management, and technological knowhow) into outputs (the goods and services produced). The simplest measure of efficiency is the quantity of inputs that it takes to produce a given output; that is, efficiency = outputs/inputs. The more efficient a company, the fewer the inputs required to produce a given output, and therefore the lower its cost structure. Put another way, an efficient company has higher productivity and therefore lower costs than its rivals. Here we review the steps that companies can take at the functional level to increase efficiency and lower cost structure.

Efficiency and Economies of Scale

economies of scale

Reductions in unit costs attributed to larger output.

Economies of scale are unit cost reductions associated with large-scale output. You will recall from the Chapter 3 that it is very important for managers to understand how the cost structure of their enterprise varies with output, because this understanding should help to drive strategy. For example, if unit costs fall significantly as output is expanded—that is, if there are significant economies of scale—a company may benefit by keeping prices down and increasing volume.

fixed costs

Costs that must be incurred to produce a product regardless of level of output.

One source of economies of scale is the ability to spread fixed costs over a large production volume. **Fixed costs** are costs that must be incurred to produce a product regardless of the level of output; examples are the costs of purchasing machinery, setting up machinery for individual production runs, building facilities, advertising, and research and development (R&D). For example, Microsoft spent approximately $5 billion to develop its Windows operating system, Windows 8. It can realize substantial scale economies by distributing the fixed costs associated with developing the new operating system over the enormous unit sales volume it expects for this system (over 90% of the world's 1.6 billion personal computers (PCs) use Windows). These scale economies are significant because of the trivial incremental (or marginal) cost of producing additional copies of Windows 8. For example, once the master copy has been produced, original equipment manufacturers (OEMs) can install copies of Windows 8 on new PCs for zero marginal cost to Microsoft. The key to Microsoft's efficiency and profitability (and that of other companies with high fixed costs and trivial incremental or marginal costs) is to increase sales rapidly enough that fixed costs can be spread out over a large unit volume and substantial scale economies realized.

Another source of scale economies is the ability of companies producing in large volumes to achieve a greater division of labor and specialization. Specialization is said to have a favorable impact on productivity, primarily because it enables employees to become very skilled at performing a particular task. The classic example of such economies is Ford's Model T automobile. The Model T Ford, introduced in 1923, was the world's first mass-produced car. Until 1923, Ford had made cars using an expensive, hand-built, craft production method. Introducing mass-production techniques allowed the company to achieve greater division of labor (it split assembly into small, repeatable tasks) and specialization, which boosted employee productivity. Ford was also able to distribute the fixed costs of developing a car and setting up production machinery over a large volume of output. As a result of these economies, the cost of manufacturing a car at Ford fell from $3,000 to less than $900 (in 1958 dollars).

The concept of scale economies is depicted in Figure 4.2, which illustrates that, as a company increases its output, unit costs decrease. This process comes to an end at an output of Q1, where all scale economies are exhausted. Indeed, at outputs of greater than Q1, the company may encounter **diseconomies of scale**, which are the unit cost increases associated with a large scale of output. Diseconomies of scale occur primarily because of the increased bureaucracy associated with large-scale enterprises and the managerial inefficiencies that can result.[1] Larger enterprises have a tendency to develop extensive managerial hierarchies in which dysfunctional political behavior is commonplace. Information about operating matters can accidentally and/or deliberately be distorted by the number of managerial layers through which the information must travel to reach top decision makers. The result is poor decision making. Therefore, past a specific point—such as Q1 in Figure 4.2—inefficiencies that result from such developments outweigh any additional gains from economies of scale. As output expands, unit costs begin to rise.

Managers must know the extent of economies of scale, and where diseconomies of scale begin to occur. At Nucor Steel, for example, the realization that diseconomies of scale exist has led to the company's decision to build plants that employ only 300 individuals or less. The belief is that it is more efficient to build two plants, each employing 300 people, than one plant employing 600 people. Although the larger plant may theoretically make it possible to reap greater scale economies, Nucor's management believes that larger plants would suffer from the diseconomies of scale associated with large organizational units.

diseconomies of scale
Unit cost increases associated with a large scale of output.

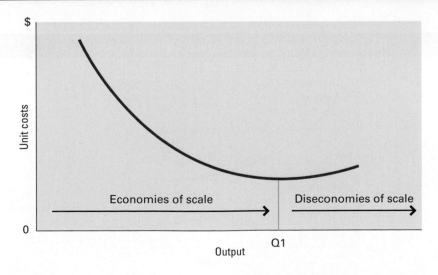

Figure 4.2 Economies and Diseconomies of Scale

Efficiency and Learning Effects

learning effects

Cost savings that come from learning by doing.

Learning effects are cost savings that result from "learning by doing." Labor, for example, learns by repetition how to best carry out a task. Therefore, labor productivity increases over time, and unit costs decrease as individuals learn the most efficient way to perform a particular task. Equally important, management in a new manufacturing facility typically learns over time how best to run the new operation. Hence, production costs decline because of increasing labor productivity and management efficiency. Put differently, over time, management and labor accumulate valuable process knowledge that leads to higher productivity. Japanese companies such as Toyota are noted for making the accumulation of process knowledge central to their operating philosophy.

Learning effects tend to be more significant when a technologically complex task is repeated because there is more to learn. Thus, learning effects will be more significant in an assembly process that has 1,000 complex steps than in a process with 100 simple steps. Although learning effects are normally associated with the manufacturing process, there is substantial evidence that they are just as important in service industries. One famous study of learning in the health-care industry discovered that more-experienced medical providers posted significantly lower mortality rates for a number of common surgical procedures, suggesting that learning effects are at work in surgery.[2] The authors of this study used the evidence to argue in favor of establishing regional referral centers for the provision of highly specialized medical care. These centers would perform many specific surgical procedures (such as heart surgery), replacing local facilities with lower volumes and presumably higher mortality rates. Another recent study found strong evidence of learning effects in a financial institution. This study looked at a newly established document-processing unit with 100 staff members and found that, over time, documents were processed much more rapidly as the staff learned the process. Overall, the study concluded that unit costs decreased every time the cumulative number of documents processed doubled.[3] Strategy in Action 4.1 looks at the determinants of differences in learning effects across a sample of hospitals performing cardiac surgery.

In terms of the unit cost curve of a company, economies of scale imply a movement along the curve (say, from A to B in Figure 4.3). The realization of learning effects implies a downward shift of the entire curve (B to C in Figure 4.3) as both labor and management become more efficient over time at performing their tasks at every

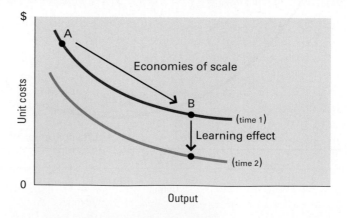

Figure 4.3 The Impact of Learning and Scale Economies on Unit Costs

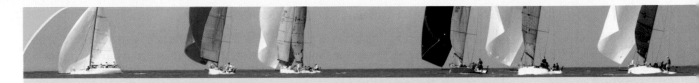

4.1 STRATEGY IN ACTION

Learning Effects in Cardiac Surgery

Researchers at the Harvard Business School carried out a study to estimate the importance of learning effects in the case of a new technology for minimally invasive heart surgery that was approved by federal regulators. The researchers looked at 16 hospitals and obtained data on operations for 660 patients who underwent surgery using the new technology. They examined how the time required to undertake the procedure varied with cumulative experience. Across the 16 hospitals, they found that average time decreased from 280 minutes for the first procedure with the new technology to 220 minutes once a hospital had performed 50 procedures (note that not all hospitals performed 50 procedures, and the estimates represent an extrapolation based on the data).

Next, the study observed differences across hospitals; here they found evidence of very large differences in learning effects. One hospital, in particular, stood out. This hospital, which they called "Hospital M," reduced its net procedure time from 500 minutes on case 1 to 132 minutes by case 50. Hospital M's 88-minute procedure time advantage over the average hospital at case 50 meant a cost savings of approximately $2,250 per case, which allowed surgeons at the hospital to complete one more revenue-generating procedure per day.

The researchers inquired into factors that made Hospital M superior. They noted that all hospitals had similar, state-of-the-art operating rooms, all used the same devices, approved by the Food and Drug Administration

(FDA), all surgeons who adopted the new technology completed the same training courses, and all surgeons came from highly respected training hospitals. Follow-up interviews, however, suggested that Hospital M differed in how it implemented the new procedure. The adopting surgeon handpicked the team that would perform the surgery. Members of the team had significant prior experience working together, which was a key criterion for member selection, and the team trained together to perform the surgery with the new technology. Before undertaking the surgery, the entire team met with the operating room nurses and anesthesiologists to discuss it. In addition, the adopting surgeon mandated that no changes would be made to either the team or the procedure in the early stages of using the technology. The initial team completed 15 procedures before members were added or substituted, and completed 20 cases before the procedure was modified. The adopting surgeon also insisted that the team meet prior to each of the first 10 cases, and after the first 20 cases, to debrief.

The picture that emerges is a core team selected and managed to maximize gains from learning Unlike other hospitals where team members and procedures were less consistent, and where there was not the same attention to briefing, debriefing, and learning, surgeons at Hospital M learned much faster and ultimately achieved higher productivity than their peers in other institutions. Clearly, differences in the implementation of the new procedure were very significant.

Source: G. P. Pisano, R. M. J. Bohmer, and A. C. Edmondson, "Organizational Differences in Rates of Learning: Evidence from the Adoption of Minimally Invasive Cardiac Surgery," Management Science 47 (2001): 752–768.

level of output. In accounting terms, learning effects in a production setting reduce the cost of goods sold as a percentage of revenues, enabling the company to earn a higher return on sales and return on invested capital.

No matter how complex the task, learning effects typically diminish in importance after a period of time. Indeed, it has been suggested that they are most important during the start-up period of a new process and become trivial after 2 or 3 years.[4] When a company's production system changes—as a result of the use of new information technology, for example—the learning process must begin again.

Efficiency and the Experience Curve

experience curve

The systematic lowering of the cost structure and consequent unit cost reductions that have been observed to occur over the life of a product.

The **experience curve** refers to the systematic lowering of the cost structure, and consequent unit cost reductions, that have been observed to occur over the life of a product.[5] According to the experience-curve concept, per-unit production costs for a product typically decline by some characteristic amount each time accumulated output of the product is doubled (accumulated output is the total output of a product since its introduction). This relationship was first observed in the aircraft industry, where it was found that each time the accumulated output of airframes doubled, unit costs declined to 80% of their previous level.[6] As such, the fourth airframe typically cost only 80% of the second airframe to produce, the eighth airframe only 80% of the fourth, the sixteenth only 80% of the eighth, and so on. The outcome of this process is a relationship between unit manufacturing costs and accumulated output similar to the illustration in Figure 4.3. Economies of scale and learning effects underlie the experience-curve phenomenon. Put simply, as a company increases the accumulated volume of its output over time, it is able to realize both economies of scale (as volume increases) and learning effects. Consequently, unit costs and cost structure fall with increases in accumulated output.

The strategic significance of the experience curve is clear: Increasing a company's product volume and market share will lower its cost structure relative to its rivals. In Figure 4.4, Company B has a cost advantage over Company A because of its lower cost structure, and because it is farther down the experience curve. This concept is very important in industries that mass-produce a standardized output—for example, the manufacture of semiconductor chips. A company that wishes to become more efficient and lower its cost structure must try to move down the experience curve as quickly as possible. This means constructing manufacturing facilities that are scaled for efficiency even before the company has generated demand for its product, and aggressively pursuing cost reductions from learning effects. It might also need to adopt an aggressive marketing strategy, cutting prices drastically and stressing heavy sales promotions and extensive advertising in order to build up demand and accumulated volume as quickly as possible. A company is likely to have a significant cost advantage

Figure 4.4 The Experience Curve

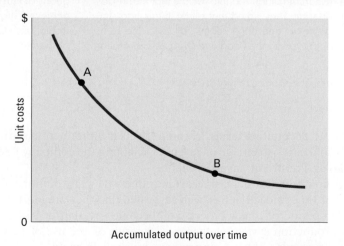

Accumulated output over time

over its competitors because of its superior efficiency once it is down the experience curve. It has been argued that Intel uses such tactics to ride down the experience curve and gain a competitive advantage over its rivals in the microprocessor market.[7]

It is worth emphasizing that this concept is just as important outside of manufacturing. For example, as it invests in its distribution network, online retailer Amazon is trying to both realize economies of scale (spreading the fixed costs of its distribution centers over a large sales volume) and improve the efficiency of its inventory-management and order-fulfillment processes at distribution centers (a learning effect). Together these two sources of cost savings should enable Amazon to ride down the experience curve ahead of its rivals, thereby gaining a low-cost position that enables it to make greater profits at lower prices than its rivals.

Managers should not become complacent about efficiency-based cost advantages derived from experience effects. First, because neither learning effects nor economies of scale are sustained forever, the experience curve will bottom out at some point; it must do so by definition. When this occurs, further unit-cost reductions from learning effects and economies of scale will be difficult to attain. Over time, other companies can lower their cost structures and match the cost leader. Once this happens, many low-cost companies can achieve cost parity with each other. In such circumstances, a sustainable competitive advantage must rely on strategic factors other than the minimization of production costs by using existing technologies— factors such as better responsiveness to customers, product quality, or innovation.

Second, cost advantages gained from experience effects can be rendered obsolete by the development of new technologies. For example, the large, "big box" book-stores Borders and Barnes & Noble may have had cost advantages that were derived from economies of scale and learning. However, those advantages diminished when Amazon, utilizing Web technology, launched its online bookstore in 1994. By selling online, Amazon was able to offer a larger selection at a lower cost than established rivals with physical storefronts. When Amazon introduced its Kindle digital reader in 2007 and started to sell eBooks, it changed the basis of competition once more, effectively nullifying the experience-based advantage enjoyed by Borders and Barnes & Noble. By 2012, Borders was bankrupt and Barnes & Noble was in financial trouble and closing stores. Amazon, in the meantime, has gone from strength to strength.

Efficiency, Flexible Production Systems, and Mass Customization

Central to the concept of economies of scale is the idea that a lower cost structure, attained through the mass production of a standardized output, is the best way to achieve high efficiency. There is an implicit tradeoff in this idea between unit costs and product variety. Wide product variety shipped from a single factory implies shorter production runs, which implies an inability to realize economies of scale and thus higher costs. That is, greater product variety makes it difficult for a company to increase its production efficiency and reduce its unit costs. According to this logic, the way to increase efficiency and achieve a lower cost structure is to limit product variety and produce a standardized product in large volumes (see Figure 4.5a).

This view of production efficiency has been challenged by the rise of flexible production technologies. The term **flexible production technology** covers a range of

flexible production technology
A range of technologies designed to reduce setup times for complex equipment, increase the use of machinery through better scheduling, and improve quality control at all stages of the manufacturing process.

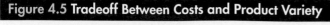

Figure 4.5 Tradeoff Between Costs and Product Variety

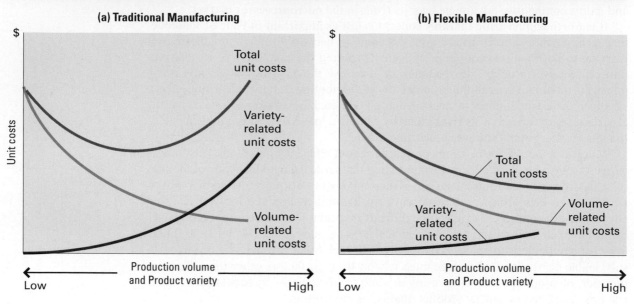

technologies designed to reduce setup times for complex equipment, increase the use of individual machines through better scheduling, and improve quality control at all stages of the manufacturing process.[8] Flexible production technologies allow the company to produce a wider variety of end products at a unit cost that at one time could be achieved only through the mass production of a standardized output (see Figure 4.5b). Research suggests that the adoption of flexible production technologies may increase efficiency and lower unit costs relative to what can be achieved by the mass production of a standardized output, while at the same time enabling the company to customize its product offering to a much greater extent than was once thought possible. The term **mass customization** has been coined to describe a company's ability to use flexible manufacturing technology to reconcile two goals that were once thought to be incompatible: low cost and differentiation through product customization.[9]

Dell Computer pursues a mass-customization strategy when it allows its customers to build their own machines online. Dell keeps costs and prices under control by allowing customers to make choices within a limited menu of options (different amounts of memory, hard-drive capacity, video card, microprocessor, and so on). The result is to create more value for customers than is possible for rivals that sell a limited range of PC models through retail outlets. Similarly, Mars offers a service, My M&Ms, that enables customers to design "personalized" M&Ms online. Customers can pick different colors and have messages or pictures printed on their M&Ms. Another example of mass customization is the Internet radio service Pandora, which is discussed in Strategy in Action 4.2.

The effects of installing flexible production technology on a company's cost structure can be dramatic. Over the last decade, the Ford Motor Company has been introducing such technologies in its automotive plants around the world. These technologies

mass customization

The use of flexible manufacturing technology to reconcile two goals that were once thought to be incompatible: low cost and differentiation through product customization.

4.2 STRATEGY IN ACTION

Pandora: Mass Customizing Internet Radio

M4OS Photos/Alamy

Pandora Media streams music to PCs and mobile devices. Customers start by typing in the kind of music that they want to listen to. With a database of over 100,000 artists, there is a good chance that Pandora has something for you, however particular your tastes. Customers can then rate the music that Pandora plays for them (thumbs up or down). Pandora takes this feedback and refines the music it streams to a customer. The company also uses sophisticated predictive statistical analysis (what do other customers who also like this song listen to?) and product analysis (what Pandora calls its Music Genome, which analyzes songs and identifies similar songs) to further customize the experience for the individual listener. The Music Genome has the added benefit of introducing listeners to new songs they might like based on an analysis of their listening habits. The result is a radio station attuned to each individual's unique listening preferences. This is mass customization at its most pure.

Launched in 2000, by late 2014 Pandora's annualized revenue run rate was 920 million. There were 250 million registered users and 77 million active users, giving Pandora a 78% share of the online radio market in the United States. Pandora's revenue comes primarily from advertising, although premium subscribers can pay $36 a year and get commercial-free music.

Despite its rapid growth—a testament to the value of mass customization—Pandora does have its problems. Pandora pays more than half of its revenue in royalties to music publishers. By comparison, satellite-radio company Sirius-XM pays out only 7.5% of its revenue in the form of royalties, and cable companies that stream music pay only 15%. The different royalty rates are due to somewhat arcane regulations under which three judges who serve on the Copyright Royalty Board, an arm of the Library of Congress, set royalty fees for radio broadcasters. This method of setting royalty rates has worked against Pandora, although the company is lobbying hard to have the law changed. Pandora is also facing growing competition from Spotify and Rdio, two customizable music-streaming services that have sold equity stakes to recording labels in exchange for access to their music libraries. There are also reports that Apple will soon be offering its own customizable music-streaming service. Whatever happens to Pandora in the long run, however, it would seem that the mass customization of Internet radio is here to stay.

Sources: A. Fixmer, "Pandora Is Boxed in by High Royalty Fees," Bloomberg Businessweek, December 24, 2012; E. Smith and J. Letzing, "At Pandora Each Sales Drives up Losses," *The Wall Street Journal*, December 6, 2012; E. Savitz, "Pandora Swoons on Weak Outlook," Forbes.com, December 5, 2012; G. Peoples, "Pandora Revenue up 40 percent, Listening Growth Softens," Billboardbiz, October 23, 2014.

have enabled Ford to produce multiple models from the same line and to switch production from one model to another much more quickly than in the past. Ford removed $2 billion out of its cost structure between 2006 and 2010 through flexible manufacturing, and is striving to remove more.[10]

Marketing and Efficiency

marketing strategy

The position that a company takes with regard to pricing, promotion, advertising, product design, and distribution.

The marketing strategy that a company adopts can have a major impact on its efficiency and cost structure. **Marketing strategy** refers to the position that a company takes with regard to market segmentation, pricing, promotion, advertising, product design, and distribution. Some of the steps leading to greater efficiency are fairly obvious. For example, moving down the experience curve to achieve a lower cost structure can be facilitated by aggressive pricing, promotion, and advertising—all of which are tasks of the marketing function. Other aspects of marketing strategy have a less obvious—but no less important—impact on efficiency. One important aspect is the relationship of customer defection rates, cost structure, and unit costs.[11]

customer defection

The percentage of a company's customers who defect every year to competitors.

Customer defection (or "churn rate") is the percentage of a company's customers who defect every year to competitors. Defection rates are determined by customer loyalty, which in turn is a function of the ability of a company to satisfy its customers. Because acquiring a new customer often entails one-time fixed costs, there is a direct relationship between defection rates and costs. For example, when a wireless service company signs up a new subscriber, it has to bear the administrative cost of opening a new account and the cost of a subsidy that it pays to the manufacturer of the handset the new subscriber chooses. There are also the costs of advertising and promotions designed to attract new subscribers. The longer a company retains a customer, the greater the volume of customer-generated unit sales that can be set against these fixed costs, and the lower the average unit cost of each sale. Thus, lowering customer defection rates allows a company to achieve a lower cost structure.

One consequence of the defection–cost relationship illustrated in Figure 4.6. Because of the relatively high fixed costs of acquiring new customers, serving customers who stay with the company only for a short time before switching to competitors often leads to a loss on the investment made to acquire those customers. The longer a customer stays with the company, the more the fixed costs of acquiring that customer can be distributed over repeat purchases, boosting the profit per customer. Thus, there is a positive relationship between the length of time that a customer stays with a company and profit per customer.

Figure 4.6 The Relationship Between Customer Loyalty and Profit per Customer

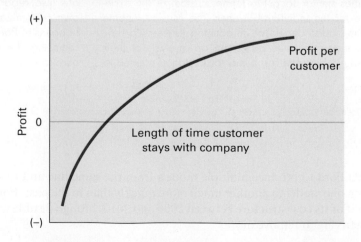

A company that can reduce customer defection rates can make a much better return on its investment in acquiring customers, and thereby boost its profitability.

For example, consider the credit card business.[12] Most credit card companies spend an average of $50 per customer for recruitment and new account setup. These costs accrue from the advertising required to attract new customers, the credit checks required for each customer, and the mechanics of setting up an account and issuing a card. These one-time fixed costs can be recouped only if a customer stays with the company for at least 2 years. Moreover, when customers stay a second year, they tend to increase their use of the credit card, which raises the volume of revenues generated by each customer over time. As a result, although the credit card business loses $50 per customer in year 1, it makes a profit of $44 in year 3 and $55 in year 6.

Another economic benefit of long-time customer loyalty is the free advertising that customers provide for a company. Loyal customers can dramatically increase the volume of business through referrals. A striking example is Britain's largest retailer, the clothing and food company Marks & Spencer, whose success is built on a well-earned reputation for providing its customers with high-quality goods at reasonable prices. The company has generated such customer loyalty that it does not need to advertise in Britain—a major source of cost savings.

The key message, then, is that reducing customer defection rates and building customer loyalty can be major sources of a lower cost structure. One study has estimated that a 5% reduction in customer defection rates leads to the following increases in profits per customer over average customer life: 75% in the credit card business, 50% in the insurance brokerage industry, 45% in the industrial laundry business, and 35% in the computer software industry.[13]

A central component of developing a strategy to reduce defection rates is to identify customers who have defected, find out why they defected, and act on that information so that other customers do not defect for similar reasons in the future. To take these measures, the marketing function must have information systems capable of tracking customer defections.

MATERIALS MANAGEMENT, JUST-IN-TIME SYSTEMS, AND EFFICIENCY

The contribution of materials management (logistics) to boosting the efficiency of a company can be just as dramatic as the contribution of production and marketing. Materials management encompasses the activities necessary to get inputs and components to a production facility (including the costs of purchasing inputs), through the production process, and out through a distribution system to the end-user.[14] Because there are so many sources of cost in this process, the potential for reducing costs through more efficient materials-management strategies is enormous. For a typical manufacturing company, materials and transportation costs account for 50 to 70% of its revenues, so even a small reduction in these costs can have a substantial impact on profitability. According to one estimate, for a company with revenues of $1 million, a return on invested capital (ROIC) of 5% and materials-management costs that amount to 50% of sales revenues (including purchasing costs), increasing total profits by $15,000 would require either a 30% increase in sales revenues or a 3% reduction in materials costs.[15] In a typical competitive market, reducing materials costs by 3% is usually much easier than increasing sales revenues by 30%.

Improving the efficiency of the materials-management function typically requires the adoption of a **just-in-time (JIT) inventory system**, which is designed to economize on inventory holding costs by scheduling components to arrive at a manufacturing plant just in time to enter the production process, or to have goods arrive at a retail store only when stock is almost depleted. The major cost saving comes from increasing inventory turnover, which reduces both inventory holding costs, such as warehousing and storage costs, and the company's need for working capital. For example, through efficient logistics, Wal-Mart can replenish the stock in its stores at least twice a week; many stores receive daily deliveries if they are needed. The typical competitor replenishes its stock every 2 weeks, so it must carry a much higher inventory, which requires more working capital per dollar of sales. Compared to its competitors, Wal-Mart can maintain the same service levels with a lower investment in inventory—a major source of its lower cost structure. Thus, faster inventory turnover has helped Wal-Mart achieve an efficiency-based competitive advantage in the retailing industry.[16]

More generally, in terms of the profitability model developed in Chapter 3, JIT inventory systems reduce the need for working capital (because there is less inventory to finance) and the need for fixed capital to finance storage space (because there is less to store), which reduces capital needs, increases capital turnover, and, by extension, boosts ROIC.

The drawback of JIT systems is that they leave a company without a buffer stock of inventory. Although buffer stocks are expensive to store, they can help a company prepare for shortages on inputs brought about by disruption among suppliers (for instance, a labor dispute at a key supplier), and can help a company respond quickly to increases in demand. However, there are ways around these limitations. For example, to reduce the risks linked to dependence on just one supplier for an important input, a company might decide to source inputs from multiple suppliers.

Recently, the efficient management of materials and inventory has been recast in terms of **supply chain management**: the task of managing the flow of inputs and components from suppliers into the company's production processes to minimize inventory holding and maximize inventory turnover. Dell, whose goal is to streamline its supply chain to such an extent that it 'replaces inventory with information,' is exemplary in terms of supply chain management.

Research and Development Strategy and Efficiency

The role of superior research and development (R&D) in helping a company achieve a greater efficiency and a lower cost structure is twofold. First, the R&D function can boost efficiency by designing products that are easy to manufacture. By cutting down on the number of parts that make up a product, R&D can dramatically decrease the required assembly time, which results in higher employee productivity, lower costs, and higher profitability. For example, after Texas Instruments redesigned an infrared sighting mechanism that it supplies to the Pentagon, it found that it had reduced the number of parts from 47 to 12, the number of assembly steps from 56 to 13, the time spent fabricating metal from 757 minutes per unit to 219 minutes per unit, and unit assembly time from 129 minutes to 20 minutes. The result was a substantial decline in production costs. Design for manufacturing requires close coordination between the production and R&D functions of the company. Cross-functional teams that contain production and R&D personnel who work jointly can best achieve this.

just-in-time (JIT) inventory system
System of economizing on inventory holding costs by scheduling components to arrive just in time to enter the production process or only as stock is depleted.

supply chain management
The task of managing the flow of inputs and components from suppliers into the company's production processes to minimize inventory holding and maximize inventory turnover.

Pioneering process innovations is the second way in which the R&D function can help a company achieve a lower cost structure. A process innovation is a new, unique way that production processes can operate more efficiently. Process innovations are often a major source of competitive advantage. Toyota's competitive advantage is based partly on the company's invention of new, flexible manufacturing processes that dramatically reduce setup times. This process innovation enabled Toyota to obtain efficiency gains associated with flexible manufacturing systems years ahead of its competitors.

Human Resource Strategy and Efficiency

Employee productivity is a key determinant of an enterprise's efficiency, cost structure, and profitability.[17] Productive manufacturing employees can lower the cost of goods sold as a percentage of revenues; a productive sales force can increase sales revenues for a given level of expenses; and productive employees in the company's R&D function can boost the percentage of revenues generated from new products for a given level of R&D expenses. Thus, productive employees lower the costs of generating revenues, increase the return on sales, and, by extension, boost the company's ROIC. The challenge for a company's human resource function is to devise ways to increase employee productivity. Among its choices are using certain hiring strategies, training employees, organizing the workforce into self-managing teams, and linking pay to performance.

Hiring Strategy

Many companies that are well known for their productive employees devote considerable attention to hiring. Southwest Airlines hires people who have a positive attitude and who work well in teams because it believes that people who have a positive attitude will work hard and interact well with customers, therefore helping to create customer loyalty. Nucor hires people who are self-reliant and goal-oriented because its employees, who work in self-managing teams, require these skills to perform well. As these examples suggest, it is important to be sure that the hiring strategy of the company is consistent with its internal organization, culture, and strategic priorities. A company's hires should have attributes that match its strategic objectives.

Employee Training

Employees are a major input into the production process. Those who are highly skilled can perform tasks faster and more accurately, and are more likely to learn the complex tasks associated with many modern production methods than individuals with lesser skills. Training upgrades employee skill levels, bringing the company productivity-related efficiency gains from learning and experimentation.[18]

Self-Managing Teams The use of **self-managing teams**, whose members coordinate their own activities and make their own hiring, training, work, and reward decisions, has been spreading rapidly. The typical team comprises 5 to 15 employees who produce an entire product or undertake an entire task. Team members learn all team tasks and rotate from job to job. Because a more flexible workforce is one result, team members can fill in for absent coworkers and take over managerial duties such as scheduling work and vacation, ordering materials, and hiring new members. The greater

self-managing teams
Teams where members coordinate their own activities and make their own hiring, training, work, and reward decisions.

responsibility delegated to team members, and the empowerment that it implies, are seen as motivators. (*Empowerment* is the process of giving lower-level employees decision-making power.) People often respond well to being given greater autonomy and responsibility. Performance bonuses linked to team production and quality targets work as an additional motivator.

The effect of introducing self-managing teams is reportedly an increase in productivity of 30% or more and a substantial increase in product quality. Further cost savings arise from eliminating supervisors and creating a flatter organizational hierarchy, which lowers the cost structure of the company. In manufacturing companies, perhaps the most potent way to lower the cost structure is to combine self-managing teams with flexible manufacturing cells. For example, after the introduction of flexible manufacturing technology and work practices based on self-managing teams, a General Electric (GE) plant in Salisbury, North Carolina, increased productivity by 250% compared with GE plants that produced the same products 4 years earlier.[19]

Still, teams are no panacea. In manufacturing companies, self-managing teams may fail to live up to their potential unless they are integrated with flexible manufacturing technology. Also, many management responsibilities are placed upon team members, and helping team members cope with these responsibilities often requires substantial training—a fact that many companies often forget in their rush to drive down costs. Haste can result in teams that don't work out as well as planned.[20]

Pay for Performance

It is hardly surprising that linking pay to performance can help increase employee productivity, but the issue is not quite as simple as just introducing incentive pay systems. It is also important to define what kind of job performance is to be rewarded and how. Some of the most efficient companies in the world, mindful that cooperation among employees is necessary to realize productivity gains, link pay to group or team (rather than individual) performance. Nucor Steel divides its workforce into teams of about 30, with bonus pay, which can amount to 30% of base pay, linked to the ability of the team to meet productivity and quality goals. This link creates a strong incentive for individuals to cooperate in pursuit of team goals; that is, it facilitates teamwork.

Information Systems and Efficiency

With the rapid spread of computers and devices, the explosive growth of the Internet and corporate intranets (internal corporate computer networks based on Internet standards), and the spread of high-bandwidth fiber-optics and digital wireless technology, the information systems function has moved to center stage in the quest for operating efficiencies and a lower cost structure.[21] The impact of information systems on productivity is wide ranging and potentially affects all other activities of a company. For example, Cisco Systems was able to realize significant cost savings by moving its ordering and customer service functions online. The company found it could operate with just 300 service agents handling all of its customer accounts, compared to the 900 it would need if sales were not handled online. The difference represented an annual savings of $20 million a year. Moreover, without automated customer service functions, Cisco calculated that it would need at least 1,000 additional service engineers, at a cost of close to $75 million.[22]

Like Cisco, many companies are using Web-based information systems to reduce the costs of coordination between the company and its customers and the company and its suppliers. By using Web-based programs to automate customer and supplier interactions, they can substantially reduce the staff required to manage these interfaces, thereby reducing costs. This trend extends beyond high-tech companies. Banks and financial-service companies are finding that they can substantially reduce costs by moving customer accounts and support functions online. Such a move reduces the need for customer service representatives, bank tellers, stockbrokers, insurance agents, and others. For example, it costs an average of about $1.07 to execute a transaction at a bank, such as shifting money from one account to another; executing the same transaction over the Internet costs $0.01.[23]

Similarly, the concept behind Internet-based retailers such as Amazon.com is that replacing physical stores and their supporting personnel with an online, virtual store and automated ordering and checkout processes allows a company to eliminate significant costs from the retailing system. Cost savings can also be realized by using Web-based information systems to automate many internal company activities, from managing expense reimbursements to benefits planning and hiring processes, thereby reducing the need for internal support personnel.

Infrastructure and Efficiency

A company's infrastructure—including its organizational structure, culture, style of strategic leadership, and control system—determines the context within which all other value creation activities take place. It follows that improving infrastructure can help a company increase efficiency and lower its cost structure. Above all, an appropriate infrastructure can help foster a companywide commitment to efficiency and promote cooperation among different functions in pursuit of efficiency goals. These issues are addressed at length in Chapter 12.

For now, it is important to note that strategic leadership is especially important in building a companywide commitment to efficiency. The leadership task is to articulate a vision that recognizes the need for all functions of a company to focus on improving efficiency. It is not enough to improve the efficiency of production, or of marketing, or of R&D in a piecemeal fashion. Achieving superior efficiency requires a companywide commitment to this goal that must be articulated by general and functional managers. A further leadership task is to facilitate the cross-functional cooperation needed to achieve superior efficiency. For example, designing products that are easy to manufacture requires that production and R&D personnel communicate; integrating JIT systems with production scheduling requires close communication between materials management and production; and designing self-managing teams to perform production tasks requires close cooperation between human resources and production.

Summary

Table 4.1 summarizes the primary roles of various functions in achieving superior efficiency. Keep in mind that achieving superior efficiency is not something that can be tackled on a function-by-function basis. It requires organizationwide commitment and the ability to ensure close cooperation among functions. Top management, by exercising leadership and influencing the infrastructure, plays a significant role in this process.

Table 4.1 Primary Roles of Value Creation Functions in Achieving Superior Efficiency

Value Creation Function	Primary Roles
Infrastructure (leadership)	1. Provide companywide commitment to efficiency.
	2. Facilitate cooperation among functions.
Production	1. Where appropriate, pursue economies of scale and learning economics.
	2. Implement flexible manufacturing systems.
Marketing	1. Where appropriate, adopt aggressive marketing to ride down the experience curve.
	2. Limit customer defection rates by building brand loyalty.
Materials management	1. Implement JIT systems.
	2. Implement supply chain coordination.
R&D	1. Design products for ease of manufacture.
	2. Seek process innovations.
Information systems	1. Use information systems to automate processes.
	2. Use information systems to reduce costs of coordination.
Human resources	1. Institute training programs to build skills.
	2. Implement self-managing teams.
	3. Implement pay for performance.

◢ACHIEVING SUPERIOR QUALITY

In Chapter 3, we noted that quality can be thought of in terms of two dimensions: *quality as reliability* and *quality as excellence*. High-quality products are reliable, do well the job for which they were designed, and are perceived by consumers to have superior attributes. We also noted that superior quality provides a company with two advantages. First, a strong reputation for quality allows a company to differentiate its products from those offered by rivals, thereby creating more value in the eyes of customers and giving the company the option of charging a premium price for its products. Second, eliminating defects or errors from the production process reduces waste, increases efficiency, lowers the cost structure of the company, and increases its profitability. For example, reducing the number of defects in a company's manufacturing process will lower the cost of goods sold as a percentage of revenues, thereby raising the company's return on sales and ROIC. In this section, we look in more depth at what managers can do to enhance the reliability and other attributes of the company's product offering.

Attaining Superior Reliability

The principal tool that most managers now use to increase the reliability of their product offering is the Six Sigma quality improvement methodology. Six Sigma is a direct descendant of the **total quality management** (TQM) philosophy that was widely adopted, first by Japanese companies and then by American companies, during the 1980s and early 1990s.[24] The TQM concept was developed by a number of American management consultants, including W. Edwards Deming, Joseph Juran, and A. V. Feigenbaum.[25]

total quality management
Increasing product reliability so that it consistently performs as it was designed to and rarely breaks down.

Originally, these consultants won few converts in the United States. However, managers in Japan embraced their ideas enthusiastically, and even named their premier annual prize for manufacturing excellence after Deming. Underlying TQM, according to Deming, are five factors:

1. Improved quality means that costs decrease because of less rework, fewer mistakes, fewer delays, and better use of time and materials.
2. As a result, productivity improves.
3. Better quality leads to higher market share and allows the company to raise prices.
4. Higher prices increase the company's profitability and allow it to stay in business.
5. Thus, the company creates more jobs.[26]

Deming identified a number of steps that should be part of any quality improvement program:

1. Management should embrace the philosophy that mistakes, defects, and poor-quality materials are not acceptable and should be eliminated.
2. Quality of supervision should be improved by allowing more time for supervisors to work with employees, and training employees in appropriate skills for the job.
3. Management should create an environment in which employees will not fear reporting problems or recommending improvements.
4. Work standards should not only be defined as numbers or quotas, but should also include some notion of quality to promote the production of defect-free output.
5. Management is responsible for training employees in new skills to keep pace with changes in the workplace.
6. Achieving better quality requires the commitment of everyone in the company.

Western businesses were blind to the importance of the TQM concept until Japan rose to the top rank of economic powers in the 1980s. Since that time, quality improvement programs have spread rapidly throughout Western industry. Strategy in Action 4.3 describes one of the most successful implementations of a quality improvement process, General Electric's Six Sigma program.

Implementing Reliability Improvement Methodologies

Among companies that have successfully adopted quality improvement methodologies, certain imperatives stand out. These are discussed in the following sections in the order in which they are usually tackled in companies implementing quality improvement programs. However, it is essential to understand that improvement in product reliability is a cross-functional process. Its implementation requires close cooperation among all functions in the pursuit of the common goal of improving quality; it is a process that works across functions. The roles played by the different functions in implementing reliability improvement methodologies are summarized in Table 4.2.

4.3 STRATEGY IN ACTION

General Electric's Six Sigma Quality Improvement Process

Six Sigma, a quality and efficiency program adopted by many major corporations, including Motorola, General Electric, and AlliedSignal, aims to reduce defects, boost productivity, eliminate waste, and cut costs throughout a company. "Sigma" refers to the Greek letter that statisticians use to represent a standard deviation from a mean: the higher the number of sigmas, the smaller the number of errors. At Six Sigma, a production process would be 99.99966% accurate, creating just 3.4 defects per million units. Although it is almost impossible for a company to achieve such precision, several companies strive toward that goal.

General Electric (GE) is perhaps the most well-known adopter of the Six Sigma program. Under the direction of long-serving CEO Jack Welch, GE spent nearly $1 billion to convert all of its divisions to the Six Sigma method.

One of the first products designed using Six Sigma processes was a $1.25-million diagnostic computer tomography (CT) scanner, the LightSpeed VCT, which produces rapid, three-dimensional images of the human body. The new scanner captured multiple images simultaneously, requiring only 20 seconds to do full-body scans that once took 3 minutes—important because patients must remain perfectly still during the scan. GE spent $50 million to run 250 separate Six Sigma analyses designed to improve the reliability and lower the manufacturing cost of the new scanner. Its efforts were rewarded when LightSpeed VCT's first customers soon noticed that it ran without downtime between patients—a testament to its reliability.

Achieving that reliability took immense work. GE's engineers deconstructed the scanner into its basic components and tried to improve the reliability of each component through a detailed step-by-step analysis. For example, the most important components of CT scanners are vacuum tubes that focus x-ray waves. The tubes that GE used in previous scanners, which cost $60,000 each, suffered from low reliability. Hospitals and clinics wanted the tubes to operate for 12 hours a day for at least 6 months, but typically they lasted only half that long. Moreover, GE was scrapping some $20 million in tubes each year because they failed preshipping performance tests, and disturbing numbers of faulty tubes were slipping past inspection, only to prove dysfunctional upon arrival.

To try to solve the reliability problem, the Six Sigma team took the tubes apart. They knew that one problem was a petroleum-based oil used in the tubes to prevent short circuits by isolating the anode (which has a positive charge) from the negatively charged cathode. The oil often deteriorated after a few months, leading to short circuits, but the team did not know why. Using statistical "what-if" scenarios on all parts of the tube, the researchers discovered that the lead-based paint on the inside of the tube was contaminating the oil. Acting on this information, the team developed a paint that would preserve the tube and protect the oil.

By pursuing this and other improvements, the Six Sigma team was able to extend the average life of a vacuum tube in the CT scanner from 3 months to over 1 year. Although the improvements increased the cost of the tube from $60,000 to $85,000, the increased cost was outweighed by the reduction in replacement costs, making it an attractive proposition for customers.

Source: C. H. Deutsch, "Six-Sigma Enlightenment," *New York Times*, December 7, 1998, p. 1; J. J. Barshay, "The Six-Sigma Story," *Star Tribune*, June 14, 1999, p. 1; D. D. Bak, "Rethinking Industrial Drives," Electrical/Electronics Technology, November 30, 1998, p. 58. G. Eckes, *The Six-Sigma Revolution* (New York: Wiley, 2000); General Electric, "What Is Six Sigma?," http://www.ge.com/en/company/companyinfo/quality/whatis.htm.

Table 4.2 Roles Played by Different Functions in Implementing Reliability Improvement Methodologies

Infrastructure (leadership)	1. Provide leadership and commitment to quality.
	2. Find ways to measure quality.
	3. Set goals and create incentives.
	4. Solicit input from employees.
	5. Encourage cooperation among functions.
Production	1. Shorten production runs.
	2. Trace defects back to the source.
Marketing	1. Focus on the customer.
	2. Provide customer feedback on quality.
Materials management	1. Rationalize suppliers.
	2. Help suppliers implement quality improvement methodologies.
	3. Trace defects back to suppliers.
R&D	1. Design products that are easy to manufacture.
Information systems	1. Use information systems to monitor defect rates.
Human resources	1. Institute quality improvement training programs.
	2. Identify and train black belts.
	3. Organize employees into quality teams

First, it is important that senior managers agree to a quality improvement program and communicate its importance to the organization. Second, if a quality improvement program is to be successful, individuals must be identified to lead the program. Under the Six Sigma methodology, exceptional employees are identified and put through a "black belt" training course on the Six Sigma methodology. The black belts are taken out of their normal job roles, and assigned to work solely on Six Sigma projects for the next 2 years. In effect, the black belts become internal consultants *and* project leaders. Because they are dedicated to Six Sigma programs, the black belts are not distracted from the task at hand by day-to-day operating responsibilities. To make a black belt assignment attractive, many companies now endorse the program as an advancement in a career path. Successful black belts might not return to their prior job after 2 years, but could instead be promoted and given more responsibility.

Third, quality improvement methodologies preach the need to identify defects that arise from processes, trace them to their source, find out what caused the defects, and make corrections so that they do not recur. Production and materials management are primarily responsible for this task. To uncover defects, quality improvement methodologies rely upon the use of statistical procedures to pinpoint variations in the quality of goods or services. Once variations have been identified, they must be traced to their respective sources and eliminated.

One technique that helps greatly in tracing defects to the source is reducing lot sizes for manufactured products. With short production runs, defects show up immediately. Consequently, they can quickly be sourced, and the problem can be rectified. Reducing lot sizes also means that defective products will not be produced in large lots, thus decreasing waste. Flexible manufacturing techniques can be used to reduce lot sizes without raising costs. JIT inventory systems also play a part. Under a JIT system, defective parts enter the manufacturing process immediately; they are not warehoused for several months before use. Hence, defective inputs can be quickly spotted. The problem can then be traced to the supply source and corrected before more defective parts are produced. Under a more traditional system, the practice of warehousing parts for months before they are used may mean that suppliers deliver large quantities of parts with defects before they are detected in the production process.

Fourth, another key to any quality improvement program is to create a metric that can be used to measure quality. In manufacturing companies, quality can be measured by criteria such as defects per million parts. In service companies, suitable metrics can be devised with a little creativity. For example, one of the metrics Florida Power & Light uses to measure quality is meter-reading errors per month.

Fifth, once a metric has been devised, the next step is to set a challenging quality goal and create incentives for reaching it. Under Six Sigma programs, the goal is 3.4 defects per million units. One way of creating incentives to attain such a goal is to link rewards such as bonus pay and promotional opportunities to the goal.

Sixth, shop floor employees can be a major source of ideas for improving product quality, so these employees must participate and be incorporated into a quality improvement program.

Seventh, a major source of poor-quality finished goods is poor-quality component parts. To decrease product defects, a company must work with its suppliers to improve the quality of the parts they supply.

Eighth, the more assembly steps a product requires, the more opportunities there are for mistakes. Thus, designing products with fewer parts is often a major component of any quality improvement program.

Finally, implementing quality improvement methodologies requires organizationwide commitment and substantial cooperation among functions. R&D must cooperate with production to design products that are easy to manufacture; marketing must cooperate with production and R&D so that customer problems identified by marketing can be acted on; and human resource management must cooperate with all the other functions of the company in order to devise suitable quality-training programs.

Improving Quality as Excellence

As we stated in Chapter 3, a product is comprised of different attributes. Reliability is just one attribute, albeit an important one. Products can also be *differentiated* by attributes that collectively define product excellence. These attributes include the form, features, performance, durability, and styling of a product. In addition, a company can create quality as excellence by emphasizing attributes of the service associated with the

Table 4.3 Attributes Associated with a Product Offering

Product Attributes	Service Attributes	Associated Personnel Attributes
Form	Ordering ease	Competence
Features	Delivery	Courtesy
Performance	Installation	Credibility
Durability	Customer training	Reliability
Reliability	Customer consulting	Responsiveness
Style	Maintenance and repair	Communication

product. Dell Inc., for example, differentiates itself on ease of ordering (via the Web), prompt delivery, easy installation, and the ready availability of customer support and maintenance services. Differentiation can also be based on the attributes of the people in the company with whom customers interact when making a purchase, such as competence, courtesy, credibility, responsiveness, and communication. Singapore Airlines enjoys an excellent reputation for quality service, largely because passengers perceive their flight attendants as competent, courteous, and responsive to their needs. Thus, we can talk about the product attributes, service attributes, and personnel attributes associated with a company's product offering (see Table 4.3).

To be regarded as being high in the excellence dimension, a company's product offering must be seen as superior to that of rivals. Achieving a perception of high quality on any of these attributes requires specific actions by managers. First, it is important for managers to collect marketing intelligence indicating which attributes are most important to customers. For example, consumers of personal computers (PCs) may place a low weight on durability because they expect their PCs to be made obsolete by technological advances within 3 years, but they may place a high weight on features and performance. Similarly, ease of ordering and timely delivery may be very important attributes for customers of online booksellers (as indeed they are for customers of Amazon.com), whereas customer training and consulting may be very important attributes for customers who purchase complex, business-to-business software to manage their relationships with suppliers.

Second, once the company has identified the attributes that are important to customers, it needs to design its products (and the associated services) in such a way that those attributes are embodied in the product. It also needs to train personnel in the company so that the appropriate attributes are emphasized during design creation. This requires close coordination between marketing and product development (the topic of the next section) and the involvement of the human resource management function in employee selection and training.

Third, the company must decide which significant attributes to promote and how best to position them in the minds of consumers; that is, how to tailor the marketing message so that it creates a consistent image in the minds of customers.[27] At this point, it is important to recognize that although a product might be differentiated on the basis of six attributes, covering all of those attributes in the company's communications may lead to an unfocused message. Many marketing experts advocate promoting only one or two central attributes. For example, Volvo consistently emphasizes the safety and durability of its vehicles in all marketing messages, creating the perception in the minds of consumers (backed by product design) that Volvos are safe and durable. Volvos are also very reliable and have high performance, but the company does not emphasize these attributes in its marketing messages. In contrast, Porsche emphasizes performance and styling in all of its marketing messages; thus, a Porsche is positioned differently in the minds of consumers than Volvo. Both are regarded as high-quality products because both have superior attributes, but each company differentiates its models from the average car by promoting distinctive attributes.

Finally, it must be recognized that competition is not stationary, but instead continually produces improvement in product attributes, and often the development of new-product attributes. This is obvious in fast-moving high-tech industries where product features that were considered leading edge just a few years ago are now obsolete—but the same process is also at work in more stable industries. For example, the rapid diffusion of microwave ovens during the 1980s required food companies to build new attributes into their frozen-food products: they had to maintain their texture and consistency while being cooked in the microwave; a product could not be considered high quality unless it could do that. This speaks to the importance of a strong R&D function within the company that can work with marketing and manufacturing to continually upgrade the quality of the attributes that are designed into the company's product offerings. Exactly how to achieve this is covered in the next section.

◤ACHIEVING SUPERIOR INNOVATION

In many ways, innovation is the most important source of competitive advantage. This is because innovation can result in new products that better satisfy customer needs, can improve the quality (attributes) of existing products, or can reduce the costs of making products that customers want. The ability to develop innovative new products or processes gives a company a major competitive advantage that allows it to: (1) differentiate its products and charge a premium price, and/or (2) lower its cost structure below that of its rivals. Competitors, however, attempt to imitate successful innovations and often succeed. Therefore, maintaining a competitive advantage requires a continuing commitment to innovation.

Successful new-product launches are major drivers of superior profitability. Robert Cooper reviewed more than 200 new-product introductions and found that of those classified as successes, some 50% achieve a return on investment in excess of 33%, half have a payback period of 2 years or less, and half achieve a market share in excess of 35%.[28] Many companies have established a track record for successful innovation. Among them are Apple, whose successes include the iPod, iPhone, and iPad; Pfizer, a drug company that during the 1990s and early 2000s produced eight new blockbuster drugs; 3M, which has applied its core competency in tapes and adhesives to developing a wide range of new products; and Intel, which has consistently managed to lead in the development of innovative microprocessors to run PCs.

The High Failure Rate of Innovation

Although promoting innovation can be a source of competitive advantage, the failure rate of innovative products is high. Research evidence suggests that only 10 to 20% of major R&D projects give rise to commercial products.[29] Well-publicized product failures include Apple's Newton, an early, handheld computer that flopped in the marketplace; Sony's Betamax format in the videocassette recorder segment; Sega's Dreamcast videogame console; and Windows Mobile, an early smartphone operating system created by Microsoft that was made obsolete in the eyes of consumers by the arrival of Apple's iPhone. Although many reasons have been advanced to explain why so many new products fail to generate an economic return, five explanations for failure repeatedly appear.[30]

First, many new products fail because the demand for innovation is inherently uncertain. It is impossible to know prior to market introduction whether the new product has tapped an unmet customer need, and if there is sufficient market demand to justify manufacturing the product. Although good market research can reduce the uncertainty about likely future demand for a new technology, that uncertainty cannot be fully eradicated; a certain failure rate is to be expected.

Second, new products often fail because the technology is poorly commercialized. This occurs when there is definite customer demand for a new product, but the product is not well adapted to customer needs because of factors such as poor design and poor quality. For instance, the failure of Microsoft to establish an enduring, dominant position in the market for smartphones, despite the fact that phones using the Windows Mobile operating system were introduced in 2003—4 years before Apple's iPhone hit the market—can be traced to its poor design. Windows Mobile phones had a physical keyboard, and a small, cluttered screen that was difficult to navigate, which made the product unattractive to many consumers. In contrast, the iPhone's large touchscreen and associated keyboard appealed to many consumers, who rushed out to buy it in droves.

Third, new products may fail because of poor positioning strategy. **Positioning strategy** is the specific set of options a company adopts for a product based upon four main dimensions of marketing: price, distribution, promotion and advertising, and product features. Apart from poor design, another reason for the failure of Windows Mobile phones was poor positioning strategy. They were targeted at business users, whereas Apple developed a mass market by targeting the iPhone at retail consumers.

Fourth, many new-product introductions fail because companies make the mistake of marketing a technology for which there is not enough demand. A company can become blinded by the wizardry of a new technology and fail to determine whether there is sufficient customer demand for it. A classic example is the Segway two-wheeled personal transporter. Despite the fact that its gyroscopic controls were highly sophisticated, and that the product introduction was accompanied by massive media hype, sales fell well below expectations when it transpired that most consumers had no need for such a conveyance.

Finally, companies fail when products are slowly marketed. The more time that elapses between initial development and final marketing—the slower the "cycle time"—the more likely it is that a competitor will beat the company to market and gain a first-mover advantage.[31] In the car industry, General Motors long suffered from being a slow innovator. Its typical product development cycle used to be about 5 years, compared with 2 to 3 years at Honda, Toyota, and Mazda, and 3 to 4 years at Ford. Because GM's offerings were based on 5-year-old technology and design concepts, they are already out of date when they reached the market.

positioning strategy
The specific set of options a company adopts for a product based upon four main dimensions of marketing: price, distribution, promotion and advertising, and product features.

Reducing Innovation Failures

One of the most important things that managers can do to reduce the high failure rate associated with innovation is to make sure that there is tight integration between R&D, production, and marketing.[32] Tight, cross-functional integration can help a company ensure that:

1. Product development projects are driven by customer needs.
2. New products are designed for ease of manufacture.
3. Development costs are not allowed to spiral out of control.
4. The time it takes to develop a product and bring it to market is minimized.
5. Close integration between R&D and marketing is achieved to ensure that product development projects are driven by the needs of customers.

A company's customers can be a primary source of new-product ideas. The identification of customer needs, particularly unmet needs, can set the context within which successful product innovation takes place. As the point of contact with customers, the marketing function can provide valuable information. Moreover, integrating R&D and marketing is crucial if a new product is to be properly commercialized—otherwise, a company runs the risk of developing products for which there is little or no demand.

Integration between R&D and production can help a company ensure that products are designed with manufacturing requirements in mind. Design for manufacturing lowers manufacturing costs and leaves less room for error; thus it can lower costs and increase product quality. Integrating R&D and production can help lower development costs and speed products to market. If a new product is not designed with manufacturing capabilities in mind, it may prove too difficult to build with existing manufacturing technology. In that case, the product will need to be redesigned, and both overall development costs and time to market may increase significantly. Making design changes during product planning can increase overall development costs by 50% and add 25% to the time it takes to bring the product to market.[33]

One of the best ways to achieve cross-functional integration is to establish cross-functional product development teams composed of representatives from R&D, marketing, and production. The objective of a team should be to oversee a product development project from initial concept development to market introduction. Specific attributes appear to be important in order for a product development team to function effectively and meet all its development milestones.[34]

First, a project manager who has high status within the organization and the power and authority required to secure the financial and human resources that the team needs to succeed should lead the team and be dedicated primarily, if not entirely, to the project. The leader should believe in the project (be a champion for the project) and be skilled at integrating the perspectives of different functions and helping personnel from different functions work together for a common goal. The leader should also act as an advocate of the team to senior management.

Second, the team should be composed of at least one member from each key function or position. Individual team members should have a number of attributes, including an ability to contribute functional expertise, high standing within their function, a willingness to share responsibility for team results, and an ability to put functional advocacy aside. It is generally preferable if core team members are 100% dedicated to the project for its duration. This ensures that their focus is on the project, not on their ongoing, individual work.

Third, team members work in proximity to one another to create a sense of camaraderie and facilitate communication. Fourth, the team should have a clear plan and clear goals, particularly with regard to critical development milestones and development budgets. The team should have incentives to attain those goals; for example, bonuses paid when major development milestones are attained. Fifth, each team needs to develop its own processes for communication, as well as conflict resolution. For example, one product development team at Quantum Corporation, a California-based manufacturer of disk drives for PCs, mandated that all major decisions would be made and conflicts resolved during meetings that were held every Monday afternoon. This simple rule helped the team meet its development goals.[35]

Finally, there is substantial evidence that developing competencies in innovation requires managers to proactively learn from their experience with product development, and to incorporate the lessons from past successes and failures into future new-product development processes.[36] This is easier said than done. To learn, managers need to undertake an objective assessment after a product development project has been completed, identifying key success factors and the root causes of failures, and allocating resources to repairing failures. Leaders also must admit their own failures if they are to encourage other team members to responsibly identify what they did wrong.

The primary role that the various functions play in achieving superior innovation is summarized in Table 4.4. The table makes two matters clear. First, top management must bear primary responsibility for overseeing the entire development process. This entails both managing the development process and facilitating cooperation among the functions. Second, the effectiveness of R&D in developing new products and processes depends upon its ability to cooperate with marketing and production.

Table 4.4 Functional Roles for Achieving Superior Innovation

Value Creation Function	Primary Roles
Infrastructure (leadership)	1. Manage overall project (i.e., manage the development function).
	2. Facilitate cross-functional cooperation.
Production	1. Cooperate with R&D on designing products that are easy to manufacture.
	2. Work with R&D to develop process innovations.
Marketing	1. Provide market information to R&D.
	2. Work with R&D to develop new products.
Materials management	No primary responsibility.
R&D	1. Develop new products and processes.
	2. Cooperate with other functions, particularly marketing and manufacturing, in the development process.
Information systems	1. Use information systems to coordinate cross-functional, cross-company product development.
Human resources	1. Hire talented scientists and engineers.

▼ACHIEVING SUPERIOR CUSTOMER RESPONSIVENESS

To achieve superior customer responsiveness, a company must give customers what they want, when they want it, and at a price they are willing to pay—and not compromise the company's long-term profitability in the process. Customer responsiveness is an important differentiating attribute that can help build brand loyalty. Strong product differentiation and brand loyalty give a company more pricing options; it can charge a premium price for its products, or keep prices low to sell more goods and services to customers. Whether prices are at a premium or kept low, the company that is most responsive to customers' needs will gain the competitive advantage.

Achieving superior responsiveness to customers means giving customers value for their money, and steps taken to improve the efficiency of a company's production process and the quality of its products should be consistent with this aim. In addition, giving customers what they want may require the development of new products with new features. In other words, achieving superior efficiency, quality, and innovation are all part of achieving superior responsiveness to customers. There are two other prerequisites for attaining this goal. First, a company must develop a competency in listening to its customers, focusing on its customers, and investigating and identifying their needs. Second, it must constantly seek better ways to satisfy those needs.

Focusing on the Customer

A company cannot respond to its customers' needs unless it knows what those needs are. Thus, the first step to building superior customer responsiveness is to motivate the entire company to focus on the customer. The means to this end are demonstrating leadership, shaping employee attitudes, and using mechanisms for making sure that customer needs are well known within the company.

Demonstrating Leadership

Customer focus must emanate from the top of the organization on down. A commitment to superior responsiveness to customers brings attitudinal changes throughout a company that can only be built through strong leadership. A mission statement that puts customers first is one way to send a clear message to employees about the desired focus. Another avenue is top management's own actions. For example, Tom Monaghan, the founder of Domino's Pizza, stayed close to the customer by eating Domino's pizza regularly, visiting as many stores as possible every week, running some deliveries himself, and insisting that top managers do the same.[37]

Shaping Employee Attitudes

Leadership alone is not enough to attain superior customer responsiveness. All employees must see the customer as the focus of their activity and be trained to concentrate on the customer—whether their function is marketing, manufacturing, R&D, or accounting. The objective should be to put employees in customers' shoes, a perspective that enables them to become better able to identify ways to improve the quality of a customer's experience with the company.

To reinforce this mindset, incentive systems should reward employees for satisfying customers. For example, senior managers at the Four Seasons hotel chain, who pride themselves on customer focus, tell the story of Roy Dyment, a doorman in Toronto who neglected to load a departing guest's briefcase into his taxi. The doorman called the guest, a lawyer, in Washington, D.C., and found that he desperately needed the briefcase for a morning meeting. Dyment hopped on a plane to Washington and returned it—without first securing approval from his boss. Far from punishing Dyment for not checking with management before going to Washington, the Four Seasons responded by naming Dyment Employee of the Year.[38] This sent a powerful message to Four Seasons employees, stressing the importance of satisfying customer needs.

Knowing Customer Needs

"Know thy customer" is one of the keys to achieving superior responsiveness to customers. Knowing the customer not only requires that employees think like customers; it also demands that they listen to what customers have to say. This involves communicating customers' opinions by soliciting feedback from customers on the company's goods and services, and by building information systems that disseminate the feedback to the relevant people.

For an example, consider clothing retailer Lands' End. Through its catalog, the Internet, and customer-service telephone operators, Lands' End actively solicits comments about the quality of its clothing and the kind of merchandise customers want Lands' End to supply. Indeed, it was customer insistence that initially prompted the company to move into the clothing segment. Lands' End formerly supplied equipment for sailboats through mail-order catalogs. However, it received so many requests from customers to include outdoor clothing in its offering that it responded by expanding the catalog to fill this need. Soon, clothing became its main business, and Lands' End ceased selling sailboat equipment. Today, the company continues to pay close attention to customer requests. Every month, data on customer requests and comments is reported to managers. This feedback helps the company fine-tune the merchandise it sells; new lines of merchandise are frequently introduced in response to customer requests.

Satisfying Customer Needs

Once customer focus is integral to the organization, the next requirement is to satisfy those customer needs that have been identified. As already noted, efficiency, quality, and innovation are crucial competencies that help a company satisfy customer needs. Beyond that, companies can provide a higher level of satisfaction if they differentiate their products by (1) customizing them, where possible, to the requirements of individual customers, and (2) reducing the time it takes to respond to or satisfy customer needs.

Customization

Customization involves varying the features of a good or service to tailor it to the unique needs or tastes of a group of customers, or—in the extreme case—individual customers. Although extensive customization can raise costs, the development of flexible manufacturing technologies has made it possible to customize products to a greater extent than was feasible 10 to 15 years ago, without experiencing a prohibitive rise in cost structure (particularly when flexible manufacturing technologies are linked with Web-based information systems). For example, online retailers such as Amazon. com have used Web-based technologies to develop a homepage customized for each individual user. When a customer accesses Amazon.com, he or she is offered a list of recommended books and music to purchase based on an analysis of prior buying history—a powerful competency that gives Amazon.com a competitive advantage.

The trend toward customization has fragmented many markets, particularly customer markets, into ever-smaller niches. An example of this fragmentation occurred in Japan in the early 1980s when Honda dominated the motorcycle market there. Second-place Yamaha was determined to surpass Honda's lead. It announced the opening of a new factory that, when operating at full capacity, would make Yamaha the world's largest manufacturer of motorcycles. Honda responded by proliferating its product line and increasing its rate of new-product introduction. At the start of what became known as the "Motorcycle Wars," Honda had 60 motorcycles in its product line. Over the next 18 months thereafter, it rapidly increased its range to 113 models, customizing them to ever-smaller niches. Because of its competency in flexible manufacturing, Honda accomplished this without bearing a prohibitive cost penalty. The flood of Honda's customized models pushed Yamaha out of much of the market, effectively stalling its bid to overtake Honda.[39]

Response Time

To gain a competitive advantage, a company must often respond to customer demands very quickly, whether the transaction is a furniture manufacturer's completion of an order , a bank's processing of a loan application, an automobile manufacturer's delivery of a spare part, or the wait in a supermarket checkout line. We live in a fast-paced society where time is a valuable commodity. Companies that can satisfy customer demands for rapid response build brand loyalty, differentiate their products, and can charge higher prices for products.

Increased speed often lets a company opt for premium pricing, as the mail delivery industry illustrates. The air-express niche of the mail delivery industry is based on the notion that customers are often willing to pay substantially more for overnight express mail than for regular mail. Another exemplar of the value of rapid response is Caterpillar, the manufacturer of heavy-earthmoving equipment, which can deliver a spare part to any location in the world within 24 hours. Downtime for heavy-construction equipment is very costly, so Caterpillar's ability to respond quickly in the event of equipment malfunction is of prime importance to its customers. As a result, many customers have remained loyal to Caterpillar despite the aggressive, low-price competition from Komatsu of Japan.

In general, reducing response time requires: (1) a marketing function that can quickly communicate customer requests to production, (2) production and materials-management functions that can quickly adjust production schedules in response to unanticipated customer demands, and (3) information systems that can help production and marketing in this process.

Table 4.5 summarizes the steps different functions must take if a company is to achieve superior responsiveness to customers. Although marketing plays a critical role in helping a company attain this goal (primarily because it represents the point of contact with the customer), Table 4.5 shows that the other functions also have major roles. Achieving superior responsiveness to customers requires top management to lead in building a customer orientation within the company.

Table 4.5 Primary Roles of Different Functions in Achieving Superior Customer Responsiveness

Value Creation Function	Primary Roles
Infrastructure (leadership)	• Through leadership by example, build a companywide commitment to responsiveness to customers
Production	• Achieve customization through implementation of flexible manufacturing • Achieve rapid response through flexible manufacturing
Marketing	• Know the customer • Communicate customer feedback to appropriate functions
Materials management	• Develop logistics systems capable of responding quickly to unanticipated customer demands (JIT)
R&D	• Bring customers into the product development process
Information systems	• Use Web-based information systems to increase responsiveness to customers
Human resources	• Develop training programs that get employees to think like customers

KEY TERMS

functional-level strategies 111
economies of scale 112
fixed costs 112
diseconomies of scale 113
learning effects 114
experience curve 116
flexible production technology 117
mass customization 118
marketing strategy 120
customer defection 120
just-in-time (JIT) inventory system 122
supply chain management 122
self-managing teams 123
total quality management 127
positioning strategy 133

TAKEAWAYS FOR STRATEGIC MANAGERS

1. A company can increase efficiency through a number of steps: exploiting economies of scale and learning effects; adopting flexible manufacturing technologies; reducing customer defection rates; implementing just-in-time systems; getting the R&D function to design products that are easy to manufacture; upgrading the skills of employees through training; introducing self-managing teams; linking pay to performance; building a companywide commitment to efficiency through strong leadership; and designing structures that facilitate cooperation among different functions in pursuit of efficiency goals.

2. Superior quality can help a company lower its costs, differentiate its product, and charge a premium price.

3. Achieving superior quality demands an organizationwide commitment to quality and a clear focus on the customer. It also requires metrics to measure quality goals and incentives that

emphasize quality; input from employees regarding ways in which quality can be improved; a methodology for tracing defects to their source and correcting the problems that produce them; a rationalization of the company's supply base; cooperation with approved suppliers to implement total quality management programs; products that are designed for ease of manufacturing; and substantial cooperation among functions.

4. The failure rate of new-product introductions is high because of factors such as uncertainty, poor commercialization, poor positioning strategy, slow cycle time, and technological shortsightedness.

5. To achieve superior innovation, a company must build skills in basic and applied research; design good processes for managing development projects; and achieve close integration between the different functions of the company, primarily through the adoption of cross-functional product development teams and partly parallel development processes.

6. Achieving superior customer responsiveness often requires that the company achieve superior efficiency, quality, and innovation.

7. Furthermore, to achieve superior customer responsiveness, a company must also give customers what they want, when they want it. It must ensure a strong customer focus, which can be attained by emphasizing customer focus through leadership; training employees to think like customers; bringing customers into the company through superior market research; customizing products to the unique needs of individual customers or customer groups; and responding quickly to customer demands.

DISCUSSION QUESTIONS

1. How are the four building blocks of competitive advantage related to each other?

2. What role can top management play in helping a company achieve superior efficiency, quality, innovation, and responsiveness to customers?

3. Over time, will the adoption of Six Sigma quality improvement processes give a company a competitive advantage, or will it be required only to achieve parity with competitors?

4. What is the relationship between innovation and competitive advantage?

CLOSING CASE

Amazon.Com

When Jeff Bezos founded Amazon.com in 1995, the online retailer focused just on selling books. Music and videos were soon added to the mix. Today, you can purchase a wide range of media and general-merchandise products from Amazon, which is now the world's largest online retailer, with over $85 billion in annual sales. According to Bezos, Amazon's success is based on three core factors: a relentless focus on delivering value to customers, operating efficiencies, and a willingness to innovate.

Amazon offers customers a much wider selection of merchandise than they can find in a physical store, and does so at a low price. Online shopping and purchasing is made easy with a user-friendly interface, product recommendations, customer wish lists, and a one-click purchasing option for repeat customers. The percentage of traffic that Amazon gets from search engines such as Google has been falling for several years, whereas other online retailers are becoming more dependent on third-party search engines. This indicates that Amazon is increasingly becoming the starting point for online purchases. As a result, its active customer base is now approaching 250 million.

To deliver products to customers quickly and accurately, Amazon has been investing heavily in a network of distribution centers. In the United States alone there are now over 40 such centers. Sophisticated software analyzes customer purchasing patterns and informs the company what to order, where to store it in the distribution network, what to charge for it, and when to mark it down to shift it. The goal is to reduce inventory-holding costs while always having product in stock. The increasingly dense network of distribution centers enables Amazon to reduce the time it takes to deliver products to consumers and to cut down on delivery costs. As Amazon grows it can support a denser distribution network, which it turn enables it to fulfill customer orders more rapidly and at a lower cost, thereby solidifying its competitive advantage over smaller rivals.

To make its distribution centers even more efficient, Amazon is embracing automation. Until recently, most picking and packing of products at Amazon distribution centers was done by hand, with employees walking as much as 20 miles per shift to pick merchandise off shelves and bring it to packing stations. Although walking 20 miles a day may be good for the physical health of employees, it represents much wasted time and hurts productivity. In 2012, Amazon purchased Kiva, a leading manufacturer of robots that service warehouses. Post the acquisition, Kiva announced that, for the next 2 to 3 years, it would take no external orders

and instead focus on automating Amazon's distribution centers. Kiva robots pick products from shelves and deliver them to packing stations. This reduces the staff needed per distribution center by 30 to 40%, and boosts productivity accordingly.

On the innovation front, Amazon has been a leader in pushing the digitalization of media. Its invention of the Kindle digital reader, and the ability of customers to use that reader either on a dedicated Kindle device or on a general-purpose device such as an iPad, turbocharged the digital distribution of books—a market segment where Amazon is the clear leader. Digitalization of books is disrupting the established book-retailing industry and strengthening Amazon's advantage in this segment. To store digital media, from books to films and music, and to enable rapid customer download, Amazon has built huge server farms. Its early investment in "cloud-based" infrastructure has turned Amazon into a leader in this field. It is now leveraging its expertise and infrastructure to build another business, Amazon Web Services (AWS), which will host websites, data, and associated software for other companies. In 2014, this new business generated over $2.5 billion in revenues, making Amazon one of the early leaders in the emerging field of cloud computing. Jeff Bezos is on record as stating that he believes AWS will ultimately match Amazon's online retail business in sales volume.

Sources: "Amazon to Add 18 New Distribution Centers," *Supply Chain Digest*, August 7, 2012; A. Lashinsky, "Jeff Bezos: The Ultimate Disrupter," *Fortune*, December 3, 2012, pp. 34–41; S. Banker, "The New Amazon Distribution Model," *Logistics Viewpoints*, August 6, 2012; G. A. Fowler, "Holiday Hiring Call: People Vs Robots," *The Wall Street Journal*, December 10, 2010, p. B1.

CASE DISCUSSION QUESTIONS

1. What functional-level strategies has Amazon pursued to boost its efficiency?
2. What functional-level strategies has Amazon pursued to boost its customer responsiveness?
3. What does product quality mean for Amazon? What functional-level strategies has Amazon pursued to boost its product quality?
4. How has innovation helped Amazon improve its efficiency, customer responsiveness, and product quality?
5. Do you think that Amazon has any rare and valuable resources? In what value creation activities are these resources located?
6. How sustainable is Amazon's competitive position in the online retail business?

NOTES

[1]G. J. Miller, *Managerial Dilemmas: The Political Economy of Hierarchy* (Cambridge: Cambridge University Press, 1992).

[2]H. Luft, J. Bunker, and A. Enthoven, "Should Operations Be Regionalized?" *New England Journal of Medicine* 301 (1979): 1364–1369.

[3]S. Chambers and R. Johnston, "Experience Curves in Services," *International Journal of Operations and Production Management* 20 (2000): 842–860.

[4]G. Hall and S. Howell, "The Experience Curve from an Economist's Perspective," *Strategic Management Journal* 6 (1985): 197–212; M. Lieberman, "The Learning Curve and Pricing in the Chemical Processing Industries," *RAND Journal of Economics* 15 (1984): 213–228; R. A. Thornton and P. Thompson, "Learning from Experience and Learning from Others," *American Economic Review* 91 (2001): 1350–1369.

[5]Boston Consulting Group, *Perspectives on Experience* (Boston: Boston Consulting Group, 1972); Hall and Howell, "The Experience Curve," pp. 197–212; W. B. Hirschmann, "Profit from the Learning Curve," *Harvard Business Review* (January–February 1964): 125–139.

[6]A. A. Alchian, "Reliability of Progress Curves in Airframe Production," *Econometrica* 31 (1963): 679–693.

[7]M. Borrus, L. A. Tyson, and J. Zysman, "Creating Advantage: How Government Policies Create Trade in the Semi-Conductor Industry," in P. R. Krugman (ed.), *Strategic Trade Policy and the New International Economics* (Cambridge, Mass.: MIT Press, 1986); S. Ghoshal and C. A. Bartlett, "Matsushita Electrical Industrial (MEI) in 1987," Harvard Business School Case #388-144 (1988).

[8]See P. Nemetz and L. Fry, "Flexible Manufacturing Organizations: Implications for Strategy Formulation," *Academy of Management Review* 13 (1988): 627–638; N. Greenwood, *Implementing Flexible Manufacturing Systems* (New York: Halstead Press, 1986); J. P. Womack, D. T. Jones, and D. Roos, *The Machine That Changed the World* (New York: Rawson Associates, 1990); R. Parthasarthy and S. P. Seith, "The Impact of Flexible Automation on Business Strategy and Organizational Structure," *Academy of Management Review* 17 (1992): 86–111.

[9]B. J. Pine, *Mass Customization: The New Frontier in Business Competition* (Boston: Harvard Business School Press, 1993); S. Kotha, "Mass Customization: Implementing the Emerging Paradigm for Competitive Advantage," *Strategic Management Journal* 16 (1995): 21–42; J. H. Gilmore and B. J. Pine II, "The Four Faces of Mass Customization," *Harvard Business Review* (January–February 1997): 91–101.

[10]P. Waurzyniak, "Ford's Flexible Push," *Manufacturing Engineering*, September 1, 2003: 47–50.

[11]F. F. Reichheld and W. E. Sasser, "Zero Defections: Quality Comes to Service," *Harvard Business Review* (September–October 1990): 105–111.

[12]Ibid.

[13]The example comes from Reichheld and Sasser.

[14]R. Narasimhan and J. R. Carter, "Organization, Communication and Coordination of International Sourcing," *International Marketing Review* 7 (1990): 6–20.

[15]H. F. Busch, "Integrated Materials Management," *IJDP & MM* 18 (1990): 28–39.

[16]G. Stalk and T. M. Hout, *Competing Against Time* (New York: Free Press, 1990).

[17]See P. Bamberger and I. Meshoulam, *Human Resource Strategy: Formulation, Implementation, and Impact* (Thousand Oaks, Calif.: Sage, 2000); P. M. Wright and S. Snell, "Towards a Unifying Framework for Exploring Fit and Flexibility in Human Resource Management," *Academy of Management Review* 23 (October 1998): 756–772.

[18]A. Sorge and M. Warner, "Manpower Training, Manufacturing Organization, and Work Place Relations in Great Britain and West Germany," *British Journal of Industrial Relations* 18 (1980): 318–333; R. Jaikumar, "Postindustrial Manufacturing," *Harvard Business Review,* November–December 1986, pp. 72–83.

[19]J. Hoerr, "The Payoff from Teamwork," *Business Week,* July 10, 1989, pp. 56–62.

[20]"The Trouble with Teams," *The Economist,* January 14, 1995, p. 61.

[21]T. C. Powell and A. Dent Micallef, "Information Technology as Competitive Advantage: The Role of Human, Business, and Technology Resource," *Strategic Management Journal* 18 (1997):

375–405; B. Gates, *Business @ the Speed of Thought* (New York: Warner Books, 1999).

[22]"Cisco@speed," *The Economist,* June 26, 1999, p. 12; S. Tully, "How Cisco Mastered the Net," *Fortune,* August 17, 1997, pp. 207–210; C. Kano, "The Real King of the Internet," *Fortune,* September 7, 1998, pp. 82–93

[23]Gates, *Business @ the Speed of Thought.*

[24]See the articles published in the special issue of the *Academy of Management Review on Total Quality Management* 19:3 (1994). The following article provides a good overview of many of the issues involved from an academic perspective: J. W. Dean and D. E. Bowen, "Management Theory and Total Quality," *Academy of Management Review* 19 (1994): 392–418. See also T. C. Powell, "Total Quality Management as Competitive Advantage," *Strategic Management Journal* 16 (1995): 15–37.

[25]For general background information, see "How to Build Quality," *The Economist,* September 23, 1989, pp. 91–92; A. Gabor, *The Man Who Discovered Quality* (New York: Penguin, 1990); P. B. Crosby, *Quality Is Free* (New York: Mentor, 1980).

[26]W. E. Deming, "Improvement of Quality and Productivity Through Action by Management," *National Productivity Review* 1 (Winter 1981–1982): 12–22.

[27]A. Ries and J. Trout, *Positioning: The Battle for Your Mind* (New York: Warner Books, 1982).

[28]R. G. Cooper, *Product Leadership* (Reading, Mass.: Perseus Books, 1999).

[29]See Cooper, *Product Leadership*; A. L. Page "PDMA's New Product Development Practices Survey: Performance and Best Practices," presentation at PDMA 15th Annual International Conference, Boston, MA, October 16, 1991; E. Mansfield, "How Economists See R&D," *Harvard Business Review* (November–December 1981): 98–106.

[30]S. L. Brown and K. M. Eisenhardt, "Product Development: Past Research, Present Findings, and Future Directions," *Academy of Management Review* 20 (1995): 343–378; M. B. Lieberman and D. B. Montgomery, "First Mover Advantages," *Strategic Management Journal* 9 (Special Issue, Summer 1988): 41–58; D. J. Teece, "Profiting from Technological Innovation: Implications for Integration, Collaboration, Licensing and Public Policy," *Research Policy* 15 (1987): 285–305; G. J. Tellis and P. N. Golder, "First to Market, First to Fail?" *Sloan Management Review,* Winter 1996, pp. 65–75; G. A. Stevens and J. Burley, "Piloting the Rocket of Radical Innovation," *Research Technology Management* 46 (2003): 16–26.

[31]G. Stalk and T. M. Hout, *Competing Against Time* (New York: Free Press, 1990).

[32]K. B. Clark and S. C. Wheelwright, *Managing New Product and Process Development* (New York: Free Press, 1993); M. A. Schilling and C. W. L. Hill, "Managing the New Product Development Process," *Academy of Management Executive* 12:3 (August 1998): 67–81.

[33]O. Port, "Moving Past the Assembly Line," *Business Week* (Special Issue, "Reinventing America," 1992): 177–180.

[34]K. B. Clark and T. Fujimoto, "The Power of Product Integrity," *Harvard Business Review* (November–December 1990): 107–118; Clark and Wheelwright, *Managing New Product and Process Development*; Brown and Eisenhardt, "Product Development"; Stalk and Hout, *Competing Against Time.*

[35]C. Christensen, "Quantum Corporation—Business and Product Teams," Harvard Business School Case, #9-692-023.

[36]H. Petroski, *Success Through Failure: The Paradox of Design* (Princeton, NJ: Princeton University Press, 2006). See also A. C. Edmondson, "Learning from Mistakes Is Easier Said Than Done," *Journal of Applied Behavioral Science* 40 (2004): 66–91.

[37]S. Caminiti, "A Mail Order Romance: Lands' End Courts Unseen Customers," *Fortune,* March 13, 1989, pp. 43–44.

[38]Sellers, "Getting Customers to Love You."

[39]Stalk and Hout, *Competing Against Time.*

sergign/Shutterstock.com

3

STRATEGIES

sergign/Shutterstock.com

OPENING CASE

Virgin America

Virgin America is consistently rated as one of the top U.S. airlines. The 7-year-old airline serves 20 destinations out of its main hub in San Francisco. Virgin America is known for its leather seats, cocktail lounge-style lighting, onboard Wi-Fi, in-seat power outlets for electronics devices, full-service meals, and that most scarce of all assets in coach class, legroom! The airline has earned a host of awards since its launch in 2007, including being named the "Best U.S. Airline" in the *Condé Nast* Traveler Readers' Choice Awards every year from 2008-2014; and "Best Domestic Airline" in the *Travel + Leisure* World's Best Awards, both for the past 7 years. Furthermore, *Consumer* Reports named Virgin America the "Best U.S. Airline" in 2013 and 2014. Industry statistics support these accolades. In 2014, Virgin was #1 in on-time arrivals in the United States, with 83.5% of aircraft arriving on time. Virgin America

Bob Riha Jr/Getty Images

also had the lowest level of denied boarding's (0.07 per 1,000 passengers), and mishandled baggage (0.87 per 1,000 passengers), and the fewest customer complaints (1.50 per 1,000 passengers).

Virgin America is an offshoot of the Virgin Group, the enterprise started by British billionaire Richard Branson. Branson got his start in the music business with Virgin Records stores (established in 1971) and the Virgin Record record label (established in 1973). In 1984, he leveraged the Virgin brand to enter an entirely new industry, airlines, with Virgin Atlantic. Virgin Atlantic became a major competitor to British Airways on a number of long-haul routes out of London, winning market share through superior customer service, innovative touches for premium travelers, and competitive pricing. Branson has also licensed the right to use the Virgin brand name across a wide array of businesses, including Virgin Media (a major U.K. cable operator), Virgin Money (a U.K. financial services company), and Virgin Mobile (a wireless brand that exists in many countries). This strategy has made Virgin one of the most recognizable brands in the world. Interestingly, Branson makes money from royalty payments irrespective of whether companies licensing the Virgin brand are profitable or not. Branson himself describes the Virgin brand as representing, "innovation, quality, and a sense of fun."

For all of its accolades and the power of the Virgin brand, Virgin America has had a hard time making money. One problem is that, as a small airline, Virgin only has a few flights a day on many routes and is unable to offer consumers the choice of multiple departure times, something that many travelers value. For example, on the popular route for tech workers between San Francisco and Austin, Texas, United offers six flights a day and Jet Blue offers two, compared with just one for Virgin America.

Another serious problem is that providing all of the extra frills necessary to deliver a high-quality experience costs money. In its first 5 years of operation, Virgin America accumulated $440 million in losses before registering a small profit of $67 million on revenues of $1.4 billion in 2013. In 2014, Virgin America went public and managed to post a respectable $150 million in net profits on revenues of close to $1.5 billion. The company was helped by an improving economy, strong demand, and lower jet fuel costs.

The key competitive issue the company faces is that it is a niche player in a much larger industry where low-cost carriers such as Southwest Airlines and Jet Blue are putting constant pressure on prices and crowding out routes with multiple flights daily. Virgin America does charge prices that are 10-20% above those of its no-frills rivals, but it cannot raise prices too far without losing customers and flying with empty seats, which is a recipe for failure in an industry where margins are slim. On the route between New York's Kennedy Airport and Los Angeles during late 2012, for example, Virgin passengers were paying an average of $305 a ticket compared to an industry average of $263. Virgin's passenger-load factor on that route was 96% of the industry average during the same period. Virgin CEO David Cush, however, is adamant that the airline "… won't get into a fare war. Our product is good; we've got good loyalty. People will be willing to pay $20 or $30 more." Is he correct? Only time will tell. History, however, is not on Virgin's side. Since airline deregulation in 1978, all but a handful of the roughly 250 new airlines have failed.

Sources: M. Richtel, "At Virgin America, a fine line between pizazz and profit," *New York Times*, September 7, 2013; B. Tuttle, "Why an airline that travelers love is failing," *Time*, October 25, 2012; T. Huddleston, "Virgin America goes public," *Fortune*, November 13, 2014; A. Levine-Weinberg, "How Richard Branson built a $5-billion fortune from scratch," *Motley Fool*, October 19, 2014, www.fool.com.

◤OVERVIEW

business-level strategy

A business's overall competitive theme; the way it positions itself in the marketplace to gain a competitive advantage, and the different positioning strategies that it can use in different industry settings.

In this chapter we look at the formulation of **business-level strategy**. As you may recall from Chapter 1, business-level strategy refers to the overarching competitive theme of a company in a given market. At its most basic, business-level strategy is about *whom* a company decides to serve (which customer segments), what customer *needs* and *desires* the company is trying to satisfy, and *how* the company decides to satisfy those needs and desires.[1] If this sounds familiar, it is because we have already discussed this in Chapter 1 when we considered how companies construct a mission statement.

The airline Virgin America provides us with an illustration of how this works (see the Opening Case). Virgin America is targeting mid- to upper-income travelers, many of them in the technology industry, who are willing to pay 10–20% extra for a more pleasant flying experience. Virgin attempts to satisfy the desires of this customer segment through excellent customer service and a range of inflight offerings that includes leather seats, more legroom, and full-service meals. As proven by the many awards that it has won, Virgin America has certainly *differentiated* itself from rival carriers. However, like many enterprises that pursue a differentiation strategy, Virgin America also has to deal with an incrementally higher cost structure than its rivals. This is particularly problematic in the airline industry, where low-cost carriers such as Southwest and Jet Blue have conditioned customers to shop for the lowest price. Unless Virgin America can fill its aircraft at higher price points, the strategy may not lead to higher profitability and a sustained competitive advantage.

In this chapter, we will look at how managers decide what business-level strategy to pursue, and how they go about executing that strategy in order to attain a sustainable competitive advantage. We start by looking at the two basic ways that companies compete in a marketplace—by *lowering costs* and by *differentiating* their goods or services from those offered by rivals so that they create more value. Next, we consider the issue of *customer choice* and *market segmentation*, and discuss the decisions that managers must make when it comes to their company's segmentation strategy. Then, synthesizing this, we discuss the various business-level strategies that an enterprise can adopt, and what must be done to successfully implement those strategies. The chapter closes with a discussion of how managers can think about formulating an innovative, business-level strategy that gives their company a unique and defendable position in the marketplace.

◤LOW COST AND DIFFERENTIATION

Strategy is about the search for competitive advantage. As we saw in Chapter 3, at the most fundamental level, a company has a competitive advantage if it can lower costs relative to rivals and/or if it can differentiate its product offering from those of rivals, thereby creating more value. We will look at lowering costs first, and then at differentiation.[2]

Lowering Costs

Imagine that all enterprises in an industry offer products that are very similar in all respects except for price, and that each company is small relative to total market demand, so that they are unable to influence the prevailing price. This is the situation that exists in commodity markets such as those for oil, wheat, aluminum, and steel. In the global oil market, for example, prices are set by the interaction of supply and demand. Even the world's largest private oil producer, Exxon Mobile, only produces around 3.5% of world output and cannot influence the prevailing price.

In commodity markets, competitive advantage goes to the company that has the lowest costs. Low costs enable a company to make a profit at price points where its rivals are losing money. Low costs can also allow a company to undercut rivals on price, gain market share, and maintain or even increase profitability. Being the low-cost player in an industry can be a very advantageous position.

Although lowering costs below those of rivals is a particularly powerful strategy in a pure commodity industry, it can also have great utility in other settings. General merchandise retailing, for example, is not a classic commodity business. Nevertheless, Wal-Mart has built a very strong competitive position in the U.S. market by being the low-cost player. Because its costs are so low, Wal-Mart can cut prices, grow its market share, and still make profits at price points where its competitors lose money. The same is true in the airline industry, where Southwest Airlines has established a low-cost position. Southwest's operating efficiencies have enabled it to make money in an industry that has been hit by repeated bouts of price warfare, and where many of its rivals have been forced into bankruptcy.

Differentiation

Now let's look at the differentiation side of the equation. Differentiation involves distinguishing your company from its rivals by offering something that they find hard to match. As we saw in the Opening Case, Virgin America has differentiated itself from its rivals through excellence in customer service and offering inflight amenities that its rivals do not. A company can differentiate itself from rivals in many ways A product can be differentiated by superior reliability (it breaks down less often, or not at all), better design, superior functions and features, better point-of-sale service, better after-sales service and support, better branding, and so on. A Rolex watch is differentiated from a Timex watch by superior design, materials, and reliability; a Toyota car is differentiated from a General Motors car by superior reliability (historically, new Toyota models have had fewer defects than new GM models); Apple differentiates its iPhone from rival offerings through superior product design, ease of use, excellent customer service at its Apple stores, and easy synchronization with other Apple products, such as its computers, tablets, iTunes, and iCloud.

Differentiation gives a company two advantages. First, it can allow the company to charge a premium price for its good or service, should it chose to do so. Second, it can help the company grow overall demand and capture market share from its rivals. In the case of the iPhone, Apple has reaped both of these benefits through its successful differentiation strategy. Apple charges more for its iPhone than people pay for rival smartphone offerings, and the differential appeal of Apple products has led to strong demand growth.

It is important to note that differentiation often (but not always) raises the cost structure of the firm. It costs Virgin America more to create a comfortable, full-service, inflight experience. It is often the case that companies pursuing a differentiation strategy have a higher cost structure than companies pursuing a low-cost strategy. On the other hand, somewhat counter intuitively, there are situations where successful differentiation, because it increases primary demand so much, can actually lower costs. Apple's iPhone is a case in point. Apple uses very expensive materials in the iPhone—Gorilla Glass for the screen and brushed aluminum for the case. It could have used cheap plastic, but then the product would not have looked as good and would have scratched easily. Although these decisions about materials originally raised the unit cost of the iPhone, the fact is that Apple has sold so many iPhones that it now enjoys economies of scale in purchasing and can effectively bargain down the price it pays for expensive materials. The result for Apple—successful differentiation of the iPhone—not only helped the company charge a premium price, it has also gown demand to the point where it can lower costs through the attainment of scale economies, thereby widening profit margins. This is why Apple captured 89% of all profits in the global smartphone business in the second half of 2014.

The Apple example points to an essential truth: Successful differentiation gives managers options. One option is to raise the price to reflect the differentiated nature of the product offering and cover any incremental increase in costs (see Figure 5.1). Many firms pursue this option, which can by itself enhance profitability as long as prices increase more than costs. For example, Four Seasons hotels are very luxurious. It certainly costs a lot to provide that luxury, but Four Seasons also charges very high prices for its rooms, and the firm is profitable as a result.

However, the Apple example also suggests that increased profitability and profit growth can come from the increased demand associated with successful differentiation, which enables the firm to use its assets more efficiently and thereby realize *lower costs* from scale economies. This leads to another option: The successful differentiator can hold prices constant, or only increase them slightly, sell more, and boost profitability through the attainment of scale economies (see Figure 5.1).[3]

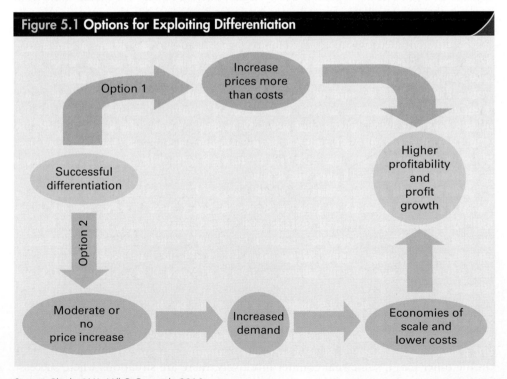

Figure 5.1 Options for Exploiting Differentiation

Source: Charles W.L. Hill © Copyright 2013.

For another example, consider Starbucks. The company has successfully differentiated its product offering from that of rivals such as Tully's by the excellent quality of its coffee-based drinks; by the quick, efficient, friendly service that its baristas offer customers; by the comfortable atmosphere created by the design of its stores; and by its strong brand image. This differentiation increases traffic volume in each Starbucks store, thereby increasing the productivity of employees (they are always busy) and the productivity of the capital invested in the store. Thus, each store realizes scale economies from greater volume, which lowers the average unit costs at each store. Spread across the 12,000 stores that Starbucks operates, this represents potentially huge cost savings that translate into higher profitability. Add this to the enhanced demand that comes from successful differentiation—which in the case of Starbucks not only enables the firm to sell more from each store, but also to open more stores—and profit growth will also accelerate.

The Differentiation–Low Cost Tradeoff

The thrust of our discussion so far is that a low-cost position and a differentiated position are two very different ways of gaining a competitive advantage. The enterprise striving for the lowest costs does everything it can to be productive and drive down its cost structure, whereas the enterprise striving for differentiation necessarily has to bear higher costs to achieve that differentiation. Put simply, one cannot be both Wal-Mart and Nordstrom, Virgin America and Southwest, Porsche and Kia, Rolex and Timex. Managers must choose between these two basic ways of attaining a competitive advantage.

However, presenting the choice between differentiation and low costs in these terms is something of a simplification. As we have already noted, the successful differentiator might be able to subsequently reduce costs if differentiation leads to significant demand growth and the attainment of scale economies. But in actuality, the relationship between low cost and differentiation is subtler than this. In reality, strategy is not so much about making discrete choices as it is about achieving the right balance is between differentiation and low costs.

To understand these issues, see Figure 5.2. The convex curve in Figure 5.2 illustrates what is known as an *efficiency frontier* (also known in economics as a production possibility frontier).[4] The efficiency frontier shows all of the different positions that a company can adopt with regard to differentiation and low cost, *assuming* that its internal functions and organizational arrangements are configured efficiently to support a particular position (note that the horizontal axis in Figure 5.2 is reverse scaled—moving along the axis to the right implies lower costs). The efficiency frontier has a convex shape because of diminishing returns. Diminishing returns imply that when an enterprise already has significant differentiation built into its product offering, increasing differentiation by a relatively small amount requires significant additional costs. The converse also holds: A company that already has a low-cost structure must relinquish much differentiation in its product offering to achieve additional cost reductions.

The efficiency frontier shown in Figure 5.2 is for the U.S. retail apparel business (Wal-Mart sells more than apparel, but that need not concern us here). As you can see, the high-end retailer Nordstrom and the low-cost retailer Wal-Mart are both shown to be on the frontier, implying that both organizations have configured their internal functions and organizations efficiently. However, they have adopted very different positions; Nordstrom has high differentiation and high costs, whereas Wal-Mart has low costs and low differentiation. These are not the only viable positions in the industry, however. The

Figure 5.2 The Differentiation–Low Cost Tradeoff

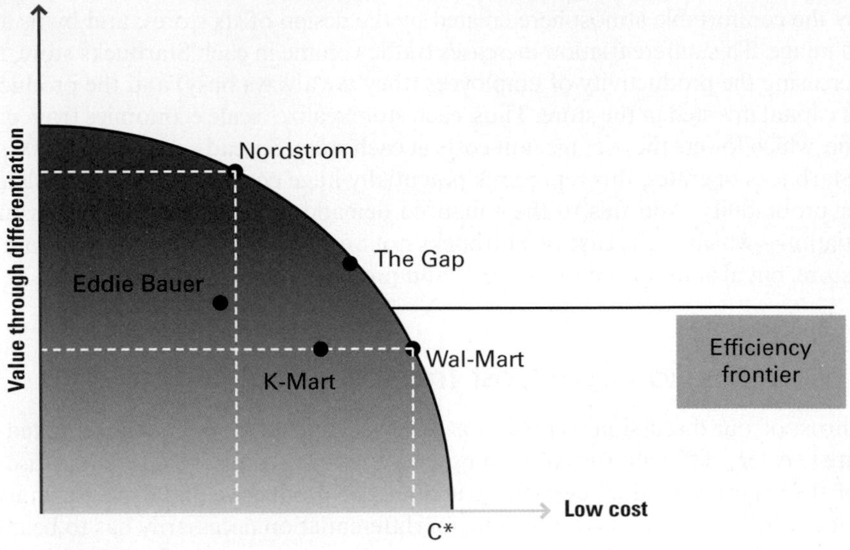

Source: Charles W.L. Hill © Copyright 2013.

Gap, too, is on the frontier. The Gap offers higher-quality apparel merchandise than Wal-Mart, sold in a more appealing environment, but its offering is nowhere near as differentiated as that of Nordstrom; it is positioned between Wal-Mart and Nordstrom. This mid-level position, offering moderate differentiation at a higher cost than Wal-Mart, makes perfect sense because there are enough consumers demanding this option. They don't want to look as if they purchased their clothes at Wal-Mart; they want fashionable, casual clothes that are more affordable than those available at Nordstrom.

The essential point is that *there are often multiple positions on the differentiation–low-cost continuum that are viable in the sense that they have enough demand to support an offering.* The task for managers is to identify a position in the industry that is viable and then configure the functions and organizational arrangements of the enterprise so that they are run as efficiently and effectively as possible, and enable the firm to reach the frontier. Not all companies are able to do this. Only those that can get to the frontier have a competitive advantage. Getting to the frontier requires excellence in strategy implementation. As has been suggested already in this chapter, business-level strategy is implemented through function and organization. Therefore, *to successfully implement a business-level strategy and reach the efficiency frontier, a company must pursue the right functional-level strategies and be appropriately organized; business-level strategy, functional-level strategy, and organizational arrangement must all be in alignment.*

It should be noted that not all positions on an industry's efficiency frontier are equally attractive. For some positions, there may not be sufficient demand to support a product offering. For other positions, there may be too many competitors going after the same basic position—the competitive space might be too crowded—and the resulting competition might drive prices below acceptable levels.

In Figure 5.2, K-Mart is inside the frontier. K-Mart is trying to position itself in the same basic space as Wal-Mart, but its internal operations are not efficient (the company was operating under bankruptcy protection in the early 2000s, although it is now out of bankruptcy). Also shown in Figure 5.2 is Seattle-based clothing retailer Eddie Bauer, which is owned by Spiegel. Like K-Mart, Eddie Bauer is not an efficiently run operation relative to its rivals. Its parent company has operated under bankruptcy protection three times in the last 20 years.

Value Innovation: Greater Differentiation at a Lower Cost

The efficiency frontier is not static; it is continually being pushed outward by the efforts of managers to improve their firm's performance through innovation. For example, in the mid-1990s, Dell pushed out the efficiency frontier in the personal computer (PC) industry (see Figure 5.3). Dell pioneered the online sale of PCs allowing customers to build their own machines and effectively creating value through customization. In other words, the strategy of selling online allowed Dell to *differentiate* itself from rivals that sold PCs through retail outlets. At the same time, Dell used order information submitted over the Web to efficiently coordinate and manage the global supply chain, driving down production costs in the process. The net result was that Dell was able to offer more value (through superior *differentiation*) at a *lower cost* than its rivals. Through its process innovations, it redefined the frontier of what was possible in the industry.

We use the term **value innovation** to describe what happens when innovation pushes out the efficiency frontier in an industry, allowing for greater value to be offered through superior differentiation at a lower cost than was previously thought possible.[5] When

value innovation
When innovations push out the efficiency frontier in an industry, allowing for greater value to be offered through superior differentiation at a lower cost than was previously thought possible.

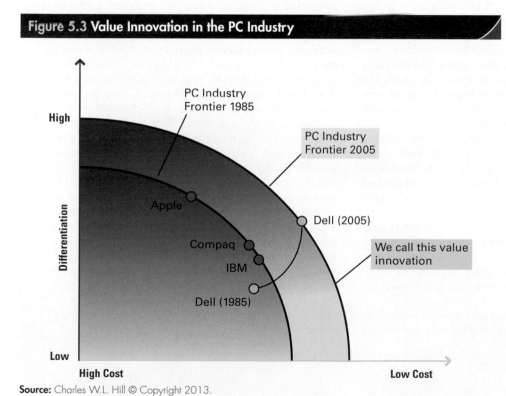

Figure 5.3 Value Innovation in the PC Industry

Source: Charles W.L. Hill © Copyright 2013.

a company pioneers process innovations that lead to value innovation, it effectively changes the game in an industry and may be able to outperform its rivals for a long period of time. This is what happened to Dell. After harnessing the power of the Internet to sell PCs online and coordinate the global supply chain, Dell outperformed its rivals in the industry for over a decade while they scrambled to catch up with the industry leader.

Toyota is another company that benefitted from value innovation. As we have discussed in Chapters 3 and 4, Toyota pioneered lean production systems that improved the quality of automobiles, while simultaneously lowering costs. Toyota *redefined what was possible in the automobile industry*, effectively pushing out the efficiency frontier and enabling the company to better differentiate its product offering at a cost level that its rivals couldn't match. The result was a competitive advantage that persisted for over two decades. For another example of value innovation, see Strategy in Action 5.1,which describes how IKEA redefined competition in the furniture business.

5.1 STRATEGY IN ACTION

IKEA: Value Innovation in Furniture Retailing

IKEA, the privately held furniture retailer, is a global colossus. The world's largest furniture retailer, in 2014 IKEA had 361 stores around the globe, 164,000 employees, revenues in excess of 30 billion Euros, and 861 million customer visits to its stores. The company started out with a single store in Sweden in 1958. The vision of the company's founder, Ingvar Kamprad, was to "democratize furniture," making stylish, functional furniture available at a low cost.

Kamprad's vision was a reaction to the existing market for furniture. Furniture was either seen as an expensive heirloom, which typically had to be ordered from the manufacturer after the consumer had made a purchase decision in a retail store, and might take 3 months to deliver, or was poorly designed, low-quality, cheap furniture sold in discount stores. As IKEAs strategy evolved, its core target market became young professionals looking to furnish their first apartments or homes with stylish but inexpensive furniture that could be disposed off when they were able to buy more traditional, heirloom-style furniture.

Over the years, Kamprad assembled a world-class team that designed stylish, quality furniture that emphasized clean, "Swedish" lines. An important goal was to make IKEA offerings 30% cheaper than comparable items produced by rivals. To drive down costs, Kamprad and his associates worked out ways to reduce the costs of making and delivering this furniture. They cooperated closely with long-term suppliers to drive down material and manufacturing costs. They designed furniture that could be flat packed, which reduced transportation and storage costs. They pushed assembly onto the consumer, but gave them lower prices as part of the bargain. They even made the consumer responsible for pulling inventory out of the warehouse, which was typically placed between the product-display areas and the cash registers. As a result of these actions, all taken at the functional level within the company, IKEA was able to offer more value to its target market than rivals, and to do so at a lower cost. Through astute market segmentation and a well-thought-out strategy of value innovation, IKEA redefined the furniture market not just in Sweden but in countries around the globe, in the process becoming the world's largest furniture retailer and making Ingvar Kamprad one of the world's richest men.

Source: C.W.L. Hill, "IKEA in 2013: Furniture Retailer to the World," in C.W.L Hill, G.R. Jones, and M. Shilling, *Strategic Management*, 11th edition (Boston: Cengage, 2015).

◤ WHO ARE OUR CUSTOMERS? MARKET SEGMENTATION

As noted in the introduction to this chapter, business-level strategy begins with deciding *who* the company is going to serve, what *needs* or *desires* it is trying to satisfy, and *how* it is going to satisfy those needs and desires. Answering these questions is not straightforward, because customers in a market are not homogenous. They often differ in fundamental ways. Some are wealthy, some are not; some are old, some are young; some are women, some are men; some are influenced by popular culture, some never watch TV; some live in cities, some in the suburbs; some care deeply about status symbols, others do not; some place a high value on luxury, others value for money; some exercise every day, others have never seen the inside of a gym; some speak English most of the time, while for others Spanish is their first language; and so on.

One fundamental decision that every company faces is whether to recognize such differences in customers, and if so, how to tailor its approach depending on which customer segment or segments it decides to serve. The first step toward answering these questions is to segment the market according to differences in customer demographics, needs, and desires.

Market segmentation refers to the process of subdividing a market into clearly identifiable groups of customers with similar needs, desires, and demand characteristics. Customers within these segments are relatively homogenous, whereas they differ in important ways from customers in other segments of the market. For example, Nike segments the athletic shoe market according to sport and gender because it believes that people participating in different sports expect different things from an athletic shoe (a shoe designed for running is not suitable for playing basketball), and that men and women desire different shoe styling and construction (most men don't want to wear pink shoes). Similarly, in the market for colas, Coca-Cola segments the market by needs—regular Coke for the average consumer, and diet cola for consumers concerned about their weight. The diet cola segment is further subdivided by gender, with Diet Coke targeted at women, and Coke Zero targeted at men.

market segmentation
The way a company decides to group customers, based on important differences in their needs, in order to gain a competitive advantage.

Three Approaches to Market Segmentation

Companies adopt one of three basic approaches to market segmentation. The first is to *not* tailor different offerings to different segments and instead produce and sell a standardized product that is targeted at the average customer in that market. This was the approach adopted by Coca-Cola until the early 1980s, before the introduction of Diet Coke and flavored cola drinks such as Cherry Cola. In those days, Coke was *the* drink for everyone. Coke was differentiated from the offerings of rivals, and particularly Pepsi Cola, by lifestyle advertising that positioned Coke as the iconic American drink, the "real thing." Some network broadcast news programs adopt this approach today. The coverage offered by ABC News, for example, is tailored toward the average American viewer. The giant retailer Wal-Mart targets the average customer in the market, although, unlike Coca-Cola, Wal-Mart's goal is to drive down costs so that it can charge everyday low prices, give its customers value for money, and still make a profit.

A second approach is to recognize differences between segments and create different product offerings for each segment. Coca-Cola has adopted this approach since the 1980s. In 1982, it introduced Diet Coke, targeting that drink at the weight and health conscious. In 2007, it introduced Coke Zero, also a diet cola, but this time targeted at men. Coca Cola did this because company research found that men tended to associate Diet Coke with women. Since 2007, Diet Coke has been repositioned as more of a women's diet drink. Similarly, in the automobile industry, Toyota has brands that address the entire market—Scion for budget-constrained, young, entry-level buyers, Toyota for the middle market, and Lexus for the luxury end of the market. In each of these segments Toyota tries to differentiate itself from rivals in the segment by the excellent reliability and high quality of its offerings.

A third approach is to target only a limited number of market segments, or just one, and to become the very best at serving that particular segment. In the automobile market, Porsche focuses exclusively on the very top end of the market, targeting wealthy, middle-aged, male consumers who have a passion for the speed, power, and engineering excellence associated with its range of sports cars. Porsche is clearly pursuing a differentiation strategy with regard to this segment, although it emphasizes a different type of differentiation than Toyota. Alternatively, Kia of South Korea has positioned itself as low-cost player in the industry, selling vehicles that are aimed at value-conscious buyers in the middle- and lower-income brackets. In the network broadcasting news business, Fox News and MSNBC have also adopted a focused approach. Fox tailors its content toward viewers on the right of the political spectrum, whereas MSNBC is differentiated toward viewers on the left.

When managers decide to ignore different segments and produce a standardized product for the average consumer, we say they are pursuing a **standardization strategy**. When they decide to serve many segments, or even the entire market, producing different offerings for different segments, we say they are pursuing a **segmentation strategy**. When they decide to serve a limited number of segments, or just one segment, we say they are pursuing a **focus strategy**. Today, Wal-Mart is pursuing a standardization strategy, Toyota a segmentation strategy, and Nordstrom a focus strategy.

Market Segmentation, Costs and Revenues

It is important to understand that these different approaches to market segmentation have different implications for costs and revenues. Consider first the comparison between a standardization strategy and a segmentation strategy.

A standardization strategy, which is typically associated with lower costs than a segmentation strategy, involves the company producing one, basic offering and trying to attain economies of scale by achieving high-volume sales. Wal-Mart pursues a standardization strategy and achieves enormous economies of scale in purchasing, driving down its cost of goods sold.

In contrast, a segmentation strategy requires that the company customize its product offering to different segments, producing multiple offerings, one for each segment. Customization can drive up costs for two reasons; first, the company may sell less of each offering, making it harder to achieve economies of scale; second, products targeted at segments at the higher-income end of the market may require more functions and features, which can raise the costs of production and delivery.

standardization strategy

When a company decides to ignore different segments and produces a standardized product for the average consumer.

segmentation strategy

When a company decides to serve many segments, or even the entire market, producing different offerings for different segments.

focus strategy

When a company decides to serve a limited number of segments, or just one segment.

On the other hand, it is important not to lose sight of the fact that advances in production technology, and particularly lean production techniques, have allowed for *mass customization*—that is, the production of more product variety without a large cost penalty (see Chapter 4 for details). In addition, by designing products that share common components, some manufacturing companies achieve substantial economies of scale in component production while still producing a variety of end products aimed at different segments. This is an approach adopted by large automobile companies, which try to utilize common components and platforms across a wide range of models. To the extent that mass customization and component sharing is possible, the cost penalty borne by a company pursuing a segmentation strategy may be limited.

Although a standardization strategy may have lower costs than a segmentation strategy, a segmentation strategy has one big advantage: It allows the company to capture incremental revenues by customizing its offerings to the needs of different groups of consumers and thus selling more in total. A company pursuing a standardization strategy where a product is aimed at the average consumer may lose sales from customers who desire more functions and features and are prepared to pay more for them. Similarly, it may lose sales from customers who cannot afford to purchase the average product but might enter the market if a more basic offering was available.

This reality was first recognized in the automobile industry back in the 1920s. The early leader in the automobile industry was Ford with its Model T offering. Henry Ford famously said that consumers could have it in "any color as long as it's black." Ford was in essence pursuing a standardization strategy. However, in the 1920s, Ford rapidly lost market share to General Motors, a company that pursued a segmentation strategy and offered a range of products aimed at different customer groups.

For a focus strategy, the impact on costs and revenues is subtler. Companies that focus on the higher-income or higher-value end of the market will tend to have a higher cost structure for two reasons. First, they have to add features and functions to their products that appeal to higher-income consumers, and this raises costs. For example, luxury retailer Nordstrom locates its stores in areas where real estate is expensive; its stores have costly fittings and fixtures and a wide-open store plan with lots of room to browse; and the merchandise is expensive and does not turn over as fast as the basic clothes and shoes sold at stores like Wal-Mart. Second, the relatively limited nature of demand associated with serving a given segment of the market may make it hard to attain economies of scale. Offsetting this, however, is the fact that the customization and exclusivity associated with a strategy of focusing on the high-income end of the market may enable a firm to charge significantly higher prices than enterprises pursuing standardization and segmentation strategies.

For companies focusing on the lower-income end of the market, or a segment that desires value for money, a different calculus comes into play. First, such companies tend to produce a more basic offering that is relatively inexpensive to produce and deliver. This may help them to drive down their cost structures. The retailer Costco, for example, focuses on consumers who seek value for money and are less concerned about brand than they are about price. Costco sells a limited range of merchandise in large, warehouse-like stores. A Costco store has about 3,750 stock-keeping units (SKUs), compared to 142,000 SKUs at the average Wal-Mart superstore. Products are stored on pallets stacked on utilitarian metal shelves. Costco offers consumers the opportunity to purchase basic goods such as breakfast cereal, dog food, and paper towels in bulk purchases and at lower prices than found elsewhere. It turns over

generic business-level strategy
A strategy that gives a company a specific form of competitive position and advantage vis-à-vis its rivals, resulting in above-average profitability.

broad low-cost strategy
When a company lowers costs so that it can lower prices and still make a profit.

broad differentiation strategy
When a company differentiates its product in some way, such as by recognizing different segments or offering different products to each segment.

focus low-cost strategy
When a company targets a certain segment or niche and tries to be the low-cost player in that niche.

focus differentiation strategy
When a company targets a certain segment or niche and customizes its offering to the needs of that particular segment through the addition of features and functions.

inventory rapidly, typically selling it before it has to pay its suppliers and thereby reducing its working capital needs. Thus, by tailoring its business to the needs of a segment, Costco is able to undercut the cost structure and pricing of a retail gain such as Wal-Mart, even though it lacks Wal-Mart's enormous economies of scale in purchasing. The drawback, of course, is that Costco offers much less choice than you will find at a Wal-Mart superstore; so, for customers looking for one-stop shopping at a low price, Wal-Mart is likely to be the store of choice.

▌BUSINESS-LEVEL STRATEGY CHOICES

We now have enough information to identify the basic, business-level strategy choices that companies make. These basic choices are sometimes called **generic business-level strategy**. The various choices are illustrated in Figure 5.4.

Companies that pursue a standardized or segmentation strategy both target a broad market. However, those pursuing a segmentation strategy recognize different segments and tailor their offering accordingly, whereas those pursuing a standardization strategy focus on serving the average consumer. Companies that target the broad market can either concentrate on lowering their costs so that they can lower prices and still make a profit, in which case they are pursuing a **broad low-cost strategy**, or they can try to differentiate their product in some way, in which case they are pursuing a **broad differentiation strategy**. Companies that decide to recognize different segments and offer different product to each one are by default pursuing a broad differentiation strategy. It is possible, however, to pursue a differentiation strategy while not recognizing different segments, as Coca-Cola did prior to the 1980s. Today, Wal-Mart pursues a broad low-cost strategy, whereas Toyota and Coca-Cola pursue a broad differentiation strategy.

Companies that target a few segments, or more typically, just one, are pursuing a focus or niche strategy. These companies can either try to be the low-cost player in that niche, as Costco has done, in which case we say they pursuing a **focus low-cost strategy**, or they can try to customize their offering to the needs of that particular segment through the addition of features and functions, as Virgin America has done, in which case we say they are pursuing a **focus differentiation strategy**.

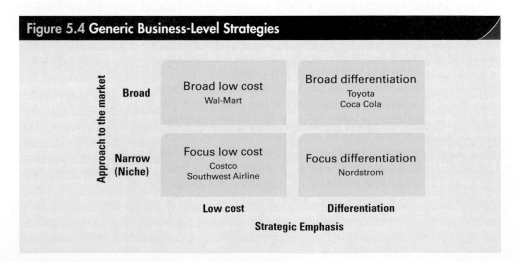

Figure 5.4 Generic Business-Level Strategies

It is important to understand that there is often no one best way to compete in an industry. Different strategies may be equally viable. Wal-Mart, Costco, and Nordstrom are all in the retail industry, all three compete in different ways, and all three have done very well financially. The important thing is that managers are confident in their business-level strategy, have clear logic for pursuing that strategy, have an offering that matches their strategy, and have aligned functional activities and organizational arrangements with that strategy in order to execute it well.

Michael Porter, the originator of the concept of generic business-level strategies, has argued that companies must make a clear choice between the different options outlined in Figure 5.4.[6] If they don't, Porter argues, they may become "stuck in the middle" and experience relatively poor performance. Central to Porter's thesis is the assertion that it is not possible to be both a differentiated company and a low-cost enterprise. According to Porter, differentiation by its very nature raises costs and makes it impossible to attain the low-cost position in an industry. By the same token, to achieve a low-cost position companies necessarily must limit spending on product differentiation.

There is certainly considerable value in this perspective. As we have noted, one company cannot be both Nordstrom and Wal-Mart, Timex and Rolex, Porsche and Kia, or Southwest and Virgin America. Low cost and differentiation are very different ways of competing—they require different functional strategies and different organizational arrangements. Trying to do both at the same time may not work. On the other hand, there are important caveats to this argument.

First—as we have already seen in this chapter when we discussed value innovation through improvements in process and product—a company can push out the efficiency frontier in its industry, redefining what is possible, and deliver more differentiation at a lower cost than its rivals. In such circumstances, a company might find itself in the fortunate position of being both the differentiated player in its industry and having a low-cost position. Ultimately its rivals might catch up, in which case it may well have to make a choice between emphasizing low cost and differentiation, but as we have seen from the case histories of Dell and Toyota, value innovators can gain a competitive advantage that lasts for years, if not decades (another example of value innovation is given in Strategy in Action 5.2, which recounts the history of Microsoft Office).

Second, it is important for the differentiated company to recognize that it cannot waver in its focus on efficiency. Similarly, the low-cost company cannot ignore product differentiation. The task facing a company pursuing a differentiation strategy is to be as efficient as possible given its choice of strategy. The differentiated company should not cut costs so deeply that it harms its capability to differentiate its offering from that of rivals. At the same time, it cannot let costs get out of control. Nordstrom, for example, is very efficient given its choice of strategic position. It is not a low-cost company by any means, but given its choice of how to compete it operates as efficiently as possible. Similarly, the low-cost company cannot totally ignore key differentiators in its industry. Wal-Mart does not provide the high level of customer service found at Nordstrom, but Wal-Mart cannot simply ignore customer service. Even though Wal-Mart has a self-service business model, employees are on hand to help customers with questions if needed. The task for low-cost companies such as Wal-Mart is to be "good enough" with regard to key differentiators. For another example of how this plays out, see Strategy in Action 5.2, which examines the competition between Google and Microsoft in the market for office-productivity software.

5.2 STRATEGY IN ACTION

Microsoft Office Versus Google Apps

Microsoft has long been the dominant player in the market for office productivity software with its Office suite of programs, which includes a word processor, spreadsheet, presentation software, and an e-mail client. Microsoft's rise to dominance in this market was the result of an important innovation—in 1989, Microsoft was the first company to bundle word processing, spreadsheet, and presentation programs together into a single offering that was interoperable. At the time, the market leader in word-processing software was Word Perfect; in spreadsheet software it was Lotus; and in presentation software it was Harvard Graphics. Microsoft was number 2 in each of these markets. However, by offering a bundle and pricing it below the price of each program purchased on its own, Microsoft grabbed share from its competitors, none of which had a full suite of offerings. In effect, Microsoft Office offered consumers more value (interoperability), at a lower price, than could be had from rivals.

As demand for Office expanded, Microsoft was able to spread the fixed costs of product development over a much larger volume than its rivals, and unit costs fell, giving Microsoft the double advantage of a differentiated product offering and a low-cost position. The results included the creation of a monopoly position in office-productivity software and two decades of extraordinary high returns for Microsoft in this market.

The landscape shifted in 2006, when Google introduced Google Apps, an online suite of office productivity software that was aimed squarely at Microsoft's profitable Office franchise. Unlike Office at the time, Google Apps was an online service. The basic programs reside on the cloud, and documents are saved on the cloud. At first, Google lacked a full suite of programs, and traction was slow, but since 2010 adoption of Google Apps has accelerated. Today, Google Apps offers the same basic programs as Office—a word processer, spreadsheet, presentation software, and an e-mail client—but far fewer features. Google's approach is not to match Office on features, but to *be good enough* for the majority of users. This helps to reduce development costs. Google also distributes Google Apps exclusively over the Internet, which is a very-low-cost distribution model, whereas Office still has a significant presence in the physical retail channel, raising costs.

In other words, Google is pursuing a low-cost strategy with regard to Google Apps. Consistent with this, Google Apps is priced significantly below Office. Google charges $50 a year for each person using its product. In contrast, Microsoft Office costs $400 per computer for business users (although significant discounts are often negotiated). Initially, Google Apps was targeted at small businesses and start-ups, but more recently, Google seems to be gaining traction in the enterprise space, which is Microsoft's core market for Office. In 2012, Google scored an impressive string of wins, including licenses with the Swiss drug company Hoffman La Roche, where over 80,000 employees use the package, and with the U.S. Interior Department, where 90,000 use it. In total, Google Apps earned approximately $1 billion in revenue in 2012. Estimates suggest that the company has more than 30 million paying subscribers. This still makes it a small offering relative to Microsoft Office, which is installed on over 1 billion computers worldwide. Microsoft Office, which generated $24 billion in revenue in 2012, remains Microsoft's most profitable business. However, Microsoft cannot ignore Google Apps.

Indeed, Microsoft is not standing still. In 2012, Microsoft rolled out its own cloud-based Office offering, Office 365. Office 365 starts at a list price of $72 a year per person, and it can cost as much as $240 per user annually in versions that offer many more features and software-development capabilities. According to a Microsoft spokesperson, demand for Office 365 is strong. Microsoft argues that Google cannot match the quality of the enterprise experience that Microsoft can provide in in areas like privacy, security, and data handling. Microsoft's message is clear—it still believes that Office is the superior product offering, differentiated by features, functions, privacy, data handing, and security. Whether Office 365 will keep Google Apps in check, however, remains to be seen.

Sources: Author interviews at Microsoft and Google; Q. Hardy, "Google Apps Moving onto Microsoft's Business Turf," *New York Times*, December 26, 2012; A. R. Hickey, "Google Apps: A $1-Billion Business?," *CRN*, February 3, 2012, www.crn.com.

BUSINESS-LEVEL STRATEGY, INDUSTRY, AND COMPETITIVE ADVANTAGE

Properly executed, a well-chosen, well-crafted business-level strategy can give a company a competitive advantage over actual and potential rivals. More precisely, it can put the company in an advantageous position relative to each of the competitive forces that we discussed in Chapter 2—specifically, the threat of entrants, the power of buyers and suppliers, the threat posed by substitute goods or services, and the intensity of rivalry between companies in the industry.

Consider first the low-cost company; by definition, the low-cost enterprise can make profits at price points that its rivals cannot profitably match. This makes it very hard for rivals to enter its market. In other words, the low-cost company can build an entry barrier into its market; it can, in effect, erect an economic moat around its business that thwarts higher-cost rivals. Amazon has done this in the online retail business. Through economies of scale and other operating efficiencies, Amazon has attained a very-low-cost structure that effectively constitutes a high entry barrier into this business. Rivals with less volume and fewer economies of scale than Amazon cannot match it on price without losing money—not a very appealing proposition.

A low-cost position and the ability to charge low prices and still make profits also protect a company against substitute goods or services. Low costs can help a company absorb cost increases that may be passed on downstream by powerful suppliers. Low costs can also enable the company to respond to demands for deep price discounts from powerful buyers and still make money. The low-cost company is often best positioned to survive price rivalry in its industry. Indeed, a low-cost company may deliberately initiate a price war in order to grow volume and drive its weaker rivals out of the industry. Dell did this during its glory days in the early 2000s, when it repeatedly cut prices for PCs to drive up sales volume and force marginal competitors out of the business. This strategy enabled Dell to become the largest computer company in the world by the mid-2000s.

Now let us consider the differentiated company. The successful differentiator is also protected against each of the competitive forces we discussed in Chapter 2. The brand loyalty associated with differentiation can constitute an important entry barrier, protecting the company's market from potential competitors. The brand loyalty enjoyed by Apple in the smartphone business has set a very high hurdle for any new entrant to match, and effectively acts as a deterrent to entry. Because the successful differentiator sells on non-price factors such as design or customer service, it is also less exposed to pricing pressure from powerful buyers. Indeed, the opposite may be the case—the successful differentiator may be able to implement price increases without encountering much, if any, resistance from buyers. The differentiated company can also fairly easily absorb price increases from powerful suppliers and pass them on downstream in the form of higher prices for its offerings, without suffering much, if any, loss in market share. The brand loyalty enjoyed by the differentiated company also protects it from substitute goods and service.

The differentiated company is protected from intense price rivalry within its industry by its brand loyalty, and by the fact that non-price factors are important to its customer set. At the same time, the differentiated company often does have to invest significant effort and resources in non-price rivalry, such as brand building through marketing campaigns or expensive product development efforts, but to the extent that it is successful, it can reap the benefits of these investments in the form of stable or higher prices.

This being said, it is important to note that focused companies often have an advantage over their broad market rivals in the segment or niche in which they compete in. For example, although Wal-Mart and Costco are both low-cost companies, Costco has a cost advantage over Wal-Mart in the segment that it serves. This primarily is due to the fact that Costco carries far fewer SKUs, and those it does are sold in bulk. However, if Costco tried to match Wal-Mart and serve the broader market, the need to carry a wider product selection (Wal-Mart has over 140,000 SKUs) means that its cost advantage would be lost.

The same can be true for a differentiated company. By focusing on a niche, and customizing the offering to that segment, a differentiated company can often outsell differentiated rivals that target a broader market. Thus, Porsche can outsell broad market companies like Toyota or General Motors in the high-end sports car niche of the market, in part because the company does not sell outside of its core niche. Porsche creates an image of exclusivity that appeals to its customer base. Were Porsche to start moving down market, it would lose this exclusive appeal and become just another broad market differentiator.

◤ IMPLEMENTING BUSINESS-LEVEL STRATEGY

As we have already suggested in this chapter, for a company's business-level strategy to translate into a competitive advantage, it must be well implemented. This means that actions taken at the functional level should support the business-level strategy, as should the organizational arrangements of the enterprise. There must, in other words, be *alignment* or *fit* between business-level strategy, functional strategy, and organization (see Figure 5.5). We have discussed functional strategy in Chapter 4; detailed discussion of organizational arrangements is postponed until Chapter 12. Notwithstanding, we will make some basic observations about the functional strategies and

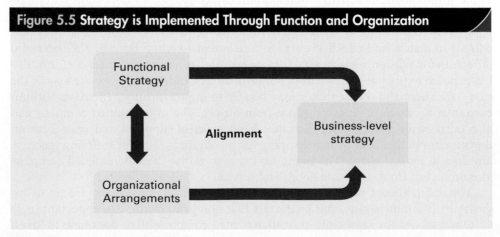

Figure 5.5 Strategy is Implemented Through Function and Organization

Functional Strategy

Alignment

Business-level strategy

Organizational Arrangements

Source: Charles W.L. Hill © Copyright 2013.

organizational arrangements required to implement the business-level strategies of low cost and differentiation.

Lowering Costs Through Functional Strategy and Organization

Companies achieve a low-cost position primarily by pursuing functional-level strategies that result in *superior efficiency* and *superior product reliability*, which we discussed in detail in Chapter 4 when we looked at functional-level strategy and the building blocks of competitive advantage. As you will recall from Chapter 4, the following are clearly important:

- Achieving economies of scale and learning effects.
- Adopting lean production and flexible manufacturing technologies.
- Implementing quality improvement methodologies to ensure that the goods or services the company produces are reliable, so that time, materials, and effort are not wasted producing and delivering poor-quality products that have to be scrapped, reworked, or reproduced from scratch
- Streamlining processes to take out unnecessary steps
- Using information systems to automate business process
- Implementing just-in-time inventory control systems
- Designing products that can be produced and delivered at as low a cost as possible
- Taking steps to increase customer retention and reduce customer churn

In addition, to lower costs the firm must be *organized* in such a way that the structure, control systems, incentive systems, and culture of the company all emphasize and reward employee behaviors and actions that are consistent with, or lead to, higher productivity and greater efficiency. As will be explained in detail in Chapter 12, the kinds of organizational arrangements that are favored in such circumstances include a flat organizational structure with very few levels in the management hierarchy, clear lines of accountability and control, measurement and control systems that focus on productivity and cost containment, incentive systems that encourage employees to work in as productive a manner as possible and empower them to suggest and pursue initiatives that are consistent with productivity improvements, and a frugal culture that emphasizes the need to control costs. Companies that operate with these organizational arrangements include Amazon and Wal-Mart.

Differentiation Through Functional-Level Strategy and Organization

As with low costs, to successfully differentiate itself a company must pursue the right actions at the functional level and organize itself appropriately. Pursuing functional-level strategies that enable the company to achieve *superior quality* in terms of both reliability and excellence are important, as is an emphasis upon *innovation* in the product offering, and high levels of *customer responsiveness*. You will recall from Chapters 3 and 4 that superior quality, innovation, and customer responsiveness are three of the four building blocks of competitive advantage, the other being *efficiency*. Remember, too, that the differentiated firm cannot ignore efficiency; by virtue of its strategic choice, the differentiated company is likely to have a higher cost structure than the low-cost player in its industry. Specific functional-level strategies designed to improve differentiation include:

- Customization of the product offering and marketing mix to different market segments
- Designing product offerings that have high perceived quality in terms of their functions, features, and performance, in addition to being reliable
- A well-developed customer-care function for quickly handling and responding to customer inquiries and problems
- Marketing efforts focused on brand building and perceived differentiation from rivals
- Hiring and employee development strategies designed to ensure that employees act in a manner that is consistent with the image that the company is trying to project to the world

As demonstrated in the opening case, Virgin America's successful differentiation is due to its excellent customer service, which is an element of customer responsiveness. Similarly, Apple has an excellent customer care function, as demonstrated by its in-store "Genius Bars," where well-trained employees are available to help customers with inquiries and problems, and provide tutorials to help them get the best value out of their purchases. Apple has also been very successful at building a brand that differentiates it from rivals such as Microsoft (for example, the long-running TV advertisements featuring "Mac," a very hip guy, and "PC," a short, overweight man in a shabby gray suit).

As regards organization, creating the right structure, controls, incentives, and culture can all help a company differentiate itself. In a differentiated enterprise, one key issue is to make sure that marketing, product design, customer service, and customer care functions all play a key role. Again consider Apple; following the return of Steve Jobs to the company in 1997, he reorganized to give the industrial design group the lead on all new product development efforts. Under this arrangement, industrial design, headed by Johnny Ive, reported directly to Jobs, and engineering reported to industrial design for purposes of product development. This meant that designers rather than engineers specified the look and feel of a new product, and engineers then had to design according to the parameters imposed by the design group. This is in contrast to almost all other companies in the computer and smartphone business, where engineering typically takes the lead on product development. Jobs felt that this organizational arrangement was necessary to ensure that Apple produced beautiful products that not only worked well, but also looked and felt elegant. Because Apple under Jobs was differentiating by design, design was given a pivotal position in the organization.[7]

Making sure that control systems, incentive systems, and culture are aligned with the strategic thrust is also extremely important for differentiated companies. We will return to and expand upon these themes in Chapter 12.

◤ COMPETING DIFFERENTLY: BLUE OCEAN STRATEGY

We have already suggested in this chapter that sometimes companies can fundamentally shift the game in their industry by figuring out ways to offer more value through differentiation at a lower cost than their rivals. We referred to this as *value innovation*, a term first coined by Chan Kim and Renee Mauborgne.[8] Kim and Mauborgne developed their ideas further in the bestselling book *Blue Ocean Strategy*.[9] Their basic proposition is that many successful companies have built their competitive advantage by redefining their product offering through value innovation and, in essence, creating a new market space. They describe the process of thinking through value innovation as searching for the blue ocean—which they characterize as a wide-open market space where a company can chart its own course.

One of their examples of a company that found its blue ocean is Southwest Airlines. From its conception, Southwest competed differently than other companies in the U.S. airline industry. Most important, Southwest saw its main competitors not as other airlines but as people who would typically drive or take a bus to travel. For Southwest, the focus was to reduce travel time for its customer set and do so in a way that was cheap, reliable, and convenient, so that they would prefer to fly rather than drive.

The first route that Southwest operated was between Houston and Dallas. To reduce total travel time, it decided to fly into the small, downtown airports in both cities, Hobby in Houston and Love Field in Dallas, rather than the large, intercontinental airports located an hour's drive outside of both cities. The goal was to reduce total travel time by eliminating the need to drive to reach a major airport outside the city before even beginning one's journey. Southwest put as many flights a day on the route as possible to make it convenient, and did everything possible to drive down operating costs so that it could charge low prices and still make a profit.

As the company grew and opened more routes, it followed the same basic strategy. Southwest always flew point to point, never routing passengers through hubs. Changing planes in a hub adds to total travel time and can hurt reliability, measured by on-time departures and arrivals, if connections are slow arriving or departing a hub due to adverse events such as bad weather delaying traffic somewhere in an airline's network. Southwest also dispensed with inflight meals, only offers coach-class seating, does not have lounges in airports for business-class passengers, and has standardized on one type of aircraft, the Boeing 737, which helps to raise reliability. The net result is that Southwest delivers more value *to its customer set* and does so at a lower cost than its rivals, enabling it to price lower than them and still make a profit. Southwest is a value innovator.

Kim and Mauborgne use the concept of a *strategy canvas* to map out how value innovators differ from their rivals. The strategy canvas for Southwest shown in Figure 5.6, shows that Southwest charges a low price and does not provide meals or lounges in airports, business-class seating, or connections through hubs (it flies point to point), but does provide friendly, quick, convenient, reliable low-cost service, *which is exactly what its customer set values.*

The whole point of the Southwest example, and other business case histories Kim and Mauborgne review, is to illustrate how many successful enterprises compete differently than their less successful rivals: They carve out a unique market space for themselves through value innovation. When thinking about how a company might redefine its market and craft a new business-level strategy, Kim and Mauborgne suggest that managers ask themselves the following questions:

1. **Eliminate**: Which factors that rivals take for granted in our industry can be eliminated, thereby reducing costs?
2. **Reduce**: Which factors should be reduced well below the standard in our industry, thereby lowering costs?
3. **Raise**: Which factors should be raised above the standard in our industry, thereby increasing value?
4. **Create**: What factors can we create that rivals do not offer, thereby increasing value?

Southwest *eliminated* lounges, business seating, and meals in flight; it *reduced* inflight refreshment to be well below industry standards; but by flying point to point it

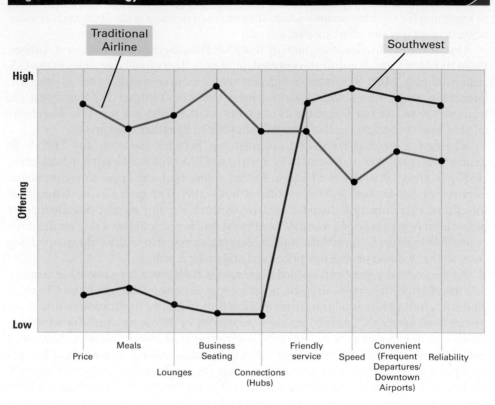

Figure 5.6 A Strategy Canvas for Southwest Airlines

raised speed (reducing travel time), convenience, and reliability. Southwest also *created* more value by flying between smaller, downtown airports whenever possible, something that other airlines did not typically do.

This is a useful framework, and it directs managerial attention to the need to think differently than rivals in order to create an offering and strategic position that are unique. If such efforts are successful, they can help a company build a sustainable advantage.

One great advantage of successful value innovation is that it can catch rivals off guard and make it difficult for them to catch up. For example, when Dell Computer started to sell direct to customers via the Internet, it was very difficult for rivals to respond because they had already invested in a different way of doing business—selling though a physical retail channel. Dell's rivals could not easily adopt the Dell model without alienating their channel, which would have resulted in lost sales. The prior strategic investment of Dell's rivals in distribution channels—which, at the time they were made, seemed reasonable—became a source of inertia that limited their ability to rapidly respond to Dell's innovations. The same holds true in the airline industry, where the prior strategic investments of traditional airlines have made it very difficult for them to respond to the threat posed by Southwest.

In sum, value innovation, because it shifts the basis of competition, can result in a sustained competitive advantage for the innovating company due to the relative inertia of rivals and their inability to respond in a timely manner without breaking prior strategic commitments.

KEY TERMS

business-level
   strategy 148
value innovation 153
market segmentation 155
standardization
   strategy 156

segmentation
   strategy 156
focus strategy 156
generic business-level
   strategy 158

broad low-cost
   strategy 158
broad differentiation
   strategy 158

focus low-cost
   strategy 158
focus differentiation
   strategy 158

TAKEAWAYS FOR STRATEGIC MANAGERS

1. Business-level strategy refers to the overarching competitive theme of a company in a given market.
2. At the most basic level, a company has a competitive advantage if it can lower costs relative to rivals and/or differentiate its product offering from those of rivals.
3. A low-cost position enables a company to make money at price points where its rivals are losing money.
4. A differentiated company can charge a higher price for its offering, and/or it can use superior value to generate growth in demand.
5. There are often multiple positions along the differentiation–low cost continuum that are viable in a market.
6. Value innovation occurs when a company develops new products, processes, or strategies that enable it to offer more value through differentiation at a lower cost than its rivals.
7. Formulating business-level strategy starts with deciding *who* the company is going to serve, what *needs* or *desires* it is trying to satisfy, and *how* it is going to satisfy those needs and desires.
8. Market segmentation is the process of subdividing a market into clearly identifiable groups of customers that have similar needs, desires, and demand characteristics.
9. A company's approach to market segmentation is an important aspect of its business-level strategy.
10. There are four generic business-level strategies: broad low cost, broad differentiation, focus low cost, and focus differentiation.
11. Business-level strategy is executed through actions taken at the functional level and through organizational arrangements.
12. Many successful companies have built their competitive advantage by redefining their product offering through value innovation and creating a new market space. The process of thinking through value innovation has been described as searching for a "blue ocean"—a wide-open market space where a company can chart its own course.

DISCUSSION QUESTIONS

1. What are the main differences between a low-cost strategy and a differentiation strategy?
2. Why is market segmentation such an important step in the process of formulating a business-level strategy?
3. How can a business-level strategy of (a) low cost and (b) differentiation offer some protection against competitive forces in a company's industry?
4. What is required to transform a business-level strategy from a concept to a reality?
5. What is meant by the term *value innovation*? Can you identify a company not discussed in the text that has established a strong competitive position through value innovation?

CLOSING CASE

Nordstrom

Nordstrom is one of American's most successful fashion retailers. John Nordstrom, a Swedish immigrant, established the company in 1901 with a single shoe store in Seattle. From the very start, Nordstrom's approach to business was to provide exceptional customer service, selection, quality, and value. This approach remains Nordstrom's hallmark today.

The modern Nordstrom is a fashion specialty chain with 240 stores in 31 states. Nordstrom generated almost $12.5 billion in sales in 2014 and makes consistently higher-than-average returns on invested capital. Its return on invested capital (ROIC) has consistently been in the mid teens to low 20s, and was 16.3% in 2014–strong performance for a retailer.

Nordstrom is a niche company. It focuses on a relatively affluent customer base that is looking for affordable luxury. The stores, located in upscale areas, have expensive fittings and fixtures that convey an impression of luxury. The stores invite browsing. Touches such as live music played on a grand piano help create an appealing atmosphere. The merchandise is fashionable and of high quality. What truly differentiates Nordstrom from many of its rivals, however, is its legendary excellence in customer service.

Nordstrom's salespeople are typically well groomed and dressed, polite and helpful, and known for their attention to detail. They are selected for their ability to interact with customers in a positive way. During the interview process for new employees, one of the most important questions asked of candidates is their definition of good customer service. Thank-you cards, home deliveries, personal appointments, and access to personal shoppers are the norm at Nordstrom. There is a no-questions-asked returns policy, with no receipt required. Nordstrom's philosophy is that the customer is always right. The company's salespeople are well compensated, with good benefits and commissions on sales that range from 6.75% to 10% depending on the department. Top salespeople at Nordstrom have the ability to earn over $100,000 a year, mostly in commissions.

The customer service ethos is central to the culture and organization of Nordstrom. The organization chart is an inverted pyramid, with salespeople on the top and the CEO at the bottom. According to CEO Blake Nordstrom, this is because "I work for them. My job is to make them as successful as possible." Management constantly shares anecdotes emphasizing the primacy of customer service at Nordstrom in order to reinforce the culture. One story relates that when a customer in Fairbanks, Alaska, wanted to return two tires (which Nordstrom does not sell), bought some time ago from another store once on the same site, a sales clerk looked up their price and gave him his money back!

Despite its emphasis on quality and luxury, Nordstrom has not neglected operating efficiency. Sales per square foot are $400 despite the large, open-plan nature of the stores, and inventory turns exceed 5 times per year, up from 3.5 times a decade ago. These are good figures for a high-end department store. Management constantly seeks ways to improve efficiency and customer service; recently, it put mobile checkout devices into the hands of 5,000 salespeople, eliminating the need for customers to wait in a checkout line.

Sources: A. Martinez, "Tale of Lost Diamond Adds Glitter to Nordstrom's Customer Service," *Seattle Times*, May 11, 2011 (www.seattletimes.com); C. Conte, "Nordstrom Built on Customer Service," *Jacksonville Business Journal*, September 7, 2012 (www.bizjournals.com/Jacksonville); W. S. Goffe, "How Working as a Stock Girl at Nordstrom Prepared Me for Being a Lawyer," *Forbes*, December 3, 2012; and P. Swinand, "Nordstrom Inc," Morningstar, February 22, 2013, www. Morningstar.com.

CASE DISCUSSION QUESTIONS

1. What is Nordstrom's segmentation strategy? Who does it serve?
2. With regard to its core segment, what does Nordstrom offer its customers?
3. Using the Porter model, which generic business-level strategy is Nordstrom pursuing?
4. What actions taken at the functional level have enabled Nordstrom to successfully implement its strategy?
5. What is the source of Nordstrom's long-term, sustainable competitive advantage? What valuable and rare resources does Nordstrom have that its rivals find difficult to imitate?
6. Is Nordstrom organized for success?

NOTES

[1]D. F. Abell, *Defining the Business: The Starting Point of Strategic Planning* (Englewood Cliffs, NJ: Prentice-Hall, 1980).

[2]M. E. Porter, *Competitive Advantage* (New York: Free Press, 1985); M. E. Porter, *Competitive Strategy* (New York, Free Press, 1980).

[3]C. W. L. Hill, "Differentiation Versus Low Cost or Differentiation and Low Cost: A Contingency Framework," *Academy of Management Review* 13 (1988): 401–412.

[4]M. E. Porter, "What Is Strategy?" *Harvard Business Review,* Onpoint Enhanced Edition Article, February 1, 2000.

[5]W.C. Kim and R. Mauborgne, "Value Innovation: The Strategic Logic of High Growth," *Harvard Business Review* (January–February 1997).

[6]Porter, *Competitive Advantage* and *Competitive Strategy*.

[7]The story was related to author Charles Hill by an executive at Apple.

[8]Kim and Mauborgne, "Value Innovation: The Strategic Logic of High Growth."

[9]W.C. Kim and R. Mauborgne, *Blue Ocean Strategy* (Boston, Mass: Harvard Business School Press, 2005).

sergign/Shutterstock.com

CHAPTER **6**

BUSINESS-LEVEL STRATEGY AND THE INDUSTRY ENVIRONMENT

OPENING CASE

Can Best Buy Survive the Rise of E-commerce?

Best Buy Co., Inc. is the world's largest retailer of consumer electronics, computers, mobile phones, and related products. In the United States it operates under the brands of Best Buy, Magnolia Audio Video, Pacific Sales, and Geek Squad. In Canada it owns the chain of stores Future Shop, and in China it operates the Five Star stores. In 2014, Best Buy was one of the top twenty retail brands in America.

The rise of e-commerce had been hard on consumer electronics stores. Many notable rivals such as Circuit City and CompUSA did not survive the pressure online shopping put on prices and margins, and liquidated their stores. In early 2015, even long-time electronics industry veteran Radio Shack announced it too would file bankruptcy and close its doors. Best Buy was the sole surviving multinational electronics retail chain.

©Vdovichenko Denis/Shutterstock.com

Globally, the consumer electronics market was maturing. The industry had experienced modest growth in the last few years—a compound annual growth rate of 0.8% from 2009-2013—and revenues of $253.9 billion in 2013. Most of that growth, however, was occurring in emerging markets. In the United States, consumer electronics spending was flat. Making things tougher for Best Buy was the fact that a growing percentage of consumer electronics spending was occurring online (over 20% in 2012) (see Figure 6.1). The online sales channel was a difficult one in which to compete. There was intense pressure on prices, almost no customer loyalty, and big, general purpose competitors such as Amazon, Target, and Wal-Mart (see Figure 6.2), along with large computer manufactures that sold in direct-to-customer channels.

Figure 6.1 U.S. Consumer Electronics Sales, Online versus Bricks and Mortar, 1999-2012

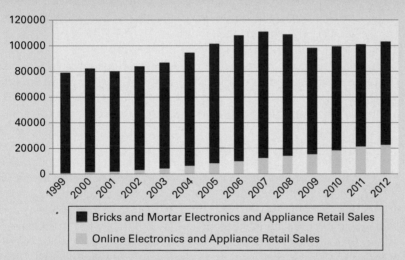

- ■ Bricks and Mortar Electronics and Appliance Retail Sales
- ▢ Online Electronics and Appliance Retail Sales

Sources: Census Bureau, Annual Trade Survey.

Figure 6.2 Major Consumer Electronics Retailers, 2013 sales (in $billions)

Best Buy	30.48
HP	29.07
Dell	24.93
Wal-Mart	22.27
Apple Stores	14.9
CDW Corp.	10.84
Staples	7.47
Target	7.4
Gamestop	7.19

Source: www.Hoovers.com

Though Best Buy had been working hard to build its web presence, online sales still only accounted for 8% of its U.S. revenues. Best Buy was thus still primarily a bricks-and-mortar retail chain that depended heavily on new product introductions in categories in which people wanted to physically compare products. When a new smartphone was introduced, for example, people often wanted to test it before committing to a purchase. Unfortunately for Best Buy, however, in many product categories people were increasingly relying on online reviews to make their purchase decisions; they could browse among various vendors to find the best price. This led to extreme price competition that made it difficult for retailers with a strong physical presence to compete, because that physical presence typically resulted in a high cost structure.

To combat online heavyweights like Amazon, Wal-Mart, and Target (and the growing threat from office-supply stores like Staples and Office Depot), Best Buy implemented a price-matching policy: If customers found a better price online, Best Buy would match it. This put intense pressure on margins, so the company engaged in several cost-cutting measures, including shuttering many stores and cutting 40,000 jobs between 2010 and 2014. It also implemented a program whereby online purchases would be shipped directly from local stores, which helped to match Amazon's speedy delivery times while simultaneously reducing inventory costs.

At the same time, Best Buy worked hard to differentiate its stores from the general purpose competitors. Best Buy salespeople underwent extensive training to ensure that they could provide knowledgeable assistance to customers, and its Geek Squad service provided advanced technical support and home installation services. Best Buy also avoided paying commissions to individual salespeople in order to prevent the use of aggressive sales tactics.

To attract shoppers, Best Buy created programs that would make their stores a destination for consumers to experience electronics products in ways that were more complex or immersive. For example, in 2014, it created "Connected Home" sections in 400 stores, where customers could experience ways of automating their homes with products like programmable lights and thermostats, and home surveillance systems that would enable them to keep an eye on the family pet. Customers found it difficult to shop for such products online; it was a product category that was still not well understood, and customers were often confused about the different components or features they might want to use. As described by Josh Will, senior vice president and general merchandise manager for cellphones, connected home products, and mobile stores, "We want to show them what's possible. That's very difficult to do in a digital-only environment."

To survive, Best Buy would have to be both lean and differentiated. By 2015, it looked like its efforts might pay off. Though the company had suffered losses in 2012 and 2013, it posted profits of $532 million for 2014, resulting in a razor-thin 1.25% profit margin. Though the company had taken a beating with the rise of online commerce, many analysts were betting that it would weather the storm, become a tougher competitor, and remain the winner in an increasingly difficult industry.

Sources: L. Gensler, "Best Buy Battered after Soft Sales Forecast, But Optimists Still Abound," *Forbes*, January 15, 2015, p. 4; J. Wieczner, "Which Fortune 500 Stocks Will Lift Off?," *Fortune*, June 16, 2014, pp. 90–92; Marketline; Hoovers.

OVERVIEW

In Chapter 2 we learned that industries go through a life cycle. Some industries are young and dynamic, with rapidly growing demand. Others are mature and relatively stable, whereas still other industries, like the bricks-and-mortar consumer electronics retailers described in the Opening Case, are in decline.

In this chapter we look at the different strategies that companies can pursue to strengthen their competitive position in each of these different stages of the industry life cycle. We will see that each stage in the evolution of its industry raises interesting challenges for a business. Managers must adopt the appropriate strategies to deal with these challenges.

For example, as illustrated in the Opening Case, many retailers that counted on having a physical presence in the form of local stores are now under intense pricing pressure from online retailers. Some, like Wal-Mart, Target, and Best Buy, have responded by investing heavily in an online presence. Others, like Circuit City, Border's bookstores, and Tower Records, succumbed to competitive pressure and disappeared. However, paradoxically, there is often still good money to be made in a declining industry if managers can figure out the right strategy. A niche strategy of focusing on market segments where demand remains strong is a classic way of making money in a declining industry. There are still many categories of products that customers want to experience in person before purchasing, for example, and Best Buy is hoping it can remain the leader in its declining industry by providing an exceptional experience to these customers.

Before we look at the different stages of an industry life cycle, we first consider strategy in a fragmented industry. We do this because fragmented industries can offer unique opportunities for enterprises to pursue strategies that result in the consolidation of those industries, often creating significant wealth for the consolidating enterprise and its owners.

STRATEGY IN A FRAGMENTED INDUSTRY

A **fragmented industry** is composed of a large number of small- and medium-sized companies. Examples of fragmented industries include the dry-cleaning, hair salon, restaurant, health club, massage, and legal services industries. There are several reasons that an industry may consist of many small companies rather than a few large ones.[1]

fragmented industry
An industry composed of a large number of small- and medium-sized companies.

Reasons for Fragmentation

There are three reasons for fragmentation. First, a lack of scale economies may mean that there are few, if any, cost advantages to large size. There are no obvious scale economies in landscaping and massage services, for example, which helps explain why these industries remain highly fragmented. In some industries customer needs are so specialized that only a small amount of a product is required; hence, there is no scope for a large, mass-production operation to satisfy the market. Custom-made jewelry and catering are examples of this. In some industries there may even be diseconomies of scale. In the restaurant business, for example, customers often prefer the unique food and style of a popular, local restaurant, rather than the standardized offerings of a national chain. This diseconomy of scale places a limit on the ability of large restaurant chains to dominate the market.

Second, brand loyalty in the industry may primarily be local. It may be difficult to build a brand through differentiation that transcends a particular location or region. Many homebuyers, for example, prefer dealing with local real estate agents, whom they perceive as having better local knowledge than national chains. Similarly, there are no large chains in the massage services industry because differentiation and brand loyalty are primarily driven by differences in the skill sets of individual massage therapists.

Third, the lack of scale economies and national brand loyalty implies low entry barriers. When this is the case, a steady stream of new entrants may keep the industry fragmented. The massage services industry exemplifies this situation. Due to the absence of scale requirements, the costs of opening a massage services business can be shouldered by a single entrepreneur. The same is true of landscaping services, which helps to keep that industry fragmented.

In industries that have these characteristics, focus strategies tend to work best. Companies may specialize by customer group, customer need, or geographic region. Many small, specialty companies may operate in local or regional markets. All kinds of specialized or custom-made products fall into this category, as do all small, service operations that cater to personalized customer needs.

Consolidating a Fragmented Industry Through Value Innovation

Business history is full of examples of entrepreneurial organizations that have pursued strategies to create meaningful scale economies and national brands where none previously existed. In the process they have consolidated industries that were once fragmented, reaping enormous gains for themselves and their shareholders in the process.

For example, until the 1980s, the office-supply business was a highly fragmented industry composed of many small, "mom-and-pop" enterprises that served local markets. The typical office-supply enterprise in those days had a limited selection of products, low inventory turnover, limited operating hours, and a focus on providing personal service to local businesses. Customer service included having a small sales force, which visited businesses and took orders, along with several trucks that delivered merchandise to larger customers. Then along came Staples, started by executives who had cut their teeth in the grocery business; they opened a big-box store with a wide product selection, long operating hours, and a self-service business model. They implemented computer information systems to track product sales and make sure that inventory was replenished just before it was out of stock, which drove up inventory turnover. True, Staples did not initially offer the same level of personal service that established office-supply enterprises did, but the managers of Staples made a bet that small-business customers were more interested in value from a wide product selection, long opening hours, and low prices—and they were right! Put differently, the managers at Staples had a different view of what was important to their customer set than did the established enterprises. Today, Staples, Office Depot, and Office Max dominate the office-supply industry, and most of their small rivals have gone out of businesses.

You may recognize in the Staples story a theme that we discussed in the Chapter 5: Staples is a *value innovator*.[2] The company's founders figured out a way to offer more value to their customer set, and to do so at a lower cost. Nor have they been alone in doing so. In the retail sector, for example, Wal-Mart and Target did a similar thing in general merchandise, Lowes and Home Depot pulled off the same trick in building materials and home improvement, and Barnes and Noble did this in book retailing. In the restaurant sector, MacDonald's, Taco Bell, Kentucky Fried Chicken, and, more recently, Starbucks have all followed a similar course. In each case, these enterprises succeeded in consolidating once-fragmented industries.

The lesson is clear: Fragmented industries are wide-open market spaces—blue oceans—just waiting for entrepreneurs to transform them through the pursuit of value innovation. A key to understanding this process is to recognize that in each case, the value innovator defines value differently than do the established companies, and finds a way to offer that value that lowers costs through the creation of scale economies. In fast food, for example, McDonald's offers reliable, quick, convenient fast food, and does so at a low cost. The low cost has two sources—first, the standardization of processes within each store, which boosts labor productivity, and second, the attainment of scale economies on the input side due to McDonald's considerable purchasing power (which grew over time as the McDonald's chain grew). McDonald's was a value innovator in its day, and through its choice of strategy it helped to drive consolidation in the fast-food segment of the restaurant industry.

Chaining and Franchising

In many fragmented industries that have been consolidated through value innovation, the transforming company often starts with a single location, or just a few locations. This was true for Best Buy, which started as a single store (called Sound of Music) in Saint Paul, Minnesota, and Starbucks, which had just three stores in Seattle, Washington, when Howard Shultz took over and started to transform the business. The key is to get the strategy right at the first few locations, and then expand as rapidly as possible to build a national brand and realize scale economies before rivals move into the market. If this is done right, the value innovator can build formidable barriers to new entry by establishing strong brand loyalty and enjoying the scale economies that come from large size (often, these scale economies are associated with purchasing power).

There are two strategies that enterprises use to *replicate* their offering once they get it right. One is chaining and the other is franchising.[3]

Chaining involves opening additional locations that adhere to one, basic formula, *and that the company owns*. Thus, Staples pursued a chaining strategy when it quickly opened additional stores after perfecting its formula at its first location in Boston. Today, Staples has over 2,000 stores worldwide. Starbuck, too, has pursued a chaining strategy, offering the same basic formula in every store that it opens. Its store count now exceeds 21,000 in 63 countries. Best Buy, Wal-Mart, Barnes & Noble, and Home Depot have also all pursued a chaining strategy.

By expanding through chaining, a value innovator can quickly build a national brand. This may be of significant value in a mobile society, such as the United States, where people move and travel frequently, and when in a new town or city they look for familiar offerings. At the same time, by rapidly opening locations, and by knitting those locations together through good information systems, the value innovator can

chaining

A strategy designed to obtain the advantages of cost leadership by establishing a network of linked merchandising outlets interconnected by information technology that functions as one large company.

realize many of the cost advantages that come from large size. Wal-Mart, for example, uses a hub-and-spoke distribution system that is monitored real-time through a satellite-based information system that enables it to tightly control the flow of inventory through its stores. This tight control allows it to customize inventory for particular regions based on sales patterns and maximize inventory turnover (a major source of cost savings). In addition, as Wal-Mart grew, it was able to exercise more and more bargaining power over suppliers, driving down the price for the goods that it then resold in its stores.

franchising

A strategy in which the franchisor grants to its franchisees the right to use the franchisor's name, reputation, and business model in return for a franchise fee and often a percentage of the profits.

Franchising is similar in many respects to chaining, except that in the case of franchising the founding company—the franchisor—licenses the right to open and operate a new location to another enterprise—franchisee—in return for a fee. Typically, franchisees must adhere to some strict rules that require them to adopt the same basic business model and operate in a certain way. Thus, a McDonald's franchisee has to have the same basic look, feel, offerings, pricing, and business processes as other restaurants in the system, and has to report standardized financial information to McDonald's on a regular basis.

There are advantages to using a franchising strategy. First, normally the franchisee puts up some or all of the capital to establish his or her operation. This helps to finance the growth of the system and can result in more rapid expansion. Second, because franchisees are the owners of their operations, and because they often put up capital, they have a strong incentive to make sure that their operations are run as efficiently and effectively as possible, which is good for the franchisor.

Third, because the franchisees are entrepreneurs who own their own businesses, they have an incentive to improve the efficiency and effectiveness of their operations by developing new offerings and/or processes. Typically, the franchisor will give them some latitude to do this, as long as they do not deviate too much from the basic business model. Ideas developed in this way may then be transferred to other locations, improving the performance of the entire system. For example, McDonald's has recently been changing the design and menu of its restaurants in the United States based on ideas first pioneered by a franchisee in France.

The drawbacks of a franchising strategy are threefold. First, it may allow less control than can be achieved through a chaining strategy, because, by definition, a franchising strategy delegates some authority to the franchisee. Howard Shultz of Starbucks, for example, decided to expand primarily via a chaining strategy rather than a franchising strategy because he felt that franchising would not give Starbucks the necessary control over customer service in each store. Second, in a franchising system the franchisee captures some of the economic profit from a successful operation, whereas in a chaining strategy it all flows to the company. Third, because franchisees are small relative to the founding enterprise, they may face a higher cost of capital, which raises system costs and lowers profitability. Given these various pros and cons, the choice between chaining and franchising depends on managers evaluating which strategy is best given the circumstances facing the founding enterprise.

Horizontal Mergers

Another way of consolidating a fragmented industry is to merge with or acquire competitors, combining them into a single, larger enterprise that is able to realize scale economies and build a compelling national brand. For example, in the aerospace and defense contracting business there are many small, niche producers that build the components installed into large products such as Boeing jets or military aircraft. Esterline, a company based in Bellevue, Washington, has been pursuing horizontal mergers and acquisitions, trying to consolidate this tier of suppliers. Esterline started off as a small supplier. Over the last decade it has acquired another 30 or so niche companies, building a larger enterprise that now has sales of almost $2 billion. Esterline's belief is that, as a larger enterprise offering a full portfolio of defense and avionic products, it can gain an edge over smaller rivals when selling to companies like Boeing and Lockheed, while its larger size enables it to realize scale economies and lowers its cost of capital.

It is worth noting that although mergers and acquisitions can help a company consolidate a fragmented industry, the road to success when pursuing this strategy is littered with failures. Some companies pay too much for the companies they acquire. Others find out after the acquisition that they have bought a "lemon" that is nowhere as efficient as they thought prior to the acquisition. Still others discover that the gains envisaged for an acquisition are difficult to realize due to a clash between the culture of the acquiring and acquired enterprises. We will consider the benefits, costs, and risks associated with a strategy of horizontal mergers and acquisitions in Chapters 9 and 10 when we look at corporate-level strategy

▼ STRATEGIES IN EMBRYONIC AND GROWTH INDUSTRIES

As Chapter 2 discusses, an embryonic industry is one that is just beginning to develop, and a growth industry is one in which first-time demand is rapidly expanding as many new customers enter the market. Choosing the strategies needed to succeed in such industries poses special challenges because new groups of customers with different needs enter the market. Managers must be aware of the way competitive forces in embryonic and growth industries change over time because they frequently need to develop new competencies and refine their business strategy in order to effectively compete in the future.

Most embryonic industries emerge when a technological innovation creates a new product opportunity. For example, in 1975, the personal computer (PC) industry was born after Intel developed the microprocessor technology that allowed companies to build the world's first PCs; this spawned the growth of the PC software industry that took off after Microsoft developed an operating system for IBM.[4]

Customer demand for the products of an embryonic industry is initially limited for a variety of reasons, including: (1) the limited performance and poor quality of the first products; (2) customer unfamiliarity with what the new product can do for them; (3) poorly developed distribution channels to get the product to customers; (4) a lack of complementary products that might increase the value of the product for customers; and (5) high production costs because of small volumes of production.

Customer demand for the first cars, for example, was limited by their poor performance (they were no faster than a horse, far noisier, and frequently broke down), a lack of important complementary products (such as a network of paved roads and gas stations), and high production costs that made these cars an expensive luxury (before Ford invented the assembly line, cars were built by hand in a craft-based production setting). Similarly, demand for electric cars is currently limited because many customers are unfamiliar with the technology and its implications for service and resale value. Customers also worry about whether there are charging stations along routes they will drive, or worry that charging will take too long. Because of such concerns, early demand for the products of embryonic industries typically comes from a small set of technologically savvy customers willing and able to tolerate, and even enjoy, the imperfections in their new purchase. Early adopters of electric cars, for example, tend to have higher-than-average incomes and are highly motivated to buy a car that is environmentally friendly.

mass market
One in which large numbers of customers enter the market.

An industry moves from the embryonic stage to the growth stage when a mass market starts to develop for its product. A **mass market** is one in which large numbers of customers enter the market. Mass markets emerge when three things happen: (1) ongoing technological progress makes a product easier to use, and increases its value for the average customer; (2) complementary products are developed that also increase its value; and (3) companies in the industry work to find ways to reduce the costs of producing the new products so they can lower their prices and stimulate high demand.[5] For example, the mass market for cars emerged and the demand for cars surged when: (1) technological progress increased the performance of cars; (2) a network of paved roads and gas stations was established; and (3) Henry Ford began to mass-produce cars using an assembly-line process, dramatically reducing production costs and enabling him to decrease prices and build consumer demand. Similarly, the mass market for PCs emerged when technological advances made computers easier to use, a supply of complementary software (such as spreadsheet and word-processing programs) was developed, and companies in the industry (such as Dell) began to use mass production to build PCs at low cost.

The Changing Nature of Market Demand

Managers who understand how the demand for a product is affected by the changing needs of customers can focus on developing new strategies that will protect and strengthen their competitive position, such as building competencies to lower production costs or speed product development. In most product markets, the changing needs of customers lead to the S-shaped growth curve in Figure 6.3.[6] This illustrates how different groups of customers with different needs enter the market over time. The curve is S-shaped because adoption is initially slow when an unfamiliar technology is introduced to the market. Adoption accelerates as the technology becomes better understood and utilized by the mass market, and eventually the market is saturated. The rate of new adoptions then declines as demand is increasingly limited to replacement demand.[7] For instance, electronic calculators were adopted upon their introduction by a relatively small pool of scientists and engineers. This group had previously used slide rules. Then, the calculator began to penetrate the larger markets of accountants and commercial users, followed by the still-larger market that included students and the general public. After these markets had become saturated, fewer opportunities remained for new adoptions. This curve has major implications for a company's differentiation, cost, and pricing decisions.

The first group of customers to enter the market is referred to as *innovators*. Innovators are "technocrats" or "gadget geeks"; people who are delighted to be the first to purchase and experiment with a product based on a new technology—even if it is imperfect and expensive. Frequently, innovators have technical talents and interests,

Figure 6.3 Market Development and Customer Groups

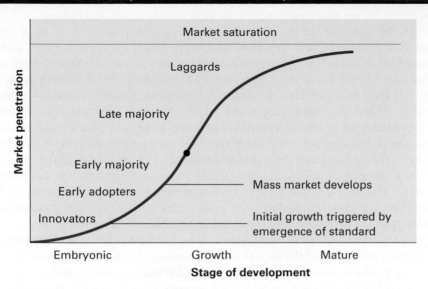

which drive them to "own" and develop new technology. They tend to be less risk averse than other customer groups, and often have greater resources to spare. Though they are not always well integrated into social networks, they are influential in new-product adoption because they are the first to bring a new idea into the social system. In the PC market, the first customers were software engineers and computer hobbyists who wanted to write computer code at home.[8]

Early adopters are the second group of customers to enter the market; they understand that the technology may have important future applications and are willing to experiment with it to see if they can pioneer new uses for the technology. They are comfortable with technical information, and will adopt products that seem appealing even if none of their peers have purchased those products. Early adopters often envision how the technology may be used in the future, and they try to be the first to profit from its use. Jeff Bezos, the founder of Amazon.com, was an early adopter of Web technology. In 1994, before anyone else, he saw that the Web could be used in innovative ways to sell books.

Innovators and early adopters alike enter the market while the industry is in its embryonic stage. The next group of customers, the *early majority*, forms the leading wave or edge of the mass market. Their entry into the market signifies the beginning of the growth stage. Customers in the early majority are practical and generally understand the value of new technology. They weigh the benefits of adopting new products against the costs, and wait to enter the market until they are confident they will benefit. When the early majority decides to enter the market, a large number of new buyers may be expected. This occurred in the PC market after IBM's introduced the PC in 1981. For the early majority, IBM's entry into the market signaled that the benefits of adopting the new PC technology would be worth the cost to purchase, and the time spent to learn how to use, a PC. The growth of the PC market was further strengthened by the development of applications that added value to the PC and transformed it from a hobby into a business-productivity tool. The same process unfolded in the smartphone market after Apple introduced its iPhone in 2007. The early majority entered the market at that point because these customers saw the value that a smartphone could deliver, and they were comfortable adopting new technology.

When the mass market reaches a critical mass, with about 30% of the potential market penetrated, the next group of customers enters the market. This group is characterized as the *late majority*, the customers who purchase a new technology or product only when many of their peers already have done so and it is obvious the technology has great utility and is here to stay. A typical late majority customer group is a somewhat "older" and more conservative set of customers. They are often unfamiliar with the advantages of new technology. The late majority can be a bit nervous about buying new technology but will do so if they see many people adopting it and finding value in it. The late majority did not start to enter the PC market until the mid-1990s, when they saw people around them engaging in email exchanges and browsing the Web, and it became clear that these technologies were here to stay. In the smartphone business, the late majority started to enter the market in 2012, when it became clear that smartphones were becoming the dominant mobile-phone technology.

Laggards, the last group of customers to enter the market, are inherently conservative and unappreciative of the uses of new technology. Laggards frequently refuse to adopt new products even when the benefits are obvious, or unless they are forced to do so by circumstances—for example, due to work-related reasons. People who use typewriters rather than computers to write letters and books are laggards. Given the fast rate of adoption of smartphones in the United States, it will not be long before the only people not in the smartphone market are laggards. These consumers will either continue to use basic wireless phones, or may reject a wireless phone altogether, relying instead on increasingly outdated, traditional, landline phones.

In Figure 6.4, the bell-shaped curve represents the total market, and the divisions in the curve show the average percentage of buyers who fall into each of these customer groups. Note that early adopters are a very small percentage of the market; hence, the

Figure 6.4 Market Share of Different Customer Segments

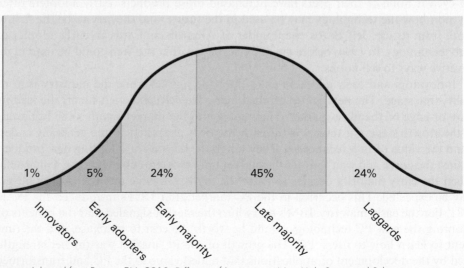

1% 5% 24% 45% 24%

Innovators   Early adopters   Early majority   Late majority   Laggards

Source: Adapted from Rogers, EM. 2010. Diffusion of Innovations. New York: Simon and Schuster.

figure illustrates a vital competitive dynamic—the highest market demand and industry profits arise when the early and late majority groups enter the market. Additionally, research has found that although early pioneering companies succeed in attracting innovators and early adopters, many of these companies often *fail* to attract a significant share of early and late majority customers, and ultimately go out of business.[9]

Strategic Implications: Crossing the Chasm

Why are pioneering companies often unable to create a business model that allows them to be successful over time and remain as market leaders? *Innovators and early adopters have very different customer needs from the early majority.* In an influential book, Geoffrey Moore argues that because of the differences in customer needs between these groups, the business-level strategies required for companies to succeed in the emerging mass market are quite different from those required to succeed in the embryonic market.[10] Pioneering companies that do not change the strategies they use to pursue their business model will therefore lose their competitive advantage to those companies that implement new strategies aimed at best serving the needs of the early and late majority. New strategies are often required to strengthen a company's business model as a market develops over time for the following reasons:

- Innovators and early adopters are technologically sophisticated customers willing to tolerate the limitations of the product. The early majority, however, values ease of use and reliability. Companies competing in an embryonic market typically pay more attention to increasing the performance of a product than to its ease of use and reliability. Those competing in a mass market need to make sure that the product is reliable and easy to use. Thus, the product development strategies required for success vary as a market develops over time.
- Innovators and early adopters are typically reached through specialized distribution channels, and products are often sold by word of mouth. They are active consumers of technical information. Reaching the early majority requires mass-market distribution channels and mass-media advertising campaigns that require a different set of marketing and sales strategies.
- Because innovators and the early majority are relatively few in number and are not particularly price sensitive, companies serving them typically pursue a focus model, produce small quantities of a product, and price high. To serve the rapidly growing mass market, large-scale mass production may be critical to ensure that a high-quality product can be reliably produced at a low price point.

In sum, the business models and strategies required to compete in an embryonic market populated by early adopters and innovators are very different from those required to compete in a high-growth, mass market populated by the early majority. As a consequence, the transition between the embryonic market and the mass market is not a smooth, seamless one. Rather, it represents a *competitive chasm* or gulf that companies must cross. According to Moore, many companies do not or cannot develop the right business model; they fall into the chasm and go out of business. Thus, although embryonic markets are typically populated by numerous small companies, once the mass market begins to develop, the number of companies sharply decreases.[11] For a detailed example of how this unfolds, see Strategy in Action 6.1, which explains how Microsoft and Research in Motion fell into the chasm in the smartphone market, whereas Apple leaped across it with its iPhone, a product designed for the early majority.

6.1 STRATEGY IN ACTION

Crossing the Chasm in the Smartphone Market

The first smartphones appeared in the early 2000s. Early market leaders included Research in Motion (RIM), with its Blackberry line of smartphones, and Microsoft, whose Windows Mobile operating system powered a number of early smartphone offerings made by companies such as Motorola. These phones were sold to business users and marketed as business productivity tools. They had small screens and a physical keyboard crammed onto a relatively small device. Although they had the ability to send and receive e-mails, browse the Web, and so on, there was no independent applications market, and consequently the utility of the phones was very limited. Nor were they always easy to use. System administrators were often required to set up basic features such as corporate e-mail access. They were certainly not consumer-friendly devices. The customers at this time were primarily innovators and early adopters.

The market changed dramatically after the introduction of the Apple iPhone in 2007 (see Figure 6.5). First,

this phone was aimed not at power business users, but at a broader consumer market. Second, the phone was easy to use, with a large, touch-activated screen and a virtual keyboard that vanished when not in use. Third, the phone was stylishly designed, with an elegance that appealed to many consumers. Fourth, Apple made it very easy for independent developers to write applications that could run on the phone, and they set up an App store that made it easy for developers to market their apps. Very quickly, new applications started to appear that added value to the phone. These included mapping applications, news feeds, stock information, and a wide array of games, several of which soon became big hits. Clearly, the iPhone was a device squarely aimed not at business users but at consumers. The ease of use and utility of the iPhone quickly drew the early majority into the market, and sales surged. Meanwhile, sales of Blackberry devices and Windows Mobile phones started to spiral downward.

Both Microsoft and Blackberry were ultimately forced to abandon their existing phone platforms and

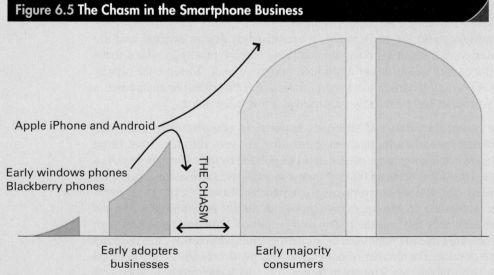

Figure 6.5 The Chasm in the Smartphone Business

Apple iPhone and Android

Early windows phones
Blackberry phones

THE CHASM

Early adopters
businesses

Early majority
consumers

Source: Adapted from Moore, GA. 2009. Crossing the Chasm: Marketing and selling high tech products to mainstream customers. New York: Harper Collins.

strategies, and reorient themselves. Both developed touch-activated screens similar to those on the iPhone, launched app stores, and targeted consumers. However, it may have been too late for them. By early 2015, both former market leaders had market shares in the single digits, whereas Apple's iPhone and Google's Android (which imitated many of the design and technical features of the iPhone) dominated the market.

Sources: Anonymous, "iPhone tops 1 Millionth Sale," *Information Today* 24 (9), 2007, p. 27; Anonymous, "The Battle for the Smart-phone's Soul," *The Economist,* November 22, 2008, pp. 76–77; L. Dignan, "Android, Apple iOS Flip Consumer, Corporate Market Share," *Between the Lines,* February 13, 2013; IDC: Smartphone OS Market Share, Q1, 2015, www.idc.com.

The implication is clear: To cross the chasm successfully, managers must correctly identify the needs of the first wave of early majority users—the leading edge of the mass market. Then they must adjust their business models by developing new strategies to redesign products and create distribution channels and marketing campaigns to satisfy the needs of the early majority. They must have a suitable product available at a reasonable price to sell to the early majority when they begin to enter the market in large numbers. At the same time, industry pioneers must abandon outdated, focused business models directed at the needs of innovators and early adopters. Focusing on an outdated model leads managers to ignore the needs of the early majority—and the need to develop the strategies necessary to pursue a differentiation or cost-leadership business model in order to remain a dominant industry competitor.

Strategic Implications of Differences in Market Growth Rates

Managers must understand a final, important issue in embryonic and growth industries: Different markets develop at different rates. The speed at which a market develops can be measured by its growth rate, that is, the rate at which customers in that market purchase the industry's product. A number of factors explain the variation in market growth rates for different products, and thus the speed with which a particular market develops. It is important for managers to understand the source of these differences because their choice of strategy can accelerate or retard the rate at which a market grows.[12]

The first factor that accelerates customer demand is a new product's *relative advantage*; that is, the degree to which a new product is perceived as being better at satisfying customer needs than the product it supersedes. For example, the early growth in demand for cell phones was partly driven by their economic benefits. Studies showed that because business customers could always be reached by cell phone, they made better use of their time—for example, by not showing up at a meeting that had been cancelled at the last minute—and saved 2 hours per week in time that would otherwise have been wasted. For busy executives—the early adopters—the productivity benefits of owning a cell phone outweighed the costs. Cell phones also rapidly diffused for social reasons, in particular, because they conferred glamour or prestige upon their users (something that also drives demand for today's most advanced smartphones).

A second factor of considerable importance is *complexity*. Products that are viewed by consumers as being complex and difficult to master will diffuse more slowly than products that are easy to master. The early PCs diffused quite slowly because many people saw the archaic command lines needed operate a PC as being very complex and intimidating. PCs did not become a mass-market device until graphical user interfaces with onscreen icons became widespread, enabling users to open programs and perform functions by pointing and clicking with a mouse. In contrast, the first cell phones were simple to use and quickly adopted.

Another factor driving growth in demand is *compatibility*, the degree to which a new product is perceived as being consistent with the current needs or existing values of potential adopters. Demand for cell phones grew rapidly because their operation was compatible with the prior experience of potential adopters who used traditional, landline phones. A fourth factor is *trialability*, the degree to which potential customers can experiment with a new product during a hands-on trial basis. Many people first used cell phones by borrowing them from colleagues to make calls, and their positive experiences helped accelerate growth rates. In contrast, early PCs were more difficult to experiment with because they were rare and expensive, and because some training was needed in how to use them. These complications led to slower growth rates for PCs. A final factor is *observability*, the degree to which the results of using and enjoying a new product can be seen and appreciated by other people. Originally, the iPhone and Android phones diffused rapidly because it became obvious that their owners were putting them to many different uses.

Thus, managers must devise strategies that educate customers about the value of their new products if they are to grow demand over time. In addition, they need to design their products to overcome barriers to adoption by making them less complex and intimidating, and easy to use, and by showcasing their relative advantage over prior technology. This is exactly what Apple did with the iPhone, which helps explain the rapid diffusion of smartphones after Apple introduced its first iPhone in 2007.

When a market is rapidly growing, and the popularity of a new product increases or spreads in a way that is analogous to a *viral model of infection*, a related strategic issue arises. Lead adopters (the first customers who buy a product) in a market become "infected" or enthused with the product, as exemplified by iPhone users. Subsequently, lead adopters infect others by telling them about the advantages of products. After observing its benefits, these people also adopt and use the product. Companies promoting new products can take advantage of viral diffusion by identifying and aggressively courting opinion leaders in a particular market—the customers whose views command respect. For example, when the manufacturers of new, high-tech medical equipment such as magnetic resonance imaging (MRI) scanners market a new product, they try to get well-known doctors at major research and teaching hospitals to use the product first. Companies may give these opinion leaders (the doctors) free machines for research purposes, and work closely with the doctors to further develop the technology. Once these opinion leaders commit to the product and give it their stamp of approval, doctors at other hospitals often follow.

In sum, understanding competitive dynamics in embryonic and growth industries is an important strategic issue. The ways in which different kinds of customer groups emerge and the ways in which customer needs change are important determinants of the strategies that need to be pursued to make a business model successful over time. Similarly, understanding the factors that affect a market's growth rate allows managers to tailor their business model to a changing industry environment. (Competition in high-tech industries is discussed further in the Chapter 7.)

STRATEGY IN MATURE INDUSTRIES

A mature industry is commonly dominated by a small number of large companies. Although a mature industry may also contain many medium-sized companies and a host of small, specialized companies, the large companies often determine the nature of competition in the industry because they can influence the six competitive forces. Indeed, these large companies hold their leading positions because they have developed the most successful business models and strategies in an industry.

By the end of the shakeout stage, companies have learned how important it is to analyze each other's business model and strategies. They also know that if they change their strategies, their actions are likely to stimulate a competitive response from industry rivals. For example, a differentiator that starts to lower its prices because it has adopted a more cost-efficient technology not only threatens other differentiators, but may also threaten cost leaders that see their competitive advantage being eroded. Hence, by the mature stage of the life cycle, companies have learned the meaning of competitive interdependence.

As a result, in mature industries, business-level strategy revolves around understanding how established companies *collectively* attempt to moderate the intensity of industry competition in order to preserve both company and industry profitability. Interdependent companies can protect their competitive advantage and profitability by adopting strategies and tactics, first, to deter entry into an industry, and second, to reduce the level of rivalry within an industry.

Strategies to Deter Entry

In mature industries, successful enterprises have normally gained substantial economies of scale and established strong brand loyalty. As we saw in Chapter 2, the economies of scale and brand loyalty enjoyed by incumbents in an industry constitute strong barriers to entry. However, there may be cases in which scale and brand, although significant, are not sufficient to deter entry. In such circumstances there are other strategies that companies can pursue to make new entry less likely. These strategies include product proliferation, limit pricing, technology upgrading, and strategic commitments.[13]

Product Proliferation   One way in which companies try to enter a mature industry is by looking for market segments or niches that are poorly served by incumbent enterprises. This strategy involves entering these segments, gaining experience, scale, and brand in that segment, and then progressively moving upmarket. This is how Japanese automobile companies first entered the U.S. market in the late 1970s and early 1980s. They targeted segments at the bottom end of the market for small, inexpensive, fuel-efficient cars. These segments were not well served by large American manufacturers such as Ford and GM. Once companies like Toyota and Honda had gained a strong position in these segments, they started to move upmarket with larger offerings and ultimately entered the pickup truck and SUV markets, which historically had been the most profitable segments of the automobile industry for American companies.

A **product proliferation strategy** involves incumbent companies attempting to forestall entry by making sure that *every* niche or segment in the marketplace is well served. Had U.S. automobile companies pursued product proliferation in the 1970s and early

product proliferation strategy
The strategy of "filling the niches" or catering to the needs of customers in all market segments to deter entry by competitors.

1980s, and produced a line of smaller, fuel-efficient cars, it may have been more difficult for Japanese automobile companies to enter the U.S. market. Another example concerns breakfast cereal companies, which are famous for pursuing a product proliferation strategy. Typically they produce many different types of cereal, so that they can cater to all likely consumer needs. The net result is that the three big breakfast cereal companies—General Mills, Post, and Kellogg—have been able to occupy all of the valuable real estate in the industry—shelf space in supermarkets—filling it with a multiplicity of offerings and leaving very little room for new entrants. Moreover, when new entry does occur—as happened when smaller companies selling granola and organic cereals entered the market —the big three have moved rapidly to offer their own versions of these products, effectively foreclosing entry. A product proliferation strategy can thus effectively deter entry because it gives new entrants very little opportunity to find an unoccupied niche in an industry.

Limit Price   A limit price strategy may be used to deter entry when incumbent companies in an industry enjoy economies of scale, but the resulting cost advantages are *not* enough to keep potential rivals out of the industry. A **limit price strategy** involves charging a price that is lower than that required to maximize profits in the short run to signal to a potential entrant that the incumbent could price the new entrant out of the market, thereby deterring entry. Though limit pricing may not be sustainable in the long run for the incumbent, new entrants often do not have full information about the incumbent's costs and thus do not know how long the incumbent can keep prices low.

For illustration, consider Figure 6.6, which shows that incumbent companies have a unit cost structure that is lower than that of potential entrants. However, if incumbents charge the price that the market will bear (Figure 6.6a), this will be above the unit cost structure of new entrants (Figure 6.6b), allowing them to enter and still make a profit under the pricing umbrella set by incumbents. In this situation, the best option for incumbents might be to charge a price that is still above their own cost structure but just below the cost structure of any potential new entrants (Figure 6.6c). Now there is no incentive for companies to attempt to enter the market, because at the lower limit price they cannot make a profit. Thus, because it deters entry, the limit price

limit price strategy
Charging a price that is lower than that required to maximize profits in the short run to signal that the incumbent has a low-cost structure that the entrant likely cannot match.

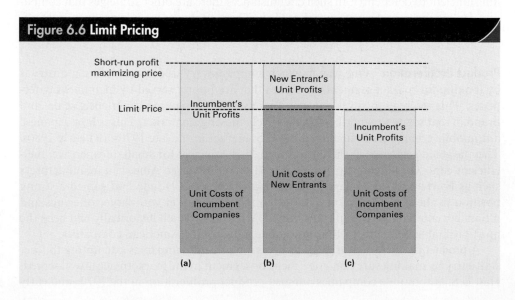

Figure 6.6 Limit Pricing

might be thought of as the long-run, profit-maximizing price. For example, in the U.S. cable industry, incumbents such as Time Warner and Comcast often have near-monopolies over the regions they serve. However, when companies attempt to enter their markets, the incumbents often engage in limit pricing to deter entry. Research by Robert Seamans showed that when new entrants came from outside industries—and thus were unlikely to have full information on the incumbent's costs (e.g., telecom companies such as Verizon FIOS)—incumbent cable companies often used limit pricing to deter their entry. On the other hand, when new entrants were city-owned and thus less sensitive to profit margins, incumbents would use large investments in technology upgrading (discussed below) that city-owned operators had difficulty matching.[14]

Technology Upgrading   If an incumbent is limited in its pricing strategies or faces potential entrants that may be willing to match its pricing, it can deter entry through investments in **technology upgrading** that the new entrant has difficulty matching. For example, though municipal cable TV entrants may be relatively insensitive to profit margins (as described above), they may have difficulty matching investments that a large incumbent can make in state-of-the-art technologies. Thus, when incumbent cable companies were threatened by potential, city-owned entrants, they invested in upgrading their cable infrastructure to provide the two-way communication needed to provide Internet service, thereby slowing municipal entry.[15]

Strategic Commitments   Incumbent companies can deter entry by engaging in strategic commitments that send a signal to potential new entrants that entry will be difficult. **Strategic commitments** are investments that signal an incumbent's long-term commitment to a market, or a segment of that market.[16] As an entry-deterring strategy, strategic commitments involve raising the perceived costs of entering a market, thereby reducing the likelihood of entry. To the extent that such actions are successful, strategic commitments can protect an industry and lead to greater long-run profits for those already in the industry.

One example of strategic commitment occurs when incumbent companies invest in excess productive capacity. The idea is to signal to potential entrants that if they do enter, the incumbents have the ability to expand output and drive down prices, making the market less profitable for new entrants. It has been argued, for example, that chemical companies may overinvest in productive capacity as a way of signaling their commitment to a particular market, and indicating that new entrants will find it difficult to compete.[17]

Other strategic commitments that might act as an entry deterrent include making significant investments in basic research, product development, or advertising beyond those necessary to maintain a company's competitive advantage over its existing rivals.[18] In all cases, for such actions to deter entry, potential rivals must be aware of what incumbents are doing, and the investments must be sufficient to deter entry.

Incumbents might also be able to deter entry if they have a history of responding aggressively to new entry through price cutting, accelerating product development efforts, increasing advertising expenditures, or some combination of these. For example, in the 1990s, when a competitor announced a new software product Microsoft would often attempt to make entry difficult by quickly announcing that it had a similar software product under development that would work well with Windows (the implication being that consumers should wait for the Microsoft product). The term "vaporware" was often used to describe such aggressive product preannouncements. Many observers believe that the practice did succeed on occasion in forestalling entry.[19]

technology upgrading
Incumbent companies deterring entry by investing in costly technology upgrades that potential entrants have trouble matching.

strategic commitments
Investments that signal an incumbent's long-term commitment to a market or a segment of that market.

A history of such actions sends a strong signal to potential rivals that market entry will not be easy and that the incumbents will respond vigorously to any encroachment on their turf. When established companies succeed in signaling this position to potential rivals through past actions, we say that they have established a *credible commitment* to respond to new entry.

One thing to note is that, when making strategic commitments, a company must be careful not to fall afoul of antitrust law. For example, it is illegal to engage in predatory pricing, or pricing a good or service below the cost of production with the express intent of driving a rival out of business and monopolizing a market. In the late 1990s, Microsoft violated antitrust laws when it informed PC manufacturers that they had to display Internet Explorer on the PC desktop if they wanted to license the company's Windows operating system. Because Windows was the only viable operating system for PCs at the time, this was basically viewed as strong-arming PC makers. The intent was to give Internet Explorer an edge over rival browsers, particularly one produced by Netscape. The U.S. Justice Department ruled that Microsoft's actions were predatory. Microsoft was forced to pay fines and change its practices.

Strategies to Manage Rivalry

Beyond seeking to deter entry, companies may wish to develop strategies to manage their competitive interdependence and decrease price rivalry. Unrestricted competition over prices reduces both company and industry profitability. Companies use several strategies to manage industry rivalry. The most important are price signaling, price leadership, non-price competition, and capacity control.

Price Signaling   A company's ability to choose the price option that leads to superior performance is a function of several factors, including the strength of demand for a product and the intensity of competition between rivals. Price signaling is a method whereby companies attempt to control rivalry among competitors to allow the *industry* to choose the most favorable pricing option. **Price signaling** is the process by which companies increase or decrease product prices to convey their intentions to other companies and influence the way other companies price their products. Companies use price signaling to improve industry profitability.

Companies may use price signaling to communicate that they will vigorously respond to hostile competitive moves that threaten them. For example, they may signal that if one company starts to aggressively cut prices, they will respond in kind. A *tit-for-tat strategy* is a well-known price signaling maneuver in which a company exactly mimics its rivals: If its rivals cut prices, the company follows; if they raise prices, the company follows. By consistently pursuing this strategy over time, a company sends a clear signal to its rivals that it will mirror any pricing moves they make; sooner or later, rivals learn that the company will always pursue a tit-for-tat strategy. Because rivals know that it will match any price reductions– and thus reduce profits–price cutting becomes less common in the industry. Moreover, a tit-for-tat strategy also signals to rivals that price increases will be imitated, growing the probability that rivals will initiate price increases to raise profits. Thus, a tit-for-tat strategy can be a useful way of shaping pricing behavior in an industry.[20]

The airline industry is a good example of the power of price signaling when prices typically rise and fall depending upon the current state of customer demand. If one carrier signals the intention to lower prices, a price war frequently ensues as carriers

price signaling

The process by which companies increase or decrease product prices to convey their intentions to other companies and influence the price of an industry's products.

copy one another's signals. If one carrier feels demand is strong, it tests the waters by signaling an intention to increase prices, and price signaling becomes a strategy to obtain uniform price increases. Nonrefundable tickets or charges for a second bag, another strategy adopted to allow airlines to charge higher prices, also originated as a market signal by one company that was quickly copied by all other companies in the industry (it is estimated that extra bag charges have so far allowed airlines to raise over $1 billion in revenues). Carriers have recognized that they can stabilize their revenues and earn interest on customers' money if they collectively act to force customers to assume the risk of buying airline tickets in advance. In essence, price signaling allows companies to exchange information that enables them to understand each other's competitive product or market strategy and make coordinated, price-competitive moves.

Price Leadership   When one company assumes the responsibility for setting the pricing option that maximizes industry profitability, that company assumes the position of price leader—a second tactic used to reduce price rivalry between companies in a mature industry. Explicit price leadership, when companies jointly set prices, is illegal under antitrust laws; therefore, the process of **price leadership** is often very subtle. In the car industry, for example, prices are set by imitation. The price set by the weakest company—that is, the company with the highest cost structure—is often used as the basis for competitors' pricing. Thus, in the past, U.S. carmakers set their prices and Japanese carmakers then set their prices in response to the U.S. prices. The Japanese are happy to do this because they have lower costs than U.S. carmakers and still make higher profits without having to compete on price. Pricing is determined by market segment. The prices of different auto models in a particular range indicate the customer segments that the companies are targeting, and the price range the companies believe each segment can tolerate. Each manufacturer prices a model in the segment with reference to the prices charged by its competitors, not with reference to competitors' costs. Price leadership also allows differentiators to charge a premium price.

Although price leadership can stabilize industry relationships by preventing head-to-head competition and raising the level of profitability within an industry, it has its dangers. It allows companies with high cost structures to survive without needing to implement strategies to become more efficient, although in the long term such behavior makes them vulnerable to new entrants that have lower costs because they have developed low-cost production techniques. This happened in the U.S. car industry. After decades of tacit price fixing, and GM as the price leader, U.S. carmakers were threatened by growing, low-cost, overseas competition. In 2009, the U.S. government bailed out Chrysler and GM, loaning them billions of dollars while forcing them to enter and then emerge from, bankruptcy. This dramatically lowered the cost structures of these companies and has made them more competitive today. (This also applies to Ford, which obtained similar benefits while managing to avoid bankruptcy.)

Non-price Competition   A third very important aspect of product and market strategy in mature industries is the use of **non-price competition** to manage rivalry within an industry. The use of strategies to try to prevent costly price cutting and price wars does not preclude competition by product differentiation. In many industries, product differentiation strategies are the principal tools companies use to deter potential entrants and manage rivalry.

Product differentiation allows industry rivals to compete for market share by offering products with different or superior features, such as smaller, more powerful,

price leadership
When one company assumes the responsibility for determining the pricing strategy that maximizes industry profitability.

non-price competition
The use of product differentiation strategies to deter potential entrants and manage rivalry within an industry.

or more sophisticated computer chips, as AMD, Intel, and NVIDIA compete to offer, or by applying different marketing techniques, as Procter & Gamble, Colgate, and Unilever do. In Figure 6.7, product and market segment dimensions are used to identify four non-price competitive strategies based on product differentiation: market penetration, product development, market development, and product proliferation. (Note that this model applies to new market *segments*, *not* new markets.)

Market Penetration   When a company concentrates on expanding market share in its existing product markets, it is engaging in a strategy of *market penetration* . Market penetration involves heavy advertising to promote and build product differentiation. For example, Intel has actively pursued penetration with its aggressive marketing campaign of "Intel Inside." In a mature industry, advertising aims to influence customers' brand choice and create a brand-name reputation for the company and its products. In this way, a company can increase its market share by attracting its rival's customers. Because brand-name products often command premium prices, building market share in this situation is very profitable.

In some mature industries—for example, soap and detergent, disposable diapers, and brewing—a market-penetration strategy becomes a long-term strategy. In these industries, all companies engage in intensive advertising and battle for market share. Each company fears that if it does not advertise it will lose market share to rivals who do. Consequently, in the soap and detergent industry, Procter & Gamble spends more than 20% of sales revenues on advertising, with the aim of maintaining, and perhaps building, market share. These huge advertising outlays constitute a barrier to entry for prospective competitors.

product development

The creation of new or improved products to replace existing products.

Product Development   **Product development** is the creation of new or improved products to replace existing ones. The wet-shaving industry depends on product replacement to create successive waves of customer demand, which then create new sources of revenue for companies in the industry. Gillette, for example, periodically unveils a new, improved razor such as its vibrating razor (which competes with Schick's four-bladed razor) to try to boost its market share. Similarly, in the car industry, each major car company replaces its models every 3 to 5 years to encourage customers to trade in old models and purchase new ones.

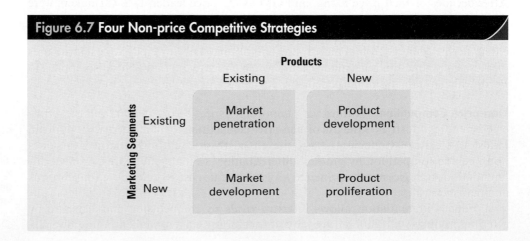

Figure 6.7 Four Non-price Competitive Strategies

	Products	
	Existing	New
Existing	Market penetration	Product development
New	Market development	Product proliferation

(Marketing Segments on vertical axis)

Product development is crucial for maintaining product differentiation and building market share. For instance, the laundry detergent Tide has gone through more than 50 changes in formulation during the past 40 years to improve its performance. The product is always advertised as Tide, but it is a different product each year. Refining and improving products is a crucial strategy companies use to fine-tune and improve their business models in a mature industry, but this kind of competition can be as vicious as a price war because it is very expensive and can dramatically increase a company's cost structure. This occurred in the computer-chip industry, where intense competition to make the fastest or most powerful chip and become the market leader has dramatically increased the cost structure of Intel, AMD, and NVIDIA, and sharply reduced their profitability.

Market Development   **Market development** seeks new market segments for a company's products. A company pursuing this strategy wants to capitalize on the brand name it has developed in one market segment by locating new market segments in which to compete—just as Mattel and Nike do by entering many different segments of the toy and shoe markets, respectively. In this way, a company can leverage the product differentiation advantages of its brand name. Japanese auto manufacturers provide an interesting example of the use of market development. When each manufacturer entered the market, it offered a car model aimed at the economy segment of the auto market, such as the Toyota Corolla and the Honda Accord. Then, these companies upgraded each model over time to target a more expensive market segment. The Honda Accord is a leading contender in the mid-sized car segment, and the Toyota Corolla fills the small-car segment. By redefining their product offerings, Japanese manufacturers have profitably developed their market segments and successfully attacked their U.S. rivals, wresting market share from them. Although the Japanese once competed primarily as cost leaders, market development has allowed them to become differentiators as well. In fact, as we noted in the previous chapter, Toyota has used market development to become a broad differentiator. Over time, it has used market development to create a vehicle for almost every segment of the car market, a tactic discussed in Strategy in Action 6.2.

market development
When a company searches for new market segments for its existing products in order to increase sales.

Product Proliferation   We have already seen how product proliferation can deter entry into an industry. The same strategy can be used to manage rivalry within an industry. As noted earlier, product proliferation generally means that large companies in an industry have a product in each market segment (or niche). If a new niche develops, such as SUVs, designer sunglasses, or shoe-selling websites, the leader gets a first-mover advantage—but soon thereafter, all the other companies catch up. Once again, competition is stabilized, and rivalry within the industry is reduced. Product proliferation thus allows the development of stable industry competition based on product differentiation, not price—that is, non-price competition based on the development of new products. The competitive battle is over a product's perceived uniqueness, quality, features, and performance, not its price. Nike, for example, was founded as a running shoe company, and early in its history it shunned markets for gear for sports such as golf, soccer, basketball, tennis, and skateboarding. However, when its sales declined Nike realized that using marketing to increase sales in a particular market segment (market penetration) could only grow sales and profits so much. The company thus directed its existing design and marketing competencies to the crafting of new lines of shoes for those market segments and others.

6.2 STRATEGY IN ACTION

Toyota Uses Market Development to Become the Global Leader

The car industry has always been one of the most competitive in the world because of the huge revenues and profits at stake. Given the difficult economic conditions in the late-2000s, it is hardly surprising that rivalry has increased as global carmakers struggle to develop new models that better satisfy the needs of particular groups of buyers. One company at the competitive forefront is Toyota.

Toyota produced its first car 40 years ago—an ugly, boxy vehicle that was, however, cheap. As the quality of its car became apparent, sales increased. Toyota, which was then a focused cost leader, reinvested its profits into improving the styling of its vehicles, and into efforts to continually reduce production costs. Over time, Toyota has taken advantage of its low-cost structure to make an ever-increasing range of reasonably priced vehicles tailored to different segments of the car market. The company's ability to begin with the initial design stage and move to the production stage in 2 to 3 years allowed it to make new models available more rapidly than its competitors, and to capitalize on the development of new market segments.

Toyota has been a leader in positioning its entire range of vehicles to take advantage of new, emerging market segments. In the SUV segment, for example, its first offering was the expensive Toyota Land Cruiser, even then priced at over $35,000. Realizing the need for SUVs in lower price ranges, it

next introduced the 4Runner, priced at $20,000 and designed for the average SUV customer; the RAV4, a small SUV in the low $20,000 range, followed; then came the Sequoia, a bigger, more powerful version of the 4Runner in the upper $20,000 range. Finally, drawing on technology from its Lexus division, it introduced the luxury Highlander SUV in the low $30,000 range. Today, it sells six SUV models, each offering a particular combination of price, size, performance, styling, and luxury to appeal to a particular customer group within the SUV segment of the car market. In a similar way, Toyota positions its sedans to appeal to the needs of different sets of customers. For example, the Camry is targeted at the middle of the market to customers who can afford to pay about $25,000 and want a balance of luxury, performance, safety, and reliability.

Toyota's broad-differentiation business model is geared toward making a range of vehicles that optimizes the amount of value it can create for different groups of customers. At the same time, the number of models it makes is constrained by the need to keep costs under strict control so that its pricing options that will generate maximum revenues and profits. Competition in every car market segment is now intense, so all carmakers must balance the advantages of showcasing more cars to attract customers against the increasing costs that result when their line of models expands to suit different customers' needs.

Capacity Control   Although non-price competition helps mature industries avoid the cutthroat price cutting that reduces company and industry levels of profitability, price competition does periodically occur when excess capacity exists in an industry. Excess capacity arises when companies collectively produce too much output; to dispose of it, they cut prices. When one company cuts prices, others quickly do the same because they fear that the price cutter will be able to sell its entire inventory and leave them with unwanted goods. The result is a developing price war.

Excess capacity may be caused by a shortfall in demand, as when a recession lowers the demand for cars and causes automakers to offer customers price incentives to purchase new cars. In this situation, companies can do nothing but wait for better times. By and large, however, excess capacity results from companies within an industry simultaneously responding to favorable conditions; they all invest in new plants to take advantage of the predicted upsurge in demand. Paradoxically, each individual company's effort to outperform the others means that, collectively, companies create industry overcapacity, which hurts all companies. Although demand is rising, the consequence of each company's decision to increase capacity is a surge in industry capacity, which drives down prices. To prevent the accumulation of costly excess capacity, companies must devise strategies that enable them to control—or at least benefit from—capacity-expansion programs. Before we examine these strategies, however, we need to consider in greater detail the factors that cause excess capacity.[21]

Factors Causing Excess Capacity   Excess capacity often derives from technological developments. New, low-cost technology sometimes can create an issue because all companies invest in it simultaneously to prevent being left behind. Excess capacity occurs as the new technology produces more efficiently than the old. In addition, new technology is often introduced in large increments, which generates overcapacity. For instance, an airline that needs more seats on a route must add another plane, thereby adding hundreds of seats even if only 50 are needed. To take another example, a new chemical process may efficiently operate at the rate of only 1,000 gallons per day, whereas the previous process was efficient at 500 gallons per day. If all companies within an industry change technologies, industry capacity may double, and enormous problems can ensue.

Competitive factors within an industry can cause overcapacity. Entry into an industry is one such factor. The economic recession of 2008-2009 caused global overcapacity and the price of steel plunged; with global recovery the price has increased. Sometimes the age of a company's physical assets is the source of the problem. For example, in the hotel industry, given the rapidity with which the quality of hotel room furnishings decline, customers are always attracted to new hotels. When new hotel chains are built alongside the old chains, excess capacity can result. Often, companies are simply making simultaneous competitive moves based on industry trends—but these moves lead to head-to-head competition. Most fast-food chains, for instance, establish new outlets whenever demographic data show population increases. However, companies seem to forget that all other chains use the same data—they do not anticipate their rivals' actions. Thus, a certain locality that has few fast-food outlets may suddenly have several new outlets being built at the same time. Whether all the outlets survive depends upon the growth rate of customer demand, but often the least popular outlets close.

Choosing a Capacity-Control Strategy   Given the various ways in which capacity can expand, companies clearly need to find means of controlling it. Companies that are always plagued by price cutting and price wars will be unable to recoup their investments in generic strategies. Low profitability caused by overcapacity forces not only the weakest companies but also sometimes major players to exit the industry. In general, companies have two strategic choices: (1) each company must try to preempt its rivals and seize the initiative, or (2) the companies must collectively find indirect means of coordinating with each other so that they are all aware of the mutual effects of their actions.

To *preempt* rivals, a company must forecast a large increase in demand in the product market and then move rapidly to establish large-scale operations that will be able to satisfy the predicted demand. By achieving a first-mover advantage, the company may deter other firms from entering the market because the preemptor will usually be able to move down the experience curve, reduce its costs, and therefore reduce its prices as well—and threaten a price war if necessary.

This strategy, however, is extremely risky, for it involves investing resources before the extent and profitability of the future market are clear. A preemptive strategy is also risky if it does not deter competitors that decide to enter the market. If competitors can develop a stronger generic strategy, or have more resources (think of Google and Microsoft), they can make the preemptor suffer. Thus, for the strategy to succeed, the preemptor must generally be a credible company with enough resources to withstand a possible advertising/price war.

To *coordinate* with rivals as a capacity-control strategy, caution must be exercised because collusion on the timing of new production capacity investments is illegal under antitrust law. However, tacit coordination is practiced in many industries as companies attempt to understand and forecast one another's competitive moves. Generally, companies use market signaling to secure coordination. They make announcements about their future investment decisions in trade journals and newspapers. In addition, they share information about their production levels and their forecasts of demand within an industry to bring supply and demand into equilibrium. Thus, a coordination strategy reduces the risks associated with investment in the industry. This is very common in the chemical refining and oil businesses, where new capacity investments frequently cost hundreds of millions of dollars.

▼ STRATEGIES IN DECLINING INDUSTRIES

Sooner or later, many industries enter into a decline stage in which the size of the total market begins to shrink. Examples are the railroad industry, the tobacco industry, the steel industry, and the newspaper business (see the Closing Case). Industries decline for many reasons, including technological change, social trends, and demographic shifts. The railroad and steel industries began to decline when technological changes brought viable substitutes for their products. The advent of the internal combustion engine drove the railroad industry into decline, and the steel industry fell into decline with the rise of plastics and composite materials. Similarly, as noted in the Closing Case, the newspaper industry is in decline because of the rise of news sites on the Web. As for the tobacco industry, changing social attitudes and warnings about the health effects of smoking have caused the decline.

The Severity of Decline

Competition tends to intensify in a declining industry, and profit rates tend to fall. The intensity of competition in a declining industry depends on four critical factors, which are depicted in Figure 6.8. First, the intensity of competition is greater in industries in which decline is rapid, as opposed to industries such as tobacco in which decline is slow and gradual.

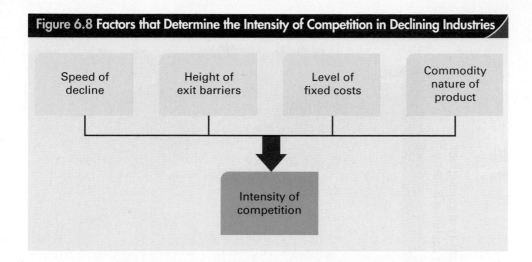

Figure 6.8 Factors that Determine the Intensity of Competition in Declining Industries

Second, the intensity of competition is greater in declining industries in which exit barriers are high. Recall from Chapter 2 that high exit barriers keep companies locked into an industry, even when demand is falling. The result is excess productive capacity and hence an increased probability of fierce price competition.

Third, and related to the previous point, the intensity of competition is greater in declining industries in which fixed costs are high (as in the steel industry). The reason is that the need to cover fixed costs such as the costs of maintaining productive capacity can drive companies to try to use excess capacity by slashing prices, which can trigger a price war.

Finally, the intensity of competition is greater in declining industries in which the product is perceived as a commodity (as it is in the steel industry) in contrast to industries in which differentiation gives rise to significant brand loyalty, as was true (until very recently) of the declining tobacco industry.

Not all segments of an industry typically decline at the same rate. In some segments, demand may remain reasonably strong despite decline elsewhere. The steel industry illustrates this situation. Although bulk steel product, such as sheet steel have suffered a general decline, demand has actually risen for specialty steels such as those used in high-speed machine tools. Vacuum tubes provide another example. Although demand for the tubes collapsed when transistors replaced them as a key component in many electronics products, vacuum tubes still had limited applications in radar equipment for years afterward. Consequently, demand in this one segment remained strong despite the general decline in demand for vacuum tubes. The point is that there may be pockets of demand in an industry in which demand is declining more slowly than in the industry as a whole—or where demand is not declining at all. Price competition may be far less intense among companies serving pockets of demand than within the industry as a whole.

Choosing a Strategy

There are four main strategies that companies can adopt to deal with decline: (1) a **leadership strategy**, by which a company seeks to become the dominant player in a declining industry; (2) a **niche strategy**, which focuses on pockets of demand that are declining more slowly than the industry as a whole; (3) a **harvest strategy**, which

leadership strategy
When a company develops strategies to become the dominant player in a declining industry.

niche strategy
When a company focuses on pockets of demand that are declining more slowly than the industry as a whole to maintain profitability.

harvest strategy
When a company reduces to a minimum the assets it employs in a business to reduce its cost structure and extract ("milk") maximum profits from its investment.

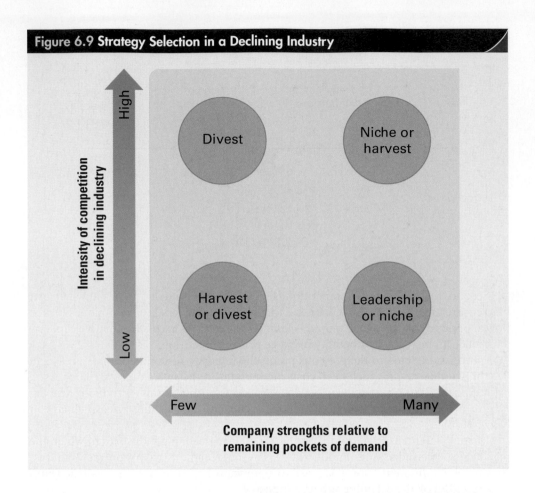

Figure 6.9 Strategy Selection in a Declining Industry

Intensity of competition in declining industry — High / Low

Divest

Niche or harvest

Harvest or divest

Leadership or niche

Few   Many

Company strengths relative to remaining pockets of demand

divestment strategy

When a company exits an industry by selling its business assets to another company.

optimizes cash flow; and (4) a **divestment strategy**, by which a company sells the business to others.[22] Figure 6.9 provides a simple framework for guiding strategic choice. Note that the intensity of competition in the declining industry is measured on the vertical axis, and a company's strengths relative to remaining pockets of demand are measured on the horizontal axis.

Leadership Strategy   A leadership strategy aims at growing in a declining industry by picking up the market share of companies that are leaving the industry. A leadership strategy makes most sense when (1) the company has distinctive strengths that allow it to capture market share in a declining industry, and (2) the speed of decline and the intensity of competition in the declining industry are moderate. Philip Morris used this strategy in the tobacco industry. While other cigarette companies were responding to slumping demand by cutting costs or exiting the market, Philip Morris increased its advertising, and subsequently its market share, in the declining industry. It earned enormous profits in the process.

The tactical steps companies might use to achieve a leadership position include using aggressive pricing and marketing to build market share, acquiring established competitors to consolidate the industry, and raising the stakes for other competitors, for example by making new investments in productive capacity. Such competitive tactics signal to rivals that the company is willing and able to stay and compete in the declining industry. These signals may persuade other companies to exit the industry, which would further enhance the competitive position of the industry leader.

Niche Strategy   A niche strategy focuses on pockets of demand in the industry in which demand is stable or declining less rapidly than the industry as a whole. This strategy makes sense when the company has unique strengths relative to those niches in which demand remains relatively strong. Consider Naval, a company that manufactures whaling harpoons (and small guns to fire them) and makes adequate profits. This might be considered rather odd because the world community has outlawed whaling. However, Naval survived the terminal decline of the harpoon industry by focusing on the one group of people who are still allowed to hunt whales, although in very limited numbers: North American Inuit, who are permitted to hunt bowhead whales provided that they do so only for food and not for commercial purposes. Naval is the sole supplier of small harpoon whaling guns to Inuit communities, and its monopoly position allows the company to earn a healthy return in this small market.

Harvest Strategy   As noted earlier, a harvest strategy is the best choice when a company wishes to exit a declining industry and optimize cash flow in the process. This strategy makes the most sense when the company foresees a steep decline and intense future competition, or when it lacks strengths relative to remaining pockets of demand in the industry. A harvest strategy requires the company to halt all new investments in capital equipment, advertising, research and development (R&D), and so forth. The inevitable result is that the company will lose market share, but because it is no longer investing in the business, initially its positive cash flow will increase. Essentially, the company is accepting cash flow in exchange for market share. Ultimately, cash flow will start to decline, and when that occurs, it makes sense for the company to liquidate the business. Although this strategy can be very appealing in theory, it can be somewhat difficult to put into practice. Employee morale in a declining business may suffer. Furthermore, if customers realize what the company is doing, they may rapidly defect, and market share may decline much faster than the company expects. Research by Professors Daniel Elfenbein and Anne Marie Knott found that U.S. banks often delayed exiting the market well past the time when it would have been rational to do so based on their profits. Elfenbein and Knott argue that banks appear to exit late in part because of rational demand uncertainty, and in part because of irrational optimism or escalating commitment that results in management overweighting positive signals that profits might rebound.[23]

Divestment Strategy   A divestment strategy rests on the idea that a company can recover most of its investment in an underperforming business by selling it early, before the industry has entered into a steep decline. This strategy is appropriate when the company has few strengths relative to whatever pockets of demand are likely to remain in the industry, and when the competition in the declining industry is likely to be intense. The best option may be to sell to a company that is pursuing a leadership strategy in the industry. The drawback of the divestment strategy is that its success depends upon the ability of the company to spot industry decline before it becomes detrimental, and to sell while the company's assets are still valued by others.

KEY TERMS

TAKEAWAYS FOR STRATEGIC MANAGERS

1. In fragmented industries composed of many small- and medium-sized companies, the principal forms of competitive strategy are chaining, franchising, and horizontal merger.
2. In embryonic and growth industries, strategy is partly determined by market demand. Innovators and early adopters have different needs than the early and the late majority, and a company must have the right strategies in place to cross the chasm and survive. Similarly, managers must understand the factors that affect a market's growth rate so that they can tailor their business model to a changing industry environment.
3. Mature industries are composed of a few large companies whose actions are so highly interdependent that the success of one company's strategy depends upon the responses of its rivals.
4. The principal strategies used by companies in mature industries to deter entry are product proliferation, price cutting, and maintaining excess capacity.
5. The principal strategies used by companies in mature industries to manage rivalry are price signaling, price leadership, non-price competition, and capacity control.
6. In declining industries, in which market demand has leveled off or is decreasing, companies must tailor their price and non-price strategies to the new competitive environment. Companies also need to manage industry capacity to prevent the emergence of capacity-expansion problems.
7. There are four main strategies a company can pursue when demand is falling: leadership, niche, harvest, and divestment. The strategic choice is determined by the severity of industry decline and the company's strengths relative to the remaining pockets of demand.

DISCUSSION QUESTIONS

1. Why are industries fragmented? What are the primary ways in which companies can turn a fragmented industry into a consolidated industry?
2. What are the key problems in maintaining a competitive advantage in embryonic and growth industry environments? What are the dangers associated with being the leader in an industry?
3. What investment strategies should be made by: (a) differentiators in a strong competitive position, and (b) differentiators in a weak competitive position, while managing a company's growth through the life cycle?
4. Discuss how companies can use: (a) product differentiation, and (b) capacity control to manage rivalry and increase an industry's profitability.
5. What strategies might these enterprises use to strengthen their business models (a) a small pizza place operating in a crowded college market, and (b) a detergent manufacturer seeking to unveil new products in an established market?

CLOSING CASE

How to Make Money in Newspaper Advertising

The U.S. newspaper business is a declining industry. Since 1990, newspaper circulation been steadily falling, with the drop accelerating in recent years. According to the Newspaper Association of America, in 1990, 62.3 million newspapers were sold every day. By 2011, this figure had dropped to 44.4 million. The fall in advertising revenue has been even steeper, with revenues peaking in 2000 at $48.7 billion, and falling to just $20.7 billion in 2013. Reasons for the decline in circulation and advertising revenue are not hard to find; digitalization has disrupted the industry; news consumption has moved to the Web, and advertising has followed suit. The online classified advertising website Craigslist has been particularly damaging to newspapers. Advertisers can post ads on Craigslist for free (in most cases) that are easy to search and update in real time, unlike a newspaper. According to research by professors Robert Seamans and Feng Zhu, Craigslist alone was responsible for over $5 billion in lost revenues in the newspaper industry between 2000-2007.

Declining demand for printed newspapers has left established players in the industry reeling and searching for responses. Gannett Co., which publishes *USA Today* and a host of local newspapers, has seen its revenues slip to $4.3 billion in 2014, down from $6.77 billion in 2008. The venerable *New York Times* has seen revenues fall from $2.9 billion to $1.6 billion over the same period. The industry has responded in multiple ways, but implementing a response has proven to be anything but easy, as a change to one side of a newspaper's business model requires changes to its other side. Newspapers traditionally relied so heavily on advertising that they subsidized the consumer news side. According to research by Professor Seamans and Zhu, without classified

advertising revenue to subsidize subscriptions, many newspapers decided to increase their subscription prices, by 5 to 10%. This led, however, to falling numbers of subscribers. In addition, some newspapers have rapidly expanded Web-based news properties at the risk of cannibalizing their offline print customers. As of 2014, almost 30% of total newspaper circulation in the United States was online, and for the fifteen largest newspapers, over 45% of their total circulation was online. Of the country's 1,380 daily newspapers, 450 had adopted digital pay plans that offered a combination of online and print subscription. The *New York Times*, for example, had a range of subscription options that included everything from online only, to select days of print in addition to online, to print only. Many newspapers increased the price of single copies, and this, combined with the digital paywall movement of charging for online content, appeared to stabilize circulation revenues and helped reduce the industry's historic dependence on advertising revenues.

Against this background, one local newspaper company is swimming against the tide, and making money at it. Community Impact Newspaper produces 13 hyperlocal editions that are delivered free each month to 855,000 homes in the Austin, Houston, and Dallas areas. The paper is the brainchild of John Garrett, who used to work as an advertising director for the *Austin Business Journal*. In 2005, Garrett noticed that the large-circulation local newspapers in Texas did not cover news that was relevant to smaller neighborhoods—such as the construction of a local toll road, or the impact of a new corporate campus for Exxon Mobil. Nor could news about these projects be gleaned from the Web. Yet Garrett believed that local people were still hungry for news about local projects and events that

(continued)

might impact them. So he launched the inaugural issue of his paper in September 2005, and financing it with $40,000 borrowed from low-interest credit cards.

Today, the paper has a staff of 30 journalists, about 35% of the total workforce. The reporting is pretty straight stuff. There is no investigative reporting, although *Impact* will run in-depth stories on controversial local issues, being careful not to take sides. "That would just lose us business," says Garrett. About half of each edition is devoted to local advertisements, and this is where *Impact* makes money. For their part, the advertisers seem happy with the paper. "We've tried everything, from Google Ads to Groupon, but this is the most effective," says Richard Hunter, who spends a few hundred dollars each month to advertise his Houston restaurant, Catfish Station. Another advertiser, Rob Sides, who owns a toy store, Toy Time, places 80% of his advertising dollars with *Impact*'s local edition in order to reach 90,000 homes in the area.

An analysis by *Forbes* estimated that each 40-page issue of *Impact* brings in about $2.50 in ad revenue per printed copy. About 50 cents of that goes to mailing and distribution costs, 80 cents to payroll, and another 80 cents to printing and overhead, leaving roughly 40 cents per copy for Garrett and his wife, who own the entire company. If this analysis is right, *Impact* is making very good money for its owners in an industry where most players are struggling just to survive.

Sources: C. Helman, "Breaking: A Local Newspaper Chain That's Actually Making Good Money," *Forbes*, January 21, 2013, www.forbes.com; News Paper Association of America, "Trends and Numbers," www.naa.org/Trends-and-Numbers/Research .aspx; J. Agnese, "Publishing and Advertising," S&P netAdvantage, April 12, 2012, http://eresources.library.nd.edu/ databases /netadvantage; R. Edmonds, E. Guskin, A. Mitchell, and M. Jurkowitz, 2013; *Newspapers by the Numbers. The State of the News Media 2014*, annual report on American journalism, Pew Research Center, New York; Yahoo Finance, finance.yahoo. com; R. Seamans and F. Zhu, "Responses to Entry in Multi-Sided Markets: The Impact of Craigslist on Local Newspapers," *Management Science*, 60 (2), 2014, pp. 476–493; R. Seamans and F. Zhu, "Repositioning and Cost Cutting: The Impact of Competition on Newspaper Strategies," NYU Stern Working Paper, 2014.

CASE DISCUSSION QUESTIONS

1. What advantages do traditional print newspapers have for entering the online news business? What disadvantages do they have?

2. What do you think determines whether people will use print, online, or both sources for their news?

3. When a print newspaper initiates an online version of its newspaper, what are the possible outcomes for its current display advertisers? Are they likely to prefer one channel over the other to reach their customers, or are they likely to select both? If both, are they likely to expect a discount for a bundle of print and online advertising? How do these outcomes affect the newspaper's bargaining power?

4. How do you think the cost structure of online advertising compares to the cost structure of print advertising?

5. Which print newspapers do you think will fare the best as online news continues to expand? Why?

NOTES

[1]M. E. Porter, *Competitive Strategy: Techniques for Analyzing Industries and Competitors* (New York: Free Press, 1980), pp. 191–200.

[2]W. C. Kim and R. Mauborgne, "Value Innovation: The Strategic Logic of High Growth," *Harvard Business Review* (January–February 1997): pp. 103–112.

[3]S. A. Shane, "Hybrid Organizational Arrangements and Their Implications for Firm Growth and Survival: A Study of New Franchisors," *Academy of Management Journal* 1 (1996): 216–234.

[4]Microsoft is often accused of not being an innovator, but the fact is that Bill Gates and Paul Allen wrote the first commercial software program for the first commercially available personal computer. Microsoft was the first mover in its industry. See P. Freiberger and M. Swaine, *Fire in the Valley* (New York: McGraw-Hill, 2000).

[5]J. M. Utterback, *Mastering the Dynamics of Innovation* (Boston: Harvard Business School Press, 1994).

[6]E. M. Rogers, *Diffusion of Innovations*, 5th ed. Free Press, 2003. Ibid.

[7]R. Brown "Managing the 'S' Curves of Innovation, "*Journal of Consumer Marketing* 9 (1992): 61–72; P. A. Geroski. "Models of Technology Diffusion," *Research Policy* 29 (2000): 603–25.

[8]Freiberger and Swaine, *Fire in the Valley.*

[9]Utterback, *Mastering the Dynamics of Innovation.*

[10]G. A. Moore, *Crossing the Chasm* (New York: HarperCollins, 1991).

[11]Utterback, *Mastering the Dynamics of Innovation.*

[12]E. Rogers, *Diffusion of Innovations* (New York: Free Press, 1995).

[13]R. J. Gilbert, "Mobility Barriers and the Value of Incumbency," in R. Schmalensee and R. D. Willig (eds.), *Handbook of Industrial Organization* (Elsevier Science Publishers, 1989).

[14]R. Seamans, "Threat of Entry, Asymmetric Information, and Pricing," *Strategic Management Journal* 34 (2013): 426–44.

[15]R. Seamans. "Fighting City Hall: Entry Deterrence and Technology Upgrades in Cable TV Markets," *Management Science* 58 (2012): 461–75.

[16]P. Ghemawat, *Commitment: The Dynamic of Strategy* (Harvard Business School Press, 1991).

[17]M. B. Lieberman, "Excess Capacity as a Barrier to Entry: An Empirical Appraisal," *Journal of Industrial Economics* 35 (1987): 607–27

[18]R. Lukach, P. M. Kort, and J. Plasmans, "Optimal R&D Investment Strategies Under the Threat of New Technology Entry," *International Journal of Industrial Organization* 25 (February 2007): 103–19.

[19]W. B. Arthur, "Increasing Returns and the New World of Business," *Harvard Business Review* (July 1996): 100–109

[20]R. Axelrod, *The Evolution of Cooperation* (New York: Basic Books, 1984).

[21]The next section draws heavily on Marvin B. Lieberman, "Strategies for Capacity Expansion," *Sloan Management Review* 8 (1987): 19–27; Porter, *Competitive Strategy*, 324–38.

[22]K. R. Harrigan, "Strategy Formulation in Declining Industries," *Academy of Management Review* 5 (1980): 599 604.

[23]D. W. Elfenbein and A. W. Knott. "Time to Exit: Rational, Behavioral, and Organizational Delays," *Strategic Management Journal* (June 2014): 957–75.

sergign/Shutterstock.com

CHAPTER 7

STRATEGY AND TECHNOLOGY

OPENING CASE

Blu-ray versus HD-DVD and Streaming: Standards Battles in Video

In 2003, Sony officially launched its Blu-ray disc, an optical disc data-storage format that could offer high-definition video, with hopes of replacing the DVD format. Sony's technology had the backing of a consortium that included Philips, Panasonic, Pioneer, Sharp, Samsung, Hitachi, and others. Toshiba, on the other hand, was not eager to let Sony dominate the market with its Blu-ray technology; Sony and Philips had controlled the original standard for compact discs (CDs), and every producer of CDs, CD players, and CD recorders, had been required to pay licensing fees to Sony and Philips—an extremely lucrative arrangement for the partners. Toshiba thus formed a consortium, the DVD Forum, which developed a competing high-definition DVD standard, HD-DVD, making it the "official" successor to the DVD format.

Both new formats were intended to deliver a theaterlike experience at home, with brilliantly clear video and surround-sound audio, on high-end LCD and plasma televisions. The formats, however, would be incompatible. Consumers, retailers, and movie producers all groaned at the prospect of a format war similar to the battle that had taken place between Sony's Betamax and JVC's VHS video standard three decades earlier. That war had left many bloodied—consumers who bought

© Nikolay Kuleshin/Shutterstock.com

Betamax players, for example, found that very few movies were ultimately made available in the format, and retailers got stuck with unwanted inventory in Betamax players and movies. The threat of another format war caused many retailers and consumers to delay their purchases of the next-generation players while they waited to see if the market would pick a winner. Fearing a lengthy, costly battle, consumer electronics producers began working on players that would be compatible with both standards, even though that would significantly increase their cost.

Initially, the HD-DVD standard had a head start. Blu-ray players were considered to be too expensive and buggy, and there were few movie titles available in the standard. Toshiba, on the other hand, already had the cooperation of several major Hollywood studios for its format, including Time Warner's Warner Brothers, Viacom's Paramount Pictures and Dreamworks Animation, and NBC Universal's Universal Pictures. Sony had only its own Sony Pictures Entertainment, Disney, News Corporation's 20th Century Fox, and Lions Gate Entertainment.

Both companies also used videogame consoles to promote their standards. Sony incorporated the Blu-ray format into its PlayStation 3, dramatically raising the cost of the devices. Though it sold the consoles at a very low price relative to cost, the consoles were still significantly more expensive than traditional videogame consoles, causing PlayStation 3 to sell only about half as many total units as PlayStation2 had sold (85.23 million versus 157.68 million, respectively). Sony was willing, however, to concede some ground in the PlayStation battle to win the Blu-ray war. Toshiba's HD-DVD was offered as an optional, add-on drive for Microsoft's Xbox 360.

However, on the eve of the Consumer Electronics Show in Las Vegas in early January 2008, Warner Brothers announced that it would no longer support the HD-DVD standard. This set off a chain reaction among content providers and retailers. By late February, New Line Cinema, Universal Studios, and Paramount announced that they would be releasing movies on the Blu-ray format, and Best Buy, Wal-Mart, Circuit City, Future Shop, Blockbuster, and Netflix all announced that they would exclusively stock Blu-ray DVDs. The blow was unexpected—and devastating—for Toshiba. On February 19, 2008, Toshiba's CEO, Atsutoshi Nishida, conceded defeat by publicly announcing that Toshiba would no longer produce HD-DVD players, recorders, or components. By late 2009, Toshiba had released its own Blu-ray disc player.

Sony's Blu-ray victory, however, was not the landslide that it expected. On September 12, 2008, a consortium of tech heavyweights (including Intel and Hewlett Packard) announced that they would collaborate with Hollywood to create standards that would make downloading movies fast and easy. If consumers were able to download high-quality movies off the Internet, it would become increasingly difficult to persuade them to spend $300 or more on a Blu-ray player. Carmi Levi, senior vice president at consulting firm AR Communications, predicted that "Blu-ray is probably going to be the last physical [product] where you walk into a store, get a movie in a box, and bring it home."

By 2012, about one-third of US households had a device that could play a Blu-ray movie (including PlayStation 3); at the same point in the DVD format's life, over half of U.S. households had a device for playing DVDs. Video streaming revenues had reached $5.7 billion in the United States by 2014 and were expected to reach $14 billion by 2018. Physical DVD and Blu-ray sales, on the other hand, were expected to drop from $12.2 billion in 2013 to $8.7 billion by 2018. Though the availability of Blu-ray format streamed content was increasing, many people preferred to stream content in standard (versus high definition) format because it was faster, reducing the buffering time necessary for watching content. In fact, one study found that nearly one-quarter of U.S. households did not have adequate bandwidth to stream high-definition content, and another study found that even in households that could stream high-definition content, many viewers still chose standard definition viewing. On May 1, 2014, Sony issued a warning to investors that it expected to take a hit on earnings because Blu-ray sales were contracting faster than it had expected.

Sources: Anonymous, "Battle of the Blue Lasers," *The Economist*, December 2, 2004, p. 16; B. Schlender, "The Trouble with Sony," *Fortune*, February 22, 2007, p. 46; C. Edwards, "R.I.P., HD DVD," *BusinessWeek Online*, February 20, 2008; K. Hall, "DVD Format Wars: Toshiba Surrenders," *BusinessWeek Online*, February 20, 2008; C. Edwards, "Blu-ray: Playing for a Limited Engagement?," *BusinessWeek Online*, September 18, 2008; M. Snider, "Blu-ray Caught in Shift to Streaming," *USA Today*, August 23, 2012, www.USAToday.com; Yahoo Finance; R. McCormick, "Video Streaming Services Could Make More Money than the U.S. Box Office by 2017," *The Verge*, June 4, 2014, www.theverge.com; M. Willens, "Home Entertainment 2014: US DVD Sales and Rentals Crater, DVD Subscriptions Soar," *International Business Times*, March 10, 2015; vgchartz.com, March 10, 2015; J. Rietveld and J. Lampel, "Nintendo: Fighting the Video Game Console Wars," in *The Strategy Process* (H. Mintzberg, Ed.) (5th ed.). FT Press, 2014.

◤ OVERVIEW

The high-stakes battle that Sony faced in video formats is typical of the nature of competition in high-technology industries (see the Opening Case). In industries where standards and compatibility are important strategic levers, a technology that gains an initial advantage can sometimes rise to achieve a nearly insurmountable position. Such industries can thus become "winner-take-all" markets. Being successful in such industries can require very different strategies than those used in more traditional industries. Firms may aggressively subsidize adoption of their preferred technology (including sometimes giving away products for free) in order to win the standards battle.

In this chapter, we will take a close look at the nature of competition and strategy in high-technology industries. Technology refers to the body of scientific knowledge used in the production of goods or services. High-technology (high-tech) industries are those in which the underlying scientific knowledge that companies in the industry use is rapidly advancing, and, by implication, so are the attributes of the products and services that result from its application. The computer industry is often thought of as the quintessential example of a high-technology industry. Other industries often considered high-tech are telecommunications, where new technologies based on wireless and the Internet have proliferated in recent years; consumer electronics, where the digital technology underlying products from high-definition DVD players to video-game terminals and digital cameras is advancing rapidly; pharmaceuticals, where new technologies based on cell biology, recombinant DNA, and genomics are revolutionizing the process of drug discovery; power generation, where new technologies based on fuel cells and cogeneration may change the economics of the industry; and aerospace, where the combination of new composite materials, electronics, and more efficient jet engines is giving birth to a new era of superefficient commercial jet aircraft such as Boeing's 787.

This chapter focuses on high-technology industries for a number of reasons. First, technology is accounting for an ever-larger share of economic activity. Estimates suggest that in the last decade, nearly 25% of growth in domestic product was accounted for by information technology industries.[1] This figure actually underestimates the true impact of technology on the economy, because it ignores the other high-technology areas we just mentioned. Moreover, as technology advances, many low-technology industries are becoming more high-tech. For example, the development of biotechnology and genetic engineering transformed the production of seed corn, long considered a low-tech business, into a high-technology business. Retailing was once considered a low-tech business, but the shift to online retailing, led by companies like Amazon.com, has changed this. In addition, high-tech products are making their way into a wide range of businesses; today, most automobiles contain more computing power than the multimillion-dollar mainframe computers used in the *Apollo* space program, and the competitive advantage of physical stores such as Wal-Mart is based on their use of information technology. The circle of high-technology industries is both large and expanding, and technology is revolutionizing aspects of the product or production system even in industries not typically considered high-tech.

Although high-tech industries may produce very different products, when developing a business model and strategies that will lead to a competitive advantage and superior profitability and profit growth, they often face a similar situation. For example, "winner-take-all" format wars are common in many high-tech industries such as the consumer electronics and computer industries. In mobile payments, for example, it is possible that a new payment system will emerge that could displace Visa, MasterCard, and American Express as the dominant firms for managing payment transactions worldwide. This could result in a tremendous windfall for the firm(s) controlling the new standard (and a tremendous loss for Visa, MasterCard, and American Express). Firms are thus carefully forging alliances and backing standards they believe will best position them to capture the billions of dollars in transactions fees that are at stake (see the Closing Case). This chapter examines the competitive features found in many high-tech industries and the kinds of strategies that companies must adopt to build business models that will allow them to achieve superior profitability and profit growth.

TECHNICAL STANDARDS AND FORMAT WARS

Especially in high-tech industries, ownership of **technical standards**—a set of technical specifications that producers adhere to when making the product, or a component of it—can be an important source of competitive advantage.[2] Indeed, in many cases product differentiation is based on a technical standard. Often, only one standard will dominate a market, so many battles in high-tech industries involve companies that compete to set the standard. For example, for the last three decades, Microsoft has controlled the market as the dominant operating system for personal computers (PCs), sometimes exceeding a 90% market share. Notably, however, Microsoft held very small shares of the tablet (roughly 4.8%) and smartphone (roughly 3.6%) operating system markets in 2014, suggesting the possibility of turbulent times ahead for the firm (see Strategy in Action 7.1).

Battles to set and control technical standards in a market are referred to as **format wars**—essentially, battles to control the source of differentiation, and thus the value

technical standards

A set of technical specifications that producers adhere to when making a product or component.

format wars

Battles to control the source of differentiation, and thus the value that such differentiation can create for the customer.

7.1 STRATEGY IN ACTION

"Segment Zero"—A Serious Threat to Microsoft?

From 1980 to 2013, Microsoft's Windows was entrenched as the dominant PC operating system, giving it enormous influence over many aspects of the computer hardware and software industries. Although competing operating systems had been introduced during that time (e.g., Unix, Geoworks, NeXTSTEP, Linux, and the Mac OS), Microsoft's share of the PC operating system market held stable at roughly 85% throughout most of that period. By 2015, however, Microsoft's position in the computing industry was under greater threat than it had ever been. A high-stakes race for dominance over the next generation of computing was well under way, and Microsoft was not in the front pack.

"Segment Zero"

As Andy Grove, former CEO of Intel, noted in 1998, in many industries—including microprocessors, software, motorcycles, and electric vehicles—technologies improve faster than customer demands of those technologies increase. Firms often add features such as speed and power to products more quickly than customers' capacity to absorb them. Why would firms provide higher performance than that required by the bulk of their customers? The answer appears to lie in the market segmentation and pricing objectives of a technology's providers. As competition in an industry drives prices and margins lower, firms often try to shift sales into progressively higher tiers of the market. In these tiers, high-performance and feature-rich products can command higher margins. Although customers may also expect to have better-performing products over time, their ability to fully utilize such performance improvements is slowed by the need to learn how to use new features and adapt their work and lifestyles accordingly. Thus, both the trajectory of technology improvement and the trajectory of customer demands are upward sloping, but the trajectory for technology improvement is steeper.

In Figure 7.1 the technology trajectory begins at a point where it provides performance close to that demanded by the mass market, but over time it increases faster than the expectations of the mass market as the firm targets the high-end market. As the price of the technology rises, the mass market may feel it is overpaying for technological features it does not value. In Figure 7.1 the low-end market is not being served; it either pays far more for technology that it does not need, or it goes without. It is this market that Andy Grove, former CEO of Intel, refers to as segment zero.

For Intel, segment zero was the market for low-end personal computers (those less than $1,000). Although segment zero may seem unattractive in terms of margins, if it is neglected, it can become the breeding ground for companies that provide lower-end versions of the technology. As Grove notes, "The overlooked, underserved, and seemingly unprofitable end of the market can provide fertile ground for massive competitive change."

As the firms serving low-end markets with simpler technologies ride up their own trajectories (which are also steeper than the slope of the trajectories of customer expectations), they can eventually reach a performance level that meets the demands of the mass market while offering a much lower price than the premium technology (see Figure 7.2). At this point, firms offering premium technology may suddenly find they are losing the bulk of their sales revenue to industry contenders that do not look so low-end anymore. For example, by 1998, the combination of rising microprocessor power and decreasing prices enabled PCs priced under $1,000 to capture 20% of the market.

The Threat to Microsoft

So where was the segment zero that could threaten Microsoft? Look in your pocket. In 2015, Apple's iPhone operating system (iOS) and Google's Android collectively controlled over 95% of the worldwide market for smartphones. Estimates put Microsoft's share

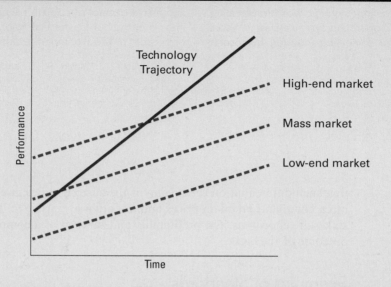

Figure 7.1 Trajectories of Technology Improvement and Customer Requirements

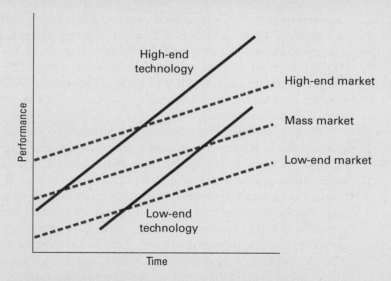

Figure 7.2 Low-End Technology's Trajectory Intersects Mass-Market Trajectory

at 3.6%. The iOS and Android interfaces offered a double whammy of beautiful aesthetics and remarkable ease of use. The applications business model used for the phones was also extremely attractive to both developers and customers, and quickly resulted in enormous libraries of applications that ranged from ridiculous to indispensable.

From a traditional economics perspective, the phone operating system market should not be that attractive to Microsoft—people do not spend as much on the applications, and the carriers have too much bargaining power, among other reasons. However, those smartphone operating systems soon became tablet operating systems, and tablets were rapidly

(*continued*)

becoming fully functional computers. Suddenly, all of the mindshare that Apple and Google had achieved in smartphone operating systems was transforming into mindshare in PC operating systems. Despite years of masterminding the computing industry, Microsoft's dominant position was at risk of evaporating. The outcome is still uncertain—in 2015, Microsoft had an impressive arsenal of capital, talent, and relationships in its armory, but for the first time, it was fighting the battle from a disadvantaged position.

Sources: Adapted from M. A. Schilling, "'Segment Zero': A Serious Threat to Microsoft?" Conceptual Note, New York University, 2013; A. S. Grove, "Managing Segment Zero," *Leader to Leader* 11 (1999); L. Dignan, "Android, Apple iOS Flip Consumer, Corporate Market Share," *Between the Lines*, February 13, 2013; J. Edwards, "The iPhone 6 Had Better Be Amazing and cheap, Because Apple Is Losing the War to Android," *Business Insider*, May 31, 2014; M. Hachman, "Android, iOS Gobble Up Even More Global Smartphone Share," *PC World*, August 14, 2014.

that such differentiation can create for the customer. Because differentiated products often command premium prices and are often expensive to develop, the competitive stakes are enormous. The profitability and survival of a company may depend on the outcome of the battle.

Examples of Standards

A familiar example of a standard is the layout of a computer keyboard. No matter what keyboard you purchase, the letters are all arranged in the same pattern.[3] The reason is quite obvious. Imagine if each computer maker changed the ways keys were arranged—if some had QWERTY on the top row of keys (which is indeed the format used, known as the QWERTY format), some had YUHGFD, and some had ACFRDS. If you learned to type on one layout, it would be irritating and time consuming to relearn on a YUHGFD layout. The standard QWERTY format makes it easy for people to move from computer to computer because the input medium, the keyboard, is standardized.

Another example of a technical standard can be seen in the dimensions of containers used to transport goods on trucks, railcars, and ships. All have the same basic dimensions of height, length, and width, and all make use of the same locking mechanisms to secure them to a surface or to bolt together. Having a standard ensures that containers can easily be moved from one mode of transportation to another— from trucks, to railcars, to ships, and back to railcars. If containers lacked standard dimensions and locking mechanisms, it would become much more difficult to deliver containers around the world. Shippers would need to make sure that they had the right kind of container to go on the ships, trucks, and railcars scheduled to carry a particular container around the world—a very complicated process.

Consider, finally, PCs. Most share a common set of features: an Intel or Intel-compatible microprocessor, random access memory (RAM), a Microsoft operating system, an internal hard drive, a DVD drive, a keyboard, a monitor, a mouse, a modem, and so on. We call this set of features the dominant design for personal computers. **Dominant design** refers to a common set of features or design characteristics. Embedded in this design are several technical standards (see Figure 7.3). For example, there is the Wintel technical standard based on an Intel microprocessor and a Microsoft operating system. Microsoft and Intel "own" that standard, which is central to the PC.

dominant design

Common set of features or design characteristics.

Figure 7.3 Technical Standards for Personal Computers

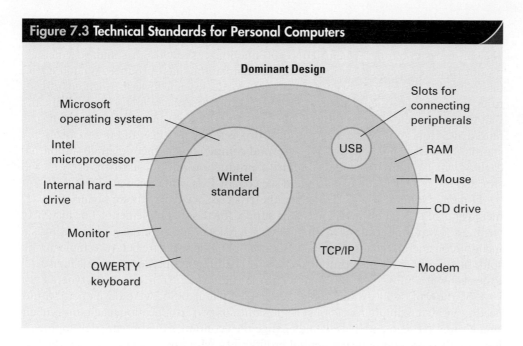

Developers of software applications, component parts, and peripherals such as printers adhere to this standard when developing their products because this guarantees that they will work well with a PC based on the Wintel standard. Another technical standard for connecting peripherals to the PC is the universal serial bus (or USB), established by an industry-standards-setting board. No one owns it; the standard is in the public domain. A third technical standard is for communication between a PC and the Internet via a modem. Known as TCP/IP, this standard was also set by an industry association and is in the public domain. Thus, as with many other products, the PC is actually based on several technical standards. It is also important to note that when a company owns a standard, as Microsoft and Intel do with the Wintel standard, it may be a source of competitive advantage and high profitability.

Benefits of Standards

Standards emerge because there are economic benefits associated with them. First, a technical standard helps to guarantee compatibility between products and their complements. For example, containers are used with railcars, trucks, and ships, and PCs are used with software applications. Compatibility has the tangible economic benefit of reducing the costs associated with making sure that products work well with each other.

Second, a standard can help reduce confusion in the minds of consumers. As noted in the opening case, when Blu-ray was launched it was competing against HD-DVD to be the dominant video standard. Players based on the different standards were incompatible; a disc designed to run on a Blu-ray player would not run on a HD-DVD player, and vice versa. The companies feared that selling these incompatible versions of the same technology would produce confusion in the minds of consumers, who would not know which version to purchase and might decide to wait and see which technology would dominate the marketplace. With lack of demand, both technologies might fail to gain traction in the marketplace and be unsuccessful. After Toshiba conceded the defeat of the HD-DVD standard, Blu-ray sales grew rapidly.

Third, a standard can help reduce production costs. Once a standard emerges, products that are based on the standard design can be mass produced, enabling the manufacturers to realize substantial economies of scale while lowering their cost structures. The fact that there is a central standard for PCs (the Wintel standard) means that the component parts for a PC can be mass produced. A manufacturer of internal hard drives, for example, can mass produce drives for Wintel PCs and thus realize substantial scale economies. If there were several competing and incompatible standards, each of which required a unique hard drive, production runs for hard drives would be shorter, unit costs would be higher, and the cost of PCs would increase.

Fourth, standards can help reduce the risks associated with supplying complementary products, and thus increase the supply for those complements. For instance, writing software applications to run on PCs is a risky proposition, requiring the investment of considerable sums of money for developing the software before a single unit is sold. Imagine what would occur if there were ten different operating systems in use for PCs, each with only 10% of the market, rather than the current situation, where over 90% of the world's PCs adhere to the Wintel standard. Software developers would need to write ten different versions of the same software application, each for a much smaller market segment. This would change the economics of software development, increase its risks, and reduce potential profitability. Moreover, because of their higher cost structure and fewer economies of scale, the price of software programs would increase.

Thus, although many people complain about the consequences of Microsoft's near-monopoly of PC operating systems, that dominance does have at least one good effect: It substantially reduces the risks facing the makers of complementary products and the costs of those products. In fact, standards lead to both low-cost and differentiation advantages for individual companies and can help raise the level of industry profitability.

Establishment of Standards

Standards emerge in an industry in three primary ways. First, when the benefits of establishing a standard are recognized, companies in an industry might lobby the government to mandate an industry standard. In the United States, for example, the Federal Communications Commission (FCC), after detailed discussions with broadcasters and consumer electronics companies, mandated a single technical standard for digital television broadcasts (DTV) and required analog television broadcasts to be terminated in 2009. The FCC took this step because it believed that without government action to set the standard, the DTV rollout would be very slow. Given a standard set by the government, consumer electronics companies have greater confidence that a market will emerge, and this should encourage them to develop DTV products.

Second, technical standards are often set by cooperation among businesses, without government help, and often through the medium of an industry association, as the example of the DVD forum illustrates. Companies cooperate in this way when they decide that competition to create a standard might be harmful because of the uncertainty that it would create in the minds of consumers or the risk it would pose to manufacturers and distributors.

Government- or association-set standards fall into the **public domain**, meaning that any company can freely incorporate the knowledge and technology upon which the standard is based into its products. For example, no one owns the QWERTY format, and therefore no company can profit from it directly. Similarly, the language that underlies the presentation of text and graphics on the Web, hypertext markup language (HTML), is in the public domain; it is free for all to use. The same is true for TCP/IP, the communications standard used for transmitting data on the Internet.

Often, however, the industry standard is selected competitively by the purchasing patterns of customers in the marketplace—that is, by market demand. In this case, the strategy and business model a company has developed for promoting its technological standard are of critical importance because ownership of an industry standard that is protected from imitation by patents and copyrights is a valuable asset—a source of sustained competitive advantage and superior profitability. Microsoft and Intel, for example, both owe their competitive advantage to their ownership of a specific technological standard or format. As noted earlier, format wars occur when two or more companies compete to get their designs adopted as the industry standard. Format wars are common in high-tech industries where standards are important. The Wintel standard became the dominant standard for PCs only after Microsoft and Intel won format wars against Apple's proprietary system, and later against IBM's OS/2 operating system. There is an ongoing format war within the smartphone business, as Apple, Google, Research in Motion, and Microsoft all battle to get their respective operating systems and phones adopted as the industry standard, as described in Strategy in Action 7.1.

Network Effects, Positive Feedback, and Lockout

There has been a growing realization that when standards are set by competition between companies promoting different formats, network effects are a primary determinant of how standards are established.[4] **Network effects** arise in industries where the size of the "network" of complementary products is a primary determinant of demand for an industry's product. For example, the demand for automobiles early in the 20th century was an increasing function of the network of paved roads and gas stations. Similarly, the demand for early telephones was an increasing function of the multitude of numbers that could be called; that is, of the size of the telephone network (the telephone network being the complementary product). When the first telephone service was introduced in New York City, only 100 numbers could be dialed. The network was very small because of the limited number of wires and telephone switches, which made the telephone a relatively useless piece of equipment. But, as an increasing number of people acquired telephones and the network of wires and switches expanded, the telephone connection gained value. This led to an upsurge in demand for telephone lines, which further increased the value of owning a telephone, setting up a positive feedback loop.

To understand why network effects are important in the establishment of standards, consider the classic example of a format war: the battle between Sony and Matsushita to establish their respective technologies for videocassette recorders (VCRs) as the standard in the marketplace. Sony was first to market with its Betamax technology, followed by JVC with its VHS technology. Both companies sold VCR recorder-players, and movie studios issued films prerecorded on VCR tapes for rental to consumers. Initially, all tapes were issued in Betamax format to play on Sony's

public domain
Government- or association-set standards of knowledge or technology that any company can freely incorporate into its product.

network effects
The network of complementary products as a primary determinant of the demand for an industry's product.

machine. Sony did not license its Betamax technology, preferring to make all player-recorders itself. Because Japan's Ministry of International Trade and Industry (MITI) appeared poised to select Sony's Betamax as a standard for Japan, JVC decided to liberally license its format and turned to Matsushita (now Panasonic) for support. Matsushita was the largest Japanese electronics manufacturer at that time. JVC and Matushita realized that to make the VHS format players valuable to consumers, they would need to encourage movie studios to issue movies for rental in VHS format. The only way to do that, they reasoned, was to increase the installed base of VHS players as rapidly as possible. They believed that the greater the installed base of VHS players, the greater the incentive for movie studios to issue films in VHS format for rental. As more prerecorded VHS tapes were made available for rental, VHS players became more valuable to consumers and demand for them increased (see Figure 7.4). JVC and Matsushita wanted to exploit a positive feedback loop.

JVC and Matsushita chose a licensing strategy under which any consumer electronics company was allowed to manufacture VHS-format players under license. This strategy worked. A large number of companies signed on to manufacture VHS players, and soon far more VHS players were available for purchase in stores than Betamax players. As sales of VHS players grew, movie studios issued more films for rental in VHS format, and this stoked demand. Before long, it was clear to anyone who entered a video rental store that there were more VHS tapes available for rent than Betamax tapes. This served to reinforce the positive feedback loop, and ultimately Sony's Betamax technology was shut out of the market. The pivotal difference between the two companies was strategy: JVC and Matsushita chose a licensing strategy; Sony did not. As a result, JVC's VHS technology became the de facto standard for VCRs.

The general principle that underlies this example is that when two or more companies compete to get technology adopted as an industry standard, and when network effects and positive feedback loops are important, *the company whose strategy best exploits positive feedback loops wins the format war*. This is a very important strategic principle in many high-technology industries, particularly computer hardware, software, telecommunications, and consumer electronics. Microsoft is where it is today because it exploited a positive feedback loop. Dolby presents us with another example of a company

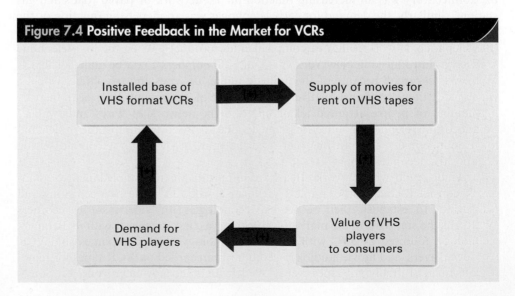

Figure 7.4 Positive Feedback in the Market for VCRs

that exploited a positive feedback loop. When Ray Dolby invented a technology for reducing the background hiss in professional tape recording, he adopted a licensing model that charged a very modest fee. He knew his technology was valuable, but he also understood that charging a high fee would encourage manufacturers to develop their own noise-reduction technology. He also decided to license the technology for use on prerecorded tapes for free, collecting licensing fees on the players only. This set up a powerful, positive feedback loop: Growing sales of prerecorded tapes encoded with Dolby technology created a demand for tape players that contained Dolby technology, and as the installed base of tape players with Dolby technology grew, the proportion of prerecorded tapes that were encoded with Dolby technology surged—further boosting demand for players incorporating Dolby technology. By the mid-1970s, virtually all prerecorded tapes were encoded with Dolby noise-reduction technology.

As the market settles on a standard, an important implication of the positive feedback process occurs: Companies promoting alternative standards can be locked out of the market when consumers are unwilling to bear the switching costs required to abandon the established standard and adopt the new standard. In this context, consumers must bear the costs of switching from a product based on one technological standard to a product based on another technological standard.

For illustration, imagine that a company developed an operating system for personal computers that was both faster and more stable than the current standard in the marketplace, Microsoft Windows. This company would be able to gain significant market share from Microsoft only with great difficulty. Consumers choose PCs not for their operating system but for the applications that run on the operating system. A new operating system would initially have a very small installed base, so few developers would be willing to take the risks involved in writing word-processing programs, spreadsheets, games, and other applications for that operating system. Because there would be very few applications available, consumers who did make the switch would have to bear the switching costs associated with giving up some of their applications, which they might be unwilling to do. Moreover, even if applications were available for the new operating system, consumers would have to bear the costs of purchasing those applications—another source of switching costs. In addition, they would have to bear the costs associated with learning to use the new operating system, yet another source of switching costs. Thus, many consumers would be unwilling to switch even if the new operating system performed better than Windows, and the company promoting the new operating system would be locked out of the market.

However, consumers will bear switching costs if the benefits of adopting the new technology outweigh the costs of switching. For example, in the late 1980s and early 1990s, millions of people switched from analog record players to digital CD players despite the fact that switching costs were significant: Consumers had to purchase the new player technology, and many people purchased CD versions of favorite musical recordings that they already owned. Nevertheless, people made the switch because, for many, the perceived benefit—the incredibly better sound quality associated with CDs—outweighed the costs of switching.

As this switching process continued, a positive feedback loop developed. The installed base of CD players grew, leading to an increase in the number of musical recordings issued on CD as opposed to, or in addition to, vinyl records. The installed base of CD players got so big that mainstream music companies began to issue recordings only in CD format. Once this occurred, even those who did not want to switch to the new technology were required to do so if they wished to purchase new music recordings. The industry standard had shifted: new technology had locked in as the standard, and the old technology was locked out.

Extrapolating from this example, it can be argued that despite its dominance, the Wintel standard for PCs could one day be superseded if a competitor finds a way of providing sufficient benefits that enough consumers are willing to bear the switching costs associated with moving to a new operating system. Indeed, there are signs that Apple and Google are chipping away at the dominance of the Wintel standard, primarily by using elegant design and ease of use as tools to get people to bear the costs of switching from Wintel computers..

STRATEGIES FOR WINNING A FORMAT WAR

From the perspective of a company pioneering a new technological standard in a marketplace where network effects and positive feedback loops operate, the key question becomes: "What strategy should we pursue to establish our format as the dominant one?"

The various strategies that companies should adopt in order to win format wars are centered upon *finding ways to make network effects work in their favor and against their competitors*. Winning a format war requires a company to build the installed base for its standard as rapidly as possible, thereby leveraging the positive feedback loop, inducing consumers to bear switching costs and ultimately locking the market to its technology. It requires the company to jump-start and then accelerate demand for its technological standard or format such that it becomes established as quickly as possible as the industry standard, thereby locking out competing formats. A number of key strategies and tactics can be adopted to try to achieve this.[5]

Ensure a Supply of Complements

It is important for a company to make sure that there is an adequate supply of complements for its product. For example, no one will purchase the Sony PlayStation 4 unless there is an adequate supply of games to run on that machine. Companies typically take two steps to ensure an adequate supply of complements.

First, they may diversify into the production of complements and seed the market with sufficient supply to help jump-start demand for their format. Before Sony produced the original PlayStation in the early 1990s, for example, it established its own in-house unit to produce videogames for the console. When it launched PlayStation, Sony also simultaneously released 16 games to run on the it, giving consumers a reason to purchase the format. Tesla is similarly constructing its own network of supercharging stations at which customers can charge its electric vehicles for free.

Second, companies may create incentives or make it easy for independent companies to produce complements. Sony also licensed the right to produce games to a number of independent game developers, charged the developers a lower royalty rate than they had to pay to competitors such as Nintendo and Sega, and provided them with software tools that made it easier for them to develop games (Apple is now doing the same thing with its smartphones). Thus, the launch of the Sony PlayStation was accompanied by the simultaneous launch of approximately 30 games, which quickly helped to stimulate demand for the machine.

Leverage Killer Applications

Killer applications are applications or uses of a new technology or product that are so compelling that they persuade customers to adopt the new format or technology in droves, thereby "killing" demand for competing formats. Killer applications often help to jump-start demand for the new standard. For example, the killer applications that induced consumers to sign up for online services such as AOL in the 1990s were e-mail, chat rooms, and Web browsers.

Ideally, the company promoting a technological standard will also want to develop its own killer applications—that is, develop the appropriate complementary products. However, it may also be able to leverage applications that others develop. For example, the early sales of the IBM PC following its 1981 introduction were primarily driven by IBM's decision to license two important software programs for the PC: VisiCalc (a spreadsheet program) and EasyWriter (a word-processing program), both developed by independent companies. IBM saw that they were driving rapid adoption of rival personal computers, such as the Apple II, so it quickly licensed software, produced versions that would run on the IBM PC, and sold these programs as complements to the IBM PC, a very successful strategy. In video games, console producers such as Microsoft, Nintendo, and Sony often award endorsements to exceptional games developed by third-party developers. For example, PlayStation designates the best games for each console generation with the award "Platinum: The Best of PlayStation." Nintendo similarly has a "Nintendo Selects" endorsement, and Microsoft has a "Microsoft Xbox 360 Classics" endorsement. These endorsements signal potential customers about the quality of the game and help to generate "buzz" about the game and the console. Endorsing a complement in this way can help to turn the complement into a blockbuster, which in turn fuels more sales of the platform.[6]

killer applications
Applications or uses of a new technology or product that are so compelling that customers adopt them in droves, killing competing formats.

Aggressive Pricing and Marketing

A common tactic used to jump-start demand is to adopt a **razor and blade strategy**: pricing the product (razor) low in order to stimulate demand and increase the installed base, and then trying to make high profits on the sale of complements (razor blades), which are priced relatively high. This strategy owes its name to Gillette, the company that pioneered this strategy to sell its razors and blades. Many other companies have followed this strategy—for example, Hewlett-Packard typically sells its printers at cost but makes significant profits on the subsequent sales of replacement cartridges. In this case, the printer is the "razor" and is priced low to stimulate demand and induce consumers to switch from their existing printer, while the cartridges are the "blades," which are priced high to make profits. The inkjet printer represents a proprietary technological format because only HP cartridges can be used with HP printers; cartridges designed for competing inkjet printers such as those sold by Canon will not work in HP printers. A similar strategy is used in the videogame industry: manufacturers price videogame consoles at cost to induce consumers to adopt their technology, while they make profits on royalties from the sales of games that run on the system.

razor and blade strategy
Pricing the product low in order to stimulate demand, and pricing complements high.

Aggressive marketing is also a key factor in jump-starting demand to get an early lead in an installed base. Substantial upfront marketing and point-of-sales promotion techniques are often used to try to attract potential early adopters who will bear the switching costs associated with adopting the format. If these efforts are successful, they can be the start of a positive feedback loop. Again, the Sony PlayStation provides a good example. Sony co-linked the introduction of the PlayStation with nationwide television advertising aimed at its primary demographic (18- to 34-year-olds) and in-store displays that allowed potential buyers to play games on the machine before making a purchase.

Cooperate with Competitors

Companies have been close to simultaneously introducing competing and incompatible technological standards a number of times. A good example is the compact disc. Initially four companies—Sony, Philips, JVC, and Telefunken—were developing CD players using different variations of the underlying laser technology. If this situation had persisted, they might have introduced incompatible technologies into the marketplace; a CD made for a Philips CD player would not play on a Sony CD player. Understanding that the nearly simultaneous introduction of such incompatible technologies can create significant confusion among consumers, and often lead them to delay their purchases, Sony and Philips decided to join forces and cooperate on developing the technology. Sony contributed its error-correction technology, and Philips contributed its laser technology. The result of this cooperation was that momentum among other players in the industry shifted toward the Sony–Philips alliances; JVC and Telefunken were left with little support. Most important, recording labels announced that they would support the Sony–Philips format but not the Telefunken or JVC format.

Telefunken and JVC subsequently abandoned their efforts to develop CD technology. The cooperation between Sony and Philips was important because it reduced confusion in the industry and allowed a single format to rise to the fore, which accelerated adoption of the technology. The cooperation was a win-win situation for both Philips and Sony, which eliminated competitors and enabled them to share in the success of the format.

License the Format

Licensing the format to other enterprises so that they too can produce products based on the format is another strategy often adopted. The company that pioneered the format gains from the licensing fees that return to it, as well as from the enlarged supply of the product, which can stimulate demand and help accelerate market adoption. This was the strategy that JVC and Matsushita adopted with the VHS format for the VCR. As discussed previously, in addition to producing VCRs at Matsushita's factory in Osaka, JVC licensed a number of other companies produce VHS format players, and so VHS players became widely available. (Sony decided not to license its competing Betamax format and produced all Betamax format players itself.)

The correct strategy to pursue in a particular scenario requires that the company consider all of these different strategies and tactics and pursue those that seem most appropriate given the competitive circumstances prevailing in the industry and the likely strategy of rivals. Although there is no single best combination of strategies and tactics, the company must keep the goal of rapidly increasing the installed base of products based on its standard at the forefront of its endeavors. By helping to jump-start demand for its format, a company can induce consumers to bear the switching costs associated with adopting its technology and leverage any positive feedback process that might exist. It is also important not to pursue strategies that have the opposite effect. For example, pricing high to capture profits from early adopters, who tend not to be as price sensitive as later adopters, can have the unfortunate effect of slowing demand growth and allowing a more aggressive competitor to pick up share and establish its format as the industry standard.

▼ COSTS IN HIGH-TECHNOLOGY INDUSTRIES

In many high-tech industries, the fixed costs of developing the product are very high, but the costs of producing one extra unit of the product are very low. This is most obvious in the case of software. For example, it reportedly cost Microsoft $5 billion to develop Windows Vista, but the cost of producing one more copy of Windows Vista is virtually zero. Once the Windows Vista program was complete, Microsoft duplicated its master disks and sent the copies to PC manufacturers, such as Dell Computer, which then installed a copy of Windows Vista onto every PC sold. Microsoft's cost was, effectively, zero, and yet the company receives a significant licensing fee for each copy of Windows Vista installed on a PC.[7] For Microsoft, the marginal cost of making one more copy of Windows Vista is close to zero, although the fixed costs of developing the product were around $5 billion.

Many other high-technology products have similar cost economics: very high fixed costs and very low marginal costs. Most software products share these features, although if the software is sold through stores, the costs of packaging and distribution will raise the marginal costs, and if it is sold by a sales force direct to end-users, this too will raise the marginal costs. Many consumer electronics products have the same basic economics. The fixed costs of developing a DVD player or a videogame console can be very expensive, but the costs of producing an incremental unit are very low. Similarly, the fixed costs of developing a new drug can are typically estimated to be at least $1.6 billion (and potentially much more if one factors in the cost of all the failed drug development efforts),[8] but the marginal cost of producing each additional pill is at most a few cents.

Comparative Cost Economics

To grasp why this cost structure is strategically important, a company must understand that, in many industries, marginal costs rise as a company tries to expand output (economists call this the *law of diminishing returns*). To produce more of a good, a company must hire more labor and invest in more plant and machinery. At the margin, the additional resources used are not as productive, so this leads to increasing marginal costs. However, the law of diminishing returns often does not apply in many high-tech settings such as the production of software or sending data through a digital telecommunications network.

Consider two companies, α and β (see Figure 7.5). Company α is a conventional producer and faces diminishing returns, so as it tries to expand output, its marginal costs rise. Company β is a high-tech producer, and its marginal costs do not rise at all as output is increased. Note that in Figure 7.5, company β's marginal cost curve is drawn as a straight line near to the horizontal axis, implying that marginal costs are close to zero and do not vary with output, whereas company α's marginal costs rise as output is expanded, illustrating diminishing returns. Company β's flat, low

Figure 7.5 Cost Structures in High-Technology Industries

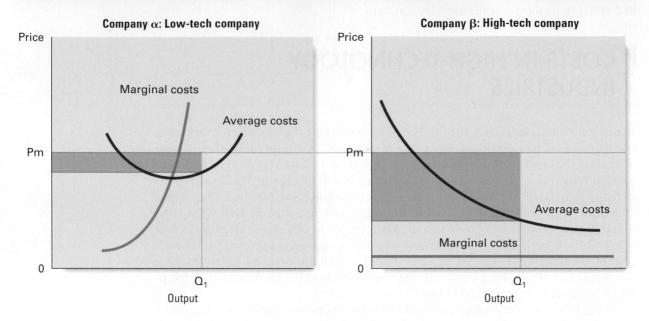

marginal cost curve means that its average cost curve will continuously fall over all ranges of output as it spreads its fixed costs out over greater volume. In contrast, the rising marginal costs encountered by company α mean that its average cost curve is the U-shaped curve familiar from basic economics texts. For simplicity, assume that both companies sell their product at the same price, Pm, and both sell exactly the same quantity of output, $0 - Q_1$. Figure 7.5 shows that, at an output of Q_1, company β has much lower average costs than company α and as a consequence is making far more profit (profit is the shaded area in Figure 7.5).

Strategic Significance

If a company can shift from a cost structure where it encounters increasing marginal costs to one where fixed costs may be high but marginal costs are much lower, its profitability may increase. In the consumer electronics industry, such a shift has been playing out for two decades. Musical recordings were once based on analog technology where marginal costs rose as output expanded due to diminishing returns (as in the case of company α in Figure 7.5). In the 1980s and 1990s, digital systems such as CD players replaced analog systems. Digital systems are software based, and this implies much lower marginal costs of producing one more copy of a recording. As a result, music companies were able to lower prices, expand demand, and see their profitability increase (their production system has more in common with company β in Figure 7.5).

This process, however, was still unfolding. The latest technology for copying musical recordings is based on distribution over the Internet (e.g., by downloading songs onto a smartphone). Here, the marginal costs of making one more copy of a recording are lower still. In fact, they are close to zero, and do not increase with output. The only problem is that the low costs of copying and distributing music recordings can lead to widespread illegal fire sharing, which ultimately leads to a very large decline in overall revenues in recorded music. According to the International Federation of the Phonographic Industry, worldwide revenues for CDs, vinyl, cassettes, and digital downloads dropped from $36.9 billion in 2000 to $15.9 billion in 2010. We discuss copyright issues in more detail shortly when we consider intellectual property rights. The same shift is now beginning to affect other industries. Some companies are building their strategies around trying to exploit and profit from this shift. For an example, Strategy in Action 7.2 looks at SonoSite.

7.2 STRATEGY IN ACTION

Lowering the Cost of Ultrasound Equipment Through Digitalization

The ultrasound unit has been an important piece of diagnostic equipment in hospitals for some time. Ultrasound units use the physics of sound to produce images of soft tissues in the human body. Ultrasounds can produce detailed, three-dimensional, color images of organs and, by using contrast agents, track the flow of fluids through them. A cardiologist, for example, can use an ultrasound in combination with contrast agents injected into the bloodstream to track the flow of blood through a beating heart. In addition to the visual diagnosis, ultrasound also produces an array of quantitative diagnostic information of great value to physicians.

Modern ultrasound units are sophisticated instruments that cost about $250,000 to $300,000 each for a top-line model. They are bulky instruments, weighing approximately 300 pounds, wheeled around hospitals on carts.

A few years ago, a group of researchers at ATL, one of the leading ultrasound companies, proposed an idea for reducing the size and cost of a basic machine. They theorized that it might be possible to replace up to 80% of the solid circuits in an ultrasound unit with software, and in the process significantly shrink the size and reduce the weight of machines, thereby producing portable ultrasound units. Moreover, by digitalizing much of the ultrasound (replacing hardware with software), they could considerably decrease the marginal costs of making additional units, and would thus be able to make a better profit at much lower price points.

The researchers reasoned that a portable, inexpensive ultrasound unit would find market opportunities in totally new niches. For example, a smaller ultrasound unit could be placed in an ambulance or carried into battle by an army medic, or purchased by family physicians for use in their offices. Although they realized that it would be some time, perhaps decades, before such a unit could attain the image quality and diagnostic sophistication of top-of-the-line machines, they saw the opportunity in terms of creating market niches that previously could not be served by ultrasound companies because of the high costs and bulk of the product.

The researchers later became part of a project team within ATL, and thereafter became an entirely new company, SonoSite. In late-1999, SonoSite introduced its first portable product, which weighed just 6 pounds and cost about $25,000. SonoSite targeted niches that full-sized ultrasound products could not reach: ambulatory care and foreign markets that could not afford the more expensive equipment. In 2010, the company sold over $275 million of product. In 2011, Fujifilm Holdings bought SonoSite for $995 million to expand its range of medical imaging products and help it overtake the dominant portable ultrasound equipment producer, General Electric.

Source: Interviews by C. W. L. Hill.

When a high-tech company faces high fixed costs and low marginal costs, its strategy should emphasize the low-cost structure option: deliberately drive down prices in order to increase volume. Figure 7.5 shows that the high-tech company's average costs fall rapidly as output expands. This implies that prices can be reduced to stimulate demand, and as long as prices fall less rapidly than average costs, per-unit profit margins will expand as prices fall. This is a consequence of low marginal costs that do not rise with output. This strategy of pricing low to drive volume and reap wider profit margins is central to the business model of some very successful high-tech companies, including Microsoft.

◤CAPTURING FIRST-MOVER ADVANTAGES

first mover

A firm that pioneers a particular product category or feature by being first to offer it to market.

In high-technology industries, companies often compete by striving to be the first to develop revolutionary new products, that is, to be a **first mover**. By definition, the first mover that creates a revolutionary product is in a monopoly position. If the new product satisfies unmet consumer needs and demand is high, the first mover can capture significant revenues and profits. Such revenues and profits signal to potential rivals that imitating the first mover makes money. Figure 7.6 implies that in the absence of strong barriers to imitation, imitators will rush into the market created by the first mover, competing away the first mover's monopoly profits and leaving all participants in the market with a much lower level of returns.

Despite imitation, some first movers have the ability to capitalize on and reap substantial first-mover advantages—the advantages of pioneering new technologies and products that lead to an enduring competitive advantage. Intel introduced the world's first microprocessor in 1971; today, it still dominates the microprocessor segment of the semiconductor industry. Xerox introduced the world's first photocopier and for a long time enjoyed a leading position in the industry. Cisco introduced the first Internet

Figure 7.6 The Impact of Imitation on Profits of a First Mover

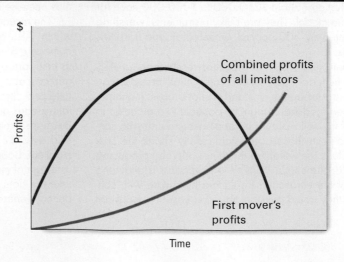

protocol network router in 1986, and still leads the market for that equipment today. Microsoft introduced the world's first software application for a personal computer in 1979, Microsoft BASIC, and it remains a dominant force in PC software.

Some first movers can reap substantial advantages from their pioneering activities that lead to an enduring competitive advantage. They can, in other words, limit or slow the rate of imitation.

But there are plenty of counterexamples suggesting that first-mover advantages might not be easy to capture and, in fact, that there might be **first-mover disadvantages**— the competitive disadvantages associated with being first. For example, Apple was the first company to introduce a handheld computer, the Apple Newton, but the product failed; a second mover, Palm, succeeded where Apple had failed (although Apple has recently had major success as a first mover with the first true tablet computer, the iPad). In the market for commercial jet aircraft, DeHavilland was first to market with the Comet, but it was the second mover, Boeing, with its 707 jetliner, that went on to dominate the market.

Clearly, being a first mover does not by itself guarantee success. As we shall see, the difference between innovating companies that capture first-mover advantages and those that fall victim to first-mover disadvantages in part incites the strategy that the first mover pursues. Before considering the strategy issue, however, we need to take a closer look at the nature of first-mover advantages and disadvantages.[9]

first-mover disadvantages
Competitive disadvantages associated with being first to market.

First-Mover Advantages

There are five primary sources of first-mover advantages.[10] First, the first mover has an opportunity to exploit network effects and positive feedback loops, locking consumers into its technology. In the VCR industry, Sony could have exploited network effects by licensing its technology, but instead the company ceded its first-mover advantage to the second mover, Matsushita.

Second, the first mover may be able to establish significant brand loyalty, which is expensive for later entrants to break down. Indeed, if the company is successful in this endeavor, its name may become closely associated with the entire class of products, including those produced by rivals. People still talk of "Xeroxing" when making a photocopy, or "FedExing" when they will be sending a package by overnight mail.

Third, the first mover may be able to increase sales volume ahead of rivals and thus reap cost advantages associated with the realization of scale economies and learning effects (see Chapter 4). Once the first mover has these cost advantages, it can respond to new entrants by cutting prices in order to retain its market share and still earn significant profits.

Fourth, the first mover may be able to create switching costs for its customers that subsequently make it difficult for rivals to enter the market and take customers away from the first mover. Wireless service providers, for example, will give new customers a "free" wireless phone, but customers must sign a contract agreeing to pay for the phone if they terminate the service contract within a specified time period such as 1 or 2 years. Because the real cost of a wireless phone may run from $100 to $200, this represents a significant switching cost that later entrants must overcome.

Finally, the first mover may be able to accumulate valuable knowledge related to customer needs, distribution channels, product technology, process technology, and so on. Knowledge so accumulated can give it an advantage that later entrants might find difficult or expensive to match. Sharp, for example, was the first mover in the commercial manufacture of active matrix liquid crystal displays used in laptop computers.

The process for manufacturing these displays is very difficult, with a high rejection rate for flawed displays. Sharp has accumulated such an advantage with regard to production processes that it has been very difficult for later entrants to match it on product quality, and therefore on costs.

First-Mover Disadvantages

Balanced against these first-mover advantages are a number of disadvantages.[11] First, the first mover has to bear significant pioneering costs that later entrants do not. The first mover must pioneer the technology, develop distribution channels, and educate customers about the nature of the product. This can be expensive and time consuming. Later entrants, by way of contrast, might be able to free-ride on the first mover's investments in pioneering the market and customer education. That is, they do not have to bear the pioneering costs of the first mover. Generic drug makers, for example, spend very little on R&D compared to the costs borne by the developer of an original drug because they can replicate the finished chemical or biological product (that is,, they do not have to explore many alternative paths to a solution), and they can bypass most of the clinical testing process.[12]

Related to this, first movers are more prone to make mistakes because there are so many uncertainties in a new market. Later entrants may learn from the mistakes made by first movers, improve on the product or the way in which it is sold, and come to market with a superior offering that captures significant market share from the first mover. For example, one reason that the Apple Newton failed was that the software in the handheld computer failed to recognize human handwriting. The second mover in this market, Palm, learned from Apple's error. When it introduced the PalmPilot, it used software that recognized letters written in a particular way, graffiti style, and then persuaded customers to learn this method of inputting data into the handheld computer.

Third, first movers run the risk of building the wrong resources and capabilities because they focus on a customer set that is not characteristic of the mass market. This is the "crossing the chasm" problem that we discussed in the previous chapter. You will recall that the customers in the early market—those we categorized as innovators and early adopters—have different characteristics from the first wave of the mass market, the early majority. The first mover runs the risk of directing its resources and capabilities to the needs of innovators and early adopters, and not being able to switch when the early majority enters the market. As a result, first movers run a greater risk of plunging into the chasm that separates the early market from the mass market.

Finally, the first mover may invest in inferior or obsolete technology. This can happen when its product innovation is based on underlying technology that is rapidly advancing. Basing its product on an early version of a technology may lock a company into a resource that rapidly becomes obsolete. In contrast, later entrants may be able to leapfrog the first mover and introduce products that are based on later versions of the underlying technology. This happened in France during the 1980s when, at the urging of the government, France Telecom introduced the world's first consumer online service, Minitel. France Telecom distributed free terminals to consumers , which connected to the phone line and could be used to browse phone directories. Other simple services were soon added, and before long the French could shop, bank, make travel arrangements, and check weather and news "online"—years before the Web was invented. The problem was that by the standards of the Web, Minitel was very crude and inflexible, and France Telecom, as the first mover, suffered. The French were very slow to adopt personal computers and the Internet primarily because Minitel had such a presence. As late as 1998, only one-fifth of French households had a computer, compared with two-fifths in the United States, and only 2% of households were connected to the Internet, compared to over 30% in the United States. As the result of a government decision, France Telecom, and the entire nation of France, was slow to adopt a revolutionary new online medium—the Web—because they were the first to invest in a more primitive version of the technology.[13]

Strategies for Exploiting First-Mover Advantages

First movers must strategize and determine how to exploit their lead and capitalize on first-mover advantages to build a sustainable, long-term competitive advantage while simultaneously reducing the risks associated with first-mover disadvantages. There are three basic strategies available: (1) develop and market the innovation; (2) develop and market the innovation jointly with other companies through a strategic alliance or joint venture; and (3) license the innovation to others and allow them to develop the market.

The optimal choice of strategy depends on the answers to three questions:

1. Does the innovating company have the complementary assets to exploit its innovation and capture first-mover advantages?
2. How difficult is it for imitators to copy the company's innovation? In other words, what is the height of barriers to imitation?
3. Are there capable competitors that could rapidly imitate the innovation?

Complementary Assets   Complementary assets are required to exploit a new innovation and gain a competitive advantage.[14] Among the most important complementary assets are competitive manufacturing facilities capable of handling rapid growth in customer demand while maintaining high product quality. State-of-the-art manufacturing facilities enable the first mover to quickly move down the experience curve without encountering production bottlenecks or problems with the quality of the product. The inability to satisfy demand because of these problems, however, creates the opportunity for imitators to enter the marketplace. For example, in 1998, Immunex was the first company to introduce a revolutionary biological treatment for rheumatoid arthritis. Sales for this product, Enbrel, very rapidly increased, reaching $750 million in 2001. However, Immunex had not invested in sufficient manufacturing capacity. In mid-2000, it announced that it lacked the capacity to satisfy demand and that bringing additional capacity on line would take at least 2 years. This manufacturing bottleneck gave the second mover in the market, Johnson & Johnson, the opportunity to rapidly expand demand for its product, which by early 2002 was outselling Enbrel. Immunex's first-mover advantage had been partly eroded because it lacked an important complementary asset, the manufacturing capability required to satisfy demand.

Complementary assets also include marketing knowhow, an adequate sales force, access to distribution systems, and an after-sales service and support network. All of these assets can help an innovator build brand loyalty and more rapidly achieve market penetration.[15] In turn, the resulting increases in volume facilitate more rapid movement down the experience curve and the attainment of a sustainable, cost-based advantage due to scale economies and learning effects. EMI, the first mover in the market for computerized tomography (CT) scanners, ultimately lost out to established medical equipment companies such as GE Medical Systems because it lacked the marketing knowhow, sales force, and distribution systems required to effectively compete in the world's largest market for medical equipment, the United States.

Developing complementary assets can be very expensive, and companies often need large infusions of capital for this purpose. That is why first movers often lose out to late movers that are large, successful companies in other industries with the resources to quickly develop a presence in the new industry. Microsoft and 3M exemplify companies that have moved quickly to capitalize on the opportunities when other companies open up new product markets, such as compact discs or floppy disks. For example, although Netscape pioneered the market for Internet browsers with the Netscape Navigator, Microsoft's Internet Explorer ultimately dominated that market.

Height of Barriers to Imitation   Recall from Chapter 3 that barriers to imitation are factors that prevent rivals from imitating a company's distinctive competencies and innovations. Although any innovation can be copied, the higher the barriers are, the longer it takes for rivals to imitate the innovation, and the more time the first mover has to build an enduring competitive advantage.

Barriers to imitation give an innovator time to establish a competitive advantage and build more enduring barriers to entry in the newly created market. Patents, for example, are among the most widely used barriers to imitation. By protecting its photocopier technology with a thicket of patents, Xerox was able to delay any significant imitation of its product for 17 years. However, patents are often easy to "invent around." For example, one study found that this happened to 60% of patented innovations within 4 years.[16] If patent protection is weak, a company might try to slow imitation by developing new products and processes in secret. The most famous example of this approach is Coca-Cola, which has kept the formula for Coke a secret for generations. But Coca-Cola's success in this regard is an exception. A study of 100 companies has estimated that rivals learn about a company's decision to develop a major new product or process and its related proprietary information within 12 to 18 months of the original development decision.[17]

Capable Competitors   Capable competitors are companies that can move quickly to imitate the pioneering company. Competitors' capability to imitate a pioneer's innovation depends primarily on two factors: (1) R&D skills; and (2) access to complementary assets. In general, the greater the number of capable competitors with access to the R&D skills and complementary assets needed to imitate an innovation, the more rapid imitation is likely to be.

In this context, R&D skills refer to the ability of rivals to reverse-engineer an innovation to find out how it works and quickly develop a comparable product. As an example, consider the CT scanner. GE bought one of the first CT scanners produced by EMI, and its technical experts reverse-engineered the machine. Despite the product's technological complexity, GE developed its own version, which allowed it to quickly imitate EMI and replace it as the major supplier of CT scanners.

Complementary assets—the access that rivals have to marketing, sales knowhow, and manufacturing capabilities—are key determinants of the rate of imitation. If would-be imitators lack critical complementary assets, not only will they have to imitate the innovation, but they may also need to imitate the innovator's complementary assets. This is expensive, as AT&T discovered when it tried to enter the PC business in 1984. AT&T lacked the marketing assets (sales force and distribution systems) necessary to support personal computer products. The lack of these assets and the time it takes to build the assets partly explains why: Four years after it entered the market, AT&T had lost $2.5 billion and still had not emerged as a viable contender. It subsequently exited this business.

Three Innovation Strategies   The way in which these three factors—complementary assets, height of barriers to imitation, and the capability of competitors—influence the choice of innovation strategy is summarized in Table 7.1. The competitive strategy of developing and marketing the innovation alone makes most sense when: (1) the innovator has the complementary assets necessary to develop the innovation, (2) the barriers to imitating a new innovation are high, and (3) the number of capable competitors is limited. Complementary assets allow rapid development and promotion of the innovation. High barriers to imitation give the innovator time to establish a competitive advantage and build enduring barriers to entry through brand loyalty or experience-based cost advantages. The fewer capable competitors there are, the less likely it is that any one of them will succeed in circumventing barriers to imitation and quickly imitating the innovation.

The competitive strategy of developing and marketing the innovation jointly with other companies through a strategic alliance or joint venture makes most sense when: (1) the innovator lacks complementary assets, (2) barriers to imitation are high, and (3) there are several capable competitors. In such circumstances, it makes sense to enter into an alliance with a company that already has the complementary assets—in other words, with a capable competitor. Theoretically, such an alliance should prove to be mutually beneficial, and each partner can share in high profits that neither could earn on its own. Moreover, such a strategy has the benefit of co-opting a potential rival. For example, had EMI teamed with a capable competitor to develop the market for CT scanners, such as GE Medical Systems, instead of going it alone, the company might have been able to build a more enduring competitive advantage and also co-opt a powerful rival into its camp.

The third strategy, licensing, makes most sense when: (1) the innovating company lacks the complementary assets, (2) barriers to imitation are low, and (3) there are many capable competitors. The combination of low barriers to imitation and many capable competitors makes rapid imitation almost certain. The innovator's lack of

Table 7.1 Strategies for Profiting from Innovation

Strategy	Does the Innovator Have the Required Complementary Assets?	Likely Height of Barriers to Imitation	Number of Capable Competitors
Going it alone	Yes	High	Very few
Entering into an alliance	No	High	Moderate number
Licensing the innovation	No	Low	Many

complementary assets further suggests that an imitator will soon capture the innovator's competitive advantage. Given these factors, because rapid diffusion of the innovator's technology through imitation is inevitable, the innovator can at least share in some benefits of this diffusion by licensing out its technology.[18] Moreover, by setting a relatively modest licensing fee, the innovator may be able to reduce the incentive that potential rivals have to develop their own competing, and possibly superior, technology. As described previously, Dolby adopted this strategy to get its technology established as the standard for noise reduction in the music and film businesses.

◤ TECHNOLOGICAL PARADIGM SHIFTS

technological paradigm shift

Shifts in new technologies that revolutionize the structure of the industry, dramatically alter the nature of competition, and require companies to adopt new strategies in order to survive.

Technological paradigm shifts occur when new technologies revolutionize the structure of the industry, dramatically alter the nature of competition, and require companies to adopt new strategies in order to survive. A good example of a paradigm shift is the evolution of photography from chemical to digital printing processes. For over half a century, the large, incumbent enterprises in the photographic industry such as Kodak and Fujifilm have generated most of their revenues from selling and processing film using traditional silver halide technology. The rise of digital photography has been a huge disruptive threat to their business models. Digital cameras do not use film, the mainstay of Kodak's and Fuji's business. In addition, these cameras are more like specialized computers than conventional cameras, and are therefore based on scientific knowledge in which Kodak and Fuji have little expertise. Although both Kodak and Fuji have heavily invested in the development of digital cameras, they are facing intense competition from companies such as Sony, Canon, and Hewlett-Packard, which have developed their own digital cameras; from software developers such as Adobe and Microsoft, which make software for manipulating digital images; and from printer companies such as Hewlett-Packard and Canon, which make printers that consumers use to print high-quality pictures from home. As digital substitution gathers speed in the photography industry, it is not clear that the traditional incumbents will survive this shift; the new competitors might rise to dominance in the new market.

Kodak and Fuji are hardly the first large incumbents to be felled by a technological paradigm shift in their industry. In the early 1980s, the computer industry was revolutionized by the arrival of personal computer technology, which gave rise to client–server networks that replaced traditional mainframe and minicomputers for many business uses. Many incumbent companies in the mainframe era, such as Wang, Control Data, and DEC, ultimately did not survive, and even IBM went through a decade of wrenching changes and large losses before it reinvented itself as a provider of e-business solutions. Instead, new entrants such as Microsoft, Intel, Dell, and Compaq rose to dominate this new computer industry.

Today, many believe that the advent of cloud computing is ushering in a paradigm shift in the computer industry. Microsoft, the dominant incumbent in the PC software business, is very vulnerable to this shift. If the center of computing does move to the cloud, with most data and applications stored there, and if all one needs to access data and run applications is a Web browser, then the value of a PC operating system such as Windows is significantly reduced. Microsoft understands this as well as anyone, which is why the company is pushing aggressively into the cloud computing market with Windows Azure.

Examples such as these raise four questions:

1. When do paradigm shifts occur, and how do they unfold?
2. Why do so many incumbents go into decline following a paradigm shift?
3. What strategies can incumbents adopt to increase the probability that they will survive a paradigm shift and emerge on the other side of the market abyss created by the arrival of new technology as a profitable enterprise?
4. What strategies can new entrants into a market adopt to profit from a paradigm shift?

We shall answer each of these questions in the remainder of this chapter.

Paradigm Shifts and the Decline of Established Companies

Paradigm shifts appear to be more likely to occur in an industry when one, or both, of the following conditions are in place.[19] First, the established technology in the industry is mature, and is approaching or at its "natural limit." Second, a new "disruptive technology" has entered the marketplace and is taking root in niches that are poorly served by incumbent companies using established technology.

Natural Limits to Technology   Richard Foster has formalized the relationship between the performance of a technology and time in terms of what he calls the technology S-curve (see Figure 7.7).[20] This curve shows the relationship over time of cumulative investments in R&D and the performance (or functionality) of a given technology. Early in its evolution, R&D investments in a new technology tend to yield rapid improvements in performance as basic engineering problems are solved. After a time, diminishing returns to cumulative R&D begin to set in, the rate of improvement in performance slows, and the technology starts to approach its natural limit, where further advances are not possible. For example, one can argue that there was more improvement in the first 50 years of the commercial aerospace business following the pioneering flight by the Wright Brothers than there has been in the second 50 years. Indeed, the venerable Boeing 747 is based on a 1960's design. In commercial aerospace, therefore, we are now in the region of diminishing returns and may be approaching the natural limit to improvements in the technology of commercial aerospace.

Figure 7.7 The Technology S-Curve

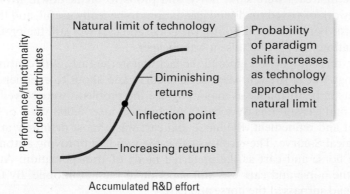

Similarly, it can be argued that we are approaching the natural limit to technology in the performance of silicon-based semiconductor chips. Over the past two decades, the performance of semiconductor chips has been increased dramatically; companies can now manufacture a larger amount of transistors in a single, small silicon chip. This process has helped to increase the power of computers, lower their cost, and shrink their size. But we are starting to approach limits to the ability to shrink the width of lines on a chip and therefore pack ever more transistors onto a single chip. The limit is imposed by the natural laws of physics. Light waves are used to etch lines onto a chip, and one cannot etch a line that is smaller than the wavelength of light being used. Semiconductor companies are already using light beams with very small wavelengths, such as extreme ultraviolet, to etch lines onto a chip, but there are limits to how far this technology can be pushed, and many believe that we will reach those limits within the decade. Does this mean that our ability to make smaller, faster, cheaper computers is coming to an end? Probably not. It is more likely that we will find another technology to replace silicon-based computing and enable us to continue building smaller, faster, cheaper computers. In fact, several exotic competing technologies are already being developed that may replace silicon-based computing. These include self-organizing molecular computers, three-dimensional microprocessor technology, quantum computing technology, and using DNA to perform computations.[21]

What does all of this have to do with paradigm shifts? According to Foster, when a technology approaches its natural limit, research attention turns to possible alternative technologies, and sooner or later one of those alternatives might be commercialized and replace the established technology. That is, the probability that a paradigm shift will occur increases. Thus, sometime in the next decade or two, another paradigm shift might shake up the foundations of the computer industry as exotic computing technology replaces silicon-based computing. If history is any guide, if and when this happens, many incumbents in today's computer industry will go into decline, and new enterprises will rise to dominance.

Foster pushes this point a little further, noting that, initially, the contenders for the replacement technology are not as effective as the established technology in producing the attributes and features that consumers demand in a product. For example, in the early years of the 20th century, automobiles were just beginning to be produced. They were valued for their ability to move people from place to place, but so was the horse and cart (the established technology). When automobiles originally appeared, the horse and cart was still quite a bit better than the automobile (see Figure 7.8). After all, the first cars were slow, noisy, and prone to break down. Moreover, they needed a network of paved roads and gas stations to be really useful, and that network didn't yet exist. For most applications, the horse and cart was still the preferred mode of transportation—in part because it was cheaper.

However, this comparison ignored the fact that in the early 20th century, automobile technology was at the very start of its S-curve and about to experience dramatic improvements in performance as major engineering problems were solved (and those paved roads and gas stations were built). In contrast, after 3,000 years of continuous improvement and refinement, the horse and cart was almost definitely at the end of its technological S-curve. The result was that the rapidly improving automobile soon replaced the horse and cart as the preferred mode of transportation. At time T_1 in Figure 7.8, the horse and cart was still superior to the automobile. By time T_2, the automobile had surpassed the horse and cart.

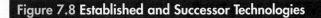

Figure 7.8 Established and Successor Technologies

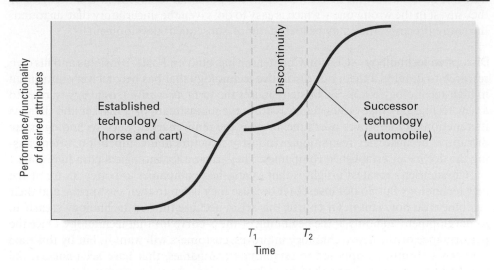

Foster notes that because successor technology is initially less efficient than established technology, established companies and their customers often make the mistake of dismissing it, only to be surprised by its rapid performance improvement. Many people are betting that this is the process unfolding in the electric vehicle industry. Although electric vehicles still have technical disadvantages to internal combustion vehicles (e.g., limited range, time spent recharging), and cost significantly more than comparable internal combustion vehicles, it is possible that dramatic improvements in battery technology could simultaneously address technical disadvantages while reducing the costs of the vehicles.

A final point is that often there is not a single potential successor technology but a swarm of potential successor technologies, only one of which might ultimately rise to the fore (see Figure 7.9). When this is the case, established companies are put at a

Figure 7.9 Swarm of Successor Technologies

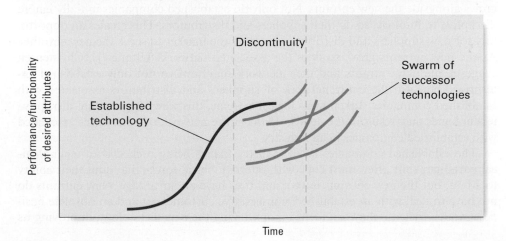

disadvantage. Even if they recognize that a paradigm shift is imminent, companies may not have the resources to invest in all the potential replacement technologies. If they invest in the wrong one—which is easy to do, given the uncertainty that surrounds the entire process—they may be locked out of subsequent development.

Disruptive Technology   Clayton Christensen has built on Foster's insights and his own research to develop a theory of disruptive technology that has become very influential in high-technology circles.[22] Christensen uses the term *disruptive technology* to refer to a new technology that originates away from the mainstream of a market and then, as its functionality improves over time, invades the main market. Such technologies are disruptive because they revolutionize industry structure and competition, often causing the decline of established companies. They cause a technological paradigm shift.

Christensen's greatest insight is that established companies are often aware of the new technology but do not invest in it because they listen to their customers, and their customers do not want it. Of course, this arises because the new technology is early in its development and only at the beginning of the S-curve for that technology. Once the performance of the new technology improves, customers will want it, but by this time it is new entrants, as opposed to established companies, that have accumulated the required knowledge to bring the new technology into the mass market.

In addition to listening too closely to their customers, Christensen also identifies a number of other factors that make it very difficult for established companies to adopt a new disruptive technology. He notes that many established companies decline to invest in new disruptive technologies because initially they serve such small market niches that it seems unlikely there would be an impact on the company's revenues and profits. As the new technology starts to improve in functionality and invade the main market, their investment can often be hindered by the difficult implementation of a new business model required to exploit the new technology.

Both of these points can be illustrated by reference to one more example: the rise of online discount stockbrokers during the 1990s such as Ameritrade and E*TRADE, which made use of a new technology—the Internet—to allow individual investors to trade stocks for a very low commission fee, whereas full-service stockbrokers such as Merrill Lynch, which required that orders be placed through a stockbroker who earned a commission for performing the transaction, did not.

Christensen also notes that a new network of suppliers and distributors typically grows alongside the new entrants. Not only do established companies initially ignore disruptive technology, so do their suppliers and distributors. This creates an opportunity for new suppliers and distributors to enter the market to serve the new entrants. As the new entrants grow, so does the associated network. Ultimately, Christensen suggests, the new entrants and their network may replace not only established enterprises, but also the entire network of suppliers and distributors associated with established companies. Taken to its logical extreme, this view suggests that disruptive technologies may result in the demise of the entire network of enterprises associated with established companies in an industry.

The established companies in an industry that is being rocked by a technological paradigm shift often must cope with internal inertia forces that limit their ability to adapt, but the new entrants do not and thus have an advantage. New entrants do not have to deal with an established, conservative customer set and an obsolete business model. Instead, they can focus on optimizing the new technology, improving its performance, and riding the wave of disruptive technology into new market segments until they invade the main market and challenge the established companies. By then, they may be well equipped to surpass the established companies.

Strategic Implications for Established Companies

Although Christensen has uncovered an important tendency, it is by no means written in stone that all established companies are doomed to fail when faced with disruptive technologies, as we have seen with IBM and Merrill Lynch. Established companies must meet the challenges created by the emergence of disruptive technologies.[23]

First, having access to the knowledge about how disruptive technologies can revolutionize markets is a valuable strategic asset. Many of the established companies that Christensen examined failed because they took a myopic view of the new technology and asked their customers the wrong question. Instead of asking: "Are you interested in this new technology?" they should have recognized that the new technology was likely to improve rapidly over time and instead have asked: "Would you be interested in this new technology if it improves its functionality over time?" If established enterprises had done this, they may have made very different strategic decisions.

Second, it is clearly important for established enterprises to invest in newly emerging technologies that may ultimately become disruptive technologies. Companies have to hedge their bets about new technology. As we have noted, at any time, there may be a swarm of emerging technologies, any one of which might ultimately become a disruptive technology. Large, established companies that are generating significant cash flows can, and often should, establish and fund central R&D operations to invest in and develop such technologies. In addition, they may wish to acquire emerging companies that are pioneering potentially disruptive technologies, or enter into alliances with others to jointly develop the technology. The strategy of acquiring companies that are developing potentially disruptive technology is one that Cisco Systems, a dominant provider of Internet network equipment, is famous for pursuing. At the heart of this strategy must be recognition on behalf of the incumbent enterprise that it is better for the company to develop disruptive technology, and then cannibalize its established sales base, than to have the sales base taken away by new entrants.

However, Christensen makes a very important point: Even when established companies undertake R&D investments in potentially disruptive technologies, they often fail to commercialize those technologies because of internal forces that suppress change. For example, managers who are currently generating the most cash in one part of the business may claim that they need the greatest R&D investment to maintain their market position, and may lobby top management to delay investment in a new technology. This can be a powerful argument when, early in the S-curve, the long-term prospects of a new technology are very unclear. The consequence, however, may be that the company fails to build competence in the new technology, and suffers accordingly.

In addition, Christensen argues that the commercialization of new disruptive technology often requires a radically different value chain with a completely different cost structure—a new business model. For example, it may require a different manufacturing system, a different distribution system, and different pricing options, and may involve very different gross margins and operating margins. Christensen argues that it is almost impossible for two distinct business models to coexist within the same organization. When companies try to implement both models, the already established model will almost inevitably suffocate the model associated with the disruptive technology.

The solution to this problem is to create an autonomous operating division devoted solely to the new technology. For example, during the early 1980s, HP built a very successful laserjet printer business. Then inkjet technology was invented. Some employees at HP believed that inkjet printers would cannibalize sales of laserjet printers, and consequently argued that HP should not produce inkjet printers. Fortunately for HP, senior management saw inkjet technology for what it was: a potential disruptive technology. Instead of choosing to not invest in inkjet technology, HP allocated significant R&D funds toward its commercialization. Furthermore, when the technology was ready for market introduction, HP established an autonomous inkjet division at a different geographical location, including manufacturing, marketing, and distribution departments. HP senior managers accepted that the inkjet division might take sales away from the laserjet division and decided that it was better for an HP division to cannibalize the sales of another HP division, than allow those sales to be cannibalized by another company. Happily for HP, inkjets cannibalize sales of laserjets only on the margin, and both laserjet and inkjet printers have profitable market niches. This felicitous outcome, however, does not detract from the message of this example: If a company is developing a potentially disruptive technology, the chances for success will be enhanced if it is placed in a stand-alone product division and given its own mandate.

Strategic Implications for New Entrants

Christensen's work also holds implications for new entrants. The new entrants, or attackers, have several advantages over established enterprises. Pressures to continue the existing, out-of-date business model do not hamstring new entrants, which do not need to worry about product cannibalization issues. They need not worry about their established customer base or about relationships with established suppliers and distributors. Instead, they can focus all their energies on the opportunities offered by the new disruptive technology, move along the S-curve of technology improvement, and rapidly grow with the market for that technology. This does not mean that the new entrants do not have problems to solve. They may be constrained by a lack of capital or must manage the organizational problems associated with rapid growth; most important, they may need to find a way to take their technology from a small, out-of-the-way niche into the mass market.

Perhaps one of the most important issues facing new entrants is choosing whether to partner with an established company or go it alone in an attempt to develop and profit from a new disruptive technology. Although a new entrant may enjoy all the advantages of the attacker, it may lack the resources required to fully exploit them. In such a case, the company might want to consider forming a strategic alliance with a larger, established company to gain access to those resources. The main issues here are the same as those discussed earlier when examining the three strategies that a company can pursue to capture first-mover advantages: go it alone, enter into a strategic alliance, or license its technology.

KEY TERMS

technical standards   205
format wars   205
dominant design   208
public domain   211

network effects   211
killer applications   215
razor and blade
    strategy   215

first mover   220
first-mover
    disadvantages   221

technological paradigm
    shift   226

TAKEAWAYS FOR STRATEGIC MANAGERS

1. Technical standards are important in many high-tech industries. They guarantee compatibility, reduce confusion in the minds of customers, allow for mass production and lower costs, and reduce the risks associated with supplying complementary products.
2. Network effects and positive feedback loops often determine which standard will dominate a market.
3. Owning a standard can be a source of sustained competitive advantage.
4. Establishing a proprietary standard as the industry standard may require the company to win a format war against a competing and incompatible standard. Strategies for doing this include producing complementary products, leveraging killer applications, using aggressive pricing and marketing, licensing the technology, and cooperating with competitors.
5. Many high-tech products are characterized by high fixed costs of development but very low or zero marginal costs of producing one extra unit of output. These cost economics create a presumption in favor of strategies that emphasize

aggressive pricing to increase volume and drive down average total costs.
6. It is very important for a first mover to develop a strategy to capitalize on first-mover advantages. A company can choose from three strategies: develop and market the technology itself, do so jointly with another company, or license the technology to existing companies. The choice depends on the complementary assets required to capture a first-mover advantage, the height of barriers to imitation, and the capability of competitors.
7. Technological paradigm shifts occur when new technologies emerge that revolutionize the structure of the industry, dramatically alter the nature of competition, and require companies to adopt new strategies in order to succeed.
8. Technological paradigm shifts are more likely to occur when progress in improving the established technology is slowing because of diminishing returns and when a new disruptive technology is taking root in a market niche.
9. Established companies can deal with paradigm shifts by investing in technology or setting up a stand-alone division to exploit technology.

DISCUSSION QUESTIONS

1. What is different about high-tech industries? Were all industries once high-tech?
2. Why are standards so important in high-tech industries? What are the competitive implications of this?
3. You work for a small company that has the leading position in an embryonic market. Your boss believes that the company's future is ensured

because it has a 60% share of the market, the lowest cost structure in the industry, and the most reliable and highest-valued product. Write a memo to your boss outlining why the assumptions posed might be incorrect.
4. You are working for a small company that has developed an operating system for PCs that is faster and more stable than Microsoft's

Windows operating system. What strategies might your company pursue to unseat Windows and establish its own operating system as the dominant technical standard in the industry?

5. You are a manager for a major record label. Last year, music sales declined by 10%, primarily because of illegal file sharing. Your boss has asked you to develop a strategy for reducing illegal file sharing. What would you suggest that the company do?

6. Reread the Strategy in Action 7.1, on Microsoft's "segment zero" threat. Do you think one operating system for smartphones or tablets will become dominant? If so, which one and why?

CLOSING CASE

A Battle Emerging in Mobile Payments

By 2014, there were 6.6 billion mobile phone subscriptions in the world, and of those, 2.3 billion had active mobile broadband subscriptions that would enable users to access the mobile web. Mobile payment systems offered the potential of enabling all of these users to perform financial transactions on their phones, similar to how they would perform those transactions using personal computers. However, in 2015, there was no dominant mobile payment system, and a battle among competing mobile payment mechanisms and standards was unfolding.

In the United States, several large players, including Apple, Samsung, and a joint venture called Softcard between Google, AT&T, T-Mobile, and Verizon Wireless, had developed systems based on near field communication (NFC) chips in smartphones. NFC chips enable communication between a mobile device and a point-of-sale system just by having the devices in close proximity. The systems being developed by Apple, Samsung, and Softcard transferred the customer's information wirelessly, and then used merchant banks and credit card systems such as Visa or MasterCard to complete the transaction. These systems were thus very much like existing ways of using credit cards, but enabled completion of the purchase without contact.

Other competitors such as Square (with Square Wallet) and PayPal did not require a smartphone with an NFC chip, but instead used a downloadable application and the Web to transmit a customer's information. Square had gained early fame by offering small, free, credit card readers that could be plugged into the audio jack of a smartphone. These readers enabled vendors that would normally only take cash (for example, street vendors and babysitters) to accept major credit cards. Square processed $30 billion in payments in 2013, making the company one of the fastest-growing tech start-ups in Silicon Valley. Square takes about 2.75 to 3% from each transaction it processes, but must split that with credit card companies and other financial institutions. In terms of installed base, however, PayPal had the clear advantage, with over 161 million active registered accounts. With PayPal, customers could complete purchases simply by entering their phone numbers and a pin number, or use a PayPal-issued magnetic stripe cards linked to their PayPal accounts. Users could opt to link their PayPal accounts to their credit cards, or directly to their bank accounts. PayPal also owned a service, Venmo, that enabled peer-to-peer exchanges with a Facebook-like interface that was growing in popularity as a way to exchange money without carrying cash. Venmo charged a 3% fee if the transaction used a major credit card, but was free if the consumer used it with a major bank card and debit card.

As noted above, some of the systems being developed did not require involvement of the major credit card companies, which potentially meant that billions of dollars in transaction fees might be avoided, or captured by a new player. PayPal, and its peer-to-peer system Venmo, for instance, did not require credit cards. A group of large merchants that included Wal-Mart, Old Navy, Best Buy, 7-Eleven, and more had also developed their own payment system –"Current-C"—a downloadable application for a smartphone that enabled purchases to be deducted directly from the customer's bank accounts. This would enable merchants to avoid the 2-4% charges that they paid on credit card transactions, amounting to billions of dollars in savings for the participating merchants.

For consumers, the key dimensions that influenced adoption were convenience (would the customer have to type in a code at the point of purchase? was it easily accessible on a device the individual already owned?), risk of fraud (was the individual's identity and financial information at risk?)n and ubiquity (could the system be used everywhere? did it enable peer-to-peer transactions?). For merchants, fraud was also a big concern, especially in situations where the transaction was not guaranteed by a third party, and cost (what were the fixed costs and transaction fees of using the system?) Apple Pay had a significant convenience advantage in that a customer could pay via their fingerprint. Current-C, by contrast, had a serious convenience disadvantage because consumers would have to open the application on their phone and get a QR code to be scanned at the checkout aisle. Both Apple Pay and Current-C also experienced fraud problems, with multiple

reports of hacked accounts emerging by early 2015.

In the United States, almost half of all consumers had used their smartphones to make a payment at a merchant location by early 2015. Mobile payments accounted for $52 billion in transactions in 2014 and were expected to be $67 billion in 2015.

In other parts of the world, intriguing alternatives for mobile banking were gaining traction even faster. In India and Africa, for example, there are enormous populations of "unbanked" or "underbanked" people (individuals who do not have bank accounts or make limited use of banking services). In these regions, the proportion of people with mobile phones vastly exceeds the proportion of those with credit cards. In Africa, for example, less than 3% of the population was estimated to have a credit card, whereas 69% of the population was estimated to have mobile phones. Notably, the maximum fixed-line phone penetration ever achieved in Africa was 1.6%—reached in 2009–demonstrating the power of mobile technology to "leapfrog" land-based technology in the developing world. The opportunity, then, of giving such people access to fast and inexpensive funds transfer is enormous.

The leading system in India is the Inter-bank Mobile Payment Service developed by National Payments Corporation of India (NPCI). NPCI leveraged its ATM network (connecting more than 65

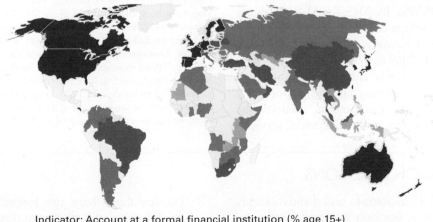

Indicator: Account at a formal financial institution (% age 15+)
Year: 2011

no data   0–16.5   16.5–28.5   23.5–50.3   50.3–81.2   81.2–99.8

Financial Inclusion around the World (data from 2011 World Bank survey)

(continued)

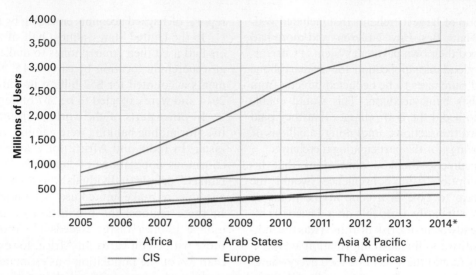

Mobile phone penetration around the world, 2005 - 2014

Sources: United Nations Telecommunications, ICT Report 2014

large banks in India) to create a person-to-person mobile banking system that works on mobile phones. The system uses a unique identifier for each individual who links directly to a bank account. In parts of Africa, where the proportion of people who are unbanked is even larger, a system called M-Pesa ("M" for mobile and "pesa," which is Kiswahili for money) enables any individual with a passport or national ID card to deposit money into his or her phone account and transfer money to other users using short message service (SMS). By 2015, the M-Pesa system had roughly12.2 million active users. The system enabled the percent of Kenyans with access to banking to rise from 41% in 2009 to 67% in 2014.

By early 2015, it was clear that mobile payments represented a game-changing opportunity that could accelerate e-commerce, smartphone adoption, and the global reach of financial services.

However, lack of compatibility between many of the mobile payment systems, and uncertainty over what type of mobile payment system will become dominant, still pose significant obstacles to consumer and merchant adoption.

Sources: J. Kent, "Dominant Mobile Payment Approaches and Leading Mobile Payment Solution Providers: A Review," *Journal of Payments Strategy & Systems* 6 (4), 2012, pp. 315–324; V. Govindarajan and M. Balakrishnan, "Developing Countries Are Revolutionizing Mobile Banking," *Harvard Business Review*, Blog Network, April 30, 2012; M. Helft, "The Death of Cash," *Fortune* 166 (2), 2012, www.fortune.com; D. Pogue, "How Mobile Payments Are Failing and Credit Cards Are Getting Better," *Scientific American*, January 20, 2015, www.scientificamerican.com; M. Isaac, "Square Expands Its Reach into Small-business Services." *New York Times*, March 8, 2015, www.nytimes.com; C. McKay and R. Mazer, "10 Myths about M-PESA: 2014 Update," *Consultative Group to Assist the Poor*, October 1, 2014; *United Nations Telecommunications Development Sector*, ICT Report, 2014.

CASE DISCUSSION QUESTIONS

1. What are the advantages and disadvantages of using mobile banking systems for individuals and businesses?

2. What are the major dimensions that make different mobile payment systems attractive or unattractive to a) consumers, b) merchants, c) banks, and d) credit card companies?

3. Do you think there are forces encouraging the adoption of a dominant design in mobile banking systems?

4. What is likely to determine which mobile banking systems succeed?

NOTES

[1]Data from Bureau of Economic Analysis, 2013, www.bea.gov.

[2]J. M. Utterback, *Mastering the Dynamics of Innovation* (Boston: Harvard Business School Press, 1994); C. Shapiro and H. R. Varian, *Information Rules: A Strategic Guide to the Network Economy* (Boston: Harvard Business School Press, 1999); M.A. Schilling, "Technology Success and Failure in Winner-take-all Markets: Testing a Model of Technological Lock Out," *Academy of Management Journal* 45 (2002): 387–398

[3]The layout is not universal, although it is widespread. The French, for example, use a different layout.

[4]For details, see C. W. L. Hill, "Establishing a Standard: Competitive Strategy and Technology Standards in Winner Take All Industries," *Academy of Management Executive* 11 (1997): 7–25; Shapiro and Varian, *Information Rules;* B. Arthur, "Increasing Returns and the New World of Business," *Harvard Business Review,* July–August 1996, pp. 100–109; G. Gowrisankaran and J. Stavins, "Network Externalities and Technology Adoption: Lessons from Electronic Payments," *Rand Journal of Economics* 35 (2004): 260–277; V. Shankar and B. L. Bayus, "Network Effects and Competition: An Empirical Analysis of the Home Video Game Industry," *Strategic Management Journal* 24 (2003): 375–394; R. Casadesus-Masanell and P. Ghemawat, "Dynamic Mixed Duopoly: A Model Motivated by Linux vs Windows," *Management Science* 52 (2006): 1072–1085.

[5]See Shapiro and Varian, *Information Rules;* Hill, "Establishing a Standard"; M. A. Schilling, "Technological Lockout: An Integrative Model of the Economic and Strategic Factors Driving Technology Success and Failure," *Academy of Management Review* 23 (2) (1998): 267–285.

[6]J. Reitveld, C. Bellavitus, & M. A. Schilling, "Relaunch and Reload: Platform Governance and the Creation and Capture of Value in Ecosystems," New York University Working Paper, 2015.

[7]Microsoft does not disclose the per-unit licensing fee that it receives from original equipment manufacturers, although media reports speculate that it is around $50 a copy.

[8]M. Herper, "The Truly Staggering Costs of Inventing New Drugs," *Forbes,* February 10, 2012; Pharmaceutical Industry 2008, *Standard & Poor's Industry Surveys;* J. A. DiMasi and H. G. Grabowski, "R&D Costs and Returns to New Drug Development: A Review of the Evidence," in P. M. Danzon and S. Nicholson (ed.), *The Oxford Handbook of the Economics of the Biopharmaceutical Industry* (Oxford, UK: Oxford University Press, 2012), chapter 2, pp. 21–46; Innovation.org, 2007; *Drug Discovery and Development: Understanding the R&D Process* (Washington, DC: PhRMA, February), www.phrma.org (accessed August 1, 2015).

[9]Much of this section is based on C. W. L. Hill, M. Heeley, and J. Sakson, "Strategies for Profiting from Innovation," in *Advances in Global High Technology Management* (3rd ed.). (Greenwich, CT: JAI Press, 1993), pp. 79–95.

[10]M. Lieberman and D. Montgomery, "First Mover Advantages," *Strategic Management Journal* 9 (Special Issue, Summer 1988): 41–58

[11]W. Boulding and M. Christen, "Sustainable Pioneering Advantage? Profit Implications of Market Entry Order?" *Marketing Science* 22 (2003): 371–386; C. Markides and P. Geroski, "Teaching Elephants to Dance and Other Silly Ideas," *Business Strategy Review* 13 (2003): 49–61.

[12]M. A. Schilling, Towards dynamic efficiency: Innovation and its implications for antitrust. *Antitrust Bulletin,* forthcoming.

[13]J. Borzo, "Aging Gracefully," *Wall Street Journal,* October 15, 2001, p. R22.

[14]The importance of complementary assets was first noted by D. J. Teece. See D. J. Teece, "Profiting from Technological Innovation," in D. J. Teece (ed.), *The Competitive Challenge* (New York: Harper & Row, 1986), pp. 26–54.

[15]M. J. Chen and D. C. Hambrick, "Speed, Stealth, and Selective Attack: How Small Firms Differ from Large Firms in Competitive Behavior," *Academy of Management Journal* 38 (1995): 453–482.

[16]E. Mansfield, M. Schwartz, and S. Wagner, "Imitation Costs and Patents: An Empirical Study," *Economic Journal* 91 (1981): 907–918.

[17]E. Mansfield, "How Rapidly Does New Industrial Technology Leak Out?" *Journal of Industrial Economics* 34 (1985): 217–223.

[18]This argument has been made in the game theory literature. See

R. Caves, H. Cookell, and P. J. Killing, "The Imperfect Market for Technology Licenses," *Oxford Bulletin of Economics and Statistics* 45 (1983): 249–267; N. T. Gallini, "Deterrence by Market Sharing: A Strategic Incentive for Licensing," *American Economic Review* 74 (1984): 931–941; C. Shapiro, "Patent Licensing and R&D Rivalry," *American Economic Review* 75 (1985): 25–30.

[19]M. Christensen, *The Innovator's Dilemma* (Boston: Harvard Business School Press, 1997); R. N. Foster, *Innovation: The Attacker's Advantage* (New York: Summit Books, 1986).

[20]Foster, *Innovation*.

[21]Ray Kurzweil, *The Age of the Spiritual Machines* (New York: Penguin Books, 1999).

[22]See Christensen, *The Innovator's Dilemma;* C. M. Christensen and M. Overdorf, "Meeting the Challenge of Disruptive Change," *Harvard Business Review* (March–April 2000): 66–77.

[23]C. W. L. Hill and F. T. Rothaermel, "The Performance of Incumbent Firms in the Face of Radical Technological Innovation," *Academy of Management Review* 28 (2003): 257–274; F. T. Rothaermel and Charles W. L. Hill, "Technological Discontinuities and Complementary Assets: A Longitudinal Study of Industry and Firm Performance," *Organization Science* 16 (1) (2005): 52–70.

8

sergign/Shutterstock.com

STRATEGY IN THE GLOBAL ENVIRONMENT

The Globalization of Starbucks

Thirty years ago, Starbucks was a single store in Seattle's Pike Place Market selling premium-roasted coffee. Today, it is a global roaster and retailer of coffee with more than 20,000 stores, 40% of which are in 50 countries outside of the United States. Starbucks set out on its current course in the 1980s, when the company's director of marketing, Howard Schultz, came back from a trip to Italy enchanted with the Italian coffeehouse experience. Schultz, who later became CEO, persuaded the company's owners to experiment with the coffeehouse format, and the Starbucks experience was born. The strategy was to sell the company's own, premium-roasted coffee and freshly brewed, espresso-style coffee beverages, along with a variety of pastries, coffee

8.1 Understand the process of globalization and how it impacts a company's strategy

8.2 Discuss the motives for expanding internationally

8.3 Review the different strategies that companies use to compete in the global marketplace

8.4 Explain the pros and cons of different modes for entering foreign markets

Nic Cleave Photography/Alamy

239

accessories, teas, and other products, in a tastefully designed coffeehouse setting. From the outset, the company focused on selling "a third-place experience" (in other words, spending significant time at a place that is neither work nor home), rather than just the coffee. The formula led to spectacular success in the United States, where, within a decade, Starbucks went from obscurity to one of the best-known brands in the country. Thanks to Starbucks, coffee stores became places for relaxation, chatting with friends, reading the newspaper, holding business meetings, or (more recently) browsing the web.

In 1995, with 700 stores across the United States, Starbucks began exploring foreign opportunities. The first target market was Japan. The company established a joint venture with a local retailer, Sazaby Inc. Each company held a 50% stake in the venture, Starbucks Coffee of Japan. Starbucks initially invested $10 million in this venture, its first foreign direct investment. The Starbucks format was then licensed to the venture, which was charged with growing Starbucks' presence in Japan.

To make sure the Japanese operations replicated the "Starbucks experience" in North America, Starbucks transferred some employees to oversee the Japanese operation. The licensing agreement required all Japanese store managers and employees to attend training classes similar to those given to U.S. employees. The agreement also required that stores adhere to the design parameters established in the United States. In 2001, the company introduced a stock option plan for all Japanese employees, making it the first company in Japan to do so. Skeptics doubted that Starbucks would be able to replicate its North American success overseas but, by 2014, Starbucks' had 1,034 stores and a profitable business in Japan.

After Japan, the company embarked on an aggressive foreign investment program. In 1998, it purchased Seattle Coffee, a British coffee chain with 60 retail stores, for $84 million. An American couple, originally from Seattle, had started Seattle Coffee with the intention of establishing a Starbucks-like chain in Britain. By 2014, there were 530 stores in the United Kingdom. In the late 1990s, Starbucks opened stores in Taiwan, China, Singapore, Thailand, New Zealand, South Korea, and Malaysia. In Asia, Starbucks' most common strategy was to license its format to a local operator in return for initial licensing fees and royalties on store revenues. As in Japan, Starbucks insisted on an intensive employee-training program and strict specifications regarding the format and layout of the store. By 2002, Starbucks was pursuing an aggressive expansion in mainland Europe, primarily through joint ventures with local companies. Its largest footprints are in Switzerland, France, and Germany.

To succeed in some countries, Starbucks has found that it has to adjust its basic formula to accommodate local differences. France, for example, has a well-established café culture. The French find Starbuck's lattes too bland, and the espresso too burnt, so Starbucks has had to change the recipe for its drinks to match French tastes. Since French consumers like to sit and chat while they drink their coffee, Starbucks has had to add more seating per store than is common elsewhere.

As it has grown its global footprint, Starbucks has also embraced ethical sourcing policies and environmental responsibility. Now one of the world's largest buyers of coffee, in 2000 Starbuck's started to purchase Fair Trade Certified coffee. The goal was to empower small-scale farmers organized in cooperatives to invest in their farms and communities, to protect the environment, and to develop the business skills necessary to compete in the global marketplace. In short, Starbucks was trying to use its influence to not only change the way people consumed coffee around the world, but also to change the way coffee was produced in a manner that benefited the farmers and the environment. By 2010, some 75% of the coffee Starbucks purchased was Fair Trade Certified, and the company has a goal of increasing that to 100% by 2015.

Sources: Starbucks 10K, various years; C. McLean, "Starbucks Set to Invade Coffee-Loving Continent," *Seattle Times*, October 4, 2000, p. E1; J. Ordonez, "Starbucks to Start Major Expansion in Overseas Market," *The Wall Street Journal*, October 27, 2000, p. B10; S. Homes and D. Bennett, "Planet Starbucks," *BusinessWeek*, September 9, 2002, pp. 99–110; "Starbucks Outlines International Growth Strategy," *Business Wire*, October 14, 2004; A. Yeh, "Starbucks Aims for New Tier in China," *Financial Times*, February 14, 2006, p. 17; C. Matlack, "Will Global Growth Help Starbucks?" *Business Week*, July 2, 2008; Liz Alderman, "In Europe, Starbucks Adjusts to a Café Culture," *New York Times*, March 30, 2012.

◢ OVERVIEW

One of the striking developments of the last 30 years has been the globalization of markets. As a result of declining barriers to cross-border trade and investment, along with the rapid economic development of countries like Brazil, Russia, India, and China, segmented national markets have increasingly merged into much larger global markets. In this chapter, we discuss the implications of this phase shift in the global competitive environment for strategic management.

The chapter begins with a discussion of ongoing changes in the global competitive environment. Next, it discusses the various ways in which global expansion can increase a company's profitability and profit growth. We then discuss the advantages and disadvantages of the different strategies companies can pursue to gain a competitive advantage in the global marketplace. This is followed by a discussion of two related strategic issues: (1) how managers decide which foreign markets to enter, when to enter them, and on what scale; and (2) what kind of vehicle or method a company should use to expand globally and enter a foreign country.

The global expansion of Starbucks, profiled in the Opening Case, gives a preview of some issues explored in this chapter. Starbucks expanded overseas to boost its profit growth by leveraging its product offering to markets that typically lacked indigenous competitors. Today, over 40% of Starbucks stores are outside of its core North American market. *Leveraging product offering* to achieve greater growth is a common motive for global expansion. For the most part, Starbucks' strategy has been to use the same basic formula that worked in the United States. We call this a *global standardization* strategy. However, in certain countries, such as France, where there already was a strong coffee/café culture, Starbucks has had to adapt its format to capture local demand. We call this a *localization* strategy. Starbucks has often favored a *joint venture* strategy for entering foreign markets, teaming up with a local company in order to learn about the unique characteristics of each national market from its venture partners, thereby increasing its chances of successful entry. As we shall see, the choice of entry strategy is an important consideration for any firm expanding globally.

We shall discuss the issues touched on in the Starbucks' case, along with many others, and by the time you have completed the chapter, you will have a good understanding of the various strategic issues that companies face when they decide to expand their operations abroad to achieve superior profitability and/or profit growth.

◤ GLOBAL AND NATIONAL ENVIRONMENTS

Fifty years ago, most national markets were isolated from one another by significant barriers to international trade and investment. In those days, managers could focus on analyzing only those national markets in which their company competed. They did not need to pay much attention to entry by global competitors, for there were few and entry was difficult. Nor did they need to pay much attention to entering foreign markets, because that was often prohibitively expensive. All of this has now changed. Barriers to international trade and investment have tumbled, huge global markets for goods and services have been created, and companies from different nations are entering each other's home markets on an unprecedented scale, increasing the intensity of competition. Rivalry can no longer be understood merely in terms of what happens within the boundaries of a nation; managers now need to consider how globalization is impacting the environment in which their company competes and what strategies their company should adopt to exploit the unfolding opportunities and counter competitive threats. In this section, we look at the changes ushered in by falling barriers to international trade and investment, and we discuss a model for analyzing the competitive situation in different nations.

The Globalization of Production and Markets

The past half-century has seen a dramatic lowering of barriers to international trade and investment. For example, the average tariff rate on manufactured goods traded between advanced nations has fallen from around 40% to under 4%. For some goods, such as information technology, tariff rates have approached zero. Similarly, in nation after nation, regulations prohibiting foreign companies from entering domestic markets and establishing production facilities, or acquiring domestic companies, have been removed. As a result of these developments, there has been a surge in both the volume of international trade and the value of foreign direct investment. The volume of world merchandise trade has been growing faster than the world economy since the 1950s. Between 1970 and 2012, the volume of world merchandise trade increased 32 times, compared to a 9-fold increase in the size of the world economy.[1] As for foreign direct investment, between 1992 and 2013, the total flow of foreign direct investment from all countries increased over 500%, while world trade by value grew by some 150% and world output by around 40%.[2] These trends have led to the globalization of production and the globalization of markets.[3]

The globalization of production has been increasing as companies take advantage of lower barriers to international trade and investment to disperse important parts of their production processes around the globe. Doing so enables them to exploit national differences in the cost and quality of factors of production such as labor, energy, land, and capital, which allows companies to lower their cost structures and boost profits. For example, foreign companies build nearly 65% by value of Boeing's 787 commercial jet aircraft. Three Japanese companies build 35% of the 787, and another 20% is allocated to companies located in Italy, Singapore, and the United Kingdom.[4] Part of Boeing's rationale for outsourcing so much production to foreign suppliers is that these suppliers are the best in the world at performing their particular activity. Therefore, the result of having foreign suppliers build specific parts is a better final product and higher profitability for Boeing.

As for the globalization of markets, it has been argued that the world's economic system is moving from one in which national markets are distinct entities, isolated from each other by trade barriers and barriers of distance, time, and culture, toward a system in which national markets are merging into one huge, global marketplace. Increasingly, customers around the world demand and use the same basic product offerings. Consequently, in many industries, it is no longer meaningful to talk about the German market, the U.S. market, or the Chinese market; there is only the global market. The global acceptance of Coca-Cola, Citigroup credit cards, Starbucks, McDonald's hamburgers, Samsung and Apple smartphones, IKEA furniture, and Microsoft's Windows operating system are examples of this trend.[5]

The trend toward the globalization of production and markets has several important implications for competition within an industry. First, industry boundaries do not stop at national borders. Because many industries are becoming global in scope, competitors and potential future competitors exist not only in a company's home market but also in international markets. Managers who analyze only their home market can be caught unprepared by the entry of efficient foreign competitors. The globalization of markets and production implies that companies around the globe are finding their home markets under attack from foreign competitors. For example, in Japan, American financial institutions such as J.P. Morgan have been making inroads against Japanese financial service institutions. In the United States, South Korea's Samsung has been battling Apple for a share of the smartphone market. In the European Union, the once-dominant Dutch company Philips has seen its market share in the customer electronics industry taken by Japan's Panasonic and Sony, and Samsung of South Korea.

Second, the shift from national to global markets has intensified competitive rivalry in many industries. National markets that once were consolidated oligopolies, dominated by three or four companies and subjected to relatively little foreign competition, have been transformed into segments of fragmented global industries in which many companies battle each other for market share in many countries. This rivalry has threatened to drive down profitability and made it more critical for companies to maximize their efficiency, quality, customer responsiveness, and innovative ability. The painful restructuring and downsizing that has been occurring at companies such as the once dominant and now bankrupt photographic company Kodak is as much a response to the increased intensity of global competition as it is to any other factor. However, not all global industries are fragmented. Many remain consolidated oligopolies, except that now they are consolidated, global (rather than national) oligopolies. In the videogame industry, for example, three companies are battling for global dominance: Microsoft from the United States, and Nintendo and Sony from Japan. In the market for smartphones, Apple is in a global battle with Samsung from South Korea and Xiaomi from China.

Finally, although globalization has increased both the threat of entry and the intensity of rivalry within many formerly protected national markets, it has also created enormous opportunities for companies based in those markets. The steady decline in barriers to crossborder trade and investment has opened up many once-protected national markets to companies based outside these nations. Thus, for example, Western European, Japanese, and U.S. companies have accelerated their investment in the nations of Eastern Europe, Latin America, and Southeast Asia as they try to take advantage of growth opportunities in those areas.

National Competitive Advantage

Despite the globalization of production and markets, many of the most successful companies in certain industries are still clustered in a small number of countries. For example, many of the world's most successful biotechnology and computer companies are based in the United States, and many of the most successful consumer electronics companies are based in Japan, Taiwan, South Korea, and China. Germany is the base for many successful chemical and engineering companies. These facts suggest that the nation-state within which a company is based may have an important bearing on the competitive position of that company in the global marketplace.

In a study of national competitive advantage, Michael Porter identified four attributes of a national or country-specific environment that have an important impact on the global competitiveness of companies located within that nation:[6]

- *Factor endowments*: A nation's position in factors of production such as skilled labor or the infrastructure necessary to compete in a given industry
- *Local demand conditions*: The nature of home demand for the industry's product or service
- *Related and supporting industries*: The presence or absence in a nation of supplier industries and related industries that are internationally competitive
- *Firm strategy, structure, and rivalry*: The conditions in the nation governing how companies are created, organized, and managed, and the nature of domestic rivalry

Porter speaks of these four attributes as constituting the "diamond," arguing that companies from a given nation are most likely to succeed in industries or strategic groups in which the four attributes are favorable (see Figure 8.1). He also argues that

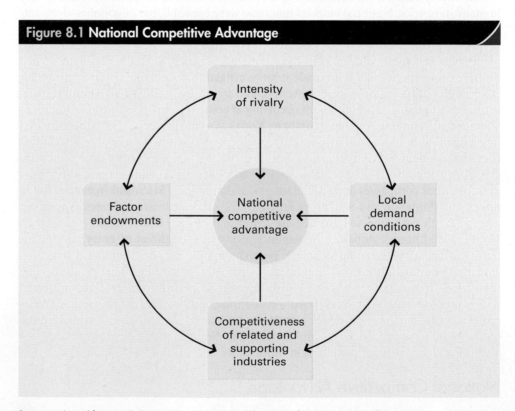

Figure 8.1 National Competitive Advantage

Source: Adapted from M. E. Porter, "The Competitive Advantage of Nations," Harvard Business Review, March–April 1990, p. 77.

the diamond's attributes form a mutually reinforcing system in which the effect of one attribute is dependent on the state of others.

Factor Endowments   Factor endowments—the cost and quality of factors of production—are a prime determinant of the competitive advantage that certain countries might have in certain industries. Factors of production include basic factors such as land, labor, capital, and raw materials, and advanced factors such as technological knowhow, managerial sophistication, and physical infrastructure (roads, railways, and ports). The competitive advantage that the United States enjoys in biotechnology might be explained by the presence of certain advanced factors of production—for example, technological knowhow—in combination with some basic factors, which might be a pool of relatively low-cost venture capital that can be used to fund risky start-ups in industries such as biotechnology.

Local Demand Conditions   Home demand plays an important role in providing the impetus for "upgrading" competitive advantage. Companies are typically most sensitive to the needs of their closest customers. Thus, the characteristics of home demand are particularly important in shaping the attributes of domestically made products and creating pressures for innovation and quality. A nation's companies gain competitive advantage if their domestic customers are sophisticated and demanding, and pressure local companies to meet high standards of product quality and produce innovative products. Japan's sophisticated and knowledgeable buyers of cameras helped stimulate the Japanese camera industry to improve product quality and introduce innovative models. A similar example can be found in the cell phone equipment industry, where sophisticated, demanding local customers in Scandinavia helped push Nokia of Finland and Ericsson of Sweden to invest in cellular phone technology long before demand for cellular phones increased in other developed nations. As a result, Nokia and Ericsson, together with Motorola, became significant players in the global cellular telephone equipment industry.

Competitiveness of Related and Supporting Industries   The third broad attribute of national advantage in an industry is the presence of internationally competitive suppliers or related industries. The benefits of investments in advanced factors of production by related and supporting industries can spill over into an industry, thereby helping it achieve a strong competitive position internationally. Swedish strength in fabricated steel products such as ball bearings and cutting tools has drawn on strengths in Sweden's specialty-steel industry. Switzerland's success in pharmaceuticals is closely related to its previous international success in the technologically related dye industry. One consequence of this process is that successful industries within a country tend to be grouped into clusters of related industries. Indeed, this is one of the most pervasive findings of Porter's study. One such cluster is the German textile and apparel sector, which includes high-quality cotton, wool, synthetic fibers, sewing machine needles, and a wide range of textile machinery.

Intensity of Rivalry   The fourth broad attribute of national competitive advantage in Porter's model is the intensity of rivalry of firms within a nation. Porter makes two important points. First, different nations are characterized by different management ideologies, which either help them or do not help them to build national competitive advantage. For example, Porter noted the predominance of engineers in top management at German and Japanese firms. He attributed this to these firms' emphasis on improving manufacturing processes and product design. In contrast, Porter noted a predominance of people with finance backgrounds leading many U.S. firms. He linked this to U.S. firms' lack of attention to improving manufacturing processes and product design. He argued that the dominance of finance led to an overemphasis on maximizing short-term financial returns. According to Porter, one consequence of these different management ideologies was a relative loss of U.S. competitiveness in those engineering-based industries where manufacturing processes and product design issues are all-important (such as the automobile industry).

Porter's second point is that there is a strong association between vigorous domestic rivalry and the creation and persistence of competitive advantage in an industry. Rivalry compels companies to look for ways to improve efficiency, which makes them better international competitors. Domestic rivalry creates pressures to innovate, improve quality, reduce costs, and invest in upgrading advanced factors. All this helps to create world-class competitors.

Using the Framework The framework just described can help managers identify where their most significant global competitors are likely to originate. For example, there is a cluster of computer service and software companies in Bangalore, India, that includes two of the fastest-growing information technology companies in the world, Infosys and Wipro. These companies have emerged as aggressive competitors in the global market. Both companies have recently opened up offices in the European Union and United States so they can better compete against Western rivals such as IBM and Hewlett Packard, and both are gaining share in the global marketplace.

The framework can also be used to help managers decide where they might want to locate certain productive activities. Seeking to take advantage of U.S. expertise in biotechnology, many foreign companies have set up research facilities in San Diego, Boston, and Seattle, where U.S. biotechnology companies tend to cluster. Similarly, in an attempt to take advantage of Japanese success in consumer electronics, many U.S. electronics companies have set up research and production facilities in Japan, often in conjunction with Japanese partners.

Finally, the framework can help a company assess how tough it might be to enter certain national markets. If a nation has a competitive advantage in certain industries, it might be challenging for foreigners to enter those industries. For example, the highly competitive retailing industry in the United States has proved to be a very difficult industry for foreign companies to enter. Successful foreign retailers such as Britain's Tesco and Sweden's IKEA have found it tough going into the United States because the U.S. retailing industry is the most competitive in the world.

◤ GLOBAL EXPANSION, PROFITABILITY, AND PROFIT GROWTH

Expanding globally allows firms to increase their profitability and rate of profit growth in ways not available to purely domestic enterprises.[7] Firms that operate internationally are able to:

1. Expand the market for their domestic product offerings by selling those products in international markets.

2. Realize location economies by dispersing individual value creation activities to those locations around the globe where they can be performed most efficiently and effectively.
3. Realize greater cost economies from experience effects by serving an expanded global market from a central location, thereby reducing the costs of value creation.
4. Earn a greater return by leveraging any valuable skills developed in foreign operations and transferring them to other entities within the firm's global network of operations.

As we will see, however, a firm's ability to increase its profitability and profit growth by pursuing these strategies is constrained by the need to customize its product offering, marketing strategy, and business strategy to differing national or regional conditions— that is, by the imperative of localization.

Expanding the Market: Leveraging Products

A company can increase its growth rate by taking goods or services developed at home and selling them internationally; almost all multinationals started out doing this. Procter & Gamble (P&G), for example, developed most of its bestselling products at home and then sold them around the world. Similarly, from its earliest days, Microsoft has focused on selling its software around the world. Automobile companies such as Ford, Volkswagen, and Toyota also grew by developing products at home and then selling them in international markets. The returns from such a strategy are likely to be greater if indigenous competitors in the nations a company enters lack comparable products. Thus, Toyota has grown its profits by entering the large automobile markets of North America and Europe and offering products differentiated from those offered by local rivals (Ford and GM) by superior quality and reliability.

The success of many **multinational companies** that expand in this manner is based not just on the goods or services that they sell in foreign nations, but also upon the distinctive competencies (i.e., unique resources) that underlie the production and marketing of those goods or services. Thus, Toyota's success is based on its distinctive competency in manufacturing automobiles. International expansion can be seen as a way for Toyota to generate greater returns from this competency. Similarly, P&G's global success was based on more than its portfolio of consumer products; it was also based on the company's competencies in mass-marketing consumer goods. P&G grew rapidly in international markets between 1950 and 1990 because it was one of the most skilled mass-marketing enterprises in the world and could "out-market" indigenous competitors in the nations it entered. Global expansion was, therefore, a way of generating higher returns from its valuable, rare, and inimitable resources in marketing.

The same can be said of companies engaged in the service sectors of an economy, such as financial institutions, retailers, restaurant chains, and hotels. Expanding the market for their services often means replicating their business model in foreign nations (albeit with some changes to account for local differences, which we will discuss in more detail shortly). Starbucks, for example, has expanded globally by taking the basic business model it developed in the United States and using that as a blueprint for establishing international operations.

multinational company
A company that does business in two or more national markets.

Realizing Cost Economies from Global Volume

In addition to growing profits more rapidly, a company can realize cost savings from economies of scale, thereby boosting profitability, by expanding its sales volume through international expansion. Such scale economies come from several sources. First, by spreading the fixed costs associated with developing a product and setting up production facilities over its global sales volume, a company can lower its average unit cost. Thus, Microsoft can garner significant scale economies by spreading the $5- to $10- billion cost of developing Windows 8 over global demand.

Second, by serving a global market, a company can potentially utilize its production facilities more intensively, which leads to higher productivity, lower costs, and greater profitability. For example, if Intel sold microprocessors only in the United States, it might only be able to keep its factories open for 1 shift, 5 days a week. But by serving a global market from the same factories, it might be able to utilize those assets for two shifts, 7 days a week. In other words, the capital invested in those factories is used more intensively if Intel sells to a global—as opposed to a national—market, which translates into higher capital productivity and a higher return on invested capital.

Third, as global sales increase the size of the enterprise, its bargaining power with suppliers increases, which may allow it to bargain down the cost of key inputs and boost profitability that way. For example, Wal-Mart has been able to use its enormous sales volume as a lever to bargain down the price it pays to suppliers for merchandise sold through its stores.

In addition to the cost savings that come from economies of scale, companies that sell to a global rather than a local marketplace may be able to realize further cost savings from learning effects. We first discussed learning effects in Chapter 4, where we noted that employee productivity increases with cumulative increases in output over time. (For example, it costs considerably less to build the 100th aircraft from a Boeing assembly line than the 10th because employees learn how to perform their tasks more efficiently over time.) Selling to a global market may enable a company to increase its sales volume more rapidly, and thus the cumulative output from its plants, which in turn should result in accelerated learning, higher employee productivity, and a cost advantage over competitors that are growing more slowly because they lack international markets.

Realizing Location Economies

location economies

The economic benefits that arise from performing a value creation activity in an optimal location.

Earlier in this chapter, we discussed how countries differ from each other along a number of dimensions, including differences in the cost and quality of factors of production. These differences imply that some locations are more suited than others for producing certain goods and services.[8] **Location economies** are the economic benefits that arise from performing a value creation activity in the optimal location for that activity, wherever in the world that might be (transportation costs and trade barriers permitting). Thus, if the best designers for a product live in France, a firm should base its design operations in France. If the most productive labor force for assembly operations is in Mexico, assembly operations should be based in Mexico. If the best marketers are in the United States, the marketing strategy should be formulated in the United States—and so on. Apple, for example, designs the iPhone and develops the associated software in California, but undertakes final assembly in China precisely because the company believes that these are the best locations in the world for carrying out these different value creation activities.

Locating a value creation activity in the optimal location for that activity can have one of two effects: (1) it can lower the costs of value creation, helping the company achieve a low-cost position; or (2) it can enable a company to differentiate its product offering, which gives it the option of charging a premium price or keeping prices low and using differentiation as a means of increasing sales volume. Thus, efforts to realize location economies are consistent with the business-level strategies of low cost and differentiation.

In theory, a company that realizes location economies by dispersing each of its value creation activities to the optimal location for that activity should have a competitive advantage over a company that bases all of its value creation activities at a single location. It should be able to better differentiate its product offering and lower its cost structure more than its single-location competitor. In a world where competitive pressures are increasing, such a strategy may well become an imperative for survival.

Introducing transportation costs and trade barriers can complicate the process of realizing location economies. New Zealand might have a comparative advantage for low-cost car assembly operations, but high transportation costs make it an uneconomical location from which to serve global markets. Factoring transportation costs and trade barriers into the cost equation helps explain why some U.S. companies have shifted production from Asia to Mexico. Mexico has three distinct advantages over many Asian countries as a location for value creation activities: low labor costs; Mexico's proximity to the large U.S. market, which reduces transportation costs; and the North American Free Trade Agreement (NAFTA), which has removed many trade barriers between Mexico, the United States, and Canada, increasing Mexico's appeal as a production site for the North American market. Thus, although the relative costs of value creation are important, transportation costs and trade barriers also must be considered in location decisions.

Leveraging the Competencies of Global Subsidiaries

You will recall from Chapter 3 that competitive advantage is based upon valuable, rare, and inimitable resources, in particular process knowledge, intellectual property, and organizational architecture. Initially, many multinational companies develop the valuable resources and competencies that underpin their competitive advantage in their home nation and then expand internationally, primarily by selling products and services based on those competencies. However, for more mature multinational enterprises that have already established a network of subsidiary operations in foreign markets, the development of valuable resources and competencies can just as well occur in foreign subsidiaries.[9] Competencies can be created anywhere within a multinational's global network of operations, wherever people have the opportunity and incentive to try new ways of doing things. The creation of resources and competencies such as unique process knowledge that helps to lower the costs of production, or to enhance perceived value and support higher product pricing, is not the monopoly of the corporate center.

Leveraging the valuable resources created within subsidiaries and applying them to other operations within the firm's global network may create value. For example, McDonald's is increasingly finding that its foreign franchisees are a source of valuable new ideas. Faced with slow growth in France, its local franchisees have begun to experiment with the menu, as well as the layout and theme of restaurants. Gone are the ubiquitous Golden Arches; gone too are many of the utilitarian chairs and tables and other plastic features of the fast-food giant. Many McDonald's restaurants in

France now have hardwood floors, exposed brick walls, and even armchairs. Half of the outlets in France have been upgraded to a level that would make them unrecognizable to an American. The menu, too, has been changed to include premier sandwiches, such as chicken on focaccia bread, priced some 30% higher than the average hamburger. In France, this strategy seems to be working. Following these changes, increases in same-store sales rose from 1% annually to 3.4%. Impressed with the impact, McDonald's executives are now considering adopting similar changes at other restaurants in markets where same-store sales growth is sluggish, including the United States.[10]

For the managers of a multinational enterprise, this phenomenon creates important new challenges. First, managers must have the humility to recognize that valuable resources such as unique process knowledge or intellectual property can arise anywhere within the firm's global network, not just at the corporate center. Second, they must establish an incentive system that encourages local employees to acquire and build new resources and competencies. This is not as easy as it sounds. Creating new competencies involves a degree of risk. Not all new skills add value. For every valuable idea created by a McDonald's subsidiary in a foreign country, there may be several failures. The management of the multinational must install incentives that encourage employees to take necessary risks, reward them for successes, and not sanction them for taking risks that did not pan out. Third, managers must have a process for identifying when valuable new resources and competencies have been created in a subsidiary. Finally, they need to act as facilitators, helping to transfer valuable resources and competencies within the firm.

COST PRESSURES AND PRESSURES FOR LOCAL RESPONSIVENESS

Companies that compete in the global marketplace typically face two types of competitive pressures: *pressures for cost reductions and pressures to be locally responsive* (see Figure 8.2).[11] These competitive pressures place conflicting demands on a company. Responding to pressures for cost reductions requires that a company attempt to minimize its unit costs. To attain this goal, it may have to base its productive activities at the most favorable low-cost location, wherever in the world that might be. It may also need to offer a standardized product to the global marketplace in order to realize the cost savings that come from economies of scale and learning effects. On the other hand, responding to pressures to be locally responsive requires that a company differentiate its product offering and marketing strategy from country to country in an effort to accommodate the diverse demands arising from national differences in consumer tastes and preferences, business practices, distribution channels, competitive conditions, and government policies. Because differentiation across countries can involve significant duplication and a lack of product standardization, it may raise costs.

Whereas some companies, such as Company A in Figure 8.2, face high pressures for cost reductions and low pressures for local responsiveness, and others, such as Company B, face low pressures for cost reductions and high pressures for local responsiveness, many companies are in the position of Company C. They face high

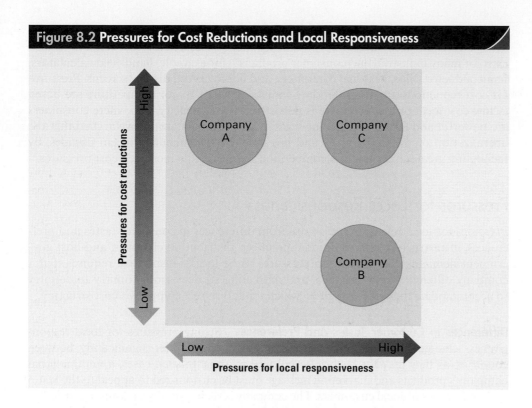

Figure 8.2 Pressures for Cost Reductions and Local Responsiveness

pressures for both cost reductions and local responsiveness. Dealing with these conflicting and contradictory pressures is a difficult strategic challenge, primarily because local responsiveness tends to raise costs.

Pressures for Cost Reductions

In competitive global markets, international businesses often face pressures for cost reductions. To respond to these pressures, a firm must try to lower the costs of value creation. A manufacturer, for example, might mass-produce a standardized product at an optimal site to realize economies of scale and location economies. Alternatively, it might outsource certain functions to low-cost foreign suppliers in an attempt to reduce costs. Thus, many computer companies have outsourced their telephone-based customer service functions to India, where qualified technicians who speak English can be hired for a lower wage rate than in the United States. In the same vein, Wal-Mart pushes its suppliers (which are manufacturers) to also lower their prices. In fact, the pressure that Wal-Mart has placed on its suppliers to reduce prices has been cited as a major cause of the trend among North American manufacturers to shift production to China.[12] A service business such as a bank might move back-office functions such as information processing to developing nations where wage rates are lower.

Cost-reduction pressures can be particularly intense in industries producing commodity-type products where meaningful differentiation on non-price factors is difficult, and price is the main competitive weapon. This tends to be the case for products that serve universal needs. Universal needs exist when the tastes and preferences of consumers in different nations are similar, if not identical, such as for bulk chemicals, petroleum, steel, sugar, and similar products. Pressures for cost reductions also exist for many industrial and consumer products—for example, hand-held calculators, semiconductor chips, personal computers, and liquid crystal display screens. Pressures for cost reductions are also intense in industries where major competitors are based in low-cost locations, where there is persistent excess capacity, and where consumers are powerful and face low switching costs. Many commentators have argued that the liberalization of the world trade and investment environment in recent decades, by facilitating greater international competition, has generally increased cost pressures.[13]

Pressures for Local Responsiveness

Pressures for local responsiveness arise from differences in consumer tastes and preferences, infrastructure and traditional practices, distribution channels, and host government demands. Responding to pressures to be locally responsive requires that a company differentiate its products and marketing strategy from country to country to accommodate these factors, all of which tend to raise a company's cost structure.

Differences in Customer Tastes and Preferences   Strong pressures for local responsiveness emerge when customer tastes and preferences differ significantly between countries, as they may for historic or cultural reasons. In such cases, a multinational company's products and marketing message must be customized to appeal to the tastes and preferences of local customers. The company is then typically pressured to delegate its production and marketing responsibilities and functions to overseas subsidiaries.

For example, the automobile industry in the 1980s and early 1990s moved toward the creation of "world cars." The idea was that global companies such as General Motors, Ford, and Toyota would be able to sell the same basic vehicle globally, sourcing it from centralized production locations. If successful, the strategy would have enabled automobile companies to reap significant gains from global-scale economies. However, this strategy frequently ran aground upon the hard rocks of consumer reality. Consumers in different automobile markets have historically had different tastes and preferences, and these require different types of vehicles. North American consumers show a strong demand for pickup trucks. This is particularly true in the South and West, where many families have a pickup truck as a second or third vehicle. But in European countries, pickup trucks are seen purely as utility vehicles and are purchased primarily by firms rather than individuals. As a consequence, the product mix and marketing message need to be tailored to take into account the different nature of demand in North America and Europe.

Some commentators have argued that customer demands for local customization are on the decline worldwide.[14] According to this argument, modern communications and transport technologies have created the conditions for a convergence of the tastes and preferences of customers from different nations. The result is the emergence of enormous global markets for standardized consumer products. The worldwide acceptance of McDonald's hamburgers, Coca-Cola, GAP clothes, the Apple iPhone, and Sony television sets, all of which are sold globally as standardized products, is often cited as evidence of the increasing homogeneity of the global marketplace.

However, this argument may not hold in many consumer goods markets. Significant differences in consumer tastes and preferences still exist across nations and cultures.

Managers in international businesses do not yet have the luxury of being able to ignore these differences, and they may not for a long time to come. For an example of a company that has discovered the importance of pressures for local responsiveness, see Strategy in Action 8.1 on MTV Networks.

Differences in Infrastructure and Traditional Practices   Pressures for local responsiveness also arise from differences in infrastructure or traditional practices among countries, creating a need to customize products accordingly. To meet this need, companies may have to delegate manufacturing and production functions to foreign subsidiaries. For example, in North America, consumer electrical systems are based on 110 volts, whereas in some European countries 240-volt systems are standard. Thus, domestic electrical appliances must be customized to take this difference in infrastructure into

8.1 STRATEGY IN ACTION

Local Responsiveness at MTV Networks

MTV Networks has become a symbol of globalization. Established in 1981, the U.S.-based TV network has been expanding outside of its North American base since 1987, when it launched MTV Europe. MTV Networks figures that, every second of every day, over 2 million people are watching MTV around the world, the majority outside the United States. Despite its international success, MTV's global expansion got off to a weak start. In the 1980s, when its main programming fare was music videos, it piped a single feed across Europe almost entirely composed of American programming with English-speaking veejays. Naively, the network's U.S. managers thought Europeans would flock to the American programming. But although viewers in Europe shared a common interest in a handful of global superstars, their tastes turned out to be surprisingly local. After losing share to local competitors that focused more on local tastes, MTV changed it strategy in the 1990s. It broke its service into "feeds" aimed at national or regional markets. Although MTV Networks

exercises creative control over these different feeds, and although all the channels have the same familiar, frenetic look and feel of MTV in the United States, a significant share of the programming and content is now local.

Today, an increasing share of programming is local in conception. Although many programming ideas still originate in the United States, with staples such as "The Real World" having equivalents in different countries, an increasing share of programming is local in conception. In Italy, "MTV Kitchen" combines cooking with a music countdown. "Erotica" airs in Brazil and features a panel of youngsters discussing sex. The Indian channel produces twenty-one homegrown shows hosted by local veejays who speak "Hinglish," a city-bred version of Hindi and English. Many feeds still feature music videos by locally popular performers. This localization push reaped big benefits for MTV, allowing the network to capture viewers back from local imitators.

Sources: M. Gunther, "MTV's Passage to India," *Fortune*, August 9, 2004, pp. 117–122; B. Pulley and A. Tanzer, "Sumner's Gemstone," *Forbes*, February 21, 2000, pp. 107–11; K. Hoffman, "Youth TV's Old Hand Prepares for the Digital Challenge," *Financial Times*, February 18, 2000, p. 8; presentation by Sumner M. Redstone, chairman and CEO, Viacom Inc., delivered to the Salomon Smith Barney 11th Annual Global Entertainment Media, Telecommunications Conference, Scottsdale, AZ, January 8, 2001, www.viacom .com; Viacom 10K Statement, 2005.

account. Traditional social practices also often vary across nations. In Britain, people drive on the left-hand side of the road, creating a demand for right-hand-drive cars, whereas in France and the rest of Europe, people drive on the right-hand side of the road (and therefore want left-hand-drive cars).

Although many differences in infrastructure are rooted in history, some are quite recent. In the wireless telecommunications industry, different technical standards are found in different parts of the world. A technical standard known as GSM is common in Europe, and an alternative standard, CDMA, is more common in the United States and parts of Asia. The significance of these different standards is that equipment designed for GSM will not work on a CDMA network, and vice versa. Thus, companies that manufacture wireless handsets and infrastructure such as switches need to customize their product offerings according to the technical standard prevailing in a given country.

Differences in Distribution Channels   A company's marketing strategies may have to be responsive to differences in distribution channels among countries, which may necessitate delegating marketing functions to national subsidiaries. In the pharmaceutical industry, for example, the British and Japanese distribution system is radically different from the U.S. system. British and Japanese doctors will not accept or respond favorably to a U.S.-style, high-pressure sales force. Thus, pharmaceutical companies must adopt different marketing practices in Britain and Japan compared with the United States—soft sell versus hard sell.

Similarly, Poland, Brazil, and Russia all have similar per capita income on the basis of purchasing-power parity, but there are big differences in distribution systems across the three countries. In Brazil, supermarkets account for 36% of food retailing; in Poland, for 18%; and in Russia, for less than 1%.[15] These differences in channels require that companies adapt their own distribution and sales strategies.

Host Government Demands   Finally, economic and political demands imposed by host-country governments may require local responsiveness. For example, pharmaceutical companies are subject to local clinical testing, registration procedures, and pricing restrictions, all of which make it necessary that the manufacturing and marketing of a drug meet local requirements. Moreover, because governments and government agencies control a significant portion of the health-care budget in most countries, they are in a powerful position to demand a high level of local responsiveness. More generally, threats of protectionism, economic nationalism, and local content rules (which require that a certain percentage of a product be manufactured locally) can dictate that international businesses manufacture locally.

The Rise of Regionalism   Typically, we think of pressures for local responsive as deriving from *national* differences in tastes and preferences, infrastructure, and the like. While this is still often the case, there is also a tendency toward the convergence of tastes, preferences, infrastructure, distribution channels, and host-government demands within a broader *region* that is composed of two or more nations.[16] We sometimes see this when there are strong pressures for convergence due to, for example, a shared history and culture, or the establishment of a trading block where there are deliberate attempts to harmonize trade policies, infrastructure, regulations, and the like.

The most obvious example of a region is the European Union (EU), and particularly the eurozone countries within that trade block, where institutional forces are pushing toward convergence. The creation of a single EU market, with a single currency, common business regulations, standard infrastructure, and so on, cannot help but result in the reduction of certain national differences between countries within the EU, and the creation of one regional rather than several national markets. Indeed, at the economic level at least, that is the explicit intent of the EU.

Another example of regional convergence is North America, which includes the United States, Canada, and to some extent in some product markets, Mexico. Canada and the United States share history, language, and much of their culture, and both are members of NAFTA. Mexico is clearly different in many regards, but its proximity to the United States, along with its membership in NAFTA, implies that for some product markets (e.g., automobiles) it might be reasonable to consider it part of a relatively homogenous regional market. In the Latin America region, shared Spanish history, cultural heritage, and language (with the exception of Brazil, which was colonized by the Portuguese) mean that national differences are somewhat moderated. One can argue that Greater China, which includes the city-states of Honk Kong and Singapore, along with Taiwan, is a coherent region, as is much of the Middle East, where a strong Arab culture and shared history may limit national differences. Similarly, Russia and some former states of the Soviet Union such as Belarus and the Ukraine might be considered part of a larger regional market, at least for some products.

Taking a regional perspective is important because it may suggest that localization at the regional rather than the national level is the appropriate strategic response. For example, rather than produce cars for each national market within Europe or North America, it makes far more sense for car manufacturers to build cars for the European or North American regions. The ability to standardize a product offering within a region allows for the attainment of greater scale economies, and hence lower costs, than if each nation required its own offering. At the same time, one should be careful about not pushing this perspective too far. There are still deep, profound, cultural differences between the United Kingdom, France, Germany, and Italy—all members of the EU—which may require some degree of local customization at the national level. Managers must thus make a judgment call about the appropriate level of aggregation given (1) the product market they are looking at, and (2) the nature of national differences and trends for regional convergence. What might make sense for automobiles might not be appropriate for packaged food products.

◤ CHOOSING A GLOBAL STRATEGY

Pressures for local responsiveness imply that it may not be possible for a firm to realize the full benefits from economies of scale and location economies. It may not be possible to serve the global marketplace from a single, low-cost location, producing a globally standardized product, and marketing it worldwide to achieve economies of scale. In practice, the need to customize the product offering to local conditions may work against the implementation of such a strategy. For example, automobile firms have found that Japanese, American, and European consumers demand different kinds of cars, and this necessitates producing products that are customized for local markets. In response, firms such as Honda, Ford, and Toyota are pursuing a strategy of establishing top-to-bottom design and production facilities in each of these regions so that they can better serve local demands. Although such customization brings benefits, it also limits the ability of a firm to realize significant scale economies and location economies.

In addition, pressures for local responsiveness imply that it may not be possible to leverage skills and products associated with a firm's distinctive competencies wholesale from one nation to another. Concessions often have to be made to local conditions. Despite being depicted as "poster child" for the proliferation of standardized, global products, even McDonald's has found that it has to customize its product offerings (its menu) in order to account for national differences in tastes and preferences.

Given the need to balance the cost and differentiation (value) sides of a company's business model, how do differences in the strength of pressures for cost reductions versus those for local responsiveness affect the choice of a company's strategy? Companies typically choose among four main strategic postures when competing internationally: a global standardization strategy, a localization strategy, a transnational strategy, and an international strategy.[17] The appropriateness of each strategy varies with the extent of pressures for cost reductions and local responsiveness. Figure 8.3 illustrates the conditions under which each of these strategies is most appropriate.

Global Standardization Strategy

global standardization strategy

A business model based on pursuing a low-cost strategy on a global scale.

Companies that pursue a **global standardization strategy** focus on increasing profitability by reaping the cost reductions that come from economies of scale and location economies; that is, they pursue a low-cost strategy on a global scale. The production, marketing, and R&D activities of companies pursuing a global strategy are

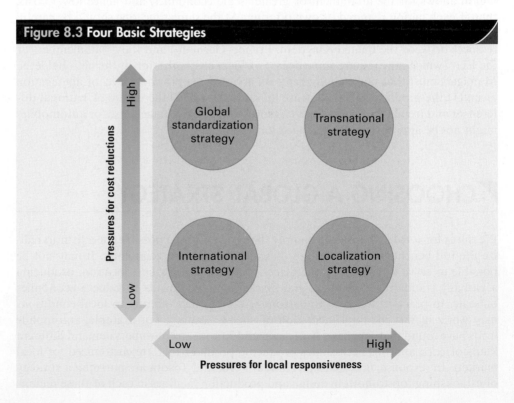

Figure 8.3 Four Basic Strategies

concentrated in a few favorable locations. These companies try not to customize their product offerings and marketing strategy to local conditions because customization, which involves shorter production runs and the duplication of functions, can raise costs. Instead, they prefer to market a standardized product worldwide so that they can reap the maximum benefits from economies of scale. They also tend to use their cost advantage to support aggressive pricing in world markets.

This strategy makes most sense when there are strong pressures for cost reductions and demand for local responsiveness is minimal. Increasingly, these conditions prevail in many industrial-goods industries, whose products often serve universal needs. In the semiconductor industry, for example, global standards have emerged, creating enormous demands for standardized, global products. Accordingly, companies such as Intel, Texas Instruments, and Motorola all pursue a global strategy.

These conditions are not always found in consumer goods markets, where demands for local responsiveness remain high. However, even some consumer goods companies are moving toward a global standardization strategy in an attempt to drive down their costs.

Localization Strategy

A **localization strategy** focuses on increasing profitability by customizing the company's goods or services so that they provide a favorable match to tastes and preferences in different national or regional markets. Localization is most appropriate when there are substantial differences across nations or regions with regard to consumer tastes and preferences, and where cost pressures are not too intense. By customizing the product offering to local demands, the company increases the value of that product in the local market. On the downside, because it involves some duplication of functions and smaller production runs, customization limits the ability of the company to capture the cost reductions associated with mass-producing a standardized product for global consumption. The strategy may make sense, however, if the added value associated with local customization supports higher pricing, which would enable the company to recoup its higher costs, or if it leads to substantially greater local demand, enabling the company to reduce costs through the attainment of scale economies in the local market.

MTV is a good example of a company that has had to pursue a localization strategy. If MTV localized its programming to match the demands of viewers in different nations, it would have lost market share to local competitors, its advertising revenues would have fallen, and its profitability would have declined. Thus, even though it raised costs, localization became a strategic imperative at MTV.

At the same time, it is important to realize that companies like MTV still have to closely monitor costs. Companies pursuing a localization strategy still need to be efficient and, whenever possible, capture scale economies from their global reach. As noted earlier, many automobile companies have found that they have to customize some of their product offerings to local market demands—for example, by producing large pickup trucks for U.S. consumers and small, fuel-efficient cars for European and Japanese consumers. At the same time, these companies try to achieve scale economies from their global volume by using common vehicle platforms and components across many different models and by manufacturing those platforms and components at efficiently scaled factories that are optimally located. By designing their products in this way, these companies have localized their product offerings and simultaneously capture some scale economies.

localization strategy
A strategy focused on increasing profitability by customizing a company's goods or services so that they provide a favorable match to tastes and preferences in different national markets.

Transnational Strategy

We have argued that a global standardization strategy makes most sense when cost pressures are intense and demands for local responsiveness limited. Conversely, a localization strategy makes most sense when demands for local responsiveness are high but cost pressures are moderate or low. What happens, however, when the company simultaneously faces both strong cost pressures and strong pressures for local responsiveness? How can managers balance out such competing and inconsistent demands? According to some researchers, pursuing a transnational strategy is the answer.

Two of these researchers, Christopher Bartlett and Sumantra Ghoshal, argue that, in today's global environment, competitive conditions are so intense that, to survive, companies must do all they can to respond to pressures for both cost reductions and local responsiveness. They must try to realize location economies and economies of scale from global volume, transfer distinctive competencies and skills within the company, and simultaneously pay attention to pressures for local responsiveness.[18]

Moreover, Bartlett and Ghoshal note that, in the modern, multinational enterprise, valuable competencies and resources do not reside just in the home country but can develop in any of the company's worldwide operations. Thus, they maintain that the flow of skills and product offerings should not be all one way, from home company to foreign subsidiary. Rather, the flow should also be from foreign subsidiary to home country, and from foreign subsidiary to foreign subsidiary. Transnational companies, in other words, must focus on leveraging subsidiary skills.

transnational strategy

A business model that simultaneously achieves low costs, differentiates the product offering across geographic markets, and fosters a flow of skills between different subsidiaries in the company's global network of operations.

In essence, companies that pursue a **transnational strategy** are trying to develop a strategy that simultaneously achieves low costs, differentiates the product offering across geographic markets, and fosters a flow of resources such as process knowledge between different subsidiaries in the company's global network of operations. As attractive as this may sound, the strategy is not easy to pursue because it places conflicting demands on the company. Differentiating the product to respond to local demands in different geographic markets raises costs, which runs counter to the goal of reducing costs. Companies such as 3M and ABB (a Swiss-based, multinational engineering conglomerate) have tried to implement a transnational strategy and found it difficult.

Indeed, how best to implement a transnational strategy is one of the most complex questions that large, global companies grapple with today. It may be that few, if any, companies have perfected this strategic posture. But some clues to the right approach can be derived from a number of companies. Consider, for example, the case of Caterpillar. The need to compete with low-cost competitors such as Komatsu of Japan forced Caterpillar to look for greater cost economies. However, variations in construction practices and government regulations across countries meant that Caterpillar also had to be responsive to local demands. Therefore, it confronted significant pressures for cost reductions and for local responsiveness.

To deal with cost pressures, Caterpillar redesigned its products to use many identical components and invested in a few large-scale, component-manufacturing facilities, sited at favorable locations, to fill global demand and realize scale economies. At the same time, the company augments the centralized manufacturing of components with assembly plants in each of its major global markets. At these plants, Caterpillar adds local product features, tailoring the finished product to local needs. Thus, Caterpillar realizes many of the benefits of global manufacturing while reacting to pressures for local responsiveness by differentiating its product among national markets.[19] Caterpillar started to pursue this strategy in the 1980s. By the 2000s, it had succeeded in doubling output per employee, significantly reducing its overall cost structure in the process. Meanwhile, Komatsu and Hitachi, which are still wedded to a Japan-centric global strategy, have seen their cost advantages evaporate and have been steadily losing market share to Caterpillar.

However, building an organization capable of supporting a transnational strategy is a complex, challenging task. Indeed, some would say it is too complex because the strategy implementation problems of creating a viable organizational structure and set of control systems to manage this strategy are immense. We return to this issue in Chapter 12.

International Strategy

Sometimes it is possible to identify multinational companies that find themselves in the fortunate position of being confronted with low cost pressures and low pressures for local responsiveness. Typically these enterprises sell a product that serves universal needs, but because they do not face significant competitors, they are not confronted with pressures to reduce their cost structure. Xerox found itself in this position in the 1960s, after its invention and commercialization of the photocopier. Strong patents protected the technology comprising the photocopier, so for several years Xerox did not face competitors—it had a monopoly. Because the product was highly valued in most developed nations, Xerox was able to sell the same basic product all over the world and charge a relatively high price for it. At the same time, because it did not face direct competitors, the company did not have to deal with strong pressures to minimize its costs.

Historically, companies like Xerox have followed a similar pattern as they developed their international operations. They tend to centralize product development functions such as R&D at home. However, companies also tend to establish manufacturing and marketing functions in each major country or geographic region in which they do business. Although they may undertake some local customization of product offering and marketing strategy, this tends to be rather limited in scope. Ultimately, in most international companies, the head office retains tight control over marketing and product strategy.

Other companies that have pursued this strategy include P&G, which had historically always developed innovative new products in Cincinnati and thereafter transferred them wholesale to local markets. Microsoft has followed a similar strategy. The bulk of Microsoft's product development work takes place in Redmond, Washington, where the company is headquartered. Although some localization work is undertaken elsewhere, it is limited to producing foreign-language versions of popular Microsoft programs such as Office.

Changes in Strategy over Time

The Achilles heel of the international strategy is that, over time, competitors inevitably emerge, and if managers do not take proactive steps to reduce their cost structure, their company may be rapidly outflanked by efficient, global competitors. This is exactly what happened to Xerox. Japanese companies such as Canon ultimately invented their way around Xerox's patents, produced their own photocopying equipment in very efficient manufacturing plants, priced the machines below Xerox's products, and rapidly took global market share from Xerox. Xerox's demise was not due to the emergence of competitors, for ultimately that was bound to occur, but rather to its failure to proactively reduce its cost structure in advance of the emergence of competitors. The message here is that an international strategy may not be viable in the long term, and to survive, companies that are able to pursue it need to shift toward a global standardization strategy, or perhaps a transnational strategy, ahead of competitors (see Figure 8.4).

The same can be said about a localization strategy. Localization may give a company a competitive edge, but if it is simultaneously facing aggressive competitors, the company will also need to reduce its cost structure—and the only way to do that may be to adopt a transnational strategy. Thus, as competition intensifies, international and localization strategies tend to become less viable, and managers need to orientate their companies toward either a global standardization strategy or a transnational strategy. Strategy in Action 8.2 describes how this process occurred at Coca-Cola.

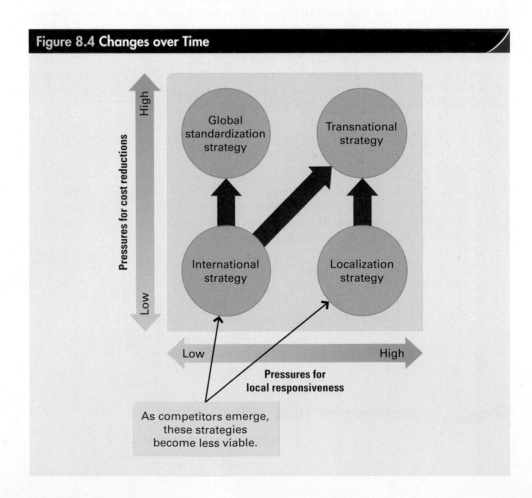

Figure 8.4 Changes over Time

8.2 STRATEGY IN ACTION

The Evolving Strategy of Coca-Cola

Coca-Cola, the iconic American soda maker, has long been among the most international of enterprises. The company made its first move outside the United States in 1902, when it entered Cuba. By 1929, Coke was marketed in 76 countries. In World War II, Coke struck a deal to supply the U.S. military with Coca-Cola wherever soldiers might be stationed. During this era, the company built 63 bottling plants around the world. Its global push continued after the war, fueled in part by the belief that the U.S. market would eventually reach maturity and by the perception that huge growth opportunities awaited overseas. By 2012, Coca Cola was operating in more than 200 countries, and over 80% of Coke's case volume was in international markets.

Up until the early 1980s, Coke's strategy could best be characterized as one of considerable localization. Local operations were granted a high degree of independence to oversee operations as managers saw fit. This changed in the 1980s and 1990s, under the leadership of Roberto Goizueta, a talented Cuban immigrant who became the CEO of Coke in 1981. Goizueta placed renewed emphasis on Coke's flagship brands, which were extended with the introduction of Diet Coke, Cherry Coke, and similar flavors. His prime belief was that the main difference between the United States and international markets was the lower level of penetration overseas, where consumption per capita of colas was only 10 to 15% of the U.S. figure. Goizueta pushed Coke to become a global company, centralizing many management and marketing activities at the corporate headquarters in Atlanta, focusing on core brands, and taking equity stakes in foreign bottlers so that the company could exert more strategic control over them. This one-size-fits-all strategy was built around standardization and the realization of economies of scale by, for example, using the same advertising message worldwide.

Goizueta's global strategy was adopted by his successor, Douglas Ivester, but by the late 1990s, the drive toward a one-size-fits-all strategy was running out of steam, as smaller, more nimble local competitors that were marketing local beverages began to halt the Coke growth engine. When Coke began failing to hit its financial targets for the first time in a generation, Ivester resigned in 2000 and was replaced by Douglas Daft. Daft instituted a 180-degree shift in strategy. His belief was that Coke needed to put more power back in the hands of local country managers. He thought that strategy, product development, and marketing should be tailored to local needs. He laid off 6,000 employees, many of them in Atlanta, and granted country managers much greater autonomy. Moreover, in a striking move for a marketing company, he announced that the company would stop using global advertisements and placed advertising budgets and control over creative content back in the hands of country managers.

Ivester's move was, in part, influenced by the experience of Coke in Japan, the company's second most profitable market, where the bestselling Coca-Cola product is not a carbonated beverage but a canned, cold coffee drink, Georgia Coffee, which is sold from vending machines. The Japanese experience seemed to signal that products should be customized to local tastes and preferences, and that Coke would do well to decentralize more decision-making authority to local managers.

However, the shift toward localization didn't produce the growth that had been expected and, by 2002, the trend was moving back toward more central coordination, with Atlanta exercising *oversight* over marketing and product development in different nations outside the United States. But this time, it was not the one-size-fits-all ethos of the Goizueta era. Under the leadership of Neville Isdell, who became CEO in March 2004, senior managers at corporate headquarters now reviewed and helped to guide local marketing and product development. However, Isdell adopted the belief that strategy (including pricing, product offerings, and marketing message) should vary from market to market to match local conditions. Isdell's position, in other words, represented a midpoint

(continued)

between the strategy of Goizueta and the strategy of Daft. Moreover, Isdell has stressed the importance of leveraging good ideas across nations—such as Georgia Coffee, for example. Having seen the success of this beverage in Japan, in 2007, Coke entered into a strategic alliance with Illycaffè, one of Italy's premier coffee makers, to build a global franchise for canned or bottled cold coffee beverages. Similarly, in 2003, the Coke subsidiary in China developed a low-cost, noncarbonated, orange-based drink that has rapidly become one of the bestselling drinks in that nation. Sensing the potential of the drink, Coke rolled it out in other Asian countries such as Thailand, where it has been a huge hit.

Sources: "Orange Gold," *The Economist*, March 3, 2007, p. 68; P. Bettis, "Coke Aims to Give Pepsi a Routing in Cold Coffee War," *Financial Times*, October 17, 2007, p. 16; P. Ghemawat, *Redefining Global Strategy* (Boston, Mass: Harvard Business School Press, 2007); D. Foust, "Queen of Pop," *Business Week*, August 7, 2006, pp. 44–47; W. J. Holstein, "How Coca-Cola Manages 90 Emerging Markets," *Strategy+Business*, November 7, 2011, www.strategy-business.com/article/00093?pg=0.

◢ THE CHOICE OF ENTRY MODE

Any firm contemplating entering a different national market must determine the best mode or vehicle for such entry. There are five primary choices of entry mode: exporting, licensing, franchising, entering into a joint venture with a host-country company, and setting up a wholly owned subsidiary in the host country. Each mode has advantages and disadvantages, and managers must weigh these carefully when deciding which mode to use.[20]

Exporting

Most manufacturing companies begin their global expansion as exporters and only later switch to one of the other modes for serving a foreign market. Exporting has two distinct advantages: It avoids the costs of establishing manufacturing operations in the host country, which are often substantial, and it may be consistent with scale economies and location economies. By manufacturing the product in a centralized location and then exporting it to other national markets, a company may be able to realize substantial scale economies from its global sales volume. That is how Sony came to dominate the global television market, how many Japanese auto companies originally made inroads into the U.S. auto market, and how Samsung gained share in the market for computer memory chips.

There are a number of drawbacks to exporting. First, exporting from the company's home base may not be appropriate if there are lower-cost locations for manufacturing the product abroad (that is, if the company can achieve location economies by moving production elsewhere). Thus, particularly in the case of a company pursuing a global standardization or transnational strategy, it may pay to manufacture in a location where conditions are most favorable from a value creation perspective and then export from that location to the rest of the globe. This is not so much an argument against exporting as it is an argument against exporting from the company's home country. For example, many U.S. electronics companies have moved some manufacturing to Asia because low-cost but highly skilled labor is available there. They export from Asia to the rest of the globe, including the United States (as Apple does with the iPhone).

Another drawback is that high transport costs can make exporting uneconomical, particularly in the case of bulk products. One way of alleviating this problem is to manufacture bulk products on a regional basis, thereby realizing some economies from large-scale production while limiting transport costs. Many multinational chemical companies manufacture their products on a regional basis, serving several countries in a region from one facility.

Tariff barriers, too, can make exporting uneconomical, and a government's threat to impose tariff barriers can make the strategy very risky. Indeed, the implicit threat from the U.S. Congress to impose tariffs on Japanese cars imported into the United States led directly to the decision by many Japanese auto companies to set up manufacturing plants in the United States.

Finally, a common practice among companies that are just beginning to export also poses risks. A company may delegate marketing activities in each country in which it does business to a local agent, but there is no guarantee that the agent will act in the company's best interest. Often, foreign agents also carry the products of competing companies and thus have divided loyalties. Consequently, agents may not perform as well as the company would if it managed marketing itself. One way to solve this problem is to set up a wholly owned subsidiary in the host country to handle local marketing. In this way, the company can reap the cost advantages that arise from manufacturing the product in a single location and exercise tight control over marketing strategy in the host country.

Licensing

International licensing is an arrangement whereby a foreign licensee purchases the rights to produce a company's product in the licensee's country for a negotiated fee (normally, royalty payments on the number of units sold). The licensee then provides most of the capital necessary to open the overseas operation.[21] The advantage of licensing is that the company does not have to bear the development costs and risks associated with opening up a foreign market. Licensing therefore can be a very attractive option for companies that lack the capital to develop operations overseas. It can also be an attractive option for companies that are unwilling to commit substantial financial resources to an unfamiliar or politically volatile foreign market where political risks are particularly high.

Licensing has three serious drawbacks, however. First, it does not give a company the tight control over manufacturing, marketing, and strategic functions in foreign countries that it needs to have in order to realize scale economies and location economies—as companies pursuing both global standardization and transnational strategies try to do. Typically, each licensee sets up its manufacturing operations. Hence, the company stands little chance of realizing scale economies and location economies by manufacturing its product in a centralized location. When these economies are likely to be important, licensing may not be the best way of expanding overseas.

Second, competing in a global marketplace may make it necessary for a company to coordinate strategic moves across countries so that the profits earned in one country can be used to support competitive attacks in another. Licensing, by its very nature, severely limits a company's ability to coordinate strategy in this way. A licensee is unlikely to let a multinational company take its profits (beyond those due in the form of royalty payments) and use them to support an entirely different licensee operating in another country.

Third, there is risk associated with licensing technological knowhow to foreign companies. For many multinational companies, technological knowhow forms the basis of their competitive advantage, and they want to maintain control over how this competitive advantage is put to use. By licensing its technology, a company can quickly lose control over it. RCA, for instance, once licensed its color television technology to a number of Japanese companies. The Japanese companies quickly assimilated RCA's technology and then used it to enter the U.S. market, where they soon gained a larger share of the U.S. market than the RCA brand holds.

There are ways of reducing this risk. One way is by entering into a cross-licensing agreement with a foreign firm. Under a cross-licensing agreement, a firm might license some valuable, intangible property to a foreign partner and, in addition to a royalty payment, also request that the foreign partner license some of its valuable knowhow to the firm. Such agreements are reckoned to reduce the risks associated with licensing technological knowhow, as the licensee realizes that if it violates the spirit of a licensing contract (by using the knowledge obtained to compete directly with the licensor), the licensor can do the same to it. Put differently, cross-licensing agreements enable firms to hold each other hostage, thereby reducing the probability that they will behave opportunistically toward each other.[22] Such cross-licensing agreements are increasingly common in high-technology industries. For example, the U.S. biotechnology firm Amgen licensed one of its key drugs, Neupogen, to Kirin, the Japanese pharmaceutical company. The license gives Kirin the right to sell Neupogen in Japan. In return, Amgen receives a royalty payment, and through a licensing agreement it gains the right to sell certain Kirin products in the United States.

Franchising

In many respects, franchising is similar to licensing, although franchising tends to involve longer-term commitments than licensing. Franchising is basically a specialized form of licensing in which the franchiser not only sells intangible property to the franchisee (normally a trademark), but also insists that the franchisee abide by strict rules governing how it does business. The franchiser will often assist the franchisee run the business on an ongoing basis. As with licensing, the franchiser typically receives a royalty payment, which amounts to a percentage of the franchisee revenues.

Whereas licensing is a strategy pursued primarily by manufacturing companies, franchising, which resembles it in some respects, is a strategy employed chiefly by service companies. McDonald's provides a good example of a firm that has grown by using a franchising strategy. McDonald's has set down strict rules as to how franchisees should operate a restaurant. These rules extend to controlling the menu, cooking methods, staffing policies, and restaurant design and location. McDonald's also organizes the supply chain for its franchisees and provides management training and financial assistance.[23]

The advantages of franchising are similar to those of licensing. Specifically, the franchiser does not need to bear the development costs and risks associated with opening up a foreign market on its own, for the franchisee typically assumes those costs and risks. Thus, using a franchising strategy, a service company can build up a global presence quickly and at a low cost.

The disadvantages of franchising are less pronounced than in licensing. Because service companies often use franchising, there is no reason to consider the need for coordination of manufacturing to achieve experience curve and location economies. But franchising may inhibit the firm's ability to take profits out of one country to support competitive attacks in another. A more significant disadvantage of franchising is quality control. The foundation of franchising arrangements is that the firm's brand name conveys a message to consumers about the quality of the firm's product. Thus, a business traveler checking in at a Four Seasons hotel in Hong Kong can reasonably expect the same quality of room, food, and service that would be received in New York, Hawaii, or Ontario, Canada. The Four Seasons name is assumed to guarantee consistent product quality. This presents a problem in that foreign franchisees may not be as concerned about quality as they are supposed to be, and the result of poor quality can cascade beyond lost sales in a particular foreign market to a decline in the firm's worldwide reputation. For example, if a business traveler has a bad experience at the Four Seasons in Hong Kong, he or she may never go to another Four Seasons hotel, and may urge colleagues to avoid the chain as well. The geographical distance of the firm from its foreign franchisees can make poor quality difficult to detect. In addition, the numbers of franchisees—in the case of McDonald's, tens of thousands—can make quality control difficult.

To reduce these problems, a company can set up a subsidiary in each country or region in which it is expanding. The subsidiary, which might be wholly owned by the company or a joint venture with a foreign company, then assumes the rights and obligations to establish franchisees throughout that particular country or region. The combination of proximity and the limited number of independent franchisees that need to be monitored reduces the quality control problem. Because the subsidiary is at least partly owned by the company, it can place its own managers in the subsidiary to ensure the level of quality monitoring it demands. This organizational arrangement has proved very popular in practice; it has been used by McDonald's, KFC, and Hilton Worldwide to expand international operations, to name just three examples.

Joint Ventures

Establishing a joint venture with a foreign company has long been a favored mode for entering a new market. The most typical form of joint venture is a 50/50 joint venture, in which each party takes a 50% ownership stake and a team of managers from both parent companies shares operating control. Some companies seek joint ventures wherein they become the majority shareholder (for example, a 51 to 49% ownership split), which permits tighter control by the dominant partner.[24]

Joint ventures have several advantages. First, a company may feel that it can benefit from a local partner's knowledge of a host country's competitive conditions, culture, language, political systems, and business systems. Second, when the development costs and risks of opening up a foreign market are high, a company might gain by sharing these costs and risks with a local partner. Third, in some countries, political considerations make joint ventures the only feasible entry mode. For example, historically, many U.S. companies found it much easier to obtain permission to set up operations in Japan if they joined with a Japanese partner than if they tried to enter on their own.

Despite the advantages, there are major disadvantages with joint ventures. First, as with licensing, a firm that enters into a joint venture risks yielding control of its technology to its partner. Thus, a proposed joint venture in 2002 between Boeing and Mitsubishi Heavy Industries to build Boeing's new, wide-body jet (the 787) raised fears that Boeing might unwittingly give its commercial airline technology to the Japanese. However, joint-venture agreements can be constructed to minimize this risk. One option is to hold majority ownership in the venture. This allows the dominant partner to exercise great control over its technology—but it can be difficult to find a foreign partner who is willing to settle for minority ownership. Another option is to "wall off" from a partner technology that is central to the core competence of the firm while sharing other technology.

A second disadvantage is that a joint venture does not give a firm the tight control over subsidiaries that it might need to realize experience-curve or location economies. Nor does it give a firm the control over a foreign subsidiary it might need for engaging in coordinated, global attacks against its rivals. Consider the entry of Texas Instruments (TI) into the Japanese semiconductor market. When TI established semiconductor facilities in Japan, it did so for the dual purpose of checking Japanese manufacturers' market share and limiting the cash they had available for invading TI's global market. In other words, TI was engaging in global strategic coordination. To implement this strategy, TI's subsidiary in Japan had to be prepared to take instructions from corporate headquarters regarding competitive strategy. The strategy also required the Japanese subsidiary to run at a loss if necessary. Few, if any, potential joint-venture partners would have been willing to accept such conditions, as it would have necessitated a willingness to accept a negative return on investment. Indeed, many joint ventures establish a degree of autonomy that would make such direct control over strategic decisions all but impossible to establish.[25] Thus, to implement this strategy, TI set up a wholly owned subsidiary in Japan.

Wholly Owned Subsidiaries

A wholly owned subsidiary is one in which the parent company owns 100% of the subsidiary's stock. To establish a wholly owned subsidiary in a foreign market, a company can either set up a completely new operation in that country or acquire an established host-country company to promote its products in the host market.

Setting up a wholly owned subsidiary offers three advantages. First, when a company's competitive advantage is based on its control of a technological competency, a wholly owned subsidiary will normally be the preferred entry mode because it reduces the company's risk of losing this control. Consequently, many high-tech companies prefer wholly owned subsidiaries to joint ventures or licensing arrangements. Wholly owned subsidiaries tend to be the favored entry mode in the semiconductor, computer, electronics, and pharmaceutical industries.

Second, a wholly owned subsidiary gives a company the kind of tight control over operations in different countries that it needs if it is going to engage in global strategic coordination—taking profits from one country to support competitive attacks in another.

Third, a wholly owned subsidiary may be the best choice if a company wants to realize location economies and the scale economies that flow from producing a standardized output from a single or limited number of manufacturing plants. When pressures on costs are intense, it may pay a company to configure its value chain in such a way that value added at each stage is maximized. Thus, a national subsidiary may specialize in manufacturing only part of the product line, or certain components of the end product, exchanging parts and products with other subsidiaries in the company's global system. Establishing such a global production system requires a high degree of control over the operations of national affiliates. Different national operations must be prepared to accept centrally determined decisions as to how they should produce, how much they should produce, and how their output should be priced for transfer between operations. A wholly owned subsidiary would have to comply with these mandates, whereas licensees or joint-venture partners would most likely shun such a subservient role.

On the other hand, establishing a wholly owned subsidiary is generally the most costly method of serving a foreign market. The parent company must bear all the costs and risks of setting up overseas operations—in contrast to joint ventures, where the costs and risks are shared, or licensing, where the licensee bears most of the costs and risks. But the risks of learning to do business in a new culture diminish if a company acquires an established host-country enterprise. Acquisitions, however, raise a whole set of additional problems, such as trying to marry divergent corporate cultures, and these may more than offset the benefits. (The problems associated with acquisitions are discussed in Chapter 10.)

Choosing an Entry Strategy

The advantages and disadvantages of the various entry modes are summarized in Table 8.1. Inevitably, there are tradeoffs in choosing one entry mode over another. For example, when considering entry into an unfamiliar country with a track record of nationalizing foreign-owned enterprises, a company might favor a joint venture with a local enterprise. Its rationale might be that the local partner will help it establish operations in an unfamiliar environment and speak out against nationalization should the possibility arise. But if the company's distinctive competency is based on proprietary technology, entering into a joint venture might mean risking loss of control over that technology to the joint venture partner, which would make this strategy unattractive. Despite such hazards, some generalizations can be offered about the optimal choice of entry mode.

Distinctive Competencies and Entry Mode   When companies expand internationally to earn greater returns from their differentiated product offerings, entering markets where indigenous competitors lack comparable products, the companies are pursuing an international strategy. The optimal entry mode for such companies depends to some degree upon the nature of their distinctive competency. In particular, we need to distinguish between companies with a distinctive competency in technological knowhow and those with a distinctive competency in management knowhow.

If a company's competitive advantage—its distinctive competency—derives from its control of proprietary technological knowhow (i.e., intellectual property), licensing and joint-venture arrangements should be avoided if possible to minimize the risk of losing control of that technology. Thus, if a high-tech company is considering setting up operations in a foreign country in order to profit from a distinctive competency in technological knowhow, it should probably do so through a wholly owned subsidiary.

However, this should not be viewed as a hard-and-fast rule. For instance, a licensing or joint-venture arrangement might be structured in such a way as to reduce the

Table 8.1 The Advantages and Disadvantages of Different Entry Modes

Entry Mode	Advantages	Disadvantages
Exporting	• Ability to realize location- and scale-based economies	• High transport costs • Trade barriers • Problems with local marketing agents
Licensing	• Low development costs and risks	• Inability to realize location- and scale-based economies • Inability to engage in global strategic coordination • Lack of control over technology
Franchising	• Low development costs and risks	• Inability to engage in global strategic coordination • Lack of control over quality
Joint Ventures	• Access to local partner's knowledge • Shared development costs and risks • Political dependency	• Inability to engage in global strategic coordination • Inability to realize location- and scale-based economies • Lack of control over technology
Wholly Owned Subsidiaries	• Protection of technology • Ability to engage in global strategic coordination • Ability to realize location- and scale-based economies	• High costs and risks

risks that licensees or joint-venture partners will expropriate a company's technological knowhow. (We consider this kind of arrangement in more detail later in the chapter when we discuss the issue of structuring strategic alliances.) Or consider a situation where a company believes its technological advantage will be short lived and expects rapid imitation of its core technology by competitors. In this situation, the company might want to license its technology as quickly as possible to foreign companies in order to gain global acceptance of its technology before imitation occurs.[26] Such a strategy has some advantages. By licensing its technology to competitors, the company may deter them from developing their own, possibly superior, technology. It also may be able to establish its technology as the dominant design in the industry, ensuring a steady stream of royalty payments. Such situations aside, however, the attractions of licensing are probably outweighed by the risks of losing control of technology, and therefore licensing should be avoided.

The competitive advantage of many service companies such as McDonald's or Hilton Worldwide is based on management knowhow (i.e., process knowledge). For such companies, the risk of losing control of their management skills to franchisees or joint-venture partners is not that great. The reason is that the valuable asset of such companies is their brand name, and brand names are generally well protected by intellectual property laws pertaining to trademarks. Given this fact, many issues that arise in the case of technological knowhow do not arise in the case of management knowhow. As a result, many service companies favor a combination of franchising and subsidiaries to control franchisees within a particular country or region. The subsidiary may be wholly owned or a joint venture. In most cases, however, service companies have found that entering into a joint venture with a local partner in order to set up a controlling subsidiary in a country or region works best because a joint venture is often politically more acceptable and brings a degree of local knowledge to the subsidiary.

Pressures for Cost Reduction and Entry Mode   The greater the pressures for cost reductions, the more likely that a company will want to pursue some combination of exporting and wholly owned subsidiaries. By manufacturing in the locations where factor conditions are optimal and then exporting to the rest of the world, a company may be able to realize substantial location economies and substantial scale economies. The company might then want to export the finished product to marketing subsidiaries based in various countries. Typically, these subsidiaries would be wholly owned and have the responsibility for overseeing distribution in a particular country. Setting up wholly owned marketing subsidiaries is preferable to a joint-venture arrangement or using a foreign marketing agent because it gives the company the tight control over marketing that might be required to coordinate a globally dispersed value chain. In addition, tight control over a local operation enables the company to use the profits generated in one market to improve its competitive position in another market. Hence companies pursuing global or transnational strategies prefer to establish wholly owned subsidiaries.

▐ GLOBAL STRATEGIC ALLIANCES

Global strategic alliances are cooperative agreements between companies from different countries that are actual or potential competitors. Strategic alliances range from formal joint ventures in which two or more companies have an equity stake, to short-term contractual agreements in which two companies may agree to cooperate on a particular problem (such as developing a new product).

global strategic alliances Cooperative agreements between companies from different countries that are actual or potential competitors.

Advantages of Strategic Alliances

Companies enter into strategic alliances with competitors to achieve a number of strategic objectives.[27] First, strategic alliances may facilitate entry into a foreign market. For example, many firms feel that if they are to successfully enter the Chinese market, they need a local partner who understands business conditions and has good connections. Thus, Warner Brothers entered into a joint venture with two Chinese partners to produce and distribute films in China. As a foreign film company, Warner found that if it wanted to produce films on its own for the Chinese market, it had to go through a complex approval process for every film. It also had to farm out distribution to a local company, which made doing business in China very difficult. Due to the participation of Chinese firms, however, the joint-venture films will require a streamlined approval process, and the venture will be able to distribute any films it produces. Moreover, the joint venture will be able to produce films for Chinese TV, something that foreign firms are not allowed to do.[28]

Second, strategic alliances allow firms to share the fixed costs (and associated risks) of developing new products or processes. An alliance between Boeing and a number of Japanese companies to build Boeing's latest commercial jetliner, the 787, was motivated by Boeing's desire to share the estimated $8-billion investment required to develop the aircraft.

Third, an alliance is a way to bring together complementary skills and assets that neither company could easily develop on its own.[29] In 2011, for example, Microsoft and Nokia established an alliance aimed at developing and marketing smartphones that used Microsoft's Windows 8 operating system. Microsoft contributed its software engineering skills, particularly with regard to the development of a version of its Windows operating system for smartphones, and Nokia contributed its design, engineering, and marketing knowhow. The first phones resulting from this collaboration reached the market in late 2012 (Microsoft subsequently purchased Nokia's mobile phone business in 2013.)

Fourth, it can make sense to form an alliance that will help firms establish technological standards for the industry that will benefit them. This was also a goal of the alliance between Microsoft and Nokia. The idea is to try to establish Windows 8 as the de facto operating system for smartphones in the face of strong competition from Apple, with its iPhone, and Google, whose Android operating system was the most widely used smartphone operating system in the world in 2012.

Disadvantages of Strategic Alliances

The advantages we have discussed can be very significant. Despite this, some commentators have criticized strategic alliances on the grounds that they give competitors a low-cost route to new technology and markets.[30] For example, a few years ago, some commentators argued that many strategic alliances between U.S. and Japanese firms were part of an implicit Japanese strategy to keep high-paying, high-value-added jobs in Japan while gaining the project engineering and production process skills that underlie the competitive success of many U.S. companies.[31] They argued that Japanese success in the machine tool and semiconductor industries was built on U.S. technology acquired through strategic alliances. And they argued that U.S. managers were aiding the Japanese by entering alliances that channel new inventions to Japan and provide a U.S. sales and distribution network for the resulting products. Although such deals may generate short-term profits, the argument goes, in the long term, the result is to "hollow out" U.S. firms, leaving them with no competitive advantage in the global marketplace.

These critics have a point; alliances have risks. Unless a firm is careful, it can give away more than it receives. But there are so many examples of apparently successful alliances between firms—including alliances between U.S. and Japanese firms—that this position appears extreme. It is difficult to see how the Boeing–Mitsubishi alliance for the 787, or the long-term Fuji–Xerox alliance, fit the critics' thesis. In these cases, both partners seem to have gained from the alliance. Why do some alliances benefit both firms while others benefit one firm and hurt the other? The next section provides an answer to this question.

Making Strategic Alliances Work

The failure rate for international strategic alliances is quite high. For example, one study of 49 international strategic alliances found that two-thirds run into serious managerial and financial troubles within 2 years of their formation, and that although many of these problems are ultimately solved, 33% are rated as failures by the parties involved.[32] The success of an alliance seems to be a function of three main factors: partner selection, alliance structure, and the manner in which the alliance is managed.

Partner Selection   One key to making a strategic alliance work is selecting the right partner. A good partner has three principal characteristics. First, a good partner helps the company achieve strategic goals such as achieving market access, sharing the costs and risks of new-product development, or gaining access to critical core competencies. In other words, the partner must have capabilities that the company lacks and that it values. Second, a good partner shares the firm's vision for the purpose of the alliance. If two companies approach an alliance with radically different agendas, the chances are great that the relationship will not be harmonious and the partnership will end.

Third, a good partner is unlikely to try to exploit the alliance for its own ends—that is, to expropriate the company's technological knowhow while giving away little in return. In this respect, firms with reputations for fair play probably make the best partners. For example, IBM is involved in so many strategic alliances that it would not pay for the company to trample over its individual alliance partners.[33] This would tarnish IBM's reputation of being a good ally and would make it more difficult for it to attract alliance partners. Because IBM attaches great importance to its alliances, it is unlikely to engage in the kind of opportunistic behavior that critics highlight. Similarly, their reputations make it less likely (but by no means impossible) that such Japanese firms as Sony, Toshiba, and Fuji, which have histories of alliances with non-Japanese firms, would exploit an alliance partner.

To select a partner with these three characteristics, a company needs to conduct comprehensive research on potential alliance candidates. To increase the probability of selecting a good partner, the company should collect as much pertinent, publicly available information about potential allies as possible; collect data from informed third parties, including companies that have had alliances with the potential partners, investment bankers who have had dealings with them, and former employees; and get to know potential partners as well as possible before committing to an alliance. This last step should include face-to-face meetings between senior managers (and perhaps middle-level managers) to ensure that the chemistry is right.

Alliance Structure   Having selected a partner, the alliance should be structured so that the company's risk of giving too much away to the partner is reduced to an acceptable level. First, alliances can be designed to make it difficult (if not impossible) to transfer technology not meant to be transferred. Specifically, the design, development, manufacture, and service of a product manufactured by an alliance can be structured to "wall off" sensitive technologies to prevent their leakage to the other participant. In the alliance between General Electric and Snecma to build commercial aircraft engines, for example, GE reduced the risk of "excess transfer" by walling off certain steps of the production process. The modularization effectively cut off the transfer of what GE regarded as key competitive technology while permitting Snecma access to final assembly. Similarly, in the alliance between Boeing and the Japanese to build the 787, Boeing walled off research, design, and marketing functions considered central to its competitive position, while allowing the Japanese to share in production technology. Boeing also walled off new technologies not required for 787 production.[34]

opportunism
Seeking one's own self-interest, often through the use of guile.

Second, contractual safeguards can be written into an alliance agreement to guard against the risk of **opportunism** by a partner. For example, TRW has three strategic alliances with large Japanese auto component suppliers to produce seat belts, engine valves, and steering gears for sale to Japanese-owned auto assembly plants in the United States. TRW has clauses in each of its alliance contracts that bar the Japanese firms from competing with TRW to supply U.S.-owned auto companies with component parts. By doing this, TRW protects itself against the possibility that the Japanese companies are entering into the alliances merely as a means of gaining access to the North American market to compete with TRW in its home market.

Third, both parties in an alliance can agree in advance to exchange skills and technologies that the other covets, thereby ensuring a chance for equitable gain. Cross-licensing agreements are one way to achieve this goal.

Fourth, the risk of opportunism by an alliance partner can be reduced if the firm extracts a significant, credible commitment from its partner in advance. The long-term alliance between Xerox and Fuji to build photocopiers for the Asian market perhaps best illustrates this. Rather than enter into an informal agreement or a licensing arrangement (which Fujifilm initially preferred), Xerox insisted that Fuji invest in a 50/50 joint venture to serve Japan and East Asia. This venture constituted such a significant investment in people, equipment, and facilities that Fujifilm was committed from the outset to making the alliance work in order to earn a return on its investment. By agreeing to the joint venture, Fuji essentially made a credible commitment to the alliance. In turn, Xerox felt secure in transferring its photocopier technology to Fuji.

Managing the Alliance   Once a partner has been selected and an appropriate alliance structure agreed upon, the task facing the company is to maximize benefits from the alliance. One important ingredient of success appears to be sensitivity to cultural differences. Many differences in management style are attributable to cultural differences, and managers need to make allowances for these when dealing with their partners. Beyond this, maximizing benefits from an alliance seems to involve building trust between partners and learning from partners.[35]

Managing an alliance successfully requires building interpersonal relationships between the firms' managers, or what is sometimes referred to as *relational capital*.[36] This is one lesson that can be drawn from the strategic alliance between Ford and Mazda. Ford and Mazda set up a framework of meetings within which their managers not only discuss matters pertaining to the alliance, but also have time to get to know one another. The belief is that the resulting friendships help build trust and facilitate harmonious relations between the two firms. Personal relationships also foster an informal management network between the firms. This network can then be used to help solve problems arising in more formal contexts (such as in joint committee meetings between personnel from the two firms).

Academics have argued that a major determinant of how much knowledge a company acquires from an alliance is its ability to learn from its alliance partner.[37]

For example, in a study of 15 strategic alliances between major multinationals, Gary Hamel, Yves Doz, and C. K. Prahalad focused on a number of alliances between Japanese companies and Western (European or American) partners.[38] In every case in which a Japanese company emerged from an alliance stronger than its Western partner, the Japanese company had made a greater effort to learn. Few Western companies studied seemed to want to learn from their Japanese partners. They tended to regard the alliance purely as a cost-sharing or risk-sharing arrangement, rather than an opportunity to learn how a potential competitor does business.

For an example of an alliance in which there was a clear learning asymmetry, consider the agreement between General Motors and Toyota Motor Corp. to build the Chevrolet Nova. This alliance was structured as a formal joint venture, New United Motor Manufacturing, in which both parties had a 50% equity stake. The venture owned an auto plant in Fremont, California. According to one of the Japanese managers, Toyota achieved most of its objectives from the alliance: "We learned about U.S. supply and transportation. And we got the confidence to manage U.S. workers." All that knowledge was then quickly transferred to Georgetown, Kentucky, where Toyota opened a plant of its own. By contrast, although General Motors (GM) got a new product, the Chevrolet Nova, some GM managers complained that their new knowledge was never put to good use inside GM. They say that they should have been kept together as a team to educate GM's engineers and workers about the Japanese system. Instead, they were dispersed to different GM subsidiaries.

When entering an alliance, a company must take measures to ensure that it learns from its alliance partner and then puts that knowledge to good use within its own organization. One suggested approach is to educate all operating employees about the partner's strengths and weaknesses and make clear to them how acquiring particular skills will bolster their company's competitive position. For such learning to be of value, the knowledge acquired from an alliance must be diffused throughout the organization—which did not happen at GM. To spread knowledge, the managers involved in an alliance should be used as a resource to educate others within the company about the skills of the alliance partner.

KEY TERMS

multinational company 247	localization strategy 257	global strategic alliances 269
location economies 248	transnational strategy 258	opportunism 272
global standardization strategy 256		

TAKEAWAYS FOR STRATEGIC MANAGERS

1. For some companies, international expansion represents a way of earning greater returns by transferring the skills and product offerings derived from their distinctive competencies to markets where indigenous competitors lack those skills. As barriers to international trade

have fallen, industries have expanded beyond national boundaries and industry competition, and opportunities have increased.

2. Because of national differences, it pays for a company to base each value creation activity it performs at the location where factor conditions are most conducive to the performance of that activity. This strategy is known as focusing on the attainment of location economies.

3. By building sales volume more rapidly, international expansion can help a company gain a cost advantage through the realization of scale economies and learning effects.

4. The best strategy for a company to pursue depends on the pressures it must cope with: pressures for cost reductions or for local responsiveness. Pressures for cost reductions are greatest in industries producing commodity-type products, where price is the main competitive weapon. Pressures for local responsiveness arise from differences in consumer tastes and preferences, as well as from national infrastructure and traditional practices, distribution channels, and host government demands.

5. Companies pursuing an international strategy transfer the skills and products derived from distinctive competencies to foreign markets, while undertaking some limited local customization.

6. Companies pursuing a localization strategy customize their product offerings, marketing strategies, and business strategies to national conditions.

7. Companies pursuing a global standardization strategy focus on reaping the cost reductions that come from scale economies and location economies.

8. Many industries are now so competitive that companies must adopt a transnational strategy. This involves a simultaneous focus upon reducing costs, transferring skills and products, and being locally responsive. Implementing such a strategy may prove difficult.

9. There are five different ways of entering a foreign market: exporting, licensing, franchising, entering into a joint venture, and setting up a wholly owned subsidiary. The optimal choice among entry modes depends on the company's strategy.

10. Strategic alliances are cooperative agreements between actual or potential competitors. The advantages of alliances are that they facilitate entry into foreign markets, enable partners to share the fixed costs and risks associated with new products and processes, facilitate the transfer of complementary skills between companies, and help companies establish technical standards.

11. The drawbacks of a strategic alliance are that the company risks giving away technological knowhow and market access to its alliance partner, while getting very little in return.

12. The disadvantages associated with alliances can be reduced if the company selects partners carefully, paying close attention to reputation, and structures the alliance in order to avoid unintended transfers of knowhow.

DISCUSSION QUESTIONS

1. Plot the position of the following companies on Figure 8.3: Microsoft, Google, Coca-Cola, Dow Chemicals, Pfizer, and McDonald's. In each case, justify your answer.

2. Are the following global standardization industries, or industries where localization is more important: bulk chemicals, pharmaceuticals, branded food products, moviemaking, television manufacture, personal computers, airline travel, fashion retailing?

3. Discuss how the need for control over foreign operations varies with the strategy and distinctive competencies of a company. What are the implications of this relationship for the choice of entry mode?

4. Licensing proprietary technology to foreign competitors is the best way to give up a company's competitive advantage. Discuss.

5. What kind of companies stand to gain the most from entering into strategic alliances with potential competitors? Why?

CLOSING CASE

Ford's Global Strategy

When Ford CEO Alan Mulally arrived at the company in 2006, after a long career at Boeing, he was shocked to learn that the company produced one Ford Focus for Europe, and a totally different one for the United-States. "Can you imagine having one Boeing 737 for Europe and one 737 for the United States?," he said at the time. Due to this product strategy, Ford was unable to buy common parts for the vehicles, could not share development costs, and couldn't use its European Focus plants to make cars for the United States, or vice versa. In a business where economies of scale are important, the result was high costs. Nor were these problems limited to the Ford Focus—the strategy of designing and building different cars for different regions was the standard approach at Ford.

Ford's long-standing strategy of regional models was based upon the assumption that consumers in different regions had different tastes and preferences, which required considerable local customization. Americans, it was argued, loved their trucks and SUVs, whereas Europeans preferred smaller, fuel-efficient cars. Notwithstanding such differences, Mulally still could not understand why small car models like the Focus or the Escape SUV, which were sold in different regions, were not built on the same platform and did not share common parts. In truth, the strategy probably had to do with the autonomy of different regions within Ford's organization, a fact that was deeply embedded in Ford's history as one of the oldest multinational corporations.

When the global financial crisis rocked the world's automobile industry in 2008-2009, and precipitated the steepest drop in sales since the Great Depression, Mulally decided that Ford had to change its traditional practices in order to get its costs under control. Moreover, he felt that there

was no way that Ford would be able to compete effectively in the large, developing markets of China and India unless Ford leveraged its global scale to produce low-cost cars. The result was Mulally's "One Ford" strategy, which aims to create a handful of car platforms that Ford can use everywhere in the world.

Under this strategy, new models—such as the 2013 Fiesta, Focus, and Escape—share a common design, are built on a common platform, use the same parts, and will be built in identical factories around the world. Ultimately, Ford hopes to have only five platforms to deliver sales of more than 6 million vehicles by 2016. In 2006, Ford had 15 platforms that accounted for sales of 6.6 million vehicles. By pursuing this strategy, Ford can share the costs of design and tooling, and it can attain much greater scale economies in the production of component parts. Ford has stated that it will take about one-third out of the $1-billion cost of developing a new car model and should significantly reduce its $50-billion annual budget for component parts. Moreover, because the different factories producing these cars are identical in all respects, useful knowledge acquired through experience in one factory can quickly be transferred to other factories, resulting in systemwide cost savings.

Ford hopes this strategy will bring down costs sufficiently to enable it to improve profit margins in developed markets and achieve good margins at lower price points in hypercompetitive developing nations such as China, now the world's largest car market, where Ford currently trails global rivals such as General Motors and Volkswagen. Indeed, the strategy is central to Mulally's goal for growing Ford's sales from $5.5 million in 2010 to $8 million by 2015.

(continued)

Sources: M. Ramsey, "Ford SUV Marks New World Car Strategy," *The Wall Street Journal*, November 16, 2011; B. Vlasic, "Ford Strategy Will Call for Stepping up Expansion, Especially in Asia," *New York Times*, June 7, 2011; "Global Manufacturing Strategy Gives Ford Competitive Advantage," Ford Motor Company, http://media.ford .com/article_display.cfm?article_id=13633.

CASE DISCUSSION QUESTIONS

1. Why do you think that Ford historically made different cars in different regions? What are the advantages of Ford's historic strategy? What are the drawbacks?
2. What global developments forced Ford to rethink its historic strategy?
3. How will the "One Ford" strategy benefit Ford? What does this strategy mean for Ford's ability to compete in established markets like the United States and Europe, and emerging markets like China?
4. Using the framework outlined in this chapter and summarized in Figure 8.3, how would you describe Ford's global strategy?

NOTES

[1] World Trade Organization (WTO), *International Trade Statistics 2013* (Geneva: WHO, 2013).

[2] Ibid.; United Nations, *World Investment Report, 2013* (New York and Geneva: United Nations, 2013).

[3] P. Dicken, *Global Shift* (New York: Guilford Press, 1992).

[4] D. Pritchard, "Are Federal Tax Laws and State Subsidies for Boeing 7E7 Selling America Short?" *Aviation Week,* April 12, 2004, pp. 74–75.

[5] T. Levitt, "The Globalization of Markets," *Harvard Business Review,* May–June 1983, pp. 92–102.

[6] M. E. Porter, *The Competitive Advantage of Nations* (New York: Free Press, 1990). See also R. Grant, "Porter's Competitive Advantage of Nations: An Assessment," *Strategic Management Journal* 7 (1991): 535–548.

[7] Empirical evidence does seem to indicate that, on average, international expansion is linked to greater firm profitability. For recent examples, see M. A. Hitt, R. E. Hoskisson, and H. Kim, "International Diversification, Effects on Innovation and Firm Performance," *Academy of Management Journal* 40 (4) (1997): 767–98; S. Tallman and J. Li, "Effects of International Diversity and Product Diversity on the Performance of Multinational Firms," *Academy of Management Journal* 39 (1) (1996): 179–196.

[8] Porter, *Competitive Advantage of Nations*.

[9] See J. Birkinshaw and N. Hood, "Multinational Subsidiary Evolution: Capability and Charter Change in Foreign Owned Subsidiary Companies," *Academy of Management Review* 23 (October 1998): 773–795; A. K. Gupta and V. J. Govindarajan, "Knowledge Flows Within Multinational Corporations," *Strategic Management Journal* 21 (2000): 473–496; V. J. Govindarajan and A. K. Gupta, *The Quest for Global Dominance* (San Francisco: Jossey-Bass, 2001); T. S. Frost, J. M. Birkinshaw, and P. C. Ensign, "Centers of Excellence in Multinational Corporations," *Strategic Management Journal* 23 (2002): 997–1018; U. Andersson, M. Forsgren, and U. Holm, "The Strategic Impact of External Networks," *Strategic Management Journal* 23 (2002): 979–996.

[10] S. Leung, "Armchairs, TVs and Espresso: Is It McDonald's?," *The Wall Street Journal,* August 30, 2002, pp. A1, A6.

[11] C. K. Prahalad and Yves L. Doz, *The Multinational Mission: Balancing Local Demands and*

Global Vision (New York: Free Press, 1987). See also J. Birkinshaw, A. Morrison, and J. Hulland, "Structural and Competitive Determinants of a Global Integration Strategy," *Strategic Management Journal* 16 (1995): 637–655.

[12]J. E. Garten, "Walmart Gives Globalization a Bad Name," *Business Week*, March 8, 2004, p. 24.

[13]Prahalad and Doz, *Multinational Mission*. Prahalad and Doz actually talk about local responsiveness rather than local customization.

[14]Levitt, "Globalization of Markets."

[15]W.W. Lewis. *The Power of Productivity* (Chicago, University of Chicago Press, 2004).

[16]For an extended discussion, see G.S. Yip and G. Tomas M. Hult, *Total Global Strategy* (Boston: Pearson, 2012); A. M. Rugman and A. Verbeke, "A perspective on regional and global strategies of multinational enterprises," *Journal of International Business Studies* 35 (1) (2004): 3–18.

[17]Bartlett and Ghoshal, *Managing Across Borders.*

[18]Ibid.

[19]T. Hout, M. E. Porter, and E. Rudden, "How Global Companies Win Out," *Harvard Business Review* (September–October 1982), pp. 98–108.

[20]This section draws on numerous studies, including C. W. L. Hill, P. Hwang, and W. C. Kim, "An Eclectic Theory of the Choice of International Entry Mode," *Strategic Management Journal* 11 (1990): 117–28; C. W. L. Hill and W. C. Kim, "Searching for a Dynamic Theory of the Multinational Enterprise: A Transaction Cost Model," *Strategic Management Journal* 9

(Special Issue on Strategy Content, 1988): 93–104; E. Anderson and H. Gatignon, "Modes of Foreign Entry: A Transaction Cost Analysis and Propositions," *Journal of International Business Studies* 17 (1986): 1–26; F. R. Root, *Entry Strategies for International Markets* (Lexington, MA: D. C. Heath, 1980); A. Madhok, "Cost, Value and Foreign Market Entry: The Transaction and the Firm," *Strategic Management Journal* 18 (1997): 39–61; K. D. Brouthers and L. B. Brouthers, "Acquisition or Greenfield Start-Up?" *Strategic Management Journal* 21 (1) (2000): 89–97; X. Martin and R. Salmon, "Knowledge Transfer Capacity and Its Implications for the Theory of the Multinational Enterprise," *Journal of International Business Studies,* July 2003, p. 356; A. Verbeke, "The Evolutionary View of the MNE and the Future of Internalization Theory," *Journal of International Business Studies,* November 2003, pp. 498–515.

[21]F. J. Contractor, "The Role of Licensing in International Strategy," *Columbia Journal of World Business,* Winter 1982, pp. 73–83.

[22]Andrew E. Serwer, "McDonald's Conquers the World," *Fortune,* October 17, 1994, pp. 103–116.

[23]For an excellent review of the basic theoretical literature of joint ventures, see B. Kogut, "Joint Ventures: Theoretical and Empirical Perspectives," *Strategic Management Journal* 9 (1988): 319–32. More recent studies include T. Chi, "Option to Acquire or Divest a Joint Venture," *Strategic Management Journal* 21 (6), 2000: 665–688; H. Merchant and D. Schendel, "How Do International Joint Ventures Create Shareholder Value?" *Strategic Management*

Journal 21 (7) (2000): 723–737; H. K. Steensma and M. A. Lyles, "Explaining IJV Survival in a Transitional Economy Through Social Exchange and Knowledge Based Perspectives," *Strategic Management Journal* 21 (8), 2000: 831–851; J. F. Hennart and M. Zeng, "Cross Cultural Differences and Joint Venture Longevity," *Journal of International Business Studies,* December 2002, pp. 699–717.

[24]J. A. Robins, S. Tallman, and K. Fladmoe-Lindquist, "Autonomy and Dependence of International Cooperative Ventures," *Strategic Management Journal,* October 2002, pp. 881–902.

[25]C. W. L. Hill, "Strategies for Exploiting Technological Innovations," *Organization Science* 3 (1992): 428–441.

[26]See K. Ohmae, "The Global Logic of Strategic Alliances," *Harvard Business Review*, March–April 1989, pp. 143–154; G. Hamel, Y. L. Doz, and C. K. Prahalad, "Collaborate with Your Competitors and Win!" *Harvard Business Review,* January–February 1989, pp. 133–139; W. Burgers, C. W. L. Hill, and W. C. Kim, "Alliances in the Global Auto Industry," *Strategic Management Journal* 14 (1993): 419–432; P. Kale, H. Singh, and H. Perlmutter, "Learning and Protection of Proprietary Assets in Strategic Alliances: Building Relational Capital," *Strategic Management Journal* 21 (2000): 217–237.

[27]L. T. Chang, "China Eases Foreign Film Rules," *The Wall Street Journal,* October 15, 2004, p. B2.

[28]B. L. Simonin, "Transfer of Marketing Knowhow in International Strategic Alliances," *Journal of International Business Studies,*

Vol 30 issue 3 1999, pp. 463–91; J. W. Spencer, "Firms' Knowledge Sharing Strategies in the Global Innovation System," *Strategic Management Journal* 24 (2003): 217–233.

[29]Kale et al., "Learning and Protection of Proprietary Assets."

[30]R. B. Reich and E. D. Mankin, "Joint Ventures with Japan Give Away Our Future," *Harvard Business Review,* March–April 1986, pp. 78–90.

[31]J. Bleeke and D. Ernst, "The Way to Win in Cross-Border Alliances," *Harvard Business Review,* November–December 1991, pp. 127–135.

[32]E. Booker and C. Krol, "IBM Finds Strength in Alliances," *B to B,* February 10, 2003, pp. 3, 27.

[33]W. Roehl and J. F. Truitt, "Stormy Open Marriages Are Better," *Columbia Journal of World Business,* Summer 1987, pp. 87–95.

[34]See T. Khanna, R. Gulati, and N. Nohria, "The Dynamics of Learning Alliances: Competition, Cooperation, and Relative Scope," *Strategic Management Journal* 19 (1998): 193–210; Kale et al., "Learning and Protection of Proprietary Assets."

[35]Kale et al., "Learning and Protection of Proprietary Assets."

[36]Hamel et al., "Collaborate with Competitors"; Khanna et al., "The Dynamics of Learning Alliances"; E. W. K. Tang, "Acquiring Knowledge by Foreign Partners from International Joint Ventures in a Transition Economy: Learning by Doing and Learning Myopia," *Strategic Management Journal* 23 (2002): 835–854.

[37]Hamel et al., "Collaborate with Competitors."

[38]B. Wysocki, "Cross Border Alliances Become Favorite Way to Crack New Markets," *The Wall Street Journal,* March 4, 1990, p. A1.

CHAPTER 9

CORPORATE-LEVEL STRATEGY: HORIZONTAL INTEGRATION, VERTICAL INTEGRATION, AND STRATEGIC OUTSOURCING

sergign/Shutterstock.com

OPENING CASE

The Proposed Merger of Comcast and Time Warner Cable

In February 2014, Comcast and Time Warner announced their intention to merge—a deal worth about $45 billion. The merger would form the largest cable TV and Internet provider in the United States and enable the company to control 27 of the top 30 markets in the United States, and three-fourths of the overall cable market. The merger first had to be approved, however, by the Department of Justice (to assess antitrust concerns) and the Federal Communications Commission (FCC, which evaluates media deals to assess their influence on the public interest).

Drew Angerer/Getty Images

9.1 Discuss how corporate-level strategy can be used to strengthen a company's business model and business-level strategies

9.2 Define horizontal integration and discuss the primary advantages and disadvantages associated with this corporate-level strategy

9.3 Explain the difference between a company's internal value chain and the industry value chain

9.4 Describe why, and under what conditions, cooperative relationships such as strategic alliances and outsourcing may become a substitute for vertical integration

Comcast and Time-Warner argued that the deal would not significantly influence competition in the cable industry because the companies operated in nonoverlapping geographic markets, so customers would not be losing an option for getting cable service. They also argued that the merger would enable the companies to make investments that would provide customers with faster broadband, greater network reliability and security, better in-home Wi-Fi, and greater Video on Demand choices. As argued by David Cohen, Comcast's executive vice president, in front of a Senate panel: "I can make you and the members of this committee one absolute commitment, which is that there is nothing in this transaction that will cause anybody's cable bills to go up."

Opponents of the merger, however, argued that the size and scale of the merged company (particularly given that Comcast had recently acquired NBC Universal) would make the company dangerously powerful. Whereas the merger might not change the cable options available for end consumers, it definitely would change the options available for content providers such as Disney or Viacom, or on-demand programming providers such as Netflix, Cinema Now, Hulu, and others. The merged company's overwhelming bargaining power over suppliers could also create cost advantages other TV or Internet providers might be unable to match, thereby enabling it to squeeze competitors out of the market. For example, satellite operator Dish Network argued that the combined company would be able to use its size to force providers of content to lower their prices, and that companies such as Dish Network would be at a competitive disadvantage. Dish also argued that the merged company might undermine video services such as Netflix or Cinema Now by altering streaming speeds either at the "last mile" of the Internet (where it is delivered into people's homes) or at interconnection points between Internet providers. In support of this, Netflix noted that Comcast had already required the Netflix to pay "terminating access fees" to ensure that customers did not get a downgraded signal. If the cable companies downgraded the signal for on-demand providers, customers would abandon services like Netflix and turn to on-demand options the cable operators themselves were providing. Senator Al Franken pointed out that when Comcast had acquired NBC Universal in 2010, it had defended that vertical integration move by referring to Time Warner as a fierce competitor. "Comcast can't have it both ways," Franken argued. "It can't say that the existence of competition among distributors, including Time Warner Cable, was a reason to approve the NBC deal in 2010 and then turn around a few years later and say the absence of competition with Time Warner Cable is reason to approve this deal."

For Brian Roberts, CEO and chairman of Comcast, the merger would be yet another milestone in the megadeal acquisition spree he had used to grow the company into a $68-billion media behemoth. The deal was a more nuanced proposition for Robert Marcus, who had been CEO at Time Warner Cable for less than 2 months when the deal was announced: he would get a $79.9-million severance payoff to walk away. The investment bankers advising the deal also stood to rake in $140 million in fees. After a year of reviewing the proposed merger, the FCC announced it needed more time and would delay its decision until at least August 2015. Many industry observers, however, still thought the deal was likely to be approved.

Sources: V. Luckerson, "Dish Network Slams Potential Comcast-Time Warner Merger," www.Time.com, July 10, 2014; A. Fitzpatrick, "Time Warner Cable Outage Raises Questions about Comcast Merger," www.Time.com, August 28, 2014; A. Rogers, "Comcast Urges Congress to Back Time Warner Cable Merger," www.Time.com, April 11, 2014; D. Pomerant, "Netflix Calls on the FCC to Deny the Time Warner Comcast Merger," www.Forbes.com, August 26, 2014, p.1; A. Timms, "Deals of the Year 2014: Comcast Faces Screen Test," *Institutional Investor*, December 2014.

◤ OVERVIEW

The overriding goal of managers is to maximize the value of a company for its shareholders. The Opening Case about the proposed merger between Comcast and Time Warner illustrates how companies might horizontally integrate to achieve greater economies of scale or bargaining power over suppliers and customers. This is likely to benefit Comcast and Time Warner's shareholders, although the net effect on consumer welfare is in question.

In general, corporate-level strategy involves choices strategic managers must make: (1) deciding in which businesses and industries a company should compete; (2) selecting which value creation activities it should perform in those businesses; and (3) determining how it should enter, consolidate, or exit businesses or industries to maximize long-term profitability. When formulating corporate-level strategy, managers must adopt a long-term perspective and consider how changes taking place in an industry and in its products, technology, customers, and competitors will affect their company's current business model and its future strategies. They then decide how to implement specific corporate-level strategies that redefine their company's business model to allow it to increase its competitive advantage in a changing industry environment by taking advantage of opportunities and countering threats. Thus, the principal goal of corporate-level strategy is to enable a company to sustain or promote its competitive advantage and profitability in its present business—*and in any new businesses or industries that it chooses to enter.*

This chapter is the first of two that describe the role of corporate-level strategy in repositioning and redefining a company's business model. We discuss three corporate-level strategies—horizontal integration, vertical integration, and strategic outsourcing—that are primarily directed toward improving a company's competitive advantage and profitability in its current business or industry. Diversification, which entails entry into new kinds of businesses or industries, is examined in the next chapter, along with guidelines for choosing the most profitable way to enter new businesses or industries, or to exit others. By the end of this chapter and the next, you will understand how the different levels of strategy contribute to the creation of a successful, profitable business or multibusiness model. You will also be able to distinguish between the types of corporate strategies managers use to maximize long-term company profitability.

◤ CORPORATE-LEVEL STRATEGY AND THE MULTIBUSINESS MODEL

The choice of corporate-level strategies is the final part of the strategy-formulation process. Corporate-level strategies drive a company's business model over time and determine which types of business- and functional-level strategies managers will choose to maximize long-term profitability. The relationship between business-level strategy and functional-level strategy was discussed in Chapter 5. Strategic managers develop a business model and strategies that use their company's distinctive competencies to strive for a cost-leadership position and/or to differentiate its products. Chapter 8 described how global strategy is an extension of these basic principles.

In this chapter and the next, we repeatedly emphasize that, to increase profitability, a corporate-level strategy should enable a company or one or more of its business divisions or units *to perform value-chain functional activities (1) at a lower cost and/or (2) in a way that results in increased differentiation*. Only when it selects the appropriate corporate-level strategies can a company choose the pricing option (lowest, average, or premium price) that will allow it to maximize profitability. In addition, corporate-level strategy will increase profitability if it helps a company reduce industry rivalry by reducing the threat of damaging price competition. In sum, a company's corporate-level strategies should be chosen to promote the success of its business-level strategies, which allows it to achieve a sustainable competitive advantage, leading to higher profitability.

Many companies choose to expand their business activities beyond one market or industry and enter others. When a company decides to expand into new industries, it must construct its business model at two levels. First, it must develop a business model and strategies for each business unit or division in every industry in which it competes. Second, it must develop a higher-level *multibusiness model* that justifies its entry into different businesses and industries. This multibusiness model should explain how and why entering a new industry will allow the company to use its existing functional competencies and business strategies to increase its overall profitability. This model should also explain any other ways in which a company's involvement in more than one business or industry can increase its profitability. IBM, for example, might argue that its entry into online computer consulting, data storage, and cloud computing enables it to offer its customers a lineup of computer services that allows it to better compete with HP, Oracle, and Amazon.com. Apple might argue that its entry into digital music and entertainment has given it a commanding lead over rivals such as Sony, Google, and Microsoft.

This chapter first focuses on the advantages of staying inside one industry by pursuing horizontal integration. It then looks at why companies use vertical integration and expand into new industries. In the next chapter, we examine two principal corporate strategies companies use to enter new industries to increase their profitability—related and unrelated diversification—and several other strategies companies use to enter and compete in new industries.

▰ HORIZONTAL INTEGRATION: SINGLE-INDUSTRY CORPORATE STRATEGY

Managers use corporate-level strategy to identify industries in which their company should compete in order to maximize its long-term profitability. For many companies, profitable growth and expansion often entail finding ways to successfully compete within a single market or industry over time. In other words, a company confines its value creation activities to just one business or industry. Examples of such single-business companies include McDonald's, with its focus on the global fast-food business, and Wal-Mart, with its focus on global discount retailing.

Staying within one industry allows a company to focus all of its managerial, financial, technological, and functional resources and capabilities on competing successfully in one area. This is important in fast-growing, changing industries in which demands on a company's resources and capabilities are likely to be substantial, but where the long-term profits from establishing a competitive advantage are also likely to be substantial.

A second advantage of staying within a single industry is that a company "sticks to the knitting," meaning that it stays focused on what it knows and does best. A company does not make the mistake of entering new industries in which its existing resources and capabilities create little value and/or where a whole new set of competitive industry forces—new competitors, suppliers, and customers—present unanticipated threats. Coca-Cola, like many other companies, has committed this strategic error in the past. Coca-Cola once decided to expand into the movie business and acquired Columbia Pictures; it also acquired a large California winemaker. It soon found it lacked the competencies to successfully compete in these new industries and had not foreseen the strong competitive forces that existed in these industries from movie companies such as Paramount and winemakers such as Gallo. Coca-Cola concluded that entry into these new industries had reduced rather than created value and lowered its profitability; it divested or sold off these new businesses at a significant loss.

Even when a company stays in one industry, sustaining a successful business model over time can be difficult because of changing conditions in the environment, such as advances in technology that allow new competitors into the market, or because of changing customer needs. Two decades ago, the strategic issue facing telecommunications providers was how to shape their landline phone services to best meet customer needs in local and long-distance telephone service. However, when wireless telephone service emerged and quickly gained in popularity, landline providers like Verizon and AT&T had to quickly change their business models, lower the price of landline service, merge with wireless companies, and offer broadband services to ensure their survival.

Even within one industry, it is very easy for strategic managers to fail to see the "forest" (changing nature of the industry that results in new product/market opportunities) for the "trees" (focusing only on how to position current products). A focus on corporate-level strategy can help managers anticipate future trends and then change their business models to position their companies to compete successfully in a changing environment. Strategic managers must not become so committed to improving their company's *existing* product or service lines that they fail to recognize *new* product or service opportunities and threats. Apple has been so successful because it recognized the increasing number of product opportunities offered by digital entertainment. The task for corporate-level managers is to analyze how emerging technologies will impact their business models, how and why these technologies might change customer needs and customer groups in the future, and what kinds of new distinctive competencies will be needed to respond to these changes.

One corporate-level strategy that has been widely used to help managers strengthen their company's business model is horizontal integration, a strategy illustrated in the Opening Case. **Horizontal integration** is the process of acquiring or merging with industry competitors to achieve the competitive advantages that arise from a large size and scope of operations. An **acquisition** occurs when one company uses capital resources such as stock, debt, or cash, to purchase another company. A **merger** is an agreement between equals to pool their operations and create a new entity.

Mergers and acquisitions are common in most industries. In the aerospace industry, Boeing merged with McDonnell Douglas to create the world's largest aerospace company; in the pharmaceutical industry, Pfizer acquired Warner-Lambert to become the largest pharmaceutical firm; and global airlines are increasingly merging their

horizontal integration
The process of acquiring or merging with industry competitors to achieve the competitive advantages that arise from a large size and scope of operations.

acquisition
When a company uses its capital resources to purchase another company.

merger
An agreement between two companies to pool their resources and operations and join together to better compete in a business or industry.

operations in order to rationalize the number of flights offered between destinations and increase their market power. The pace of mergers and acquisitions has been rising as companies try to gain a competitive advantage over their rivals. This is because horizontal integration often significantly improves the competitive advantage and profitability of companies whose managers choose to stay within one industry and focus on managing its competitive position to keep the company at the value creation frontier.

Benefits of Horizontal Integration

In pursuing horizontal integration, managers invest their company's capital resources to purchase the assets of industry competitors to increase the profitability of its single-business model. Profitability increases when horizontal integration (1) lowers the cost structure, (2) increases product differentiation, (3) leverages a competitive advantage more broadly, (4) reduces rivalry within the industry, and (5) increases bargaining power over suppliers and buyers.

Lower Cost Structure   Horizontal integration can lower a company's cost structure because it creates increasing *economies of scale*. Suppose five major competitors exist, each of which operates a manufacturing plant in some region of the United States, but none of the plants operate at full capacity. If one competitor buys another and closes that plant, it can operate its own plant at full capacity and reduce its manufacturing costs. Achieving economies of scale is very important in industries that have a high-fixed-cost structure. In such industries, large-scale production allows companies to spread their fixed costs over a large volume, and in this way drive down average unit costs. In the telecommunications industry, for example, the fixed costs of building advanced 4G and LTE broadband networks that offer tremendous increases in speed are enormous, and to make such an investment profitable, a large volume of customers is required. Thus, AT&T and Verizon purchased other telecommunications companies to acquire their customers, increase their customer base, increase utilization rates, and reduce the cost of servicing each customer. In 2011, AT&T planned to acquire T-Mobile, but abandoned the deal in response to antitrust concerns raised by the U.S. Department of Justice and the FCC. Similar considerations were involved in the hundreds of acquisitions that have taken place in the pharmaceutical industry in the last decade because of the need to realize scale economies in research and development (R&D) and sales and marketing. The fixed costs of building a nationwide pharmaceutical sales force are enormous, and pharmaceutical companies such as Pfizer and Merck must possess a wide portfolio of drugs to sell to effectively make use of their sales forces.

A company can also lower its cost structure when horizontal integration allows it to *reduce the duplication of resources* between two companies, such as by eliminating the need for two sets of corporate head offices, two separate sales teams, and so forth. Notably, however, these cost savings are often overestimated. If two companies are operating a function such as a call center, for example, and both are above the minimum efficient scale for operating such a center, there may be few economies from consolidating operations: If each center was already optimally utilized, the consolidated call center could require just as many service people, computers, phone lines, and real estate as the two call centers previously required. Similarly, one justification made for banks consolidating during the late 1990s was that they could save by consolidating their information technology (IT) resources. Ultimately, however, most merged banks realized that their potential savings were meager at best, and the costs of attempting to harmonize their information systems were high; thus, most of them continued to run the separate legacy systems they had prior to merging.

Increased Product Differentiation   Horizontal integration may also increase profitability when it increases product differentiation; for example, by increasing the flow of innovative products that a company's sales force can sell to customers at premium prices. Desperate for new drugs to fill its pipeline, for example, Eli Lilly paid $6.5 billion to ImClone Systems to acquire its new, cancer-preventing drugs in order to outbid rival Bristol-Myers Squibb. Google, anxious to provide its users with online coupons, offered to pay $6 billion for Groupon to fill this niche in its online advertising business in order to increase its differentiation advantage—and reduce industry rivalry. Similarly, in the opening case, Comcast argued to the FCC that a merger with Time Warner Cable would enable the companies to offer faster, more reliable, more secure internet service to their customers.

Horizontal integration may also increase differentiation when it allows a company to combine the product lines of merged companies so that it can offer customers a wider range of products that can be bundled together. **Product bundling** involves offering customers the opportunity to purchase a range of products at a single, combined price. This increases the value of a company's product line because customers often obtain a price discount when purchasing a set of products at one time, and customers become used to dealing with only one company and its representatives. A company may obtain a competitive advantage from increased product differentiation.

Another way to increase product differentiation is through **cross-selling**, which is when a company takes advantage of or leverages its established relationship with customers by way of acquiring additional product lines or categories that it can sell to them. In this way, a company increases differentiation because it can provide a "total solution" and satisfy all of a customer's specific needs. Cross-selling and becoming a total-solution provider is an important rationale for horizontal integration in the computer sector, where IT companies attempt to increase the value of their offerings by satisfying all of the hardware and service needs of corporate customers. Providing a total solution saves customers' time and money because they do not have to work with several suppliers, and a single sales team can ensure that all the components of a customer's IT seamlessly work together. When horizontal integration increases the differentiated appeal and value of the company's products, the total solution provider gains market share.

Leveraging a Competitive Advantage More Broadly   For firms that have resources or capabilities that could be valuably deployed across multiple market segments or geographies, horizontal integration may offer opportunities to become more profitable. In the retail industry, for example, Wal-Mart's enormous bargaining power with suppliers and its exceptional efficiency in inventory logistics enabled it to have a competitive advantage in other discount retail store formats, such as its chain of Sam's Clubs (an even-lower-priced warehouse segment). It also expanded the range of products it offers customers when it entered the supermarket business and established a nationwide chain of Wal-Mart supercenters that sell groceries as well as all the clothing, toys, and electronics sold in regular Wal-Mart stores. It has also replicated its business model globally, although not always with as much success as it has had in the United States because many of its efficiencies in logistics (such as its hub-and-spoke distribution system and inventory tracked by satellite) employ fixed assets that are geographically limited (see the Strategy in Action 9.1 for more on this).

product bundling
Offering customers the opportunity to purchase a range of products at a single, combined price; this increases the value of a company's product line because customers often obtain a price discount when purchasing a set of products at one time, and customers become used to dealing with only one company and its representatives.

cross-selling
When a company takes advantage of or leverages its established relationship with customers by way of acquiring additional product lines or categories that it can sell to them. In this way, a company increases differentiation because it can provide a "total solution" and satisfy all of a customer's specific needs.

9.1 STRATEGY IN ACTION

Wal-Mart's Expansion into Other Retail Formats

In 2014, Wal-Mart was the largest firm in the world, with sales of $485.7 billion, more than 11,000 stores worldwide, and employing 2.2 million people. However, as the U.S. discount retail market was mature (where Wal-Mart earned 70% of its revenues), it looked for other opportunities to apply its exceptional retailing power and expertise. In the United States it had expanded into supercenters that sold groceries in addition to general merchandise and even-lower-priced warehouse store formats (Sam's Club), both of which were doing well. These stores could directly leverage Wal-Mart's bargaining power over suppliers (for many producers of general merchandise, Wal-Mart accounted for more than 70% of their sales, giving it unrivaled power to negotiate prices and delivery terms), and benefitted from its exceptionally efficient system for transporting, managing, and tracking inventory. Wal-Mart had invested relatively early in advanced information technology: it adopted radio frequency identification (RFID) tagging well ahead of its competitors, and satellites tracked inventory in real time. Wal-Mart knew where each item of inventory was at all times and when it had sold, enabling it to simultaneously minimize its inventory holding costs while optimizing the inventory mix in each store. As a result, it had higher sales per square foot and inventory turnover than either Target or Kmart. It handled inventory through a massive, hub-and-spoke distribution system that included more than 140 distribution centers that each served approximately 150 stores within a 150-mile radius. As supercenters and Sam's Clubs were also approaching saturation, however, growth had become harder and harder to sustain. Wal-Mart began to pursue other types of expansion opportunities. It expanded into smaller-format neighborhood stores, international stores (many of which were existing chains that were acquired), and was considering getting into organic foods and trendy fashions. While expansion into contiguous geographic regions (e.g., Canada and Mexico) had gone well, its success at overseas expansions was spottier. Wal-Mart's forays into Germany and South Korea, for example, resulted in large losses, and it ultimately exited the markets. Wal-Mart's entry into Japan was also not as successful as hoped, resulting in many years of losses and never gaining a large share of the market. The challenge was that many of these markets already had tough competitors by the time Wal-Mart entered—they weren't the sleepy, underserved markets that had initially helped it grow in the United States. Furthermore, Wal-Mart's IT and logistics advantages could not easily be leveraged into overseas markets—they would require massive, upfront investments to replicate, and it would be hard to break even on those investments without achieving massive scale in those markets. This rasied important questions such as: "Which of Wal-Mart's advantages could be leveraged overseas and to which markets?" "Was Wal-Mart better off trying to diversify its product offerings within North America?" "Should it perhaps reconsider its growth objectives altogether?"

Source: www.walmart.com.

Reduced Industry Rivalry　Horizontal integration can help to reduce industry rivalry in two ways. First, acquiring or merging with a competitor helps to *eliminate excess capacity* in an industry, which, as we discuss in Chapter 6, often triggers price wars. By taking excess capacity out of an industry, horizontal integration creates a more benign environment in which prices might stabilize—or even increase.

Second, by reducing the number of competitors in an industry, horizontal integration often makes it easier to implement *tacit price coordination* between rivals; that is, coordination reached without communication. (Explicit communication to fix prices is illegal in most countries.) In general, the larger the number of competitors in an industry, the more difficult it is to establish informal pricing agreements—such as price leadership by the dominant company—which increases the possibility that a price war will erupt. By increasing industry concentration and creating an oligopoly, horizontal integration can make it easier to establish tacit coordination among rivals.

Both of these motives seem to have been behind Oracle's many software acquisitions. There was significant excess capacity in the corporate software industry, and major competitors were offering customers discounted prices that had led to a price war and falling profit margins. Oracle hoped to eliminate excess industry capacity, which would reduce price competition.

Increased Bargaining Power   Finally, horizontal integration allows some companies to obtain bargaining power over suppliers or buyers and increase profitability at their expense. By consolidating the industry through horizontal integration, a company becomes a much larger buyer of suppliers' products and uses this as leverage to bargain down the price it pays for its inputs, thereby lowering its cost structure. Wal-Mart, for example, is well known for pursuing this strategy, and it may also have been a major motivation for the proposed merger of Comcast and Time Warner described in the Opening Case. Consolidation among competitors also gives companies more bargaining power over customers: By gaining control over a greater percentage of an industry's product or output, a company can increase its power to raise prices and profits because customers have less choice of suppliers and are more dependent on the company for their products. When a company has greater ability to raise prices to buyers or bargain down the price paid for inputs, it has obtained increased market power.

Problems with Horizontal Integration

Although horizontal integration can strengthen a company's business model in several ways, there are problems, limitations, and dangers associated with pursuing this corporate-level strategy. Implementing a horizontal integration strategy is no easy task for managers. As we discuss in Chapter 10, there are several reasons why mergers and acquisitions may fail to result in higher profitability: problems associated with merging very different company cultures; high management turnover in the acquired company when the acquisition is a hostile one; and a tendency of managers to overestimate the potential benefits from a merger or acquisition and underestimate the problems involved in merging their operations.

When a company uses horizontal integration to become a dominant industry competitor in the United States, it may come into conflict with the Federal Trade Commission (FTC) or the Department of Justice (DOJ), two government agencies that help to enforce antitrust laws. Antitrust authorities are concerned about the potential for abuse of market power; more competition is generally better for consumers than less competition. Antitrust authorities are likely to intervene when a few companies within one industry try to make acquisitions that will allow them to raise consumer prices above the level that would exist in a more competitive situation, and thus abuse their market power. The FTC and DOJ try to prevent dominant companies from using their market power to crush potential competitors, for example, by cutting prices when a new competitor enters the industry and forcing the competitor out of business, then raising prices after the threatening company has been eliminated.

Because of these concerns, any merger or acquisition the FTC perceives as creating too much consolidation, and the *potential* for future abuse of market power, may, for antitrust reasons, be blocked. The proposed merger between the two dominant satellite radio companies Sirius and XM was blocked for months until it became clear that customers had many other options to obtain high-quality radio programming—for example, through their computers and cell phones—so substantial competition would still exist in the industry. Similarly, as discussed in the Opening Case, in 2015 the FTC was still in the process of reviewing the Comcast/Time Warner merger to evaluate whether it would harm the public interest.

VERTICAL INTEGRATION: ENTERING NEW INDUSTRIES TO STRENGTHEN THE "CORE" BUSINESS MODEL

Many companies that use horizontal integration to strengthen their business model and improve their competitive position also use the corporate-level strategy of vertical integration for the same purpose. When pursuing vertical integration, however, a company is entering new industries to support the business model of its "core" industry, that is, the industry which is the primary source of its competitive advantage and profitability. At this point, therefore, a company must formulate a multibusiness model that explains how entry into a new industry using vertical integration will enhance its long-term profitability. The model that justifies the pursuit of vertical integration is based on a company entering industries that *add value* to its core products because this increases product differentiation and/or lowers its cost structure, thus increasing its profitability.

vertical integration
When a company expands its operations either backward into an industry that produces inputs for the company's products (backward vertical integration) or forward into an industry that uses, distributes, or sells the company's products (forward vertical integration).

A company pursuing a strategy of **vertical integration** expands its operations either backward into an industry that produces inputs for the company's products (*backward vertical integration*) or forward into an industry that uses, distributes, or sells the company's products (*forward vertical integration*). To enter an industry, it may establish its own operations and build the value chain needed to compete effectively, or it may acquire a company that is already in the industry. A steel company that supplies its iron ore needs from company-owned iron ore mines illustrates backward integration. A maker of personal computers (PCs) that sells its laptops through company-owned retail outlets illustrates forward integration. For example, Apple entered the retail industry in 2001 when it decided to establish a chain of Apple stores to sell, promote, and service its products. IBM is a highly vertically integrated company; it integrated backward into the chip and memory disk industry to produce the components that work inside its mainframes and servers, and integrated forward into the computer software and consulting services industries.

Figure 9.1 illustrates four *main* stages in a typical raw-materials-to-customer value-added chain. For a company based in the final assembly stage, backward integration means moving into component parts manufacturing and raw materials production.

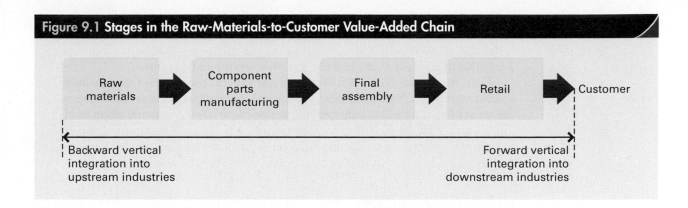

Figure 9.1 Stages in the Raw-Materials-to-Customer Value-Added Chain

Forward integration means moving into distribution and sales (retail). At each stage in the chain *value is added* to the product, transforming it in such a way that it is worth more to the company at the next stage in the chain and, ultimately, to the customer. It is important to note that each stage of the value-added chain involves a separate industry, or industries, in which many different companies compete. Moreover, within each industry, each company has a value chain composed of the value creation activities we discussed in Chapter 3: R&D, production, marketing, customer service, and so on. In other words, we can think of a value chain that runs *across* industries, and embedded within that are the value chains of companies *within* each industry.

As an example of the value-added concept, consider how companies in each industry involved in the production of a PC contribute to the final product (Figure 9.2). The first stage in the chain includes raw-materials companies that make specialty ceramics, chemicals, and metal, such as Kyocera of Japan, which manufactures the ceramic substrate for semiconductors. Companies at the first stage in the chain sell their products to the makers of PC component products such as Intel and AMD, which transform the ceramics, chemicals, and metals they purchase into PC components such as microprocessors, disk drives, and memory chips. In the process, companies *add value* to the raw materials they purchase. At the third stage, the manufactured components are sold to PC makers such as Apple, Dell, and HP, and these companies decide which components to purchase and assemble to *add value* to the finished PCs (that they make or outsource to a contract manufacturer). At stage four, the finished PCs are then either

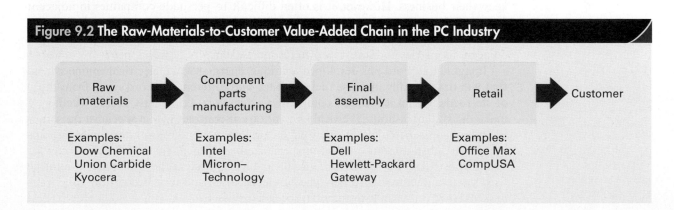

Figure 9.2 The Raw-Materials-to-Customer Value-Added Chain in the PC Industry

sold directly to the final customer over the Internet, or sold to retailers such as Best Buy and Staples, which distribute and sell them to the final customer. Companies that distribute and sell PCs also *add value* to the product because they make the product accessible to customers and provide customer service and support.

Thus, companies in different industries add value at each stage in the raw-materials-to-customer chain. Viewed in this way, vertical integration presents companies with a choice about within which industries in the raw-materials-to-customer chain to operate and compete. This choice is determined by the degree to which establishing operations at a given stage in the value chain will increase product differentiation or lower costs—and therefore increase profitability—as we discuss in the following section.

Increasing Profitability Through Vertical Integration

As noted earlier, a company pursues vertical integration to strengthen the business model of its original or core business and to improve its competitive position.[1] Vertical integration increases product differentiation, lowers costs, or reduces industry competition when it (1) facilitates investments in efficiency-enhancing, specialized assets, (2) protects product quality, and (3) results in improved scheduling.

Facilitating Investments in Specialized Assets   A specialized asset is one that is designed to perform a specific task and the value of which is significantly reduced in its next-best use.[2] The asset may be a piece of equipment that has a firm-specific use or the knowhow or skills that a company or employees have acquired through training and experience. Companies invest in specialized assets because these assets allow them to lower their cost structure or to better differentiate their products, which facilitates premium pricing. A company might invest in specialized equipment to lower manufacturing costs, as Toyota does, for example, or it might invest in an advanced technology that allows it to develop better-quality products than its rivals, as Apple does. Thus, specialized assets can help a company achieve a competitive advantage at the business level.

Just as a company invests in specialized assets in its own industry to build competitive advantage, it is often necessary that suppliers invest in specialized assets to produce the inputs that a specific company needs. By investing in these assets, a supplier can make higher-quality inputs that provide its customers with a differentiation advantage, or inputs at a lower cost so it can charge its customers a lower price to keep their business. However, it is often difficult to persuade companies in adjacent stages of the value chain to invest in specialized assets. Often, to realize the benefits associated with such investments, a company must vertically integrate and enter into adjacent industries and invest its own resources. Why does this happen?

Imagine that Ford has developed a unique, energy-saving, electrical engine system that will dramatically increase fuel efficiency and differentiate Ford's cars from those of its rivals, giving it a major competitive advantage. Ford must decide whether to make the system in-house (vertical integration) or contract with a specialist outsourcing manufacturer to make the new engine system. Manufacturing these new systems requires a substantial investment in specialized equipment that can be used only for this purpose. In other words, because of its unique design, the equipment cannot be used to manufacture any other type of electrical engine for Ford or any other carmaker. Thus, this is an investment in specialized assets.

Consider this situation from the perspective of the outside supplier deciding whether or not to make this investment. The supplier might reason that once it has made the investment, it will become dependent on Ford for business because *Ford is the only possible customer for the electrical engine made by this specialized equipment.* The supplier realizes that this puts Ford in a strong bargaining position, and that Ford might use its buying power to demand lower prices for the engines. Given the risks involved, the supplier declines to make the investment in specialized equipment.

Now consider Ford's position. Ford might reason that if it outsources production of these systems to an outside supplier, it might become too dependent on that supplier for a vital input. Because specialized equipment is required to produce the engine systems, Ford cannot switch its order to other suppliers. Ford realizes that this increases the bargaining power of the supplier, which might demand higher prices.

The situation of *mutual dependence* that would be created by the investment in specialized assets makes Ford hesitant to allow outside suppliers to make the product and makes suppliers hesitant to undertake such a risky investment. The problem is a lack of trust—neither Ford nor the supplier can trust the other to operate fairly in this situation. The lack of trust arises from the risk of **holdup**—that is, being taken advantage of by a trading partner *after* the investment in specialized assets has been made.[3] Because of this risk, Ford reasons that the only cost-effective way to get the new engine systems is for it to invest in specialized assets and manufacture the engine in-house.

To generalize from this example, if achieving a competitive advantage requires one company to make investments in specialized assets so it can trade with another, *the risk of holdup* may serve as a deterrent, and the investment may not take place. Consequently, the potential for higher profitability from specialization will be lost. To prevent such loss, companies vertically integrate into adjacent stages in the value chain. Historically, the problems surrounding specific assets have driven automobile companies to vertically integrate backward into the production of component parts, steel companies to vertically integrate backward into the production of iron, computer companies to vertically integrate backward into chip production, and aluminum companies to vertically integrate backward into bauxite mining. Often such firms practice **tapered integration**, whereby the firm makes some input and buys some input. Purchasing part or most of its needs for a given input from suppliers enables the firm to tap the advantages of the market (e.g., choosing from suppliers that are competing to improve quality or lower the cost of the product). At the same time, meeting some of its needs for input through internal production improves the firm's bargaining power by reducing the likelihood of holdup by its supplier. A firm that is engaged in production of an input is also better able to evaluate the cost and quality of external suppliers of that input.[4]

Enhancing Product Quality   By entering industries at other stages of the value-added chain, a company can often enhance the quality of the products in its core business and strengthen its differentiation advantage. For example, the ability to control the reliability and performance of complex components such as engine and transmission systems may increase a company's competitive advantage in the luxury-sedan market and enable it to charge a premium price. Conditions in the banana industry also illustrate the importance of vertical integration in maintaining product quality. Historically, a problem facing food companies that import bananas has been the variable quality of delivered bananas, which often arrive on the shelves of U.S. supermarkets too ripe or not ripe enough. To correct this problem, major U.S. food companies such as Del Monte have integrated backward and now own banana plantations, putting them in control of the

holdup
When a company is taken advantage of by another company it does business with after it has made an investment in expensive specialized assets to better meet the needs of the other company.

tapered integration
When a firm uses a mix of vertical integration and market transactions for a given input. For example, a firm might operate limited semiconductor manufacturing while also buying semiconductor chips on the market. Doing so helps to prevent supplier holdup (because the firm can credibly commit to not buying from external suppliers) and increases its ability to judge the quality and cost of purchased supplies.

banana supply. As a result, they can distribute and sell bananas of a standard quality at the optimal time to better satisfy customers. Knowing they can rely on the quality of these brands, customers are also willing to pay more for them. Thus, by vertically integrating backward into plantation ownership, banana companies have built customer confidence, which has, in turn, enabled them to charge a premium price for their product.

The same considerations can promote forward vertical integration. Ownership of retail outlets may be necessary if the required standards of after-sales service for complex products are to be maintained. For example, in the 1920s, Kodak owned the retail outlets that distributed its photographic equipment because the company felt that few existing retail outlets had the skills necessary to sell and service its complex equipment. By the 1930s, new retailers had emerged that could provide satisfactory distribution and service for Kodak products, so it left the retail industry.

McDonald's has also used vertical integration to protect product quality and increase efficiency. In the 1990s, McDonald's faced a problem: After decades of rapid growth, the fast-food market was beginning to show signs of market saturation. McDonald's responded to the slowdown by rapidly expanding abroad. In 1980, 28% of the chain's new restaurant openings were abroad; in 1990, it was 60%, and by 2000, 70%. In 2014, McDonalds had 14,350 restaurants in the United States, and 21,908 restaurants in 110 countries outside the United States.[5] Replication of its value creation skills was the key to successful global expansion and spurred the growth of McDonald's in the countries and regions in which it operates. McDonald's U.S. success was built on a formula of close relations with suppliers, nationwide marketing might, and tight control over store-level operating procedures.

The biggest problem McDonald's has faced is replicating its U.S. supply chain in other countries; its domestic suppliers are fiercely loyal to the company because their fortunes are closely linked to its success. McDonald's maintains very rigorous specifications for all the raw ingredients it uses—the key to its consistency and quality control. Outside of the United States, however, McDonald's has found suppliers far less willing to make the investments required to meet its specifications. In Great Britain, for example, McDonald's had problems getting local bakeries to produce the hamburger bun. After experiencing quality problems with two local bakeries, McDonald's had to vertically integrate backward and build its own bakeries to supply its British stores. When McDonald's decided to operate in Russia, it found that local suppliers lacked the capability to produce ingredients of the quality it demanded. It was then forced to vertically integrate through the local food industry on an epic scale, importing potato seeds and bull semen and indirectly managing dairy farms, cattle ranches, and vegetable plots. It also needed to construct the world's largest food-processing plant at a huge cost. In South America, McDonald's purchased huge ranches in Argentina upon which it could raise its own cattle. In short, vertical integration has allowed McDonald's to protect product quality and reduce its global cost structure.[6]

Improved Scheduling   Sometimes important strategic advantages can be obtained when vertical integration makes it quicker, easier, and more cost-effective to plan, coordinate, and schedule the transfer of a product such as raw materials or component parts between adjacent stages of the value-added chain.[7] Such advantages can be crucial when a company wants to realize the benefits of just-in-time (JIT) inventory systems. For example, in the 1920s, Ford profited from the tight coordination and scheduling that backward vertical integration made possible. Ford integrated backward into steel foundries, iron ore shipping, and iron ore production—it owned mines in

Upper Michigan. Deliveries at Ford were coordinated to such an extent that iron ore unloaded at Ford's steel foundries on the Great Lakes was turned into engine blocks within 24 hours, which lowered Ford's cost structure.

Problems with Vertical Integration

Vertical integration can often be used to strengthen a company's business model and increase profitability. However, the opposite can occur when vertical integration results in (1) an increasing cost structure, (2) disadvantages that arise when technology is changing fast, and (3) disadvantages that arise when demand is unpredictable. Sometimes these disadvantages are so great that vertical integration, rather than increasing profitability, may actually reduce it—in which case a company engages in **vertical disintegration** and exits industries adjacent to its core industry in the industry value chain. For example, Ford, which was highly vertically integrated, sold all its companies involved in mining iron ore and making steel when more efficient and specialized steel producers emerged that were able to supply lower-priced steel.

vertical disintegration
When a company decides to exit industries, either forward or backward in the industry value chain, to its core industry to increase profitability.

Increasing Cost Structure   Although vertical integration is often undertaken to lower a company's cost structure, it can raise costs if, over time, a company makes mistakes such as continuing to purchase inputs from company-owned suppliers when low-cost independent suppliers that can supply the same inputs exist. For decades, for example, GM's company-owned suppliers made more than 60% of the component parts for its vehicles; this figure was far higher than that for any other major carmaker, which is why GM became such a high-cost carmaker. In the 2000s, it vertically disintegrated by selling off many of its largest component operations, such as Delhi, its electrical components supplier. Thus, vertical integration can be a major disadvantage when company-owned suppliers develop a higher cost structure than those of independent suppliers. Why would a company-owned supplier develop such a high cost structure?

In this example, company-owned or in-house suppliers know that they can always sell their components to the car-making divisions of their company—they have a "captive customer." Because company-owned suppliers do not have to compete with independent, outside suppliers for orders, they have much less *incentive* to look for new ways to reduce operating costs or increase component quality. Indeed, in-house suppliers simply pass on cost increases to the car-making divisions in the form of higher **transfer prices**, the prices one division of a company charges other divisions for its products. Unlike independent suppliers, which constantly need to increase their efficiency to protect their competitive advantage, in-house suppliers face no such competition and the resulting rising cost structure reduces a company's profitability.

transfer pricing
The price that one division of a company charges another division for its products, which are the inputs the other division requires to manufacture its own products.

The term *bureaucratic costs* refers to the costs of solving the transaction difficulties that arise from managerial inefficiencies and the need to manage the handoffs or exchanges between business units to promote increased differentiation, or to lower a company's cost structure. Bureaucratic costs become a significant component of a company's cost structure because considerable managerial time and effort must be spent to reduce or eliminate managerial inefficiencies such as those that result when company-owned suppliers lose their incentive to increase efficiency or innovation.

Technological Change   When technology is changing fast, vertical integration may lock a company into an old, inefficient technology and prevent it from changing to a new one that would strengthen its business model.[8] Consider Sony, which had integrated back-ward to become the leading manufacturer of now-outdated cathode ray tubes (CRTs) used in TVs and computer monitors. Because Sony was locked into the outdated CRT technology, it was slow to recognize that the future was in liquid crystal display (LCD) flatscreens and it did not exit the CRT business. Sony's resistance to change in technol-ogy forced it to enter into a strategic alliance with Samsung to supply the LCD screens that are used in its BRAVIA TVs. As a result, Sony lost its competitive advantage and ex-perienced a major loss in TV market share. Thus, vertical integration can pose a serious disadvantage when it prevents a company from adopting new technology, or changing its suppliers or distribution systems to match the requirements of changing technology.

Demand Unpredictability   Suppose the demand for a company's core product, such as cars or washing machines, is predictable, and the company knows how many units it needs to make each month or year. Under these conditions, vertical integration al-lows a company to schedule and coordinate efficiently the flow of products along the industry value-added chain, which may result in major cost savings. However, sup-pose the demand for cars or washing machines wildly fluctuates and is unpredictable. If demand for cars suddenly plummets, the carmaker may find itself burdened with warehouses full of component parts it no longer needs, which is a major drain on profitability—something that has hurt major carmakers during the recent recession. Thus, vertical integration can be risky when demand is unpredictable because it is hard to manage the volume or flow of products along the value-added chain.

For example, a PC maker might vertically integrate backward to acquire a supplier of memory chips so that it can make exactly the number of chips it needs each month. However, if demand for PCs falls because of the popularity of mobile computing de-vices, the PC maker finds itself locked into a business that is now inefficient because it is not producing at full capacity, and therefore its cost structure starts to rise. In gen-eral, high-speed environmental change (e.g., technological change, changing customer demands, and major shifts in institutional norms or competitive dynamics) provides a disincentive for integration, as the firm's asset investments are at greater risk of rapid obsolescence.[9] It is clear that strategic managers must carefully assess the advantages and disadvantages of expanding the boundaries of their company by entering adja-cent industries, either backward (upstream) or forward (downstream), in the industry value-added chain. Moreover, although the decision to enter a new industry to make crucial component parts may have been profitable in the past, it may make no economic sense today because so many low-cost, global, component parts suppliers exist that compete for the company's business. The risks and returns on investing in vertical inte-gration must be continually evaluated, and companies should be as willing to vertically disintegrate as to vertically integrate in order to strengthen their core business model.

◤ALTERNATIVES TO VERTICAL INTEGRATION: COOPERATIVE RELATIONSHIPS

Is it possible to obtain the differentiation and cost-savings advantages associated with vertical integration without having to bear the problems and costs associated with this strategy? In other words, is there another corporate-level strategy that managers can use to obtain the advantages of vertical integration while allowing other companies to perform upstream and downstream activities? Today, companies have found that they can realize many of the benefits associated with vertical integration by entering into *long-term cooperative relationships* with companies in industries along the value-added chain, also known as **quasi integration**. Such moves could include, for example, sharing the expenses of investment in production assets or inventory, or making long-term supply or purchase guarantees. Apple's decision to invest in production equipment for its suppliers is a prime example (in the Closing Case).

Short-Term Contracts and Competitive Bidding

Many companies use short-term contracts that last for a year or less to establish the price and conditions under which they will purchase raw materials or components from suppliers or sell their final products to distributors or retailers. A classic example is the carmaker that uses a *competitive bidding strategy*, in which independent component suppliers compete to be chosen to supply a particular component, such as brakes, made to agreed-upon specifications, at the lowest price. For example, GM typically solicits bids from global suppliers to produce a particular component and awards a 1-year contract to the supplier that submits the lowest bid. At the end of the year, the contract is once again put out for competitive bid, and once again the lowest-cost supplier is most likely to win the bid.

The advantage of this strategy for GM is that suppliers are forced to compete over price, which drives down the cost of its components. However, GM has no long-term commitment to outside suppliers—and it drives a hard bargain. For this reason, suppliers are unwilling to make the expensive, long-term investments in specialized assets that are required to produce higher-quality or better-designed component parts over time. In addition, suppliers will be reluctant to agree upon the tight scheduling that makes it possible to use a JIT inventory system because this may help GM lower its costs but will increase a supplier's costs and reduce its profitability.

As a result, short-term contracting does not result in the specialized investments that are required to realize differentiation and cost advantages *because it signals a company's lack of long-term commitment to its suppliers*. Of course, this is not a problem when there is minimal need for cooperation, and specialized assets are not required to improve scheduling, enhance product quality, or reduce costs. In this case, competitive bidding may be optimal. However, when there is a need for cooperation—something that is becoming increasingly significant today—the use of short-term contracts and competitive bidding can be a serious drawback.

Strategic Alliances and Long-Term Contracting

Unlike short-term contracts, **strategic alliances** between buyers and suppliers are long-term, cooperative relationships; both companies agree to make specialized investments and work jointly to find ways to lower costs or increase product quality so that they both gain from their relationship. A strategic alliance becomes a *substitute* for vertical integration because it creates a relatively stable, long-term partnership that allows both companies to obtain the same kinds of benefits that result from vertical integration. However, it also avoids the problems (bureaucratic costs) that arise from managerial inefficiencies that result when a company owns its own suppliers, such as

quasi integration
The use of long-term relationships, or investment in some activities normally performed by suppliers or buyers, in place of full ownership of operations that are backward or forward in the supply chain.

strategic alliances
Long-term agreements between two or more companies to jointly develop new products or processes that benefit all companies that are a part of the agreement.

those that arise because of a lack of incentives, or when a company becomes locked into an old technology even when technology is rapidly changing.

Consider the cooperative relationships that often were established decades ago, which many Japanese carmakers have with their component suppliers (the *keiretsu* system). Japanese carmakers and suppliers cooperate to find ways to maximize the value added they can obtain from being a part of adjacent stages of the value chain. For example, they do this by jointly implementing JIT inventory systems, or sharing future component-parts designs to improve quality and lower assembly costs. As part of this process, suppliers make substantial investments in specialized assets to better serve the needs of a particular carmaker, and the cost savings that result are shared. Thus, Japanese carmakers have been able to capture many of the benefits of vertical integration without having to enter the component industry.

Similarly, component suppliers also benefit because their business and profitability grow as the companies they supply grow, and they can invest their profits in investing in ever more specialized assets.[10] An interesting example of this is the computer chip outsourcing giant Taiwan Semiconductor Manufacturing Company (TSMC), which makes chips for many companies such as NVIDIA, Acer, and AMD. The cost of investing in the machinery necessary to build a state-of-the-art chip factory can exceed $10 billion. TSMC is able to make this huge (risky) investment because it has developed cooperative, long-term relationships with its computer-chip partners. All parties recognize that they will benefit from this outsourcing arrangement, which does not preclude some hard bargaining between TSMC and the chip companies, because all parties want to maximize their profits and reduce their risks.

Building Long-Term Cooperative Relationships

How does a company create a long-term strategic alliance with another company when the fear of holdup exists, and the possibility of being cheated arises if one company makes a specialized investment with another company? How do companies such as GM or Nissan manage to develop such profitable, enduring relationships with their suppliers?

There are several strategies companies can adopt to promote the success of a long-term, cooperative relationship and lessen the chance that one company will renege on its agreement and cheat the other. One strategy is for the company that makes the specialized investment to demand a *hostage* from its partner. Another is to establish a *credible commitment* from both companies that will result in a trusting, long-term relationship.[11]

hostage taking

A means of exchanging valuable resources to guarantee that each partner to an agreement will keep its side of the bargain.

Hostage Taking   **Hostage taking** is essentially a means of guaranteeing that each partner will keep its side of the bargain. The cooperative relationship between Boeing and Northrop Grumman illustrates this type of situation. Northrop is a major subcontractor for Boeing's commercial airline division, providing many components for its aircraft. To serve Boeing's special needs, Northrop has had to make substantial investments in specialized assets, and, in theory, because of this investment Northrop has become dependent on Boeing—which can threaten to change orders to other suppliers as a way of driving down Northrop's prices. In practice, Boeing is highly unlikely to change suppliers because it is, in turn, a major supplier to Northrop's defense division and provides many parts for its Stealth aircraft; it also has made major investments in specialized assets to serve Northrop's needs. Thus, the companies are *mutually dependent*; each company holds a hostage—the specialized investment the other has made. Thus, Boeing is unlikely to renege on any pricing agreements with Northrop because it knows that Northrop would respond the same way.

Credible Commitments   A **credible commitment** is a believable promise or pledge to support the development of a long-term relationship between companies. Consider the way GE and IBM developed such a commitment. GE is a major supplier of advanced semiconductor chips to IBM, and many of the chips are customized to IBM's requirements. To meet IBM's specific needs, GE has had to make substantial investments in specialized assets that have little other value. As a consequence, GE is dependent on IBM and faces a risk that IBM will take advantage of this dependence to demand lower prices. In theory, IBM could back up its demand by threatening to switch its business to another supplier. However, GE reduced this risk by having IBM enter into a contractual agreement that committed IBM to purchase chips from GE for a 10-year period. In addition, IBM agreed to share the costs of the specialized assets needed to develop the customized chips, thereby reducing the risks associated with GE's investment. Thus, by publicly committing itself to a long-term contract and putting money into the chip development process, IBM made a *credible commitment* that it would continue to purchase chips from GE. When a company violates a credible commitment with its partners, the results can be dramatic, as discussed in Strategy in Action 9.2.

credible commitment
A believable promise or pledge to support the development of a long-term relationship between companies.

Maintaining Market Discipline   Just as a company pursuing vertical integration faces the problem that its company-owned suppliers might become inefficient, a company that forms a strategic alliance with an independent component supplier runs the risk that its alliance partner might become inefficient over time, resulting in higher component costs or lower quality. This also happens because the outside supplier knows it does not need to compete with other suppliers for the company's business. Consequently, a company seeking to form a mutually beneficial, long-term strategic alliance needs to possess some kind of power that it can use to discipline its partner should the need arise.

A company holds two strong cards over its supplier partner. First, all contracts, including long-term contracts, are periodically renegotiated, usually every 3 to 5 years, so the supplier knows that if it fails to live up to its commitments, its partner may refuse to renew the contract. Second, many companies that form long-term relationships with suppliers use a **parallel sourcing policy**—that is, they enter into long-term contracts with at least *two* suppliers for the *same* component (this is Toyota's policy, for example).[12] This arrangement protects a company against a supplier that adopts an uncooperative attitude because the supplier knows that if it fails to comply with the agreement, the company can switch *all* its business to its other supplier partner. When both the company and its suppliers recognize that the parallel sourcing policy allows a supplier to be replaced at short notice, most suppliers behave because the policy brings market discipline into their relationship.

parallel sourcing policy
A policy in which a company enters into long-term contracts with at least two suppliers for the same component to prevent any incidents of opportunism.

The growing importance of JIT inventory systems as a way to reduce costs and enhance quality and differentiation is increasing the pressure on companies to form strategic alliances in a wide range of industries. The number of strategic alliances formed each year, especially global strategic alliances, is increasing, and the popularity of vertical integration is falling because so many low-cost global suppliers exist in countries such as Malaysia, Korea, and China.

9.2 STRATEGY IN ACTION

eBay's Changing Commitment to Its Sellers

Since its founding in 1995, eBay has cultivated good relationships with the millions of sellers that advertise their goods for sale on its website. Over time, however, to increase its revenues and profits, eBay has steadily increased the fees it charges sellers to list their products on its sites, to insert photographs, to use its PayPal online payment service, and for other additional services. Although this has caused grumbling among sellers because it reduces their profit margins, eBay increasingly engages in extensive advertising to attract millions more buyers to its website, so sellers can receive better prices and increase their total profits. As a result, they remained largely satisfied with eBay's fee structure.

These policies changed when a new CEO, John Donohue, took the place of eBay's long-time CEO, Meg Whitman, who had built the company into a dot.com giant. By 2008, eBay's profits had not increased rapidly enough to keep its investors happy, and its stock price plunged. To increase performance, one of Donohue's first moves was to announce a major overhaul of eBay's fee structure and feedback policy. The new fee structure would reduce upfront seller listing costs but increase back-end commissions on completed sales and payments. For smaller sellers that already had thin profit margins, these fee hikes were painful. In addition, in the future, eBay announced it would block sellers from leaving negative feedback about buyers—feedback such as buyers didn't pay for the goods they purchased, or buyers took too long to pay for goods. The feedback system that eBay had originally developed had been a major source of its success; it allowed buyers to be certain they were dealing with reputable sellers, and vice versa. All sellers and buyers have feedback scores that provide them with a reputation as good—or bad—individuals with whom to do business, and these scores helped reduce the risks involved in online transactions. Donohue claimed this change was implemented in order to improve the buyer's experience because many buyers had complained that if they left negative feedback on a seller, the seller would in turn leave negative feedback for the buyer.

Together, however, throughout 2009, these changes resulted in conflict between eBay and its millions of sellers, who perceived they were being harmed by these changes. Their bad feelings resulted in a revolt. Blogs and forums all over the Internet were filled with messages claiming that eBay had abandoned its smaller sellers, and was pushing them out of business in favor of high-volume "powersellers" who contributed more to eBay's profits. Donohue and eBay received millions of hostile e-mails, and sellers threatened they would do business elsewhere, such as on Amazon.com and Yahoo!, two companies that were both trying to break into eBay's market. Sellers also organized a 1-week boycott of eBay during which they would list no items with the company to express their dismay and hostility! Many sellers did shut down their eBay online storefronts and moved to Amazon.com, which claimed in 2011 that its network of sites had overtaken eBay in monthly unique viewers or "hits" for the first time. The bottom line was that the level of commitment between eBay and its sellers had fallen dramatically; the bitter feelings produced by the changes eBay had made were likely to result in increasing problems that would hurt its future performance.

Realizing that his changes had backfired, Donohue reversed course and eliminated several of eBay's fee increases and revamped its feedback system; sellers and buyers can now respond to one another's comments in a fairer way. These changes did improve hostility and smooth over the bad feelings between sellers and eBay, but the old "community relationship" it had enjoyed with sellers in its early years largely disappeared. As this example suggests, finding ways to maintain cooperative relationships—such as by testing the waters in advance and asking sellers for their reactions to fee and feedback changes—could have avoided many of the problems that arose.

Source: www.ebay.com.

STRATEGIC OUTSOURCING

Vertical integration and strategic alliances are alternative ways of managing the value chain *across industries* to strengthen a company's core business model. However, just as low-cost suppliers of component parts exist, so today many *specialized companies* exist that can perform one of a company's *own value-chain activities* in a way that contributes to a company's differentiation advantage or that lowers its cost structure. For example, as noted in the Closing Case, Apple found that using Foxconn factories in China to assemble its iPhones enabled it to not only benefit by lower costs, but to also much more rapidly incorporate design changes and scale up production.

Strategic outsourcing is the decision to allow one or more of a company's value-chain activities or functions to be performed by independent specialist companies that focus all their skills and knowledge on just one kind of function, such as the manufacturing function, or on just one kind of activity that a function performs. For example, many companies outsource the management of their pension systems while keeping other human resource management (HRM) activities within the company. When a company chooses to outsource a value-chain activity, it is choosing to focus on a *fewer* number of value creation activities to strengthen its business model.

strategic outsourcing
The decision to allow one or more of a company's value-chain activities to be performed by independent, specialist companies that focus all their skills and knowledge on just one kind of activity to increase performance.

There has been a clear move among many companies to outsource activities that managers regard as being "noncore" or "nonstrategic," meaning they are not a source of a company's distinctive competencies and competitive advantage.[13] The vast majority of companies outsource manufacturing or some other value-chain activity to domestic or overseas companies today; some estimates are that over 60% of all global product manufacturing is outsourced to manufacturing specialists because of pressures to reduce costs. Some well-known companies that outsource include Nike, which does not make its athletic shoes; Gap Inc., which does not make its jeans and clothing; and Microsoft, which does not make its Xbox consoles. These products are made under contract at low-cost, global locations by contract manufacturers that specialize in low-cost assembly.

Although manufacturing is the most common form of strategic outsourcing, as we noted earlier, many other kinds of noncore activities are also outsourced. Microsoft has long outsourced its entire customer technical support operation to an independent company, as does Dell. Both companies have extensive customer support operations in India staffed by skilled operatives who are paid a fraction of what their U.S. counterparts earn. British Petroleum outsourced almost all of its human resource function to Exult, a San Antonio company, in a 5-year deal worth $600 million; a few years later, Exult won a 10-year, $1.1 billion contract to handle HRM activities for Bank of America's 150,000 employees. Similarly, American Express outsourced its entire IT function to IBM in a 7-year deal worth $4 billion. In 2006, IBM announced it was outsourcing its purchasing function to an Indian company to save $2 billion a year, and it has steadily increased its use of outsourcing ever since. For example, in 2009, IBM announced it would lay off 5,000 IT employees in the United States and move their jobs to India.[14]

Companies engage in strategic outsourcing to strengthen their business models and increase their profitability. The process of strategic outsourcing typically begins with strategic managers identifying the value-chain activities that form the basis of a company's competitive advantage; these are obviously kept within the company to protect them from competitors. Managers then systematically review noncore functions to assess whether independent companies that specialize in those activities can perform them more effectively and efficiently. Because these companies specialize in

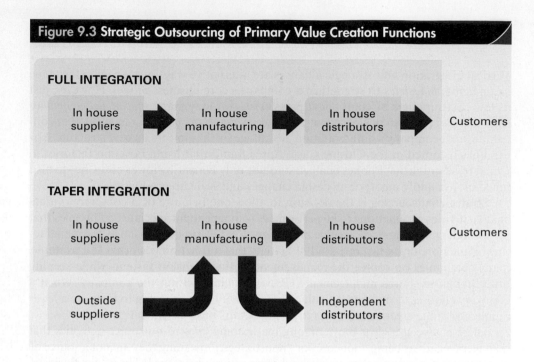

Figure 9.3 Strategic Outsourcing of Primary Value Creation Functions

FULL INTEGRATION

In house suppliers → In house manufacturing → In house distributors → Customers

TAPER INTEGRATION

In house suppliers → In house manufacturing → In house distributors → Customers

Outside suppliers → ↑ In house manufacturing → Independent distributors

particular activities, they can perform them in ways that lower costs or improve differentiation. If managers determine that there are differentiation or cost advantages, these activities are outsourced to those specialists.

This is illustrated in Figure 9.3, which shows the primary value-chain activities and boundaries of a company before and after it has pursued strategic outsourcing. In this example, the company decided to outsource its production and customer service functions to specialist companies, leaving only R&D and marketing and sales within the company. Once outsourcing has been executed, the relationships between the company and its specialists are then often structured as long-term contractual relationships, with rich information sharing between the company and the specialist organization to which it has contracted the activity. The term **virtual corporation** has been coined to describe companies that have pursued extensive strategic outsourcing.[15]

virtual corporation
When companies pursued extensive strategic outsourcing to the extent that they only perform the central value creation functions that lead to competitive advantage.

Benefits of Outsourcing

Strategic outsourcing has several advantages. It can help a company (1) lower its cost structure, (2) increase product differentiation,[16] and (3) focus on the distinctive competencies that are vital to its long-term competitive advantage and profitability.

Lower Cost Structure Outsourcing will reduce costs when the price that must be paid to a specialist company to perform a particular value-chain activity is less than what it would cost the company to perform that activity in-house. Specialists are often able to perform an activity at a lower cost than the company because they are able to realize scale economies or other efficiencies not available to the company. For example, performing HRM activities such as managing benefit and pay systems requires a significant investment in sophisticated HRM IT; purchasing these IT systems represents a considerable fixed cost for one company. But, by aggregating the HRM IT needs of many individual companies, companies that specialize in HRM such as Exult and Paychex can obtain huge economies of scale in IT that any single company could not hope to achieve. Some of these cost savings are then passed to the client companies in the form of lower prices, which reduces their cost structure. A similar dynamic is at work in the contract manufacturing business. Manufacturing specialists like Foxconn, Flextronics, and Jabil Circuit make large capital investments to build efficient-scale manufacturing facilities, but then are able to spread those capital costs over a huge volume of output and drive down unit costs so that they can make a specific product— an Apple iPod or Motorola XOOM, for example—at a lower cost than the company.

Specialists are also likely to obtain the cost savings associated with learning effects much more rapidly than a company that performs an activity just for itself (see Chapter 4 for a review of learning effects). For example, because a company like Flextronics is manufacturing similar products for several different companies, it is able to build up *cumulative* volume more rapidly, and it learns how to manage and operate the manufacturing process more efficiently than any of its clients could. This drives down the specialists' cost structure and also allows them to charge client companies a lower price for a product than if they made that product in-house.

Specialists are also often able to perform activities at lower costs than a specific company because of lower wage rates in those locations. For example, many workers at the Foxconn factory that assembles iPhones in China earn less than $17 a day; moving production of iPhones to the United States would, according to estimates, raise the cost of an iPhone by $65.[17] Similarly, Nike outsources the manufacture of its running shoes to companies based in China because of much lower wage rates. Even though wages have doubled in China since 2010, a Chinese-based specialist can assemble shoes (a very labor-intensive activity) at a much lower cost than could be done in the United States. Although Nike could establish its own operations in China to manufacture running shoes, it would require a major capital investment and limit its ability to switch production to an even lower-cost location later—for example, Vietnam; many companies are moving to Vietnam because wage rates are lower there. So, for Nike and most other consumer goods companies, outsourcing manufacturing activities lowers costs and gives companies the flexibility to switch to a more favorable location if labor costs change is the most efficient way to handle production.

Enhanced Differentiation   A company may also be able to differentiate its final products better by outsourcing certain noncore activities to specialists. For this to occur, the *quality* of the activity performed by specialists must be greater than if that same activity was performed by the company. On the reliability dimension of quality, for example, a specialist may be able to achieve a lower error rate in performing an activity precisely because it focuses solely on that activity and has developed a strong, distinctive competency in it. Again, this is one advantage claimed for contract manufacturers. Companies like Flextronics have adopted Six Sigma methodologies (see Chapter 4) and driven down the defect rate associated with manufacturing a product. This means they can provide more reliable products to their clients and differentiate their products on the basis of their superior quality.

A company can also improve product differentiation by outsourcing to specialists when they stand out on the excellence dimension of quality. For example, the excellence of Dell's U.S. customer service is a differentiating factor, and Dell outsources its PC repair and maintenance function to specialist companies. A customer who has a problem with a product purchased from Dell can get excellent help over the phone, and if there is a defective part in the computer, a maintenance person will be dispatched to replace the part within a few days. The excellence of this service differentiates Dell and helps to guarantee repeat purchases, which is why HP has worked hard to match Dell's level of service quality. In a similar way, carmakers often outsource specific vehicle component design activities such as microchips or headlight, to specialists that have earned a reputation for design excellence in this particular activity.

Focus on the Core Business   A final advantage of strategic outsourcing is that it allows managers to focus their energies and their company's resources on performing the core activities that have the most potential to create value and competitive advantage. In other words, companies can enhance their core competencies and are able to push out the value frontier and create more value for their customers. For example, Cisco Systems remains the dominant competitor in the Internet router industry because it has focused on building its competencies in product design, marketing and sales, and supply-chain management. Companies that focus on the core activities essential for competitive advantage in their industry are better able to drive down the costs of performing those activities and thus better differentiate their final products.

Risks of Outsourcing

Although outsourcing noncore activities has many benefits, there are also risks associated with it, risks such as holdup and the possible loss of important information when an activity is outsourced. Managers must assess these risks before they decide to outsource a particular activity, although, as we discuss the following section, these risks can be reduced when the appropriate steps are taken.

Holdup   In the context of outsourcing, holdup refers to the risk that a company will become too dependent upon the specialist provider of an outsourced activity and that the specialist will use this fact to raise prices beyond some previously agreed-upon rate. As with strategic alliances, the risk of holdup can be reduced by outsourcing to several suppliers and pursuing a parallel sourcing policy, as Toyota and Cisco do. Moreover, when an activity can be performed well by any one of several different providers, the threat that a contract will not be renewed in the future is normally sufficient to keep the chosen provider from exercising bargaining power over the company. For example, although IBM enters into long-term contracts to provide IT services to a wide range of companies, it would be unadvisable for those companies to attempt to raise prices after the contract has been signed because it knows full well that such an action would reduce its chance of getting the contract renewed in the future. Moreover, because IBM has many strong competitors in the IT services business, such as Accenture, Capgemini, and HP, it has a very strong incentive to deliver significant value to its clients.

Increased Competition   As firms employ contract manufacturers for production, they help to build an industrywide resource that lowers barriers to entry in that industry. In industries that have efficient, high-quality contract manufacturers, large firms may find that their size no longer affords them protection against competitive pressure; their high investments in fixed assets can become a constraint rather than a source of advantage.[18] Furthermore, firms that use contract manufacturing pay, in essence, for the contract manufacturer to progress down its own learning curve. Over time, the contract manufacturer's capabilities improve, putting it at a greater manufacturing advantage over the firm. Contract manufacturers in many industries increase the scope of their activities over time, adding a wider range of services (e.g., component purchasing, redesign-for-manufacturability, testing, packaging, and after-sales service) and may eventually produce their own end products in competition with their customers. Contracts to manufacture goods for U.S. and European electronics manufacturers, for example, helped to build the electronics manufacturing giants that exist today in Japan and Korea.

Loss of Information and Forfeited Learning Opportunities   A company that is not careful can lose important competitive information when it outsources an activity. For example, many computer hardware and software companies have outsourced their customer technical support function to specialists. Although this makes good sense from a cost and differentiation perspective, it may also mean that a critical point of contact with the customer, and a source of important feedback, is lost. Customer complaints can be useful information and valuable inputs into future product design, but if those complaints are not clearly communicated to the company by the specialists performing the technical support activity, the company can lose the information. Similarly, a firm that manufactures its own products also gains knowledge about how to improve their design in order to lower the costs of manufacturing or produce more reliable products. Thus, a firm that forfeits the development of manufacturing knowledge could unintentionally forfeit opportunities for improving its capabilities in product design. The firm risks becoming "hollow."[19] These are not arguments against outsourcing; rather, they are arguments for ensuring that there is appropriate communication between the outsourcing specialist and the company. At Dell, for example, a great deal of attention is paid to making sure that the specialist responsible for providing technical support and onsite maintenance collects and communicates all relevant data regarding product failures and other problems to Dell, so that Dell can design better products.

KEY TERMS

horizontal integration   283
acquisition   283
merger   283
product bundling   285

cross-selling   285
vertical integration   288
holdup   291
tapered integration   291
vertical disintegration   293

transfer pricing   293
quasi integration   295
strategic alliances   295
hostage taking   296
credible commitment   297

parallel sourcing policy   297
strategic outsourcing   299
virtual corporation   300

TAKEAWAYS FOR STRATEGIC MANAGERS

1. A corporate strategy should enable a company, or one or more of its business units, to perform one or more of the value creation functions at a lower cost or in a way that allows for differentiation and a premium price.

2. The corporate-level strategy of horizontal integration is pursued to increase the profitability of a company's business model by (a) reducing costs, (b) increasing the value of the company's products through differentiation, (c) replicating

the business model, (d) managing rivalry within the industry to reduce the risk of price warfare, and (e) increasing bargaining power over suppliers and buyers.

3. There are two drawbacks associated with horizontal integration: (a) the numerous pitfalls associated with making mergers and acquisitions and (b) the fact that the strategy can bring a company into direct conflict with antitrust authorities.

4. The corporate-level strategy of vertical integration is pursued to increase the profitability of a company's "core" business model in its original industry. Vertical integration can enable a company to achieve a competitive advantage by helping build barriers to entry, facilitating investments in specialized assets, protecting product quality, and helping to improve scheduling between adjacent stages in the value chain.

5. The disadvantages of vertical integration include (a) increasing bureaucratic costs if a company-owned or in-house supplier becomes lazy or inefficient, (b) potential loss of focus on those resources and capabilities that create the most value for the firm, and (c), reduced flexibility to adapt to a fast-changing environment. Entering into a long-term contract can enable a company to realize many of the benefits associated with vertical integration without having to bear the same level of bureaucratic costs. However, to avoid the risks associated with becoming too dependent upon its partner, it needs to seek a credible commitment from its partner or establish a mutual hostage-taking situation.

6. The strategic outsourcing of noncore value creation activities may allow a company to lower its costs, better differentiate its products, and make better use of scarce resources, while also enabling it to respond rapidly to changing market conditions. However, strategic outsourcing may have a detrimental effect if the company outsources important value creation activities or becomes too dependent upon the key suppliers of those activities.

DISCUSSION QUESTIONS

1. Under what conditions might horizontal integration be inconsistent with the goal of maximizing profitability?

2. What is the difference between a company's internal value chain and the industry value chain? What is the relationship between vertical integration and the industry value chain?

3. Why was it profitable for GM and Ford to integrate backward into component-parts manufacturing in the past, and why are both companies now buying more of their parts from outside suppliers?

4. What value creation activities should a company outsource to independent suppliers? What are the risks involved in outsourcing these activities?

5. What steps would you recommend that a company take to build mutually beneficial, long-term, cooperative relationships with its suppliers?

CLOSING CASE

Outsourcing and Vertical Integration at Apple

At a dinner for Silicon Valley luminaries in February 2011, U.S. President Barack Obama asked Steve Jobs of Apple, "What would it take to make iPhones in the United States?" Jobs replied, "Those jobs aren't coming back." Apple's management had concluded that overseas factories provided superior scale, flexibility, diligence, and access to industrial skills—"Made in the U.S.A." just did not make sense for Apple anymore.

As an example of the superior responsiveness of Chinese factories to Apple's needs, an executive described a recent event when Apple wanted to revamp its iPhone manufacturing just weeks before it was scheduled for delivery to stores. At the last minute, Apple had redesigned the screen, and new screens arrived at the Chinese factory at midnight. Fortunately, the 8,000 workers slept in dormitories at the factory—they were woken, given a cookie and a cup of tea, and were at work fitting glass screens into their beveled frames within 30 minutes. Soon the plant was producing 10,000 iPhones per day. The executive commented, "The speed and flexibility is breathtaking . . . There's no American plant that can match that."

"Foxconn City," a complex where the iPhone is assembled, has 230,000 employees, many of whom work 6 days a week and up to 12 hours a day. It is owned by Foxconn Technology, which has dozens of factories in Asia, Eastern Europe, Mexico, and Brazil. It is estimated that Foxconn assembles 40% of the world's consumer electronics. It boasts a customer list that includes Amazon, Dell, Hewlett-Packard, Motorola, Nintendo, Nokia, Samsung, and Sony, in addition to Apple. Foxconn can hire thousands of engineers overnight and house them in dorms—something no American firm could do. Nearly 8,700 industrial engineers were needed to oversee the 200,000 assembly-line workers required to manufacture iPhones. Apple's analysts estimated that it could take 9 months to find that many qualified engineers in the United States. It only took 15 days in China. Moreover, China's advantage was not only in assembly; it offered advantages across the entire supply chain. As noted by an Apple executive, "The entire supply chain is in China now. You need a thousand rubber gaskets? That's the factory next door. You need a million screws? That factory is a block away. You need that screw made a little bit different? It will take three hours." Of Apple's 64,000 employees, nearly one-third are outside of the United States. In response to criticisms about failing to support employment

in its home country, Apple executives responded, "We sell iPhones in over a hundred countries. . . . Our only obligation is making the best product possible."

Although Apple epitomizes the opportunities for strategic outsourcing, it is also—paradoxically, perhaps—more vertically integrated than most computer or smartphone firms. Apple's decision to produce its own hardware and software—and tie them tightly together and sell them its own retail stores—was widely known and hotly debated. However, the vertical integration did not end there. Apple also spends billions of dollars buying production equipment that is used to outfit new and existing Asian factories that will be run by others (an example of quasi vertical integration), and then requires those factories to commit to producing for Apple exclusively. By providing the upfront investment, Apple removes most of the risk for its suppliers in investing in superior technology or scale. For decades, the computer and mobile phone industries have been characterized by commoditization and rapid cost reduction. Suppliers had to work hard to reduce costs to win competitive bids, and standardized production facilities trumped specialized facilities as they enabled suppliers to smooth out volatility in scale by working with multiple buyers. This meant that most suppliers to the computer and phone industry could produce cost-efficient hardware, but not "insanely great" hardware. Apple's strategy of paying upfront for both the technology and capacity enabled it to induce its suppliers to make specialized investments in technologies that were well beyond the industry standard, and to hold excess capacity that would enable rapid scaling. The net result is that Apple develops superior flexibility and technological sophistication that its competitors cannot match.

Seeming to acknowledge the advantages of Apple's strategy of controlling device design and production, Microsoft announced on June 18, 2012, that it too would design and produce its own tablet, the Surface. It also launched its own chain of dedicated Microsoft retail stores that looked remarkably similar to Apple stores. The success of this strategy

(continued)

is far from assured, however. Although Microsoft can imitate some of the individual integration strategies of Apple, it lacks both the tightly woven ecosystem that Apple has developed around those strategies, and its decades of experience in implementing them.

Sources: C. Duhigg and K. Bradsher, "How the U.S. Lost Out on iPhone Work," *New York Times*, January 21, 2012, p. 1; C. Guglielmo, "Apple's Secret Plan for Its Cash Stash," *Forbes*, May 7, 2012, pp. 116–120.

CASE DISCUSSION QUESTIONS

1. What are the advantages and disadvantages to Apple of outsourcing its production to factories in China?
2. What factors influence the choice of countries to which a firm might outsource its production?
3. Is there anything that might cause Apple to eventually shift production back to the United States?
4. Why is Apple more vertically integrated than many other computer makers?
5. What factors will help or impede Microsoft in matching the advantages Apple gains from its vertical integration strategies?

NOTES

[1] This is the essence of Chandler's argument. See A. D. Chandler, *Strategy and Structure* (Cambridge: MIT Press, 1962). The same argument is also made by J. Pfeffer and G. R. Salancik, *The External Control of Organizations* (New York: Harper & Row, 1978). See also K. R. Harrigan, *Strategic Flexibility* (Lexington: Lexington Books, 1985); K. R. Harrigan, "Vertical Integration and Corporate Strategy," *Academy of Management Journal* 28 (1985): 397–425; F. M. Scherer, *Industrial Market Structure and Economic Performance* (Chicago: Rand McNally, 1981).

[2] O. E. Williamson, *The Economic Institutions of Capitalism* (New York: Free Press, 1985). For another empirical work that uses this framework, see L. Poppo and T. Zenger, "Testing Alternative Theories of the Firm: Transaction Cost, Knowledge Based, and Measurement Explanations for Make or Buy Decisions in Information Services," *Strategic Management Journal* 19 (1998): 853–878.

[3] Williamson, *Economic Institutions of Capitalism*.

[4] J. M. deFigueiredo and B. S. Silverman, "Firm Survival and Industry Evolution in Vertically Related Populations," *Management Science* 58 (2012): 1632–1650.

[5] www.mcdonalds.com.

[6] Ibid.

[7] A. D. Chandler, *The Visible Hand* (Cambridge: Harvard University Press, 1977).

[8] Harrigan, *Strategic Flexibility*, pp. 67–87. See also A. Afuah, "Dynamic Boundaries of the Firm: Are Firms Better Off Being Vertically Integrated in the Face of a Technological Change?" *Academy of Management Journal* 44 (2001): 1121–1228

[9] K. M. Gilley, J. E. McGee, and A. A. Rasheed, "Perceived Environmental Dynamism and Managerial Risk Aversion as Antecedents of Manufacturing Outsourcing: The Moderating Effects of Firm Maturity," *Journal of Small Business Management* 42 (2004): 117–134; M. A. Schilling and H. K. Steensma, "The Use of Modular Organizational Forms: An Industry-Level Analysis," *Academy of Management Journal* 44 (2001): 1149–1169.

[10] X. Martin, W. Mitchell, and A. Swaminathan, "Recreating and

Extending Japanese Automobile Buyer-Supplier Links in North America," *Strategic Management Journal* 16 (1995): 589–619; C. W. L. Hill, "National Institutional Structures, Transaction Cost Economizing, and Competitive Advantage," *Organization Science* 6 (1995): 119–131.

[11]Williamson, *Economic Institutions of Capitalism*. See also J. H. Dyer, "Effective Inter-Firm Collaboration: How Firms Minimize Transaction Costs and Maximize Transaction Value," *Strategic Management Journal* 18 (1997): 535–556.

[12]Richardson, "Parallel Sourcing."

[13]W. H. Davidow and M. S. Malone, *The Virtual Corporation* (New York: Harper & Row, 1992).

[14]J. Krane, "American Express Hires IBM for $4 Billion," *Columbian*, February 26, 2002, p. E2; www .ibm.com.

[15]Davidow and Malone, *The Virtual Corporation*.

[16]Ibid.; see also H. W. Chesbrough and D. J. Teece, "When Is Virtual Virtuous? Organizing for Innovation," *Harvard Business Review*, January–February 1996, pp. 65–74;

J. B. Quinn, "Strategic Outsourcing: Leveraging Knowledge Capabilities," *Sloan Management Review*, Summer 1999, pp. 9–21.

[17]C. Duhigg and K. Bradsher, "How the U.S. Lost Out on iPhone Work," *New York Times*, January 21, 2012, p. 1.

[18]Schilling and Steensma, "The Use of Modular Organizational Forms."

[19]R. Venkatesan, "Strategic Sourcing: To Make or Not to Make," *Harvard Business Review*, November–December 1992, pp. 98–107.

sergign/Shutterstock.com

CHAPTER 10

CORPORATE-LEVEL STRATEGY: RELATED AND UNRELATED DIVERSIFICATION

10.1 Differentiate between multibusiness models based on related and unrelated diversification

10.2 Explain the five primary ways in which diversification can increase company profitability

10.3 Discuss the conditions that lead managers to pursue related diversification versus unrelated diversification, and explain why some companies pursue both strategies

10.4 Describe the three methods companies use to enter new industries—internal new venturing, acquisitions, and joint ventures—and discuss the advantages and disadvantages associated with each method

OPENING CASE

LVMH: Getting Big While Staying Beautiful

In 1854, Louis Vuitton founded a trunk-making company in Paris. He had observed that most trunks could not be easily stacked because they had rounded tops; he thus began producing trunks with flat bottoms and tops out of trianon canvas, which was lightweight and airtight. The style became extremely popular, and soon competitors were imitating his design. To deter imitation, he began creating trunks with special patterns and a logo—creating the iconic look that distinguishes Louis Vuitton products today. After his death, his son, Georges Vuitton, took over the company and began to expand it worldwide. He exhibited the trunks at the Chicago World's Fair in 1893, and toured cities such as New York, Chicago, and Philadelphia, selling the trunks to retailers. Over the next 80 years, Louis Vuitton stores opened all over the world, including Bombay, London, Washington DC, Buenos Aires, Taipei, Tokyo, and Seoul. In 1987, Moët Hennessy and Louis Vuitton merged to create the LVMH group, one of the world's largest and best-known luxury goods companies.

Many brands that came to be owned by the LVMH group were even older than Louis Vuitton: Moët & Chandon, the champagne company, had been founded in 1743; Veuve Clicquot Ponsardin dated back to 1772; Hennessy (maker of fine cognac) was originally formed in 1765, and perfumery Guerlain dated back to 1829. The oldest company in the group, Château d'Yquem, began making wine in 1593. Each company

Mandritoiu/Shutterstock.com   CFimages/Alamy   iStockphoto.com/TkKurikawa   PETIT Philippe/Getty images   Bloomberg/Getty Images

brought a legacy of craftsmanship and a loyal following of customers. However, LVMH's biggest brand by far has continued to be the Louis Vuitton brand, which accounts for about one-third of its sales and almost half of its profit.

Much of LVMH's growth into the diversified, luxury goods group that it has become can be attributed to Bernard Arnault. Arnault's career in luxury goods began in 1984, when he bought Dior in the bankruptcy sale of an industrial group. A few years later, he bought Luis Vuitton, which at the time had 125 stores. He subsequently transformed the group into a luxury conglomerate with over 60 brands. One of his first moves was to take production and distribution back from license-holders to begin restoring the exclusivity of the brands. In the years that followed, he bought Celine, Givenchy, Fendi, Kenzo, Bulgari, Sephora, Tag Heuer, and more. In 2014, LVMH also opened a stunning new arts center in Paris, the Foundation Louis Vuitton. The center, designed by world- renowned architect Frank Gehry, generated a flurry of publicity for the group.

Perhaps ironically, luxury goods benefit from economies of scale: A large luxury group can help a new brand grow faster through its distribution reach and expertise in brand management. "Key money" to open a shop on a prestigious, high-traffic location such as London's Bond Street can cost as much as $16 million. On top of that, a vendor must pay to outfit the shop, and may pay annual rent of $1.5 million. A large luxury group can make such investments and wait for them to pay off; small brands usually cannot. Furthermore, large luxury groups have more bargaining power with fashion magazines, more access to important fashion shows, and more influence with "key opinion leaders." They can also better attract and retain managers because they offer a deep, broad career path. At LVMH, for example, managers can move from fashion to wine to jewelry, and can live in a range of the world's biggest cities, vastly increasing their experience and marketability.

According to Bain & Company, over the past 20 years the number of luxury-goods consumers has more than tripled to 330 million, and their spending on luxury goods has risen at double the rate of global GDP. Most new buyers are not superwealthy but rather are "merely prosperous," earning up to $188,000 annually. As luxury-goods makers have raced to capture this market, they have had to carefully balance growth on a global scale while preserving an artisan image and exclusivity. Expanding too fast or too far can tarnish a luxury brand by making it seem too accessible.

By 2014, LVMH was earning almost $31 billion in revenues and had a net profit margin of 18.4%. It operated over 400 stores under the Louis Vuitton name alone. LVMH had proven that a company could be big and global, yet have prestigious and exclusive brands. As noted by Arnault, "People said in 1989 that Louis Vuitton was already too big. Now it's ten times the size."

Sources: www.lvmh.com; Anonymous, "Beauty and the Beasts: The Business Case," *The Economist*, December 13, 2014, pp. 6–8; Anonymous, "Exclusively for Anybody," *The Economist*, December 13, 2014, pp. 3–5; Yahoo Finance.

◤ OVERVIEW

Diversification can create, and destroy, value. As shown in the Opening Case, diversification enabled Louis Vuitton to leverage its branding expertise, distribution reach, influence, and capital resources to help new brands grow more profitably than they would grow on their own. However, as shown in the Closing Case, overdiversification at Citibank led the company away from its key strengths in consumer retail banking and made it difficult for managers to provide adequate oversight within the organization. Diversification can be very alluring to managers, and it is easy to overestimate potential synergies. It is much harder to realize them.

In this chapter, we continue to discuss both the challenges and opportunities created by corporate-level strategies of related and unrelated diversification. A diversification strategy is based upon a company's decision to enter one or more new industries to take advantage of its existing distinctive competencies and business model. We examine the different kinds of multibusiness models upon which related and unrelated diversification are based. Then, we discuss three different ways companies can implement a diversification strategy: internal new ventures, acquisitions, and joint ventures. By the end of this chapter, you will understand the advantages and disadvantages associated with strategic managers' decisions to diversify and enter new markets and industries.

◤ INCREASING PROFITABILITY THROUGH DIVERSIFICATION

diversification

The process of entering new industries, distinct from a company's core or original industry, to make new kinds of products for customers in new markets.

diversified company

A company that makes and sells products in two or more different or distinct industries.

Diversification is the process of entering new industries, distinct from a company's core or original industry, to make new kinds of products that can be sold profitably to customers in these new industries. A multibusiness model based on diversification aims to find ways to use a company's existing strategies and distinctive competencies to make products that are highly valued by customers in the new industries it enters. A **diversified company** is one that makes and sells products in two or more different or distinct industries (industries *not* in adjacent stages of an industry value chain, as in vertical integration). As in the case of the corporate strategies discussed in Chapter 9, a diversification strategy should enable a company or its individual business units to perform one or more value-chain functions: (1) at a lower cost, (2) in a way that allows for differentiation and gives the company pricing options, or (3) in a way that helps the company manage industry rivalry better—*in order to increase profitability*.

Most companies consider diversification when they are generating *free cash flow;* that is, cash in excess of that required to fund new investments in the company's current business and meet existing debt commitments.[1] In other words, free cash flow is cash beyond that needed to make profitable new investments in the existing business. When a company's successful business model is generating free cash flow and profits, managers must decide whether to return that cash to shareholders in the form of higher dividend payouts or to invest it in diversification. In theory, any free cash flow belongs to the company's owners—its shareholders. So, for diversification to create value, a company's return on investing free cash flow to pursue diversification opportunities—that is, its future ROIC—*must* exceed the value shareholders would reap by returning the cash to them. When a firm does not pay out its free cash flow to its shareholders, the shareholders bear an opportunity cost equal to their next best use of those funds (i.e., another investment that pays a similar return at a similar risk, an investment that pays a higher return at a higher risk, or an investment that pays a lower return but at a lower risk). Thus, a diversification strategy must pass the "better off" test: The firm must be more valuable than it was before the diversification, and that value must not be fully capitalized by the cost of the diversification move (i.e., the cost of entry into the new industry must be taken into account when assessing the value created by the diversification). Thus managers might defer paying dividends now to invest in diversification, but they should do so only when this is expected to create even greater cash flow (and thus higher dividends) in the future.

There are five primary ways in which pursuing a multibusiness model based on diversification can increase company profitability. Diversification can increase profitability when strategic managers (1) transfer competencies between business units in different industries, (2) leverage competencies to create business units in new industries, (3) share resources between business units to realize synergies or economies of scope, (4) use product bundling, and (5) utilize *general* organizational competencies that increase the performance of *all* a company's business units.

Transferring Competencies Across Businesses

Transferring competencies involves taking a distinctive competency developed by a business unit in one industry and implanting it in a business unit operating in another industry. The second business unit is often one a company has acquired. Companies that base their diversification strategy on transferring competencies aim to use one or more of their existing distinctive competencies in a value-chain activity—for example, in manufacturing, marketing, materials management, or research and development (R&D)—to significantly strengthen the business model of the acquired business unit or company. For example, over time, Philip Morris developed distinctive competencies in product development, consumer marketing, and brand positioning that had made it a leader in the tobacco industry. Sensing a profitable opportunity, it acquired Miller Brewing, which at the time was a relatively small player in the brewing industry. Then, to create valuable new products in the brewing industry, Philip Morris transferred some of its best marketing experts to Miller, where they applied the skills acquired at Philip Morris to turn around Miller's lackluster brewing business (see Figure 10.1). The result was the creation of Miller Light, the first "light" beer, and a marketing campaign that helped to push Miller from number 6 to number 2 in market share in the brewing industry.

Companies that base their diversification strategy on transferring competencies tend to acquire new businesses *related* to their existing business activities because of commonalities between one or more of their value-chain functions. A **commonality** is a skill or attribute that, when shared or used by two or more business units, allows both businesses to operate more effectively and efficiently and create more value for customers.

For example, Miller Brewing was related to Philip Morris's tobacco business because it was possible to create important marketing commonalities; both beer and tobacco are mass-market consumer goods in which brand positioning, advertising, and

transferring competencies
The process of taking a distinctive competency developed by a business unit in one industry and implanting it in a business unit operating in another industry.

commonality
A skill or competency that, when shared by two or more business units, allows them to operate more effectively and create more value for customers.

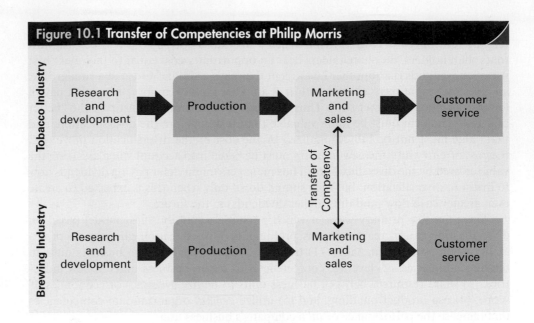

Figure 10.1 Transfer of Competencies at Philip Morris

product development skills are crucial to create successful new products. In general, such competency transfers increase profitability when they either (1) lower the cost structure of one or more of a diversified company's business units or (2) enable one or more of its business units to better differentiate their products, both of which give business-unit pricing options to lower a product's price to increase market share, or to charge a premium price.

To increase profitability, transferred competencies must involve value-chain activities that become an important source of a specific business unit's competitive advantage in the future. In other words, the distinctive competency being transferred must have real strategic value. However, all too often, companies assume that *any* commonality between their value chains is sufficient for creating value. When they attempt to transfer competencies, they find the anticipated benefits are not forthcoming because the different business units did not share some important attribute in common. For example, Coca-Cola acquired Minute Maid, the fruit juice maker, to take advantage of commonalities in global distribution and marketing, and this acquisition has proved to be highly successful. On the other hand, Coca-Cola once acquired the movie studio Columbia Pictures because it believed it could use its marketing prowess to produce blockbuster movies. This acquisition was a disaster that cost Coca-Cola billions in losses, and Columbia was eventually sold to Sony, which was then able to base many of its successful PlayStation games on the hit movies the studio produced.

Leveraging Competencies to Create a New Business

leveraging competencies
The process of taking a distinctive competency developed by a business unit in one industry and using it to create a new business unit in a different industry.

By **leveraging competencies a company** can develop a new business in a different industry. For example, Apple leveraged its competencies in personal computer (PC) hardware and software to enter the smartphone industry. Once again, the multibusiness model is based on the premise that the set of distinctive competencies that are the source of a company's competitive advantage in one industry might be applied to create a differentiation or cost-based competitive advantage for a new business unit or division in a different industry. For example, Canon used its distinctive competencies in precision mechanics, fine optics, and electronic imaging to produce laserjet printers, which, for Canon, was a new business in a new industry. Its competencies enabled it to produce high-quality (differentiated) laser printers that could be manufactured at a low cost, which created its competitive advantage, and made Canon a leader in the printer industry.

Many companies base their diversification strategy on leveraging their competencies to create new business units in different industries. Microsoft leveraged its long-time experience and relationships in the computer industry, skills in software development, and its expertise in managing industries characterized by network externalities to create new business units in industries such as videogames (with its Xbox videogame consoles and game), online portals and search engines (e.g., MSN and Bing), and tablet computers (the Surface).

Sharing Resources and Capabilities

A third way in which two or more business units that operate in different industries can increase a diversified company's profitability is when the shared resources and capabilities result in economies of scope, or synergies.[2] **Economies of scope** arise when one or more of a diversified company's business units are able to realize cost-saving or differentiation synergies because they can more effectively pool, share, and utilize expensive resources or capabilities such as skilled people, equipment, manufacturing facilities, distribution channels, advertising campaigns, and R&D laboratories. If business units in different industries can share a common resource or function, they can collectively lower their cost structure; the idea behind synergies is that 2 + 2 = 5, not 4, in terms of value created.[3] As shown in the Opening Case, LVMH can utilize its distribution channels and its influence with fashion editors to help newer brands reach a global market more quickly and cost effectively. Similarly, GE can leverage its consumer-products advertising, sales, and service activities across a wide range of products such as light bulbs, appliances, air conditioners, and furnaces, thereby reducing the average cost of these activities for each product line. There are two major sources of cost reductions.

There are two major sources of cost reductions. First, when companies can share resources or capabilities across business units, it lowers their cost structure compared to a company that operates in only one industry and bears the full costs of developing resources and capabilities. For example, P&G makes disposable diapers, toilet paper, and paper towels, which are all paper-based products that customers value for their ability to absorb fluids without disintegrating. Because these products need the same attribute—absorbency—P&G can share the R&D costs associated with developing and making even more advanced absorbent, paper-based products across the three distinct businesses (only two are shown in Figure 10.2). Similarly, because all of these products are sold to retailers, P&G can use the same sales force to sell its whole array of products (see Figure 10.2). In contrast, P&G competitors that make only one or two of these products cannot share these costs across industries, so their cost structures are higher. As a result, P&G has lower costs; it can use its marketing function to better differentiate its products, and it achieves a higher ROIC than companies that operate only in one or a few industries—which are unable to obtain economies of scope from the ability to share resources and obtain synergies across business units.

economies of scope
The synergies that arise when one or more of a diversified company's business units are able to lower costs or increase differentiation because they can more effectively pool, share, and utilize expensive resources or capabilities.

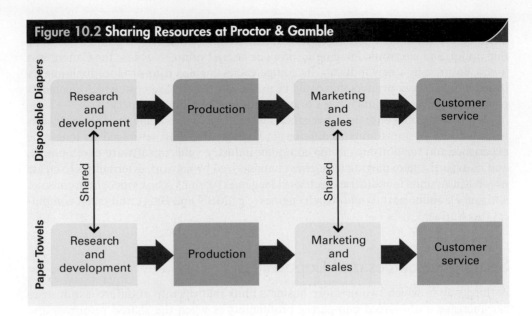

Figure 10.2 Sharing Resources at Proctor & Gamble

Similarly, Nike, which began strictly as a maker of running shoes, realized that its brand image, and its relationships with athletes and sports events, could be profitably leveraged into other types of athletic footwear, athletic apparel, and accessories such as sunglasses and headphones. Those products were more differentiated because of the Nike brand name and had better exposure because Nike was able to place them in suitable endorsement spots via its relationships with athletes and events, and Nike is able to amortize the cost of its brand-building activities across a wider range of products, thus achieving economies of scope.

To reiterate, diversification to obtain economies of scope is possible only when there are *significant* commonalities between one or more value-chain functions in a company's different business units or divisions that result in synergies which increase profitability. In addition, managers must be aware that the costs of coordination necessary to achieve synergies or economies of scope within a company may sometimes be *higher* than the value that can be created by such a strategy.[4] As noted in the Closing Case, although Citibank had anticipated major cost savings from consolidating operations across its acquisitions, and revenue-increasing opportunities from cross-selling, some synergies turned out to be small or difficult to reap. In retrospect, the coordination costs that Citi bore (in the form of massive losses due to inadequate oversight over its investment activities) probably vastly exceeded the synergies it gained. Consequently, diversification based on obtaining economies of scope should be pursued only when the sharing of competencies will result in *significant* synergies that will achieve a competitive advantage for one or more of a company's new or existing business units.

Using Product Bundling

In the search for new ways to differentiate products, more and more companies are entering into industries that provide customers with new products that are connected or related to their existing products. This allows a company to expand the range of products it produces in order to satisfy customers' needs for a complete package of related products. This is currently happening in telecommunications, in which customers are increasingly seeking package prices for wired phone service, wireless phone service, high-speed access to the Internet, television programming, online gaming, video on demand, or any combination of these services. To meet this need, large phone companies such as AT&T and Verizon have been acquiring other companies that provide one or more of these services, and cable companies such as Comcast have acquired or formed strategic alliances with companies that can offer their customers a package of these services. In 2010, for example, Comcast acquired GE's NBC division to gain control of its library of content programming. The goal, once again, is to bundle products to offer customers lower prices and/or a superior set of services.

Just as manufacturing companies strive to reduce the number of their component suppliers to reduce costs and increase quality, final customers want to obtain the convenience and reduced price of a bundle of related products—such as from Google or Microsoft's cloud-based commercial, business-oriented online applications. Another example of product bundling comes from the medical equipment industry, in which companies that, in the past, made one kind of product such as operating theater equipment, ultrasound devices, or magnetic imaging or X-ray equipment, have now merged with or been acquired by other companies to allow a larger, diversified company to provide hospitals with a complete range of medical equipment. This industry consolidation has also been driven by hospitals and health maintenance organizations (HMOs) that wish to obtain the convenience and lower prices that often follow from forming a long-term contract with a single supplier.

It is important to note that product bundling often does not require joint ownership. In many instances, bundling can be achieved through market contracts. For example, McDonald's does not need to manufacture toys in order to bundle them into Happy Meals—it can buy them through a supply contract. Disney does need to own airline services to offer a package deal on a vacation—an alliance contract will serve just as well. For product bundling to serve as a justification for diversification, there must be a strong need for coordination between the producers of the different products that cannot be overcome through market contracts.

Utilizing General Organizational Competencies

General organizational competencies transcend individual functions or business units and are found at the top or corporate level of a multibusiness company. Typically, **general organizational competencies** are the result of the skills of a company's top managers and functional experts. When these general competencies are present—and many times they are not—they help each business unit within a company perform at a higher level than it could if it operated as a separate or independent company. This increases the profitability of the entire corporation.[5] Three general organizational competencies help a company increase its performance and profitability: (1) entrepreneurial capabilities, (2) organizational design capabilities, and (3) strategic capabilities.

Entrepreneurial Capabilities A company that generates significant excess cash flow can take advantage of it only if its managers are able to identify new opportunities and act on them to create a stream of new and improved products, in its current industry and in new industries. Companies such as Apple, 3M, Google, and Samsung

general organizational competencies

Competencies that result from the skills of a company's top managers and that help every business unit within a company perform at a higher level than it could if it operated as a separate or independent company.

are able to promote entrepreneurship because they have an organizational culture that stimulates managers to act entrepreneurially.[6] As a result, they create new, profitable business units more quickly than do other companies, and this allows them to take advantage of profitable opportunities for diversification. We discuss one of the strategies required to generate new, profitable businesses later in this chapter: internal new venturing. For now, it is important to note that, to promote entrepreneurship, a company must (1) encourage managers to take risks, (2) give managers the time and resources to pursue novel ideas, (3) not punish managers when a new idea fails, and (4) make sure that the company's free cash flow is not wasted in pursuing too many risky ventures that have a low probability of generating a profitable return on investment. Strategic managers face a significant challenge in achieving all four of these objectives. On the one hand, a company must encourage risk taking; on the other hand, it must limit the number of risky ventures in which it engages.

Companies that possess strong entrepreneurial capabilities achieve this balancing act. For example, 3M's goal of generating 40% of its revenues from products introduced within the past 4 years focuses managers' attention on the need to develop new products and enter new businesses. 3M's long-standing commitment to help its customers solve problems also ensures that ideas for new businesses are customer focused. The company's celebration of employees who have created successful new businesses reinforces the norm of entrepreneurship and risk taking. Similarly, there is a norm that failure should not be punished but instead viewed as a learning experience.

Capabilities in Organizational Design   Organizational design skills are a result of managers' ability to create a structure, culture, and control systems that motivate and coordinate employees to perform at a high level. Organizational design is a major factor that influences a company's entrepreneurial capabilities; it is also an important determinant of a company's ability to create the functional competencies that give it a competitive advantage. The way strategic managers make organizational design decisions, such as how much autonomy to give to managers lower in the hierarchy, what kinds of norms and values should be developed to create an entrepreneurial culture, and even how to design its headquarters to encourage the free flow of ideas, is an important determinant of a diversified company's ability to profit from its multibusiness model. Effective organizational structure and controls create incentives that encourage business-unit (divisional) managers to maximize the efficiency and effectiveness of their units. Moreover, good organizational design helps prevent strategic managers from missing out on profitable new opportunities, as happens when employees become so concerned with protecting their company's competitive position in *existing* industries that they lose sight of new or improved ways to do business and gain profitable opportunities to enter new industries.

Chapters 11 and 12 of this book look at organizational design in depth. To profit from pursuing the corporate-level strategy of diversification, a company must be able to continuously manage and change its structure and culture to motivate and coordinate its employees to work at a high level and develop the resources and capabilities upon which its competitive advantage depends. The need to align a company's structure with its strategy is a complex, never-ending task, and only top managers with superior organizational design skills can do it.

Superior Strategic Management Capabilities   For diversification to increase profitability, a company's top managers must have superior capabilities in strategic

organizational design skills

The ability of a company's managers to create a structure, culture, and control systems that motivate and coordinate employees to perform at a high level.

management. They must possess the intangible, hard-to-define governance skills that are required to manage different business units in a way that enables these units to perform better than they would if they were independent companies.[7] These governance skills are a rare and valuable capability. However, certain CEOs and top managers seem to have them; they have developed the aptitude of managing multiple businesses simultaneously and encouraging the top managers of those business units to devise strategies that achieve superior performance. Examples of CEOs famous for their superior strategic management capabilities include Jeffrey Immelt at GE, Steve Jobs at Apple, and Larry Ellison at Oracle.

An especially important governance skill in a diversified company is the ability to diagnose the underlying source of the problems of a poorly performing business unit, and then to understand how to proceed to solve those problems. This might involve recommending new strategies to the existing top managers of the unit, or knowing when to replace them with a new management team that is better able to fix the problems. Top managers who have such governance skills tend to be very good at probing business-unit managers for information and helping them think through strategic problems, as the example of United Technologies Corporation (UTC) discussed in Strategy in Action 10.1 suggests.

10.1 STRATEGY IN ACTION

United Technologies Has an "ACE" in Its Pocket

United Technologies Corporation (UTC), based in Hartford, Connecticut, is a *conglomerate*, a company that owns a wide variety of other companies that operate separately in many different businesses and industries. UTC has businesses in two main groups, aerospace and building systems. Its aerospace group includes Sikorsky aircraft, Pratt & Whitney Engines, and UTC Aerospace systems, which was formed through the merger of Hamilton Sundstrand and Goodrich. Its building systems group includes Otis elevators and escalators; Carrier and Noresco heating and air-conditioning solutions; fire-detection and security businesses that include Chubb, Kidde, Edwards, Fenwal, Marioff, Supra, and Interlogix; and business that develop business automation systems (such as automatically controlled lighting and temperature) that include AutomatedLogic, Onity, Lenel, and UTEC.

Today, investors frown upon companies like UTC that own and operate companies in widely different industries. There is a growing perception that managers can better manage a company's business model when the company operates as an independent or stand-alone entity. How can UTC justify holding all these companies together in a conglomerate? Why would this lead to a greater increase in total profitability than if they operated as independent companies? In the last decade, the boards of directors and CEOs of many conglomerates such as Tyco and Textron have realized that by holding diverse companies together they were reducing, not increasing, the profitability of their companies. As a result, many conglomerates have been broken up, and their individual companies spun off to allow them to operate as separate, independent entities.

(continued)

UTC's CEO George David claims that he has created a unique, sophisticated, multibusiness model that adds value across UTC's diverse businesses. David joined Otis Elevator as an assistant to its CEO in 1975, but within a year, UTC acquired Otis. The 1970s was a decade when a "bigger is better" mindset ruled corporate America, and mergers and acquisitions of all kinds were seen as the best way to grow profits. UTC sent David to manage its South American operations and later gave him responsibility for its Japanese operations. Otis had formed an alliance with Matsushita to develop an elevator for the Japanese market, and the resulting "Elevonic 401," after being installed widely in Japanese buildings, proved to be a disaster. It broke down far more often than elevators made by other Japanese companies, and customers were concerned about the reliability and safety of this model.

Matsushita was extremely embarrassed about the elevator's failure and assigned one of its leading total quality management (TQM) experts, Yuzuru Ito, to head a team of Otis engineers to find out why it performed so poorly. Under Ito's direction, all employees—managers, designers, and production workers—who had produced the elevator analyzed why it was malfunctioning. This intensive study led to a total redesign of the elevator, and when the new, improved elevator was launched worldwide, it met with great success. Otis's share of the global elevator market dramatically increased, and David was named president of UTC in 1992. He was given the responsibility to cut costs across the entire corporation, including its important Pratt & Whitney division, and his success in reducing UTC's cost structure and increasing its ROIC led to his appointment as CEO in 1994.

Now responsible for all of UTC's diverse companies, David decided that the best way to increase UTC's profitability, which had been declining, was to find ways to improve efficiency and quality in *all* its constituent companies. He convinced Ito to move to Hartford and take responsibility for championing the kinds of improvements that had by now transformed the Otis division. Ito began to develop UTC's TQM system, also known as "Achieving Competitive Excellence," or ACE.

ACE is a set of tasks and procedures used by employees, from the shop floor to top management, to analyze all aspects of the way a product is made. The goal is to find ways to improve *quality and reliability*, to *lower the costs* of making a product, and, especially, to find ways to make the next generation of a particular product perform better—in other words, to encourage *technological innovation*. David makes every employee in every function at every level personally responsible for achieving the incremental, step-by-step gains that result in state-of-the-art, innovative, efficient products that allow a company to dominate its industry.

David calls these techniques "process disciplines," and he has used them to increase the performance of all UTC companies. Through these techniques, he has created the extra value for UTC that justifies it owning and operating such a diverse set of businesses. David's success can be seen in the performance that his company has achieved in the decade since he took control: he has quadrupled UTC's earnings per share, and its sales and profits have soared. UTC has been in the top three performers of the companies that make up the Dow Jones industrial average for most of the 2000s, and the company has consistently outperformed GE, another huge conglomerate, in its return to investors.

David and his managers believe that the gains that can be achieved from UTC's process disciplines are never-ending because its own R&D—in which it invests more than $2.5 billion a year—is constantly producing product innovations that can help all its businesses. Recognizing that its skills in creating process improvements are specific to manufacturing companies, UTC's strategy is to only acquire companies that make products that can benefit from the use of its ACE program—hence its Chubb acquisition. At the same time, David invests only in companies that have the potential to remain leading companies in their industries and can therefore charge above-average prices. His acquisitions strengthen the competencies of UTC's existing businesses. For example, he acquired Sundstrand, a leading aerospace and industrial systems company, and combined it with UTC's Hamilton Aerospace Division to create Hamilton Sundstrand, which is now a major supplier to Boeing and makes products that command premium prices. In October 2011, UTC acquired Goodrich, a major supplier of airline components, for over $22 billion in order to strengthen its aircraft division.

Source: http://utc.com.

Related to strategic management skills is the ability of the top managers of a diversified company to identify inefficient, poorly managed companies in other industries and then acquire and restructure them to improve their performance—and thus the profitability of the total corporation. This is known as a **turnaround strategy**.[8] There are several ways to improve the performance of an acquired company. First, the top managers of the acquired company are replaced with a more aggressive top-management team. Second, the new top-management team sells off expensive assets such as underperforming divisions, executive jets, and elaborate corporate headquarters; it also terminates staff to reduce the cost structure. Third, the new management team devises new strategies to improve the performance of the operations of the acquired business and improve its efficiency, quality, innovativeness, and customer responsiveness.

Fourth, to motivate the new top-management team and the other employees of the acquired company to work toward such goals, a companywide, pay-for-performance bonus system linked to profitability is introduced to reward employees at all levels for their hard work. Fifth, the acquiring company often establishes "stretch" goals for employees at all levels; these are challenging, hard-to-obtain goals that force employees at all levels to work to increase the company's efficiency and effectiveness. The members of the new top-management team clearly understand that if they fail to increase their division's performance and meet these stretch goals within some agreed-upon amount of time, they will be replaced. In sum, corporate managers of the acquiring company establish a system of rewards and sanctions that incentivize new top managers of the acquired unit to develop strategies to improve their unit's operating performance.

turnaround strategy
When managers of a diversified company identify inefficient, poorly managed companies in other industries and then acquire and restructure them to improve their performance—and thus the profitability of the total corporation.

TWO TYPES OF DIVERSIFICATION

The last section discussed five principal ways in which companies use diversification to transfer and implant their business models and strategies into other industries and so increase their long-term profitability. The two corporate strategies of *related diversification* and *unrelated diversification* can be distinguished by how they attempt to realize the five profit-enhancing benefits of diversification.[9]

Related Diversification

Related diversification is a corporate-level strategy based on the goal of establishing a business unit (division) in a new industry that is *related* to a company's existing business units by some form of commonality or linkage between the value-chain functions of the existing and new business units. As you might expect, the goal of this strategy is to obtain benefits from transferring competencies, leveraging competencies, sharing resources, and bundling products, as just discussed.

The multibusiness model of related diversification is based on taking advantage of strong technological, manufacturing, marketing, and sales commonalities between new and existing business units that can be successfully "tweaked" or modified to increase the competitive advantage of one or more business units. Figure 10.3 illustrates the commonalities or linkages possible among the different functions of three different business units or divisions. The greater the number of linkages that can be formed among business units, the greater the potential to realize the profit-enhancing benefits of the five reasons to diversify discussed previously.

related diversification
A corporate-level strategy based on the goal of establishing a business unit in a new industry that is related to a company's existing business units by some form of commonality or linkage between their value-chain functions.

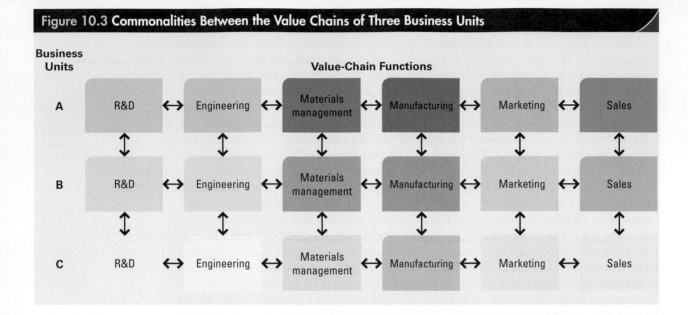

Figure 10.3 Commonalities Between the Value Chains of Three Business Units

Another advantage of related diversification is that it can allow a company to use any general organizational competency it possesses to increase the overall performance of *all* its different industry divisions. For example, strategic managers may strive to create a structure and culture that encourages entrepreneurship across divisions, as Google, Apple, and 3M have done; beyond these general competences, these companies all have a set of distinctive competences that can be shared among their different business units and that they continuously strive to improve.

Unrelated Diversification

unrelated diversification

A corporate-level strategy based on a multibusiness model that uses general organizational competencies to increase the performance of all the company's business units.

internal capital market

A corporate-level strategy whereby the firm's headquarters assesses the performance of business units and allocates money across them. Cash generated by units that are profitable but have poor investment opportunities within their business is used to cross-subsidize businesses that need cash and have strong promise for long-run profitability.

Unrelated diversification is a corporate-level strategy whereby firms own unrelated businesses and attempt to increase their value through an internal capital market, the use of general organizational competencies, or both. Business organizations that operate in many diverse industries are often called *conglomerates*. An **internal capital market** refers to a situation whereby corporate headquarters assesses the performance of business units and allocates money across them. Cash generated by units that are profitable but have poor investment opportunities within their business is used to cross-subsidize businesses that need cash and have strong promise for long-run profitability. A large, diverse firm may have free cash generated from its internal businesses, or readier access to cheap cash on the external capital market than an individual business unit might have. For example, GE's large capital reserves and excellent credit rating enable it to provide funding to advanced-technology businesses within its corporate umbrella (e.g., solar power stations, subsea oil-production equipment, avionics, photonics) that would otherwise pay a high price (either in interest payments or equity shares) for funding due to their inherent uncertainty.

The benefits of an internal capital market are limited, however, by the efficiency of the external capital market (banks, stockholders, venture capitalists, angel investors, and so on). If the external capital market were perfectly efficient, managers could not create additional value by cross-subsidizing businesses with internal cash. An internal capital market is, in essence, an arbitrage strategy whereby managers make money by making better investment decisions within the firm than the external capital market would, often because they possess superior information. The amount of value that can be created through an internal capital market is thus directly proportional to the inefficiency of the external capital market. In the United States, where capital markets have become fairly efficient due to (1) reporting requirements mandated by the Securities and Exchange Commission (SEC), (2) large numbers of research analysts, (3) an extremely large and active investment community, (4) strong communication systems, and (5) strong contract law, it is not common to see firms create significant value through an internal capital market. As a result, few large conglomerates have survived, and many of those that do survive trade at a discount (that is, their stock is worth less than the stock of more specialized firms operating in the same industries). On the other hand, in a market with a less efficient capital market, conglomerates may create significant value. Tata Group, for example, is an extremely large, diverse, business-holding group in India. Founded during the 1800s, it took on many projects that its founders felt were crucial to India's development (for example, developing a rail transportation system, hotels, and power production). The lack of a well-developed investment community and poor contract law to protect investors and bankers meant that funds were often not available to entrepreneurs in India, or were available only at a very high cost. Tata Group was thus able to use cross-subsidization to fund projects much more cheaply than independent businesses could. Furthermore, the reputation of the company served as a strong guarantee that it would fulfill its promises (which was particularly important in the absence of strong contract law), and its long, deep relationships with the government gave it an advantage in securing licenses and permits.

Companies pursuing a strategy of unrelated diversification have *no* intention of transferring or leveraging competencies between business units or sharing resources other than cash and general organizational competencies. If the strategic managers of conglomerates have the special skills needed to manage many companies in diverse industries, the strategy can result in superior performance and profitability; often they do not have these skills, as is discussed later in the chapter. Companies such as UTC (discussed in Strategy in Action 10.1) have top managers who do possess these special skills.

◤ THE LIMITS AND DISADVANTAGES OF DIVERSIFICATION

Many companies, such as 3M, Samsung, UTC, and Cisco, have achieved the benefits of pursuing either or both of the two diversification strategies just discussed, and they have sustained their profitability over time. On the other hand, GM, Tyco, Textron, and Philips failed miserably and became unprofitable when they pursued diversification. There are three principal reasons why a business model based on diversification may lead to a loss of competitive advantage: (1) changes in the industry or inside a company that occur over time, (2) diversification pursued for the wrong reasons, and (3) excessive diversification that results in increasing bureaucratic costs.

Changes in the Industry or Company

Diversification is a complex strategy. To pursue it, top managers must have the ability to recognize profitable opportunities to enter new industries and implement the strategies necessary to make diversification profitable. Over time, a company's top-management team often changes; sometimes its most able executives join other companies and become CEOs, and sometimes successful CEOs retire or step down. When the managers who possess the hard-to-define skills leave, they often take their vision with them. A company's new leaders may lack the competency or commitment necessary to pursue diversification successfully over time; thus, the cost structure of the diversified company increases and eliminates any gains the strategy may have produced.

In addition, the environment often changes rapidly and unpredictably over time. When new technology blurs industry boundaries, it can destroy the source of a company's competitive advantage. For example, by 2011, it was clear that Apple's iPhone and iPad had become a direct competitor with Nintendo's and Sony's mobile gaming consoles. When such a major technological change occurs in a company's core business, the benefits it has previously achieved from transferring or leveraging distinctive competencies disappear. The company is then saddled with a collection of businesses that have all become poor performers in their respective industries because they are not based on the new technology—something that has happened to Sony. Thus, a major problem with diversification is that the future success of a business is hard to predict when this strategy is used. For a company to profit from it over time, managers must be as willing to divest business units as they are to acquire them. Research suggests managers do not behave in this way, however.

Diversification for the Wrong Reasons

As we have discussed, when managers decide to pursue diversification, they must have a clear vision of how their entry into new industries will allow them to create new products that provide more value for customers and increase their company's profitability. Over time, however, a diversification strategy may result in falling profitability for reasons noted earlier, but managers often refuse to recognize that their strategy is failing. Although they know they should divest unprofitable businesses, managers "make up" reasons to keep their collection of businesses together.

In the past, for example, one widely used (and false) justification for diversification was that the strategy would allow a company to obtain the benefits of risk pooling. The idea behind risk pooling is that a company can reduce the risk of its revenues and profits rising and falling sharply (something that sharply lowers its stock price) if it acquires and operates companies in several industries that have different business cycles. The business cycle is the tendency for the revenues and profits of companies in an industry to rise and fall over time because of "predictable" changes in customer demand. For example, even in a recession, people still need to eat—the profits earned by supermarket chains will be relatively stable; sales at Safeway, Kroger, and also at "dollar stores," actually rise as shoppers attempt to get more value for their dollars. At the same time, a recession can cause demand for cars and luxury goods to plunge. Many CEOs argue that diversifying into industries that have different business cycles would allow the sales and revenues of some of their divisions to rise, while sales and revenues in other divisions would fall. A more stable stream of revenue and profits is the net result over time. An example of risk pooling occurred when U.S. Steel diversified into the oil and gas industry in an attempt to offset the adverse effects of cyclical downturns in the steel industry.

This argument ignores two important facts. First, stockholders can eliminate the risk inherent in holding an individual stock by diversifying their own portfolios, and they can do so at a much lower cost than a company can. Thus, attempts to pool risks through diversification represent an unproductive use of resources; instead, profits should be returned to shareholders in the form of increased dividends. Second, research suggests that corporate diversification is not an effective way to pool risks because the business cycles of different industries are *inherently difficult to predict,* so it is likely that a diversified company will find that an economic downturn affects *all* its industries simultaneously. If this happens, the company's profitability plunges.[10]

When a company's core business is in trouble, another mistaken justification for diversification is that entry into new industries will rescue the core business and lead to long-term growth and profitability. One company that made this mistake is Kodak. In the 1980s, increased competition from low-cost, Japanese competitors such as Fuji, combined with the beginnings of the digital revolution, soon led its revenues and profits to plateau and then fall. Its managers should have done all they could to reduce its cost structure; instead, they took its huge free cash flow and spent tens of billions of dollars to enter new industries such as health care, biotechnology, and computer hardware in a desperate and mistaken attempt to find ways to increase profitability.

This was a disaster because every industry Kodak entered was populated by strong companies such as 3M, Canon, and Xerox. Also, Kodak's corporate managers lacked any general competencies to give their new business units a competitive advantage. Moreover, the more industries Kodak entered, the greater the range of threats the company encountered, and the more time managers had to spend dealing with these threats. As a result, they could spend much less time improving the performance of their core film business, which continued to decline.

In reality, Kodak's diversification was solely for growth, but *growth does not create value for stockholders*; growth is the by-product, not the objective, of a diversification strategy. However, in desperation, companies diversify for reasons of growth alone rather than to gain any well-thought-out, strategic advantage.[11] In fact, many studies suggest that too much diversification may reduce rather than improve company profitability.[12] That is, the diversification strategies many companies pursue may *reduce* value instead of creating it.[13]

The Bureaucratic Costs of Diversification

A major reason why diversification often fails to boost profitability is that, very often, the *bureaucratic costs* of diversification exceed the benefits created by the strategy (that is, the increased profit that results when a company makes and sells a wider range of differentiated products and/or lowers its cost structure). As we mention

bureaucratic costs

The costs associated with solving the transaction difficulties between business units and corporate headquarters as a company obtains the benefits from transferring, sharing, and leveraging competencies.

in the previous chapter, **bureaucratic costs** are the costs associated with solving the transaction difficulties that arise between a company's business units and between business units and corporate headquarters, as the company attempts to obtain the benefits from transferring, sharing, and leveraging competencies. They also include the costs associated with using general organizational competencies to solve managerial and functional inefficiencies. The level of bureaucratic costs in a diversified organization is a function of two factors: the number of business units in a company's portfolio, and the degree to which coordination is required between these different business units to realize the advantages of diversification.

Number of Businesses   The greater the number of business units in a company's portfolio, the more difficult it is for corporate managers to remain informed about the complexities of each business. Managers simply do not have the time to assess the business model of each unit. This problem occurred at GE in the 1970s, when its growth-hungry CEO Reg Jones acquired many new businesses. As he commented:

> I tried to review each plan [of each business unit] in great detail. This effort took untold hours and placed a tremendous burden on the corporate executive office. After a while I began to realize that no matter how hard we would work, we could not achieve the necessary in-depth understanding of the 40-odd business unit plans.[14]

The inability of top managers in extensively diversified companies to maintain control over their multibusiness models over time often leads them to base important resource-allocation decisions on a superficial analysis of each business unit's competitive position. For example, a promising business unit may be starved of investment funds, while other business units receive far more cash than they can profitably reinvest in their operations. Furthermore, because they are distant from the day-to-day operations of the business units, corporate managers may find that business-unit managers try to hide information on poor performance to save their own jobs. For example, business-unit managers might blame poor performance on difficult competitive conditions, even when it is the result of their inability to craft a successful business model. As such organizational problems increase, top managers must spend an enormous amount of time and effort to solve them. This increases bureaucratic costs and cancels out the profit-enhancing advantages of pursuing diversification, such as those obtained from sharing or leveraging competencies.

Coordination Among Businesses   The amount of coordination required to realize value from a diversification strategy based on transferring, sharing, or leveraging competencies is a major source of bureaucratic costs. The bureaucratic mechanisms needed to oversee and manage the coordination and handoffs between units, such as cross-business-unit teams and management committees, are a major source of these costs. A second source of bureaucratic costs arises because of the enormous amount of managerial time and effort required to accurately measure the performance and unique profit contribution of a business unit that is transferring or sharing resources with another. Consider a company that has two business units, one making household products (such as liquid soap and laundry detergent) and another making packaged food products. The products of both units are sold through supermarkets. To lower the cost structure, the parent company decides to pool the marketing and sales functions

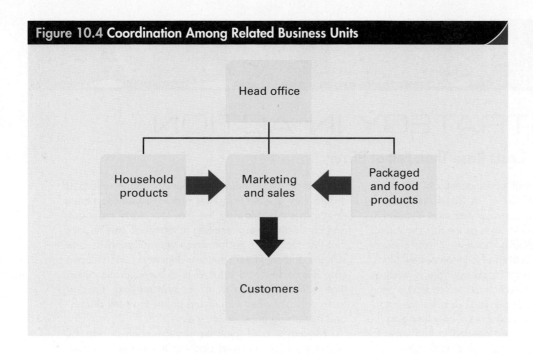

Figure 10.4 Coordination Among Related Business Units

Head office

Household products → Marketing and sales ← Packaged and food products

↓

Customers

of each business unit, using an organizational structure similar to that illustrated in Figure 10.4. The company is organized into three divisions: a household products division, a food products division, and a marketing division.

Although such an arrangement may significantly lower operating costs, it can also give rise to substantial control problems, and hence bureaucratic costs. For example, if the performance of the household products business begins to slip, identifying who is to be held accountable—managers in the household products division or managers in the marketing division—may prove difficult. Indeed, each may blame the other for poor performance. Although such problems can be resolved if corporate management performs an in-depth audit of both divisions, the bureaucratic costs (managers' time and effort) involved in doing so may once again cancel out any value achieved from diversification. The need to reduce bureaucratic costs is evident from the experience of Pfizer, discussed in Strategy in Action 10.2.

In sum, although diversification can be a highly profitable strategy to pursue, it is also the most complex and difficult strategy to manage because it is based on a complex, multibusiness model. Even when a company has pursued this strategy successfully in the past, changing conditions both in the industry environment and within a company can quickly reduce the profit-creating advantages of this strategy. For example, such changes may result in one or more business units losing their competitive advantage, as happened to Sony. Or, changes may cause the bureaucratic costs associated with pursuing diversification to rise sharply and cancel out its advantages. Thus, the existence of bureaucratic costs places a limit on the amount of diversification that a company can profitably pursue. It makes sense for a company to diversify only when the profit-enhancing advantages of this strategy exceed the bureaucratic costs of managing the increasing number of business units required when a company expands and enters new industries.

10.2 STRATEGY IN ACTION

How Bureaucratic Costs Rose Then Fell at Pfizer

Pfizer is the largest global pharmaceuticals company, with sales of almost $50 billion in 2014. Its research scientists have innovated some of the most successful, profitable drugs in the world, such as the first cholesterol reducer, Lipitor. In the 2000s, however, Pfizer encountered major problems in its attempt to innovate new blockbuster drugs while its current blockbuster drugs, such as Lipitor, lost their patent protection. Whereas Lipitor once earned $13 billion in profits per year, its sales were now fast declining. By 2012, Lipitor was only bringing in $3.9 billion. Pfizer desperately needed to find ways to make its product development pipeline work. One manager, Martin Mackay, believed he knew how to do it.

When Pfizer's R&D chief retired, Mackay, his deputy, made it clear to CEO Jeffrey Kindler that he wanted the job. Kindler made it equally clear he thought the company could use some new talent and fresh ideas to solve its problems. Mackay realized he had to quickly devise a convincing plan to change the way Pfizer's scientists worked to develop new drugs, gain Kindler's support, and get the top job. He created a detailed plan for changing the way Pfizer's thousands of researchers made decisions, ensuring that the company's resources, talent, and funds would be put to their best use. After Kindler reviewed the plan, he was so impressed he promoted Mackay to the top R&D position. What was Mackay's plan?

As Pfizer had grown over time as a result of mergers with two large pharmaceutical companies, Warner Lambert and Pharmacia, Mackay noted how decision-making problems and conflict between the managers of Pfizer's different drug divisions had increased. As it grew, Pfizer's organizational structure had become taller and taller, and the size of its headquarters staff grew. With more managers and levels in the company's hierarchy there was a great need for committees to integrate across activities. However, in meetings, different groups of managers fought to promote the development of the drugs in which they had the most interest, and increas-

ingly came into conflict with one another in efforts to ensure they got the resources needed to develop these drugs. In short, Mackay felt that too many managers and committees were resulting in too much conflict, and that the company's performance was suffering as a result. In addition, Pfizer's success depended upon innovation, but conflict had resulted in a bureaucratic culture that reduced the quality of decision making, creating more difficulty when identifying promising new drugs—and increasing bureaucratic costs.

Mackay's bold plan to reduce conflict and bureaucratic costs involved slashing the number of management layers between top managers and scientists from fourteen to seven, which resulted in the layoff of thousands of Pfizer's managers. He also abolished the product development committees whose wrangling he believed was slowing down the process of transforming innovative ideas into blockbuster drugs. After streamlining the hierarchy, he focused on reducing the number of bureaucratic rules scientists had to follow, many of which were unnecessary and promoted conflict. He and his team eliminated every kind of written report that was slowing the innovation process. For example, scientists had been in the habit of submitting quarterly and monthly reports to top managers explaining each drug's progress; Mackay told them to choose one report or the other.

As you can imagine, Mackay's efforts caused enormous upheaval in the company, as managers fought to keep their positions and scientists fought to protect the drugs they had in development. However, a resolute Mackay pushed his agenda through with the support of the CEO, who defended his efforts to create a new R&D product development process that empowered Pfizer's scientists and promoted innovation and entrepreneurship. Pfizer's scientists reported that they felt "liberated" by the new work flow; the level of conflict decreased, and they felt hopeful that new drugs would be produced more quickly.

Source: www.pfizer.com.

CHOOSING A STRATEGY

Related Versus Unrelated Diversification

Because related diversification involves more sharing of competencies, one might think it can boost profitability in more ways than unrelated diversification, and is therefore the better diversification strategy. However, some companies can create as much or more value from pursuing unrelated diversification, so this strategy must also have some substantial benefits. An unrelated company does *not* need to achieve coordination between business units; it has to cope only with the bureaucratic costs that arise from the number of businesses in its portfolio. In contrast, a related company must achieve coordination *among* business units if it is to realize the gains that come from utilizing its distinctive competencies. Consequently, it has to cope with the bureaucratic costs that arise *both* from the number of business units in its portfolio *and* from coordination among business units. Although it is true that related diversified companies can create value and profit in more ways than unrelated companies, they also have to bear higher bureaucratic costs to do so. These higher costs may cancel out the greater benefits, making the strategy no more profitable than one of unrelated diversification.

How, then, does a company choose between these strategies? The choice depends upon a comparison of the benefits of each strategy against the bureaucratic costs of pursuing it. It pays for a company to pursue related diversification when (1) the company's competencies can be applied across a greater number of industries and (2) the company has superior strategic capabilities that allow it to keep bureaucratic costs under close control—perhaps by encouraging entrepreneurship or by developing a value creating organizational culture.

Using the same logic, it pays for a company to pursue unrelated diversification when (1) each business unit's functional competencies have few useful applications across industries, but the company's top managers are skilled at raising the profitability of poorly run businesses and (2) the company's managers use their superior strategic management competencies to improve the competitive advantage of their business units and keep bureaucratic costs under control. Well-managed companies such as UTC (discussed in Strategy in Action 10.1) have managers who can successfully pursue unrelated diversification and reap its rewards.

The Web of Corporate-Level Strategy

Finally, it is important to note that although some companies may choose to pursue a strategy of related or unrelated diversification, there is nothing that stops them from pursuing both strategies at the same time. The purpose of corporate-level strategy is to increase long-term profitability. A company can pursue multiple strategies as long as strategic managers have weighed the advantages and disadvantages of those strategies and arrived at a multibusiness model that justifies them. Figure 10.5 illustrates how Sony developed a web of corporate strategies to compete in many industries—a program that proved a mistake and reduced its differentiation advantage and increased its cost structure in the 2000s.

Sony's core business is in electronic products, and in the past, it was well known for innovative products that made it a leading, global brand. To protect the quality of its electronic products, Sony decided to manufacture a high percentage of the component

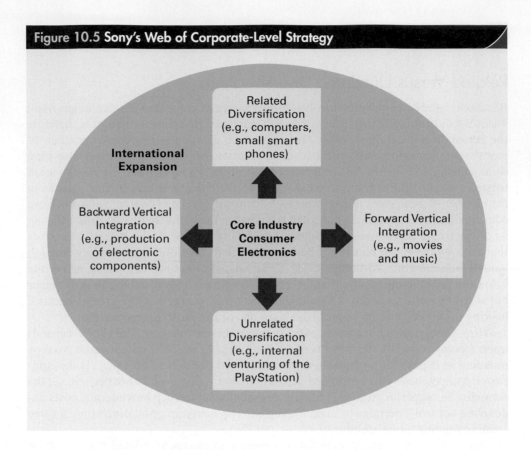

Figure 10.5 Sony's Web of Corporate-Level Strategy

parts for its televisions, DVD players, and other units and pursued a strategy of backward vertical integration. Sony also engaged in forward vertical integration: for example, it acquired Columbia Pictures and MGM to enter the movie or "entertainment software" industry, and it opened a chain of Sony stores in shopping malls (to compete with Apple). Sony also shared and leveraged its distinctive competencies by developing its own business units to operate in the computer and smartphone industries, a strategy of related diversification. Finally, when it decided to enter the home videogame industry and develop its PlayStation to compete with Nintendo, it was pursuing a strategy of unrelated diversification. In the 2000s, this division contributed more to Sony's profits than its core electronics business—but the company has not been doing well.

As this discussion suggests, Sony's profitability has fallen dramatically because its multibusiness model led it to diversify into too many industries, in each of which the focus was upon innovating high-quality products. As a result, its cost structure increased so much it swallowed up all the profits its businesses were generating. Sony's strategy of individual-business-unit autonomy also resulted in each unit pursuing its own goals at the expense of the company's multibusiness model—which escalated bureaucratic costs and drained its profitability. In particular, because its different divisions did not share their knowledge and expertise, this incongruence allowed competitors such as Samsung to supersede Sony, especially with smartphones and flatscreen, LCD TV products.

ENTERING NEW INDUSTRIES: INTERNAL NEW VENTURES

We have discussed the sources of value managers seek through corporate-level strategies of related and unrelated diversification (and the challenges and risks these strategies also impose). Now we turn to the three main methods managers employ to enter new industries: internal new ventures, acquisitions, and joint ventures. In this section, we consider the pros and cons of using internal new ventures. In the following sections, we look at acquisitions and joint ventures.

The Attractions of Internal New Venturing

Internal new venturing is typically used to implement corporate-level strategies when a company possesses one or more distinctive competencies in its core business model that can be leveraged or recombined to enter a new industry. **Internal new venturing** is the process of transferring resources to, and creating a new business unit or division in, a new industry. Internal venturing is used often by companies that have a business model based upon using their technology or design skills to innovate new kinds of products and enter related markets or industries. Thus, technology-based companies that pursue related diversification—for example, DuPont, which has created new markets with products such as cellophane, nylon, Freon, and Teflon—are most likely to use internal new venturing. 3M has a near-legendary knack for creating new or improved products from internally generated ideas, and then establishing new business units to create the business model that enables it to dominate a new market. Similarly, HP entered into the computer and printer industries by using internal new venturing.

A company may also use internal venturing to enter a newly emerging or embryonic industry—one in which no company has yet developed the competencies or business model to give it a dominant position in that industry. This was Monsanto's situation in 1979, when it contemplated entering the biotechnology field to produce herbicides and pest-resistant crop seeds. The biotechnology field was young at that time, and there were no incumbent companies focused on applying biotechnology to agricultural products. Accordingly, Monsanto internally ventured a new division to develop the required competencies necessary to enter and establish a strong competitive position in this newly emerging industry.

internal new venturing
The process of transferring resources to, and creating a new business unit or division in, a new industry to innovate new kinds of products.

Pitfalls of New Ventures

Despite the popularity of internal new venturing, there is a high risk of failure. Research suggests that somewhere between 33 and 60% of all new products that reach the marketplace do not generate an adequate economic return,[15] and that most of these products were the result of internal new ventures. Three reasons are often put forward to explain the relatively high failure rate of internal new ventures: (1) market entry on too small a scale, (2) poor commercialization of the new-venture product, and (3) poor corporate management of the new-venture division.[16]

Scale of Entry Research suggests that large-scale entry into a new industry is often a critical precondition for the success of a new venture. In the short run, this means that a substantial capital investment must be made to support large-scale entry; thus, there is a risk of major losses if the new venture fails. But, in the long run—which can be as long as 5 to 12 years (depending on the industry)—such a large investment results in far greater returns than if a company chooses to enter on a small scale to limit its investment and reduce potential losses.[17] Large-scale entrants can more rapidly realize scale economies, build brand loyalty, and gain access to distribution channels in the new industry, all of which increase the probability of new-venture success. In contrast, small-scale entrants may find themselves handicapped by high costs due to lack of scale economies and lack of market presence, which limits the entrant's ability to build brand loyalty and gain access to distribution channels. These scale effects are particularly significant when a company is entering an established industry in which incumbent companies possess scale economies, brand loyalty, and access to distribution channels. In that case, the new entrant must make a major investment to succeed.

Figure 10.6 plots the relationship between scale of entry and profitability over time for successful small-scale and large-scale ventures. The figure shows that successful small-scale entry is associated with lower initial losses, but in the long term, large-scale entry generates greater returns. However, because of the high costs and risks associated with large-scale entry, many companies make the mistake of choosing a small-scale entry strategy, which often means they fail to build the market share necessary for long-term success.

Commercialization   Many internal new ventures are driven by the opportunity to use a new or advanced technology to make better products and outperform competitors in a market. To succeed commercially, the products under development must be tailored to meet the needs of customers. New ventures often fail because the company ignores these needs; its managers become so focused on the technological possibilities of the new product that customer requirements are forgotten.[18] Thus, a new venture may fail because it is marketing a product based on a technology for which there is no demand, or the company fails to correctly position or differentiate the product in the market to attract customers.

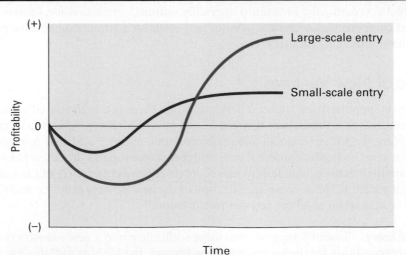

Figure 10.6 Scale of Entry and Profitability

For example, consider the desktop PC marketed by NeXT, a company started by Apple founder Steve Jobs. The NeXT system failed to gain market share because the PC incorporated an array of expensive technologies that consumers simply did not want, such as optical disk drives and hi-fidelity sound. The optical disk drives, in particular, turned off customers because it was difficult to move work from PCs with floppy drives to NeXT machines with optical drives. In other words, NeXT failed because its founder was so dazzled by leading-edge technology that he ignored customer needs. However, Jobs redeemed himself and was named "CEO of the Decade" by *Fortune* magazine in 2010, after he successfully commercialized Apple's iPod, which dominates the MP3 player market. Also, the iPhone set the standard in the smartphone market, and the iPad quickly dominated the tablet computer market following its introduction in 2010.

Poor Implementation   Managing the new-venture process, and controlling the new-venture division, creates many difficult managerial and organizational problems.[19] For example, one common mistake companies make to try to increase their chances of introducing successful products is to establish too many internal new-venture divisions at the same time. Managers attempt to spread the risks of failure by having many divisions, but this places enormous demands upon a company's cash flow. Sometimes, companies are forced to reduce the funding each division receives to keep the entire company profitable, and this can result in the most promising ventures being starved of the cash they need in order to succeed.[20] Another common mistake is when corporate managers fail to do the extensive advanced planning necessary to ensure that the new venture's business model is sound and contains all the elements that will be needed later if it is to succeed. Sometimes corporate managers leave this process to the scientists and engineers championing the new technology. Focused on the new technology, managers may innovate new products that have little strategic or commercial value. Corporate managers and scientists must work together to clarify how and why a new venture will lead to a product that has a competitive advantage, and jointly establish strategic objectives and a timetable to manage the venture until the product reaches the market.

The failure to anticipate the time and costs involved in the new-venture process constitutes a further mistake. Many companies have unrealistic expectations regarding the time frame and expect profits to flow in quickly. Research suggests that some companies operate with a philosophy of killing new businesses if they do not turn a profit by the end of the third year, which is unrealistic given that it can take 5 years or more before a new venture generates substantial profits.

Guidelines for Successful Internal New Venturing

To avoid these pitfalls, a company should adopt a well-thought-out, structured approach to manage internal new venturing. New venturing is based on R&D. It begins with the *exploratory research* necessary to advance basic science and technology (the "R" in R&D) and *development research* to identify, develop, and perfect the commercial applications of a new technology (the "D" in R&D). Companies with strong track records of success at internal new venturing excel at both kinds of R&D; they help to advance basic science and discover important commercial applications for it.[21] To advance basic science, it is important for companies to have strong links with universities, where much of the scientific knowledge that underlies new technologies is discovered. It is also important to make sure that research funds are being controlled by scientists who understand the importance of both "R" and "D" research. If the "D" is lacking, a company will probably generate few successful commercial ventures no matter how well it does basic research. Companies can take a number of steps to ensure that good science ends up with good, commercially viable products.

First, many companies must place the funding for research into the hands of business-unit managers who have the skill or knowhow to narrow down and then select the optimal set of research projects—those that have the best chance of a significant commercial payoff. Second, to make effective use of its R&D competency, top managers must work with R&D scientists to continually develop and improve the business model and strategies that guide their efforts, and make sure that all its scientists and engineers understand what they have to do to make it succeed.[22]

Third, a company must foster close links between R&D and marketing to increase the probability that a new product will be a commercial success in the future. When marketing works to identify the most important customer requirements for a new product and then communicates these requirements to scientists, it ensures that research projects meet the needs of their intended customers. Fourth, a company should also foster close links between R&D and manufacturing to ensure that it has the ability to make a proposed new product in a cost-effective way. Many companies successfully integrate the activities of the different functions by creating cross-functional project teams to oversee the development of new products from their inception to market introduction. This approach can significantly reduce the time it takes to bring a new product to market. For example, while R&D is working on design, manufacturing is setting up facilities, and marketing is developing a campaign to show customers how much the new product will benefit them.

Finally, because large-scale entry often leads to greater long-term profits, a company can promote the success of internal new venturing by "thinking big." A company should construct efficient-scale manufacturing facilities and allocate marketing a large budget to develop a future product campaign that will build market presence and brand loyalty quickly and well in advance of that product's introduction. Also, corporate managers should not panic when customers are slow to adopt the new product; they need to accept the fact there will be initial losses and recognize that as long as market share is expanding, the product will eventually succeed.

▮ ENTERING NEW INDUSTRIES: ACQUISITIONS

In Chapter 9, we explained that acquisitions are the main vehicle that companies use to implement a horizontal integration strategy. Acquisitions are also a principal way companies enter new industries to pursue vertical integration and diversification, so it is necessary to understand both the benefits and risks associated with using acquisitions to implement a corporate-level strategy.

The Attraction of Acquisitions

In general, acquisitions are used to pursue vertical integration or diversification when a company lacks the distinctive competencies necessary to compete in a new industry, and so uses its financial resources to purchase an established company that has those competencies. A company is particularly likely to use acquisitions when it needs to move rapidly to establish a presence in an industry, commonly an embryonic or growth industry. Entering a new industry through internal venturing is a relatively slow process; acquisition is a much quicker way for a company to establish a significant market presence. A company can purchase a leading company with a strong competitive position in months, rather than waiting years to build a market leadership position by engaging in internal venturing. Thus, when speed is particularly important, acquisition is the favored entry mode. Intel, for example, used acquisitions to build its communications chip business because it sensed that the market was developing very quickly, and that it would take too long to develop the required competencies.

In addition, acquisitions are often perceived as being less risky than internal new ventures because they involve less commercial uncertainty. Because of the risks of failure associated with internal new venturing, it is difficult to predict its future success and profitability. By contrast, when a company makes an acquisition it acquires a company with an already established reputation, and it knows the magnitude of the company's market share and profitability.

Finally, acquisitions are an attractive way to enter an industry that is protected by high barriers to entry. Recall from Chapter 2 that barriers to entry arise from factors such as product differentiation, which leads to brand loyalty, and high market share, which leads to economies of scale. When entry barriers are high, it may be very difficult for a company to enter an industry through internal new venturing because it will have to construct large-scale manufacturing facilities and invest in a massive advertising campaign to establish brand loyalty—difficult goals that require huge capital expenditures. In contrast, if a company acquires another company already established in the industry, possibly the market leader, it can circumvent most entry barriers because that company has already achieved economies of scale and obtained brand loyalty. In general, the higher the barriers to entry, the more likely it is that acquisitions will be the method used to enter the industry.

Acquisition Pitfalls

For these reasons, acquisitions have long been the most common method that companies use to pursue diversification. However, as we mentioned earlier, research suggests that many acquisitions fail to increase the profitability of the acquiring company and may result in losses. A study of 700 large acquisitions found that although 30% of these resulted in higher profits, 31% led to losses, and the remainder had little impact.[23] Research suggests that many acquisitions fail to realize their anticipated benefits.[24] One study of the postacquisition performance of acquired companies found that their profitability and market share often decline, suggesting that many acquisitions destroy rather than create value.[25]

Acquisitions may fail to raise the performance of the acquiring companies for four reasons: (1) companies frequently experience management problems when they attempt to integrate a different company's organizational structure and culture into their own; (2) companies often overestimate the potential economic benefits from an acquisition; (3) acquisitions tend to be so expensive that they do not increase future profitability; and (4) companies are often negligent in screening their acquisition targets and fail to recognize important problems with their business models.

Integrating the Acquired Company   Once an acquisition has been made, the acquiring company must integrate the acquired company and combine it with its own organizational structure and culture. Integration involves the adoption of common management and financial control systems, the joining together of operations from the acquired and the acquiring company, the establishment of bureaucratic mechanisms to share information and personnel, and the need to create a common culture.[26] Experience has shown that many problems can occur as companies attempt to integrate their activities. When the processes and cultures of two companies are very different, integration can be extremely challenging. For example, when Daimler Benz acquired Chrysler, the two companies discovered that the more formal and hierarchical culture at Daimler chafed Chrysler employees, who were used to a looser, more entrepreneurial culture. Furthermore, though Daimler had hoped to benefit from Chrysler's more rapid new-product development processes, they soon realized that to do so they would have to adopt a more modular approach to developing cars, for instance by re-using platforms across different car models. This contrasted sharply with Daimler's historic emphasis on holistic "ground up" development of car designs. In the end, few of the anticipated advantages of the acquisition materialized. After paying roughly $36 billion for Chrysler (through a stock swap), Daimler ended up having to *pay out* another $650 million to Cerberus Capital Management to shed the Chrysler group.[27]

Many acquired companies experience high management turnover because their employees do not like the acquiring company's way of operating—its structure and culture.[28] Research suggests that the loss of management talent and expertise, and the damage from constant tension between the businesses, can materially harm the performance of the acquired unit.[29] Moreover, companies often must take on an enormous amount of debt to fund an acquisition, and they are frequently unable to pay it once the management problems (and sometimes the weaknesses) of the acquired company's business model surface.

Overestimating Economic Benefits   Even when companies find it easy to integrate their activities, they often overestimate the combined businesses' future profitability. Managers often overestimate the competitive advantages that will derive from the acquisition and so pay more for the acquired company than it is worth. One reason is that top managers typically overestimate their own general competencies to create valuable new products from an acquisition (this is known as the "hubris hypothesis").[30] The very fact that they have risen to the top of a company gives some managers an exaggerated sense of their own capabilities and a self-importance that distorts their strategic decision making. Coca-Cola's acquisition of a number of mid-sized winemakers illustrates this. Reasoning that a beverage is a beverage, Coca-Cola's then-CEO decided he would be able to mobilize his company's talented marketing managers to develop the strategies needed to dominate the U.S. wine industry. After purchasing three wine companies and enduring 7 years of marginal profits because of failed marketing campaigns, he subsequently decided that wine and soft drinks are very different products; in particular, they have different kinds of appeal, pricing systems, and distribution networks. Coca-Cola eventually sold the wine operations to Joseph E. Seagram and took a substantial loss.[31]

The Expense of Acquisitions   Perhaps the most important reason for the failure of acquisitions is that acquiring a company with stock that is publicly traded tends to be very expensive—and the expense of the acquisition can more than wipe out the value of the stream of future profits that are expected from the acquisition. One reason is that the top managers of a company that is "targeted" for acquisition are likely to resist any takeover attempt unless the acquiring company agrees to pay a substantial premium above its current market value. These premiums are often 30 to 50% above the usual value of a company's stock. Similarly, the stockholders of the target company are unlikely to sell their stock unless they are paid major premiums over market value prior to a takeover bid. Collectively, this means that it is far easier to overpay for an acquisition target than to "get a bargain," and research shows that managers do regularly overpay for acquisitions.[32]

To pay such high premiums, the acquiring company must be certain it can use its acquisition to generate the stream of future profits that justifies the high price of the target company. This is frequently difficult to do given how fast the industry environment can change and other problems discussed earlier such as integrating the acquired company. This is a major reason why acquisitions are frequently unprofitable for the acquiring company.

The reason why the acquiring company must pay such a high premium is that the stock price of the acquisition target increases enormously during the acquisition process as investors speculate on the final price the acquiring company will pay to capture it. In the case of a contested bidding contest, where two or more companies simultaneously bid to acquire the target company, its stock price may surge. Also, when many acquisitions are occurring in one particular industry, investors speculate that the value of the remaining industry companies that have *not* been acquired has increased, and that a bid for these companies will be made at some future point. This also drives up their stock price and increases the cost of making acquisitions. This happened in the telecommunications sector when, to make sure they could meet the needs of customers who were demanding leading-edge equipment, many large companies went on acquisition "binges." Nortel and Alcatel-Lucent engaged in a race to purchase smaller, innovative companies that were developing new telecommunications equipment. The result was that the stock prices for these companies were bid up by investors, and they were purchased at a hugely inflated price. When the telecommunications boom turned to bust, the acquiring companies found that they had vastly overpaid for their acquisitions and had to take enormous accounting write-downs. Nortel was forced to declare bankruptcy and sold off all its assets, and the value of Alcatel-Lucent's stock plunged almost 90%.

Inadequate Pre-acquisition Screening   As the problems of these companies suggest, top managers often do a poor job of pre-acquisition screening—that is, evaluating how much a potential acquisition may increase future profitability. Researchers have discovered that one important reason for the failure of an acquisition is that managers make the decision to acquire other companies without thoroughly analyzing potential benefits and costs.[33] In many cases, after an acquisition has been completed, many acquiring companies discover that instead of buying a well-managed business with a strong business model, they have purchased a troubled organization. Obviously, the managers of the target company may manipulate company information or the balance sheet to make their financial condition look much better than it is. The acquiring company must be wary and complete extensive research. In 2009, IBM was in negotiations to purchase chip-maker Sun Microsystems. After spending 1 week examining its books, IBM reduced its offer price by 10% when its negotiators found its customer base was not as solid as they had expected. Sun Microsystems was eventually sold to

Oracle in 2010 for $7.4 billion. For the next 5 years, Sun Microsystems was a drain on Oracle's profit, but Ellison persevered in investing in Sun's technologies, and by 2015 it appeared his investment finally might be paying off.[34]

Guidelines for Successful Acquisition

To avoid these pitfalls and make successful acquisitions, companies need to follow an approach to targeting and evaluating potential acquisitions that is based on four main steps: (1) target identification and pre-acquisition screening, (2) bidding strategy, (3) integration, and (4) learning from experience.[35]

Identification and Screening Thorough pre-acquisition screening increases a company's knowledge about a potential takeover target and lessens the risk of purchasing a problem company—one with a weak business model. It also leads to a more realistic assessment of the problems involved in executing a particular acquisition so that a company can plan how to integrate the new business and blend organizational structures and cultures. The screening process should begin with a detailed assessment of the strategic rationale for making the acquisition, an identification of the kind of company that would make an ideal acquisition candidate, and an extensive analysis of the strengths and weaknesses of the prospective company's business model compared to other possible acquisition targets.

Indeed, an acquiring company should select a set of top potential acquisition targets and evaluate each company using a set of criteria that focus on revealing (1) its financial position, (2) its distinctive competencies and competitive advantage, (3) changing industry boundaries, (4) its management capabilities, and (5) its corporate culture. Such an evaluation helps the acquiring company perform a detailed strength, weakness, opportunities, and threats (SWOT) analysis that identifies the best target, for example, by measuring the potential economies of scale and scope that can be achieved between the acquiring company and each target company. This analysis also helps reveal potential problems that might arise when it is necessary to integrate the corporate cultures of the acquiring and acquired companies. For example, managers at Microsoft and SAP, the world's leading provider of enterprise resource planning (ERP) software, met to discuss a possible acquisition by Microsoft. Both companies decided that despite the strong, strategic rationale for a merger—together they could dominate the software computing market, satisfying the need of large global companies—they would have challenges to overcome. The difficulties of creating an organizational structure that could successfully integrate their hundreds of thousands of employees throughout the world, and blend two very different cultures, were insurmountable.

Once a company has reduced the list of potential acquisition candidates to the most favored one or two, it needs to consult expert third parties such as investment bankers like Goldman Sachs and Merrill Lynch. These companies provide valuable insights about the attractiveness of a potential acquisition, assess current industry competitive conditions, and handle the many other issues surrounding an acquisition such as how to select the optimal bidding strategy for acquiring the target company's stock and keep the purchase price as low as possible.

Bidding Strategy The objective of the bidding strategy is to reduce the price that a company must pay for the target company. The most effective way a company can acquire another is to make a friendly takeover bid, which means the two companies decide upon an amicable way to merge the two companies, satisfying the needs of each company's stockholders and top managers. A friendly takeover prevents speculators from bidding up stock prices. By contrast, in a hostile bidding environment, such as existed between Oracle and PeopleSoft, and between Microsoft and Yahoo!, the price of the target company often gets bid up by speculators who expect that the offer price will be raised by the acquirer, or by another company with a higher counteroffer.

Another essential element of a good bidding strategy is timing. For example, Hanson PLC, one of the most successful companies to pursue unrelated diversification, searched for sound companies suffering from short-term problems because of the business cycle or because performance was being seriously impacted by one underperforming division. Such companies are often undervalued by the stock market and can be acquired without paying a high stock premium. With good timing, a company can make a bargain purchase.

Integration Despite good screening and bidding, an acquisition will fail unless the acquiring company possesses the essential organizational-design skills needed to integrate the acquired company into its operations and quickly develop a viable multibusiness model. Integration should center upon the source of the potential strategic advantages of the acquisition; for instance, opportunities to share marketing, manufacturing, R&D, financial, or management resources. Integration should also involve steps to eliminate any duplication of facilities or functions. In addition, any unwanted business units of the acquired company should be divested.

Learning from Experience Research suggests that organizations that acquire many companies over time become expert in this process and can generate significant value from their experience of the acquisition process.[36] Their past experience enables them to develop a "playbook" they can follow to execute an acquisition efficiently and effectively. One successful company, Tyco International, never made hostile acquisitions; it audited the accounts of the target companies in detail, acquired companies to help it achieve a critical mass in an industry, moved quickly to realize cost savings after an acquisition, promoted managers one or two layers down to lead the newly acquired entity, and introduced profit-based, incentive-pay systems in the acquired unit.[37] Over time, however, Tyco tended to become too large and diversified, leading both investors and management to suspect it was not generating as much value as it could. In 2007, Tyco's health-care and electronics divisions were spun off. In 2012, Tyco was split again into three parts that would each have their own stock: Tyco Fire and Security, ADT (which provided residential and small-business security installation), and Flow Control (which sold water and fluid valves and controls).[38]

ENTERING NEW INDUSTRIES: JOINT VENTURES

Joint ventures, where two or more companies agree to pool their resources to create new business, are most commonly used to enter an embryonic or growth industry. Suppose a company is contemplating the creation of a new-venture division in an embryonic industry. Such a move involves substantial risks and costs because the company must make the huge investment necessary to develop the set of value-chain activities required to make and sell products in the new industry. On the other hand, an acquisition can be a dangerous proposition because there is rarely an established leading company in an emerging industry; even if there is, it will be extremely expensive to purchase.

In this situation, a joint venture frequently becomes the most appropriate method to enter a new industry because it allows a company to share the risks and costs associated with establishing a business unit in the new industry with another company. This is especially true when the companies share *complementary* skills or distinctive competencies, because this increases the probability of a joint venture's success. Consider the 50/50 equity joint venture formed between UTC and Dow Chemical to build plastic-based composite parts for the aerospace industry. UTC was already involved in the aerospace industry (it builds Sikorsky helicopters), and Dow Chemical had skills in the development and manufacture of plastic-based composites. The alliance called for UTC to contribute its advanced aerospace skills, and for Dow to contribute its skills in developing and manufacturing plastic-based composites. Through the joint venture, both companies became involved in new product markets. They were able to realize the benefits associated with related diversification without having to merge their activities into one company or bear the costs and risks of developing new products on their own. Thus, both companies enjoyed the profit-enhancing advantages of entering new markets without having to bear the increased bureaucratic costs.

Although joint ventures usually benefit both partner companies, under some conditions they may result in problems. First, although a joint venture allows companies to share the risks and costs of developing a new business, it also requires that they share in the profits if it succeeds. So, if one partner's skills are more important than the other partner's skills, the partner with more valuable skills will have to "give away" profits to the other party because of the 50/50 agreement. This can create conflict and sour the working relationship as time passes. Second, the joint-venture partners may have different business models or time horizons, and problems can arise if they start to come into conflict about how to run the joint venture; these kinds of problems can disintegrate a business and result in failure.

Third, while one advantage of joint ventures is that they allow frequent and close contact between companies, which facilitates learning and transfer of knowledge, this also creates a risk that a joint venture can lead to the unintentional leak of proprietary information across companies.[39] Even when collaboration agreements have extensive contractual clauses designed to protect the proprietary knowledge possessed by each partner or developed through the collaboration, it is still very difficult to prevent that knowledge from being expropriated. Secrecy clauses are very difficult to enforce when knowledge is dispersed over a large number of employees.[40] A company that enters into a joint venture thus runs the risk of giving away important, company-specific knowledge to its partner, which might then use it to compete with its other partner in the future. For example, having gained access to Dow's expertise in plastic-based composites, UTC might have dissolved the alliance and produced these materials on its own. As the previous chapter discussed, this risk can be minimized if Dow gets a *credible commitment* from UTC, which is what Dow did.

UTC had to make an expensive, asset-specific investment to make the products the joint venture was formed to create.

Restructuring

Many companies expand into new industries to increase profitability. Sometimes, however, companies need to exit industries to increase their profitability and split their existing businesses into separate, independent companies. **Restructuring** is the process of reorganizing and divesting business units and exiting industries to refocus upon a company's core business and rebuild its distinctive competencies.[41] Why are so many companies restructuring, and how do they do it?

Why Restructure?

One main reason that diversified companies have restructured in recent years is that the stock market has valued their stock at a *diversification discount*, meaning that the stock of highly diversified companies is valued lower, relative to their earnings, than the stock of less-diversified companies.[42] Investors see highly diversified companies as less attractive investments for four reasons. First, as we discussed earlier, investors often feel these companies no longer have multibusiness models that justify their participation in many different industries. Second, the complexity of the financial statements of highly diversified enterprises disguises the performance of individual business units; thus, investors cannot determine if their multibusiness models are succeeding. The result is that investors perceive the company as being riskier than companies that operate in one industry, whose competitive advantage and financial statements are more easily understood. Given this situation, restructuring can be seen as an attempt to boost returns to shareholders by splitting up a multibusiness company into separate, independent parts.

The third reason for the diversification discount is that many investors have learned from experience that managers often have a tendency to pursue too much diversification or diversify for the wrong reasons: Their attempts to diversify *reduce* profitability.[43] For example, some CEOs pursue growth for its own sake; they are empire builders who expand the scope of their companies to the point where fast-increasing bureaucratic costs become greater than the additional value that their diversification strategy creates. Restructuring thus becomes a response to declining financial performance brought about by overdiversification.

A final factor leading to restructuring is that innovations in strategic management have diminished the advantages of vertical integration or diversification. For example, a few decades ago, there was little understanding of how long-term cooperative relationships or strategic alliances between a company and its suppliers could be a viable alternative to vertical integration. Most companies considered only two alternatives for managing the supply chain: vertical integration or competitive bidding. As we discuss in Chapter 9, in many situations long-term cooperative relationships can create the most value, especially because they avoid the need to incur bureaucratic costs or dispense with market discipline. As this strategic innovation has spread throughout global business, the relative advantages of vertical integration have declined.

restructuring
The process of reorganizing and divesting business units and exiting industries to refocus upon a company's core business and rebuild its distinctive competencies.

KEY TERMS

TAKEAWAYS FOR STRATEGIC MANAGERS

1. Strategic managers often pursue diversification when their companies are generating free cash flow; that is, financial resources they do not need to maintain a competitive advantage in their company's core industry and so can be used to fund new, profitable business ventures.

2. A diversified company can create value by (a) transferring competencies among existing businesses, (b) leveraging competencies to create new businesses, (c) sharing resources to realize economies of scope, (d) using product bundling, (e) taking advantage of general organizational competencies that enhance the performance of all business units within a diversified company, and (f) operating an internal capital market. The bureaucratic costs of diversification rise as a function of the number of independent business units within a company and the extent to which managers must coordinate the transfer of resources between those business units.

3. Diversification motivated by a desire to pool risks or achieve greater growth often results in falling profitability.

4. The three methods companies use to enter new industries are internal new venturing, acquisition, and joint ventures.

5. Internal new venturing is used to enter a new industry when a company has a set of valuable competencies in its existing businesses that can be leveraged or recombined to enter a new business or industry.

6. Many internal ventures fail because of entry on too small a scale, poor commercialization, and poor corporate management of the internal new venturing process. Guarding against failure involves a carefully planned approach to project selection and management, integration of R&D and marketing to improve the chance new products will be commercially successful, and entry on a scale large enough to result in competitive advantage.

7. Acquisitions are often the best way to enter a new industry when a company lacks the competencies required to compete in the new industry, and it can purchase a company that does have those competencies at a reasonable price. Acquisitions are also the method chosen to enter new industries when there are high barriers to entry and a company is unwilling to accept the time frame, development costs, and risks associated with pursuing internal new venturing.

8. Acquisitions are unprofitable when strategic managers (a) underestimate the problems associated with integrating an acquired company, (b) overestimate the profit that can be created from an acquisition, (c) pay too much for the acquired company, and (d) perform inadequate pre-acquisition screening to ensure the acquired company will increase the profitability of the whole company. Guarding against acquisition failure requires careful pre-acquisition screening, a carefully selected bidding strategy, effective organizational design to successfully integrate

the operations of the acquired company into the whole company, and managers who develop a general managerial competency by learning from their experience of past acquisitions.

9. Joint ventures are used to enter a new industry when (a) the risks and costs associated with setting up a new business unit are more than a company is willing to assume on its own and (b) a company can increase the probability that its entry into a new industry will result in a successful new business by teaming up with another company with skills and assets that complement its own.

10. Restructuring is often required to correct the problems that result from (a) a business model that no longer creates competitive advantage, (b) the inability of investors to assess the competitive advantage of a highly diversified company from its financial statements, (c) excessive diversification because top managers desire to pursue empire building that results in growth without profitability, and (d) innovations in strategic management such as strategic alliances and outsourcing that reduce the advantages of vertical integration and diversification.

DISCUSSION QUESTIONS

1. When is a company likely to choose (a) related diversification and (b) unrelated diversification?

2. What factors make it most likely that (a) acquisitions or (b) internal new venturing will be the preferred method to enter a new industry?

3. Imagine that IBM has decided to diversify into the telecommunications business to provide on-line cloud-computing data services and broadband access for businesses and individuals. What method would you recommend that IBM pursue to enter this industry? Why?

4. Under which conditions are joint ventures a useful way to enter new industries?

5. Identify Honeywell's portfolio of businesses, which can be found by exploring its website (www.honeywell.com). In how many different industries is Honeywell involved? Would you describe Honeywell as a related or an unrelated diversification company? Has Honeywell's diversification strategy increased profitability over time?

CLOSING CASE

Citigroup: The Opportunities and Risks of Diversification

In 2015, Citigroup was a $70.1-billion, diversified financial-services firm known around the world. However, its history had not always been smooth. From the late 1990s through 2010, the company's diversification moves, and its role in the mortgage crisis, combined to bring the company to its knees, raising fears that the venerable bank—one of the oldest and largest in the United States—would not survive.

Citigroup traces its history all the way back to 1812, when it was formed by a group of merchants in response to the abolishment of the First Bank of the United States (the First Bank's charter had been permitted to lapse due to Thomas Jefferson's arguments about the dangers of centralized control of the economy). The merchants, led by Alexander Hamilton, created the City Bank of New York in 1812, which they hoped would be large enough to replicate the scale advantages that had been offered by the First Bank. The bank played some key roles in the rise of the United States as a global power, including lending money

(continued)

to support the purchasing of armaments for the War of 1812, financing the Union war effort in the mid-1800s, and later pioneering foreign-exchange trading, which helped to bring the United States to the world stage in the early 1900s. By 1929, it was the largest commercial bank in the world.

The bank's capital resources and its trusted brand name enabled it to successfully diversify into a range of consumer banking services. The highly innovative company was, for example, the first to introduce savings accounts with compound interest, unsecured personal loans, checking accounts, and 24-hour ATMs, among other things. However, its business remained almost entirely within traditional, retail-banking services. That would soon change with the rise of a new concept: the "financial supermarket."

During the 1990s, there was much buzz in the financial industry about the value of having a wide range of financial services within the same bank. Why have your savings account in New Jersey, your stock broker in California, and your insurance agent in Maryland, when you could have them all under one roof? Merging such services would enable numerous "cross-selling" opportunities: Each company's customer bases could be more fully leveraged by promoting other financial products to them. Furthermore, cost savings might be realized by consolidating operations such as information technology, customer service and billing, and so forth. In 1998, Sanford "Sandy" Weill, who had already begun creating his own financial supermarket, which included Travelers insurance, Aetna, Primerica, Salomon Brothers, and Smith Barney Holdings, convinced Citicorp chairman and CEO John Reed that the two companies should merge. Travelers Group purchased all of Citicorp's shares for $70 billion, and issued 2.5 new Citigroup shares for each Citicorp Share. Existing shareholders of each company thus owned approximately half of the new firm. The merger created a $140-billion firm with assets of $700 billion. Renamed Citigroup, it was now the largest financial-services organization in the world.

Unfortunately, at almost exactly the same time, the Internet rendered the bricks-and-mortar financial supermarket obsolete: The best deals were to be found at the financial supermarket on the Web. To make matters worse, rather than cross-selling, the different divisions of Citi and Travelers began battling each other to protect their turf. Savings in consolidating back-office operations also turned out to be meager and costly to realize. Harmonizing each company's information technology systems, for example, was going to be so expensive that ultimately the legacy systems were left intact. Additionally, though the merged company shed more than 10,000 employees, it was harder to part with executives—indeed, the company kept so many pairs of executives with "co" titles (including co-CEOs Weill and Reed) that some people compared Citi to Noah's Ark. According to Meredith Whitney, a banking analyst who was an early critic of Citi's megabank model, Citi had become "a gobbledygook of companies that were never integrated... The businesses didn't communicate with each other. There were dozens of technology systems and dozens of financial ledgers."

To boost earnings Citi began investing in subprime loans, the risk of which was camouflaged by bundling the loans into mortgage-backed securities known as collateralized debt obligations (CDOs). Trouble began brewing before even Citi knew the scale of risk it had undertaken. Loose lending policies had resulted in a large number of poor-quality mortgages, the vast majority of which were adjustable-rate mortgages (i.e., the initial rate was very low, but would increase over time). This combined with a steep decline in housing prices that made it next to impossible for homebuyers to refinance their mortgages as their interest rates climbed—their homes were now worth less than what they owed. Delinquencies and foreclosures soared, meaning that banks holding those mortgages had assets whose value was rapidly declining. A lawsuit by Citi's shareholders in 2006 accused the company of using a "CDO-related quasi-Ponzi scheme" to falsely give the appearance that it had a healthy asset base and to conceal the true risks the company was facing, but even Citi's CEO at the time, Charles O. Prince III, did not know how much the company had invested in mortgage-related assets. Prince found out at a September 2007 meeting that the company had $43 billion in mortgage related assets, but was assured by Thomas Maheras (who oversaw trading at the bank) that everything was fine. Soon, the company was posting billions in losses, and its stock price fell to the lowest it had been in a decade (see the accompanying figures). To Lynn Turner, a former chief accountant with the Securities and Exchange Commission, Citi's crisis was no surprise. He pointed out that Citi was too large, did not have the right controls, and lacked sufficient accountability for individuals undertaking risks on the company's behalf, making such problems inevitable.

The amalgamation of businesses had created conflicts of interest, and Citi's managers lacked the ability to accurately gauge the risk of the exotic financial instruments that were proliferating. As the true scope of the problem was revealed, Citi found itself in very dire circumstances. The losses from writing down its mortgage assets threatened to destroy the entire company, bringing down even its profitable lines of business.

Citigroup's Revenues and Net Income (in $US millions), 2003–2014

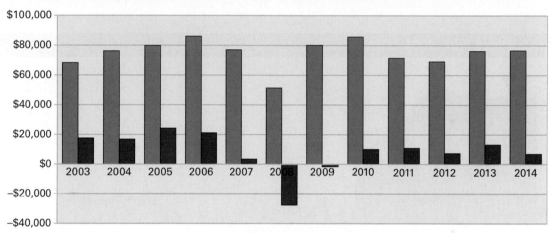

■ Revenue ■ Net Income

While the U.S. government kept the bank from failing with a $45-billion bailout (out of fear that Citi's failure would cause an even greater economic collapse—giving rise to the phrase "too big to fail"), Citigroup began reducing its workforce and selling off everything it could, dismantling its financial supermarket. Over the next 2 years, it slashed over 80,000 jobs and sold Smith Barney, Phibro (its commodities-trading unit), Diner's Club (a credit card), its Japanese brokerage operations, Primerica, and more. Furthermore, to raise capital it sold 5% of its equity to the Abu Dhabi Investment authority for $7.5 billion, and then raised another $12 billion by selling shares to a group of investors that included Prince Alwaleed Bin Talal of Saudi Arabia in 2008. It also restructured into two operating units: Citicorp for retail and institutional client business, and Citi Holdings for its brokerage and asset management.

This reorganization would help isolate Citi's banking operations from the riskier assets it wished to sell.

In 2010, Citigroup finally returned to profitability. It repaid its U.S. government loans, and its managers and the investment community breathed a sigh of relief, optimistic that the worst was over. In 2014, Citi posted $76.9 billion in revenues and $7.3 billion in net income. Today, roughly 50% of its revenues come from its consumer businesses (retail banking, credit cards, mortgages, and commercial banking for small-to-medium businesses); just over 40% comes from its Institutional Clients group (which provides investment and banking services for corporations, governments, institutions and ultra-high-net-worth individuals); and Citi Holdings accounts for just under 10% of revenues.

The saga of Citi seriously undermined the investment community's faith in the financial supermarket

(*continued*)

model, although in the wake of the mortgage crisis it was difficult to assess how much had been gained and lost through the diversification of the firm. One thing was clear, however: Having a very large, complex organization had made it more difficult to provide sufficient, and effective, oversight within the firm. This, in turn, allowed problems to grow very threatening before being detected. Citi's managers knew they would have to think much more carefully about their business choices in the future, and about how to manage the interdependencies between those businesses.

Sources: R. Wile, "Dramatic Highlights from Citi's 200-Year History," *Business Insider*, April 4, 2012, www. businessinsider.com/presenting-a-history-of-citi-2012-4?op=1); "About Citi—Citibank, N.A.," www.citigroup.com; M. Martin, "Citicorp and Travelers Plan to Merge in Record $70 Billion Deal," *New York Times*, April 7, 1998, p. 1; A. Kessler, "The End of Citi's Financial Supermarket," *The Wall Street Journal*, January 16, 2009, p. A11; "Fall Guy," *The Economist*, November 5, 1998; E. Dash and J. Creswell, "Citigroup Saw No Red Flags Even as It Made Bolder Bets," *New York Times*, November 22, 2008, p. 14; P. Hurtado and D. Griffin, "Citigroup Settles Investors' CDO Suit for $590 Million," Bloomberg.com, August 29, 2012; D. Ellis, "Citi Plunges 26%–Lowest in 15 Years," CNNMoney .com, November 20, 2008; Citigroup 2014 10-K.

Citigroup's Stock Price, 2004–2015

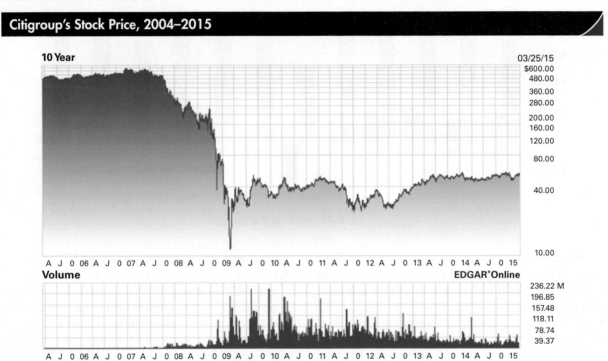

CASE DISCUSSION QUESTIONS

1. What advantages did Citigroup's managers think would result from creating a "financial supermarket"?
2. Why didn't the "financial supermarket" concept pay off the way Citi's managers had anticipated?
3. Why do you think it was so hard to integrate the different companies that were merged?
4. What are some challenges involved with managing a very large, diverse financial-services company?

NOTES

[1]This resource-based view of diversification can be traced to Edith Penrose's seminal book, *The Theory of the Growth of the Firm* (Oxford: Oxford University Press, 1959).

[2]D. J. Teece, "Economies of Scope and the Scope of the Enterprise," *Journal of Economic Behavior and Organization* 3 (1980): 223–247. For more recent empirical work on this topic, see C. H. St. John and J. S. Harrison, "Manufacturing Based Relatedness, Synergy and Coordination," *Strategic Management Journal* 20 (1999): 129–145.

[3]Teece, "Economies of Scope." For more recent empirical work on this topic, see St. John and Harrison, "Manufacturing Based Relatedness, Synergy and Coordination."

[4]For a detailed discussion, see C. W. L. Hill and R. E. Hoskisson, "Strategy and Structure in the Multiproduct Firm," *Academy of Management Review* 12 (1987): 331–341.

[5]See, for example, G. R. Jones and C. W. L. Hill, "A Transaction Cost Analysis of Strategy Structure Choice," *Strategic Management Journal* 2 (1988): 159–172; O. E. Williamson, *Markets and Hierarchies, Analysis and Antitrust Implications* (New York: Free Press, 1975), pp. 132–175.

[6]R. Buderi, *Engines of Tomorrow* (New York: Simon & Schuster, 2000).

[7]See, for example, Jones and Hill, "A Transaction Cost Analysis," and Williamson, *Markets and Hierarchies*.

[8]C. A. Trahms, H. A. Ndofor, and D. G. Sirmon, "Organizational Decline and Turnaound: A Review and Agenda for Future Research," *Journal of Management*, 39 (2013): 1277–1307.

[9]The distinction goes back to R. P. Rumelt, *Strategy, Structure and Economic Performance* (Cambridge: Harvard Business School Press, 1974).

[10]For evidence, see C. W. L. Hill, "Conglomerate Performance over the Economic Cycle," *Journal of Industrial Economics* 32 (1983): 197–212; D. T. C. Mueller, "The Effects of Conglomerate Mergers," *Journal of Banking and Finance* 1 (1977): 315–347.

[11]For reviews of the evidence, see V. Ramanujam and P. Varadarajan, "Research on Corporate Diversification: A Synthesis," *Strategic Management Journal* 10 (1989): 523–551; G. Dess, J. F. Hennart, C. W. L. Hill, and A. Gupta, "Research Issues in Strategic Management," *Journal of Management* 21 (1995): 357–392; D. C. Hyland and J. D. Diltz, "Why Companies Diversify: An Empirical Examination," *Financial Management* 31 (Spring 2002): 51–81.

[12]M. E. Porter, "From Competitive Advantage to Corporate Strategy," *Harvard Business Review* (May–June 1987): 43–59.

[13]For reviews of the evidence, see Ramanujam and Varadarajan, "Research on Corporate Diversification"; Dess et al., "Research Issues in Strategic Management"; Hyland and Diltz, "Why Companies Diversify."

[14]C. R. Christensen et al., *Business Policy Text and Cases* (Homewood: Irwin, 1987), p. 778.

[15]See Booz, Allen, and Hamilton, *New Products Management for the 1980s* (New York: Booz, Allen and Hamilton, 1982); A. L. Page, "PDMA's New Product Development Practices Survey: Performance and Best Practices" (presented at the PDMA 15th Annual International Conference, Boston, October 16, 1991); E. Mansfield, "How Economists See R&D," *Harvard Business Review* (November–December 1981): 98–106.

[16]See R. Biggadike, "The Risky Business of Diversification," *Harvard Business Review* (May–June 1979): 103–111; R. A. Burgelman, "A Process Model of Internal Corporate Venturing in the Diversified Major Firm," *Administrative Science Quarterly* 28 (1983): 223–244; Z. Block and I. C. MacMillan, *Corporate Venturing* (Boston: Harvard Business School Press, 1993).

[17]Biggadike, "The Risky Business of Diversification"; Block and Macmillan, *Corporate Venturing*.

[18]Buderi, *Engines of Tomorrow*.

[19]I. C. MacMillan and R. George, "Corporate Venturing: Challenges for Senior Managers," *Journal of Business Strategy* 5 (1985): 34–43.

[20]See R. A. Burgelman, M. M. Maidique, and S. C. Wheelwright, *Strategic Management of Technology and Innovation* (Chicago: Irwin, 1996), pp. 493–507. See also Buderi, *Engines of Tomorrow*.

[21]Buderi, *Engines of Tomorrow*.

[22]See Block and Macmillan, *Corporate Venturing*; Burgelman et al., *Strategic Management of Technology and Innovation,* and Buderi, *Engines of Tomorrow*.

[23]For evidence on acquisitions and performance, see R. E. Caves,

"Mergers, Takeovers, and Economic Efficiency," *International Journal of Industrial Organization* 7 (1989): 151–174; M. C. Jensen and R. S. Ruback, "The Market for Corporate Control: The Scientific Evidence," *Journal of Financial Economics* 11 (1983): 5–50; R. Roll, "Empirical Evidence on Takeover Activity and Shareholder Wealth," in J. C. Coffee, L. Lowenstein, and S. Rose (eds.), *Knights, Raiders and Targets* (Oxford: Oxford University Press, 1989), pp. 112–127; A. Schleifer and R. W. Vishny, "Takeovers in the 60s and 80s: Evidence and Implications," *Strategic Management Journal* 12 (Special Issue, Winter 1991): 51–60; T. H. Brush, "Predicted Changes in Operational Synergy and Post Acquisition Performance of Acquired Businesses," *Strategic Management Journal* 17 (1996): 1–24; T. Loughran and A. M. Vijh, "Do Long-Term Shareholders Benefit from Corporate Acquisitions?" *Journal of Finance* 5 (1997): 1765–1787.

[24]Ibid.

[25]D. J. Ravenscraft and F. M. Scherer, *Mergers, Sell-offs, and Economic Efficiency* (Washington, DC: Brookings Institution, 1987).

[26]F. Bauer and K. Matzler, "Antecedents of M&A Success: The Role of Strategic Complementarity, Cultural Fit, and Degree and Speed of Integration," *Strategic Management Journal* 35 (2014): 269–291.

[27]C. Isidore, "Daimler Pays to Dump Chrysler," *CNNMoney* (May 14, 2007).

[28]See J. P. Walsh, "Top Management Turnover Following Mergers and Acquisitions," *Strategic Management Journal* 9 (1988): 173–183.

[29]See A. A. Cannella and D. C. Hambrick, "Executive Departure and Acquisition Performance," *Strategic Management Journal* 14 (1993): 137–152.

[30]R. Roll, "The Hubris Hypothesis of Corporate Takeovers," *Journal of Business* 59 (1986): 197–216.

[31]"Coca-Cola: A Sobering Lesson from Its Journey into Wine," *Business Week* (June 3, 1985): 96–98.

[32]J. Harford, M. Humphery-Jenner, and R. Powell, "The Sources of Value Destruction in Acquisitions by Entrenched Managers," *Journal of Financial Economics* 106 (2012): 247–161; F. Fu, L. Lin, and M. C. Officer, "Acquisitions Driven by Stock Overvaluation: Are They Good Deals?" *Journal of Financial Economics* 109 (2013): 24–39.

[33]P. Haspeslagh and D. Jemison, *Managing Acquisitions* (New York: Free Press, 1991).

[34]J. Burt, "Oracle Continues to Grow Hardware Business 5 Years After Sun Deal," *eWeek* (February 16, 2015): 1.

[35]For views on this issue, see L. L. Fray, D. H. Gaylin, and J. W. Down, "Successful Acquisition Planning," *Journal of Business Strategy* 5 (1984): 46–55; C. W. L. Hill, "Profile of a Conglomerate Takeover: BTR and Thomas Tilling," *Journal of General Management* 10 (1984): 34–50; D. R. Willensky, "Making It Happen: How to Execute an Acquisition," *Business Horizons* (March–April 1985): 38–45; Haspeslagh and Jemison, *Managing Acquisitions*; and P. L. Anslinger and T. E. Copeland, "Growth Through Acquisition: A Fresh Look," *Harvard Business Review* (January–February 1996): 126–135.

[36]M. L. A. Hayward, "When Do Firms Learn from Their Acquisition Experience? Evidence from 1990–1995," *Strategic Management Journal* 23 (2002): 21–39; K. G. Ahuja, "Technological Acquisitions and the Innovation Performance of Acquiring Firms: A Longitudinal Study," *Strategic Management Journal* 23 (2001): 197–220; H. G. Barkema and F. Vermeulen, "International Expansion Through Startup or Acquisition," *Academy of Management Journal* 41 (1998): 7–26.

[37]Hayward, "When Do Firms Learn from Their Acquisition Experience?"

[38]N. Zieminski, "Tyco Shareholders Approve Three-Way Break-Up," Reuters, September 17, 2012.

[39]A. C. Inkpen and S. C. Currall, "The Coevolution of Trust, Control, and Learning in Joint Ventures," *Organization Science* 15 (2004): 586–599; D. C. Mowery, J. E. Oxley, and B. S. Silverman, "Strategic Alliances and Interfirm Knowledge Transfer," *Strategic Management* 17 (1996): 77–91.

[40]M. A. Schilling, "Technology Shocks, Technological Collaboration, and Innovation Outcomes," *Organization Science* 26: 668–686.

[41]For a review of the evidence and some contrary empirical evidence, see D. E. Hatfield, J. P. Liebskind, and T. C. Opler, "The Effects of Corporate Restructuring on Aggregate Industry Specialization," *Strategic Management Journal* 17 (1996): 55–72.

[42]A. Lamont and C. Polk, "The Diversification Discount: Cash Flows Versus Returns," *Journal of Finance* 56 (October 2001): 1693–1721; R. Raju, H. Servaes, and L. Zingales, "The Cost of Diversity: The Diversification Discount and Inefficient Investment," *Journal of Finance* 55 (2000): 35–80.

[43]For example, see Schleifer and Vishny, "Takeovers in the '60s and '80s."

Igor Sokolov (breeze)/Shutterstock.com

4

IMPLEMENTING STRATEGY

Chapter 11 Corporate Governance, Social
Responsibility, and Ethics

Chapter 12   Implementing Strategy Through
Organization

Igor Sokolov (breeze)/Shutterstock.com

11

CORPORATE GOVERNANCE, SOCIAL RESPONSIBILITY, AND ETHICS

OPENING CASE

Starbucks: Taking a Stand on Social Issues

When Howard Schultz founded Starbucks in 1987, he wanted to create a company that would genuinely care for the well-being of its employees. He had been very influenced by his memories of his father, noting that his father "struggled a great deal and never made more than $20,000 a year, and his work was never valued, emotionally or physically, by his employer ... This was an injustice ... I want our employees to know we value them." He also believed that happy employees are the key to competitiveness and growth. As he stated: "We can't achieve our strategic objectives without a work force of people who are immersed in the same commitment as management. Our only sustainable advantage is the quality of our work force. We're building a national retail company by creating pride in—and stake in—the outcome of our labor."

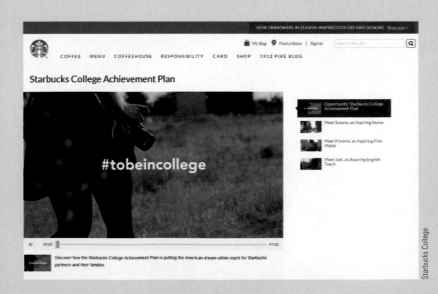

Starbucks College

Schulz set out to accomplish his goals by creating an empowering corporate culture, exceptional employee benefits, and employee stock ownership programs. While Starbucks enforces almost fanatical standards of coffee quality and customer service, the culture at Starbucks towards employees is laid back and supportive. Employees are empowered to make decisions without constant referral to management, and are encouraged to think of themselves as partners in the business. Starbucks wants employees to use their best judgment in making decisions and will stand behind them. This is reinforced through generous compensation and benefits packages.

In 2000, Schultz announced that he was resigning as CEO and left the firm to pursue other ventures (though he remained chairman of the board of directors). However, after Starbucks began to suffer from slumping net income and decreasing share price, Schultz returned to the helm in 2008. Rather than cutting costs and reducing the work force, Schulz announced his "Transformation Agenda"—a controversial plan to invest in Starbucks' employees, environment, and community. Schultz's plan included:

Competitive employee compensation plans that include equity-based compensation for nonexecutive partners. In 2013, $230 million was paid out in equity awards. In 2015, Starbucks gave all baristas and supervisors a pay raise and increased starting pay rates across the United States. In 2015, Starbucks's U.S. baristas earned between $7.59 and $10.92 an hour, plus $.33 to $1.91 an hour in tips, depending on location and experience.

Industry-leading health care benefits and 401K benefits for both part-time and full-time workers. Other companies that offer health benefits to part-time workers typically only do so for employees who work at least 30 hours a week. Starbucks broke with industry norms by creating benefits for employees who work at least 20 hours a week.

Tuition reimbursement for students. In June 2014, Starbucks unveiled a "College Achievement Plan" wherein employees who work more than 20 hours a week can work towards a bachelor's degree through an online program from Arizona State University.

An ethical sourcing plan. Starbucks' coffee must be purchased from suppliers that adhere to Starbucks' "C.A.F.E." standards. These standards include practices related to *product quality, economic accountability and transparency* (e.g., suppliers must provide evidence to demonstrate that the price Starbucks pays reaches the farmer), *social responsibility* (e.g., third-party verifiers provide audits to ensure that suppliers are using safe, fair, and humane working and living conditions, including minimum-wage requirements and the prohibition of child and forced labor), and *environmental leadership* (e.g., measures to manage waste, protect water quality, and reduce use of agrochemicals).

Whether investors and consumers were inspired by the Agenda, were encouraged by Schultz's return, or just floated up with the recovering economy is unclear, but Starbuck's stock price and balance sheet roared back to life. Revenues and net income began to climb again and, by September 2014, Starbucks' sales had reached $16.4 billion—160% of what sales had been when Schultz returned as CEO and an all-time high for the company. With a 12.6% net margin and 19.2% return on assets, Starbucks was one of the most profitable food retailers in the world.

In late 2014 and early 2015, Schultz decided to leverage the company's influence in the world by beginning to speak out on such issues as gay marriage (Schultz supports it), gun carrying laws (Starbucks requests that people not carry guns into their locations, even in states that permit it), and treatment of veterans (in March 2014, Schultz committed $30 million of his own money to posttraumatic stress disorder programs and other initiatives to help veterans, and vowed to hire 10,000 veterans and military spouses by 2018).

The company drew some ire in taking on issues that bear little relationship to its core activities. Critics admonished that such initiatives risked alienating some consumers and investors, and creating elevated expectations that the company might not always be able to meet. As Schultz noted, "I can tell you the organization is not thrilled when I walk into a room and say we're now going to take on veterans (issues)." But he adds, "The size and the scale of the company and the platform that we have allows us, I think, to project a voice into the debate, and hopefully that's for good … We are leading [Starbucks] to try to redefine the role and responsibility of a public company."

Sources: C. Birkner, "Taking Care of Their Own," *Marketing News*, February, pp. 44–49; M. Rothman, "Into the Black," *Inc.*, January, 1993, p. 58; D. Ritter, "3 Reasons It's Hard to Hate Starbucks," *Wall Street Cheat Sheet*, July 6, 2014; www.usatoday.com, A. Gonzalez, "Starbucks as Citizen: Schultz Acts Boldly on Social, Political Issues," *Seattle Times*, March 15, 2015; www.seattletimes.com, www.starbucks.com (accessed April 28, 2015); Yahoo Finance, Hoovers.

◤ OVERVIEW

We open this chapter with a close look at the governance mechanisms that shareholders implement to ensure that managers act in the company's interest and pursue strategies that maximize shareholder value. We also discuss how managers need to pay attention to other stakeholders such as employees, suppliers, and customers. The Opening Case on Starbucks is a good illustration of how some companies incorporate a wide range of stakeholder needs into their strategy. Balancing the needs of different stakeholder groups is in the long-term interests of the company's owners, its shareholders. Good governance mechanisms recognize this truth. In addition, we will review the ethical implications of strategic decisions, and discuss how managers can make sure that their strategic decisions are founded upon strong ethical principles.

◤ STAKEHOLDERS AND CORPORATE PERFORMANCE

stakeholders

Individuals or groups with an interest, claim, or stake in the company—in what it does and in how well it performs.

internal stakeholders

Stockholders and employees, including executive officers, other managers, and board members.

external stakeholders

All other individuals and groups that have some claim on the company.

A company's **stakeholders** are individuals or groups with an interest, claim, or stake in the company, in what it does, and in how well it performs.[1] They include stockholders, creditors, employees, customers, the communities in which the company does business, and the general public. Stakeholders can be divided into two groups: internal stakeholders and external stakeholders (see Figure 11.1). **Internal stakeholders** are stockholders and employees, including executive officers, other managers, and board members. **External stakeholders** are all other individuals and groups that have some

Figure 11.1 Stakeholders and the Enterprise

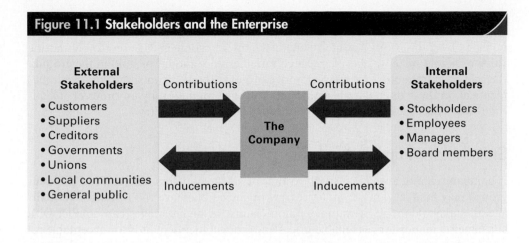

claim on the company. Typically, this group comprises customers, suppliers, creditors (including banks and bondholders), governments, unions, local communities, and the general public.

All stakeholders are in an exchange relationship with their company. Each stakeholder group listed in Figure 11.1 supplies the organization with important resources (or contributions), and in exchange each expects its interests to be satisfied (by inducements).[2] Stockholders provide the enterprise with risk capital and expect management to attempt to maximize the return on their investment. Creditors, particularly bondholders, also provide the company with capital in the form of debt, and they expect to be repaid on time, with interest. Employees provide labor and skills and in exchange expect commensurate income, job satisfaction, job security, and good working conditions. Customers provide a company with its revenues, and in exchange want high-quality, reliable products that represent value for money. Suppliers provide a company with inputs and in exchange seek revenues and dependable buyers. Governments provide a company with rules and regulations that govern business practice and maintain fair competition. In exchange they want companies to adhere to these rules. Unions help to provide a company with productive employees, and in exchange they want benefits for their members in proportion to their contributions to the company. Local communities provide companies with local infrastructure, and in exchange want companies that are responsible citizens. The general public provides companies with national infrastructure, and in exchange seeks some assurance that the quality of life will be improved as a result of the company's existence.

A company must take these claims into account when formulating its strategies, or stakeholders may withdraw their support. For example, stockholders may sell their shares, bondholders may demand higher interest payments on new bonds, employees may leave their jobs, and customers may buy elsewhere. Suppliers may seek more dependable buyers, and unions may engage in disruptive labor disputes. Government may take civil or criminal action against the company and its top officers, imposing fines and, in some cases, jail terms. Communities may oppose the company's attempts to locate its facilities in their area, and the general public may form pressure groups, demanding action against companies that impair the quality of life. Any of these reactions can have a damaging impact on an enterprise. A study by Witold Henisz, Sinziana Dorobantu and Lite Nartey on the impact of stakeholder opposition to gold mines, for example, found that the value of cooperative relationships with external stakeholders was worth twice as much as the market value of the gold itself.[3] As articulated by Yani Roditis, former COO of Gabriel Resources, "It used to be that the value of a gold mine was based on three variables: the amount of gold in the ground, the cost of extraction, and the world price of gold. Today, I can show you two mines identical on these three variables that differ in their valuation by an order of magnitude. Why? Because one has local support and the other doesn't."

Stakeholder Impact Analysis

A company cannot always satisfy the claims of all stakeholders. The goals of different groups may conflict, and, in practice, few organizations have the resources to manage all stakeholders.[4] For example, union claims for higher wages can conflict with consumer demands for reasonable prices and stockholder demands for acceptable returns. Often, the company must make choices, and t do so it must identify the most important stakeholders and give highest priority to pursuing strategies that satisfy their needs. Stakeholder impact analysis can provide such identification. Typically, stakeholder impact analysis follows these steps:

1. Identify stakeholders.
2. Identify stakeholders' interests and concerns.
3. As a result, identify the claims stakeholders are likely to make on the organization.
4. Identify the stakeholders who are most important from the organization's perspective.
5. Identify the resulting strategic challenges.[5]

Such an analysis enables a company to identify the stakeholders most critical to its survival and to make sure that the satisfaction of their needs is paramount. Most companies that have gone through this process quickly come to the conclusion that three stakeholder groups must be satisfied above all others if a company is to survive and prosper: customers, employees, and stockholders.

The Unique Role of Stockholders

risk capital

Capital that cannot be recovered if a company fails and goes bankrupt.

A company's stockholders are usually put in a different class from other stakeholder groups, and for good reason. Stockholders are the legal owners and the providers of **risk capital**, a major source of the capital resources that allow a company to operate its business. The capital that stockholders provide to a company is seen as risk capital because there is no guarantee that stockholders will recoup their investments and/or earn a decent return.

Recent history demonstrates all too clearly the nature of risk capital. For example, many investors who bought shares in Washington Mutual, the large, Seattle-based bank and home loan lender, believed that they were making a low-risk investment. The company had been around for decades and paid a solid dividend, which it increased every year. It had a large branch network and billions in deposits. However, during the 2000s, Washington Mutual was also making increasingly risky mortgage loans, reportedly giving mortgages to people without properly verifying if they had the funds to pay back those loans on time. By 2008, many borrowers were beginning to default on their loans, and Washington Mutual had to take multibillion-dollar write-downs on the value of its loan portfolio, effectively destroying its once-strong balance sheet. The losses were so large that customers with deposits at the bank started to worry about its stability, and they withdrew nearly $16 billion in November 2008 from accounts at Washington Mutual. The stock price collapsed from around $40 at the start of 2008 to under $2 a share, and with the bank teetering on the brink of collapse, the federal government intervened, seized the bank's assets, and engineered a sale to JP Morgan. Washington Mutual's shareholders got absolutely nothing: They were wiped out.

Over the past decade, maximizing returns to stockholders has taken on significant importance as an increasing number of employees have become stockholders in the companies for which they work through employee stock ownership plans (ESOPs). At Wal-Mart, for example, all employees who have worked for more than 1 year are eligible for the company's ESOP. Under an ESOP, employees are given the opportunity to purchase stock in the company, sometimes at a discount or less than the market value of the stock. The company may also contribute a certain portion of the purchase price to the ESOP. By making employees stockholders, ESOPs tend to increase the already strong emphasis on maximizing returns to stockholders, for they now help to satisfy two key stakeholder groups: stockholders and employees.

Profitability, Profit Growth, and Stakeholder Claims

Because of the unique position assigned to stockholders, managers normally seek to pursue strategies that maximize the returns that stockholders receive from holding shares in the company. As we noted in Chapter 1, stockholders receive a return on their investment in a company's stock in two ways: from dividend payments and from capital appreciation in the market value of a share (that is, by increases in stock market prices). The best way for managers to generate the funds for future dividend payments and keep the stock price appreciating is to pursue strategies that maximize the company's long-term profitability (as measured by the return on invested capital, ROIC) and grow the profits of the company over time.[6]

As we saw in Chapter 3, ROIC is an excellent measure of the profitability of a company. It tells managers how efficiently they are using the capital resources of the company (including the risk capital provided by stockholders) to generate profits. A company that is generating a positive ROIC is covering all of its ongoing expenses and has money left over, which is then added to shareholders' equity, thereby increasing the value of a company and thus the value of a share of stock in the company. The value of each share will increase further if a company can grow its profits over time, because then the profit that is attributable to every share (that is, the company's earnings per share) will also grow. As we have seen in this book, to grow profits, companies must be doing one or more of the following: (a) increasing the margins earned on their products and services, (b) maintaining margins and share while participating in a market that is growing, (b) maintaining margins while taking market share from competitors, (c) or (d) developing new markets through innovation, geographic expansion, or diversification.

Although managers should strive for profit growth if they are trying to maximize shareholder value, the relationship between profitability and profit growth is a complex one because attaining future profit growth may require investments that reduce the current rate of profitability. The task of managers is to find the right balance between profitability and profit growth.[7] Too much emphasis on current profitability at the expense of future profitability and profit growth can make an enterprise less attractive to shareholders. Too much emphasis on profit growth can reduce the current profitability of the enterprise and have the same effect. In an uncertain world where the future is unknowable, finding the right balance between profitability and profit growth is as much art as it is science, but it is something that managers must try to do.

In addition to maximizing returns to stockholders, boosting a company's profitability and profit growth rate is also consistent with satisfying the claims of several other key stakeholder groups. When a company is profitable and its profits are continuing to grow, it can pay higher salaries to productive employees and can also afford benefits such as health insurance coverage, all of which help to satisfy employees. In addition, companies with a high level of profitability and profit growth have no problem meeting their debt commitments, which provides creditors, including bondholders, with a measure of security. Profitable organizations are also better able to undertake philanthropic investments, which can help to satisfy some of the claims that local communities and the general public place on a company. Pursuing strategies that maximize the long-term profitability and profit growth of the company is therefore generally consistent with satisfying the claims of various stakeholder groups.

Stakeholder management requires consideration of how the firm's practices affect the cooperation of stakeholders in the short term, the benefits of building trust and a knowledge-sharing culture with stakeholders in the long run, and the firm's profitability and growth that will enable it to serve stakeholder interests in the future.[8] The company that overpays its employees in the current period, for example, may have very happy employees for a short while, but such action will raise the company's cost structure and limit its ability to attain a competitive advantage in the marketplace, thereby depressing its long-term profitability and hurting its ability to award future pay increases. As far as employees are concerned, the way many companies deal with this situation is to make future pay raises contingent upon improvements in labor productivity. If labor productivity increases, labor costs as a percentage of revenues will fall, profitability will rise, and the company can afford to pay its employees more and offer greater benefits.

Of course, not all stakeholder groups want the company to maximize its long-run profitability and profit growth. Suppliers are more comfortable about selling goods and services to profitable companies because they can be assured that the company will have the funds to pay for those products. Similarly, customers may be more willing to purchase from profitable companies because they can be assured that those companies will be around in the long term to provide after-sales services and support. But neither suppliers nor customers want the company to maximize its profitability at their expense. Rather, they would like to capture some of these profits from the company in the form of higher prices for their goods and services (in the case of suppliers), or lower prices for the products they purchase from the company (in the case of customers). Roberto Garcia-Castro and Ruth Aguilera capture this dynamic nicely by breaking the traditional explanation of value creation and value capture (discussed in Chapter 3) down into more fine-grained categories that show how value is created and captured by multiple stakeholders, similar to Figure 11.2.[9] As shown, the total value that is created is the spread between the opportunity costs of the resources it employs and the willingness-to-pay of its customers. However, value is created and captured by different stakeholders. Suppliers create and capture value in the form of goods and services they sell to the firm; employees and management create value through their labor and capture value in the form of salaries and other benefits; government creates value in the form of providing the broad infrastructure in which the firm operates and

Figure 11.2 Value Creation and Capture with Multiple Stakeholder Groups

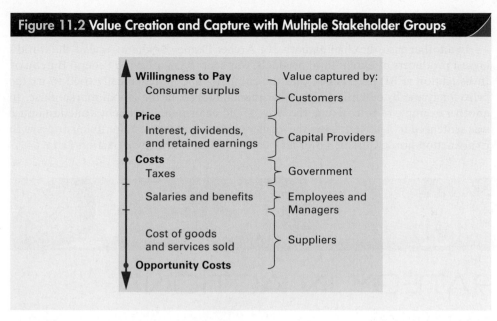

Source: Adapted from R. Garcia-Castro and R. Aguilera, "Increasing Value Creation and Appropriation in a World with Multiple Stakeholders," *Strategic Management Journal*, 36 (2015): 137–147.

captures value in the form of taxes; debt providers and stockholders create value by providing capital to the firm that it can use to finance its operations, and they capture value in the form of interest, dividends, and capital gains. Finally, customers capture value in the form of consumer surplus–the difference between the price they pay for goods and their true willingness-to-pay.

Despite the argument that maximizing long-term profitability and profit growth is the best way to satisfy the claims of several key stakeholder groups, it should be noted that a company must do so within the limits set by the law and in a manner consistent with societal expectations. The unfettered pursuit of profit can lead to behaviors that are outlawed by government regulations, opposed by important public constituencies, or simply unethical. Governments have enacted a wide range of regulations to govern business behavior, including antitrust laws, environmental laws, and laws pertaining to health and safety in the workplace. It is incumbent on managers to make sure that the company is in compliance with these laws when pursuing strategies.

Unfortunately, there is plenty of evidence that managers can be tempted to cross the line between legal and illegal in their pursuit of greater profitability and profit growth. For example, in mid-2003, the U.S. Air Force stripped Boeing of $1 billion in contracts to launch satellites when it was discovered that Boeing had obtained thousands of pages of proprietary information from rival Lockheed Martin. Boeing had used that information to prepare its winning bid for the satellite contract. This was followed by the revelation that Boeing's CFO, Mike Sears, had offered a government official, Darleen Druyun, a lucrative job at Boeing while Druyun was still involved in evaluating whether Boeing should be awarded a $17-billion contract to build tankers for the Air Force. Boeing won the contract against strong competition from Airbus and hired Druyun. It was clear that the job offer may have had an impact on the Air Force decision. Boeing fired Druyun and the CFO, and shortly thereafter, Boeing

CEO Phil Condit resigned in a tacit acknowledgment that he bore responsibility for the ethics violations that had occurred at Boeing during his tenure as leader.[10]

In another case, the chief executive of Archer Daniels Midland, one of the world's largest producers of agricultural products, was sent to jail after the Federal Bureau of Investigation (FBI) determined that the company had systematically tried to fix the price for lysine by colluding with other manufacturers in the global marketplace. In another example of price fixing, the 76-year-old chairman of Sotheby's auction house was sentenced to a jail term, and the former CEO to house arrest, for fixing prices with rival auction house Christie's over a 6-year period (see Strategy in Action 11.1).

11.1 STRATEGY IN ACTION

Price Fixing at Sotheby's and Christie's

Sotheby's and Christie's are the two largest fine-art auction houses in the world. In the mid-1990s, the two companies controlled 90% of the fine-art auction market, which at the time was worth approximately $4 billion annually. Traditionally, auction houses earn their profits by the commissions they charge on auction sales. In good times, these commissions can be as high as 10% on some items, but in the early 1990s, the auction business was in a slump, with the supply of art for auction shriveling. With Sotheby's and Christie's desperate for works of art, sellers played the two houses against each other, driving commissions down to 2%, or sometimes lower.

To try to control this situation, Sotheby's CEO, Dede Brooks, met with Christie CEO Christopher Davidge in a series of clandestine meetings held in parking lots that began in 1993. Brooks claimed that she was acting on behalf of her boss, Alfred Taubman, the chairman and controlling shareholder of Sotheby's. According to Brooks, Taubman had agreed with the chairman of Christie's, Anthony Tennant, to work together in the weak auction market and limit price competition. In their meetings, Brooks and Davidge agreed to a fixed and nonnegotiable commission structure. Based on a sliding scale, the commission structure would range from 10% on a $100,000 item to 2%

on a $5-million item. In effect, Brooks and Davidge were agreeing to eliminate price competition between them, thereby guaranteeing both auction houses higher profits. The price-fixing agreement started in 1993 and continued unabated for 6 years, until federal investigators uncovered the arrangement and brought charges against Sotheby's and Christie's.

With the deal out in the open, lawyers filed several class-action lawsuits on behalf of the sellers that had been defrauded. Ultimately, at least 100,000 sellers signed on to the class-action lawsuits, which the auction houses settled with a $512-million payment. The auction houses also pleaded guilty to price fixing and paid $45 million in fines to U.S. antitrust authorities. As for the key players, the chairman of Christie's, as a British subject, was able to avoid prosecution in the United States (price fixing is not an offense for which someone can be extradited). Davidge struck a deal with prosecutors, and in return for amnesty turned over incriminating documents to the authorities. Brooks also cooperated with federal prosecutors and avoided jail (in April 2002, she was sentenced to 3 years of probation, 6 months of home detention, 1,000 hours of community service, and a $350,000 fine). Taubman, ultimately isolated by all his former coconspirators, was sentenced to 1 year in jail and fined $7.5 million.

Sources: S. Tully, "A House Divided," *Fortune*, December 18, 2000, pp. 264–275; J. Chaffin, "Sotheby's Ex CEO Spared Jail Sentence," *Financial Times*, April 30, 2002, p. 10; T. Thorncroft, "A Courtroom Battle of the Vanities," *Financial Times*, November 3, 2001, p. 3.

Examples such as these beg the question of why managers would engage in such risky behavior. A body of academic work collectively known as agency theory provides an explanation for why managers might engage in behavior that is either illegal or, at the very least, not in the interest of the company's shareholders.

AGENCY THEORY

Agency theory looks at the problems that can arise in a business relationship when one person delegates decision-making authority to another. It offers a way of understanding why managers do not always act in the best interests of stakeholders and why they might sometimes behave unethically, and, perhaps, also illegally.[11] Although agency theory was originally formulated to capture the relationship between management and stockholders, the basic principles have also been extended to cover the relationship with other key stakeholders, such as employees, as well as relationships between different layers of management within a corporation.[12] Although the focus of attention in this section is on the relationship between senior management and stockholders, some of the same language can be applied to the relationship between other stakeholders and top managers, and between top management and lower levels of management.

Principal–Agent Relationships

The basic propositions of agency theory are relatively straightforward. First, an agency relationship is held to arise whenever one party delegates decision-making authority or control over resources to another. The principal is the person delegating authority, and the agent is the person to whom authority is delegated. The relationship between stockholders and senior managers is the classic example of an agency relationship. Stockholders, who are the principals, provide the company with risk capital but delegate control over that capital to senior managers, and particularly to the CEO, who, as their agent, is expected to use that capital in a manner consistent with the best interests of stockholders. As we have seen, this means using capital to maximize the company's long-term profitability and profit growth rate.

The agency relationship continues down the hierarchy within the company. For example, in a large, complex, multibusiness company, top managers cannot possibly make all the important decisions; therefore, they delegate some decision-making authority and control over capital resources to business-unit (divisional) managers. Thus, just as senior managers such as the CEO are the agents of stockholders, business-unit managers are the agents of the CEO (and in this context, the CEO is the principal). The CEO entrusts business-unit managers to use the resources over which they have control in the most effective manner in order to maximize the performance of their units. This helps the CEO ensure that he or she maximizes the performance of the entire company, thereby discharging agency obligation to stockholders. More generally, whenever managers delegate authority to managers below them in the hierarchy and give them the right to control resources, an agency relation is established.

The Agency Problem

Although agency relationships often work well, problems may arise if agents and principals have different goals, and if agents take actions that are not in the best interests of their principals. Sometimes this occurs because an **information asymmetry** exists between the principal and the agent: Agents almost always have more information about the resources they are managing than principals do. Unscrupulous agents can take advantage of such information asymmetry to mislead principals and maximize their own interests at the expense of principals.

In the case of stockholders, the information asymmetry arises because they delegate decision-making authority to the CEO, their agent, who, by virtue of his or her position inside the company, is likely to know far more than stockholders do about the company's operations. Indeed, there may be certain information about the company that the CEO is unwilling to share with stockholders because that information would also help competitors. In such a case, withholding information from stockholders may be in the best interest of all. More generally, the CEO, involved in the day-to-day operations of the company, is bound to have an information advantage over stockholders, just as the CEO's subordinates may have an information advantage over the CEO with regard to the resources under their control.

The information asymmetry between principals and agents is not necessarily a bad thing, but it can make it difficult for principals to measure an agent's performance and thus hold the agent accountable for how well he or she is using the entrusted resources. There is a certain amount of performance ambiguity inherent in the relationship between a principal and agent. Principals cannot know for sure if the agent is acting in his or her best interests. They cannot know for sure if the agent is using the resources to which he or she has been entrusted as effectively and efficiently as possible. This ambiguity is amplified by the fact that agents must engage in behavior that has outcomes for different time horizons. For example, investing in research and development may lower profits today but help to ensure the firm is profitable in the future. Principals who reward only immediate performance outcomes could induce myopic ("short-sighted") behavior on the part of the agent. To an extent, principals must trust the agent to do the right thing.

Of course, this trust is not blind: principals do put mechanisms in place with the purpose of monitoring agents, evaluating their performance, and, if necessary, taking corrective action. As we shall see shortly, the board of directors is one such mechanism, for, in part, the board exists to monitor and evaluate senior managers on behalf of stockholders. In Germany, the codetermination law (*Mitbestimmungsgesetz*) requires that firms with over 2,000 employees have boards of directors that represent the interests of employees—just under half of a firm's supervisory board members must represent workers. Other mechanisms serve a similar purpose. In the United States, publicly owned companies must regularly file detailed financial statements with the Securities and Exchange Commission (SEC) that are in accordance with generally agreed-upon accounting principles (GAAP). This requirement exists to give stockholders consistent, detailed information about how well management is using the capital with which it has been entrusted. Similarly, internal control systems within a company help the CEO ensure that subordinates are using the resources with which they have been entrusted to the best possible advantage.

Despite the existence of governance mechanisms and comprehensive measurement and control systems, a degree of information asymmetry will always remain between

information asymmetry

A situation where an agent has more information about the resources he or she is managing than the principal has.

principals and agents, and there is always an element of trust involved in the relationship. Unfortunately, not all agents are worthy of this trust. A minority will deliberately mislead principals for personal gain, sometimes behaving unethically or breaking laws in the process, or engaging in behaviors that the principals would never condone.

The interests of principals and agents are not always the same; they diverge. For example, some authors argue that, like many other people, senior managers are motivated by desires for status, power, job security, and income.[13] By virtue of their position within the company, certain managers, such as the CEO, can use their authority and control over corporate funds to satisfy these desires at the cost of returns to stockholders. CEOs might use their position to invest corporate funds in various perks that enhance their status—executive jets, lavish offices, and expense-paid trips to exotic locales—rather than investing those funds in ways that increase stockholder returns. Economists have termed such behavior **on-the-job consumption**.[14]

Aside from engaging in on-the-job consumption, CEOs, along with other senior managers, might satisfy their desire for greater income by using their influence or control over the board of directors to persuade the compensation committee of the board to grant pay increases. Critics of U.S. industry claim that extraordinary pay has now become an endemic problem, and that senior managers are enriching themselves at the expense of stockholders and other employees. They point out that CEO pay has been increasing far more rapidly than the pay of average workers, primarily because of very liberal stock option grants that enable a CEO to earn huge pay bonuses in a rising stock market, even if the company underperforms the market and competitors.[15] In 1980, the average CEO in *Business Week's* survey of CEOs of the largest 500 American companies earned 42 times what the average blue-collar worker earned. By 1990, this figure had increased to 85 times. In 2013, the AFL-CIO's Executive PayWatch database reported that American CEOs made 331 times the pay of average workers.[16]

What rankles critics is the size of some CEO pay packages and their apparent lack of relationship to company performance.[17] In 2010, a study by Graef Crystal evaluated the relationship between CEO pay and performance and concluded that there virtually is none. For example, if CEOs were paid according to shareholder return, the CEO of CBS Corporation, Leslie Moonves, who earned an impressive $43.2 million in 2009, should have gotten a $28 million pay cut, according to Crystal.[18] Critics argue that CEO compensation is disproportionate to achievement, representing a clear example of the agency problem. However, in response to shareholder pressure, in recent years more companies have begun adopting compensation practices that more closely tie CEO pay to performance. For example, at Air Products & Chemicals, when the earnings per share fell short of its 9% growth target in 2012, CEO John McGlade paid the price in the form of a 65% cut in his annual bonus. His stock grants and stock options decreased as well, reducing his total direct compensation 19%, to 9.1 million.[19]

A further concern is that in trying to satisfy a desire for status, security, power, and income, a CEO might engage in empire building—buying many new businesses in an attempt to increase the size of the company through diversification.[20] Although such growth may depress the company's long-term profitability and thus stockholder returns, it increases the size of the empire under the CEO's control and, by extension, the CEO's status, power, security, and income (there is a strong relationship between company size and CEO pay). Instead of trying to maximize stockholder returns by seeking the right balance between profitability and profit growth, some senior managers may trade long-term profitability for greater company growth via new business

on-the-job consumption
A term used by economists to describe the behavior of senior management's use of company funds to acquire perks (lavish offices, jets, and the like) that will enhance their status, instead of investing the funds to increase stockholder returns.

purchases. For example, in the mid-1970s, Compagnie Générale des Eaux was primarily a water utility and waste-management company, operating "near-monopolies" in local municipalities in France and generating strong, stable cash flows for its shareholders. However, a series of audacious, debt-funded acquisitions in the 1980s and 1990s, first by CEO Guy DeJouany and later by his successor, Jean-Marie Messier, rapidly transformed the company into one of the world's largest media and telecom empires, renamed "Vivendi." Then, in the 2000s, as the tech, media, and telecom bubble burst, the Vivendi empire came crashing down under the weight of its debt burden. Jean-Marie Messier was investigated by both French and U.S. courts and accused of misleading shareholders, misappropriating funds, and worsening the company's precarious position. He was fined and forced to resign.[21]

Figure 11.3 graphs long-term profitability against the rate of growth in company revenues. A company that does not grow is likely missing out on profitable opportunities.[22] A moderate revenue growth rate of G^* allows a company to maximize long-term profitability, generating a return of π^*. Thus, a growth rate of $G1$ in Figure 11.3 is not consistent with maximizing profitability ($\pi1 < \pi^*$). By the same token, however, attaining growth in excess of $G2$ requires moving into market segments that earn lower profit margins or diversification into areas that the company knows little about. Consequently, it can be achieved only by sacrificing profitability; that is, past G^*, the investment required to finance further growth does not produce an adequate return, and the company's profitability declines. Yet $G2$ may be the growth rate favored by an empire-building CEO, for it will increase his or her power, status, and income. At this growth rate, profitability is equal only to $\pi2$. Because $\pi^* > \pi2$, a company growing at this rate is clearly not maximizing its long-run profitability or the wealth of its stockholders.

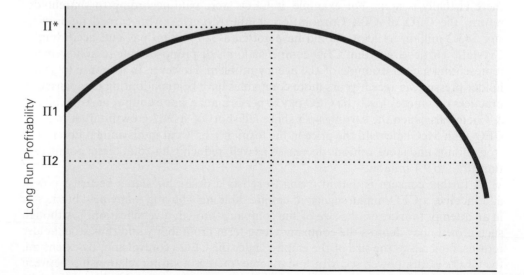

Figure 11.3 The Tradeoff Between Profitability and Revenue Growth Rates

The magnitude of agency problems was emphasized in the early 2000s, when a series of scandals swept through the corporate world, many of which could be attributed to self-interest-seeking senior executives and a failure of corporate governance mechanisms to hold the largess of those executives in check. In 2003, an investigation revealed that the CEO of Hollinger, Conrad Black, had used "tunneling" to divert over $400 million in company funds to his family and friends (see the Strategy in Action 11.2 for more details on Hollinger and Black). Between 2001 and 2004, accounting scandals also unfolded at a number of major corporations, including Enron, WorldCom, Tyco, Computer Associates, HealthSouth, Adelphia Communications, Dynegy, Royal Dutch Shell, and Parmalat, a major Italian food company. At Enron, $27 billion in debt was hidden from shareholders, employees, and regulators in special partnerships that were removed from the balance sheet. At Parmalat, managers apparently "invented" $8 to $12 billion in assets to shore up the company's balance sheet—assets that never existed. In the case of Royal Dutch Shell, senior managers knowingly inflated the value of the company's oil reserves by one-fifth, which amounted to 4 billion barrels of oil that never existed, making the company appear much more valuable than it was. At the other companies, earnings were systematically overstated,

11.2 STRATEGY IN ACTION

Self-Dealing at Hollinger International Inc.

From 1999 to 2003, Conrad Black, CEO, and F. David Radler, chief operating officer (COO), of Hollinger International Inc. illegally diverted cash and assets to themselves, family members, and other corporate insiders. Hollinger International was a global publishing empire that owned newspapers around the world, such as the *Chicago Sun-Times*, the *Daily Telegraph* (in London), the *National Post* (in Toronto), and the *Jerusalem Post* (in Israel), among others. According to Stephen Cutler, the director of the SEC's Division of Enforcement, "Black and Radler abused their control of a public company and treated it as their personal piggy bank. Instead of carrying out their responsibilities to protect the interest of public shareholders, the defendants cheated and defrauded these shareholders through a series of deceptive schemes and misstatements." In a practice known as "tunneling," Black and Radler engaged in a series of self-dealing transactions such as selling some of Hollinger's newspapers at below-market prices to companies privately held by Black and Radler themselves—sometimes for a price as low as one dollar. They also directly channeled money out of the firm under the guise of "noncompetition payments." The managers abused corporate perks, using a company jet to fly to the South Pacific for a vacation and spending corporate funds on a swanky, New York apartment on Park Avenue and a lavish, $62,000 birthday party for Black's wife. Black's ill-gotten gains are thought to total more than $400 million, and fallout from the scandal resulted in a loss of $2 billion in shareholder value. Although Black was sentenced to 6½ years in jail, he ultimately only served 42 months.

Sources: S. Taub, "SEC Charges Hollinger, Two Executives," *CFO*, November 16, 2004; www.cfo.com, U.S. Department of Justice, "Former Hollinger Chairman Conrad Black and Three Other Executives Indicted in U.S.–Canada Corporate Fraud Schemes," indictment released November 17, 2005; "Ex-Media Mogul Black Convicted of Fraud," Associated Press, July 13, 2007; A. Stern, "Ex-Media Mogul Conrad Black Sent Back to Prison," Reuters, June 24, 2011.

often by hundreds of millions of dollars, or even billions of dollars in the case of Tyco and WorldCom, which understated its expenses by $3 billion in 2001. In all of these cases, the prime motivation seems to have been an effort to present a more favorable view of corporate affairs to shareholders than was the case, thereby securing senior executives significantly higher pay packets.[23]

It is important to remember that the agency problem is not confined to the relationship between senior managers and stockholders. It can also bedevil the relationship between the CEO and subordinates, and between them and their subordinates. Subordinates might use control over information to distort the true performance of their unit in order to enhance their pay, increase their job security, or make sure their unit gets more than its fair share of company resources.

Confronted with agency problems, the challenge for principals is to (1) shape the behavior of agents so that they act in accordance with the goals set by principals, (2) reduce information asymmetry between agents and principals, and (3) develop mechanisms for removing agents who do not act in accordance with the goals of principals and mislead them. Principals deal with these challenges through a series of governance mechanisms.

◤ GOVERNANCE MECHANISMS

Principals put governance mechanisms in place to align incentives between principals and agents and to monitor and control agents. The purpose of governance mechanisms is to reduce the scope and frequency of the agency problem; that is, to help ensure that agents act in a manner that is consistent with the best interests of their principals. In this section, the primary focus is on governance mechanisms that exist to align the interests of senior managers (as agents) with their principals, stockholders. It should not be forgotten, however, that governance mechanisms also exist to align the interests of business-unit managers with those of their superiors, and likewise down the hierarchy within the organization.

Here we look at four main types of governance mechanisms for aligning stockholder and management interests: the board of directors, stock-based compensation, financial statements, and the takeover constraint. The section closes with a discussion of governance mechanisms within a company to align the interest of senior and lower-level managers.

The Board of Directors

The board of directors is the centerpiece of the corporate governance system. Board members are directly elected by stockholders, and under corporate law they represent the stockholders' interests in the company. Hence, the board can be held legally accountable for the company's actions. Its position at the apex of decision making within the company allows it to monitor corporate strategy decisions and ensure that they are consistent with stockholder interests. If the board believes that corporate strategies are not in the best interest of stockholders, it can take measures such as voting against management nominations to the board of directors or submitting its own nominees. In addition, the board has the legal authority to hire, fire, and compensate corporate employees, including, most importantly, the CEO.[24] The board is also responsible for making sure that the company's audited financial statements present a true picture of its financial situation. Thus, the board exists to reduce the information asymmetry between stockholders and managers, and to monitor and control management actions on behalf of stockholders.

The typical board of directors is composed of a mix of inside and outside directors. **Inside directors** are senior employees of the company, such as the CEO. They are required on the board because they have valuable information about the company's activities. Without such information, the board cannot adequately perform its monitoring function. But because insiders are full-time employees of the company, their interests tend to be aligned with those of management. Hence, outside directors are needed to bring objectivity to the monitoring and evaluation processes. **Outside directors** are not full-time employees of the company. Many of them are full-time, professional directors who hold positions on the boards of several companies. They need to maintain a reputation for competency and so are motivated to perform their role as objectively and effectively as possible.[25]

There is little doubt that many boards perform their assigned functions admirably. For example, when the board of Sotheby's discovered that the company had been engaged in price fixing with Christie's, board members moved quickly to oust both the CEO and the chairman of the company (see Strategy in Action 11.1). But not all boards perform as well as they should. The board of now-bankrupt energy company Enron approved the company's audited financial statements, which were later discovered to be grossly misleading.

Critics of the existing governance system charge that inside directors often dominate the outsiders on the board. Insiders can use their position within the management hierarchy to exercise control over the company-specific information that the board receives. Consequently, they can present information in a way that puts them in a favorable light. In addition, because insiders have intimate knowledge of the company's operations, and because superior knowledge and control over information are sources of power, they may be better positioned than outsiders to influence boardroom decision making. The board may become the captive of insiders and merely rubber-stamp management decisions instead of guarding stockholder interests.

Some observers contend that many boards are dominated by the company CEO, particularly when the CEO is also the chairman of the board.[26] To support this view, they point out that both inside and outside directors are often the CEO's nominees. The typical inside director is subordinate to the CEO in the company's hierarchy and therefore unlikely to criticize the boss. Nor can outside directors nominated by the CEO be expected to evaluate the CEO objectively. Sometimes CEOs sit on each other's boards as outside directors, forming "interlocking directorates" that may induce them to act in each other's interests. Thus, the loyalty of the board may be biased toward the CEO, not the stockholders. Moreover, a CEO who is also chairman of the board may be able to control the agenda of board discussions in such a manner as to deflect criticisms of his or her leadership. Notably, although shareholders ostensibly vote on board members, board members are not legally required to resign if they do not receive a majority of the vote. The Council of Institutional Investors (which represents pension funds, endowments, and other large investors) published a list of "zombie directors" in 2012—directors who were retained on boards despite being rejected by shareholders. The list includes a wide range of companies, from Boston Beer Company to Loral Space and Communications to Cablevision. In fact, Cablevision

inside directors
Senior employees of the company, such as the CEO.

outside directors
Directors who are not full-time employees of the company, needed to provide objectivity to the monitoring and evaluation of processes.

was listed as having three directors who lost their shareholder votes twice between 2010 and 2012, yet remained on the board.[27]

In the aftermath of the wave of scandals that hit the corporate world in the early 2000s, there are clear signs that many corporate boards are moving away from merely rubber-stamping top-management decisions and are beginning to play a much more active role in corporate governance. In part, they have been prompted by new legislation such as the 2002 Sarbanes-Oxley Act in the United States, which tightened rules regulating corporate reporting and corporate governance. A growing trend on the part of the courts to hold directors liable for corporate misstatements has also been important. Powerful institutional investors such as pension funds have also been more aggressive in exerting their power, often pushing for more outside representation on the board of directors and for a separation between the roles of chairman and CEO—with the chairman role going to an outsider. Partly as a result, 43% of firms on the Standard & Poor's 500 index split the chairman and CEO jobs as of November 2012—up from 25% 10 years earlier.[28] Separating the role of chairman and CEO limits the ability of corporate insiders, particularly the CEO, to exercise control over the board. Regardless, it must be recognized that boards of directors do not work as well as they should in theory, and other mechanisms are needed to align the interests of stockholders and managers.

Stock-Based Compensation

According to agency theory, one of the best ways to reduce the scope of the agency problem is for principals to establish incentives for agents to behave in the company's best interest through pay-for-performance systems. In the case of stockholders and top managers, stockholders can encourage top managers to pursue strategies that maximize a company's long-term profitability and profit growth, and thus the gains from holding its stock, by linking the pay of those managers to the performance of the stock price.

stock options

The right to purchase company stock at a predetermined price at some point in the future, usually within 10 years of the grant date.

Giving managers **stock options**— the right to purchase the company's shares at a predetermined (strike) price at some point in the future, usually within 10 years of the grant date—has been the most common pay-for-performance system. Typically, the strike price is the price at which the stock was trading when the option was originally granted. Ideally, stock options will motivate managers to adopt strategies that increase the share price of the company, for in doing so managers also increase the value of their own stock options. Granting managers stock if they attain predetermined performance targets is another stock-based, pay-for-performance system.

Several academic studies suggest that stock-based compensation schemes such as stock options and stock grants can align executive and stockholder interests. For instance, one study found that managers were more likely to consider the effects of their acquisition decisions on stockholder returns if they were significant shareholders.[29] According to another study, managers who were significant stockholders were less likely to pursue strategies that would maximize the size of the company rather than its profitability.[30] More generally, it is difficult to argue with the proposition that the chance to get rich from exercising stock options is the primary reason for the 14-hour days and 6-day workweeks that many employees of fast-growing companies experience.

However, the practice of granting stock options has become increasingly controversial. Many top managers earn huge bonuses from exercising stock options that were granted several years prior. Critics claim that these options are often too generous but do not deny that they motivate managers to improve company performance. A particular cause for concern is that stock options are often granted at such low strike prices that the CEO can hardly fail to make a significant amount of money by exercising them, even if the company underperforms in the stock market by a significant margin. A serious example of the agency problem emerged in 2005 and 2006, when the SEC investigated a number of companies that had granted stock options to senior executives and apparently "backdated" the stock to a time when the price was lower, enabling executives to earn more money than if those options had simply been dated on the day they were granted.[31] By late 2006, the SEC had investigated nearly 130 companies for possible fraud related to stock-option backdating. Major corporations such as Apple, Jabil Circuit, United Healthcare, and Home Depot were included in the list.[32]

Other critics of stock options, including the famous investor Warren Buffett, complain that huge stock-option grants increase the outstanding number of shares in a company and therefore dilute the equity of stockholders; accordingly, they should be shown in company accounts as an expense against profits. Under accounting regulations that were enforced until 2005, stock options, unlike wages and salaries, were not expensed. However, this has since changed, and as a result many companies are beginning to reduce their use of options. Microsoft, for example, which had long given generous stock-option grants to high-performing employees, replaced stock options with stock grants in 2005. Requiring senior management to hold large numbers of shares in the company also has its downside: Managers who hold a large portion of their personal wealth in the company they manage are likely to be underdiversified. This can lead to excessively risk-averse behavior, or overdiversification of the firm.

Financial Statements and Auditors

Publicly traded companies in the United States are required to file quarterly and annual reports with the SEC that are prepared according to GAAP. The purpose of this requirement is to give consistent, detailed, and accurate information about how efficiently and effectively the agents of stockholders—the managers—are running the company. To make sure that managers do not misrepresent financial information, the SEC also requires that the accounts be audited by an independent and accredited accounting firm. Similar regulations exist in most other developed nations. If the system works as intended, stockholders can have a lot of faith that the information contained in financial statements accurately reflects the state of affairs at a company. Among other things, such information can enable a stockholder to calculate the profitability (ROIC) of a company in which he or she invests and to compare its ROIC against that of competitors.

Unfortunately, this system has not always worked as intended in the United States. Despite the fact that the vast majority of companies do file accurate information in their financial statements, and although most auditors review that information accurately, there is substantial evidence that a minority of companies have abused the system, aided in part by the compliance of auditors. This was clearly an issue at bankrupt energy trader Enron, where the CFO and others misrepresented the true financial state of the company to investors by creating off-balance-sheet partnerships that hid the true state of Enron's indebtedness from public view. Enron's auditor, Arthur Andersen, was complicit with this deception and in direct violation of its fiduciary duty. Arthur Anderson had lucrative consulting contracts with Enron that it did not want to jeopardize by questioning the accuracy of the company's financial statements. The losers in this mutual deception were shareholders, who relied completely upon inaccurate information to make their investment decisions.

There have been numerous examples in recent years of managers' gaming of financial statements to present a distorted picture of their company's finances to investors (see the accusations made by HP about Autonomy in the Closing Case, for example). The typical motive has been to inflate the earnings or revenues of a company, thereby generating investor enthusiasm and propelling the stock price higher, which gives managers an opportunity to cash in stock-option grants for huge personal gain, obviously at the expense of stockholders, who have been misled by the reports.

The gaming of financial statements by companies such as Enron raises serious questions about the accuracy of the information contained in audited financial statements. In response, Congress passed the Sarbanes-Oxley Act in 2002, representing the most far-reaching overhaul of accounting rules and corporate governance procedures since the 1930s. Among other things, Sarbanes-Oxley established an oversight board for accounting firms, required CEOs and CFOs to endorse their company's financial statements, and barred companies from hiring the same accounting firm for both auditing and consulting services.

The Takeover Constraint

Given the imperfections in corporate governance mechanisms, it is clear that the agency problem persists at some companies. However, stockholders do have residual power—they can always sell their shares. If stockholders sell in large numbers, the price of the company's shares will decline. If the share price falls far enough, the company might be worth less on the stock market than the actual value of its assets. At this point, the company may become an attractive acquisition target and runs the risk of being purchased by another enterprise, against the wishes of the target company's management.

takeover constraint
The risk of being acquired by another company.

The risk of being acquired by another company is known as the **takeover constraint**—it limits the extent to which managers can pursue strategies and take actions that put their own interests above those of stockholders. If they ignore stockholder interests and the company is acquired, senior managers typically lose their independence, and likely their jobs as well. Therefore, the threat of takeover can constrain management action and limit the worst excesses of the agency problem.

During the 1980s and early 1990s, the threat of takeover was often enforced by corporate raiders: individuals or corporations that purchase large blocks of shares in companies that appear to be pursuing strategies inconsistent with maximizing stockholder wealth. Corporate raiders argue that if these underperforming companies pursued different strategies, they could create more wealth for stockholders. Raiders purchase stock in a company either to take over the business and run it more efficiently or to precipitate a change in top management, replacing the existing team with one more likely to maximize stockholder returns. Raiders are motivated not by altruism but by gain. If they succeed in their takeover bid, they can institute strategies that create value for stockholders, including themselves. Even if a takeover bid fails, raiders can still earn millions, for their stockholdings will typically be bought out by the defending company for a hefty premium. Called **greenmail**, this source of gain has stirred much controversy and debate about its benefits. Whereas some claim

greenmail
A source of gaining wealth whereby corporate raiders either push companies to change their corporate strategy to one that will benefit stockholders, or charge a premium for stock when the company wants to buy it back.

that the threat posed by raiders has had a salutary effect on enterprise performance by pushing corporate management to run companies better, others counter that there is little evidence of this.[33]

Although the incidence of hostile takeover bids has fallen off significantly since the early 1990s, this should not imply that the takeover constraint has ceased to operate. Unique circumstances existed in the early 2000s that made it more difficult to execute hostile takeovers. The boom years of the 1990s left many corporations with excessive debt (corporate America entered the new century with record levels of debt on its balance sheets), limiting the ability to finance acquisitions, particularly hostile acquisitions, which are often particularly expensive. In addition, the market valuation of many companies became misaligned with underlying fundamentals during the stock market bubble of the 1990s, and after a substantial fall in certain segments of the stock market, such as the technology sector, present valuations are still high relative to historic norms—making the hostile acquisition of even poorly run and unprofitable companies expensive. However, takeovers tend to occur in cycles, and it seems likely that once excesses are worked out of the stock market and off corporate balance sheets, the takeover constraint will reassert itself. It should be remembered that the takeover constraint is the governance mechanism of last resort and is often invoked only when other governance mechanisms have failed.

Governance Mechanisms Inside a Company

Thus far, this chapter has focused on the governance mechanisms designed to reduce the agency problem that potentially exists between stockholders and managers. Agency relationships also exist within a company, and the agency problem can arise between levels of management. In this section, we explore how the agency problem can be reduced within a company by using two complementary governance mechanisms to align the incentives and behavior of employees with those of upper-level management: strategic control systems and incentive systems.

Strategic Control Systems   Strategic control systems are the primary governance mechanisms established within a company to reduce the scope of the agency problem between levels of management. These systems are the formal target-setting, measurement, and feedback systems that allow managers to evaluate whether a company is executing the strategies necessary to maximize its long-term profitability and, in particular, whether the company is achieving superior efficiency, quality, innovation, and customer responsiveness. They are discussed in more detail in Chapter 12.

The purpose of strategic control systems is to (1) establish standards and targets against which performance can be measured, (2) create systems for measuring and monitoring performance on a regular basis, (3) compare actual performance against the established targets, and (4) evaluate results and take corrective action if necessary. In governance terms, their purpose is to ensure that lower-level managers, as the agents of top managers, act in a way that is consistent with top managers' goals, which should be to maximize the wealth of stockholders, subject to legal and ethical constraints.

One increasingly influential model that guides managers through the process of creating the right kind of strategic control systems is the balanced scorecard model.[34] Managers have traditionally emphasized financial measures of performance such as ROIC to gauge and evaluate organizational performance. According to the balanced scorecard model financial information is extremely important, but it alone is not enough. If managers are to obtain a true picture of organizational performance, financial information must be supplemented with performance measures that indicate how well an organization has been achieving the four building blocks of competitive advantage: efficiency, quality, innovation, and responsiveness to customers. This is because financial results simply inform managers about the results of strategic decisions they have already taken; the other measures balance this picture of performance by informing managers about how reliably the organization has in place the building blocks to drive future performance.[35]

One version of the way the balanced scorecard operates is presented in Figure 11.4. Based on an organization's mission and goals, strategic managers develop a set of criteria for assessing performance according to multiple perspectives such as:

- *The financial perspective:* for example, ROIC, cash flow, and revenue growth
- *The customer perspective:* for example, satisfaction, product reliability, on-time delivery, and level of service

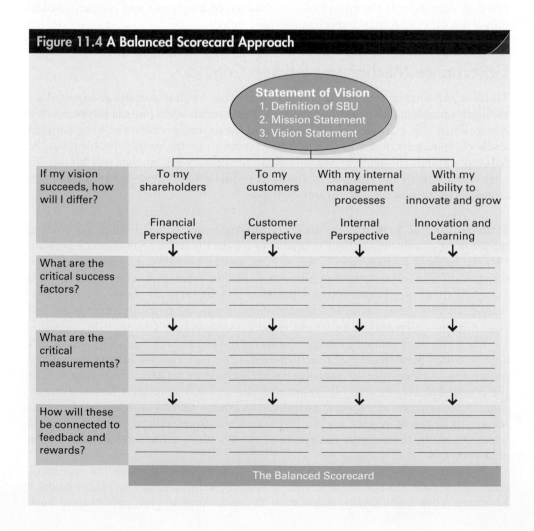

Figure 11.4 A Balanced Scorecard Approach

- *The internal perspective:* for example, efficiency, timeliness, and employee satisfaction
- *Innovation and learning:* for example, the number of new products introduced, the percentage of revenues generated from new products in a defined period, the time taken to develop the next generation of new products versus the competition, and the productivity of research and development (R&D)—how much R&D spending is required to produce a successful product

As Kaplan and Norton, the developers of this approach, suggest, "Think of the balanced scorecard as the dials and indicators in an airplane cockpit. For the complex task of navigating and flying an airplane, pilots need detailed information about many aspects of the flight. They need information on fuel, air speed, altitude, learning, destination, and other indicators that summarize the current and predicted environment. Reliance on one instrument can be fatal. Similarly, the complexity of managing an organization today requires that managers be able to view performance in several areas simultaneously."[36]

Based on an evaluation of the complete set of measures in the balanced scorecard, strategic managers are in a good position to reevaluate the company's mission and goals and take corrective action to rectify problems, limit the agency problem, or exploit new opportunities by changing the organization's strategy and structure—which is the purpose of strategic control.

Employee Incentives   Control systems alone may not be sufficient to align incentives between stockholders, senior management, and the organization as a whole. To help do this, positive incentive systems are often put into place to motivate employees to work toward goals that are central to maximizing long-term profitability. As already noted, ESOPs are one form of positive incentive, as are stock-option grants. In the 1990s, ESOPs and stock-ownership grants were pushed down deep within many organizations, meaning that employees at many levels of the firm were eligible for the plans. The logic behind such systems is straightforward: Recognizing that the stock price, and therefore their own wealth, is dependent upon the profitability of the company, employees will work toward maximizing profitability.

In addition to stock-based compensation systems, employee compensation can be tied to goals that are linked to the attainment of superior efficiency, quality, innovation, and customer responsiveness. For example, the bonus pay of a manufacturing employee might depend upon attaining quality and productivity targets, which, if reached, will lower the costs of the company, increase customer satisfaction, and boost profitability. Similarly, a salesperson's bonus pay might depend upon surpassing sales targets, and an R&D employee's bonus pay may be contingent upon the success of new products he or she had worked on developing.

ETHICS AND STRATEGY

The term **ethics** refers to accepted principles of right or wrong that govern the conduct of a person, the members of a profession, or the actions of an organization. **Business ethics** are the accepted principles of right or wrong governing the conduct of businesspeople. Ethical decisions are in accordance with those accepted principles, whereas unethical decisions violate accepted principles. This is not as straightforward

ethics
Accepted principles of right or wrong that govern the conduct of a person, the members of a profession, or the actions of an organization.

business ethics
Accepted principles of right or wrong governing the conduct of businesspeople.

ethical dilemmas

Situations where there is no agreement over exactly what the accepted principles of right and wrong are, or where none of the available alternatives seems ethically acceptable.

as it sounds. Managers may be confronted with **ethical dilemmas**, which are situations where there is no agreement over exactly what the accepted principles of right and wrong are, or where none of the available alternatives seems ethically acceptable.

In our society, many accepted principles of right and wrong are not only universally recognized but also codified into law. In the business arena, there are laws governing product liability (tort laws), contracts and breaches of contract (contract law), the protection of intellectual property (intellectual property law), competitive behavior (antitrust law), and the selling of securities (securities law). Not only is it unethical to break these laws, it is illegal.

In this book we argue that the preeminent goal of managers in a business should be to pursue strategies that maximize the long-term profitability and profit growth of the enterprise, thereby boosting returns to stockholders. Strategies, of course, must be consistent with the laws that govern business behavior: Managers must act legally while seeking to maximize the long-term profitability of the enterprise. Unfortunately, as we have already seen in this chapter, managers do break laws. Moreover, managers may take advantage of ambiguities and gray areas in the law, of which there are many in our common law system, to pursue actions that are at best legally suspect and, in any event, clearly unethical. It is important to realize, however, that behaving ethically surpasses staying within the bounds of the law. In the Opening Case, for example, we described how Starbucks goes well beyond legal requirements to ensure that its coffee is purchased from suppliers that use safe, fair, humane working and living conditions, including minimum-wage requirements and the prohibition of child and forced labor. On the other hand, research by Surroca, Tribó, and Zahra on 110 multinational firms found that often multinational firms deal with stakeholder pressures and legal concerns in their home country by simply transferring their socially irresponsible practices to their overseas subsidiaries. The researchers found that this was particularly likely when it was not overtly apparent that the subsidiary had a connection to the multinational, suggesting that managers knew the behavior was unethical and did not want to be associated with it, yet continued the practice anyway.[37]

In this section, we take a closer look at the ethical issues that managers may confront when developing strategy, and at the steps managers can take to ensure that strategic decisions are not only legal, but also ethical.

Ethical Issues in Strategy

The ethical issues that strategic managers confront cover many topics, but most are due to a potential conflict between the goals of the enterprise, or the goals of individual managers, and the fundamental rights of important stakeholders, including stockholders, customers, employees, suppliers, competitors, communities, and the general public. Stakeholders have basic rights that must be respected; it is unethical to violate those rights.

Stockholders have the right to timely and accurate information about their investments (in accounting statements), and it is unethical to violate that right. Customers have the right to be fully informed about the products and services they purchase, including the right to information about how those products might cause them harm, and it is unethical to restrict their access to such information. Employees have the right to safe working conditions, fair compensation for the work they perform, and just treatment by managers. Suppliers have the right to expect contracts to be respected, and the company should not take advantage of a power disparity between it and a supplier to opportunistically rewrite a contract. Competitors have the right to expect that the firm will abide by the rules of competition and not violate the basic principles of antitrust laws. Communities and the general public, including their political representatives in government, have the right to expect that a firm will not violate the basic expectations that society places on enterprises—for example, by dumping toxic pollutants into the environment, or overcharging for work performed on government contracts.

Those who take the stakeholder view of business ethics often argue that it is in the enlightened self-interest of managers to behave in an ethical manner that recognizes and respects the fundamental rights of stakeholders, because doing so will ensure the support of stakeholders and, ultimately, benefit the firm and its managers. Others go beyond this instrumental approach to ethics and argue that, in many cases, acting ethically is simply the right thing to do. They argue that businesses need to recognize their *noblesse oblige*, a French term that refers to honorable and benevolent behavior that is considered the responsibility of people of high (noble) birth, and give something back to the society that made their success possible. In a business setting, it is understood that benevolent behavior is the moral responsibility of successful enterprises.

Unethical behavior often arises in a corporate setting when managers decide to put the attainment of their own personal goals, or the goals of the enterprise, above the fundamental rights of one or more stakeholder groups (in other words, unethical behavior may arise from agency problems). The most common examples of such behavior involve self-dealing, information manipulation, anticompetitive behavior, opportunistic exploitation of other players in the value chain in which the firm is embedded (including suppliers, complement providers, and distributors), the maintenance of substandard working conditions, environmental degradation, and corruption.

Self-dealing occurs when managers find a way to feather their own nests with corporate monies, as we have already discussed in several examples in this chapter (such as Conrad Black at Hollinger). **Information manipulation** occurs when managers use their control over corporate data to distort or hide information in order to enhance their own financial situation or the competitive position of the firm, such as HP accused Autonomy of in the Closing Case. As we have seen, many accounting scandals have involved the deliberate manipulation of financial information. Information manipulation can also occur with nonfinancial data. An example of this is when managers at the tobacco companies suppressed internal research that linked smoking to health problems, violating the right of consumers to accurate information about the dangers of smoking. When this evidence came to light, lawyers filed class-action suits against the tobacco companies, claiming that they had intentionally caused harm to smokers; they had broken tort law by promoting a product that they knew was seriously harmful to consumers. In 1999, the tobacco companies settled a lawsuit brought by the states that sought to recover health-care costs associated with tobacco-related illnesses; the total payout to the states was $260 billion.

Anticompetitive behavior covers a range of actions aimed at harming actual or potential competitors, most often by using monopoly power, and thereby enhancing the long-run prospects of the firm. For example, in the 1990s, the Justice Department claimed that Microsoft used its monopoly in operating systems to force PC makers to bundle Microsoft's Web browser, Internet Explorer, with the Windows operating system, and to display the Internet Explorer logo prominently on the computer desktop. Microsoft reportedly told PC makers that it would not supply them with Windows

self-dealing
Managers using company funds for their own personal consumption

information manipulation
When managers use their control over corporate data to distort or hide information in order to enhance their own financial situation or the competitive position of the firm.

anticompetitive behavior
A range of actions aimed at harming actual or potential competitors, most often by using monopoly power, and thereby enhancing the long-run prospects of the firm.

unless they did this. Because the PC makers needed Windows to sell their machines, this was a powerful threat. The alleged aim of the action, which exemplifies "tie-in sales"—which are illegal under antitrust laws—was to drive a competing browser maker, Netscape, out of business. The courts ruled that Microsoft was indeed abusing its monopoly power in this case and, under a 2001 consent decree, the company was forced to cease this practice.

Legality aside, the actions Microsoft managers allegedly engaged in are unethical on at least three counts; first, by violating the rights of end-users by unfairly limiting their choice; second, by violating the rights of downstream participants in the industry value chain, in this case PC makers, by forcing them to incorporate a particular product in their design; and third, by violating the rights of competitors to free and fair competition.

opportunistic exploitation

Unethical behavior sometimes used by managers to unilaterally rewrite the terms of a contract with suppliers, buyers, or complement providers in a way that favors to the firm.

Opportunistic exploitation of other players in the value chain in which the firm is embedded is another example of unethical behavior. Exploitation of this kind typically occurs when the managers of a firm seek to unilaterally rewrite the terms of a contract with suppliers, buyers, or complement providers in a way that is more favorable to the firm, often using their power to force a revision to the contract. For example, in the late 1990s, Boeing entered into a $2-billion contract with Titanium Metals Corporation to purchase certain amounts of titanium annually for 10 years. In 2000, after Titanium Metals had already spent $100 million to expand its production capacity to fulfill the contract, Boeing demanded that the contract be renegotiated, asking for lower prices and an end to minimum-purchase agreements. As a major purchaser of titanium, managers at Boeing probably thought they had the power to push this contract revision through, and Titanium's investment meant that it would be unlikely that the company walk away from the deal. Titanium promptly sued Boeing for breach of contract. The dispute was settled out of court, and under a revised agreement Boeing agreed to pay monetary damages to Titanium Metals (reported to be in the $60-million range) and entered into an amended contract to purchase titanium.[38] This action was arguably unethical because it violated the supplier's right to have a purchaser do business in a fair and open way, regardless of any issues of legality.

substandard working conditions

Arise when managers underinvest in working conditions, or pay employees below-market rates, in order to reduce their production costs.

Substandard working conditions arise when managers underinvest in working conditions, or pay employees below-market rates, in order to reduce their production costs. The most extreme examples of such behavior occur when a firm establishes operations in countries that lack the workplace regulations found in developed nations such as the United States. For example, The Ohio Art Company ran into an ethical storm when newspaper reports alleged that it had moved production of its popular Etch A Sketch toy from Ohio to a supplier in Shenzhen Province where employees—mostly teenagers—work long hours for $0.24 per hour, below the legal minimum wage of $0.33 per hour. Moreover, production reportedly started at 7:30 a.m. and continued until 10 p.m., with breaks only for lunch and dinner. Furthermore, Saturdays and Sundays were treated as normal workdays, meaning that employees worked 12 hours per day, 7 days per week, or 84 hours per week—well above the standard 40-hour week authorities set in Shenzhen. Working conditions such as these clearly violate employees' rights in China, as specified by local regulations (which are poorly enforced). Is it ethical for the Ohio Art Company to use such a supplier? Many would say it is not.[39]

environmental degradation

Occurs when a company's actions directly or indirectly result in pollution or other forms of environmental harm.

Environmental degradation occurs when a company's actions directly or indirectly result in pollution or other forms of environmental harm. Environmental degradation can violate the right of local communities and the general public to clean air and water, land that is free from pollution by toxic chemicals, and properly managed forests.

Finally, **corruption** can arise in a business context when managers pay bribes to gain access to lucrative business contracts. For example, it was alleged that Halliburton was part of a consortium that paid nearly $180 million in bribes to win a lucrative contract to build a natural gas plant in Nigeria.[40] Similarly, between 2006 and 2009, Siemens was found guilty of paying hundreds of millions of dollars in bribes to secure sales contracts; the company was ultimately forced to pay hefty fines, and one Chinese executive who accepted $5.1 million in bribes was sentenced to death by Chinese courts.[41] Corruption is clearly unethical because it violates many rights, including the right of competitors to a level playing field when bidding for contracts, and, when government officials are involved, the right of citizens to expect that government officials will act in the best interest of the local community (or nation) and not in response to corrupt payments.

corruption

Can arise in a business context when managers pay bribes to gain access to lucrative business contracts.

The Roots of Unethical Behavior

Why do some managers behave unethically? What motivates managers to engage in actions that violate accepted principals of right and wrong, trample on the rights of one or more stakeholder groups, or simply break the law? Although there is no simple answer to this question, a few generalizations can be made.[42] First, it is important to recognize that business ethics are not divorced from **personal ethics**, which are the generally accepted principles of right and wrong governing the conduct of individuals. As individuals we are taught that it is wrong to lie and cheat, and that it is right to behave with integrity and honor and stand up for what we believe to be true. The personal ethical code that guides behavior comes from many sources, including parents, schools, religion, and the media. A personal ethical code will exert a profound influence on the way an individual behaves as a businessperson. An individual with a strong sense of personal ethics is less likely to behave in an unethical manner in a business setting; in particular, he or she is less likely to engage in self-dealing and more likely to behave with integrity.

personal ethics

Generally accepted principles of right and wrong governing the conduct of individuals.

Second, many studies of unethical behavior in a business setting have come to the conclusion that businesspeople sometimes do not realize that they are behaving unethically, primarily because they simply fail to ask the relevant question: Is this decision or action ethical? Instead, they apply straightforward business calculus to what they perceive to be a business decision, forgetting that the decision may also have an important ethical dimension.[43] The fault here is within the processes that do not incorporate ethical considerations into business decision making. This may have been the case at Nike and other textile companies when managers originally made subcontracting arrangements with contractors that operated factories as "sweatshops," with long hours, low pay, and poor working conditions. Those decisions were probably made on the basis of good economic logic. Subcontractors were probably chosen on the basis of business variables such as cost, delivery, and product quality, and key managers simply failed to ask: "How does this subcontractor treat its workforce?" If managers pondered this question at all, they probably reasoned that it was the subcontractor's concern, not the company's.

Unfortunately, the climate in some businesses does not encourage people to think through the ethical consequences of business decisions. This brings us to the third cause of unethical behavior in businesses: an organizational culture that de-emphasizes business ethics and considers all decisions to be purely economic ones. Individuals may believe their decisions within the workplace are not subject to the same ethical principles that govern their personal lives, or that their decisions within the firm do not really "belong" to them, but rather that they are merely acting as agents of the firm. A related fourth cause of unethical behavior may be pressure from top management to meet performance goals that are unrealistic and can only be attained by cutting corners or acting in an unethical manner. Thus the pressure to perform induces individuals to behave in ways they otherwise would not.

An organizational culture can "legitimize" behavior that society would judge as unethical, particularly when this is mixed with a focus upon unrealistic performance goals such as maximizing short-term economic performance regardless of the costs. In such circumstances, there is a greater-than-average probability that managers will violate their own personal ethics and engage in behavior that is unethical. By the same token, an organization's culture can do just the opposite and reinforce the need for ethical behavior. Recreational Equipment Inc. (REI), for example, has a strong culture around valuing environmental sustainability, respect for individuals, and trustworthiness. The firm backs up this belief system with such policies as producing an annual environmental stewardship report and providing health-care benefits for all workers (including part-time employees), a retirement plan that does not require individual contributions, and grants for employees to contribute to their communities or to buy gear to pursue personal outdoor challenges. The company has made *Fortune*'s "100 Best Companies to Work For" list every year since 1998.

This brings us to a fifth root cause of unethical behavior: *unethical leadership*. Leaders help to establish the culture of an organization, and they set the example that others follow. Other employees in a business often take their cues from business leaders, and if those leaders do not behave in an ethical manner, employees may not either. It is not what leaders say that matters, but what they do. A good example is Ken Lay, the former CEO of the failed energy company Enron. While constantly referring to Enron's code of ethics in public statements, Lay simultaneously engaged in behavior that was ethically suspect. Among other things, he failed to discipline subordinates who had inflated earnings by engaging in corrupt energy-trading schemes. Such behavior sent a very clear message to Enron's employees—unethical behavior would be tolerated if it could boost earnings.

Behaving Ethically

What is the best way for managers to ensure that ethical considerations are taken into account? In many cases, there is no easy answer to this question, for many of the most vexing ethical problems involve very real dilemmas and suggest no obvious right course of action. Nevertheless, managers can and should do at least seven things to ensure that basic ethical principles are adhered to and that ethical issues are routinely considered when making business decisions. They can (1) favor hiring and promoting people with a well-grounded sense of personal ethics, (2) build an organizational culture that places a high value on ethical behavior, (3) make sure that leaders within the business not only articulate the rhetoric of ethical behavior but also act in a manner that is consistent with that rhetoric, (4) put decision-making processes in place that require people to consider the ethical dimension of business decisions, (5) use ethics officers, (6) put strong governance processes in place, and (7) act with moral courage.

Hiring and Promotion It seems obvious that businesses should strive to hire people who have a strong sense of personal ethics and would not engage in unethical or illegal behavior. Similarly, you would rightly expect a business to not promote people, and perhaps fire people, whose behavior does not match generally accepted ethical standards. But doing this is actually very difficult.

Is there anything that businesses can do to ensure they do not hire people who have poor personal ethics, particularly given that people have an incentive to hide this from public view (indeed, unethical people may well lie about their nature)? Businesses can give potential employees psychological tests to try to discern their ethical predisposition, and they can check with prior employees regarding someone's reputation, such as by asking for letters of reference and talking to people who have worked with the prospective employee. The latter approach is not uncommon and does influence the hiring process. Promoting people who have displayed poor ethics should not occur in a company where the organizational culture values ethical behavior and where leaders act accordingly.

Organization Culture and Leadership   To foster ethical behavior, businesses must build an organizational culture that places high value on ethical behavior. Three actions are particularly important. First, businesses must explicitly articulate values that place a strong emphasis on ethical behavior. Many companies now do this by drafting a **code of ethics**, a formal statement of the ethical priorities to which a business adheres—in fact, both the New York Stock Exchange and Nasdaq listing services require listed companies to have a code of ethics that identifies areas of ethical risk, provides guidance for recognizing and dealing with ethical issues, provides mechanisms for reporting unethical conduct, and notes procedures to ensure prompt action against violations.[44] Firms also sometimes incorporate ethical statements into documents that articulate the values or mission of the business. For example, the food and consumer products giant Unilever's code of ethics includes the following points: "We will not use any form of forced, compulsory or child labor" and "No employee may offer, give or receive any gift or payment which is, or may be construed as being, a bribe. Any demand for, or offer of, a bribe must be rejected immediately and reported to management."[45] Unilever's principles send a very clear message to managers and employees within the organization. Data from the National Business Ethics Survey, administered by the Ethics Resource Center, a U.S. nonprofit, has found that firms with strong, well-implemented ethics programs have significantly fewer cases of ethical misconduct.

Having articulated values in a code of ethics or some other document, it is important that leaders in the business give life and meaning to those words by repeatedly emphasizing their importance and then acting on them. This means using every relevant opportunity to stress the importance of business ethics and making sure that key business decisions not only make good economic sense but also are ethical. Many companies have gone a step further and hired independent firms to audit them and make sure that they are behaving in a manner consistent with their ethical codes. Nike, for example, has in recent years hired independent auditors to ensure that its subcontractors are adhering to Nike's code of conduct.

Finally, building an organization culture that places a high value on ethical behavior requires incentive and reward systems, including promotional systems that reward people who engage in ethical behavior and sanction those who do not.

Decision-Making Processes   In addition to establishing the right kind of ethical culture in an organization, businesspeople must be able to think through the ethical

code of ethics
Formal statement of the ethical priorities to which a business adheres.

implications of decisions in a systematic way. To do this, they need a moral compass, and beliefs about what determines individual rights and justice. Some experts on ethics have proposed a straightforward practical guide, or ethical algorithm, to determine whether a decision is ethical. A decision is acceptable on ethical grounds if a business-person can answer "yes" to each of these questions:

1. Does my decision fall within the accepted values or standards that typically apply in the organizational environment (as articulated in a code of ethics or some other corporate statement)?
2. Am I willing to see the decision communicated to all stakeholders affected by it— for example, by having it reported in newspapers or on television?
3. Would the people with whom I have a significant personal relationship, such as family members, friends, or even managers in other businesses, approve of the decision?

Ethics Officers   To make sure that a business behaves in an ethical manner, a number of firms now have ethics officers. These individuals are responsible for making sure that all employees are trained to be ethically aware, that ethical considerations enter the business decision-making process, and that employees adhere to the company's code of ethics. Ethics officers may also be responsible for auditing decisions to ensure that they are consistent with this code. In many businesses, ethics officers act as an internal ombudsperson with responsibility for handling confidential inquiries from employees, investigating complaints from employees or others, reporting findings, and making recommendations for change.

United Technologies, a large aerospace company with worldwide revenues of about $60 billion, has had a formal code of ethics since 1990. There are now some 450 "business practice officers" (the company's name for ethics officers) within United Technologies who are responsible for making sure that employees adhere to the code. United Technologies also established an ombudsperson program in 1986 that allows employees to inquire anonymously about ethics issues.[46]

Strong Corporate Governance   Strong corporate governance procedures are needed to ensure that managers adhere to ethical norms, in particular, that senior managers do not engage in self-dealing or information manipulation. Strong corporate governance procedures require an independent board of directors that is willing to hold top managers accountable for self-dealing and is capable of verifying the information managers provide. If companies like Tyco, WorldCom, and Enron had had strong boards of directors, it is unlikely that these companies would have experienced accounting scandals or that top managers would have been able to access the funds of these corporations as personal treasuries.

There are five cornerstones of strong governance. The first is a board of directors that is composed of a majority of outside directors who have no management responsibilities in the firm, who are willing and able to hold top managers accountable, and who do not have business ties with important insiders. Outside directors should be individuals of high integrity whose reputation is based on their ability to act independently. The second cornerstone is a board where the positions of CEO and chairman are held by separate individuals and the chairman is an outside director. When the CEO is also chairman of the board of directors, he or she can control the agenda, thereby furthering his or her own personal agenda (which may include self-dealing) or limiting criticism against current corporate policies. The third cornerstone is a compensation committee formed by the board that is composed entirely of outside directors. It is the compensation committee that sets the level of pay for top managers, including stock-option grants and additional benefits. The scope of self-dealing is reduced by making sure that the compensation committee is independent of managers. Fourth, the audit committee of the board, which reviews the financial statements of the firm, should also be composed of outsiders, thereby encouraging vigorous independent questioning of the firm's financial statements. Finally, the board should use outside auditors that are truly independent and do not have a conflict of interest. This was not the case in many recent accounting scandals, where outside auditors were also consultants to the corporation and therefore less likely to ask management hard questions for fear that doing so would jeopardize lucrative consulting contracts.

Moral Courage It is important to recognize that sometimes managers and others need significant moral courage. It is moral courage that enables managers to walk away from a decision that is profitable but unethical, that gives employees the strength to say no to superiors who instruct them to behave unethically, and that gives employees the integrity to contact the media and "blow the whistle' on persistent unethical behavior in a company. Moral courage does not come easily; there are well-known cases where individuals have lost their jobs because they were whistleblowers on unethical corporate behaviors.

Companies can strengthen the moral courage of employees by making a commitment to refuse to seek retribution against employees who exercise moral courage, say no to superiors, or otherwise complain about unethical actions. For example, Unilever's code of ethics includes the following:

> Any breaches of the Code must be reported in accordance with the procedures specified by the Joint Secretaries. The Board of Unilever will not criticize management for any loss of business resulting from adherence to these principles and other mandatory policies and instructions. The Board of Unilever expects employees to bring to their attention, or to that of senior management, any breach or suspected breach of these principles. Provision has been made for employees to be able to report in confidence and no employee will suffer as a consequence of doing so.

This statement gives "permission" to employees to exercise moral courage. Companies can also set up an ethics hotline that allows employees to anonymously register a complaint with a corporate ethics officer.

Final Words The steps discussed here can help to ensure that when managers make business decisions, they are fully cognizant of the ethical implications and do not violate basic ethical prescripts. At the same time, not all ethical dilemmas have a clean and obvious solution—that is why they are dilemmas. At the end of the day, there are things that a business should not do, and there are things that a business should do, but there are also situations that present managers with true predicament. In these cases a premium is placed upon the ability of managers to make sense out of complex, messy situations and to make balanced decisions that are as just as possible.

KEY TERMS

TAKEAWAYS FOR STRATEGIC MANAGERS

1. Stakeholders are individuals or groups that have an interest, claim, or stake in the company—in what it does and in how well it performs.

2. Stakeholders are in an exchange relationship with the company. They supply the organization with important resources (or contributions) and in exchange expect their interests to be satisfied (by inducements).

3. A company cannot always satisfy the claims of all stakeholders. The goals of different groups may conflict. The company must identify the most important stakeholders and give highest priority to pursuing strategies that satisfy their needs.

4. A company's stockholders are its legal owners and the providers of risk capital–a major source of capital resources that allow a company to operate its business. As such, they have a unique role among stakeholder groups.

5. Maximizing long-term profitability and profit growth is the route to maximizing returns to stockholders, and it is also consistent with satisfying the claims of several other key stakeholder groups.

6. When pursuing strategies that maximize profitability, a company has the obligation to do so within the limits set by the law and in a manner consistent with societal expectations.

7. An agency relationship is said to exist whenever one party delegates decision-making authority or control over resources to another party.

8. The essence of the agency problem is that the interests of principals and agents are not always the same, and some agents may take advantage of information asymmetries to maximize their own interests at the expense of principals.

9. Numerous governance mechanisms serve to limit the agency problem between stockholders and managers. These include the board of directors, stock-based compensation schemes, financial statements and auditors, and the threat of a takeover.

10. The term *ethics* refers to accepted principles of right or wrong that govern the conduct of a person, the members of a profession, or the actions of an organization. Business ethics are the accepted principles of right or wrong governing the conduct of businesspeople, and an ethical strategy is one that does not violate these accepted principles.

11. Unethical behavior is rooted in poor personal ethics; the inability to recognize that ethical issues are at stake; failure to incorporate ethical issues into strategic and operational decision making; a dysfunctional culture; and failure of leaders to act in an ethical manner.

12. To make sure that ethical issues are considered in business decisions, managers should (a) favor hiring and promoting people with a well-grounded sense of personal ethics, (b) build an organizational culture that places high value on ethical behavior, (c) ensure that leaders within

the business not only articulate the rhetoric of ethical behavior but also act in a manner that is consistent with that rhetoric, (d) put decision-making processes in place that require people to consider the ethical dimension of business decisions, (e) use ethics officers, (f) have strong corporate governance procedures, and (g) be morally courageous and encourage others to be the same.

DISCUSSION QUESTIONS

1. How prevalent has the agency problem been in corporate America during the last decade? During the late 1990s, there was a boom in initial public offerings of Internet companies (dot. com companies). The boom was supported by sky-high valuations, often assigned to Internet start-ups that had no revenues or earnings. The boom came to an abrupt end in 2001, when the Nasdaq stock market collapsed, losing almost 80% of its value. Who do you think benefited most from this boom: investors (stockholders) in those companies, managers, or investment bankers?

2. Why is maximizing ROIC consistent with maximizing returns to stockholders?

3. How might a company configure its strategy-making processes to reduce the probability that managers will pursue their own self-interest at the expense of stockholders?

4. In a public corporation, should the CEO of the company also be allowed to be the chairman of the board (as allowed for by the current law)? What problems might this present?

5. Under what conditions is it ethically defensible to outsource production to companies in the developing world that have much lower labor costs when such actions involve laying off long-term employees in the firm's home country?

6. Is it ethical for a firm faced with a labor shortage to employ illegal immigrants to meet its needs?

CLOSING CASE

HP's Disastrous Acquisition of Autonomy

In 2011, HP was churning on many fronts simultaneously. It had decided to abandon its tablet computer and was struggling with a decision about whether to exit its $40 billion-a-year personal computer (PC) business altogether. It also had a new CEO, Leo Apotheker (formerly the head of German software company SAP AG), who was intent on making a high-impact acquisition that would transform the firm from being primarily a hardware manufacturer into a fast-growing software firm. The firm also had a new chairman of the board, Ray Lane, who was also a software specialist as well as former president of Oracle.

Leo Apotheker had proposed buying two mid-sized software companies, but both deals fell through. The first was nixed by the board's finance committee, and the second fell apart during negotiations over price. In frustration, Apotheker told Lane, "I'm running out of software companies."

Then, in the summer of 2011, Apotheker proposed looking at Autonomy, a British company that makes software firms use to search for information

(continued)

in text files, video files, and other corporate documents. Lane was enthusiastic about the idea. When Apotheker brought the proposal to the board members in July 2011, half of them were already busy analyzing the decision to jettison the PC business, so only half of the board evaluated the acquisition proposal. The board approved a price for Autonomy that was about a 50% premium over its market value, which was already high at about 15 times its operating profit. HP announced the acquisition on August 18, 2011--the same day that it announced it would abandon its tablet computer and was considering exiting the PC industry. The price of the acquisition was $11.1 billion—12.6 times Autonomy's 2010 revenue. Notably, Oracle had already considered acquiring Autonomy and decided that, even if the numbers Autonomy was presenting were taken at face value, it was not worth buying even at a $6-billion price tag. HP's stock fell by 20% the next day.

In the days following the announcement, HP's stock continued to tumble, and backlash from shareholders and others in the investment community was scathing. Ray Lane asked HP's advisers if the company could back out of the deal and was told that, according to U.K. takeover rules, backing out was only possible if HP could show that Autonomy engaged in financial impropriety. HP began frantically examining the financials of Autonomy, hoping for a way to get out of the deal. In the midst of harsh disapproval from HP's largest stockholders and other senior executives within the firm, HP fired Leo Apotheker on September 22, 2012, less than a month after the acquisition's announcement, and only 11 months into his tenure as CEO.

By May 2012, it was clear that Autonomy was not going to hit its revenue targets, and Michael Lynch, Autonomy's founder (who had been asked to stay on and run the company) was fired. In late November 2012, HP wrote down $8.8 billion of the acquisition, essentially admitting that the company was worth 79% less than it had paid for it. Then the finger pointing began in earnest. HP attributed more than $5 billion of the write-down to a "willful

effort on behalf of certain former Autonomy employees to inflate the underlying financial metrics of the company in order to mislead investors and potential buyers. . . . These misrepresentations and lack of disclosure severely impacted management's ability to fairly value Autonomy at the time of the deal."

Michael Lynch denied the charges, insisting he knew of no wrongdoing at Autonomy, arguing that auditors from Deloitte had approved its financial statements, and pointing out that the firm followed British accounting guidelines, which differ in some ways from American rules. Lynch also accused HP of mismanaging the acquisition, saying "Can HP really state that no part of the $5-billion write-down was, or should be, attributed to HP's operational and financial mismanagement of Autonomy since acquisition? ... Why did HP senior management apparently wait six months to inform its shareholders of the possibility of a material event related to Autonomy?"

Many shareholders and analysts also pointed their fingers at HP, saying that the deal was shockingly overpriced. Sanford C. Bernstein & Company analyst Toni Sacconaghi wrote, "We see the decision to purchase Autonomy as value-destroying," and Richard Kugele, an analyst at Needham & Company, wrote, "HP may have eroded what remained of Wall Street's confidence in the company" with the "seemingly overly expensive acquisition of Autonomy for over $10B." Apotheker responded by saying, "We have a pretty rigorous process inside HP that we follow for all our acquisitions, which is a D.C.F.-based model…. Just take it from us. We did that analysis at great length, in great detail, and we feel that we paid a very fair price for Autonomy." However, when Ray Lane was questioned, he seemed unfamiliar with any cash flow analysis done for the acquisition. He noted instead that he believed the price was fair because Autonomy was unique and critical to HP's strategic vision.

According to an article in *Fortune*, Catherine A. Lesjak, the chief financial officer at HP, had spoken out against the deal before it transpired, arguing that it was not in the best interests of the shareholders and that HP could not afford it. Furthermore, outside auditors for Autonomy apparently informed HP (during a call in the days leading up to the announcement) that an executive at Autonomy had raised allegations of improper accounting at the firm, but a review had deemed the allegations baseless and they were never passed on to HP's board or CEO.

In the third quarter of 2012, HP lost $6.9 billion, largely because of the Autonomy mess. Its stock was trading at $13—almost 60% less than it had been worth when the Autonomy deal was announced. By April 4, 2013, Ray Lane stepped down as chairman of the board (although he continued on as a board member).

Did Autonomy intentionally inflate its financial metrics? Did Apotheker and Lane's eagerness for a "transformative acquisition" cause them to be sloppy in their valuation of Autonomy? Or was the value of Autonomy lost due to the more mundane cause of integration failure? Financial forensic investigators are trying to answer these questions, but irrespective of the underlying causes, Sacconaghi notes that Autonomy "will arguably go down as the worst, most value-destroying deal in the history of corporate America."

Sources: J. Bandler, "HP Should Have Listened to Its CFO," *Fortune*, November 20, 2012; www.fortune.com, J. B. Stewart, "From HP, a Blunder That Seems to Beat All," *New York Times*, November 30, 2012; www.nytimes.com, M. G. De La Merced, "Autonomy's Ex-Chief Calls on HP to Defend Its Claims," *New York Times*, Dealbook, November 27, 2012, www.nytimes.com/pages/business/dealbook; B. Worthen and J. Scheck, "Inside H-P's Missed Chance to Avoid a Disastrous Deal," *The Wall Street Journal*, January 21, 2013, pp. A1–A16.

CASE DISCUSSION QUESTIONS

1. Why do you think Apotheker was so eager to make an acquisition?
2. Why do most acquisitions result in paying a premium over the market price? Was the 50% premium for Autonomy reasonable?
3. Was it unethical for Apotheker to propose the acquisition at the 50% premium? Was it unethical for Autonomy to go along with the price at a 50% premium? Who suffers the consequences of an overpriced acquisition?
4. Is there anything HP and Autonomy could have done differently to avoid the public backlash and share price drop the company suffered?

NOTES

[1] E. Freeman, *Strategic Management: A Stakeholder Approach* (Boston: Pitman Press, 1984).

[2] C. W. L. Hill and T. M. Jones, "Stakeholder-Agency Theory," *Journal of Management Studies* 29 (1992): 131–154, and J. G. March and H. A. Simon, *Organizations* (New York: Wiley, 1958).

[3] W. Henisz, S. Dorobantu, and L. Nartey, L. "Spinning Gold: The Financial Returns to Stakeholder Engagement," *Strategic Management Journal*, 35 (2014):1727–1748.

[4] Hill and Jones, "Stakeholder-Agency Theory,; and C. Eesley and M. J. Lenox, "Firm Responses to Secondary Stakeholder Action," *Strategic Management Journal* 27 (2006): 13–24.

[5] I. C. Macmillan and P. E. Jones, *Strategy Formulation: Power and Politics* (St. Paul: West, 1986).

[6] T. Copeland, T. Koller, and J. Murrin, *Valuation: Measuring and Managing the Value of Companies* (New York: Wiley, 1996).

[7] R. S. Kaplan and D. P. Norton, *Strategy Maps* (Boston: Harvard Business School Press, 2004).

[8] J. S. Harrison, D. A. Bosse, and R. A. Phillips, "Managing for Stakeholders, Stakeholder Utility Functions, and Competitive Advantage," *Strategic Management Journal* 31 (2010): 58–74.

[9] R. Garcia-Castro, and R. Aguilera, "Increasing Value Creation and Appropriation in a World with Multiple Stakeholders," *Strategic Management Journal*, 36 (2015): 137–147.

[10] A. L. Velocci, D. A. Fulghum, and R. Wall, "Damage Control," *Aviation Week*, December 1, 2003, pp. 26–27.

[11] M. C. Jensen and W. H. Meckling, "Theory of the Firm: Managerial Behavior, Agency Costs and Ownership Structure," *Journal of Financial Economics* 3 (1976): 305–360, and E. F. Fama, "Agency Problems and the Theory of the Firm," *Journal of Political Economy* 88 (1980): 375–390.

[12] Hill and Jones, "Stakeholder-Agency Theory."

[13] For example, see R. Marris, *The Economic Theory of Managerial Capitalism* (London: Macmillan, 1964), and J. K. Galbraith, *The New Industrial State* (Boston: Houghton Mifflin, 1970).

[14] Fama, "Agency Problems and the Theory of the Firm."

[15] A. Rappaport, "New Thinking on How to Link Executive Pay with Performance," *Harvard Business Review,* March–April 1999, pp. 91–105.

[16] AFL-CIO's Executive Pay-Watch Database, www.aflcio.org/Corporate-Watch/CEO-Pay-and-You.

[17] For academic studies that look at the determinants of CEO pay, see M. C. Jensen and K. J. Murphy, "Performance Pay and Top Management Incentives," *Journal of Political Economy* 98 (1990): 225–264; Charles W. L. Hill and Phillip Phan, "CEO Tenure as a Determinant of CEO Pay," *Academy of Management Journal* 34 (1991): 707–717; H. L. Tosi and L. R. Gomez-Mejia, "CEO Compensation Monitoring and Firm Performance," *Academy of Management Journal* 37 (1994): 1002–1016; and J. F. Porac, J. B. Wade, and T. G. Pollock, "Industry Categories and the Politics of the Comparable Firm in CEO Compensation," *Administrative Science Quarterly* 44 (1999): 112–144.

[18] J. Silver-Greenberg and A. Leondis, "CBS Overpaid Moonves $28 Million, Says Study of CEO Pay," *Bloomberg News*, May 6, 2010.

[19] "'Pay for Performance' No Longer a Punchline," *The Wall Street Journal*, March 20, 2013.

[20] For research on this issue, see P. J. Lane, A. A. Cannella, and M. H. Lubatkin, "Agency Problems as Antecedents to Unrelated Mergers and Diversification: Amihud and Lev Reconsidered," *Strategic Management Journal* 19 (1998): 555–578.

[21] M. Saltmarsh and E. Pfanner, "French Court Convicts Executives in Vivendi Case," *New York Times*, January 21, 2011.

[22] E. T. Penrose, *The Theory of the Growth of the Firm* (London: Macmillan, 1958).

[23] G. Edmondson and L. Cohn, "How Parmalat Went Sour," *Business Week*, January 12, 2004, pp. 46–50; and "Another Enron? Royal Dutch Shell," *Economist,* March 13, 2004, p. 71.

[24] O. E. Williamson, *The Economic Institutions of Capitalism* (New York: Free Press, 1985).

[25] Fama, "Agency Problems and the Theory of the Firm."

[26] S. Finkelstein and R. D'Aveni, "CEO Duality as a Double Edged Sword," *Academy of Management Journal* 37 (1994): 1079–1108; B. Ram Baliga and R. C. Moyer, "CEO Duality and Firm Performance," *Strategic Management Journal* 17 (1996): 41–53; M. L. Mace, *Directors: Myth and Reality* (Cambridge: Harvard University Press, 1971); and S. C. Vance, *Corporate Leadership: Boards of Directors and Strategy* (New York: McGraw-Hill, 1983).

[27] J. B. Stewart, "When Shareholder Democracy Is a Sham," *New York Times*, April 12, 2013.

[28] "Goldman Union Deal Lets Blankfein Keep Dual Roles," *Reuters*, April 11, 2013.

[29] W. G. Lewellen, C. Eoderer, and A. Rosenfeld, "Merger Decisions and Executive Stock Ownership in Acquiring Firms," *Journal of Accounting and Economics* 7 (1985): 209–231.

[30] C. W. L. Hill and S. A. Snell, "External Control, Corporate Strategy, and Firm Performance," *Strategic Management Journal* 9 (1988): 577–590.

[31] The phenomenon of back dating stock options was uncovered by academic research, and then picked up by the SEC. See Erik Lie, "On the Timing of CEO Stock Option Awards," *Management Science* 51 (2005): 802–812.

[32] G. Colvin, "A Study in CEO Greed," *Fortune*, June 12, 2006, pp. 53–55.

[33] J. P. Walsh and R. D. Kosnik, "Corporate Raiders and Their Disciplinary Role in the Market for Corporate Control," *Academy of Management Journal* 36 (1993): 671–700.

[34] R. S. Kaplan and D. P. Norton, "The Balanced Scorecard—Measures That Drive Performance," *Harvard Business Review,* January–February 1992, pp. 71–79, and Kaplan and Norton, *Strategy Maps* (Boston: Harvard Business School Press, 2004).

[35] R. S. Kaplan and D. P. Norton, "Using the Balanced Scorecard as a Strategic Management System," *Harvard Business Review,* January–February 1996, pp. 75–85, and Kaplan and Norton, *Strategy Maps.*

[36] Kaplan and Norton, "The Balanced Scorecard," p. 72.

[37] J. Surroca, J. A, Tribó, and S. A. Zahr, "Stakeholder Pressure on MNEs and the Transfer of Socially Irresponsible Practices to Subsidiaries," *Academy of Management Journal,* 56 (2015): 549–572.

[38] "Timet, Boeing Settle Lawsuit," *Metal Center News* 41 (June 2001): 38–39.

[39] Joseph Kahn, "Ruse in Toyland: Chinese Workers Hidden Woe," *New York Times,* December 7, 2003, pp. A1, A8.

[40] N. King, "Halliburton Tells the Pentagon Workers Took Iraq Deal Kickbacks," *The Wall Street Journal,* 2004, p. A1; "Whistleblowers Say Company Routinely Overcharged," *Reuters,* February 12, 2004; and R. Gold and J. R. Wilke, "Data Sought in Halliburton Inquiry," *The Wall Street Journal,* 2004, p. A6.

[41] L. Jieqi and Z. Hejuan, "Siemens Bribery Scandal Ends in Death Sentence," *Caixin Online,* June 30, 2011.

[42] S. W. Gellerman, "Why Good Managers Make Bad Ethical Choices," *Ethics in Practice: Managing the Moral Corporation,* ed. K. R. Andrews (Harvard Business School Press, 1989).

[43] Ibid.

[44] S. Hopkins, "How Effective Are Ethics Codes and Programs?," *Financial Executive,* March 2013.

[45] www.unilever.com/company/ourprinciples/.

[46] www.utc.com/governance/ethics.

Igor Sokolov (breeze)/Shutterstock.com

12.1 Explain the concept of organizational architecture

12.2 Articulate how strategy is implemented through the right combination of organizational structure, controls, incentives, process, culture, and people

12.3 Discuss how effective organizational design enables a company to implement its business-level strategy

12.4 Discuss how effective organization design enables a company to implement its corporate-level strategy

OPENING CASE

Organization Change at Google

In April 2011, Larry Page, one of Google's two founders, became CEO of the company. Page had been CEO of Google from its establishment in 1998 through 2001, when Eric Schmidt took over. After 10 years, Schmidt decided to step down and handed the reins back to Page. One of Page's first actions was to reorganize the company into business units.

Under Schmidt, Google operated with a functional structure that was split into two main entities—an engineering function and a product management function. The engineering group was responsible for creating, building, and maintaining Google's products. The product management group focused on selling Google's offerings, particularly its advertising services. There were, however, two main exceptions to this structure: YouTube and the Android group. These were both acquisitions, and both were left to run their own operations in a largely autonomous manner. Notably, both had been more successful than many of Google's own internally generated new-product ideas.

The alleged great virtue of Google's functional structure was that it was flat, with very few layers in the hierarchy and wide spans of control.

©Yeamake/Shutterstock.com

384

Innovation was encouraged. Indeed, numerous articles were written about Google's "bottom-up" new product development process. Engineers were encouraged to spend 20% of their time on projects of their own choosing. They were empowered to form teams to flesh out product ideas, and could get funding to take those products to market by going through a formal process that ended with a presentation in front of Page and Google cofounder Sergey Brin. The products that emerged from this process included Google News, Google Earth, Gmail, and Google Apps.

By 2011, it was becoming increasingly clear that there were limitations to this structure. There was a lack of accountability for products once they had been developed. The core engineers might move on to other projects. Projects could stay in the beta stage for years, essentially unfinished offerings. No one was really responsible for taking products and making them into stand-alone businesses. Many engineers complained that the process for approving new products had become mired in red tape. It was too slow. A structure that had worked well when Google was still a small start-up was no longer scaling. Furthermore, the structure did not reflect the fact that Google had become a multibusiness enterprise, albeit one in which search-based advertising income was still the main driver of the company's revenues. Indeed, that in itself was viewed as an issue, for despite creating many new-product offerings, Google was still dependent upon search-based advertising for the bulk of its income.

Page's solution to this problem was to reorganize Google into seven core business units: Search, Advertising, YouTube, Mobile (Android), Chrome, Social (Google + and Blogger), and Commerce (Google Apps). Senior vice presidents who report directly to Page head each unit. Each VP has full responsibility (and accountability) for the fate of his or her unit. Getting a new product started no longer requires convincing executives from across the company to get on board. And once a product ships, engineers and managers can't jump to the next thing and leave important products like Gmail in unfinished beta for years. "Now you are accountable not only for delivering something, but for revising and fixing it," said one Google spokesperson.

Sources: Miguel Helft, "The Future According to Google's Larry Page," *CNNMoney,* January 3, 2013; Liz Gannes, "GoogQuake: The Larry Page Reorg Promotes Top Lieutenants to SVP," *All Things Digital,* April 7, 2011; Jessica Guynn, "Google CEO Larry Page Completes Major Reorganization of Internet Search Giant," *Los Angeles Times,* April 7, 2011.

▛OVERVIEW

Earlier in this book we noted that strategy is implemented through the organizational arrangements of a firm and through actions taken at the functional level. We discussed the functional actions required to implement different *business-level strategies* in Chapters 4 and 5. In this chapter, we look at how organizational arrangements are used to implement the business-, corporate-, and global-level strategies of an enterprise.

The Opening Case illustrates some of the issues that we shall be discussing in this chapter. Like most new enterprises, Google started out with a functional organization. Processes within Google's organization were also configured to encourage product innovation. This arrangement worked well when the company was relatively small and focused on the single business of providing a search engine. But as the company started to grow and diversify, it found that many of its new products were not as profitable as it had hoped. In an attempt to boost the performance of its new businesses, CEO Larry Page created a *multidivisional structure* at Google, with each business unit or "division" being given full responsibility to run its own operations, and being held accountable for its own performance.

Google is not the first company to wrestle with the problem of how best to manage a company as it grows and starts to generate new-product offerings; there is in fact a long history of companies moving from a functional toward a multidivisional structure as they grow and diversify. Organizational arrangements that are appropriate for managing a single business turn out to be inappropriate for managing a more diversified, multibusiness enterprise, which Google has become. By reorganizing itself, Google hopes to promote more profitable business diversification.

ORGANIZATIONAL ARCHITECTURE

In this chapter, we use the term **organizational architecture** to refer to the totality of a firm's organizational arrangements, including its formal organizational structure, control systems, incentive systems, organizational culture, organizational processes, and people (or human capital).[1] Figure 12.1 illustrates these different elements.

By **organizational structure**, we mean three things: First, the location of decision-making responsibilities in the firm (e.g., centralized or decentralized); second, the formal division of the organization into subunits such as functions, product divisions, and national operations; and third, the establishment of integrating mechanisms to coordinate the activities of subunits.

organizational architecture
The totality of a firm's organizational arrangements, including its formal organizational structure, control systems, incentive systems, organizational culture, organizational processes, and human capital.

organizational structure
The combination of the location of decision-making responsibilities, the formal division of the organization into subunits, and the establishment of integrating mechanisms to coordinate the activities of the subunits.

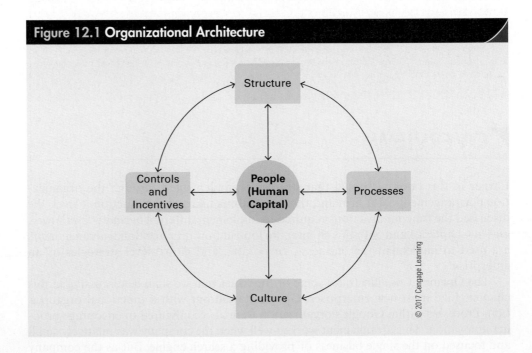

Figure 12.1 Organizational Architecture

© 2017 Cengage Learning

Controls are the metrics used to measure the performance of subunits and make judgments about how well managers are running those subunits. **Incentives** are the devices used to encourage desired employee behavior. Incentives are very closely tied to performance metrics. For example, the incentives of a manager in charge of General Electric's lighting business might be linked to the performance of that division.

Organizational processes refer to the manner in which decisions are made and work is performed within the organization. Examples include the processes for formulating strategy, for deciding how to allocate resources within a firm, for developing new products, and for evaluating the performance of managers and giving feedback. Processes are conceptually distinct from the location of decision-making responsibilities within an organization, although both involve decisions. For example, while the CEO might have ultimate responsibility for deciding what the strategy of the firm should be (that is, the decision-making responsibility is centralized), the *process* he or she uses to make that decision might include the solicitation of ideas and criticism from lower-level managers and employees.

Organizational culture refers to the norms and value systems that are shared among the employees of an organization. Just as societies have cultures, so do organizations. Organizations are societies of individuals who come together to perform collective tasks. They have their own distinctive patterns of culture and subculture.[2] As we shall see, organizational culture can have a profound impact on how a firm performs.

Finally, by **people** we mean not just the employees of the organization, but also the strategy used to recruit, compensate, motivate, and retain those individuals and the type of people that they are in terms of their skills, values, and orientation. Collectively, the people within an organization, the employees, constitute the human capital of an enterprise. We have already discussed the role of human resources in recruiting, training, developing, and compensating employees in order to execute the strategy of the firm in Chapters 3 and 4. We will not repeat that discussion here. However, it is important to note that the value of an organization's human capital is more than the sum of each individual employee's skills and capabilities. Much of the value is *contextual* in the sense that employees can achieve things within an organization that would not be possible if they were working as independent contractors. Put differently, the other elements of the architecture of an organization may create an environment within which it is possible for people to do extraordinary things.

For example, Johnny Ive, the head of product design at Apple, is clearly a remarkably skilled individual. However, Ive probably could not have had the impact that he has without the benefit of working within Apple, where the structure, control systems, incentives, decision-making processes, and culture all supported what he was trying to do in terms of developing elegantly designed digital devices that are as much a fashion statement as they are a computing tool. Much of Ive's human capital, in other words, is the result of the *combination* of his skills and Apple's organizational architecture.

As suggested by this example, and illustrated by the arrows in Figure 12.1, the various components of organization architecture are not independent of each other: Each component shapes, and is shaped by, other components of architecture. Again, an obvious example is the strategy regarding people. Human resources can proactively hire individuals whose internal values are consistent with those that the firm emphasizes in its organizational culture. The people component of architecture can be used to reinforce the prevailing culture of the organization. A business enterprise endeavoring to attain a competitive advantage and maximize its performance must pay close

controls
The metrics used to measure the performance of subunits and make judgments about how well managers are running them.

incentives
The devices used to encourage desired employee behavior.

organizational processes
The manner in which decisions are made and work is performed within the organization.

organizational culture
The norms and value systems that are shared among the employees of an organization.

people
The employees of an organization, as well as the strategy used to recruit, compensate, motivate, and retain those individuals; also refers to employees' skills, values, and orientation.

attention to achieving internal consistency between the various components of its architecture, and the architecture must support the strategy and functional activities of the enterprise.

ORGANIZATIONAL STRUCTURE

Organizational structure can be thought of in terms of three dimensions. The first is **vertical differentiation**, which refers to the location of decision-making responsibilities within a structure (that is, centralization or decentralization) and also to the number of layers in a hierarchy (that is, whether the organizational structure is tall or flat). The second is **horizontal differentiation**, which refers to the formal division of the organization into subunits. The third is the establishment of **integrating mechanisms**, which are mechanisms for coordinating subunits. We will discuss each of these in turn.

Centralization and Decentralization

A firm's vertical differentiation determines where in its hierarchy decision-making power is concentrated.[3] Are production and marketing decisions centralized in the offices of upper-level managers, or are they decentralized to lower-level managers? Where does the responsibility for R&D decisions lie? Are important strategic and financial decisions pushed down to operating units, or are they concentrated in the hands of top management? And so on. There are arguments for centralization, and other arguments for decentralization. **Centralization** is a condition where decision-making authority is concentrated at a high level in a management hierarchy. **Decentralization** is a condition where decision-making authority is vested in lower-level managers or other employees.

Arguments for Centralization   There are four main arguments for centralization. First, centralization can facilitate coordination. For example, consider a firm that that has a component manufacturing operation in California and a final assembly operation in Seattle. The activities of these two operations may need to be coordinated to ensure a smooth flow of products from the component operation to the assembly operation. This might be achieved by centralizing production scheduling at the firm's head office.

Second, centralization can help ensure that decisions are consistent with organizational objectives. When decisions are decentralized to lower-level managers, those managers may make decisions at variance with top management's goals. Centralization of important decisions minimizes the chance of this occurring. Major strategic decisions, for example, are often centralized in an effort to make sure that the entire organization is pulling in the same direction. In this sense, centralization is a way of controlling the organization.

Third, centralization can avoid the duplication of activities that occurs when similar activities are carried on by various subunits within the organization. For example, many firms centralize their R&D functions at one or two locations to ensure that R&D work is not duplicated. Similarly, production activities may be centralized at key locations to eliminate duplication, attain economies of scale, and lower costs. The same may also be true of purchasing decisions. Wal-Mart, for example, has centralized all purchasing decisions at its headquarters in Arkansas. By wielding its enormous

---

vertical differentiation

The location of decision-making responsibilities within a structure, referring to centralization or decentralization, and also the number of layers in a hierarchy, referring to whether to organizational structure is tall or flat.

horizontal differentiation

The formal division of the organization into subunits.

integrating mechanisms

Processes and procedures used for coordination subunits.

centralization

Structure in which decision-making authority is concentrated at a high level in the management hierarchy.

decentralization

Structure in which decision-making authority is distributed to lower-level managers or other employees.

bargaining power, purchasing managers at the head office can drive down the costs that Wal-Mart pays for the goods it sells in its stores. It then passes on those savings to consumers in the form of lower prices, which enables the company to grow its market share and profits.

Fourth, by concentrating power and authority in one individual or a management team, centralization can give top-level managers the means to bring about needed major organizational changes. Often times, firms seeking to transform their organizations centralize power and authority in a key individual, or group, who then sets the new strategic direction for the firm and redraw organizational architecture. Once the new strategy and architecture have been decided upon, however, greater decentralization of decision making normally follows. Put differently, the *temporary* centralization of decision-making power is often an important step in organization change.

Arguments for Decentralization   There are five main arguments for decentralization. First, top management can become overburdened when decision-making authority is centralized. Centralization increases the amount of information that senior managers have to process, and this can result in information overload and poor decision making.[4] Decentralization gives top management time to focus on critical issues by delegating more routine issues to lower-level managers and reducing the amount of information top managers have to process.

Second, motivational research favors decentralization. Behavioral scientists have long argued that people are willing to give more to their jobs when they have a greater degree of individual freedom and control over their work. The idea behind employee empowerment is that if you give employees more responsibility for their jobs they will work harder, which increases productivity and reduces costs.

Third, decentralization permits greater flexibility—more rapid response to environmental changes. In a centralized firm, the need to refer decisions up the hierarchy for approval can significantly impede the speed of decision making and inhibit the ability of the firm to adapt to rapid environmental changes.[5] This can put the firm at a competitive disadvantage. Managers deal with this by decentralizing decisions to lower levels within the organization. Thus, at Wal-Mart, while purchasing decisions are centralized so that the firm can realize economies of scale in purchasing, routine pricing and stocking decisions are decentralized to individual store managers who have some control over pricing and decide upon the products to stock depending on local conditions. This enables store managers to respond quickly to changes in their local environment, such as a drop in demand or actions by a local competitor.

Fourth, decentralization can result in better decisions. In a decentralized structure, decisions are made closer to the spot by individuals who (presumably) have better information than managers several levels up a hierarchy. It might make little sense for the CEO of Procter & Gamble to make marketing decisions for the detergents business in Germany because he is unlikely to have the relevant expertise and information. Instead, those decisions are decentralized to local marketing managers, who are far more likely to be in tune with the German market.

Fifth, decentralization can increase control. Decentralization can be used to establish relatively autonomous, self-contained subunits within an organization. An **autonomous subunit** is one that has all of the resources and decision-making power required to run the operation on a day-to-day basis. Managers of autonomous subunits can be held accountable for subunit performance. The more responsibility subunit

autonomous subunit
A subunit that has all the resources and decision-making power required to run the operation on a day-to-day basis.

managers have for decisions that impact subunit performance, the fewer excuses they have for poor performance and the more accountable they are. Thus, by giving store managers the ability to set prices and make stocking decisions, Wal-Mart's top managers are able to hold local store managers accountable for the performance of their stores, and this increases the ability of top managers to control the organization. Just as centralization is one way of maintaining control in an organization, decentralization is another.

The Choice Between Decentralization and Centralization The choice between centralization and decentralization is not absolute. Frequently it makes sense to centralize some decisions and decentralize others, depending on the type of decision and the firm's strategy. We have already noted how Wal-Mart centralized purchasing decisions and decentralized pricing and stocking decisions. Similarly, Microsoft has centralized major development activities for its Windows operating system at its Redmond corporate campus, but has decentralized responsibility for marketing and sales to local managers in each country and region where it does business. Although the choice between centralization and decentralization depends upon the circumstances being considered, a few important generalizations can be made.

First, decisions regarding overall firm strategy, major financial expenditures, financial objectives, and legal issues are centralized at the senior-management level in most organizations. Functional decisions relating to production, marketing, R&D, and human resource management may or may not be centralized depending on the firm's strategy and environmental conditions.

Second, when the realization of economies of scale is an important factor, there tends to be greater centralization. Purchasing and manufacturing decisions are often centralized in an attempt to eliminate duplication and realize scale economies. In contrast, sales decisions tend to be more decentralized because economies of scale are less of a consideration here.

Third, when local adaptation is important, decentralization is typically favored. When there are substantial differences between conditions in local markets, marketing and sales decisions will often be decentralized to local marketing and sales managers. Multinational, consumer products firms such as Unilever centralize decisions about manufacturing and purchasing in order to realize scale economies, but decentralize marketing and sales decisions to local brand managers in different countries precisely because competitive conditions differ from country to country and local adaptation is required.[6]

Finally, decentralization is favored in environments characterized by high uncertainty and rapid change. When competitive conditions in a firm's market are changing rapidly, with new technologies and competitors emerging in ways that are difficult to anticipate, centralization, because it slows down decision making, can put a firm at a competitive disadvantage. Due to this, many high-tech firms operate with a greater degree of decentralization than firms operating in more stable and predictable environments.[7] At Google, for example, lower-level employees are given the ability to develop new business ideas and the right to lobby top managers for the funds to develop those ideas (see the Opening Case). Such decentralization of strategy making might not be found in firms operating in a more stable and predictable environment, such as the automobile industry. For a vivid example of the costs of making the wrong choice between centralization and decentralization, see Strategy in Action 12.1 on FEMA and Hurricane Katrina.

12.1 STRATEGY IN ACTION

FEMA and Hurricane Katrina

A vivid example of the costs of making the wrong choice between centralization and decentralization occurred in 2005, when the Federal Emergency Management Agency (FEMA) responded to the devastating impact that Hurricane Katrina had on New Orleans. The hurricane flooded much of the city and resulted in a mandatory evacuation. However FEMA, the Federal agency responsible for disaster relief, was widely criticized for being very slow to respond to the plight of the hundreds of thousands of mostly poor people who had been made homeless. For several days, while thousands of homeless people huddled in the New Orleans Superdome, lacking food and adequate sanitary facilities, FEMA was nowhere to be seen.

A postmortem revealed that one reason for FEMA's slow response was that the once-autonomous agency had been placed under the direct supervision of the Department of Homeland Security after September 11,

2001. FEMA officials apparently felt that they had to discuss relief efforts with their superiors before proceeding. This cost the agency crucial time in the early hours of the disaster and significantly slowed its response, meaning that the relief effort was less effective than it might have been. In addition, FEMA was poorly managed. Its head, Mike Brown, a political appointee, had no experience in disaster relief. Moreover, the agency had been gutted by budget cuts.

In a report that was highly critical of FEMA, the U. S. Senate Committee charged with reviewing the response to Katrina cited a "failure of agility" and concluded that response plans at all levels of government lacked flexibility and adaptability, which often delayed response. In other words, decision making was too centralized, bureaucratic, and inflexible. Decentralization would have helped enormously in this case.

Sources: "A failure to innovate: Final report of the select bipartisan committee to investigate the preparation for and response to Hurricane Katrina". United States Government Printing Office, February 17th, 2006. *The Economist*, "When Government Fails – Katrina's aftermath", September 2005, page 25.

Tall Versus Flat Hierarchies

A second aspect of vertical differentiation refers to the number of levels in an organization hierarchy. **Tall hierarchies** have many layers of management, while **flat hierarchies** have very few layers (see Figure 12.2). Most firms start out small, often with only one or at most two layers in the hierarchy. As they grow, management finds that there is a limit to the amount of information they can process and the control they can exert over day-to-day operations. To avoid being stretched too thin and losing control, they tend to add another layer to the management hierarchy, hiring more managers and delegating some decision-making authority to them. In other words, as an organization gets larger it tends to become taller. In addition, growing organizations often undertake more activities, expanding their product line, diversifying into adjacent activities, vertically integrating, or expanding into new regional or national markets. This too creates problems of coordination and control, and once again the organization's response often is to add another management layer. Adding levels in the

tall hierarchies
An organizational structure with many layers of management.

flat hierarchies
An organizational structure with very few layers of management.

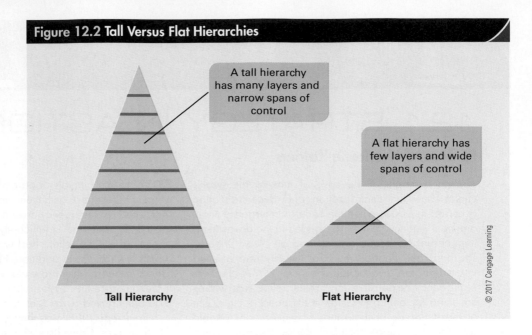

Figure 12.2 Tall Versus Flat Hierarchies

A tall hierarchy has many layers and narrow spans of control

A flat hierarchy has few layers and wide spans of control

Tall Hierarchy   **Flat Hierarchy**

© 2017 Cengage Learning

hierarchy is a problem that mounts when managers have too much work to do. The number of layers added is also partly determined by the span of control that managers can effectively handle.

span of control

The number of a manager's direct reports.

Span of Control   The term **span of control** refers to the number of direct reports that a manager has. At one time it was thought that the optimal span of control was six subordinates.[8] The argument was that, if a manager was responsible for more than six subordinates, he would soon lose track of what was going on and control loss would occur. Now we recognize that the relationship is not this simple. The number of direct reports a manger can handle depends upon (1) the nature of the work being supervised, (2) the extent to which the performance of subordinates is visible, and (3) the extent of decentralization within the organization. Generally, if the work being performed by subordinates is routine, if the performance of subordinates is visible and easy to measure, and if the subordinates are empowered to make many decision by themselves, and do not have to refer up the hierarchy for approval or consultation, managers can operate with a wide span of control. How wide is the subject of debate, but it does seem as if managers can effectively handle as many as 20 direct reports if the circumstances are right.

In sum, as organizations grow and undertake more activities, the management hierarchy tends to be come taller, but how tall depends upon the span of control that is feasible, and that in turn depends upon the nature of the work being performed, the visibility of subordinate performance, and the extent of decentralization within the organization. It is important to note that managers can influence the visibility of subunit performance and the extent of decentralization through organization design, thereby limiting the impact of organization size and diversity on the size of a management hierarchy. This is significant because we know that while adding layers to an organization can reduce the workload of higher-level managers and attenuate control loss, tall hierarchies have their own problems.

Problems in Tall Hierarchies   Several problems can occur in tall hierarchies that may result in lower organizational efficiency and effectiveness. First, there is a tendency for information to get *accidentally distorted* as it passes through layers in a hierarchy. The phenomenon is familiar to anyone who has played the game "telephone," in which players sit in a circle and each whispers a message to the person sitting next to them, who then whispers the message to the next person, and so on around the room. Often, by the time the message has been transmitted through all the players, it has become distorted and its meaning has changed (this can have very funny consequences, which of course is the point of the game). Human beings are not adept at transmitting information; they tend to embellish or omit data. In a management context, if critical information has to pass through many layers in a tall hierarchy before it reaches critical decision makers, it may well get distorted in the process, resulting in a message that differs from the one originally sent. As a result, decisions may be made based on inaccurate information and poor performance may result.

In addition to the accidental distortion of information as it travels through a management hierarchy, there is also the problem of *deliberate distortion* by mid-level managers trying to curry favor with their superiors or pursue a personal agenda. For example, the manager of a division might suppress negative information, while exaggerating positive information, in an attempt to "window dress" the performance of the unit under his control to higher-level managers and win their approval. By doing so he may gain access to more resources, earn performance bonuses, or avoid sanctions for poor performance. All things being equal, the more layers in a hierarchy, the more opportunities exist for people to deliberately distort information. To the extent that information is distorted, once again it implies that senior managers will be making important decisions on the basis of inaccurate information, which can result in poor performance. Economists refer to the loss of efficiency that arises from deliberate information distortions for personal gain within an organization as **influence costs**, and they argue that influence costs can be a major source of low efficiency.[9]

An interesting case of information distortion in a hierarchy concerned the quality of pre-war intelligence information on weapons of mass destruction in Iraq prior to the 2003 invasion by the United States and allied forces. The information on biological weapons that was used to help justify the invasion of Iraq was derived from a single Iraq defector, code named "Curveball," who was an alcoholic and, in the view of the one person who had interviewed him, a Pentagon analyst, "utterly useless as a source." However, higher-level personnel in the intelligence community took the information provided by Curveball, stripped out the reservations expressed by the Pentagon analyst, and passed it on as high-quality intelligence to U.S. Secretary of State, Colin Powell, who included the information in a speech he made to the United Nations to justify the war. Powell was apparently unaware of the highly questionable nature of the data. Had he been, he probably would not have included it in his speech. Apparently, gatekeepers who stood between Powell and the Pentagon analyst deliberately distorted the information, presumably to further their own agenda, or the agenda of other parties whose favor they were trying to curry.[10]

A third problem with tall hierarchies is that they are expensive. The salaries and benefits of multiple layers of mid-level managers can add up to significant overhead, which can increase the cost structure of the firm. Unless there is a commensurate benefit, a tall hierarchy can put a firm at a competitive disadvantage.

A final problem concerns the inherent inertia associated with a tall hierarchy. Organizations are inherently inert—that is, they are difficult to change. One cause of

influence costs

The loss of efficiency that arises from deliberate information distortions for personal gain within an organization.

inertia in an organization is that, in order to protect their turf, and perhaps their jobs, managers often argue for the maintenance of the status quo. In tall hierarchies there is more turf, more centers of power and influence, and more voices arguing against change. Thus, tall hierarchies tend to be slow to change.

Delayering–Reducing the Size of a Hierarchy   Many firms attempt to limit the size of the management hierarchy. **Delayering** to reduce the number of levels in a management hierarchy has become a standard component of many attempts to boost a firm's performance.[11] Delayering is based on the assumption that when times are good, many firms tend to expand their management hierarchies beyond the point at which it is efficient to do so. However, the bureaucratic inefficiencies associated with a tall hierarchy become evident when the competitive environment becomes tougher, at which time managers seek to delayer the organization. Delayering, and simultaneously widening spans of control, is also seen as a way of enforcing greater decentralization within an organization and reaping the associated efficiency gains.

The process of delayering was a standard feature of Jack Welch's tenure at General Electric, during which time he laid off 150,000 people and reduced the number of layers in the hierarchy from nine to five, while simultaneously growing General Electric's profits and revenues. Welch believed that GE had become too top heavy during the tenure of his successors. A key element of his strategy was to transform General Electric into a leaner, faster-moving organization, which required delayering. Welch himself had a wide span of control, with some 20 subordinates reporting directly to him, including the heads of GE's 15 top businesses. Similarly, Jeffery Immelt, the head of GE's medical-systems business under Welch, had 21 direct reports (Immelt eventually replaced Welch as CEO).[12]

Structural Forms

Most firms begin with no formal structure and are run by a single entrepreneur or a small team of individuals. As they grow, the demands of management become too great for one individual or a small team to handle. At this point, the organization is split into functions that represent different aspects of the firm's value chain (see Chapter 3).

Functional Structure   In a **functional structure**, the structure of the organization follows the obvious *division of labor* within the firm with different functions focusing on different tasks. There might be a production function, an R&D function, a marketing function, a sales function, and so on (see Figure 12.3). A top manager, such as the CEO, or a small top-management team oversees these functions. Most single businesses of any scale are organized along functional lines.

While a functional structure can work well for a firm that is active in a single line of business, problems develop once the firm expands into different businesses. Google began as a search company, but has expanded into operating systems (Android and Chrome), software applications (Google Apps, Gmail), digital media distribution (Google Play), and social products (Google Plus, Blogspot). As noted in the Opening Case, trying to manage these different businesses within the context of a functional structure creates problems of accountability, coordination, and control.[13]

With regard to control, it becomes difficult to identify the profitability of each distinct business when the activities of those businesses are scattered across various

---

delayering

The process of reducing the number of levels in a management hierarchy.

functional structure

The organizational structure is built upon the division of labor within the firm, with different functions focusing on different tasks.

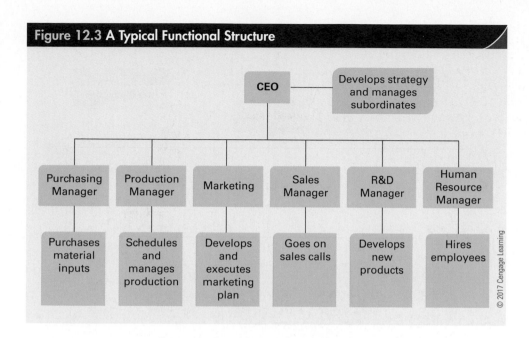

Figure 12.3 A Typical Functional Structure

© 2017 Cengage Learning

functions. It is hard to assess whether a business is performing well or poorly. More-over, because no one individual or management team is responsible for the perfor-mance of each business, there is a lack of accountability within the organization, and this too can result in poor control. As for coordination, when the different activities that constitute a business are embedded in different functions, such as production and marketing, that are simultaneously managing multiple businesses, it can be difficult to achieve the tight coordination between functions needed to effectively run a business. Moreover, it is difficult to run a functional department if it is supervising the value creation activities of several business areas.

Multidivisional Structure   The problems that we have just discussed were first recog-nized in the 1920s by one of the pioneers of American management thinking, Alfred Sloan, who at the time was CEO of General Motors, then the largest company in the world.[14] Under Sloan, GM had diversified into multiple businesses. In addition to making cars under several distinct brands, it made trucks, airplane engines, and re-frigerators. After struggling to run these different businesses within the framework of a functional structure, Sloan realized that a fundamentally different structure was re-quired. His solution, which has since become the classic way to organize a diversified, multibusiness enterprise, was to adopt a multidivisional structure (see Figure 12.4).

In a **multidivisional structure**, the firm is divided into different divisions, each of which is responsible for a distinct business area. The multidivisional structure has be-come the standard structural form for managing a diversified enterprise. Thus, as we saw in the Opening Case, in 2011 Google created seven core business divisions: Search, Advertising, YouTube, Mobile (Android), Chrome, Social (Google + and Blogger), and Commerce (Google Apps). In most multidivisional enterprises, each division is set up as a self-contained, largely autonomous entity with its own functions. Respon-sibility for functional decisions and business-level strategy is typically decentralized to the divisions, which are then held accountable for their performance. Headquarters is

multidivisional structure

An organizational structure in which a firm is divided into divisions, each of which is responsible for a distinct business area.

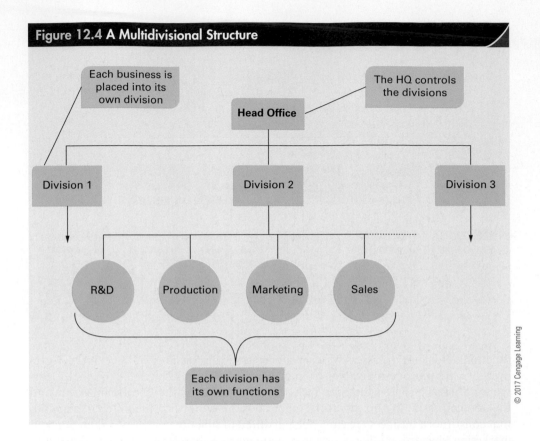

Figure 12.4 A Multidivisional Structure

Each business is placed into its own division

The HQ controls the divisions

Head Office

Division 1   Division 2   Division 3

R&D   Production   Marketing   Sales

Each division has its own functions

© 2017 Cengage Learning

responsible for the overall strategic development of the firm (corporate-level strategy), for the control of the various divisions, for allocating capital between divisions, for supervising and coaching the managers who run each division, and for transferring valuable knowledge between divisions.

The divisions are generally left alone to run day-to-day operations as long as they hit performance targets, which are typically negotiated on an annual basis between the head office and divisional management. Headquarters, however, will often help divisional managers think through their strategy. Thus, while Jeff Immelt does not develop strategy for the various businesses within GE's portfolio (that is decentralized to divisional managers), he does probe the thinking of divisional managers to see if they have thought through their strategy. In addition, he devotes much effort to getting managers to share best practices across divisions, and to the formulation and implementation of strategies that span multiple businesses.

One of the great virtues claimed for the multidivisional structure is that it creates an internal environment where divisional managers focus on efficiency.[15] Because each division is a self-contained entity, its performance is highly visible. The high level of responsibility and accountability implies that divisional managers have few alibis for poor performance. This motivates them to focus on improving efficiency. Base pay, bonuses, and promotional opportunities for divisional managers can be tied to how well the division does. Capital is also allocated by top management between the competing divisions depending upon how effectively top management thinks the division managers can invest that capital. The desire to get access to capital to grow their businesses, and to gain pay increases and bonuses, creates further incentives for divisional managers to focus on improving the competitive position of the businesses under their control.

On the other hand, too much pressure from the head office on divisional managers to improve performance can result in some of the worst practices of management. These can include cutting necessary investments in plant, equipment, and R&D to boost short-term performance, even though such action can damage the long-term competitive position of the enterprise.[16] To guard against this possibility, top managers need to develop a good understanding of each division, set performance goals that are attainable, and have personnel who can regularly audit the accounts and operations of divisions to ensure that each division is not being managed for short-term results or in a way that destroys its long-term competitiveness.

Matrix Structure   High-technology firms based in rapidly changing environments sometimes adopt a **matrix structure**, in which they try to achieve tight coordination between functions, particularly R&D, production, and marketing.[17] Tight coordination is required so that R&D designs products that (a) can be manufactured efficiently, and (b) are designed with customer needs in mind—both of which increase the probability of successful product commercialization (see Chapter 4). Tight coordination between R&D, manufacturing, and marketing has also been shown to result in a quicker product development effort, which can enable a firm to gain an advantage over its rivals.[18] As illustrated in Figure 12.5, in such an organization an employee may belong to two subunits within the firm. For example, a manager might be a member of the manufacturing function and a product development team.

matrix structure

An organizational structure in which managers try to achieve tight coordination between functions, particularly R&D, production, and marketing.

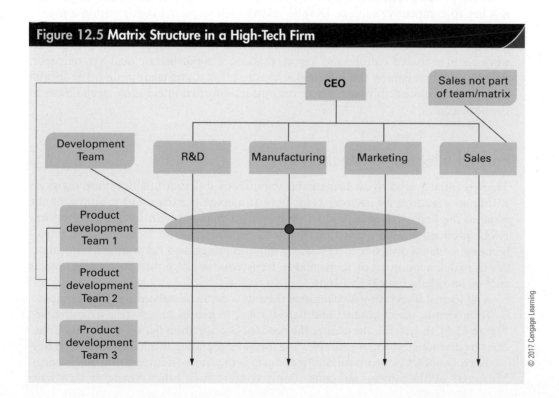

Figure 12.5 Matrix Structure in a High-Tech Firm

© 2017 Cengage Learning

A matrix structure looks nice on paper, but the reality can be very different. Unless this structure is managed very carefully it may not work well.[19] In practice, the matrix can be clumsy and bureaucratic. It can require so many meetings that it is difficult to get any work done. The dual-hierarchy structure can lead to conflict and perpetual power struggles between the different sides of the hierarchy. In one high-tech firm, for example, the manufacturing manager was reluctant to staff a product development team with his best people because he felt that would distract them from their functional work. The result was that the product development team did not work as well it might have.

To make matters worse, it can prove difficult to ascertain accountability in a matrix structure. When all critical decisions are the product of negotiation between different hierarchies, one side can always blame the other when things go wrong. As a manager in one high-tech matrix structure said to the author when reflecting on a failed product launch, "Had the engineering (R&D) group provided our development team with decent resources, we would have got that product out on time and it would have been successful." For his part, the head of the engineering group stated that "We did everything we could to help them succeed but the project was not well managed. They kept changing their requests for engineering skills, which was very disruptive." The result of such finger pointing can be that accountability is compromised and conflict escalated, and senior management can lose control over the organization.

Despite these problems, there is evidence that a matrix structure can work.[20] Making a matrix work requires clear lines of responsibility. Normally this means that one side of the matrix must be given the primary role, while the other is given a support role. In a high-tech firm, for example, the product development teams might be given the primary role, because getting good products to market as quickly as possible is a key to competitive success. Despite taking such steps, managing within a matrix structure is difficult. In light of these problems, managers sometimes try to build "flexible" matrix structures based more on enterprisewide management knowledge networks, and a shared culture and vision, than on a rigid, hierarchical arrangement. Within such companies, the informal structure plays a greater role than the formal structure. We discuss this issue when we consider informal integrating mechanisms in the next section.

Formal Integrating Mechanisms

There is often a need to coordinate the activities of different functions and divisions within an organization in order to achieve strategic objectives. For example, at the *business level* effective new product development requires tight integration between R&D, production, and marketing functions. Similarly, at the *corporate level*, implementing a related diversification strategy requires integration between divisions in order to realize economies of scope and to transfer or leverage rare, valuable resources such as knowledge across divisions.

The formal integrating mechanisms used to coordinate subunits vary in complexity from simple, direct contact and liaison roles, to teams, to a matrix structure (see Figure 12.6). In general, the greater the need for coordination between subunits (functions or divisions), the more complex the formal integrating mechanisms need to be.[21]

Direct contact between subunit managers is the simplest integrating mechanism: Managers of the various subunits simply contact each other whenever they have

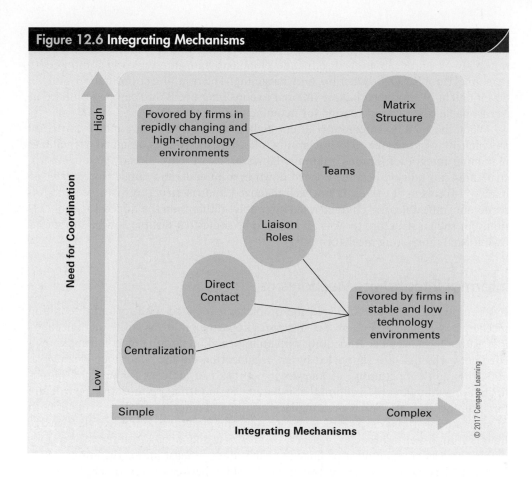

Figure 12.6 Integrating Mechanisms

Need for Coordination

High

Low

Fovored by firms in repidly changing and high-technology environments

Matrix Structure

Teams

Liaison Roles

Direct Contact

Fovored by firms in stable and low technology environments

Centralization

Simple   Complex

Integrating Mechanisms

© 2017 Cengage Learning

a common concern. Direct contact may not be effective, however, if the managers have differing orientations that impede coordination, partly because they have different tasks. For example, production managers are typically concerned with issues such as capacity utilization, cost control, and quality control, whereas marketing managers are concerned with issues such as pricing, promotions, distribution, and market share. These differences can inhibit communication between managers. Managers from different functions often do not "speak the same language." Managers can also become entrenched in their own "functional silos," and this can lead to a lack of respect between subunits (for example, marketing managers "looking down on" production managers, and vice versa). This further inhibits the communication required to achieve cooperation and coordination. For these reasons, direct contact is rarely sufficient to achieve coordination between subunits when the need for integration is high.

Liaison roles are a bit more complex than direct contact. As the need for coordination between subunits increases, integration can be improved by giving one individual in each subunit responsibility for coordinating with other subunits on a regular basis. Through these roles, the employees involved establish a permanent relationship. This helps attenuate the impediments to coordination discussed above.

When the need for coordination is greater still, firms often use temporary or permanent teams composed of individuals from the subunits that need to achieve coordination. Teams are often used to coordinate product development efforts, but they can be useful when any aspect of operations or strategy requires the cooperation of two or more subunits. Product development teams are typically composed of personnel from R&D, production, and marketing. The resulting coordination aids the development of products that are tailored to consumer needs and can be produced at a reasonable cost (through design for manufacturing).

When the need for integration is very high, firms may institute a matrix structure in which all roles are viewed as integrating roles. The structure is designed to facilitate maximum integration among subunits. However, as we have already noted, matrix structures can quickly become bogged down in a bureaucratic tangle that creates as many problems as it solves. If not well managed, matrix structures can become bureaucratic, inflexible, and characterized by conflict rather than the hoped-for cooperation. For such a structure to work, it needs to be somewhat flexible and be supported by informal integrating mechanisms.[22]

Informal Integrating Mechanisms

In attempting to alleviate or avoid the problems associated with formal integrating mechanisms in general, and matrix structures in particular, firms with a high need for integration have been experimenting with an informal integrating mechanism: knowledge networks that are supported by an organization culture that values teamwork and cross-unit cooperation.[23] A **knowledge network** is a network for transmitting information within an organization that is based not on formal organizational structure but on informal contacts between managers within an enterprise.[24] The great strength of such a network is that it can be used as a nonbureaucratic conduit for knowledge flows within an enterprise.[25] For a network to exist, managers at different locations within the organization must be linked to each other, at least indirectly. For example, Figure 12.7 shows the simple network relationships between seven managers within a multinational firm. Managers A, B, and C all know each other personally, as do Managers D, E, and F. Although Manager B does not know Manager F personally, they are linked through common acquaintances (Managers C and D). Thus, Managers A through F are all part of the network; Manager G is not.

knowledge network

A network for transmitting information within an organization that is based not on formal organization structure but on informal contacts between managers within an enterprise and on distributed-information systems.

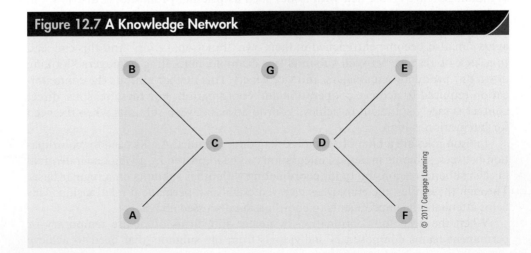

Figure 12.7 A Knowledge Network

© 2017 Cengage Learning

Imagine Manager B is a marketing manager in Spain and needs to know the solution to a technical problem to better serve an important European customer. Manager F, an R&D manager in the United States, has the solution to Manager B's problem. Manager B mentions her problem to all of her contacts, including Manager C, and asks if they know of anyone who might be able to provide a solution. Manager C asks Manager D, who tells Manager F, who then calls Manager B with the solution. In this way, coordination is achieved informally through the network, rather than by formal integrating mechanisms such as teams or a matrix structure.

For such a network to function effectively, it must embrace as many managers as possible. For example, if Manager G had a problem similar to manager B's, he would not be able to utilize the informal network to find a solution; he would have to resort to more formal mechanisms. Establishing firmwide knowledge networks is difficult. Although network enthusiasts speak of networks as the "glue" that binds complex organizations together, it is far from clear how successful firms have been at building companywide networks. The techniques that have been used to establish knowledge networks include information systems, management development policies, and conferences.

Firms are using their distributed computer and telecommunications information systems to provide the foundation for informal knowledge networks.[26] Email, videoconferencing, intranets, and Web-based search engines make it much easier for managers scattered over the globe to get to know each other, to identify contacts who might help to solve a particular problem, and to publicize and share best practices within the organization. Wal-Mart, for example, uses its intranet system to communicate ideas about merchandizing strategy between stores located in different countries.

Firms are also using their management development programs to build informal networks. Tactics include rotating managers through various subunits on a regular basis so they build their own informal network, and using management education programs to bring managers of subunits together in a single location so they can become acquainted. In addition, some science-based firms use internal conferences as a way to establish contacts between people in different units of the organization. At 3M, regular, multidisciplinary conferences bring together scientists from different business units and get them talking to each other. Apart from the benefits of direct interaction in the conference setting, the idea is that once the conference is over, the scientists may continue to share ideas, and this will increase knowledge flows within the organization. 3M has many stories of product ideas that were the result of such knowledge flows, including the ubiquitous Post-it Notes, whose inventor, Art Fry, first learned about the adhesive that he would use on the product from a colleague working in another division of 3M, Spencer Silver, who had spent several years shopping his adhesive around 3M.[27]

Knowledge networks alone may not be sufficient to achieve coordination if subunit managers persist in pursuing subgoals that are at variance with firmwide goals. For a knowledge network to function properly—and for a formal matrix structure to work as well—managers must share a strong commitment to the same goals. To appreciate the nature of the problem, consider again the case of Manager B and Manager F. As before, Manager F hears about Manager B's problem through the network. However, solving Manager B's problem would require Manager F to devote considerable time to the task. Insofar as this would divert Manager F away from his regular tasks—and the pursuit of subgoals that differ from those of Manager B—he may be unwilling to do it. Thus, Manager F may not call Manager B, and the informal network would fail to provide a solution to Manager B's problem.

To eliminate this flaw, an organization's managers must adhere to a common set of norms and values that override differing subunit orientations.[28] In other words, the firm must have a strong organizational culture that promotes teamwork and cooperation. When this is the case, a manager is willing and able to set aside the interests of his own subunit when doing so benefits the firm as a whole. If Manager B and Manager F are committed to the same organizational norms and value systems, and if these organizational norms and values place the interests of the firm as a whole above the interests of any individual subunit, Manager F should be willing to cooperate with Manager B on solving her subunit's problems.

▼ ORGANIZATION CONTROLS AND INCENTIVES

One critical management task is to control an organization's activities. Controls are an integral part of an enterprise's organizational architecture. They are necessary to ensure that an organization is operating efficiently and effectively, and in a manner that is consistent with its intended strategy. Without adequate controls, *control loss* occurs and the organization's performance will suffer.

Control Systems

control

The process through which managers regulate the activities of individuals and units so that they are consistent with the goals and standards of the organization.

Control can be viewed as the process through which managers *regulate* the activities of individuals and units so that they are consistent with the goals and standards of the organization.[29] A **goal** is a desired future state that an organization attempts to realize. A **standard** is a performance requirement that the organization is meant to attain on an ongoing basis. Managers can regulate the activities of individuals and units in several different ways to assure that they are consistent with a firm's goals and standards. Before considering these, we need to review the workings of a typical control system. As illustrated in Figure 12.8, this system has five main elements; establishing goals and standards, measuring performance, comparing performance against goals and standards, taking corrective action, and/or providing reinforcement.[30]

goal

A desired future state that an organization attempts to realize.

Most organizations operate with a hierarchy of goals. In the case of a business enterprise, the major goals at the top of the hierarchy are normally expressed in terms of profitability and profit growth. These major goals are typically translated into subgoals that can be applied to individuals and units within the organization. A **subgoal** is an *objective*, the achievement of which helps the organization attain or exceed it major goals. Goals and subgoals should be precise, measurable, address important issues, be challenging but realistic, and specify a time period.

standard

A performance requirement that the organization is meant to attain on an ongoing basis.

To illustrate the concept of a goal hierarchy, suppose that the retailer Nordstrom has a goal of attaining a 15% return on invested capital (ROIC) in the coming year. This is the company's major profitability goal. One way of achieving it is to reduce the amount of capital needed to generate a dollars' worth of sales, and a good way of doing that is to reduce the amount of capital that Nordstrom has tied up in inventory. How does the company do that? By turning over inventory more rapidly. Thus, Nordstrom might operate with a subgoal of turning over inventory five times in the next year. If it hits that subgoal, which is precise, measurable, challenging, and has to be achieved

subgoal

An objective, the achievement of which helps the organization attain or exceed it major goals.

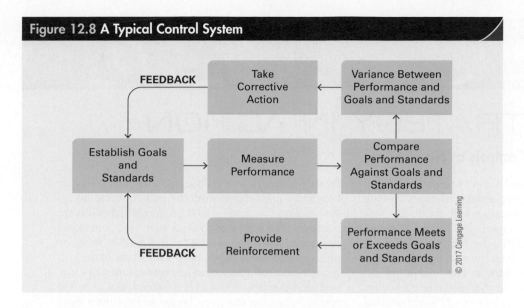

Figure 12.8 A Typical Control System

within a prespecified time period, the company's profitability, measured by ROIC, will increase. In fact, as explained in Strategy in Action 12.2, Nordstrom has done something very much along these lines.

Standards are similar to goals but tend to be objectives that the organization is expected to achieve as a part of its routine operations, rather than a challenging goal it is striving to attain. For example, an organization might operate with standards specifying that vendors should be paid within 30 days of submitting an invoice, that customer inquiries should be answered within 24 hours, that all employees should have a formal performance review and be given written feedback once a year, that safety checks should be performed on production equipment every six months, or that employees should fly coach when traveling on business trips.

A key element in the control process is generating the right goals, subgoals, and standards. Managers need to choose goals and standards carefully to avoid motivating the wrong behavior. There is a saying, "You get what you measure." If you chose the wrong goals and standards, you get the wrong behavior. Dysfunctional controls will generate dysfunctional behavior. A few years ago, a placement agency decided to start evaluating and rewarding its staff based on how many job seekers they sent to a job interviews. This productivity measure seemed to produce the desired results; over the next few months; more job seekers got interviews. However, after a while the numbers started to drop off quite alarmingly. When management looked into the issue, they found that several prospective employers would no longer interview people referred to them by the placement agency. The problem: In an effort to hit their numbers, staff members had been sending people to interview for jobs for which they were not qualified. This had damaged the reputation of the placement agency among prospective employers, and led to a fall-off in business for the agency—the opposite of what managers had been trying to achieve. Managers subsequently changed the measure to reflect the number of job seekers who were actually hired.

The next step in the control process is to compare actual performance against goals and standards. If performance is in line with goals or standards, that is good. However, the point made earlier still holds: Management needs to make sure that the reported

12.2 STRATEGY IN ACTION

Goal Setting and Controls at Nordstrom

A few years ago, Nordstrom, the venerable, high-end department store, was facing some challenges. Despite industry-leading sales per square foot, profits had fallen short of the company's goals for 3 years in a row and were down some 35%. The root of the problem was that poor inventory controls meant that Nordstrom either had too much merchandise that was in low demand, or too little of the merchandise that consumers wanted. To get rid of excess inventory, Nordstrom had to hold frequent sales, marking down produce and selling it at a lower profit margin. Moreover, the failure to stock popular items meant that Nordstrom was losing high-margin sales.

To correct this problem, Nordstrom revamped its inventory-control systems. The company invested heavily in information technology so that it could track its inventory on a real-time basis. It also built electronic links to

provide suppliers with visibility of what was selling at Nordstrom and what the reorder pattern would be, so the suppliers could adjust their production schedules accordingly. The goal was to stock only what consumers demanded by having inventories delivered to stores on an as-needed basis. To measure the success of this program, Nordstrom focused on two metrics–inventory turnover and average inventory per square foot of selling space. When the company began to implement these systems it was turning over its inventory 3.73 times a year, and on average throughout the year had $60 of inventory for every square foot of selling space in a store. Three years later, as a result of better inventory controls, inventory was turning over 4.51 times a year, and the company held $52.46 of inventory for every square foot of selling space. Due to improved operating efficiency, net profits tripled over this time period.[31]

Endnote Crediting: J. Batsell, "Cost Cutting, Inventory Control Help Boost Nordstrom's Quarterly Profit", *Knight Ridder Tribune News*, Feburary 22, 2002, page 1. Nordstrom's 2004 10K statement.

performance is being achieved in a manner that is consistent with the values of the organization. If reported performance falls short of goals and standards, management needs to start digging to find out the reason for the variance. This typically requires collecting more information, much of which might be qualitative data gleaned from face-to-face meetings and detailed probing to get behind the numbers. The same is true if reported performance *exceeds* goals or standards. Management needs to find out the reason for such favorable variance, and doing so requires collecting more information.

Variances from goals (and standards) require that managers take corrective action. When actual performance easily exceeds the goal, corrective action might include raising the goal. When actual performance falls short of the goal, depending on what further investigation reveals, management might make changes in strategy, operations, or personnel. Radical adjustment is not always the appropriate response when an organization fails to hit a major goal. Investigation might reveal that the original goal was too aggressive, or that changes in market conditions outside the control of management accounted for the poor performance. In such cases, the response to a shortfall might be to adjust the goal downward.

If the goals and standards are meet, or exceeded, management needs to provide timely, positive reinforcement to those responsible. This can run from congratulations for a job well done, to awards, pay increases, bonuses, and enhanced career prospects for those responsible. Providing positive reinforcement is every bit as import an aspect of a control system as is taking corrective action. Behavioral scientists have long known that positive reinforcement increases the probability that those being acknowledged will continue to pursue the rewarded behavior in the future.[32] Without positive reinforcement, people become discourage, feel underappreciated, may not be willing to work as hard, and might look for other employment opportunities where they are better appreciated.

Methods of Control

There are several main ways of achieving control within an organization including personal controls, bureaucratic controls, output controls, incentive controls, market controls, and control through culture (which we consider in the next section on organizational culture).[33]

Personal Controls   As the term suggests, **personal control** is control by personal contact with and direct supervision of subordinates. Personal control consists of making sure, through personal inspection and direct supervision, that individuals and units behave in a way that is consistent with the goals of the organization. Personal control can be very subjective, with the manager assessing how well subordinates are performing by observing and interpreting their behavior. As an overarching philosophy for control within an organization, personal control tends to be found primarily in small firms where the activities of a few people might be regulated through direct oversight. By its very nature, personal control tends to be associated with the centralization of power and authority in a key manager, who is often the owner of the small business. Personal control may work best when this key manager is a charismatic individual who can command the personal allegiance of subordinates.

Personal control has several serious limitations. For one thing, excessive supervision can be demotivating. Employees may resent being closely supervised and may perform better if given a greater degree of personal freedom. Moreover, the subjective nature of personal control can lead to a feeling that there is a lack of objectivity and procedural justice in the performance review process. Subordinates may feel that favoritism, personal likes and dislikes, and individual idiosyncrasies may be as important in performance reviews as actual performance. Personal control is also costly in that managers must devote considerable time and attention to the direct supervision of subordinates, which takes their attention away from other important issues. The real Achilles heel of personal control, however, is that it starts to break down as an overarching control philosophy when an organization grows in size and complexity. As this occurs, the key manager has no choice but to decentralize decision making to others within the hierarchy if the enterprise is to continue growing. Doing so effectively requires the adoption of different control philosophies.

Bureaucratic Control   **Bureaucratic control** is defined as control through a formal system of written rules and procedures.[34] As a strategy for control, bureaucratic control methods rely on prescribing what individuals and units can and cannot do; that is, on establishing bureaucratic standards. At the University of Washington, for example, there is a bureaucratic standard specifying that faculty members can perform no more

personal control
Control by personal contact with and direct supervision of subordinates.

bureaucratic control
Control through a formal system of written rules and procedures.

than 1 day a week of outside work. Other standards articulate the steps to be taken when hiring faculty and promoting faculty, purchasing computer equipment for faculty, and so on.

Almost all organizations use bureaucratic controls. Familiar examples are budgetary controls and controls over capital spending. Budgets are essentially a set of rules for allocating an organization's financial resources. A subunit's budget specifies with some precision how much the unit may spend, and how that spending should be allocated across different areas. Senior managers in an organization use budgets to control the behavior of subunits. For example, an R&D budget might specify how much cash an R&D unit may spend on product development in the coming year. R&D managers know that if they spend too much on one project, they will have less to spend on other projects, so they modify their behavior to stay within the budget. Most budgets are set by negotiation between headquarters management and subunit management. Headquarters management can encourage the growth of certain subunits and restrict the growth of others by manipulating their budgets.

Although the term "bureaucratic" often has negative connotations, bureaucratic control methods can be very useful in organizations. They allow managers to decentralize decision making within the constraints specified by formal rules and procedures. However, too great a reliance on bureaucratic rules can lead to problems. Excessive formal rules and procedures can be stifling, limiting the ability of individuals and units to respond in a flexible way to specific circumstances. This can result in poor performance and sap the motivation of those who value individual freedom and initiative. As such, extensive bureaucratic control methods are not well suited to organizations facing dynamic, rapidly changing environments, or to organizations that employ skilled individuals who value autonomy. The costs of monitoring the performance of individuals and units to make sure that they comply with bureaucratic rules can also be significant and may outweigh the benefits of establishing extensive rules and standards.

Bureaucratic standards can also lead to unintended consequences if employees try to find ways around rules that they think are unreasonable. An interesting and controversial case in point concerns rules on forced school busing in the United States. In the 1970s, school districts around America started to bus children to schools outside of their immediate neighborhood in order to achieve a better racial mix. This well-intentioned bureaucratic rule was designed to speed racial integration in a society characterized by significant racial discrimination. Unfortunately, the rule had unintended consequences. Parents of all races objected to their children being bused to distant schools in order to comply with a bureaucratic rule. In many large cities where forced busing was practiced, white families with children responded by fleeing to the suburbs, where there were few minorities and busing was not practiced, or by sending their children to expensive, private schools within the city. The result: Far from advancing racial integration, busing had the opposite effect. A case in point was Seattle, where the percentage of white students in city schools dropped from 60 to 41% over the 20 years during which forced busing was enforced.[35] In the 1990s, most school districts ended forced busing.

Output Controls   Output controls can be used when managers can identify tasks that are complete in the sense of having a measurable output or meeting a criterion of overall achievement.[36] For example, the overall achievement of an automobile factory might be measured by the number of employee hours it takes to build a car (a measure of productivity) and the number of defects found per 100 cars produced by the factory (a measure of quality). Nordstrom measures the overall achievement of the unit responsible for inventory management by the number of inventory turns per year. FedEx measures the "output" of each of its local stations in its express delivery network by the percentage of packages delivered before 10:30 a.m. In a multibusiness company such as GE or 3M, senior management might measure the "output" of a product division in terms of that division's profitability, profit growth, and market share.

When complete tasks can be identified, **output controls** involve setting goals for units or individuals and monitoring performance against those goals. The performance of unit managers is then judged by their ability to achieve the goals.[37] If goals are met or exceeded, unit managers will be rewarded (an act of reinforcement). If goals are not met, senior management will normally intervene to find out why and take corrective action. Thus, as in a classic control system, control is achieved by comparing actual performance against targets, providing reinforcement, and intervening selectively to take corrective action.

The goals assigned to units depend on the unit's role in the firm. Self-contained product divisions are typically given goals for profitability and profit growth. Functions are more likely to be given goals related to their particular activity. Thus, R&D will be given product development goals, production will be given productivity and quality goals, marketing will be given market-share goals, and so on.

The great virtue of output controls is that they facilitate decentralization and give individual managers within units much greater autonomy then either personal controls or bureaucratic controls. This autonomy enables managers within a unit to configure their own work environment in a way that best matches the particular contingencies they face, rather than having a work environment imposed upon them from above. Thus, output controls are useful when units have to respond rapidly to changes in the markets they serve. Output controls also involve less extensive monitoring than either bureaucratic or personal controls. Senior managers can achieve control by comparing actual performance against targets, and intervening selectively. As such, they reduce the workload on senior executives and allow them to mange a larger, more diverse organization with relative ease. Thus, many large, multiproduct, multinational enterprises rely heavily upon output controls to manage their various product divisions and foreign subsidiaries.

Output controls have limitations. Senior managers need to look behind the numbers to make sure that unit managers are not only achieving goals, but are doing so in a way that is consistent with the values of the organization. Managers also need to make sure that they choose the right criteria to measure output. Failure to select the right criteria might result in dysfunctional behavior. Moreover, output controls do not always work well when extensive interdependencies exist between units.[38]

The performance of a unit may be ambiguous if it is based upon cooperation with other units. For example, if the performance of a unit is declining, it may be because of poor management within that unit, or it may be because a unit with which it is cooperating is not doing its part. In general, interdependence between units within an organization can create performance ambiguities that make output controls more difficult to interpret. Resolving these ambiguities requires managers to collect more information, which places more demands on top management and raises the monitoring costs associated with output controls. It also increases the possibility that managers will become overloaded with information and, as a result, make poor decisions.

output controls

Goals that are set for units or individuals and monitoring performance against those goals.

market controls

The regulation of the
behavior of individuals
and units within an
enterprise by setting up
an internal market for
valuable resource such as
capital.

Market Controls   Market controls involve regulating the behavior of individuals and units within an enterprise by setting up an *internal market* for valuable resource such as capital.[39] Market controls are usually found within diversified enterprises organized into product divisions, where the head office might act as an internal investment bank, allocating capital funds between the competing claims of the different product divisions based upon an assessment of their likely future performance. Within this internal market, all cash generated by the divisions is viewed as belonging to the head office. The divisions then have to compete for access to the capital resources controlled by the head office. Insofar as they need that capital to grow their divisions, the assumption is that this internal competition will drive divisional managers to find ways to improve the efficiency of their units. One of the first companies in the world to establish an internal capital market was Japanese electronics manufacturer Matsushita, which introduced such systems in the 1930s.[40]

In addition, in some enterprises divisions compete with each other for the right to develop and sell new products. Again, Japan's Matsushita has a long history of letting different divisions develop similar new products, and then assigning overall responsibility for producing and selling the product to the division that seems to be furthest along in the commercialization process. While some might view such duplication of product development effort as wasteful, Matsushita's legendary founder, Konosuke Matsushita, believed that the creation of an internal market for the right to commercialize technology drove divisional managers to maximize the efficiency of product development efforts within their unit. Similarly, within Samsung, the Korean electronics company, senior management will often set up two different teams within different units to develop new products such as new memory chips. The purpose of the internal competition between the two teams is to accelerate the product development process, with the winning team earning significant accolades and bonuses.[41]

The main problem with market controls is that fostering internal competition between divisions for capital and the right to develop new products can make it difficult to establish cooperation between divisions for mutual gain.[42] If two different divisions are racing against each other to develop very similar new products, and are competing against each other for limited capital resources, they may be unwilling to share technological knowhow with each other, perhaps to the determinant of the entire corporation. Companies like Samsung deal with this problem by using integrating mechanisms such as liaison role, and by assigning the responsibility for leveraging technological knowhow across divisions to key individuals.

Incentives Control   Incentives are the devices used to encourage and reward appropriate employee behavior. Many employees receive incentives in the form of annual bonus pay. Incentives are usually closely tied to the performance metrics used for output controls. For example, setting targets linked to profitability might be used to measure the performance of a subunit such as a product division. To create positive incentives for employees to work hard to exceed those targets, they may be given a share of any profits over above those targeted. If a subunit has set a goal of attaining a 15% ROIC and actually attains a 20% return, unit employees may be given a share in the profits generated in excess of the 15% target in the form of bonus pay.

The idea is that giving employees incentives to work productively reduces the need for other control mechanisms. Control through incentives is designed to facilitate *self-control*. Employees regulate their own behavior in a manner consistent with organizational goals in order to maximize their chance of earning incentive-based pay.

Although paying out bonus and the like costs the organization money, well-designed incentives pay for themselves. That is, the increase in performance due to incentives more than offsets the costs of financing them.

The type of incentive used may vary depending on the employees and their tasks. Incentives for employees working on the factory floor may be very different from the incentives for senior managers. The incentives must be matched to the type of work being performed. The employees on the factory floor of a manufacturing plant may be broken into teams of 20 to 30 individuals, and they may have their bonus pay tied to the ability of their team to hit or exceed targets for output and product quality. In contrast, the senior managers of the plant may be rewarded according to metrics linked to the output of the entire operation. The basic principle is to make sure the incentive scheme for an individual employee is linked to an output target that he or she has some control over and can influence. Individual employees on the factory floor may not be able to exercise much influence over the performance of the entire operation, but they can influence the performance of their team, so their incentive pay is tied to output at this level.

When incentives are tied to team performance, as is often the case, they have the added benefit of encouraging cooperation between team members and fostering a degree of peer control. **Peer control** occurs when employees pressure others within their team or work group to perform up to or in excess of the expectations of the organization.[43] Thus, if the incentive pay of a 20-person team is linked to team output, members can be expected to pressure those in the team who are perceived as slacking off and freeloading on the efforts of others, urging them to pick up the pace and make an equal contribution to team effort. When peer control is functioning well within an organization, it reduces the need for direct supervision of a team and can facilitate attempts to move toward a flatter management hierarchy.

peer control
The pressure that employees exert on others within their team or work group to perform up to or in excess of the expectations of the organization.

In sum, incentives can reinforce output controls, induce employees to practice self-control, increase peer control, and lower the need for other control mechanisms. Like all other control methods discussed here, controls through incentives have limitations. Since incentives are typically linked to the metrics used in output controls, the points made with regard to output controls also apply here. Specifically, managers need to make sure that incentives are not tied to output metrics that result in unintended consequences or dysfunctional behavior.

ORGANIZATIONAL CULTURE

Organizational culture refers to the values, norms, and assumptions that are shared among employees of an organization. By **values** we mean abstract ideas about what a group believes to be good, right, and desirable. Put differently, values are shared assumptions about how things ought to be. By **norms**, we mean social rules and guidelines that prescribe the appropriate behavior in particular situations.

values
The ideas or shared assumptions about what a group believes to be good, right, and desirable.

Culture can exert a profound influence on the way people behave within an organization, on the decisions that are made, on the things that the organization pays attention to, and ultimately, on the firm's strategy and performance.

An organization's culture has several sources. There seems to be wide agreement that founders or important leaders can have a profound impact on organizational culture, often imprinting their own values upon it. In addition, the culture of an enterprise can be shaped by landmark events in its history. Culture is maintained and

norms
Social rules and guidelines that prescribe the appropriate behavior in particular situations.

transmitted over time through formal and informal socialization mechanisms. These include hiring practices, procedures regarding rewards, pay, and promotions, and the informal rules of behavior that employees are expected to adopt if they want to fit in and succeed within the organization.[44]

Microsoft, for example, has a strong culture that was influenced by the company's founder and long-time CEO, Bill Gates. Gates always placed a high value on a technical brilliance, competitiveness, and a willingness to work long hours, something that he himself did. Gates hired and promoted people who shared these characteristics, and he led by example. He also had a tendency to dismiss the opinions of people who lacked technical brilliance. Talented engineers often "walked taller" within Microsoft, and they had a disproportionate impact on strategic decisions. The employees who gained Gates's confidence themselves hired and promoted individuals who were technically strong, competitive, and hardworking. The culture of the company was thus transmitted and enforced throughout the organization. As a result, Microsoft became a company where technical brilliance, competitiveness, and working long hours were highly valued attributes of behavior. New employees were socialized into these norms by coworkers who themselves had been similarly socialized.

History also shaped the culture at Microsoft. Most notably, it took three versions and 6 years before sales of Windows started to take off with the introduction of Windows 3.1 (Windows 1.0 and 2.0 did not do well). The lesson that Microsoft gained from this was that persistence can pay off. "We will get it right by version 3" is a phrase that is still used frequently at Microsoft. This culturally embedded value influences strategic decisions regarding investments such as Microsoft's long running commitment to its money-losing Bing search business. Reflecting the culture of Microsoft, many employees believe that if they stick with it, Bing will eventually turn profitable.

Culture as a Control Mechanism   Given that organizational culture shapes behavior within an organization, culture can be viewed as a control mechanism that mandates expected behaviors. At Microsoft, under the leadership of Gates, staff worked long hours not because bureaucratic rules told them to do so, and not because supervisors explicitly required them to do so, but because that was the cultural norm. In this sense, culture shaped behavior, thereby reducing the need for bureaucratic and personal controls. The company could trust people to work hard and behave in a competitive manner, because those norms were such a pervasive aspect of the culture.

Although cultural controls can mitigate the need for other controls, thereby reducing monitoring costs, they are not universally beneficial. Cultural controls can have dysfunctional aspects. The hard-driving, competitive aspect of Microsoft's culture was arguably a contributing factor in the antitrust violations that the company was found to have made in the 1990s (the U.S. Justice Department, which brought the antitrust case against Microsoft in the United States, used as evidence internal e-mails where one senior manager stated that Microsoft would "cut off a competitor's air supply"). Moreover, Microsoft's culture of working long hours clearly had a downside: Many good employees burned out and left the company. In the post-Gates era, the company has become attuned to this. As its work force has aged and started families, it has become more accommodating, stressing that the output produced is more important than the hours worked.

Implementing Strategy Through Culture   Given that culture can have such a profound impact upon the way in which people behave within organizations, it is important for managers to get culture right. The right culture can help a company execute its strategy; the wrong culture can hinder strategy execution.[45] In the 1980s, when IBM was performing very well, several management authors sang the praises of its culture, which among other things placed a high value on consensus-based decision making.[46] These authors argued that such a decision-making process was appropriate given the substantial financial investments that IBM routinely made in new technology. However, this process turned out to be a weakness in the fast-moving computer industry of the late 1980s and 1990s. Consensus-based decision making was slow, bureaucratic, and not particularly conducive to corporate risk taking. While this was fine in the 1970s, IBM needed rapid decision making and entrepreneurial risk taking in the 1990s, but its culture discouraged such behavior. IBM was outflanked by then-small enterprises such as Microsoft, almost went bankrupt, and had to go through a massive change to shift its organizational culture.

One academic study concluded that firms that exhibited high performance over a prolonged period tended to have strong but adaptive cultures. According to this study, in an adaptive culture most managers care deeply about and value customers, stockholders, and employees. They also strongly value people and processes that create useful change in a firm.[47] While this is interesting, it does reduce the issue to a very high level of abstraction; after all, what company would say that it doesn't care deeply about customers, stockholders, and employees? A somewhat different perspective is to argue that the culture of the firm must match the rest of its architecture, its strategy, and the demands of the competitive environment for superior performance to be attained. All these elements must be consistent with each other. Lincoln Electric provides a useful example (see Strategy in Action 12.3). Lincoln competes in a business that is very competitive, where cost minimization is a key source of competitive advantage. Lincoln's culture and incentive systems both encourage employees to strive for high levels of productivity, which translates into the low costs that are critical for its success. These aspects of Lincoln's organizational architecture are aligned with the low-cost strategy of the company.

ORGANIZATION PROCESSES

Processes, defined as the manner in which decisions are made and work is performed within an organization,[48] are found at many different levels within an organization. There are processes for formulating strategy, allocating resources, evaluating new-product ideas, handling customer inquiries and complaints for improving product quality, evaluating employee performance, and so on. Often, a firm's core competencies or valuable, knowledge-based resources are embedded in its processes. Efficient, effective processes can lower the costs of value creation and add additional value to a product. For example, the global success of many Japanese manufacturing enterprises in the 1980s was based in part on their early adoption of processes for improving product quality and operating efficiency, including total quality management and just-in-time inventory systems. Today, the competitive success of General Electric can in part be attributed to a number of processes that have been widely promoted within the company. These include the company's Six Sigma process for quality improvement, its process for "digitalization" of business (using corporate intranets and the Internet to automate activities and reduce operating costs), and its process for idea generation,

12.3 STRATEGY IN ACTION

Organizational Culture at Lincoln Electric

Lincoln Electric is one of the leading companies in the global market for arc welding equipment. Lincoln's success has been based on extremely high levels of employee productivity. The company attributes its productivity to a strong organizational culture and an incentive scheme based on piecework. Lincoln's organizational culture dates back to James Lincoln. Lincoln had a strong respect for the ability of the individual and believed that, correctly motivated, ordinary people could achieve extraordinary performance. He emphasized that Lincoln should be a meritocracy where people were rewarded for their individual effort. Strongly egalitarian, Lincoln removed barriers to communication between "workers" and "managers," practicing an open-door policy. He made sure that all who worked for the company were treated equally; for example, everyone ate in the same cafeteria, there were no reserved parking places for "managers," and so on. Lincoln also believed that gains in productivity should be shared with consumers in the form of lower prices, with employees in the form of higher pay, and with shareholders in the form of higher dividends.

The organizational culture that grew out of Lincoln's beliefs was reinforced by the company's incentive system. Production workers receive no base salary but are paid according to the number of pieces they produce. The piecework rates at the company enable an employee working at a normal pace to earn an income equivalent to the average wage for manufacturing workers in the area where a factory is based. Workers have responsibility for the quality of their output and must repair defects spotted by quality inspectors before the pieces are included in the piecework calculation. Production workers are awarded a semiannual bonus based on merit ratings. These ratings are based on objective criteria (such as an employee's level and quality of output) and subjective criteria (such as an employee's attitudes toward cooperation and his or her dependability). These systems give Lincoln's employees an incentive to work hard and generate innovations that boost productivity, for doing so influences their level of pay. Lincoln's factory workers have been able to earn a base pay that often exceeds the average manufacturing wage in the area by more than 50% and receive a bonus on top of this which, in good years, could double their base pay. Despite high employee compensation, its workers are so productive that Lincoln has a lower cost structure than its competitors.[49]

Endnote Crediting: J. O'Connell, "Lincoln Electric: Venturing Abroad," Harvard Business School Case No. 9-398-095, April 1998; and www.lincolnelectric.com.

referred to within the company as "workouts," where managers and employees gather for intensive sessions over several days to identify and commit to ideas for improving productivity.

An organization's processes can be summarized by means of a flow chart, which illustrates the various steps and decision points involved in performing work. A detailed consideration of the nature of processes and strategies for process improvement and reengineering is beyond the scope of this book. However, it is important to make two basic remarks about managing processes, particularly in the context of an international business.[50]

First, many processes cut across functions, or divisions, and require cooperation between individuals in different subunits. For example, product development processes require employees from R&D, manufacturing, and marketing to work in a cooperative manner to make sure new products are developed with market needs in mind and designed in such a way that they can be manufactured at a low cost. Because they cut across organizational boundaries, performing processes effectively often require the establishment of formal integrating mechanisms and incentives for cross-unit cooperation.

Second, it is particularly important for an enterprise to recognize that valuable new processes that might lead to a competitive advantage can be developed anywhere within the organization's network of operations.[51] Valuable and rare new processes may be developed within a team, function, product division, or foreign subsidiary. Those processes might then be valuable to other parts of the enterprise. The ability to create valuable processes matters, but it is also important to leverage those processes, and this requires both formal and informal integrating mechanisms such as knowledge networks.

IMPLEMENTING STRATEGY THROUGH ORGANIZATIONAL ARCHITECTURE

We are now in a position to make observations about the kind of organizational arrangements required to implement different strategies. Rather than construct an exhaustive list, we will focus on a limited number of business- and corporate-level strategies. We start by considering strategy and organization within the single-business firm. Then we look at strategy and organization within the diversified firm.

Strategy and Organization in the Single-Business Enterprise

As noted earlier, single-business enterprises are typically organized along functional lines (see Figure 12.3). However, the need for integration between functions will vary depending upon (1) the business-level strategy of the firm, and (2) the nature of the environment in which the firm competes (see Figure 12.9).

Strategy, Environment, and the Need for Integration   In general, the need for integration between functions is greater for firms that are competing through product

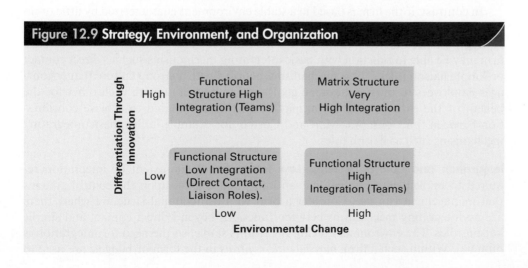

Figure 12.9 Strategy, Environment, and Organization

		Low	High
Differentiation Through Innovation	High	Functional Structure High Integration (Teams)	Matrix Structure Very High Integration
	Low	Functional Structure Low Integration (Direct Contact, Liaison Roles).	Functional Structure High Integration (Teams)
		Environmental Change	

development and innovation.[52] This is typically the case when an organization's business-level strategy involves differentiation through the introduction of new and/ or improved product offerings. Apple, Google, Ford, Microsoft, Tesla, and Toyota, for example, all try to differentiate themselves through product development and innovation. As discussed earlier, in such organizations there is an ongoing need to coordinate the R&D, production, and marketing functions of the firm to ensure that (1) new products are developed in a timely manner, (2) that they can be efficiently produced and delivered, and (3) that they match consumer demands. We saw that a matrix structure is one way of achieving such coordination (see Figure 12.5). Another, more common, solution is to form temporary teams to oversee the development and introduction of a new product. Once the new product has been introduced, the team is disbanded and employees return to their functions or move to another team.

Firms that face an uncertain, highly turbulent, competitive environment,where rapid adaptation to changing market conditions is required, need coordination in order to survive.[53] Environmental change, such as that which occurs when an industry is disrupted by radical innovations, may require a change in product, process, business model, and strategy. In such cases, it is critical to make sure that the different functions of the firm all pull in the same direction, so that the firm's response to a changing environment is coherent and organizationwide. Temporary teams are often used to effect such coordination.

For example, in the mid-1990s, the World Wide Web emerged with stunning speed and in a way that almost no one anticipated. The rise of the Web produced a profound change in the environment facing computer software firms such as Microsoft, where managers quickly shifted their strategy so as to make their products Web enabled, and position their marketing and sales activities to compete in this new landscape. This shift required very tight coordination between different software engineering groups, such as those working on the software code for Windows, Office and MSN, so that all products not only were Web enabled but also worked seamlessly with each other. Microsoft achieved this by forming cross-functional teams.

In addition to using formal integrating mechanisms such as cross-functional teams, firms with a crucial need for coordination between subunits—for instance, those based in turbulent, high-tech environments—would do well to foster informal knowledge networks, for they too can facilitate coordination between subunits.

In contrast, if the firm is based in a stable environment characterized by little or no change, and if developing new products is not a central aspect of the firm's business strategy, the need for coordination between functions may be lower. In such cases, a firm may be able to function with basic integrating mechanisms such as direct contact or simple liaison roles. These mechanisms, coupled with a strong culture that encourages employees to pursue the same goals, and to cooperate with each other for the benefit of the entire organization, may be all that is required to achieve coordination between functions. Wal-Mart and Costco, for example, utilize basic integrating mechanisms such as liaison roles.

Integration and Control Systems: Low Integration   The extent of integration required to implement a strategy has an important impact upon the control systems that management can use. Consider a firm with a functional structure where there are no integrating mechanisms between functions beyond direct contact and simple liaison roles. The environment facing the firm is stable, so the need for integration is minimal. Within such a firm, *bureaucratic controls* in the form of budgets are used to allocate financial resources to each function and control spending by the functions. *Output controls* will then be used to assess how well a function is performing. Different functions will be assigned different output targets, depending on their specific tasks. The procurement function might be assigned an output target based on procurement costs as a percentage of sales; a manufacturing function might be given productivity and product quality targets such as output per employee and defects per thousand products; the logistics function might be given an inventory turnover target; the marketing and sales function might be given sales-growth and market-share goals; and the success of the service function might be measured by the time it takes to resolve a customer problem. To the extent that each function hits these targets, the overall performance of the firm will improve, and its profitability will increase.

Output controls might also be pushed further down within functions. A production process might be subdivided into discrete tasks, each of which has a measurable output. Employee teams might be formed and empowered to take ownership over each discrete task. Each team will be assigned an output target. To the extent that functions can be divided into teams, and output controls applied to those teams, this will facilitate (1) decentralization within the organization, (2) wider spans of control (since it is relatively easy to control a team by monitoring its outputs, as opposed to regulating behavior through bureaucratic rules), and (3) a flatter organization structure.

Within such a structure, the CEO will monitor the heads of the functions. They in turn will exercise control over units or teams within their function. There may also be some degree of *personal control,* with the CEO using personal supervision to influence the behavior of functional heads; they in turn do the same for their direct reports. *Incentives* will be tied to output targets. The incentive pay of the head of manufacturing might be linked to the attainment of predetermined productivity and quality targets for the manufacturing function; the incentive pay of the head of logistic might be linked to increases in inventory turnover; the pay of the head of marketing and sales to gains in market share, and so on. Incentives might also be pushed further down within the organization, with members of teams within functions being rewarded on the basis of the ability of their team to hit or exceed predetermined targets. A portion of the incentive pay for managers—and perhaps all employees—might be tied to the overall performance of the enterprise to encourage cooperation and knowledge sharing within the organization.

Finally, it is possible for such an enterprise to have strong *cultural controls.* Cultural controls may reduce the need for personal controls and bureaucratic rules. Individuals might be trusted to behave in the desired manner because they "buy into" the prevailing culture. Thus, cultural controls might allow the firm to operate with a flatter organization structure and wider spans of control, and generally increase the effectiveness of output controls and incentives, because employees may buy into the underlying philosophy upon which such controls are based.

Integration and Control Systems: High Integration   A functional structure where the strategy and/or environment requires a high degree of integration presents managers with a complex control problem. The problem is particularly severe if the firm adopts a matrix structure. As noted earlier, a firm based in a dynamic environment where competition centers on product development might adopt such a structure. Within such an enterprise, *bureaucratic controls* will again be used for financial budgets and as before *output controls* will be applied to the different functions. *Output controls* will also be applied to cross-functional product development teams. Thus a team might be assigned output targets covering development time, production costs of the new product, and the features the product should incorporate. For functional managers, *incentive controls* might be linked to output targets for their functions, whereas for the members of a product development team, incentives will be tied to the performance of the team.

The problem with such an arrangement is that the performance of the product development team is dependent upon the support the team gets from the various functions. The support needed includes people and information from production, marketing, and R&D. Consequently, significant performance ambiguity might complicate the process of using output controls to assess the performance of a product development team. **Performance ambiguity** arises when it is difficult to identify with precision the reason for the high (or low) performance of a subunit such as a function or team. In this context, the failure of a cross-functional product development team to hit predetermined output targets might be due to the poor performance of team members, but it could just as well be due to the failure of the functions to provide an appropriate level of support to the team. Senior management cannot determine which explanation is correct simply by observing output controls tied to team performance, because such outputs are not an unambiguous indicator of performance. Identifying the true cause of performance variations requires senior managers to collect information, much of it subjective, which increases the time and energy they must devote to the control process, diverts their attention from other important issues, and hence increases the costs of monitoring and controlling the organization. Other things being equal, this reduces the span of control that senior managers can handle, suggesting the need for a taller hierarchy which, as we saw earlier, gives rise to all kinds of additional problems.

The nature of the performance ambiguity problem in such an enterprise raises the question of whether there is a better solution to the control problem. In fact, there is. One step is to make sure that the incentives of all key personnel are aligned; that is, to use *incentive controls* in a discriminating way. The classic way of doing this is to tie incentives to a higher level of organization performance. Thus, in addition to being rewarded on the basis of the performance of their function, functional heads might also be rewarded on the basis of the overall performance of the firm. Insofar as the success of product development teams increases firm performance, this gives functional heads an incentive to make sure that the product development teams receive adequate support from the functions. In addition, strong *cultural controls* can be very helpful in establishing company wide norms and values that emphasize the importance of cooperation between functions and teams for their mutual benefit.

Strategy and Organization in the Multibusiness Enterprise

As discussed earlier, multibusiness enterprises typically organize themselves along divisional lines (see Figure 12.4). Within each division, there will be a functional organization. The extent of integration between functions *within divisions* may differ from division to division depending upon the business-level strategy and the nature of the environment. The need for integration *between divisions*, on the other hand, depends upon the specific corporate strategy the firm is pursuing. This will have an impact not only on the integrating mechanisms used, but also on the type of control and incentive systems employed.[54]

performance ambiguity
The difficulty of identifying with precision the reason for the high (or low) performance of a subunit such as a function or team.

If the firm is pursuing a strategy of related diversification and trying to realize economies of scope by sharing inputs across product divisions, or is trying to boost profitability by transferring or leveraging valuable competencies across divisions, it will have a need for integrating mechanisms to coordinate the activities of the different product divisions. Liaison roles, temporary teams, and permanent teams can all be used to ensure such coordination. On the other hand, if top management is focusing primarily on boosting profitability through superior internal governance, and if each division is managed on a stand-alone basis, with no attempt to leverage competencies or realize economies of scope, as is the case in firms pursuing a strategy of unrelated diversification, the firm may well operate well with minimal or no integrating mechanisms between divisions.

Controls in the Diversified Firm with Low Integration   In firms that focus primarily on boosting performance through superior internal governance where the strategy is one of unrelated diversification, the need for integration between divisions is low. Firms pursuing a strategy of unrelated diversification are not trying to share resources or leverage core competencies across divisions, so there is no need for complex integrating mechanisms, such as cross-divisional teams, to coordinate the activities of different divisions. In these enterprises, the head office typically controls the divisions in four main ways.[55]

First, they use *bureaucratic controls* to regulate the financial budgets and capital spending of the divisions. Typically each division will have to have its financial budgets approved for the coming year by the head office. In addition, capital expenditures in excess of a certain amount have to be approved by the head office; for example, any item of spending by a division in excess of $50,000 might have to be approved by the head office.

Second, the head office will use *output controls*, assigning each division output targets that are normally based on measurable financial criteria such as the profitability, profit growth, and cash flow produced by each division. Typically targets for the coming year are set by negotiation between divisional heads and senior managers at the head office. As long as the divisions hit their targets, they are left alone to run their own operations. If performance falls short of targets, however, top managers will normally audit a division to discover why this occurred, and take corrective action if necessary by instituting a change in strategy and/or personnel.

Third, *incentive controls* will be used, with the incentives for divisional managers being tied to the financial performance of their divisions. To earn pay bonuses, divisional managers have to hit or exceed the performance targets previously negotiated between the head office and the divisions. To make sure that divisional managers do not try to "talk down" their performance targets for the year, making it easy for them to hit their targets and earn bonuses, the head office will normally benchmark a product division against its competitors, take a close look at industry conditions, and use this information to establish performance targets that are challenging but attainable.

Fourth, the head office will use *market controls* to allocate capital resources between different divisions.[56] As noted earlier, in multidivisional enterprises the cash generated by product divisions is normally viewed as belonging to the head office, which functions as an internal capital market, reallocating cash flows between the competing claims of different divisions based on an assessment of likely future performance. The competition between divisions for access to capital, which they need to grow their businesses, is assumed to create further incentives for divisional managers to run their operations as efficiently and effectively as possible. In addition, the head office might use market controls to allocate the right to develop and commercialize new products between divisions.

Within divisions, the control systems used will be those found within single-business enterprises. It should also be noticed that head office managers might utilize some *personal controls* to influence the behavior of divisional heads. In particular, the CEO might exercise control over divisional heads by meeting with them on a regular basis and probing them to get rich feedback about the operations of the entity for which they are responsible.

Controls in the Diversified Firm with High Integration   The control problem is more complex in diversified firms pursuing a strategy of related diversification where they are trying to improve performance not only through superior internal governance, but also proactively attempting to leverage competencies across product divisions and realize economies of scope. Consider, for example, 3M, a highly diversified enterprise with multiple product divisions. The company devotes great effort trying to leverage core technology across divisions (for instance, by establishing internal knowledge networks). In addition, 3M tries to realize economies of scope, particularly in the areas of marketing and sales, where a marketing and sales division might sell the products of several 3M divisions. More generally, when a multidivisional enterprise tries to improve performance through the attainment of economies of scope, and via the leveraging of core competencies across divisions, the need for integration between divisions is high.

In such organizations, top managers use the standard repertoire of control mechanisms discussed in the last section (e.g. bureaucratic, output, incentive, and market controls). However, in addition, they have to deal with two control problems that are not found in multidivisional firms pursuing a strategy of unrelated diversification where there is no cooperation and integration between divisions. First, they have to find a control mechanism that induces divisions to cooperate with each other for mutual gain. Second, they need to find a way to deal with the performance ambiguities that arise when divisions are tightly coupled with each other, share resources, and the performance on one cannot be understood in isolation but depends upon how well it cooperates with others.

The solution to both problems is in essence the same as that adopted by single-business firms with high integration between functions. Specifically, the firm needs to adopt incentive controls for divisional managers that are linked to higher-level performance, in this case the performance of the entire enterprise. Insofar as improving the performance of the entire firm requires cooperation between divisions, such incentive controls should facilitate that cooperation. In addition, strong cultural controls can be helpful in creating values and norms that emphasize the importance of cooperation between divisions for mutual gain. At 3M there is a long-established cultural norm that, while products belong to the divisions, the technology underlying those products belongs to the entire company. Thus, the surgical tape business might utilize adhesive technology developed by the office supply business to improve its own products.

Despite such solutions to control problems, there is no question that top managers in firms where divisions are tightly integrated have to deal with greater performance ambiguities than top managers in less complex multidivisional organizations. Integration between various product divisions means that it is hard for top managers to judge the performance of each division just by monitoring objective output criteria. To accurately gauge performance and achieve adequate controls, they probably have to spend time auditing the affairs of operating divisions, and talking to divisional managers to get a comprehensive, qualitative picture of performance than can help them "dig behind" objective output numbers. Other things being equal, this might limit the span of control managers can effectively handle, and thus the scope of the enterprise.[57]

KEY TERMS

organizational
   architecture 386
organizational
   structure 386
controls 387
incentives 387
organizational
   processes 387
organizational
   culture 387
people 387

vertical
   differentiation 388
horizontal
   differentiation 388
integrating
   mechanisms 388
centralization 388
decentralization 388
autonomous subunit 389
tall hierarchies 391
flat hierarchies 391

span of control 392
influence costs 393
delayering 394
functional structure 394
multidivisional
   structure 395
matrix structure 397
knowledge network 400
control 402
goal 402
standard 402

subgoal 402
personal control 405
bureaucratic control 405
output controls 407
market controls 408
peer control 409
values 409
norms 409
performance
   ambiguity 416

TAKEAWAYS FOR STRATEGIC MANAGERS

1. Strategy is implemented through the organizational architecture of the enterprise.

2. It is useful to think of organizational architecture as a system that encompasses structure, controls, incentives, processes, culture, and human capital.

3. In general, a flat organizational structure where the performance of each subunit is visible, unambiguous, and can be measured by objective output controls, is preferable.

4. Implementing strategy may require cooperation between functions and product divisions. The need for cooperation requires integrating mechanisms. Extensive use of integrating mechanisms may lead to performance ambiguity, and require more complex and varied control mechanisms.

5. At the business level, the need for integrating mechanisms to coordinate functional activities is greater for firms whose business-level strategy requires ongoing product development efforts and product innovation, and for firms based in rapidly changing market environments.

6. At the corporate level, the need for integrating mechanisms to coordinate the activities of different divisions is greater for companies pursuing a strategy of related diversification than for those pursuing a strategy of unrelated diversification.

DISCUSSION QUESTIONS

1. What is the relationship among organizational structure, control systems, incentives, and culture? Give some examples of when and under what conditions a mismatch among these components might arise.
2. What kind of structure best describes the way your (a) business school and (b) university operate? Why is the structure appropriate? Would another structure be better?
3. When would a company choose a matrix structure? What are the problems associated with managing this type of structure? How might these problems be mitigated?
4. What kind of structure, controls, incentives, and culture would you be likely to find in (a) a small manufacturing company based in a stable environment, (b) a high-tech company based in a rapidly changing market, and (c) a Big Four accounting firm?
5. When would a company decide to change from a functional to a multidivisional structure?
6. How would you design structure, controls, incentives, processes, and culture to encourage entrepreneurship in a large, established corporation? How might the desire to encourage entrepreneurship influence your hiring and management development strategy?

CLOSING CASE

Organization at Apple

Apple has a legendary ability to produce a steady stream of innovative new products and product improvements that are differentiated by design elegance and ease of use. Product innovation is in many ways the essence of what the company has always done, and what it strives to continue doing. Innovation at Apple began with the Apple II in 1979. The original Macintosh computer, the first personal computer (PC) to use a graphical user interface, a mouse, and onscreen icons, followed in 1984. After the late founder and former CEO Steve Jobs returned to the company in 1997, the list of notable innovations expanded to include the iPod and iTunes, the Mac Airbook, the iPhone, the Apple App store, and the iPad.

Unlike most companies of its size, Apple has a functional structure. The employees reporting directly to current CEO Tim Cook include the senior vice presidents of operations, Internet software and services, industrial design, software engineering, hardware engineering, and worldwide marketing, along with the CFO and company general council. This group meets every Monday morning to review the strategy of the company, its operations, and ongoing product development efforts.

The industrial design group takes the lead on new-product development efforts, dictating the look and feel of a new product, and the materials that must be used. The centrality of industrial design is unusual—in most companies engineers first develop products, with industrial design coming into the picture quite late in the process. The key role played by industrial design at Apple, however, is consistent with the company's mission of designing beautiful products that change the world. The industrial design group works closely with hardware and software engineering to develop features and functions for each new product, with operations to ensure that manufacturing can be rapidly scaled up following a product launch, and with worldwide marketing to plan the product launch strategy.

Thus, product development at Apple is a cross-functional effort that requires intense coordination. This coordination is achieved through a centralized command and control structure, with the top-management group driving collaboration and the industrial design group setting key parameters. During his long tenure as CEO, Jobs was well known for clearly articulating who was responsible for what in the product development process, and for holding people accountable if they failed to meet his high standards. His management style could be unforgiving and harsh—there are numerous stories of people being fired on the spot for failing to meet his standards—but it did get the job done.

Even though Jobs passed away in 2011, the focus on accountability persists at Apple. Each task is given a "directly responsible individual," or DRI in "Apple-speak." Typically, the DRI's name will appear on an agenda for a meeting, so everyone knows who is responsible. Meetings at Apple have an action list, and next to each action item will be a DRI. By such clear control processes, Apple pushes accountability down deep within the ranks.

A key feature of the Apple culture is the secrecy surrounding much of what the company does. Information that reaches the outside world tightly controlled, and so is the flow of information within the company. Many employees are kept in the dark about new-product development efforts and frequently do not know what others are working on. Access to buildings where teams are developing new products or features is tightly controlled, with only team members allowed in. Cameras monitor sensitive workspaces to make sure that this is restriction is not violated. Disclosing what the company is doing to an outside source, or an unauthorized inside source, is grounds for termination—as all employees are told when they join the company. The goal is to keep new products under very tight wraps until launch day. Apple wants to control the message surrounding new products. It does not want to give the competition time to respond, or media critics time to bash products under development.

Sources: J. Tyrangiel, "Tim Cook's Freshman Year: The Apple CEO Speaks," *Bloomberg Businessweek*, December 6, 2012; A. Lashinsky, "The Secrets Apple Keeps," *CNNMoney*, January 10, 2012; and B. Stone, "Apple's Obsession with Secrecy Grows Stronger," *New York Times*, June 23, 2009.

CASE DISCUSSION QUESTIONS

1. Describe as best you can the organizational architecture at Apple, and specifically, its organizational structure, control systems, incentives, product development processes, and culture.
2. What do you think is different about the way Apple is organized compared to most high-tech firms?
3. What is Apple trying to achieve with its current organizational architecture? What are the strengths of this architecture? What are the potential weaknesses?
4. Are there changes that you think Apple should make in its organizational architecture? What are these changes? How might they benefit Apple?

NOTES

[1] D. Naidler, M. Gerstein, and R. Shaw, *Organization Architecture* (San Francisco: Jossey-Bass, 1992).

[2] G. Morgan, *Images of Organization* (Beverly Hills, CA: Sage Publications, 1986).

[3] The material in this section draws on J. Child, *Organizations* (London: Harper & Row, 1984).

Recent work addressing the issue includes J. R. Baum and S. Wally, "Strategic Decision Speed and Firm Performance," *Strategic Management Journal* 24 (2003): 1107–1120; D. I. Jung and B. J. Avolio, "Effects of Leadership Style and Followers Cultural Orientation on Performance in Groups and Individual Task Conditions," *Academy of Management Journal* 42 (1999): 208–218.

[4] This is a key tenet of the information-processing view of organizations. See J. Galbraith. *Designing Complex Organizations* (Reading, MA: Addison-Wesley, 1972).

[5] J. Kim and R. M. Burton, "The Effects of Uncertainty and Decentralization on Project Team Performance," *Computational & Mathematical Organization Theory* 8 (2002): 365–384.

[6] J. Birkinshaw, N. Hood, and S. Jonsson, "Building Firm Specific Advantages in Multinational Corporations: The Role of Subsidiary Initiatives," *Strategic Management Journal* 19 (1998): 221–241.

[7] K. M. Eisenhardt, "Making Fast Strategic Decisions in High Velocity Environments," *Academy of Management Journal* 32 (1989): 543–575.

[8] G. P. Hattrup and B. H. Kleiner, "How to Establish a Proper Span of Control for Managers", *Industrial Management* 35 (1993): 28–30

[9] The classic statement was made by P. Milgrom and J. Roberts, "Bargaining Costs, Influence Costs and the Organization of Economic Activity", in J. E. Alt and K. A. Shepsle (eds.), *Perspectives in Positive Political Economy*, (Cambridge: Cambridge University Press, 1990). Also see R. Inderst, H. M. Muller, and K. Warneryd, "Influence Costs and Hierarchy," *Economics of Governance* 6 (2005): 177–198.

[10] D. Priest and D. Linzer, "Panel Condemns Iraq Prewar Intelligence," *The Washington Post*, July 10, 2004, page A1; D. Jehl, "Senators Assail CIA Judgments of Iraq's Arms as Deeply Flawed," *New York Times*, July 10, 2004, page A1; M. Isikoff, "The Dots Never Existed," *Newsweek*, July 19, 2004, pp. 36–40.

[11] C. R. Littler, R. Wiesner and R. Dunford, "The Dynamics of Delayering," *Journal of Management Studies* 40 (2003): 225–240.

[12] J. A. Byrne, "Jack: A Close-up Look at How America's #1 Manager Runs GE," *Business Week*, June 8, 1998, pp 90-100. Also see *Harvard Business School Press*, "GE's Two Decade Transformation."

[13] A. D. Chandler, *Strategy and Structure: Chapters in the History of the Industrial Enterprise* (Cambridge, MA: MIT Press, 1962). Also see O.E. Williamson, *Markets and Hierarchies: Analysis and Anti-Trust Implications* (New York: Free Press, 1975).

[14] A. P. Sloan, *My Years at General Motors* (New York: Bantum Books, 1996). Originally published in 1963.

[15] C. W. L. Hill, M. A. Hitt, and R. E. Hoskisson. "Cooperative versus Competitive Structures in Related and Unrelated Firms," *Organization Science* 45 (1992): 501–521; O. E. Williamson, *Markets and Hierarchies: Analysis and Anti-Trust Implications* (New York: Free Press, 1975).

[16] C. W. L. Hill, M. A. Hitt, and R. E. Hoskisson, "Declining U.S. Competitiveness: Reflections on a Crisis," *Academy of Management Executives* 2 (1988): 51–60.

[17] P. R. Lawrence and J. Lorsch, *Organization and Environment* (Boston, MA: Harvard University Press, 1967).

[18] K. B. Clark and S. C. Wheelwright, *Managing New Product and Process Development* (New York: Free Press, 1993); M. A. Schilling and C. W. L. Hill, "Managing the New Product Development Process," *Academy of Management Executive* 12 (3) (August 1998): 67–68; S. L. Brown and K. M. Eisenhardt, "Product Development: Past Research, Present Findings, and Future Directions," *Academy of Management Review* 20 (1995): 343–378.

[19] L. R. Burns and D. R. Whorley, "Adoption and Abandonment of Matrix Management Programs: Effects of Organizational Characteristics and Interorganizational Networks," *Academy of Management Journal* (February 1993), pp. 106–138; C. A. Bartlett and S. Ghoshal, "Matrix Management: Not a Structure, a Frame of Mind," *Harvard Business Review* (July-August 1990), pp. 138–145.

[20] S. Thomas and L. S. D'Annunizo, "Challenges and Strategies of Matrix Organizations," *HR Human Resource Planning* 28 (2005): 39–49.

[21] See J. R. Galbraith, *Designing Complex Organizations* (Reading, MA: Addison-Wesley, 1977).

[22] M. Goold and A. Campbell, "Structured Networks: Towards the Well Designed Matrix," *Long Range Planning* (October 2003), pp. 427–460.

[23] Bartlett and Ghoshal, *Managing across Borders*; F. V. Guterl, "Goodbye, Old Matrix," *Business Month* (February 1989), pp. 32–38; I. Bjorkman, W. Barner-Rasussen, and L. Li, "Managing Knowledge Transfer in MNCs: The Impact

of Headquarters Control Mechanisms," *Journal of International Business* 35 (2004): 443–460.

[24]M. S. Granovetter, "The Strength of Weak Ties," *American Journal of Sociology* 78 (1973): 1360–1380.

[25]A. K. Gupta and V. J. Govindarajan, "Knowledge Flows within Multinational Corporations," *Strategic Management Journal* 21 (4) (2000): 473–496; V. J. Govindarajan and A. K. Gupta, *The Quest for Global Dominance* (San Francisco: Jossey-Bass, 2001); U. Andersson, M. Forsgren, and U. Holm, "The Strategic Impact of External Networks: Subsidiary Performance and Competence Development in the Multinational Corporation," *Strategic Management Journal* 23 (2002): 979–996.

[26]For examples, see W. H. Davidow and M. S. Malone, *The Virtual Corporation* (New York: Harper Collins, 1992).

[27]3M. A Century of Innovation, the 3M Story. 3M, 2002. www.3m.com/about3m/century/index.jhtml.

[28]W. G. Ouchi, "Markets, Bureaucracies, and Clans," *Administrative Science Quarterly* 25 (1980): 129–144.

[29]J. Child, *Organization: A Guide to Problems and Practice* (Harper & Row: London, 1984).

[30]S. G. Green and M. A. Welsh. "Cybernetics and Dependence: Reframing the Control Concept," *Academy of Management Review* 13 (2) (1988): 287–301.

[31]J. Batsell, "Cost Cutting, Inventory Control Help Boost Nordstrom's Quarterly Profit," Knight Ridder Tribune News, Feburary 22, 2002, p. 1; Nordstrom 2004 10K statement.

[32]For a recent summary, see D. M. Wiegand and E. S. Geller. "Connecting Positive Psychology and Organization Behavior Management," *Journal of Organization Behavior Management* 24 (12) (2004/2005): 3–20.

[33]J. Child, "Strategies of Control and Organization Behavior," *Administrative Science Quarterly* 18 (1973): 1–17; K. Eisenhardt, "Control: Organizational and Economic Approaches," *Management Science* 31 (1985): 134–149; S. A. Snell, "Control Theory in Human Resource Management," *Academy of Management Review* 35 (1992): 292–328; W. G. Ouchi, "The Transmission of Control Through Organizational Hierarchy," *Administrative Science Quarterly* 21 (1978): 173–192.

[34]J. Child, *Organization: A Guide to Problems and Practice* (Harper & Row: London, 1984).

[35]R. Teichroeb, "End to Forced Busing Creates New Problems for Seattle's Schools," *Seattle Post Intelligencer*, June 3, 1999, online edition. www.seattlepi.com

[36]J. Child, *Organization: A Guide to Problems and Practice* (Harper & Row: London, 1984).

[37]Hill, Hitt, and Hoskisson, "Cooperative versus Competitive Structures in Related and Unrelated Diversified Firms."

[38]J. D. Thompson, *Organizations in Action* (New York: McGraw Hill, 1967).

[39]O. E. Wiliamson. *The Economic Institutions of Capitalism* (Free Press, New York, 1985).

[40]C. Bartlett. "Philips versus Matsushita: A New Century, a New Round," *Harvard Business School Press* Case No. 9–302–049, 2005.

[41]L. Kim. "The Dynamics of Samsung's Technological Learning in Semiconductors," *California Management Review* 39 (3) (1997): 86–101.

[42]Hill, Hitt, and Hoskisson, "Cooperative versus Competitive Structures in Related and Unrelated Diversified Firms."

[43]Peer control has long been argued to be a characteristic of many Japanese organizations. See M. Aoki, *Information, Incentives and Bargaining in the Japanese Economy* (Cambridge, UK: Cambridge University Press, 1988).

[44]E. H. Schein, *Organizational Culture and Leadership,* 2nd ed. (San Francisco: Jossey-Bass, 1992).

[45]J. P. Kotter and J. L. Heskett, *Corporate Culture and Performance* (New York: Free Press, 1992); M. L. Tushman and C. A. O'Reilly, *Winning through Innovation* (Boston, MA: Harvard Business School Press, 1997).

[46]The classic song of praise was produced by T. Peters and R. H. Waterman, *In Search of Excellence* (New York: Harper & Row, 1982). Ironically, IBM's decline began shortly after their book was published.

[47]Kotter and Heskett, *Corporate Culture and Performance.*

[48]J. O'Connell, "Lincoln Electric: Venturing Abroad," Harvard Business School Press Case No. 9–398–095, April 1998, and www.lincolnelectric.com.

[49]M. Hammer and J. Champy, *Reengineering the Corporation* (New York: Harper Business, 1993).

[50]T. Kostova, "Transnational Transfer of Strategic Organizational Practices: A Contextual Perspective," *Academy of Management Review* 24 (2) (1999): 308–324.

[51]Andersson, Forsgren, and Holm, "The Strategic Impact of External Networks: Subsidiary Performance and Competence

Development in the Multinational Corporation."

[52] Ulf Anderson, Mats Forsgren, and Ulf Holm, "The strategic impact of external networks: Subsidiary performance and competence development in the multinational corporation," *Strategic Management Journal*, Vol 23(11), pp. 979–996.

[53] P. R Lawrence and J. Lorsch, *Organization and Environment.* (Boston, MA: Harvard University Press, 1967).

[54] Hill, Hitt, & Hoskisson, "Cooperative versus Competitive Structures in Related and Unrelated Firms."

[55] Ibid.

[56] C. W. L. Hill, "The Role of Corporate Headquarters in the Multidivisional Firm," in R. Rumelt, D. J. Teece, and D. Schendel (eds), *Fundamental Issues in Strategy Research*. (Cambridge, Mass: Harvard Business School Press, 1994), pp. 297–321.

[57] C. W. L. Hill and R. E. Hoskisson. "Strategy and Structure in the Multiproduct Firm," *Academy of Management Review* 12 (1988): 331–341.

5

CASES IN STRATEGIC MANAGEMENT

CASES

CASES	Chapter 2	Chapter 3	Chapter 4	Chapters 5 and 6	Chapter 7	Chapter 8	Chapters 9 and 10	Chapter 11	Chapter 12
Short Cases									
The U.S. Airline Industry	Yes								
Lean Production at Virginia Mason			Yes						
Consolidating Dry Cleaning	Yes						Yes		
General Electric's Ecomagination Strategy		Yes					Yes		
Avon Products		Yes			Yes				
Organizational Change at Unilever		Yes			Yes	Yes		Yes	
The Evolution of Strategy at Procter & Gamble		Yes			Yes	Yes		Yes	
VF Corp. Acquires Timberland to Realize the Benefits from Related Diversification		Yes				Yes	Yes		
Disaster in Bangladesh					Yes				Yes
Did Goldman Sachs Commit Fraud?									Yes

Long Cases	Industry Analysis	Competitive Advantage	Functional Strategy	Business Level Strategy	Technology Strategy	Global Strategy	Corporate Strategy	Ethics/Social Responsibility	Implementation through Organization
Boeing Commercial Aircraft	Yes	Yes	Yes	Yes					
Staples in 2015	Yes	Yes	Yes	Yes					
Trader Joe's: A Remarkably Quirky—and Successful!—Grocery Retailer	Yes	Yes	Yes	Yes					
Getting an Inside Look: Given Imaging's Camera Pill	Yes	Yes	Yes	Yes					
Skullcandy	Yes	Yes	Yes	Yes					
Toyota: Lean Production and the Rise of the World's Largest Automobile Manufacturer		Yes	Yes	Yes		Yes			
Uber: Driving Global Disruption	Yes	Yes	Yes	Yes	Yes	Yes		Yes	
The Home Videogame Industry: The First Four Decades	Yes	Yes		Yes	Yes				
Google in 2015	Yes	Yes		Yes			Yes		Yes
Microsoft: From Gates to Satya Nadella	Yes	Yes		Yes	Yes		Yes		Yes
Satellite Radio (A): XM versus Sirius	Yes	Yes	Yes	Yes	Yes				
Satellite Radio (B): The Sirius XM Merger and its Aftermath		Yes		Yes	Yes		Yes		
Ending HIV? Sangamo Biosciences and Gene Editing	Yes	Yes	Yes	Yes	Yes		Yes		
Genzyme's Focus on Orphan Drugs	Yes	Yes		Yes	Yes		Yes		
Starbucks, 2015	Yes	Yes	Yes	Yes			Yes	Yes	
Dell Inc.—Going Private	Yes	Yes	Yes	Yes			Yes		
3M—The First 110 years		Yes			Yes	Yes	Yes		Yes
The Tata Group, 2015	Yes	Yes				Yes	Yes		
Tesla Motors, 2015	Yes	Yes	Yes	Yes	Yes		Yes		
The Heinz and Kraft Merger		Yes					Yes		

INTRODUCTION
ANALYZING A CASE STUDY AND WRITING A CASE STUDY ANALYSIS

WHAT IS CASE STUDY ANALYSIS?

Case study analysis is an integral part of a course in strategic management. The purpose of a case study is to provide students with experience of the strategic management problems that actual organizations face. A case study presents an account of what happened to a business or industry over a number of years. It chronicles the events that managers had to deal with, such as changes in the competitive environment, and charts the managers' response, which usually involved changing the business- or corporate-level strategy. The cases in this book cover a wide range of issues and problems that managers have had to confront. Some cases are about finding the right business-level strategy to compete in changing conditions. Some are about companies that grew by acquisition, with little concern for the rationale behind their growth, and how growth by acquisition affected their future profitability. Each case is different because each organization is different. The underlying thread in all cases, however, is the use of strategic management techniques to solve business problems.

Cases prove valuable in a strategic management course for several reasons. First, cases provide you, the student, with experience of organizational problems that you probably have not had the opportunity to experience firsthand. In a relatively short period of time, you will have the chance to appreciate and analyze the problems faced by many different companies and to understand how managers tried to deal with them.

Second, cases illustrate the theory and content of strategic management. The meaning and implications of this information are made clearer when they are applied to case studies. The theory and concepts help reveal what is going on in the companies studied and allow you to evaluate the solutions that specific companies adopted to deal with their problems. Consequently, when you analyze cases, you will be like a detective who, with a set of conceptual tools, probes what happened and what or who was responsible and then marshals the evidence that provides the solution. Top managers enjoy the thrill of testing their problem-solving abilities in the real world. It is important to remember that no one knows what the right answer is. All that managers can do is to make the best guess. In fact, managers say repeatedly that they are happy if they are right only half the time in solving strategic problems. Strategic management is an uncertain game, and using cases to see how theory can be put into practice is one way of improving your skills of diagnostic investigation.

Third, case studies provide you with the opportunity to participate in class and to gain experience in presenting your ideas to others. Instructors may sometimes call on students as a group to identify what is going on in a case, and through classroom discussion the issues in and solutions to the case problem will reveal themselves. In such a situation, you will have to organize your views and conclusions so that you can present them to the class. Your classmates may have analyzed the issues differently from you, and they will want you to argue your points before they will accept your conclusions, so be prepared for debate. This mode of discussion is an example of the dialectical approach to decision making. This is how decisions are made in the actual business world.

Instructors also may assign an individual, but more commonly a group, to analyze the case before the whole class. The individual or group probably will be responsible for a 30 to 40 minute presentation of the case to the class. That presentation must cover the issues posed, the problems facing the company, and a series of recommendations for resolving the problems. The discussion then will be thrown open to the class, and you will have to defend your ideas. Through such discussions and presentations, you will experience how to convey your ideas effectively to others. Remember that a great deal of managers' time is spent in these kinds of situations: presenting their ideas and engaging in discussion with other managers who have their own views about what is going on. Thus, you will experience in the classroom the actual process of strategic management, and this will serve you well in your future career.

If you work in groups to analyze case studies, you also will learn about the group process involved in working as a team. When people work in groups, it is often difficult to schedule time and allocate responsibility for the case analysis. There are always group members who shirk their responsibilities and group members who are so sure of their own ideas that they try to dominate the group's analysis. Most of the strategic management takes place in groups, however, and it is best if you learn about these problems now.

ANALYZING A CASE STUDY

The purpose of the case study is to let you apply the concepts of strategic management when you analyze the issues facing a specific company. To analyze a case study, therefore, you must examine closely the issues confronting the company. Most often you will need to read the case several times—once to grasp the overall picture of what is happening to the company and then several times more to discover and grasp the specific problems.

Generally, detailed analysis of a case study should include eight areas:

1. The history, development, and growth of the company over time
2. The identification of the company's internal strengths and weaknesses
3. The nature of the external environment surrounding the company
4. A SWOT analysis
5. The kind of corporate-level strategy that the company is pursuing
6. The nature of the company's business-level strategy
7. The company's structure and control systems and how they match its strategy
8. Recommendations

To analyze a case, you need to apply the concepts taught in this course to each of these areas. To help you further, we next offer a summary of the steps you can take to analyze the case material for each of the eight points we just noted:

1. *Analyze the company's history, development, and growth.* A convenient way to in-vestigate how a company's past strategy and structure affect it in the present is to

chart the critical incidents in its history—that is, the events that were the most unusual or the most essential for its development into the company it is today. Some of the events have to do with its founding, its initial products, how it makes new-product market decisions, and how it developed and chose functional competencies to pursue. Its entry into new businesses and shifts in its main lines of business are also important milestones to consider.

2. *Identify the company's internal strengths and weaknesses*. Once the historical profile is completed, you can begin the SWOT analysis. Use all the incidents you have charted to develop an account of the company's strengths and weaknesses as they have emerged historically. Examine each of the value creation functions of the company, and identify the functions in which the company is currently strong and currently weak. Some companies might be weak in marketing; some might be strong in research and development. Make lists of these strengths and weaknesses. The SWOT Checklist (Table 1) gives examples of what might go in these lists.

Table 1 A SWOT Checklist

Potential Internal Strengths	Potential Internal Weaknesses
Many product lines?	Obsolete, narrow product lines?
Broad market coverage?	Rising manufacturing costs?
Manufacturing competence?	Decline in R&D innovations?
Good marketing skills?	Poor marketing plan?
Good materials management systems?	Poor material management systems?
R&D skills and leadership?	Loss of customer good will?
Information system competencies?	Inadequate human resources?
Human resource competencies?	Inadequate information systems?
Brand name reputation?	Loss of brand name capital?
Portfolio management skills?	Growth without direction?
Cost of differentiation advantage?	Bad portfolio management?
New-venture management expertise?	Loss of corporate direction?
Appropriate management style?	Infighting among divisions?
Appropriate organizational structure?	Loss of corporate control?
Appropriate control systems?	Inappropriate organizational
Ability to manage strategic change?	structure and control systems?
Well-developed corporate strategy?	High conflict and politics?
Good financial management?	Poor financial management?
Others?	Others?

Potential Environmental Opportunities	Potential Environment Threats
Expand core business(es)?	Attacks on core business(es)?
Exploit new market segments?	Increases in domestic competition?
Widen product range?	Increase in foreign competition?
Extend cost or differentiation advantage?	Change in consumer tastes?
Diversify into new growth businesses?	Fall in barriers to entry?
Expand into foreign markets?	Rise in new or substitute products?
Apply R&D skills in new areas?	Increase in industry rivalry?
Enter new related businesses?	New forms of industry competition?
Vertically integrate forward?	Potential for takeover?
Vertically integrate backward?	Existence of corporate raiders?
Enlarge corporate portfolio?	Increase in regional competition?
Overcome barriers to entry?	Changes in demographic factors?
Reduce rivalry among competitors?	Changes in economic factors?
Make profitable new acquisitions?	Downturn in economy?
Apply brand name capital in new areas?	Rising labor costs?
Seek fast market growth?	Slower market growth?
Others?	Others?

© Cengage Learning 2013

3. *Analyze the external environment.* To identify environmental opportunities and threats, apply all the concepts on industry and macroenvironments to analyze the environment the company is confronting. Of particular importance at the industry level are the Competitive Forces Model, adapted from Porter's Five Forces Model and the stage of the life-cycle model. Which factors in the macroenvironment will appear salient depends on the specific company being analyzed. Use each factor in turn (for instance, demographic factors) to see whether it is relevant for the company in question.

   Having done this analysis, you will have generated both an analysis of the company's environment and a list of opportunities and threats. The SWOT Checklist table also lists some common environmental opportunities and threats that you may look for, but the list you generate will be specific to your company.

4. *Evaluate the SWOT analysis.* Having identified the company's external opportunities and threats as well as its internal strengths and weaknesses, consider what your findings mean. You need to balance strengths and weaknesses against opportunities and threats. Is the company in an overall strong competitive position? Can it continue to pursue its current business- or corporate-level strategy profitably?

What can the company do to turn weaknesses into strengths and threats into opportunities? Can it develop new functional, business, or corporate strategies to accomplish this change? *Never merely generate the SWOT analysis and then put it aside.* Because it provides a succinct summary of the company's condition, a good SWOT analysis is the key to all the analyses that follow.

5. *Analyze corporate-level strategy.* To analyze corporate-level strategy, you first need to define the company's mission and goals. Sometimes the mission and goals are stated explicitly in the case; at other times, you will have to infer them from available information. The information you need to collect to find out the company's corporate strategy includes such factors as its lines of business and the nature of its subsidiaries and acquisitions. It is important to analyze the relationship among the company's businesses. Do they trade or exchange resources? Are there gains to be achieved from synergy? Alternatively, is the company just running a portfolio of investments? This analysis should enable you to define the corporate strategy that the company is pursuing (for example, related or unrelated diversification, or a combination of both) and to conclude whether the company operates in just one core business. Then, using your SWOT analysis, debate the merits of this strategy. Is it appropriate given the environment the company is in? Could a change in corporate strategy provide the company with new opportunities or transform a weakness into a strength? For example, should the company diversify from its core business into new businesses?

Other issues should be considered as well. How and why has the company's strategy changed over time? What is the claimed rationale for any changes? Often, it is a good idea to analyze the company's businesses or products to assess its situation and identify which divisions contribute the most to or detract from its competitive advantage. It is also useful to explore how the company has built its portfolio over time. Did it acquire new businesses, or did it internally venture its own? All of these factors provide clues about the company and indicate ways of improving its future performance.

6. *Analyze business-level strategy.* Once you know the company's corporate-level strategy and have done the SWOT analysis, the next step is to identify the company's business-level strategy. If the company is a single-business company, its business-level strategy is identical to its corporate-level strategy. If the company is in many businesses, each business will have its own business-level strategy. You will need to identify the company's generic competitive strategy—differentiation, low-cost, or focus—and its investment strategy, given its relative competitive position and the stage of the life cycle. The company also may market different products using different business-level strategies. For example, it may offer a low-cost product range and a line of differentiated products. Be sure to give a full account of a company's business-level strategy to show how it competes.

Identifying the functional strategies that a company pursues to build competitive advantage through superior efficiency, quality, innovation, and customer responsiveness and to achieve its business-level strategy is very important. The SWOT analysis will have provided you with information on the company's functional competencies. You should investigate its production, marketing, or research and development strategy further to gain a picture of where the company is going. For example, pursuing a low-cost or a differentiation strategy successfully requires very different sets of competencies. Has the company developed the right ones? If it has, how can it exploit them further? Can it pursue both a low-cost and a differentiation strategy simultaneously?

The SWOT analysis is especially important at this point if the industry analysis, particularly Porter's model, has revealed threats to the company from the environment. Can the company deal with these threats? How should it change its business-level strategy to counter them? To evaluate the potential of a company's business-level strategy, you must first perform a thorough SWOT analysis that captures the essence of its problems.

Once you complete this analysis, you will have a full picture of the way the company is operating and be in a position to evaluate the potential of its strategy. Thus, you will be able to make recommendations concerning the pattern of its future actions. However, first you need to consider strategy implementation, or the way the company tries to achieve its strategy.

7. *Analyze structure and control systems.* The aim of this analysis is to identify what structure and control systems the company is using to implement its strategy and to evaluate whether that structure is the appropriate one for the company. Different corporate and business strategies require different structures. You need to determine the *degree of fit between the company's strategy and structure.* For example, does the company have the right level of vertical differentiation (e.g., does it have the appropriate number of levels in the hierarchy or decentralized control?) or horizontal differentiation (does it use a functional structure when it should be using a product structure?)? Similarly, is the company using the right integration or control systems to manage its operations? Are managers being appropriately rewarded? Are the right rewards in place for encouraging cooperation among divisions? These are all issues to consider.

In some cases, there will be little information on these issues, whereas in others there will be a lot. In analyzing each case, you should gear the analysis toward its most salient issues. For example, organizational conflict, power, and politics will be important issues for some companies. Try to analyze why problems in these areas are occurring. Do they occur because of bad strategy formulation or because of bad strategy implementation?

Organizational change is an issue in many cases because the companies are attempting to alter their strategies or structures to solve strategic problems. Thus, as part of the analysis, you might suggest an action plan that the company in question could use to achieve its goals. For example, you might list in a logical sequence the steps the company would need to follow to alter its business-level strategy from differentiation to focus.

8. *Make recommendations.* The quality of your recommendations is a direct result of the thoroughness with which you prepared the case analysis. Recommendations are directed at solving whatever strategic problem the company is facing and increasing its future profitability. Your recommendations should be in line with your analysis; that is, they should follow logically from the previous discussion. For example, your recommendation generally will center on the specific ways of changing functional, business, and corporate strategies and organizational structure and control to improve business performance. The set of recommendations will be specific to each case, and so it is difficult to discuss these recommendations here. Such recommendations might include an increase in spending on specific research and development projects, the divesting of certain businesses, a change from a strategy of unrelated to related diversification, an increase in the level of integration among divisions by using task forces and teams, or a move to a different kind of structure to implement a new business-level strategy. Make sure your recommendations are mutually consistent and written in the form of an action plan. The plan might contain a timetable that sequences the actions for changing the company's strategy

and a description of how changes at the corporate level will necessitate changes at the business level and subsequently at the functional level.

After following all these stages, you will have performed a thorough analysis of the case and will be in a position to join in class discussion or present your ideas to the class, depending on the format used by your professor. Remember that you must tailor your analysis to suit the specific issue discussed in your case. In some cases, you might completely omit one of the steps in the analysis because it is not relevant to the situation you are considering. You must be sensitive to the needs of the case and not apply the framework we have discussed in this section blindly. The framework is meant only as a guide, not as an outline.

◤ WRITING A CASE STUDY ANALYSIS

Often, as part of your course requirements, you will need to present a written case analysis. This may be an individual or a group report. Whatever the situation, there are certain guidelines to follow in writing a case analysis that will improve the evaluation your work will receive from your instructor. Before we discuss these guidelines and before you use them, make sure that they do not conflict with any directions your instructor has given you.

The structure of your written report is critical. Generally, if you follow the steps for analysis discussed in the previous section, *you already will have a good structure for your written discussion*. All reports begin with an *introduction* to the case. In it, outline briefly what the company does, how it developed historically, what problems it is experiencing, and how you are going to approach the issues in the case write-up. Do this sequentially by writing, for example, "First, we discuss the environment of Company. . . . Third, we discuss Company X's business-level strategy. . . . Last, we provide recommendations for turning around Company X's business."

In the second part of the case write-up, the *strategic analysis* section, do the SWOT analysis, analyze and discuss the nature and problems of the company's business-level and corporate strategies, and then analyze its structure and control systems. Make sure you use plenty of headings and subheadings to structure your analysis. For example, have separate sections on any important conceptual tool you use. Thus, you might have a section on the Competitive Forces Model as part of your analysis of the environment. You might offer a separate section on portfolio techniques when analyzing a company's corporate strategy. Tailor the sections and subsections to the specific issues of importance in the case.

In the third part of the case write-up, present your *solutions and recommendations*. Be comprehensive, and make sure they are in line with the previous analysis so that the recommendations fit together and move logically from one to the next. The recommendations section is very revealing because your instructor will have a good idea of how much work you put into the case from the quality of your recommendations.

Following this framework will provide a good structure for most written reports, though it must be shaped to fit the individual case being considered. Some cases are about excellent companies experiencing no problems. In such instances, it is hard to write recommendations. Instead, you can focus on analyzing why the company is doing so well, using that analysis to structure the discussion. Following are some minor suggestions that can help make a good analysis even better:

1. Do not repeat in summary form large pieces of factual information from the case. The instructor has read the case and knows what is going on. Rather, use the

information in the case to illustrate your statements, defend your arguments, or make salient points. Beyond the brief introduction to the company, you must avoid being *descriptive*; instead, you must be *analytical*.

2. Make sure the sections and subsections of your discussion flow logically and smoothly from one to the next. That is, try to build on what has gone before so that the analysis of the case study moves toward a climax. This is particularly important for group analysis, because there is a tendency for people in a group to split up the work and say, "I'll do the beginning, you take the middle, and I'll do the end." The result is a choppy, stilted analysis; the parts do not flow from one to the next, and it is obvious to the instructor that no real group work has been done.

3. Avoid grammatical and spelling errors. They make your work look sloppy.

4. In some instances, cases dealing with well-known companies end in 1998 or 1999 because no later information was available when the case was written. If possible, do a search for more information on what has happened to the company in subsequent years.

   Many libraries now have comprehensive web-based electronic data search facilities that offer such sources as *ABI/Inform, The Wall Street Journal Index,* the *F&S Index,* and the *Nexis-Lexis* databases. These enable you to identify any article that has been written in the business press on the company of your choice within the past few years. A number of nonelectronic data sources are also useful. For example, *F&S Predicasts* publishes an annual list of articles relating to major companies that appeared in the national and international business press. *S&P Industry Surveys* is a great source for basic industry data, and *Value Line Ratings and Reports* can contain good summaries of a firm's financial position and future prospects. You will also want to collect full financial information on the company. Again, this can be accessed from Web-based electronic databases such as the *Edgar* database, which archives all forms that publicly quoted companies have to file with the Securities and Exchange Commission (SEC; e.g., 10-K filings can be accessed from the SEC's *Edgar* database). Most SEC forms for public companies can now be accessed from Internet-based financial sites, such as Yahoo's finance site (http://finance.yahoo.com/).

5. Sometimes instructors hand out questions for each case to help you in your analysis. Use these as a guide for writing the case analysis. They often illuminate the important issues that have to be covered in the discussion.

If you follow the guidelines in this section, you should be able to write a thorough and effective evaluation.

THE ROLE OF FINANCIAL ANALYSIS IN CASE STUDY ANALYSIS

An important aspect of analyzing a case study and writing a case study analysis is the role and use of financial information. A careful analysis of the company's financial condition immensely improves a case write-up. After all, financial data represent the concrete results of the company's strategy and structure. Although analyzing financial statements can be quite complex, a general idea of a company's financial position can be determined through the use of ratio analysis. Financial performance ratios can be calculated from the balance sheet and income statement. These ratios can be classified into five subgroups: profit ratios, liquidity ratios, activity ratios, leverage ratios, and shareholder-return ratios. These ratios should be compared with the industry average or the company's prior years of performance. It should be noted, however, that deviation from the average is not necessarily bad; it simply warrants further investigation. For example, young companies will have purchased assets at a different price and will likely have a different capital structure than older companies do. In addition to ratio analysis, a company's cash flow position is of critical importance and should be assessed. Cash flow shows how much actual cash a company possesses.

Profit Ratios

Profit ratios measure the efficiency with which the company uses its resources. The more efficient the company, the greater is its profitability. It is useful to compare a company's profitability against that of its major competitors in its industry to determine whether the company is operating more or less efficiently than its rivals. In addition, the change in a company's profit ratios over time tells whether its performance is improving or declining.

A number of different profit ratios can be used, and each of them measures a different aspect of a company's performance. Here, we look at the most commonly used profit ratios.

Return on Invested Capital (ROIC)   This ratio measures the profit earned on the capital invested in the company. It is defined as follows:

$$\text{Return on invested capital (ROIC)} = \frac{\text{Net profit}}{\text{Invested capital}}$$

Net profit is calculated by subtracting the total costs of operating the company away from its total revenues (total revenues − total costs). Total costs are the (1) costs of goods sold, (2) sales, general, and administrative expenses, (3) R&D expenses, and (4) other expenses. Net profit can be calculated before or after taxes, although many financial analysts prefer the before-tax figure. Invested capital is the amount that is invested in the operations of a company—that is, in property, plant, equipment, inventories, and other assets. Invested capital comes from two main sources: interest-bearing debt and shareholders' equity. Interest-bearing debt is money the company borrows from banks and from those who purchase its bonds. Shareholders' equity is the money raised from selling shares to the public, *plus* earnings that have been retained by the company in prior years and are available to fund current investments. ROIC measures the effectiveness with which a company is using the capital funds that it has available for investment. As such, it is recognized to be an excellent measure of the value a company is creating.1 Remember that a company's ROIC can be decomposed into its constituent parts.

Return on Total Assets (ROA)   This ratio measures the profit earned on the employment of assets. It is defined as follows:

$$\text{Return on total assests} = \frac{\text{Net profit}}{\text{Total assets}}$$

Return on Stockholders' Equity (ROE)   This ratio measures the percentage of profit earned on common stockholders' investment in the company. It is defined as follows:

$$\text{Return on stockholders equity} = \frac{\text{Net profit}}{\text{Stockholders equity}}$$

If a company has no debt, this will be the same as ROIC.

Liquidity Ratios

A company's liquidity is a measure of its ability to meet short-term obligations. An asset is deemed liquid if it can be readily converted into cash. Liquid assets are current assets such as cash, marketable securities, accounts receivable, and so on. Two liquidity ratios are commonly used.

Current Ratio   The current ratio measures the extent to which the claims of short-term creditors are covered by assets that can be quickly converted into cash. Most companies should have a ratio of at least 1, because failure to meet these commitments can lead to bankruptcy. The ratio is defined as follows:

$$\text{Current ratio} = \frac{\text{Current assets}}{\text{Current liabilities}}$$

Quick Ratio   The quick ratio measures a company's ability to pay off the claims of short-term creditors without relying on selling its inventories. This is a valuable measure since in practice the sale of inventories is often difficult. It is defined as follows:

$$\text{Quick ratio} = \frac{\text{Current assets} - \text{inventory}}{\text{Current liabilities}}$$

Activity Ratios

Activity ratios indicate how effectively a company is managing its assets. Two ratios are particularly useful.

Inventory Turnover   This measures the number of times inventory is turned over. It is useful in determining whether a firm is carrying excess stock in inventory. It is defined as follows:

$$\text{Inventory turnover} = \frac{\text{Cost of goods sold}}{\text{Inventory}}$$

Cost of goods sold is a better measure of turnover than sales because it is the cost of the inventory items. Inventory is taken at the balance sheet date. Some companies choose to compute an average inventory, beginning inventory, and ending inventory, but for simplicity, use the inventory at the balance sheet date.

Days Sales Outstanding (DSO) or Average Collection Period   This ratio is the average time a company has to wait to receive its cash after making a sale. It measures how effective the company's credit, billing, and collection procedures are. It is defined as follows:

$$DSO = \frac{\text{Accounts receivable}}{\text{Total sales}/360}$$

Accounts receivable is divided by average daily sales. The use of 360 is the standard number of days for most financial analysis.

Leverage Ratios

A company is said to be highly leveraged if it uses more debt than equity, including stock and retained earnings. The balance between debt and equity is called the *capital structure*. The optimal capital structure is determined by the individual company. Debt has a lower cost because creditors take less risk; they know they will get their interest and principal. However, debt can be risky to the firm because if enough profit is not made to cover the interest and principal payments, bankruptcy can result. Three leverage ratios are commonly used.

Debt-to-Assets Ratio   The debt-to-assets ratio is the most direct measure of the extent to which borrowed funds have been used to finance a company's investments. It is defined as follows:

$$\text{Debt-to-assets ratio} = \frac{\text{Total debt}}{\text{Total assets}}$$

Total debt is the sum of a company's current liabilities and its long-term debt, and total assets are the sum of fixed assets and current assets.

Debt-to-Equity Ratio   The debt-to-equity ratio indicates the balance between debt and equity in a company's capital structure. This is perhaps the most widely used measure of a company's leverage. It is defined as follows:

$$\text{Debt-to-equity ratio} = \frac{\text{Total debt}}{\text{Total equity}}$$

Times-Covered Ratio   The times-covered ratio measures the extent to which a company's gross profit covers its annual interest payments. If this ratio declines to less than 1, the company is unable to meet its interest costs and is technically insolvent. The ratio is defined as follows:

$$\text{Times-covered ratio} = \frac{\text{Profit before interest and tax}}{\text{Total interest charges}}$$

Shareholder-Return Ratios

Shareholder-return ratios measure the return that shareholders earn from holding stock in the company. Given the goal of maximizing stockholders' wealth, providing shareholders with an adequate rate of return is a primary objective of most companies. As with profit ratios, it can be helpful to compare a company's shareholder returns against those of similar companies as a yardstick for determining how well the company is satisfying the demands of this particularly important group of organizational constituents. Four ratios are commonly used.

Total Shareholder Returns Total shareholder returns measure the returns earned by time $t + 1$ on an investment in a company's stock made at time t. (Time t is the time at which the initial investment is made.) Total shareholder returns include both dividend payments and appreciation in the value of the stock (adjusted for stock splits) and are defined as follows:

$$\text{Total shareholder returns} = \frac{\text{Stock price } (t+1) - \text{stock price } (t) + \text{sum of annual dividends per share}}{\text{Stock price } (t)}$$

If a shareholder invests $2 at time t and at time $t + 1$ the share is worth $3, while the sum of annual dividends for the period t to $t + 1$ has amounted to $0.20, total shareholder returns are equal to $(3 - 2 + 0.2)/2 = 0.6$, which is a 60% return on an initial investment of $2 made at time t.

Price-Earnings Ratio The price-earnings ratio measures the amount investors are willing to pay per dollar of profit. It is defined as follows:

$$\text{Price-earnings ratio} = \frac{\text{Market price per share}}{\text{Earnings per share}}$$

Market-to-Book Value Market-to-book value measures a company's expected future growth prospects. It is defined as follows:

$$\text{Market-to-book value} = \frac{\text{Market price per share}}{\text{Earnings per share}}$$

Dividend Yield The dividend yield measures the return to shareholders received in the form of dividends. It is defined as follows:

$$\text{Dividend} = \frac{\text{Dividend per share}}{\text{Market price per share}}$$

Market price per share can be calculated for the first of the year, in which case the dividend yield refers to the return on an investment made at the beginning of the year. Alternatively, the average share price over the year may be used. A company must decide how much of its profits to pay to stockholders and how much to reinvest in the company. Companies with strong growth prospects should have a lower dividend payout ratio than mature companies. The rationale is that shareholders can invest the money elsewhere if the company is not growing. The optimal ratio depends on the individual firm, but the key decider is whether the company can produce better returns than the investor can earn elsewhere.

Cash Flow

Cash flow position is cash received minus cash distributed. The net cash flow can be taken from a company's statement of cash flows. Cash flow is important for what it reveals about a company's financing needs. A strong positive cash flow enables a company to fund future investments without having to borrow money from bankers or investors. This is desirable because the company avoids paying out interest or dividends. A weak or negative cash flow means that a company has to turn to external sources to fund future investments. Generally, companies in strong-growth industries often find themselves in a poor cash flow position (because their investment needs are substantial), whereas successful companies based in mature industries generally find themselves in a strong cash flow position.

A company's internally generated cash flow is calculated by adding back its depreciation provision to profits after interest, taxes, and dividend payments. If this figure is insufficient to cover proposed new investments, the company has little choice but to borrow funds to make up the shortfall or to curtail investments. If this figure exceeds proposed new investments, the company can use the excess to build up its liquidity (that is, through investments in financial assets) or repay existing loans ahead of schedule.

◤CONCLUSION

When evaluating a case, it is important to be *systematic*. Analyze the case in a logical fashion, beginning with the identification of operating and financial strengths and weaknesses and environmental opportunities and threats. Move on to assess the value of a company's current strategies only when you are fully conversant with the SWOT analysis of the company. Ask yourself whether the company's current strategies make sense given its SWOT analysis. If they do not, what changes need to be made? What are your recommendations? Above all, link any strategic recommendations you may make to the SWOT analysis. State explicitly how the strategies you identify take advantage of the company's strengths to exploit environmental opportunities, how they rectify the company's weaknesses, and how they counter environmental threats. Also, do not forget to outline what needs to be done to implement your recommendations.

Endnote

1. Tom Copeland, Tim Koller, and Jack Murrin, *Valuation: Measuring and Managing the Value of Companies* (New York: Wiley, 1996).

CASE

1

THE U.S. AIRLINE INDUSTRY

The U.S. airline industry has long struggled to make a profit. In the 1990s, investor Warren Buffet famously quipped that investors in the airline industry would have been more fortunate if the Wright Brothers had crashed at Kitty Hawk. Buffet's point was that the airline industry had cumulatively lost more money than it had made—it has always been an economically losing proposition. Buffet once made the mistake of investing in the industry when he took a stake in US Airways. A few years later, he was forced to write off 75% of the value of that investment. He told his shareholders that if he ever invested in another airline, they should shoot him.

The 2000s have not been kinder to the industry. The airline industry lost $35 billion between 2001 and 2006. It managed to earn meager profits in 2006 and 2007, but lost $24 billion in 2008 as oil and jet fuel prices surged throughout the year. In 2009, the industry lost $4.7 billion as a sharp drop in business travelers—a consequence of the deep recession that followed the global financial crisis—more than offset the beneficial effects of falling oil prices. The industry returned to profitability in 2010–2012, and in 2012 actually managed to make $13 billion in net profit on revenues of $140.5 billion.

Analysts point to a number of factors that have made the industry a difficult place in which to do business. Over the years, larger carriers such as United, Delta, and American have been hurt by low-cost budget carriers entering the industry, including Southwest Airlines, Jet Blue, AirTran Airways, and Virgin America. These new entrants have used nonunion labor, often fly just one type of aircraft (which reduces maintenance costs), have focused on the most lucrative routes, typically fly point-to-point (unlike the incumbents, which have historically routed passengers through hubs), and compete by offering very low fares. New entrants have helped to create a situation of excess capacity in the industry, and have taken share from the incumbent airlines, which often have a much higher cost structure (primarily due to higher labor costs).

The incumbents have had little choice but to respond to fare cuts, and the result has been a protracted industry price war. To complicate matters, the rise of Internet travel sites such as Expedia, Travelocity, and Orbitz has made it much easier for consumers to comparison shop, and has helped to keep fares low.

Beginning in 2001, higher oil prices also complicated matters. Fuel costs accounted for 32% of total revenues in 2011 (labor costs accounted for 26%; together they are the two biggest variable expense items). From 1985 to 2001, oil prices traded in a range between $15 and $25 a barrel. Then, prices began to rise due to strong demand from developing nations such as China and India, hitting a high of $147 a barrel in mid-2008. The price for jet fuel, which stood at $0.57 a gallon in December 2001, hit a high of $3.70 a gallon in July 2008, plunging the industry deep into the red. Although oil prices and fuel prices subsequently fell, they remain far above historic levels. In late 2012, jet fuel was hovering around $3.00 a gallon.

Many airlines went bankrupt in the 2000s, including Delta, Northwest, United, and US Airways. The larger airlines continued to fly, however, as they reorganized under Chapter 11 bankruptcy laws, and excess capacity persisted in the industry. These companies came out of bankruptcy protection with lower labor costs, but generating revenue still remained challenging for them.

The late 2000s and early 2010s were characterized by a wave of mergers in the industry. In 2008, Delta and Northwest merged. In 2010, United and Continental merged, and Southwest Airlines announced plans to acquire AirTran. In late 2012, American Airlines put itself under Chapter 11 bankruptcy protection. US Airways subsequently pushed for a merger agreement with American Airlines, which was under negotiation in early 2013. The driving forces behind these mergers include the desire to reduce excess capacity and lower costs by eliminating duplication. To the extent that they are successful, they could lead to a more stable pricing environment in the industry, and higher profit rates. That, however, remains to be seen.

Sources: J. Corridore, "Standard & Poors Industry Surveys: Airlines," June 28, 2012; B. Kowitt, "High Anxiety," *Fortune*, April 27, 2009, p. 14; "Shredding Money," *The Economist*, September 20, 2008.

CASE DISCUSSION QUESTIONS

1. Conduct a competitive forces analysis of the U.S. airline industry. What does this analysis tell you about the causes of low profitability in this industry?

2. Do you think there are any strategic groups in the U.S. airline industry? If so, what might they be? How might the nature of competition vary from group to group?

3. The economic performance of the airline industry seems to be very cyclical. Why do you think this is the case?

4. Given your analysis, what strategies do you think an airline should adopt in order to improve its chances of being persistently profitable?

CASE 2

LEAN PRODUCTION AT VIRGINIA MASON

In the early 2000s, Seattle's Virginia Mason Hospital was not performing as well as it should have been. Financial returns were low, patient satisfaction was subpar, too many errors were occurring during patient treatment, and staff morale was suffering. Gary Kaplan, the CEO, was wondering what to do about this when he experienced a chance encounter with Ian Black, the director of lean thinking at Boeing. Black told Kaplan that Boeing had been implementing aspects of Toyota's famous lean production system in its aircraft assembly operations, and Boeing was seeing positive results. Kaplan soon became convinced that the same system that had helped Toyota build more reliable cars at a lower cost could also be applied to health care to improve patient outcomes at a lower cost.

In 2002, Kaplan and a team of executives began annual trips to Japan to study the Toyota production system. They learned that "lean" meant doing without things that were not needed; it meant removing unnecessary steps in a process so that tasks were performed more efficiently. It meant eliminating waste and elements that didn't add value. Toyota's system applied to health care meant improving patient outcomes through more rapid treatment the elimination of errors in the treatment process.

Kaplan and his team returned from Japan believing in the value of lean production. They quickly set about applying what they had learned to Virginia Mason. Teams were created to look at individual processes in what Virginia Mason called "rapid process improvement workshops." The teams, which included doctors as well as other employees, were freed from their normal duties for 5 days. They learned the methods of lean production, analyzed systems and processes, tested proposed changes, and were empowered to implement the chosen changes the following week.

The gains appeared quickly, reflecting the fact that there was a lot of inefficiency in the hospital. One of the first changes involved the delay between a doctor's referral to a specialist and the patient's first consultation with that specialist. By examining the process, it was found that secretaries, whose job it was to arrange these referrals, were not needed. Instead, the doctor would send a text message to the consultant the instant he or she decided that a specialist was required. The specialist then needed to respond within 10 minutes, even if only to confirm the receipt of the message. Delays in referral-to-treatment time dropped by 68% as a consequence of this simple change, which improved patient satisfaction.

On another occasion, a team in the radiation oncology department mapped out the activities that the department performed when processing a patient with the intention of eliminating time wasted in performing those activities. By removing unnecessary workflow activities, patient time spent in the department fell from 45 minutes to just 15 minutes. A similar exercise at Virginia Mason's back clinic cut treatment time from an average of 66 days to just 12.

By 2012, Virginia Mason was claiming that lean production had transformed the hospital into a more efficient, customer-responsive organization where medical errors during treatment had been significantly reduced. Among other gains, lean processes reduced annual inventory costs by more than $1 million, reduced the time it took to report lab tests to a patient by more than 85%, freed up the equivalent of 77 full-time employee positions through more efficient processes,

and reduced staff walking distance by 60 miles a day, giving both doctors and nurses more time to spend with patients. These, and many other similar changes, lowered costs, increased the organization's customer responsiveness, improved patient outcomes, and increased the financial performance of the hospital.

Sources: C. Black, "To Build a Better Hospital, Virginia Mason Takes Lessons from Toyota Plants," *Seattle PI*, March 14, 2008; P. Neurath, "Toyota Gives Virginia Mason Docs a Lesson in Lean," *Puget Sound Business Journal*, September 14, 2003; K. Boyer and R. Verma, *Operations and Supply Chain Management for the 21st Century* (New York: Cengage, 2009).

CASE DISCUSSION QUESTIONS

1. What do you think were the *underlying* reasons for the performance problems that Virginia Mason Hospital was encountering in the early 2000s?
2. Which of the four building blocks of competitive advantage did lean production techniques help improve at Virginia Mason?
3. What do you think was the key to the apparently successful implementation of lean production techniques at Virginia Mason?

4. Lean production was developed at a manufacturing firm, Toyota, yet it is being applied in this case at a hospital. What does that tell you about the nature of the lean production philosophy for performance improvement?

3

CONSOLIDATING DRY CLEANING

No large companies dominate the U.S. dry-cleaning industry. The industry has some 30,000 individual businesses employing around 165,000 people. Most establishments are very small. The top 50 enterprises in the industry are estimated to account for no more than 40% of industry revenues. According to the Drycleaning & Laundry Institute, the median annual sales for a commercial dry cleaner are less than $250,000. The industry is a favored starting point for many immigrants, who are attracted by the low capital requirements. More than 80% of industry revenues can be attributed to individual retail customers, with hospitals, hotels, and restaurants accounting for much of the balance. The larger companies in the industry tend to focus on serving larger establishments such as hospitals and hotels.

Total industry revenues are estimated to be around $9 billion. Between 2007 and 2012 demand shrunk at 2.5% per annum. A weak economy with persistently high unemployment, the rise of "business casual" dress norms in many companies, and the development of new clothing materials that do not need dry cleaning or pressing are all cited as reasons for the weak demand conditions.

Demand for dry-cleaning services is very local. All dry cleaners within a 10-minute drive of each other are often viewed as direct competitors. Convenience seems to be one of the major factors leading a consumer to pick one dry cleaner over another. Dry cleaning has been described as a classic low-interest category—there is very little about dry cleaning that excites consumers.

The industry has defied efforts to consolidate it. The largest national dry-cleaning chain in the United States is Martinizing. Started more than 60 years ago, in 2012, Martinizing had some 160 franchisees that operate more than 456 stores. However, as recently as 2001 its franchisees operated almost 800 stores, so the company seems to have been shrinking steadily over the last decade.

In the late 1990s the founders of Staples, the office-supply superstore, entered the dry-cleaning industry, establishing a Boston-based chain known as Zoots. Backed with up to $40 million in capital, they had visions of transforming the dry-cleaning industry (as they had done with office supplies), consolidating a fragmented industry and creating enormous economic value for themselves in the process. They created of cluster of 7 to 10 stores around a central cleaning hub. Each store had a drive-through window, self-service lockers for leaving and picking up clothes, and one or two full-time staff members on hand to help customers. The hub had about 40 employees engaged in cleaning processes. Zoots promised to get dry cleaning done right, reliably, and conveniently, and to do this at a reasonable price. Unfortunately, Zoots found that the service-intensive nature of dry cleaning and the very high variability of clothing made it all but impossible to standardize processes. Costs were significantly higher than anticipated, quality was not as good as management hoped, employee turnover was high, and demand came in below forecasts. Today, Zoots has less than 40 stores and remains concentrated in the Boston area. The founders are no longer involved in the business and, clearly, it did not come close to transforming the industry.

Sources: IBIS World, "Dry Cleaners in the US: Market Research Report," October 2012; Myra M. Hart and Sharon Peyus, "Zoots: The Cleaner Cleaner," *Harvard Business School*, September 20, 2000; Fulcrum Inquiry, "Valuation Guide: Dry Cleaners," www.fulcrum.com/drycleaning_appraisal.htm.

CASE DISCUSSION QUESTIONS

1. Why do you think that the dry-cleaning industry has a fragmented structure?
2. The larger enterprises in the industry seem to serve large customers with standardized needs, such as hotels and hospitals. Why do you think this is the case?

3. Why do you think that Zoots was unable to consolidate the dry-cleaning industry, despite adequate capital and the managerial talent that created Staples?
4. If you were to try to consolidate the dry-cleaning industry, what strategy would you pursue and why?

CASE 4

GENERAL ELECTRIC'S ECOMAGINATION STRATEGY

Back in 2004, GE's top-management team was going through its annual strategic planning review when the management team came to a sudden realization: six of the company's core businesses were deeply involved in environmental and energy-related projects. The appliance business was exploring energy conservation. The plastics business was working on the replacement of PCBs, once widely used in industrial compounds, which had been found to have negative consequences for human health and the environment. The energy business was looking into alternatives to fossil fuels, including wind, solar, and nuclear power. Other businesses were looking at ways to reduce emissions and use energy more efficiently. What was particularly striking was that GE had initiated almost all of these projects in response to requests from its customers.

When these common issues surfaced across different lines of business, the team members realized that something deeper was going on that they needed to understand. They initiated a data-gathering effort. They made an effort to educate themselves on the science behind energy and environmental issues, including greenhouse gas emissions. As CEO Jeff Immelt later explained, "We went through a process of really understanding and coming to our own points of view on the science." Immelt himself became convinced that climate change was a technical fact. GE executives engaged in "dreaming sessions" with customers

in energy and heavy-industry companies to try to understand their concerns and desires. What emerged was a wish list from customers that included cleaner ways to burn coal, more efficient wastewater treatment plants, better hydrogen fuel cells, and so on. At the same time, GE talked to government officials and regulators to get a sense for where public policy might be going.

This external review led to the conclusion that energy prices would likely increase going forward, driven by rising energy consumption in developing nations and creating demand for energy-efficient products. The team also saw tighter environmental controls, including caps on greenhouse gas emissions, as all but inevitable. At the same time, team members looked inside GE. Although the company had already been working on numerous energy-efficiency and environmental projects, the team realized there were gaps in technological capabilities and there was a lack of overarching strategy.

From these efforts emerged the realization that GE could build strong businesses by helping its customers to improve their energy efficiency and environmental performance. As Immelt soon became fond of saying, "green is green." Thus was born GE's ecomagination strategy.

First rolled out in 2005, the ecomagination strategy cut across businesses. Immelt tapped one of the company's promising young leaders to head the program. GE established targets for doubling investments in clean technology to $1.5 billion per year by 2010 and growing annual revenues from eco-products to $20 billion from $10 billion in 2004, twice the growth rate of its overall revenues. In its own operations, GE set out to cut greenhouse gas emissions per unit of output by 30% by 2008, and to cut absolute emissions by 1% by 2010 (as opposed to a forecasted increase of 40% due to the growth of the business). These corporate goals were broken into subgoals and handed down to the relevant businesses. Performance against goals was reviewed on a regular basis, and the compensation of executives was tied to their ability to meet these goals.

The effort soon started to bear fruit: a new generation of energy-efficient appliances, more-efficient fluorescent and LED lights, a new jet engine that burned 10% less fuel, a hybrid locomotive that burned 3% less fuel and put out 40% lower emissions than its immediate predecessor, lightweight plastics to replace the steel in cars, and technologies for turning coal into gas in order to drive electric turbines, while stripping most of the carbon dioxide (CO_2) from the turbine exhaust.

By the end of its first 5-year plan, GE had met or exceeded most of its original goals, despite the global financial crisis that hit in 2008. Not only did GE sell more than $20 billion worth of eco-products in 2010, but, according to management, these products were among the most profitable in GE's portfolio. In total, GE reported that its ecomagination portfolio included over 140 products and solutions that had generated $105 billion in revenues by 2011. One of the great growth stories in the company has been its wind turbine business, which it bought from Enron in 2002. In that year, it sold $200 million worth of wind turbines. By 2008, this was a $6-billion business that had installed 10,000 turbines. By 2012, GE had installed over 20,000 turbines worldwide and was predicting a surge in orders from developing nations. Sales from Brazil alone were forecasted to be in the range of $1 billion a year for the next decade. GE plans to double cleantech R&D to $10 billion 2015, grow ecomagination revenues at twice the rate of overall revenues, reduce its energy intensity by 50% and its greenhouse gas emissions by 25%, and reduce its water use by 25%.

Sources: D. Fisher, "GE Turns Green," *Forbes,* August 8, 2005, pp. 80–85; R. Kauffeld, A. Malhotra, and S. Higgins, "Green Is a Strategy," *Strategy + Business,* December 21, 2009; J. L. Bower, H. B. Leonard, and L. S. Paine, "Jeffrey Immelt and the Reinvention of GE," *Reuters* (October 14, 2011); General Electric, "Progress: Ecomagination Report 2011," http://files.gecompany.com/ecomagination/progress/GE_ecomagination_2011AnnualReport.pdf.

CASE DISCUSSION QUESTIONS

1. Where did the original impetus for GE's ecomagination strategy come from? What does this tell you about strategy making?
2. To what extent did GE follow a classic SWOT model when formulating its ecomagination strategy?
3. GE's CEO Jeff Immelt often states that "green is green." What does he mean by this? Is the ecomagination strategy in the best interests of GE's stockholders?
4. By most reports, GE's ecomagination strategy has been successfully implemented. Why do you think this is the case? What did GE do correctly? What are the key lessons here?
5. If GE had not pursued an ecomagination strategy, where do you think it would be today? Where might it be 10 years from now?

CASE 5

AVON PRODUCTS

For 6 years after Andrea Jung became CEO in 1999 of Avon Products, the beauty products company famous for its direct sales model, revenues grew in excess of 10% a year. Profits tripled, making Jung a Wall Street favorite. Then, in 2005, the success story started to turn ugly. Avon, which derives as much as 70% of its revenues from international markets, mostly in developing nations, suddenly began losing sales across the globe. A ban on direct sales had hurt its business in China (the Chinese government had accused companies that used a direct sales model of engaging in pyramid schemes and of creating "cults"). To compound matters, economic weakness in Eastern Europe, Russia, and Mexico, all drivers of Avon's success, stalled growth there. The dramatic turn of events took investors by surprise. In May 2005, Jung had told investors that Avon would exceed Wall Street's targets for the year. By September, she was rapidly backpedaling, and the stock fell 45%.

With her job on the line, Jung began to reevaluate Avon's global strategy. Until this point, the company had expanded primarily by replicating its U.S. strategy and organization in other countries. When it entered a nation, it gave country managers considerable autonomy. All used the Avon brand name and adopted the direct sales model that has been the company's hallmark. The result was an army of 5 million Avon representatives around the world, all independent contractors, who sold the company's skin care and makeup products. However, many country managers also set up their own local manufacturing operations and supply chains, were responsible for local marketing, and developed their own new products. In Jung's words, "they were the king or queen of every decision." The result was a lack of consistency in marketing strategy from nation to nation, extensive duplication of manufacturing operations and supply chains, and a profusion of new products, many of which were not profitable. In Mexico, for example, the roster of products for sale had ballooned to 13,000. The company had 15 layers of management, making accountability and communication problematic. There was also a distinct lack of data-driven analysis of new-product opportunities, with country managers often making decisions based on their intuition or gut feeling.

Jung's turnaround strategy involved several elements. To help transform Avon, she hired seasoned managers from well-known global consumer products companies such as P&G and Unilever. She flattened the organization to improve communication, performance visibility, and accountability, reducing the number of management layers to just eight and laying off 30% of managers. Manufacturing was consolidated in a number of regional centers, and supply chains were rationalized, eliminating duplication and reducing costs by more than $1 billion a year. Rigorous return-on-investment criteria were introduced to evaluate product profitability. As a consequence, 25% of Avon's products were discontinued. New-product decisions were centralized at Avon's headquarters. Jung also invested in centralized product development.

The goal was to develop and introduce blockbuster new products that could be positioned as global brands. And Jung pushed the company to emphasize its value proposition in every national market, which could be characterized as high quality at a low price.

By 2007, this strategy was starting to yield dividends. The company's performance improved and growth resumed. It didn't hurt that Jung, a Chinese-American who speaks Mandarin, was instrumental in persuading Chinese authorities to rescind the ban on direct sales, allowing Avon to recruit 400,000 new representatives in China. Then, in 2008 and 2009, the global financial crisis hit. Jung's reaction: This was an opportunity for Avon to expand its business. In 2009, Avon ran ads around the world aimed at recruiting sales representatives. In the ads, female sales representatives talked about working for Avon. "I can't get laid off, I can't get fired," one said. Phones started to ring of the hook, and Avon was quickly able to expand its global sales force. She also instituted an aggressive pricing strategy, and packaging was redesigned for a more elegant look at no additional cost. The idea was to emphasize the "value for money" the Avon products represented. Media stars were used in ads to help market the company's products, and Avon pushed its representatives to use online social networking sites as a medium for representatives to market themselves.

The result of all this was initially good: In the difficult years of 2008 and 2009, Avon gained global market share and its financial performance improved. However, the company started to stumble again in 2010 and 2011. The reasons were complex. In many of Avon's important emerging markets the company found itself increasingly on the defensive against rivals such as P&G that were building a strong retail presence there. Meanwhile, sales in developed markets sputtered in the face of persistently slow economic growth. To complicate matters, there were reports of numerous operational mistakes—problems with implementing information systems, for example—that were costly for the company. Avon also came under fire for a possible violation of the Foreign Corrupt Practices Act when it was revealed that some executives in China had been paying bribes to local government officials. Under pressure from investors, in December 2011 Andrea Jung relinquished her CEO role, although she will stay on as Chairman until at least 2014.

_____

Sources: A. Chang, "Avon's Ultimate Makeover Artist," *Market-Watch,* December 3, 2009; N. Byrnes, "Avon: More Than Cosmetic Change," *Businessweek,* March 3, 2007, pp. 62–63; J. Hodson, "Avon 4Q Profit Jumps on Higher Overseas Sales," *The Wall Street Journal* (online), February 4, 2010; M. Boyle, "Avon Surges After Saying That Andrea Jung Will Step Down as CEO," *Bloomberg Businessweek*, December 15, 2011.

CASE DISCUSSION QUESTIONS

1. What strategy was Avon pursuing until the mid-2000s? What were the advantages of this strategy? What were the disadvantages?
2. What changes did Andrea Jung make in Avon's strategy after 2005? What were the benefits of these changes? Can you see any drawbacks?
3. In terms of the framework introduced in this chapter, what strategy was Avon pursuing by the late 2000s?
4. Do you think that Avon's problems in 2010 and 2011 were a result of the changes in its strategy, or were there other reasons for this?

CASE 6

ORGANIZATIONAL CHANGE AT UNILEVER

Unilever is one of the world's oldest multinational corporations, with extensive product offerings in the food, detergent, and personal care businesses. It generates annual revenues in excess of $50 billion and sells a wide range of branded products in virtually every country. Detergents, which account for about 25% of corporate revenues, include well-known names such as Omo, which is sold in more than 50 countries. Personal care products, which account for about 15% of sales, include Calvin Klein Cosmetics, Pepsodent toothpaste brands, Faberge hair care products, and Vaseline skin lotions. Food products account for the remaining 60% of sales and include strong offerings in margarine (where Unilever's market share in most countries exceeds 70%), tea, ice cream, frozen foods, and bakery products.

Historically, Unilever was organized on a decentralized basis. Subsidiary companies in each major national market were responsible for the production, marketing, sales, and distribution of products in that market. In Western Europe, for example, the company had 17 subsidiaries in the early 1990s, each focused on a different national market. Each was a profit center and each was held accountable for its own performance. This decentralization was viewed as a source of strength. The structure allowed local managers to match product offerings and marketing strategy to local tastes and preferences and to alter sales and distribution strategies to fit the prevailing retail systems. The U.S. subsidiary (Lever Brothers) was run by Americans, the Indian subsidiary by Indians, and so on.

By the mid-1990s, this decentralized structure was increasingly out of step with a rapidly changing competitive environment. Unilever's global competitors, which include the Swiss firm Nestlé and Procter & Gamble from the United States, had been more successful than Unilever on several fronts—building global brands, reducing cost structure by consolidating manufacturing operations at a few choice locations, and executing simultaneous product launches in several national markets. Unilever's decentralized structure worked against efforts to build global or regional brands. It also meant lots of duplication, particularly in manufacturing; a lack of scale economies; and a high-cost structure. Unilever also found that it was falling behind rivals in the race to bring new products to market. In Europe, for example, while Nestlé and Procter & Gamble moved toward pan-European product launches, it could take Unilever 4 to 5 years to "persuade" its 17 European operations to adopt a new product.

Unilever began to change all this in the late 1990s. It introduced a new structure based on regional business groups. Within each business group were a number of divisions, each focusing on a specific category of products. Thus, in the European Business Group, a division focused on detergents, another on ice cream and frozen foods, and so on. These groups and divisions coordinated the activities of national subsidiaries within their regions to drive down operating costs and speed up the process of developing and introducing new products.

For example, Lever Europe was established to consolidate the company's detergent operations. The 17 European companies reported directly to Lever Europe. Using its newfound organizational clout, Lever Europe consolidated the production of detergents in Europe in a few key locations to reduce costs and speed up new-product introduction. Implicit in this new approach was a bargain: the 17 companies relinquished autonomy in their traditional markets in exchange for opportunities to help develop and execute a unified pan-European strategy. The number of European plants manufacturing soap was cut from 10 to 2, and some new products were manufactured at only one site. Product sizing and packaging were harmonized to cut purchasing costs and to accommodate unified, pan-European advertising. By taking these steps, Unilever estimated it saved as much as $400 million a year in its European detergent operations.

By the early 2000, however, Unilever found that it was still lagging its competitors, so the company embarked upon another reorganization. This time the goal was to cut the number of brands that Unilever sold from 1,600 to just 400 that could be marketed on a regional or global scale. To support this new focus, the company reduced the number of manufacturing plants from 380 to about 280. The company also established a new organization based on just two global product divisions—a food division and a home and personal care division. Within each division are a number of regional business groups that focus on developing, manufacturing, and marketing either food or personal care products within a given region. For example, Unilever Bestfoods Europe, which is headquartered in Rotterdam, focuses on selling food brands across Western and Eastern Europe, while Unilever Home and Personal Care Europe does the same for home and personal care products. A similar structure can be found in North America, Latin America, and Asia. Thus, Bestfoods North America, headquartered in New Jersey, has a similar charter to Bestfoods Europe, but in keeping with differences in local history, many of the food brands marketed by Unilever in North America are different from those marketed in Europe.

Sources: H. Connon, "Unilever's Got the Nineties Licked," The Guardian, May 24, 1998, p. 5; "Unilever: A Networked Organization," Harvard Business Review, November–December 1996, p. 138; C. Christensen and J. Zobel, "Unilever's Butter Beater: Innovation for Global Diversity," Harvard Business School Case No. 9-698-017, March 1998; M. Mayer, A. Smith, and R. Whittington, "Restructuring Roulette," Financial Times, November 8, 2002, p. 8; www.unilever.com.

CASE DISCUSSION QUESTIONS

1. Why did Unilever's decentralized structure make sense in the 1960s and 1970s? Why did this structure start to create problems for the company in the 1980s?

2. What was Unilever trying to do when it introduced a new structure based on business groups in the mid-1990s? Why do you think that this structure failed to cure Unilever's ills?

3. In the 2000s, Unilever switched to a structure based on global product divisions. What do you think is the underlying logic for this shift? Does the structure make sense given the nature of competition in the detergents and food business?

CASE

7

THE EVOLUTION OF STRATEGY AT PROCTER & GAMBLE

Founded in 1837, Cincinnati-based Procter & Gamble (P&G) has long been one of the world's most international companies. Today, P&G is a global colossus in the consumer products business with annual sales in excess of $80 billion, some 54% of which are generated outside of the United States. P&G sells more than 300 brands—including Ivory soap, Tide, Pampers, IAMS pet food, Crisco, and Folgers—to consumers in 180 countries. Historically, the strategy at P&G was well established. The company developed new products in Cincinnati and then relied on semiautonomous foreign subsidiaries to manufacture, market, and distribute those products in different nations. In many cases, foreign subsidiaries had their own production facilities and tailored the packaging, brand name, and marketing message to local tastes and preferences. For years, this strategy delivered a steady stream of new products and reliable growth in sales and profits. By the 1990s, however, profit growth at P&G was slowing.

The essence of the problem was simple: P&G's costs were too high because of extensive duplication of manufacturing, marketing, and administrative facilities in different national subsidiaries. The duplication of assets made sense in the world of the 1960s, when national markets were segmented by barriers to cross-border trade. Products produced in Great Britain, for example, could not be sold economically in Germany due to high tariff duties levied on imports into Germany. By the 1980s, however, barriers to cross-border trade were falling rapidly worldwide, and fragmented national markets were merging into larger regional or global markets. Also, the retailers through which P&G distributed its products were growing larger and more globalized. Wal-Mart, Tesco (from the United Kingdom), and Carrefour (from France) were demanding price discounts from P&G.

In the 1990s, P&G embarked on a major reorganization in an attempt to control its cost structure and recognize the new reality of emerging global markets. The company shut down some 30 manufacturing plants around the globe, laid off 13,000 employees, and concentrated production in fewer plants that could better realize economies of scale and serve regional markets. It wasn't enough. Profit growth remained sluggish, so in 1999, P&G launched its second reorganization of the decade, "Organization 2005," with the goal of transforming P&G into a truly global company. P&G replaced its old organization, which was based on countries and regions, with one

C-29

based on seven self-contained, global business units, ranging from baby care to food products. Each business unit was given complete responsibility for generating profits from its products and for manufacturing, marketing, and product development. Each business unit was told to rationalize production, concentrating it in a few large facilities; to try to build global brands wherever possible, thereby eliminating marketing differences among countries; and to accelerate the development and launch of new products. P&G announced that, as a result of this initiative, it would close another 10 factories and lay off 15,000 employees, mostly in Europe where there was still extensive duplication of assets. The annual cost savings were estimated to be about $800 million. P&G planned to use the savings to cut prices and increase marketing spending in an effort to gain market share, and thus further lower costs through the attainment of scale economies. This time, the strategy seemed to work. For most of the 2000s, P&G reported strong growth in both sales and profits. Significantly, P&G's global competitors such as Unilever, Kimberly-Clark, and Colgate-Palmolive were struggling during the same time period.

Sources: J. Neff, "P&G Outpacing Unilever in Five-Year Battle," *Advertising Age,* November 3, 2003, pp. 1–3; G. Strauss, "Firm Restructuring into Truly Global Company," *USA Today,* September 10, 1999, p. B2; Procter & Gamble 10K Report, 2005; M. Kolbasuk McGee, "P&G Jump-Starts Corporate Change," *Information Week,* November 1, 1999, pp. 30–34.

CASE DISCUSSION QUESTIONS

1. How did global expansion by P&G create economic value for the company and its shareholders?
2. What multinational strategy was P&G pursuing when it first expanded overseas?
3. What were the problems with this strategy? Why do you think these problems didn't become evident until the 1990s?
4. What were the goals of the reorganization that P&G embarked upon in the late 1990s? What multinational strategy is the company now pursuing? How should this benefit the company? Can you see any drawbacks?

CASE 8

VF CORP. ACQUIRES TIMBERLAND TO REALIZE THE BENEFITS FROM RELATED DIVERSIFICATION

In June 2011, U.S.-based VF Corp., the global apparel and clothing maker, announced that it would acquire Timberland, the U.S.-based global footwear maker, for $2 billion, which was a 40% premium on Timberland's stock price. VF is the maker of such established clothing brands as Lee and Wrangler Jeans, Nautica, lucy, 7 For All Mankind, Vans, Kipling, and outdoor apparel brands such as The North Face, JanSport, and Eagle Creek. Timberland is well known for its tough waterproof leather footwear, such as its bestselling, hiking, boots and its classic boat shoes; it also licenses the right to make clothing and accessories under its brand name. Obviously, Timberland's stockholders were thrilled that they had made a 40% profit overnight on their investment; but why would a clothing maker purchase a footwear company that primarily competes in a different industry?

The reason, according to VF's CEO Eric Wiseman, is that the Timberland deal would be a "transformative" acquisition that would add footwear to VF's fastest-growing division, the outdoor and action sports business, which had achieved a 14% gain in revenues in 2010 and contributed $3.2 billion of VF's total revenues of $7.7 billion. By combining the products of the clothing and footwear division, Wiseman claimed that VF could almost double Timberland's profitability by increasing its global sales by at least 15%. At the same time, the addition of the Timberland brand would increase the sales of VF's outdoor brands such as The North Face by 10%. The result would be a major increase in VF's revenues and profitability—an argument its investors agreed with because, whereas the stock price of a company that acquires another company normally declines after the announcement, VF's stock price soared by 10%.

Why would this merger of two very different companies result in so much more value being created? The first reason is that it would allow the company to offer an extended range of outdoor products—clothing, shoes, backpacks, and accessories—which could all be packaged together, distributed to retailers, and marketed and sold to customers. The result would be substantial cost savings because purchasing, distribution, and marketing costs would now be shared between the different brands or product lines in VF's expanded portfolio. In addition, VF would be able to increasingly differentiate its outdoor products by, for example, linking its brand The North Face with the Timberland brand, so customers purchasing outdoor clothing would be more likely to purchase Timberland hiking boots and related accessories such as backpacks offered by VF's other outdoor brands.

In addition, although Timberland is a well-known, popular brand in the United States, it generates more than 50% of its revenues from global sales (especially in high-growth markets such as China), and it has a niche presence in many countries such as the United Kingdom and Japan. In 2011, VF was only generating 30% of its revenues from global sales; by taking advantage of the commonalities between its outdoor brands, VF argued that purchasing Timberland would increase its sales in overseas markets and also increase the brand recognition and sales of its other primary brands such as Wrangler Jeans and Nautica. For example, hikers could wear VF's Wrangler or Lee Jeans, as well as The North Face clothing, at the same time they put on their Timberland hiking boots. In short, Timberland's global brand cachet and the synergies between the two companies' outdoor-lifestyle products would result in major new value creation. Thus, the acquisition would allow VF to increase the differentiated appeal of all its brands, resulting in lower costs. VF would be able to negotiate better deals with specialist outsourcing companies abroad, and economies of scale would result from reduced global shipping and distribution costs.

In a conference call to analysts, Wiseman said that: "Timberland has been our Number 1 acquisition priority. It knits together two powerful companies into a new global player in the outdoor and action sports space."

After the acquisition, the combined companies had more than 1,225 VF-operated retail stores, of which most were single-brand shops. VF also operated 80 U.S. outlet stores that sold a wide range of excess VF products. VF also sold to specialty stores, department stores, national chains, and mass merchants such as Wal-Mart (Wal-Mart accounted for 8% of VF's total sales in 2012—primarily due to its purchases of jeanswear). The Timberland acquisition increased the range of products VF could distribute and sell through its many channels, resulting in synergies and cost savings. VF's organizational structure leveraged the advantage of centralized purchasing, distribution, and IT to reduce costs across the organization.

Timberland's 2010 sales (prior to the acquisition) had been $1.4 billion, and its net income had been $96 million—a net profit margin of just under 7%. VF's sales in 2010 had been $7.7 billion with net income of $571 million, for a net profit margin of 7.4%. After the acquisition, VF Corporation posted revenues of $9.4 billion and $10.9 billion while also showing an increase in net profit margin to 9.4% and 10.0% in 2011 and 2012, respectively. Although it is difficult to know how much of these gains could be directly attributable to the Timberland acquisition, VF's strategy of related diversification appeared to be paying off.

_____

Sources: www.vfc.com and www.timberland.com.

CASE DISCUSSION QUESTIONS

1. What kinds of resources can likely be shared across different brands between an apparel maker and a footwear maker? What kinds of resources are unlikely to be shared?
2. How much does being a larger, more diversified apparel and footwear company increase VF's market power over its suppliers or customers? How could we assess how much this is worth?
3. If VF had increased its sales only by the amount of Timberland's sales and had not reaped an increase in profitability, would you consider the acquisition successful?
4. How might you compare VF's increase in profits to the premium it paid for Timberland?

DISASTER IN BANGLADESH

On the morning of Wednesday April 24, 2013, an eight-story industrial and commercial building in Bangladesh collapsed, killing over 1,100 people, most of them workers in one of the five garment factories that occupied six floors of the building. This was not the first high-profile accident in the Bangladesh garment industry. The prior November, a factory fire had killed 112 garment workers. Just days after the building collapse, a fire in another garment factory killed eight people. The spate of accidents led to calls for Western clothing retailers to do more to improve working conditions and safety in Bangladesh and other poor nations from which they source production. Some interest groups went further, arguing that Western companies should refuse to source production from countries where working conditions were so bad. One prominent Western company, Walt Disney, had already made this decision. In March 2013, Disney removed Bangladesh from the list of countries where it authorized partners to produce clothing and other merchandise. Politicians in Bangladesh responded to the Disney announcement with dismay. They argued that the economy of Bangladesh was very dependent upon the garment industry, and that "the whole nation should not be made to suffer" because of these accidents.

THE GARMENT INDUSTRY IN BANGLADESH

Bangladesh, one of the world's poorest countries, has long depended heavily upon exports of textile products to generate income, employment, and economic growth. Most of these exports are low-cost, finished garments sold to a wide range of retailers in the West such as Wal-Mart, The Gap, H&M, and Zara. For decades, Bangladesh was able to take advantage of a quota system for textile exports that gave it, and other poor countries, preferential access to rich markets such as the United States and the European Union. On January 1, 2005, that system was scrapped in favor of one based on free-trade principles. From 2005 on, exporters in Bangladesh would have to compete for business against producers from other nations such as China and Indonesia. Many analysts foresaw the quick collapse of Bangladesh's textile industry. They predicted a sharp jump in unemployment, a decline in the country's balance of payments accounts, and a negative impact on economic growth.

The collapse didn't happen. Bangladesh's exports of textiles continued to grow, even as the rest of the world plunged into an economic crisis in 2008.

Bangladesh's exports of garments rose to around $20 billion in 2012, up from $8.9 billion in 2006, making it the largest export industry in the country and a primary driver of economic growth. By 2012, the textile industry in Bangladesh comprised some 5,000 factories, which were the source of employment for 3 million people, 85% of whom were women with few alternative employment opportunities.

As a deep economic recession took hold in developed nations during 2008–2009, major importers such as Wal-Mart increased their purchases of low-cost garments from Bangladesh to better serve their customers, who were looking for low prices. Li & Fung, a Hong Kong company that handles sourcing and apparel manufacturing, saw its production in Bangladesh jump 25% in 2009, while production in China, its biggest supplier, slid 5%.

Bangladesh's advantage is based on a number of factors. First, labor costs are low, in part due to low hourly wage rates and in part due to investments by textile manufacturers in productivity-boosting technology during the past decade. The minimum wage rate in Bangladesh is currently $38 a month, compared to a minimum wage in China of $138 a month. Wage rates in the textile industry are about $50 to $60 a month, less than a fifth of the going rate in China. Textile workers may have to work 12-hour shifts and can work 7 days a week during busy periods. While the pay rate is dismally low by Western standards, in a country where the gross national income per capita is only $850 a year the pay is better than that available in many other unskilled and low-skilled occupations.

Second, there are few regulations in Bangladesh, and as one foreign buyer says, "there are no rules whatsoever that cannot be bent." The lack of effective regulations keeps costs down. Another advantage for Bangladesh is that it has an established network of supporting industries that supply inputs to its garment manufacturers. Some three-quarters of all inputs are made locally. This saves garment manufacturers transport and storage costs, import duties, and the long lead times that come with the imported woven fabrics used to make shirts and trousers.

Bangladesh also has the advantage of being an alternative to China. Many importers in the West have grown cautious about becoming too dependent upon China for imports of specific goods, fearing that if there was a disruption, economic or otherwise, their supply chains would be decimated unless they had an alternative source of supply. Thus, Bangladesh has benefited from the trend by Western importers to diversify their supply sources. Although China remains the world's largest exporter of garments, Bangladesh is now second. Moreover, Chinese wages are now rising fast, suggesting that the trend to shift textile production away from China may continue.

Bangladesh, however, does have disadvantages; most notable are constant disruptions in electricity because the government has underinvested in power generation and distribution infrastructure. Roads and ports are also inferior to those found in China.

The demand for garments from low-cost sources such as Bangladesh has been driven by intense competition among Western clothing retailers. U.S. consumers, for example, have become accustomed to spending relatively little on clothing. In 2012, U.S. consumers devoted just 3% of their annual spending to clothing and footwear, compared to around 7% in 1970. One reason Americans now spend so little on clothing is that real prices have fallen significantly over the last two decades. Since 1990, clothing prices in the United States have risen by just 10% in nominal terms, compared to an 82% jump in nominal food prices during the same period. Adjusted for price inflation, clothing prices have fallen. The sluggish U.S. economy and stagnant wage growth have increased pressure on clothing retailers by capping consumers' disposable income. At the same time, the desire to shop for fashionable new outfits remains strong. The result has been strong price competition among retail apparel chains.

◤ FACTORY COLLAPSE

The building that collapsed on April 24 was an eight-story complex, the Rana Plaza, named after its owner, Sohel Rana, a local politician and member of the ruling political party. The builders of the Rana Plaza only had approval for the construction of a five-story structure, but in Bangladesh rules can be bent, so the builders added three extra floors. Five garment factories occupied six floors in the building. At the time of the collapse, it is estimated that they were making clothes for some 30 Western apparel brands.

In retrospect, the building collapse should not have been a total surprise. Parts of the complex had been built on a pond filled with sand, making for an unstable foundation. The entire building vibrated whenever its diesel generator was working. The day before the collapse, visible cracks had appeared in the building, promoting some workers to run out. Both the local police and the Bangladesh Garment Manufacturers and Exporters Association warned Sohel Rana that the building was unsafe. Rana disagreed, and the complex stayed open for business. Two inspectors were in the building when it collapsed. Both died. Some survivors stated that their employees had pressured them to turn up for work as usual on Wednesday, the day of the incident. After the collapse Sohel Rana fled. He was arrested four days later on the border with India and charged with criminal negligence.

The death toll from the factory collapse was initially pegged at 250, but over the following days and weeks it kept increasing. By mid-May it was clear that over 1,100 people had died in the collapse, making it the second-worst industrial disaster in the history of South Asia, after the infamous Bhopal disaster in 1984. The Bangladesh government stated that it would pay $250 in compensation to each family that lost a member in the building collapse.

AFTERMATH

The building collapse prompted soul searching on the part of Western retailers who sourced production from Bangladesh. Critics were quick to point out that desires to drive prices down may have contributed to the situation in Bangladesh. Factory owners might bid low to get business from Western companies. While these factories might meet the standards required by Western companies, such as they are, it is commonplace for them to outsource production to a shadow economy of subcontractors where regulations are routinely ignored and workers are paid less than the legal minimum wage. Indeed, this is how they make a profit. That being said, all of the factories operating in the Rana Plaza seem to have been among the country's 1,500 or so regular exporters.

Some Western companies had already taken steps to improve working conditions in Bangladesh prior to the collapse of the Rana Plaza building. In October 2012, The Gap announced a $22-million fire and building safety plan with its suppliers in Bangladesh, without identifying which factories it was using there or how many factories would be improved under the plan. In early April, in response to the factory fire the prior November that had killed 112, Wal-Mart pledged $1.8 million to train 2,000 Bangladesh factory managers about fire safety. Critics noted that these commitments represented a drop in the bucket. Some nongovernmental organizations estimated that it would cost some $3 billion to make the needed fire safety and building improvements to ensure that Bangladesh's 5,000 garment factories were safe.

Three weeks after the building collapse, several of the world's largest apparel companies–including the retailer H&M, Inditex, the owner of the Zara chain, and Tesco–signed a legally binding agreement designed to improve safety conditions in Bangladesh's garment factories. Under the 5-year agreement, the signatories agreed not to hire manufacturers whose factories fail to meet safety standards and committed to help pay for necessary repairs and renovations. Signatories will form a governing board to oversee safety inspections of up to 5,000 factories over 2 years, with results being made public. The governing board will include three representatives from retailers, three labor representatives, and a chairman chosen by the UN International Labor Organization. Participation will cost each company a maximum of $2.5 million over the 5-year period of the agreement.

Several major U.S. retailers, including Wal-Mart, Gap Inc., Sears, and JC Penny, did not initially sign the pact. Gap Inc. stated that it would not sign the pact because the language makes it legally binding in U.S. courts. Instead it put forward an amendment calling for retailers to be publically expelled from the group if they fail to comply with arbitration. Wal-Mart declined to comment on why it did not sign, but stated that it will continue to work with industry groups, suppliers, and the Bangladesh government "to come up with an appropriate resolution for this matter and develop broad based solutions." Wal-Mart, which has had a sourcing office in Bangladesh for at least a decade and is one of the largest garment importers from the country, has long resisted legally binding agreements. For its part, the government of

Bangladesh stated that it would raise the minimum wage for garment workers in the country and tighten building and fire regulations.

Sources: S. Banjo, "Promises in Bangladesh," *The Wall Street Journal*, May 14, 2013; K. Bradsher, "Jobs Vanish as Exports Fall in Asia," *New York Times*, January 22, 2009, p. B1; "Knitting Pretty," *The Economist*, July 18, 2008, p. 54; "The New Collapsing Building," *The Economist*, April 25, 2013; "Rags in the Ruins," *The Economist*, May 4, 2013; K. Bradsher, "Competition Means Learning to Offer More Than Just Low Wages," *New York Times*, December 14, 2004, p. C1; V. Bajaj, "As Labor Costs Rise in China, Textile Jobs Shift Elsewhere," *New York Times*, July 17, 2010, pp. 1, 3; S. Greenhouse, "Bangladesh Fears Exodus of Apparel Firms," *New York Times*, May 2, 2013; S. Greenhouse, "Major Retailers Join Bangladesh Safety Plan," *New York Times*, May 13, 2013; A. Zimmerman and N. Shah, "American Tastes Fuel Boom in Bangladesh," *Wall Street Journal*, May 13, 2013.

CASE DISCUSSION QUESTIONS

1. From an economic perspective, was the shift to a free-trade regime in the textile industry good for Bangladesh?
2. Economically who benefits when retailers in Europe and the United States source textiles from low-wage countries such as Bangladesh? Who might lose? Do the gains outweigh the losses?
3. What are the causes of the weak safety record of the Bangladesh garment industry? Do Western companies that import garments from Bangladesh bear any responsibility for what happened at the Rana Plaza and other workplace accidents?
4. Do you think the legally binding agreement signed by H&M, Zara, Tesco and others will make a difference? Does it go far enough? What else might be done?
5. What do you think about Walt Disney's decision not to purchase merchandise from Bangladesh? Is this an appropriate way of dealing with the problem?
6. What do you think of Wal-Mart's approach to this problem? Is the company doing enough? What else could it do?

CASE 10

DID GOLDMAN SACHS COMMIT FRAUD?

In the mid-2000s, when housing prices in the United States were surging, hedge fund manager John Paulson approached Goldman Sachs. Paulson believed that housing prices had risen too much. There was, he felt, a speculative bubble in housing. In his view, the bubble had been fueled by cheap money from banks. The banks were enticing people to purchase homes with adjustable-rate mortgages with very low interest rates for the first 1 to 3 years. Many of the borrowers, however, could probably not afford their monthly payments once higher rates would later begin. Paulson thought that homeowners would start to default on their mortgage payments in large numbers. When that happened, the housing market would be flooded with distressed sales and housing prices would collapse. Paulson wanted to find a way to make money from this situation.

Goldman Sachs devised an investment vehicle that would allow Paulson to do just this. During the early 2000s, mortgage originators had started to pool thousands of individual mortgages together into bonds known as collateralized debt obligations, or CDOs. They then sold the bonds to institutional investors. The underlying idea was simple: The pool of mortgage payments generated income for the bondholders. As long as people continued to make their mortgage payments, the CDOs would generate good income and their price would be stable. Many

of these bonds were given favorable ratings from the two main rating agencies, Moody's and Standard & Poor's, suggesting that they were safe investments. At the time, institutional investors were snapping up CDOs. Paulson, however, took a very different view. He believed that the rating agencies were wrong and that many CDOs were far more risky than investors thought. He believed that when people started to default on their mortgage payments, the price of these CDOs would collapse.

Goldman Sachs decided to offer bonds for sale to institutional investors that were a collection of 90 or so CDOs. They asked Paulson to identify the CDOs that he thought were very risky and grouped them together into *synthetic CDOs*. Goldman then sold these very same bonds to institutional investors—many of them long-time Goldman Sachs clients. Goldman did not tell investors that Paulson had helped to pick the CDOs that were pooled into the bonds, nor did the company tell investors that the underlying CDOs might be a lot more risky than the rating agencies thought. Paulson then took a short position in these synthetic CDOs. Short selling is a technique whereby the investor will make money if the price of the asset goes down over time. Paulson was effectively betting against the synthetic CDOs, a fact that Goldman knew, while he was actively marketing these bonds to institutions.

Shortly thereafter, Paulson was proved correct. People did start to default on their housing payments, the price of houses did fall, and the value of CDOs and the synthetic CDOs that Goldman had created plunged. Paulson made an estimated $3.7 billion in 2007 alone from this event. Goldman Sachs, too, made over $1 billion by betting against the very same bonds that it had been selling.

The SEC soon started to investigate the transactions. Some at the SEC believed that Goldman had knowingly committed fraud by failing to inform buyers that Paulson had selected the CDOs. The SEC's case was strengthened by internal Goldman e-mails. In one, a senior executive described the synthetic CDOs it was selling as "one shitty deal." In another, a colleague applauded the deal for making "lemonade from some big old lemons."

In April 2010, the SEC formally charged Goldman Sachs with civil fraud, arguing that the company had knowingly mislead investors about the risk and value of the synthetic CDOs, and failed to inform them of John Paulson's involvement in selecting the underlying CDOs. Goldman provided a vigorous defense; it argued that a market maker like Goldman Sachs owes no fiduciary duty to clients and offers no warranties—it is up to clients to make their own assessment of the value of a security. However, faced with a barrage of negative publicity, Goldman opted to settle the case out of court and pay a $550-million fine. In doing so, Goldman admitted no legal wrongdoing, but did say that the company had made a "mistake" in not disclosing Paulson's role, and vowed to raise its standards in the future.

Sources: L. Story and G. Morgenson, "SEC Accuses Goldman of Fraud in Housing Deal," *New York Times*, April 16, 2010; J. Stempel and S. Eder, "Goldman Sachs Charged with Fraud by SEC," *Reuters*, April 16, 2010; "Sachs and the Shitty," *The Economist*, May 1, 2010.

CASE DISCUSSION QUESTIONS

1. Did Goldman Sachs break the law by not telling investors that Paulson had created the synthetic CDOs and was betting against them? Was it unethical for Goldman Sachs to market the CDOs?
2. Would your answer to the question above change if Goldman had not made billions from selling the CDOs? Would your answer to the question above change if Paulson had been wrong, and the CDOs had increased in value?
3. If opinions vary about the quality or riskiness of an investment, does a firm like Goldman Sachs owe a fiduciary duty to its clients to try to represent all of those opinions?
4. Is it unethical for a company like Goldman to permit its managers to trade on the company's account (i.e., invest on the company's behalf rather than an external client's behalf)? If not, how should compensation policies be designed to prevent conflicts of interest from arising between trades on behalf of the firm and trades on behalf of clients?

CASE 11

BOEING COMMERCIAL AIRCRAFT

INTRODUCTION

The first 15 years of the 21st century were a period of ups and downs for Boeing Commercial Airplane, the commercial aircraft division of the world's largest aerospace company. In the late 1990s and early 2000s, Boeing had struggled with a number of ethics scandals and production problems that had tarnished the reputation of the company and led to subpar financial performance. To make matters worse, its global rival, Airbus, had been gaining market share. Between 2001 and 2005, the European company regularly garnered more new orders than Boeing.

Boeing started to gain an edge over its rival in 2003, when it formally launched its next-generation jet, the 787. Built largely out of carbon-fiber composites, the wide-bodied 787 was billed as the most fuel-efficient large jetliner in the world. The 787 was forecast to consume 20% less fuel than Boeing's older wide-bodied jet, the 767. By 2006, the 787 was logging significant orders. This, together with strong interest in Boeing's bestselling narrow-bodied jet, the 737, helped the company recapture the lead in new commercial jet aircraft orders. Moreover, in 2006, Boeing's rival Airbus was struggling with significant production problems and weak orders for its new

aircraft, the A380 super-jumbo. Airbus was also late to market with a rival for the 787, the wide-bodied Airbus A350, which would also be built largely out of carbon fiber. While the 787 was scheduled to enter service in 2008, the A350 would not do so until 2012, giving Boeing a significant lead.

Over the next few years, Boeing encountered a number of production problems and technical design issues with the 787 that resulted in the introduction of the 787 being delayed five times. The 787 finally entered service in 2011, more than 3 years later than planned. From that point on, production ramped up rapidly. By the end of 2014, Boeing had delivered 225 787s, helping to propel the company to record revenues and earnings. Boeing also had a very healthy backlog of over 843 firm orders for 787. Airbus has encountered production problems of its own with the A350, and did not deliver its first A350 until late 2014, more than 2 years behind schedule. Still, Airbus had grown its order book for the A350, and by 2014 had 779 firm orders.

By 2011, Boeing had to make another important decision regarding its venerable narrow-bodied 737 aircraft family, which accounts for some 60% of Boeing's total aircraft deliveries. The main competitor for the 737 has long been Airbus's A320. In late 2010, Airbus announced that it would build a new version of the A320 designed to use advanced engines from Pratt & Whitney that are estimated to be 10 to 15% more efficient than existing engines. Known as the A320neo (neo stands for "new engine option"), by August 2011 the aircraft had garnered an impressive 1,029 orders. Airbus's success forced Boeing's hand. Boeing too stated that they would offer a version of the 737, known as the 737 MAX, using new engines (which required some redesign of the 737, driving up Boeing's R&D costs). Initially, the company was considering a complete redesign of the 737 to incorporate the carbon-fiber technology used in the 787. However, it opted not to go down this road on the grounds that the redesign would have pushed out delivery of the new plane too far, enabling Airbus to gain a lead in the narrow-bodied market. By March 2015, Boeing had assembled a backlog of 2,715 orders for the 737 MAX. The first planes are scheduled to enter service in late 2017. However, by January 2015, Airbus had a backlog of 3,621 orders for the A320neo.

To complicate matters, for the first time in a generation, there are several new entrants of the horizon. The Canadian regional jet manufacturer, Bombardier, is booking orders for 110- to 130-seat narrow-bodied CSeries jet, which would place it in direct competition with the smallest of the 737 and A320 family. In addition, the Commercial Aircraft Corporation of China (Comac) has announced that it will build a 170- to 190-seat narrow-bodied jet.

THE COMPETITIVE ENVIRONMENT

By the 2000s, the market for large commercial jet aircraft was dominated by just two companies, Boeing and Airbus. A third player in the industry, McDonnell Douglas, had been significant historically but had lost share during the 1980s and 1990s. In 1997, Boeing acquired McDonnell Douglas, primarily for its strong military business. Since the mid-1990s, Airbus has been gaining orders at Boeing's expense. By the mid-2000s, the two companies were splitting the market, a situation that has continued to the present day.

Both Boeing and Airbus have a full range of aircraft. Boeing offers five aircraft "families" that range in size from 100 to over 500 seats. They are the narrow-bodied 737 and the wide-bodied 747, 767, 777, and 787 families. Each family comes in various forms. For example, there are currently four main variants of the 737 aircraft. They vary in size from 110 to 215 seats, and in range from 2,000 to over 5,000 miles. List prices vary from $47 million for the smallest member of the 737 family, the 737-600, to $282 million for the largest Boeing aircraft, the 747-8. The newest member of the Boeing family, the 787, lists for between $138 million and $188 million depending upon the model.[1]

Similarly, Airbus offers five families: the narrow-bodied A320 family, and the wide-bodied A300/310, A330/340, A350, and A380 families. These aircraft vary in size from 100 to 550 seats. The range of list prices is similar to Boeing's. The A380 super-jumbo lists for between $282 million to $302 million, while the smaller A320 lists for between $62 million and $66.5 million.[2] Both companies also offer freighter versions of their wide-bodied aircraft.

Airbus, a relatively recent entrant into the market, began as a consortium between a French company and Germany company in 1970. Later, a British and Spanish company joined the consortium. Initially, few people gave Airbus much chance for success, but the consortium gained ground by innovating. It was the first aircraft maker to build planes that "flew by wire," made extensive use of composites, had only two flight crew members (most had three), and used a common cockpit layout across models. It also gained sales by being the first company to offer a wide-bodied twin-engine jet, the A300, which was positioned between smaller, single-aisle planes like the 737 and large aircraft like the Boeing 747.

In 2001, Airbus became a fully integrated company. The European Defense and Space Company (EADS), formed by a merger between French, German, and Spanish interests, acquired 80% of the shares in EADS, and BAE Systems, a British company, took a 20% stake.

Development and Production

The economics of development and production in the industry are characterized by several factors. First, the R&D and tooling costs associated with developing a new airliner are very high. Boeing spent some $5 billion to develop the 777. Its latest aircraft, the 787, was initially expected to cost $8 billion to develop, but delays increased that to at least $15 billion. Development costs for Airbus' A380 super-jumbo reportedly exceeded $15 billion.

Second, given the high upfront costs, in order to break even a company has to capture a significant share of projected world demand. The breakeven point for the Airbus super-jumbo, for example, has been estimated to be between 250 and 270 aircraft. While it was being developed, estimates of the total potential market for this aircraft varied widely. Boeing suggested that the total world market would be for no more than 320 aircraft over the first 20 years of its existence—Airbus believed that there would be demand for some 1,250 aircraft of this size. In the event, by the end of 2014 Airbus had only delivered 152 A380s, and its order backlog was just 165, suggesting that Boeing's demand estimates may have been closer to the mark. It now looks as if the A380 won't break even until the 2020s, and that on top of years of negative cash flow during development.[3]

Third, there are significant learning effects in aircraft production.[4] On average, unit costs fall by about 20 percent each time *cumulative* output of a specific model is doubled. The phenomenon occurs because managers and shop floor workers learn over time how to assemble a particular model of plane more efficiently, reducing assembly time, boosting productivity, and lowering the marginal costs of producing subsequent aircraft.

Fourth, the assembly of aircraft is an enormously complex process. Modern planes have over 1 million component parts that have to be designed to fit with each other, and then produced and assembled at the right time in order to produce the engine. At several times in the history of the industry, problems with the supply of critical components have held up production schedules and resulted in losses. In 1997, Boeing took a charge of $1.6 billion against earnings when it had to halt the production of its 737 and 747 models due to a lack of component parts. In 2008, Boeing had to delay production of the 787 due to a shortage of fasteners.

Historically, airline manufacturers tried to manage the supply process through vertical integration, making many of the component parts that went into an aircraft (engines were long the exception to this). Over the last two decades, however, there has been a trend to contract out production of components and even entire subassemblies to independent suppliers. On the 777, for example, Boeing outsourced about 65 % of the aircraft production, by value, excluding the engines.[5] While helping to reduce costs, contracting out places enormous demands on airline manufacturers to work closely with suppliers to coordinate the entire production process.

Finally, all new aircraft are now designed digitally and assembled virtually before a single component is produced. Boeing was the first to do this with its 777 in the early 1990s, and its new version of the 737 in the late 1990s.

Customers

Demand for commercial jet aircraft is very volatile and tends to reflect the financial health of the commercial airline industry, which is prone to boom-and-bust cycles (see Figures 1, 2, and 3). The airline industry

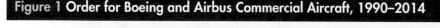

Figure 1 Order for Boeing and Airbus Commercial Aircraft, 1990–2014

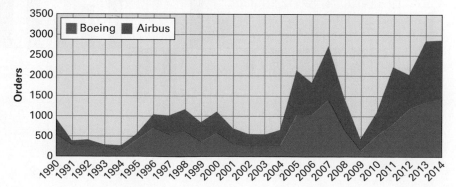

Source: Boeing and Airbus websites.

Figure 2 World Airline Industry Revenues

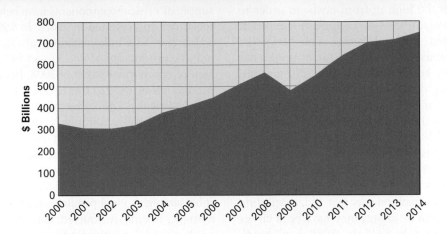

Source: IATA Data.

has long been characterized by excess capacity, intense price competition, and a perception among the travelling public that airline travel is a commodity. After a moderate boom during the 1990s, the airline industry went through a nasty downturn during 2001–2005. The downturn started in early 2001, due to a slowdown in business travel after the boom of the 1990s. It

was compounded by a dramatic slump in airline travel after the terrorist attacks on the United States in September 2001. Between 2001 and 2005, the entire global airline industry lost some $40 billion—more money than it had made since its inception.[6]

The industry recovered in 2006 and 2007, only to rack up big losses again in 2008 and 2009 due to

Figure 3 World Airline Industry Net Profit 2000–2014

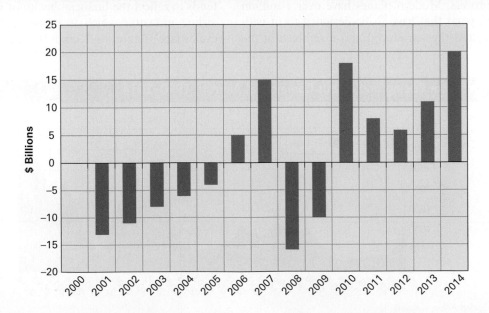

Source: IATA Data.

the recession that was ushered in by the 2008–2009 global financial crisis. High fuel prices since the early 2000s have made matters worse. The bill for jet fuel represented over 25% of the industry's total operating costs in 2006, compared to less than 10% in 2001.[7] By 2014, as a result of high prices for oil and jet fuel, fuel accounted for 33% of operating expenses for U.S. airlines. Wages and benefits were the second biggest operating expense, accounting for 25% of costs in 2014.[8]

During the 2001–2005 period, losses were particularly severe among the big six airlines in the world's largest market, the United States (American Airlines, United, Delta, Continental, US Airways, and Northwest). Three of these airlines (United, Delta, and Northwest) were forced to seek Chapter 11 bankruptcy protection. Even though demand and profits plummeted at the big six airlines, some carriers continued to make profits during 2001–2005, most notably the budget airline Southwest. In addition, newer budget airlines including AirTran and Jet Blue (which was started in 2000) gained market share during this period. Indeed, between 2000 and 2003, the budget airlines in the United States expanded capacity by 44% even as the majors slashed their carrying capacity and parked unused planes in the desert. In 1998, the budget airlines held a 16% share of U.S. market; by mid-2004, their share had risen to 29%.[9]

The key to the success of the budget airlines is a strategy that gives them a 30 to 50% cost advantage over traditional airlines. The budget airlines all follow the same basic script. They purchase just one type of aircraft (some standardize on Boeing 737s, others on Airbus 320s). They hire nonunion labor and cross-train employees to perform multiple jobs (e.g., to help meet turnaround times, the pilots might help check tickets at the gate). As a result of flexible work rules, Southwest needs only 80 employees to support and fly an aircraft, compared to 115 at traditional airlines. The budget airlines also favor flying "point to point" rather than through hubs, and often use cheaper secondary airports rather than major hubs. They focus on large markets with lots of traffic (e.g., up and down the east coast). There are no frills on the flights; no inflight food or complementary drinks. And prices are set low to fill the seats.

In contrast, the operations of major airlines are based on the network or "hub-and-spoke" system. Under this system, the network airlines route their flights through major hubs. Often, a single airline will dominate a hub (thus, United dominates Chicago O'Hare airport, American Airlines dominates Dallas, and so on). This system was developed for good reason: It was a way of efficiently using airline capacity when there wasn't enough demand to fill a plane flying point to point. By using a hub-and-spoke system, the major network airlines have been able to serve some 38,000 city pairs, some of which generate fewer than 50 passengers per day. But by focusing a few hundred city pairs where there is sufficient demand to fill their planes, and flying directly between them (point to point), the budget airlines seem to have found a way around this constraint. The network carriers also suffer from a higher cost structure due to their legacy of a unionized workforce. In addition, their costs are pushed higher by their superior inflight service. In good times, the network carriers can recoup their costs by charging higher prices than the discount airlines, particularly for business travelers, who pay more to book late and to fly business or first class. In the competitive environment of the 2000s, however, this was no longer the case. Indeed, between 2000 and 2010, the price of an average, round-trip, domestic ticket in the United States increased from $317 to $338—an increase of 6.7% over the decade—while the consumer price index increased 26.6% (that is, in real terms, prices fell).[10]

Due to the effect of increased competition, the real yield that U.S. airlines got from passengers fell from 8.70 cents per mile in 1980 to 6.37 cents per mile in 1990, 5.12 cents per mile in 2000, and 4.00 cents per mile in 2005 (these figures are expressed in constant 1978 cents).[11] Real yields are also declining elsewhere. With real yields declining, the only way that airlines can become profitable is to reduce their operating costs.

Outside of the United States, competition has intensified as deregulation has allowed low-cost airlines to enter local markets and capture share from long-established, national airlines that utilize the hub-and-spoke model. In Europe, for example, Ryan Air and Easy Jet have adopted the business model of Southwest and used it to grow aggressively.

By the mid-2000s, large airlines in the United States were starting to improve their operating efficiency, helped by growing traffic volumes, higher load factors, and reductions in operating costs, particularly labor costs. Load factor refers to the percentage of a plane that is full on average, which hit a record 86%

in mid-2006 in the United States, and 81% in international markets. Load factors have remained reasonably high since then, moving between 75 and 85% on a monthly basis between 2006 and 2015.

Demand Projections

Both Boeing and Airbus issue annual projects of likely future demand for commercial jet aircraft. These projections are based upon assumptions about future global economic growth, the resulting growth in demand for air travel, and the financial health of the world's airlines.

In its 2014 report, Boeing assumed that the world economy would grow by 3.2% per annum over the next 20 years, which should generate growth in passenger traffic of 5.0% and growth in cargo traffic of 4.7% per annum. On this basis, Boeing forecast demand for some 36,770 new aircraft valued at more $5.2 trillion over the next 20 years. In 2033, Boeing estimates that the total global fleet of aircraft will be 42,180, up from 17,330 in 2005. Boeing believes that North America will account for 21% of all new orders by unit share, Asia Pacific for 37%, and Europe for 20%. Passenger traffic is projected to grow at 6.3% per annum in Asia, versus 2.9% in North America and 3.9% in Europe.[12]

Regarding the mix of orders, Boeing believes that 70% of all orders by units will be for narrow-bodied aircraft such as the 737 and A320, 22% will be for wide-bodied, twin-aisle jets such as the 787 and 747, and less than 2% for large aircraft such as the 747 and A380, with regional jets accounting for the balance.

The latest Airbus forecast covers 2014–2033. Over that period, Airbus forecasts world passenger traffic to grow by 4.7% per annum and predicts demand for 31,358 new aircraft worth $4.6 trillion. (Note that Airbus excludes regional jets from its forecast; there are some 2,400 regional jet deliveries included in Boeing's forecasts). Airbus believes that demand for very large aircraft will be more robust, amounting to 1,501 large passenger aircraft and freighters in the 747 and A380 range and above, or 4% of the total units of aircraft delivered.[13]

The difference in the mix of orders projected by Boeing and Airbus reflect different views of how future demand will evolve. Airbus believes that hubs will continue to play an important role in airline travel, particularly international travel, and that very large

jets will be required to transport people between hubs. Airbus bases this assumption partly on an analysis of data over the last 20 years, which shows that traffic between major airline hubs has grown faster than traffic between other city pairs. Airbus also assumes that urban concentrations will continue to grow. Airbus states that demand is simply a function of where people want to go, and most people want to travel between major urban centers. The company notes, for example, that 90% of travelers from the United States to China go to three major cities. Fifty other cities make up the remaining 10%, and Airbus believes that very few of these cities will have demand large enough to justify nonstop service from North America or Europe. Based on this assumption, Airbus sees continued demand for very large aircraft, particularly its A380 offering.

Boeing has a different view of the future. The company has theorized that hubs will become increasingly congested, and that many travelers will seek to avoid them. Boeing thinks that passengers prefer frequent, nonstop service between the cities they wish to visit. Boeing also sees growth in travel between city pairs as being large enough to support an increasing number of direct, long-haul flights. The company notes that continued liberalization of regulations governing airline routes around the world will allow for the establishment of more direct flights between city pairs. As in the United States, the company believes that long-haul, low-cost airlines will emerge that focus on serving city pairs and avoid hubs.

In sum, Boeing believes that airline travelers will demand more frequent nonstop flights, not larger aircraft.[14] It cites data showing that all growth in airline travel since 1995 has been met by the introduction of new, nonstop flights between city pairs, and by an increased frequency of flights between city pairs, and not by an increase in airplane size. For example, Boeing notes that following the introduction of the 767, airlines introduced more flights between city pairs in North America and Europe, and more frequent departures. In 1984, 63% of all flights across the North Atlantic were made by the 747. By 2004, the figure had declined to 13%, with smaller, wide-bodied aircraft such as the 767 and 777 dominating traffic. Following the introduction of the 777, which can fly nonstop across the Pacific and is smaller than the 747, the same process occurred in the North Pacific. In 2006, there were 72 daily flights serving 26 city pairs in North America and Asia.

BOEING'S HISTORY[15]

William Boeing established the Boeing Company in 1916 in Seattle. In the early 1950s, Boeing took an enormous gamble when it decided to build a large jet aircraft that could be sold both to the military as a tanker and to commercial airlines as a passenger plane. Known as the Dash 80, the plane had swept-back wings and four jet engines. Boeing invested $16 million to develop the Dash 80, two-thirds of the company's entire profits during the postwar years. The Dash 80 was the basis for two aircraft—the KC-135 Air Force tanker and the Boeing 707. Introduced into service in 1957, the 707 was the world's first commercially successful passenger jet aircraft. Boeing went on to sell some 856 Boeing 707s, along with 820 KC-135s. The final 707, a freighter, rolled off the production line in 1994 (production of passenger planes ended in 1978). The closest rival to the 707 was the Douglas DC 8, of which some 556 were ultimately sold.

The 707 was followed by a number of other successful jetliners, including the 727 (entered service in 1962), the 737 (entered service in 1967), and the 747 (entered service in 1970). The single-aisle 737 went on to become the workhorse of many airlines. In the 2000s, a completely redesigned version of the 737 that could seat between 110 and 180 passengers was still selling strong. Cumulative sales of the 737 totaled 6,500 by mid-2006, making it by far the most popular commercial jet aircraft ever sold.

It was the 747 "jumbo jet," however, that probably best defined Boeing. In 1966, when Boeing's board took the decision to develop the 747, they were widely viewed as betting the company on the jet. The 747 was born out of the desire of Pan Am, then America's largest airline, for a 400-seat passenger aircraft that could fly 5,000 miles. Pan Am believed that the aircraft would ideal for the growing volume of transcontinental traffic. However, beyond Pan Am, which committed to purchasing 25 aircraft, demand was very uncertain. Moreover, the estimated $400 million in development and tooling costs placed a heavy burden on Boeing's financial resources. To make a return on its investment, the company estimated it would have to sell close to 400 aircraft. To complicate matters further, Boeing's principal competitors, Lockheed and McDonnell Douglas, were each developing 250-seat jumbo jets.

Boeing's big bet turned out to be auspicious. Pan Am's competitors feared being left behind, and by the end of 1970 almost 200 orders for the aircraft had been placed. Successive models of the 747 extended the range of the aircraft. The 747-400, introduced in 1989, had a range of 8,000 miles and a maximum seating capacity of 550 (although most configurations seated around 400 passengers). By this time, both Douglas and Lockheed had exited the market, giving Boeing a lucrative monopoly in the very large commercial jet category. By 2005, the company had sold some 1,430 747s, and was actively selling its latest version of the 747 family, the 747-8, which was scheduled to enter service in 2008.

By the mid-1970s, Boeing was past the breakeven point on all of its models (707, 727, 737, and 747). The positive cash flow helped to fund investment in two new aircraft, the narrow-bodied 757 and the wide-bodied 767. The 757 was designed as a replacement to the aging 727, while the 767 was a response to a similar aircraft from Airbus. These were the first Boeing aircraft to be designed with two-person cockpits (rather than three-person). Indeed, the cockpit layout was identical, allowing crew to shift from one aircraft to the other. The 767 was also the first aircraft for which Boeing subcontracted a significant amount of work to a trio of three Japanese manufacturers—Mitsubishi, Kawasaki, and Fuji—that supplied about 15% of the airframe. Introduced in 1981, both aircraft were successful. Some 1049 757s were sold during the life of the program (which ended in 2003). Over 950 767s had been sold by 2006, and the program was still ongoing.

The next Boeing plane was the 777. A two-engine, wide-bodied aircraft with seating capacity of up to 400 and a range of almost 8,000 miles, the 777 program was initiated in 1990. The 777 was seen as a response to Airbus' successful A330 and A340 aircraft. Development costs were estimated at some $5 billion. The 777 was the first wide-bodied, long-haul jet to have only two engines. It was also the first to be designed virtually. To develop the 777, for the first time Boeing used cross-functional teams composed of engineering and production employees. It also brought major suppliers and customers into the development process. As with the 767, a significant amount of work was outsourced to foreign manufacturers, including the Japanese trio of Mitsubishi, Kawasaki, and Fuji, who supplied 20% of the 777 airframe. In total, some 60% of parts for the 777 were outsourced. The 777 proved to be another successful venture: By mid-2006, 850 777s had been ordered—far greater than the 200 or so required to break even.

In December 1996, Boeing stunned the aerospace industry by announcing it would merge with long-time rival McDonnell Douglas in a deal estimated to be worth $13.3 billion. The merger was driven by Boeing's desire to strengthen its presence in the defense and space side of the aerospace business areas, where McDonnell Douglas was traditionally strong. On the commercial side of the aerospace business, Douglas had been losing market share since the 1970s. By 1996, Douglas accounted for less than 10% of production in the large commercial jet aircraft market and only 3% of new orders placed that year. The dearth of new orders meant the long-term outlook for Douglas's commercial business was increasingly murky. With or without the merger, many analysts felt that it was only a matter of time before McDonnell Douglas would be forced to exit from the commercial jet aircraft business. In their view, the merger with Boeing merely accelerated that process.

The merger transformed Boeing into a broad based aerospace business within which commercial aerospace accounted for 40 to 60% of total revenue depending upon the stage of the commercial production cycle. In 2001, for example, the commercial aircraft group accounted for $35 billion in revenues out of a corporate total of $58 billion, or 60%. In 2005, with the delivery cycle at a low point (but the order cycle rebounding), the commercial airplane group accounted for $22.7 billion out of a total of $54.8 billion, or 41%. The balance of revenue was made up by a wide range of military aircraft, weapons and defense systems, and space systems.

In the early 2000s, in a highly symbolic act, Boeing moved its corporate headquarters from Seattle to Chicago. The move was an attempt to put some distance between top corporate officers and the commercial aerospace business, the headquarters of which remained in Seattle. The move was also intended to signal to the investment community that Boeing was far more than its commercial businesses.

To some extent, the move to Chicago may have been driven by a number of production missteps in the late 1990s that hit the company at a time when it should have been enjoying financial success. During the mid-1990s, orders had boomed as Boeing cut prices in an aggressive move to gain share from Airbus. However, delivering these aircraft meant that Boeing had to more than double its production schedule between 1996 and 1997. As it attempted to do this, the company ran into some server production bottlenecks.[16] It scrambled to hire and train some 41,000 workers, recruiting many from suppliers—a move it came to regret when many of the suppliers could not meet Boeing's demands and shipments of parts were delayed. In the Fall 1997, things got so bad that Boeing shut down its 747 and 737 production lines so that workers could catch up with out-of-sequence work and wait for back ordered parts to arrive. Ultimately, the company had to take a $1.6-billion charge against earnings to account for higher costs and penalties paid to airlines for the late delivery of jets. As a result, Boeing made very little money out of its mid-1990s order boom. The head of Boeing's commercial aerospace business was fired, and the company committed itself to a major acceleration of its attempt to overhaul its production system, elements of which dated back half a century.

BOEING IN THE 2000s

In the 2000s, three things dominated the development of Boeing Commercial Aerospace. First, the company accelerated a decade long project aimed at improving the company's production methods by adopting the lean production systems initially developed by Toyota and applying them to the manufacture of large jet aircraft. Second, the company considered and then rejected the idea of building a successor to the 747. Third, Boeing decided to develop a new wide-bodied long-haul jetliner, the 787.

Lean Production at Boeing

Boeing's attempt to revolutionize the way planes are built dates back to the early 1990s. Beginning in 1990, the company started to send teams of executives to Japan to study the production systems of Japan's leading manufacturers, particularly Toyota. Toyota had pioneered a new way of assembling automobiles, known as lean production (in contrast to conventional mass production).

Toyota's lean production system was developed by one of the company's engineers, Ohno Taiichi.[17] After working at Toyota for 5 years and visiting Ford's U.S. plants, Ohno became convinced that the mass-production philosophy for making cars was flawed. He saw numerous problems, including three major drawbacks. First, long production runs created massive inventories, which had to be stored in large warehouses. This was expensive because of the cost of warehousing and because inventories tied up capital in unproductive uses. Second, if the initial machine settings were wrong, long production runs resulted in the production of a large number of defects (that is, waste). And third, the mass-production system was unable to accommodate consumer preferences for product diversity.

In looking for ways to make shorter production runs economical, Ohno developed a number of techniques designed to reduce setup times for production equipment, a major source of fixed costs. By using a system of levers and pulleys, he was able to reduce the time required to change dies on stamping equipment from a full day in 1950 to 3 minutes by 1971. This advance made small production runs economical, which allowed Toyota to respond better to consumer demands for product diversity. Small production runs also eliminated the need to hold large inventories, thereby reducing warehousing costs. Furthermore, small production runs and the lack of inventory meant that defective parts were produced only in small numbers and entered the assembly process immediately. This reduced waste and made it easier to trace defects to their source and fix the problem. In sum, Ohno's innovations enabled Toyota to produce a more diverse product range at a lower unit cost than was possible with conventional mass production.

Impressed with what Toyota had done, in the mid-1990s, Boeing started to experiment with applying Toyota-like lean production methods to the manufacture of aircraft. Production at Boeing used to be all about producing parts in high volumes, and then storing them in warehouses until they were ready to be used in the assembly process. After visiting Toyota, engineers realize that Boeing was drowning in inventory. A huge amount of space and capital was tied up in items that didn't add value. Moreover, expensive, specialized machines often took up a lot of space and were frequently idle for long stretches of time.

Like Ohno at Toyota, the company engineers started to think about how they could modify equipment and processes at Boeing to reduce waste. Boeing set aside space and time for teams of creative plant employees—design engineers, maintenance technicians, electricians, machinists, and operators—to experiment with machinery. They called these teams "moonshiners." The term "moonshine" was coined by Japanese executives who visited the United States after World War II. They were impressed by two things in the United States—supermarkets and the stills built by people in the Appalachian hills. They noticed that people built these stills with no money. They would use salvaged parts to make small stills that produced alcohol that they sold for money. The Japanese took this philosophy home with them and applied it to industrial machinery—which is where Boeing executives saw the concept in operation in the 1990s. With the help of Japanese consultants, they decided to apply the moonshine creative philosophy at Boeing to produce new, "right-sized" machines with very little money which then could be used to make money.

The moonshine teams were trained in lean production techniques, given a small budget, and then set loose. Initially many moonshine teams focused on redesigning equipment to produce parts. Underlying this choice was a Boeing study which showed that more than 80% of the parts manufactured for aircraft are less than 12 inches long, and yet the metalworking machinery is huge, inflexible, and could only economically produce parts in large lots.[18]

Soon empowered moonshine teams were designing their own equipment—small-scale machines with wheels on that could be moved around the plant and took up little space. A case in point: One team replaced a large stamping machine that cost six figures and was used to produce L-shaped metal parts in batches of 1,000 with a miniature stamping machine powered by a small, hydraulic motor that could be wheeled around the plant. With the small machine, which cost a couple of thousand dollars, parts could be produced very quickly in small lots, eliminating the need for inventory. They also made a sanding machine and a parts cleaner of equal size. Now the entire process—from stamping the raw material to the finished part—is completed in minutes (instead of hours or days) just by configuring these machines into a small cell and having them serviced by a single person. The small scale and quick turnaround now make it possible to produce these parts just in time, eliminating the need to produce and store inventory.[19]

Another example of a moonshine innovation concerns the process for loading seats onto a plane during assembly. Historically, this was a cumbersome process. After the seats would arrive at Boeing from a supplier, wheels were attached to each seat, and then the seats were delivered to the factory floor in a large container. An overhead crane lifted the container up to the level of the aircraft door. Then the seats were unloaded and rolled into the aircraft before being installed. The process was repeated until all of the seats had been loaded. For a single-aisle plane, this could take 12 hours. For a wide-bodied jet, it would take much longer. A moonshine team adapted a hay elevator to perform the same job. It cost a lot less, delivered seats quickly through the passenger door, and took just 2 hours, while eliminating the need for cranes.[20]

Multiply such examples and soon you start to have a very significant impact on production costs. A drill machine was built for 5% of the cost of a full-scale machine from Ingersoll-Rand; portable routers were built for 0.2% of the cost of a large, fixed router; one process that took 2,000 minutes for a 100-part order (20 minutes per part because of setup, machining, and transit) now takes 100 minutes (1 minute per part); employees building 737 floor beams reduced labor hours by 74%, increased inventory turns from 2 to 18 per year, and reduced manufacturing space by 50%; employees building the 777 tail cut lead time by 70% and reduced space and work in progress by 50%; and production of parts for landing gear support used to take 32 moves from machine to machine and required 10 months—now it takes 3 moves and 25 days.[21]

In general, Boeing found that it was able to produce smaller lots of parts economically, often from machines that it had built, which were smaller and cost less than the machines available from outside vendors. In turn, these innovations enabled Boeing to switch to just-in-time inventory systems and reduce waste. Boeing was also able to save on space. By eliminating large production machinery at its Auburn facility, replacing much of it with smaller more flexible machines, Boeing was able to free up 1.3 million square feet of space, and sold seven buildings.[22]

In addition to moonshine teams, Boeing adopted other process improvement methodologies, using them when deemed appropriate. Six Sigma quality improvement processes are widely used within Boeing. The most wide-reaching process change, however, was the decision to switch from a static assembly line to a moving line. In traditional aircraft manufacture, planes are docked in angled stalls. Ramps surround each plane, and workers go in and out to find parts and install them. Moving a plane to the next workstation was a complex process. The aircraft had to be down jacked from its workstation, a powered cart was bought in, the aircraft was towed to the next station, and then it was jacked up. This could take two shifts. Much time was wasted bringing parts to a stall, and moving a plane from one stall to the next.

In 2001, Boeing introduced a moving assembly line into its Renton plant near Seattle, which manufactures the 737. With a moving line each aircraft is attached to a "sled" that rides a magnetic strip embedded in the factory floor, pulling the aircraft at a rate of 2 inches per minute, moving past a series of stations where tools and parts arrive at the moment needed, allowing workers to install the proper assemblies. The setup eliminates wandering for tools and parts, as well as expensive tug pulls or crane lifts (just having tools delivered to workstations, rather than having workers fetch them, was found to save 20 to 45 minutes on every shift). Preassembly tasks are performed on feeder lines. For example, inboard and outboard flaps are assembled on the wing before it arrives for joining to the fuselage.[23]

Like a Toyota assembly line, the moving line can be stopped if a problem arises. Lights are used to indicate the state of the line. A green light indicates a normal work flow, the first sign of a stoppage brings a yellow warning light, and if the problem isn't solved within 15 minutes, a purple light indicates that the line has stopped. Each work area and feeder line has its own lights, so there is no doubt where the problem is.[24]

The cumulative effects of these process innovations have been significant. By 2005, assembly time for the 737 had been cut from 22 days to just 11 days. In addition, work-in-process inventory had been reduced by 55 percent and stored inventory by 59 percent.[25] By 2006, all of Boeing's production lines except that for the 747 had shifted from static bays to a moving line. The 747 shifted to a moving line in the late 2000s.

The Super-Jumbo Decisions

In the early 1990s, Boeing and Airbus started to contemplate new aircraft to replace Boeing's aging 747.

The success of the 747 had given Boeing a monopoly in the market for very large jet aircraft, making the plane one of the most profitable in the jet age, but the basic design dated back to the 1960s, and some believed there might be sufficient demand for a super-jumbo aircraft with as many as 900 seats.

Initially, the two companies considered establishing a joint venture to share the costs and risks associated with a developing a super-jumbo aircraft, but Boeing withdrew in 1995 citing costs and uncertain demand prospects. Airbus subsequently concluded that Boeing was never serious about the joint venture, and the discussions were nothing more than a ploy to keep Airbus from developing its own plane.[26]

After Boeing withdrew, Airbus started to contemplate a competitor to the 747. The plane, dubbed the A3XX, was to be a super-jumbo with capacity for over 500 passengers. Indeed, Airbus stated that some versions of the plane might carry as many as 900 passengers. Airbus initially estimated that there would be demand for some 1,400 planes of this size over 20 years, and that development costs would total around $9 billion (estimates ultimately increased to some $15 billion). Boeing's latest 747 offering—the 747-400—could carry around 416 passengers in three classes.

Boeing responded by drafting plans to develop new versions of the 747 family, the 747-500X and the 747-600X. The 747-600X was to have a new (larger) wing, a fuselage almost 50 feet longer than the 747-400, would carry 550 passengers in three classes, and have a range of 7,700 miles. The smaller 747-500X would have carried 460 passengers in three classes and had a range of 8,700 miles.

After taking a close look at the market for a super-jumbo replacement to the 747, in early 1997 Boeing announced that it would not proceed with the program. The reasons given for this decision included the limited market and high development costs, which at the time were estimated to be $7 billion. There were also fears that the wider wing span of the new planes would mean that airports would have to redesign some of their gates to accommodate the aircraft. Boeing, McDonnell Douglas (prior to the merger with Boeing), and the major manufacturers of jet engines all forecast demand for about 500–750 such aircraft over the next 20 years. Airbus alone forecast demand has high as 1,400 aircraft. Boeing stated that the fragmentation of the market due to the rise of "point-to-point" flights across oceans would limit demand for a super-jumbo. Instead of focusing on the super-jumbo category, Boeing stated that it would develop new versions of the 767 and 777 aircraft that could fly up to 9,000 miles and carry as many as 400 passengers.

Airbus, however, continued to push forward with plans to develop the A3XX. In December 2000, with more than 50 orders in hand, the board of EADS, Airbus' parent company, approved development of the plane, which was now dubbed the A380. Development costs at this point were pegged at $12 billion, and the plane was forecast to enter service in 2006 with Singapore Airlines. The A380 was to have two passenger decks, more space per seat, and wider aisles. It would carry 555 passengers in great comfort, something that passengers would appreciate on long transoceanic flights. According to Airbus, the plane would carry up to 35% more passengers than the most popular 747-400 configuration, yet cost per seat would be 15 to 20% lower due to operating efficiencies. Concerns were raised about turnaround time at airport gates for such a large plane, but Airbus stated that dual boarding bridges and wider aisles meant that turnaround times would be no more than those for the 747-400.

Airbus also stated that the A380 was also designed to operate on existing runways and within existing gates. However, London's Heathrow airport found that it had to spend some $450 million to accommodate the A380, widening taxiways and building a baggage reclaim area for the plane. Similarly, 18 U.S. airports had reportedly spent some $1 billion just to accommodate the A380.[27]

The 787

While Airbus pushed forward with the A380, Boeing announced, in March 2001, the development of a radically new aircraft. Dubbed the sonic cruiser, the plane would carry 250 passengers 9,000 miles and fly just below the speed of sound, cutting 1 hour of transatlantic flights and 3 hours of transpacific flights. To keep down operating costs, the sonic cruiser would be built out of low-weight, carbon-fiber "composites." Although the announcement created considerable interest in the aviation community, in the wake of the recession that hit the airline industry after September 11, 2001, both Boeing and the airlines became considerably less enthusiastic. In March 2002, the program was cancelled. Instead, Boeing said that it would develop a more conventional aircraft using composite technology. The plane was initially known as the 7E7, with the E standing for "efficient" (the plane was renamed the 787 in early 2005).

In April 2004, the 7E7 program was formally launched with an order for 50 aircraft worth $6 billion from All Nippon Airlines of Japan. It was the largest launch order in Boeing's history. The 7E7 was a twin-aisle, wide-bodied, two-engine plane designed to carry 200 to 300 passengers up to 8,500 miles, making the 7E7 well suited for long-haul, point-to-point flights. The range exceeded all but the longest range plane in the 777 family, and the 7E7 could fly 750 miles more than Airbus' closest competitor, the mid-sized A330-200. With a fuselage built entirely out of composites, the aircraft was lighter and would use 20% less fuel than existing aircraft of comparable size.

The plane was also designed with passenger comfort in mind. The seats would be wider, as would the aisles, and the windows were larger than in existing aircraft. The plane would be pressurized at 6,000 feet altitude, as opposed to 8,000 feet, which is standard industry practice. Airline cabin humidity was typically kept at 10% to avoid moisture buildup and corrosion, but because composites don't corrode, humidity would be closer to 20 to 30%.[28]

Initial estimates suggested that the jet would cost some $7–8 billion to develop and enter service in 2008. Boeing decided to outsource more work for the 787 than on any other aircraft to date. Some 35% of the plane's fuselage and wing structure would be built by Boeing. The trio of Japanese companies that worked on the 767 and 777, Mitsubishi Heavy Industries, Kawasaki Heavy Industries, and Fuji Heavy Industries, would build another 35%, and some 26% would be built by Italian companies, particularly Alenia.[29] For the first time, Boeing asked its major suppliers to bear some of the development costs for the aircraft.

The plane was to be assembled at Boeing's wide-bodied plant in Everett, Washington. Large sub-assemblies were to be built by major suppliers, and then shipped to Everett for final assembly. The idea was to "snap together" the parts in Everett in three days, cutting down on total assembly time. To speed up transportation, Boeing would adopt air freight as its major transportation method for many components.

Airbus' initial response was to dismiss Boeing's claims of cost savings as inconsequential. They pointed out that even if the 787 used less fuel than the A330, that was equivalent to just 4% of total operating costs.[30] However, even by Airbus' calculations, as fuel prices starting to accelerate, the magnitude of the savings rose. Moreover, Boeing quickly started to snag some significant orders for the 787. In 2004, Boeing booked 56 orders for the 787 and, in 2005, some 232 orders. Another 85 orders were booked in the first 9 months of 2006 for a running total of 373—well beyond the breakeven point.

In December 2004, Airbus announced that it would develop a new model, the A350, to compete directly with the 787. The planes were to be long-haul, twin-aisle jets, seating 200 to 300 passengers, and constructed of composites. The order flow, however, was slow, with airlines complaining that the A350 did not match the Boeing 787 on operating efficiency, range, or passenger comfort. Airbus went back to the drawing board, and in mid-2006 it announced a new version of the A350, the A350 XWB (for extra wide body). Airbus estimated that the A350 XWB would cost $10 billion to develop and enter service in 2012, several years behind the 787. The two-engine A350 XWB will carry between 250 and 375 passengers and fly up to 8,500 miles. The largest versions of the A350 XWB will be competing directly with the Boeing 777, not the 787. Like the 787, the A350 XWB will be built primarily of composite materials. The "extra wide body" is designed to enhance passenger comfort. To finance the A350 XWB, Airbus stated that it would seek launch aid from Germany, France, Spain, and the United Kingdom, all countries where major parts of Airbus are based.[31]

TRADE TENSIONS

It is impossible to discuss the global aerospace industry without touching on trade issues. Over the last 3 decades, both Boeing and Airbus have charged that their competitor benefited unfairly from government subsidies. Until 2001, Airbus functioned as a consortium of four European aircraft manufacturers: one British (20.0% ownership stake), one French (37.9% ownership), one German (37.9% ownership), and one Spanish (4.2% ownership). In the 1980s and early 1990s, Boeing maintained that subsidies from these nations allow Airbus to set unrealistically low prices, to offer concessions and attractive financing terms to airlines, write off development costs, and use state-owned airlines to obtain orders. According to a study by the United States Department of Commerce, Airbus received more than $13.5 billion in government subsidies between 1970 and 1990 ($25.9 billion if commercial interest rates are applied). Most of these subsidies were in the form of loans at below-market interest rates and tax breaks. The subsidies financed research and development and provided attractive financing terms for Airbus's customers. Airbus responded by pointing out that Boeing had benefited for years from hidden U.S. government subsidies, particularly Pentagon R&D grants.

In 1992, the two sides appeared to reach an agreement that put to rest their longstanding trade dispute. The 1992 pact, which was negotiated by the European Union on behalf of the four member states, limited direct government subsidies to 33% of the total costs of developing a new aircraft and specified that and such subsidies had to be repaid with interest within 17 years. The agreement also limited indirect subsidies such as government-supported military research that has applications to commercial aircraft to 3% of a country's annual total commercial aerospace revenues, or 4% of commercial aircraft revenues of any single company on that country. Although Airbus officials stated that the controversy had now been resolved, Boeing officials argued that they would still be competing for years against subsidized products.

The trade dispute heated up again in 2004, when Airbus announced the first version of the A350 to compete against Boeing's 787. Signs from Airbus that it would apply for $1.7 billion in launch aid to help fund the development of the A350 raised a red flag for the U.S. government. As far as the United States was concerned, this was too much. In late 2004, U.S. Trade Representative Robert Zoellick issued a statement formally renouncing the 1992 agreement and calling for an end to launch subsidies. According to Zoellick, "Since its creation 35 years ago, some Europeans have justified subsidies to Airbus as necessary to support an infant industry. If that rationalization were ever valid, its time has long passed. Airbus now sells more large civil aircraft than Boeing." Zoellick went on to claim that Airbus has received some $3.7 billion in launch aid for the A380, plus another $2.8 billion in

indirect subsidies including $1.7 billion in taxpayer-funded infrastructure improvements, for a total of $6.5 billion.

Airbus shot back that Boeing too continued to enjoy lavish subsidies, and that the company had received some $12 billion from NASA to develop technology, much of which has found its way into commercial jet aircraft. The Europeans also contended that Boeing would receive as much as $3.2 billion in tax breaks from Washington State, where the 787 is to be assembled, and more than $1 billion in loans from the Japanese government to three Japanese suppliers, who will build over one-third of the 787. Moreover, Airbus was quick to point out that a trade war would not benefit either side, and that Airbus purchased some $6 billion a year in supplies from companies in the United States.

In January 2005, both the United States and the European Union (EU) agreed to freeze direct subsidies to the two aircraft makers while talks continued. However, in May 2005 news reports suggested, and Airbus confirmed, that the jet maker had applied to four EU governments for launch aid for the A350, and that the British government would announce some $700 million in aid at the Paris Air Show in mid-2005. Simultaneously, the EU offered to cut launch aid for the A350 by 30%. Dissatisfied, the U.S. side decided that the talks were going nowhere, and on May 31 the United States formally filed a request with the World Trade Organization (WTO) for the establishment of a dispute resolution panel to resolve the issues. The EU quickly responded by filing a countersuit with the WTO claiming that U.S. aid to Boeing exceeded the terms set out in the 1992 agreement.[32]

In early 2011, the WTO ruled on the complaint by Boeing and on Airbus's counterclaim. The WTO stated that Airbus had indeed benefited from some $15 billion in improper launch aid subsidies over the prior 40 years, and that this practice must stop. Boeing, however, had little time to celebrate. In a separate ruling, the WTO stated that Boeing too had benefited from improper subsidies, including $5.3 billion from the United States government to develop the 787 (the WTO stated that most of these subsidies were in the form of payments from NASA to develop space technology that subsequently had commercial applications). Both sides in the dispute appealed these rulings, a process that could drag out for years.[33]

THE NEXT CHAPTER

Huge financial bets have been placed on somewhat different visions of the future of airline travel, Airbus with the A380 and Boeing with the 787. By mid-2011, Airbus had delivered 51 A380s and had a backlog of 236 or order. The rate of new orders had been slow, however. Boeing has a backlog of 827 787s on order. Airbus also hedged its bets by announcing the A350 XWB, and after a slow start the aircraft has amassed some 567 orders as compared to 827 for the 787.

Both companies have had substantial production problems and faced significant delays. In mid-2006, Airbus announced that deliveries for the A380 would be delayed by 6 months while the company dealt with "production issues" arising from problems installing the wiring bundles in the A380. Estimates suggested that the delay would cost Airbus some $2.6 billion over the next 4 years.[34] Within months, Airbus had revised the expected delay to 18 months and stated that the number of A380s it now needed to sell in order to break even had increased from 250 to 420. The company also stated that, due to production problems, it would only be able to deliver 84 A380 planes by 2010, compared to an original estimate of 420 (in fact, it delivered only half of this amount).[35]

Boeing ran into a number of production and design problems with the 787 that resulted in five delay announcements, pushing out the first deliveries more than 3 years. For the 787, Boeing outsourced an unprecedented amount of work to suppliers. This was seen at the time as a risky move, particularly given the amount of new technology incorporated into the 787. As it turned out, several suppliers had problems meeting Boeing's quality specifications, supplying substandard parts that had to be reworked or redesigned. The issues included a shortage of fasteners, a misalignment between the cockpit section and the fuselage, and microscopic wrinkles in the fuselage skin. In addition, Boeing found that it had to redesign parts of the section where the wing meets the fuselage. Boeing executives complained that their engineers were often fixing problems "that should not have come to us in the first place."[36]

Some company sources suggested that Boeing erred by not managing its supplier relationships as well as it should have done. In particular, there may have been a lack of ongoing communication between Boeing and key suppliers. Boeing tended to throw design specifications "over the wall" to suppliers, and then was surprised when they failed to comply fully with the company's expectations. In addition, Boeing's dependency on single suppliers for key components meant that a problem with any one of those suppliers could create a bottleneck that would hold up production.

In an attempt to fix some of the supply-chain issues, in 2009 Boeing purchased a Vought Industries Aircraft plant for $580 million. Vought had been in a joint venture with the Italian company, Alenia Aeronautical, to make fuselage parts for the 787. Vought had not been able to keep up with the demands of the program, and Boeing's acquisition has seen as a move to exert more control over the production process, and inject capital into Vought.

In another development, Boeing quietly launched the 747-8 program in November 2005. This plane is a completely redesigned version of the 747 and incorporates many of the technological advances developed for the 787, including significant use of composites. It is offered in both a freighter and intercontinental passenger configuration that carries 467 passengers in a three-seat configuration and has a range of 8,000 miles (the 747-400 can carry 416 passengers). The 747-8 uses the fuel-efficient engines developed for the 787, and has the same cockpit configuration as the 737, 777, and 787. Development costs were estimated to be around $4 billion. By July 2011, Boeing had orders for 78 747-8 freighters and 36 passenger planes. The first deliveries of the freighter version were made in 2011, and the passenger version in 2012. Demand for the aircraft has been slow to build, however, with the passenger version in particular failing to garner sales due to the 787. At the end of 2014, Boring only had 36 orders for the 747-8 on its books, most of which were freighters.

By 2010, the main issue confronting both Airbus and Boeing is what to do about their aging narrow-bodied planes, the A320 and the 737. These aircraft are the workhorses of many airlines, comprising some 70% of all units produced by the two manufacturers. Strong demand is expected for this category going forward. Both Boeing and Airbus would probably prefer to wait for a few more years before bearing the R&D costs associated with new product development. The argument often made is that this will give time for new technologies to mature, and make for a better aircraft at the end of the day. However, events have conspired to force their hands.

First, new engine technologies developed by Pratt & Whitney reportedly increase fuel efficiency by 10 to 15%. Airlines want the new engines on their aircraft, but this requires some redesign of the A320 and 737. The wings of the 737, in particular, are too low slung to take the new engines, so Boeing would have to do some major redesign work.

Second, there are several potential new entrants into the narrow-bodied segment of the market. The Canadian regional jet manufacturer, Bombardier, is developing a 110- to 150-seat aircraft that makes extensive use of composites to reduce weight. This will reduce operating costs by about 15% compared to the older 737 and A320 models. Known as the CSeries, as of early 2015 Bombardier had 243 firm orders for this aircraft plus options for another 162. The first CSeries aircraft are expected to enter service in 2015.

In addition, the Commercial Aircraft Corporation of China (Comac) has announced that it will build a 170- to 190-seat narrow-bodied jet. Scheduled for introduction in 2016, this will compete with the larger 737 and A320 models. The European low-cost airline, Ryanair, has entered into a codevelopment agreement with Comac and has talked about a 200+ plane order that could go as high as 400. Up until this point Ryanair has been a Boeing customer. Boeing must decide how to confront these growing threats.

Responding to these threats, Airbus in late 2010 announced that it would introduce a redesigned version of the A320 that utilizes the Pratt & Whitney engine. Known as the A320neo ("new engine option"), the offering has garnered strong interest from airlines, racking up over 1,000 orders by August 2011.

These developments presented Boeing with a major strategic dilemma. Should they continue to evaluate what to do with the 737, perhaps waiting a few more years before making the heavy investment associated with redesign? This would allow them to design a high-technology successor to the 737 that would incorporate many of the technologies developed for the 787. Alternatively, should they jump into the fray immediately and offer a redesigned version of the 737 that can utilize new engine technology? Ultimately, Boeing's hand was forced by demands from longstanding customers such as Southwest Airlines for an updated version of the 737 that would match the A320neo (reportedly, Southwest threatened to start ordering Airbus planes if Boeing did not move forward with the 737MAX program).

The 737MAX is now in development at Boeing, with the first planes expected to enter service at the end of 2017.[37]

NOTES

1. www.boeing.com
2. www.airbus.com
3. J. Palmer, "Big Bird," *Barron's*, December 19, 2005, pp. 25-29; www.yeald.com/Yeald/a/33941/both_a380_and_787_have_bright_futures.html.
4. G. J. Steven. "The Learning Curve: From Aircraft to Spacecraft," *Management Accounting,* May 1999, pp. 64–66.
5. D. Gates, "Boeing 7E7 Watch: Familiar Suppliers Make Short List," *Seattle Times.*
6. The figures are from the International Airline Travelers Association (IATA).
7. IATA press release, "2006 Loss Forecast Drops to US$1.7 Billion," August 31, 2006.
8. Air Transport Association, Industry Review and Outlook, April 29, 2015.
9. Anonymous, "Turbulent Skies: Low Cost Airlines," *The Economist,* July 10, 2004, pp. 68–72; Anonymous, "Silver Linings, Darkening Clouds," *The Economist,* March 27, 2004, pp. 90–92.
10. Air Transport Association, "The Economic Climb Out for U.S. Airlines," ATA Economics, August 3, 2011. Accessed on www.airlines.org
11. Data from the Air Transport Association, www.airlines.org.
12. Boeing, Current Market Outlook, 2014. Archived on www.boeing.com
13. www.airbus.com/en/myairbus/global_market_forcast.html.
14. Presentation by Randy Baseler, vice president of Boeing Commercial Airplanes, Farnborough Air Show, July 2006. Archived at www.boeing.com/nosearch/exec_pres/CMO.pdf.
15. This material is drawn from an earlier version of the Boeing case written by Charles W. L. Hill. See C. W. L. Hill, "The Boeing Corporation: Commercial Aircraft Operations," in C. W. L. Hill and G. R. Jones (eds.), *Strategic Management*, 3rd ed. (Boston: Houghton Mifflin, 1995). Much of Boeing's history is described in R. J. Sterling, *Legend and Legacy* (St Martin's Press, New York, 1992).

16. S. Browder, "A Fierce Downdraft at Boeing," *Businessweek*, January 26, 1988, p. 34.

17. M. A. Cusumano, *The Japanese Automobile Industry* (Cambridge, Mass.: Harvard University Press, 1989); Ohno Taiichi, *Toyota Production System* (Cambridge, Mass.: Productivity Press, 1990); J. P. Womack, D. T. Jones, and D. Roos, *The Machine That Changed the World* (New York: Rawson Associates, 1990).

18. J. Gillie, "Lean Manufacturing Could Save Boeing's Auburn Washington Plant," *Knight Ridder Tribune Business News*, May 6, 2002, p. 1.

19. P. V. Arnold, "Boeing Knows Lean," *MRO Today*, February 2002.

20. Boeing press release, "Converted Farm Machine Improves Production Process," July 1, 2003.

21. P. V. Arnold, "Boeing Knows Lean"; "Build in Lean: Manufacturing for the Future," www.boeing.com /aboutus/environment/create_build.htm; J. Gillie, "Lean Manufacturing Could Save Boeing's Auburn Washington Plant."

22. J. Gillie, "Lean Manufacturing Could Save Boeing's Auburn Washington Plant."

23. P. V. Arnold, "Boeing Knows Lean."

24. M. Mecham, "The Lean, Green Line," *Aviation Week*, July 19, 2004, pp. 144–148.

25. Boeing press release, "Boeing Reduces 737 Airplane's Final Assembly Time by 50 Percent," January 27, 2005.

26. Anonymous, "A Phony War," *The Economist,* May 5, 2001, pp. 56–57.

27. J. D. Boyd, "Building Room for Growth," *Traffic World*, August 7, 2006, p. 1.

28. W. Sweetman, "Boeing, Boeing, Gone," *Popular Science*, June 2004, p. 97.

29. Anonymous, "Who Will Supply the Parts?," *Seattle Times*, June 15, 2003.

30. W. Sweetman, "Boeing, Boeing, Gone."

31. D. Michaels and J. L. Lunsford, "Airbus Chief Reveals Plans for New Family of Jetliners," *The Wall Street Journal,* July 18, 2006, p. A3.

32. J. Reppert-Bismarck, and W. Echikson, "EU Countersues Over U.S. Aid to Boeing," *The Wall Street Journal*, June 1, 2005, p. A2; United States Trade Representative Press Release, "United States Takes Next Steps in Airbus WTO Litigation," May 30, 2005.

33. N. Clark, "WTO Rules U.S. Subsidies for Boeing Unfair," *New York Times*, March 31, 2011.

34. Anonymous, "Airbus Agonistes," *The Wall Street Journal*, September 6, 2006, p. A20.

35. Anonymous, "Forecast Dimmer for Profit on Airbus' A380," *Seattle Times*, October 20, 2006, Web Edition.

36. J. Weber, "Boeing to Rein in Dreamliner Outsourcing," *Bloomberg Businessweek*, January 16, 2009.

37. Staff reporter, "American Airlines Orders 200 Boeing 737s, 260 More From Airbus," Associated Press, July 19, 2011.

12

STAPLES IN 2015

INTRODUCTION

It was 1985, and 36-year-old retailer Tom Stemberg was being interviewed by the CEO of the Dutch-based warehouse club, Makro, for the top job at Makro's nascent U.S. operation. Stemberg didn't think Makro's concept would work in the United States, but he was struck by one thing as he toured Makro's first U.S. store in Langhorne, Pennsylvania: office supplies were flying off the shelves. "It was obvious that this merchandise was moving very fast," he later recalled, "That aisle (where the office supplies were located) was just devastated."[1] Stemberg began to wonder whether a supermarket selling just office supplies could do to the office supplies business what Toys R Us had done to the fragmented toy retailing industry—consolidate it, and create enormous economic value in the process.

Within a year, Stemberg had founded Staples, the first office supplies supermarket. Thirty years later, Staples was the leading retailer in the office supplies business, with 1,679 stores in the United States and Canada, and another 284 internationally in 23 countries. Although the company had performed well for most of its history, the 2008–2014 period proved to be extremely challenging. Demand fell in the face of a sharp economic pullback following the 2008–2009 global financial crisis. The period was characterized by intense price competition between Staples and its rivals, which depressed profitability. To compound matters, retailers such as Walmart, Costco, and Amazon.com had expanded their office supplies offerings and were becoming increasingly tough competitors for Staples. In 2007, before the crisis hit, Staples' return on invested capital stood at 19.16%, but it declined to 9.11% by 2014. Staples revenues peaked in 2013 at $25 billion. By 2014, they had fallen to $22.5 billion as Staples closed poorly performing stores. Net income dropped from $974 million to $135 million over the same period.

Faced with an increasingly tough competitive environment, in early 2015 Staples announced that it had reached a deal to merge with its largest rival, Office Depot. Federal regulators had disallowed a similar proposed merger in 1997, but Staples and Office Depot believed that this time the merger would be approved given the significant change in market dynamics since then.[2]

THE FOUNDING OF STAPLES

Tom Stemberg

By 1985, despite his young age, Tom Stemberg had assembled an impressive resume in retailing. He had been born in Los Angeles but spent much of his teens in Austria, where his parents were originally from. He moved back to the United States to enter Harvard University, ultimately graduating with an MBA from Harvard Business School in 1973. Stemberg was hired out of Harvard by the Jewel Corporation, which put him to work at Star Market, the company's supermarket grocery division in the Boston area.

Henry Nasella, Stemberg's first boss at Jewel, who would later work for Stemberg at Staples, remembers meeting Stemberg on his first day at Jewel: "He came in 15 minutes late, his hair too long, his tie over his shoulder, his shirt hanging out over the back of his pants. I thought, what in the world do I have here?"[3] What he had in the disheveled Stemberg, in turns out, was a brilliant marketer. Stemberg started out on the store floor, bagging groceries, stocking the aisle, and ringing up sales at the checkout counter. However, he rose rapidly. By the time he was 28, he had been named vice president of sales and marketing at Star Market, the youngest VP in the history of the Jewel Corporation.

Stemberg became known as an aggressive marketer, competing vigorously on price and introducing generic brands (he developed and launched the first line of "generic" foods sold in the country).[4] According to Stemberg, "It was a nutso thing we were trying to do, and the fact that it worked out well was a miracle. We opened all these big stores, and we were trying to take market share away from people who were much better financed than we were. They retaliated and lowered prices . . . I learnt to experience the challenges of rapid growth. There was no better experience to have been through. It taught me the necessity of having infrastructure and putting it in place."[5]

One supermarket that Stemberg battled with was Heartland Food Warehouse, the first successful, deep-discount warehouse supermarket in the country. Leo Kahn, one of the country's leading supermarket retailers, ran Heartland. Kahn had started the Purity Supreme supermarket chain in the late 1940s, making him one of the founding fathers of the supermarket business. Stemberg and Kahn fought relentless marketing battles with each other. In a typical example of their tussles, at one point Kahn ran ads guaranteeing that his customers would get the best price on Thanksgiving turkeys. Stemberg responded with his own ads promising that Star would match the lowest advertised price on turkeys. Technically that made Kahn's claim incorrect—a point that Stemberg made to the Massachusetts attorney general's office, which told Kahn to pull his ad.

In 1982, Stemberg left Jewel to run the grocery division of another retailer, First National Supermarkets, Inc. To build market share, he decided to take the company into the warehouse food business, imitating Kahn's Heartland chain. Stemberg soon came into conflict with the CEO at First National. As he later admitted, "I probably didn't do a very good job, in a corporate political sense, of making sure he understood the risks in what we were trying to do. The situation was very stressful."[6] In January 1985, things came to a head and Stemberg was fired. It was probably the best thing that ever happened to him.

When Kahn heard that Stemberg had been fired, he quickly got in touch. Kahn had just sold his own business for $80 million, and he was looking for investment opportunities. He had developed great respect for his old adversary, and wanted to back him in a new retailing venture. As Stemberg paraphrases it, Kahn said "I want to back you in a business, kid, what have you got in mind?"[7] Kahn agreed to put up $500,000 in seed money to help Stemberg develop a new venture opportunity. He also took on the role of mentor, evaluating Stemberg's ideas.

Initially, Kahn and Stemberg looked at the business they both knew best, supermarket grocery retailing. But they were put off by the intense competition now raging and the high price they would have to pay for properties. At this juncture, Bob Nakasone, the then president of Toys R Us, stepped into the picture. Nakasone had worked at Jewel alongside Stemberg before moving to Toys R Us. It was Nakasone who urged Stemberg to "think outside of the food box." Nakasone told Stemberg that there were more similarities than differences across product categories, and that profit margins were much better outside of the grocery business.

While mulling over possible entrepreneurial opportunities, Stemberg continued to explore other options, including working for an established retailer. This parallel search took him to Makro for a job interview, and it was there that he suddenly realized there was a possible opportunity to be had in starting the Toys R Us of office supplies.

THE FOUNDING OF STAPLES

Hot on the heels of his trip to Makro, Stemberg started to think about his idea. The first thing was to get a handle on the nature of the market. Stemberg started by asking people if they knew how much they spent on office supplies. In his words:

> There was this lawyer I knew in Hartford, which is where I lived then. If ever there was a cheap bastard in this world, he was a cheap bastard. And I said, "Gee, how much do you spend on office supplies?" He said, "Oh I don't know, I guess about a couple of hundred bucks a person, 40 people in the office, I bet you we spend ten grand." I said, "Do me a favor will you? You've got good records. Go through your records and tell me exactly how much you spend." He calls me up the next day. "Son of a bitch, I spend $1,000 apiece! But I'm getting a discount, I'm paying 10% of list." I said, "Toys R Us is paying 60% of list." He says, "Are you kidding me? You mean I could save like half? I could save like twelve grand?" In his mind, this is the payment on his new Jaguar.[8]

Stemberg began to think that this idea had potential. He reasoned that people want to save money—and in this case the savings might be substantial—but they didn't even know they were paying too much. Small businesses in particular, he thought, might be a viable target market. While working on the idea, the printer ribbon on his printer ran out. It was a weekend. He drove to the local office supply store in Hartford, which was closed. He went to another, but that was also closed. He ended up going to BJ's Wholesale Club, a deep-discount warehouse club. BJ's was open, and they sold office supplies at low prices, but the selection was limited and they didn't carry the type of ribbon Stemberg wanted. Stemberg immediately saw the opportunity.

Around the same time, Stemberg went to see another mentor of his, Walter Salmon, who taught retailing at Harvard Business School. Over lunch they discussed the supermarket business and Stemberg's quest. Salmon asked Stemberg if he had thought of applying his retailing skills to a product category that was growing faster than the grocery business, and was not well served by modern retailers. Stemberg replied that he had been thinking about office supplies. Salmon responded, "Gee, this is a really big idea."

Scoping Out the Opportunity

Stemberg ended up hiring a former teaching assistant of Salmon's for $20,000 to do some basic market research on the industry and validate the market. As he tells the story:

> I never forget the night I went to her house and we went through the slide deck. I always want to jump ahead. And she puts her hand on my hand and says, "Wait, we will walk through it." She's teasing us! Finally she said it was a $45-billion market growing at 15% per year. And it turns out she was lying. That was actually at the manufacturer level. It was actually more than $100 billion already if you looked at retail. She confirmed that the pricing umbrellas were as big as we thought they were, and that small businesses victimized the way we had said they were. I was pretty damn excited during the long drive home.[9]

The market growth was being driven by favorable demographic trends. The United States economy was recovering from the recessions of the late 1970s and early 1980s, and underlying economic growth was strong. A wave of new technology was finding its way into American businesses, including personal computers, printers, faxes, and small copiers, and this was driving demand for office supplies, including basic equipment and consumables like paper, printer ink, diskettes, and toner.

The wave of downsizing that had swept corporate America in the early 1980s had a beneficial side effect—unemployed people were starting their own businesses. The rate of new-business formation was the highest in years. There were 11 million small businesses in the country—Stemberg's proposed target market—the vast majority of which had less than 20 employees. This sector was the engine of job growth in the economy: Between 1980 and 1986, small enterprises had been responsible for a net increase of 10.5 million jobs. Many of these new jobs were in the service sector, which was a major consumer of office supplies. Each new white-collar job meant another $1,000 a year in office supplies.

Stemberg's research started to uncover an industry that was highly fragmented at the retail level, but had some huge participants. Upstream in the value chain were the manufacturers. This was a very diverse collection of companies including paper manufacturers such as Boise Cascade, office furniture makers, manufacturers of pencils and pens, the Bic Corporation, 3M (which supplied Post-it Notes and much more besides), office equipment companies like Xerox and Canon (manufacturers of copiers and consumables), and manufacturers of PCs, printers, and faxes such as Apple, Compaq, and Hewlett Packard.

Then there were the wholesalers, some of which were very large, such as United Stationers and McKesson. The wholesalers bought in bulk and sold to business clients and smaller retail establishments, either directly or through a network of dealers. The dealers often visited businesses to collect orders and arrange for delivery. The dealers themselves ranged in scale from small, one-person enterprises to large firms that sold through central warehouses. Some dealers also had a retail presence, while others did not. Manufacturers and wholesalers would also sell directly to large business through catalogs or a direct-sales presence.

The retailers fell into two main categories. There were the local office supply retailers, generally small business themselves, and there were the general merchandise discounters, such as BJ's Wholesale and Wal-Mart. The smaller retailers had an intrinsically high cost structure. They were full-service retailers who purchased in small lots, and delivered in trucks or sold out of the store. The general merchandise discounters purchased from wholesalers or direct from manufacturers, and their prices were much lower, but they did not carry a wide range of product.

On the consumer side, most large businesses had dedicated personnel for purchasing office supplies. They either bought from dealers, who purchased directly from manufacturers or through wholesalers, or bought direct from the manufacturer themselves. Large firms were able to negotiate on price and received discounts that could be as large as 80% of the list price on some items. Businesses of fewer than 100 people did not generally have someone dedicated to managing office supplies, and they tended to rely primarily on dealers. For these companies, product availability, not price, was viewed as key. In even smaller firms, the convenience of being able to get office supplies seemed to matter more than anything else.

Consistent with his initial insight, Stemberg found that the big dealers ignored smaller firms. To verify this he called Boise Cascade, which operated as both a dealer and a manufacturer, to see what service they might offer. First he called on behalf of Ivy Satellite Network, a small company that Stemberg owned that broadcast events of Ivy League schools to alumni around the world. Boise wouldn't even bother to send a catalog to this company. Then he called Boise back, this time representing the 100-person office of a friend of his who was a food broker. This time Boise was happy to send a representative to the food broker. The representative offered the broker deep discounts. A Bic pen from Boise that cost Ivy $3.68 cents from the local stationary store was offered for just $0.85. More generally, Stemberg found that while an office manager in a company with more than 1,000 employees could often obtain discounts averaging 50% from dealers, small businesses with fewer than 20 employees were lucky to get a 10% discount and often had to pay full price.[10]

Stemberg also found a study produced by researchers at the Wharton School that seemed to confirm his suspicions:

> Essentially they first asked dealers, "What does the customer want?" Ninety percent of the dealers said better service, and 10% said other. Then they asked customers, and 90% of the customers said what they really wanted was lower prices. Ha! The dealers were totally out of touch. They were making 40% to 50%, the wholesalers were making 30%, and the manufacturers were making huge margins. Everybody's rich, fat, and happy, and they're all going: "What's wrong with this?"[11]

Creating the Company

Stemberg knew from experience that for Staples to succeed it would have to execute well, and do to that it needed experienced management. Stemberg turned to people he knew, managers who, like him, had risen quickly through the ranks at the Jewel Corporation or other Boston-area retailers. From Jewel came Myra Hart, who was to become the Staples group vice president for growth and development; Todd Krasnow, who became vice president for marketing; Paul Korian, Staples's vice president of merchandising, and Henry Nasella, Stemberg's mentor at Star market who subsequently became president of Staples. The CFO was

Bob Leombruno, who had bought Mammoth Mart, a failed retail operation, out of bankruptcy for a group of investors. Stemberg took on the CEO role, while Kahn became chairman. Most of these people started working full time on January 1, 1986. They gave up secure jobs, high salaries, and annual bonuses for reduced compensation and 14-hour days.

According to Stemberg, the pitch to prospective managers was this:

> I'm going to give you a big chunk of stock in this thing. This is your chance. We're all going to work our tails off. We're going to work crazy hours. But here you'll be part of a retailing revolution. If you own 2% of the company and it gets to be worth $100 million, you're going to make $2 million.[12]

In the end, each member of the top management team got a 2.5% stake in the company.

By now Stemberg had a name for this nascent company, Staples. Reflecting on how it came about years later, he noted:

> I'm driving between Hartford and Boston. I'm thinking about names. Pencils? Pens? 8 ½ by 11? Staples? Staples! Staples, the Office Superstore. That was it. The bad thing about the name was that when we started out, we had to explain to everybody what it was. Office Depot basically copied Home Depot and put the "office" in front. It was Home Depot for the office, and it lived off the Home Depot name. Office Club was a Price Club for the office. It lived off the Price Club name. In the early days ours was actually a problem. But those other names aren't a brand. Ours is a brand.[13]

With the management team in place, the next steps were to refine the concept and raise capital. The concept was straightforward; implementing it would not be. The plan was to offer a wide selection of merchandise in a warehouse-type setting with prices deeply discounted from those found at smaller retailers. Because it was to be a supermarket, the idea was to move from a full-service to a self-service format. At the same time, they recognized that staff would need to be trained in office supplies so that they could provide advice when asked.

To make the concept viable, a number of issues had to be dealt with. Where should they locate the store? How big a population base would be needed to support a store? What kind of selection was required? How many stock keeping units (SKUs) should the store offer? And there was the problem of educating customers: If potential customers currently didn't know that they were paying excessive prices for office supplies, and consistently underestimated how much they spent on the category, what could Staples do to change this?

To keep prices low, Staples would need to cut costs to the bone and be managed very efficiently. They would have to get manufacturers or wholesalers to deliver directly to Staples. How could this be done? Wouldn't wholesalers and manufacturers create channel conflict with dealers and established retailers by delivering straight to Staples? How was this to be resolved? Staples also needed to minimize its inventory, thereby reducing its working capital needs. Management knew that if they could turn inventory over 12 times a year, and delay payment to vendors for 30 days, then vendors would essentially finance Staples's inventory. Pulling that off would require state-of-the-art information systems, and the state of the art at the time in office supplies did not include barcoding on individual items. How was Staples to deal with this?

There was also the potential competition to worry about. Stemberg was sure that once Staples unveiled its concept, others would follow quickly. To preempt competitors, the plan called for rapid rollout of the concept, with sales ramping up from nothing to $42 million after 3 years. This would require considerable capital. It also required that the concept be easy to replicate, so that once the first store was opened, others could be opened in quick succession. This meant that the systems that were put in place for the first store had to be the right ones, and be able to support rapid expansion. There wasn't much room for error.

As the management team refined the concept, they came to the realization that information systems were key to the entire venture. With the right information systems in place, Staples could track sales and inventory closely at the level of individual items and figure out its gross profit on each item sold, and adjust its merchandising mix accordingly. This would be a departure from existing retailers, the majority of which lacked the ability to calculate profit on each item sold and could only calculate the average gross profit across a range of items. The right information systems could also be used to collect data on customers at the point of sales, and this would assist greatly in market research and direct marketing to customers.

On the other hand, raising capital proved to be easier than anticipated. Stemberg valued Staples at $8 million, even though it was still little more than a concept, a management team, and a business plan full of unanswered questions. He went looking for $4 million, which he would exchange for 50% of the company. The venture capitalists were initially reluctant. They held back, waiting to see who would commit first. They also valued Staples at $6 million and wanted a 67% stake for the $4 million in first-round financing. Stemberg balked at that, and instead focused his efforts on one firm that seemed more willing to break away from the pack. The firm was Bain Venture Capital, whose managing general partner, Mitt Romney, later observed that "A lot of retailing startups come by, but a lot of them are a twist on an old theme, or a better presentation . . . Stemberg wasn't proposing just a chain of stores, but an entirely new retailing category. That really captures you attention. It slaps you in the face with the idea that this could be big." (Romney later became governor of Massachusetts).[14]

To validate the business concept, Romney's firm surveyed 100 small businesses after being urged to do so by Stemberg. Auditing invoices from these companies for office supplies, Romney discovered what Stemberg already knew—the companies were spending about twice what they estimated. Romney then ran the numbers on his own company and found that his firm would save $117,000 a year by purchasing supplies at the discount that Stemberg promised. That was enough for Romney, and he committed to investing. Others followed and Staples raised $4.5 million in its first round of financing, which closed on January 23rd, 1986. This gave the company enough capital to go ahead with the first store. In return for the financing, Staples had to give the VCs a 54% stake in the company. To get the money, however, Staples had to commit to opening its first store on May 1st, 1986, and to meet a plan for rolling out additional stores as quickly as possible.

The First Store

With just 4 months to open their first store, the management team went into overdrive. They would meet every morning at about 7 a.m. in a session that could run from 30 minutes to 2 hours. Someone would rush out to get sandwiches for lunch, and they would keep working. The workday came to a close at 9:00 or 10:00 p.m. There was no template for what they were doing; they knew they had to put a system in place that would allow them to quickly roll out additional stores.

One of the most difficult tasks fell on the shoulders of Leombruno, the CFO. In addition to setting up an accounting system, he was put in charge of installing the entire information system for Staples. The system had to be able to track customer purchases so that Staples could reorder products. The cash registers, which were to be connected individually to the system, had to be easy to operate so that there would be no congestion at the checkout stands. Stemberg was adamant that the register receipts indicate the list price of each item, as well as a much lower Staples price, and an even lower price for customers who became Staples members. He also wanted the system to collect detailed demographics on each customer.

Leombruno insisted that the system be able to do two things. The first was to calculate the gross profit margin Staples made on each item sold. Most retailers at the time could only calculate the average profit margin across the mix of inventory. Second, Leombruno wanted to make sure that inventory turned over at least 12 times a year, and good information systems were the key. With most vendors requiring payment in 30 days, an inventory turnover of greater than 12 would allow Staples to cut its working capital requirements.

As the wish list for the information systems grew, it soon became apparent that it would not be possible to do everything in the allotted time span. No existing software package did what the management team wanted, so they had to hire consultants to customize existing packages. In the end, several proposed features were dropped. However, at Stemberg's insistence, the three-way price requirements remained. To track sales and inventory levels, Staples assigned a six-digit look-up code for each item. While entering the codes was a slower process than scanning items, most manufacturers in the office supplies business were still not marking their products with barcodes, which meant scanning was not feasible.

Another problem was to get suppliers to ship products to the first Staples store. The company was asking suppliers to bypass the existing distribution system, and risk alienating longtime customers in the established channel of distribution. To get suppliers on board, Staples used a number of tactics. One was a visionary pitch. The company told suppliers that they were out to revolutionize the retail end of the industry. Staples would be very big, they said, and it was in the best interests of the suppliers to back the start-up. Stemberg's punchline was simple: "I'm going to be very loyal to those who stick their necks out for us. But it's going to cost you a lot more to get in later."[15] Connections also helped to get suppliers to deliver to Staples. One of the venture capitalist backers of Staples, Bessemer Venture Partners, also owned a paper manufacturer, Ampad. Bessemer told Ampad to start selling to Staples, which they did, even though existing distributors complained bitterly about the arrangement.

Finding real estate also presented a problem. As an enterprise with no proven track record, Staples found it difficult to rent decent real estate large enough to stock and display the 5,000 SKUs that it was planning for its first store, and to do so at a decent price. Most landlords wanted sky-high rent from Staples. In the end, the best that Staples could do was a site in Brighton, Massachusetts, that was within sight of a housing project and had failed as a site for several different retailers. The one redeeming feature of the site was that it was smack in the middle of a high concentration of small businesses.

Despite all the problems, Staples opened its first store on May 1, 1996. The opening day was busy, but only because everybody who worked at Staples had invited everybody they knew. On the second day, just 16 people came through the store. On the third day, it was the same number. A few weeks of this, and Staples would have to shut its doors. Desperate, Krasnow decided to bribe customers to get them into the store. The company sent $25 to each of 35 office managers, inviting them to shop in the store and pass along their reactions. According to Krasnow, "A week later we called them back. They had all taken the money, but none of them had come into the store. I was apoplectic."[16] In the end, nine of them finally came in, and they gave Staples rave reviews. Slowly the momentum started to build and, by August, lines were starting to form at the cash registers at lunchtime.

THE 1990s: GROWTH, COMPETITION, AND CONSOLIDATION

Growth

Staples had set of target of $4 million in first-year sales from its Brighton store, but within a few months the numbers were tracking up toward a $6-million annual run rate. The concept was starting to work. The number of customers coming through the door every month was growing, but it was not only customers that were coming. One day Joe Antonini, the CEO of K-Mart, was spotted walking around the Staples store. Around the same time, Stemberg heard from contacts that Staples had been mentioned at a Wal-Mart board meeting. He realized that if other discount retailers were noticing Staples when it had just one store, competition could not be far behind.

Within 5 months of the opening of the first Staples store, a clone had appeared in the Southeast: Office Depot. Needing money fast to fund expansion and lock in Staples territory, Stemberg went back to the venture capitalists. While the initial backers were only willing to value Staples at $15 million, Stemberg held out for and got a valuation of $22 million, raising another $14 million. He pulled off this trick by finding institutional investors who were willing to invest on a valuation of $22 million. He then went back to the original VCs and told them that the deal was closing fast, which persuaded them to commit.

By May 1987, Staples had three stores open and planned to increase the number to 20 by the end of 1988 (in the event, it opened 22). Sales were running at anywhere from $300 to $800 per square foot. In contrast, high volume discount stores were lucky to get $300 per square foot. By mid-1989, 3 years after its first store opened, Staples had 27 stores open in the Northeast and an annual sales run rate of $120 million, way above the original 3-year target of $42 million. The stores now averaged 15,000 square feet and stocked 5,000 items.

Explaining the success, Stemberg noted; "From a value perspective, I think there is no question that we have been a friend to the entrepreneur. If you look at the average small town merchant, we've lowered the costs of his office products—where he was once paying say $4,000 to $5,000 a year, now he's paying $2,000 or $3,000. We've made him more efficient."[17]

Helping to driving sales growth was the development of a direct marketing pitch. Every time Staples opened a store, it purchased a list of small businesses within 15 minutes driving distance. A group of telemarketers would go to work, calling up the buyer of office supplies at the businesses. The telemarketers would tell them Staples was opening up a store like Toys R Us for office supplies, ask them how much they spent on office supplies every year (often they did not know), cite typical cost savings at small businesses, and sent them a coupon for a free item such as copy paper. Slowly at first the customers would come in, but momentum would build as customers realized the scale of their savings.

Every time a customer redeemed a coupon at a store, they were given a free Staples Card. This "membership" card entitled cardholders to even deeper discounts on select items. The card quickly became the lynchpin of Staples direct marketing effort. From the card application, Staples gathered information about the customer—what type of business they were in, how many employees they had, where they were located, and so on. This information was entered into a customer database, and every time a member used that card, the card number and purchases were logged into the database via the cash register. This gave Staples real-time information about what was being purchased and by whom. This information then allowed Staples to target promotions at certain customer groups—for example, card holders who were not making purchases. The goal was to get existing customers to spend more at Staples, a goal that over time was attained.

Because Staples started to reach so many of its customers through direct marketing (about 80% of its sales were made to cardholders), it was able to spend less on media ads; in some areas, it dropped media advertising altogether, saving on costs. This was an important source of cost savings in the Northeast, where media is expensive.

A problem that continued the bedevil Staples as it expanded was a shortage of good real estate locations that could be rented at a reasonable price, particularly in the Northeast. Finding a good site in the early days required flexibility; at various times Staples converted anything and everything from restaurants to massage parlors into Staples stores. As the company grew, its real estate strategy started took on a defensive aspect, with Staples bidding for prime sites in order to preempt competitors.

The high cost of real estate in the Northeast led Staples to establish its first distribution center in 1987 (it now has some 65 "delivery fulfillment centers" and larger "distribution centers" in North America). This decision was hotly debated within the company and opposed by some investors who thought that the capital should be used to build more stores, but Stemberg prevailed. The distribution center was located off an interstate highway in an area of rural Connecticut where land was cheap. The facility cost $6 million to build, and tied up a total of $10 million in working capital, almost $0.29 out of every dollar that the company had raised to that point. But Stemberg saw this as a necessary step. The inventory storage capacity at the distribution center enabled the company to operate with smaller stores than many of its rivals, but still offer the same variety of goods. By 1989, the average Staples store was 35% smaller than the Office Depot outlets that were then opening up all over the Southeast, saving on real estate costs. The distribution center also helped save labor costs, because wages are lower in rural areas. Equally important, inventory storage at the distribution centers allowed the stores to remain fully stocked. A Stemberg noted: "In competition with the clones, it will come down to who has the lowest costs and the best in-stock position.[18]"

The expansion strategy at Staples was very methodical. Stores were clustered together in a region, even to the extent that they cannibalized each other on the margin, so that Staples could become the dominant supplier in that market. The early focus was on major metropolitan areas such as Boston, New York, Philadelphia, and Los Angeles. Although high real estate and labor costs in these areas were a disadvantage, strong demand from local businesses helped compensate, as did the distribution centers. In 1990, Staples open its second distribution center, in California, to support expansion there.

The expansion at Staples was fueled by the proceeds from a 1989 IPO, which raised $61.7 million of capital—enough for Staples to accelerate its store openings. By mid-1991, Staples's store count passed 100.

Competition

A rash of imitators to Staples soon appeared on the market. The first of these, Office Depot, focused on the Southeast. By the end of 1988, Office Depot had 26 stores, Office Club had opened 15, Biz Mart had established 10, and Office Max about 12. More than a dozen other office supplies superstores had sprung up. Venture capitalist looking to repeat the success of Staples financed some of these businesses. Others were financed by established retailers, or even started by them. For example, Ben Franklin started Office Station in 1987, but shut it down in 1989 as it failed to gain traction.

Initially, most of the competitors focused in unique regions—Office Depot on the Southeast, Office Club on California, Office Max on the Midwest, BizMart on the Southwest—but as the number of entrants increased, head-to-head competition became more frequent. Stemberg's belief had always been that competition was inevitable, and that the winners in the competitive race would not necessarily be those that grew the fastest, but those that executed best. This philosophy underpinned Stemberg's insistence that the company grow by focusing on key urban areas and achieving a critical mass of stores served by a central distribution system.

Not everyone agreed with this recipe for success. Office Depot did the opposite: The company grew as fast as possible, entering towns quickly to preempt competitors. Office Depot lacked centralized distribution systems, but made up for that by locating in less-expensive areas than Staples, persuading suppliers to ship directly to stores and keeping more backup inventory on the premises. Although this meant larger stores, the lower rental costs in Office Depot's markets offset this.

It soon became apparent that the rash of entrants included a number of companies that simply could not execute. Very quickly a handful of competitors emerged in the forefront of the industry: Staples, Office Depot, Office Max, and Office Club. As the market leaders grew, they increasingly came into contact with each other. The result was price wars. These first broke out in California. Staples entered the market in 1990, and initially focused on pricing not against Office Club, but against Price Club. Although Price Club was a warehouse store selling food and general merchandise, it had the largest share of the office supplies market in California. Staples positioned itself as having the same low prices as Price Club, but a wider selection of office supplies and no membership fee.

Todd Krasnow, the executive VP of marketing at Staples, describes what happened next: "What we failed to realize was that Price Club was very worried about Office Club and was pricing against Office Club. So when we went and matched Price Club, we were matching Office Club. And Office Club was saying: 'We are not going to let anybody have the same prices as us.'"[19] Office Club lowered its prices, causing Price Club to lower prices, and Staples followed. Not willing to be beat, Office Club cut prices again, and so continued the downward spiral. The price war drove profit margins down by as much as 8%.

As Krasnow noted, "We realized that by engaging in this price war, we were focusing on our competitors, not our customers. Our customers weren't paying attention to this spat. So we raised our prices a little. You feel like you're just doing absolutely the wrong thing, because your whole position is: We have the lowest price."[20] Be that as it may, Office Club and Price club followed suit, and prices started to rise again. Ultimately, the three companies carved out different prices niches, each unwilling to be undercut on about 20 or so top-selling items, but in general they were not the same items.

What happened in California occurred elsewhere. When Office Max entered the Boston market in 1992, a price war broke out. There was an unanticipated effect this time, though—the price cuts apparently broadened the market by making buying from Staples attractive to customers with between 25 and 100 employees, who previously bought directly from mail-order and retail stationers.[21]

Price wars such as those that started to break out in California and Boston started to moderate. "We finally realized that it's not in any company's self-interest to have a price war because you can get lots of market share without having a price war. And having a price war among low-priced competitors doesn't get you more market share. It doesn't serve any purpose."[22] Other factors that may have contributed toward more rational pricing behavior in the market were the strong economy of the 1990s and industry consolidation.

Industry Consolidation

At its peak in 1991, there were 25 chains in the office supply industry.[23] Industry consolidation started when some of the clones began to fall by the wayside, filing for bankruptcy. U.S. Office Supply, itself the result of a merger between two office supplies chains, filed for bankruptcy in 1991, as did Office Stop. Consolidation was also hastened by acquisitions. In 1991,

Office Depot acquired Office Club, giving the primary rival of Staples more than twice the number of stores. For its part, Staples acquired HQ Office Supplies Warehouse in 1991 and, in 1992, it purchased another smaller chain, Workplace.[24]

These trends continued and, by the mid-1990s, it became apparent that three players were rising to dominance in the industry: Office Depot, Staples, and Office Max. By mid-1996, Office Depot led the industry with 539 stores, followed by Staples with 517, and Office Max with around 500 stores. In terms of revenues, Office Depot had a clear lead with $5.3 billion in 1996, Staples was second with $3.07 billion, and Office Max third with $2.6 billion. Staples remained concentrated in the Northeast and California, with numerous stores in dense urban areas. Office Depot's stores were concentrated in the South, and the company continued to stay clear of congested cities. Office Max was still strongest in the Midwest.[25]

The consolidation phase peaked in September 1996, when Staples announced an agreement to purchase its larger rival, Office Depot, for $3.36 billion. The executives of the two companies had apparently been talking about merger possibilities for years, while continuing to pursue their own independent growth strategies. If the merger went through, Tom Stemberg would step into the CEO role. The two companies sold the merger to the investment community of the basis of cost savings. The combined firm would have almost 1,100 stores and revenues of $8.5 billion. The combination, Stemberg argued, would attain terrific economies of scale that would allow it to significantly lower costs, saving an estimated $4.9 billion over 5 years, including $2.2 billion in product cost savings.

In a move to preempt a possible investigation by the Federal Trade Commission (FTC), the companies claimed that, because their stores focused on different territories, the combination would not reduce competition. They also noted that Staples still faced intense competition not only from Office Max, but also from the likes of Wal-Mart, Circuit City, and mail-order outlets. Indeed, Stemberg claimed that the combined company would still only account for 5% of the total sales of office supplies in the nation.[26]

The FTC didn't buy the arguments, quickly started an investigation, and, in May 1997, sought an injunction to block the deal. The FTC claimed that the deal would stifle competition and raise prices for office supplies, especially in those markets where

the two firms competed head to head. To buttress its case, the FTC released a report of pricing data showing that nondurable office supplies such as paper were 10 to 15% higher in markets where Staples faced no direct rivals. Staples claimed that the FTC's pricing surveys were done selectively and were biased.

In July 1997, a federal judge granted the FTC's request for an injunction to halt the merger. Staples realized that it was in a losing fight, and pulled its bid for Office Depot. But the failure had a silver lining— not anticipating much interference from the FTC, Office Depot had put most of its expansion plans on hold, opening just two stores in 8 months. In comparison, Staples opened 43, allowing the company to close the gap between itself and its larger rival.

STAPLES'S EVOLVING STRATEGY

Moving into Small Towns

Stemberg has described Staples's initial strategy to deal with the high costs of doing business in the Northeast as follows: "Establish superstores that were smaller than most, save on rent and operating costs, cluster them in densely populated areas to justify paying for expensive advertisements, and stock the stores from a distribution center."[27] The drawback with this strategy was that Staples ignored many potentially lucrative markets in smaller towns. While Office Depot was barnstorming into towns with populations of just 75,000, Staples could not see how they made it pay. Surely towns of that size were just too small to support an office supplies superstore?

It turned out they were not. The mistake Staples made was to assume that a store would serve customers within a 10- to 15-minute drive. But in smaller cities customers would drive much further to get good prices. The revelation did not hit home until Staples opened its first store in Portland, Maine. With a population of 200,000, the town was smaller than most areas focused on by Staples, but within a few months the store was doing very well. To test the hypothesis, in 1992 and 1993, Staples opened stores in a number of smaller towns. The results were surprising. Many of the stores generated higher sales per square foot than those located in large cities. Sales were helped by the fact that in many of these small towns the only competitors were small "mom and pop" stationers, and that many small towns also lacked supermarket electronic retailers, such as Circuit City, selling low-priced office equipment, allowing Staples to pick up a much larger share of that business. Moreover, the lower rent, labor costs, advertising costs, and shrinkage made these stores significantly more profitable.

From that point on, Staples moved into small towns and suburban locations, where the same economics apply. Stemberg has described not moving into small towns earlier as "one of the dumbest mistakes I made." In 1994, some 10% of Staples stores were in small towns; by 1998, that figure had risen to 28%, and some of the most profitable stores in Staples network were located in small towns.[28]

Selling Direct

Established as a retailer, Staples initially turned its back on customer requests for delivery and mail- or telephone-order service. The reason for doing this was simple: Staples saw itself as a low-cost retailer, and a delivery service would probably raise costs. However, Staples's competitors started to offer mail-order and delivery service, and customers continued to ask for the service; so, in 1988, Staples began to experiment with this, albeit halfheartedly. Store managers were not enthusiastic about supporting a delivery service that they believed decreased store sales, and Staples discouraged delivery by tacking a 5% delivery charge onto the order price. Moreover, the company questioned whether it could generate the volume of business to cover the costs of a delivery service and make a decent return on capital.

This all changed when a study undertaken for Staples by a management-consulting firm found that the customers who purchased via a catalog and required delivery were not always the same ones who brought directly from the store. While there was a lot of cross-shopping, the mail-order customers tended to be bigger and somewhat more interested in service, whereas those buying from the store were often buying for home offices. Staples also could not help but notice that its major rivals were offering a delivery service, and that business seemed to be thriving.

In 1991, Staples set up an independent business unit within the company to handle the mail- and telephone-order and delivery service, known as Contract and Commercial. The core of this business unit was Staples Direct (now called Staples Business Delivery). The man put in charge of this business, Ronald Sargent, would replace Stemberg as CEO of Staples in 2003.

One issue that had to be dealt with was the potential conflict between Staples Direct and the stores. The stores didn't want to push business the way of Staples Direct because they would not get credit for the sale. As Sargent commented later, "We were like the bad guys inside Staples, because the feeling was that if customers got products delivered they wouldn't shop inside our stores."[29] To align incentives, Staples changed the compensation systems so that (a) the store would get credit if a delivery order was placed through the store, and (b) the annual bonus of store employees would be partly based on how well they met goals for generating delivery sales.

As Staples Direct started to grow, the company also discovered that the delivery infrastructure they put in place could be used to serve clients in addition to the company's established, small-business customers, which typically had less than 50 employees. Increasingly, medium-sized businesses (with 50 to 100 employees), and larger businesses (with more than 100 employees) started to utilize Staples Direct. To support this new business, Staples started to grow by acquisition, purchasing a number of regional stationary companies with established customers and delivery systems. Typically, Staples kept the owners of these businesses on as Staples employees, often because they had long-established relationships with key accounts in large organizations such as Xerox, Ford, and Pepsi Cola. Staples, however, established a consistent product line, brand image, and computer and accounting systems across all of its acquisitions.

Between 1991 and 1996, Staples Direct grew from a $30-million business to almost $1 billion. As sales volume ramped up, Staples gained greater efficiencies out of its distribution network, which helped to drive down the costs of doing business through this channel. Staples used a network of regional distribution centers to hold an inventory of some 15,000 SKUs for delivery, compared to 8,000 SKUs in a typical store. In 1998, a web-based element was added to Staples Direct, Staples.com. Through the web or catalog, Staples customers could access some 130,000 SKUs, many of which were shipped directly from manufacturers with Staples acting as an intermediary and consolidator.

To continue building the direct business, in 1988, Staples acquired Quill Corporation for $685 million in Staples stock. Established in 1956, Quill is a direct-mail catalog business with a targeted approach to servicing the business products needs of around a million small- and medium-sized businesses in the United States. Quill differentiated itself through excellent customer service. Staples decided to let Quill keep its own organization, setting it up as a separate division within the Contract and Commercial business unit, but integrated Quill's purchasing with that of the rest of the organization to gain economies of the input side. Quill now operates under two brands—Staples National Advantage, which focuses upon large multiregional businesses, and Staples Business Advantage, which focuses upon large- and medium-sized regional companies, and has the flexibility to handle smaller accounts (although these are mostly handled via Staples Direct). In justifying the acquisition of Quill, Stemberg noted that the direct business amounted to a $60-billion industry annually, but it was highly fragmented, with the top eight players accounting for less than 20% of the market.[30]

By 2014, the combined North American delivery business had grown to represent 40% of total sales, with some two-thirds of the *Fortune* 100 being counted as customers of Staples delivery business.[31]

Going International

Staples first foray into international markets occurred in the early 1990s. A Canadian retailer, Jack Bingleman, who wanted to start a Staples-type chain north of the border, approached the company. Bingleman also approached Office Depot and Office Max, but had a preference for Staples because of the close geographic proximity. Board members at Staples initially opposed expansion into Canada, arguing that scarce resources should be dedicated toward growth in the much larger U.S. market, but Stemberg liked Bingleman's vision and pushed the idea. Ultimately, in 1991, Staples agreed to invest $2 million in Bingleman's start-up for a 16% equity stake.

Known as Business Depot, the Canadian venture expanded rapidly, modeling itself on Staples. Between 1991 and 1994, the number of Canadian Business Depot stores expanded to 30 stores, and the

enterprise turned profitable in 1993. In 1994, Staples announced an agreement to purchase Business Depot outright for $32 million.[32] By 2014, there were 315 stores in Canada.

The Canadian venture was soon followed by investments in Europe. Staples entered the U.K. market in 1992, partnering with Kingfisher PLC, a large retailer that operated home improvement and consumer electronics stores, among other things. The Canadian venture had taught Staples that a local partner was extremely valuable. As one Staples executive noted later:

> You absolutely cannot do it yourself. There are too many cultural impediments for you to know where the booby traps lie. In a retail start-up, the most important task is to generate locations. There's no way a U.S. national can go into any country and generate the real estate it needs. That person will be chasing his tail for a long time.[33]

On the heels of entry into the United Kingdom, Staples purchased MAXI-Papier, a German company that was attempting to copy what Staples had done in the United States. This was followed by entry into the Netherlands and Portugal. In late 2002, Staples purchased the mail-order business of a French company, Guilbert, for nearly $800 million, which boosted delivery sales in Europe from $50 million a year to $450 million a year almost overnight.[34] In 2008, Staples purchased Corporate Express NV, a Dutch office supplies company with a substantial direct-delivery business in Europe. By 2014, Staples had stores in 23 countries outside of North America, including 112 stores in the United Kingdom, 59 in Germany, 41 in the Netherlands, and 34 in Portugal. At this point, around 20% of total sales were generated by the international operations, with half of that total coming from direct delivery and the remainder from retail sales.

Changing the Shopping Experience

By the 2000s, Staples started to realize that its stores looked very similar to those of its two main competitors, Office Depot and Office Max. As the number of markets where all three companies competed grew, head-to-head competition increased. Management started to look for ways to differentiate their stores from those of competitors. A new store design, known as "Dover," emerged. The core of "Dover" was a customer-centric philosophy known as "Easy." Rolled out across the company in 2005, "Easy" is all about making the shopping experience for customers as easy as possible—through store design and layout, through a merchandising strategy that aims to ensure that items are never out of stock, and through superior in-store customer service. The idea is to complete transactions as expeditiously as possible.

To execute "Easy," Staples had to redesign its store layout, invest in upgrading the knowledge level of its sales associates, and improve its supply-chain management processes.[35] Staples started a big push to improve the efficiency of its supply-chain management process in 2003, and that is still ongoing today. Elements of this push include better use of information systems to link Staples with its suppliers, and extensive use of "cross-docking" techniques at distribution centers, so that merchandise spends less time in distribution centers. As a consequence of this strategy, Staples has increased inventory turnover, reduced inventory holdings, and improved the in-stock experience for its customers.

STAPLES TODAY

In February 2002, Tom Stemberg announced that he was stepping down as CEO and passing the baton to Ron Sargent. Stemberg would remain on as chairman. Upon taking over as CEO, Sargent put the brakes on store expansion, declaring that Staples would open no more than 75 new stores a year, down from over 130 in 2000. He used the slowdown to refocus attention upon internal operating efficiencies. The product line within stores was rationalized, with Staples cutting back on stocking low-margin items such as PCs. He also set up a task force to look for ways to remove every excess cent out of the cost structure. As a result, operating margins at Staples stores came in at 5.9% of sales in 2002—the best in the industry, and up from 4.5% in 2000.

By 2003, Sargent was refocusing on attaining profitable growth for the company. Although by this point Staples or one of its competitors operated in all major markets in North America, the company's management decided that Staples was in a strong enough position to go head to head with major competitors.

In 2005, Staples pushed into Chicago, a market previously served by Office Depot and Office Max, opening 25 stores. The Chicago experience proved to be a pivotal one for Staples. In the words of COO, Mike Miles, "What we found in Chicago was we can come into a two-player market and make it a three-player market successfully. There was a little trepidation about that because the model in the first 10 to 15 years was that office superstores were interchangeable."[36]

Outside of the retail market, Sargent turned his attention to the direct-delivery business, where he had made his name. He points out that, although the number of independent office supplies dealers is down to 6,000 from 15,000 a decade ago, the delivery market is still highly fragmented and very large. Sargent believes that direct delivery from warehouses can be as big a business as Staples's office supplies stores. He also sees huge potential for growth in Europe, which is the second-largest office supplies market in the world and still years behind the United States in terms of consolidation.

At the same time, Staples continues to face strategic challenges. Additional expansion by Staples in North America is bringing it into direct competition with Office Depot and Office Max. Staples also faces continued competition from Sam's Club and Costco, both of which are focusing on small businesses and continue to sell office supplies. In addition, FedEx Kinko's, which has a nationwide network of 1,000 copying and printing stores, is now offering more office supplies in a new store layout.

The 2008–2009 global financial crisis triggered a deep economic recession in the United States and elsewhere. The U.S. office supplies industry was hit by price discounting which, resulting in much slower top-line growth for Staples and a decline in net profit. Sargent responded by cutting back on expansion plans and reducing capital spending going forward. Staples, however, continued to be the strongest of the big three office supplies retailers.

While the economy started to recover from the recession in 2010, Staples and its peers did not. The recession seemed to usher in a permanent change in buyer behavior. As Ron Sargent noted in 2014, "Our customers are using less office supplies, shopping less often in our stores and more often online, and the focus on value has made the marketplace even more competitive."[37] Amazon, Wal-Mart, and Costco had all expanded their office supplies offerings since the mid-2000s, and online sales from all three were cutting into demand for product from physical stores. Staples, too, saw its online sales grow even as sales from its physical stores stagnated or declined. By 2015, over half of all of Staples sales in North America were online.

Staples responded to this trend by announcing in March 2014 that it would close up to 225 of its North American stores by the end of 2015 as part of a corporate goal to reduce its annual operating costs by $500 million. At the same time, the company would continue to expand its online offerings. In 2013 and 2014, it increased the number of products sold on its website, Staples.com, from 100,000 to 500,000. Ron Sargent expected this number to reach 1.5 million by the end of 2015. Most products will be shipped directly from the manufacturer to the customer, with Staples acting as an intermediary, much as Amazon does.[38]

With their sales also falling, Office Depot and Office Max completed a $1.2-billion merger in late 2013. The two companies cited the growth of Internet sales as a prime reason for the merger. The FTC, which had opposed the proposed merger between Staples and Office Depot in 1997, blessed this merger, noting that the deal "was unlikely to substantially lessen competition."[39] The merger was expected to reduce the costs of the combined entity by $400 to $600 million per year, primarily by closing duplicate stores.

In late 2014, the hedge fund Starboard Value announced that it had taken a position in both Staples and Office Depot. Jeffrey Smith, the CEO of Starboard Value, has emerged as a powerful activist investor over the last few years, taking large positions in companies and then urging them to change their strategy. Smith urged Staples and Office Depot to merge, stating that if they did not, he would mount a proxy battle to get board seats in both companies and push a merger through. As it turned out, neither company needed much encouragement. In February 2015, the two companies announced a $6.3-billion merger agreement. If the deal goes through, it will create a company with $34 billion in revenues and 4,400 stores worldwide. Both Staples and Office Depot argue that the proposed merger is necessary to compete in a world where bigger store chains and online competitors have reduced prices and provided new competition. Reflecting on these developments, Sargent noted; "I think Amazon just launched a business-to-business office products initiative, so I'm sure they are knocking on the door."[40] It remains to be seen whether the FTC will agree.

NOTES

1. S. D. Solomon, "Born to Be Big," *Inc.*, June 1989, p. 94.
2. M. de la Merced and D. Gelles, "Staples and Office Depot Say Merger Will Keep Them Competitive," *New York Times*, February 25, 2015.
3. S. D. Solomon, "Born to Be Big," p. 96.
4. T. Stemberg, "Staples for Success," Knowledge Exchange, Santa Monica, California, 1996.
5. M. Barrier, "Tom Stemberg Calls the Office," *Nation's Business*, July 1990, p. 42.
6. Ibid, p. 44.
7. Ibid.
8. T. Stember and D. Whiteford, "Putting a Stop to Mom and Pop," *Fortune Small Business*, October 2002, p. 39.
9. Ibid.
10. T. Stemberg, "Staples for Success."
11. T. Stember and D. Whiteford, "Putting a Stop to Mom and Pop," p. 40.
12. T. Stemberg, "Staples for Success," p. 17.
13. T. Stember and D. Whiteford, "Putting a Stop to Mom and Pop," p. 41.
14. S. D. Solomon, "Born to Be Big," pp. 94–95.
15. T. Stemberg, "Staples for Success," p. 24.
16. Ibid.
17. T. Stember and D. Whiteford, "Putting a Stop to Mom and Pop," p. 40.
18. S. D. Solomon, "Born to be Big," p. 100.
19. T. Stemberg, "Staples for Success," p. 97.
20. Ibid.
21. N. Alster, "Penney Wise," *Forbes*, February 1, 1993, pp. 48–51.
22. T. Stemberg, "Staples for Success," p. 97.
23. R. C. Rouland, "And Then There Were Three," *Discount Merchandiser*, December 1994, p. 27.
24. L. Montgomery, "Staples: Buy the Laggard," *Financial World*, November 9, 1993, p. 22. Anonymous, "The New Plateau in Office Supplies," *Discount Merchandiser*, November 1991, pp. 50–54. NEEDS #

25. J. S. Hirsch and E. de Lisser, "Staples to Acquire Archrival Office Depot," *The Wall Street Journal*, September 5, 1996, p. A3.

26. J. Pereira and J. Wilke, "Staples Faces FTC in Antitrust Showdown on Merger," *The Wall Street Journal*, May 19, 1997, p. B4.

27. T. Stemberg, "Staples for Success," p. 128.

28. W. M. Bulkeley, "Office Supplies Superstores Find Bounty in the Boonies," *The Wall Street Journal*, September 1, 1998, p. B1.

29. W. C. Symonds, "Thinking Outside the Big Box," *Businessweek*, August 11, 2003, p. 62.

30. W. M. Bulkeley, "Staples, Moving Beyond Superstores, Will Buy Quill for $685 Million in Stock," *The Wall Street Journal*, April 8, 1998, p. A1.

31. J. MacKay, "Staples Achieves Impressive Operating Margins Relative to Peers Due to Scale Advantages," *Morningstar Research Report*, May 19, 2011.

32. S. Gelston, "Staples Goes on Buying Spree to Acquire Business Depot, National Office Supply Company," *The Boston Herald*, January 25, 1994, p. 24.

33. T. Stemberg, "Staples for Success," p. 90.

34. W. C. Symonds, "Thinking Outside the Big Box," *Businessweek*, August 11, 2003, pp. 62–64.

35. M. Troy, "Office Supplies: Staples Positioned as the Architect of "Easy," *Retailing Today*, August 7, 2006, p. 30.

36. Anonymous, "Moving in on Major Markets," *DSN Retailing Today*, May 22, 2006, p. 10.

37. Anonymous, "Citing Shift to Online Sales, Staples Says it Will Close Up to 225 Stores by the End of 2015," *Reuters*, March 6, 2015.

38. Ibid.

39. M. de la Merced and D. Gelles, "Staples and Office Depot Say Merger Will Keep Them Competitive," *New York Times*, February 25, 2015.

40. Ibid.

TRADER JOE'S: A REMARKABLY QUIRKY– AND SUCCESSFUL!– GROCERY RETAILER

In the mid-1960s, Joe Coulombe owned a chain of "Pronto Market" convenience stores in the greater Los Angeles area, but they were under heavy competitive pressure from 7-11. He began to ponder the idea of opening up a new kind of store, one with more unusual goods for people who had acquired more diverse tastes while traveling and yearned for flavors they could not get at home. He went on vacation in the Caribbean and came home inspired: He opened up his first Trader Joe's store (named after himself) in 1967. His store would focus on delivering innovative, hard-to-find foods with prices that would deliver great value. He also made a point of carrying every California wine available. He imbued his new store with a distinctive South Seas theme, lining the walls with cedar planks, creating displays out of fishing nets, and having employees wear Hawaiian shirts.

The formula was a hit. By the late 1970s, there were 20 Trader Joe's in southern California, and by the late 1970s the chain had attracted the attention of the German Albrecht family, owners of a chain of discount supermarkets called Aldi Nord. In 1979, Theo Albrecht offered to buy Trader Joe's, keeping Joe on to run the business. Coulombe continued to run the company until 1987. He then retired and was succeeded by his friend, John Shields, who expanded the company into Arizona, the Pacific Northwest, and Brookline and Cambridge (near Boston). When Shields retired in 2001, Dan Bane succeeded him and continued to expand the chain. By May 2014, the company had 418 stores in nearly 40 states, more than 10,000 employees, and an estimated $12 billion in annual sales.

◤ A DISTINCTIVE PRODUCT STRATEGY

From the beginning, Trader Joe's had a distinctive product strategy. Whereas a typical grocery store might carry 50,000 different items, Trader Joe's carried closer to 4,000, and most products (roughly 80%) bore one of Trader Joe's own brand names. Many of the names are a fun twist on the name Trader Joe but modified to reflect the nature of the food, such as "Trader Jose's" (for Mexican food), "Trader Ming's" (for Asian food), and "Pilgrim Joe" (for New England favorites such as clam chowder). The company focused on gourmet and organic foods, vegetarian offerings, and imported foods, as well as wines and interesting frozen entrees.

Trader Joe's is very selective about the products it stocks. Its biggest R&D expense is for its top buyers to travel the world looking for new, trendsetting items such as the wildly successful Trader Joe's cookie butter, which is a gooey, Belgian spread known as "Speculoos" in its home country. The company does not charge slotting fees to suppliers to get on the shelves; instead, it makes them compete to demonstrate they can sell in high enough volumes and at low enough prices to keep their shelf space. Trader Joe's routinely discontinues products that fail to deliver on these dimensions, cutting the 10% worst performers to make room for new items. Customers do not seem to mind the narrower selection—in fact, analysts speculated that customers actually felt *better* about their choices when there were fewer options. Trader Joe's had cultivated a reputation of choosing products very carefully, which in turn inspired customer faith in the company's offerings. As articulated by a former employee, "If they're going to get behind only one jar of Greek olives, then they're sure as heck going to make sure it's the most fabulous jar of Greek olives they can find for the price."

Trader Joe's also took a fairly strict stance on issues pertaining to the environment, humane practices, and food safety. For example, products sold under the Trader Joe's brand name could not contain artificial colors, flavors, preservatives, or genetically modified ingredients; Trader Joe eggs could only come from cage-free hens; and Trader Joe dairy products had to come from cows that were not given artificial hormones. In 2007, it announced that it would discontinue stocking most products from China due to concerns about inadequate monitoring of food safety.

The carefully curated product line turned out to have big economic advantages. Selling a narrower selection of high-volume products helped drive down supply costs because Trader Joe's could negotiate deep discounts on each item. At the same time, managing a narrower product line lowered inventory carrying costs, and stocking only items that turned quickly boosted sales per square foot. Trader Joe's stores sell roughly $1,750 per square foot—more than double that of Whole Foods. As a result, many analysts speculated that Trader Joe's was significantly more popular than typical grocery retailers (actual profits were unknown; Trader Joe's, a privately-held company, did not share its income figures).

LOGISTICS AND MARKETING

Most Trader Joe's store locations were leased, and about two-thirds operated out of existing buildings rather than being newly built. The stores ranged from 8,000 to 15,000 square feet, and were typically opened in nonprime locations (though its Manhattan stores were notable exceptions). From its inception, Coulombe recognized that the stores would fare better in communities that had adventurous, educated people, and thus he targeted college towns and other educated communities.

Rather than working with national or regional distributors, Trader Joe's purchased directly from manufacturers, which shipped their products straight to Trader Joe's distribution centers. This process streamlined the distribution process and reduced costs, but also limited where, and how quickly, Trader Joe's was able to expand. For example, it took Trader Joe's longer to enter Texas and Florida (despite entreaties from customers in those locations who had become familiar with Trader Joe's stores) because they were not easily accessible through its distribution centers.

Trader Joe's spends very little on advertising, instead relying on regional radio advertising, word of mouth, and its newsletter, the "Fearless Flyer." The newsletter is customized by region and offers detailed, witty write-ups of new products that emphasize their authenticity and uniqueness.

UNIQUELY FRIENDLY EMPLOYEES

A big part of Trader Joe's strategy (and image) is the friendliness of the experience in the stores. Employees are encouraged to interact with customers, getting to know the names of regulars, and generating a fun, informal vibe. Store employees can work in any function in the store, and all are expected to be knowledgeable about the products and be able to make recommendations. If a customer asks a Trader Joe employee about a product, the employee will typically enthusiastically share their own experience with the product, will often accompany the customer to the location where the product is shelved, and may open a package to offer the customer a sample.

Management at Trader Joe's believed that a significant reason why people shop in stores is not about food at all—it's about interacting with people, sharing a smile or a joke, and feeling welcomed. Trader Joe's therefore did not offer online ordering, nor did management feel particularly threatened by the growth of online grocery shopping. The Trader Joe's experience was distinctive enough, and fun enough, that online shopping was not direct competition. However, creating this fun and friendly vibe in the stores had become a growing challenge as the chain grew: how would Trader Joe's ensure that its distinctive store culture of friendly interaction would be retained when stores and employees were being added to the chain quickly? Protecting and reinforcing this culture was a priority that Trader Joe's management took seriously.

One way Trader Joe's attempted to preserve the employee culture was through its pay policies. When Joe Coulombe founded Trader Joe's, he decided to pay full-time employees the median California family income rather than the much lower salaries typically offered to workers at convenience and grocery stores. Today, store managers and full-time crew members at Trader Joe's are still paid better than typical store employees. According to Glassdoor, a company that gathers pay and benefits information from employees at over 300,000 companies, hourly store employees at Trader Joe's earned an average of $14/hour in 2014, and store managers earned over $100K. Trader Joe's also contributes 15.4% of employees' gross income to tax-deferred retirement accounts.

COMPETITION

The traditional grocery retail industry was mature and had famously slim margins. Firms relied on rapid turnover and tight cost control, while also selling premium items such as made-to-order sandwiches, imported cheeses, and cut flowers to bolster earnings. Whole Foods, which was strongly differentiated by its focus on high-quality, organic foods, had somewhat higher margins than other industry-leading grocery chains, but even Whole Foods had net margins of only 4%. Wal-Mart's net margins hovered in the 3.5% range, and most grocers had net margins under 2% (see Table 1). This meant there was little room for waste or error in the grocery industry.

Table 1: Revenues and Net Profit Margin at Select U.S. Grocery Chains

Grocery Retailer	Gross Revenues ($millions)	Net Profit Margin
Costco	112,640	1.96%
Kroger	108,465	1.59%
Safeway	36,330	0.31%
H-E-B	15,600	–
Whole Foods	14,194	4.04%
Stop & Shop	11,554	–
Trader Joe's	10,500*	
A&P	8,078	−6.95%

*Sales for Trader Joe's are estimated.

Though many customers were attracted to Trader Joe's because of its strong focus on value and its low prices, its emphasis on gourmet and healthy foods caused many people to view the store as being more like Whole Foods than a discounter grocer like Costco. Being a lower-cost Whole Foods was a valuable and unique niche position. However, there was growing risk that this particular niche would become more crowded as new, alternative grocers emerged. One such competitor was Sprouts Farmers Market. In 2014, Sprouts Farmers Market was primarily located in the Southwestern states, but it was growing far faster than any other retailer in the country (see Figure 1). Its business model focused heavily on fresh produce, sold at 20 to 30% discounts to conventional competitors. Its low-cost strategy was simple: whereas conventional grocery stores piled produce high in aesthetically attractive displays that connoted abundance, Sprout Farmers Market used smaller

"low displays," which resulted in far less than the nearly 15% of produce that is typically discarded by a grocery store.

REMARKABLY SUCCESSFUL, FAMOUSLY SECRETIVE

In 2013 and 2014, a survey conducted by Market Force Information found that Trader Joe's was ranked as America's favorite supermarket chain. Perhaps not coincidentally, this was just two spots ahead of Aldi, its lesser known sibling. Both chains were praised for their courteous, fast service, and their high-quality, private-label lines. Trader Joe's success could also be observed in the growth in the number of its stores and its estimated revenues. It was unknown, however, just

Figure 1: Retail Sales Growth, Selected Chains, 2008–2013

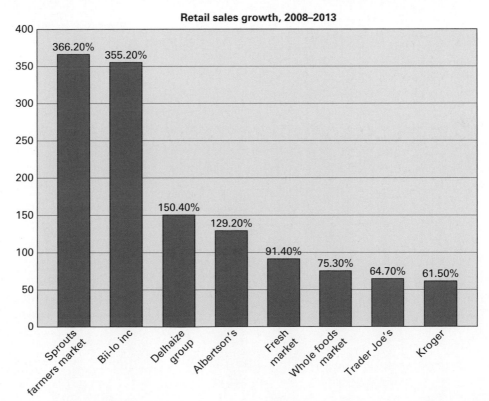

Source: Euromonitor.

how much the company earned on those revenues. Was Trader Joe's remarkably profitable?

Trader Joe's had always been privately held and famously secretive. It did not reveal its sourcing, and made suppliers sign contracts forbidding them to publicize their relationship with Trader Joe's. There were no signs with the company's name or logo at the Monrovia California headquarters, and management routinely denied requests for interviews from magazines and newspapers. Such secrecy made it hard for competitors to know what profits Trader Joe's earned or how it generated those profits. It also facilitated suppliers' ability to sell products at a lower cost to Trader Joe's without alienating their other retailers.

Remaining privately held, however, came at a price. By not franchising or accessing capital through the stock market, Trader Joe's forfeited opportunities to grow faster. Some analysts expressed concern that this left a lot of opportunity for competitors to imitate Trader Joe's business model and product strategy and seize geographic regions that Trader Joe's had left unserved. This left many wondering: How much more profitable was Trader Joe's than other grocery retailers? Should the company grow faster? And if it did, how could it preserve its company culture and store culture?

Sources: B. Kowitt, "Inside Trader Joe's," *Fortune,* 162 (4) (2010): 86–96; E. Z, "Trader Joe's Doubles Its Growth Rate," *SN: Supermarket News* 62 (9) (2014): 24–26; Anonymous, "America's Favorite Super: Trader Joe's," *MMR* 31 (9) (2014): 87; M. Gustafson, "Trader Joe's Remarkable Journey," *Private Label Buyer* (November 2008), pp. 42–46; M. Nisen, "The Secret to America's Most 'Disruptive' Supermarket–Fruits and Vegetables," *Reuters,* June 30, 2014; Hoovers; www.traderjoes.com, accessed May 25, 2015.

GETTING AN INSIDE LOOK: GIVEN IMAGING'S CAMERA PILL[1]

Founded in 1998, Given Imaging is an Israeli medical-device company that developed the "camera pill"—a tiny, capsule-shaped electronic device that, after being swallowed by a patient, sends visual images of the gastrointestinal tract to a video pack worn around the patient's waist. These images can be evaluated to diagnose numerous small-intestine problems that have been hitherto very difficult to locate and diagnose.

Though Given's product offered numerous advantages in terms of both effectiveness and patient comfort, it was somewhat difficult to get doctors to adopt the product. Many physicians and hospitals already had the equipment and training required for traditional endoscopy techniques, and were also risk averse about trying the new method. Analysts wondered if Given would be able to overcome physicians' aversion and reluctance to switching costs. Further complicating matters, new competitors had emerged: Japanese camera companies were developing their own camera pills, some with intriguing special features that Given's system did not possess. The race was on: How fast would the market emerge, and who would end up as leader?

THE HISTORY OF THE CAMERA PILL

Gavriel Iddan was an electro-optical engineer at Israel's Rafael Armament Development Authority, the Israeli authority for the development of weapons and military technology. One of Iddan's projects was to develop the "eye" that leads a guided missile to its target. In 1981, Iddan traveled to Boston on sabbatical to work for a company that produced x-ray tubes and ultrasonic probes. While there, he befriended a gastroenterologist (a physician who focuses on digestive diseases), Eitan Scapa. During long conversations in which they discussed their respective fields, Scapa taught Iddan about the technologies used to view the interior lining of the digestive system. Scapa pointed out that the existing technologies had a number of significant limitations, particularly with respect to viewing the small intestine.[2] The small intestine is the locale of a number of serious disorders. In the United States alone, approximately 19 million people suffer from disorders of the small intestine (including bleeding,

Crohn's disease, celiac disease, chronic diarrhea, irritable bowel syndrome, and small-bowel cancer).[3] Furthermore, the nature of the small intestine makes it difficult to diagnose and treat such disorders. The small intestine (or "small bowel") is about 5 to 6 meters long in a typical person and is full of twists and turns (see Figure 1). X-rays do not enable a physician to view the lining of the intestine, and endoscopes (small cameras attached to long, thin, flexible poles) can only reach the first third of the small intestine and can be quite uncomfortable for the patient. The remaining option, surgery, is very invasive and can be impractical if the physician does not know which part of the small intestine is affected. Scapa thus urged Iddan to come up with a better way to view the small intestine, but at that time Iddan had no idea how to do it.

Ten years later, Iddan visited the United States again, and his old friend Scapa again inquired whether there was a technological solution that would provide a better solution for viewing the small intestine. By this time, very small charge-coupled device (CCD) image sensors had been developed in the quest to build small videocameras. Iddan wondered if perhaps it would be possible to create a very small, missilelike device that could travel through the intestine

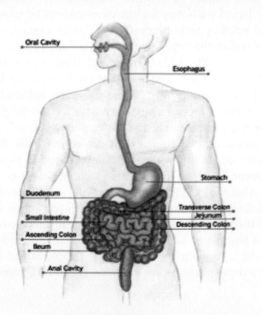

Figure 1 The Gastrointestinal Tract

without a lifeline leading to the outside of the body. Like the missiles Iddan developed at Rafael, this device would have a camera "eye." If designed well, the body's natural peristaltic action would propel the camera through the length of the intestine.

When Iddan returned to Israel, he began working on a way to have a very small CCD camera introduced into the digestive system and transmit images wirelessly to a receiver outside of the body. Initially unsure whether images could be transmitted through the body wall, he conducted a rudimentary experiment with a store-bought chicken. He placed a transmitting antenna inside the chicken and a receiving antenna outside of it. The results indicated that it was possible to transmit a clear video image. Encouraged by this, he set about overcoming the battery-life problem: The CCD sensors consumed so much energy that their batteries were often depleted within 10 minutes. Fortunately, advancements in semiconductors promised to replace CCD imagers with a new generation of complementary metal oxide semiconductors (CMOS), which would consume a fraction of the power of CCD imagers. Iddan began developing a prototype based on CMOS technology, and applied for an initial patent on the device in 1994. In 1995, he presented his product idea to Gavriel Meron, CEO of Applitect Ltd., a company that made small, endoscopic cameras. Meron thought the project was a fascinating idea and founded Given Imaging ("Gi" for gastrointestinal, "v" for video, and "en" for endoscopy) to develop and market the technology.[4]

Unbeknownst to Iddan or Meron, a team of scientists in the United Kingdom was also working on a method for wireless endoscopy. This team included a physician, C. Paul Swain, a bioengineer, Tim Mills, and a doctoral student, Feng Gong. Swain, Mills, and Gong were exploring using commercially available miniature videocameras and processors. They scouted out miniature camera technology at "spy shops" in London that supplied small video cameras and transmitters to private detectives and other users.[5] By 1994, they were developing crude devices to see if they could transmit moving images from within the gut using microwave frequencies. By 1996, they had succeeded in their first live animal trial. They surgically inserted their prototype device into a pig's stomach, and demonstrated that they could see the pylorus valve of the stomach open and close. Their next hurdle was to develop a device that could be swallowed instead of being surgically inserted.

In Fall 1997, Meron met Dr. Swain at a conference in Birmingham, England, and the teams concluded that their progress would accelerate if they joined forces. Swain's team had superior expertise in anatomy and the imaging needs of diagnosing small-intestine disorders, while Iddan's CMOS-based sensors enabled the production of a smaller device with lower power requirements. The teams thus had complementary knowledge that each knew would be crucial to producing a successful capsule endoscope.

In 1999, the team got permission from the ethics committee at the Royal London Hospital to conduct their first human trial. Dr. Swain would be the patient, and Dr. Scapa (whose initial urgings had motivated Iddan to develop the wireless endoscope) would be the surgeon who would oversee the procedure. In October 1999, in Scapa's clinic near Tel Aviv, Israel, Dr. Swain swallowed the 11 × 33 mm (.43 inches × 1.3 inches) capsule. The first images were of poor quality due to the team's inexperience at holding the receiving antenna in an optimal position. The team was not sure how far the capsule had traveled so they used a radiograph to find the position of the capsule. The radiograph revealed that the device had reached Swain's colon, and thus had successfully traversed the entire length of the small intestine. The team was thrilled at this victory, and urged Swain to swallow another capsule, which he did the next morning. Now that the team was more practiced at optimizing the receiving antennae, and they achieved much better quality images. Swain remarked that he "enjoyed watching the lovely sea view" of his lower intestine. Though the first capsule had only transmitted for approximately 2 hours before its battery life was depleted, the second capsule transmitted for more than 6 hours, and the team knew they had obtained quality images of a substantial length of small intestine.[6]

Over the next few months, the team conducted several animal and human trials. By April 2000, they had used the device to find a small-intestinal bleeding source in three patients with "obscure recurrent gastrointestinal bleeding" (a difficult problem to diagnose and treat). An article on the device published that year in *Nature* (a prestigious scientific journal) was titled "The Discomfort of Internal Endoscopy May Soon Be a Thing of the Past."[7] By August 2001, the device had received Food and Drug Administration (FDA) clearance, and by October 2001 Given Imaging had gone public, raising $60 million in its initial public offering.

Given Imaging marketed its device as a system that included its proprietary "RAPID" software, wearable video recording packs, and the capsules (called PillCams). After swallowing the $500 PillCam, the patient goes about his or her day while the PillCam broadcasts images to a video recording pack the patient wears around the waist. When the patient returns the pack to the physician, the physician uploads the images and can both view them directly and utilize Given software that employs algorithms to automatically examine pixels in the images to identify possible locations of bleeding. The software also enables physicians to collect the data at remote sites and then send it (or transport it on a USB device) to a central location for diagnostic interpretation if needed. The PillCam exits the patient naturally.

Encouraged by their success, developers at Given Imaging began working on PillCams for the esophagus (PillCam ESO) and for the colon (PillCam COLON). Whereas Given estimated the global market potential for small-bowel capsule endoscopy (PillCam SB) was $1 billion, it believed the global market opportunity for PillCam COLON could be a multibillion dollar opportunity due to widespread routine screening for colon cancer. By 2013, Given had also developed PillCam SB3, which offered sharper images and adaptive frame-rate technology that enables it to snap more pictures, more quickly. These improvements would enable clinicians to better spot lesions indicating Crohn's disease that would go undetected by traditional endoscopic methods.[8] Crohn's disease is an autoimmune disorder in

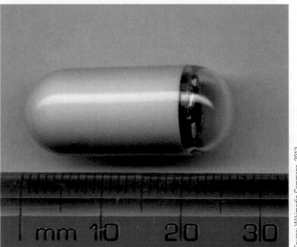

The PillCam

Source: Wikimedia Commons, 2013.

which the digestive tract attacks itself, leading to pain, diarrhea, and vomiting. More than 1 million people have been diagnosed worldwide, and many more cases were thought to be undiagnosed.

By 2015, numerous studies had shown that Pill-Cams compared favorably to traditional endoscopy in terms of safety. While use of capsule endoscopy could result occasionally in the camera becoming lodged and not exiting the body naturally (roughly eight cases of this happening had been identified by 2015), traditional endoscopy bore a risk of tearing the gastrointestinal wall, which could quickly lead to deadly infections. At $500, PillCams were also less expensive than traditional gastrointestinal endoscopy procedures, which ran from $800 to $4,000 or more.

◤ COMPETITION IN THE ENDOSCOPY MARKET

Until 2005, Given enjoyed the benefits of offering a medical technology with tremendous advantages over the alternatives and having no competitors. However, in 2005, Japanese optics giant Olympus introduced its own camera pill—the Endo Capsule. As awareness of the benefits of capsule endoscopy began to grow, new competitors in this space began to emerge, including Chongqing Jinshan Science & Technology, IntroMedic, and others.

Olympus

Olympus was founded in 1919 in Japan. Though known by most people as a camera maker, Olympus has a well-established history in medical devices, having developed and marketed medical microscopes, ultrasound equipment, and endoscopes. In 1949, a Tokyo doctor asked Olympus to develop a camera that could photograph the inside of a patient's stomach. By 1950, Olympus had developed a prototype of an endoscope, too primitive for clinical use but with clear potential for further development. Over the next several decades, Olympus was very active in the development of endoscopes, eventually introducing a wide range of endoscopic devices intended for diagnosis and endosurgery and achieving a leading global position.[9] It had legions of salespeople with well-developed relationships with gastroenterologists.

Olympus's Endo Capsule was launched into the European market in 2006, and into the U.S. market in 2007. It offered higher-resolution imaging than the PillCam and real-time viewing, but the latter was seen as both an advantage and a disadvantage. On the one hand, immediacy can be important in some diagnostic situations; on the other hand, taking advantage of real-time viewing meant sitting with a gastroenterologist for the 8 to 12 hours it took the camera to traverse the patient's GI tract. Though Olympus was estimated to have only a 10% share of the global capsule endoscopy market, its size ($6.18 billion in revenues in 2014) meant it had far greater resources to deploy than did Given.

Chongqing Jinshan Science & Technology

Based in China, Chongqing Jinshan Science & Technology was founded in 1998 to produce digital medical devices and, as of 2015, primarily produced capsule endoscopy products and PH monitoring systems.[10] It sold its products in more than 60 countries in 2014, and held the majority share of the capsule endoscopy market in China.[11]

IntroMedic

Korea-based IntroMedic was founded in 2004 to focus entirely on the development of capsule endoscopes.[12] It had locations in the United States, Africa, Asia, Europe, Oceania, and the Middle East.[13] Its capsule endoscopy product, MicroCam, received FDA approval in 2012. It had revenues of $6.69 billion in 2014.[14]

Fujifilm Holdings

Like Olympus, Fujifilm was founded in Japan in 1919, and was an early entrant into film production. By the 1930s, it was producing 35 mm photographic film, 16 mm motion picture film, and x-ray film, and by the 1960s it had offices in Brazil, the United States, and Japan. By the 1980s, the company was aggressively developing medical diagnostic equipment and artificial "eyes" for robots, in addition to copiers, printers, and film. In 1999, Fuji developed the Sapientia, a digital endoscope system, followed by other endoscope products. In 2007,

Fujinon, a division of Fujifilm, signed a strategic R&D agreement with Given Imaging permitting Fujinon to distribute Given's PillCam in various countries, including China. In October 2012, Fujinon entered talks to acquire Given Imaging for $750 million. Given Imaging purportedly needed the cash, but ultimately announced that it would not sell (and Fujinon agreed to continue distributing Given's PillCam).

MANUFACTURING

Given manufactured the PillCam capsules in Yoqneam, Israel. The process included a number of steps in which components were assembled into subassemblies, then into the final product, and then inspected, tested, and packaged. Most processes were fully or semiautomated with machines that enabled high-volume manufacturing. A few products such as sensor arrays and computer workstations (for customers that purchased Given's software preloaded on a workstation) were purchased from external vendors and tested and customized at Given's facilities. While many of its inputs could be obtained from multiple suppliers, Given relied on sole suppliers for inputs such as its imaging sensor and transmitter for the PillCam.

MARKETING

Given's products were sold primarily to hospitals and gastroenterology offices. Though Given spent very little on advertising, the company benefited from significant free press due to the nature of its intriguing product. Articles compared the product to the movie *Fantastic Voyage*. On one occasion, in 2005, Katie Couric shared footage of her gastrointestinal system with viewers on the *Today Show*.[15] Similarly, in July 2012, BBC reporter Michael Mosley spent the entire day having live pictures of his gastrointestinal system transmitted to a public screen as an exhibit at the Science Museum in London.[16]

In 2013, Given launched its first ever direct-to-consumer marketing campaign. The center of the campaign is a website that attempts to explain Crohn's disease and the PillCam in a user-friendly way. Jonathan Huber, Given's vice president of global marketing, noted that one obstacle to getting customers to adopt the product

for use in identifying and managing Crohn's disease is that most people are unaware such a product exists. Many physicians already had training and equipment for traditional endoscopy methods rather than capsule endoscopy, and they were unlikely to volunteer information about the PillCam to patients if they did not already use the system. The PillCam, however, was significantly more comfortable than traditional endoscopy methods; Huber was confident that if patients knew about the PillCam alternative, they would bring it up with their doctor.

Given also employed a force of roughly 100 salespeople to call on gastrointestinal physicians, and offered free training programs and webinars for doctors and staff to teach them how to read the PillCam video output. Given routinely held 50 or more "physician events" annually to promote its products. Given also focused on generating clinical evidence of the effectiveness of the PillCam in diagnosing and monitoring Crohn's disease.

DISTRIBUTION

Given operated its own direct sales and marketing organizations in the United States, Germany, France, Australia, Brazil, Canada, Japan, Hong Kong, and Israel. It also used third-party distributors or independent sales representatives to sell in other countries (75 countries in total). Typically such distributors would be granted the exclusive right to sell Given's products in a particular country or region as long as they met minimum sales targets. Given would then be very reliant on that distributor for marketing the product in that region and ensuring that regulatory and reimbursement approvals were met.

A VIEW TO THE FUTURE

In early 2014, Given's PillCam COLON received regulatory approval in the United States and Japan (the world's second-largest health-care market), opening up the possibility for tremendous growth.[17] Colonoscopy was the largest category of the endoscopy market—in the United States alone, 14 million patients a year undergo a colonoscopy, and it was believed that even more people would undergo screening if it were more comfortable. Given thus had the potential to grow the market.

As of 2015, U.S. approval for the PillCam COLON was limited to "patients who had undergone incomplete colonoscopies," with regulators citing results that indicated the images from the camera pill were less clear than those produced by traditional colonoscopy. Many in the industry, however, suspected that the camera pill would eventually supplant all traditional colonoscopy.

In February 2014, Dublin-based medical device maker Covidien acquired Given Imaging for roughly $860 million,[18] and in early 2015 medical equipment giant Medtronic acquired Covidien for $49.9 billion (see financials for Given and Medtronic financials in Figures 2–5).[19] Given would now have access to much greater capital resources and larger (and more geographically distributed) salesforces: If it could continue to get its PillCams approved for more applications and in more countries, it was positioned to transform the market for gastrointestinal endoscopy.

Figure 2 Given Imaging's Revenues and Net Income, in $US Millions, 2003 to 2012

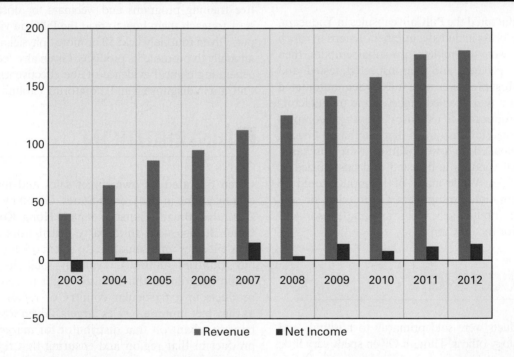

Figure 3 Given Imaging's Income Statement Data, in $US Thousands, 2008–2012

	2012	2011	2010	2009	2008
Revenues	180,501	177,955	157,809	141,763	125,108
Cost of revenues	(42,971)	(41,466)	(37,629)	(33,145)	(33,001)
Gross profit	**137,530**	**136,489**	**120,180**	**108,618**	**92,107**

	2012	2011	2010	2009	2008
Operating expenses:					
Research and development, gross	(25,627)	(26,129)	(21,695)	(17,842)	(15,126)
In-process research and development acquired in a business combination	—	—	—	—	(4,700)
Government grants	1,439	1,113	1,477	1,109	1,530
Research and development, net	(24,188)	(25,016)	(20,218)	(16,733)	(18,296)
Sales and marketing	(76,272)	(75,014)	(67,114)	(61,428)	(60,902)
General and administrative	(22,746)	(23,078)	(25,138)	(18,919)	(19,320)
Termination of marketing agreement	—	—	—	—	5,443
Other, net	(455)	(397)	(759)	(1,220)	(867)
Total operating expenses	**(123,661)**	**(123,505)**	**(113,229)**	**(98,300)**	**(93,942)**
Operating profit (loss)	13,869	12,984	6,951	10,318	(1,835)
Financial income, net	847	1,343	2,599	1,584	4,004
Profit before taxes on income	14,716	14,327	9,550	11,902	2,169
Income tax benefit (expense)	(459)	(2,158)	(1,362)	1,542	(250)
Net profit	**14,257**	**12,169**	**8,188**	**13,444**	**1,919**

Sources: Given Imaging, 20-F filing, 2013.

Figure 4 Given Imaging's Balance Sheet Data, in $US Thousands, 2008–2012

	2012	2011	2010	2009	2008
Cash and cash equivalents	35,442	24,285	34,619	46,458	31,697
Short term investments	58,446	64,762	51,973	31,736	28,509
Working capital	122,282	116,613	105,339	100,586	85,154
Long term marketable securities	30,188	16,003	3,873	16,956	30,063
Total assets	274,314	248,265	222,200	185,720	177,915
Long-term liabilities	14,552	13,202	13,266	5,886	5,084

(continued)

Figure 4 Given Imaging's Balance Sheet Data, in $US Thousands, 2008–2012 [*continued*]

	2012	2011	2010	2009	2008
Total liabilities	51,366	50,340	49,412	33,114	31,751
Retained earnings (accumulated deficit)[1]	1,621	(12,729)	(24,707)	(33,185)	(31,721)
Total shareholders' equity	222,948	197,634	172,688	151,928	144,171

[1] In March 2009, Given paid a dividend of approximately $15.8 million.
Sources: Given Imaging, 20-F filing, 2013.

Figure 5 Selected Financial Data for Medtronic, 2010–2014 (in $millions, except per-share data and additional information)

Operating Results for the Fiscal Year	2014	2013	2012	2011	2010
Net sales	$17,005	$16,590	$16,184	$15,508	$15,392
Cost of products sold	4,333	4,126	3,889	3,700	3,582
Gross margin percentage	74.5%	75.1%	76.0%	76.1%	76.7%
Research and development expense	$1,477	$1,557	$1,490	$1,472	$1,424
Selling, general, and administrative expense	5,847	5,698	5,623	5,427	5,282
Special charges	40				
Restructuring charges, net	78	172	87	259	50
Certain litigation charges, net	770	245	90	245	374
Acquisition-related items	117	(49)	12	14	23
Amortization of intangible assets	349	331	335	339	317
Other expense, net	181	108	364	110	150
Interest expense, net	108	151	149	278	246
Provision for income taxes	640	784	730	609	861
Earnings from continuing operations	3,065	3,467	3,415	3,055	3,083
Earnings from disc. operations, net of tax	—	—	202	41	16
Net earnings	$3,065	$3,467	$3,617	$3,096	$3,099

Sources: Medtronic 2014 10-K.

NOTES

1. This case was developed through a combination of publicly available materials and documents provided by Given Imaging. The author is grateful for the valuable assistance of Sharon Koninsky of Given Imaging.
2. G. J. Iddan and C. P. Swain, "History and Development of Capsule Endoscopy," *Gastrointestinal Endoscopy Clinics of North America* 14 (2004): 1–9.
3. Given Imaging Prospectus, 2004.
4. Anonymous, "Given Imaging," *Wall Street Transcript-Bear, Stearns & Co. 15th Annual Healthcare Special,* September 2002, pp. 203–206.
5. G. J. Iddan and C. P. Swain, "History and Development of Capsule Endoscopy."
6. Ibid.
7. G. Iddan, G. Meron, A. Glukhovsky, and P. Swain, "Wireless Capsule Endoscopy," *Nature* 405 (2000): 417.
8. M. Arnold, "A View to a Pill," *Medical Marketing & Media* June 1, 2013, pp. 27–30.
9. www.olympus.com.
10. www.jinshangroup.com, accessed March 10, 2015.
11. C. Pallardy, "4 Key Players in the U.S. Capsule Endoscopy Market," *Becker's GI & Endoscopy*, August 7, 2014. http://www.beckersasc.com/.
12. www.intromedic.com, accessed March 12, 2015.
13. C. Pallardy, "4 Key Players in the U.S. Capsule Endoscopy Market."
14. Hoovers.com, accessed March 10, 2015.
15. M. Arnold, "A View to a Pill."
16. M. Mosley, "The Second Brain in Our Stomachs," *BBC*, July 12, 2012. www.bbc.com.
17. www.accessdata.fda.gov/cdrh_docs/pdf12/K123666.pdf, accessed March 8, 2015.
18. J. Walker, "PillCam Maker Given Imaging to Be Bought by Covidien," *The Wall Street Journal*, December 8, 2013. www.wsj.com.
19. C. Riley, "Medtronic Buys Covidien for $2.9 Billion," *CNN Money*, June 15, 2014. www.cnnmoney.com.

SKULLCANDY

Founded in 2003 by Rick Alden, Skullcandy grew from a simple idea to a company with products distributed in approximately 80 countries and generating over $200 million in revenues annually. The company's core products, headphones with an extreme sport aesthetic, were sold in both specialty shops (e.g., skateboard, surf, and snowboard shops) and mass-market channels such as Target, Best Buy, college bookstores, and more, and its iconic skull logo was recognizable by its core youth market worldwide. Rather than the simplistic and streamlined ear buds that dominated the headphone category throughout the 1990s, many of Skullcandy's designs had large ear cups with integrated amplifiers, akin to those worn by disc jockeys. As Alden notes, one of their first set of headphones, the Skullcrushers, pro-

vided sound that "rattles your head and bleeds through your eyes. It's a damage-your-hearing kind of bass."[1] The headphones also came in bold colors and patterns (see Figure 1). Skullcandy had reinvented the headphone category from a commodity-like product to one that was highly differentiated and branded, with distinct designs that became as much about fashion and identity as functionality. As a result, Skullcandy headphones commanded much higher prices, and greater brand loyalty than typical headphones.

After the company's 2011 initial public offering, however, Skullcandy's founder Rick Alden left the company to pursue other entrepreneurial ventures (starting, among other projects, the company Stance, which makes high-performance sports socks with unique designs). This worried the young company's new stockholders. Furthermore, competitors began to eagerly imitate the Skullcandy strategy by developing large-ear-cup headphones with bolder aesthetics and higher prices. Analysts began to wonder just how far Skullcandy could go.

CREATING AN ACTION SPORTS BRAND

In 2001, veteran snowboarder Rick Alden was riding up a ski lift and listening to music on an MP3 player when he heard his phone ringing, muffled in

Figure 1 Skullcandy Product Examples

Style	In Ear	On Ear	Over Ear
Product			
Price Range	$10–80 MSRP	$20–100 MSRP	$60–300 MSRP
Models	Jib Ink'd 2 Riot Chops Smokin' Buds Titan 50/50 Fix Heavy Medal	Icon 3 Uprock Lowrider Cassette Navigator	Hesh Agent Skullcrusher Crusher Aviator Mix Master

Source: Skullcandy 10-K, 2013.

the pocket of his ski jacket. He fumbled around with his gloved hands, trying to get to the phone before it stopped ringing, worrying that he would drop either his gloves or his phone into the snow 30 feet below. At that moment he thought, "Why not have headphones that connect to both a cell phone and an MP3 player?"[2] In January 2002, he had his first prototype of a device called the "Link," built by a Chinese manufacturer. The device could plug into a cellphone and an MP3 player at the same time, and had a control switch on the cord with a microphone, a button that could switch between the phone and the MP3 player, and a volume control. The device was a hit. By January 2003, he had taken out two mortgages on his home to launch his company, Skullcandy, in Park City, Utah.[3]

Alden had an extensive background in the snowboarding industry, having previously founded National Snowboard Incorporated (one of the first companies to promote snowboarding) and having developed and marketed his own line of snowboard bindings. His father, Paul Alden, had played many roles in the industry, including serving as the president of the North American Snowboard Association, which helped open up ski resorts to snowboarders. His brother, David Alden, had been a professional

snowboarder for Burton and a sales representative for several snowboard lines. Thus, when Alden began creating an image and brand for the headphones, it only made sense to have a dynamic edginess that would attract snowboarders and skateboarders. Alden could also use his deep connections in the snowboarding and skateboarding worlds to line up endorsements by pro riders and distribution by skate and snowboard shops. As Alden notes, "I'd walk into snowboarding and skateboarding shops that I'd sold bindings to or that I'd known for 15 years," and say, "Hey, man, I think you ought to sell headphones." Soon he was developing headphones that were integrated into Giro ski and snowboard helmets, and MP3-equipped backpacks and watches. The graphic imagery of the brand—which draws from hip-hop culture and features a prominent skull—helped turn a once-placid product category into an exciting, important fashion accessory for action-sports enthusiasts.

The company grew quickly. By 2005, it broke $1 million in sales, and in the following year sold almost $10 million worth of headphones and accessories. In 2007, Alden pitched Skullcandy's products to Best Buy, Target, and Circuit City, never dreaming that all three would say "Yes" and place orders for their

U.S. stores. Suddenly the challenge was not selling, but production: Could the company deliver enough product on time? Alden's team went to China and quickly figured out a way to increase the tooling cavities used to produce the headphones so that they could get more units out of each production run. Remarkably, they were able to deliver to all three chains by their deadlines.[4] By the end of the year, Skullcandy had achieved $35 million in revenue, greatly exceeding even the stretch targets the company was shooting for. In 2008, almost 10 million people purchased Skullcandy headphones, for total sales of $86.5 million, and by 2009, it had already broken $100 million in sales. In the same year, Alden was named *Entrepreneur* magazine's "Entrepreneur of the Year."

Competition

Though Skullcandy had pioneered the market for action-sports headphones sold through specialty sports channels, in the mass-market channels it faced competition from major consumer-electronics brands that produced traditional headphones (e.g., Sony, Sennheiser, Bose) and new entrants that entered directly in response to Skullcandy's success (e.g., Beats by Dr. Dre). The former category had the advantage of greater financial and distribution resources, and greater economies of scale. The latter had benefited mostly by observing Skullcandy's strategies to fine-tune their own market entry. For example, whereas Alden had not originally thought people would be willing to pay hundreds of dollars for headphones, managers at Beats by Dr. Dre had correctly surmised that if people are willing to pay hundreds of dollars for designer sunglasses, they might be willing to do so also with headphones. Alden conceded, "We have to give them a lot of credit for figuring out that one."[5] In addition, some sports brands (e.g., Nike and Adidas) had begun offering headphones bearing their brands.

The functionality and style trends in headphones were relatively easy to quickly imitate. The key source of advantage, then, was to create brand loyalty among consumers and distributors. Alden noted that, though he had initially patented some individual headphone models or technologies, given the time lag between patent application and patent granting, and the expense involved in using patent attorneys, patenting didn't make much sense in his industry—he preferred to just beat his competitors to market with great products.[6]

Skullcandy Distribution

Alden was careful in his approach to selling to the mass market, vigilantly distinguishing between products that were sold to the core channel versus to big-box retailers.[7] Even though the core market only accounted for 10% of sales, they were disproportionately important to the reputation of the brand. Alden's philosophy was that "Conservative guys buy core products, but core guys will never buy conservative. In other words, we've got to be edgy and keep our original consumer happy, because without him, we'll lose people like me–old guys who want to buy cool young products too."[8] To achieve this, Skullcandy restricted sale of some of its products with the highest performance or edgiest designs to specialty action-sports retailers such as dedicated skateboard, snowboard, or surf shops, while releasing the rest of the product lineup to broader channels. This helped to ensure that snowboarders and skaters who bought the latest products at their local board shop were unlikely to see other types of customers with the same headphones, thus preserving some of the exclusivity of the brand. In 2013, it also dramatically cut distribution to discount channels, resulting in a major drop in sales for the year. The company's managers felt, however, that protecting the exclusivity of the brand was more important in the long run than preserving short-term revenue growth.

Marketing at Skullcandy

Skullcandy's marketing relied primarily on in-store advertising, trade shows, and sponsoring highly visible sports events, action-sports athletes, and music celebrities. Typical sponsorship contracts had a 1- to 3-year term, required sponsored individuals to maintain a visible and exclusive association with Skullcandy headphones, and granted Skullcandy the right to use their names and likenesses in its other marketing. These Skullcandy "ambassadors" also received cash payments for wearing Skullcandy products during public appearances, in magazine photo shoots, or on the podium after a sports victory. The company also made extensive use of social media such as Twitter, Instagram, Facebook, and YouTube to promote its products.

New Product Development at Skullcandy

To develop a new headphone line, Skullcandy put together teams that included knowledgeable end users, industrial designers, and "creatives." For example, in 2009, the company began to develop a headphone line that would target the hip hop music aficionado market by partnering with key music industry veterans such as Calvin "Snoop Dogg" Broadus and Michael "Mix Master Mike" Schwartz of the Beastie Boys. The collaboration with Snoop Dogg resulted in the "Skullcrusher"—a headphone with extreme bass amplification perfect for listening to rap music. The collaboration with Mix Master Mike was intended to produce the "ultimate DJ headphone," which would target disk jockeys/turntablists.

To develop the new product, a design team was assembled that included Mix Master Mike (who would lend insight into the key factors that would make the "ideal" DJ headphone, as well as lending his own personal design inspirations), Skullcandy's director of industrial design, Pete Kelly (who would translate the desired features into engineering specifications), an external industrial design company that could quickly transform the team's ideas into photorealistic renderings, product manager Josh Poulsen (who would manage the project milestones and communicate directly to the factory in China where the product would be manufactured), and team members with backgrounds in graphic arts or fine arts who would explore potential color palettes, materials, and form factors.

Skullcandy's small size and informal atmosphere ensured close contact between team members, and between the team and other Skullcandy personnel. For example, the director of industrial design and the art director shared an office, and all of the graphic designers worked in a common bullpen.[9] The team would schedule face-to-face meetings with Mix Master Mike and the external industrial design company. Josh Poulsen would travel to China for similar face-to-face meetings with the manufacturer.

In the first phase, the team met to analyze what functionalities would be key to making a compelling product. For the DJ headphones, the team identified the following key factors that would significantly improve headphone design[10]:

- Tough, replaceable, and/or washable ear pads made of antimicrobial materials (ear pads were prone to getting soiled or torn)
- Headphones that could be worn by "righty" or "lefty" DJs (DJs typically have a preference for leaning on one side while they work, and this side determines the optimal cable location)

- Sound quality that was not too clear, not too bass, and not too muddy (DJs typically were not looking for the clear quality of studio sound)
- Coiled cord or straight cord options (many DJs preferred coiled cords, whereas mass-market consumers typically preferred straight cords)

Above all, the team had the mandate given by Alden to create "headphones that don't look like headphones."

The product's aesthetic design was heavily influenced by Mix Master Mike. As noted by Dan Levine, "When you attach yourself to someone iconic, you try to figure out what inspires their form sensibilities. For example, Mike likes transformers, Japanese robots, Lamborghinis, furniture by B&B Italia . . . we use these design elements to build inspiration boards."[11] The team initially met for 3 straight days in Mix Master Mike's studio. Then, after the team had created 6 to 12 initial sketches, they worked to narrow the list down to three of the best, and then fine-tuned those until they had one best sketch. The external industrial design firm created photorealistic renderings that precisely portrayed what the end product was to look like. At this point, marketing people could be brought into the team to begin developing a marketing strategy around the product. The marketing team used "sneak peaks" of renderings and nonfunctioning prototypes to gain initial sales contracts.

The next phase was an iterative process of commercialization and design refinement. According to Levine, "That's when it feels like you're swimming in glue because it never happens fast enough. The design phase is exciting. Once you have that design you get impatient for it to come to market, but you can only work as fast as manufacturing capabilities dictate, and building technical products takes time."[12] First, CAD files would be brought to China, where a manufacturer would use a stereolithography apparatus (SLA) to create prototypes of each part of the headphone in a wax resin. As described by Alden, "You can't see the lasers–the part just rises up out of this primordial ooze. Then you can sand it down, paint it, screw it to your other parts. This part will end up costing $300 compared to the 30 cents the part will eventually cost when its mass produced using injection molding, but it's worth creating these SLA parts to make sure they're accurate."[13] SLA versions of the products were also often taken to the trade shows to solicit customer feedback and generate orders. Every week or two, the product manager would talk to the Chinese factory about building or modifying SLA parts, until eventually a 100% complete SLA product was achieved. At that point, it was time to begin "tooling" (the process of building molds that would be used to mass produce the product). This phase took 4 to 6 weeks to complete and was expensive. Several samples would be produced while final modifications were made, and then, once a perfect sample was obtained, the tools would be hardened and mass production would begin. As Alden described, "After you've got everything in place–after you've made the first one, then it's just like making doughnuts."[14]

All of the steps of the project were scheduled using a Gantt chart (a type of chart commonly used to depict project elements and their deadlines). Project deadlines were determined by working backward from a target market release date and the time required to manufacture the product in China.[15] In general, the firm sought to release new products in September (before the big Christmas sales season), which required having the tooling complete in July.

Team Roles and Management Product manager Josh Poulsen was responsible for coordinating all of the team members and making sure all deadlines were met. Every major design decision was passed up to Dan Levine for approval, and when the design was ready for tooling (being handed off to manufacturing), it had to be approved by Rick Alden, as this phase entailed large, irreversible investments. Most of the people at Skullcandy were involved with many projects simultaneously. As Levine emphasized, "This is a lean organization. At Nike you can work on a single or a few projects; when you have a brand that's small and growing fast, you work on a tremendous number of projects, and you also hire outside talent for some tasks."[16] According to Rick Alden, "We used to try to manage everything in-house, but we just don't have enough bodies. We've discovered that the fastest way to expand our development capacity is to use outside developers for portions of the work. We'll develop the initial idea, and then bring it to one of our trusted industrial design firms to do the renderings, for example."[17]

According to Alden, the biggest challenge associated with new product development is managing three different development cycles simultaneously:

You have your new stuff that you're coming out with that you haven't shown anyone yet–that's the really exciting stuff that everyone focuses on. Then you have the products you have just shown at the last show but that aren't done yet–maybe the manufacturing process isn't approved or the packaging isn't finished. You're taking orders but you haven't yet finished the development. Finally, you have all of the products you've been selling already but that require little improvements (e.g., altering how something is soldered, improving a cord, changing the packaging). We have so little bandwidth in product development that the big challenge has been managing all of these cycles. We just showed a product in January of this year [2009] that we still haven't delivered and its now May. We were just too excited to show it. But that's risky. If you don't deliver on time to a retailer, they get really angry and they won't keep your product on the shelf.[18]

Employee Reviews and Rewards

Team members did not receive financial rewards from individual projects. Instead, their performance was rewarded through recognition at monthly "Skullcouncil" meetings, and through quarterly "one touch" reviews. For the quarterly reviews, each employee would prepare a one-page "brag sheet" about what they had accomplished in the previous quarter, what they intended accomplish in the next quarter, and what their strengths and weaknesses were. These reviews were used to provide feedback to the employee and to determine the annual bonus: 75% of the annual bonus was based on the individual's performance, and 25% was based on overall company performance. According to Rick Alden, "In the early days, we did things very differently than we do now. Everyone received bonuses based on overall performance–there were so few of us that we all had a direct attachment to the bottom line. Now with a bigger staff, we have to rely more on individual metrics, and we have to provide quarterly feedback so that the amount of the annual bonus doesn't come as a surprise."[19] The company also relied on less conventional incentives. Each year, the board of directors would set an overarching stretch target for revenues, and if the company surpassed it,

Alden took the whole company on a trip. In 2006, he took everyone heli-boarding (an extreme sport where snowboarders are brought to the top of a snow-covered peak by helicopter). When the company achieved nearly triple its 2007 sales goal (earning $35 million instead of the targeted $13 million), Alden took the entire staff and their families to Costa Rica to surf.[20]

THE FUTURE OF SKULLCANDY

Alden had always been, first and foremost, an entrepreneur. Chafing under the direction of others, Alden had early in his life concluded that he was "completely unemployable" and set about creating his own economic opportunities. As an archetypal serial entrepreneur, he was happier creating new companies than managing established companies. In 2009, as the IPO process was unfolding, he noted to Jeremy Andrus (who had been with the company since 2005 and served as COO since 2008), "There are other entrepreneurial enterprises I'd like to focus on. I don't think I'll be sitting in public CEO seat for the next five years–it's time to do something different."[21] Thus, 1 month after the IPO filing in January 2009, Alden startled the investment community by resigning as the CEO of Skullcandy (though he remained on the board of directors). Andrus initially replaced Alden at the helm of Skullcandy, as Alden left to work closely with his new start-up, Stance socks. In 2013, Hoby Darling joined the company as chief executive officer. Darling had deep brand, product, and distribution experience, having previously worked with Nike+ (the digital innovation group at Nike) and Volcom apparel company. He was also a "tough-minded optimist" who got up every morning at 4:30 a.m. to do CrossFit, and he was eager to take on the challenge of running Skullcandy.[22]

In the years that followed, management at Skullcandy sought to expand both its product portfolio and its global reach. Though Skullcandy generated the vast majority of its revenues from headphones, the company also offered branded apparel, smartphone cases, and docking stations. Skullcandy also began to sell headphones designed specifically for videogaming (and acquired gaming handset manufacturer Astro Gaming for $10 million in early 2011),

and worked with partners to incorporate Skullcandy-branded technology into computers (with Toshiba), helmets, and bags. It also formed partnerships with rapper Jay-Z's Roc Nation, the NBA, the NCAA, and the Hard Rock Hotel and Casino.[23]

The company also began to expand more aggressively internationally. Though prior to 2011 the company had only worked with third-party distributors to sell product into international markets, Skullcandy's management believed that such distributors were not invested in stewarding the brand. They thus used some of the capital raised through the IPO to buy Skullcandy's European distributor (Kungsbacka 57 AB, which held an exclusive distribution license to sell Skullcandy products in Europe), and began making investments in brand, marketing, and infrastructure in order to accelerate growth in Europe. Skullcandy also began marketing directly to Mexico, Japan, and China, and began sponsoring international athletes, musicians, and artists. By 2015, Skullcandy products could be found in roughly 80 countries, and the company was earning roughly 25% of its sales in markets outside of North America.

Though the Skullcandy name was becoming more and more well known, and its products were available in an ever-wider range of outlets, investors still had concerns. Though revenues had continued to increase, so had competition, and Skullcandy's net margin had decreased from 18% and 17% in 2007 and 2008, respectively, to 4% in 2014 (see Figure 2).[24] Furthermore, as noted previously, a decision to cut its sales to low-price channels resulted in a significant drop in sales in 2013 that resulted in the company posting losses for the year. Apple's 2014 announcement that it would acquire Beats by Dre also had analysts questioning what impact this would have on Skullcandy—Apple's reach and branding expertise was unparalleled.[25] As a result, Skullcandy's stock price had fallen from its IPO price of $20 per share to $10.75 per share in March 2015 (see Figure 3). The young, fast-growing company was making the transition to adulthood, and it was anyone's guess what that adulthood look like. Would it continue to grow and diversify, leveraging the brand profitably to more product categories? Would it stay focused and lean, deepening its presence primarily in action-sports headphones and accessories? Or would it stumble, enabling competitors to displace it in the market it had pioneered? The next few years would be pivotal ones as the answers to these questions emerged.

Figure 2 Skullcandy Revenues and Net Income, 2005–2014

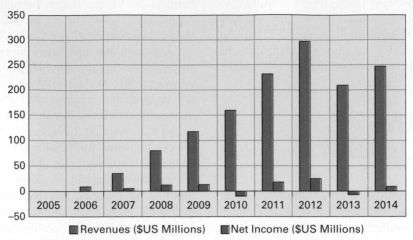

Source: Skullcandy 10-K, 2013, 2014; Rick Alden for early revenue numbers.

Figure 3 Skullcandy Stock Price and Trading Volume, September 2012–March 2015

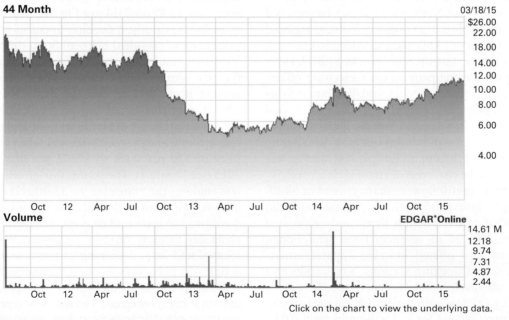

Click on the chart to view the underlying data.

Source: Nasdaq.com.

NOTES

1. R. Alden, "How I Did It," *Inc.,* September 2008.
2. A. Osmond, "Rick Alden: Founder & CEO of Skullcandy," *Launch*, March/April 2007.
3. Interview with Rick Alden, May 5, 2009.
4. R. Alden, "How I Did It."
5. R. Alden, "Breakthrough Strategic Thinking," speech given at New York University Executive Education Seminar, October 2012.
6. Interview with Rick Alden, February 2012.
7. Anonymous, "Caught on Tape: Rick Alden, CEO of Skullcandy," *Transworld Business*, October 24, 2008.
8. R. Alden, "How I Did It."
9. Interview with Dan Levine, May 2, 2009.
10. Ibid.
11. Ibid.
12. Ibid.
13. Ibid.
14. Ibid.
15. Ibid.
16. Ibid.
17. Ibid.
18. Ibid.
19. Ibid.
20. Ibid.
21. M. Lewis, "Skullcandy CEO Jeremy Andrus Breaks the Silent Period," *Transworld Business,* August 29, 2011.
22. C. Bessette, "10 Questions: Hoby Darling, CEO, Skullcandy," fortune.com, July 18, 2014.
23. Hoovers.com, accessed March 13, 2015.
24. Skullcandy 10-K Reports, 2013 and 2015.
25. B. Geier, "Where Does Apple Deal Leave Beats' Rivals?" fortune.com, April 12, 2014.

16

TOYOTA: LEAN PRODUCTION AND THE RISE OF THE WORLD'S LARGEST AUTOMOBILE MANUFACTURER

▰ INTRODUCTION

The growth of Toyota has been one of the great success stories of Japanese industry during the last half century. In 1947, the company was a little-known domestic manufacturer producing around 100,000 vehicles a year. In 2012, Toyota sold 9.4 million light vehicles globally, making it the largest automobile manufacturer in the world, ahead of Volkswagen with 9.1 million units sold and GM with 7.7 million units.

For all of its success, however, recent years have been challenging for Toyota. As a consequence of the global financial crisis, demand for vehicles fell sharply in 2008 and 2009, pushing most of the world's major automobile companies into the red. GM, one of Toyota's main global rivals, filed for Chapter 11 bankruptcy protection in 2009. However, the GM that emerged from Chapter 11 2 years later was a leaner, more viable competitor to Toyota. At the same time, the South Korean company, Hyundai-Kia, emerged from the financial crisis in a strong position as the fourth-largest automobile manufacturer in the world and the most profitable. Volkswagen too was strength-

ening its position and closing in on Toyota in terms of sales volume.

Not only did Toyota face stronger global rivals than hitherto, its own position was damaged when a series of product recalls, mostly in the United States, tarnished its brand and corporate image. The most infamous of these was the "sticky accelerator pedal" issue that allegedly led to sudden uncontrolled vehicle acceleration and in some cases serious accidents. Toyota recalled some 9 million vehicles to in 2009–2010, the largest product recall in industry history, and temporarily suspended some sales while it tried to identify and solve the issue. An investigation by the U.S. National Highway Transport & Safety Agency found no electronic fault with Toyota's "drive-by-wire" throttle system, which was initially blamed for the issue, and instead attributed the problem to mechanical causes (including pedals caught under floor mats), and "driver error." Irrespective of the failure to identify a clear cause, in 2012 Toyota agreed to pay $1.1 billion to settle a class action lawsuit related to the issue. More importantly perhaps, Toyota's legendary reputation for product quality had taken a major blow. The questions facing Toyota's management were, how could they reestablish the company as the undisputed leader in quality, and how could they fend off stronger competitors in a rapidly globalizing marketplace?

THE ORIGINS OF TOYOTA

The original idea behind the founding of the Toyota Motor Company came from the fertile mind of Toyoda Sakichi.[1] The son of a carpenter, Sakichi was an entrepreneur and inventor whose primary interest lay in the textile industry, but he had been intrigued by automobiles since a visit to the United States in 1910. Sakichi's principal achievement was the invention of an automatic loom that held the promise of being able to lower the costs of weaving high-quality cloth. In 1926, Sakichi set up Toyoda Automatic Loom to manufacture this product. In 1930, he sold the patent rights to a British textile concern, Platt Brothers, for about 1 million yen, a considerable sum in those days. Sakichi urged his son, Toyoda Kiichiro, to use this money to study the possibility of manufacturing automobiles in Japan. In 1930, Kiichiro, a mechanical engineer with a degree from the University of Tokyo, became managing director of loom production at Toyoda Automatic Loom.

Kiichiro was at first reluctant to invest in automobile production. The Japanese market was at that time dominated by Ford and General Motors, both of which imported knock-down car kits from the United States and assembled them in Japan. Given this, the board of Toyoda Automatic Loom, including Kiichiro's brother-in-law and the company's president, Kodama Risaburo, opposed the investment on the grounds that it was too risky. Kiichiro probably would not have pursued the issue further had not his father made a deathbed request in 1930 that Kiichiro explore the possibilities of automobile production. Kiichiro had to push but, in 1933, he secured permission to set up an automobile department within Toyoda Automatic Loom.

Kiichiro's belief was that he would be able to figure out how to manufacture automobiles by taking apart U.S.-made vehicles and examining them piece by piece. He also felt that it should be possible to adapt U.S. mass-production technology to manufac-

ture cost efficiently at lower volumes. His confidence was based in large part upon the already considerable engineering skills and capabilities at his disposal through Toyoda Automatic Loom. Many of the precision engineering and manufacturing skills needed in automobile production were similar to the skills required to manufacture looms.

Kiichiro produced his first 20 vehicles in 1935, and in 1936 the automobile department produced 1,142 vehicles—910 trucks, 100 cars, and 132 buses. At this time, however, the production system was essentially craft based rather than a modern assembly line. Despite some progress, the struggle might still have been uphill had not fate intervened in the form of the Japanese military. Japan had invaded Manchuria in 1931 and quickly found American-made trucks useful for moving men and equipment. As a result, the military felt that it was strategically important for Japan to have its own automobile industry. The result was the passage of an automobile manufacturing law in 1936 that required companies producing more than 3,000 vehicles per year in Japan to get a license from the government. Moreover, to get a license, over 50% of the stock had to be owned by Japanese investors. The law also placed a duty on imported cars, including the knock-down kits that Ford and GM brought into Japan. As a direct result of this legislation, both GM and Ford exited the Japanese market in 1939.

Once the Japanese government passed this law, Kodama Risaburo decided that the automobile venture could be profitable and switched from opposing to proactively supporting Kiichiro (in fact, Risaburo's wife, who was Kiichiro's elder sister, had been urging him to take this step for some time). The first priority was to attract the funds necessary to build a mass-production facility. In 1937, Risaburo and Kiichiro decided to incorporate the automobile department as a separate company in order to attract outside investors—which they were successful in doing. Kiichiro Toyoda was appointed president of the new company. The company was named the Toyota Motor Company. (The founding family's name, "Toyoda," means "abundant rice field" in Japanese. The new name had no meaning in Japanese.)

Upon incorporation, Risaburo and Kiichiro's vision was that Toyota should expand its passenger car production as quickly as possible. However, once again fate intervened in the form of the Japanese military. Toyota had barely begun passenger car production when war broke out; in 1939, the Japanese government, on advice from the military, prohibited passenger car production and demanded that the company specialize in the production of military trucks.

THE EVOLUTION OF THE TOYOTA PRODUCTION SYSTEM

After the end of World War II, Kiichiro was determined that Toyota should reestablish itself as a manufacturer of automobiles.[2] Toyota, however, faced a number of problems in doing this:

1. The Japanese domestic market was too small to support efficient-scale, mass-production facilities such as those common in America by that time.
2. The Japanese economy was starved for capital, which made it difficult to raise funds to finance new investments.
3. New labor laws introduced by the American occupiers increased the bargaining power of labor and made it difficult for companies to lay off workers.
4. North America and Western Europe were full of large auto manufacturers eager to establish operations in Japan.

In response to the last point, in 1950, the new Japanese government prohibited direct foreign investment in the automobile industry and imposed high tariffs on the importation of foreign cars. This protection, however, did little to solve the other problems facing the company at this time.

Limitations of Mass Production

At this juncture, a remarkable mechanical engineer entered the scene: Taiichi Ohno. More than anyone else, it was Ohno who was to work out a response to the above problems. Ohno had joined Toyoda Spinning and Weaving in 1932 as a production engineer in cotton thread manufacture and entered Toyota when the former company was absorbed into the latter in

1943. Ohno worked in auto production for 2 years, was promoted and managed auto assembly and machine shops between 1945 and 1953, and in 1954 was appointed a company director.

When Taiichi Ohno joined Toyota, the mass-production methods pioneered by Ford had become the accepted method of manufacturing automobiles. The basic philosophy behind mass production was to produce a limited product line in massive quantities to gain maximum economies of scale. The economies came from spreading the fixed costs involved in setting up the specialized equipment required to stamp body parts and manufacture components over as large a production run as possible. Since setting up much of the equipment could take a full day or more, the economies involved in long production runs were reckoned to be considerable. Thus, for example, Ford would stamp 500,000 right-hand door panels in a single production run, and then store the parts in warehouses until they were needed in the assembly plant, rather than stamp just those door panels that were needed immediately and then change the settings and stamp out left-hand door panels or other body parts.

A second feature of mass production was that each assembly worker should perform only a single task, rather than a variety of tasks. The idea was that, as the worker became completely familiar with a single task, he could perform it much faster, thereby increasing labor productivity. Assembly-line workers were overseen by a foreman who did not perform any assembly tasks but instead ensured that workers followed orders. In addition, a number of specialists were employed to perform nonassembly operations such as tool repair, die changes, quality inspection, and general "housecleaning."

After working at Toyota for 5 years and visiting Ford's U.S. plants, Ohno became convinced that the basic mass-production philosophy was flawed. He saw five problems with the mass-production system:

1. Long production runs created massive inventories that had to be stored in large warehouses. This was expensive both because of the cost of warehousing and because inventories tied up capital in unproductive uses.
2. If the initial machine settings were wrong, long production runs resulted in the production of a large number of defects.

3. The sheer monotony of assigning assembly-line workers to a single task generated defects, since workers became lax about quality control. In addition, since workers were not responsible for quality control, they had little incentive to minimize defects.

4. The extreme division of labor resulted in the employment of specialists such as foremen, quality inspectors, and tooling specialists, whose jobs logically could be performed by assembly-line workers.

5. The mass-production system was unable to accommodate consumer preferences for product diversity.

In addition to these flaws, Ohno knew that the small domestic market in Japan and the lack of capital for investing in mass-production facilities made the American model unsuitable for Toyota.

Reducing Setup Times

Given these flaws and the constraints that Toyota faced, Ohno decided to take a fresh look at the techniques used for automobile production. His first goal was to try to make it economical to manufacture auto body parts in small batches. To do this, he needed to reduce the time it took to set up the machines for stamping out body parts. Ohno and his engineers began to experiment with a number of techniques to speed up the time it took to change the dies in stamping equipment. This included using rollers to move dies in and out of position, along with a number of simple adjustment mechanisms to fine-tune the settings. These techniques were relatively simple to master, so Ohno directed production workers to perform the die changes themselves. This in itself reduced the need for specialists and eliminated the idle time that workers previously had enjoyed while waiting for the dies to be changed.

Through a process of trial and error, Ohno succeeded in reducing the time required to change dies on stamping equipment from a full day to 15 minutes by 1962, and to as little as 3 minutes by 1971. By comparison, even in the early 1980s, many American and European plants required anywhere between 2 and 6 hours to change dies on stamping equipment. As a consequence, American and European plants found it economical to manufacture in lots equivalent to 10 to 30 days' supply and to reset equipment only every other day. In contrast, since Toyota could change the dies on stamping equipment in a matter of minutes, it manufactured in lots equivalent to just 1 day's supply, while resetting equipment three times per day.

Not only did these innovations make small production runs economical, but they also had the added benefit of reducing inventories and improving product quality. Making small batches eliminated the need to hold large inventories, thereby reducing warehousing costs and freeing up scarce capital for investment elsewhere. Small production runs and the lack of inventory also meant that defective parts were produced only in small numbers and entered the assembly process almost immediately. This had the added effect of making workers in the stamping shops far more attentive to quality. In addition, once it became economical to manufacture small batches of components, much greater variety could be included in the final product at little or no cost penalty.

Organization of the Workplace

One of Ohno's first innovations was to group the workforce into teams. Each team was given a set of assembly tasks to perform, and team members were trained to perform each task for which the team was responsible. Each team had a leader who was also an assembly-line worker. In addition to coordinating the team, the team leader was expected to perform basic assembly-line tasks and to fill in for any absent worker. The teams were given the job of housecleaning, minor tool repair, and quality inspection (along with the training required to perform these tasks). Time was also set aside for team members to discuss ways to improve the production process (the practice now referred to as "quality circles").

The immediate effect of this approach was to reduce the need for specialists in the workplace and to create a more flexible workforce in which individual assembly-line workers were not treated simply as human machines. All of this resulted in increased worker productivity.

None of this would have been possible had it not been for an agreement reached between management and labor after a 1950 strike. The strike was brought on by management's attempt to cut the workforce by 25% (in response to a recession in Japan). After lengthy negotiations, Toyota and the union worked out a compromise. The workforce was cut by 25%, as originally proposed, but the remaining employees were given two guarantees: one for lifetime employment and the other for pay graded by seniority and tied to company profitability through bonus payments. In exchange for these guarantees, employees agreed to be flexible in work assignments. In turn, this allowed for the introduction of the team concept.

Improving Quality

One standard practice in the mass-production auto assembly plants was to fix errors that occurred during assembly in a rework area at the end of the assembly line. Errors routinely occurred in most assembly plants either because bad parts were installed or because good parts were installed incorrectly. The belief was that stopping an assembly line to fix such errors would cause enormous bottlenecks in the production system. Thus, it was thought to be more efficient to correct errors at the end of the line.

Ohno viewed this system as wasteful for three reasons: (1) since workers understood that any errors would be fixed at the end of the line, they had little incentive to correct errors themselves; (2) once a defective part had been embedded in a complex vehicle, an enormous amount of rework might be required to fix it; and (3) since defective parts were often not discovered until the end of the line when the finished cars were tested, a large number of cars containing the same defect may have been built before the problem was found.

In an attempt to eliminate this practice, Ohno sought ways to reduce the amount of rework at the end of the line. His approach involved two elements. First, he placed a cord above every workstation and instructed workers to stop the assembly line if a problem emerged that could not be fixed. It then became the responsibility of the whole team to work on the problem. Second, team members were taught to trace every defect back to its ultimate cause and then to ensure that the problem was fixed so that it would not reoccur.

Initially, this system produced enormous disruption. The production line was stopping all the time, and workers became discouraged. However, as team members gained experience in identifying problems and tracing them back to their root cause, the number of errors began to drop dramatically and stops in the line became much rarer. Today, in most Toyota plants, the line virtually never stops.

Developing the Kanban System

Once reduced setup times had made small production runs economical, Ohno began to look for ways to coordinate the flow of production within the Toyota manufacturing system so that the amount of inventory in the system could be reduced to a minimum. Toyota produced about 25% of its major components in-house (the rest were contracted out to independent suppliers). Ohno's initial goal was to arrange for components and/or subassemblies manufactured in-house to be delivered to the assembly floor only when they were needed, and not before (this goal was later extended to include independent suppliers).

To achieve this, in 1953, Ohno began experimenting with what came to be known as the kanban system. Under the kanban system, component parts are delivered to the assembly line in containers. As each container is emptied, it is sent back to the previous step in the manufacturing process. This then becomes the signal to make more parts. The system minimizes work in progress by increasing inventory turnover. The elimination of buffer inventories also means that defective components show up immediately in the next process. This facilitates the process of tracing defects back to their source and correcting the problem before too many defects are made. Moreover, the elimination of buffer stocks, by removing all safety nets, makes it imperative that problems be solved before they become serious enough to jam up the production process, thereby creating a strong incentive for workers to ensure that errors are corrected as quickly as possible. In addition, by decentralizing responsibility for coordinating the manufacturing process to lower-level employees, the kanban system does away with the need for extensive centralized management to coordinate the flow of parts between the various stages of production.

After perfecting the kanban system in one of Toyota's machine shops, Ohno had a chance to apply the system broadly in 1960 when he was made general manager of the Motomachi assembly plant. Ohno already had converted the machining, body stamping, and body shops to the kanban system, but since many parts came from shops that had yet to adopt the system, or from outside suppliers, the impact on inventories was initially minimal. However, by 1962, he had extended kanban to forging and casting, and between 1962 and 1965, he began to bring independent suppliers into the system.

Organizing Suppliers

Assembly of components into a final vehicle accounts for only about 15% of the total manufacturing process in automobile manufacture. The remaining 85% of the process involves manufacturing more than 10,000 individual parts and assembling them into about 100 major components such as engines, suspension systems, transaxles, and so on. Coordinating this process so that everything comes together at the right time has always been a problem for auto manufacturers. Historically, the response at Ford and GM to this problem was massive vertical integration. The belief was that control over the supply chain would allow management to coordinate the flow of component parts into the final assembly plant. In addition, American firms held the view that vertical integration made them more efficient by reducing their dependence on other firms for materials and components and by limiting their vulnerability to opportunistic overcharging.

As a consequence of this philosophy, even as late as the mid-1990s, General Motors made 68% of its components in-house, while Ford made 50% (in the late 1990s, both GM and Ford de-integrated, spinning off many of their in-house supply operations as independent enterprises). When they didn't vertically integrate, U.S. auto companies historically tried to reduce the procurement costs that remain through competitive bidding—several companies to submit contracts and placing orders with suppliers offering the lowest price.

Under the leadership of Kiichiro Toyoda during the 1930s and 1940s, Toyota followed the American model and pursued extensive vertical integration into the manufacture of component parts. In fact, Toyota had little choice in this matter, because only a handful of Japanese companies were able to make the necessary components. However, the low volume of production during this period meant that the scale of integration was relatively small. In the 1950s, however, the volume of auto production began to increase dramatically. This presented Toyota with a dilemma: Should the company increase its capacity to manufacture components in-house, in line with the growth in auto production, or should it contract out?

In contrast to American practice, the company decided that, while it should increase in-house capacity for essential subassemblies and bodies, it would do better to contract out for most components. Four reasons seemed to bolster this decision:

1. Toyota wanted to avoid the capital expenditures required to expand capacity to manufacture a wide variety of components.
2. It wanted to reduce risk by maintaining a low factory capacity in case factory sales slumped.
3. It wanted to take advantage of the lower wage scales in smaller firms.
4. Toyota managers realized that in-house manufacturing offered few benefits if it was possible to find stable, high-quality, low-cost external sources of component supply.

At the same time, Toyota managers felt that the American practice of inviting competitive bids from suppliers was self-defeating. While competitive bidding might achieve the lowest short-run costs, the practice of playing suppliers off against each other did not guarantee stable supplies, high quality, or cooperation beyond existing contracts to solve design or engineering problems. Ohno and other Toyota managers believed that real efficiencies could be achieved if the company entered into long-term relationships with major suppliers. This would allow them to introduce the kanban system, thereby further reducing inventory holding costs and realizing the same kind of quality benefits that Toyota was already beginning to encounter with its in-house supply operations. In addition, Ohno wanted to bring suppliers into the design process because he believed they might suggest ways of improving the design of component parts based upon their own manufacturing experience.

As it evolved during the 1950s and 1960s, Toyota's strategy toward its suppliers had several elements. The company spun off some of its in-house supply operations into quasi-independent entities in which it took a minority stake, typically holding between 20 and 40% of the stock. It then recruited a number of independent companies with a view to establishing a long-term relationship with them for the supply of critical components. Sometimes, but not always, Toyota took a minority stake in these companies as well. All of these companies were designated as "first-tier suppliers." First-tier suppliers were responsible for working with Toyota as an integral part of the new product development team. Each first tier was responsible for the formation of a "second tier" of suppliers under its direction. Companies in the second tier were given the job of fabricating individual parts.

Both first- and second-tier suppliers were formed into supplier associations.

By 1986, Toyota had three regional supply organizations in Japan with 62, 135, and 25 first-tier suppliers. A major function of the supplier associations was to share information regarding new manufacturing, design, or materials management techniques among themselves. Concepts such as statistical process control, total quality control, and computer-aided design were rapidly diffused among suppliers by this means.

Toyota also worked closely with its suppliers, providing them with management expertise, engineering expertise, and sometimes capital to finance new investments. Critical to this relationship were the incentives that Toyota established to encourage its suppliers to focus on realizing continuous process improvements. The basic contract for a component would be for 4 to 5 years, with the price being agreed upon in advance. If by joint efforts the supplier and Toyota succeeded in reducing the costs of manufacturing the components, the additional profit would be shared between the two. If the supplier by its own efforts came up with an innovation that reduced costs, the supplier would keep the additional profit that the innovation generated for the lifetime of the contract.

As a consequence of this strategy, Toyota outsourced more production than almost any other major auto manufacturer. By the late 1980s, Toyota was responsible for only about 27% of the value going into a finished automobile, with the remainder coming from outside suppliers. In contrast, at the time General Motors was responsible for about 70% of the value going into a finished automobile. Other consequences included long-term improvements in productivity and quality among Toyota's suppliers that were comparable to the improvements achieved by Toyota itself. In particular, extension of the kanban system to include suppliers, by eliminating buffer inventory stocks, in essence forced suppliers to focus more explicitly on the quality of their product.

Consequences

The consequences of Toyota's production system included a surge in labor productivity and a decline in the number of defects per car. Figure 1 compares the number of vehicles produced per worker at General Motors, Ford, Nissan, and Toyota between 1965 and 1983.

These figures are adjusted for the degree of vertical integration pursued by each company. As can be seen, in 1960, productivity at Toyota already outstripped that of Ford, General Motors, and its main Japanese competitor, Nissan. As Toyota refined its production system over the next 18 years, productivity doubled. In comparison, productivity essentially stood still at General Motors and Ford during the same period.

Figure 2 provides another way to assess the superiority of Toyota's production system. Here the performance of Toyota's Takaoka plant is compared

Figure 1 Vehicles Produced per Worker (adjusted for vertical integration), 1965–1983

Year	General Motors	Ford	Nissan	Toyota
1965	5.0	4.4	4.3	8.0
1970	3.7	4.3	8.8	13.4
1975	4.4	4.0	9.0	15.1
1979	4.5	4.2	11.1	18.4
1980	4.1	3.7	12.2	17.8
1983	4.8	4.7	11.0	15.0

Source: M. A. Cusumano, *The Japanese Automotive Industry* (Cambridge, Mass.: Harvard University Press, 1989), p. 197.

Figure 2 General Motors's Framingham Plant versus Toyota's Takaoka Plant, 1987

	GM Framingham	Toyota Takaoke
Assembly hours per car	31	16
Assembly defects per 100 cars	135	45
Inventory of parts	2 weeks	2 hours

Source: J. P. Womack, D. T. Jones, and D. Roos, *The Machine That Changed the World* (New York: Macmillan, 1990), p. 83.

with that of General Motors's Framingham plant in 1987. As can be seen, the Toyota plant was more productive, produced far fewer defects per 100 cars, and kept far less inventory on hand.

A further aspect of Toyota's production system is that the short setup times made it economical to manufacture a much wider range of models than is feasible at a traditional mass-production assembly plant. In essence, Toyota soon found that it could supply much greater product variety than its competitors with little in the way of a cost penalty. In 1990, Toyota was offering consumers around the world roughly as many products as General Motors (about 150), even though Toyota was still only half GM's size. Moreover, it was doing this at a lower cost than GM.

DISTRIBUTION AND CUSTOMER RELATIONS

Toyota's approach to its distributors and customers as it evolved during the 1950s and 1960s was in many ways just as radical as its approach toward suppliers. In 1950, Toyota formed a subsidiary, Toyota Motor Sales, to handle distribution and sales. The new subsidiary was headed by Kaymiya Shotaro from its inception until 1975. Kaymiya's philosophy was that dealers should be treated as "equal partners" in the Toyota family. To back this up, he had Toyota Motor Sales provide a wide range of sales training and service training for dealership personnel.

Kaymiya then used the dealers to build long-term ties with Toyota's customers. The ultimate aim was to bring customers into the Toyota design and

production process. To this end, through its dealers, Toyota Motor Sales assembled a huge database on customer preferences. Much of the data came from monthly or semiannual surveys conducted by dealers asking Toyota customers about their preferences for styling, model types, colors, prices, and other features. Toyota also used these surveys to estimate the potential demand for new models. This information was then fed directly into the design process.

Kaymiya began this process in 1952, when the company was redesigning its Toyopet model. The Toyopet was primarily used by urban taxi drivers. Toyota Motor Sales surveyed taxi drivers to try to find out what type of vehicle they preferred. They wanted something reliable, inexpensive, and with good city fuel mileage—which Toyota engineers then set about designing. In 1956, Kaymiya formalized this process when he created a unified department for planning and market research whose function was to coordinate the marketing strategies developed by researchers at Toyota Motor Sales with product planning by Toyota's design engineers. From this time on, marketing information played a critical role in the design of Toyota's cars and in the company's strategy. In particular, it was the research department at Toyota Motor Sales that provided the initial stimulus for Toyota to start exporting during the late 1960s after predicting, correctly, that growth in domestic sales would slow down considerably during the 1970s.

Expanding Internationally

Large-scale overseas expansion did not become feasible at Toyota until the late 1960s, for one principal reason: Despite the rapid improvement in productivity, Japanese cars were still not competitive.[3] In 1957, for example, the Toyota Corona sold in Japan for the equivalent of $1,694. At the same time, the Volkswagen Beetle sold for $1,111 in West Germany, while Britain's Austin company was selling its basic model for the equivalent of $1,389 in Britain. Foreign companies were effectively kept out of the Japanese market, however, by a 40% value-added tax and shipping costs.

Despite these disadvantages, Toyota tried to enter the U.S. market in the late 1950s. The company set up a U.S. subsidiary in California in October 1957 and began to sell cars in early 1958, hoping to capture the American small-car market (which at that time was poorly served by the U.S. automobile companies). The result was a disaster. Toyota's cars performed poorly in road tests on U.S. highways. The basic problem was that the engines of Toyota's cars were too small for prolonged, high-speed driving and tended to overheat and burn oil, while the poorly designed chassis resulted in excessive vibration. Sales were slow and, in 1964, Toyota closed its U.S. subsidiary and withdrew from the market.

The company was determined to learn from its U.S. experience and quickly redesigned several of its models based on feedback from American consumer surveys and U.S. road tests. As a result, by 1967, the picture had changed considerably. The quality of Toyota's cars was now sufficient to make an impact in the U.S. market, while production costs and retail prices had continued to fall and were now comparable with international competitors in the small-car market.

In the late 1960s, Toyota reentered the U.S. market. Although sales were initially slow, they increased steadily. Then the OPEC-engineered, four-fold increase in oil prices that followed the 1973 Israeli-Arab conflict gave Toyota an unexpected boost. U.S. consumers began to turn to small, fuel-efficient cars in droves, and Toyota was one of the main beneficiaries. Driven primarily by a surge in U.S. demand, worldwide exports of Toyota cars increased from 157,882 units in 1967 to 856,352 units by 1974 and to 1,800,923 units by 1984. Put another way, in 1967 exports accounted for 19% of Toyota's total output. By 1984, they accounted for 52.5%.

Success brought its own problems. By the early 1980s, political pressures and talk of local content regulations in the United States and Europe were forcing an initially reluctant Toyota to rethink its exporting strategy. Toyota already had agreed to "voluntary" import quotas with the United States in 1981. The consequence for Toyota was stagnant export growth between 1981 and 1984. Against this background, in the early 1980s Toyota began to think seriously about setting up manufacturing operations overseas.

Transplant Operations

Toyota's first overseas operation was a 50-50 joint venture with General Motors established in February 1983 under the name New United Motor Manufacturing, Inc. (NUMMI). NUMMI, based in Fremont, California, began producing Chevrolet Nova cars for GM in December 1984.[4] The maximum capacity of the Fremont plant is about 250,000 cars per year.

For Toyota, the joint venture provided a chance to find out whether it could build quality cars in the United States using American workers and American suppliers. It also provided Toyota with experience dealing with an American union (the United Auto Workers Union) and with a means of circumventing "voluntary" import restrictions. For GM, the venture provided an opportunity to observe in full detail the Japanese approach to manufacturing. While GM's role was marketing and distributing the plant's output, Toyota designed the product and designed, equipped, and operated the plant. At the venture's start, 34 executives were loaned to NUMMI by Toyota, and 16 by General Motors. The chief executive and chief operating officer were both Toyota personnel.

By Fall 1986, the NUMMI plant was running at full capacity and early indications were that the NUMMI plant was achieving productivity and quality levels close to those achieved at Toyota's major Takaoka plant in Japan. For example, in 1987, it took the NUMMI plant 19 assembly hours to build a car, compared to 16 hours at Takaoka, while the number of defects per 100 cars was the same at NUMMI as at Takaoka—45.[5]

Encouraged by its success at NUMMI, Toyota announced in December 1985 that it would build an automobile manufacturing plant in Georgetown, Kentucky. The plant, which came on stream in May 1988, officially had the capacity to produce 200,000 Toyota Camrys a year. Such was the success of this plant, however, that by early 1990 it was producing the equivalent of 220,000 cars per year. This success was followed by an announcement in December 1990 that Toyota would build a second plant in Georgetown with a capacity to produce a further 200,000 vehicles per year.[6]

By 2012, Toyota had 14 vehicle assembly plants in North America, 10 of them in the United States, which collectively produced 7 out of every 10 Toyota cars sold in the region. In addition, the company had six other plants producing a range of components, including engines and transmissions. The company also has two R&D and design centers in the United States, its only such facilities outside of Japan. By 2012, Toyota's cumulative investment in the United States exceeded $19.5 billion. In April 2013, Toyota announced that it would move production of one of its luxury Lexus vehicles from Japan to the United States, marking the first time that the company had produced a luxury vehicle outside of Japan. At the same time, Toyota announced that it would invest another $2.5 billion to expand U.S. production capacity.[7]

In addition to its North American transplant operations, Toyota moved to set up production in Europe in anticipation of the 1992 lowering of trade barriers among the 12 members of the European Economic Community. In 1989, the company announced that it would build a plant in England with the capacity to manufacture 200,000 cars per year by 1997. It opened a second plant in France in 2001, and by 2008, Toyota had four assembly plants in Europe with a total production capacity of 800,000 vehicles.

The company also expanded into China during the first decade of the 20th century. In China, it had three assembly plants by 2008 that were capable of producing over 440,000 vehicles a year. In the rest of Southeast Asia, Toyota had another 10 plants that could produce almost 1 million vehicles. There were also sizable assembly plants in South Africa, Australia, and South America.

Despite Toyota's apparent commitment to expand global assembly operations, it was not all smooth sailing. One problem was building an overseas supplier network comparable to Toyota's Japanese network. For example, in a 1990 meeting of Toyota's North American suppliers' association, Toyota executives informed their North American suppliers that the defect ratio for parts produced by 75 North American and European suppliers was 100 times greater than the defect ratio for parts supplied by 147 Japanese suppliers—1,000 defects per million parts versus 10 defects per million among Toyota's Japanese suppliers. Moreover, Toyota executives pointed out that parts manufactured by North American and European suppliers tend to be significantly more expensive than comparable parts manufactured in Japan.

Because of these problems, Toyota had to import many parts from Japan for its U.S. assembly operations. However, for political reasons, Toyota was being pushed to increase the local content of cars assembled in North America. By the mid-2000s, the local content of cars produced in North America was over 70%. To improve the efficiency of its U.S.-based suppliers, Toyota embarked upon an aggressive supplier education process. In 1992, it established the Toyota Supplier Support Center to teach its suppliers the basics of the Toyota production system. By the mid-2000s, over 100 supplier companies had been through the center. Many had reportedly seen double- and triple-digit productivity growth as a result, as well as dramatic reductions in inventory levels.[8]

Product Strategy

Toyota's initial production was aimed at the small-car/basic transportation end of the automobile market. This was true both in Japan and of its export sales to North America and Europe. During the 1980s, however, Toyota progressively moved up market and abandoned much of the lower end of the market to new entrants such as the South Koreans. Thus, the company's Camry and Corolla models, which initially were positioned toward the bottom of the market, have been constantly upgraded and now are aimed at the middle-income segments of the market. This upgrading reflects two factors: (1) the rising level of incomes in Japan and the commensurate increase in the ability of Japanese consumers to purchase mid-range and luxury cars and (2) a desire to hold on to its U.S. consumers, many of whom initially purchased inexpensive Toyotas in their early 20S and who have since traded up to more expensive models.

The upgrading of Toyota's models reached a logical conclusion in September 1989, when the company's Lexus division began marketing luxury cars to compete with Jaguars, BMWs, and the like. Although the Lexus brand initially got off to a slow start—in large part due to an economic recession—by 2001, Toyota was selling over 200,000 Lexus models a year in the United States, making it the bestselling luxury brand in the country.

In the mid-1990s, Toyota's U.S. research suggested that the company was losing younger buyers to hipper brands like Volkswagen. The result was a brand designed especially for the U.S. market, the Scion. Established with its own dealer network, the Scion has been a hit for Toyota.

TOYOTA IN 2000–2012

The first 8 years of the 21st century were ones of solid growth for Toyota. In 2004, it overtook Ford to become the second-largest car company in the world. The company surpassed GM in 2008, and seemed on track to meet its goal of capturing 15% of the global automobile market by 2010. Toyota was now a truly international company. Its overseas operations had grown from 11 production facilities in 9 countries in 1980 to 48 production facilities in 26 countries around the world.[9] In the important United States market, the world's largest, Toyota held an 18.4% share of passenger car sales in mid-2008, up from 11% in 2000. Ford's share was 15.4%, while GM held on to a 19.3% share.[10]

The company was very profitable. In the financial year ending March 2008, it earned $17.5 billion in net profits on sales of $183 billion. Both GM and Ford lost money that year.

According to data from J. D. Power, Toyota was the quality leader in the U.S. market in 2008. For cars that had been on the market for over 3 years, Toyota's Lexus brand led the pack for the 14th consecutive year, with 120 problems per 100 vehicles, compared to an industry average of 206 problems per 100 vehicles. The Toyota brand had 159 problems per 100 vehicles, compared to 177 for Honda, 204 for Ford, 226 for GMC, 229 for Chrysler, and 253 for Volkswagen. Toyota also had a strong record in the industry when measured by problems reported in the first 90 days after a sale—99 problems per 100 cars for the Lexus brand and 104 for the Toyota brand, versus an industry average of 118 problems per 100 cars.[11]

J. D. Power also found that Toyota led the market in Japan. A survey found that for vehicles purchased in 2002, Toyota had 89 problems per 100 vehicles compared to an industry average of 104. Honda was next, with 91 problems per 100 vehicles, followed by Nissan, with 108 problems per 100 vehicles.[12]

On the productivity front, Toyota's lead seemed to have narrowed. While it was clearly the productivity leader in the United States in 2003, where it took an average of 30.1 hours to make a car, compared to 35.2 hours at General Motors and 38.6 hours at Ford, by 2007 Toyota was taking 30.37 hours to build a car, compared to 32.29 hours at GM and 33.88 hours at Ford.[13] On the other hand, according to J.D. Power, Toyota had the three most efficient assembly plants in the world, all located in Japan.[14]

Higher quality and greater productivity helped Toyota make far more money per car than its large rivals. In 2007, Toyota made a pretax profit of $922 per vehicle in the United States, compared with losses of $729 and $1,467 at GM and Ford, respectively. These losses also reflect the fact that Ford and GM still pay more for health care, pensions, and sales incentives than does Toyota. Also, Ford and GM support more dealers relative to their market share than does Toyota.[15]

Toyota's ability to stay on top of productivity and quality rankings can be attributed to a companywide obsession with continuing to improve the efficiency and effectiveness of its manufacturing operations. The latest round of these was initiated in 2000, by Toyota President Fujio Cho. Cho, who worked for a while under Toyota's legendary engineer, Taiichi Ohno, introduced an initiative known as "Construction of Cost Competitiveness for the 21st Century," or CCC21. The initiative has as a goal slashing component part

Figure 3 Total Manufacturing Productivity in the U.S. Automobile Industry (total labor hours per unit)

Company	2003	2007
Ford	38.6	33.88
Chrysler	37.42	30.37
General Motors	35.2	32.39
Nissan	32.94	32.96
Honda	32.36	31.33
Toyota	30.01	30.37

Note: Includes assembly, stamping, engine, and transmission plants.
Source: O. Wyman, *Oliver Wyman's Harbour Report*, June 2008.

costs by 30% on all new models. Attaining this goal necessitated Toyota working closely with suppliers—something it has long done.

By the mid-2000s, Toyota was close to attaining its CCC21 goal. In implementing CCC21, no detail has been too small. For example, Toyota took a close look at the grip handles mounted above the doors inside most cars. By working closely with suppliers, they managed to reduce the number of parts in these handles from 34 to 5, which cut procurement costs by 40% and reduced the time need for installation from 12 seconds to 3 seconds.[16]

More generally, Toyota continues to refine its lean production system. For example, in die making, by 2004 Toyota had reduced the lead time to engineer and manufacture die sets for large body panels to 1.7 months, down from 3 months in 2002. By reducing lead time, Toyota reduced the startup costs associated with producing a new model, as well as the development time.[17]

In welding, Toyota developed and installed a simplified assembly process known as the "Global Body Line" or GBL. First developed in a low-volume, Vietnamese assembly plant in 1996, and introduced into its first Japanese plant in 1998, by 2004 the GBL was operating in some 20 of the company's 50 assembly plants and was found in all plants by 2007. The GBL system replaced Toyota's Flexible Body Line assembly philosophy that had been in place since 1985. The GBL system is based upon a series of programmable, robotic wielding tools. Under the old FBL system each car required three pallets to hold body parts in place during the welding process, each gripping either a major body side assembly or the roof assembly. The GBL system replaces these three pallets with a single pallet that holds all three major body panels in place from the inside as welding proceeds.[18]

According to Toyota, the GLB system has the following consequences:

- 30% reduction in the time a vehicle spends in the body shop
- 70% reduction in the time required to complete a major body change
- 50% cut in the cost to add or switch models
- 50% reduction in the investment to set up a line for a new model
- 50% reduction in assembly-line footprint

The floor space freed up by the GLB allows two assembly lines to be placed in the space traditionally required for one, effectively doubling plant capacity. Moreover, using GLB technology, as many as eight different models can be produced on a single assembly line. To achieve this, Toyota has pushed for consistency in design across model ranges, particularly with regard to the "hard points" that are grasped by the single master pallet.

Meanwhile, Toyota has been accelerating the process of moving toward fewer vehicle platforms, the goal being to build a wide range of models on a limited range of platforms that use many of the same component parts or modules. The company is reportedly working toward a goal of having just 10 platforms, down from over 20 in 2000.[19]

While Toyota is undoubtedly making progress refining its manufacturing efficiency, the fact remains that the productivity and quality gap between Toyota and its global competitors has narrowed. General Motors and Ford have both made significant strides in improving their quality and productivity in recent years. Moreover, in the American market at least, Toyota has suffered from the perception that its product offerings lack design flair and are not always as well attuned to consumer tastes as they might be. Here too, however, there are signs that Toyota is improving matters—interestingly enough, by listening more to its American designers and engineers.

A pivotal event in the changing relationship between Toyota and its American designers occurred in the late 1990s. Japanese managers had resisted their U.S. colleagues' idea that the company should produce a V8 pickup truck for the American market. To change their minds, the U.S. executives flew their Japanese counterparts over from Japan and took them to a Dallas Cowboys football game—with a pit stop in the Texas Stadium parking lot. There the Japanese saw row upon row of full-size pickups. Finally, it dawned on them that Americans see the pickup as more than a commercial vehicle, considering it primary transportation. The result of this was Toyota's best selling V8 pickup truck, the Tundra.[20]

American designers also pushed Toyota to redesign the Prius, its hybrid car first introduced in Japan in 1997. The Americans wanted a futuristic design change so that people would notice the technology. The result, the new Prius, became a surprise hit, with global sales of over 1 million vehicles by mid-2008.

By 2010, Toyota was manufacturing more than 1 million hybrid vehicles annually.[21]

Toyota's Americanization runs deeper than just product design issues. On the sales front, the company now sells more cars and trucks in North American than it does in Japan, and 70 to 80% of Toyota's global profits come from North America. On the personnel front, President Cho had made his reputation by opening Toyota's first U.S. production plant in Georgetown, Kentucky, in 1988. Another senior executive, Yoshi Inaba, spent 8 years in the United States and has an MBA from Northwestern University. Americans are also starting to make their way into Toyota's top ranks.[22]

Another concern of Toyota has been the aging of its customer base. According to J. D. Power, the average Toyota customer is 44 years old, compared with 38 for Volkswagen and 41 for Honda. Concerned that it was losing its cache with the younger generation, some 60 million of whom will reach driving age over the next few years, Toyota introduced a new car brand, the Scion, into America in June 2004. The Scion, targeted at young, entry-level buyers, could be purchased over the Web or through traditional Toyota dealers. Toyota's initial sales goals for the brand were 100,000 cars in 2005, but, in October 2004 it raised that target to 170,000. The average buyer in the months following launch was 31 years old.[23]

THE 2008–2009 CRISIS AND ITS AFTERMATH

Starting in mid-2008, sales in the global automobile industry collapsed at unprecedented rates, falling by around 40%. The sales collapse was a direct consequence of the global financial crisis that started in the American mortgage market, and then spilled over into other sectors. A combination of tight credit and uncertainty about the future caused consumers to buy far fewer new cars. For an industry with high fixed costs, a sales decline of this level was catastrophic.

Toyota was caught flat-footed by the decline. Toyota had been adding to its production capacity in the United States, its largest market, and pushing into the full-size pickup truck segment, when the storm hit. It had also been adding significant capacity elsewhere, a move that seemed sensible only 12 months earlier given that the company had been struggling to keep up with demand for its vehicles. Indeed, between 2001 and 2007, Toyota added about 500,000 cars' worth of production capacity per year, a pace that now seems to be aggressive.[24]

By April 2009, Toyota's sales in the United States were down 42% compared to the same month a year earlier. Moreover, there were sales declines in all other major national markets as well, including China, where Toyota sales fell by 17% in the first quarter of 2009, even though that market was one of the few that continued to grow. Toyota's problems in China reflected a slow response to increasing demand outside of China's big cities for small, affordable cars. Toyota exports from Japan were also hit hard by a rise in the value of the Japanese yen against the dollar and the euro during 2008 and early 2009.

In the United States, Toyota responded to the recession by placing the planned addition of a new production plant in Mississippi on hold and idling a production line in Texas. In Japan, production was cut by as much as 40% in some factories. These actions created a huge problem for Toyota, which adheres to a policy of lifetime employment and has not made significant workforce reductions since the 1950s. Toyota's initial response was to send underutilized employees to training sessions, and to have them work on identifying ideas for cost savings. However, the company did start to lay off temporary workers, and many questioned whether Toyota would be able to stick to its commitment of lifetime employment, particularly if the recession was prolonged.

Toyota also launched an "Emergency Profit Improvement Committee" tasked with finding $1.4 billion in savings in 2009. These cost savings came upon some $3.3 billion in cost reductions attained during the preceding few years. In typical Toyota style, no action seemed too small. Employees were been encouraged to take the stairs rather than use elevators to save electricity. The heat in factories was turned down. Teams of workers looked for ways to shave costs out of a production system that is already the world's most efficient.[25]

Trying to boost sales in the United States, Toyota introduced 0% financing in late 2008, but sales continued to falter. Ironically, one of Toyota's bestselling cars in the United States during much of 2007 and 2008, the fuel-efficient Prius, which carries a relative high price sticker, also saw steep sales declines in early 2009 as gasoline prices fell. Consumers who did purchase switched to low-priced, small cars from Kia and Ford.

Meanwhile, Toyota was changing its senior management ranks. In June 2009, Akio Toyoda, grandson of the company's founder, succeeded outgoing CEO Katsuaki Watanabe. With an MBS from Babson College in the United States, and time working in both New York and London, Toyoda is without question the most cosmopolitan CEO to take the helm at Toyota. He did so at a particularly challenging time for the company. His major challenge was to weather the storm and return the company to its growth path.

By 2012, it looked as if he had succeeded. Toyota had regained the mantel of the world's largest automobile company. Its reputation for quality, which had been badly tarnished by the sudden-acceleration problems in the United States, was again riding high. Accordingly to J. D. Power's annual Vehicle Dependency Study, after slipping in 2009 and 2010, Toyota brands regained the top spot in 2011 and 2012. That being said, Toyota faced invigorated competitors who were fast closing in on the company. Most notably, Hyundai-Kia of South Korea had grown its output from just 2.4 million units in 2000 to 7.1 million in 2012, making it the fourth-largest automaker in the world. Hyundai was more profitable than Toyota and produced more vehicles per employee, suggesting that Toyota might be losing its crown as the most productive automobile company in the world. In addition, Volkswagen was investing aggressively in capacity, particularly in China—now the world's largest national automobile market—and was well positioned to challenge Toyota for global market-share leadership. Rounding out the top four global automakers was General Motors, which had emerged from bankruptcy a smaller but stronger company. Indeed, on global measures of labor productivity, GM surpassed Toyota. Moreover, GM was well positioned in the large and rapidly growing Chinese market, where Toyota had struggled due to anti-Japanese sentiment. The future thus presented numerous challenges for Toyota.[26]

NOTES

1. This section is based primarily on the account given in M. A. Cusumano, *The Japanese Automobile Industry* (Cambridge, Mass: Harvard University Press, 1989).

2. The material in this section is drawn from three main sources: M. A. Cusumano, *The Japanese Automobile Industry* (Cambridge, Mass.: Harvard University Press, 1989); Taiichi Ohno, *Toyota Production System* (Cambridge, Mass.: Productivity Press, 1990; Japanese Edition, 1978); J. P. Womack, D. T. Jones, and D. Roos, *The Machine That Changed the World* (New York: Macmillan, 1990).

3. The material in this section is based on M. A. Cusumano, *The Japanese Automobile Industry*.

4. N. Powell, "U.S.-Japanese Joint Venture: New United Motor Manufacturing, Inc.," *Planning Review*, January–February 1989, pp. 40–45.

5. J. P. Womack, D. T. Jones, and D. Roos, *The Machine That Changed the World*.

6. J. B. Treece, "Just What Detroit Needs: 200,000 More Toyotas a Year," *Businessweek*, December 10, 1990, p. 29.

7. P. Eisensteon, "Toyota Investing Over $500 Million to Launch US Lexus Production," *NBC News*, April 19, 2013.

8. P. Strozniak, "Toyota Alters the Face of Production," *Industry Week*, August 13, 2001, pp. 46–48.

9. Anonymous, "The Car Company Out in Front," *The Economist*, January 29, 2005, pp. 65–67.

10. R. Newman, "How Toyota Could Become the US Sales Champ," *US News and World Reports*, June 9, 2008.

11. J. D. Power press release, "Lexus Ranks Highest in Vehicle Dependability for 14th Consecutive Year," August 7, 2008; J. D. Power press release, "Overall Initial Quality Improves Considerably," June 4, 2008.

12. J. D. Power press release, "Toyota Ranks Highest in Japan's First Long Term Vehicle Dependability Study," September 2, 2004.

13. *Oliver Wyman's Harbour Report*, Oliver Wyman, June 2008.

14. Ibid.

15. Ibid.

16. B. Bremner and C. Dawson, "Can Anything Stop Toyota?" *Businessweek*, November 17, 2003, pp. 114–117.

17. M. Hara, "Moving Target," *Automotive Industries*, June 2004, pp. 26–29.

18. B. Visnic, "Toyota Adopts New Flexible Assembly Process," *Wards Auto World*, November

2002, pp. 30–31; M. Bursa, "A Review of Flexible Automotive Manufacturing," *Just Auto*, May 2004, p. 15.

19. M. Hara, "Moving Target," *Automotive Industries*, June 2004, pp. 26–29.

20. C. Dawson and L. Armstrong, "The Americanization of Toyota," *Businessweek*, April 15, 2002, pp. 52–54.

21. C. Squatriglia, "Prius Sales Top 1 Million," *Autopia*, May 15, 2008.

22. A. Taylor, "The Americanization of Toyota," *Fortune*, December 8, 2004, p. 165.

23. N. Shirouzu, "Scion Plays Hip-Hop Impresario to Impress Young Drivers," *The Wall Street Journal*, October 5, 2004, p. B1.

24. Y. Takahashi, "Toyota Record $7.74 Billion Quarterly Loss," *The Wall Street Journal*, May 11, 2009, p. 3.

25. I. Rowly, "Toyota's Cost Cutting Drive," *Businessweek*, January 1, 2009, p. 15.

26. S. Pearson, et al., "Global Autos: A Clash of Titans," *Morgan Stanley Blue Paper*, January 22, 2013.

17

UBER: DRIVING GLOBAL DISRUPTION

"Uber is software eats taxis."

Marc Andreesen[1]

"I have had some terrible experiences with the taxi service; twice this past year I ordered a taxi to my house to go to the airport and they just didn't show up."

Kevin Kane[2]

"Cab driver robbed, stabbed overnight in Salt Lake City."

KUTV News headline.[3]

INTRODUCTION

In June 2014, 5-year-old company, Uber Technologies, the developer of the car-hailing smartphone app, secured $1.2 billion in funding from a consortium of investors led by mutual-fund giant Fidelity Investments. On the basis of the funding, Uber was valued at $18.2 billion, making it one of the world's most valuable privately held companies. This placed Uber's valuation above that of the rental car companies Hertz and Avis, as well as other well known, private technology companies such as Airbnb and Dropbox. In justifying the valuation, CEO Travis Kalanick noted that Uber was already using its app to offer ride-for-hire services in 130 cities in 36 countries, and that revenues were "at least doubling every 6 months."[4]

At the same time, Uber was facing challenges from incumbent taxi services around the globe that argued Uber was circumventing existing regulations and competing against them unfairly. On June 12, 2014, European taxi drivers protested the rise of Uber, stopping in the middle of streets and shutting down major portions of several major European cities including London, Lyon, Madrid, and Milan. Uber responded by offering discounts to stranded commuters in major cities. The day after the protests, Uber reported that its ridership in London had soared by 850%.[5] In the United States, regulators in numerous cities have issued cease-and-desist orders against Uber, which the company has generally ignored and, in several high-profile instances, overturned.

THE "RIDE-FOR-HIRE" MARKETPLACE IN THE UNITED STATES

Historically in the United States, two different types of provider have operated in the ride-for-hire marketplace: taxicab services and limousine services, each of which operates under a different set of rules. Both taxicab and limousine services are regulated by the states and/or cities in which they operate. In most cases, taxicabs are regulated at the municipal level, whereas limousine services are regulated at the city or state level. The regulations that apply to taxicab and limousine services are roughly similar from jurisdiction to jurisdiction, although they may differ in detail.[6]

Regulations typically address who can operate a taxicab or limousine, how service providers are contacted, the fare structure, and the labeling and appearance of vehicles. The motive for regulation is to ensure that services are safe, reliable, and affordable, and that owners and drivers are adequately compensated.

Customers can contact ride providers in two ways: by hailing on the street, or by prearrangement. In general, only licensed taxicabs can be hailed on the street; limousine services must be prearranged. Moreover, unlike taxicabs, in many cities limousine services cannot respond immediately to pick-up requests—they typically have a minimum prearrangement time, often at least an hour. This requirement works to protect taxicabs from direct competition from limousine services.

Most large urban markets are served by a significant number of local taxicab companies operating fleets of cars. For example, there are 31 cab companies in San Francisco and 10 taxi dispatch companies that schedule rides. No one firm is dominant. There are about 1,500 licensed taxicabs within the city. Some 57% of taxi drivers in San Francisco are immigrants, a pattern repeated in many other cities. The average mean wage of a San Francisco driver was reported to be $22,440 in 2013.[7]

In New York, which has the largest ride for hire fleet in the USA, licenses have been issued for 13,437 taxicabs. There are an estimated 42,000 drivers in the city, with a licensed vehicle being used by 2–3 drivers a day. In 2014, only 6% of cab drivers in New York were born in the USA, and 36% came from Bangladesh and Pakistan.

The New York taxi fleet picks up 600,000 passengers per day. There are also an estimated 25,000 livery cars that provide for hire service by pre arrangement, and carry 500,000 passengers per day. There are 10,000 "black cars" that provide services mostly for corporate clients.[8]

Regulators have long required that taxicabs available to be hailed on the street be licensed. The license is to ensure that the taxi service is safe and reliable, and that fares are fair. For hire vehicles must be insured to cover drivers and passengers, meet safety standards, and (if taxicabs) have a sealed meter. Regulations also require that licensed cabs be quickly and easily identifiable. This is normally achieved by a distinctive color (e.g., yellow cabs). Cabs must also display whether they are in service or not.

Taxicabs charge a regulated fare, set by a government agency, based on the time and distance of the trip as measured by a meter. Some trips to and from established destinations such as an airport may have a fixed price that will displayed in the cab. Taxicabs are required to carry standardized meters that must be prominently displayed, sealed, and periodically checked to ensure that the proper fare is being charged. Limousine services are generally prohibited from charging fares based on time and distance, and they do not carry a meter. Typically, fees are based on time, often with a minimum billed time. The fee normally has to be agreed upon in advance.

In many jurisdictions, the licensing system limits the supply of taxicabs. One common variant of licensing is the medallion system that is used in cities such as New York, Boston, Chicago, and San Francisco. Medallions are small, metal plates attached to the hood of a taxi certifying it for passenger pickup throughout a defined area (normally metropolitan boundaries). When the medallion system was first introduced in New York in 1937, the idea was to make sure that taxi driver was not a criminal luring passengers into his vehicle. To get a medallion, the taxi service has to adhere to the regulatory requirements in that jurisdiction and be approved by the appropriate regulatory agency. Medallions may be given to individual taxi drivers who own their own cars, but more typically taxi companies that own fleets of cars acquire them. The taxi companies then lease cars and medallions to drivers on a daily or weekly basis. In some locations the driver may own the car, but lease or purchase the medallion from an agent who has acquired it. An example would be Medallion Financial, a publically traded company that owns hundreds of medallions in New York, sells them to aspiring young cabbies, and arranges for loans to finance their purchase.

In cities that utilize a medallion system, the supply of medallions has often been limited. The rationalizations for doing this include ensuring quality, guaranteeing a fair return to taxi companies, and helping to support demand for other forms of public transportation such as buses, trains, and the subway. It has also been argued that limiting the number of cabs helps reduce congestion and pollution.[9]

In practice, the supply of medallions has often not kept pace with growing populations. In New York, Chicago, and Boston, for example, the number of medallions issued has barely budged since the 1930s. In New York, there were 11,787 medallions issued after World War II, a number that remained constant until 2004. By 2014, there were 13,437 medallions issued in New York.

Medallions can be traded. Thus over time, a secondary market in medallions has developed. In this market, the price is not set by the agency issuing them but by the laws of supply and demand. The effect of limited supply has been to drive up the price of medallions. In New York, taxi medallions were famously selling for over $1 million in 2012. In Boston, the price was $625,000. In San Francisco, the price was $300,000 and the city took a $100,000 commission on the sale of medallions.[10] The average annual price of medallions surged during the 2000s. In New York, prices increased 260% between 2004 and 2012. The inflation-adjusted annualized return for medallions over this time period in New York was 19.5%, compared to a 3.9% annual return for the S&P 500.[11]

As noted above, drivers often do not own the medallions. There are three players in many taxi markets: the medallion holders (often taxi companies) who have acquired the right to operate a taxi from the regulatory agency; the taxi driver; and taxi dispatch companies. A taxi dispatch company typically matches available cabs with customers and takes a fee for its scheduling services.

In New York, about 18% of cabs were owner operated in 2014, putting most medallions in the hands of taxi companies. In New York, regulations allow medallion owners to lease them out to drivers for 12-hour shifts. The critical problem facing drivers is that they must get access to a medallion in order to make a living. Due to this, companies that own medallions can extract high fees from drivers. There are also reports that some taxi dispatch companies use their position as schedulers to extract payment in the form of bribes from drivers in return for preferred shifts.[12]

Drivers, who legally are viewed as "independent contractors," can begin a 12-hour shift owing as much as $130 to their medallion-leasing company. They may not break even until halfway through their shift. One consulting company report found that, in 2006, a driver's take-home pay in New York for a 12-hour shift averaged $158. In 2011, the New York transportation authority calculated that it was $96.[13] A study of taxi drivers in Los Angeles found that drivers worked on average 72 hours a week for a median take-home wage of $8.39 an hour. The LA drivers were paying $2,000 in leasing fees per month to taxi companies. None of the drivers in the LA study had health insurance provided by their companies, and 61% were completely without health insurance.[14] Given the compensation, it is perhaps not surprising that some drivers can be rude, impatient, and prone to drive fast and take poor care of their cabs.

The LA study noted that, because City officials heavily regulate the taxi business, taxi companies are active politically, paying lobbyist to advocate for their interests and contributing to the campaign funds of local politicians. The same is true in New York City, where the medallion owners' trade association, the Metropolitan Taxi Board of Trade, lobbies hard to influence public policy. In 2011, for example, medallion owners were initially able to block plans to create a fleet of "Boro" cabs (painted green) to serve New York's outer boroughs. They argued that doing so would drive down the price of their medallions. In June 2013, however, the New York Supreme Court overruled lower court rulings and allowed the licensing of Boro cabs to proceed. The intention now is to issue 18,000 new licenses to green cabs. These cabs, however, will not be able to pick up passengers in lower Manhattan, which remains the territory of yellow cabs.[15]

THE RIDE-FOR-HIRE MARKET IN OTHER COUNTRIES

Many regulations in the U.S. ride-for-hire marketplace have analogs in other countries. In London, for example, there are 22,000 black cabs (taxis that can be hailed) and 49,000 vehicles licensed for private hire that cannot be hailed on the street. Although there is no regulatory limit on the number of taxis in London, before London taxi drivers can join the work force they must navigate byzantine licensing procedures that include memorizing the city's street maps, which is referred to as "the knowledge." Acquiring "the knowledge" constitutes the most demanding taxi driver training program in the world. On average it takes 12 attempts at the final test and 34 months of preparation to pass the knowledge exam. The effect of "the knowledge" requirement is to limit the supply of taxis in London. Similar, though less demanding, knowledge tests are found in Austria, Brussels, Finland, Germany, and Hungary.[16]

In Paris, the number of taxi permits was capped at 14,000 in 1937. By 2014, a much bigger and vastly richer Paris was receiving 27 million tourist visits a year, yet the number of cabs had edged up just 14%, to 15,900. The result: Parisians must stand in long lines for cabs that never come. In 2007, the Government of Nicolas Sarkozy proposed to license 6,500 new cabs in Paris. The proposal triggered a strike among transportation workers that shut the city down for a day and frightened Sarkozy into surrender.[17]

Italy is another country with a restrictive licensing system for taxis. This has been a problem in Milan, for example. In 2002, the ratio of taxis to inhabitants was 1 for every 1,094 inhabitants, compared to 1 for every 387 in London and 1 for every 414 in Paris. At the time, there were 4,571 taxis in Milan, a number that had been frozen for 20 years. The shortage of taxis resulted in long waiting periods at peak demand times. The price of taxi licenses on the secondary market had risen to between EUR 100,000 and EUR 130,000. In 2002, the city government moved to alleviate the cab shortage, announcing that it would issue 500 new cab licenses. Milan's taxi drivers mounted a vigorous campaign against this. The city responded by reducing the number of proposed new licenses to 300. The taxi drivers still objected and protested by forming "go-slow" convoys of taxis that paralyzed city traffic for 2 days. The city effectively backed off.[18]

In contrast, Dublin offers a view of what can happen when regulations are relaxed. Due to the limited availability of licenses, between 1979 and 1998 the number of licenses in Dublin barely budged even though demand had soared as the population grew. Deregulation in 2000 reduced the cost of entry (car plus license) by 74%. The result was more than three times as many cabs on the road, shorter waiting times,

better cab quality, and higher passenger satisfaction— all in 2 years.[19]

Interestingly, Tehran, the capital of Iran, has a highly deregulated ride-for-hire market. In addition to private taxis, a shared taxi system allows any private car to pick up passengers. Since travelers can hop on and off as they please, a driver can carry passengers travelling to different destinations at the same time, which increases utilization of the vehicle. The system also means that the supply of taxis is very fluid, increasing during rush hour as commuters pick up passengers on their way home.[20]

UBER'S SERVICE

Uber was founded in San Francisco, in 2009, by Garrett Camp and Travis Kalanick to develop a smartphone app that would facilitate the creation of a new ride-for-hire service. The company raised $1.25 million in angel investments in 2010 to help fund the initial service rollout. From the outset, the goal was to overcome common frustrations that customers often experience when trying to find a taxi. Passengers can find taxicabs to be unpleasant, poorly maintained, dirty, and recklessly driven. Taxicabs can be difficult to find in certain areas—many drivers avoid areas of a city where there are few passengers, or where they are unlikely to find a return fare. There can also be a shortage of cabs at peak commute times, or at special events, such as New Year's Eve, which leads to long wait times. Sometimes taxicabs just don't turn up, leaving a traveler stranded. This author once missed a plane flight because a taxicab booked the day before didn't appear. On another occasion, a scheduled ride turned up very late because the taxi driver got lost.

Business Model

Uber exploited the opportunity created by customer frustrations to develop a smartphone application that effectively enables customers to hail a car immediately from the comfort of a couch or a barstool, rather than standing on a cold street and waiting for a cab to drive by. The app also shows customers the location of cars. In general, a car will arrive a few minutes after being hailed. The fare, including a tip, is charged directly to the customer's credit card. This means that no cash changes hands, which is a major plus for drivers who did not like to carry large quantities of cash (there is a long history of taxi drivers being robbed by riders). The fee is based on time and distance, as determined by the Uber application using the GPS capability of the driver's mobile device. Under the initial model, the fee was split between the driver, who kept 80%, and Uber, which got 20%. When Uber started its service in 2010, the company was charging 40 to 100% more than a similar trip using a taxicab. However, over time, the price differential between Uber cars and regular taxicabs fares has declined substantially.

Uber does not own cars. Instead it relies upon a network of established, licensed limousine drivers and companies that wish to be part of its system. In effect, the Uber app allows limousine's to be transformed into a service that can be hailed from any location, albeit by an app rather than hand signaling. Uber relies greatly on data analytics to determine the best locations for drivers to wait in order to speed up response time to customer requests for rides. The more data Uber gathers, the better its predictive models, the more optimal its placement of vehicles, and the higher its vehicle utilization.

Uber also used data analytics to pioneer the use of what it calls "surge pricing."[21] Instead of using fixed pricing as do conventional taxi services, Uber adjusts prices for a ride depending upon the state of demand. For example, prices have been known to surge on New Year's Eve. Similarly, if there is an unforeseen event such as a snowstorm that makes everyone want a car at the same time, prices will go up, often dramatically. There have been reports of Uber fares increasing to as much as seven times the normal level during periods of peak demand. In turn, the higher prices attract more Uber vehicles onto the road, and prices drop back down toward normal levels. Uber argues that a benefit of this system is that it encourages more supply at periods of peak demand, and visa-versa. However, there have been some reports of grumbling on the part of customers who find that they are paying unexpectedly high prices. Conversely, if Uber's network of drivers responds quickly to price signals, dramatic prices surges should be a very transitory phenomenon.

An added benefit of the Uber app is a feature that allows riders to rate drivers, which translates into an implicit guarantee of driver reliability based on prior reputation. There is a corresponding feature on the driver's app, which enables them to rate customers and red flag and avoid troublesome clients.

Limousine and other private car owners have been attracted to the Uber model by a number of factors. First, the Uber app has enabled limo drivers to circumvent regulations that prohibit them from being hailed on the street. As such, it has increased demand for their services. Second, the app increases vehicle utilization, which drives more revenues to the vehicle owner. Third, owners of the vehicle benefit from the surge-pricing methodology that enables them to charge more than regulated fares at times of peak demand. Fourth, the fact that no cash changes hands and that payment is guaranteed when a ride is booked increases the safety of the driver, as does the client-rating feature on the driver's app. Fifth, the Uber system means that drivers can work flexible hours, driving when they want to rather than when a taxi company tells them they must take a shift.

There have been reports of Uber drivers earning multiples of what the driver of a regulated taxicab could earn. In early 2014, Uber suggested that while a typical taxicab driver could earn $30,000 a year, an Uber driver working a 40-hour-week could earn nearly $91,000 a year in New York, and $74,000 in San Francisco.[22] Attracted by such financial inducements, in 2014, the company claimed that 20,000 drivers a month were signing up with Uber worldwide.

Some financial journalists have questioned Uber's claims about driver income. Uber's estimates were based on a sample of drivers who drove over 40 hours a week. The earnings figures also excluded the cost of gas, insurance, parking, maintenance, repairs, and paying for tolls. One journalist concluded that in order to earn $75,000 a year driving for Uber in San Francisco, a driver would have to work 58 hours a week.[23]

Expansion Strategy

Uber began offering its service in June 2010 in San Francisco under the name UberCab. New York was added in May 2011. By April 2012, the company was in seven U.S. cities, Paris, and Toronto. Two years later, Uber was operating in 130 cities in 36 countries around the world. Initially, Uber limited its service to drivers with high-end, limo-type cars. In San Francisco, Uber explicitly targeted members of the tech community in its early marketing efforts, sponsoring local tech and venture capital events and providing free rides to attendees. Uber's bet was that its service would immediately resonate with this demographic, who would rapidly spread the news via word of mouth and social networks. According to CEO Travis Kalanick:

> Uber spends virtually zero dollars on marketing, spreading almost exclusively via word of mouth. I'm talking old-school word of mouth, you know at the water cooler in the office, at a restaurant when you're paying the bill, at a party with friends–"Who's Ubering home?" Ninety-five percent of all our riders have heard about Uber from other Uber riders. Our virality is almost unprecedented. For every 7 rides we do, our users' big mouths generate a new rider.[24]

One of Uber's business development managers elaborated on this:

> With Uber everything is very local-focused as transportation is a local topic. For that reason we have an operations team on the ground in all the cities where Uber exists, and that team is working with both local drivers and local clients to grow the business there.
>
> We've also found that our growth is driven substantially by word of mouth. When someone sees the ease of use, the fact that they press a button on their phone and in under 5 minutes a car appears, they inevitably become a brand advocate. We've also done our best to reach out to folks who are influencer in our markets, who obviously have a stronger reach and bigger audience.[25]

To drive rapid growth, Uber picked cities that have what Kalanick refers to as "accelerants." These accelerants indicate a concentrated need for Uber's service and include (1) lots of restaurants and nightlife, (2) holidays and events, (3) weather, and (4) sports.[26] For example, in Chicago, a city with lots of nightlife, intense weather, and numerous sporting events, Uber's initial viral growth was double what they normally experienced. Special events and holidays also provided an opportunity to showcase Uber's model. Uber's ability to deliver rides on New Year's Eve in San Francisco, a city notorious for its lack of taxis, drove spikes in new ridership. Kalanick has also noted that Uber is getting better at local market entry over time:

> Every city, every subsequent city that we go to we're getting better at rolling the city out and growing the city faster. And so a lot of the cities where there's a constrained number of taxis, no liquid black car market, those are the cities where we launch and things explode from the start. We have other cities where there's tons of taxis, in some cases way too many and in those situations often the quality of service being delivered is really poor, so we go in there and explode as well. But there's all kinds of different cities in terms of regulatory, and in terms of what the industry looks like, an industry which we're disrupting in a substantial way.
>
> We think that cities deserve to have another transportation alternative. It sounds crazy to have to say that but you have to do that because you have incumbent interests which are often trying to curtail innovation and curtail the sort of transportation alternatives that might compete with their existing business. And, because of that, it requires us to take a very local approach to how we go after a city. We have launchers that go into [cities] . . . and turn nothing into something. I like to say they drop in with parachutes and machetes [and] get highly involved with the suppliers, people who own cars and run car services, and really just make sure that we can launch a service that is high quality from the start. Being local and speaking with a local voice is important when you're doing transportation and means you know what's going on for the city.[27]

To achieve rapid expansion, Uber needs to be able to quickly build a network of drivers in each city it enters. The company certainly touts the financial and safety advantages of working for Uber, but it is also taking other actions to make sure there are plenty of drivers available. Most notably, in December 2013, Uber lined up $2.5 billion in outside financing for low-interest-rate loans for Uber X drivers with Toyota and GM (more on Uber X later in this case).

This should make it possible for up to 200,000 drivers to buy their own cars at very low interest rates, under the condition that they use those cars on the Uber network for the duration of the loan. In effect, drivers are lock in for the duration of the loan unless they want to see their interest rates balloon. Reportedly, drivers have to agree to two financing rates, one that reflects the cost savings of them partnering with Uber, and one that doesn't.[28]

Regulatory Responses

Uber had not been operating in San Francisco long before there was rumbling among taxicab companies that Uber might not be legal. A taxi driver raised objections against Uber at a city Taxi Advisory Council meeting. Among the concerns were the following:[29]

- Uber operates much like a cab company but does not have a taxi license.
- Its cars don't have insurance equivalent to taxi insurance.
- Uber may threaten taxi dispatchers' way of making a living.
- Limos usually have to book an hour in advance, by law, while only licensed taxis can pick someone up right away, but Uber picks people up immediately, without a license to do so.

On October 20, the San Francisco Metro Transit Authority and the Public Utilities Commission of California issued a cease-and-desist order against the company. Uber, however, continued its service under threat of penalties including fines of up to $5,000 per instance of operation, and potentially 90 days in jail for each day the company remained in operation past the order.

Undeterred, Uber stated that it would work with the agencies involved to understand their exact concerns and make sure that the service was in compliance. On the company blog, the following statement was posted:

> Uber is a first to market, cutting edge transportation technology and it must be recognized that the regulations from both city and state regulatory bodies have not been written with these innovations in mind. As such, we are happy to help educate the regulatory bodies on this new generation of technology, and work closely with both agencies to ensure our compliance and keep our service available.

However, the company did quietly change the name of its service from UberCab to Uber.

The dispute between Uber and regulatory authorities in California simmered on for 3 years. During this time, Uber continued to operate, and indeed dramatically expanded its service. At one point, CEO Kalanick joked that he probably had 20,000 years of jail time in front of him.[30] In 2013, influenced by evidence of strong public demand for Uber's service, the California Public Utilities Commission stuck a deal with Uber, lifted the (ignored) cease-and-desist order, and eliminated fines.

As Uber expanded its service, what had happened in California occurred in cities around the United States, and then the globe. In Washington D.C., for example, where existing taxi services were rated as poor by many residents, demand for Uber cars rapidly took off after the company started service in December 2011. The local regulatory authority, The DC Taxicab Commission, deemed the service illegal. True to form, Uber continued to operate. At one point, the Commission conducted sting operations against Uber, hailing cars via the Uber app, then impounding the cars and ticketing the drivers. Responding to intense lobbying from D.C.'s 150 taxicab companies, in mid-2012 the City Council drafted legislation to fix the price for Uber's service so that it would be five times the minimum cost of cabs. Uber CEO Kalanick responded with a social media campaign, urging D.C. customers to sign a petition and email council members to protest the legislation. The council members, swamped with thousands of emails, quickly withdrew the legislation. In a major victory for Kalanick, in short order a new bill was drafted and passed that exempted Uber from regulation by the Taxicab Commission.[31]

In Seattle, after initially ignoring Uber, the City Council responded to its increasing popularity by passing an ordinance that limited the number of Uber drivers to 150. At the time, Uber already had 1,000 drivers in the city. The City Council said that it was concerned about the safety and insurance coverage of Uber cars. Council member Kshama Sawant, the Council's only socialist, argued in favor of the cap as a means to protect traditional taxi drivers. However, in Seattle, city ordinances can be suspended if enough citizens sign a petition requesting this. The day after the ordinance was passed, a group that received some $400,000 in funding from Uber and similar services submitted more than 36,000 signatures to the city clerk's office, more than double the required number to suspend an ordinance. In July 2014, the City Council voted 8-1 in favor of legislation that legalized Uber and similar services, and removed any caps on the number of drivers.[32]

In New York, a city with a long tradition of limo services, Uber initially operated unimpeded. However, when it tried to expand operations to include New York's traditional yellow cabs, the city's Taxi and Limousine Commission (TLC) stepped in, telling cab owners that it had "not authorized any electronic hailing of payment applications for use in New York City taxicabs," and further that "drivers and owners are reminded that violations of Commission rules can lead to fines, and in some cases, the suspension or revocation of their license."[33] Interestingly, the TLC took this position despite strong interest among taxi drivers. Uber responded by withdrawing its yellow taxi service, but its limo service continued to operate.

In London, taxi drivers responded to the growing popularity of Uber with a day of protests, stopping in the middle of streets and causing significant congestion. The protests backfired, as Uber reported a surge in app downloads and registration by London residents. In Paris, where similar protests by taxi drivers also took place, the Senate passed a bill that requires online car service drivers to return to their headquarters or a parking garage between each client, unless they have a prior reservation—a requirement that would substantially reduce Uber's ability to respond in a timely manner. The bill would also prevent companies from showing live locations of their cars on a map. The bill was scheduled for a full vote in the National Assembly in Fall 2014. In Brussels, Uber was banned after a court ruled it did not have the appropriate permits to operate in the city. In Berlin, the chairman of the Berlin Taxi Association won an injunction against Uber in April 2014, barring the company from operating there. However, the ruling is not being enforced in Berlin while Uber awaits the outcome of an appeal.[34]

Commenting on legal attempts to stop Uber, CEO Kalanick argues that they are classic example of regulators trying to stifle innovation. Kalanick also asserts that Uber's strategy of marching into new cities without asking permission is necessary. "If you put yourself in the position to ask for something that is already legal, you'll never be able to roll it out . . . the corruption of the taxi industries will make it so you will never get to market."[35] At the time of writing, Uber is fighting multiple cease-and-desist orders in cities across the United States and around the world, as well as regulatory attempts to ban or hamstring the service. Despite the sustained legal assault, Uber has so far only exited one city, Vancouver, Canada.

Competition

No good idea goes long without imitation, and Uber soon found itself facing several rivals, including most notably Lyft. Lyft is a privately held company based in San Francisco backed by venture capital. By mid-2014, it had raised over $300 million in financing. Logan Green and John Zimmer launched Lyft in Summer 2012. It was originally conceived as a local service of Zimride, a ridesharing service the two founded in 2007 that was focused on long-distance ride sharing, typically between cities. Lyft uses a smartphone app that facilitates peer-to-peer ride sharing and electronic hailing by enabling passengers who need a ride to request one from the available community of drivers nearby.

Lyft differs from Uber in that its drivers are regular citizens using their own cars. Lyft drivers are distinguished by a pink, fuzzy mustache placed on the front of their vehicles. Drivers and passengers can rate each other on a five-star scale after each ride. The ratings establish the reputations of both drivers and passengers within the Lyft network. Ratings are displayed on the Lyft smartphone app, enabling drivers to avoid bad customers, and customers to avoid drivers with poor ratings. Lyft initially did not charge fixed prices, but instead relied upon voluntary donations to the driver. This changed in November 2013, when the company said that it would institute a fixed price schedule, with a 25% surcharge for peak periods. As with Uber, payment is automatic, made through the Lyft app, and Lyft takes 20% of the fare.[36]

By mid-2014, Lyft had established itself in 60 cities in the United States. Like Uber, Lyft has run into significant regulatory headwinds. Indeed, if anything, Lyft has faced more regulatory opposition because its drivers use their own cars. To counter claims regarding safety, Lyft insures each driver with a $1-million "excess" liability policy. Any driver with an average user rating of less than 4.5 out of 5 stars is also dropped from the service.

Lyft faced the same headwinds as Uber in California, and stuck a similar deal with regulators in mid-2013. In New York City, the TLC, which had declared Lyft an unauthorized service that had not demonstrated compliance with safety and licensing requirements, initially blocked it from operating. The restriction was lifted in July 2014 after Lyft agreed to use licensed, commercial drivers within the city. To grow its network in New York, Lyft was reportedly offering a guaranteed $10,000 a month to drivers with a license from the TLC who would agree to work 60 hours a week, and $5,000 to those willing to work 40 hours a week.[37]

A smaller competitor, Sidecar, began in San Francisco in 2012. Sidecar, a peer-to-peer ridesharing service, is similar to Lyft in many respects. It, too, uses a smartphone app to facilitate matching drivers to customers. One major difference is that Sidecar lets drivers set their own prices, while riders can select the car they want based on price and vehicle model. In mid-2014, Sidecar was operating in eight U.S. cities.

PRODUCT EXTENSIONS AND PRICE CUTS: UBER X

Uber started out using traditional, black limousines. In July 2012, it created a new service category, Uber X, which allowed Uber drivers to use vehicles such as Toyota Prius Hybrids and SUVs like the Cadillac Escalade. By 2014, Uber X drivers were also using basic sedans like the Toyota Camry or Honda Accord. Initially, the pricing for Uber X cars was a $5 base fee, with a $3.25 per mile charge thereafter, making Uber X 35% cheaper than Uber's "black car" rates. The introduction of Uber X was seen as a competitive response to the emergence of Lyft as a low-cost competitor.[38]

In June 2013, Uber reduced the price of its Uber X service in San Francisco by 25%. In October 2013, it announced similar fare reductions in Los Angeles, San Diego, and Washington, D.C. At the time, Uber stated that its fares were 18 to 37% cheaper than hailing a traditional taxicab, depending upon location. Although Uber compares its prices to traditional taxicabs, its price reductions have often come in cities where Lyft has recently launched its service.

For example, Uber launched its Uber X service in Indianapolis and St. Paul just a week after Lyft introduced its service to riders in those cities. Uber also offered a free month of service to riders in those cities.

Uber dropped its prices again in January 2014. To push back against resistance from drivers, it argued that the price cuts meant more rides, and thus greater revenue. Uber announced a further round of 25% price cuts in Summer 2014 for its Uber X service in select cities, including San Francisco. These cuts are meant to be for a limited time only. However, Uber also stated that drivers would still pocket 80% of the original fare *before* the cut. This implies that, in some cases, Uber was now paying drivers more than they earned. For example, a 25% cut implies that a rider will now pay $11.25 for a ride that previously cost $15. But the driver will still keep 80% of the original $15 fee, which means that Uber has to pay the driver $0.75 to make up the $12 salary for the driver. Under the new pricing scheme, Uber X is now cheaper than taxicab service in many locations. For example, a fare from Union Square to the Mission District in San Francisco costs $11 via taxicab, and $6 by Uber X.[39] On July 7, 2014, Uber dropped its New York City fare by 20%, making Uber X cheaper than a taxi in that market.

CONCLUSION

Uber is a private company. Its financials remain a closely guarded secret and the source of some speculation. In August 2013, well-known tech writer Kara Swisher reported that Uber was on track to make $125 million in revenue in 2013. In December 2013, a news source gained access to what appeared to be a leaked screenshot of Uber's financials dated November 20, 2013. This suggested that the company was on track to generate revenues around $210 million in 2013. The same screenshot indicated that Uber had received 12 million ride requests and processed 89,976 new signups in the last 7 days.[40] In June 2014, Kalanick stated that revenues were at least doubling every 6 months. If true, Uber may be on track to having an annual revenue run rate of $800 million by the end of 2014.

The company declined to comment on these numbers, but with private investors valuing the company at around $18 billion in mid-2014, this kind of rapid growth does not seem unreasonable. Indeed, in mid-2014 Uber's global rollout seemed to be accelerating. Early August brought launches in Dusseldorf in Germany, Ft. Lauderdale, West Palm Beach, and Richmond in the United States, San Paulo in Brazil, and Saigon in Vietnam. With the San Paulo launch, Uber was now available in the 10 largest cities of the 10 largest economies in the world. By early 2015, Uber was claiming that it served more than 200 cities in 54 countries.

In December 2014, Uber announced that it had raised an additional $1.2 billion in financing from a consortium of hedge funds and wealthy private investors. The new round of funding valued the company at a staggering $40 billion—higher than the market capitalization of three-quarters of the S&P 500. This was followed by an announcement on January 21, 2015, that Uber had raised an additional $1.6 billion in convertible debt from wealth management clients of Goldman Sachs. Uber indicated that the funds were to be used for "strategic investments."

As Uber expanded, it continued to run into regulatory headwinds. Following allegations that an Uber driver had raped a passenger in India, the Indian Government issued an order asking local authorities to stop all app-based taxi services until they are registered with local transportation departments. Authorities in Thailand and Vietnam also declared that Uber was an illegal service, although it continued to operate in both countries. In December, a judge temporarily banned Uber from operating in Spain following complaints from local taxi drivers that the service was damaging their industry.

As 2015 began, numerous questions swirled around Uber. Was the private valuation reasonable? How big could the company ultimately get, and how profitable would it be? Would regulators be able to keep Uber at bay, or would the victories it had won in California, Seattle, and Washington D.C., become commonplace? How would incumbent taxicab companies respond? Would Lyft and other competitors emerge as a strong threat to Uber? And perhaps most tantalizingly, could Uber grow the way Amazon had, starting in one category (books), before branching out into other sectors? As several commentators have noted, Uber is potentially far more than a ride-for-hire service. It's really a logistics company with the ability to digitally connect customers with commercial transportation to move not just people, but a range of physical goods.[41] Once Uber has you summoning cars from your phone, the logic goes, it can use that same technology to arrange for all sorts of other deliveries such as food, clothes, and Christmas trees (which it experimented with in 2013). What then, is the true upside here, and what are the risks?

NOTES

1. P. Sloan "Marc Andreesen: Predictions for 2012 and Beyond," CNET, December 19, 2011.
2. J. Kartch, "Uber Battle of New Orleans Pits Old Guard vs New," Forbes, July 7, 2014.
3. http://kutv.com/news/features/archive-10/stories/vid_650.shtml.
4. E.Rusli, "Uber CEO Travis Kalanick: We're Doubling Revenue Every Six Months," The Wall Street Journal, June 6, 2014.
5. G. Sullivan, "Uber Said Ridership Up 850% after Taxis Hold London to "Ransom," Morning Mix blog, Washington Post, June 12, 2014.
6. D. Hoyt and S. Callander, "Uber: 21st Century Technology Confronts 20th Century Regulation," Stanford Business School Case, September 25, 2012.
7. D. Bond-Graham, "Uber and Lyft Get a Lot of Hype But Ridesharing in a Parasitic Business Model," AlterNet, October 22, 2013.
8. New York City Taxi and Limousine Commission, 2014 Taxicab Factbook.
9. M. W. Frankena and P. Pautler, "An Economic Analysis of Taxicab Regulation," Federal Trade Commission, Bureau of Economics Staff Report, May 1984.
10. R. Dhar, "The Tyranny of the Taxi Medallions," Priceonomics blog, April 10, 2013. http://blog.priconomics.com.
11. New York City Taxi and Limousine Commission, 2014 Taxicab Factbook.
12. Globe Staff Reporters, "For Boston Cabbies, a Losing Battle Against the Numbers," Boston Globe, March 31, 2013.
13. J. Horwitz and C. Cumming, "Taken for a Ride," Slate, June 6, 2012.
14. J. Leavitt and G. Blasi, "The Los Angeles Taxi Workers Alliance," University of California

Transportation Center, UCTC Research paper No. 893, Fall 2009.

15. D. Wiessner, "Court OKs Plan That Will Double the Number of Cabs in New York," *Reuters*, June 6, 2013.

16. J. T. Bekken, "Experiences with Regulatory Changes of the Taxi Industry," 9th Conference on Competition and Ownership in Land Transportation. www.thredbo-conference-series.org/downloads /thredbo9_papers/thredbo9-workshopD-Bekken .pdf.

17. D. Frum, "Paris Taxi Shortage: It's About Jobs," *CNN Opinion*, July 10, 2012.

18. D. Coletto and R. Pedersini, "Milan Taxi Drivers Protest Against Increased Licenses," EIR Online, March 7, 2003. www.eurofound.europa.eu/eiro /2003/02/feature/it0302206f.htm.

19. "A Fare Fight," *The Economist*, February 11, 2011.

20. Ibid.

21. "Pricing the Surge," *The Economist*, May 29, 2014.

22. M. McFarland, "Ubers Remarkable Growth Could End the Era of Poorly Paid Cab Drivers," *Washington Post*, May 27, 2014.

23. M. R. Dickey, "Here's How Much Money You Can Really Earn as an Uber Driver," *Business Insider*, June 28, 2014.

24. T. Kalanick, "Chicago: Uber's Biggest Launch Date?" Uber blog, September 22, 2011.

25. S. Ellis, E. Taylor, and D. La Com, "Uber: What's Fueling Uber's Growth Engine?" GrowthHackers. http://growthhackers.com/companies/uber/.

26. Ibid.

27. N. Carter and T. Rice, "How Uber Rolls Out, City by City," *Inc.*, April 25, 2012.

28. K. Rose, "Uber Might Be More Valuable than Facebook Someday. Here's Why," *New York Magazine*, December 6, 2013.

29. L. Kolodny, "Uber Ordered to Cease and Desist," techcrunch.com, October 24, 2010.

30. M. G. Siegler, "Uber CEO: I Think I've Got 20,000 Years of Jail Time in Front of Me," techcrunch.com, May 25, 2011.

31. B. X. Chen, "Uber, Maker of Summon a Car App, Wins in Washington," Bits, July 10, 2012.

32. Z. Miners, "Seattle City Council Legalizes Uber, Lyft, Sidecar without Caps," *PC World*, July 14, 2014.

33. C. Albanesius, "Uber Drops Taxi-hailing App in New York," *PC Magazine*, October 16, 2012.

34. M. Scott, "European Taxi Drivers Snarl Traffic in Protest Against Car-paging Service," *New York Times*, June 12, 2014, p. B3.

35. B. X. Chen, "A Feisty Startup Is Met with Regulatory Snarl," *New York Times*, December 2, 2012.

36. D. Bond-Graham, "Uber and Lyft Get a Lot of Hype–But Ridesharing Is a Parasitic Business Model," *AlterNet*, October 22, 2013.

37. Staff reporter, "Lyft Offers $10K a Month to Lure Drivers in NYC," *Crain's New York Business*, August 1, 2014.

38. R. Lawler, "See Uber–This Is What Happens When You Cannibalize Yourself," TechCrunch, March 15, 2013.

39. E. Huet, "Uber's Newest Tactic: Pay Drivers More Than They Earn," *Forbes*, July 2, 2014.

40. N. Tiku, "Leaked: Uber's Internal Revenue and Ride Request Numbers," Valleywag, December 4, 2013.

41. K. Rose, "Uber Might Be More Valuable than Facebook Someday. Here's Why."

18

THE HOME VIDEOGAME INDUSTRY: THE FIRST FOUR DECADES

AN INDUSTRY IS BORN

In 1968, Nolan Bushell, the 24-year-old son of a Utah cement contractor, graduated from the University of Utah with a degree in engineering.[1] Bushnell then moved to California, where he worked briefly in the computer graphics division of Ampex. At home, Bushnell turned his daughter's bedroom into a laboratory. There, he created a simpler version of Space War, a computer game that had been invented in 1962 by an MIT graduate student, Steve Russell. Bushnell's version of Russell's game, which he called Computer Space, was made of integrated circuits connected to a 19-inch, black-and-white television screen. Unlike a computer, Bushnell's invention could do nothing but run the game, which meant that, unlike a computer, it could be produced cheaply.

Bushnell envisioned videogames like his standing next to pinball machines in arcades. With hopes of having his invention put into production, Bushnell left Ampex to work for a small pinball company that manufactured 1,500 copies of his videogame. The game never sold, primarily because the player had to read a full page of directions before playing—way too complex for arcade gaming. Bushnell left the pinball company and with a friend, Ted Dabney, put up $500 to start a company that would develop a simpler videogame. They wanted to call the company Syzygy, but the name was already taken, so they settled on Atari, a Japanese word that is the equivalent of "check in the go."

In his home laboratory, Bushnell built the simplest game he could think of. People knew the rules immediately, and it could be played with one hand. The game was modeled on table tennis, and players batted a ball back and forth with paddles that could be moved up and down sides of a court by twisting knobs. He named the game Pong after the sonarlike sound that was emitted every time the ball connected with a paddle.

In Fall 1972, Bushnell installed his prototype for Pong in Andy Capp's tavern in Sunnyvale, California. The only instructions were "avoid missing the ball for a high score." In the first week, 1,200 quarters were deposited in the casserole dish that served for a coin box in Bushnell's prototype. Bushnell was ecstatic; his simple game had brought in $300 in a week. The pinball machine that stood next to it averaged $35 a week.

Lacking the capital to mass produce the game, Bushnell approached established amusement game companies, only to be repeatedly shown the door. Down but hardly out, Bushnell cut his hair, put on a suit, and talked his way into a $50,000 line of credit from a local bank. He set up a production line in an abandoned roller-skating rink and e-hired people to assemble machines while Led Zeppelin and the Rolling Stones were played at full volume over the speaker system of the rink. Among his first batch of employees was a skinny, 17-year-old named Steve Jobs, who would later found Apple Computer, NeXT, and Pixar. Like others, Jobs had been attracted by a classified ad that read "Have Fun and Make Money."

In no time at all, Bushnell was selling all the machines that his small staff could make—about 10 per day—but to grow, he needed additional capital. While the ambience at the rink, with its mix of rock music and marijuana fumes, put off most potential investors, Don Valentine, one of the country's most astute and credible venture capitalists, was impressed with the growth story. Armed with Valentine's money, Atari began to increase production and expand their range of games. New games included Tank and Breakout; the latter was designed by Jobs and a friend of his, Steve Wozniak, who had left Hewlett-Packard to work at Atari.

By 1974, 100,000 Ponglike games were sold worldwide. Although Atari manufactured only 10% of the games, the company still made $3.2 million that year. With the Pong clones coming on strong, Bushnell decided to make a Pong system for the home. In fact, Magnavox had been marketing a similar game for the home since 1972, although sales had been modest.[2] Bushnell's team managed to compress Atari's coin-operated Pong game down to a few inexpensive circuits that were contained in the game console. Atari's Pong had a sharper picture and more sensitive controllers than Magnavox's machine; it also cost less. Bushnell then went on a road show, demonstrating Pong to toy buyers, but he received an indifferent response and no sales. A dejected Bushnell returned to Atari with no idea of what to do next. Then the buyer for the sporting goods department at Sears came to see Bushnell, examined the machine, and offered to buy every home

Pong game Atari could make. With Sears's backing, Bushnell boosted production. Sears ran a major television ad campaign to sell home Pong, and Atari's sales soared, hitting $450 million in 1975. The home videogame had arrived.

BOOM AND BUST

Nothing attracts competitors like success. By 1976, about 20 different companies were crowding into the home videogame market, including National Semiconductor, RCA, Coleco, and Fairchild. Recognizing the limitations of existing home videogame designs, Fairchild came out in 1976 with a home videogame system capable of playing multiple games. The Fairchild system consisted of three components—a console, controllers, and cartridges. The console was a small computer optimized for graphics-processing capabilities. It was designed to receive information from the controllers, process it, and send signals to a television monitor. The controllers were handheld devices used to direct on-screen action. The cartridges contained chips encoding the instructions for a game. The cartridges were designed to be inserted into the console.

In 1976, Bushnell sold Atari to Warner Communications for $28 million. Bushnell stayed on to run Atari. Backed by Warner's capital, in 1977, Atari developed and brought out its own cartridge-based system, the Atari 2600. The 2600 system sold for $200, and associated cartridges retailed for $25 to $30. Sales surged during the 1977 Christmas season. However, a lack of manufacturing capacity on the part of market leader Atari, and a very cautious approach to inventory by Fairchild, led to shortages and kept sales significantly below what they could have been. Fairchild's cautious approach was the result of prior experience in consumer electronics. A year earlier, it had increased demand for its digital watches only to accumulate a buildup of excess inventory that caused the company to take a $24.5 million write-off.[3]

After the 1977 Christmas season, Atari claimed to have sold about 400,000 units of the 2600 VCA, about 50% of all cartridge-based systems in American homes. Atari had also earned more than $100 million in sales of game cartridges. By this point, second-place Fairchild sold around 250,000 units of its system. Cartridge sales for the year totaled about 1.2 million units, with an average selling price of $20. Fresh from this success and fortified by market forecasts predicting sales of 33 million cartridges and an installed base of 16 million machines by 1980, Bushnell committed Atari to manufacturing 1 million units of the 2600 for the 1978 Christmas season. Atari estimated that total demand would reach 2 million units. Bushnell was also encouraged by signals from Fairchild that it would again be limiting production to around 200,000 units. At this point, Atari had a library of 9 games; Fairchild had 17.[4]

Atari was not the only company excited by the growth forecasts. In 1978, a host of other companies, including Coleco, National Semiconductor, Magnavox, General Instrument, and a dozen other companies, entered the market with incompatible cartridge-based home systems. The multitude of choices did not entice consumers, however, and the 1978 Christmas season brought unexpectedly low sales. Only Atari and Coleco survived an industry shakeout. Atari lost Bushnell, who was ousted by Warner executives. (Bushnell went on to start Chuck E. Cheese Pizza Time Theater, a restaurant chain that had 278 outlets by 1981.) Bushnell later stated that part of the problem was a disagreement over strategy. Bushnell wanted Atari to price the 2600 at cost and make money on sales of software; Warner wanted to continue making profits on hardware sales.[5]

Several important developments occurred in 1979. First, several game producers and programmers defected from Atari to set up their own firm, Activision, and to make games compatible with the Atari 2600. Their success encouraged others to follow suit. Second, Coleco developed an expansion module that allowed its machine to play Atari games. Atari and Mattel (which entered the market in 1979) did likewise. Third, three new games were introduced to the home market—Space Invaders, Asteroids, and PacMan. All three were adapted from popular arcade games, and all three helped drive demand for players.

Demand recovered strongly in late 1979 and kept growing for the next three years. In 1981, U.S. sales of home videogames and cartridges hit $1 billion. In 1982, they surged to $3 billion, with Atari accounting for half of this amount. It seemed as if Atari could do no wrong; the 2600 was everywhere. About

20 million units were sold, and by late 1982, numerous independent companies, including Activision, Imagic, and Epyx, were producing hundreds of games for the 2600. Second-place Coleco was also doing well, partly because of a popular arcade game, Donkey Kong, which it had licensed from the Japanese company Nintendo.

Atari was also in contact with Nintendo. In 1982, the company very nearly licensed the rights to Nintendo's Famicom, a cartridge-based videogame system machine that was a big hit in Japan. Atari's successor to the 2600, the 5200, was not selling well; the Famicom seemed like a good substitute. Negotiations broke down, however, when Atari discovered that Nintendo had extended its Donkey Kong license to Coleco. This allowed Coleco to port a version of the game to its home computer, which was a direct competitor to Atari's 800 home computer.[6]

After a strong 1982 season, the industry hoped for continued growth in 1983. Then the bottom dropped out of the market. Sales of home videogames plunged to $100 million. Atari lost $500 million in the first 9 months of the year, causing the stock of parent company Warner Communications to drop by half. Part of the blame for the collapse was laid at the feet of an enormous inventory overhang of unsold games. About 15 to 20 million surplus game cartridges were left over from the 1982 Christmas season (in 1981, there were none). On top of this, some 500 new games hit the market in 1993. The average price of a cartridge plunged from $30 in 1979 to $16 in 1982, and then to $4 in 1983. As sales slowed, retailers cut back on the shelf space allocated to video games. It proved difficult for new games to make a splash in a crowded market. Atari had to dispose of 6 million "ET: The Extraterrestrial" games. Meanwhile, big hits from previous years such as Pac Man were bundled with consoles and given away free to try to encourage system sales.[7]

Surveying the rubble, commentators claimed that the videogame industry was dead. The era of dedicated game machines was over, they claimed. Personal computers were taking their place.[8] It seemed to be true. Mattel sold off its game business, Fairchild moved on to other things, Coleco folded, and Warner decided to break up Atari and sell its constituent pieces—at least, those pieces for which it could find a buyer. No one in America seemed to want to have anything to do with the home videogame business—no one, that is, except for Minoru Arakawa, the head of Nintendo's U.S. subsidiary, Nintendo of America (NOA). Picking through the rubble of the industry, Arakawa noticed that there were people who still packed video arcades, bringing in $7 billion a year, more money than the entire movie industry. Perhaps it was not a lack of interest in home videogames that had killed the industry. Perhaps it was bad business practice.

▌ THE NINTENDO MONOPOLY

Nintendo was a century-old Japanese company that had built up a profitable business making playing cards before diversifying into the videogame business. Based in Kyoto and still run by the founding Yamauchi family, the company diversified into the videogame business in the late 1970s. The first step was to license videogame technology from Magnavox. In 1977, Nintendo introduced a home videogame system in Japan based on this technology that played a variation of Pong. In 1978, the company began to sell coin-operated videogames. It had its first hit with Donkey Kong, designed by Sigeru Miyamoto.

The Famicom

In the early 1980s, the company's boss, Hiroshi Yamauchi, decided that Nintendo had to develop its own videogame machine. He pushed the company's engineers to develop a machine that combined superior graphics-processing capabilities and low cost. Yamauchi wanted a machine that could sell for $75, less than half the price of competing machines at the time. He dubbed the machine the Family Computer, or Famicom. The machine that his engineers designed was based on the controller, console, and plug-in cartridge format pioneered by Fairchild. It contained two custom chips—an 8-bit central processing unit and a graphics-processing unit. Both chips had been scaled down to perform only essential functions. A 16-bit processor was available at the time, but to keep costs down Yamauchi refused to use it.

Nintendo approached Ricoh, the electronics giant, which had spare semiconductor capacity. Employees at Ricoh said that the chips had to cost no more that 2,000 yen. Ricoh thought that the 2,000-yen price point was absurd. Yamauchi's response was to guarantee Ricoh a 3-million-chip order within 2 years. Since the leading companies in Japan were selling, at most, 30,000 video games per year at the time, many within the company viewed this as an outrageous commitment, but Ricoh went for it.[9]

Another feature of the machine was its memory—2,000 bytes of random access memory (RAM), compared to the 256 bytes of RAM in the Atari machine. The result was a machine with superior graphics-processing capabilities and faster action, which could handle far more complex games than Atari's. Nintendo engineers also built a new set of chips into the game cartridges. In addition to chips that held the game program, they developed memory map controller (MMC) chips that took over some of the graphics-processing work from the chips in the console and enabled the system to run more complex games. With the addition of the MMC chips, the potential for more sophisticated, more complex games had arrived. Over time, Nintendo engineers developed increasingly powerful MMC chips, enabling the basic 8-bit system to perform in ways that originally seemed out of reach. The engineers also figured out a way to include a battery backup system in cartridges that allowed some games to store information independently—to keep track of where a player had left off or to track high scores.

The Games

Yamauchi recognized that great hardware would not sell itself. The key to the market, he reasoned, was great games. Yamauchi had instructed the engineers developing the hardware to make sure that "it was appreciated by software engineers." Nintendo decided that it would become a haven for game designers. "An ordinary man," Yamauchi said, "cannot develop good games no matter how hard he tries. A handful of people in this world can develop games that everyone wants. Those are the people we want at Nintendo."[10]

Yamauchi had an advantage in the person of Sigeru Miyamoto. Miyamoto had joined Nintendo at the age of 24. Yamauchi had hired Miyamoto, a graduate of Kanazawa Munici College of Industrial Arts, as a favor to his father and an old friend, although he had little idea what he would do with an artist. For 3 years, Miyamoto worked as Nintendo's staff artist. Then, in 1980, Yamauchi called Miyamoto into his office. Nintendo had started selling coin-operated videogames, but one of the new games, Radarscope, was a disaster. Could Miyamoto come up with a new game? Miyamoto was delighted. He had always spent a lot of time drawing cartoons, and as a student he had played videogames constantly. Miyamoto believed that videogames could be used to bring cartoons to life.[11]

The game Miyamoto developed was nothing short of a revelation. At a time when most coin-operated videogames lacked characters or depth, Miyamoto created a game around a story that had both. Most games involved battles with space invaders or heroes shooting lasers at aliens; Miyamoto's game did neither. Based loosely on *Beauty and the Beast* and *King Kong,* Miyamoto's game involved a pet ape who runs off with his master's beautiful girlfriend. His master is an ordinary carpenter called Mario, who has a bulbous nose, a bushy mustache, a pair of large, pathetic eyes, and a red cap (which Miyamoto added because he was not good at hairstyles). He does not carry a laser gun. The ape runs off with the girlfriend to get back at his master, who was not especially nice to the beast. The man, of course, has to get his girlfriend back by running up ramps, climbing ladders, jumping off elevators, and the like, while the ape throws objects at the hapless carpenter. Since the main character is an ape, Miyamoto called him Kong; because the main character is as stubborn as a donkey, he called the game Donkey Kong.

Released in 1981, Donkey Kong was a sensation in the world of coin-operated video arcades and a smash hit for Nintendo. In 1984, Yamauchi again summoned Miyamoto to his office. He needed more games, this time for Famicom. Miyamoto was named the head of a new research and development (R&D) group and told to come up with the most imaginative videogames ever.

Miyamoto began with Mario from Donkey Kong. A colleague had told him that Mario looked more like a plumber than a carpenter, so a plumber he became. Miyamoto gave Mario a brother, Luigi, who was as tall and thin as Mario was short and fat. They became the Super Mario Brothers. Plumbers spend their time working on pipes; so large, green sewer pipes became obstacles and doorways into secret worlds. Mario and Luigi's task was to search for the captive Princess Toadstool. Mario and Luigi are endearing bumblers, unequal to their tasks yet surviving. They shoot, squash, or evade their enemies—including flying turtles, stinging fish, maneating flowers, and fire-breathing dragons—while they collect gold coins, blow air bubbles, and climb vines into smiling clouds.[12]

Super Mario Brothers was introduced in 1985. For Miyamoto, this was just the beginning. Between 1985 and 1991, Miyamoto produced eight Mario games. About 60 to 70 million were sold worldwide, making Miyamoto the most successful game designer in the world. After adapting Donkey Kong for Famicom, he went on to create other top-selling games, including another classic, The Legend of Zelda. While Miyamoto drew freely from folklore, literature, and pop culture, the main source for his ideas was his own experience. The memory of being lost among a maze of sliding doors in his family's home was recreated in the labyrinths of the Zelda games. The dog that attacked him when he was a child attacks Mario in Super Mario. As a child, Miyamoto had once climbed a tree to catch a view of far-off mountains and had become stuck. Mario gets himself in a similar fix. Once Miyamoto went hiking without a map and was surprised to stumble across a lake. In the Legend of Zelda, part of the adventure is in walking into new places without a map and being confronted by surprises.

Nintendo in Japan

Nintendo introduced Famicom into the Japanese market in May 1983. Famicom was priced at $100, more than Yamauchi wanted but significantly less than the products of competitors. When he introduced the machine, Yamauchi urged retailers to forgo profits on the hardware because it was just a tool to sell software, and that is where they would make their money. Backed by an extensive advertising campaign, 500,000 units of Famicom were sold in the first 2 months. Within a year, the figure stood at 1 million, and sales were still expanding rapidly. With the hardware quickly finding its way into Japanese homes, Nintendo was besieged with calls from desperate retailers frantically demanding more games.

At this point Yamauchi told Miyamoto to come up with the most imaginative games ever. However, Yamauchi also realized that Nintendo alone could not satisfy the growing thirst for new games, so he initiated a licensing program. To become a Nintendo licensee, companies had to agree to an unprecedented series of restrictions. Licensees could issue only five Nintendo games per year, and they could not write those titles for other platforms. The licensing fee was set at 20% of the wholesale price of each cartridge sold (game cartridges wholesaled for around $30). It typically cost $500,000 and took around 6 months to develop a game. Nintendo insisted that games contain no excessively violent or sexually suggestive material, and they reviewed every game before allowing it to be produced.[13]

Despite these restrictions, six companies (Bandai, Capcom, Konami, Namco, Taito, and Hudson) agreed to become Nintendo licensees, not least because millions of customers were now clamoring for games. Bandai was Japan's largest toy company. The others already made either coin-operated videogames or computer software games. Because of these licensing agreements, they saw their sales and earnings surge. For example, Konami's earnings went from $10 million in 1987 to $300 million in 1991.

After the six licensees began selling games, reports of defective games began to reach Yamauchi. The original six licensees were allowed to manufacture their own game cartridges. Realizing that he had given away the ability to control the quality of the cartridges, Yamauchi decided to change the contract for future licensees. Future licensees were required to submit all manufacturing orders for cartridges to Nintendo. Nintendo charged licensees $14 per cartridge, required that they place a minimum order for 10,000 units (later the minimum order was raised to 30,000), and insisted on cash payment in full when the order was placed. Nintendo outsourced all manufacturing to other companies, using the volume of its orders to get rock bottom prices. The cartridges were estimated to cost Nintendo between $6 and $8 each. The licensees then picked up the cartridges from Nintendo's loading dock and were responsible for distribution. In 1985, there were 17 licensees. By 1987, there were 50. By this point, 90% of the home videogame systems sold in Japan were Nintendo systems.

Nintendo in America

In 1980, Nintendo established a subsidiary in America to sell its coin-operated videogames. Yamauchi's American-educated son-in-law, Minoru Arakawa, headed the subsidiary. All of the other essential employees were Americans, including Ron Judy and Al Stone. For its first 2 years, Nintendo of America (NOA), based originally in Seattle, struggled to sell second-rate games such as Radarscope. The subsidiary seemed on the brink of closing. NOA could not even make the rent payment on the warehouse. Then they received a large shipment from Japan: 2,000 units of a new, coin-operated videogame. Opening the box, they discovered Donkey Kong. After playing the game briefly, Judy proclaimed it a disaster. Stone walked out of the building, declaring that "it's over."[14] The managers were appalled. They could not imagine a game less likely to sell in video arcades. The only promising sign was that a 20-year employee, Howard Philips, rapidly became enthralled with the machine.

Arakawa, however, knew he had little choice but to try to sell the machine. Judy persuaded the owner of the Spot Tavern near Nintendo's office to take one of the machines on a trial basis. After one night, Judy discovered $30 in the coin box, a phenomenal amount. The next night there was $35, and $36 the night after that. NOA had a hit on its hands.

By the end of 1982, NOA had sold over 60,000 copies of Donkey Kong and had booked sales in excess of $100 million. The subsidiary had outgrown its Seattle location. They moved to a new site in Redmond, a Seattle suburb, where they located next to a small but fast-growing software company run by an old school acquaintance of Howard Philips, Bill Gates.

By 1984, NOA was riding a wave of success in the coin-operated videogame market. Arakawa, however, was interested in the possibilities of selling Nintendo's new Famicom system in the United States. Throughout 1984, Arakawa, Judy, and Stone met with numerous toy and department store representatives to discuss the possibilities, only to be repeatedly rebuffed. Still smarting from the 1983 debacle, the representatives wanted nothing to do with the home videogame business. They also met with former managers from Atari and Caloco to gain their insights. The most common response they received was that the market had collapsed because the last generation of games were awful.

Arakawa and his team decided that if they were going to sell Famicom in the United States, they would have to find a new distribution channel. The obvious choice was consumer electronics stores.

Thus, Arakawa asked the R&D team in Kyoto to re-design Famicom for the U.S. market so that it looked less like a toy (Famicom was encased in red and white plastic), and more like a consumer electronics device. The redesigned machine was renamed the Nintendo Entertainment System (NES).

Arakawa's big fear was that illegal, low-quality Taiwanese games would flood the U.S. market if NES was successful. To stop counterfeit games being played on NES, Arakawa asked Nintendo's Japanese engineers to design a security system into the U.S. version of Famicom so that only Nintendo-approved games could be played on NES. The Japanese engineers responded by designing a security chip to be embedded in the game cartridges. NES would not work unless the security chips in the cartridges unlocked—or "shook hands with"—a chip in NES. Since the code embedded in the security chip was proprietary, the implication of this system was that no one could manufacture games for NES without Nintendo's specific approval.

To overcome the skepticism and reluctance of retailers to stock a home videogame system, Arakawa decided in late 1985 to make an extraordinary commitment. Nintendo would stock stores and set up displays and windows. Retailers would not have to pay for anything they stocked for 90 days. After that, retailers could pay Nintendo for what they sold and return the rest. NES was bundled with Nintendo's bestselling game in Japan, Super Mario Brothers. It was essentially a risk-free proposition for retailers, but even with this, most were skeptical. Ultimately, 30 Nintendo personnel descended on the New York City area. Referred to as the Nintendo SWAT team, they persuaded some stores to stock NES after an extraordinary blitz that involved 18-hour days. To support this product launch, Nintendo committed itself to a $5-million advertising campaign aimed at the 7- to 14-year-old boys who seemed to be Nintendo's likely core audience.

By December 1985, between 500 and 600 stores in the New York City area were stocking Nintendo systems. Sales were moderate—about half of the 100,000 NES machines shipped from Japan were sold—but enough to justify going forward. The SWAT team then moved to Los Angeles, then Chicago, then Dallas. As in New York, sales started at a moderate pace but, by late 1986, they started to accelerate rapidly and Nintendo went national with NES.

In 1986, around 1 million NES units were sold in the United States. In 1987, the figure increased to 3 million. In 1988, it jumped to over 7 million. In the same year, 33 million game cartridges were sold. Nintendo mania had arrived in the United States. To expand the supply of games, Nintendo licensed the rights to produce up to five games per year to 31 American software companies. Nintendo continued to use a restrictive licensing agreement that gave it exclusive rights to any games, required licensees to place their orders through Nintendo, and insisted on a 30,000-unit minimum order.[15]

By 1990, the home videogame market was worth $5 billion worldwide. Nintendo dominated the industry, with a 90% share of the market for game equipment. The parent company was, by some measures, now the most profitable company in Japan. By 1992, it was netting over $1 billion in gross profit annually, or more than $1.5 million for each employee in Japan. The company's stock market value exceeded that of Sony, Japan's premier consumer electronics firm. Indeed, the company's net profit exceeded that of all the American movie studios combined. Nintendo games, it seemed, were bigger than the movies.

As of 1991, there were over 100 licensees for Nintendo, and over 450 titles were available for NES. In the United States, Nintendo products were distributed through toy stores (30% of volume), mass merchandisers (40% of volume), and department stores (10% of volume). Nintendo tightly controlled the number of game titles and games that could be sold, quickly withdrawing titles as soon as interest appeared to decline. In 1988, retailers requested 110 million cartridges from Nintendo. Market surveys suggested that perhaps 45 million could have been sold, but Nintendo allowed only 33 million to be shipped.[16] Nintendo claimed that the shortage of games was in part due to a worldwide shortage of semiconductor chips.

Several companies had tried to reverse-engineer the code embedded in Nintendo's security chip, which competitors characterized as a lockout chip. Nintendo successfully sued them. The most notable was Atari Games, one of the successors of the original Atari, which in 1987 sued Nintendo of America for anti-competitive behavior. Atari claimed that the purpose of the security chip was to monopolize the market. At the same time, Atari announced that it had found a way around Nintendo's security chip and would begin to sell unlicensed games.[17] NOA responded with a countersuit. In a March 1991 ruling, Atari was found to have obtained Nintendo's security code illegally and was ordered to stop selling NES-compatible games. However, Nintendo did not always have it all its own way. In 1990, under pressure from Congress, the Department of Justice, and several lawsuits, Nintendo rescinded its exclusivity requirements, freeing up developers to write games for other platforms. However, developers faced a real problem: What platform could they write for?

◢ SEGA'S SONIC BOOM

Back in 1954, David Rosen, a 20-year-old American, left the U.S. Air Force after a tour of duty in Tokyo.[18] Rosen had noticed Japanese citizens needed many photographs for ID cards, but that local photo studios were slow and expensive. He formed Rosen Enterprises and went into the photo-booth business, which was a big success. By 1957, Rosen had established a successful, nationwide chain. At this point, the Japanese economy was booming, so Rosen decided it was time to get into another business—entertainment. As his vehicle, he chose arcade games, which were unknown in Japan at the time. He picked up used games on the cheap from America and set up arcades in the same Japanese department stores and theaters that typically housed his photo booths. Within a few years, Rosen had 200 arcades nationwide. His only competition came from another American-owned firm, Service Games (Sega), whose original business was jukeboxes and fruit machines.

By the early 1960s, the Japanese arcade market had caught up with the U.S. market. The problem was that game makers had run out of exciting new games to offer. Rosen decided that he would have to get into the business of designing and manufacturing games, but to do that he needed manufacturing facilities. Sega manufactured its own games, so in 1965 Rosen approached the company and suggested a merger. The result was Sega Enterprises, a Japanese company with Rosen as its CEO.

Rosen himself designed Sega's first game, Periscope, in which the objective was to sink chain-mounted cardboard ships by firing torpedoes, represented by lines of colored lights. Periscope was a big success not only in Japan, but also in the United States and Europe, and it allowed Sega to build up a respectable export business. Over the years, the company continued to invest heavily in game development, always using the latest electronic technology.

Gulf and Western, a U.S. conglomerate, acquired Sega in 1969, with Rosen running the subsidiary. In 1975, Gulf and Western (G&W) took Sega public in the United States, but left Sega Japan as a G&W subsidiary. Hayao Nakayama, a former Sega distributor, was drafted as president. In the early 1980s, Nakayama pushed G&W to invest more in Sega Japan so that the company could enter the then-booming home videogame market. When G&W refused, Nakayama suggested a management buyout. G&W agreed and, in 1984, for the price of just $38 million, Sega became a Japanese company once more. (Sega's Japanese revenues were around $700 million, but by now the company was barely profitable.)

Sega was caught off guard by the huge success of Nintendo's Famicom. Although it released its own 8-bit system in 1986, the machine never commanded more than 5% of the Japanese market. Nakayama, however, was not about to give up. From years in the arcade business, he understood that great games drove sales. Nevertheless, he also understood that more powerful technology gave game developers the tools to develop more appealing games. This philosophy underlay Nakayama's decision to develop a 16-bit game system, Genesis.

Sega took the design of its 16-bit arcade machine and adapted it for Genesis. Compared to Nintendo's 8-bit machine, the 16-bit machine featured an array of superior technological features, including high-definition graphics and animation, a full spectrum of colors, two independent, scrolling backgrounds that created an impressive depth of field, and near-CD quality sound. The design strategy also made it easy to port Sega's catalog of arcade hits to Genesis.

Genesis was launched in Japan in 1989, and in the United States in 1990. In the United States, the machine was priced at $199. The company hoped that sales would be boosted by the popularity of its arcade games, such as the graphically violent Altered Beast. Sega also licensed other companies to develop games for the Genesis platform. In an effort to recruit licensees, Sega asked for lower royalty rates than Nintendo, and it gave licensees the right to manufacture their own cartridges. Independent game developers were slow to climb on board, however, and the $200 price tag for the player held back sales.

One of the first independent game developers to sign up with Sega was Electronic Arts. Established by Trip Hawkins, Electronic Arts had focused on designing games for PCs and consequently had missed the Nintendo 8-bit era. Now Hawkins was determined to get a presence in the home videogame market, and aligning his company with Sega seemed to be the best option. The Nintendo playing field was already crowded, and Sega offered a far less restrictive licensing deal than Nintendo. Electronic Arts subsequently wrote several popular games for Genesis, including John Madden Football and several gory combat games.[19]

Nintendo had not been ignoring the potential of its 16-bit system, Super NES, which was ready for market introduction in 1989—at the same time as Sega's Genesis. Nintendo introduced Super NES in Japan in 1990, where it quickly established a strong market presence and beat Sega's Genesis. In the United States, however, the company decided to hold back longer to reap the full benefits of the dominance it enjoyed with the 8-bit NES system. Yamauchi was also worried about the lack of backward compatibility between Nintendo's 8-bit and 16-bit systems. (The company had tried to make the 16-bit system so that it could play 8-bit games, but concluded that the cost of doing so was prohibitive.) These concerns may have led the company to delay market introduction until the 8-bit market was saturated.

Meanwhile, in the United States, the Sega bandwagon was beginning to gain momentum. One development that gave Genesis a push was the introduction of a new Sega game, Sonic the Hedgehog. Developed by an independent team that was contracted to Sega, the game featured a cute hedgehog that impatiently tapped his paw when the player took too long to act. Impatience was Sonic's central feature—he had places to go, and quickly. He zipped along, collecting brass rings when he could find them, before rolling into a ball and flying down slides with loops and underground tunnels. Sonic was Sega's Mario.

In mid-1991, in an attempt to jump-start slow sales, Tom Kalinske, head of Sega's American subsidiary, decided to bundle Sonic the Hedgehog with the game player. He also reduced the price for the bundled unit to $150 and relaunched the system with an aggressive advertising campaign aimed at teenagers. The campaign was built around the slogan "Genesis does what Nintendon't." The shift in strategy worked, and sales accelerated sharply.

Sega's success prompted Nintendo to launch its 16-bit system, Super NES, at $200. However, Sega now had a 2-year head start in games. By the end of 1991, about 125 game titles were available for Genesis, compared to 25 for Super NES. In May 1992, Nintendo reduced the price of Super NES to $150. At this time, Sega was claiming a 63% share of the 16-bit market in the United States, and Nintendo claimed a 60% share. By now, Sega was cool. It began to take more chances with mass-media-defined morality. When Acclaim Entertainment released its bloody Mortal Kombat game in September 1992, the Sega version let players rip off heads and tear out hearts. Reflecting Nintendo's image of their core market, its version was sanitized. The Sega version outsold Nintendo's two to one.[20] Therefore, the momentum continued to run in Sega's favor. By January 1993, there were 320 titles available for Sega Genesis, and 130 for Super NES. In early 1994, independent estimates suggested that Sega had 60% of the U.S. market and Nintendo had 40%, figures Nintendo disputed.

3DO

Trip Hawkins, whose first big success was Electronic Arts, founded 3DO in 1991.[21] Hawkins's vision for 3DO was to shift the home videogame business away from the existing cartridge-based format and toward a CD-ROM-based platform. The original partners in 3DO were Electronic Arts, Matsushita, Time Warner, AT&T, and the venture-capital firm Kleiner Perkins. Collectively they invested over $17 million in 3DO, making it the richest start-up in the history of the home videogame industry. 3DO went public in May 1993 at $15 per share. By October of that year, the stock had risen to $48 per share, making 3DO worth $1 billion—not bad for a company that had yet to generate a single dollar in revenues.

The bases for 3DO's $1-billion market cap were its patented computer system architecture and a copyrighted operating system that allowed for much richer graphics and audio capabilities. The system was built around a 32-bit, RISC microprocessor and proprietary graphics processor chips. Instead of a cartridge, the 3DO system stored games on a CD-ROM that was capable of holding up to 600 megabytes of content, sharply up from the 10 megabytes of content found in the typical game cartridge of the time. The slower access time of a CD-ROM compared to a cartridge was alleviated somewhat by the use of a double-speed CD-ROM drive.[22]

The belief at 3DO—a belief apparently shared by many investors—was that the superior storage and graphics-processing capabilities of the 3DO system would prove very attractive to game developers, allowing them to be far more creative. In turn, better games would attract customers away from Nintendo and Sega. Developing games that used the capabilities of a CD-ROM system altered the economics of game development. Estimates suggested that it would cost approximately $2 million to produce a game for the 3DO system and could take as long as 24 months to develop. However, at $2 per disc, a CD-ROM cost substantially less to manufacture than a cartridge.

The centerpiece of 3DO's strategy was to license its hardware technology for free. Game developers paid a royalty of $3 per disc for access to the 3DO operating code. Discs typically retailed for $40 each.

Matsushita introduced the first 3DO machine into the U.S. market in October 1993. Priced at $700, the machine was sold through electronic retailers that carried Panasonic high-end electronics products. Sega's Tom Kalinsky noted, "It's a noble effort. Some people will buy 3DO, and they'll have a wonderful experience. It's impressive, but it's a niche. We've done the research. It does not become a large market until you go below $500. At $300, it starts to get interesting. We make no money on hardware. It's a cutthroat business. I hope Matsushita understands that."[23] CD-ROM discs for the 3DO machine retailed for around $75. The machine came bundled with Crash n Burn, a high-speed, combat racing game. However, only 18 3DO titles were available by the crucial Christmas period, although reports suggested that 150 titles were under development.[24]

Sales of the hardware were slow, reaching only 30,000 by January 1994.[25] In the same month, AT&T and Sanyo both announced that they would begin to manufacture the 3DO machine. In March, faced with continuing sluggish sales, 3DO announced that it would give hardware manufacturers two shares of 3DO stock for every unit sold at or below a certain retail price. Matsushita dropped the price of its machine to $500. About the same time, Toshiba, LG, and Samsung all announced that they would start to produce 3DO machines.

By June 1994, cumulative sales of 3DO machines in the United States stood at 40,000 units. Matsushita announced plans to expand distribution beyond the current 3,500 outlets to include the toy and mass-merchandise channels. Hawkins and his partners announced that they would invest another $37 million in 3DO. By July, there were 750 3DO software licensees, but only 40 titles were available for the format. Despite these moves, sales continued at a very sluggish pace, and the supply of new titles started to dry up.[26]

In September 1996, 3DO announced that it would either sell its hardware system business or move it into a joint venture.[27] The company announced that some 150 people, one-third of the work force, would probably lose their jobs in the restructuring. According to Hawkins, 3DO would now focus on developing software for online gaming. Hawkins stated that the Internet and Internet entertainment constituted a huge opportunity for 3DO. The stock dropped $1.375, to $6.75.

SONY PLAYSTATION

In Fall 1995, Sony entered the fray with the introduction of its PlayStation.[28] PlayStation used a 32-bit, RISC microprocessor running at 33 MHz and using a double-speed CD-ROM drive. PlayStation cost an estimated $500 million to develop. The machine had actually been under development since 1991, when Sony decided that the home videogame industry was getting too big to ignore. Initially, Sony was in an alliance with Nintendo to develop the machine. Nintendo walked away from the alliance in 1992, however, after a disagreement over who owned the rights to future CD-ROM games. Sony moved forward alone.[29]

A consumer electronics giant with a position in the Hollywood movie business and the music industry (Sony owned Columbia Pictures and the Columbia record label), Sony believed from the start that it had access to significant intellectual property that could form the basis of many popular games.

In 1991, Sony established a division in New York: Sony Electronic Publishing. The division was to serve as an umbrella organization for Sony's multimedia offerings. Headed by Iceland native Olaf Olafsson, then just 28 years old, this organization ultimately took the lead role in both the market launch of PlayStation and in developing game titles.[30] In 1993, as part of this effort, Sony purchased a well-respected British game developer, Psygnosis. By Fall 1995, this unit had 20 games ready to complement PlayStation: The Halde-man Diaries, Mickey Mania (developed in collaboration with Disney), and Johnny Mnemonic, based on the William Gibson short story. To entice independent game developers such as Electronic Arts, Namco, and Acclaim Entertainment, Olafsson used the promise of low royalty rates. The standard royalty rate was set at $9 per disc, although developers that signed on early enough were given a lower royalty rate. Sony also provided approximately 4,000 game development tools to licensees in an effort to help them speed games to market.[31]

To distribute PlayStation, Sony set up a retail channel separate from Sony's consumer electronics sales force. It marketed the PlayStation as a hip, powerful alternative to the outdated Nintendo and Sega cartridge-based systems. Sony worked closely with retailers before the launch to determine how it could help them sell the PlayStation. To jump-start demand, Sony set up in-store displays to allow potential consumers to try the equipment. Just before the launch, Sony had lined up an impressive 12,000 retail outlets in the United States.[32]

Sony targeted its advertising for PlayStation at males in the 18 to 35 age range. The targeting was evident in the content of many games. One big hit for PlayStation was Tomb Raider, whose central character, Lara Croft, combined sex appeal and savvy and helped to recruit an older generation to PlayStation.[33] PlayStation was initially priced at $299, and games retailed for as much as $60. Sony's Tokyo-based executives had reportedly been insisting on a $350–$400 price for PlayStation, but Olafsson pushed hard for the lower price. Because of the fallout from this internal battle, in January 1996, Olafsson resigned from Sony. By then, however, Sony was following Olafsson's script.[34]

Sony's prelaunch work was rewarded with strong early sales. By January 1996, more than 800,000 PlayStations had been sold in the United States, plus another 4 million games. In May 1996, with 1.2 million PlayStations shipped, Sony reduced the price of PlayStation to $199. Sega responded with a similar price cut for its Saturn. The prices on some of Sony's initial games were also reduced to $29.99. The weekend after the price cuts, retailers reported that PlayStation sales were up by between 350 and 1,000% over the prior week.[35] The sales surge continued through 1996. By the end of the year, sales of PlayStation and associated software amounted to $1.3 billion, out of a total for U.S. sales at $2.2 billion for all videogame hardware and software. In March 1997, Sony cut the price of PlayStation again, this time to $149. It also reduced its suggested retail price for games by $10 to $49.99. By this point, Sony had sold 3.4 million units of PlayStation in the United States, compared to Saturn's 1.6 million units.[36] Worldwide, PlayStation had outsold Saturn by 13 million to 7.8 million units, and Saturn sales were slowing.[37] The momentum was clearly running in Sony's favor, but the company now had a new challenge to deal with: Nintendo's latest generation game machine, the N64.

NINTENDO STRIKES BACK

In July 1996, Nintendo launched Nintendo 64 (N64) in the Japanese market. This release was followed by a late Fall introduction in the United States. N64 is a 64-bit machine developed in conjunction with Silicon Graphics. Originally targeted for introduction a year earlier, N64 had been under development since 1993. The machine used a plug-in cartridge format rather than a CD-ROM drive. According to Nintendo, cartridges allow for faster access time and are far more durable than CD-ROMs (an important consideration with children).[38]

The most striking feature of the N64 machine, however, was its 3D graphics capability. N64 provides fully rounded figures that can turn on their heels and rotate through 180 degrees. Advanced ray-tracing techniques borrowed from military simulators and engineering workstations added to the sense of realism by providing proper highlighting, reflections, and shadows.

N64 was targeted at children and young teenagers. It was priced at $200 and launched with just four games. Despite the lack of games, initial sales were very strong. Indeed, 1997 turned out to be a banner year for both Sony and Nintendo. The overall U.S. market was strong, with sales of hardware and software combined reaching a record $5.5 billion. Estimates suggest that PlayStation accounted for 49% of machines and games by value. N64 captured a 41%

share, leaving Sega trailing badly with less than 10% of the market. During the year, the average price for game machines had fallen to $150. By year-end there were 300 titles available for PlayStation, compared to 40 for N64. Games for PlayStation retailed for $40, on average, compared to over $60 for N64.[39]

By late 1998, PlayStation was widening its lead over N64. In the crucial North American market, PlayStation was reported to be outselling N64 by a two-to-one margin, although Nintendo retained a lead in the under-12 category. At this point, there were 115 games available for N64 versus 431 for PlayStation.[40] Worldwide, Sony had now sold close to 55 million PlayStations. The success of PlayStation had a major impact on Sony's bottom line. In fiscal 1998, PlayStation business generated revenues of $5.5 billion for Sony, 10% of its worldwide revenues, but accounted for $886 million, or 22.5%, of the company's operating income.[41]

THE 128-BIT ERA

When Nintendo launched its 64-bit machine in 1996, Sony and Sega didn't follow, preferring instead to focus on the development of even more powerful 128-bit machines.

Sega was the first to market a 128-bit console, which it launched in Japan in late 1998 and in the United States in late 1999. The Dreamcast came equipped with a 56-kilobit modem to allow for online gaming over the Internet. By late 2000, Sega had sold around 6 million Dreamcasts worldwide, accounting for about 15% of console sales since its launch. Sega nurtured Dreamcast sales by courting outside software developers who helped develop new games, including Crazy Taxi, Resident Evil, and Quake III Arena. The company had a goal of shipping 10 million units by March 2001—a goal it never reached.[42]

Despite its position as first mover with a 128-bit machine, and despite solid technical reviews, by late 2000 the company was struggling. Sega was handicapped first by product shortages due to constraints on the supply of component parts, and then by a lack of demand as consumers waited to see whether Sony's 128-bit offering, the much-anticipated PlayStation 2 (PS2), would be a more attractive machine. In September 2000, Sega responded to the impending U.S. launch of Sony's PS2 by cutting the price for its console from $199 to $149. In late October, Sega announced that, due to this price cut, it would probably lose over $200 million in the fiscal year ending March 2001.[43]

Sony's PlayStation 2

PlayStation 2 was launched in Japan in mid-2000 and in the United States at the end of October 2000. Initially priced at $299, PlayStation 2 was a powerful machine. At its core was a 300-megahertz graphics-processing chip that was jointly developed with Toshiba and consumed about $1.3 billion in R&D. Referred to as the Emotion Engine processor, the chip allowed the machine to display stunning graphic images previously found only on supercomputers. The chip made the PlayStation 2 the most powerful videogame machine yet.

It was designed play different CD and DVD formats, as well as proprietary game titles. As was true with the original PlayStation, PlayStation 2 could play audio CDs. The system was also compatible with the original PlayStation; any PlayStation title could be played on the PlayStation 2. To help justify the initial price tag, the unit doubled as a DVD player with picture quality as good as dedicated players. PlayStation 2 did not come equipped with a modem, but it had networking capabilities, and a modem could be attached using one of two USB ports.[44]

Nintendo GameCube

Nintendo had garnered a solid position in the industry with its N64 machine by focusing on its core demographic, 7- to 12-year-olds. In 1999, Nintendo took 33% of the hardware market and 28% of the game market. Nintendo's next-generation videogame machine, GameCube, packed a modem and a powerful, 400-megahertz, 128-bit processor made by IBM into a compact cube. GameCube marked a shift away from Nintendo's traditional approach of using proprietary cartridges to hold game software. Instead, software for the new player came on 8-centimeter CDs, which are smaller than music compact disks. The disks held 1.5 gigabytes of data each—far greater storage capacity than the old game cartridges. Players could control GameCube using wireless controllers.[45]

Nintendo tried to make the GameCube easy for developers to work with rather than focusing on raw peak performance. While developers no doubt appreciated this, by the time GameCube hits store shelves in late 2001, PlayStation 2 had been on the market for eighteen months and boasted a solid library of games. Despite its strong brand and instantly recognized intellectual property, which included Donkey Kong, Super Mario Brothers, and the Pokemon characters, Nintendo was playing catch up to Sony. Moreover, another new entrant into the industry—Microsoft—launched its 128-bit offering at around the same time.

Microsoft Xbox

Microsoft was first rumored to be developing a videogame console in late 1999. In March 2000, Bill Gates made it official when he announced that Microsoft would enter the home videogame market in fall 2001 with a console code named Xbox. In terms of sheer computing power, the 128-bit Xbox had the edge over competitors. Xbox had a 733-megahertz Pentium III processor, a high-powered graphics chip from Nvidia Corp, a built-in broadband cable modem to allow for online game playing and high-speed Internet browsing, 64 megabytes of memory, CD and DVD drives, and an internal hard disk drive. The operating system was a stripped-down version of Microsoft's popular Windows system optimized for graphics-processing capabilities. Microsoft claimed that because the Xbox was based on familiar PC technology, it would be much easier for software developers to write games for, and it would be relatively easy to convert games from the PC to run on the Xbox.[46]

Although Microsoft was a new entrant to the videogame industry, it was no stranger to games. Microsoft had long participated in the PC gaming industry and was one of the largest publishers of PC games, with hits such as Microsoft Flight Simulator and Age of Empires I and II to its credit. Sales of Microsoft's PC games increased 50% annually between 1998 and 2001, and the company controlled about 10% of the PC game market in 2001. Microsoft had also offered online gaming for some time, including its popular MSN Gaming Zone site. Started in 1996, by 2001 the website had become the largest online PC gaming hub on the Internet, with nearly 12 million subscribers paying $9.95 a month to play premium games such as Asheron's Call or Fighter

Ace. Nor was Microsoft new to hardware; its joysticks and game pads outsold all other brands, and it had an important mouse business.

To build the Xbox, Microsoft chose Flextronics, a contract manufacturer that already made computer mice for Microsoft. Realizing that it would probably have to cut Xbox prices over time, Microsoft guaranteed Flextronics a profit margin, effectively agreeing to subsidize Flextronics if selling prices fell below a specified amount. By 2003, Microsoft was thought to be losing $100 on every Xbox sold. To make that back and turn a profit, Microsoft reportedly had to sell between six and nine videogames per Xbox.[47]

Analysts speculated that Microsoft's entry into the home videogame market was a response to a potential threat from Sony. Microsoft was worried that Internet-ready consoles like PlayStation 2 might take over many Web-browsing functions from the personal computer. Some in the company described Internet-enabled videogame terminals as Trojan horses in the living room. In Microsoft's calculation, it made sense to get in the market to try to keep Sony and others in check. With annual revenues in excess of $20 billion worldwide, the huge home videogame market was an important source of potential growth for Microsoft. Still, by moving away from its core market, Microsoft was taking a big risk, particularly given the scale of investments required to develop the Xbox, reported to run as high as $1.5 billion.

Mortal Combat: Microsoft Versus Sony

The launch of Xbox and Game Cube helped propel sales of videogame hardware and software to a record $9.4 billion in 2001, up from $6.58 billion in 2000. Although both Xbox and Nintendo initially racked up strong sales, the momentum slowed significantly in 2002. Microsoft in particular, found it very difficult to penetrate the Japanese market. By September 2002, Sony had sold 11.2 million units of PS2 in the United States, versus 2.2 million units of Xbox and 2.7 million units of Nintendo's game Cube. Unable to hold onto market share in the wake of the new competition, Sega withdrew from the console market, announcing that henceforth it would focus on developing games for other platforms.

In June 2002, Sony responded to the new entry by cutting the price for PS2 from $299 to $199. Microsoft quickly followed, cutting the price for Xbox from

$299 to $199, while Nintendo cut its price from $299 to $149.[48] A year later, Sony cut prices again, this time to $179. Microsoft followed with a similar price cut and, in March 2004, it took the lead, cutting Xbox prices to $149. Sony followed suit two months later.[49]

Microsoft's strategy, however, involved far more than just cutting prices. In November 2002, Microsoft announced that it would introduce a new service for gamers, Xbox Live. For $50 a year, Xbox Live subscribers with broadband connections would be able to play online enabled versions of Xbox games with other online subscribers. To support Xbox Live, Microsoft invested some $500 million in its own data centers to host online game playing.

Online game playing was clearly a strategic priority from the outset. Unlike the PS2 and Game Cube, Xbox came with built-in broadband capability. The decision to make the Xbox broadband capable had been made in 1999, when less than 5% of U.S. homes were linked to the Internet with a broadband connection. Explaining the decision to build broadband capabilities into the Xbox at a time when rivals lacked them, the head of Xbox, Jay Allard, noted that "my attitude has always been to bet on the future, not against it."[50] While Sony's PS2 can be hooked up to the Internet via a broadband connection, doing so requires purchase of a special network adapter for $40.

By mid-2003, Xbox live had some 500,000 subscribers, versus 80,000 who had registered to play PlayStation 2 games online. By this point in time, there were 28 online games for Xbox, and 18 for PS2. By January 2004, the comparative figures stood at 50 for Microsoft and 32 for Sony. By mid-2004, Xbox live reportedly had over 1 million subscribers, with Sony claiming a similar number of online players.[51] In May 2004, Microsoft struck a deal with Electronic Arts, the world's largest video game publisher, to bring EA games, including its bestselling John Madden Football, to the Xbox live platform. Until this point, EA had only produced live games for Sony's platform.

In spite of these strategic moves, by late 2004, Xbox was still a distant second of PS2 in the video-game market, having sold 14 million consoles against Sony's 70 million (Nintendo had sold 13 million Game Cube consoles by this point). While Sony was making good money from the business, Microsoft was registering significant losses. In fiscal 2004, Microsoft's home and entertainment division, of which Xbox is the major component, registered $2.45 billion in revenues but lost $1.135 billion. By way of contrast, Sony's game division had $7.5 billion of sales in fiscal 2004 and generated operating profits of $640 million.

Microsoft, however, indicated that it was in the business for the long term. In late 2004, the company got a boost from the release of Halo 2, the sequel to Halo, one of its bestselling games. As first-day sales for Halo 2 were tallied, executives at Sony had to be worried. Microsoft announced that Halo 2 had sales of $125 million in its first 24 hours on the market in the United States and Canada, an industry record. These figures represented sales of 2.38 million units, and put Halo 2 firmly on track to be one of the biggest video games ever, with a shot at surpassing Nintendo's Super Mario 64, which had sold $308 million in the United States since its September 1996 debut. Moreover, the company was rumored to be ahead of Sony by as much as a year to bring the next-generation video game console to market. In late 2004, reports suggested that Xbox 2 would be on the market in time for the 2005 Christmas season, probably a full year ahead of Sony's PlayStation 3. Sony was rumored to be running into technical problems as it tried to develop PlayStation 3.[52]

THE NEXT GENERATION

As the battle between PS2 and Xbox drew to a close, it was clear that clear that Sony was the big winner. From 2001 through Fall 2006, when PlayStation 3 (PS3) hit the market, Sony had sold around 110 million PS2 consoles, versus 25 million for Microsoft's Xbox and 21 million for Nintendo's Game Cube.[53] Sony's advantage translated into a huge lead in number of games sold—some 1.08 billion for PS2 by mid-2006, versus 200 million for the Xbox.[54] With the console companies reportedly making an average royalty on third-party software of $8 per game sold, the financial implications of Sony's lead with PS2 are obvious.[55] Indeed, in 2005, Sony's games division contributed to 6.24% of the company's total revenue, but 38% of operating profit. In contrast, Microsoft's home and entertainment division lost $4 billion between the launch of Xbox and mid-2006.

However, by 2006, this was all history. In November 2005, Microsoft introduced its next-generation machine, Xbox 360, beating Sony and Nintendo to the market by a solid year. The Xbox 360 represented a big technological advance over the original Xbox. To deliver improved picture quality, the Xbox 360 could execute 500 million polygons/sec—a four-fold increase over the Xbox. The main microprocessor was 13 times faster than the chip in the Xbox. Xbox 360 had 512 megabytes of memory, an eight-fold increase, and a 20-gigabyte hard drive, 2.5 times bigger than that found on the Xbox. Xbox 360 is, of course, enabled for a broadband connection to the Internet.

The machine itself was made by Flextronics and Wistron, two contract manufactures (a third started production after launch). Priced at $299, Xbox 360 was sold at a loss. The cost of making Xbox 360 was estimated to be as high as $500 at launch, falling to $350 by late 2006. Microsoft's goal was to ultimately break even on sales of the hardware as manufacturing efficiencies drove down unit costs.

To seed the market with games, Microsoft took a number of steps. Taking a page out of its Windows business, Microsoft provided game developers with tools designed to automate many of the key software programming tasks and reduce development time and costs. The company had also expanded its own in-house game studios, in part by purchasing several independent game developers including Bungie Studios, makers of Halo. This strategy enabled Microsoft to offer exclusive content for the Xbox 360, something that third-party developers were reluctant to do.

With the costs of game development increasing to between $10 and $15 million for more complex games, and development time stretching out to between 24 and 36 months, Microsoft also had to provide an inducement to get third-party developers onboard. Although details of royalty terms are kept private, it is believed that Microsoft offered very low royalty rates, and perhaps even zero royalties, for a specified period of times to game developers who committed early to Xbox 360. One of those to commit early was Electronic Arts, the leading independent game development company, which reportedly budgeted as much as $200 million to develop some 25 versions of its bestselling games, such as its sports games, for Xbox 360. Microsoft budgeted a similar amount to develop games on its own.[56]

Some 18 games were available for the November 2005 launch of Xbox 360, and by the end of 2006, this figure had increased to around 160. Halo 3, which was expected to be one of the biggest games for Xbox

360, was released in September 2007. Exclusive to the Xbox 360, Halo 3 racked in first-day sales of $170 million, which was an industry record. Grand Theft Auto 4, the most popular franchise on PS2, was also launched simultaneously for both Xbox 360 and PS3 in 2007—a major coup for Microsoft.

The initial launch of Xbox 360 was marred by shortages of key components, which limited the number of machines that Microsoft could bring to market. Had Sony been on time with its launch of PS3, this could have been a serious error, but in the event Sony delayed its launch of PS3, first until Spring of 2006, and then November 2006. By the time Sony launched PS3 in November 2006, some 6 million Xbox 360 consoles had been sold, and Microsoft was predicting sales of 10 million by the end of 2006.

As with Xbox, Microsoft is pushing Xbox Live with Xbox 360. The company invested as much as $1 billion in Live from its inception. By late 2006, Microsoft was claiming that some 60% of Xbox 360 customers had also signed on for Xbox Live, and that the service had 4 million subscribers. By early 2008, there were over 10 million subscribers. Xbox Live allows gamers to play against each other online, and to download digital content from the Xbox Live Marketplace. Looking forward, there is little doubt that Microsoft sees Xbox Live as a critical element of its strategy, enabling Xbox owners to download any digital content—games, film, music—onto their consoles, which could become the hub of a home digital entertainment system.

The business model for Xbox 360 depends upon the number of games sold per console, the percentage of console owners who sign up for Xbox Live, sales of hardware accessories (e.g., controllers, an HD-DVD drive, wireless networking adapter), and the console itself achieving break even production costs. Reports suggest that Microsoft will break even if each console owners buys 6 to 7 games and 2 or 3 accessories, and if some 10 million sign on to Xbox Live (Microsoft splits Xbox Live revenues with game developers). By the end of 2006, it was estimated that some 33 million games had been sold for Xbox 360.[57]

Sony finally introduced PS3 on November 11 in Japan, and on November 17 in the United States. The delay in the launch of PS3 was due to Sony's decision to bundle a Blu-ray drive with PS3, and to problems developing the "cell" processor that sits at the core of the PS3. Blu-ray is Sony's proprietary, high-definition DVD format. The company is currently locked in a format war with Toshiba, which is pushing its rival HD-DVD format (which can be purchased as an accessory for the Xbox 360). Sony has argued that the combination of its cell processor and Blu-ray DVD drive will give PS3 a substantial performance edge over Xbox 360. While this is true in a technical sense (the Blu-ray discs have five times the storage capacity of the DVD discs for Xbox 360), few reviewers have noticed much in the way of difference from a game-playing perspective—perhaps because few games were initially available that showed the true power of the PS3.

What is certain is that incorporating Blu-ray drives in the PS3 has significantly raised the costs of the machine. Sony is selling its stand-alone Blu-ray drives for $999, which suggests that the PS3, initially priced at between $500 and $600 depending upon configuration, is in a sense a subsidized Blu-ray player. Shortages of blue diodes, a critical component in high-definition DVD drives, also limited supply of the PS3 after its launch. Only 93,000 PS3 players were available for the Japanese launch. At launch, there were some 20 games available for the PS3. Sony also announced its own Live offering to compete with Xbox Live, and stated that it would be free to PS3 users.

Nintendo also got back in the fray. In November 2006, it launched its own next-generation offering, Wii. When developing the Wii, Nintendo made a number of interesting strategic decisions. First, they decided not to compete with Microsoft and Sony on graphics-processing power. Instead of developing a high-powered machine crammed full of expensive, custom-built components, they used off-the-shelf components to assemble a much cheaper machine that could be sold at a much lower price point (the initial price was $250). While this machine did not offer the graphics-processing capabilities of Xbox 360 or PS3, the games were cheaper to develop, around $5 million each as opposed to as much as $20 million for the PS3. Second, Nintendo decided to target a new demographic, indifferent people who had no interest in video games, as opposed to the stereotypical game player. Nintendo already had some evidence that this market could be tapped, and that it was extremely lucrative. In 2004, Nintendo had introduced a game for its handheld player, the DS, that was aimed not at its core 7- to 12-year-old demographic, but a much wider market. The game, Brain Age, based on a brain training regime developed by a Japanese neuroscientist, was a huge hit in Japan, with sales of more than

12 million units. It made the DS a hit in such unlikely places as nursing homes. Third, rather than processing power, Nintendo decided to focus on developing a motion-sensitive, wireless controller that could detect arm and hand motions and transfer them to the screen. This enabled the development of interactive games, with players physically controlling the action on screen by moving their arms, whether by swinging an imaginary bat, driving a go kart, or slashing a sword through the air.[58]

By early 2007, it was clear that the Wii was turning into a surprise hit. The combination of low price, innovative design, and a portfolio of recognizable games based on Nintendo's long-established franchises such as Mario Brothers and Pokeman helped drive sales forward. Moreover, as planned, the Wii seemed to appeal to a broad range of age groups and to both genders. Soon, articles appeared explaining how retirement homes were buying the Wii so that residents could play virtual baseball with their visiting grandchildren, and sales stated to accelerate.

By 2010, it was clear that the Wii had been the major success story of this generation of gaming consoles. Since their respective launches, the Wii had sold 74.5 million units, compared to 43.8 million for Xbox 360 and 38.7 million of PlayStation 3. Nintendo also had a strong lead in the popular handheld market, with 135 million units sold worldwide, compared to 60.5 million for the PSP, Sony's handheld game player (Microsoft did not have a handheld player).[59] On the other hand, a key to the success of a console is the number of games sold per box, and on this measure Xbox 360 had the best performance. After each console had been on the market for 29 months, Xbox had sold 7.5 games per box, compared to 6.5 for PlayStation and 6.2 for Nintendo. By October 2010, the ratio had risen to around 9.0 games per box for Xbox 360 (these figures are for the United States only).[60]

Total industry sales in the United States peaked in 2008 at $22.11 billion, before declining to $20.2 billion as the recession cut into demand (worldwide sales were $54 billion in 2008). Despite the recession, all three players in the market were profitable on an operating basis in 2009 and 2010. Worldwide sales are expected to exceed $60 billion in 2012. Both Microsoft and Sony had shot themselves in the foot with quality problems and component shortages early in the product cycle (Microsoft had to take a $1.05-billion write-off in 2007 for replacing poor-quality consoles), but were now performing well. Microsoft is predicting that this generation of console will last about 10 years, making it the longest generation ever.

Looking forward, any number of factors may change the industry. In November 2010, Microsoft released its response to Nintendo's motion sensor with a device known as Kinect. Kinect may fundamentally alter the way users interact with digital content. Kinect combines technologies such as body movement detection, facial recognition, and voice recognition, to let gamers use natural motions and voice to control games. The input device is a camera and depth sensor mounted on top of the TV. In essence, Kinect is a potentially revolutionary step forward in human-machine interface design that could have implications that go way beyond videogames. To start with, Microsoft will use Kinect to go after the casual gamers that flocked to the Nintendo Wii has. As always with a new game technology, the success of Kinect will hinge crucially upon the quality of the games available. While it will take some time until games utilize the full power of Kinect, the early sales figures bode well for the device. Between launch and the start of March 2011, Microsoft sold over 10 million Kinect devices, making it the fastest-selling consumer electronics device of all time.[61]

Online gaming continues to gain traction. Xbox Live has turned into a big hit for Microsoft, and now has some 25 million subscribers who use it for everything from playing multiplayer games to streaming movies from Netflix and browsing Facebook. It is estimated that about 50% of Xbox Live subscribers are paying Gold Member subscribers. In fiscal 2009 (which ended June 30, 2010), Microsoft generated over $1.2 billion in revenues of Xbox Live subscriptions and services. This seems to be a growth engine going forward. Microsoft has announced the Xbox Live will be fully integrated into Windows 8, the next version of its Windows operating system now under development.

Interestingly enough, the largest multiplayer online game has no connection with any of the console platforms. This is World of Warcraft, the massive, multiplayer, online game with 12 million paying subscribers and annual revenues in excess of $1.2 billion—the bestselling game of all time.

This case is intended to be used as a basis for class discussion rather than as an illustration of either effective or ineffective handling of the situation. Reprinted by permission of Charles W. L. Hill.

NOTES

1. A good account of the early history of Bushnell and Atari can be found in S. Cohen, *Zap! The Rise and Fall of Atari*, New York: McGraw-Hill, 1984.
2. R. Isaacs, "Video Games Race to Catch a Changing Market," *Businessweek*, December 26, 1977, p. 44B.
3. P. Pagnano, "Atari's Game Plan to Overwhelm Its Competitors," *Businessweek*, May 8, 1978, p. 50F.
4. R. Isaacs, "Video Games Race to Catch a Changing Market," *Businessweek*, December 26, 1977, p. 44B.
5. P. Pagnano, "Atari's Game Plan to Overwhelm Its Competitors," *Businessweek*, May 8, 1978, p. 50F; D. Sheff, *Game Over*, New York: Random House, 1993.
6. S. Cohen, *Zap! The Rise and Fall of Atari*.
7. L. Kehoe, "Atari Seeks Way Out of Video Game Woes," *Financial Times*, December 14, 1983, p. 23.
8. M. Schrage, "The High Tech Dinosaurs: Video Games, Once Ascendant, Are Making Way," *Washington Post*, July 31, 1983, p. F1.
9. D. Sheff, *Game Over*.
10. Ibid, p. 38.
11. D. Sheff, *Game Over*.
12. D. Golden, "In Search of Princess Toadstool," *Boston Globe*, November 20, 1988, p. 18.
13. N. Grossand and G. Lewis, "Here Come the Super Mario Bros." *Businessweek*, November 9, 1987, p. 138.
14. D. Sheff, *Game Over.*.
15. D. Golden, "In Search of Princess Toadstool," *Boston Globe*, November 20, 1988, p. 18.
16. Staff reporter, "Marketer of the Year," *Adweek*, November 27, 1989, p. 15.
17. C. Lazzareschi, "No Mere Child's Play," *Los Angeles Times*, December 16, 1988, p. 1.
18. For a good summary of the early history of Sega, see J. Battl and B. Johnstone, "The Next Level: Sega's Plans for World Domination," *Wired*, December 1993.
19. D. Sheff, *Game Over*.
20. J. Battle and B. Johnstone, "The Next Level: Sega's Plans for World Domination."
21. For background details, see J. Flower, "3DO: Hip or Hype?" *Wired*, May/June 1993.
22. R. Brandt, "3DO's New Game Player: Awesome or Another Betamax?" *Businessweek*, January 11, 1993, p. 38.

23. J. Flower, "3DO: Hip or Hype?"

24. S. Jacobs, "Third Time's a Charm (They Hope)," *Wired*, January 1994.

25. A. Dunkin, "Video Games: The Next Generation," *Businessweek*, January 31, 1994, p. 80.

26. J. Greenstein, "No Clear Winners, Though Some Losers: The Video Game Industry in 1995," *Businessweek*, December 22, 1995, p. 42.

27. Staff reporter, "3DO Says 'I Do' on Major Shift of Its Game Strategy," *Los Angeles Times*, September 17, 1996, p. 2.

28. S. Taves, "Meet Your New Playmate," *Wired*, September 1995.

29. I. Kunni, "The Games Sony Plays," *Businessweek*, June 15, 1998, p. 128.

30. C. Platt, "WordNerd," *Wired*, October 1995.

31. I. Kunni, "The Games Sony Plays," *Businessweek*, June 15, 1998, p. 128.

32. J. A. Trachtenberg, "Race Quits Sony Just Before U.S. Rollout of Its PlayStation Video-Game System," *The Wall Street Journal*, August 8, 1995, p. B3.

33. S. Beenstock, "Market Raider: How Sony Won the Console Game," *Marketing*, September 10, 1998, p. 26.

34. J. A. Trachtenberg, "Olafsson Calls It Quits as Chairman of Sony's Technology Strategy Group," *The Wall Street Journal*, January 23, 1996, p. B6.

35. J. Greenstein, "Price Cuts Boost Saturn, PlayStation Hardware Sales," *Video Business*, May 31, 1996, p. 1.

36. J. Greenstein, "Sony Cuts Prices of PlayStation Hardware," *Video Business*, March 10, 1997, p. 1.

37. D. Hamilton, "Sega Suddenly Finds Itself Embattled," *The Wall Street Journal*, March 31, 1997, p. A10.

38. Staff reporter, "Nintendo Wakes Up," *The Economist*, August 3, 1996, pp. 55–56.

39. D. Takahashi, "Game Plan: Video Game Makers See Soaring Sales Now—And Lots of Trouble Ahead," *The Wall Street Journal*, June 15, 1998, p. R10.

40. D. Takahashi, "Sony and Nintendo Battle for Kids Under 13," *The Wall Street Journal*, September 24, 1998, p. B4.

41. I. Kunni, "The Games Sony Plays."

42. R. A. Guth, "Sega Cites Dreamcast Price Cuts for Loss Amid Crucial Time for Survival of Firm," *The Wall Street Journal*, October 30, 2000, p. A22.

43. Ibid.

44. T. Oxford and S. Steinberg, "Ultimate Game Machine Sony's PlayStation 2 Is Due on Shelves Oct. 26. It Brims with Potential—But at This Point Sega's Dreamcast Appears a Tough Competitor," *Atlanta Journal/Atlanta Constitution*, October 1, 2000, p. P1.

45. R. A. Guth, "New Players from Nintendo Will Link to Web," *The Wall Street Journal*, August 25, 2000, p. B1.

46. D. Takahashi, "Microsoft's X-Box Impresses Game Developers," *The Wall Street Journal*, March 13, 2000, p. B12.

47. K. Powers, "Showdown", *Forbes*, August 11, 2003, pp. 86–87.

48. "Console Wars," *The Economist*, June 22, 2002, p. 71.

49. R. A. Guth, "Game Gambit: Microsoft to cut Xbox Price," *The Wall Street Journal*, March 19, 2004, p. B1.

50. K. Powers, "Showdown."

51. E. Taub, "No Longer a Solitary Pursuit: Video Games Move Online," *New York Times*, July 5, 2004, p. C4.

52. J. Greene and C. Edwards, "Microsoft Plays Video Leapfrog," *Businessweek*, May 10, 2004, pp. 44–45.

53. "Playing a Long Game," *The Economist*, November 18, 2006, pp. 63–65.

54. B. Thill, "Microsoft: Got Game? Update on Vista, Xbox and the Tender," *Citigroup Capital Markets*, August 30, 2006.

55. Ibid.

56. D. Takahashi, *The Xbox 360 Uncloaked*, Spider Works, 2006.

57. B. Thill, "Microsoft: Got Game? Update on Vista, Xbox and the Tender."

58. J.M. O'Brian and C. Tkaczyk, "Wii Will Rock You," *Fortune*, June 11, 2007, pp. 82–92.

59. D. Takahashi, "The Video Game Console War Could End in a Three Way Tie," June 9, 2010, Venturebeat.com.

60. M. Matthews, "Console Tie Rations Reveal Market Dynamics," April 22, 2009, www.gamasutra.com.

61. S. Kessler, "Microsoft Kinect Sales Top 10 million," mashable.com, March 9, 2011.

GOOGLE IN 2015

INTRODUCTION

In the early 2000s, many Internet users started to gravitate toward a new search engine. It was called Google, and it delivered remarkable results. Type in a keyword and in the blink of an eye the search engine would return a list of links, with the most relevant links appearing at the top of the page. People quickly realized that Google was an amazing tool, enabling users to quickly find almost anything they wanted on the Web—to effortlessly sort through the vast sea of information contained in billions of webpages and retrieve the precise information they desired. It seemed like magic. Before long, "to Google" became a verb (in June 2006, the verb Google was added to the *Oxford English Dictionary*). To find out more about a person, you would "Google them." To find out more about a subject, good, or service you would "Google it." For many users, Google quickly became the "go-to" page every time they wanted information about anything.

What captured the attention of the business community, however, was Google's ability to monetize its search results. Google's core business model was the essence of simplicity. The company auctioned off the keywords used in searches to advertisers. The highest bidders would have links to their sites placed on the right-hand side of a page returning search results. The advertisers would then pay Google every time someone clicked on a link and was directed to their site.

Thus, when bidding for a keyword, advertisers would bid for the price per click. Interestingly, Google did not necessarily place the advertiser who bid the highest amount per click at the top of the page. Rather, the top spot was determined by the amount per click multiplied by Google's statistical estimate of the likelihood that someone would actually click on the advertisement. This refinement maximized the revenue that Google earned from its valuable real estate.

By November 2014, some 67% all U.S. Internet searches were conducted through Google sites.[1] Behind Google were Microsoft (19.6% share) and Yahoo (10.2% share). Google had been gaining ground; in 2006, its share had stood at 45%.[2] Outside of the United States, Google had a monopoly position in many countries, with a share of greater than 95% in much of Europe, India, and Brazil. In China and Russia, however, where Google faced entrenched local competitors (Yandex and Baidu), its share is closer to 20%.[3] In an effort to catch up with Google, Microsoft and Yahoo had joined forces. Yahoo had agreed to use Microsoft's Bing search engine. In late 2010, Bing-powered search was implemented throughout Yahoo properties, making Bing's combined share almost 30%. The belief at Microsoft was that adding Yahoo search queries to the mix would enable Bing to gain scale economies and boost revenues per search.

As more users gravitated to Google's search engine, more advertisers were attracted to it, and Google's revenues and profits took off. From a standing start in 2001, by 2014 Google had 56,000 employees; revenues had grown to $66 billion, and net income to $14.4 billion. While the bulk of revenues still came from Google's pay-for-click search business, Google was also making significant revenues from display advertising, and the company was the leader in the rapidly growing market for mobile search revenues. Estimates suggest that, in 2014, Google captured 41% of the $32-billion in mobile ad revenue generated globally (both search and display advertising). Facebook was second with 28%.[4]

Flushed by this success, Google introduced a wave after wave of new products, including mapping services (Google Maps and Google Earth), an e-mail service (gmail), Google Apps, which include free online word processing, spread sheet and presentation programs that have much of the look, feel, and functionality of Microsoft's Office suite, its own Web browser, Google Drive (cloud storage), the Chrome browser, and its mobile operating system, Android. These products suggested that Google's ambitions extended outside search, and that the company was trying to position itself as a platform company that supported an ecosystem that would rival that fostered by Microsoft, long the dominant player in the software industry.

SEARCH ENGINES[5]

A search engine connects the keywords that users enter (queries) to a database it has created of webpages (an index). It then produces a list of links to pages (and summaries of content) most relevant to the query.

Search engines consist of four main components—a Web crawler, an index, a runtime index, and a query processor (the interface that connects users to the index). The Web crawler software that goes from link to link on the Web, collecting the pages it finds and sending them back to the index. Once in the index, sophisticated algorithms that look for statistical patterns analyze webpages. Among other variables, for example, Google's page rank algorithm looks at the links on a page, the text around those links, and the popularity of the pages that link to that page, to determine how relevant a page is to a particular query (in total, Google's algorithm looks at more than 100 factors to determine a page's relevance to a query term).

Once analyzed, pages are tagged. The tag contains information about the pages—for example, whether it is porn or spam, written in a certain language, or updated infrequently. Tagged pages are then dumped into a runtime index, which is a database that is ready to serve users. The runtime index forms a bridge between the back end of an engine, the Web crawler and index, and the front end, the query processor and user interface. The query processor transports a keyword to the runtime index, where an algorithm matches the keyword to pages, ranking them by relevance, and then transports the results back to the user, where they are displayed on the user interface.

The computing and data-storage infrastructure required to support a search engine is significant. It must scale with the continued growth of the Web and with demands on the search engine. In 2013, Google had $9 billion in information technology assets on its balance sheet, and another $7.5 billion tied up in land and buildings. A significant chunk of these assets were in 13 data centers, each of which contained up to 50,000 servers configured in large-scale clusters dedicated to the job of running its search engine.[6]

THE EARLY DAYS OF SEARCH

The first Internet search engine was Archie. Created in 1990, before the World Wide Web had burst onto the scene, Archie connected users through queries to the machines on which documents they wanted were stored. The users then had to dig through the public files on those machines to find what they wanted. The next search engine, Veronica, improved on Archie in that it did allow searchers to connect directly to the document they had queried.

The Web started to take off after 1993, with the number of websites expanding from 130 to more than 600,000 by 1996. As this expansion occurred, the problem of finding the information on the Web became more difficult. The first Web-based search engine was the WWW Wanderer, developed by Matthew Gray at MIT. This was soon surpassed by Web Crawler, a search engine developed by Brian Pinkerton of the University of Washington. Web Crawler was the first search engine to index the full text of webpages, as opposed to just the title. Web Crawler was sold to AOL for $1 million in 1995. This marked the first time any company had ascribed an economic value to a search engine.

In December 1995, the next search engine appeared on the scene, Alta Vista. Developed by an employee at Digital Equipment (DEC), Louis Monier, Alta Vista, like Web Crawler, indexed the entire text of a webpage. Unlike Web Crawler, Alta Vista sent out thousands of Web crawlers, which enabled it to build the most complete index of the Web to date. Avid users soon came to value the service. However, two things handicapped the search engine. First, it was a stepchild within DEC, which saw itself as a hardware-driven business and didn't really know what to do with Alta Vista. Second, there was no obvious way for Alta Vista to make much money, which meant that it was difficult for Monier to get the resources required for Alta Vista to keep up with the rapid growth of the Web. Ultimately, Compaq Computer acquired DEC. Compaq then sold Alta Vista and related Internet properties to an Internet firm, CMGI, at the height of the Internet boom in 1999 for $2.3 billion in CMGI stock. CMGI did have plans to spin off Alta Vista in an initial public offering, but it never happened. The NASDAQ stock market collapsed in 2000, taking CMGI's stock down with it, and the market had no appetite for another dot.com IPO.

Around the same time that Alta Vista was gaining traffic, two other companies introduced search engines, Lycos and Excite. Both search engines represented further, incremental improvement. Lycos was the first search engine to use algorithms to try to determine the relevance of a webpage for a search query. Excite utilized similar algorithms. However, neither company developed a way of making money directly from search; instead they saw themselves as portal companies, like Yahoo, AOL, and MSN. Search was just a tool to increase the value of their portal as a destination site, enabling them to capture revenues from banner ads, ecommerce transactions, and the like. Both Lycos and Excite went public and then squandered much of the capital raised on acquiring other Internet properties, before seeing their value implode as the Internet bubble burst in 2000–2001.

Another company that tried to make sense out of the Web was Yahoo, but Yahoo did not use a search engine. Instead it created a hierarchical directory of webpages. This helped drive traffic to its site. Yahoo emerged as one of the most popular portals on the Web. In contrast to many of its smaller competitors, Yahoo's industry-leading scale allowed it to make good money from advertising on its site. Yahoo did add a search engine to its offering, but until 2003 it always did so through a partner. At one time, Alta Vista powered Yahoo's search function, then Inktomi, and ultimately Google. Yahoo's managers did consider developing their own search engine, but they saw it as too capital intensive—search required a lot of computing power, storage, and bandwidth. Besides, there was no business model for monetizing search. That, however, was all about to change, and it wasn't Google that pioneered the way. It was serial entrepreneur Bill Goss.

GoTo.com: A BUSINESS MODEL EMERGES[7]

Bill Gross made his first million with Knowledge Adventure, which developed software to help kids learn. After he sold Knowledge Adventure to Cendant for $100 million, Gross created IdeaLab, a business incubator that subsequently generated a number of Internet start-ups, including GoTo.com.

GoTo.com was born of Gross' concern that a growing wave of spam was detracting from the value of search engines such as Alta Vista. Spam arose because publishers of websites realized that they could drive traffic to their sites by including commonly used search keywords such as "used cars" or "airfares" on their sites. Often the words were in the same color as the background of the website (e.g., black words on a black background), so that users, who would suddenly wonder why their search for used cars had directed them to a porn site, could not see them.

Gross also wanted a tool that would help drive good traffic to the websites of a number of Internet businesses being developed by IdeaLab. In Gross' view, much of the traffic arriving at websites was undifferentiated—people had come to a site because of spam, bad portal real estate deals, or poor search engine results. Gross established GoTo.com to build a better search engine that would defeat spam, produce highly relevant results, and eliminate bad traffic.

Gross concluded that a way to limit spam was to charge for search. He realized that it was unworkable to charge the Internet user, so why not charge the advertiser? This led to his key insight—the keywords that Internet users typed into a search engine were inherently valuable to the owners of websites. They drove traffic to their sites, and many sites made money from that traffic, so why not charge for the keywords? Moreover, Gross realized that if a search engine directed higher quality traffic to a site, it would be possible to charge more for relevant keywords.

By this time, GoTo.com had decided to license search engine technology from Inktomi and focus its efforts on developing the paid search model. However, GoTo.com faced a classic chicken-and-egg problem: to launch a service, the company needed both audience and advertisers, but it had neither.

To attract advertisers, GoTo.com adopted two strategies.[8] First, GoTo.com would only charge advertisers when somebody clicked on a link and was directed to their website. To Gross' way thinking, for merchants this pay-per-click model would be more efficient than advertising through traditional media, or through banner ads on webpages. Second, GoTo.com initially priced keywords as low as $0.01 per click (although they could of course be bid above that).

To capture an audience, a website alone would not be enough. GoTo.com needed to tap into the traffic already visiting established websites. One approach was to pay the owners of high-traffic websites to place banner ads that would direct traffic to GoTo.com's website. A second approach, which ultimately became the core of GoTo.com's business, was to syndicate its service, allowing affiliates to place a co-branded GoTo.com search box on their site, or to use GoTo.com's search engine and identify the results as "partner results." GoTo.com would then split the revenues from search with them. GoTo.com had to pay an upfront fee to significant affiliates, who viewed their websites as valuable real estate. For example, in late 2000, GoTo.com paid AOL $50 million to syndicate GoTo.com's listings on its sites, which included AOL, Compuserve, and Netscape.

To finance its expansion, GoTo.com raised some $53 million in venture capital funding—a relatively easy proposition in the heady days of the dot.com boom. In June 1999, GoTo.com raised another $90 million through an initial public offering.[9]

GoTo.com launched its service in June 1998 with just 15 advertisers. Initially GoTo.com was paying more to acquire traffic than it was earning from click-through ad revenue. According to its initial IPO filing, in its first year of operation GoTo.com was paying 5.5 cents per click to acquire traffic from Microsoft's MSN sites, and around 4 cents per click to acquire traffic from Netscape. The average yield from this traffic, however, was still less than the cost of acquisition, resulting in red ink—not an unusual situation for a dot.com in the 1990s.

However, the momentum was beginning to shift toward the company. As traffic volumes grew, and as advertisers began to understand the value of keywords, yields improved. By early 1999, the price of popular keywords was starting to rise. The highest bidder for the keyword "software" was $0.59 per click, "books" was $0.38 per click, "vacations" $0.36 per click, and "porn," the source of so much spam, $0.28 per click.[10]

The turning point was the AOL syndication deal signed in September 2000. Prior to signing with AOL, GoTo.com was reaching 24 million users through its affiliates. After the deal, it was reaching 60 million unique users, or some 75% of the United States Internet audience (AOL itself had 23 million subscribers, CompuServe 3 million, and Netscape—which was owned by AOL—another 31 million registered users).[11] With over 50,000 advertisers now in its network and a large audience pool, both keyword prices and click through rates increased. GoTo.com turned profitable shortly after the AOL deal was put into effect. In 2001, the company earned net profits $20.2 million on revenues of $288 million. In 2002, it earned $73.1 million on revenues of $667.7 million, making it one of the few dot.com companies to break into profitability.

In 2001, GoTo.com changed its name to Overture Services. The name change reflected the results of a strategic shift. By 2001, the bulk of revenues were coming from affiliate sites, with the GoTo.com website only garnering 5% of the company's total traffic.[12] Still, the fact that GoTo.com had its own website that was in effect competing with traffic going to affiliates created potential channel conflict. Many in the company feared that channel conflict might induce key affiliates such as AOL to switch their allegiance. After much internal debate, the company decided to phase out the GoTo.com website, focusing all of its attention on the syndication network.

Around the same time, Bill Gross talked to the founders of another fast-growing search engine, Google, about whether they would be interested in merging the two companies. At the time Google had no business model.

Gross was paying attention to the fast growth of traffic going to Google's website. He saw a merger as an opportunity to merge a superior search engine with Overture's advertising and syndication network. The talks stalled, however, reportedly because Google's founders stated that they would never be associated with a company that mixed paid advertising with organic results.[13]

Within months, Google had introduced its own advertising service using a pay-per-click model that looked very similar in conception to Overture's. Overture sued Google for patent infringement. To make matters worse, in 2002, AOL declined to renew its deal with Overture and instead switched to Google for search services.

By 2003, it was clear that, although still growing and profitable, Overture was losing traction to Google (Overture's revenues were on track to hit $1 billion in 2003, and the company had 80,000 advertisers in its network)[14]. Moreover, Overture was invisible to many of its users, who saw the service as a part of the offering of affiliates, many of whom were powerful brands in their own right, including Yahoo and Microsoft's MSN. Yahoo and Microsoft were also waking up to the threat posed by Google. Realizing that paid search was becoming a highly profitable market, both began to eye Overture to jump-start their own paid search services. While Microsoft decided to build its own search engine and ad service from scratch, Yahoo decided to bid for Overture. In June 2003, a deal was announced, with Overture being sold to Yahoo for $1.63 billion in cash. The payday was bittersweet for Bill Gross. IdeaLab had done very well with Overture, but Gross couldn't help but feel that a bigger opportunity had slipped through his fingers and into the palms of Google's founders.

The patent case was settled in 2004, when Google agreed to hand over 2.7 million shares to Yahoo. This represented about 1% of the outstanding stock, which at the time was valued at $330. After Google's IPO, the value of those shares was closer to $1 billion.[15]

THE GENESIS OF GOOGLE

Google started as a research project undertaken by Larry Page while he was a computer science PhD student at Stanford in 1996. Called BackRub, the goal of the project was to document the link structure of the Web. Page had observed that while it was easy to follow links from one page to another, it was much more difficult to discover links *back*. Put differently, just by looking at a page, it was impossible to know who was linking to that page. Page reasoned that this might be very important information. Specifically, one might be able to rank to value of a webpage by discovering which pages were linking to it, and if those pages were themselves linked to by many other pages.

To rank pages, Page knew that he would have to send out a Web crawler to index pages and archive links. At this point, another PhD student, Sergey Brin, became involved in the project. Brin, a gifted mathematician, was able to develop an algorithm that ranked webpages according not only to the number of links into that site, but also the number of links into each of the linking sites. This methodology had the virtue of discounting links from pages that had few if any links into them.

Brin and Page noticed that the search results generated by this algorithm were superior to those returned by Alta Vista and Excite, both of which often returned irrelevant results, including a fair share of spam. They had stumbled onto the key ingredient for a better search engine: rank search results according to their relevance using a back-link methodology. Moreover, they realized that the bigger the Web became, the better the results would be.

With the basic details of what was now a search engine worked out, Brin and Page released it on the Stanford website in August 1996. They christened their new search engine Google after googol, the term for the number 1 followed by 100 zeros. Early on, Brin and Page talked to several companies about the possibility of licensing Google. Executives at Excite took a look but passed, as did executives at Infoseek and Yahoo. Many of these companies were embroiled in the portal wars—and portals were all about acquiring traffic, not about sending it away via search. Search just didn't seem central to their mission.

By late 1998, Google was serving some 10,000 queries a day and was rapidly outgrowing the computing resources available at Stanford. Brin and Page realized that to get the resources required to keep scaling Google they needed capital, and that meant starting a company. Here Stanford's deep links into Silicon Valley came in useful. Before long they found themselves sitting together with Andy Bechtolsheim, one of the founders of another Stanford start-up, Sun Microsystems. Bechtolsheim watched a demo of Google and wrote a check on the spot for $100,000.

Google was formally incorporated on September 7, 1998 with Page as CEO and Brin as president. From this point on, things accelerated rapidly. Traffic was growing by nearly 50% a month, enough to attract the attention of several "angel investors" (including Amazon founder Jeff Bezos), who collectively put in another million.

That was not enough; search engines have a voracious appetite for computing resources. To run its search engine, Brin and Page had custom designed a low-cost, Linux-based server architecture that was modular and could be scaled rapidly. But to keep up with the growth of the Web and return answers to search queries in a fraction of second, they needed ever more machines (by late 2005, the company was using over 250,000 Linux servers to handle more than 3,000 searches a second).[16]

To finance growth of their search engine, in early 1999, Brin and Page started to look for venture capital funding. It was the height of the dot.com boom and money was cheap. Never mind that there was no business model; Google's growth was enough to attract considerable interest. By June 1999, the company had closed its first round of venture capital financing, raising $25 million from two of the premier firms in Silicon Valley, Sequoia Capital and Kleiner Perkins Caufield & Byers. Just as importantly, perhaps, the legendary John Doerr, one of Silicon Valley's most successful investors and a Kleiner Perkins partner, took a seat on Google's board.

By late 1999, Google had grown to around 40 employees and was serving some 3.5 million searches a day. However, the company was burning through $500,000 a month, and there was still no business model. They had some licensing deals with companies that used Google as their search technology, but they were not bringing in enough money to stem the flow of red ink. At this point, Google started to experiment with ads, but they were not yet pay-per-click ads. Rather, Google began selling text-based ads to clients that were interested in certain keywords. The ads would then appear on the page returning search results, but *not* in the list of relevant sites. For example, if someone typed in "Toyota Corolla," an ad would appear at the top of the page, above the list of links for Toyota Corolla cars. These ads were sold on a "cost per thousand impressions" basis, or CPM (M being the Roman numeral for thousand). In other words, the cost of an ad was determined by how many people were estimated to have viewed it, not how many clicked on it. It didn't work very well.

The management team also started to ponder placing banner ads on Google's website as a way of generating additional revenue, but before they made that decision the dot.com boom imploded, the NASDAQ crashed, and the volume of online advertising dropped precipitously. Google clearly needed to figure out a different way to make money.

GOOGLE GETS A BUSINESS MODEL

Brin and Page now looked closely at the one search company that seemed to be making good money, GoTo.com. They could see the value of the pay-per-click model, and of auctioning off keywords, but there were things about GoTo.com that they did not like. GoTo.com would give guarantees that websites would be included more frequently in Web crawls, making sure they were updated, provided that the owners were prepared to pay more. Moreover, the purity of GoTo.com's search results was biased by the desire to make money from advertisers, with those who paid the most being ranked highest. Brin and Page were ideologically attached to the idea of serving up the best possible search results to users, uncorrupted by commercial considerations. At the same time, they needed to make money.

Although Bill Gross pitched the idea of GoTo.com teaming up with Google, Brin and Page decided to go it alone. They believed they could do as good a job as GoTo.com, so why share revenues with the company?[17]

The approach that Google ultimately settled on combined the innovations of GotTo.com with Google's superior relevance-based search engine. Brin and Page had always believed that Google's webpage should be kept as clean and elegant as possible—something that seemed to appeal to users. Moreover, they knew that users valued the fact that Google served up relevant search results that were unbiased by commercial considerations. The last thing they wanted to do was alienate their rapidly growing user base. So they decided to place text-based ads on the right-hand side of a page, clearly separated from search results by a thin line.

Like GoTo.com, they decided to adopt a pay-per-click model. Unlike GoTo.com, Brin and Page decided that, in addition to the price an advertiser had paid for a keyword, ads should also be ranked according to relevance. Relevance was measured by how frequently users clicked on ads. More popular ads rose to the top of the list, less popular ones fell. In other words, Google allowed their users to rank ads. This had a nice economic advantage for Google, since an ad that is generating $1.00 a click but is being clicked on three times as much as an ad generating $1.50 a click would make significantly more money for Google. It also motivated advertisers to make sure that their ads were appealing.

The system that Google used to auction off keywords was also different than that used by GoTo.com. Google used a *Vickery second price auction* methodology. Under this system, the winner pays only 1 cent more than the bidder below them. Thus, if there are bids of $1, $0.50, and $0.25 for a keyword, the winner of the top place pays just $0.51 cents, not $1; the winner of the second place pays $0.26; and so on. The auction is nonstop, with the price for a keyword rising or falling depending upon bids at any given moment. Although the minimum bid for a keyword was set at $0.05, most were above that and the range was wide. One of the most expensive search terms was reputed to be "mesothelioma," a type of cancer caused by exposure to asbestos. Bids around $30 per click came from lawyers vying for a chance to earn lucrative fees by representing clients in suits against asbestos producers.[18]

While developing this service, Google continued to grow like wildfire. In mid-2000, the service was dealing with 18 million search queries a day, and the index surpassed 1 billion documents, making it by far the largest search engine on the Web. By late 2000, when Google introduced the first version of its new service, AdWords, the company was serving up 60 million search queries a day—a scale that GoTo.com never came close to achieving. In February 2002, Google introduced a new version of AdWords that included for the first time the full set of pay-per-click advertising, keyword auctions, and advertising links ranked by relevance. Ad sales immediately accelerated. Google

had hit on the business model that would propel the company into the big league.

In 2003, Google introduced a second product, AdSense. AdSense allowed third-party publishers large and small to access Google's massive network of advertisers on a self-service basis. Publishers could sign up for AdSense in a matter of minutes. AdSense would then scan the publisher's site for content and place contextually relevant ads next to that content. As with AdWords, this is a pay-per-click service, but with AdSense Google splits the revenues with the publishers. In addition to large publishers such as online news sites, AdSense has been particularly appealing to many small publishers, such as Web bloggers. Small publishers found that by adding a few lines of code to their site, they could suddenly monetize their content. However, many advertisers felt that AdSense was not as effective as AdWords in driving traffic to their sites. Google allowed advertisers to opt out of AdSense in 2004. Despite this, AdSense soon grew into a respectable business, accounting for 15% of Google's revenues in 2005, or close to $1 billion.

GOOGLE GROWS UP

Between 2001 and 2014, Google changed in a number of ways. First, in mid-2001, the company hired a new CEO, Eric Schmidt, to replace Larry Page. Schmidt had been the chief technology officer of Sun Microsystems, and then CEO of Novell. Schmidt was brought on to help manage the company's growth with the explicit blessing of Brin and Page. Both Brin and Page were still in their 20s, and the board felt they needed a "grown up" who had run a large company to help Google transition to the next stage (Google turned a profit the month after Schmidt joined). Brin and Page became the presidents of technology and products, respectively. When Schmidt was hired, Google had over 200 employees and was handling over 100 million searches a day.

According to knowledgeable observers, Schmidt, Brin, and Page acted as a triumvirate, with Brin and Page continuing to exercise strong influence over strategies and policies at Google. Schmidt may have been CEO, but Google was still very much Brin and Page's company.[19] Working closely together, the three drove the development of a set of values and an organization that would come to define the uniquely Google way of doing things. In January 2011, Schmidt retired from the CEO position, passing the reins back to Larry Page. Schmidt remained Chairman, while Brin turned his attention to overseeing Google's experimental technologies division, Google X.

Vision and Values

As Google expanded, there was concern that rapid hiring would quickly dilute the vision, values, and principles of the founders. In mid-2001, Brin and Page asked a core group of early employees to come up with a policy for ensuring that the company's culture did not fracture as the company added employees. From this group, and subsequent discussions, emerged a vision and list of values that have continued to shape the evolution of the company. These were not new; rather, they represented the formalization of principles that Brin and Page felt they had always adhered to.

The central vision of Google is to "organize the world's information, and make it universally acceptable and useful."[20] The team also articulated a set of 10 core philosophies (values), which are listed on its website.[21] Perhaps the most significant and certainly the most discussed value is captured by the phrase "Don't be evil." The central message underlying this phrase was that Google should never compromise the integrity of its search results. Google would never let commercial considerations bias its rankings. "Don't be evil," however, has become more than that at Google; it has become a central organizing principle of the company, albeit one that is far from easy to implement. Google got positive press from libertarians when it refused to share its search data with the U.S. government, which wanted the data to help fight child porn. However, the same constituency reacted with dismay when the company caved to the Chinese government, and removed from its Chinese service offending results for search terms such as "human rights" and "democracy." Brin justified the Chinese decision by saying that "it will be better for Chinese web users, because ultimately they will get more information, though not quite all of it."[22]

Another core value at Google is "Focus on the user, and all else will follow." In many ways, this value captures what Brin and Page initially did. They focused on giving the user the best possible search experience: highly relevant results, delivered with lightning speed to an uncluttered, elegant interface. The value also reflects a belief at Google that it is okay to deliver value to users first, and then figure out the business model for monetizing that value. This belief seems to reflect Google's own early experience.

Yet another key principle, although not written down anywhere, is captured by the phrase "Launch early and often." This seems to underpin Google's approach to product development. Google has introduced a stream of new products over the years, not all of which were initially that compelling, but through rapid upgrades it has subsequently improved the efficacy of many of these products.

Google also prides itself on being a company where decisions are data driven. Opinions are said to count for nothing unless they are backed up by hard data. It is not the loudest voice that wins the day in arguments over strategy, it is the data. In some meetings, people are not allowed to say "I think . . .", instead, they say "The data suggests . . ."[23]

Finally, Google devotes considerable resources to making sure that its employees are working in a supportive and stimulating environment. To quote from the company's website:

> Google Inc. puts employees first when it comes to daily life in our Googleplex headquarters. There is an emphasis on team achievements and pride in individual accomplishments that contribute to the company's overall success. Ideas are traded, tested and put into practice with an alacrity that can be dizzying. Meetings that would take hours elsewhere are frequently little more than a conversation in line for lunch and few walls separate those who write the code from those who write the checks. This highly communicative environment fosters a productivity and camaraderie fueled by the realization that millions of people rely on Google results. Give the proper tools to a group of people who like to make a difference, and they will.[24]

Organization

Google has always operated with a flat organization. By the mid-2000s, Google had one manager for every 20 line employees. At times, the ratio has been as high as 1:40. For a while, one manager had 180 direct reports.[25] Until 2011, the structure was organized around five main functions: engineering, products, sales, legal, and finance. Within and across functions there were numerous teams. Big projects were (and still are) broken down and allocated to small, tightly focused teams. Hundreds of projects could be going on at the same time. Teams often release new software in 6 weeks or less and look at how users respond hours later. Google can try a new user interface, or some other tweak, with just 0.1% of its users and get massive feedback very quickly, letting it decide a project's fate in weeks.[26]

In 2011, shortly after assuming the CEO position, Page modified the organization, creating a structure with six product groups, each with its own functions and headed by a senior VP who reported directly to him. The product groups were mobile, social (e.g. Google+), Chrome browser and operating system, You Tube, Search, and Ads.[27] Another division, Google X, was created to oversee the exploration and development of experimental technologies. Sergey Brin leads this division.

The reorganization was undertaken to increase accountability and control, speed up innovation, and reduce bureaucracy. Prior to the reorganization, there were reports that the company's freewheeling culture had led to an anarchic resource-allocation process, extensive duplication, with multiple teams working on the same project, and increasingly dysfunctional political behavior.[28] There were also reports that Google's organization was not scaling that well, that the firm's personnel department was "collapsing," and that "absolute chaos reigns." One former employee noted that when she was hired, nobody knew when or where she was suppose to work.[29] Page has remarked that he is very pleased with the way the reorganization has worked out, and he believes it has helped Google to scale.

One aspect of Google's organization that has garnered considerable attention is the company's approach to product development. Employees are expected to spend 20% of their time on something that interests them, away from their main jobs. Seemingly based on 3M's famous 15% rule, Google's 20% rule is designed to encourage creativity. The company has set up forums on its internal network where anyone can post ideas, discuss them, and solicit help from other employees. As a natural part of this process, talent tends to gravitate to those projects that seem most promising, giving those who post the most interesting ideas the ability to select a talented team to take them to the next level.

Like 3M, Google set up a process by which projects coming out of 20% time can be evaluated, receive feedback from peers, and ultimately garner funding. Until 2011, Marissa Myer, one of Google's early employees and now CEO of Yahoo, acted as a gatekeeper. She helped decide when projects were ready to be pitched to Brin and Page. Once in front of the founders, advocates have 20 minutes, no more, to make their pitch.[30] Myer articulated a number of other principals that guide product development at Google.[31] These include:

1. Ideas come from everywhere. Set up a system where good ideas rise to the top.
2. Focus on users, not money. Money follows consumers. Advertisers follow consumers. If you amass consumers, you will find ways to monetize your ideas.
3. Innovation, not instant perfection. Put products on the market, learn, and iterate.
4. Don't kill projects, morph them. If an idea has managed to make its way out the door, there is usually some kernel of truth to it. Don't walk away from ideas, think of ways to replace or rejuvenate them.

One of the early products to come out 20% time was Google News, which returns news articles ranked by relevance in response to a keyword query. Search the term "oil prices" in Google News, for example, and the search will return news dealing with changes in oil prices, with the most relevant at the top of the list. A sophisticated algorithm determines relevance on a real-time basis by looking at the quality of the news source (e.g., the *New York Times* rates higher than local newspapers), publishing date, the number of other people who click on that source, and numerous other factors. Krishna Bharat, a software engineer from India, who in response to the events of September 11, 2001, had a desire to learn what was being written and said around the world, initiated the project. Two other employees worked with Bharat to construct a demo that was released within Google. Positive reaction soon got Bharat in front of Brin and Page, who, impressed, gave the project a green light. Bharat started to work full time on the project.[32] Other products to come out of 20% time include Google Maps, Gmail, and AdSense.

Another feature of Google's organization is its hiring strategy. Like Microsoft, Google has made a virtue out of hiring people with a high IQ. The hiring process is very rigorous. Each prospect has to take an "exam" to test their conceptual abilities. This is followed by interviews with eight or more people, each of who rate the applicant on a 1 to 4 scale (4 being "I would hire this person"). Applicants also undergo detailed background checks to find out what they are like to work with. Reportedly, some brilliant prospects don't get hired when background checks find out that they are difficult to work with. In essence, all hiring at Google is by committee, and while this can take considerable time, the company insists that the effort yields dividends.

While accounts of Google's organization and culture tend to emphasize their positive aspects, not everyone has such a sanguine view. Brain Reid, who was recruited into senior management at Google in 2002, and fired 2 years later, told author John Battelle "Google is a monarchy with two kings, Larry and Sergey. Eric is a puppet. Larry and Sergey are arbitrary, whimsical people . . . they run the company with an iron hand . . . Nobody at Google from what I could tell had any authority to do anything of consequence except Larry and Sergey."[33] According to Battelle, several other former employees made similar statements to him. Some former employees noted that, in practice, 20% time can turn out to be 120% time, since people still have their regular workload. There are also complaints that the culture is one of long workdays and seven-day workweeks, with little consideration for family issues.

The IPO

As Google grew, the question of if and when to undertake an IPO became more pressing. There were two obvious reasons for doing an IPO—gaining access to capital and providing liquidity for early backers and the large number of employees who had equity positions. On the other hand, from 2001 onward, the company was profitable, generating significant cash flows, and could fund its expansion internally. Moreover, management felt that the longer they could keep the details of what was turning out to be an extraordinarily successful business model private, the better. In the end, the company's hand was forced by an obscure SEC regulation that required companies that give stock options to employees to report as if they were a public company by as early as April 2004. Realizing that the cat would be out of the bag anyway, Google informed its employees in early 2004 that it would go public.

The IPO gave the first public glimpse of Google's financials, which were contained in the offering document. They were jaw dropping. The company had generated revenues of $1.47 billion in 2003, an increase of 230% over 2002. Google earned net profits of $106 million in 2003, but accountants soon figured out that the number was depressed by certain one-time accounting items, and that cash flow in 2003 had exceeded $500 million.

Google's went public on August 19, 2004 at $85 a share. The company's first quarterly report showed sales doubling over the prior year, and by November the price was $200. In September 2005, with the stock close to $300 a share, Google undertook a secondary offering, selling 14 million shares to raise $4.18 billion. With positive cash flow adding to this, by June 2008, Google was sitting on $12.8 billion in cash and short-term investments, prompting speculation as to the company's strategic intentions.

Strategy

Since 2001, Google has endeavored to keep enhancing the efficacy of its search engine, continually improving the search algorithms and investing heavily in computing resources. The company has branched out from being a text-based search engine. One strategic thrust has been to extend search to as many digital devices as possible. Google started out on PCs, but its fastest-growing revenue stream is now on mobile devices. A second strategy has been to widen the scope of search to include different sorts of information. Google quickly pushed beyond text into indexing and offered up searches of images, news reports, books, maps, apps, scholarly papers, a blog search, a shopping network, and videos.

Not all of this has gone smoothly. Book publishers were angered by Google's book project, which seeks to create the world's largest, searchable, digital library of books by systematically scanning books from the libraries of major universities (e.g., Stanford). The publishers argued that Google had no right to do this without first getting permission from the publishers, and was violating copyright. Several publishers filed a complaint with the U.S. District Court in New York. Google responded that users would not be able to download entire books, and that in any event creating an easy-to-use index of books is fair use under copyright law and will increase the awareness and sales of books, directly benefiting copyright holders. On another front, the World Association of News Paper Publishers formed a task force to examine the exploitation of content by search engines.[34]

Since going public, Google has introduced a rash of product offerings, many of which seem to represent diversification away from the company's core search business. Most of these products grew out of the company's new product-development process, including Gmail, Google Apps, Blogger, the Google + social networking site, the Chrome browser and operating system, the Android operating system for mobile devices (smartphones and tablets), and city-wide, fiber-optic networks (Google Fiber).

Google Apps, a cloud-based offering, seemed aimed squarely at Microsoft's Office franchise. Google Apps includes word-processing, spreadsheet, and presentation programs. Google Apps is designed for online collaboration. Users can save files in formats used by Microsoft products, although they lack the full feature set of Microsoft's Office. Google has stated that the company is not trying to match the features of Office, and that "90% of users don't necessarily need 90% of the functions that are in there."[35] For an annual licensing fee of $50 a head, Google provides corporate customers with an Apps service that includes Gmail and its Office like offerings.

In late 2007, Google announced a suite of software for smart phones that include an operating system, Android, and applications that work with it. Android was aimed squarely at Apple's iPhone and Research in Motion's Blackberry, which at the time were the leaders in the smartphone space. Apple's iPhone, introduced in 2007, was redefining the market for smart phones. Like Apple's iPhone, Android phones had a touch screen, a virtual keyboard, Apps displayed as onscreen icons, and an ability to download third-party apps from an App Store that Google established. The attraction for Google was that advertising was increasingly being inserted into content viewed on mobile handsets. Google decided to give Android to device manufacturers for free, aiming to make money through mobile search traffic.

The free model turned out to be remarkably successful. Android was very appealing to smartphone manufacturers such as Samsung, HTC, and Motorola, all of which needed an operating systems that would help them build phones that could compete with Apple's iPhone. When Apple introduced the iPad in 2010, Google quickly followed with a version of Android that could run tablets.

By 2014, Android had emerged as the dominant operating system for smartphones. Estimates suggest that some 1.28 billion Android phones were sold in 2014, and that Android captured 81% of the global market. Apple shipped 193 million smartphones and captured 15% of the global market. Microsoft, with its Windows Phone operating system, captured 3% of the global market.[36] In an attempt to gain share from Android, in 2014, Microsoft started giving the Windows Phone operating system to device manufacturers for free.

In October 2010, Google reported that its mobile advertising revenues were growing strongly due to the adoption of Android, and that it now had hit an annualized run rate of $1 billion.[37] By 2014, estimates suggested that Google was generating more than $13 billion from mobile search. Its share of mobile ad revenues stood at 41%. Facebook was second in the mobile space, with 18% of the market.[38]

Google's App store was renamed Google Play in 2012. Like Apple's iTunes, Google Play allows users to download applications and digital media including music, video (movies, TV programs, and so on), and books. By mid-2013, Google Play had 1.3 million Apps available and registered over 50 billion downloads. Google Play is now the second largest distribution channel in the world for apps and digital media by revenues, and it may surpass iTunes by 2018.[39]

Another remarkably successful new product from Google has been its Chrome browser. Released at the end of 2008, Chrome has steadily gained share. By January 2015, it was the most widely used Web browser in the world, with a 51% market share. In the all-important U.S. market, Chrome held 36% of the market in January 2015. Microsoft's once-dominant Internet Explorer had a 21% share.[40]

On the acquisition front, until 2006, Google stuck to purchasing small technology firms. This changed in October 2006, when Google announced that it would purchase YouTube for $1.64 billion in stock. YouTube is a simple, fun website to which anybody can upload video clips in order to share them. In October 2006, some 65,000 video clips were being uploaded every day, and 100 million were being viewed. Like Google in its early days, YouTube initially had no business model. The thinking was that Google would find ways to sell advertising that is linked to video clips on YouTube.[41]

By 2015, YouTube had more than 1 billion users. Every day, hundreds of millions of hours of video were being watched on YouTube, generating billions of views. Although Google does not break out You-Tube ad revenues, estimates suggest that, in 2013, YouTube generated gross revenues of $5.6 billion. After paying back advertising partners and video content creators, YouTube was estimated to have generated $1.9 billion in net revenue in 2013.[42]

Another notable Google acquisition was its $3.1-billion purchase of DoubleClick in 2007. DoubleClick is a specialist on online display advertising such as banner ads that are targeted at building brand awareness. Internet publishers pay DoubleClick to insert display ads as users visit their websites. While display advertising has not grown as rapidly as search-based advertising, it is a big business accounting for around a quarter of all Internet advertising revenue, with significant upside potential as companies begin to apply demographic technology to increase the effectiveness of Internet display ads.[43] The Double-Click deal was criticized by Google's rivals, including Microsoft, on antitrust grounds, but regulators in the United States and the European Union approved the deal which closed in 2008. By 2014, estimates suggested that Google generated about $4 billion in display ad revenues. Facebook, however, had surpassed Google and was earning close to $5 billion in display ad revenues.[44]

In May 2012, Google acquired Motorola's mobile handset business, Motorola Mobility, for $12.5 billion. Motorola Mobility made smartphones and tablets that used the Android operating system. Google reportedly purchased Motorola Mobility for its portfolio of some 17,000 patents so that it could protect itself and other Android vendors from lawsuits launched by Apple, Microsoft, and others, who claimed that Android infringed upon their patents. In late 2014, Google sold off Motorola Mobility (minus the patent portfolio, which it kept), to the Chinese PC and device maker, Lenovo, for $2.91 billion.

Critics argue that as Google moves into these additional areas its profit margins will be compressed. Henry Blodget of Cherry Hill Research notes that in its core pay-per-click search business, Google makes profit margins of about 60%. In its more recent business of placing advertisements on webpages belonging to other parties such as bloggers, its profit margins are 10 to 20%, because it is harder to make the advertisements as relevant to the audience and Google must share the resulting revenues. Display advertising also offers lower returns. Google, not surprisingly, does not see things this way. The company argues that since its costs are mostly fixed, and incremental revenue is profit, it makes good sense to push into other markets, even if its average revenue per viewer is only 1 cent (compared with 50 cents per click on the Web).[45]

THE ONLINE ADVERTISING MARKET IN 2014

There is an old adage in advertising that half of all the money spent on advertising is wasted—advertisers just don't know which half. Estimates suggest that approximately half of the $500 billion spent worldwide on advertising is wasted because the wrong message is sent to the wrong audience.[46] The problem is that traditional media advertising is indiscriminate. Consider a 30-second ad spot on broadcast TV. Advertisers pay a rate for such a spot called CPM (costs per thousand). The CPM is based on estimates of how many people are watching a show. There are numerous problems with this system. The estimates of audience numbers are only approximations at best. The owners of the TV may have left the room while the commercials are airing. They may channel surf during the commercial break, be napping, or talking on the telephone. The viewer may not be among the intended audience—a Viagra commercial might be wasted on a teenage girl, for example. Or the household might be using TiVo or a similar digital video recorder that skips commercials.

By contrast, new advertising models based on pay-per-click are more discriminating. Rather than sending out ads to a large audience, only a few of whom will be interested in the products being advertised, consumers "select in" to search-based ads.

They do this twice; first, by entering a keyword in a search engine, and second, by scanning the search results as well as the sponsored links and clicking on a link. In effect, potential purchasers pull the ads toward them through the search process. Advertisers only pay when someone clicks on their ad. Consequently, the conversion rate for search-based ads is far higher than the conversion rate for traditional media advertising.

Moreover, traditional advertising is so wasteful that most firms only advertise 5 to 10% of their products in the mass media, hoping that other products will benefit from a halo effect. In contrast, the targeted nature of search-based advertising makes it cost effective to advertise products that only sell in small quantities. In effect, search-based Internet advertising allows producers to exploit the economics of the long tail. Pay-per-click models also make it economical for small merchants to advertise their wares on the Web.

The Growth Story

Powered by the rapid growth of search-based, pay-per-click advertising, and the increasing amount of time people spend online, total advertising spending on the Internet continues to expand rapidly. In 2013, Internet ad revenues in the United States hit $42.8 billion, up 17% from the prior year. For the first time, Internet advertising exceeded advertising revenues from broadcast TV, which stood at $40.1 billion.[47] U.S. Internet ad revenues in 2014 were estimated to have been close to $48 billion.[48] Globally, Internet ad revenues hit $117 billion in 2013, and they were estimated to reach $195 billion by 2018.[49]

Paid search advertising, a business dominated by Google, continues to account for the largest share of online advertising. In 2014, in the United States, paid search was accounting for about 38% of all online ad revenue; display ads accounted for 28%; and mobile revenues for 16%. Globally, paid search accounted for 41% of all Internet ad revenue in 2013. Forecasts suggest that mobile and video advertising will experience the strongest growth going forward, although traditional paid search is still expected to grow strongly, amounting to $74 billion globally in 2018, up from $48 billion in 2013.[50]

Google's dominance is reflected in its increased share of all Internet traffic. In mid-2006, Google's websites had the fourth-largest unique audience on the Web, close behind the longer-established portal sites maintained by Microsoft (MSN), Yahoo, and Time Warner (AOL). By late 2014, Google's sites were ranked first, followed by Yahoo sites, Facebook, AOL, Microsoft, and Amazon.[51]

Google's Competitors

Google's most significant competitors include Microsoft and Yahoo in search, and Facebook is mobile display advertising. Both Yahoo and Microsoft spent several years and hundreds of millions in R&D spending trying to improve their search engine technology and gain market share at the expense of Google. Yahoo failed, and its shares have declined, while Microsoft recorded moderate market share gains after it launched its Bing search engine in 2008, reaching almost 20% of the U.S. search market by 2014. However, Microsoft has never made any money in the online search arena; in fact, it has lost billions. Although Microsoft does not break out figures for Bing, annualized run-rate losses in this business are believed to be around $2 billion, and the company may have racked up cumulative losses of over $15 billion in search.[52]

In February 2008, Microsoft launched an unsolicited takeover bid for Yahoo. After months of difficult negotiations, Microsoft withdrew its offer. In rationalizing its decision, Microsoft argued that Yahoo's continuing market-share erosion during the months of negotiations had made the acquisition far less compelling. Yahoo's managers, for their part, continued to argue that Microsoft was not offering enough.

Yahoo continued to lose market share. After top management changes at Yahoo, in June 2009, Microsoft and Yahoo announced a 10-year, broad-based partnership in the search area. Under the terms of the agreement, Bing will be the exclusive search platform at Yahoo. Yahoo will be the exclusive seller to both companies' Premium Search advertisers, while Microsoft's AdCenter will handle self-service advertising. Each company will continue to manage their own display advertising business. Yahoo also has the option to use Bing on its mobile properties. The partnership received regulatory approval in mid-2010, and both companies began to implement the agreement in late 2010. The deal does not make money directly for Microsoft—it hands over 90% of the revenue generated from searches through Yahoo to Yahoo.

To succeed, the partnership must (a) increase search query volume, and (b) drive greater revenues per search. In 2009, estimates suggested that Google was generating $36.37 of revenue per thousand search queries, Yahoo $17.06, and Microsoft $14.31. Search query volume could increase if the greater traffic improves the relevance of search results served up by Bing, and if consumers and advertisers notice this. Revenues per search could increase if advertisers are willing to bid more for keywords on Bing given the greater traffic volume of the search engine.

Another significant strategic partner for Microsoft is Facebook, the leading social network site, with over a billion registered users. Microsoft invested $240 million in Facebook in 2007 for a 1.6% stake. Since then, the two companies have worked together to introduce advertisements on Facebook. In 2010, the two companies announced an extended deal that will incorporate Facebook data into Bing search results. Bing results will now include a Facebook module offering users the likes, images, comments, and other public data from their network of friends. Thus, for example, you can see if any of your friends liked or recommended a certain restaurant. There is no question that the evolving partnership between Microsoft and Facebook is in part a response to their common rival, Google.

In November 2014, Yahoo pulled off something of a coup when it inked a deal with Mozilla to replace Google as the default search engine of the Firefox Web browser. The deal integrated Yahoo search into Firefox's browser for digital devices, including PCs, tablets, and smartphones (the searches will still be powered by Bing). Firefox at the time had 10% of the U.S. browser market. By January 2015, Yahoo's share of U.S. search traffic had reportedly jumped 2%.[53] Yahoo was also rumored to be negotiating a similar deal with Apple to be the default search engine on its Safari browser, replacing Google.

◢ LOOKING FORWARD

With online advertising predicted to grow strongly, Google seems to be in the driver's seat. It has the largest market share in search, the greatest name recognition, and is capturing a proportionately greater share of search based advertising, than its rivals.

However, despite market share losses, Microsoft and Yahoo cannot be dismissed. As their partnership in search progresses, will they be able to leverage their substantial assets and capabilities to gain ground of Google? As for Google, what is its long-term game plan? Recent strategic moves suggest that it is attempting to expand beyond search, but where will this take the company, and what will that mean for other Internet companies?

◢ NOTES

1. "comScore Releases November 2014 Search Engine Rankings," comScore press release, December 16, 2015.
2. "Google Accounts for Half of all U.S. Searches," Nielsen/Net Ratings, May 25, 2006.
3. "2013 Search Engine Market Share by Country," returnonnow.com.
4. "Driven by Facebook and Google, Mobile ad market soars 105%," www.emarketer.com, March 19, 2014.
5. This section draws heavily upon the excellent description of search given by J. Battelle in *The Search* (Penguin Portfolio, New York, 2005).
6. Google 10K for 2013.
7. The basic story of GoTo.com is related in J. Battelle, *The Search* (Penguin Portfolio, New York, 2005).
8. K. Greenberg, "Pay-for-Placement Search Services Offer Ad Alternatives," *Adweek*, September 25, 2000, p. 60.
9. M. Gannon, "GoTo.Com Inc.," *Venture Capital Journal*, August 1, 1999, p. 1.
10. T. Jackson, "Cash is the Key to a True Portal," *Financial Times*, February 2, 1999, p. 16.
11. K. Greenberg, "Pay-for-Placement Search Services Offer Ad Alternatives," *Adweek*, September 25, 2000, p. 60.
12. S. Heim, "GoTo.Com Changes to Overture Services, Launches Campaign," *Adweek*, September 10, 2001, p. 7.
13. J. Battelle, *The Search*. There is no independent confirmation of the story.
14. Anonymous, "Yahoo to Acquire Overture Services for 2.44 Times Revenues," *Weekly Corporate Growth Service*, July 21, 2003, p. 8.
15. R. Waters, "Google Settles Yahoo Case with Shares," *Financial Times*, August 19, 2004, p. 29.

16. F. Vogelstein, "Gates vs Google: Search and Destroy," *Fortune*, May 2, 2005, pp. 72–82.

17. D. A. Vise, *The Google Story* (Random House, New York, 2004).

18. Ibid.

19. J. Battelle, *The Search*. There is no independent confirmation of the story.

20. www.google.com/corporate/index.html.

21. www.google.com/corporate/tenthings.html.

22. A. Kessler, "Sellout.com," *The Wall Street Journal*, January 31, 2006, p. A14.

23. Q. Hardy, "Google Thinks Small," *Fortune*, November 14, 2005, pp. 198–199.

24. www.google.com/corporate/tenthings.html.

25. Q. Hardy, "Google Thinks Small"; D. A. Garvin, "How Google Sold its Engineers on Management," *Harvard Business Review*, December 2013.

26. Q. Hardy, "Google Thinks Small."

27. B. Ortutay, "Google CEO Larry Page Completes Major Reorganization," *Huffington Post*, January 30, 2015.

28. B. Lashinsky and Y. W. Yen, "Where Does Google Go Next?" *Fortune*, May 26, 2008, pp. 104–110.

29. Anonymous, "Inside the Googleplex," *The Economist*, September 1, 2007, pp. 53–56.

30. B. Elgin, "Managing Google's Idea Factory," *Businessweek*, October 3, 2005, pp. 88–90.

31. M. Krauss, "Google's Mayer Tells How Innovation Gets Done," *Marketing News*, April 1, 2007, pp. 7–8.

32. D. A. Vise, *The Google Story*.

33. J. Battelle, *The Search*, p. 233.

34. J. Doherty, "In the Drink," *Barrons*, February 13, 2006, pp. 31–36.

35. K. J. Delaney and R. A. Guth, "Google's Free Web Services Will Vie with Microsoft Office," *The Wall Street Journal*, October 11, 2006, p. B1.

36. "One Billion Android Phones Shipped Last Year," developer.com, January 29, 2015.

37. Citigroup Global Markets, Google Inc, October 14, 2010.

38. B. Womack, "Google Revenue Falls Short as Mobile Competition Intensifies," *Global and Mail*, January 29, 2015. PAGE #S

39. S. M. Patterson, "Revenue From the Google Play Store will Overtake Apple's App Store in 2018," *Quartz,* July 17, 2014.

40. I. Lunden, "Google's U.S. Ex-Mobile Drops Below 75% as Yahoo Makes More Firefox Gains," *Tech Crunch*, February 2, 2015.

41. Anonymous, "Two Kings Get Together; Google and YouTube," *The Economist*, October 14, 2006, pp. 82–83.

42. "Advertisers to spend $5.6 billion on YouTube in 2013 worldwide," www.emarketer.com, December 11, 2013.

43. R. Hof, "Ad Wars: Google's Green Light," *Businessweek,* March 3, 2008, pp. 22.

44. K. Likakasa, "Facebook Pulls Ahead of Google in US Digital Display Ad Revenues," *Ad Exchanger,* March 11, 2014.

45. Anonymous, "Inside the Googleplex," *The Economist,* September 1, 2007, pp. 53–56.

46. Anonymous, "The Ultimate Marketing Machine," *The Economist,* July 8, 2006, pp. 61–64; K. J. Delaney, "Google Push to Sell Ads on YouTube Hits Snag," *The Wall Street Journal*, July 9, 2008, p. A1.

47. "2103 Internet Ad Revenues Soar to $42.8 Billion," IAB, April 10, 2014.

48. "Q3 2014 Internet Advertising Revenues Hit $12.4 Billion," IAB, December 18, 2014.

49. "Global Entertainment and Media Outlook, 2014–2018," www.pwc.com.

50. Ibid.

51. "U.S. Broadband Composition Reaches 72 Percent at Home," Nielsen/Net Ratings press release June 21, 2006; "comScore Ranks the Top 50 US Digital Media Properties for September 2014," comScore press release, October 22, 2014.

52. S. Cleland, "What If Microsoft Exited the Search Business?" *The Daily Caller*, January 14, 2013.

53. I. Lunden, "Google's U.S. Ex-Mobile Drops Below 75% as Yahoo Makes More Firefox Gains," *Tech Crunch,* February 2, 2015.

MICROSOFT: FROM GATES TO SATYA NADELLA

▌INTRODUCTION

On February 4, 2014, Satya Nadella became CEO of Microsoft. Nadella, a native of Hyderabad, India, was only the third CEO in Microsoft's 39-year history. Cofounder Bill Gates was CEO from Microsoft's establishment in April 1975 through January 2000 when he passed the reins to Steve Ballmer. Gates remained chairman though until February 2014. The Gates years were characterized by dramatic growth as Microsoft expanded from a small start-up to become the largest and most dominant software company on the planet, in the process making Gates the world's richest man. The foundations of Microsoft's success during this period were its two monopolies: the Windows operating system, which at its peak was used on 95% of the world's personal computers (PCs), and Office, which had a 90% market share in 2012.[1]

Microsoft continued to expand both revenues and profits under the leadership of Steve Ballmer. During his tenure, revenues expanded from $25 billion to $70 billion while net income grew 215% to $23 billion. One area that did particularly during the Ballmer years was the Windows server business, a division that Nadella ran prior to becoming CEO.

Servers sit at the center of networks of PCs, and are used to perform a variety of functions including database hosting, file services, Web services, print services, and applications services. Microsoft makes a version of Windows, Windows Server, which runs servers. The Windows server business was a $20-billion division by 2014. Microsoft gained share from competitors such as IBM, which promoted the rival Linux operating system. By 2014, 75% of servers built around Intel microprocessors used Windows Server as their operating system, as did around 50% of all servers.[2] The Linux and Unix operating systems took the number 2 and 3 spots.

Despite impressive growth, Microsoft's stock price stagnated during the Ballmer era. This reflected a growing concern that Microsoft had lost its leadership in the computer industry to three firms, Google, Apple, and Amazon. Google had grown dramatically during the 2000s on the back of its dominant Internet search business. Along the way, Google had developed an operating system for smartphones (Android) and laptops (Chrome) that were now challenging Windows on computing devices, a category that had expanded beyond traditional PCs to included smartphones and tablets. Google was also offering a "cloud-based" suite of productivity tools, Google Docs, which competed directly with Office.

Apple, a firm that was nearly bankrupt in 1997, had done more than any other company to expand the definition of computing devices to include smartphones and tablets. Apple had introduced the first version of its smartphone, the iPhone, in 2007. Differentiated by elegant design and ease of use, two Apple hallmarks, the iPhone was a sensation that redefined what a smartphone should look like and do. Apple followed the iPhone with the 2010 introduction of the iPad, a tablet device that created an entirely new computing category, and one that cannibalized sales of laptop PCs. Both devices ran Apple's iOS operating system, further reducing the relevance of Windows.

As smartphones and tablets gained popularity, more and more computing was being done using these mobile devices—accessing applications and data stored on servers "in the cloud" rather than on a traditional PC. According to Microsoft's own estimate, by mid- 2014, while 90% of traditional desktop and laptop PCs still used Windows, only 14% of *all* computing devices (a definition which included PCs, smartphones, and tablets), used Windows.[3] Although under Ballmer's leadership Microsoft had tried to grow its share by introducing a Windows smartphone and the Surface tablet, these offerings failed to gain traction. By 2014, Windows Phone had less than 3% of the global smartphone operating system market, while Apple's iOS held 15.2%, and Android 81.1%.[4] In the tablet market, Android had a 65.8% share, Apple's iOS had 28.4%, and Windows tablets had 5.8%.[5] Microsoft was assumed to be losing significant amounts of money on its phone and tablet businesses. To compound matters, after three decades of sustained growth, PC sales were declining: PC sales fell by 4% in 2012 and by 9.8% in 2013, although demand stabilized in 2014.[6]

Amazon, the world's largest Internet retailer, was challenging Microsoft from another direction. By the mid-2000s, tens of thousands of servers were being grouped together into "server farms" located in the cloud to host high-traffic Internet websites. Google had built server farms to host its Internet search business, Microsoft likewise had server farms for its Bing search business and MSNBC Web offerings, and Amazon had built server farms to host its large online retail business. In 2005, Amazon leveraged the knowledge and capacity it had accumulated building server farms to start a new business, Amazon Web Services

(AWS). AWS hosted data, Web services, and applications for paying customer. These data, services, and applications could be accessed from anywhere by a user with a computing device and an appropriate wireless or hardwire connection. By 2014, AWS was viewed as the market-share leader in the emerging cloud-computing business.

Microsoft entered the cloud-computing business in 2010 with Azure (later renamed Microsoft Cloud). Azure was founded within the Windows Server division that Nadella ran prior to becoming CEO. In addition to hosting data and websites, Azure allows clients to build and run applications that reside on Microsoft's cloud. By 2014, Azure was thought to be number two in the emerging cloud business, with Google and IBM rounding out the top four. Industry wide, the cloud-computing business generated $16 billion in sales in 2014, but it was growing very rapidly and was thought by many to represent the future of computing.[7]

Commenting on Microsoft's overall competitive position in 2014, the general manger of one business unit noted that: "I think we have about 18 to 24 months to get it right. If we don't, Microsoft is finished."[8] This statement reflected a widespread belief within the company that the computer industry was undergoing a massive paradigm shift, away from the client-server world based on PC architecture in which Microsoft had been so dominant, and toward a world of mobile devices and cloud computing in which Microsoft faced significant competitive challenges. Nadella was as cognizant of this as anyone. By March 2014, he had already honed his vision for the company. Microsoft, he said, was competing in a "mobile-first, cloud-first" world.[9] The task facing Nadella was deciding what actions to take to ensure that Microsoft survived and prospered in this brave new mobile-first, cloud-first world. He knew he had to act fast.

BILL GATES AND THE EARLY HISTORY OF MICROSOFT

Bill Gates and Paul Allen established Microsoft in 1975. Gates was a 19-year-old Harvard dropout.[10] Allen, who was 22, had dropped out of Washington

State University to work as a programmer at Honeywell in Boston. Gates and Allen had both attended Seattle's elite Lakeside high school, where they had bonded over their common interest in computers.

By all accounts, the young Bill Gates was extremely intelligent, hypercompetitive, ambitious, hardworking, and a gifted programmer. One of his former teachers at Lakeside described him as the most intelligent student she had ever had. He could also be dismissive of people who lacked his technical acumen, abrasive, and hypercritical. One story widely circulated in Microsoft is that if he disagreed with the technical or product presentations of Microsoft employees, he would interject with sharp comments along the lines of "that's the stupidest thing I have ever heard" or that the idea was "brain damaged." Legend has it that on more than one occasion Gates reduced a presenter to tears, although Gates would argue that it was never the person he criticized, just the idea. Gates respected people who were smart and hardworking like him, who marshaled their facts, and who stuck to their guns when challenged by him if they knew they had the facts on their side. Gates ultimately relied upon such people to lead projects and businesses within Microsoft.

In 1975, Allen persuaded Gates to drop out of Harvard and start Microsoft to write a version of the computer programming language, BASIC, to run on the world's first commercially available PC, the MITS Altair 8800, which used an Intel 8080 microprocessor. Gates and Allen met with the founder of MITS and demonstrated their version of BASIC for the Altair 8800. This resulted in a deal under which MITS distributed Microsoft BASIC for the Altair 8800, making Microsoft the first company to sell software to run on a personal computer. Microsoft subsequently wrote versions of Microsoft BASIC that ran on other PCs of the time, including Apple's first successful offering, the legendary Apple II, introduced in 1979.

In June 1980, Steve Ballmer joined Microsoft. Ballmer had been a friend of Gates at Harvard, and was the only person who had outscored Gates on mathematics and microeconomics classes at Harvard. Ballmer had worked at Procter & Gamble after Harvard, and then moved on to Stanford Business School. Gates persuaded Ballmer to drop out of Stanford and manage business operations at Microsoft. He was employee number 30.

In July 1980, IBM approached Microsoft about using a version of Microsoft BASIC for the IBM PC, which was then in development. Gates persuaded IBM to adopt a 16-bit Intel processor (originally, IBM had been considering a less-powerful, 8-bit processor). Gates was also instrumental is pushing IBM to adopt an open architecture, arguing that IBM would benefit from the software and peripherals that other companies could make.

Initially, IBM was intent on licensing the CP/M operating system, produced by Digital Research, for the IBM PC. However, the current version of CP/M was designed to work on an 8-bit processor, and Gates had persuaded IBM that it needed a 16-bit processor. In a series of quick moves, Gates purchased a 16-bit operating system from a nearby company, Seattle Computer, for $50,000. Gates then hired the designer of the operating system, Tim Paterson, renamed the system MS-DOS, and offered to license it to IBM. In what turned out to be a masterstroke, Gates persuaded IBM to accept a nonexclusive license for MS-DOS (which IBM called PC-DOS). MS-DOS had a command-line, text-based interface and could only run one program at a time, but, for 1981, it was state of the art.

To drive sales, IBM commissioned developers to build a number of applications for the IBM PC. In addition to Microsoft Basic, these included a version of VisiCalc, an early spreadsheet that was a popular application for the Apple II, a word processor, EasyWriter, and a well-known series of business programs from Peachtree Software. Introduced in August 1981, the IBM PC was an instant success. Over the next 2 years, IBM would sell more than 500,000 PCs, seizing leadership from Apple, which had dominated the PC market with the Apple II. IBM had what Apple lacked—an ability to sell into corporate America. As sales of the IBM PC mounted, more independent software developers started to write programs to run on the IBM PC. These included two applications that drove adoptions of the IBM PC: word processing (WordStar and WordPerfect) and a spreadsheet (Lotus 1-2-3).

The success of IBM gave birth to clone manufacturers who made "IBM-compatible" PCs that also utilized an Intel microprocessor and Microsoft's MS-DOS operating system. The "clone" industry was born when engineers at Compaq Computer reverse engineered the BIOS chip in the original IBM PC. The BIOS chip converted the operating system into machine language, and was integral to the operation of the PC. It was the only key component of the IBM PC that IBM had not bought off the shelf from other manufacturers. Compaq's BIOS chip was functionally equivalent to the chip in the IBM PC, but used different code and thus did not violate IBM's copyright. Other PC companies soon followed Compaq's lead, including Tandy, Zenith, Leading Edge, and Dell. The birth of the clone industry was a huge boon to Microsoft. By virtue of its nonexclusive license with IBM, Microsoft had the ability to sell MS-DOS to a growing number of clone makers.

In 1983, Microsoft expanded its product offering with the introduction of Word for MS-DOS, the company's first word processor. Word was differentiated from other word processors at the time by being the first to use a mouse. In 1985, Microsoft introduced a version of Word to run on Apple's latest machine, the Macintosh. In 1985, Microsoft released the first version of Excel, the company's spreadsheet offering, which competed with the bestselling Lotus 1-2-3. In 1987, Microsoft purchased a start-up company that had developed presentation software for the Macintosh. This product ultimately became PowerPoint, the first version of which was introduced in 1990.

The lead developer for Word and Excel was Charles Simonyi, a key hire at Microsoft who had formerly worked at PARC, Xerox's legendary research center, which had pioneered the development of the computer mouse, on-screen icons, a graphical user interface (GUI), object-oriented programming, and the laser printer. In a quirk of business history, senior management at Xerox had passed on the opportunity to commercialize these innovations, which opened the doors to Apple and Microsoft to pick up the ideas and run with them.

In 1982, with business booming, Paul Allen was diagnosed with Hodgkin's lymphoma. His cancer was successfully treated with radiation therapy, but he took an extended leave and never again held an operating position at Microsoft. In 2000, he resigned from the company's board of directors.

▌BUILDING THE DOUBLE MONOPOLY

By the mid-1980s, Microsoft was doing very well. It became apparent that the MS-DOS business had some compelling economics. While Microsoft bore the costs of developing successive versions of MS-DOS, the incremental or marginal costs of producing individual copies of MS-DOS were very low. In the case of new PCs, Microsoft simply gave the master code to the manufacturer, who installed MS-DOS on every machine built, and paid Microsoft a licensing fee per machine. This resulted in gross margins as high as 90%. In contrast, the gross margins of PC makers at the time were closer to 40%.

The Development of Windows and Office

In 1986, Microsoft went public. The IPO raised $61 million and valued Microsoft at $650 million. Microsoft now had over 700 employees. The company's position, however, was not secure. Although MS-DOS was the most widely used operating system for PCs, Apple had shown what the future looked like in 1984 when it introduced the Macintosh. Borrowing many ideas from Xerox PARC, the Mac had a graphical user interface (GUI) which displayed programs as on screen icons. It also used a computer mouse with its point-and-click methodology for selecting tasks. This intuitive interface was a big improvement in usability over the clunky command-line interface of MS-DOS, which could be intimidating for people without a computing background.

Gates realized that a GUI interface was the future. Microsoft worked closely with Apple to develop the first version of Word for the Mac, which took full advantage of the Mac's GUI interface and mouse capabilities. Word for the Mac soon became one of the bestselling Mac applications. At the same time, Microsoft took what it learnt from Apple and used it to start developing its own GUI interface, which was christened Windows.

Apple inadvertently helped Microsoft in two ways. First, it licensed its "visual displays" to Microsoft in 1985, enabling Microsoft to legally develop a GUI that had a similar look and feel to the Mac. Second, it was difficult to develop applications for the Mac. Apple did a poor job of providing tools to help third-party software developers write programs for it. In contrast, Gates often said that the most important strategic business unit at Microsoft was its tools business. Microsoft invested heavily in the development of tools to boost developer productivity. This made it easy for third-party developers to write applications for MD-DOS, and later Windows, and drove adoption of Microsoft's operating system offerings.

The first version of Windows was introduced in November 1985. It was a GUI shell that displayed programs as on-screen icons allowed for multitasking (using more than one program at a time). Windows sat on top of MS-DOS. It was commercial failure. Many users lacked sufficiently powerful hardware to run Windows, and there were few programs available that took advantage of its features. Nevertheless, Microsoft continued development work on Windows.

IBM, too, saw the importance of a GUI interface. IBM was losing market share to the clone makers, so it decided to replace MS-DOS with its own GUI operating system, OS/2. IBM contracted with Microsoft to develop OS/2. However, the arrangement was a difficult one. IBM resented the fact that Microsoft had facilitated the emergence of the clone businesses by licensing MS-DOS to IBM's competitors. IBM was also concerned that Microsoft continued to work on Windows even while it developed OS/2. For its part, Microsoft knew that IBM was also investing in the UNIX operating systems, and had licensed a UNIX based PC operating system, NeXTSTEP, from NeXT, a PC company that Apple founder Steve Jobs established after he left Apple in 1985. Microsoft knew it would be in trouble if IBM scrapped OS/2 in favor of a UNIX alternative. The pivotal event was IBM's announcement that it would release two versions of OS/2, a powerful version that would be exclusive to IBM machines, and a basic version for other PC makers. That wasn't news that Microsoft wanted to hear. Gates decided to sever links with IBM and go for broke on Windows.

The fruit of this effort, Windows 3.0, was introduced in 1990. Windows 3.0 was a big improvement over earlier versions. It was well reviewed and became a major commercial success. IBM's OS/2, meanwhile, garnered mixed reviews and limited market traction. PC manufacturers, seeing a chance to deliver a body blow to IBM, which after all was a direct competitor, adopted Windows 3.0, bundling it with most new PCs. Market momentum toward Windows was also helped by the introduction versions of Microsoft's increasingly popular applications products, Word, Excel, and PowerPoint, for Windows 3.0. At the time, each of these products was number 2 in its market space (Word was behind WordPerfect, Excel behind Lotus 1-2-3, and PowerPoint trailed Harvard Graphics). Microsoft's rivals, however, were slow to introduce versions of their products for Windows, resulting in big market-share gains for Microsoft's offerings. To further drive adoption of Windows, Microsoft redoubled its efforts to provide developers with the best tools, and to persuade them that Windows was best platform for which to develop applications.

In 1992, Microsoft combined its three leading application programs—Word, Excel, and PowerPoint—into a single offering for Windows, which it called Office. Office was priced slightly below the combined price of each individual offering. Microsoft also promised interoperability between the three programs, although this took several versions to perfect. Microsoft's rivals, including most notably WordPerfect and Lotus, lacked a comparable suite of offerings and were unable to match Office. From this point on, Office became the dominant suite of productivity programs for information workers.

During the late 1980s, Microsoft started an operating system development project targeted primarily at servers. Servers were specialized PCs that sat at the heart of corporate networks of "client" PCs and "served" those "clients," holding shared files and applications programs used by many machines, such as email systems. Dubbed Windows NT, this was a powerful, 32-bit operating system that could run on servers. Unlike Windows 3.0, it was not DOS based ("NT" stood for new technology). To develop Windows NT, Microsoft hired a team of software developers led by Dave Cutler from Digital Equipment Corporation (DEC). Cutler's team drew on their prior experience developing 32-bit systems for DEC to develop Windows NT.

The move into the server OS business represented recognition by Microsoft of the growing importance of client-server systems within large enterprises. The development of Windows NT constituted a strategic shift by Microsoft toward the enterprise market, where the primary demand for client-server systems resided. Windows NT was an attempt to make secure, stable software that could run "mission-critical" applications within enterprises. Client-server networks were taking business away from the mainframes and minicomputers sold by the likes of IBM, DEC, and Hewlett Packard. Microsoft wanted a piece of this business, and with Windows NT it intended to get it. Introduced in 1993, Windows NT was a solid, stable, secure system that gained increasing acceptance within enterprises. Windows NT marked the beginning of Microsoft's server business.

To gain further enterprise business, Microsoft added an email client to its Office suite, Outlook, which could connect with corporate email hosted on severs. By the time Windows NT was introduced, Microsoft was also selling a relational database offering, Microsoft SQL Server. A relational database is a product whose primary function is to store and retrieve data as requested by other software applications, be they on the same computer or running on another computer across a network. Microsoft SQL Server was the company's entry into the enterprise-level database market, and it pitted Microsoft against Oracle and IBM, both of which had relational database offerings.

The 32-bit technology underlying Windows NT was subsequently incorporated into the next two releases of Windows for PCs, Windows 95, and then Windows XP (introduced in 1995 and 1998, respectively). Increasingly, this made Windows more than just a GUI that sat on top of MS-DOS. Windows was becoming a fully-fledged operating system in its own right. By the time Windows 2000 was introduced, Windows had effectively shed it DOS heritage.

Windows 95 was a landmark release. Its enhanced graphics effectively closed the gap between Windows and Apple's Macintosh. Since the introduction of the IBM PC, Apple had been a niche player in the PC business, focused primarily on the education, graphic artist, and desktop publishing markets, where its graphic displays and ease of use gave it maximum advantage. With Windows 95, however, the differential appeal of the Mac all but vanished. By 1997, Apple was facing bankruptcy.

The Internet Tidal Wave

One other event occurred during the 1990s that helped to cement the dominance of Microsoft: the explosive growth of the World Wide Web (WWW). Tim Berners Lee, a British researcher at CERN in Europe, invented the Web during the early 1990s. The WWW sits on top of the Internet, which itself had been developed by American researchers during the 1960s and 1970s. As Berners Lee conceived it, the Web used hypertext markup language (HTML) and hypertext transfer protocol (HTTP) to enable links to be made to information anywhere the Internet, thereby creating an enormous "web" of information. In 1993, a team at the University of Illinois led by a 22-year-old student, Marc Andreessen, developed the Mosaic Web browser. Mosaic could display information on the Web graphically. This was the beginning of the enormous growth of the WWW. After graduation, Andreessen joined up with Jim Clark, the former CEO of Silicon Graphics, to form Netscape. Netscape further developed the Mosaic Browser, releasing its version, Netscape Navigator, in November 1994. Netscape Navigator quickly became the dominant Web browser. In August 1995, Netscape held an IPO. The stock was offered at $28 a share, but closed its first day at $75, valuing Netscape at $2.9 billion.

Prior to the explosive growth of the Web, Microsoft's Internet strategy involved the creation of a dial-up online service, MSN, which was developed to be included with Windows 95. MSN was similar in conception to early versions of AOL, with email capabilities, message boards, chat rooms, and some news and weather offerings. The first version of MSN did not have a Web browser and users could not connect to the Internet. With MSN and Windows 95 in late development, Gates became aware of the rapid growth of the Web. Microsoft legend has it that the WWW was brought to the attention of Gates by memos from two junior engineers, Steve Sinofsky and Jay Allard. Gates immediately saw its strategic significance. In May 1995, Gates wrote a memo to his executive staff and direct reports, calling the growth of the Internet a "tidal wave." Gates wrote that the Internet "is crucial to every part of our business" and "the most important single development to come along since the IBM PC was introduced in 1981". In his memo, Gates went on to say that Netscape was a "new competitor", and that Microsoft's strategy should be to make it clear that "Windows machines are the best choice for the Internet."[11]

To fulfill Gates's vision, Microsoft acted rapidly. It licensed a version of the Mosaic Web browser from a company called Spyglass, improved on it and released it as Internet Explorer (IE) version 1.0 in August 1995. IE 1.0 was bundled with Windows 95 and appeared as an icon on the start screen. Although it was too late to change MSN in time for the release on Windows 95, MSN was reworked to utilize HTML and HTTP and give users access to the Web. In late 1996, the new version of MSN, MSN 2.0, was released. Microsoft also quickly added the ability to insert hypertext links into Office documents, allowing readers of those documents to navigate away to websites.

Antitrust Issues

All of these moves were successful for Microsoft. However, the bundling of IE with Windows bought Microsoft to the attention of the U.S. Department of Justice (DOJ). The DOJ argued that the bundling strategy put Netscape at a competitive disadvantage and was a deliberate attempt on Microsoft's part to "squash" their rival. Whereas Netscape charged consumers for their browser, IE was perceived as being a "free" product. Moreover, the DOJ contented that Microsoft configured the Windows code such that it was slow and difficult for users to download Netscape Navigator and install it on the Windows desktop. For its part, Microsoft claimed that IE was part of the operating system and that users expected it to be there.

In the end, the DOJ prevailed. The judge in the case ruled that Microsoft was a monopoly, and that the bundling strategy represented an abuse of Microsoft's monopoly power. In 2002, Microsoft and the DOJ reached a settlement that required Microsoft to share its application programming interfaces (APIs) with third-party companies, so that they could write programs that worked well with Windows. Microsoft, however, was allowed to continue bundling IE and other products with Windows. For Netscape, this was a Pyrrhic victory. The company continued to lose market share against IE, and was not helped by reports that its products were inferior in quality to IE. In 1999, Netscape was sold to AOL for $10 billion, a price tag that left many scratching their heads. AOL discontinued the Netscape browser in 2008. At the time it had less than a 1% share of the browser market, down from over 90% in 1995.

MANAGING THE COMPANY

From the outset, Gates made a point of hiring people who were like him—young, bright, driven, competitive, technically sharp, and able to argue effectively for what they believed in. A small but influential number of these hires came from Xerox PARC, including Charles Simonyi, who led the development of the first versions of Word and Excel. Ballmer hired some of sales personnel. One of these was an aggressive salesman named Vern Raeburn. Gates had insisted that Microsoft should not sell directly to end-users, but Raeburn marshaled his arguments and persuaded Gates to change course. Raeburn quickly pulled together a team to market and sell Microsoft's products to consumers.

This was the genesis of a split within Microsoft into two distinct functions that persist to this day: an engineering function that develops products, and a sales and marketing function that sells them. For years, Gates was the de facto head of engineering with responsibility for product development, whereas Ballmer was responsible for sales and marketing. Although Microsoft went on to create different business units—Windows, Windows Server & Tools, and Office all had their own business units, for example—the engineering and sales and marketing functions would cut across these units, creating a loose, matrix organization. Finance, legal, and human relations functions also cut across business units.

To motivate key employees and encourage them to work long hours and commit to the company, Microsoft gave them stock options. When the company did well, and the stock price rose, these employees made substantial sums of money. As the stock price surged after the IPO in 1986, Microsoft stock options became a major draw, enabling Microsoft to hire the best and the brightest. By 2000, it is estimated that the surging stock price had created over 10,000 millionaires among Microsoft employees.[12] Paradoxically, by the mid-1990s, some early employees were so secure financially that their competitive edge had been blunted. Some were said to have retired on the job. Many other key employees simply left the company to pursue other interests.

Another notable feature of Microsoft that emerged over time was the tendency for people to circulate within the company. It was not unusual for people to change jobs every 18 months, and move from business to business.

Formalizing Management Processes

As the company's growth began to accelerate in the early 1980s, Gates brought in people with business experience to help take the load of his shoulders and manage the day-to-day operations and finance side of the business, leaving him to focus on product development, technology, and strategy, and Ballmer to focus on sales. A key early hire was John Shirley. Shirley worked for Tandy Corporation, the parent company of Radio Shack. Shirley joined Microsoft as president in 1983 and stayed through 1990. He remained on the board until 2008. People within the company would joke that Shirley was there to provide some adult supervision.

In 1994, Gates hired Bob Herbold as chief operating officer (COO). Herbold had a PhD in computer science and had worked at Procter & Gamble for 25 years, where he was responsible for P&Gs worldwide marketing and brand management. Herbold stayed at Microsoft until 2001. Another "adult" in charge of day-to-day operational issues, Herbold saw it as his job to bring discipline to the company without undermining the characteristics that had made it competitive. Herbold describes arriving at a company that was chaotic: "Incompatible systems and divergent practices companywide were causing all kinds of problems. Bills from suppliers weren't being paid on time. We never knew precisely how many people worked for the company. Business units set projections using incompatible frameworks and measures that prevented a comparison of their performance."[13]

Much of this chaos was the result of rapid revenue growth often exceeding 30% a year. Herbold notes "a balkanized system had grown up because, for years, Bill had focused on product development and Steve had focused on sales. Meanwhile, business and geographical units had relatively free rein to create local functional staffs, set business practices, and build stand-alone information systems. They weren't particularly interested in giving up their autonomy."[14]

Herbold moved fast to standardized, basic businesses processes at Microsoft, including financial reporting, vendor payments, and human resources policies. He also found a company with no formal strategic planning process in place. Herbold developed a rolling, 3-year planning process based on a standardized format that included historic and future projections of market share, revenues, costs, and profits. The process distinguished between established products, such as Windows and Office, and new products where there was a much greater degree of uncertainty. The plans were modified and streamlined every year based on new data.

Herbold also formalized a human resources performance-appraisal process that had originally been developed by Gates. The appraisal process required managers to evaluate their direct reports, and it utilized a forced curve, such that some members of a team would always end up being classified as star performers, and others as poor performers. The star performers would get big pay increases, whereas the underperformers would be "encouraged to find a job outside of the company" if they couldn't bring up their rating over time. Critics of this system, known as stack ranking, noted that it pitted employees on a team against each other, encouraged backstabbing, and created a real problem for managers who had built strong teams, because they were forced to classify some of their team as underperformers, even though in an absolute sense they might be good.[15]

The Product Development Process

Given the nature of Microsoft's business, a key aspect of the company's organization and management structure relates to the way it formalizes development of its software products. In the early years "superprogrammers" such as Simonyi and Gates drove the vision for products. Gates came to the realization that this model would not scale well. Superprogrammers were in short supply, had little interest in updating a product once it had been created, might not understand the market well, and were prone to clash with other superprogrammers. In response a formal system for developing, testing, and releasing products emerged in the mid-980s.[16]

The process starts with a *program manager*, who is responsible for specifying the vision of the product, its key features, development schedule, development process, and implementation tradeoffs. The program manager works closely with senior software developers and with product managers in marketing to achieve all of this. His or her role, in other words, is to coordinate engineering and marketing and distill out of this what the product should do, what its key features should be, and a schedule to achieve these. The program manger is then responsible for managing the overall development effort, and must make the call on features to add or cut in order to hit goals such as schedule. On complex products such as Windows and Office there is a hierarchy of program managers. For example, while there may be an overall program manager for a new version of Office, there will also be program managers for each constituent program— Word, Excel, PowerPoint, and so on.

It is important to understand that many of the ideas for a product's features come from developers and marketers. Program managers are leaders and facilitators of the process, rather than bosses, and they must work through persuasion and negotiation. In part, this may be due to the high status that developers in particular have within Microsoft's culture, something that can be traced back to Gates and Simonyi. Indeed, most program managers were themselves star developers who rose through the engineering ranks.

Once the product vision, key features, schedules, and the like have been mapped out, it is up to software *developers* to implement the vision and features. Developers write the code. Typically, a small team of senior developers and program managers will take charge of the product architecture, and developer leads (first-line managers) will provide detailed guidance to their teams of programmers. While developers may be the source of ideas for new features, they are required to clarify what each feature accomplishes, and to help program managers decide what to include in a product, and what to cut in order to stay on schedule.

Testing the code is the responsibility of developers and *testers*. Developers are meant to test their own code frequently (typically every day). They also work in pairs with testers and are required to hand their code over to a tester for testing before adding their work to the "official build." The goal in this process is to reduce the bug count to zero. Microsoft also has a specially trained group of people who perform final tests on a completed product to see if it is ready for shipment. As part of this process, beta versions of the product will be released to key customers for feedback, and the product will be tested in a usability lab. Microsoft has approximately one tester for every developer, an unusually high ratio but one that is consistent with the goal of producing stable, secure software that can run mission-critical applications for enterprises.

Over time, Microsoft routinized this process, with offering such as Windows, Office, and SQL Server going through 3- to 5-year definition, development, test, and release schedules. As these products have grown in complexity and features, there was a tendency for the process to become more bureaucratic and harder to manage. This was made more challenging by the fact that many program managers, senior developers, and development leads were people who had excelled in a technical sense but had little management training or experience. In the mid-2000s, this led to

serious issues when Microsoft ran over budget and over schedule while trying to develop Windows Vista (discussed later in the case).

THE BALLMER YEARS

When Bill Gates handed the CEO role over to Steve Ballmer in February 2000, the company was at the top of its game. Windows and Office dominated their respective markets, generating prodigious amounts of free cash flow. The stock price had hit an all-time high of $58.72 on December 23, 1999. Microsoft was the most valuable company on the planet, and Gates the world's richest man. Gates continued to work full time at Microsoft until 2008, assuming the role of chief software architect, with primary oversight for product development. He also remained chairman of the company.

During the Ballmer era, revenues increased 280%, to $70 billion, while net profit expanded by 215%, to $23 billion. The stock price, however, dropped below $40 a share in mid-2000, and did not break through that level again until 2014, after Ballmer had resigned. The failure of the stock price to advance despite growing top and bottom lines reflected a widely held belief among investors that Microsoft had lost its leadership position in the industry. Moreover, critics believed that the company was destroying economic value by investing in businesses that did not generate a positive ROI. These included the Xbox videogame business, Internet search, and the device businesses that encompassed the Zune music player, smartphones, and tablet computers. By the end of the Ballmer era, it was widely believed that the shift to a world characterized by mobile devices and cloud computing presented an existential threat to Microsoft's core operating system business.

One of the first problems that Ballmer had to confront was the risk of a slowdown in the rate of growth of both Windows and Office. The markets for both products were now mature in most developed nations, implying that revenues would increasingly come from replacement rather than first-time demand. Although there was still plenty of room for growth in developing nations, those markets were also characterized by extremely high levels of piracy—as much as 90% in markets like China and Vietnam. Indeed, even in developed markets such as the United States, piracy rates for software products are as high as 20 to 25%.[17]

Two trends helped Microsoft weather the maturation of its two primary product offerings. First, a significant number of consumers in developed markets purchased multiple devices: a laptop and a desktop for example. Second, Microsoft continued to grow its share of the enterprise markets for Windows Server and SQL Server, taking business from UNIX, LINUX, Oracle, and IBM. Microsoft's success in the enterprise space reflected the fact that to a considerable extent, the company had succeeded in building stable, secure software that could run mission-critical applications in enterprises. Given that Windows for the client and Office were also widely used within enterprises, Microsoft was increasingly focused on its enterprise business. Indeed, by the early 2000s, Microsoft was more of an enterprise company than a consumer company.

Product Diversification: Xbox

Under Ballmer, Microsoft continued to diversify its product offerings, entering into new markets. The first was the videogame market. By the late 1990s, Sony dominated this market with its PlayStation console and related game offerings. The market was worth $20 billion globally and was growing. Microsoft saw the PlayStation as a threat. The PlayStation was a specialized computer that ran a non-Microsoft operating system, and could theoretically be connected to the Internet via a TV cable. Moreover, the PlayStation was often located in the living room. Bill Gates had long dreamed of having Internet-enabled computing devices in the living room that operated interactive TV, and could also be used for Web browsing, playing games, and online shopping; but Gates wanted those devices to run Windows.

Microsoft had capabilities that persuaded management that the gaming market was a viable target. Microsoft had produced one of the bestselling PC games of all time—Microsoft Flight Simulator—and had published another, Age of Empires. Through MSN it also had the world's largest online gaming site, MSN Gaming Zone, which had 12 million subscribers in the early 2000s. Moreover, Microsoft intended to use a customized version of the Windows operating system to power Xbox. This would save development costs and make it easier for developers to write games for the Xbox, because many were already familiar with Windows programming APIs and tools.

Microsoft lacked the ability to produce hardware, so it decided to outsource this to a contract manufacturer, Flextronics. Microsoft's strategy was to price the Xbox at or below cost to drive adoption, and then make money on the sales of games, either directly in the case of games developed in house, or from royalty fees in the case of games developed by third parties. For this strategy to work, it had to guarantee Flextronics a profit margin, which meant paying Flextronics a subsidy on every machine manufactured.

Xbox was introduced in late 2001, after $1.5 billion in development costs. The company faced tough competition from Sony's new offering, PlayStation 2 (PS2). To drive adoption, it cut prices for hardware aggressively. By 2003, Microsoft was thought to be losing $100 on every Xbox it sold. To make that back and turn a profit, Microsoft reportedly had to sell six to nine games per Xbox.[18] By late 2004, Xbox was still a distant second to PS2 in the videogame market, having sold 14 million consoles against Sony's 70 million. While Sony was making good money from the business, Microsoft was registering losses. Microsoft's home and entertainment division, of which Xbox was a part, lost $4 billion between the launch of Xbox and mid-2006.

In November 2005, Microsoft introduced its next-generation console, Xbox 360. Again, contract manufacturers made the machine, and again Microsoft paid them a subsidy to ensure their profit margins. Sony followed a year later with its PS3 console, as did Nintendo with the Wii console. The Wii was a less powerful machine than either Xbox 360 or PS3, but it came with a motion sensor controller than changed the way players interacted with games. The Wii bought a new generation of casual gamers into the market and turned into a surprise hit for Nintendo. Meanwhile, Microsoft and Sony slugged it out in the hard core gaming market. Demand for Xbox was helped by Microsoft's enormously popular Halo franchise. As the market expanded, all three companies were able to make profit on an operating basis in the business. However, both Microsoft and Sony hurt themselves with quality problems and component shortages early in the product cycle (Microsoft had to take a $1.05 billion write off in 2007 for replacing poor-quality consoles).

Although Microsoft did achieve profitability on an operating basis for Xbox business by late in the Xbox 360 cycle, on a cumulative basis the return on investment was still believed to be negative. One bright spot for Microsoft was the growth of its online game subscription service, Xbox Live. Introduced in 2002, by mid-2013, Xbox Live had around 45 million paying subscribers who used it for everything from playing multiplayer games online to streaming movies from Netflix and browsing Facebook. At the time, Microsoft was thought to be generating annual revenues in excess of $3 billion from Xbox Live.[19] Microsoft also garnered strong reviews and sales for its Kinect motion sensor controller. Introduced in late 2010 for the Xbox 360, Kinect was developed as a response to Nintendo's Wii controller.

In late 2013, Microsoft launched its third-generation game console, Xbox One. Sony matched with the launch of its PS4 system. At launch, Microsoft positioned Xbox One as an all-purpose entertainment system for the living room, controlling TV, music, and film streaming services through the Kinect motion and voice sensor, in addition to being a game console. Sony focused its marketing for the PS4 on the core gaming market. By mid-2014, Sony was believed to have sold 7 million PS4 consoles, versus 5 million Xbox One consoles. With Satya Nadella now in charge, Microsoft changed the marketing strategy for Xbox One, emphasizing its capabilities as a gaming machine and co- promoting it with new iterations of its popular Halo and Call of Duty franchises.

Product Diversification: Internet Search

Another hallmark of the Ballmer era was Microsoft's expansion into Internet search. Microsoft had long had primitive Internet search functionality on its MSN service, but it had never seen search as a central feature. This changed with the rise of Google, a company that didn't even exist until 1998. At the core of Google's rise was a search algorithm that cleverly ranked the relevance of a page for a search query according to the number of pages that linked into that page. Google went to great lengths to make sure that its search results were "pure." It did not mix organic and paid search results, thereby improving relevance to the user (paid search results were originally placed on the right hand side of a search page, separate from organic search results).

What made Google a valuable company was its combination of highly relevant search results with a business model that made money out of search activity—lots of money. This was the 'pay-for-click'

model, where advertisers paid Google every time someone clicked on an advertiser's link. From a standing start in 2001, by 2014 Google had grown into a colossus with $68 billion in revenues, almost $21 billion in net profits, 67% of the market for Internet search in the United States, and an estimated 70% of worldwide search marketing spend.

Along the way, Google had moved aggressively into Microsoft's turf. Reasoning that with the growth of smartphones, ever more search would come through mobile devices, Google had pushed into the smartphone business with its Android operating system, which it licensed to hardware manufacturers for free. The economic logic was that Google would be the default search engine on Android phones, so every time someone search for something on an Android phone, and clicked on an advertising link, Google would make money. Google also developed its own Web browser, Chrome, which it distributed for free. The economic reasoning was similar. Since search is conducted within a Web-browser environment, and Google was the default search engine on Chrome, Google would capture more search based advertising collars if its own browser were widely used. Both of these products were phenomenally successful. By mid 2014, Android was found on 85% of the world's smartphones, and Chrome was the browser of choice on 46% of all desktops and tablets (relegating Microsoft's Internet Explorer, the long time market leader, to second place with 20%).[20]

Microsoft tried to counter Google's rise in the Internet search business, but its success was limited,—and very expensive. Microsoft adopted Google's pay for click search model, and developed a similar search algorithm, but was unable to gain much market traction and its market share remained stuck under 10%. Part of the problem was brand confusion. Microsoft's search feature was initially known as MSN Search, sounded dull and uninspiring next to Google. In 2006, MSN search was rebranded as Windows Live Search, and given some new features. A year later, the name was changed again to Live Search. Ultimately, Microsoft came to the realization that the "Live" brand was not resonating with consumers, who found it confusing. In June 2009, Microsoft's search engine was rebranded Bing. Microsoft supported the Bing launch with a $100-million ad campaign.

In 2008, in an attempt to grow its share of the U.S. paid-search market, Microsoft launched an unsolicited takeover bid for Yahoo. Yahoo was number 2 in the US search market. Microsoft was number 3. Yahoo rejected the bid. A year later, however, following management changes at Yahoo, Microsoft and Yahoo entered into a 10-year partnership under which Bing would be the exclusive search platform on Yahoo. Although the precise terms of the deal were not made public, it is known that Microsoft pays Yahoo for search traffic. In 2013, 31% of Yahoo's revenue apparently came from Microsoft payments.[21]

Product Diversification: Smartphones and Tablets

Microsoft was an early leader in the smartphone business. It first offered an operating system for smartphones, Windows Mobile, in 2002. By 2007, 42% of all smartphones used the Windows Mobile operating system. Smartphone manufactures such as Motorola and HTC paid a licensing fee to Microsoft to use Windows Mobile. As was normal at the time, Windows Mobile powered smartphones had a physical keyboard and a small screen. The devices were primarily sold to enterprise customers, who used the phones for email, appointments, text messaging, and Web browsing.

In 2007, Apple introduced the first iPhone, which revolutionized the smartphone market and significantly expanded demand (see Table 1). The combination of a touch screen, virtual keyboard, larger screen size, elegant design, and ease of use made the iPhone a huge hit in the consumer marketplace. Business people too, bought iPhones in droves, leading many companies to adopt a policy of "bring your own device" with regard to smartphones. Growth of the iPhone got a further boost from the development of third-party applications and the opening of the Apple App store in 2008, which made it easy for users to find and download apps onto their phones. The supply of Apps was facilitated by efforts on Apple's part to make it easy for third-party developers to write Apps for the iPhone. In 2010, Apple introduced its tablet offering, the iPad. The iPad used the same iOS operating system as the iPhone and had most of the same attributes, including elegant design, a touch screen, and access to the App store through wireless connectivity. All of this helped drive rapid growth in consumer demand.

When Apple released the iPhone, Google already had its own operating systems for a touch screen phone in development. Google had acquired the original developer, Android Inc., in 2005. The first smartphones running on Android appeared in 2008. Google's business model was to offer Android for free and make money from advertising linked to mobile search. By 2013, Android was the dominant smartphone OS, followed by Apple's iOS (see Table 1). Tablets that ran on Android stated to appear soon after the launch of the iPad in 2010, and by 2014 Android was also dominating the tablet OS market (see Table 2).

Table 1 Global Smartphone Sales (millions) 2007–2013

Year	Android	iOS (Apple)	Microsoft	BlackBerry	Nokia
2007		3	15	12	78
2008		11	17	23	73
2009	7	25	15	34	81
2010	67	47	12	47	112
2011	220	89	9	52	93
2012	451	130	17	34	0
2013	759	151	31	19	0

Source: Gartner.com, various press releases.

Table 2 Global Tablet Sales (millions) 2010–2014			
Year	Android	iOS (Apple)	Microsoft
2011	17	40	0
2012	53	61	1
2013	121	70	4
2014	160	65	11

Source: Gartner.com, various press releases.

The introduction of the iPhone, and then Android phones, decimated Microsoft's market share (see Table 1). By 2011, Microsoft's OS was found on just 9 million smartphones shipped that year. Android was on 220 million phones, and Apple sold 89 million iOS phones. The situation in the tablet market was no better, where Microsoft was caught completely flat-footed by the introduction of the iPad. Google, on the other hand, adapted very quickly and soon gained market leadership.

In response to the rapid emergence of Apple and Android, Microsoft developed a new operating system for touch screen smartphones, Windows Phone. Windows Phone had an active-tile, "Metro" interface, rather than the on-screen icons used by Apple and Android. The first Windows Phones started to appear in late 2010. Microsoft also established its own App store, the Windows Phone Store.

In early 2011, Microsoft entered into an alliance with Nokia to jointly develop Windows Phones. Like Microsoft, Nokia had been caught off guard by the emergence of the iPhone and had seen its market share slide. Nokia had used its own Symbian operating system in its smartphones. Like Windows Mobile, Symbian was a primitive, first-generation smartphone OS that lacked the full features and functions of Android and iOS, including touch screen capability, a virtual keyboard, and a supply of third-party apps that could be downloaded onto the device. Under the alliance, Nokia agreed to phase out Symbian and switch to Microsoft's Windows Phone OS. The first products of this alliance, Nokia's Lumina phones, were introduced in late 2011.

Despite some favorable reviews, the Lumina phones grew more slowly than the market, and

Microsoft's market share remained in the low single digits in most nations. Reasons given to explain this included the lack of appeal of the Metro interface and relative paucity of third-party apps for Windows Phone.

In September 2013, Microsoft announced its intention to acquire Nokia's mobile phone business for $7 billion. In justifying the acquisition, Ballmer argued that merging the two companies would streamline product development processes, lower costs, and result in better phones and higher gross profit margins.[22] It was also noted that Nokia was the only company still willing to make Windows phones, and if Nokia pulled out, what would happen to Microsoft's phone business? Critics wondered whether an acquisition that made Microsoft a phone maker might not alienate other phone makers, such as HTC, who would now see Microsoft as a direct competitor.

In addition to the phone business, Microsoft entered the tablet business with its Surface offering. The Surface was positioned as a cross over between a conventional laptop and a tablet. Introduced in late 2012, it used a Windows 8.1 operating system, which by that time was also being used for Windows Phone. Like the Windows Phone, the Surface garnered some favorable reviews, but sales were slow to pick up and the product initially failed to make a dent in the dominance of Android and iOS in the tablet market. However, following the introduction of the Surface Pro 3 in mid 2014, sales appeared to be accelerating. In the last 6 months of 2014, Microsoft sold $2 billion worth of Surface tablets.

Windows Offerings Under Ballmer

Windows Vista was the first version of Windows completely developed under Ballmer's leadership (although Bill Gates oversaw the project). Vista started out as a more ambitious project with the code name of Longhorn, but when that ran into difficulties, it was recast as Vista. A primary goal for Vista was to increase security. Released in January 2007, more than 5 years after its predecessor, Windows XP, it was not well received by the marketplace. Vista took 2 years longer than expected to develop and it was several billion dollars over budget. It was a huge program—with 50 million plus lines of code—and utilized a lot of computer memory to run, resulting in unacceptably slow performance for many users. It quickly drained battery life on laptop computers. Moreover, it irritated users with constant popup authorization prompts for user account control. Many potential adopters simply stuck with Windows XP rather than switch to the much-maligned Vista. By October 2009, Windows Vista had 19% of the PC operating system marketplace, while Windows XP, an 8-year-old OS, still enjoyed a 63% share.

Many insiders blamed the poor performance of Vista on a development process that got out of hand. One problem was "too many VPs in reporting structures too narrow." There were 12 layers of management between Bill Gates and a developer at the base of the Windows organization. As one former Windows development lead noted:

> "I once sat in a scheduled review meeting with at least six VPs and ten general managers. When that many people have a say, things get confusing. Not to mention, since so many bosses are in the room, there are often negotiations between project managers prior to such meetings to make sure no one looks bad . . . In general, Windows suffers from a proclivity for action control, not results control. Instead of clearly stating desired outcomes, there is a penchant for telling people exactly what steps they must take."[23]

Other insiders complained about a lack of accountability, constant churning of features and specifications, with new features often being added without adequate testing, leading to system crashes and further development delays. Several people also noted that with Gates heading Vista, CEO Steve Ballmer was unwilling to step in and resolve problems that were resulting in delays and cost overruns.

Once Vista shipped, many of the top engineers on the project retired. Steve Sinofsky, who had been running Office, was bought in the run Windows. At Office, Sinofsky had run a very tight ship, releasing new versions on schedule like clockwork. The Office organization was also much flatter than the Windows division, with only four levels of management.

Sinofsky flattened the Windows organization, reducing the number of levels of management from 12 to 5. He pushed developers to get Vista's successor, Windows 7, to market quickly. Originally conceived as an incremental update to Vista, Windows 7 was a more streamlined program that fixed many of the performance problems and irritations with Vista. Introduced in 2009, reviewers saw Windows 7 as a big improvement over Vista, and the operating system sold well.

Once Windows 7 shipped, Sinofsky and his team turned their attention to Windows 8. Released in 2012, Windows 8 was positioned as an operating system for the new era of digital devices. Windows 8 used the same Metro-style, tile-based interface that had first been used on Windows Phone. Despite the lukewarm reception of the Metro interface on the phone, Microsoft saw the interface as an important differentiator. Sinofsky was a major advocate of the Metro interface, going so far as to push Microsoft to kill a competing interface for tablets being developed within the company because it was inconsistent with the Metro theme that he wanted on all devices.[24] Known as the Courier, the tablet was the brainchild of a group within Microsoft's Entertainment and Devices Division, headed by Jay Allard. The Courier was on track to hit the market in 2010, just months behind the iPad. Widely admired within Microsoft, Allard was the force behind the creation of the Xbox business and was instrumental in pushing Microsoft to embrace the Web back in 1995.

The Courier was a two-screen tablet that folded like a book and had a touch screens. Early prototypes had elicited rave reviews from outsiders who had seen it, some preferring what they saw to prototypes of the iPad, which was then under development. But the Courier used a modified version of Windows as its operating system, and the interface departed substantially from the Windows norm.

When the Courier dispute surfaced, Ballmer found himself in the position of having to choose between two of his best managers. Unable to make up his mind, he brought Gates into the decision. Gates, who by now had given up all day-to-day operating responsibility, met with Allard and his team. His criticism was that Courier didn't align with Microsoft's key Windows and Office franchises. Not only did it use a customized version of Windows, and a nonstandard interface, but it also did not include an Outlook email client (Allard pointed out that users could get email through an onboard Web browser). For Gates, this was a fatal flaw, and the Courier was cancelled. Within months, Allard had left Microsoft along with his boss, Robbie Bach. It would be another 2 years before Microsoft had a tablet offering, the Surface.

In addition to the Metro interface, Windows 8 also supported touch screen technology and could be used on a tablet in addition to desktop and laptop PCs. Released in 2012, Windows 8 received decidedly mixed reviews. Although reaction toward its performance improvements, security enhancements, and improved support for touchscreen devices was positive, the new user interface of the operating system was widely criticized for being potentially confusing and difficult to learn. Many users particularly disliked the fact that Microsoft had removed the start menu.

Market take-up of Windows 8 was slower than Microsoft had hoped. Sinofsky abruptly left Microsoft in December 2012. Recognizing that the Metro interface was not resonating with many users, Microsoft announced that it would release an update, Windows 8.1, in October 2013. Windows 8.1 tried to address some of the criticisms, and gave users to ability to dispense with the Metro interface and revert to the traditional start button and menu. Despite this, adoption continued to be slow. By mid-2014, only 12.5% of PCs were using Windows 8 or 8.1. Most consumers and corporation stuck with Windows 7.

The Cloud Computing Initiative

By the mid-2000s, serious conversations about cloud computing were taking place within Microsoft. The "cloud" referred to the idea that data, operating systems, and applications could be hosted on server farms comprising of thousands of machines, rather than on servers and PCs within an enterprise. These conversations were based on a realization that in a world where computing device users were always connected to the Internet through wired or wireless links, there were compelling economic reasons for moving computing power and programs off servers located within enterprises and onto server farms. Specifically, the cloud could deliver more value to users at a lower cost than traditional client-server networks.

On the value side, there was clearly great utility associated with storing files on the cloud and being able to access those files anywhere anytime through any connected device. The files could be in the form of documents, music, video, or databases. Moreover, by reaching out and accessing programs and data stored on the cloud, users with simple devices such as smartphones and tablets could theoretically access vast amounts of computing power when they needed it.

On the cost side, it was apparent that moving computing resources onto the cloud could save businesses a lot of money. Corporate IT departments traditionally shouldered the costs of buying and maintaining computer hardware and software, activities that accounted for almost 90% of all IT costs. Servers, however, often only ran at 5 to 10% capacity, while much of the software installed on corporate servers and PCs was only rarely used. By moving data and applications onto a server farm, demand for computing resources could be aggregated and servers could be run at closer to 90% capacity. This implied significant economies of scale in the costs of computation. Microsoft's estimates suggested that, under optimal conditions, shifting to a cloud-based model could reduce IT costs by as much as 80%.[25] Moreover, instead of paying for software that was rarely used, corporations might be able to pay for software only when they used it.

Microsoft proposed to build a cloud-computing business that would host data and applications for corporations, taking the burden of infrastructure and maintenance costs off their hands. In return, corporations would pay a fee for storing data, and either a subscription or runtime fee for executing applications. As early as 2006, Steve Ballmer had stated that Microsoft had no choice but to go "all in" on the cloud.[26] By 2010, this commitment had developed into Microsoft's Azure cloud-computing initiative, which was located within the company's Server & Tools Division.

Cloud computing was seen as comprising of three segments; infrastructure as a service (IaaS), platform as a service (PaaS), and software as a service (SaaS). IaaS refers to basic hosting of data, websites, and the like. Amazon's AWS is primarily an IaaS offering. PaaS refers to the idea of building a software platform upon which software applications can be built and run. Microsoft's Azure platform is essentially a PaaS offering that uses Windows Server technology. Think of Azure as Windows for a server farm of 10,000 machines. SaaS is the idea that software applications can be hosted and run on the cloud. Salesforce.com was an early leader in SaaS with its customer relationship management (CRM) software.

By 2011, Microsoft was committed to competing in all three segments. The company would host data for enterprises and consumers (IaaS), it would continue to develop Azure so that enterprises could write applications that would run well on the cloud (PaaS), and it would reposition many of its products such as Office, SQL Server, and Dynamics, as software as a service (SaaS) offerings. In June 2011, Microsoft introduced Office 365 to enterprise users. Office 365 was a cloud version of its bestselling Office suite. In 2013, Office 365 was offered to consumers. Enterprises paid a licensing fee and consumers an annual subscription fee for Office 365. Users could download the program to multiple devices (for consumers the limit was five). They could also store Office documents on Microsoft's Cloud using its One Drive storage offering. Microsoft shifted to a rolling—release model for developing Office 365, updating the program on a quarterly basis—a marked departure from the historic 3- to 5-year development schedule at Microsoft.

One problem Microsoft had to grapple with in shifting toward a cloud-computing model was that it represented a change in the underlying economics of its business. In the traditional model, most of Microsoft's costs were associated with the fixed costs of developing programs such as Windows and Office. The marginal costs of producing more versions of a program were very low, so that at high volumes Microsoft earned gross margins in the 90% range on Windows and Office. In the cloud-computing model, however, Microsoft had to build and maintain server farms, which could cost anywhere from $500 million to $2 billion each in fixed costs, and which consumed large amounts of electricity. There was a general belief that even at high volumes, the gross margins associated with a cloud-computing business would be significantly lower than what Microsoft was accustomed to. As people within the company were fond of saying, "in the cloud business we actually have costs of goods sold."

On the other hand, while cloud computing was still a small business in 2013, generating perhaps less than $10 billion in revenues industrywide, rapid growth was predicted going forward. Industry revenues were projected to balloon to $150 billion by 2020. Clearly Microsoft had to embrace this business.

SATAY NADELLA TAKES CHARGE

By early 2013, Ballmer was coming under increasing pressure from Microsoft's board of directors. Despite robust revenue and earnings growth under his leadership, Microsoft's stock price had stagnated. Microsoft had lost its technological leadership in the industry to Apple and Google. The company's problems with Vista and Windows 8, and its failures in the smartphone, tablet, and Internet search businesses, had led directors to question the direction of the company. Ballmer agreed that it was time for someone else to take the helm, and the board started to look for his successor.

Satay Nadella was picked to succeed Ballmer and took charge on February 4, 2014. Nadella was a native of Hyderabad, India. In 1988, he received an engineering degree from the Manipal Institute of Technology. He then travelled to the United States and earned a Masters in computer science from the University of Wisconsin. Later, while working full time at Microsoft, he earned an Executive MBA from the University of Chicago. Nadella had worked at Microsoft since 1992. He was senior VP of R&D for the Online Service Division from March 2007 until February 2011, when he was appointed president of the Server and Tools Division. This division grew at a healthy pace under his leadership. Moreover, the Azure cloud-computing initiative was based within this division. Nadella was credited for his adept leadership of the nascent cloud-computing business.

Nadella moved quickly to put his stamp on Microsoft. Emphasizing a break with the past, Microsoft, he said, was competing in a "mobile-first, cloud-first" world. In this world, said Nadella, Microsoft must empower people to get things done. By June 2014, he was talking about Microsoft being the premier "productivity and platform company for the mobile-first, cloud-first world."

In March 2014, Nadella announced that Microsoft would offer a version of Office 365 for the iPad. A version had been in the works for some time, but release had been delayed because of fears that it would boost demand for the iPad and hurt Microsoft's Surface tablet. Nadella asserted that in a world where Android and iOS are widely used, Microsoft had to make its applications run on those platforms too. By Fall 2014, Office for the iPad had over 30 million downloads. Also in March 2014, Nadella announced that Windows would be free for devices smaller than 9 inches, meaning smartphones and tablets. Clearly this was an attempt to jump-start adoption of Windows on digital devices, and to match Google's strategy of giving away Android for free.

In June 2014, Nadella sent a long letter to employees stating that the company would be taking "important steps to visibly change our culture." He talked about the need to obsess over customers, to streamline engineering processes and reduce the time and energy it takes to get things done, to limit the number of people involved in making decisions, to drive greater accountability, and to flatten the organization. In making these statements, Nadella was implicitly acknowledging that Microsoft's culture had been too bureaucratic and political, and that there had not been sufficient accountability. He also announced that, as part of its efforts to streamline the organization, Microsoft would lay off 18,000 employees, 12,500 of them in the newly acquired Nokia unit. These were the most significant layoffs in Microsoft's history. Coming at a time when the company was still making very healthy profits, they sent a clear signal that Nadella believed company needed to become more efficient to compete effectively going forward.

In January 2015, Microsoft unveiled Windows 10, which would be available in late 2015 (Microsoft decided to skip the Windows 9 designation). Windows 10 represents a move away from the tile-based, Metro interface. The traditional start menu that was in Windows 7 is back. Windows 10 will run on all devices, from desktops and laptops to tablets and smartphones. Applications written to run on Windows 10 should run on any device, which promises to remove a major headache for app developers. Moreover, the ability to tap into the wider Windows ecosystem might create an incentive for developers to write more apps for Windows devices. In a bold departure from its prior strategy, Microsoft announced that Windows 10 would be free to any Windows 7 or 8 users that downloaded it for the first year after its release. Estimates suggest that this would result in $500 million in lost revenue for the first year Windows 10 is on the market.

Also in January, Microsoft announced its earnings for the last quarter of 2014. Among the highlights on the consumer side of Microsoft's business, sales of the Surface tablet were accelerating and hit $1.1 billion during the quarter. Search and advertising revenues jumped 23% over the same quarter a year ago. Bing's U.S. market share increased and was up 150 basis points to 19.7%. Office 365 consumer subscribers also jumped 30% over the prior quarter, to 9.2 million. On the enterprise side of the business, cloud revenue grew by 114%, driven by strong enterprise adoption of Office 365, Azure, and Dynamics CRM online. Microsoft's cloud business was now generating annualized revenues of $5.5 billion and growing rapidly. On the other hand, sales of traditional Windows and Office products to consumers and businesses were either flat or down. Clearly, the shift to the cloud was rapidly gaining momentum, and Microsoft was starting to cannibalize its own businesses.

NOTES

1. A. Covert, "Will Google Docs Kill Off Microsoft Office," *CNN Money*, November 13, 2013.
2. International Data Corporation press release, "Worldwide Server Market Revenues Declines −3.7% in the Third Quarter," February 24, 2014.
3. K. Mackie, "Microsoft Admits Windows Use at 14%," redmondmag.com, July 14, 2014.
4. International Data Corporation press release, "Smartphone OS Market Share, Q1 2014."
5. E. Protalinski, "Strategy Analytics: Android Tablet Shipments Up to 65.8% in Q1 2014," thenextweb.com, April 28, 2014, http://thenextweb.com/insider/2014/04/28/strategy-analytics-android-tablet-shipments-65-8-q4-2014-ios-fell-28-4-windows-secured-5-8/.
6. International Data Corporation press release, "IDC Expects PC Shipments to Fall by 6% and Decline Through 2018," March 4, 2014.
7. J. D'onfro, "Here's a Reminder of How Massive Amazon's Web Services Business Is," *Business Insider*, June 16, 2014.
8. Comment made to the author.
9. S. Nadella, "Mobile First, Cloud First" press briefing, San Francisco, March 27, 2014.
10. Much of the material in this section is drawn from P. Freiberger and M. Swaine, *Fire in the Valley: The Making of the Personal Computer* (McGraw Hill, 2000); A. R. Harris, *Microsoft: The Company and Its Founders* (ABDO Publishing Company, 2013); J. Wallace and J. Erickson, *Hard Drive: Bill Gates and the Making of the Microsoft Empire* (New York: Harper Business, 1992); information gleaned by the author during nearly two decades of teaching in-house executive education courses at Microsoft.

11. The full Gates memo is archived at www.wired.com/2010/05/0526bill-gates-internet-memo/.

12. J. Bick, "The Microsoft Millionaires Come of Age," *New York Times,* May 29, 2005.

13. B. Herbold, "Inside Microsoft: Balancing Creativity and Discipline," *Harvard Business Review,* January 2002.

14. Ibid.

15. J. Brustein, "Microsoft Kills Its Hated Stack Rankings. Does Anyone do Employee Reviews Right?" *Bloomberg Businessweek*, November 13, 2013.

16. The best description of this process can be found in M. Cusumano and R. Selby, *Microsoft Secrets: How the World's Most Powerful Software Company Creates Technology, Shapes Markets and Manages People* (New York: Free Press: Touchstone Edition, 1998).

17. Business Software Alliance, Ninth Annual BSA Global Software Piracy Study, May 2010.

18. K. Powers, "Showdown," *Forbes*, August 11, 2003, pp. 86–87.

19. A. Wilhelm, "Inside Microsoft's Earnings: Windows 8 and the Xbox Money Machine," thenextweb.com, April 19, 2013, http://thenextweb.com/microsoft/2013/04/19/inside-microsofts-earnings-windows-8-and-the-xbox-money-machine/.

20. P. Dekho, "Google Android Lords Over 85% of Smartphone OS Market Share," Financial Express, September 1, 2014; C. Buckler, "Browser Trends September 2014," Site Point, September 2, 2014.

21. R. Nieve, "Yahoo Gets 31% of Search Revenue from Microsoft Deal," CBET, December 10, 2013.

22. T. B. Lee, "Here's Why Microsoft is Buying Nokia's Phone Business," *The Washington Post,* September 3, 2013.

23. Cited at http://blogs.msdn.com/b/philipsu/archive/2006/06/14/631438.aspx.

24. J. Greene, "The Inside Story of how Microsoft Killed Its Courier Tablet," CNET, November 1, 2011.

25. The Economics of the Cloud, Microsoft White Paper, November 2010.

26. The author was an observer at a Microsoft strategy conference when Ballmer made this comment in response to a presentation suggesting that Microsoft take a cautious approach to the cloud. "No," said Ballmer, "this is wrong, we have to go all in on this one."

CASE 21

SATELLITE RADIO (A): XM VERSUS SIRIUS

THE BIRTH OF A MARKET

More than anyone else, Canadian-born David Margolese was the key player in the creation of the satellite radio business. In 1978, at the age of 20, Margolese dropped out of college to create a Vancouver-based paging company. He soon turned his attention to the nascent cellular telephone business. When he tried to obtain funding to establish a cellular telephone business in Canada, he was initially rebuffed by venture capitalists who told him that the industry would never amount to much. At best, they said, cellular phones would only be used by a few CEOs and diplomats. Undeterred, Margolese persisted in his fundraising efforts. In 1980, when cellular was still little more than a dream, he convinced Ameritech to invest in his company, Cantel.

Using these funds he acquired licenses to cellular phone rights in Canada. Along the way, he joined forces with others, including Ted Rodgers of Rodgers Communications, to create what became Rogers Wireless, which by 2001 was Canada's largest cellular telephone company. In the late 1980s, while he was still just 31, Margolese sold his stake for $2 billion in cash and set himself up as a venture capitalist.

It was in that capacity that Margolese met Robert Briskman, a former NASA engineer and the operations chief at Geostar, a satellite messaging company that went bankrupt in 1991. Briskman had designed the core technology for satellite radio, called the unified S-band. He and other former Geostar employees had established a company named Satellite Radio CD to commercialize the technology, but they were without funding and needed to overcome numerous regulatory hurdles.

Initially, Margolese invested just $1 million in the business (its name was changed to CD Radio), but he soon decided that this was the best business he had ever seen. What attracted Margolese was the fact that radio programs beamed from satellite using the unified S-band technology and digital signals could deliver nationwide coverage and CD-quality sound. Established radio was local, the quality of the analog signal was often poor, and it faded quickly outside of its area. Moreover, the local markets served by established radio businesses were too small to support niche programming such as stations devoted to jazz, classical music, or reggae, but this might not be the case for a radio company that could serve a nationwide market.

However, numerous hurdles stood in the way of establishing a viable satellite radio business. It would be very expensive to put satellites into space, easily several hundred million dollars. The Federal Communication Commission (FCC) had to be persuaded to allocate radio spectrum to satellite radio. Receiving the radio signal from space would require special

radios, and how could potential customer be persuaded to purchase these when they already had radios in their cars and at home? Moreover, it would be difficult to get advertisers to support a service that initially had no listeners—it was a classic chicken-and-egg problem: without the advertisers, how would the service generate revenues?

By 1994, Margolese was estimating that satellite radio would be operational by 1997 and cost some $500 million, but CD Radio faced substantial roadblocks. Despite lobbying from Margolese, the FCC had not yet decided if it would license radio spectrum for satellite radio. Fierce opposition from the National Association of Broadcasters (NAB), which represented existing radio stations, was slowing things down. Among other things, NAB filings with the FCC argued that satellite radio would lead to the demise of local radio service, hundreds of which would close, to the detriment of local communities that relied on AM and FM radio for important local news.

It wasn't until 1997 that the FCC finally auctioned off the spectrum for satellite radio. There were four bidders for the spectrum. The FCC decided to license two providers, creating a duopoly. CD Radio and XM Radio won the auction, paying $83.3 million and $89.8 million, respectively. Established in 1992, XM Radio was a development-stage company backed by American Mobile Satellite Corp, which was owned by Hughes Electronics (then a subsidiary of General Motors) and McCaw Cellular. With spectrum in hand, CD Radio (which, in 1999, changed its name to Sirius) and XM Radio now had to deliver on their promise to establish a nationwide satellite radio service. If they did not, the FCC would not renew the licenses when they came up for review in 2007. If not renewed, the licenses would expire on February 14, 2010.

THE RADIO INDUSTRY

The radio industry dates back to 1921, when the first radio station was licensed. Radio involves the transmission of sound waves, which are sent from amplitude-modulated (AM) or frequency-modulated (FM) stations. AM radio operates on relatively low frequencies and was the earliest broadcast service. FM radio, which was first patented in 1933, operates at much higher frequencies but was very slow to catch

on because of heavy investment by stations and listeners in AM equipment.

Radios are ubiquitous; they can be found in 99 out of 100 American households. The average number of radios per household is 5.6, including radios in cars (there are approximately 150 million radios in vehicles). Some 95.4% of radio owners listen to the radio during any given week. The typical adult listener tunes in for 3 hours and 12 minutes every weekday, and 5 hours 30 minutes on weekends. On a typical weekday, the average person of 12 years or older spends 41.7% of radio listening time in a car or truck, 37.3% while at home, and 21% at work or other places. On weekends, car listening jumps to 47.3%, home listening to 40.5%, and listening elsewhere falls to 12.1%. On average, some 13 to 17% of airtime every hour is devoted to advertising on FM/AM radio stations.[1]

Encouraged by broadcast deregulation, the number of radio stations in the United States increased from 10,500 in 1985 to roughly 13,000 by the end of 2001.[2] In 1996, the Telecommunications Act removed limits on the number of radio stations that a company could own in a given market (a "market" is generally defined as discrete geographical area such as a city or county). Prior to 1996, a company could only own two FM and two AM stations in any one market, no matter how populated that market. Under the new regulations, a company may own or operate up to eight stations in any one market, with up to five in one service (AM or FM). These new rules have facilitated consolidation in the industry and led to the growth of large radio broadcasting companies that own many stations. The leader among these, Clear Channel Communications, owned 1,182 U.S. radio stations at the end of 2003, reached an audience of 180 million, and generated $3.70 billion in revenues from radio advertising.[3] The next largest radio broadcasting company in terms of revenues, Infinity Broadcasting, owned 180 radio stations, which were concentrated in the most populated markets in the United States. By 2002, the 10 largest broadcasters owned about 17% of all U.S. stations and accounted for over 40% of radio industry advertising revenues (the largest broadcasters are focused on the largest markets where advertising revenues are greater). Most analysts believe that the industry will continue to consolidate over the next few years.

Due to the limited range of their signal, radio stations focus on the market in which they are located.

Figure 1 Radio Advertising Spending ($billion)

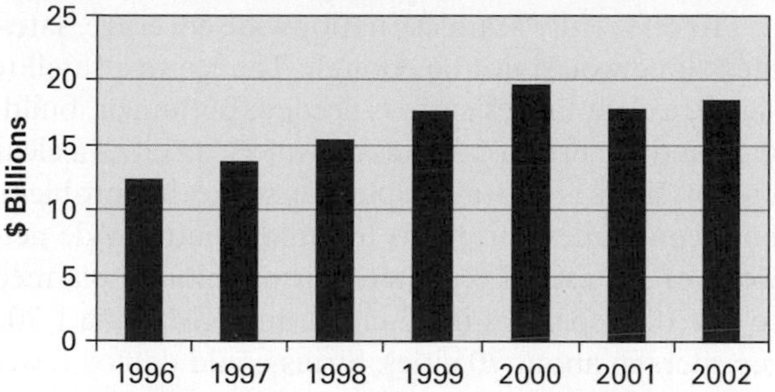

Source: Standard & Poor's Industry Survey, Broadcasting and Cable Industry, July 2002.

Radio stations earn their revenues from advertising. Advertising rates are a function of a station's ability to attract an audience that has certain demographic characteristics. Stations offer programs of a specific format in order to attract the demographic that advertisers are targeting. Popular formats include news/talk radio, rock, oldies, sports, country, and jazz. The ability of radio to offer different programs that target different demographics is a big selling point, attracting advertisers pursuing narrowly defined audiences. Also important are the number of other stations and advertising media competing in that market. Advertising rates are normally highest during morning and evening drive time hours.

In 2002, advertising revenues for radio stations was $18.6 billion, an increase from $12.41 billion in 1996 (see Figure 1). Advertising revenues dropped by almost $2 billion in 2001 compared to 2000 due to a week national economy and the impact of September 11, 2001. The cost structure of radio broadcasters is largely fixed, making the profitability of radio stations sensitive to the overall level of advertising revenues.

THE BUSINESS PLAN FOR SATELLITE RADIO

The Business Case

The business case for Sirius and XM was based on the argument that the number of radio stations in local markets is limited, most of these stations focus on the same five formats, and the geographic range of service is also limited with the signal fading outside of the market area. According to market data, over 48% of all commercial radio stations use one of only three general programming formats—country, news/talk/sports, and adult contemporary, and over 71% of all commercial radio stations use one of only five general formats—the same three, plus oldies and religion.[4] The small number of available programming choices means that artists representing other niche music formats are likely to receive little or no airtime in many markets. Radio stations prefer featuring artists they believe appeal to the broadest market. Meanwhile, according to the Recording Industry Association of America, recorded music sales of niche music formats such as classical, jazz, movie and Broadway soundtracks, religious programming, new age, children's programming, and others comprised up to 27% of total recorded music sales in 2001.

Both Sirius and XM planned to offer around 100 channels. Sirius planned to keep 50 channels of music commercial free, while selling advertising spots on the remaining news, sports, and information channels. XM planned to have 15 to 20 channels commercial free, while limiting advertising sports to just 7 minutes an hour on other channels. The channels would focus on a wide range of different music formats and news/information/talk formats. For example, XM planned to offer music channels focusing on each decade from the 1940s to the 1990s, plus contemporary music channels, several different country formats (e.g., bluegrass, Nashville), Christian rock channels, numerous news formats, information formats, and so on. Both Sirius and XM also planned to enter into agreements with established broadcasters to offer satellite radio formats of their services. These formats included MTV, VH1, CNN, the BBC, ESPN, Court TV, C-Span, and Playboy. XM also partnered with Clear Channel Communications, the largest owner of FM and AM stations in the nation, to offer Clear Channel program formats, such as the KISS pop music station, over XM Satellite radio.

To generate revenues, in addition to advertising fees both Sirius and XM decided to charge a subscription-based fee for their services that would run about $10 to $12 per month. When it was pointed out that existing radio is offered for free to consumers, executives at Sirius and XM noted that the same is true for traditional broadcast TV, but nevertheless consumers have been more than willing to pay a monthly subscription fee for cable TV service and satellite TV service. Penetration data relating to cable, satellite television, and premium movie channels suggest that consumers are willing to pay for services that expand programming choice or enhance quality. There were more than 22.9 million digital cable subscribers and 22.3 million satellite television subscribers in early 2004. As of 2004, some 69% of TV households subscribed to basic cable television, and 20% of TV households subscribed to satellite television.[5]

Infrastructure

Although the technology used by Sirius and XM Radio differs in important ways, both companies followed the same basic business plan. Sirius and XM decided to place satellites in orbit to serve the United States. Sirius planned to put three satellites in elliptical orbits 23,000 miles above the earth, while XM planned to put a pair of more powerful satellites in geostationary orbits at 22,300 miles. The satellites were expected to have a useful life of up to 15 years. Both Sirius and XM planned to keep a spare satellite in storage that could be launched quickly in the event of failure of one of their satellites. If an orbiting satellite were to fail, it would take approximately 6 months to get a replacement into space. Service would be partially interrupted during this time. Initial plans called for Sirius to launch its satellites in 1999 and XM in 2000, with service starting soon thereafter.

The satellites broadcast a digital signal that can be converted into CD-quality sound by radios fitted with the appropriate chip set and receivers that decode, decompress, and output digital signals from a satellite. The S-band signal used by both companies can be picked up by moving vehicles and will not be "weathered out" by dense cloud cover. The radios were expected to cost between $200 and $400. The digital signal cannot be picked up by a standard radio, requiring customers to invest in new equipment.

At least initially, a radio with a Sirius receiver would not pick up XM Radio, and visa a versa. On February 16, 2000, XM and Sirius signed an agreement to develop a unified standard for satellite radios enabling consumers to purchase one radio capable of receiving both Sirius and XM services. The technology relating to this unified standard was jointly developed and funded by the two companies, who share ownership of it. The unified standard was mandated by the FCC, which required interoperability with both licensed satellite radio systems. Radios based on the unified standard became available late in 2004.

To offer truly seamless nationwide coverage, satellites alone would not be enough. To receive a satellite signal, a clear line of sight is needed. In tunnels, buildings, and the urban canyons of American cities a clear line of sight is not available. To solve this problem, both companies had plans to build a nationwide network of terrestrial repeaters. Sirius initially planned to put 105 repeaters in 42 cities, and XM some 1,700 repeaters in about 70 cities. Sirius could deploy fewer repeaters because the orbits of its satellites allowed for a better coverage of the United States—but it had to put three satellites in space, not two, placing them in figure-eight orbits that have two of the three satellites high in the sky over North America at any time during the day. In contrast, XM Radio's two satellites are in geostationary orbits. Consequently, the chip sets required to pick up Sirius signals are more expensive than those for XM Radio.

In addition to satellites and repeaters, the third infrastructure element required to offer the service is recording studios. XM established three recording studios, one in Washington D.C., one in New York City, and one in Nashville. Taken together, the three studios compromise an all-digital radio complex that is one of the largest in the world, with over 80 soundproof studios of different configurations. Sirius built a single studio complex in New York City.

By mid-2000, Sirius was expecting to spend $1.2 billion and XM Radio $1.1 billion to develop this infrastructure. These estimates had increased considerably from the initial estimates made in the mid-1990s, which were around $500 million. Given the infrastructure, operational, and advertising costs, the companies estimated that they each needed 2 to 3 million subscribers to make a profit. In 2000, forecasts by market research agencies and securities analysts suggested that, in total, satellite radio could have as many as 15 million subscribers by 2006, 36 million by 2010, and around 50 million by 2014.[6]

Distribution

Both Sirius and XM believed that installation in cars and trucks was likely to drive early growth for satellite radio. In the early 2000s, 17 to 18 million new cars and light trucks were sold in the United States each year. Some 30 million car radios were sold, either installed in new cars or in the aftermarket. In total there were over 210 million vehicles on American roads. Both companies made deals with major automobile manufacturers to install satellite radios in new cars as optional—and ultimately standard—equipment. Plans called for satellite radio to be offered as an option on certain models, with the offering to be increased to more models over time. The price of the radio is folded into the price of the car, with the customer signing up for service at the time of purchase. XM has an exclusive deal with General Motors and Honda, and Sirius with Ford and Daimler Chrysler. Both companies have now entered into an agreement with the FCC under which they pledge to refrain from making further exclusive deals.

The exclusive deals with automobile companies do not come cheap. As part of its arrangement with Daimler Chrysler, Sirius reimburses the automaker for some advertising expenses and hardware costs, and has issued to DaimlerChrysler a warrant to purchase 4,000,000 shares of Sirius common stock at an exercise price of $3.00 per share. The deal with Ford was very similar. The deal between Sirius and Daimler Chrysler expires in October 2007, while the Ford deal expires May 2007.

The agreement between XM and General Motors requires XM to guarantee annual, fixed payment obligations to GM. However, the agreement is subject to renegotiation if General Motors does not achieve and maintain specified installation levels, starting with 1,240,000 by November 2005 and installations of 600,000 per year thereafter. The GM agreement expires September 2013. For its part, Honda has committed to shipping 400,000 cars with XM Radios in 2005.

The companies also lined up manufacturers of aftermarket car receivers and signed retail arrangements with the Best Buy and Circuit City chains to distribute them.

Capital Requirements and Investors

Financing these two ventures was not trivial. XM Radio raised some $2.6 billion in equity and debt proceeds through January 2004 from investors and strategic partners to fund its infrastructure build out and operations. Strategic investors in XM Radio included General Motors, Hughes Electronics/DIRECTV, Clear Channel Communications, American Honda, and Hearst Communications. Financial investors in XM included Columbia Capital, Madison Dearborn Partners, AEA Investors, BayStar Capital, and Eastbourne Capital. XM Radio went public in late 1999. Honda and General Motors are major investors in XM Radio, with stakes of 13% and 8.6%, respectively, in late 2004.[7] Similarly, Sirius, which went public in 1995, had raised around $2.5 billion by 2004.

Much of the financing went into building out the infrastructure. At the end of 2003, XM Radio reported that it had spent $470 million to put its two satellites in orbit and purchase a spare satellite, $267 million to set up a system of ground repeaters covering 60 cities, and $130 million on satellite control facilities and studios. Sirius is believed to have spent similar amounts.

Competition

Satellite radio faces competition from three main sources. Traditional AM/FM radio stations are obvious competitors. The big advantage of AM/FM radio is local content such as news, sports, and weather, which listeners do want. Although AM/FM radio is predominantly local, the emergence of consolidators such as Clear Channel Communications is beginning to change this. Clear Channel has made an effort to realize scale economies by developing a nationwide branded format for radio shows, most notably its pop format that goes under the KISS brand. KISS offers standard programming developed in a national studio. Local content such as news, weather, sports, and some dialog is spliced into KISS programming to make it seems as if the broadcast is local.[8] There are also signs that traditional AM/FM radio will ultimately move toward digital broadcasting, although doing so will require that consumers purchase radios capable of receiving a digital signal.

Internet radio is a second potential competitor. A number of FM and AM radio stations are now broadcasting digital signals over the Internet that can be accessed anywhere in the world for users with the appropriate equipment (a computer, an Internet connection, and a media player).

A third competitor comes in the form of satellite TV and cable TV systems. Both satellite and cable TV providers offering digital radio services as part of a package of digital services, with the radio being bundled with TV service, typically at no additional cost to the consumer.

LAUNCHING THE SERVICES

Initially, Sirius was thought to have the lead over XM Radio, but this changed when technical problems with their chip sets delayed the launch of Sirius' service for 2 years (the receivers, which were built by Lucent, did a poor job of picking up the digital signal and had to be redesigned).

XM Radio had delays due to problems with the Boeing rockets that were to launch its satellites, but was able to launch its two satellites—named "Rock" and "Roll"—in early 2001, more than a year behind its initial schedule. XM started offering national service in November 2001 for a monthly fee of $9.95. XM Radio's launch was supported by an advertising campaign that cost in excess of $100 million.

Beset by technical problems, Sirius did not launch its final satellite until early 2002, and did not start offering service until July 2002. Sirius charged $12.95 a month, justifying its price premium over XM by the fact that all of Sirius' 60 music channels run without commercials. XM has limited commercials of about 2 minutes per hour on 35 of its 70 music channels (see Table 1 for a comparison between XM and Sirius).

Table 1 XM Versus Sirius in 2003

	XM Satellite	Sirius
Monthly cost	$9.99	$12.95
Radio cost	$325 factory installed radio, $400-$500 for dealer installed $200-$299 for home radio	$400-$500 for dealer installed radio No home radio
Programming	101 channels 70 music 30 talk, sports, news 1 premium channel (Playboy)	100 channels 60 music 40 sports, talk, news
Commercials	None on 35 music channels Limited commercials on rest (about 2 minutes per hour)	None on music channels
Key formats	Classical (3 channels) Pop (10 channels) Jazz/Blues (7 channels) Country (6 channels) Rock (12 channels) Latin (5 channels) Franks' Place The Joint (reggae) Broadway Old-Time Radio Classics	Classical (3 channels) Pop (9 channels) Jazz standards (5 channels) Hip Hop (5 channels) Country (5 channels) Dance (6 channels) R&B (4 channels) Rock (13 channels) Broadway Radio Classics
News	Fox, CNN, CNBC, ESPN, Others	Fox, CNN, CNBC, ESPN, Others
Automotive partners	GM, Honda	Ford, Daimler Chrysler, BMW
Subscribers as of mid-2003	692,253	105,186

Sirius has stated that it will depend upon subscriptions for about 85% of its revenues. XM initially expected to rely somewhat more on advertising revenues.

By the end of 2003, Sirius had 133 terrestrial repeaters in 92 urban markets where high buildings interfere with line of sight. XM had some 800 repeaters in 60 markets.

The 9-month lead that XM gained as a result of Sirius' problems proved to be invaluable. By the end of 2002, XM had 347,000 subscribers, while Sirius had just 30,000. XM passed the 500,000-subscriber milestone in April 2003, and was projecting that it would end 2003 with over 1 million subscribers. This rapid subscriber accrual helped XM Radio sell faster than CD and DVD players did in their first year on the market.[9] Sirius, meanwhile, was aiming to end 2003 with some 300,000 subscribers and had just over 100,000 by mid-year. Both companies were now estimating that they needed 2 to 3 million subscribers to break even, with XM predicting that it would be cash-flow positive by late 2004.

In addition to XM's 9-month lead in the market, analysts attribute much of the company's early gains to an aggressive push by General Motors. GM rolled out XM's satellite radio as optional, factory-installed equipment in 25 of its 57 car, light truck, and sports utility models, including the entire Cadillac line. GM planned to increase that figure to 44 models for the 2004 model year, and the company expected to sell some 800,000 cars autos with XM's radio installed during 2004, and 1.1 million during 2005. The GM installed radio, which is built by GM supplier Delphi, costs $325 and is bundled into the price of the vehicle. In addition to being a shareholder of XM, GM is believed to receive about $100 from XM for every radio it installs.

In early 2003, Honda stated that it planned to include XM radios as standard equipment in the 2004 Acura RL, and as a factory-installed option in the 2004 Accord. In September 2003, Honda announced that XM radios would be installed as standard equipment in certain Honda Accord models. An XM Satellite Radio spokesman said that between the Accord, Pilot, and S2000 models, Honda will release about 200,000 automobiles that have the XM radio as a factory-installed feature during the 2004 model year, and 400,000 during the 2005 model year.[10] In addition to GM and Honda, XM radios became available as dealer-installed options

on certain offerings from Toyota, Volkswagen, and Audi, among others.

In contrast, Sirius' main partners were not as far along putting Sirius radios into their vehicles. Daimler and BMW offered Sirius radios as a dealer-installed option, as opposed to factory installed, meaning that a buyer had to request that the dealer install the equipment. In 2004, Daimler committed to factory-install 550,000 radios by mid-2007. Ford reportedly planned to offer factory-installed radios in select models for the 2004 model year, but that did not transpire. Ford announced that it would begin factory-installing Sirius Radios in the 2006 model year and would be factory-installing Sirius radios in 20 of its 21 car lines by 2007.[11]

The wild card in the industry, Toyota, had not aligned itself with either XM or Sirius by late 2004, although Toyota did offer XM Radio as a dealer-installed option on some models. Nor had Nissan aligned itself with either company; but it offered either XM or Sirius radios as a dealer-installed option.

Both XM and Sirius offered an array of satellite radios for home use. The bestselling of these in 2002 and 2003 was the Delphi XM SkyFi radio, which was made by Delphi for XM and sold through major consumer-electronics chains for between $199 and $230 a unit. By mid-2003, some 80,000 Delphi XM SkyFi units had been sold, and Wal-Mart, the nation's largest retailer, stocked the item. The SkyFi radio could be used at home, where it slotted into an audio player, and also be adapted for use in a car. In late 2004, XM Radio and Delphi announced that they would start selling a handheld portable radio, The Delphi MyFi, in December 2004.

Early surveys suggested high customer satisfaction with satellite radio. Surveys carried out by GM reportedly a 90% satisfaction rate among customers who chose satellite radio as an option, with 70 to 75% saying that they were likely to order satellite radio for their next vehicle.[12] Several consumer products reporters gave satellite strong reviews, although some complained that the sound quality was not quite CD quality.[13]

Sirius's late entry into the market and relatively low traction left it in a very shaky financial condition. In October 2001, CEO David Margolese abruptly resigned, presumably a casualty of the company's failure to launch its service on time. Margolese continued as nonexecutive chairman of Sirius. The delay in the launch of its service resulted in Sirius running down its cash reserves, and by mid-2002 it looked almost certain that the company would default on debt payments and file for Chapter 11 bankruptcy protection. However, at the last minute, in October 2002, Sirius was able to pull of something of a coup, converting $700 million in debt and $525 million in preferred stock into common equity. In addition, three of the original investors in Sirius agreed to supply the company with another $200 million in cash. As a result of the recapitalization plan, the existing holders of the company's common stock ended up owning just 8% of the recapitalized company. It remained to be seen whether these funds would be sufficient to see the company through to profitability.

XM Radio also returned to the capital markets in early 2003, lining up an additional $475 million in funding. Of the $475 million, $225 million came from new investors, and the remainder from General Motors in the form of deferred payments and credit facilities. Critical to the deal's success was the agreement by more than 90% of the holders of $325 million in XM bonds to swap them for newly issued debt that pays no interest until 2006.

Although XM did launch on schedule, is too experienced technological problems that represented a potential cloud on the horizon. XM's two satellites, "Rock" and "Roll," are experiencing unexpected degradation of their solar-power panels. The degradation prompted XM to cut their useful life to 2008 from 2015. However, XM believed that it would be able to launch additional satellites by the time the degradation impacts signal strength. XM felt that its insurance policies covered this problem, and that it would be able to claim sufficient funds from insurance to be able to launch additional satellites.

By mid-2003, some analysts remained very bullish about the potential of XM Radio, although the future of Sirius was somewhat hazy. A May 2002 study by the Yankee Group projected satellite radio would achieve 15 million subscribers by 2006. Other market studies conducted for XM Radio projected that as many as 50 million people might subscribe to satellite radio by 2012. More conservative investment analysts were suggesting that satellite radio might garner 4 to 5 million subscribers by mid-decade, and that the ultimate total would be closer to 40 to 50 million. According to some projections made in early 2003, if XM hit 10 million subscribers in 2007, it could earn $500 million, or $1.50 a share. If XM Radio were

ultimately to garner 30 million subscribers, it could earn $7 or more a share.[14]

SIGNIFICANT DEVELOPMENTS IN 2004

As 2004 drew to a close, subscription data suggested that XM Radio was continuing to capitalize on its early lead over Sirius in the industry. Analysts were now expecting XM to end 2004 with 3.11 million subscribers versus around 1 million for Sirius (see Figure 2). During 2004, XM Radio's net subscriber additions (gross additions less cancellations) were 1.75 million, versus 0.76 million for Sirius. XM was forecast to have 5.31 million subscribers in 2005, versus 2.14 million for Sirius.

Sirius tried to differentiate itself by aggressively signing valuable branded content. In December 2003, it signed a 7-year, exclusive deal with the NFL to broadcast football games, beginning with the 2005–2006 season. The deal cost Sirius $188 million in cash over the course of the contract, plus $32 million in warrants. In early October 2004, Sirius signed up "shock jock" Howard Stern to an exclusive, 5-year deal for $500 million, which would start to air on January 1, 2006. The branded content was used by Sirius to justify its premium subscription price.

XM Radio responded to these moves with deals of its own. In October 2004, XM signed an 11-year, $650 million deal with Major League Baseball (MBL), giving XM exclusive rights to the satellite broadcast of MLB games beginning 2005, including the World Series. Also in October 2004, XM launched a premium channel dedicated to shockjocks Opie and Anthony, who had previously been removed from the air due to profanity. The Opie and Anthony channel will cost subscribers an additional $1.99 a month.

By late 2004, the business models at XM Radio and Sirius were starting to crystallize. It was now clear that earlier statements regarding breakeven subscription levels were too low. A detailed research report on XM Radio by Salmon Smith Barney suggested that the company would not start to generate positive earnings before interest, tax, depreciation, and amortization (EBITDA) until 2007, when the subscriber base was forecast to be around 11 million (see Table 2).[15]

Figure 2 Forecasted Subscriber Growth (Millions)

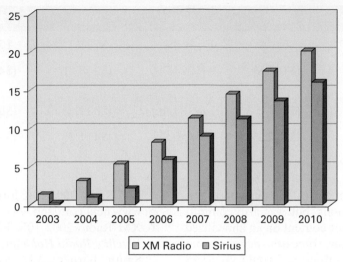

Source: Salmon Smith Barney Estimates. 2003 Figures are actual figures.

On the same basis, Sirius was not expected to start generating a positive EBITDA until 2008.

The key variables in analysts' estimation of break-even volume were subscription revenues, fixed costs, variable costs, customer acquisition costs, and customer churn rates. For 2004, Smith Barney estimated that XM Radio would have revenues of $243 million, with only $6 million of those being attributed to advertising revenues. Fixed costs—which included costs related to equipment, broadcasting, programming and content, and customer support—were estimated to be around $175 million. Variable costs—including revenue sharing with partners such as GM, royalties paid for the right to broadcast songs, and customer care costs—amounted to $96.5 million. The average cost of acquiring a customer—including advertising, marketing, and subsidies given to equipment suppliers—was pegged at $130/customer, and forecast to hit $279.9 million in 2004. In its 2003 10K, XM Radio estimated that 1.3% of its paying customers left the service every month. However, if nonpaying customers who get the service on a trial basis through automobile companies are counted, the churn rate rises to 3.5% per month.

Sirius had a revenue and cost structure similar to that of XM Radio, although accounting differences make a direct comparison difficult (see Table 3). The

Table 2 Financial Performance and Forecasts for XM Radio

$(million)	2003	2004E	2005E	2006E	2007E
Revenue	$91.8	$243.5	$469.7	$790	$1,183.2
Variable costs	($52.4)	($96.5)	($150.9)	($231.5)	($324.3)
Fixed costs	($143.1)	($175.9)	($248.7)	($281.1)	($299.6)
Customer acquisition costs	($192.4)	($279.9)	($347.4)	($412.5)	($508.1)
EBITDA	($296.1)	($308.8)	($277.2)	($135.7)	$51.1

Source: Company Reports and Salmon Smith Barney.

Table 3 Financial Performance and Forecasts for Sirius

$(million)	2003	2004	2005	2006	2007
Revenue	$12.9	$68.2	$186.7	$520.7	$1383.4
Nonmarketing operating expenses	($160.9)	($224.7)	($258.3)	($469.6)	($614.4)
Marketing expenses	($194.1)	($294.4)	($339.8)	($542.5)	($489.5)
EBITDA	($342.2)	($450.9)	($411.3)	($513.7)	$154.2)

Source: Company reports and Salomon Smith Barney.

largest difference was that Sirius still charged a premium price for subscriptions, but was also committed to paying higher fees for content on an annualized basis. In 2006, for example, forecasts suggested that programming costs per subscriber would be $3.88 at Sirius, and $1.31 at XM Radio.[16] Sirius also had a larger customer churn rate than XM Radio in 2004, around 1.7% a month, and larger customer acquisitions cost, which were forecast to be around $247 per customer in 2005. The higher customer acquisition costs relative to XM Radio were because Sirius paid a larger subsidy to equipment manufacturers, and it had a small base over which to spread its marketing costs. In Table 3, customer acquisition costs are bundled in with marketing expenses.

NOTES

1. Standard & Poor's Industry Survey, Broadcasting and Cable, July 25, 2002.
2. Ibid.
3. Clear Channel Communications 2002 10K Form.
4. XM Radio 2003 10K form.
5. www.ncta.com and www.skyreport.com.
6. XM Radio 2002 10K Form; Smith Barney, *XM Satellite Radio Holdings*, October 26, 2004.
7. Smith Barney, *XM Satellite Radio Holdings*, October 26, 2004.
8. A. W. Mathews, "From a Distance," *The Wall Street Journal*, February 25, 2002, p. A1.
9. Anonymous, "Outstanding Subscriber Growth for XM," *Dealerscope*, June 2003, p. 5.
10. Anonymous, "XM Satellite Radio to Be Standard Equipment on Honda Accord Models," *Dow Jones News Wire*, September 9, 2003.
11. Smith Barney, *XM Satellite Radio Holdings*, October 26, 2004.
12. A. Barry, "A Sound Idea," *Barrons*, February 17, 2003, pp. 17–19.
13. K. Batchman, "Reaching for the Stars," *Mediaweek*, March 25, 2003, pp. 22–30.
14. A. Barry, "A Sound Idea."
15. Smith Barney, *XM Satellite Radio Holdings*, October 26, 2004.
16. Smith Barney, *Sirius Satellite Radio*, October 26, 2004.

CASE 22

SATELLITE RADIO (B): THE SIRIUS XM MERGER AND ITS AFTERMATH

◢ INTRODUCTION

As 2005 unfolded, good times seemed to be just around the corner for the satellite radio business. XM Radio ended 2005 with almost 6 million subscribers, and Sirius with a shade over 3.3 million, both surpassing forecasts made a year earlier. Moreover, with churn rates only 1.5% a month—the lowest for any major subscription business—both companies could argue that their users clearly placed a high value on the product offering. Mel Karmazin, CEO of Sirius, argued this was because, "Our programming is so compelling, so strong, and so sticky."[1] Forecasts now called for the two companies to have a combined subscriber base of 44 million by 2010, divided more or less evenly between the two companies. For 2006, the subscriber base was expected to reach 15 million.

◢ GROWTH RATES SLOW

Late 2005 proved to be the high point of expectations for satellite radio. As 2006 progressed, the growth rate started to decelerate. The two companies ended the year with 14 million subscribers, one million less than forecast (Sirius had 6 million and XM Radio 8 million subscribers). Moreover, both companies continued to lose money; Sirius lost $513 million in 2006, and XM Radio lost $719 million. As investors fretted about whether the companies would ever gain enough subscribers to cover their fixed costs, the stock prices of both fell sharply. Despite subscriber growth throughout 2007—XM ended the year with 9 million subscribers, and Sirius with 8.3 million— losses continued to mount. Sirius lost $327 million in 2007, and XM $682 million. The 44 million subscribers forecast for 2010 now seemed out of reach. One analyst forecast 32 million subscribers for the two companies by 2011.

Various reasons were offered to explain the slowing growth rate. One was competition from other formats for listening to music. By 2007, some 57 million Americans were listening to some form of Web radio every week, and analysts worried that in the near future, Web radio might be streamed to cars using WiMax technology. Of more immediate concern was that, increasingly, people were listening to music using iPods, over 200 million of which had been sold by 2007. Many cars were now fitting with racks for iPods (about 40% of cars sold in 2007 came with sound systems that were compatible with iPods).

Another problem: The core demographic for satellite radio seemed to be middle aged. Many younger people would rather listen to their own playlists downloaded from iTunes and played on iPods. While satellite radio offered music programming, people with iPods preferred to program their own music. A study by Forrester Research estimated that only about 13% of the population actually wanted satellite radio, and that the percentage would shrink significantly if satellite radio channels started to run advertising.

Compounding matters, the auto business was facing a sharp downturn. Since auto dealers were the major distribution channel for satellite radio, as car sales shrank so did the number of new subscribers. What was a slowdown in sales became a major crisis in 2008, as tight credit in the United States led to a sharp contraction in auto sales. Auto sales for 2008 were expected to total only 13.5 million, down from 16.1 million in 2007.

MERGER PROPOSAL

In February 2007, Sirius and XM Radio announced plans to merge. Under the merger agreement, Sirius offered 4.6 of its shares for each XM share, leaving each side with 50% of the new venture. Sirius closed on the day before the announcement at $3.70 a share while XM was at $13.98. The merger valued the combined companies at $13 billion. The stock price of both companies dropped following the merger announcement, knocking $2 billion off the market capitalization of the combined entity.

The main benefit claimed for the merger was cost reduction, particularly marketing and programming costs. About 34% of XM's revenue in 2006 went to programming and marketing expenses, while 47% of Sirius' revenue was eaten up by these costs, many of which were fixed. The costly war for content between the two companies, exemplified by Sirius's $50-million deal with Howard Stern, would also come to an end. One analyst estimated that the combined company could save up to $4 billion through cost reductions over 6 years.

The merger would also enable the new company to offer a wider range of channels. Duplicate channels would be eliminated; no longer, for example, would the National Football League be exclusive to one provider, and Major League Baseball to another. This could help with subscriber retention and growth.

Implementation problems included making radio receivers that were compatible with both satellite systems—something that the companies had already been working on under a Federal Communications Commission (FCC) mandate—and in the long run, rationalizing the satellite system. From a practical point of view, many subscribers might balk at having to replace their radios with ones that can receive signals from both satellites, which could stretch out the implementation over years.

The proposed merger faced two regulatory hurdles. The Department of Justice had to agree to the merger, which created a monopoly in satellite radio, and the FCC also had to sign off. The FCC would have to reverse its mandate in 1995 (when it allocated satellite radio spectrum) that "one (satellite radio) licensee will not be permitted to acquire control of the other remaining" one.

Opposition to the merger quickly emerged from the National Association of Broadcasters (NAB), which represented conventional radio broadcasters. The NAB argued that a national satellite radio monopoly could overwhelm local broadcasters. They claimed that the new company might win additional business in the biggest markets by offering channels with local news, weather, and information.

In the end, the key issues centered on the definition of the "relevant market" for Sirius and XM Radio. If the relevant market was defined narrowly as the market for satellite radio, then the merger seemed doomed on antitrust grounds. Alternatively, the satellite radio companies argued that the relevant market was all broadcast radio, of which satellite radio was just a small segment. The satellite companies pointed out that 240 million people listened to conventional radio, and that satellite radio in total comprised less than 5% of the combined satellite and terrestrial broadcast market. They also argued that their service was competing with Internet radio and other ways of consuming music, such as the iPod.

In March 2008, the Justice Department gave the go-ahead to the merger, and the FCC followed with a green light in July 2008. Both government bodies agreed on a broad definition of the relevant market.

However, as part of the price for allowing the merger to proceed, the FCC required the new company to offer *a la carte* pricing schemes, with lower-priced subscriptions for access to limited content and higher priced subscriptions for access to premium content. This raised the possibility that many subscribers might opt for a less-expensive monthly subscription rate, which could materially impact the revenues of the new company. The FCC also mandated that there be no increase in the price of the base subscription plan, which stood at $12.95 a month, for 3 years.

The Immediate Aftermath

The merger was consummated on July 29, 2008. The new company was called Sirius XM. Mel Karmazin, CEO of Sirius, became CEO of the combined entity. In early September 2008, Sirius XM estimated that the net synergies from the merger would total $425 million, $25 million more than originally thought, and that the company would generate positive cash flow in 2009. Sirius forecast that it would end 2008 with 19.5 million subscribers, and 2009 with 21.5 million. However, rapid contraction in the U.S. automobile industry, a result of the 2008 U.S. financial crisis, raised questions about the attainability of those goals. Some 80% of all new subscriptions came though sales at auto dealers in 2007, and sales of new cars were imploding.

Having lost some $4 billion between 2005 and 2007, and with no prospect of becoming profitable soon, Sirius XM faced substantial funding issues. The company had $1.05 billion of debt that was due in 2009. Its cash on hand, which stood at $442 million in September 2008, was forecast to fall substantially in 2009 as it paid down debt and spent $100 million on new satellites. Karmazin pledged to not issue new equity to pay down debt, so a significant portion of the debt coming due in 2009 needed to be refinanced— not an easy prospect given the credit crunch in U.S. financial markets at that time.

By October 2008, the stock of the new company was trading at under $0.40 a share, down from a high $3.40. The market capitalization of the new company was down to $1.2 billion. If the stock traded at under $1 for 30 consecutive days, Sirius XM would face possible delisting from the NASDAQ stock exchange, which would have adverse consequences on its ability to raise capital. To avoid this possibility, in December 2008, following shareholder approval Sirius XM executed a 10-for-1 reverse stock split. At the same time, shareholders approved a proposal to increase the number of authorized shares by nearly 80%, giving the company some flexibility as it sought ways to refinance the $1 billion in debt that was due in 2009.

LIBERTY MEDIA INVESTS

On February 17, 2009, with bankruptcy looming, the media conglomerate built by John Malone, Liberty Media, stepped in with emergency financing. Liberty Media pledged to loan $530 million to Sirius XM, $280 million of it immediately, enabling Sirius XM to pay off $172 million in debt that had come due on February 16. The remaining $250 million would be paid later in the year to the XM subsidiary, enabling it to meet its short-term debt commitments. The loan from Liberty Media was set to mature in December 2012 and carried a 15% interest rate. Liberty Media also received 40% of Sirius XM's common stock and two seats on the company's board of directors.

While these loans would help keep Sirius XM afloat for the time being, analysts still saw significant risks of bankruptcy down the road. However, most also acknowledged that Liberty Media's John Malone was a shrewd dealmaker. Perhaps he saw value where others did not? In any event, the 15% interest rate attached to the Liberty Media loan to some extent mitigated the investment risks here, assuming Sirius XM could stay solvent until December 2012. It was also probably true that as the largest single shareholder, Liberty Media would have more protection than other shareholders should Sirius XM subsequently file for bankruptcy.

TURNAROUND

Early 2009 proved to be a low point for Sirius XM. With its short-term finances stabilized, the company was able to focus once more on building its subscriber base and improving its average revenue per subscriber, both keys to the long-term viability of the enterprise.

Sales of new cars and light trucks in the United States bottomed out in 2009 at 10.4 million, down from 16.1 million in 2007. Despite this sales implosion in its major distribution channel, Sirius XM ended 2009 with 18.8 million subscribers. Between 2010 and 2014, sales of new cars and light trucks improved every year, reaching 16.5 million units in 2014, the best number since 2007.

Subscriber numbers at Sirius XM followed the recovery in auto sales, growing from 20.2 million at the end of 2010 to 27.31 million at the end of 2014 (see Table 1). Moreover, Sirius XM was able to increase its average revenue per subscriber from a low of $11.58 per month in 2011 to $12.38 per month in 2014. Meanwhile, the monthly churn rate (the number of subscribers who leave the service every month) remained relatively stable at around 1.9%. The growth in average revenue per unit (ARPU) reflected both the introduction of more pricing plans and programming choices, and the ability of Sirius XM to initiate increases in annual subscription prices. For example, Sirius XM was able to increase its base subscription rate from $12.95 a month in 2011 to $14.49 a month in 2012, and the company still witnessed a steady rise in the number of subscribers.

These improved operating metrics drove a financial recovery in the company. Sirius XM recorded a small net income before tax in 2010 of $43 million on revenues of $2.8 billion. By 2014, the company was generating $830.8 million in net income before tax on revenues of $4,181 billion. Moreover, free cash flow had increased from $210 million in 2010 to $1.157 billion in 2014,

improving the financial position of the enterprise. The improvement in Sirius XM's financial performance was also helped by reductions in operating costs and improved efficiency. For example, when Sirius XM renewed its contract with Howard Stern in 2010 for another 5 years, Stern took a $400-million fee, as opposed to $500 million the first time around.

CURRENT STRATEGY

The bullish case for Sirius XM going forward is that the company still has only 27 million subscribers, and there are 260 million cars and light trucks in America. Sirius estimates that, by 2018, over 100 million cars will have radios capable of receiving Sirius XM signals, up from 50 million in 2012. The key is to get owners to activate those radios through subscriptions. If the company can grow its penetration rate from the current 10 to 15%, that would represent another 13 to 14 million subscribers. To do this, Sirius XM has been pursuing a number of strategies.

First, the company continues to expand its relationship with major carmakers, which preinstall Sirius XM radios in new vehicles. By 2014, Sirius XM claimed that it had relationships with every major company selling cars in the United States. Second, since the merger Sirius XM has gone aggressively after the used car market, seeking to get customers to activate the Sirius XM radio in their preowned vehicles. The company has been targeting used car

Table 1 Key Statistics

Year	2010	2011	2012	2013	2014
Revenues ($millions)	2,816	3,015	3,402	3,799	4,181
Net income before tax ($millions)	43	441	474	637	831
Free cash flow ($ millions)	210	416	709	928	1,157
Subscribers (millions)	20.2	21.9	23.9	25.6	27.3
ARPU/month	$12	$11.5	$12	$12.23	$12.38
Monthly churn	1.9%	1.9%	1.9%	1.8%	1.9%

buyers with a 2-week free subscription and low introductory prices. It also has a program that authorizes dealers to offer Sirius XM subscriptions to used car buyers. In 2010, there were only 100 dealers enrolled in the program. By mid-2014 this number had swelled to 12,500.

Third, Sirius XM continues to distinguish itself from free radio and streaming Internet radio alternatives by the lack of advertising on many of its channels, including music and news (Sirius XM does now have advertising on some non-music and news channels). Fourth, Sirius XM's key selling point remains its diverse, unique content spread over numerous channels including music, sports, talk shows, and news stations. While Internet radio offerings such as Pandora, Beats Music, Google Play, and iHeartRadio do offer free streaming music customized to a listener's tastes, they do not offer the broad range of content that can be found on Sirius XM. Moreover, some of this content, such as the Howard Stern show, is exclusive to Sirius XM. The company has also made efforts to target customer segments that are not well served by established AM/FM radio, or Internet radio, creating channels targeted at Hispanics and women among others. In 2014, it added shows from Ellen DeGeneres, Jenny McCarthy, and Hoda Koth is an effort to woo female car buyers. Also, Sirius has developed apps that enable subscribers to listen to Sirius XM content on smartphones, tablets, laptops, and desktop computers.

Challenges

On the other hand, Sirius XM continues to have challenges. Internet radio offerings such as Pandora are gaining traction and are potentially potent competitors. Pandora has 250 million registered users worldwide, 76 million of which are active each month. Many carmakers are now integrating Pandora's app into their in vehicle entertainment systems, allowing drivers to listen to Pandora radio as long as they can get a wireless signal. Since 2009, Pandora has partnered with 26 auto brands. By 2015, at least 145 vehicle models had Pandora software accessible their dashboards. Some 7 million Pandora users have now listened to music though an integrated app in their car—and that doesn't count the users who simply plug in their smartphone to listen to streaming

music. In 2015, only about 8% of vehicles of U.S. roads have any Internet capability, but that projected to grow to 22% by 2020, making Pandora and its ilk stronger competitors to Sirius XM, at least for music listening.

Recent Events

By 2014, Liberty Media had increased its ownership stake in Sirius XM from 40% it gained in 2009 to 53%, effectively giving the company a controlling interest and making Sirius XM a subsidiary of Liberty. The Liberty Media investment had been a major success. Liberty's stake was initially worth less than $1 billion; by 2014, it was worth more than $10 billion.

In January 2014, Liberty announced an all-stock deal valued at more than $10 billion to purchase the remaining shares in Sirius that it did not own. The idea was to facilitate the creation of two tracking stocks for Liberty Media, one of which, the "Liberty Media Group," would include Sirius XM as well as various other entertainment businesses owned by Liberty Media. Liberty Media stated that the deal would simplify Liberty's capital structure, clear up questions about its commitment to Sirius XM, and increase the financial flexibility of both companies.

In March 2014, Liberty Media dropped its bid to acquire Sirius XM's remaining outstanding shares after a lukewarm reception from investors and analysts who questioned whether this was the best use of Liberty's stock. Many questioned the long-term viability of Sirius XM, despite recent successes, given the growing threat from in-vehicle Internet radio in connected vehicles. The market reacted positively to the March announcement, sending Liberty Media's stock up 7%.

For its part, Sirius XM claims it is fully aware of the threat posed by Internet-enabled cars and claims it is already positioning itself for a future where all cars will be fully Internet connected. In 2013, Sirius paid $530 million to purchase the connected-vehicle division of automotive services company Agero, which makes software that constantly updates drivers on roadside assistance or tracks stolen vehicles, for example. The motivation behind the acquisition is for Sirius XM to build the required capabilities to stream its content wirelessly to Internet-enabled cars.

NOTES

1. Anonymous, "Howard's Way," *The Economist*, January 14, 2006, p. 65.

2. Anonymous, "They Cannot Be Sirius," *The Economist*, February 24, 2007, p. 77.

3. J.C. Anselmo and M.A. Taverna, "Urge to Merge," *Aviation Week and Space Technology*, February 26, 2007, p. 92.

4. Argus Research, *Sirius XM Radio Inc*, September 15, 2008.

5. C. Holahan and A. Hesseldahl, "Sirius and XM Get the Justice Go-Ahead," *Businessweek Online*, March 26, 2008.

6. O. Kharif, "The FCC Approves the XM-Sirius Merger," *Businessweek Online*, July 28, 2008.

7. O. Kharif, "Sirius XM is in a Serious Bind," *Businessweek Online*, September 18, 2008.

8. T. Lowry and P. Lehman, "XM and Sirius: What a Merger Won't Fix," *Businessweek*, March 5, 2007, p. 31.

9. C. Kang, "Liberty Extends $530 Million Loan to Bail Out Sirius XM," *Washington Post*, February 18, 2009.

10. F. Gillette, "Can Sirius XM Survive without Howard Stern?" *Bloomberg Businessweek*, March 11, 2015.

11. Sirius XM 10-K annual reports, multiple years.

ENDING HIV? SANGAMO BIOSCIENCES AND GENE EDITING

Sangamo Biosciences was founded in 1995 by Edward Lanphier, a man with 25 years of experience in the pharmaceutical and biotechnology industries who had held senior management positions at Somatix Therapy Corporation, BioGrowth, Biotherapeutics, and Synergen. Sangamo's focus was the development of zinc-finger nucleases (ZFNs), which offer the potential for "editing" the genetic code of a living individual to correct genetically based diseases (e.g., hemophilia, sickle cell anemia, Huntington's disease, and many others), or to confer genetic resistance to non-genetically-based diseases.

ZFNs work by cutting DNA in a chosen spot. The cell then typically attempts to repair the cut either by polishing the two ends of DNA and sealing them back together, or by copying the corresponding section of DNA in the other half of the chromosome pair. Since many diseases occur because of a gene on a single half of the chromosome pair, this "homologous substitution" from the other chromosome corrects the faulty gene. Alternatively, scientists can provide a template gene sequence that they want to use to substitute for the cleaved portion of the DNA (see Figure 1).

Gene editing offered a radical new way to cure or prevent diseases, but it required a significant amount of R&D work both to develop ZFNs that were precise and reliable enough to safely edit human genes, and to develop a delivery mechanism that would ensure the ZFNs penetrated enough of cells to make a difference. Clinical trials to establish the treatment's safety and efficacy to get FDA approval would also be a huge hurdle to overcome.

Because Sangamo had no commercially available products, the company was entirely reliant upon grants and funding from partners for its survival. Though Sangamo had signed collaboration agreements with Shire AG and Biogen IDEC for several of its treatment areas, it had ambitions to develop its revolutionary treatment for HIV on its own, establishing itself as a fully integrated biopharmaceutical company.

Figure 1 Gene Editing with Nucleases

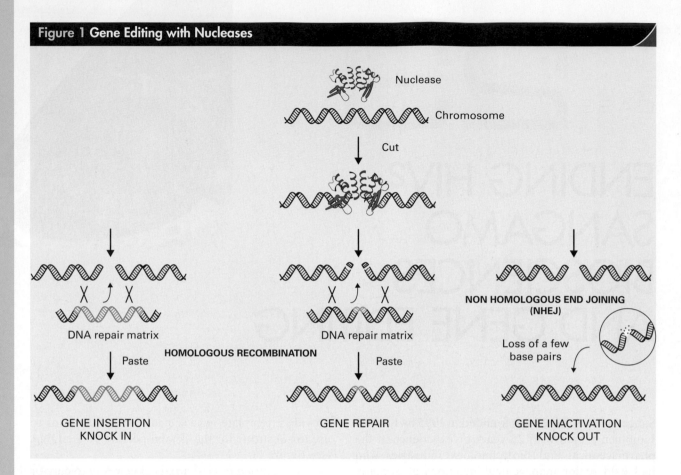

CORRECTING MONOGENIC DISEASES

Monogenic diseases are caused by a defect in a single gene. One example is hemophilia. People with hemophilia lack sufficient clotting factors in their blood, resulting in longer bleeding after an injury. Internal bleeding, in particular, can cause significant damage and be life threatening. Individuals with hemophilia need regular infusions to replace the clotting factor in their blood. Sangamo's ZFN treatment offered the hope of a cure, rather than lifelong treatment.[1] Sangamo had already demonstrated that its ZFN method for treating hemophilia worked in mice, and was preparing to file an application to begin clinical trials. Sangamo also had developed treatments for sickle cell anemia and beta-thalassemia, also monogenic diseases. Normally, patients with sickle cell anemia or beta-thalassemia require lifelong care or bone marrow transplants, at great expense and risk. Sangamo, however, had shown in the laboratory that its treatment could knock out the BCL11A gene causing these diseases.

Another example of a monogenic disease is Huntington's disease (HD). HD is a devastating neurologic disease in which people lose their motor coordination, cognition, and memory. The disease is progressive and usually fatal within 10 to 20 years of onset. It is caused by a mutation in a single gene, the Huntington gene, which results in a greater-than-usual number of repeats of the CAG DNA sequence; this in turn results in a mutant form of the Huntington protein accumulating in cells. Most individuals inherit only one copy of the faulty gene, and it only takes one copy to produce the disease. Furthermore, 50% of the children of an HD sufferer inherit the disease. Though previous research had explored ways to decrease the Huntington protein in

Figure 2 The New Product Development Funnel in Pharmaceuticals

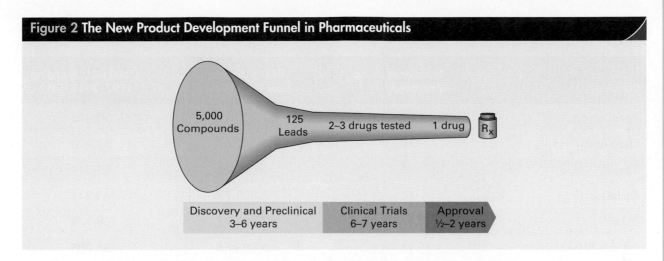

5,000 Compounds   125 Leads   2–3 drugs tested   1 drug   R$_x$

Discovery and Preclinical   Clinical Trials   Approval
3–6 years   6–7 years   ½–2 years

cells, it turned out that the normal form of the protein is essential, and mice lacking the normal Huntington protein died before birth. Sangamo, however, developed a ZFN method to identify and "turn off" only the faulty gene. This meant that an individual would have only one operational copy of the gene, which would continue to produce the normal form of the Huntington protein.

Whereas there were treatments available that could at least stop or slow the progression of hemophilia, sickle cell anemia, and beta-thalassemia, there were no such treatments for Huntington's: Nothing had been found that could halt its progression. Thus, Sangamo's presentation of promising results for its HD treatment was big news. Its success could mean the difference between life and death for sufferers of HD.

DRUG DEVELOPMENT AND CLINICAL TRIALS

Drug development is hugely expensive and risky. Most studies indicate that it costs at least $1.5 billion and a decade of research to bring a new Food and Drug Administration (FDA)-approved pharmaceutical product to market.[2] The statistics on drug development costs are, in fact, an understatement because they do not fully account for the costs of the many failed drugs that are abandoned earlier in the development process. In the pharmaceutical industry, only one out of every 5,000 compounds tested makes it to the pharmacist's shelf, and only one-third of those will be successful enough to recoup the investment in researching and developing the original 5,000 compounds (see Figure 2).[3]

Accounting for investment in failed drug efforts suggests that the cost of drug development is much higher than is typically reported. A study of R&D spending and new drug approvals published in *Forbes* in 2012, for example, found that firms spent over $6 billion per approved drug (see Table 1).[4,5]

Most studies suggested that the biggest cost in drug development was the cost of clinical trials—a cost that is borne by the sponsoring organization (usually the company that developed the drug). To be approved by the FDA in the United States, most drugs have to go through several phases of trials. First, in preclinical studies, the company will usually assess the safety and efficacy of the drug using animals. In Phase 0 trials, a single dose (smaller than what would be used to provide the therapeutic treatment) is given to a small number (10 to 15) of human subjects to evaluate what the drug does to the body. If successful, the drug may be entered into Phase 1 clinical trials, whereby the drug is given to a somewhat larger group of people (20 to 80) to evaluate its safety, determine dosage ranges, and identify side effects. Phase 1 trials primarily assess the safety of the drug. In Phase 2 trials, the drug is given to larger groups of people (100 to 300) to evaluate its effectiveness and further evaluate its safety and side effects. Finally, in Phase 3, the drug is given to very large groups of subjects (1,000 to 3,000) to confirm its effectiveness compared to alternatives and gather still further information on its safety.

Table 1 Research Spending and New Drug Approvals[6]

Company	Number of Drugs Approved	R&D Spending per Drug ($Mil)	Total R&D Spending 1997–2011 ($Mil)
AstraZeneca	5	11,790.93	58,955
GlaxoSmithKline	10	8,170.81	81,708
Sanofi	8	7,909.26	63,274
Roche Holding	11	7,803.77	85,841
Pfizer	14	7,727.03	108,178
Johnson & Johnson	15	5,885.65	88,285
Eli Lilly & Co	11	4,577.04	50,347
Abbott Laboratories	8	4,496.21	35,970
Merck & Co Inc	16	4,209.99	67,360
Bristol-Myers Squibb Co	11	4,152.26	45,675
Novartis	21	3,983.13	83,646
Amgen Inc	9	3,692.14	33,229
Average:	**11.58**	**6,199.85**	**66,872.33**

Sources: InnoThink Center for Research in Biomedical Innovation; Thomson Reuters Fundamentals via FactSet Research Systems.

Finally, if the drug successfully makes it through Phase 3 clinical trials, the sponsoring organization can apply for a new drug approval from the FDA. The entire process typically takes at least 10 to 12 years, costs hundreds of millions of dollars, and, as shown in Figure 2, the vast majority of new drug projects do not make it through the process successfully.

COMPETING TECHNOLOGIES

As if drug development was not risky enough, Sangamo also faced the threat that its ZFN technology would be rendered obsolete by other gene-editing alternatives. In early 2015, two alternatives were gaining traction: TALENs (transcription activator-like effector nucleases), and CRISPRs (clustered regularly interspaced short palindromic repeats). TALENs are like ZFNs in that they are special nucleases that identify and bind to a specific part of the DNA and cut the genome at a desired spot. The main difference between the two is how they identify the right DNA binding location. By 2015, ZFN technology was more mature and better developed, but TALEN technology was considered more straightforward to design treatments with, and thus many considered it to have an advantage in the longer term.[7] According to Stephen Ekker, director of the Mayo Addiction Research Center at the Mayo Clinic Cancer Center, while ZFNs had established the proof of principle for genome-editing technology, "TALENs ... do most of what ZFNs do, but cheaper, faster and better."[8] On the other hand, TALEN molecules were larger, which made them more difficult to deliver to certain regions of the body (a particular challenge was getting gene-editing nucleases past the blood-brain barrier for treatment of diseases such as Huntington's). Since both technologies had advantages and disadvantages, their sponsors would have to race to get effective treatments to market first.

CRISPRs were somewhat different. CRISPR technology harnessed a natural defense system of bacteria that has evolved to recognize and eliminate foreign DNA, giving bacteria "adaptive immunity." CRISPRs were even more simple and efficient than TALENs, fueling enormous excitement over their potential. However, because CRISPRs used a very short RNA sequence to guide their activity, some people worried that their effects wouldn't be precise enough; that is, they could result in "off-target" cleavages—a highly undesirable result.

As of early 2015, there remained great uncertainty about which gene-editing technology would pay off. This uncertainty, unfortunately, dampened investor support for all three technologies.

◤ SANGAMO'S PARTNERSHIPS

Biotechnology firms can spend years accumulating losses while they develop their treatments. Sangamo was no exception—it had yet to make any money from sale of its products. All of its revenues came from research grants and collaboration agreements (see financials in Figures 5 and 6), and it outspent those revenues in R&D, accumulating losses in each year. This highlights the challenging nature of drug development: Though the company had developed groundbreaking treatments that could radically improve the lives of several different patient populations, it was financially quite vulnerable.

As of 2015, Sangamo had only 84 full-time employees; it did not have the resources to do its own clinical testing, manufacturing, or marketing. For these stages of drug development, Sangamo would be reliant on partnerships with much larger firms.

Biogen Idec.

Biogen Idec was a Cambridge, Massachusetts based biotech giant, with almost $10 billion in revenues for 2014. Most of its treatments focused on immunology and neurology, and it was probably best known for its best selling Avonex (for multiple sclerosis), Tysabri (for multiple sclerosis and Crohn's disease), and Rituxan (a monoclonal antibody treatment for non-Hodgkin's lymphoma and rheumatoid arthritis). Biogen earned the majority (70%) of its revenues in North America, and had direct sales operations in about 30 countries, and used distribution partners to reach another 60 countries.

Biogen was excited by Sangamo's prospects with its zinc-finger technology, and entered into a partnership with the company to develop treatments for sickle cell anemia and beta-thalassemia. Under the terms of the deal, Biogen would give Sangamo $20 million upfront, and Sangamo would be responsible for performing all of the R&D on the treatments until they could be proven to work on humans. Then Biogen would take over with clinical trials, manufacturing, and marketing, and Sangamo would get milestone payments of up to $300 million and double-digit royalties if the products earned sales.

Shire AG

Shire was one of the United Kingdom's largest specialty biopharmaceutical companies, with almost $5 billion in revenues in 2013. It operated in three main segments: specialty pharmaceuticals, human genetic therapies, and regenerative medicine. The company had a large, well-established, global marketing and sales infrastructure. Though the company earned the majority (70%) of its sales in North America, it had direct operations in about 30 countries and sold products to more than 50 countries. Shire was known for being a highly acquisitive company, having acquired NPS pharmaceuticals, ViroPharma, Janssen Pharmaceuticals, and Advanced BioHealing just in the last few years. Its two most well-known drugs were treatments for attention deficit disorder (ADD): Vyvanse and Adderall.

In January 2012, Sangamo entered into an agreement with Shire AG to further develop its ZNF treatments for hemophilia, Huntington's disease, and other diseases. Like the Biogen deal, Shire agreed to pay Sangamo an upfront fee, plus milestone fees of up to $213.5 million, for each of seven targets.[9]

A WORLD-CHANGING OPPORTUNITY: CREATING IMMUNITY TO HIV

One of the most exciting potential applications of ZFNs was creating a treatment that could cure HIV. In 2013, approximately 35 million people were living with HIV/AIDS worldwide (see Figure 3). However, a small percentage of people have a mutation in their CCR5 gene—a gene that makes a protein found on the surface of cells. The mutation makes it difficult for HIV to enter their cells. Individuals receive their genes in pairs—one on a specific chromosome from one parent, and another on the paired chromosome from the other parent. Individuals with one copy of the mutated gene have some protection against HIV infection, and experience a less severe form of the disease if infection occurs. Individuals with two copies of the mutated CCR5 gene are typically immune to HIV. These gene mutations appear in up to 20% of people of European descent (scientists hypothesize that the gene mutation conferred resistance to the Bubonic plague or smallpox epidemics, leading this gene to be more prevalent in populations that survived such epidemics). People with the mutation appear to suffer no health problems from the mutation.

The potential for exploiting the CCR5 mutation gained widespread attention when a study published in 2011 revealed that an AIDS patient with leukemia had received a bone marrow stem-cell transplant from a donor with the CCR5 mutation, and subsequently appeared to be cured of AIDS. After the bone marrow transplant, the patient was able to discontinue all antiretroviral therapy and the virus did not reappear in his blood.[10]

Finding a bone marrow match with a CCR5 mutation is extremely unlikely, and getting a bone marrow transplant is risky. Sangamo thus decided to use its ZFN technology to develop a simpler method by which individuals could be given the mutation. Early results released by Sangamo in 2014 were promising: the treatment appeared to be well tolerated and reduced the viral load of several patients who had been taken off of their antiretroviral therapy for 12 weeks during the study.[11] However, the percent of cells showing the mutation declined over time, which meant further work needed to be done to find a way to modify enough of the patients' genes for the therapy to be a reliable and permanent treatment.

Figure 3 HIV/AIDS Worldwide, 2013

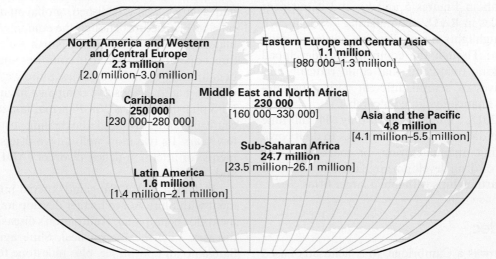

Adults and children estimated to be living with HIV | 2013

North America and Western and Central Europe
2.3 million
[2.0 million–3.0 million]

Eastern Europe and Central Asia
1.1 million
[980 000–1.3 million]

Caribbean
250 000
[230 000–280 000]

Middle East and North Africa
230 000
[160 000–330 000]

Asia and the Pacific
4.8 million
[4.1 million–5.5 million]

Sub-Saharan Africa
24.7 million
[23.5 million–26.1 million]

Latin America
1.6 million
[1.4 million–2.1 million]

Total: 35.0 million [33.2 million–37.2 million]

Source: *UNAIDS*

Figure 4 Summary of Sangamo's Research Programs and Drug Pipeline

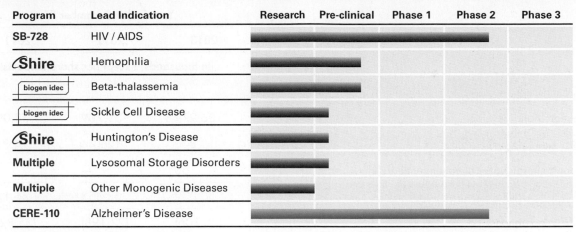

Program	Lead Indication	Research	Pre-clinical	Phase 1	Phase 2	Phase 3
SB-728	HIV / AIDS					
Shire	Hemophilia					
biogen idec	Beta-thalassemia					
biogen idec	Sickle Cell Disease					
Shire	Huntington's Disease					
Multiple	Lysosomal Storage Disorders					
Multiple	Other Monogenic Diseases					
CERE-110	Alzheimer's Disease					

Source: www.sangamo.com.

THE FUTURE

Sangamo clearly had a lot on its plate (see Figure 4). It had revolutionary treatments in clinical trials for several major diseases, including the potential to create a cure for HIV. In the short term, its business was focused on developing treatments through early-stage clinical trials that it would hand over to partners who had deeper pockets and were better positioned to conduct late-stage clinical trials, production, and marketing. However, in the long run, Sangamo wanted to be able to do all of its own clinical testing, production, and marketing, to better capture the value of its innovative technologies. Currently, Sangamo had no revenues from actual products—only grants from research foundations and cash from upfront fees paid by its licensing partners. It was also spending over $30 million a year on R&D, and posting huge losses, year after year. Sangamo thus had to carefully weigh the pros and cons of developing its HIV treatment alone.

Figure 5 Sangamo Consolidated Statements of Operations

SANGAMO BIOSCIENCES, INC.
CONSOLIDATED STATEMENTS OF OPERATIONS

	Year Ended December 31,		
	2013	**2012**	**2011**
	(In thousands, except per share amounts)		
Revenues:			
Collaboration agreements	$ 21,678	$ 18,186	$ 6,110
Research grants	2,455	3,469	4,209
Total revenues	24,133	21,655	10,319

(continued)

Figure 5 Sangamo Consolidated Statements of Operations [*continued*]

	Year Ended December 31,		
	2013	2012	2011
	(In thousands, except per share amounts)		
Operating expenses:			
Research and development	36,979	31,709	32,098
General and administrative	13,800	12,144	14,042
Change in fair value of contingent liability	60	—	—
Total operating expenses	50,839	43,853	46,140
Loss from operations	(26,706)	(22,198)	(35,821)
Other income (expense), net	82	(66)	71
Net loss	$ (26,624)	$ (22,264)	$ (35,750)
Basic and diluted net loss per share	$ (0.48)	$ (0.42)	$ (0.71)
Shares used in computing basic and diluted net loss per share	55,974	52,741	50,512

Figure 6 Sangamo Consolidated Balance Sheets

SANGAMO BIOSCIENCES, INC.
CONSOLIDATED BALANCE SHEETS

	December 31,	
	2013	2012
	(In thousands, except share and per share amounts)	
ASSETS		
Current assets:		
Cash and cash equivalents	$ 10,186	$ 21,679
Marketable securities	82,627	41,868
Interest receivable	338	190
Accounts receivable	3,155	4,129
Prepaid expenses	457	296
Restricted cash	320	—
Other current assets	191	203
Total current assets	97,274	68,365

	December 31,	
	2013	**2012**
	(In thousands, except share and per share amounts)	
Marketable securities, non-current	38,663	12,584
Property and equipment, net	1,406	1,543
Intangible assets, in-process research and development	1,870	—
Goodwill	1,585	—
Other assets	40	41
Total assets	$ 140,838	$ 82,533
LIABILITIES AND STOCKHOLDERS' EQUITY		
Current liabilities:		
Accounts payable and accrued liabilities	$ 4,380	$ 4,013
Accrued compensation and employee benefits	3,194	2,473
Escrow liability	275	—
Deferred revenue	2,282	2,304
Total current liabilities	10,131	8,790
Deferred revenue, non-current	6,679	8,847
Contingent consideration liability	1,570	—
Deferred tax liability	748	—
Total liabilities	19,128	17,637
Commitments and contingencies		
Stockholders' equity:		
Common stock, $0.01 par value; 80,000,000 shares authorized, 62,243,892 and 53,058,525 shares issued and outstanding at -December 31, 2013 and 2012, respectively	622	531
Additional paid-in capital	423,209	339,848
Accumulated deficit	(302,133)	(275,509)
Accumulated other comprehensive income	12	26
Total stockholders' equity	121,710	64,896
Total liabilities and stockholders' equity	$ 140,838	$ 82,533

NOTES

1. R. Hersher, "A Whole Clot of Hope for New Hemophilia Therapies," *Nature Medicine,* February 2, 2012. blogs.nature.com

2. J. A. DiMasi and H. G. Grabowski, "The Costs of Biopharmaceutical R&D: Is Biotech Different?" *Managerial & Decision Econ*, 28 (2007), p. 469–479.

3. "Pharmaceutical Industry, 2008," Standard & Poor's Industry Surveys; H. Grabowski, J. Vernon, and J. A. DiMasi, "Returns on Research and Development for 1990s New Drug Introductions," *Pharmacoeconomics* (2002) Suppl. 3: 11–29; "Drug Discovery and Development: Understanding the R&D Process," Washington, D.C.: PhRMA, February 2007, www.innovation.org/drug_discovery/objects/pdf/RD_Brochure.pdf.

4. M. Herper, "The Truly Staggering Costs of Inventing New Drugs," *Forbes*, February 10, 2012. www.forbes.com.

5. According to a study by the Manhattan Institute for Policy Research, the majority of the drug development expense is due to the extremely costly and time-consuming process of clinical trials. If analysis is limited to drugs that are ultimately approved by the FDA, phase III clinical trials represented over 90% of the total cost of development. *Project FDA Report*, Manhattan Institute for Policy Research, No. 5, April 2012.

6. M. Herper, "The Truly Staggering Costs of Inventing New Drugs."

7. T. Gaj, C. A. Gersbach, and C. F. Barbas III, "ZFN, TALEN, and CRISPR/Cas-based Methods for Genome Engineering," *Trends Biotechnol* 31 (July 2013): 397–405; E. Pennisi, "The CRISPR Craze," *Science*, 341 (August 2013): 833–836.

8. J. M. Perkel, "Genome Editing with CRISPRs, TALENs and ZFNs," *Biocompare*, August 27, 2013. www.biocompare.com

9. C. Renauer, "How Sangamo BioSciences, Inc. Is Partnering to Success," *The Motley Fool*, January 29, 2014. www.motleyfool.com.

10. K. Allers, et al., "Evidence for the Cure of HIV Infection by CCR5Δ32/Δ32 Stem Cell Transplantation," *Blood* 117 (2011), March 10: 2791–2799.

11. "Gene Editing of CCR5 in Autologous CD4 T-cells of Persons Infected with HIV," *New England Journal of Medicine* 370 (2014): 897–906. http://www.nejm.org/doi/full/10.1056/NEJMoa1300662.

24

GENZYME'S FOCUS ON ORPHAN DRUGS[1]

In 2015, Genzyme, a subsidiary of Sanofi, was one of the world's leading biotech companies. Genzyme's products and services were focused on rare, inherited disorders and diseases, and multiple sclerosis. The company was consistently recognized as a leader across many dimensions of its operations. It had been named to numerous national "best places to work" lists, and the journal *Science* had regularly named Genzyme a "Top Employer" in its annual survey of scientists.[2] The company had also won numerous awards for practicing environmental sustainability and ethical responsibility. In 2007, Genzyme received the National Medal of Technology, the highest honor awarded by the President of the United States for technological innovation.

Genzyme's focus on rare diseases had made it very unique in its early history. However, by 2015, many competitors were beginning to explore the "orphan drug" opportunity ("orphan drugs" are those that receive special government protection to target rare diseases). Many large pharmaceutical companies were falling off a "patent cliff"—the patents of large numbers of blockbuster drugs were expiring, leaving companies scrambling to refill their drug pipelines. As a result of this, and the fact that orphan drugs could be sold for extremely high prices and received special protection and incentives, "Big Pharma" companies were now actively pursuing orphan drugs, making the drug market for rare diseases a more hotly contested one.

HUMBLE BEGINNINGS

Genzyme was founded in Boston, in 1981, by a small group of scientists who were researching genetically inherited enzyme diseases. People with these rare disorders (for example, Gaucher disease, Fabry disease, MPS-1) lack key enzymes that regulate the body's metabolism, causing sugar, fats, or proteins to build up in the body and resulting in constant pain and early death. In 1983, the scientists were working out of the 15th floor of an old building in Boston's seedy "Combat Zone," when they were joined by Henri Termeer, who took the role of president and eventually chief executive officer of the company. Termeer had left a well-paying, executive vice president position at Baxter to join the 2-year-old start-up, and many people thought he was crazy to do so.[3] However, Termeer thought Genzyme was well positioned to pursue a novel strategy in the drug industry: target the small markets for rare diseases. Focusing on rare diseases was close to heresy in the pharmaceutical industry. Developing a drug takes 10 to 14 years and costs an average of $1.9 billion to perform the research, run the clinical trials, get Food and Drug Administration (FDA) approval, and bring a drug to market.[4] Pharmaceutical companies thus focused on potential "blockbuster" drugs that would serve a market that numbered in the millions. A drug was considered a "blockbuster" if it earned revenues of $1 billion or more, and achieving this level required many thousands of patients with chronic diseases such as hypertension, diabetes, or high cholesterol. Genzyme, however, challenged the notion that a firm needed a blockbuster drug to succeed. Genzyme would focus on drugs that were needed by only a few thousand patients with severe, life-threatening diseases.[5] Though there would be few patients for these drugs, there would also be few competitors. Furthermore, the small number of patients and the severity of the diseases would make insurance companies less likely to actively resist reimbursement. Both of these factors suggested that drugs for rare diseases might support higher margins than typical drugs. Additionally, whereas pharmaceutical companies typically needed large sales forces and considerable marketing budgets to promote their drugs, a company focusing on drugs for rare diseases could have a much smaller, more targeted sales approach. There were only a small number of physicians specializing in rare diseases, so Genzyme could go directly to those doctors rather than funding a large sales force and expensive ad campaigns. Finally, therapies with significant clinical value in smaller populations required much smaller clinical trials (though it was more difficult to find the study candidates).

THE ORPHAN DRUG ACT

Genzyme's timing was auspicious. In 1983, the FDA established the Orphan Drug Act to induce development of drugs for rare diseases. The act provides significant tax breaks on research costs and 7 years of market exclusivity to any company putting an orphan drug on the market. This market exclusivity amounted to significantly more protection from rivalry than a typical patent. When a firm secures a patent on a drug, that patent only prevents another firm from marketing the same drug; it does not prevent another firm from marketing a drug that achieves the same or similar action through other means. Thus, when a firm introduced a patented drug that met an

important medical need, the race was on by competitors to introduce a different (hopefully improved) version of the drug that could also be patented and compete with the original drug. Drugs for orphan diseases would be shielded from such competition for 7 years, potentially permitting them to recoup their development costs and earn a rate of return that would make the venture attractive.

To qualify for orphan drug status in the United States, a disease had to afflict less than 200,000 people worldwide. Big Pharma was typically uninterested because of the small market sizes and high risks of developing therapies for them. Even most biotech firms failed to see the opportunity inherent in the Orphan Drug Act that might suit their rapidly evolving technologies. Genzyme's eventual success, however, would ultimately attract their attention to this small but lucrative market.

THE FIRST BIG SUCCESS

Genzyme's first commercial product was Ceredase—a replacement protein designed to treat fewer than 10,000 people afflicted with a deadly, rare, genetic disorder called Gaucher's disease. Children born with this disease rarely live past their 10th birthday, and adults who develop this fatal disease suffer from chronic, liver, kidney, heart, and spleen damage. Clinical trials for Ceredase began in 1984, and in March 1985 the FDA designated Ceredase an orphan drug. Genzyme was first allowed to make Ceredase available to patients outside of the United States in 1990, and was approved by the FDA to market Ceredase in the United States in 1991.

Creating a therapy to treat a patient with Gaucher's disease required extracting proteins from human tissue, and the most productive source of these proteins was found in human placentas. The expense and difficulty of this provided a substantial barrier to competitive entrants. Not many experts believed Genzyme could be commercially successful with this product. As Termeer noted, "The FDA thought we were out of our minds." In an interview, he explained:

> The hurdles to raise more finance for the trials were formidable. Not least was the fact that human placentas were the source of the enzyme

and to provide a year's dose for just one patient, more than 22,000 placentas were needed. To overcome this, Genzyme built a plant in France to take unwanted placental tissue which would have otherwise been burnt and extracted the enzyme. At one point 35% of all placentas from the United States were passing through the French plant. Ceredase was the only drug made from placentas that the U.K. government allowed to be used in Britain.[6]

By 1991, Genzyme was collecting a million placentas a year, and knew it could not produce enough of the enzyme to treat all the patients who needed it. Fortunately, by 1993, Genzyme had developed a recombinant form of the enzyme, Cerezyme, which obviated the need for human tissue and made efficient production possible. In the meantime, Genzyme had also begun work on gene therapies and begun investigating potential treatments for another rare enzyme disorder, Fabry disease.

REMAINING INDEPENDENT

Genzyme also broke with industry norms in its decision to *not* work with large pharmaceutical companies. Whereas most biotech companies licensed their technologies to large pharmaceutical firms to tap the larger companies' greater capital resources, manufacturing capabilities and marketing and distribution assets, Termeer felt strongly that the company should remain independent, stating, "If we worked with a very large corporation, we would lose our strategic direction and be dependent … we've tried to stay as self-sufficient as we possibly can."[7] Performing its own testing, manufacturing, and sales meant incurring much greater risks, but it also meant that the company would keep all of the profits its drugs earned. To generate revenues to fund the research, Termeer entered into a number of side ventures, including a chemical supplies business, a genetic counseling business, and a diagnostic testing business. He also took the company public in 1986, raising $27 million. Termeer's gamble paid off: Patients taking Cerezyme paid an average of $170,000 a year for their medication, and with about

4,500 patients committed to taking the drug for life, this amounted to more than $800 million in annual revenue from Cerezyme alone.[8]

THE COMPETITION IN BIOTECH

The global biotechnology industry included about 10,000 companies in 2015, with total revenues of about $289 billion.[9] Major players included U.S-based Gilead Sciences ($24.9 billion), Amgen ($20 billion), Monsanto ($15.9 billion), Biogen Idec ($9.7 billion), and Genentech (owned by Switzerland-based Roche, $50.4 billion), as well as Australia's CSL ($5.3 billion), Germany's Merck KGaA ($15.3 billion), Denmark's Novo Nordisk ($15.4 billion), and the biotech research arms of major international pharmaceutical companies.[10] Genentech was the oldest, formed in 1976; Amgen and Genzyme were established in the early 1980s. Many competitors were small, emerging companies with less than 500 employees. In fact, more than 50 percent of biotech companies had fewer than 50 employees.[11]

Most biotech start-ups followed a similar path of evolution. The firm would begin as a research and development firm, with employees coming from university science labs or Big Pharma. If the start-up survived the lean years and had prospects for producing a commercially viable therapy, it would seek alliances with large firms for late-stage development, manufacturing, and marketing. For example, both Genentech and Gilead formed relationships with Roche, and Amgen formed a relationship with Abbott Laboratories. If a firm's drugs achieved commercial success, it could negotiate higher royalties and attract capital investment.

Genzyme differed from all its peers and from later biotech companies by being profitable early on (Genzyme posted a profit of just over $20 million in 1991, losses in 1992 and 1993, and a profit of over $16 million in 1994), and until only recently, remaining independent of partners. "We wanted a diversified company that could use technology to make a difference for people with serious diseases, and to get profitable so we can continue to develop new medicines," Termeer said.[12] In the late 2000s, most analysts believed that no other developer was likely to pursue

Genzyme's strategic path, even with the benefits offered under the Orphan Drug Act. While both Amgen and Genentech had produced orphan drugs, it had not been their strategic focus.

THE GROWING COMPETITION IN ORPHAN DRUGS

It is estimated that there are between 5,000 and 8,000 known rare diseases in the world. In the decade leading up to 1983, only 10 orphan drugs entered the market according to the FDA. However, from passage of the act until the end of 2013, 447 orphan drugs were approved by the FDA (see Figure 1). The European Union passed similar legislation protecting "orphan medicinal products," granting them market exclusivity for 10 years after approval. Japan, Singapore, and Australia also began offering subsidies and other incentives to develop drugs for rare diseases. As of 2010, roughly 200 orphan diseases had become treatable.[13]

Genzyme had proven that a business could be built around small disease populations and demonstrated its ability to profitably serve markets that seemed financially unjustified. Even large pharmaceutical companies struggling due to the "patent cliff" began to pay more attention to the orphan drug opportunity.

While this was good news for sufferers of rare diseases, it meant significantly more competition for Genzyme. Companies such as Pfizer, Isis Pharmaceutical, NPS Pharmaceuticals, GlaxoSmithKline, and Shire were all beginning to target orphan drugs. As noted by Francois Nader, chief executive of NPS Pharmaceuticals, shifts in science and economics had made the orphan drug market more viable. Researchers could identify ahead of time "the patients that would benefit from a particular drug, rather than using the shotgun approach we used in the past."[14] Ironically, despite the small numbers of patients served, high prices enabled almost one-third of orphan drugs to achieve $1 billion in sales[15]—making them the new blockbusters.

INDEPENDENCE NO MORE

Growing competition wasn't the only challenge Genzyme was facing. A series of manufacturing problems created shortages that impaired its sales of Cerezyme and Fabrazyme in 2009 and 2010. To make matters worse, plant contamination problems caught the FDA's attention in 2010, resulting in fines and sending the stock into a tumble, making the company vulnerable to a takeover. Switzerland-based pharmaceutical company Sanofi, one of the largest

Figure 1 Cumulative Number of U.S. FDA Orphan Drug Approvals, 1983–2013

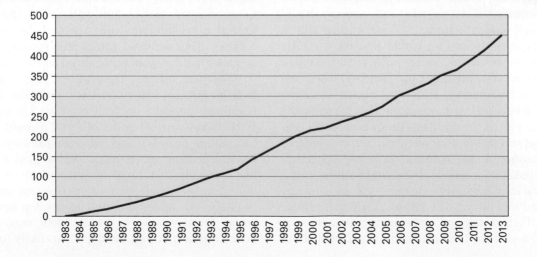

pharmaceutical companies in the world,[16] began making overtures. Genzyme rebuffed the initial offers,[17] but after months of negotiation Genzyme was acquired by Sanofi for $20.1 billion in February 2011, ending its 30-year run as an independent biotechnology drug maker. Henri Termeer resigned, and Sanofi CEO Christopher Viehbacher took over. The company retained its name and its facilities in Cambridge, Massachusetts, becoming Sanofi's new headquarters for rare diseases. With the backing of Sanofi, Genzyme was able to expand its manufacturing capabilities, opening up a manufacturing plant in the United States and expanding its production facility in Ireland.

In September 2012, the FDA approved Genzyme's first multiple sclerosis drug, Aubagio, a once-daily oral drug, and in November 2014 the FDA approved Genzyme's second multiple sclerosis drug, Lemtrada, an intravenous drug delivered through two sets of injections, a year apart.[18] Unlike Genzyme's other targeted diseases, multiple sclerosis was not rare: 2.3 million people were estimated to suffer from it worldwide, including 400,000 in the United States.[19] The two drugs made Genzyme—and parent Sanofi—among the most visible competitors in multiple sclerosis treatments. Genzyme had also proven to be among the fastest-growing holdings of Sanofi, rapidly earning far more than the $20.1 billion Sanofi had paid for it, and significantly boosting Sanofi's stock price. When Sanofi had acquired Genzyme in February 2011, its stock had traded at roughly $34 a share; by late 2014, the stock was trading at over $50 a share.[20] As noted by Sanofi CEO Chris Viehbacher, "Once we had Genzyme, that changed investor perception about Sanofi . . . It significantly increased the visibility of Sanofi in the United States. It signaled that Sanofi was a company that was serious about biotechnology and research and development."[21]

NOTES

1. Adapted from a New York University Teaching Case by Jane Cullen and Melissa A. Schilling.

2. Company website: http://www.genzyme.com/corp/structure/awards_genz.

3. S. Calabro, "The Price of Success," *Pharmaceutical Executive* 26 (3) (2006): 64–80.

4. Standard & Poor's Industry Surveys, 2013.

5. N. Watson, "This Dutchman Is Flying," *Fortune* (Europe) 148 (1) (2003): 55–57.

6. "Ten Years of Enzyme Replacement Therapy," www.gaucher.org.uk/tenyearsapr03.htm, retrieved April 21, 2006.

7. N. Watson, "This Dutchman Is Flying."

8. D. Shook, "Biotechs Adopt the Orphan-Drug Market," *Businessweek* Online, December 13, 2002.

9. Global Biotechnology: Market Research Report. IBIS World, January 2015.

10. Hoovers, accessed March 12, 2015.

11. "Top Biotech Companies by 2005 Revenue," www.bioworld.com/img/TopDrugs_sample.pdf.

12. C. Robbins-Roth, *From Alchemy to IPO: The Business of Biotechnology* (New York: Basic Books, 2000), p. 44.

13. W. Armstrong, "Pharma's Orphans," *Pharmaceutical Executive*, May 2010. www.pharmcxec.com

14. J. D. Rockoff, "The Big Business of Orphan Drugs," *The Wall Street Journal*, January 31, 2013, p. B.1.

15. Ibid.

16. A. K. Fathima, "Forbes Global 2000: Biggest Drug Companies in the World; Pfizer Tops List," *Forbes*, June 25, 2014. www.forbes.com

17. J. Jannarone, "Genzyme's Time Out with Sanofi," *The Wall Street Journal*, September 28, 2010, p. C.10.

18. www.fda.gov, accessed March 19, 2015.

19. J. Walker, "Sanofi's Genzyme Gets FDA Approval for MS Drug; Lemtrada Will Only Be Available in the U.S. Through a Restricted Distribution Program," *The Wall Street Journal Online*, November 15, 2014.

20. Finance.Yahoo.com, accessed March 9, 2015.

21. R. Weisman, "Sanofi Chief Says Genzyme Purchase Paid Off," *Boston Globe*, September 19, 2013. www.bostonglobe.com

STARBUCKS, 2015

In 2015, Starbucks was the undisputed world leader in specialty coffee retail, with over $16 billion in annual revenues (see Table 1). Starbucks had nearly 200,000 employees and over 21,000 Starbucks-branded cafes in 60 countries (about 10,700 of those were owned and operated by Starbucks itself, while 10,600 were operated by licensees and franchisees). In addition, Starbucks owned the Seattle's Best Coffee, Torrefazione Italia, Teavana's Heaven of Tea brands, and more.[1]

The company had grown remarkably fast over its short life and was still exceptionally profitable, with a 23.1% return on assets in 2014 (compared to 6.8% at Peet's Coffee and Tea, 14.0% at Keurig Green Mountain Coffee, 13.4% at McDonald's, and 5.5% at Dunkin' Donuts). However, its growth had not always been smooth; in fact, Starbucks had shuttered about 900 stores during 2008 and 2009. As its domestic market appeared to be approaching saturation, Starbucks began to focus on growing its international locations and diversifying into other product lines where its now-iconic brand could create value.

THE HISTORY OF STARBUCKS

In 1971, three Seattle entrepreneurs, Jerry Baldwin, Zev Siegl, and Gordon Bowher, started selling whole-bean coffee in Seattle's Pike Place Market. They named their store Starbucks, after the first mate in *Moby Dick*. By 1982, the business had grown to five bustling stores, a small roasting facility, and a wholesale business selling coffee to local restaurants. At the same time, Howard Schultz had been working as VP of U.S. operations for Hammarplast, a Swedish housewares company in New York, marketing coffee makers to a number of retailers, including Starbucks. Through selling to Starbucks, Schultz was introduced to the three founders, who recruited him to bring marketing savvy to the loosely run company. Schultz, 29 years old, recently married, and eager to leave New York, moved to Seattle and joined Starbucks as manager of retail sales and marketing.

One year later, Schultz visited Italy for the first time on a buying trip. As he strolled through the piazzas of Milan one evening, he was inspired by a vision. Coffee is an integral part of the romantic culture in Italy; Italians start their day at an espresso bar, and return with their friends later. There were 200,000 coffee bars in Italy, and 1,500 in Milan alone. Schultz believed that given the chance, Americans would pay good money for a premium cup of coffee and a stylish, romantic place to enjoy it. Enthusiastic about his idea, Schultz rushed back to tell the Starbucks owners of his plan for a national chain of Starbucks cafes stylized on the Italian coffee bar. The owners, however, were less enthusiastic, and said that they did not want to be in the restaurant business. Undaunted, Schultz wrote a business plan, videotaped dozens of Italian coffee bar, and began to look for investors. By April 1986, he had opened his first coffee bar, II Giornale (named after the Italian newspaper), where he served

Table 1 Selected Data for Starbucks, McDonald's, and Dunkin' Donuts, 2014

	Starbucks	McDonald's	Dunkin'	Industry Median
Stores	21,100	36,000	11,000	
Annual sales	$16.40B	$27.44B	$748.71M	
Employees	191,000	420,000	1,134	
Market cap	$112.68B	$90.22B	$4.43B	
Gross profit margin	58.84%	44.29%	86.03%	32.38%
Pre-tax profit margin	19.73%	26.90%	32.17%	0.06%
Net profit margin	14.57%	17.34%	23.55%	2.53%
Return on equity	47.08%	32.97%	45.49%	0.09%
Return on assets	23.14%	13.42%	5.50%	0.04%
Days sales outstanding	13.52	16.15	51.22	0.72
Inventory turnover	17.56	234.84	—	1.35
Asset turnover	1.59	0.77	0.23	1.24
Current ratio	1.21	1.52	1.24	1.12
Quick ratio	—	—	—	0.77
Leverage ratio	0.34	1.17	4.93	0.24
Total debt/equity	0.34	1.17	4.94	0.24
Interest coverage	—	13.71	4.78	7.35

Starbucks coffee. Following II Giornale's immediate success, Schultz opened a second coffee bar in Seattle, and then a third in Vancouver, Canada. In 1987, the owners of Starbucks finally agreed to sell to Schultz for $4 million. The II Giornale coffee bars took on the name of Starbucks, and a star was born.

Convinced that Starbucks would one day be in every neighborhood in America, Schultz was intent on growing the company slowly, with a very solid foundation. He hired top executives away from corporations such as PepsiCo, and he was determined that future profits would be well worth early losses. At first, the company's losses almost doubled, to $1.2 million from fiscal 1989 to 1990, as overhead and operating expenses ballooned with the expansion.[2] Starbucks lost money for 3 years running. The stress was hard on Schultz, but he stuck to his conviction not to "sacrifice long-term integrity and values for short-term profit."[3] In 1991, sales shot up 84%, and the company broke into the black. Everywhere Starbucks opened, people flocked to pay upward of $2.00 and more for a cup of coffee. Enthusiastic analysts began to predict that Starbucks would top $1 billion by the year 2000, but Schultz preferred to play the company's early successes down, asserting that it is better to "underpromise and overdeliver." The analysts, it turned out, had *underestimated* Starbucks' success— by 2000, it was taking in over $2 billion in revenues. In the 22 years between 1993 and 2015, Starbucks averaged an annual revenue growth rate of 26% a year.

COMPETITION IN THE SPECIALTY COFFEE SEGMENT

In the United States in 2012, specialty coffee accounted for 37% of all cups of coffee consumed, and for nearly 50% of all coffee revenue. Though the United States was the single largest buyer of unroasted coffee in the world in 2012, emerging markets were exhibiting strong growth, and many experts anticipated that Brazil would surpass the United States in coffee consumption sometime between 2014 and 2016.

Worldwide, independent coffee shops still make up the majority of coffeehouse locations, though prominent chains have emerged in many regions. Starbucks has long held a leading position in its home market, selling over 50% of the specialty coffee purchased in cafes in the United States over the last several decades, and easily dominating local specialty coffee competitors such as Caribou Coffee and Peet's Coffee & Tea. However, in recent years, Both Dunkin' Donuts and McDonald's began targeting Starbucks' growing customer base with coffee offerings based on high-quality, Arabica brews at a lower cost than Starbucks' beverages. With a very large number of existing stores (see Table 1), both competitors posed big threats if they were effective in wooing customers away from Starbucks. Furthermore, Starbucks faced other, more entrenched competition in many of its international markets (see Figure 1 for a breakdown of market share by regional areas).

Caribou Coffee

Founded in 1992, Caribou Coffee operates 470 coffeehouses in about 20 states and in many international markets (particularly in the Middle East and South Korea). Its 2012 sales were $326.5 million, and then the company was taken private in 2013. Its stores are designed to look like mountain lodges and sell only specialty coffee, baked goods, and coffee brewing supplies. However, like Starbucks, the company also sells roasted coffee to grocery stores and has a licensing agreement to make single-serve K-cups for home brewing using Keurig machines.

McDonald's

Founded in 1948 in San Bernardino, California, McDonald's grew to become the world's largest quick-service restaurant. Boasting about 36,000 restaurants in 119 countries and $27.4 billion in sales (see Table 1), McDonald's is probably the best-known restaurant in the world. Though its menu is most famous for hamburgers and fries, in the last 2 decades McDonald's has developed healthier food items in response to social pressure mounted against burger chains. In 1993, a McDonald's licensee, Ann Brown, created the McCafé—a coffeehouse style outlet that would offer high-end coffee beverages similar to Starbucks'. In response to its early success, McDonald's also introduced a line of special coffee drinks called McCafé into its other restaurants.

Dunkin' Donuts

Originally founded as the Open Kettle Doughnut shop in Quincy, Massachusetts, in 1948, founder William Rosenburg changed its name to Dunkin' Donuts in 1950 and began franchising the shops 5 years later. The popular franchise became famous for its wide variety of doughnuts, and expanded to become the world's leading doughnut chain, with 11,000 outlets in about 30 countries. Dunkin' Brands Group also owns Baskin Robbins and Togo Sandwiches, and collectively the chains earned $748.7 million in sales in 2014 (see Table 1). Though it had long offered coffee, the company did not begin offering espresso drinks until 2003.

REDEFINING "A CUP OF JOE"

Starbucks' coffee quality begins with bean procurement. Whereas historically Americans had drunk a commoditylike coffee composed of Arabica beans mixed with less-expensive Robusta filler beans, Starbucks coffee is strictly specialty varietals of Arabica beans, and the company goes to great lengths to ensure that only the highest-quality beans are used. Starbucks' bean procurement standards are demanding, and the company conducts exacting experiments in order to get the

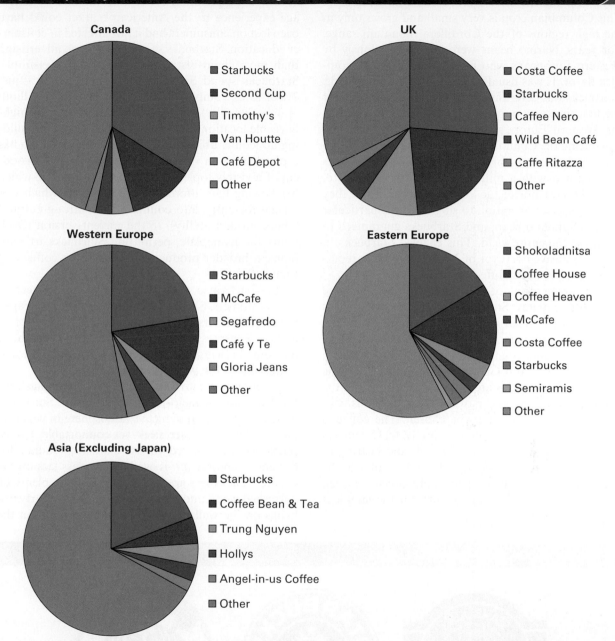

Figure 1 Specialty Coffee Market Shares by Region

Canada
- Starbucks
- Second Cup
- Timothy's
- Van Houtte
- Café Depot
- Other

UK
- Costa Coffee
- Starbucks
- Caffee Nero
- Wild Bean Café
- Caffe Ritazza
- Other

Western Europe
- Starbucks
- McCafe
- Segafredo
- Café y Te
- Gloria Jeans
- Other

Eastern Europe
- Shokoladnitsa
- Coffee House
- Coffee Heaven
- McCafe
- Costa Coffee
- Starbucks
- Semiramis
- Other

Asia (Excluding Japan)
- Starbucks
- Coffee Bean & Tea
- Trung Nguyen
- Hollys
- Angel-in-us Coffee
- Other

Data from 2008 Bernstein Research Report, "Starbucks: Getting Its Buzz Back."

proper balance of flavor, body, and acidity. Brews are subjected to "cupping"—a process similar to wine tasting that involves inhaling the steam ("the strike" and "breaking the crust"), tasting the coffee, and spitting it out ("aspirating" and "expectorating")—to evaluate aroma and taste.

From the company's inception, it has worked on developing relationships with the countries from which it buys coffee beans. Prior to Starbucks' rise, Americans were notorious for buying poor-quality coffee beans—most of the premium coffee beans were bought by Europeans and Japanese. In 1992, however,

Starbucks set a new precedent by outbidding European buyers for the exclusive Narino Supremo Bean crop. This Columbian crop is very small and grows only in the high regions of the Cordillera mountain range. For years, Narino beans were guarded zealously by Western Europeans who prized their colorful, complex flavor. It was usually used for upgrading blends. Starbucks was determined to make them available for the first time as a pure varietal. This required breaking Western Europe's monopoly over the beans by convincing the Columbian growers that it intended to use "the best beans for a higher purpose." Starbucks collaborated with a mill in the tiny town of Pasto, located on the side of the Volcano Galero. There they set up a special operation to single out the particular Narino Supremo bean, and Starbucks guaranteed to purchase the entire yield. This enabled Starbucks to be the exclusive purveyor of Narino Supremo, reputedly one of the best coffees in the world.

Procurement is not the only area where extreme care differentiates Starbucks' product: roasting is close to an art form at Starbucks. Unlike most specialty coffee retailers, Starbucks roasts its own beans in its private roasting facilities in California, Nevada, Pennsylvania, South Carolina, Washington, and the Netherlands. Roasters are promoted from within the company and trained for over a year, and it is considered quite an honor to be chosen. The coffee is roasted in a powerful, gas oven for 12 to 15 minutes while roasters use their sight, smell, and hearing to judge when beans are perfectly done. The color of the beans is even tested in an Agtron blood-cell analyzer, with the whole batch being discarded if the sample is not deemed perfect.

Despite the attention to quality, Starbucks' effort at bringing a premium coffee and Italian-style beverage experience to the American market could have been lost on consumers had it not invested in consumer education. Starbucks spends far less on advertising than most chain restaurants (in 2014, for example, Starbucks spend $315 million on advertising—just 2% of sales, compared to McDonald's' $808 million, or 3% of its sales).[4] Instead, it invests in securing highly visible locations, innovating in its menu, and building an iconic, ubiquitous brand. Starbucks' logo has evolved from an original, 16th-century Norse woodcut of a visibly topless mermaid to a version in which her flowing hair afforded more modesty (which was crucial for entry into countries with strong cultural taboos around nudity), to the current version which omits the nameplate, permitting Starbucks to symbolize a broader product range than just coffee (see Figure 2).

Starbucks also seeks to develop a close connection with customers. Starbucks employees are encouraged to help customers make decisions about beans, grind, and coffee/espresso machines and instruct customers on home brewing. The objective is to create a long-term relationship with customers.

In order to create American coffee enthusiasts with the dedication of their Italian counterparts, Starbucks needed to provide a seductive atmosphere in which to imbibe. The stores are sleek yet comfortable. Coffee preparers are referred to as "baristas," Italian for bartender, and *biscotti* is available in glass jars on the counter. The stores are well lighted, feature plenty of burnished wood and brass, and sophisticated artwork hangs on the walls. Jazz or opera plays softly in the

Figure 2 Evolution of the Starbucks Logo

1971–1987

1992–2011

2011–Present

background. According to Schultz, "We're not just selling a cup of coffee, we are providing an experience."

Many of the stores offer light lunch fare including sandwiches and salads, and an assortment of pastries, bottled waters, and juices. Starbucks also launched a line of packaged and prepared teas in 1995 in response to growing demand for teahouses and packaged tea. Tea is a highly profitable beverage for restaurants, costing only 2 to 4 cents per cup to produce.

PAMPERING EMPLOYEES

Schultz believes that happy employees are the key to competitiveness and growth. He states, "We can't achieve our strategic objectives without a work force of people who are immersed in the same commitment as management. Our only sustainable advantage is the quality of our work force. We're building a national retail company by creating pride in—and stake in—the outcome of our labor."[5] Starbucks has accomplished this through an empowering corporate culture, exceptional employee benefits, and employee stock ownership programs. While Starbucks enforces almost fanatical standards about coffee quality and service, the culture at Starbucks toward employees is laid back and supportive. Employees are empowered to make decisions without constant referral to management, and are encouraged to think of themselves as partners in the business. Starbucks wants employees to use their best judgment in making decisions and will stand behind them. This is reinforced through generous compensation and benefits packages.

Starbucks offers an industry-leading benefits package to both part-time and full-time employees. The package includes medical, dental, vision, and short-term disability insurance, as well as paid vacation, paid holidays, mental health/chemical dependency benefits, an employee assistance program, a 401 (k) savings plan, and a stock option plan. They also offer career counseling and product discounts. The decision to offer benefits even to part-time employees garnered the firm a great deal of attention in the press. It was difficult to get companies to insure Starbucks, because they did not understand why Starbucks would want to cover part-timers. However, while many companies scrimp on these essentials, Schultz believes that without these benefits, people do not feel financially or spiritually tied to their jobs. The stock options and the complete benefits package increase employee loyalty and encourage attentive service to the customer. Bradley Honeycutt (director of compensation and benefits) also points out that "part-timers are on the front line with our customers. If we treat them right, we feel they will treat [the customers] well."[6]

Employee turnover is also discouraged by Starbucks' stock option plan (known as the Bean Stock Plan). Implemented in August 1991, the plan made Starbucks the first company to offer stock options unilaterally to all employees, including part-time workers. After one year, employees may join a 401 (k) plan. There is a vesting period of 5 years; it starts 1 year after the option is granted, then vests the employee at 20% every year. In addition, every employee receives a new stock option award each year, and a new vesting period begins. This plan required the then privately-held Starbucks to get an exemption from the Security Exchange Commission, because any company with more than 500 shareholders must report its financial performance publicly—a costly process that reveals valuable information to competitors.

The option plan did not go uncontested by the venture capitalists and shareholders on the board. Craig Foley, a director and managing partner of Chancellor Capital Management Inc. (and the largest shareholder before the public offering) says, "Increasing the shareholders substantially dilutes our interest. We take that very seriously." In the end they were won over by a study conducted by Orin Smith that revealed the positive relationship between employee ownership and productivity rates, and a scenario analysis of how many employees would be vested. Foley conceded that the company's culture was a major component of its profitability. "The grants are tied to overachieving. If you just come to work and do your job, that isn't as attractive as if you beat the numbers." In 2013, Starbucks paid over $230 million in equity awards.

Training programs are extensive at Starbucks. Each employee takes at least 24 hours' worth of classes, covering everything from coffee history to a 7-hour workshop called Brewing the Perfect Cup at Home. Starbucks employees even undergo rigorous training about how to respond to cranky customers through the "Latte Method" of responding to unpleasant situations: "We Listen to the customer, Acknowledge their complaint, Take action by solving the problem, Thank them, and then Explain why the problem occurred."[7] Store managers (who have gone through facilitation workshops and are certified by the company as trainers) teach the classes. The classes emphasize the empowering culture at Starbucks and teach the employees to make decisions that will enhance customer satisfaction without requiring manager authorization. For example, if a customer comes into the store complaining about a how their beans were ground, the employee is authorized to replace them on the spot. While most restaurants use on-the-job training, Starbucks holds bar classes where employees practice taking orders and preparing beverages in a company training room. This allows employees to hone their skills in a low-stress environment, and also protects Starbucks' quality image by allowing only experienced baristas to serve customers.

Schultz is also known for his sensitivity to the well-being of employees. Once, when an employee had come to tell Schultz that he had AIDS, Schultz reassured him that he could work as long as he wanted to, and when he left Starbucks would continue to cover his insurance. After the employee left the room, Schultz sat down and wept. Schultz attributes his concern for his employees to his memories of his father. According to Schultz, his father "struggled a great deal and never made more than $20,000 a year, and his work was never valued, emotionally or physically, by his employer . . . This was an injustice . . . I want our employees to know we value them."

In 1995, Starbucks demonstrated that its concern for employee welfare extended beyond U.S. borders. After a human-rights group leafleted the stores, complaining that Guatemalan coffee pickers received less than $3 a day, Starbucks became the first agricultural commodity importer to implement a code for minimal working conditions and pay for foreign subcontractors. The company's guidelines called for overseas suppliers to pay wages and benefits that "address the basic needs of workers and their families" and to allow child labor only when it does not interrupt required education. This move set a precedent for other importers of agricultural commodities and received high praise from global human-rights activists.

In 2000, Schulz transitioned to being the chairman and chief global strategist, but continued to stay very actively involved in the company's operations and taking a strong stance on ethical business. Working in combination with Conservation International, Starbucks introduced new, ethical coffee-sourcing guidelines in 2001, and began actively promoting its Coffee and Farmer Equity (CAFE) Practices that provide measurable standards for such factors as economic transparency, fair and humane working conditions, and water and energy conservation.

GROWTH, DIVERSIFICATION, AND INTERNATIONAL EXPANSION

In Starbucks' early years, Schultz had professed a strict, slow-growth policy. While other coffeehouses or espresso bars were being franchised, Starbucks owned all of its stores outright with the exception of key locations where the only way in was through a license agreement (e.g., airports, stadiums). Hundreds of willing investors would call every day, but Schultz turned them all down, arguing that it was important to the company's integrity to keep all stores company owned. Furthermore, in each market that Starbucks entered, imitators would rapidly emerge. Thus, rather than creating outposts in all the potential markets as soon as possible, Starbucks went into a market and completely dominated it before setting its sights further abroad. Despite this, the company was consistently one of the fastest-growing companies in the United States (see Figure 3). Over time, Starbucks loosened its licensing policy and began accelerating the rate at which it permitted licensed stores. Licensing was particularly important for many international markets in which having a foreign partner reduced both the difficulty and risk of entry (see Figure 1).

The combination of the high-quality products and services, well-managed branding, and a reputation for social responsibility made the company attractive to both consumers and investors. By 2007, the company had over 15,000 stores. However, a combination of competition, the recession, and Starbucks' own saturation of many markets began to spell trouble for the company. Sales declined for the first time ever in 2009. From 2007 to 2010, many Wall Street analysts were whispering that the company's best days were behind it.[8] Feeling that the company was in

Figure 3 Starbucks Growth in Stores and Revenues, 1993–2014

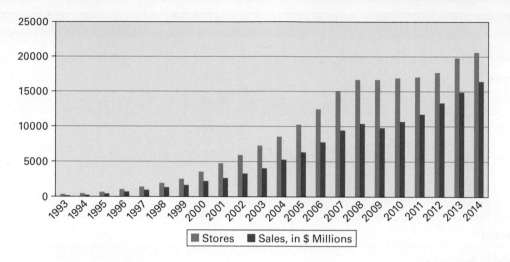

Stores ■   Sales, in $ Millions ■

crisis, Schultz decided to return to the role of chief executive officer in 2008, noting "This has been my life's work, as opposed to a job. I didn't come back to save the company–I hate that description–I came back to rekindle the emotion that built it." Though Schultz was advised to lower prices and cut benefits to employees, he opted instead to invest in a 2-year transformation of Starbucks that he called "the company's holistic restoration."[9] Although Starbucks closed about 900 company-operated stores in 2009–2010, Schultz focused most of his effort on reinvigorating what he saw as the heart of the company—its commitment to exceptional service and quality. He invested in developing new product lines and line extensions, and he even closed all U.S. stores for 3 hours on the evening of February 26, 2010, to retrain about 135,000 in-store employees. His gambles paid off, and the company began to again climb to new sales and profitability highs. In 2014, Starbucks announced that all employees would get significant pay raises, and Schultz unveiled an even more ambitious "College Achievement Plan" wherein employees who work more than 20 hours a week can also work toward a bachelor's degree through an online program from Arizona State University.[10]

In addition to expanding its menu selection to include more food products and drink options, Starbucks has begun diversifying in other ways. It now offers a range of cafe formats (including expanding the number of drive-through service locations),

and, in 2009, Starbucks introduced single-serve coffee packets targeted at the home brewing, office, and hotel coffee markets. The single-serve packs are designed to be brewed in Green Mountain Coffee's Keurig brewers, and are distributed by Green Mountain. In 2012, Starbucks acquired Bay Bread and its La Boulange bakery brand, marking its entry into the French-style bakery market. It also acquired Evolution Fresh, a fruit and vegetable juice beverage company.

By 2015, Starbucks had also expanded well beyond its U.S. origins. The company's international presence had expanded from a single store opened in Japan in 1996 to a well-diversified presence around the world by 2015 (see Table 2). Recognizing that the U.S. market was maturing, Schultz acknowledged that most of the future growth would come from emerging markets. In 2015, Schultz was focusing most of his attention on Brazil, China, India, and Vietnam.

Perhaps more importantly, Schultz no longer thinks of Starbucks as just a coffee company. As he explains, the next great challenge is to deepen the company's involvement in health and wellness. In late 2014 and early 2015, Schultz decided to leverage the company's influence in the world by beginning to speak out on such issues as gay marriage (Schultz supports it), gun carrying laws (Starbucks requests that people not carry guns into Starbucks even in those states that would otherwise permit it), and treatment of veterans (in March 2014, Schultz committed $30 million of his own money to posttraumatic stress programs and

Table 2 Starbucks Stores Open as of 2014 by Geographical Area

	Company-Operated Stores	Licensed Stores
Americas:		
United States	7049	4408
Canada	940	397
Brazil	70	
Puerto Rico	19	
Mexico		403
Other		207
Total Americas	**8078**	**5415**
Europe/Middle East/Africa		
United Kingdom	522	242
Germany	157	
France	72	
Switzerland	52	
Austria	16	
Netherlands	7	
Turkey		193
United Arab Emirates		107
Spain		82
Kuwait		69
Saudi Arabia		62
Russia		65
Other		323
Total EMEA	**826**	**1143**
China/Asia Pacific		
China	614	403
Thailand	174	
Singapore	94	

	Company-Operated Stores	Licensed Stores
Japan		1000
South Korea		559
Taiwan		297
Philippines		216
Other		525
Total China/Asia Pacific	**882**	**3000**
Totals Across Regions	**10143**	**9624**

other initiatives to help veterans, and vowed to hire 10,000 veterans and military spouses by 2018).

The company drew some ire in taking on issues that bear little relationship to its core activities. Critics admonished that such initiatives risked alienating some consumers and investors, and creating elevated expectations that the company might not always be able to meet. As Schultz noted, "I can tell you the organization is not thrilled when I walk into a room and say we're now going to take on veterans [issues]." But he adds, "The size and the scale of the company and the platform that we have allows us, I think, to project a voice into the debate, and hopefully that's for good ... We are leading [Starbucks] to try to redefine the role and responsibility of a public company."[11]

NOTES

1. Data compiled from Starbucks SEC filings, 1996–2015, and Hoovers, May, 2015. Interviews conducted with Susan Mecklenberg, Director of Environmental Affairs at Starbucks, and Troy Alstead, Director of International Planning and Finance at Starbucks.
2. M. Rothman, "Into the Black," *Inc.*, January 1993. www.inc.com.
3. I. Abramovitch, "Miracles of Marketing: How to Reinvent Your Product," *Success Magazine*, April 1993. www.success.com.
4. M. Morrison, "Starbucks: Forging a Moment of Connection," *Advertising Age* 82 (40) (2011): 30; M. Morrison, "Bang for Its Starbucks: Hits No. 3 Despite Limited Spend," *Advertising Age* 82 (18) (2011): 1–100.
5. M. Rothman, "Into the Black."
6. S. Roberts, "Working Part Time Pays Off at Starbucks Coffee," *Business Insurance*, March 27, 1995. www.businessinsurance.com.
7. C. Duhigg, *The Power of Habit: Why We Do What We Do in Life and in Business*. New York: Random House, 2012.
8. J. Gertner, "The World's 50 Most Innovative Companies: Starbucks–For Infusing a Steady Stream of New Ideas to Revive Its Business," *Fast Company*, 163 (2012): 112–149.
9. J. H. Ostdick, "Rekindling the Heart & Soul of Starbucks," *Success Magazine*, 2012, March, www.success.com.
10. M. Rothman, "Into the Black"; D. Ritter, "3 Reasons It's Hard to Hate Starbucks," *USA Today*, July 6, 1993. www.usatoday.com.
11. D. Ritter, "3 Reasons It's Hard to Hate Starbucks"; A. Gonzalez, "Starbucks as Citizen: Schultz Acts Boldly on Social, Political Issues," *Seattle Times*, March 15, 2015. .www.seattletimes.com.

26

DELL INC.—GOING PRIVATE

▼INTRODUCTION

The rise of Dell Inc. is the stuff of business legend. Founded by Michael Dell in 1984, when he was still an undergraduate at the University of Texas, Dell grew to become the largest personal computer manufacturer in the world. At its peak in 2005, the company accounted for 16.8% of all PC shipments globally (see Figure 1). The company was also phenomenally profitable. Between the mid-1990s and 2007, Dell's average return on invested capital (ROIC) was a staggering 48.3%, making it by far the best-performing enterprise in the industry. From 2007 onward, however, Dell faced increasing headwinds. By 2013, its global market share had fallen to 11.6%, putting it behind Hewlett Packard and Lenovo. The company's financial situation had also deteriorated. In 2011, Dell generated net income of $3.5 billion on revenues of $62 billion. In 2012, net income fell to $2.4 billion, revenues declined to $56.9 billion, and Dell's ROIC had contracted to 14.9%, less than half of where it was in the mid-2000s. The company's stock price closed out 2012 at $10 a share, down from an all-time high of $42 at the end of 2004.

Underlying the decline in Dell's performance was a seismic shift in the PC industry. After growing robustly for 2 decades, PC sales plateaued in 2010–2012, and then fell significantly in 2013 (see Figure 2). From 2010 onward, consumer spending migrated away from PCs toward smartphones and tablets (see Figure 3). To compound matters, low-cost producers such as Lenovo of

China and Acer of Taiwan were taking business from Dell in the market for Windows PCs. At the high end of the market, a resurgent Apple was capturing an increasing share of desktop and laptop computers with its stylishly designed iMac offerings. By late 2014, Apple's share of global PC shipments had risen to over 6%, while its share of the U.S. market stood at a record 13.4%.[1]

Dell was also struggling in the corporate market, where companies like IBM and Hewlett Packard (HP) were gaining business by bundling computer hardware with value-added information technology (IT) service offerings. IBM and HP would offer hardware, including PCs and servers at cost, and make money from multi-year service contracts that could encompass everything from basic maintenance to premium IT consulting services. In 2008, HP strengthened its position by acquiring for $13.9 billion the IT consulting company, Electronic Data Systems. Dell lacked a big consulting arm, which put the company at a clear disadvantage. To try to rectify this, after 22 years with no acquisitions, in 2007 Dell started to acquire small IT service companies.[2] In 2009, Dell made its largest acquisition ever, purchasing Perot Systems for $3.9 billion.[3] Perot Systems was a provider of information technology services with a strong position in the market for electronic health-care information. Michael Dell's strategy was clear: to move the company upstream into higher value-added IT consulting services. This strategy, however, could take years to execute. Investors were not impressed, focusing instead on Dell's inability to offer attractive smartphones and tablets, and the increasing commoditization of the company's PC business. By

Figure 1 Global Market Share of PC Manufacturers, 2004–2014 (%)

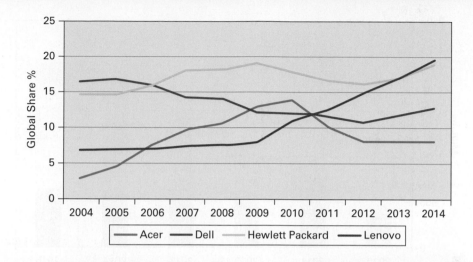

Figure 2 PC Unit Shipments Globally, 1996–2014 (Millions)

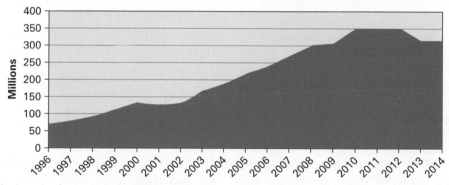

Source: Constructed by the author from multiple Gartner Press Reports.

2012, Dell was feeling the heat from the slowdown in global PC sales. Revenues and profits were down, the stock price was slumping, and investors were grumbling about the company's inability to decouple itself from the commodity PC business. Michael Dell's response was to propose to take the company private.

ESTABLISHMENT OF DELL

In 1983, a young Michael Dell was conducting a lucrative business selling upgraded PCs out of his dormitory room at the University of Texas.[4] This wasn't Dell's first business. Like many entrepreneurs, he started early. When he was 12, he set up a business selling stamps that he and his friends had collected. He quickly made $2,000. At 16, he got a summer job selling newspaper subscriptions for the *Houston Post*. Not satisfied with calling people at random, he developed a methodology for identifying who was most likely to pay for a new subscription using publically available data on mortgage applications. He targeted those people, creating personalized letters and offering subscriptions. His income that year was $18,000—not bad for a high school student in 1981. When he got his driver's license, he bought a BMW.[5]

Figure 3 Global Shipments of Digital Devices 2010–2015 (millions)

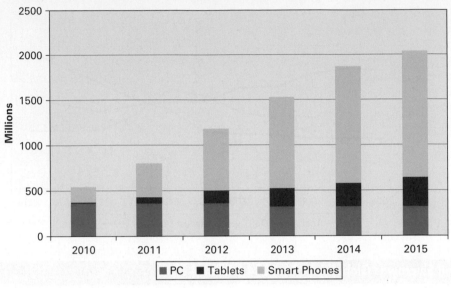

Source: Constructed by the author from multiple Gartner and IDC Press Reports.

Computers, however, were Dell's passion. Dell's first was an Apple II. Much to the horror of his parents, as soon as he got his brand-new machine, he took it apart to see how it was made. When the IBM PC was introduced in 1981, he bought one. He opened it up, added all of the enhancements he could, and sold it for a tidy profit. And so a business was born. Dell quickly noticed an interesting fact: while an IBM PC sold for about $3,000, the components were made by other companies and could be purchased off the shelf for around $700. So what accounted for the other $2,300? Sales and marketing expenses, IBM's profit margin, and the markup taken by retailers. To Dell, this screamed profit opportunity. He realized that by selling direct—something that he was already doing—he could eliminate the retailer's markup, price lower, and still make a nice profit.

By early 1984, Dell was selling $50,000 to $80,000 a month worth of upgraded PCs and add-on components to people in the Austin area. In May of that year, he incorporated the rapidly growing business as Dell Computer Corporation. He soon dropped out of school to concentrate full time on building the business. As he described it later, the original facility was a 1,000-square-foot office space in Austin. Dell's manufacturing "consisted of three guys with screwdrivers sitting at 6-foot tables upgrading machine."

THE GROWTH YEARS

Dell was riding a wave of demand for PCs. The market had transitioned from an embryonic one and was now experiencing hypergrowth. Penetration into the business and consumer segments was proceeding rapidly. By selling direct, eliminating middlemen, and using the savings to price aggressively, Dell was able to ramp up sales. By late 1986, the company was doing $60 million in annualized sales. In 1988, Dell went public. Michael Dell was just 23. The 1990s, however, were the beginning of a magic decade for the company. In 1990, Dell was ranked 25th in the world among computer companies. By 1999, it was the largest PC maker in the United States, and the second largest globally. Moreover, 17 out of the top 25 computer companies in 1990 no longer existed by 1999. Dell had ridden to the top of a highly dynamic and turbulent industry, while many more venerable enterprises had failed. IBM, the dominant computer enterprise of the 1970s and 1980s, had a near-death experience in the early 1990s, recording larger losses than any other company in history, while Dell went from strength to strength.

One of Dell's greatest strengths was the fact that it built to order. It did not have to stuff a channel with inventory. It did not have to make educated guesses about demand. It did not have to worry that it might have built too few of a certain model, and too many of another. It built only what it had already sold.

The rocket fuel that propelled Dell to the top of the industry was the Internet. The development of hypertext transfer protocol by Tim Berners-Lee gave birth to the World Wide Web. The subsequent introduction of Web browsers democratized the Internet, transforming it from a haven for computer nerds into a mainstream communications network. This enabled Dell to start direct selling over the Internet beginning in June 1994. By 2010, more than 85% of Dell's computers were sold online. According to Michael Dell: "As I saw it, the Internet offered a logical extension of the direct (selling) model, creating even stronger relationships with our customers. The Internet would augment conventional telephone, fax, and face-to-face encounters, and give our customers the information they wanted faster, cheaper, and more efficiently." Customers could now build their own machine online, add the mix of components that best suited them, put in their credit card information, and then hit the purchase button. In effect, the Internet allowed Dell to almost perfectly segment the market, creating value for customers in the process.

Moreover, Dell could transfer the real-time order flow at lightning speed via the Internet to its suppliers. This information allowed the players in Dell's globally dispersed supply chain to optimize their production and shipping schedules so that parts arrived at one of Dell's assembly plants just in time. By the late 1990s, Dell was turning over its inventory in a matter of days, reducing its working capital requirements to a minimum.

Internet-based customer ordering and procurement systems also allowed Dell to synchronize demand and supply to an extent that its rivals could not. For example, if Dell found out that it was running out of a particular component—say 17-inch monitors from Panasonic—it could manipulate demand by offering a 19-inch model at a lower price until Panasonic delivered more 17-inch monitors. By taking steps to fine-tune the balance between demand and supply, Dell could meet customers' expectations and maintain its

differential advantage. Moreover, balancing supply and demand allowed the company to minimize excess and obsolete inventory. By the early 2000s, Dell was writing off between 0.05 and 0.1% of total material costs as excess or obsolete inventory. Its competitors were writing off between 2 and 3%, which gave Dell a significant cost advantage.

By the late 1990s, Dell was starting to work some financial magic. It could take an order over the Internet, build the machine, and ship it to customers in a matter of days. The customer was billed when the machine shipped. Its suppliers, however, were paid net 30 days. The implication: Dell could use money destined for its suppliers to finance its working capital requirements, including its inventory. This reduced the need for outside capital; you don't need to borrow capital from a bank, or from investors, when you can borrow at a zero interest rate from your own suppliers.

This strategy had interesting implications for a key measure of profitability—return on invested capital (ROIC), which is defined as net profit over the capital on the enterprise's balance sheet. If you are using other people's capital, at zero cost, to finance your inventory, you can pair down the amount of working capital on your balance sheet. This reduces the denominator for ROIC, which boosts the profitability of the enterprise. By the late 1990s, Dell was earning an ROIC in the 40% range, a remarkable level of profitability by any measure. Moreover, the high ROIC was not a short-term phenomenon. Dell continued to earn similar returns on its invested capital through until 2007. Equally impressive, Dell grew both sales and earnings per share at double-digit rates for most of this time period as it surged to the top of the industry.

Dell was by no means the only company that pursued a direct-selling strategy—Gateway was another—but it was the first, and it was the best at doing it. Dell was operationally efficient. Michael Dell avoided founder's disease, a well-known phenomenon that occurs when entrepreneurs sink the businesses they created by failing to professionalize management and delegate responsibility. Dell hired skilled operators and learned how to delegate to them. The company built core skills in managing the direct-selling model and coordinating a globally dispersed supply chain.

Dell's main rivals during the period of rapid market growth included Compaq, IBM, Hewlett Packard, Packard Bell, and Toshiba. Issues arising from channel conflict made it hard for these companies to imitate

Dell's model. All of these companies had already committed to selling through a channel, and fully embracing a direct-sell model might well have led to a loss of sell-through via their existing channel.

THE GLOBAL PC INDUSTRY

The global PC industry is very competitive.[6] At the end of 2014, Lenovo was market leader with a global share of 19.4%, followed by Hewlett Packard with 18.8%, and Dell Inc. with 12.7%. Apple had 6% of the market, although in the United States its share was 13.4% (among U.S. consumers, Apple's market share is thought to be much higher, coming in at over 30%).

There was some consolidation in the industry during the 2000s. Hewlett Packard acquired the large PC vendor Compaq in 2002. Lenovo, the fast-growing Chinese firm, acquired IBM's ThinkPad consumer PC business in 2005. In 2014, Lenovo entered into a deal to buy part of IBM's server business. Meanwhile, in late 2014, HP announced plans to split into two companies, HP Inc. and HP Enterprise. HP Inc. would sell PCs and printers, while HP Enterprise would focus on providing software and services to corporations.

A long tail of small companies accounts for some 35% of the global market. Some of these companies focus on local markets and make unbranded "white box" computers. The long tail of small companies reflects relatively low start-up costs for entering the business. The standard architecture of the PC means that key components such as an Intel compatible microprocessor, a Windows operating system, memory chips, a hard drive, and other similar hardware can be purchased on the open market. Assembly is easy, requiring little capital equipment or technical skills, and economies of scale in production are moderate. Although small entrants lack the brand-name recognition and distribution reach of the market-share leaders, they survive in the industry by pricing their machines a few hundred dollars below market leaders and capturing the demand of price-sensitive consumers. This puts pressure on brand-name companies and the prices they can charge.

Most buyers view the product offerings of different branded companies as very close substitutes for each other, so competition between them often defaults to price. Due to a combination of competition and technological improvements, the average selling price of a PC fell from around $1,700 in 1999 to under $750 by 2010. The downward pressure on prices makes it hard for PC companies to achieve large gross margins and results in lower profitability. The exception is Apple, which has successfully differentiated its iMac offerings by design, operating system software, and brand.

Slowing demand growth in many developed nations, including the world's largest market, the United States, where the market is now mature and demand is limited to replacement demand, has intensified the downward pressure on prices. There is also a pronounced cyclical aspect to demand from businesses. Demand growth was just 4% in 2009, for example, due to a global recession, but it jumped to 14% in 2010 as the economy recovered. The rise of powerful substitutes in the form of tablets and smartphones has depressed demand since 2010 (see Figures 2 and 3).

Personal computer companies have long had to deal with two very powerful suppliers—Microsoft, which supplies the industry-standard operating system, Windows, and Intel, the supplier of the industry-standard microprocessor. Microsoft and Intel have been able to charge relatively high prices for their products, which has raised input costs for PC manufacturers and reduced their profitability. In late 2012, Microsoft introduced a new version of its Windows operating system, Windows 8. Windows 8 featured a different user interface that the one consumers had grown used to. It was not well received by many consumers and businesses. Some industry observers believe that the poor reception for Windows 8 hurt demand for PCs, as many people decided not to upgrade, instead sticking with Windows 7.

From the early 1990s onward, servers became an increasingly important part of the PC business. Servers are specialized PCs that sit at the heart of corporate networks and are used to store data and provide applications such as e-mail to a network of connected PCs. Client-server architecture was the dominant computing paradigm in enterprises both large and small for most of the 1990s through to the present day. By 2014, severs were accounting for about $50 billion in annual sales industrywide. The three largest server vendors were HP, IBM, and Dell, which had 27%, 18.5%, and 17.7% of this market, respectively, in the third quarter of 2014. Cisco was fourth in the market, with a 6.2% share.[7]

DELL'S GLOBAL OPERATIONS

The PC market is global, and Dell has been expanding its presence outside of the United States since the early 1990s. By 2010, over 40% of Dell's revenue was generated outside of the United States. Dell does not alter its business model from country to country—it uses the same direct-selling, supply-chain model that worked so well in the United States.

Dell's basic approach to global expansion has been to serve foreign markets from a handful of regional manufacturing facilities, each established as a wholly-owned subsidiary. To support its global business, it operates three final-assembly facilities in the United States, and one each in Brazil (serving South America), Poland (serving Europe), Malaysia (serving Southeast Asia), China (serving China), and India. Each plant is large enough to attain significant economies of scale. When demand in a region gets large enough, Dell considers opening a second plant—thus its three plants in the United States to serve North America, and its three in Asia.

Each plant uses exactly the same supply-chain management processes that have made Dell famously efficient. Taking advantage of its supply-chain management software, Dell schedules production of every line in every factory around the world every 2 hours. Every factory is run with no more than a few hours of inventory on hand, including work in progress. To serve Dell's global factories, many of Dell's largest suppliers have also located their facilities close to Dell's manufacturing plants so that they can better meet the company's demands for just-in-time inventory.

Dell has set up customer service centers in each region to handle phone and online orders and provide technical assistance. In general, each center serves an entire region, which Dell has found to be more efficient than locating a customer service center in each country where the company does business. Dell has experimented with outsourcing some of its customer service functions for English-language customers to call centers in India. Although the move helped the

company lower costs, it also led to dissatisfaction from customers, particularly in the United States, who could not always follow the directions given over the phone from someone with a thick, regional accent. Subsequently, Dell moved its call centers for English-language businesses back to the United States and the United Kingdom. Dell continues to invest in Indian call centers for its retail customers.

GOING PRIVATE

Michael Dell had stepped down as CEO in March 2004 to devote more time to his family's charitable foundation and personal investments. He passed the reins to Kevin Rollins, who had been chief operating officer, and whom Michael Dell credited with transforming Dell into an efficient manufacturer. Dell remained on as chairman. In January 2007, Rollins resigned and Dell returned as CEO.

The catalyst for Rollins's resignation was Dell's declining market share in the PC industry (see Figure 1). After 10 years of strong performance, in 2006, Dell lost its leadership position to HP, and the company's growth rate fell below that of the industry. A compounding factor was that, also in 2006, the Securities and Exchange Commission (SEC) announced that it was investigating Dell for possible accounting regularities. Rollins's resignation was seen by many as an attempt to deflect attention away from Michael Dell. According to the SEC, Dell received some $6 billion in "exclusivity payments" from Intel to use only Intel microprocessors. The SEC asserted that these payments, which were not disclosed to investors, had a material impact on Dell's performance between 2001 and 2005, allowing the company to meet or exceed analysts' earnings expectations. When the payments from Intel were cut, this negatively impacted Dell's profitability, but again the company did not disclose the reason for falling profits to investors. In 2010, Dell Inc. agreed to pay a $100-million penalty to settle the charges. Dell and Rollins both paid a $4-million fine.[8]

As he stepped back into the CEO position, Michael Dell was confronted with a number of problems, which only intensified over the next 6 years. Dell's rivals had become more efficient, eroding the cost advantage that Dell once enjoyed. Moreover, the growth rate in the PC market was slowing. The market plateaued in 2010–2012, and in 2013 it shrank (Figure 2). This triggered intense price competition. To compound matters, the rise of smartphones and tablets left traditional PC companies like Dell out in the cold (see Figure 3). Dell did enter both the smartphone and tablet markets. A mobility group was established within Dell, and Ron Garriques, who joined Dell from Motorola, was appointed to lead the unit. The division released a number of products, but they were not well received.[9] A "pocket tablet" running Android with a 5-inch screen and dubbed "The Streak" was released in August 2010. It was a year behind schedule and ran on an old version of Android. Streak it did not. It really had no chance against the runaway success of Apple's iPad, which had been released in January of that year. The mobile division also released a smartphone that used the Windows Phone 7 operating system. The phone had battery and WiFi problems. It did not sell well. In November 2010, Garriques resigned from the company, and Dell shut its mobile division down, rolling its mobile products into the broader business. The company continued to make Android smartphones until 2012, when it pulled out of the business, citing low sales and large investment requirements.

Michael Dell also pushed the company into the information technology services business. The service business encompasses a number of different product offerings including installing and maintaining IT hardware, installing and customizing software applications such ERP and database offerings, application development, business process outsourcing, and business process analysis. Steve Shuckenbrock was hired from the IT consulting services company EDS to lead the initiative. His task was to establish Dell as a viable competitor to IBM and HP. Both companies were pursuing a razor-and-blade strategy, pricing commoditized hardware at close to cost and then making money from multiyear service contracts. Dell aimed to do the same.

To build its services business, Dell made some 20 acquisitions for a total of $13 billion. These included the 2009 acquisition of Perot Systems for $3.9 billion, the largest in the company's history. The price that Dell paid for Perot Systems represented a 68% premium over the company's prior market value. Commenting on the acquisition binge, Dell noted: "At the scale of Dell, the only way you are going to move the needle quicker was acquisitions."[10] By the financial year ending February 1, 2013, "services" was

a $12-billion revenue business at Dell. In the same year, Dell made $45 billion in revenues from hardware products (mostly PCs and servers). Dell's net income in 2013 was $2.37 billion, down from $3.49 billion a year earlier. While services were growing the top line, this was not yet translating into bottom-line growth. Investors were clearly not satisfied with the lack of progress at Dell. The company's stock price, which had been trading at around $25 when Dell reassumed the CEO role in early 2007, was trading below $10 a share in mid-2012. It was against this background that, in February 2013, Dell announced that he had partnered with the private equity fund, Silver Lake, to take Dell private in a $25-billion deal.

Dell first contemplated taking his company private in mid-2012, after a conversation with Southeastern Asset Management, the company's second-biggest shareholder. Southern Asset Management was underwater on its investment in Dell and saw little upside. However, the investment company said that it would be willing to back an effort to take the company private if the price were right. This started a chain of events that culminated with Michael Dell and partners from Silver Lake and another investment firm, Kohlberg Kravis and Roberts (KKR), talking about a possible private buyout of Dell.

At this point, Dell informed the board of directors about his conversations. The board formed a special committee, from which Dell was excluded, to consider the idea along with other options. Reportedly these other options included (1) splitting Dell up into a PC business and a services business; (2) making more "transformative" acquisitions; (3) increasing the dividend payout and stock buybacks to boost the share price; and (4) selling Dell to a "strategic buyer." The board then told Dell that it was open to considering a transaction that would take Dell private.

By October 2012, KKR had submitted bids for Dell at around $12 a share. Dell had pledged that he would participate with whichever sponsor was willing to pay the highest price. At the time, the stock price was around $10 a share. Then the November earnings report came out, earnings came in below management forecasts, and the stock price fell below $9 a share. At this point KKR, citing structural weakness in the PC business, withdrew from the bidding process.

On December 6, 2012, the CFO provided updates on Dell's business, and gave the board of directors projections through 2016. He told the board that fully implementing the plan to shift from PCs to a service business would take another 3 to 5 years. It would also require more capital investments. This was a big concern given that cash flows from the PC business were declining. The board asked another private-equity firm, Texas Pacific Group, if it was interested in bidding for Dell, but the company declined.

By early February 2013, the board had come to the conclusion that a private buyout of Dell was probably the best option. With rumors of a buyout starting to appear in the media, the board needed to make a statement. They agreed that a buyout would inject needed capital into the company, and take it out of the glare of the public markets, enabling management to make long-term investments that could in the short run depress earnings. Convinced that there would be no other bidders, the board gave Michael Dell and Silver Lake the go ahead to make a formal offer to take Dell Inc. private. Dell recused himself from all board discussions and from voting on any transaction.

On February 5, the board announced that it had reached an agreement with Silver Lake and Michael Dell to take the company private. Shareholders would now have to vote on the deal. Under the terms of the agreement, Dell stockholders were to receive $13.65 in cash for every share of Dell they held—a transaction that valued the company at $24.4 billion.[11] The offer price represented a premium of 25% over the closing share price of $10.88 on January 11, the last day before rumors of a possible private-equity buyout started to appear in the media, and a premium of 37% over the average closing share price during the previous 90 calendar days ending on January 11, 2013. The buyers would acquire all outstanding shares of Dell not held by Michael Dell and certain other members of management. The buyout deal included a 45-day "go-shop" provision during which the special committee would actively solicit, receive, evaluate, and potentially enter in to negotiations with parties offering alternative proposals.

To finance the deal, Silver Lake put up $1.4 billion in cash, and Michael Dell committed another $750 million in cash, along with his existing 14% stake in the company. A consortium of banks including Bank of America, Credit Suisse, and RBC, provided loans totaling $13.75 billion. Microsoft added another $2 billion in loans. Dell was to remain CEO of the company after privatization. Without the need to pay out dividends and make stock buybacks, Dell

and Silver Lake felt that they could adequately cover the interest payments on the debt from cash flow. Moreover, privatization would give management the flexibility to pursue longer-term investments.

Enter Carl Icahn

At this point, Carl Icahn entered the field. Icahn had first made his name during the 1980s as an activist investor. He had specialized in taking a substantial or controlling positions in companies that he claimed were poorly managed, and pushing for changes in management and strategy. He would make money from selling out after the stock price had made substantial gains.

One high point of Icahn's career was a takeover of the venerable airline, TWA. TWA was in financial trouble. Icahn raised debt capital from a group of investors to finance the takeover. To sway TWA's board, management, and employees, he told them he wanted to make TWA profitable again. He ended up with a 20% stake in the company and the chairman's position. After the takeover, he sold off some of the company's assets in order to pay down the debt. In 1988, Icahn took TWA private in a leveraged buyout, which made him a profit of $469 million from selling his personal stake. The buyout left TWA with $540 million in debt. Icahn paid down the debt by selling off TWA's prized London routes to American Airlines for $445 million in 1991.

Stripped of its most valuable routes, a year later the airline went into Chapter 11 bankruptcy proceedings. Icahn resigned as chairman but remained involved in TWA, this time as a creditor. TWA emerged from bankruptcy in 1993. As part of the restructuring, TWA owed Carl Icahn $180 million. Desperate to get rid of Icahn, TWA's new management cut a deal that allowed him to buy any ticket that connected through TWA's St Louis hub for 55 cents, and then resell it at a discount price. The deal blocked Icahn from selling through travel agents, but it didn't mention a rapidly emerging new distribution channel, the Internet. Icahn set up Lowestfare.com to resell TWA tickets. Icahn put downward pressure on the amount TWA could sell tickets for, because the company was essentially competing with itself. Estimates suggest that the deal cost TWA $100 million a year. In 1995, TWA went bankrupt.[12]

Icahn reportedly became interested in Dell after some large investors contacted him. In a March 5 letter to Dell's board, Icahn let it be known that he had quietly purchased $1 billion in Dell shares, and that he thought the Dell-Silver lake bid was too low. Privately, Icahn reportedly believed that Dell was worth $20 a share. In June 2013, Icahn purchased another $1 billion in shares from Southeastern Asset Management at $13.52 a share, giving him a 9% stake in Dell Inc. Icahn did not pull any punches; he barraged investors with messages that the deal undervalued Dell, often using Twitter to communicate. He stated emphatically that Michael Dell's strategy was a failure, and that he should be fired and the board be replaced. He painted a picture of Dell's board as beholden to Michael Dell and lacking independence. Icahn urged shareholders to vote against the buyout. Icahn and Southeastern Asset Management proposed to replace Dell's board with their own slate of directors, who would then push the company into buying back 1.1 billion shares at $14 each.[13]

Michael Dell and Silver Lake responded to Icahn by boosting their bid to $13.75 a share, plus a 13-cent special dividend, up from the $13.65 a share they had originally offered in February. It was not a big concession. Dell's board backed the revised offer. Icahn pushed for shareholders to seek "appraisal rights," which is a process by which a judge determines the value of the shares. Appraisal rights are available to companies like Dell that are incorporated in Delaware, but the process can take months. There were risks involved, because while the judge might rule that Dell was worth more than $13.65 a share, the judge could also rule that it was worth less.

Dell's board scheduled a vote to approve the buyout offer to be held on September 12, 2013. Within 15 minutes the meeting was over. With roughly 65% of the votes cast for the transaction, Icahn lacked sufficient support to derail the buyout. Initially, Icahn continued to push for his own Dell shares to be appraised by a Delaware judge, but on October 4, he announced that he was withdrawing his request.[14] Icahn was left with a (for him) small $70-million profit on his Dell investments, but he wasn't beyond taking one last swipe at the company. Icahn stated that his attempt to block the buyout was "too difficult" given the lack of progress with the board, which he likened to a "dictatorship." Icahn complained that the board would just not listen to his arguments. We need better corporate governance in U.S. companies, he stated.[15]

Aftermath

The transaction to take Dell private closed on October 28, 2013. The final value of the transaction was $24.8 billion. A year later, Michael Dell told attendees at an Inc. 5000 conference that his company was "quite a bit" more profitable than it had been a year ago, without offering any specifics, and 60% of its business came from PCs. Despite media reports at the time of the Dell buyout speculating that the company might get into mobile, Dell didn't sound interested in that. Asked to respond to the criticism that Dell "missed the boat" on mobile, Dell shrugged.

"Enormous sums are being lost" in that sector, he said. "Every 3 years, the leader of the mobile space has changed. I guess all those guys missed it, too."[16]

In an open letter published in *The Wall Street Journal* on November 25, 2014, Dell again asserted that the buyout was the right move. He noted that:

> Shareholders increasingly demanded short-term results to drive returns; innovation and investment too often suffered as a result. Shareholder and customer interests Decoupled ... As a private company, Dell now has the freedom to take a long-term view ... No more pulling R&D and growth investments to make in-quarter numbers. No more having a small group of vocal investors hijack the public perception of our strategy while we're fully focused on building for the future. No more trade-offs between what's best for a short-term return and what's best for the long-term success of our customers.[17]

NOTES

1. K. Hodgkins, "Apple Grabs Record U.S. Market Share on Strong Mac Sales in Q3 2014," MacRomors, November 7, 2014.
2. A. Vance, "Dell Trails Its Rivals in the Worst of Times," *New York Times*, December 15, 2008.
3. S. Hansell and A. Vance, "Dell to Spend $3.9 Billion to Acquire Perot Systems," *New York Times*, September 21, 2009.

4. The historical material in this section is drawn from Michael Dell's autobiography, M. Dell and C. Fredman, *Direct from Dell*. New York, NY: Harper Business, 1999.

5. Ibid.

6. T. W. Smith, "Standard & Poor's Industry Surveys, Computers: Hardware," April 21, 2011.

7. Gartner press release, "Gartner Says Worldwide Server Shipments Grew 1% in the Third Quarter of 2014," December 3, 2014.

8. Security and Exchange Commission press release, "SEC Charges Dell and Senior Executives with Disclosure and Accounting Fraud," July 22, 2010.

9. E. Sherman, "Dell Mobile Is Gone, a Victim of Incompetence," CBS Money Watch, November 18, 2010.

10. C. Guglielmo, "Dell Officially Goes Private: Inside the Nastiest Tech Buyout Ever," *Forbes*, October 30, 2013.

11. Dell Inc. press release, "Dell Enters into an Agreement to Be Acquired by Michael Dell and Silver Lake," February 5, 2013.

12. J. D'Onfro, "Marc Andressen: Carl Icahn Killed an Entire Airline," *Business Insider*, March 18, 2014.

13. M. de La Merced, "Icahn's Latest Gamble at Dell: Appraisal Rights," *New York Times*, July 10, 2013.

14. M. J. de La Merced, "Icahn Gives Up Fight over Dell Appraisal Rights," *New York Times*, October 4, 2013.

15. D. Sandholm, "Carl Icahn Slams Dell Board After Dropping Fight," *CNBC*, September 9, 2013.

16. J. Fine, "Michael Dell on Carl Icahn, Hewlett Packard, and the Entrepreneurs He Most Admires", *Inc*, October 17, 2014.

17. D. H. Kass, "Michael Dell on Privatization One Year Later: 'We Got It Right,'" *The Var Guy*, November 25, 2014.

3M—THE FIRST 110 YEARS

Established in 1902, by 2012, 3M was one of the largest technology-driven enterprises in the United States, with annual sales of almost $30 billion, two-thirds of which were outside the United States. The company was solidly profitable, earning $6.5 billion in net income in 2012 and generating a return on invested capital of 19.5%. Throughout its history, 3M researchers had driven much of the company's growth. In 2012, the company sold over 50,000 products, including Post-it Notes, Flex Circuits, various kinds of Scotch tape, abrasives, specialty chemicals, Thinsulate insulation products, Nexcare bandages, optical films, fiber optic connectors, drug delivery systems, and much more. Approximately 7,350 of the company's 80,000 employees were technical employees. 3M's annual R&D budget exceeded $1.6 billion. The company had garnered over 8,000 patents since 1990. 3M was organized into 35 different business units grouped together into six main areas: consumer and office products; displays and graphics; electronics and telecommunications; health care; industrial and transportation; and safety, security, and protection services (see Figure 1 for details).

The company's 100th anniversary in 2002 was a time for celebration, but also one for strategic reflection. During the prior decade, 3M had grown profits and sales by between 6 and 7% per annum—a respectable figure, but one that lagged behind the growth rates achieved by other technology-based enterprises and diversified industrial enterprises like General Electric. In 2001, 3M took a step away from

its past when the company hired the first outsider to become CEO, James McNerney, Jr. McNerney, who joined 3M after heading up GE's fast-growing medical equipment business (and losing out in the race to replace legendary GE CEO, Jack Welch) was quick to signal that he wanted 3M to accelerate its growth rate. McNerney set an ambitious target for 3M—to grow sales by 11% per annum and profits by 12% per annum. Many wondered if McNerney could achieve this without damaging the innovation engine that had propelled 3M to its current stature. In the event, the question remained unanswered, as McNerney left to run the Boeing Company in 2005. His successor, George Buckley, another outsider, seemed committed to continuing on the course McNerney had set for the company.

THE HISTORY OF 3M: BUILDING INNOVATIVE CAPABILITIES

The 3M story dates back to 1902, when five Minnesota businessmen established the Minnesota Mining and Manufacturing Company to mine a mineral that they thought was corundum, which is ideal for making sandpaper. The mineral, however, turned out to be low-grade anorthosite, which is nowhere near as suitable for making sandpaper, and the company nearly failed. Trying to salvage the business, 3M turned to making the sandpaper using materials purchased from another source.

In 1907, 3M hired a 20-year-old business student, William McKnight, as assistant bookkeeper. This turned out to be a pivotal move in the history of the company. The hardworking McKnight soon made his mark. By 1929, he was CEO; in 1949, he became chairman of 3M's board of directors, a position that he held through until 1966.

From Sandpaper to Post-it Notes

It was McKnight, then 3M's president, who hired the company's first scientist, Richard Carlton, in 1921. Around the same time, McKnight's interest had been peaked by an odd request from a Philadelphian printer by the name of Francis Okie for samples of every sandpaper grit size that 3M made. McKnight dispatched 3M's East Coast sales manager to find out what Okie was up to. The sales manager discovered that Okie had invented a new kind of sandpaper that he had patented. It was waterproof sandpaper that could be used with water or oil to reduce dust and decrease the friction that marred auto finishes. In addition, it reduced the poisoning associated with inhaling paint dust with a high lead content. Okie had a problem, though; he had no financial backers to commercialize the sandpaper. 3M quickly stepped into the breach, purchasing the rights to Okie's Wetordry waterproof sandpaper, and hiring the young printer to join Richard Carlton in 3M's lab. Wetordry sandpaper went on to revolutionize the sandpaper industry, and was the driver of significant growth at 3M.

Another key player in the company's history, Richard Drew, also joined 3M in 1921. Hired straight out of the University of Minnesota, Drew would round out the trio of scientists, Carlton, Okie, and Drew, who under McKnight's leadership would do much to shape 3M's innovative organization.

McKnight charged the newly hired Drew with developing a stronger adhesive to better bind the grit paper to the sandpaper backing. While experimenting with adhesives, Drew accidentally developed a weak adhesive that had an interesting quality—if placed on the back of a strip of paper and stuck to a surface, the strip of paper could be pealed off the surface without leaving any adhesive residue on that surface. This discovery gave Drew an epiphany.

He had been visiting auto-body paint shops to see how 3M's wet and dry sandpaper was used, and he noticed that there was a problem with paint running. His epiphany was to cover the back of a strip of paper with his weak adhesive, and use it as "masking tape" to cover parts of the auto body that were not to be painted. An excited Drew took his idea to McKnight, and explained how masking tape might create an entirely new business for 3M. McKnight reminded Drew that he had been hired to fix a specific problem, and pointedly suggested that he concentrate on doing just that.

Chastised, Dew went back to his lab, but he could not get the idea out of his mind, so he continued to work on it at night, long after everyone else had gone home. Drew succeeded in perfecting the masking tape product, and then went to visit several auto-body shops to show them his innovation. He quickly received several commitments for orders. Drew then went to see McKnight again. He told him that he had continued to work on the masking tape idea on his own time, had perfected the product, and got several customers interested in purchasing it. This time it was McKnight's turn to be chastised. Realizing that he had almost killed a good business idea, McKnight reversed his original position and gave Drew the go ahead to pursue the idea.[1]

Introduced into the market in 1925, Drew's invention of masking tape represented the first significant product diversification at 3M. Company legend has it that this incident was also the genesis for 3M's famous 15% rule. Reflecting on Drew's work, both McKnight and Carlton both agreed that technical people could disagree with management, and should be allowed to do some experimentation on their own. The company then established a norm that technical people could spend up to 15% of their own workweek on projects that might benefit the consumer, without having to justify the project to their manager.

Drew himself was not finished. In the late 1920s, he was working with cellophane, a product that had been invented by Du Pont, when lightning struck a second time. Why, Drew wondered, couldn't cellophane be coated with an adhesive and used as a sealing tape? The result was Scotch Cellophane Tape. The first batch was delivered to a customer in September 1930, and Scotch Tape went on to become one of 3M's bestselling products. Years later, Drew noted that "Would there have been any masking or cellophane tape if it hadn't been for earlier 3M research on adhesive binders for 3M Wetordry Abrasive Paper? Probably not!"[2]

Over the years, other scientists followed Drew's footsteps at 3M, creating a wide range of innovative products by leveraging existing technology and applying it to new areas. Two famous examples illustrate how many of these innovations occurred—the invention of Scotch Guard, and the development of the ubiquitous Post-it Notes.

The genesis of Scotch Guard was in 1953, when a 3M scientist named Patsy Sherman was working on a new kind of rubber for jet aircraft fuel lines. Some of the latex mixture splashed onto a pair of canvas tennis shoes. Over time, the spot stayed clean while the rest of the canvas soiled. Sherman enlisted the help of fellow chemist Sam Smith. Together they began to investigate polymers, and it didn't take long for them to realize that they were on to something. They had discovered an oil- and water-repellant substance, based on the fluorocarbon fluid used in air conditioners, with enormous potential for protecting fabrics from stains. It took several years before the team perfected a means to apply the treatment using water as the carrier, thereby making it economically feasible for use as a finish in textile plants.

Three years after the accidental spill, the first rain- and stain-repellent for use on wool was announced. Experience and time revealed that one product could not, however, effectively protect all fabrics, so 3M continued working, producing a wide range of Scotch Guard products that could be used to protect all kinds of fabrics.[3]

The story of Post-it Notes began with Spencer Silver, a senior scientist studying adhesives.[4] In 1968, Silver had developed an adhesive with properties like no other: a pressure-sensitive adhesive that would adhere to a surface but was weak enough to easily peel off the surface and leave no residue. Silver spent several years shopping his adhesive around 3M, to no avail. It was a classic case of a technology in search of a product. Then one day in 1973, Art Fry, a new-product development researcher who had attended one of Silver's seminars, was singing in his church choir. He was frustrated that his bookmarks kept falling out of his hymn book, when he had a "Eureka" moment. Fry realized that Silver's adhesive could be used to make a wonderfully reliable bookmark.

Fry went to work next day, and using 15% time, started to develop the bookmark. When he started using sample bookmarks to write notes to his boss, Fry suddenly realized that he had stumbled on a much bigger potential use for the product. Before it could be commercialized, however, Fry had to solve a host of technical and manufacturing problems. With the support of his boss, Fry persisted and, after 18 months, the product development effort moved from 15% time to a formal development effort funded by 3M's seed capital.

The first Post-it Notes were test marketed in 1977 in four major cities, but customers were lukewarm at best. This did not gel with the experience within 3M, where people in Fry's division were using samples all the time to write messages to each other. Further research revealed that the test marketing effort, which focused on ads and brochures, didn't resonate well with consumers, who didn't seem to value Post-it Notes until they had the actual product in their hands. In 1978, 3M tried again, this time descending on Boise Idaho, and handing out samples. Follow-up research revealed that 90% of consumers who tried the product said they would buy it. Armed with this knowledge, 3M rolled out the national launch of Post-it Notes in 1980. The product subsequently went on to become a bestseller.

Institutionalizing Innovation

Early on, McKnight set an ambitious target for 3M—a 10% annual increase in sales and a 25% profit target. He thought that should be achieved with a commitment to plow 5% of sales back into R&D every year. The question though, was how to ensure that 3M would continue to develop new products?

The answer was not apparent all at once, but rather evolved over the years from experience. A prime example was the 15% rule, which emerged from McKnight's experience with Drew. In addition to the 15% rule and the continued commitment to push money back into R&D, a number of other mechanisms evolved at 3M to spur innovation.

Initially, research took place in the business units that made and sold products, but by the 1930s, 3M had already diversified into several different fields thanks in large part to the efforts of Drew and others. McKnight and Carlton realized that there was a need for a central research function. In 1937, they established a central research laboratory charged with supplementing the work of product divisions and undertaking long-run, basic research. From the outset, the researchers at the lab were multidisciplinary, with people from different scientific disciplines often working next to each other on research benches.

As the company grew, it became clear that there was a need for some mechanism to knit together its increasingly diverse business operations. This led to the establishment of the 3M Technical Forum in 1951. The goal of the Technical Forum was to foster idea sharing, discussion, and problem solving between technical employees located in different divisions and the central research laboratory. The Technical Forum sponsored "problem-solving sessions" at which businesses would present their most recent technical nightmares in the hope that somebody might be able to suggest a solution—and that often was the case. The forum also established an annual event in which each division put up a booth to show off its latest technologies. Chapters were also created to focus on specific disciplines such as polymer chemistry or coating processes.

During the 1970s, the Technical Forum cloned itself, establishing forums in Australia and England. By 2001, the forum had grown to 9,500 members in 8 U.S. locations and 19 other countries, becoming an international network of researchers who could share ideas, solve problems, and leverage technology.

According to Marlyee Paulson, who coordinated the Technical Forum from 1979 to 1992, the great virtue of the Technical Forum is to cross pollinate ideas:

> 3M has lots of polymer chemists. They may be in tape; they may be medical or several other divisions. The forum pulls them across 3M to share what they know. It's a simple but amazingly effective way to bring like minds together.[5]

In 1999, 3M created another unit within the company, 3M Innovative Properties (3M, IPC) to leverage technical knowhow. 3M IPC is explicitly charged with protecting and leveraging 3M's intellectual property around the world. At 3M there has been a long tradition that, while divisions "own" their products, the company as a whole "owns" the underlying technology, or intellectual property. One task of 3M IPC is to find ways in which 3M technology can be applied across business units to produce unique, marketable products.

Historically, the company has been remarkably successful at leveraging company technology to produce new product ideas (see Figure 1 for examples).

Another key to institutionalizing innovation at 3M has been the principle of "patient money." The basic idea is that producing revolutionary new products requires substantial, long-term investments—and often repeated failure—before a major payoff occurs. The principle can be traced back to 3M's early days. It took the company 12 years before its initial sandpaper business started to show a profit, a fact that drove home the importance of taking the long view. Throughout the company's history, similar examples can be found. Scotchlite reflective sheeting, now widely used on road signs, didn't show much profit for 10 years. The same was true of flurochemicals and duplicating products. Patient money doesn't mean substantial funding for long periods of time, however. Rather, it might imply that a small group of five researchers is supported for 10 years while they work on a technology.

More generally, if researchers create a new technology or idea, they can work on it using 15% time. If the idea shows promise, they may request seed capital from their business unit managers to develop it further. If that funding is denied, which can occur, they are free to take the idea to any other 3M business unit. Unlike the case in many other companies, requests for seed capital do not require that researchers draft detailed business plans that are reviewed by top management. That comes later in the process. As one former senior technology manager noted, "In the early stages of a new product or technology, it shouldn't be overly managed. If we start asking for business plans too early and insist on tight financial evaluations, we'll kill an idea or surely slow it down."[6]

Explaining the patient money philosophy, Ron Baukol, a former executive vice president of 3M's international operations, and a manager who started as a researcher, has noted:

> You just know that some things are going to be worth working on, and that requires technological patience. ... you don't put too much money into the investigation, but you keep one to five people working on it for twenty years if you have to. You do that because you know that, once you have cracked the code, it's going to be big.[7]

Figure 1 Examples of Leveraging Technology at 3M[8]

Richard Miller, a corporate scientist in 3M Pharmaceuticals, began experimental development of an antiherpes medicinal cream in 1982. After several years of development, his research team found that the interferon-based materials they were working with could be applied to any skin-based virus. The innovative chemistry they were working with was applied topically and was more effective than other compounds on the market. They found that the cream was particularly effective in interfering with the growth mechanism of genital warts. Competitive products on the market at the time were caustic and tended to be painful. Miller's team obtained Food and Drug Administration (FDA) approval for its Aldara (imiquimod) line of topical, patient-applied creams in 1997.

Miller then applied the same Aldara-based chemical mechanism to basal cell carcinomas, and found that here too it was particularly effective in restricting the growth of the skin cancer. "The patient benefit is quite remarkable," says Miller. New results in efficacy have been presented for treating skin cancers. His team recently completed phase III clinical testing and expects to apply later this year for FDA approval for this disease preventative. This material is already FDA-approved for use in the treatment of genital warts. Doctors are free to use it to treat patients with skin cancers.

Andrew Ouderkirk is a corporate scientist in 3M's Film & Light Management Technology Center. 3M has been working in light management materials applied to polymer-based films since the 1930s, according to Ouderkirk. Every decade since then, 3M has introduced a unique, thin-film structure for specific customer applications ranging from high-performance safety reflectors for street signs to polarized lighting products. And every decade, 3M's technology base has become more specialized and more sophisticated. Their technology has now reached the point where they can produce multiple-layer interference films to 100-nm thicknesses each and hold the tolerances on each layer to within $+/- 3$ nm. "Our laminated films are now starting to compete with vacuum-coated films in some applications," says Ouderkirk.

Rick Weiss is technical director of 3M's Microreplication Technology Center, one of 3M's 12 core technology centers. The basic microreplication technology was discovered in the early-1960s, when 3M researchers were developing fresnel lenses for overhead projectors. 3M scientists have expanded this technology to a wide variety of applications including optical reflectors for solar collectors, and adhesive coatings with air-bleed ribs that allow large area films to be applied without having the characteristic "bubbles" appear. Weiss is currently working on development of dimensionally precise barrier ribs that can be applied to separate the individual "gas" cells on new, high-resolution, large-screen commercial plasma displays. Other applications include fluid management where capillary action can be used in biological testing systems to split a drop of blood into multiple parts.

An internal review of 3M's innovation process in the early 1980s concluded that, despite the liberal process for funding new product ideas, some promising ideas did not receive funding from business units or the central research budget. This led to the establishment in 1985 of Genesis Grants, which provides up to $100,000 in seed capital to fund projects that do not get funded through 3M's regular channels. About a dozen of these grants are awarded every year. One recipient of the grant, a project that focused on creating a multilayered, reflective film, has produced a breakthrough reflective technology that may have applications in a wide range of businesses, from better reflective strips on road signs to computer displays and the reflective linings in light fixtures. Company estimates in 2002 suggest that the commercialization of this technology might ultimately generate $1 billion in sales for 3M.

Underlying the patient money philosophy is the recognition that innovation is a very risky business. 3M has long acknowledged that failure is an accepted and essential part of the new-product development process. As former 3M CEO Lew Lehr once noted, "We estimate that 60% of our formal new-product development programs never make it. When this happens, the important thing is to not punish the people involved."[9]

In the 1960s, in an effort to reduce the probability of failure, 3M started to establish a process for auditing the product development efforts ongoing in the company's business units. The idea has been to provide a peer review, or technical audit, of major development projects taking place in the company. A typical technical audit team is composed of 10 to 15 business and technical people, including technical directors and senior scientists from other divisions.

The audit team looks at the strengths and weaknesses of a development program, and its probability of success, both from a technical standpoint and a business standpoint. The team then makes nonbinding recommendations, but these are normally taken very seriously by the project managers. For example, if an audit team concludes that a project has enormous potential but is terribly underfunded, managers of the unit would often increase the funding level. Of course, the converse can also happen; in many instances the audit team can provide useful feedback and technical ideas that help a development team improve their project's chance of success.

By the 1990s, 3M's continued growth produced a company that was simultaneously pursuing a vast array of new product ideas. This was a natural outcome of 3M's decentralized, bottom-up approach to innovation, but it was problematic in one crucial respect: The company's R&D resources were being spread too thinly over a wide range of opportunities, resulting in potentially major projects being underfunded. In 1994, to channel R&D resources into projects that had blockbuster potential, 3M introduced what was known as the Pacing Plus Program.

The program asked businesses to select a small number of programs that would receive priority funding, but 3M's senior executives made the final selections for the Pacing Plus Program. An earlier attempt to do this in 1990 had met with limited success, because each sector in 3M submitted as many as 200 programs. The Pacing Plus Program narrowed the list down to 25 key programs that, by 1996, were receiving some 20% of 3M's entire R&D funds (by the early 2000s, the number of projects funded under the Pacing Plus Program had grown to 60). The focus was on "leapfrog technologies," revolutionary ideas that might change the basis of competition and lead to entirely new technology platforms that might, in typical 3M fashion, spawn an entire range of new products.

To further foster a culture of entrepreneurial innovation and risk taking, over the years 3M established a number of reward and recognition programs to honor employees who make significant contributions to the company. These include the Carton Society award, which honors employees for outstanding career scientific achievements, and the Circle of Technical Excellence and Innovation Award, which recognizes people who have made exceptional contributions to 3M's technical capabilities.

Another key component of 3M's innovative culture has been an emphasis on duel career tracks. From its early days, many key players in 3M's history, like Richard Drew, chose to stay in research, turning down opportunities to go into the management side of the business. Over the years, this became formalized in a dual career path. Today, technical employees can choose to follow a technical career path or a management career path, with equal advancement opportunities. The idea is to let researchers develop their technical professional interests without being penalized financially for not going into management.

Although 3M's innovative culture emphasizes the role of technical employees in producing innovations, the company also has a strong tradition of emphasizing that new product ideas often come from watching customers at work. Richard Drew's original idea for masking tape, for example, came from watching workers use 3M wet and dry sandpaper in auto-body shops. As with much else at 3M, the tone was set by McKnight, who insisted that salespeople needed to "get behind the smokestacks" of 3M customers, go to the factory floor, and talk to workers about problems. Over the years, this theme became ingrained in 3M's culture, with salespeople often requesting time to watch customer work, and then bringing their insights about customer problems back into the organization.

By the mid 1990s, McKnight's notion of getting behind the smokestacks had evolved into the idea that 3M could learn a tremendous amount from what were termed "lead users," who were customers working in very demanding conditions. Over the years, 3M had observed that, in many cases, these customers were innovators, developing new products to solve problems that they faced in their work setting. This was most likely to occur when customers were working in very demanding conditions. To take advantage of this process, 3M has instituted a lead-user process in the company in which cross-functional teams from a business unit observe how customers work in demanding situations.

For example, 3M has a $100-million business selling surgical drapes, which are drapes backed with adhesive used to cover parts of a body during surgery and help prevent infection. As an aid to new product development, 3M's surgical drapes business formed a cross-functional team that observed surgeons at work in very demanding situations—including on the battlefield, in hospitals in developing nations, and in veterinarians' offices. The result was a new set of product ideas, including low-cost surgical drapes that were affordable in developing nations, and devices for coating a patient's skin and surgical instruments with antimicrobial substances that would reduce the chance of infection during surgery.[10]

Driving the entire innovation machine at 3M has been a series of stretch goals set by top managers. The goals date back to 3M's early days and McKnight's ambitious growth targets. In 1977, the company established "Challenge 81," which called for 25% of sales to come from products that had been on the market for less than 5 years by 1981. By the 1990s, the goal had been raised to the requirement that 30% of sales should come from products that had been on the market less than four years.

The flip side of these goals was that, over the years, many products and businesses that had been 3M staples were phased out. More than 20 of the businesses that were 3M mainstays in 1980, for example, had been phased out by 2000. Analysts estimate that sales from mature products at 3M generally fall by 3 to 4% per annum. The company has a long history of inventing businesses, leading the market for long periods of time, and then shutting those businesses down or selling them off when they can no longer meet 3M's own demanding growth targets. Notable examples include the duplicating business, a business 3M invented with Thermo Fax copiers (which were ultimately made obsolete my Xerox's patented technology), and the video and audio magnetic tape business. The former division was sold off in 1985, and the later in 1995. In both cases the company exited these areas because they had become low-growth, commodity businesses that could not generate the top-line growth that 3M was looking for.

Still, 3M was by no means invulnerable in the realm of innovation and on occasion squandered huge opportunities. A case in point was the document copying business. 3M invented this business in 1951 when it introduced the world's first commercially successful Thermo Fax copier (which used specially coated 3M paper to copy original typed documents). 3M dominated the world copier business until 1970, when Xerox overtook the company with its revolutionary xerographic technology, which used plain paper to make copies. 3M saw Xerox coming, but rather than develop its own plain-paper copier, the company invested funds in trying to improve its (increasingly obsolete) copying technology. In 1975, 3M finally introduced its own plain-paper copier, but by then it was too late. Ironically, 3M had turned down the chance to acquire Xerox's technology 20 years earlier, when the company's founders had approached 3M.

Building the Organization

McKnight, a strong believer in decentralization, organized the company into product divisions in 1948, making 3M one of the early adopters of this organizational form. Each division was set up as an individual profit center that had the power, autonomy, and resources to run independently. At the same time, certain significant functions remained centralized, including R&D, human resources, and finance.

McKnight wanted to keep the divisions small enough that people had a chance to be entrepreneurial and focus on the customer. A key philosophy of McKnight's was "divide and grow." Put simply, when a division became too big, some of its embryonic businesses were spun of into a new division. Not only did this new division then typically attain higher growth rates, but the original division had to find new drivers of growth to make up for the contribution of the businesses that had gained independence. This drove the search for further innovations.

At 3M the process of organic diversification by splitting divisions became known as "renewal." Examples of renewal within 3M are legion. A copying machine project for Thermo Fax copiers grew to become the Office Products Division. When Magnetic Recording Materials was spun off from the Electrical Products division, it grew to become its own division and in turn spawned a spate of divisions.

However, this organic process was not without its downside. By the early 1990s, some of 3M's key customers were frustrated that they had to do business with a large number of different 3M divisions. In some cases, there could be representatives from 10 to 20 3M divisions calling on the same customer. To cope with this problem, starting in 1992, 3M assigned key account representatives to sell 3M products directly to major customers. These representatives typically worked across divisional lines. Implementing the strategy required many of 3M's general managers to give up some autonomy and power, but the solution seemed to work well, particularly for 3M's consumer and office divisions.

Underpinning the organization that McKnight put in place was his own management philosophy. As explained in a 1948 document, his basic management philosophy consisted of the following values:[11]

> As our business grows, it becomes increasingly necessary to delegate responsibility and to encourage men and women to exercise their initiative. This requires considerable tolerance. Those men and women to whom we delegate authority and responsibility, if they are good people, are going to want to do their jobs in their own way.
>
> Mistakes will be made. But if a person is essentially right, the mistakes he or she makes are not as serious in the long run as the mistakes management will make if it undertakes to tell those in authority exactly how they must do their jobs.
>
> Management that is destructively critical when mistakes are made kills initiative. And it's essential that we have many people with initiative if we are to continue to grow.

At just 3% per annum, employee turnover rate at 3M has long been among the lowest in corporate America—a fact that is often attributed to the tolerant, empowering, familylike corporate culture that McKnight helped to establish. Reinforcing this culture has been a progressive approach toward employee compensation and retention. In the depths of the Great Depression, 3M avoided laying off employees while many others did because the company's innovation engine was able to keep building new businesses even through the worst of times.

In many ways, 3M was ahead of its time in management philosophy and human resource practices. The company introduced its first profit-sharing plan in 1916, and McKnight instituted a pension plan in 1930 and an employee stock purchase plan in 1950. McKnight himself was convinced that people would be much more likely to be loyal to a company if they had a stake in it. 3M also developed a policy of promoting from within and giving its employees a plethora of career opportunities within the company.

Going International

The first steps abroad occurred in the 1920s. There were limited sales of Wet and Dry sandpaper in Europe during the early 1920s. These increased after 1929 when 3M joined the Durex Corporation, a joint venture for international abrasive-product sales in which 3M was involved along with eight other U. S. companies. In 1950, however, the Department of Justice alleged that the Durex Corporation was a mechanism for achieving collusion among U.S. abrasive-product manufacturers, and a judge ordered that the corporation be broken up. After the Durex Corporation was dissolved in 1951, 3M was left with a sandpaper factory in Britain, a small plant in France, a sales office in Germany, and a tape factory in Brazil. International sales at this point amounted to no more than 5% of 3M's total revenues.

Although 3M opposed the dissolution of the Durex Corporation, in retrospect it turned out to be one of the most important events in the company's history, for it forced the corporation to build its own international operations. By 2010, international sales amounted to 63% of total revenues.

In 1952, Clarence Sampair was put in charge of 3M's international operations and charged with getting them off the ground. He was given considerable strategic and operational independence. Sampair and his successor, Maynard Patterson, worked hard to protect the international operations from getting caught up in the red tape of a major corporation. As Patterson recounts:

> I asked Em Monteiro to start a small company in Columbia. I told him to pick a key person he wanted to take with him. "Go start a company", I said, "and no one from St Paul is going to visit you unless you ask for them. We'll stay out of your way, and if someone sticks his nose in your business you call me."[12]

The international businesses were grouped into an International Division that Sampair headed. From the get-go the company insisted that foreign ventures pay their own way. In addition, 3M's international companies were expected to pay a 5 to 10% royalty to the corporate head office. Starved of working capital, 3M's International Division relied heavily on local borrowing to fund local operations—a fact that forced those operations to quickly pay their own way.

The international growth at 3M typically occurred in stages. The company would start by exporting to a country and working through sales subsidiaries. In that way, it began to understand the country, the local marketplace, and the local business environment. Next, 3M established warehouses in each nation, and stocked those with goods paid for in local currency. The next phase involved converting products to the sizes and packaging forms that the local market conditions, customs, and culture dictated. 3M would ship jumbo rolls of products from the United States, which were then broken up and repackaged for each country. The next stage was designing and building plants, buying machinery, and getting operations up and running. Over the years, R&D functions were often added, and by the 1980s considerable R&D was being done outside of the United States.

Sampair and Patterson set an innovative, entrepreneurial framework that, according to the company, still guides 3M's International Division today. The philosophy can be reduced to several simple, key commitments: (1) get in early (within the company, the strategy is known as FIDO—"First in Defeats Others"); (2) hire talented, motivated local people; (3) become a good corporate citizen of the country; (4) grow with the local economy; (5) tailor products to fit local needs; and (6) enforce patents in foreign countries.

As 3M stepped into the international market vacuum, foreign sales surged from less than 5% in 1951 to 42% by 1979. By the end of the 1970s, 3M was beginning to understand how important it was to integrate its international operations more closely with U.S. operations, and to build innovative capabilities overseas. It expanded the company's international R&D presence (there are now more than 2,200 technical employees outside the United States), built closer ties between the United States and foreign research organizations, and started to transfer more managerial and technical employees between businesses in different countries.

In 1978, the company started the Pathfinder Program to encourage new product and new business initiatives born outside the United States. By 1983, products developed under the initiative were generating sales of over $150 million a year. 3M Brazil invented a low-cost, hot-melt adhesive from local raw materials, 3M Germany teamed up with Sumitomo 3M of Japan (a joint venture with Sumitomo) to develop electronic connectors with new features for the worldwide electronics industry, 3M Philippines developed a Scotch-Brite cleaning pad shaped like a foot after learning that Filipinos polished floors with their feet, and so on. On the back of such developments, in 1992

international operations exceeded 50% for the first time in the company's history.

By the 1990s, 3M started to shift away from a country-by-country management structure to more regional management. Drivers behind this development included the fall of trade barriers, the rise of trading blocks such as the European Union and NAFTA, and the need to bring down costs in the face of intense global competition. The first European Business Center (EBC) was created in 1991 to manage 3M's chemical business across Europe. The EBC was charged with product development, manufacturing, sales, and marketing for Europe, but also with paying attention to local country requirements. Other EBCs soon followed, such as one for disposable products and pharmaceuticals.

As the millennium ended, 3M was transforming into a transnational organization characterized by an integrated network of businesses that spanned the globe. The goal was to achieve the global scale necessary to deal with competitive pressures, while at the same time maintaining 3M's traditional focus on local market differences and decentralized R&D capabilities.

THE NEW ERA

The DeSimone Years

In 1991, Desi DeSimone became CEO of 3M. A longtime 3M employee, the Canadian-born DeSimone was the epitome of a 21st-century manager. He had made his name by building 3M's Brazilian business and spoke five languages fluently. Unlike most prior 3M CEOs, DeSimone came from the manufacturing side of the business rather than the technical aide. He soon received praise for managing 3M through the recession of the early 1990s. By the late 1990s, however, his leadership had come under fire both inside and outside the company.

In 1998 and 1999, the company missed its earnings targets, and the stock price fell as disappointed investors sold. Sales were flat, profit margins fell, and earnings slumped by 50%. The stock had underperformed the widely tracked S&P 500 stock index for most of the 1980s and 1990s.

One cause of the earnings slump in the late 1990s was 3M's sluggish response to the 1997 Asian crisis.

During the Asian crisis, the value of several Asian currencies fell by as much as 80% against the U.S. dollar in a matter of months. 3M generated a quarter of its sales from Asia, but it was slow to cut costs there in the face of slumping demand following the collapse of currency values. At the same time, a flood of cheap Asian products cut into 3M's market share in the United States and Europe as lower currency values made Asian products much cheaper.

Another problem was that, for all of its vaunted innovative capabilities, 3M had not produced a block-buster product since Post-it Notes. Most products released during the 1990s were improvements over existing products, not truly new products.

DeSimone was also blamed for not pushing 3M hard enough earlier in the decade to reduce costs. An example was the company's supply-chain excellence program. In 1995, 3M's inventory was turning over just 3.5 times a year—subpar for manufacturing. An internal study suggested that every half-point increase in inventory turnover could reduce 3M's working capital needs by $700 million and boost its return on invested capital. But by 1998, 3M had made no progress on this front.[13]

By 1998, there was also evidence of internal concerns. Anonymous letters from 3M employees were sent to the board of directors, claiming that DeSimone was not committed to research as he should have been. Some letters complained that DeSimone was not funding important projects for future growth, others that he had not moved boldly enough to cut costs, and still others that the company's duel career track was not being implemented well, and that technical people were underpaid. Critics argued that he was a slow and cautious decision maker in a time that required decisive strategic decisions. For example, in August 1998, DeSimone announced a restructuring plan that included a commitment to cut 4,500 jobs, but reports suggest that other senior managers wanted 10,000 job cuts, and DeSimone had watered down the proposals.[14]

Despite the criticism, 3M's board, which included four previous 3M CEOs among its members, stood behind DeSimone until he retired in 2001. However, the board began a search for a new top executive in February 2000 and signaled that it was looking for an outsider. In December 2000, the company announced that it had found the person it wanted: Jim McNerney, a 51-year-old General Electric veteran who ran GE's medical equipment businesses, and before that GE's

Asian operations. McNerney was one of the front-runners in the race to succeed Jack Welsh as CEO of General Electric, but lost out to Jeffrey Immelt. One week after that announcement, 3M hired him.

McNerney's Plan for 3M

In his first public statement days after being appointed, McNerney said that his focus would be on getting to know 3M's people and culture and its diverse lines of business: "I think getting to know some of those businesses and bringing some of GE here to overlay on top of 3M's strong culture of innovation will be particularly important."[15] It soon became apparent that McNerney's game plan was exactly that: to bring the GE playbook to 3M and use it to try to boost 3M's results, while simultaneously not destroying the innovative culture that had produced the company's portfolio of 50,000 products.

The first move came in April 2001, when 3M announced that the company would cut 5,000 jobs, or about 7% of the workforce, in a restructuring effort that would zero in on struggling businesses. To cover severance and other costs of restructuring, 3M announced that it would take a $600-million charge against earnings. The job cuts were expected to save $500 million a year. In another effort to save costs, the company streamlined its purchasing processes, for example, by reducing the number of packaging suppliers on a global basis from 50 to 5, saving another $100 million a year in the process.

Next, McNerney introduced the Six Sigma process, a rigorous, statistically based quality-control process that was one driver of process improvement and cost savings at General Electric. At heart, Six Sigma is a management philosophy, accompanied by a set of tools, that is rooted in identifying and prioritizing customers and their needs, reducing variation in all business processes, and selecting and grading all projects based on their impact on financial results. Six Sigma breaks every task (process) in an organization down into increments to be measured against a perfect model.

McNerney called for Six Sigma to be rolled out across 3M's global operations. He also introduced a Six Sigma-like performance evaluation system at 3M under which managers were asked to rank every single employee who reported to them

In addition to boosting performance from existing business, McNerney quickly signaled that he wanted to play a more active role in allocating resources between new business opportunities. At any given time, 3M has some 1,500 products in the development pipeline. McNerney stated that was too many; he wanted to funnel more cash to the most promising ideas, those with a potential market of $100 million a year or more, while cutting funding to weaker-looking development projects.

In the same vein, he signaled that he wanted to play a more active role in resource allocation than had traditionally been the case for a 3M CEO, using cash from mature businesses to fund growth opportunities elsewhere. He scrapped the requirement that each division get 30% of its sales from products introduced in the past four years, noting that "To make that number, some managers were resorting to some rather dubious innovations, such as pink Post- it Notes. It became a game, what could you do to get a new SKU?"[16]

Some longtime 3M watchers, however, worried that by changing resource-allocation practices McNerney might harm 3M's innovative culture. If the company's history proves anything, they say, it's that it is hard to tell which of today's unheralded products will become tomorrow's home runs. No one predicted that Scotch Guard or Post-it Notes would earn millions. They began as minor experiments that evolved without planning into big hits. McNerney's innovations all sound fine in theory, they say, but there is a risk that he will lose what is valuable in the process.

In general though, securities analysts greeted McNerney's moves favorably. One noted that "McNerney is all about speed," and that there will be "no more Tower of Babel, everyone speaks one language." This "one company" vision was meant to replace the program under which 3M systematically spun off successful new products into new business centers. The problem with this approach, according to the analyst, was that there was no leveraging of best practices across businesses.[17]

McNerney also signaled that he would reform 3M's regional management structure, replacing it with a global business-unit structure that would be defined by either products or markets.

At a meeting for investment analysts held on September 30, 2003, McNerney summarized a number of achievements.[18] At the time, the indications seemed to suggest that McNerney was helping to revitalize 3M. Profitability, measured by return on invested capital, had risen from 19.4% in 2001 and

was projected to hit 25.5% in 2003. 3M's stock price had risen from $42 just before McNerney was hired to $73 in October 2003 (see Figure 5 for details).

Like his former boss, Jack Welsh at GE, McNerney seemed to place significant value on internal executive education programs as a way of shifting to a performance-oriented culture. McNerney noted that some 20,000 employees had been through Six Sigma training by the third quarter of 2003. Almost 400 higher-level managers had been through an advanced leadership development program set up by McNerney and offered by 3M's own internal executive education institute. Some 40% of participants had been promoted on graduating. All of the company's top managers had graduated from an executive leadership program offered by 3M.

McNerney also emphasized the value of the five initiatives he had put in place at 3M: indirect cost control, global sourcing, e-productivity, Six Sigma, and the 3M Acceleration program. With regard to indirect cost control, some $800 million had been taken out of 3M's cost structure since 2001, primarily by reducing employee numbers, introducing more efficient processes that boost productivity, benchmarking operations internally, and leveraging best practices. According to McNerney, internal benchmarking highlighted another $200 to $400 million in potential cost savings over the next few years.

On global sourcing, McNerney noted that more than $500 million had been saved since 2000 by consolidating purchasing, reducing the number of suppliers, switching to lower-cost suppliers in developing nations, and introducing duel sourcing policies to keep price increases under control.

The e-productivity program at 3M embraced the entire organization and all functions. It involves the digitalization of a wide range of processes, from customer ordering and payment, through supply-chain management and inventory control, to managing employee process. The central goal is to boost productivity by using information technology to more effectively manage information within the company, and between the company and its customers and suppliers. McNerney cited some $100 million in annual cost savings from this process.

The Six Sigma program, which overlays the entire organization, focuses on improving processes to boost cash flow, lower costs (through productivity enhancements), and boost growth rates. By late 2003, there were some 7,000 Six Sigma projects in process at 3M. By using working capital more efficiently, Six Sigma programs had helped to generate some $800 million in cash, with the total expected to rise to $1.5 billion in by the end of 2004. 3M has applied the process to the company's R&D process, enabling researcher to engage customer information in the initial stages of a design discussion. According to Jay Inlenfeld, VP of R&D, Six Sigma tools "... allow us to be more closely connected to the market and give us a much higher probability of success in our new product designs."[19]

Finally, the 3M Acceleration program is aimed at boosting the growth rate from new products through better resource allocation, particularly by shifting resources from slower-growing to faster-growing markets. As McNerney noted:

3M has always had extremely strong competitive positions, but not in markets that are growing fast enough. The issue has been to shift emphasize into markets that are growing faster.[20] Part of this program is a tool termed 2X/3X. 2X is an objective for two times the number of new products that were introduced

in the past, and 3X is a business objective for three times as many winning products as there were in the past (see Figure 2). 2X focuses on generating "major" product initiatives, and 3X on improving the commercialization of those initiatives. The process illustrated in Figure 3 is 3M's "stage gate" process, where each gate represents a major decision point in the development of a new product, from idea generation to postlaunch.

Other initiatives aimed at boosting 3M's organization growth rate through innovation include Six Sigma process, leadership development programs, and technology leadership (see Figure 3). The purpose of these initiatives was to help implement the 2X/3X strategy.

As a further step in the Acceleration Program, 3M decided to centralize its corporate R&D effort. Prior to the arrival of McNerney, there were 12 technology centers staffed by 900 scientists that focused on core technology development. The company is replacing these with one central research lab, staffed by 500 scientists, some 120 of whom will be located outside the United States. The remaining 400 scientists will be relocated to

Figure 2 The New Product Development Process at 3M[21]

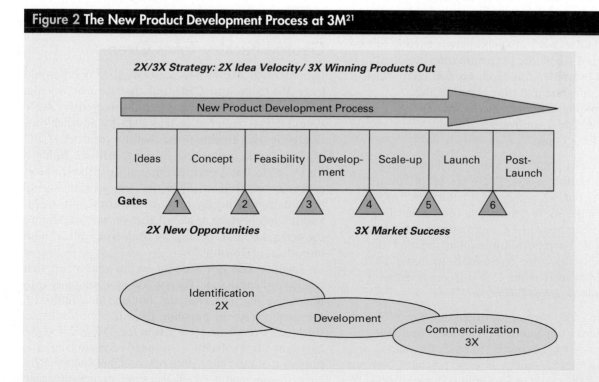

2X/3X Strategy: 2X Idea Velocity/ 3X Winning Products Out

New Product Development Process

| Ideas | Concept | Feasibility | Development | Scale-up | Launch | Post-Launch |

Gates: 1 2 3 4 5 6

2X New Opportunities   3X Market Success

Identification 2X

Development

Commercialization 3X

Figure 3 R&D's Role in Organic Growth[22]

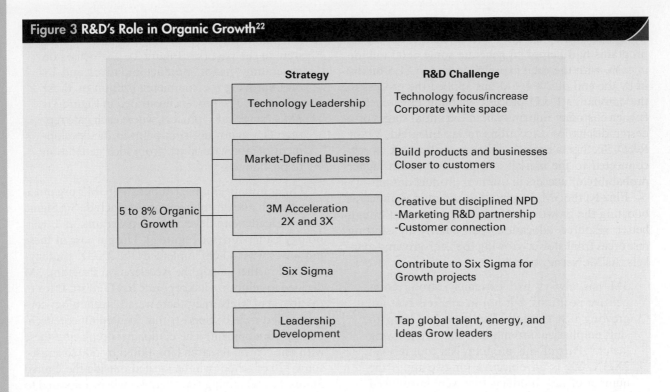

R&D centers in the business units. The goal of this new corporate research lab is to focus on developing new technology that might fill high growth "white spaces", which are areas where the company currently has no presence, but where the long term market potential is great. An example is research on fuel cells, which is currently a big research project within 3M.

Responding to critics' charges that such changes might alter 3M's innovative culture, VP of R&D Inlenfeld noted that:

> We are not going to change the basic culture of innovation at 3M. There is a lot of culture in 3M, but we are going to introduce more systematic, more productive tools that allow our researchers to be more successful.[23] For example, he repeatedly emphasized that the company remains committed to basic 3M principles such as the 15% rule and leveraging technology across businesses.

By late 2003, McNerney noted that some 600 new product ideas were underdevelopment and that collectively, they were expected to reach the market and generate some $5 billion in new revenues between 2003 and 2006, up from $3.5 billion 18 months earlier.

Approximately $1 billion of these gains were expected in 2003.

George Buckley Takes Over

In mid-2005, McNerney announced that he would leave 3M to become CEO and chairman of Boeing, a company on whose board he had served for some time. He was replaced in late 2005 by another outsider, George Buckley, the highly regarded CEO of Brunswick Industries. Buckley, British, holds a Ph.D. in electrical engineering and describes himself as a scientist at heart. Over the next year, in several presentations, Buckley outlined his strategy for 3M, and it soon became apparent that he was sticking to the general course laid out by McNerney, albeit with important corrections.[24]

Buckley did not see 3M as an enterprise that needed radical change. He saw 3M as a company with impressive internal strengths, but one that had been too cautious about pursuing growth opportunities.[25] Buckley's overall strategic vision for 3M was that the company must solve its customers' needs through the provision of innovative, differentiated products that increase those customers' efficiency and competitiveness.

Consistent with long-term 3M strategy, he saw this being achieved by applying 3M's multiple technology platforms to different market opportunities.

Controlling costs and boosting productivity through Six Sigma continued to be a major thrust under Buckley. This was hardly a surprise; Buckley had pushed Six Sigma at Brunswick. By late 2006, some 55,000 3M employees had been trained in Six Sigma methodology, 20,000 projects had been completed, and some 15,000 were underway. 3M was also adding techniques gleaned from Toyota's lean production methodology to its Six Sigma tool kit. As a result of Six Sigma and other cost control methods, between 2001 and 2005 productivity measured by sales per employee increased from $234 to $311, and some $750 million were taken out of overhead costs.

However, Buckley departed from McNerney's playbook in one significant way: He removed Six Sigma from the labs. The feeling of many at 3M was that Six Sigma rules choked those working on innovation. As one 3M researcher noted, "It's really tough to schedule innovation."[26] When McNerney left 3M in 2005, the percentage of sales from new products introduced in the last 5 years had fallen to 21%, down from the company's long-term goal of 30%. By 2010, after 5 years of Buckley's leadership, the percentage was back up to 30%. According to many in the company, Buckley has been a champion of researchers at 3M, devoting much of his personal time to empowering researchers and urging them to restore the luster of 3M.

Buckley stressed the need for 3M to more aggressively pursue growth opportunities. He wanted the company to use its differentiated brands and technology to continue to develop core businesses and extend those core business into adjacent areas. In addition, like McNerney, Buckley wanted the company to focus R&D resources on emerging business opportunities, and he too seemed prepared to play a proactive role in this process. Areas of focus include filtration systems, track and trace information technology, energy and mineral extraction, and food safety. 3M made a number of acquisitions since 2005 to achieve scale and acquire technology and other assets in these areas. In addition, it increased its investment in technologies related to these growth opportunities, particularly nanotechnology.

Buckley made selective divestures of businesses not seen as core. Most notably, in November 2006,

3M reached an agreement to sell its pharmaceutical business for $2.1 billion. 3M took this step after deciding that a combination of slow growth and high regulatory and technological risk made the sector an unattractive one that would dampen the company's growth rate.

Finally, Buckley was committed to continuing internationalization at 3M. 3M doubled its capital investment in the fast-growing markets of China, India, Brazil, Russia, and Poland between 2005 and 2010. All of these markets were seen as expanding two to three times as fast as the United States.

Judged by the company's financial results, the McNerney and Buckley eras did seem improve 3M's financial performance. The first decade of the 21st century was a difficult one, marked by sluggish growth in the United States and, in 2008–2009, a steep recession triggered by a global financial crisis. 3M weathered this storm better than most, bouncing out of the recession in 2010 with strong revenue and income growth, helped in large part by its new products and exposure to expanding international markets. For the decade, revenues expanded from $16 billion in 2001 to $26.66 billion in 2010, earnings per share expanded from $1.79 to $5.63, while ROIC increased from the mid-teens in the 1990s to the mid-20s.

Inge Thulin: Back to the Future

In early 2012, Georg Buckley retired after a successful tenure during which he had skillfully navigated 3M through the great financial crisis of 2008–2009. The company's COO, Inge Thulin replaced him. Thulin, born in Sweden, first joined 3M in 1979. Fluent in five languages, Thulin has worked for 3M in Europe, the Middle East, Canada, and Hong Kong. Within the company he is seen as one of the chief architects of 3Ms successful international business, which he oversaw as executive vice president for international operations. He is also seen as an insider who knows 3M's culture intimately and places a high value on innovation. In his first shareholder meeting, he reaffirmed this, stating that "innovation is the center of our plan" and committing the company to increasing R&D spending to 6% of company sales by 2017, up from 5.4% of sales in 2012. More generally, Thulin has stated that he would be continuing to follow the roadmap laid out by George Buckley, with whom he worked closely.

REFERENCES

J. C. Collins and J. I. Porras. *Built to Last*, Harper Business, New York, 1994.

M. Conlin. "Too Much Doodle?" *Forbes*, October 19, 1998, pp. 54–56.

M. Dickson. "Back to the Future," *Financial Times*, 1994, May 30, p. 7.

J. Hallinan. "3M's Next Chief Plans to Fortify Results with Discipline He Learned at GE Unit," *The Wall Street Journal*, December 6, 2000, p. B17.

E. Von Hippel et al., "Creating Breakthroughs at 3M," *Harvard Business Review*, September-October 1999.

R. Mullin, "Analysts Rate 3M's New Culture," *Chemical Week,* September 26, 2001, pp. 39–40.

A Century of Innovation: The 3M Story. 3M, 2002. Available at www.3m.com/about3m/century/index.jhtml.

3M Investor Meeting, September 30, 2003. Available at www.corporate-ir.net/ireye/ir_site.zhtml?ticker=MMM&script=2100.

T. Studt, "3M–Where Innovation Rules," *R&D Magazine* 45 (April 2003): 20–24.

D. Weimer, "3M: The Heat Is on the Boss," *Businessweek*, March 15, 1999, pp. 82–83.

Jerry Useem, "(Tape) + (Light Bulb) = ?" *Fortune*, August 12, 2002, pp. 127–131.

M. Gunther, M. Adamo, and B. Feldman, "3M's Innovation Revival," *Fortune*, September 27, 2010, pp. 73–76.

NOTES

1. M. Dickson, "Back to the Future," *Financial Times*, 1994, May 30, p. 7. www.3m.com/profile/looking/mcknight.jhtml.
2. www.3m.com/about3M/pioneers/drew2.jhtml.
3. www.3m.com/about3M/innovation/scotchgard50/index.jhtml.
4. *A Century of Innovation: The 3M Story*. 3M, 2002. Available at www.3m.com/about3m/century/index.jhtml.
5. Ibid, p. 33.
6. *A Century of Innovation: The 3M Story*, p. 78.
7. Ibid.
8. "3M–Where Innovation Rules," *R&D* Magazine 45 (April 2003): 20–24.
9. Ibid, p. 42.
10. E. Von Hippel et al., "Creating Breakthroughs at 3M," *Harvard Business Review* (September-October 1999).
11. www.3m.com/about3M/history/mcknight.jhtml.
12. *A Century of Innovation: The 3M Story*, pp. 143–144.
13. M. Conlin, "Too Much Doodle?" *Forbes*, October 19, 1998, pp. 54–56.
14. D. Weimer, "3M: The Heat Is on the Boss," *Businessweek*, March 15, 1999, pp. 82–83.
15. J. Hallinan, "3M's Next Chief Plans to Fortify Results with Discipline He Learned at GE Unit," *The Wall Street Journal*, December 6, 2000, p. B17.
16. J. Useem, "(Tape) + (Light Bulb) = ?" *Fortune*, August 12, 2002, pp. 127–131.
17. R. Mullin, "Analysts Rate 3M's New Culture," *Chemical Week*, September 26, 2001, pp. 39–40.
18. 3M Investor Meeting, September 30th, 2003. Archived at www.corporate-ir.net/ireye/ir_site.zhtml?ticker=MMM&script=2100.
19. T. Studt, "3M–Where Innovation Rules," *R&D Magazine* 45 (April 2003): 20–24.
20. 3M Investor Meeting, September 30, 2003.
21. Adapted from presentation by J. Inlenfeld, 3M Investor Meeting, September 30, 2003. Archived at www.corporate-ir.net/ireye/ir_site.zhtml?ticker=MMM&script=2100.
22. Ibid.
23. T. Studt, "3M—Where Innovation Rules."
24. Material drawn from G. Buckley's presentation to Prudential's investor conference, "Inside Our Best Ideas," September 28, 2006. This and other relevant presentations are archived at http://investor.3m.com/ireye/ir_site.zhtml?ticker=MMM&script=1200.
25. J. Sprague, "MMM: Searching for Growth with New CEO Leading," *Citigroup Global Markets*, May 2, 2006.
26. M. Gunther, M. Adamo, and B. Feldman, "3M's Innovation Revival," *Fortune*, September 27, 2010, p. 74.

28

THE TATA GROUP, 2015

Melissa A. Schilling & Nora Scott

The Tata Group is India's largest industrial conglomerate, and one of India's oldest and most revered business groups. Throughout its 147-year history the growth of the company has advanced in parallel with the Indian economy, increasing both the scope of businesses in which it participates, and its scale in those businesses. By 2015, the company had sales of over $100 billion a year, and operated more than 100 companies in sectors as diverse as automobiles, steel, tea, hotels, telecommunications, chemicals, and more. More remarkable still was that despite its immense size and diversification, the company had maintained a return on assets of 7% or more throughout most of its history, in contrast to the conventional wisdom that giant conglomerates typically underperform more specialized companies.

The Tata Group is managed by the holding company, Tata Sons. The original Tata family owns about 3% of Tata Sons, and a large portion of the rest of the equity of the group is held by charitable trusts that were created by the family. Since its inception in 1868, the Tata Group has had only six chairmen, two for negligible amounts of time. Tata's expansion into the massive holding company that it is today was shaped by both the evolution of the economic and political climate of India, as well as the vision of the four major chairmen who steered the group. To understand Tata's evolution and performance, it is necessary to understand both the business context of India, and the mission of its founding family.

THE HISTORY OF THE HOUSE OF TATA

Tata's storied history began in 1868, when Jamsetji Nusserwanji Tata founded a textile trading company in Mumbai. Though he had come from a long line of Parsi Zoroastrian priests, and his family intended for him to join the priesthood as well, the nonconforming young man decided to instead become a businessman. He eventually rose to almost legendary status, known as the "Father of Indian industry."

In 1869, he expanded his fledgling company into textile manufacturing through the purchase of a bankrupt mill, which he later sold for a profit after improving its efficiency. His professed goals for the company were to help industrialize India by establishing an iron and steel company that would supply the expanding railroads, a hydroelectric power plant, a luxury hotel, and a world-class learning and research institution.[1] Only one of those goals was fulfilled within his lifetime: The Taj Mahal Hotel in Bombay was opened (1903), at the time the only hotel in India to have electricity.

After his death in 1904, Jamsetji Tata's was succeeded by his eldest son, Dorabji Tata. Dorabji Tata actualized his father's remaining goals and opened India's first private steel company in 1907 (one hundred years later, it would be the country's largest private-sector steel company), the Indian Institute of Science in 1909, and a hydroelectric power plant in 1911.[2] Dorabji Tata further diversified the Tata Group when he created the New India Assurance Company in 1919, which became the largest general insurance company in India. These companies became the cash pillars of Tata Group and allowed the company to re-invest in new projects without having to borrow capital from lending institutions.

In 1932, J. R. D. Tata (the son of Dorabji's cousin) took the helm of the Tata Group. Under J. R. D. Tata, the Tata Group continued to be at the forefront of India's development, opening India's first airline in 1932, Tata Chemicals in 1939, and Tata Engineering & Locomotive in 1945. Tata Engineering & Locomotive had been founded to make steam locomotives, but after collaborating with Daimler-Benz in 1954 to enter truck production, it began producing commercial vehicles in earnest. In 1968, Tata founded India's first software firm. In total, under J. R. D. Tata's control, the Tata portfolio expanded from 14 to 95 businesses that they had either started or in which Tata held a controlling interest. If one includes subsidiary and associate companies, Tata was involved in over 300 businesses. The assets of the Tata Group rose from US $100 million to over US $5 billion under J. R. D.'s chairmanship.

Many of the sectors the Tata Group entered were new for India at the time. Whereas in the U.S. or Western Europe entrepreneurs could access investor funds or debt to found new ventures or scale up businesses, India did not have strong capital markets. Weak investing norms and infrastructure, poor enforcement of contracts, and corruption meant that capital came at too high of a price or was not available at all. However, because Tata owned so many different kinds of businesses with different levels of maturity, capital needs, and cash flow, it could subsidize new businesses with cash generated from its mature, high-income businesses. This allowed the Tata Group to expand in ways that independent companies could not. For example, by internally funding new ventures, this giant conglomerate was able to create large infrastructure projects without having to issue bonds or borrow from banks.

In 1991, Ratan Tata (great-grandson of Jamsetji Tata) took over as chairman from J. R. D. Tata. He had studied architecture at Cornell before returning to India to work, shoveling limestone at Tata Steel.[3]

While the economic setting in India leading up to the 1990s had led J. R. D. Tata to create an insular system of companies that were able to cross fund each other without having to seek external capital, by the early 1990s things were changing in India. By the time that Ratan Tata assumed the position as chairman, India's government had begun to relax its regulation of both domestic industry and the licensing regime that protected Indian industry from foreign investment. The loosening of restrictions gave Indian businesses more autonomy, but also exposed them to more foreign competition. Indian regulations mandated that foreign firms could enter India only by collaborating with a domestic company. The Tata Group's prominence and reputation for high ethical standards made it an attractive partner. As a result, Tata companies created alliances with AT&T, Cummings Engine, IBM, Honeywell, Mercedes-Benz, Silicon Graphics, and others during the 1990s. Tata's involvement with these companies enhanced its global exposure and strengthened its ability to expand into foreign markets.

Ratan Tata sought to increase the competitiveness of Tata's operating companies by cutting costs as well as employee ranks. One example of this approach is Tata Steel (the world's sixth largest producer after the $12.1-billion acquisition of U.K. based Corus in 2007). Tata Steel's output per worker increased eightfold in just over a decade. Tata Steel cut costs to improve the production of blast furnaces by continually adjusting them to burn at maximum efficiency based on the incoming coal blends. This example of improved industrial efficiency is paralleled in Tata Power's decision to lower its capital expenditures by identifying inexpensive designs for large-scale projects. For example, when planning a new, 4,000-megawatt facility, Tata engineers used cheaper welded tubes instead of seamless ones in feed-water heaters, and redesigned the layout of the turbine generator station. By making these types of adjustments, Tata Power saved more than $100 million in capital expenditures while preserving the base capacity of the plant and still meeting India's safety standards. Cutting employee ranks at Tata Steel served to reduce the number of management layers from 13 to 5, thus increasing employee accountability. These organizational changes improved the competitiveness and the quality of products and services.

Under Ratan's stewardship, Tata engaged in a series of international acquisitions, including the Corus steel deal, the purchase of U.K. teabag maker Tetley, iconic automakers Land Rover and Jaguar (which were purchased from Ford), and Singapore's National Steel. By 2008, it was earning a majority of its profits from outside of India. Though the Tata Group had been founded with a mission to serve India through economic and industrial development, it was now being transformed into a truly global company. The acquisition of the two luxury brand vehicles (Jaguar and Land Rover) particularly increased international awareness of the Tata Group, while simultaneously giving Tata Motors access to new technology and markets. At his 2012 retirement, Ratan Tata was replaced as Chairman by Cyrus Mistry, the first non-Indian to head the Tata Group and only the second without the surname Tata.

THE INDIAN BUSINESS CONTEXT

When Jamsetji Tata founded his company, India was under British rule. Tata Group had already existed for 79 years before India gained its independence in 1947. Since its independence, India's government has developed into a federation system with a parliament. Post-independence India still adhered to socialist policies with economic policies that leaned toward protectionism and state monitoring of industrialization, import substitution, and state intervention. High tariffs and the need for an import license worked to prevent foreign goods from reaching India's market. Firms were required to obtain a license in order to invest or develop their products.[4] These economic policies are what caused J.R.D. Tata to structure the Tata Group in such an insular fashion. Following an economic crisis, however, in which the Indian government was close to default, the government passed the Liberalization Act of 1991. This act opened India's economy to trade and investment, broke the state monopolies, and eased the licensing requirements. The effect of the liberalization act enabled foreign direct investment to increase dramatically, both inwardly and outwardly (see Figure 1). Unshackling Indian businesses from the cumbersome regulation allowed new businesses to more rapidly form and productivity to accelerate. As shown in Figure 2, while the population in India shows linear growth, the gross domestic product (GDP) began to increase exponentially. By 2014, India's economy was worth over $2 trillion, making it the world's tenth largest by nominal GDP and the third largest by purchasing power parity.[5]

Figure 1 India's Foreign Direct Investment (Inward and Outward), 1985–2013

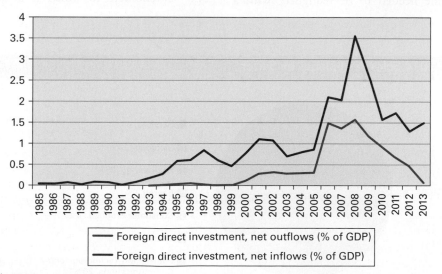

— Foreign direct investment, net outflows (% of GDP)
— Foreign direct investment, net inflows (% of GDP)

Sources: World Bank, 2015.

Figure 2 India's Population and GDP, 1985–2012

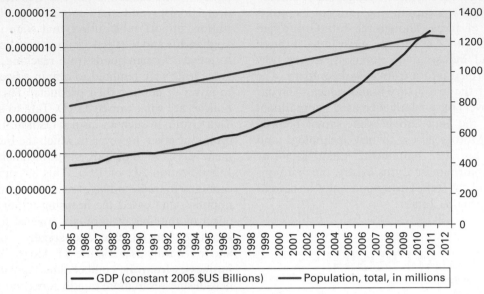

Sources: World Bank, 2015.

TATA INDUSTRIES IN 2015

Before his 2012 retirement, Ratan Tata began an initiative to streamline and consolidate the Tata Group. Ratan Tata felt that the myriad companies tied only by the Tata name needed to be realigned, with a stronger and more unified focus. He divested some operating companies while consolidating the others into seven categories: consumer products; energy; engineering; information systems and communications; services; chemicals; and materials (see Figure 3). Every Tata company has its own board of directors and shareholders to which it is accountable. The

Figure 3 2013–2014 Sales Percentages by Sector

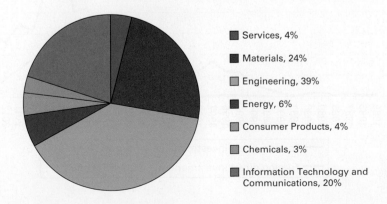

- Services, 4%
- Materials, 24%
- Engineering, 39%
- Energy, 6%
- Consumer Products, 4%
- Chemicals, 3%
- Information Technology and Communications, 20%

largest Tata companies are Tata Steel, Tata Motors, Tata Consultancy Services, Tata Power, Tata Chemicals, Tata Global Beverages, Tata Teleservices, Titan, Tata Communications, and Indian Hotels.

Consumer Products

This sector made up 4% of Tata Group's sales in 2013–14. From high-end designer furniture to bottled water, the various companies have an array of products priced to appeal to those of varied income. One company offers fine-bone china (selling to Wedgewood, Royal Doulton, and the like) and also sells industrial china to institutional customers. Titan Industries and Tata Global Beverages (the largest tea company in the world) are part of this group.

Energy

The energy sector represented 6% of sales for 2013–14. Tata Power, now 104 years old and the parent company of all others in the energy division, has a presence in all segments of the power sector from power generation, such as thermal, hydro, solar, wind, geothermal and waste gas, to the transmission, distribution, and trading of power. Its areas of focus are power generation, green energy, transmission and distribution, fuel assets, shipping and logistics, trading, and power project-related services. Tata Power has interests in Australia, South Africa, Nepal, and Bhutan, and fuel assets and geothermal projects in Indonesia as well as logistics operations in Singapore.

Engineering

Engineering made up 39% of Tata Group's sales for 2013–14, making it Tata's largest sector. The various business in this sector offer consulting services, precision tool design and manufacturing, automation, construction, and temperature engineering (essential in a country where temperatures can reach 104 in the summer months). Tata Motors is one of the businesses within the engineering sector. Established (as Tata Engineering and Locomotive Company, or TELCO) in 1945, it is South Asia's largest auto manufacturer and produces passenger cars, commercial vehicles, vans, and coaches. Jaguar and Land Rover are also part of this group.

Information Systems and Communications

This was the Tata Group's third largest sector in 2013–14, bringing in 20% of the sales for Tata Group. The range of businesses clustered in this division offer services such as industrial automation, telecommunications, software, and information systems. Notably, India has seen massive growth in the penetration of communication technologies such as mobile cellular subscriptions and Internet use in the last decade (see Figure 4). Tata's information technologies consulting company, Tata Consultancy Services, was the largest source of revenue for the group in 2014. Tata Consultancy Services employees over 300,000 consultants.

Services

The services sector comprises Tata's interests in hospitality, insurance, realty, and financial services primarily. This sector made up 4% of the Tata Group's sales for 2013–14. Indian Hotels, Taj Air, Tata Capital, Tata AIG General Insurance, among others, are part of this group.

Chemicals

Chemicals was the smallest Tata sector, comprising 3% of the company's sales. The Tata Group is one of the largest producers of soda ash (sodium carbonate) in the world. Among its plethora of uses, soda ash can be used as a water softener, a food additive, and a stabilizer in glass production. The businesses in this sector also have interests in fertilizers and pharmaceuticals.

Materials

This sector accounts for 24% of the Tata Group's sales for 2013–14. Tata Steel has investments in Corus (U.K.; renamed Tata Steel Europe), Millennium Steel (renamed Tata Steel Thailand), and NatSeel Holdings (in Singapore). It operates in over 20 countries, has a commercial presence in over 50, and has the capacity to produce over 30 million tons of crude steel every year, making it one of the largest steel producers in the world.

Figure 4 India's Growth in Penetration of Communication Technologies, 1985–2013

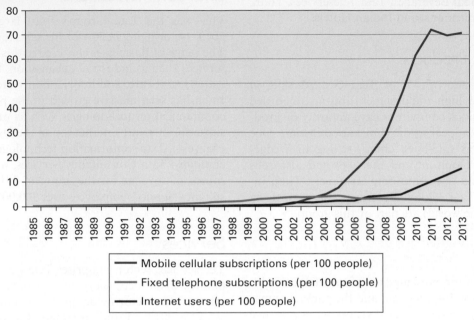

— Mobile cellular subscriptions (per 100 people)
— Fixed telephone subscriptions (per 100 people)
— Internet users (per 100 people)

Sources: World Bank, 2015.

THE NANO PROJECT

On a rainy day in 2002, Ratan Tata, Chairman of India's Tata Group, was driving to the airport in Bangalore. In front of him was a typical sight: an entire family on a two-wheel scooter. The father drove the scooter with a young child standing in front of him, and his wife held a small baby in back. Suddenly the scooter skidded and overturned, sending the family tumbling. Tata and his driver narrowly escaped running over the poor family.[6] At that moment, Ratan Tata conceived of a dream that would take five years and the help of a global network of 800 suppliers to realize: a car that was affordable by the masses of India. In a seemingly offhanded comment Tata mentioned to a reporter that the car would be priced at around Rs. 1 lakh (approximately $2200). As noted by Ratan Tata, "It was never meant to be a Rs. 1 lakh car; that happened by circumstance. I was interviewed by the *Financial Times* at the Geneva Motor Show and I talked about this future product as an affordable car. I was asked how much it would cost and I said about Rs. 1 lakh. The next day the *Financial Times* had a

headline to the effect that the Tatas are to produce a Rs. 100,000 car."[7] Despite extreme difficulties in meeting this price point, and increases in both parts and commodity prices during its development, Tata upheld what he viewed as a promise to the Indian public: to produce a Rs. Lakh car.

Developing the Nano

Ratan Tata decided to stay personally involved in the Nano project, and also put Ravi Kant, the Vice Chairman of Tata Motors, in charge of the project to ensure that the project had senior support. At the time Tata began developing the Nano, the least expensive car in the world was the Chinese QQ3, priced at $5,000. It quickly became clear that trying to make a Rs. 1 Lakh car by benchmarking against existing cars and trying to make them less expensive was not going to be successful, so Tata and Kant decided to instead benchmark many of the systems in the car against two-wheel scooters.

Many things that were taken for granted about producing a car had to be challenged. For example, rather than an engine with at least three cylinders, the

Nano would be designed with two cylinders, which would both reduce the cost and weight of the car. The car would not have electric windows or locks, antilock brakes, or airbags. Its tires would have inner tubes, its seats would have a simple, three-position recline, and there would be only one windshield wiper and one rearview mirror.

Meeting the design challenges of the car was incredibly difficult, but many of Tata's suppliers looked at the project as an exciting challenge. Rather than being given a design dictated by Tata, they were given weight and cost objectives and free reign to find a way to meet them. Many suppliers came up with startlingly unique ways of lowering the cost of the car, such as a hollow steering column and a single fuel-injection valve for both of the engines cylinders. Power steering was unnecessary due to the low weight of the car. Radios were not included with the base model of the car, but could be purchased as an optional accessory.

Everything about car design had to be reconceptualized to realize the Nano, from the car's frame to its major power systems—even its trim. As summarized by Girish Wagh, head of the Tata team, "The entire system was being reinvented. Innovation at the aggregate level trickled down to system, then to subsystems, then to parts. We went through a tremendous amount of iteration in the design process. The entire engine was redesigned thrice, the entire body was redesigned twice, and the floor plan of the car redesigned around 10 times, the wiper system designed more than 11 times."[8]

The Launch

The Nano was officially launched in March 2009, at its intended price of Rs. 1 Lakh, and meeting all of the Indian's government's safety and emissions standards. It weighed 1,320 pounds, and was rated at 50 miles to the gallon.[9] Ratan Tata, who is exceptionally tall, even sat in the car (to demonstrate that the Nano had ample interior space despite its small size), and remarked, "We made a promise to the world and we kept it." Initial demand for the Nano was very strong, but the car suffered several early obstacles. First, plans to manufacture the car in West Bengal met with resistance by farmers, forcing a costly move of both Tata's manufacturing and many suppliers.[10] Then several

Nanos caught fire, leading to extremely bad publicity for the car. Tata reinforced the exhaust systems of the car to avoid such problems in the future, but it would take some time for the car's reputation to recover. By 2010, the company was selling about 5,000 Nanos a month, though it had capacity to produce 15,000 a month. Ratan Tata had said that the car needed to sell one million units a year to be worth doing—and it was definitely not hitting this goal.[11]

The low price of the car turned out to be one of its problems: it was perceived as "cheap." According to marketing strategist Jack Trout, "Nobody wants to tell his friends and neighbors he has bought a cheap car. The brand is damaged."[12] People who were trading up from a two-wheeler did not want a no-frills, low-status, potentially unreliable car—they wanted a car of which they could be proud. Wagh and team heard the message loud and clear. They developed a new version of the Nano with power steering, better suspension, and an antiroll bar. They increased the car's power and torque, and began to offer vibrant colors like "Damsel purple." The Nano was given a glove compartment, a modern stereo system with Bluetooth connectivity, and keyless entry. You can now even get a Nano with an automatic transmission. The new Nano's price now ranges from Rs. 1.4 lakh to Rs. 2.6 lakh.[13]

▚ THE FUTURE FOR TATA GROUP

As Tata Group navigates its new global role, it must strike a balance between economic growth and investment in its country of origin. When Jamsetji Tata founded the company, his goals of growing India's economy were complemented by his desire to give back to the Indian people. This was why he wanted to create a world-class learning facility, the Indian Institute of Science. The Nano was emblematic of these goals: It aligned perfectly with Tata's mission to serve the bottom of the financial pyramid in India. Many of the company's other businesses, however, faced pressures of a global nature (see Table 1). Did Tata's mission-based management make sense for a company that earned the majority of its profits abroad? Furthermore, analysts questioned whether Tata's

Table 1 2015 Market Capitalization for Listed Tata Group Companies

Company	$ Billion
TCS	83.73
Tata Motors	25.94
Tata Steel	5.39
Titan Company	5.70
Tata Power	3.40
Tata Communications	2.07
Tata Chemicals	1.83
Tata Global Beverages	1.51
Voltas	1.56
Indian Hotels	1.51
CMC	0.99
Trent	0.76
Rallis	0.70
Tata Investment Corporation	0.52
Tata Elxsi	0.67
Tata Coffee	0.28
Tata Teleservices (Maharashtra)	0.25
Tata Sponge Iron	0.21

large and diversified holding group would continue to make sense in an increasingly modern India. India's capital markets were becoming more robust, lessening the value to be gained through cross-subsidization of businesses. Furthermore, since many of Tata's businesses could now easily access global capital markets, any constraints remaining in India's capital markets

were becoming less relevant. Would Tata ultimately be split apart? What were the advantages and costs of keeping so many businesses united under a single family name, and under the watchful eye of Tata Sons? On a tactical level, what should be Tata's plans for the Nano? Did it have the viable chance of succeeding in the international markets that Ratan had imagined? How could the learning that the company had reaped in its development be harnessed for future advantage?

NOTES

1. N. Sivakumar, "The Business Ethics of Jamsetji Nusserwanji Tata: A Forerunner in Promoting Stakeholder Welfare," *Journal of Business Ethics* 83 (2008): 353–361.
2. Hoovers, April 1, 2013.
3. W. Raynal, "The Smartest Guy in the Room," *Automotive News* 87 (6546) (2012). www.autonews.com.
4. India: The Economy, *BBC*, December, 3, 1998.
5. World Bank, 2014; International Monetary Fund, 2014.
6. K. Freiburg, J. Freiburg, and D. Dunston, *Nanovation: How a Little Car Can Teach the World to Think Big and Act Bold.* Nashville, TN: Thomas Nelson (2011).
7. S. Sinha and S. Sen, "The New Nano Promise," *Business Today*, March 30, 2014, www.businesstoday.com.
8. K. Palepu, B. Anand, and R. Tahilyani, "Tata Nano: The People's Car," Harvard Business School Case 9-710-420, 2011, p. 8.
9. A. Taylor, "Tata Takes on the World: Building an Auto Empire in India," *Fortune* 163 (6) (2011): 86–92.
10. Ibid.
11. S. Sinha and S. Sen, "The New Nano Promise," *Business Today*, March 30, pp. 62–74.
12. Ibid.
13. Ibid.

CASE 29

TESLA MOTORS, 2015

In 2015, Tesla Motors was a $3.2-billion company on track to set history. It had created two cars that most people agreed were remarkable. *Consumer Reports* had rated Tesla's Model S the best car it had ever reviewed. Though it was not yet posting profits (see Figures 1 and 2), sales were growing rapidly and analysts were hopeful that profits would soon follow. It had repaid its government loans ahead of the major auto conglomerates. Most importantly, it looked like it might *survive*—perhaps even thrive. This was astonishing, because there had been no other successful auto manufacturing start-up in the United States since the 1920s.

The road leading up to Tesla's position in 2015 had not always been smooth, and many doubts still lingered. Tesla had benefited from the enthusiasm of the "eco-wealthy"—a rather narrow portion of the market. How would Tesla fare when it was in direct competition with General Motors, Ford, and Nissan for the mass market? Would it be able to turn a sustainable profit on its auto-making operations? Furthermore, some questioned whether Tesla's goals to sell to the mass market even made sense. In the niche market, it had a privileged position with customers who were relatively price insensitive and seeking a stylish, high-performance car that made an environmental statement. To compete for the mass market, the car would have to provide good value for the money (involving trade-offs that might conflict with Chairman Elon Musk's ideals), and the obstacles to charging would have to be overcome.

◢ HISTORY OF TESLA

In 2003, an engineer named Martin Eberhard was looking for his next big project. A tall, slim man with a mop of gray hair, Eberhard was a serial entrepreneur who had launched a number of start-ups, including a company called NuvoMedia, which he sold to Gemstar in a $187-million deal. Eberhard was also looking for a sports car that would be environmentally friendly—he had concerns about global warming and U.S. dependence on the Middle East for oil. When he didn't find the car of his dreams on the market, he began contemplating building one himself, even though he had zero experience in the auto industry. Eberhard noticed that many of the driveways that had a Toyota Prius hybrid electric vehicle (or "dorkmobile" as he called it) also had expensive sports cars in them, making him speculate that there could be a market for a high-performance, environmentally friendly car. As Eberhard explained: "It was clear that people weren't buying a Prius to save money on gas. Gas was selling close to inflation-adjusted all-time lows. They were buying them to make a statement about the environment."[1]

Eberhard began to consider a range of alternative fuel options for his car: hydrogen fuel cells, natural gas, diesel. However, he soon concluded that the highest efficiency and performance would come from an entirely electric vehicle. Luckily for Eberhard, Al Cocconi (founder of AC Propulsion and one of the original engineers for GM's ill-fated EV-1) had concluded

Figure 1 Tesla Income Statement, in $US Thousands

	2014	2013	2012
Revenues			
Automotive sales	$3,192,723	$1,997,786	$385,699
Development services	5,633	15,710	27,557
Total revenues	3,198,356	2,013,496	413,256
Cost of revenues			
Automotive sales	2,310,011	1,543,878	371,658
Development services	6,674	13,356	11,531
Total cost of revenues	2,316,685	1,557,234	383,189
Gross profit	881,671	456,262	30,067
Operating expenses			
Research and development	464,700	231,976	273,978
Selling, general and administrative	603,660	285,569	150,372
Total operating expenses	1,068,360	517,545	424,350
Loss from operations	(186,689)	(61,283)	(394,283)
Interest income	1,126	189	288
Interest expense	(100,886)	(32,934)	(254)
Other income (expense), net	1,813	22,602	(1,828)
Loss before income taxes	(284,636)	(71,426)	(396,077)
Provision for income taxes	9,404	2,588	136
Net loss	**(294,040)**	**(74,014)**	**(396,213)**

Figure 2 Tesla Balance Sheet, in $US Thousands

	2014	2013
Assets		
Current assets		
Cash and cash equivalents	$1,905,713	$ 845,889

	2014	2013
Restricted cash and marketable securities	17,947	3,012
Accounts receivable	226,604	49,109
Inventory	953,675	340,355
Prepaid expenses and other current assets	94,718	27,574
Total current assets	3,198,657	1,265,939
Operating lease vehicles, net	766,744	382,425
Property, plant and equipment, net	1,829,267	738,494
Restricted cash	11,374	6,435
Other assets	43,209	23,637
Total assets	$5,849,251	$2,416,930
Liabilities and stockholders' equity		
Current liabilities		
Accounts payable	$ 777,946	$303,969
Accrued liabilities	268,884	108,252
Deferred revenue	191,651	91,882
Capital lease obligations, current portion	9,532	7,722
Customer deposits	257,587	163,153
Convertible senior notes	601,566	182
Total current liabilities	2,107,166	675,160
Capital lease obligations, less current portion	12,267	12,855
Deferred revenue, less current portion	292,271	181,180
Convertible senior notes, less current portion	1,806,518	586,119
Resale value guarantee	487,879	236,299
Other long-term liabilities	173,244	58,197
Total liabilities	4,879,345	1,749,810

the same thing and produced a car called the tzero. The tzero could go from zero to 60 miles per hour in 4.1 seconds, but it was powered with extremely heavy lead-acid batteries, limiting its range to about 60 miles between charges. Eberhard approached Cocconi with the idea of using lighter, lithium ion batteries, which offered six times more energy per pound. Cocconi was eager to try out the idea (he had, in fact, been experimenting with lithium ion batteries), and the resulting lithium ion-powered tzero accelerated to 60 miles per hour in 3.6 seconds and could travel more than 300 miles. Eberhard licensed the electric-drivetrain technology from AC Propulsion, and founded his company, Tesla Motors (named after Nikola Tesla, an early 20th-century inventor who developed, among other things, the AC electrical systems used in the United States today).[2]

Another entrepreneur—one with much deeper pockets—was also interested in developing electric vehicles based on the tzero: Elon Musk. In 2002, Musk was a 31-year-old South African living in California, who had founded a company that ultimately became PayPal. After selling PayPal to eBay in 2002 for $1.5 billion, he started a company called SpaceX with the ambitious goal of developing cheap, consumer space travel. (SpaceX's Dragon spacecraft ultimately made history in May 2012 by becoming the first commercial vehicle to launch and dock at the International Space Station.[3]) Musk was also the chairman of a high-profile, clean-tech venture in Northern California, Solar City. Musk's assertive style and astonishing record of high-tech entrepreneurship made him one of the inspirations for the Tony Stark character in Jon Favreau's *Iron Man* movies.

Like Eberhard, Musk thought electric cars were the key to the U.S. achieving energy independence, and he approached Cocconi about buying the tzero. Tom Gage, who was then AC Propulsion's CEO, suggested that Musk collaborate with Eberhard. After a 2- hour meeting in February 2004, Musk agreed to fund Eberhard's plan with $6.3 million. He would be the company's chairman; Eberhard would serve as CEO.

The first Tesla prototype, the Roadster, was based on the $45,000 Lotus Elise, a fast, light sports car that seemed perfect for the creation of Eberhard and Musk's grand idea (see Figure 3a). The car would have 400 volts of electric potential, liquid-cooled, lithium ion batteries, and a series of silicon transistors that would give the car acceleration so powerful the driver

Figure 3a Tesla Roadster

would be pressed back against the seat.[4] It would be nearly as fast as a Porsche 911 Turbo, would not create a single emission, and would get about 220 miles on a single charge from the kind of outlet you would use to power a washing machine.[5]

While the men at first worked well together, personality clashes soon emerged. Both were technically savvy and vigorously addressed problems within the company. As described by Laurie Yoler, Eberhard was "just brilliant, and he has this tenacity that is unbelievable … He is the guy you want around in those early days when you have naysayers all around." However, Eberhard could also be abrasive and critical. Musk, in turn, was not content to just financially back the company. He began to get intimately involved in decisions about the car's design and the operation of the company. Soon Musk and Eberhard were at odds over decision making. Eberhard preferred to stick with the fiberglass body panels used in the original Elise; Musk wanted to use the lighter, stronger—and more expensive—carbon fiber. Eberhard had approved the hiring of PR professionals to build publicity for the car before its launch; Musk fired them, believing his own involvement and the car itself would generate enough publicity. Eberhard wanted to reap the cost savings of sticking with the Elise's original crash-tested, off-the-rack chassis; Musk wanted to lower the doorsills by two inches to make the car easier to enter and exit. Musk also wanted to redesign the headlights and door latches, and replace the Elise's seats with more comfortable—and again, more expensive—custom seats.[6]

In each case, Musk prevailed. He insisted that "you can't sell a $100,000 car that looks like crap." Musk's views were hard to ignore given that, by 2007, he had put $55 million of his own money into the company and had also raised money from wealthy friends, including eBay's second employee, Jeff Skoll, and Google founders Sergey Brin and Larry Page.

Musk's insistence on the best materials and parts, however, combined with Eberhard's inexperience as the manager of a major firm, resulted in delays and runaway costs. At a staff meeting in June 2007, Tom Colson, head of manufacturing, revealed a cost analysis suggesting that the average cost of the cars would be over $100,000 for the first 50, and would decline only slightly with increased volume. Eberhard could not answer the financial questions of the venture capitalists on Tesla's board, and their confidence in him was eroded even further by his defense: "In any other company it's the CFO that provides those numbers … I'm an engineer, not a finance guy." In August 2007, the board removed him as CEO and demoted him to president of technology. Then, in October 2007, Musk arranged for Eberhard to be ousted from the company entirely. Furious, Eberhard started a blog detailing what he called the "Stealth Bloodbath" going on at Tesla, and he would later sue Musk for libel, slander, and breach of contract.[7]

Meanwhile, Eberhard's temporary replacement was Michael Marks, former CEO of Flextronics. Marks immediately created a priority list that identified items with potential to delay the car. He mothballed any plans for side projects and focused the entire business on streamlining costs and launching the Roadster. Despite his efforts, the Roadster missed its deadline for beginning production at the Lotus facility, triggering a penalty built into the manufacturing contract Eberhard had signed with Lotus: a $4-million fee.

By the beginning of 2008, morale was at an all-time low. In March, however, production began on the Roadster, and by July 2008, most of the production problems had been forgotten as the first seven Roadsters (the "Founder's Series") hit the road. Enthusiasm for the cars was astonishing—an all-star list of celebrities made reservations to buy one, and everywhere a Roadster appeared, people (albeit mostly men) stopped to stare.[8]

Musk's ambitions did not stop at a niche high-end car, however. He wanted to build a major U.S. auto company—a feat that had not been successfully accomplished since the 1920s. To do so, he knew he needed to introduce a less expensive car that could attract a higher volume of sales, if not quite the mass market. In June 2008, Tesla announced the Model S, a high-performance, all-electric sedan that would sell for a price ranging from $57,400 to $77,400 and compete against cars like the BMW 5-series (see Figure 3b). The car would have an all-aluminum body and a range of up to 300 miles per charge.[9] The Model S cost $500 million to develop; however, offsetting that cost was a $465-million loan Tesla received from the U.S. government to build the car, part of the U.S. government's initiative to promote the development of technologies that would help the United States achieve energy independence.

By May 2012, Tesla reported that it already had 10,000 reservations for customers hoping to buy the Model S, and Musk confidently claimed the company would soon be producing and selling 20,000 Model S cars per year. Musk also noted that after ramping up production, he expected to see "at least 10,000 units a year from demand in Europe and at least 5,000 in Asia."[10] The production of the Model S went more smoothly than that of the Roadster and, by June 2012, the first Model S cars rolled off the factory floor. The very first went to Jeff Skoll, eBay's first president, and a major investor in Tesla. On the day of the launch, Skoll talked with Musk about whether it was harder to build a rocket or a car (referring to Musk's SpaceX company): "We decided it was a car. There isn't a lot of competition in space."[11]

To build the car, Tesla bought a recently closed automobile factory in Fremont, California, that had

Figure 3b Tesla Model S

been used for the New United Motor Manufacturing Inc. (NUMMI) venture between Toyota and General Motors. The factory, which was capable of producing 1,000 cars a week, was far bigger than Tesla's immediate needs and would give the company room to grow. Furthermore, though the plant and the land it was on had been appraised at around $1 billion before NUMMI was shut down, Tesla was able to snap up the idled factory for $42 million.[12] Tesla also used the factory to produce battery packs for Toyota's RAV4 and a charger for a subcompact Daimler AG electric vehicle. These projects would supplement Tesla's income while also helping it build scale and learning-curve efficiencies in its technologies.

In the first quarter of 2013, Tesla announced its first quarterly profit. The company had taken in $562 million in revenues and reported an $11.2-million profit. Then more good news came: The Model S had earned *Consumer Reports'* highest rating and had outsold similarly priced BMW and Mercedes models in the first quarter.[13] In May 2013, the company raised $1 billion by issuing new shares, and then surprised investors by announcing that it had paid back its government loan. After repaying the loan, Tesla had some $679 million in cash. Musk had announced confidently that he felt it was his obligation to pay back taxpayer money as soon as possible, and that the company had sufficient funds now to develop its next generation of automobiles without the loan and without issuing further shares.[14]

By 2015, Tesla Motors was also in the process of developing a sport utility vehicle that seats seven, the Model X (see Figure 3c), which cost $250 million to

Figure 3c Tesla Model X

Darren Brode/Shutterstock.com

develop and would be available in 2016.[15] This SUV was part of Musk's longer-term ambition to tap a more mainstream market for the cars.

OBSTACLES TO THE ADOPTION OF ELECTRIC VEHICLES

A number of obstacles slowed the adoption of electric vehicles. The first was the price: Electric vehicles were, typically, significantly more expensive than comparable internal-combustion models. Complicating matters further, most consumers had a very difficult time estimating the cost of ownership of an electric car. How much would they pay to charge at home? How much would they pay to charge away from home? What would the maintenance and repairs of an electric vehicle cost? How long would the battery and/or car last? Would it have resale value? To lessen these concerns, Elon Musk set out to make the cost of owning a Tesla as certain as possible. First, he created a "Supercharger" network that Model S owners could use for free, for the life of the car. As noted by Musk, "The clearest way to convey the message that electric cars are actually better than gasoline cars is to say charging is free."[16] The hitch was that a user had to be within range of a Supercharger station. Second, Musk announced an unprecedented price-protection guarantee that permitted a Model S owner to trade in their car for a designated residual value anytime within the first 3 years of the cars life. Musk also announced plans to offer free repairs, and a free replacement car while a customer's car was being repaired. Needless to say, analysts scratched their heads at the potential costs of these guarantees.

The second major obstacle to the adoption of electric vehicles was their limited range and associated "range anxiety" (concerns about driving in places where owners were not sure they would be able to charge their cars). These concerns were not so much of an issue for the Tesla cars due to their exceptionally long range. Other "mass-market" electric vehicles faced tougher hurdles. For example, though a Nissan Leaf could be charged at an ordinary, 110-volt household outlet, a full charge by this method could take 8 hours. Level 2 charging with a

220-volt outlet could shorten that time to 4 hours, but this was still completely impractical for recharging during a trip. DC Fast Chargers and Tesla's "Superchargers" promised to fully charge a vehicle in 30 minutes or less. While this is still significantly longer than the typical 6-minute gasoline fill-up, it meant that charging could be feasible if it were co-located with other services that drivers might appreciate, such as restaurants or coffee shops. DC Fast Chargers and Tesla's Supercharging stations were expensive to purchase and install—up to $250,000 depending on the location—and they had to be close to heavy-duty electricity transformers. By May 2015, there were 425 Tesla Supercharger stations worldwide, with a total of 2,338 Superchargers.[17]

COMPETITION IN THE ELECTRIC VEHICLE MARKET

Hybrid electric vehicles (HEVs) such as the Toyota Prius made their appearance in the U.S. auto market in 2000. These vehicles were readily adopted by consumers because they require no change in typical consumer usage habits; they use gasoline and automatically switch between electric miles and gasoline miles. Most HEVs, however, have extremely limited electric range. For many, 10 miles of electric driving before switching over to gas is the norm. This limits their ability to reduce carbon emissions or influence energy usage. All-electric vehicles, also called plug-in electric vehicles, known alternatively as AEV or PEV, get all of their energy from electricity. They are thus considered true zero-emission vehicles. Plug-in hybrid electric vehicles (PHEVs) such as the Chevy Volt plug in to charge but can also use gas.

By 2015, a number of automakers were producing electric vehicles, in large part due to California's standards mandating that, for automobiles to be sold in California, a certain portion of an automaker's fleet had to be emission free. As a result, some automakers were willing to produce all-electric vehicles at a loss in order to also sell more lucrative internal-combustion models. These zero-emission mandates spurred a flurry of introductions of electric vehicles in the early 1990s. The subsequent downscaling of California's zero-emission mandate in the late 1990s led GM, Toyota, Honda, and Ford to shut down their loss-making EV programs, including most notoriously GM's EV-1s, which were literally torn from their owners and crushed, as shown in the film *Who Killed the Electric Car?* Other automakers opted to buy zero-emission credits from those companies that sold more than their required proportion of zero-emission vehicles. Other states had adopted similar programs, and at the federal level firms could earn greenhouse gas (GHG) emission credits by exceeding the U.S. Environmental Protection Agency's greenhouse gas standards. Tesla was one such automaker who had surplus credits (since it produced no internal combustion vehicles), and as a result Tesla earned $40.1 million in 2012, $194.4 million in 2013, and $216.3 million in 2014 selling its surplus credits to other automakers.[18]

Several companies had attempted to enter the all-electric vehicle market, but had run out of cash and ceased operations. These included Fisker, Coda, Azure Dynamics, Bright Automotive, and others. The more serious competition was coming from established automakers that had deeper pockets to withstand the losses of building the electric vehicle market. Among these, there were a few competing cars that had sold significant (though still small) numbers of cars into the market. The Nissan Leaf, for example, retailed for about $35,000, and had a range of about 90 to 100 miles per charge. By the end of 2014, it had sold 72,322 units in the United States and over 140,000 worldwide. The Chevy Volt was a plug-in hybrid that could travel about 40 all-electric miles per charge, and an additional 340 miles on gasoline (making it a good solution for individuals who primarily made short commutes but also wanted to drive the car long distances without "range anxiety"). It also retailed for about $35,000, and, including its rebadged "Ampera" versions, it had sold over 88,000 of the cars worldwide by the end of 2014.

TESLA'S STRATEGIES

Automated Manufacturing

In 2015, nearly all of Tesla's manufacturing was done at its plant in Freemont, California, though it had plans to build a manufacturing center in Tilburg, the Netherlands, where it had an assembly facility.[19] Tesla's manufacturing process was highly automated, with extensive use of 8- to 10-foot-tall red robots, reminiscent of Iron Man. Each robot had a single, multijointed arm. While typical auto factory robots perform only one function, Tesla's robots perform up to four tasks: welding, riveting, bonding, and installing a component. Eight robots might work on a single car at each station of the assembling line in a choreographed pattern, like ballet. The robots produce up to 83 cars a day and can be reprogrammed to produce the Model X on the same assembly line.[20]

Distribution

Musk saw the franchise-dealership arrangements that U.S. car companies use to sell cars as an expensive, margin-killing model. Furthermore, selling an electric vehicle is more complicated than selling an internal combustion vehicle. Because consumers are less familiar with electric vehicles, they required more explanation about the electricity costs, service issues, potential resale value issues, and more. Musk thus chose to sell direct to consumers with boutique-like stores in upscale shopping malls where salespeople could provide high-touch service and answer customer questions without using high-pressure sales tactics. The company also sold direct to consumers on the Internet.

Musk's decision to own and operate Tesla dealerships himself was a controversial move that provoked the ire of dealership networks. In the 1950s, regulation had been passed in the United States to protect dealers from exploitation by what were then very powerful auto manufacturers. This regulation prohibited auto manufacturers from competing with their own dealers by directly selling cars to consumers. The industry, however, had become increasingly competitive due to globalization, thereby lowering the power of auto manufacturers. Though most economic analysis suggested that the industry would be more efficient if the dealership restrictions were removed, the regulation remained largely unchallenged until Tesla's entry.[21] Tesla was chipping away at them one by one. In 2015, there were still 28 states that banned direct sales, making it extremely difficult for Tesla to enter.

Marketing

Tesla spends no money on advertising, nor does it have any plans to hire advertising agencies or run ads in the future. Its in-house marketing team has only seven people on staff, and an internal team runs the website. Nissan, by contrast, spent $25 million advertising the Leaf in 2012. According to Tesla spokesperson Alexis Georgeson, "Right now, the stores are our advertising. We're very confident we can sell 20,000-plus cars a year without paid advertising … It may be something we'll do years down the road. But it's certainly not something we feel is crucial for sales right now."[22]

◤ LOOKING TO THE FUTURE

In 2014, Tesla announced it would be opening a "gigafactory"—a giant, lithium-ion battery factory—with its partner Panasonic. The factory, located in Nevada after the state offered $1.1 billion in abatements, was slated to produce 500,000 lithium-ion battery packs per year by 2020.[23] That number exceeded total global production of lithium-ion batteries in 2014. Musk believed he could drive battery production costs down by as much as 30% at the factory, but many industry observers were puzzled by the move. If there were a major innovation in battery technology—advances in aluminum air batteries for example—the massive technological investment could be rendered obsolete.

In 2015, Tesla also introduced the "Powerwall"—a home energy-storage battery that would store electricity generated by solar panels during the day to then be used whenever needed by the consumer. Within a week of announcing the Powerwall, the company had orders for all of its production through 2016—roughly $800 million worth of revenues.[24]

Tesla's moves have been bold and risky, and its success thus far is inspiring. The company had survived its infancy, appeared to be solvent, and was meeting its sales objectives even though serious obstacles remained for electric vehicles. It was also competing against companies with far greater scale. As noted by O'Dell, a senior editor at auto information sites

Edmunds.com, on Tesla's success, "A lot of people have been very, very skeptical … when you want to be an automaker, you are competing with multibillion-dollar conglomerates … It's entrepreneurism on steroids … They had a huge learning curve but they've powered through it." Theo O'Neill, an analyst at Wunderlich Securities, adds that "It's going to prove everybody in Detroit wrong … They all say what Tesla is doing isn't possible."[25]

NOTES

1. M. V. Copeland, "Tesla's Wild Ride," *Fortune* 158 (2)(2008), pp. 82–94.
2. Ibid.
3. J. Boudreau, "In a Silicon Valley Milestone, Tesla Motors Begins Delivering Model S Electric Cars," *Oakland Tribune*, June 24, 2012, Breaking News Section. www.insidebayarea.com/oaklandtribune /localnews/ci_20919723/silicon-valley-milestone -tesla-motors-begins-delivering-model.
4. M. V. Copeland, "Tesla's Wild Ride."
5. A. Williams, "Taking a Tesla for a Status Check in New York," *New York Times*, July 19, 2009. ST.7.www.nytimes.com.
6. M. V. Copeland, "Tesla's Wild Ride."
7. J. Garthwaite, "Tesla Sues 'Top Gear,'" *New York Times*, April 3, 2011, AU.2.www.nytimes.com.
8. A. Williams, "Taking a Tesla for a Status Check in New York."
9. M. Ramsey, "Tesla Sets 300-Mile Range for Second Electric Car," *The Wall Street Journal (Online)*, March 7, 2011.
10. C. Sweet, "Tesla Posts Its First Quarterly Profit," *The Wall Street Journal (Online)*, May 9, 2013.
11. J. Boudreau, "In a Silicon Valley Milestone, Tesla Motors Begins Delivering Model S Electric Cars,"
12. Anonymous, "Idle Fremont Plant Gears Up for Tesla," *The Wall Street Journal (Online)*, October 20, 2010.
13. M. Levi, "How Tesla Pulled Ahead of the Electric-Car Pack," *The Wall Street Journal*, June 21, 2013, p. A.11.
14. J. B. White, "Corporate News: Electric Car Startup Tesla Repays U.S. Loan," *The Wall Street Journal*, May 23, 2013, p. B.3.
15. Caranddriver.com, accessed May 11, 2015.
16. T. Woody, "Billionaire Car Wars," *Forbes*, December 10, 2012, pp. 90–98.
17. Ibid.
18. Tesla Motors 10-K, 2015.
19. www.Teslamotors.com, accessed May 17, 2015.
20. J. Markoff, "Skilled Work, without the Worker," *New York Times*, August 19, 2012, p. A.1.
21. D. A. Crane, "Tesla and the Car Dealers Lobby," *Regulation* (Summer 2014), pp. 10–14.
22. M. McCarthy, "Tesla Generates Small Sales, Huge Buzz without Paid Ads," *Advertising Age*, June 10, 2013, p. 9.
23. P. Elkind, "Inside Elon Musk's $1.4 Billion Score," *Fortune*, December 1, 2014. www.fortune.com.
24. S. Hanley, "Tesla PowerWall Sells Out through 2016; Brings in $800 Million," www.Gas2.org, accessed may 17, 2015.
25. J. Boudreau, "In a Silicon Valley Milestone, Tesla Motors Begins Delivering Model S Electric Cars," *Oakland Tribune*, June 24, 2012, Breaking News Section. www.insidebayarea.com/oaklandtribune /localnews/ci_20919723/silicon-valley-milestone -tesla-motors-begins-delivering-model.

30

THE HEINZ AND KRAFT MERGER

On March 25, 2015, Heinz and Kraft announced a merger that would make the combined companies the third-largest food company in the United States, and the fifth-largest food company in the world. It would be called the Kraft Heinz Company. Kraft was the number-one producer of packaged macaroni and cheese (with an 80% share), and was among the top four companies that made mayonnaise, salad dressing, pickles, cottage cheese, sour cream, and lunch meat. Heinz was the number-one maker of ketchup (with a 60% share), and was among the top four companies that produce meat sauces, pasta sauces, and frozen appetizers. Together, the two companies accounted for $22.2 billion in annual revenues.

According to the terms of the deal, a 51% stake in the new company would go to shareholders of Heinz and 49% would go to Kraft shareholders. Furthermore, Kraft shareholders would get a one-time cash dividend of $16.50 per share (just over 25% of Kraft's stock price at the time of the announcement)—a total payout of $10 billion that would be paid by 3G Capital and Berkshire Hathaway. Heinz's CEO, Bernardo Hees, would be the CEO of the new company, Heinz's chairman of the board, Alex Behring, would become the chairman of the new company, and Kraft's CEO, John Cahill, would become the vice chairman.

The announcement was met with responses that varied from enthusiasm to puzzlement. Both companies were already giant food companies with significant economies of scale and bargaining power over suppliers

Scott Olson/Staff

and buyers. Furthermore, there was very little overlap in their product lines, making it unclear whether and how product lines or activities might be consolidated. Was this merger going to make the combined companies more valuable than they were individually? If so, how? Would that additional value be worth more than the coordination costs and loss of flexibility that the merger caused?

▼ HEINZ

Heinz was founded by Henry John Heinz in Sharpsburg, Pennsylvania, in 1869. He had been peddling extra vegetables from his mother's garden from the time he was 8 years old. When the company was founded, it primarily produced horseradish, pickles, sauerkraut, and vinegar, all delivered via horse-drawn wagons to grocers in and around Pittsburgh. Ketchup, the product with which the Heinz Company would become so closely associated, was not added to the product line until 1876. In 1886, Heinz packed his bags with seven varieties of Heinz products and sailed with his family to England, marking the company's first global venture.

Heinz acquired a reputation as an advertising genius. His creative marketing ideas included New York City's first large, electric advertising sign: a 40-foot pickle. He was also known for the set of principles that became lynchpins of his company's culture:

- Every profit should be fairly earned (his motto was "Deal with the seller so justly that he will want to sell to you again").
- Despise any kind of waste (he inspired employees not to waste materials, time or opportunities).
- Respect all others, rich or poor, weak or powerful (his mother's favorite rule for life was "Always remember to place yourself in the other person's shoes").

As an outcome of this, his manufacturing facility became famous for its progressive benefits plans: free medical care, a swimming pool and gym, and classes for women in cooking and dressmaking.

After his death in 1919, his son (and later his grandson) expanded upon the company's traditional product lines. The company grew and became more diversified with each subsequent leader. By 2015, Heinz had $11.5 billion in revenues (see Figures 1 and 2), and its products were sold in 200 companies around the world. Roughly 47% of its sales came from ketchup and sauces, 37% came from meals and snacks, and the remaining 16% came from other products such as infant formula and baby food. Its iconic Heinz ketchup brand held the number-one or number-two position in 50 countries, and it was also well-known for brands such as Classico pasta sauces, Lea & Perrins Worcestershire sauce, Ore-Ida frozen potatoes, and frozen foods made under the Boston Market, T.G.I. Fridays and Weight Watchers brands. Its strongest 15 brands accounted for more than two-thirds of the company's sales.

Figure 1 Heinz's Income Statement, 2009–2013 ($US millions)

	Apr 13	Apr 12	Apr 11	Apr 10	Apr 09
Revenue	11,528.89	11,649.08	10,706.59	10,494.98	10,148.08
Cost of Goods Sold	7,333.42	7,649.55	6,754.05	6,700.68	6,564.45
Gross Profit	4,195.47	3,999.53	3,952.54	3,794.31	3,583.64
Gross Profit Margin	36.39%	34.33%	36.92%	36.15%	35.31%
SG&A Expense	2,533.82	2,548.36	2,304.35	2,235.08	2,089.98
Depreciation & Amortization	—	—	—	—	—
Operating Income	1,661.65	1,451.17	1,648.19	1,559.23	1,493.65
Operating Margin	14.41%	12.46%	15.39%	14.86%	14.72%
Nonoperating Income	—	—	—	—	—
Nonoperating Expenses	—	—	—	—	—
Income Before Taxes	1,343.64	1,183.44	1,374.17	1,290.45	1,296.20
Income Taxes	241.59	243.54	368.22	358.51	373.13
Net Income After Taxes	1,027.33	939.91	1,005.95	931.94	923.07
Net Profit Margin	8.91%	8.07%	9.40%	8.88%	9.10%

Figure 2 Heinz's Balance Sheet, 2009–2013 ($US millions)

Assets	Apr 13	Apr 12	Apr 11	Apr 10	Apr 09
Current Assets					
Cash	2,458.99	1,330.44	724.31	483.25	373.15
Net Receivables	1,344.18	993.51	1,265.03	1,045.34	1,171.80
Inventories	1,435.40	1,329.35	1,451.55	1,249.13	1,237.61
Other Current Assets	60.46	54.14	153.13	142.59	36.70
Total Current Assets	5,444.13	3,882.24	3,753.54	3,051.13	2,945.02
Net Fixed Assets	2,663.49	2,484.14	2,505.08	2,091.80	1,978.30
Other Noncurrent Assets	1,305.02	932.70	1,074.80	864.16	757.91
Total Assets	38,972.35	11,983.29	12,230.65	10,075.71	9,664.18
Liabilities	**Dec 13**	**Apr 12**	**Apr 11**	**Apr 10**	**Apr 09**
Current Liabilities					
Accounts Payable	1,192.07	1,202.40	1,337.62	1,007.52	1,113.31
Short Term Debt	251.45	246.71	1,534.93	59.02	65.64
Other Current Liabilities	202.19	101.54	98.33	30.59	73.90
Total Current Liabilities	2,924.86	2,647.96	4,161.46	2,175.36	2,062.85
Long Term Debt	14,617.65	4,779.98	3,078.13	4,559.15	5,076.19
Other Noncurrent Liabilities	725.80	812.84	786.74	727.62	900.30
Total Liabilities	22,674.93	9,224.70	9,121.68	8,184.37	8,444.25
Shareholder's Equity	**Dec 13**	**Apr 12**	**Apr 11**	**Apr 10**	**Apr 09**
Preferred Stock Equity	—	0.06	0.07	0.07	0.07
Common Stock Equity	16,140.00	107.77	107.77	107.77	107.77
Total Equity	16,297.42	2,758.59	3,108.96	1,891.35	1,219.94
Shares Outstanding (M)	0.10	320.23	321.28	317.69	314.86

Manufacturing and Distribution

In 2015, Heinz had 63 food-processing factories: 15 in North America, 17 in Europe, 24 in Asia/Pacific, and 7 in the rest of the world. It had developed and patented many of its own manufacturing processes and machines. Its products were sold through its own sales force and independent brokers, and were sold primarily to wholesalers, foodservice distributors, and directly to large retail accounts such as Wal-Mart. Wal-Mart, its largest customer, accounted for 10% of its sales.

KRAFT

Kraft Foods began in 1903, when James L. Kraft started buying and selling cheese out of a horse-drawn wagon in Chicago. Soon he was producing his own cheese and became primarily known for processed cheese sold in tins and loaves (the loaves are now known as Velveeta). The company grew and expanded its product line over the years, developing products such as Kraft Macaroni and Cheese Dinner, Miracle Whip, Philadelphia Cream Cheese, and more.

Then, through a series of acquisitions and spinoffs orchestrated by Philip Morris (the cigarette company), several important product lines from General Foods, Oscar Mayer, and Nabisco were merged into Kraft's product portfolio. These included Jell-o and Maxwell House (from General Foods), Oscar Mayer Meats, Oreo cookies from Nabisco, and more.

By the end of 2014, it had revenues of $18.2 billion (see Figures 3 and 4), with 33% of revenues coming from cheese and dairy (brands like Philadelphia cream cheese, Kraft singles, and Velveeta), 15% from meats (e.g., Oscar Mayer hot

Figure 3 Kraft's Income Statement, 2010–2014 ($US millions)

	Dec 14	Dec 13	Dec 12	Dec 11	Dec 10
Revenue	18,205.00	18,218.00	18,339.00	18,655.00	17,797.00
Cost of Goods Sold	13,360.00	11,395.00	12,499.00	12,761.00	11,778.00
Gross Profit	4,845.00	6,823.00	5,840.00	5,894.00	6,019.00
Gross Profit Margin	26.61%	37.45%	31.84%	31.59%	33.82%
SG&A Expense	2,956.00	2,124.00	3,029.00	2,973.00	3,066.00
Depreciation & Amortization	—	—	—	—	—
Operating Income	1,890.00	4,591.00	2,670.00	2,923.00	2,961.00
Operating Margin	10.38%	25.20%	14.56%	15.67%	16.64%
Nonoperating Income	—	—	—	46.00	36.00
Nonoperating Expenses	—	—	—	46.00	36.00
Income Before Taxes	1,406.00	4,090.00	2,453.00	2,969.00	2,997.00
Income Taxes	363.00	1,375.00	811.00	1,130.00	1,110.00
Net Income After Taxes	1,043.00	2,715.00	1,642.00	1,839.00	1,887.00
Continuing Operations	1,043.00	2,715.00	1,642.00	1,839.00	1,887.00
Discontinued Operations	—	—	—	—	1,644.00
Total Operations	1,043.00	2,715.00	1,642.00	1,839.00	3,531.00
Total Net Income	1,043.00	2,715.00	1,642.00	1,839.00	3,531.00
Net Profit Margin	5.73%	14.90%	8.95%	9.86%	19.84%

Figure 4 Kraft's Balance Sheet, 2010–2014 ($US millions)

Assets	Dec 14	Dec 13	Dec 12	Dec 11	Dec 10
Current Assets					
Cash	1,293.00	1,686.00	1,255.00	—	2.00
Net Receivables	1,080.00	1,048.00	1,089.00	903.00	1,196.00
Inventories	1,775.00	1,616.00	1,928.00	1,943.00	1,773.00
Other Current Assets	259.00	198.00	131.00	194.00	165.00
Total Current Assets	4,791.00	4,908.00	4,823.00	3,272.00	3,307.00
Net Fixed Assets	4,192.00	4,115.00	4,204.00	4,278.00	4,283.00
Other Noncurrent Assets	326.00	391.00	325.00	29.00	23.00
Total Assets	22,947.00	23,148.00	23,329.00	21,539.00	21,598.00
Liabilities	**Dec 14**	**Dec 13**	**Dec 12**	**Dec 11**	**Dec 10**
Current Liabilities					
Accounts Payable	1,537.00	1,548.00	1,556.00	1,447.00	1,285.00
Short Term Debt	1,405.00	—	5.00	8.00	8.00
Other Current Liabilities	641.00	483.00	579.00	300.00	322.00
Total Current Liabilities	4,773.00	3,410.00	3,606.00	2,572.00	2,366.00
Long Term Debt	8,627.00	9,976.00	9,966.00	27.00	31.00
Other Noncurrent Liabilities	338.00	428.00	405.00	621.00	583.00
Total Liabilities	18,582.00	17,961.00	19,757.00	4,940.00	4,559.00
Shareholder's Equity	**Dec 14**	**Dec 13**	**Dec 12**	**Dec 11**	**Dec 10**
Preferred Stock Equity	—	—	—	—	—
Common Stock Equity	—	—	4,240.00	—	—
Total Equity	4,365.00	5,187.00	3,572.00	16,599.00	17,039.00
Shares Outstanding (M)	587.33	596.23	592.76	—	—

dogs and bacon, Lunchables), 11% from packaged meals (e.g., Macaroni and Cheese, Shake 'n Bake coatings), 10% from beverages (e.g., Maxwell House coffee, Kool-Aid, and CapriSun), and 9% from condiments (e.g., Miracle Whip, Mayonnaise, salad dressings, and A.1. sauces).

Manufacturing and Distribution

Kraft has 36 manufacturing and processing plants: 34 in the United States and three in Canada. Kraft sells its products primarily to wholesalers, distributors, convenience stores, and large retail chains. Its five largest customers accounted for 42% of its revenues, and Wal-Mart (Kraft's largest customer) accounted for 26% of its sales in 2014. In North America, the company used a combination of a direct sales force and third-parties sales agencies to promote its products to its customers; outside of North America, Kraft primarily used exporters and distributors to promote its products.

ARGUMENTS FOR AND AGAINST THE DEAL

The merger had been organized by 3G Capital (a Brazilian private investment group) and Warren Buffet's Berkshire Hathaway. Those supporting the deal argued that it would enable cost cuts of $1.5 billion through greater economies of scale in North America, and through using Kraft's better credit rating to refinance Heinz's debt. It was also argued that the combined company would have more market power over retailers, giving it greater access to shelf space and the ability to raise prices. Other argued, however, that the companies were already so big, and their brands already so powerful, there was likely little bargaining power left on the negotiating table.

Perhaps more convincingly, Bernardo Hees and Alex Behring had implemented dramatic cost-cutting practices at Heinz that included cutting jobs by 4%, closing several factories, and grounding corporate jets. It was thus reasonable to expect that the team would now impose these measures at Kraft, potentially yielding significant savings. Furthermore, many thought there was significant potential for Heinz to help Kraft sell more broadly in international markets. Whereas Heinz earned 40% of its sales outside of North America and had extensive manufacturing and distribution facilities abroad, Kraft earned only 2% of its sales outside of North America and had no manufacturing or distribution facilities outside of the continent. On the other hand, the potential to broaden Kraft's international presence was limited: In 2012, the company had struck a deal with former Kraft subsidiary, Mondelez International, that gave the latter company exclusive rights to sell many Kraft brands in international markets.

Both companies operated primarily in mature markets, and their revenues had been flat for years. Both companies were also seen as "old-school" brands that were facing serious challenges as customer tastes evolved to favor fresh, natural foods over those processed and packaged. "Both are stodgy, old brands that haven't kept up with the times in terms of shifting consumer appetites," according to Lou Biscotti, global practice leaders for WeiserMazars. Gary Stibel, CEO of New England Consulting, adds that the companies should have started reinventing their brands years ago, noting, "They've both played lip service to better-for-you (food trends) for over a decade." Would the merger help the companies better position themselves for the future?

Sources: L. Douglas, "Why You Should Pay Attention to the Heinz/Kraft Merger," Time.com, April 8, 2015; Anonymous, "Analysis of the Kraft-Heinz Merger," Forbes.com, March 30, 2015; B. Horovitz and J. Onyanga-Omara, "Heinz, Kraft to Create World's No. 5 Food Company," USAToday.com, March 25, 2015; S. Ovide, "The Long, Strange History of Kraft," *The Wall Street Journal,* August 4, 2011; Heinz 2014 10-K; Kraft 2015 10-K; Hoovers; www.heinz.com; www.kraft.com.

GLOSSARY

A

acquisition When a company uses its capital resources to purchase another company.

anticompetitive behavior A range of actions aimed at harming actual or potential competitors, most often by using monopoly power, and thereby enhancing the long-run prospects of the firm.

autonomous subunit A subunit that has all the resources and decision-making power required to run the operation on a day-to-day basis.

availability error A bias that arises from our predisposition to estimate the probability of an outcome based on how easy the outcome is to imagine.

B

broad differentiation strategy When a company differentiates its product in some way, such as by recognizing different segments or offering different products to each segment.

broad low-cost strategy When a company lowers costs so that it can lower prices and still make a profit.

bureaucratic control Control through a formal system of written rules and procedures.

bureaucratic costs The costs associated with solving the transaction difficulties between business units and corporate headquarters as a company obtains the benefits from transferring, sharing, and leveraging competencies.

business ethics Accepted principles of right or wrong governing the conduct of businesspeople.

business-level strategy The business's overall competitive theme, the way it positions itself in the marketplace to gain a competitive advantage, and the different positioning strategies that can be used in different industry settings.

business model The conception of how strategies should work together as a whole to enable the company to achieve competitive advantage.

business unit A self-contained division that provides a product or service for a particular market.

C

capital productivity The sales produced by a dollar of capital invested in the business.

centralization Structure in which the decision-making authority is concentrated at a high level in the management hierarchy.

chaining A strategy designed to obtain the advantages of cost leadership by establishing a network of linked merchandising outlets interconnected by information technology that functions as one large company.

code of ethics Formal statement of the ethical priorities to which a business adheres.

cognitive biases Systematic errors in decision making that arise from the way people process information.

commonality A skill or competency that, when shared by two or more business units, allows them to operate more effectively and create more value for customers.

competitive advantage The achieved advantage over rivals when a company's profitability is greater than the average profitability of firms in its industry.

control The process through which managers regulate the activities of individuals and units so that they are consistent with the goals and standards of the organization.

controls The metrics used to measure the performance of subunits and make judgments about how well managers are running them.

corruption Can arise in a business context when managers pay bribes to gain access to lucrative business contracts.

credible commitment A believable promise or pledge to support the development of a long-term relationship between companies.

cross-selling When a company takes advantage of or leverages its established relationship with customers by way of acquiring additional product lines or categories that it can sell to them. In this way, a company increases differentiation because it can provide a "total solution" and satisfy all of a customer's specific needs.

customer response time Time that it takes for a good to be delivered or a service to be performed.

D

decentralization Structure in which the decision-making authority is distributed to lower-level managers or other employees.

delayering The process of reducing the number of levels in a management hierarchy.

devil's advocacy A technique in which one member of a decision-making team identifies all the considerations that might make a proposal unacceptable.

dialectic inquiry The generation of a plan (a thesis) and a counterplan (an antithesis) that reflect plausible but conflicting courses of action.

distinctive competencies Firm-specific strengths that allow a company to differentiate its products and/or achieve substantially lower costs to achieve a competitive advantage.

diversification The process of entering new industries, distinct from a company's core or original industry, to make new kinds of products for customers in new markets.

diversified company A company that makes and sells products in two or more different or distinct industries.

divestment strategy When a company decides to exit an industry by selling off its business assets to another company.

dominant design Common set of features or design characteristics.

E

economies of scope The synergies that arise when one or more of a diversified company's business units are able to lower costs or increase differentiation because they can more effectively pool, share, and utilize expensive resources or capabilities.

employee productivity The output produced per employee.

environmental degradation Occurs when a company's actions directly or indirectly result in pollution or other forms of environmental harm.

escalating commitment A cognitive bias that occurs when decision makers, having already committed significant resources to a project, commit even more resources after receiving feedback that the project is failing.

ethical dilemmas Situations where there is no agreement over exactly what the accepted principles of right and wrong are, or where none of the available alternatives seems ethically acceptable.

ethics Accepted principles of right or wrong that govern the conduct of a person, the members of a profession, or the actions of an organization.

external stakeholders All other individuals and groups that have some claim on the company.

F

first mover A firm that pioneers a particular product category or feature by being first to offer it to market.

first-mover disadvantages Competitive disadvantages associated with being first to market.

flat hierarchies An organizational structure with very few layers of management.

focus differentiation strategy When a company targets a certain segment or niche, and customizes its offering to the needs of that particular segment through the addition of features and functions.

focus low-cost strategy When a company targets a certain segment or niche, and tries to be the low-cost player in that niche.

focus strategy When a company decides to serve a limited number of segments, or just one segment.

format wars Battles to control the source of differentiation, and thus the value that such differentiation can create for the customer.

fragmented industry An industry composed of a large number of small-and medium-sized companies.

functional managers Managers responsible for supervising a particular function; that is, a task, an activity, or an operation such as accounting, marketing, research and development (R&D), information technology, or logistics.

franchising A strategy in which the franchisor grants to its franchisees the right to use the franchisor's name, reputation, and business model in return for a franchise fee and often a percentage of the profits.

functional structure The organizational structure is built upon the division of labor within the firm with different functions focusing on different tasks.

G

general managers Managers who bear responsibility for the overall performance of the company or for one of its major, self-contained subunits or divisions.

general organizational competencies Competencies that result from the skills of a company's top managers and that help every business unit within a company perform at a higher level than it could if it operated as a separate or independent company.

generic business-level strategy A strategy that gives a company a specific form of competitive position and advantage vis-à-vis its rivals that results in above-average profitability.

global standardization strategy A business model based on pursuing a low-cost strategy on a global scale.

global strategic alliances Cooperative agreements between companies from different countries that are actual or potential competitors.

goal A desired future state that an organization attempts to realize.

greenmail source of gaining wealth whereby corporate raiders either push companies to change their corporate strategy to one that will benefit stockholders, or charge a premium for stock when the company wants to buy it back.

H

harvest strategy When a company reduces to a minimum the assets it employs in a business to reduce its cost structure and extract or "milk" maximum profits from its investment.

holdup When a company is taken advantage of by another company it does business with after it has made an investment in expensive specialized assets to better meet the needs of the other company.

horizontal differentiation The formal division of the organization into subunits.

horizontal integration The process of acquiring or merging with industry competitors to achieve the competitive advantages that arise from a large size and scope of operations.

hostage taking A means of exchanging valuable resources to guarantee that each partner to an agreement will keep its side of the bargain.

I

illusion of control A cognitive bias rooted in the tendency to overestimate one's ability to control events.

incentives The devices used to encourage desired employee behavior.

influence costs The loss of efficiency that arises from deliberate information distortions for personal gain within an organization.

information asymmetry A situation where an agent has more information about resources he or she is managing than the principal has.

information manipulation When managers use their control over corporate data to distort or hide information in order to enhance their own financial situation or the competitive position of the firm.

inside directors Senior employees of the company, such as the CEO.

integrating mechanisms Processes and procedures used for coordination subunits.

internal capital market A corporate-level strategy whereby the firm's headquarters assesses the performance of business units and allocates money across them. Cash generated by units that are profitable but have poor investment opportunities within their business is used to cross-subsidize businesses that need cash and have strong promise for long-run profitability.

internal new venturing The process of transferring resources to, and creating a new business unit or division in, a new industry to innovate new kinds of products.

internal stakeholders Stockholders and employees, including executive officers, other managers, and board members.

K

killer applications Applications or uses of a new technology or product that are so compelling that customers adopt them in droves, killing competing formats.

knowledge network A network for transmitting information within an organization that is based not on formal organizational structure, but on informal contacts between managers within an enterprise and on distributed information systems.

L

leadership strategy When a company develops strategies to become the dominant player in a declining industry.

leveraging competencies The process of taking a distinctive competency developed by a business unit in one industry and using it to create a new business unit in a different industry.

limit price strategy Charging a price that is lower than that required to maximize profits in the short run to signal new entrants that the incumbent has a low cost structure that the entrant likely cannot match.

localization strategy A strategy focused on increasing profitability by customizing a company's goods or services so that they provide a favorable match to tastes and preferences in different national markets.

location economies The economic benefits that arise from performing a value creation activity in an optimal location.

M

market controls The regulation of the behavior of individuals and units within an enterprise by setting up an internal market for valuable resource such as capital.

market development When a company searches for new market segments for a company's existing products to increase sales.

market segmentation The way a company decides to group customers based on important differences in their needs to gain a competitive advantage.

mass market One in which large numbers of customers enter the market.

matrix structure An organizational structure in which managers try to achieve tight coordination between functions, particularly R&D, production, and marketing.

merger An agreement between two companies to pool their resources and operations and join together to better compete in a business or industry.

mission The purpose of the company, or a statement of what the company strives to do.

multidivisional company A company that competes in several different businesses and has created a separate, self-contained division to manage each.

multidivisional structure An organizational structure in which a firm is divided into divisions, each of which is responsible for a distinct business area.

multinational company A company that does business in two or more national markets.

N

network effects The network of complementary products as a primary determinant of the demand for an industry's product.

niche strategy When a company focuses on pockets of demand that are declining more slowly than the industry as a whole to maintain profitability.

non-price competition The use of product differentiation strategies to deter potential entrants and manage rivalry within an industry.

norms Social rules and guidelines that prescribe the appropriate behavior in particular situations.

O

on-the-job consumption A term used by economists to describe the behavior of senior management's use of company funds to acquire perks (such as lavish offices, jets, etc.) that will enhance their status, instead of investing it to increase stockholder returns.

organizational design skills The ability of a company's managers to create a structure, culture, and control systems that motivate and coordinate employees to perform at a high level.

opportunism Seeking one's own self-interest, often through the use of guile.

opportunistic exploitation Unethical behavior sometimes used by managers to unilaterally rewrite the terms of a contract with suppliers, buyers, or complement providers in a way that favors to the firm.

organizational architecture The totality of a firm's organizational arrangements, including its formal organizational structure, control systems, incentive systems, organizational culture, organizational processes, and human capital.

organizational culture The norms and value systems that are shared among the employees of an organization.

organizational processes The manner in which decisions are made and work is performed within the organization.

organizational structure The combination of the location of decision-making responsibilities, the formal division of the organization into subunits, and the establishment of integrating mechanisms to coordinate the activities of the subunits.

output controls Goals that are set for units or individuals to achieve and monitoring performance against those goals.

outside directors Directors who are not full-time employees of the company, needed to provide objectivity to the monitoring and evaluation of processes.

outside view Identification of past successful or failed strategic initiatives to determine whether those initiatives will work for project at hand.

P

parallel sourcing policy A policy in which a company enters into long-term contracts with at least two suppliers for the same component to prevent any incidents of opportunism.

peer control The pressure that employees exert on others within their team or work group to perform up to or in excess of the expectations of the organization.

people The employees of an organization, as well as the strategy used to recruit, compensate, motivate, and retain those individuals; also refers to employees' skills, values, and orientation.

performance ambiguity The difficulty of identifying with precision the reason for the high (or low) performance of a subunit such as a function or team.

personal ethics Generally accepted principles of right and wrong governing the conduct of individuals.

personal control Control by personal contact with and direct supervision of subordinates.

price leadership When one company assumes the responsibility for determining the pricing strategy that maximizes industry profitability.

price signaling The process by which companies increase or decrease product prices to convey their intentions to other companies and influence the price of an industry's products.

primary activities activities related to the design, creation, and delivery of the product, its marketing, and its support and after-sales service.

prior hypothesis bias A cognitive bias that occurs when decision makers who have strong prior beliefs tend to make decisions on the basis of these beliefs, even when presented with evidence that their beliefs are wrong.

process innovation Development of a new process for producing and delivering products to customers.

product development The creation of new or improved products to replace existing products.

product bundling Offering customers the opportunity to purchase a range of products at a single, combined price; this increases the value of a company's product line because customers often obtain a price discount when purchasing a set of products at one time, and customers become used to dealing with only one company and its representatives.

product innovation Development of products that are new to the world or have superior attributes to existing products.

product proliferation strategy The strategy of "filling the niches," or catering to the needs of customers in all market segments to deter entry by competitors.

profitability The return a company makes on the capital invested in the enterprise.

public domain Government- or association-set standards of knowledge or technology that any company can freely incorporate into its product.

Q

quasi integration The use of long-term relationships, or investment in some activities normally performed by suppliers or buyers, in place of full ownership of operations that are backward or forward in the supply chain.

R

razor and blade strategy Pricing the product low in order to stimulate demand, and pricing complements high.

reasoning by analogy Use of simple analogies to make sense out of complex problems.

related diversification A corporate-level strategy based on the goal of establishing a business unit in a new industry that is related to a company's existing business units by some form of commonality or linkage between their value-chain functions.

representativeness A bias rooted in the tendency to generalize from a small sample or even a single, vivid anecdote.

restructuring The process of reorganizing and divesting business units and exiting industries to refocus upon a company's core business and rebuild its distinctive competencies.

risk capital Equity capital invested with no guarantee that stockholders will recoup their cash or earn a decent return if a company fails and goes bankrupt.

S

scenario planning Formulating plans that are based upon "what-if" scenarios about the future.

segmentation strategy When a company decides to serve many segments, or even the entire market, producing different offerings for different segments.

self-dealing Managers using company funds for their own personal consumption, as done by Enron, for example, in previous years.

shareholder value Returns that shareholders earn from purchasing shares in a company.

span of control The number of direct reports that a manager has.

stakeholders Individuals or groups with an interest, claim, or stake in the company—in what it does and in how well it performs.

standard A performance requirement that the organization is meant to attain on an ongoing basis.

stock options The right to purchase company stock at a predetermined price at some point in the future, usually within 10 years of the grant date.

strategic alliances Long-term agreements between two or more companies to jointly develop new products or processes that benefit all companies that are a part of the agreement.

strategic commitments Investments that signal an incumbent's long-term commitment to a market, or a segment of that market.

strategic leadership Creating competitive advantage through effective management of the strategy-making process.

strategic outsourcing The decision to allow one or more of a company's value-chain activities to be performed by independent, specialist companies that focus all their skills and knowledge on just one kind of activity to increase performance.

strategy A set of related actions that managers take to increase their company's performance.

strategy formulation Selecting strategies based on analysis of an organization's external and internal environment.

strategy implementation Putting strategies into action.

standardization strategy When a company decides to ignore different segments, and produce a standardized product for the average consumer.

subgoal An objective, the achievement of which helps the organization to attain or exceed it major goals.

substandard working conditions Arise when managers underinvest in working conditions, or pay employees below-market rates, in order to reduce their production costs.

support activities Activities of the value chain that provide inputs that allow the primary activities to take place.

sustained competitive advantage A company's strategies enable it to maintain above-average profitability for a number of years.

SWOT analysis The comparison of strengths, weaknesses, opportunities, and threats.

T

takeover constraint The risk of being acquired by another company.

tall hierarchies An organizational structure with many layers of management.

tapered integration When a firm uses a mix of vertical integration and market transactions for a given input. For example, a firm might operate limited semiconductor manufacturing while also buying semiconductor chips on the market. Doing so helps to prevent supplier holdup (because the firm can credibly commit to not buying from external suppliers) and increases its ability to judge the quality and cost of purchased supplies.

technical standards A set of technical specifications that producers adhere to when making a product or component.

technological paradigm shift Shifts in new technologies that revolutionize the structure of the industry, dramatically alter the nature of competition, and require companies to adopt new strategies in order to survive.

technology upgrading Incumbent companies can deter entry by investing in costly technology upgrades that potential entrants have trouble matching.

transfer pricing The price that one division of a company charges another division for its products, which are the inputs the other division requires to manufacture its own products.

transferring competencies The process of taking a distinctive competency developed by a business unit in one industry and implanting it in a business unit operating in another industry.

transnational strategy A business model that simultaneously achieves low costs, differentiates the product offering across geographic markets, and fosters a flow of skills between different subsidiaries in the company's global network of operations.

turnaround strategy When managers of a diversified company identify inefficient, poorly managed companies in other industries and then acquire and restructure them to improve their performance—and thus the profitability of the total corporation.

U

unrelated diversification A corporate-level strategy based on a multibusiness model that uses general organizational competencies to increase the performance of all the company's business units.

V

value chain The concept that a company consists of a chain of activities that transforms inputs into outputs.

value innovation When innovations push out the efficiency frontier in an industry, allowing for greater value to be offered through superior differentiation at a lower cost than was previously thought possible.

values A statement of how employees should conduct themselves and their business to help achieve the company mission; ideas or shared assumptions about what a group believes to be good, right, and desirable.

vertical differentiation The location of decision-making responsibilities within a structure, referring to centralization or decentralization, and number of layers in a hierarchy, referring to whether to organizational structure is tall or flat.

vertical disintegration When a company decides to exit industries, either forward or backward in the industry value chain, to its core industry to increase profitability.

vertical integration When a company expands its operations either backward into an industry that produces inputs for the company's products (backward vertical integration) or forward into an industry that uses, distributes, or sells the company's products (forward vertical integration).

virtual corporation When companies pursued extensive strategic outsourcing to the extent that they only perform the central value creation functions that lead to competitive advantage.

vision The articulation of a company's desired achievements or future state.